The World Book Encyclopedia

So-Sz Volume 18

World Book, Inc.

a Scott Fetzer company

Chicago London Sydney Toronto

The World Book Encyclopedia

Copyright © 1984, U.S.A.
by
World Book, Inc.

SOAP. See DETERGENT AND SOAP.

SOAP BOX DERBY is a coasting race for small motorless racing cars. The derby received its name because at one time many of the cars were built from wooden soap boxes. Young people from 10 to 15 years old may enter the derby. Contestants who are 10 or 11 must compete in the Junior Division. Youngsters from 13 to 15 must race in the Senior Division. A 12-year-old can enter either division. The contestants must build their own cars. Rules govern the size, weight, and cost of the racer. Contestants first compete in local races. Winners qualify for the All-American Soap Box Derby held every August in Akron, Ohio. Racers from the United States, Canada, and several other countries enter the derby each year. Critically reviewed by the

ALL-AMERICAN SOAP BOX DERBY

SOAP OPERA. See RADIO (The Golden Age of Broadcasting); TELEVISION (Commercial Television).

SOAP PLANT is a tall herb of California which reaches a height of about 5 feet (1.5 meters). It grows from a bulb and has tufted leaves and white flowers streaked with purple. The leaves may be about $1\frac{1}{2}$ feet (46 centimeters) long. The flowers spread open in the afternoon. Indians used the bulb as a kind of soap.

Scientific Classification. Soap plants belong to the lily family, *Liliaceae*. They are genus *Chlorogalum*, species *C. pomeridianum*. JULIAN A. STEYERMARK

SOAP SCULPTURE is the art of carving figures from soap. It is best performed with a bar of soft white soap. A hard soap chips and leaves rough edges.

Scrape off all lettering or raised designs on the soap. Then, on paper, draw an outline of the shape that will appear on each side of the bar. Transfer the outline onto each side, using carbon paper under the design you drew on paper. Cut through the soap about $\frac{1}{4}$ inch (6.4 millimeters) outside the outline. It is best to start at the top and work downward. When you have cut away the excess soap, you have a flat piece in the general shape of your design. Work carefully, taking a little soap with each cut, until you reach the outline, molding and shaping the figure as you work. An orange stick, used in fingernail care, makes a good tool for scraping out small areas and shaping angles and curves. Use your thumb or your fingers to smooth out rough surfaces.

Set the finished carving aside for several days to dry. Then polish it with a soft paper tissue. Use your finger tips and the palm of your hand to bring out highlights.

Soap sculpture can take on the lovely look of old ivory. You can preserve the carving with a coat of transparent lacquer, or you may paint it with colors.

Beginners should start off with simple designs and should practice cutting the soap until they become acquainted with this art medium. JACK WAX

SOAPBERRY is the name of a group, or genus, of trees and shrubs that bear fruit containing a soapy substance called *saponin*. Soapberry trees and shrubs grow in tropical regions, and as ornamental plants in the southern United States. The fruit has a fleshy or leathery berry. People in the tropics use the saponin from the berries for cleaning purposes. Soapberry plants are reproduced by seeds or by cuttings in early spring. They grow well in dry, sandy soil.

One type of soapberry is an evergreen tree that grows in India and Japan. This tree is about 60 feet (18 meters) in height. It has an orange-brown fruit which

Walter Dawn

Soapberry Fruit contains *saponin*, which can irritate the skin and inflame the stomach and intestines.

contains much saponin. Another species, grown in the tropical regions of the United States, has small white flowers with orange-brown fruit. It grows about 30 feet (9 meters) high. A third species grows in the U.S. from Missouri to Mexico. It has yellowish-white flowers and sheds its leaves in winter.

Scientific Classification. Soapberries belong to the soapberry family, *Sapindaceae*. It makes up the genus *Sapindus*. The evergreen trees are classified as species *S. mukorossi*, and *S. saponaria*. The deciduous tree is classified as *S. drummondii*. J. J. LEVISON

See also TREE (Familiar Broadleaf and Needleleaf Trees [picture]).

SOAPSTONE, also known as *steatite*, is a soft rock composed mostly of the mineral talc. It feels soapy or oily and varies from white to gray and grayish-green.

Soapstone has many industrial uses. It is a good electric insulator and can easily be cut into various shapes. Because soapstone is not affected by high temperatures or acids, it is used for laboratory table tops, sinks, and some chemical equipment. Powdered soapstone is added to cosmetics, paper, and paint as a filler to improve these products. For example, soapstone gives paper a smooth surface. Tailors use pieces of soapstone called *French chalk* to mark cloth.

Soapstone is formed in the earth by changes in the structure and composition of an *igneous* rock such as peridotite (see IGNEOUS ROCK). These changes occur at low temperature and moderate pressure in the presence of water. Other kinds of rock that usually occur along with soapstone include dolomite and serpentinite. Soapstone, a *metamorphic* rock, forms in layers that vary greatly in thickness.

The United States ranks among the leading soapstone producers. Deposits occur in several states, including California, New York, North Carolina, and Virginia. Other countries that produce soapstone include Canada, France, and Italy. WILLIAM C. LUTH

See also TALC; METAMORPHIC ROCK.

SOARING SOCIETY OF AMERICA. See GLIDER (introduction).

SOBIESKI, JOHN. See JOHN III SOBIESKI.

© Diego Goldberg, Sygma   © Alan R. Jacques, Image Finders Photo Agency

Soccer is the most popular sport in the world. Every four years, teams from many countries compete in the World Cup Championship, the main international soccer tournament, *left*. Teams of the North American Soccer League, *right*, represent various U.S. and Canadian cities.

SOCCER

SOCCER is the world's most popular sport. It is the national sport of most European and Latin-American countries, and of many other nations. Millions of people in more than 140 countries play soccer. Soccer's most famous international competition, the World Cup Championship, is held every four years.

In a soccer game, two teams of 11 players try to kick or hit a ball into each other's goal. The team that scores the most goals wins. All the players except the goalkeepers must kick the ball or hit it with their head or body. Only the goalies can touch the ball with their hands.

Soccer as it is played today developed in England during the 1800's and quickly spread to many other countries. Until the mid-1900's, the game was not greatly popular in the United States. But today, it is one of the nation's fastest-growing sports.

In Great Britain and many other countries, soccer is called *football* or *association football*. The word *soccer* comes from *assoc.*, an abbreviation for *association*.

The Field and Equipment

The Field is rectangular and may vary in size. In international competition, it measures from 100 to 130 yards (91 to 119 meters) long and from 50 to 100 yards (46 to 91 meters) wide. The boundary lines on the sides of the field are called *touch lines*. Those on each end are called *goal lines*. The goals stand in the center of the goal line. Each goal measures 24 feet (7.3 meters) wide and 8 feet (2.4 meters) high. The *penalty area* is a rectangle in front of each goal. It is 132 feet (40.2 meters)

Richard Rottkov, the contributor of this article, is Director of Public Relations for the United States Soccer Federation.

---

wide and extends 54 feet (16.5 meters) in front of the goal. Defending players are penalized if they break certain rules while in their own penalty area. The *goal area* is a smaller rectangle that measures 60 feet (18 meters) wide and extends 18 feet (5.5 meters) in front of the goal. Attacking players cannot come into contact with the goalkeeper in this area unless the goalie is holding the ball and has both feet on the ground. For the names and sizes of other sections of a soccer field, and the names of other lines, see the field diagram with this article.

The Ball is made of leather or other approved material and inflated with air. A soccer ball used for adult games measures from 27 to 28 inches (69 to 71 centimeters) in circumference and weighs from 14 to 16 ounces (396 to 453 grams). Children generally use a ball with a circumference of about 25 inches (64 centimeters).

The Uniform consists of a shirt, shorts, calf-length socks, and shoes with cleats. Some players wear shin guards. The goalkeeper's shirt differs in color from those of other players of both sides.

Players and Officials

The players of a soccer team—except for the goalkeeper, who normally remains within the penalty area—use certain formations for offensive or defensive strategy. The score of the game often determines a team's strategy. For example, a team that is ahead will probably use a formation based on defense. A team that is behind will choose one that emphasizes offense. Some formations are designed to take advantage of the weaknesses of the opposing team. Other formations center around the special abilities of a star player.

At the start of a game, most teams line up in a 5-3-2 formation. The first line of this formation has five forwards—the center forward, the left and right inside forwards, and the left and right outside forwards, sometimes called *wingers*. The second line consists of the left, center, and right midfielders. The third line is made up of the left and right defenders, who play in front of the goalie.

Many teams shift to a 4-2-4 formation after a game begins. The first line has four forwards, two *strikers* flanked by two wingers. The second line has two midfielders, and the third line consists of four defenders. This formation provides a tight defense.

Another popular formation, the 4-3-3, uses four forwards, three midfielders, and three defenders. This formation gives a team a stronger offense than the 4-2-4. Other formations are also used.

International soccer rules allow a team to substitute two players during a game. College teams in the United States and Canada may substitute five players, and high schools have unlimited substitution. Under international soccer rules, players who leave the game cannot return.

The Forwards must be shifty and extremely fast. They have to pass the ball accurately and *dribble* (nudge the ball ahead) with their feet while racing down the field. A good forward can fake an opponent out of position and shoot well with either foot or with the head. Forwards score most of a team's goals, but they must also help break up plays of the opposing team.

The Midfielders, also called *halfbacks* or *linkmen,* unite the offense and the defense. These players have a role in every play and require exceptional physical endurance. Midfielders sometimes score goals, but they must always be in position to help the defense.

The Defenders, sometimes called *fullbacks,* form the last line of defense in front of the goalkeeper. A defender tries to take the ball away from the other team and pass it to a midfielder to start an attack. If the goalkeeper is out of position, one defender may stand directly in front of the goal to protect it against shots. A defender called a *sweeper* tries to intercept passes by roaming behind or in front of the other defenders. Defenders seldom score, but their passes may set up goals.

The Goalkeeper has perhaps the most difficult job. A goalie must move quickly to all parts of the penalty area to stop shots or take the ball from an opponent. After stopping a shot, a good goalkeeper controls the ball and starts an attack by kicking or throwing the ball to a teammate. The goalie is the only player who may touch the ball with the hands or arms.

The Officials. A referee and two linesmen officiate international games and games in the North American Soccer League (NASL). In high school and college games in the United States, two referees or a referee and two linesmen may be used. The referee serves as the timekeeper and enforces the rules. This official decides all disputes and may put a player out of the game for repeated fouling. The linesmen determine which team gets possession of the ball after it goes out of bounds. The linesmen also notify the referee when they see a player commit a foul.

How Soccer Is Played

Soccer games played according to international rules are divided into two 45-minute halves, with a brief rest period between halves. College games in the United States also consist of two 45-minute periods. Leagues of younger teams adjust the length of games according to the physical abilities of the players.

In some leagues, the teams play an overtime period

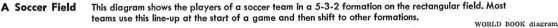

A Soccer Field This diagram shows the players of a soccer team in a 5-3-2 formation on the rectangular field. Most teams use this line-up at the start of a game and then shift to other formations.

WORLD BOOK diagram

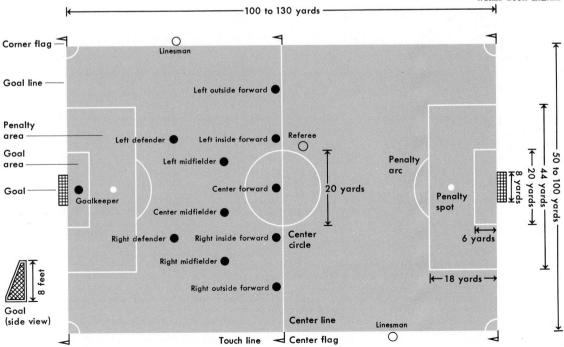

if the score is tied at the end of regulation time. If the teams are still tied after the overtime, each may shoot a series of *penalty kicks* at the goal. The team that scores the most goals wins. In the NASL, a *sudden death overtime* decides tie games. The first team to score in the overtime wins. If neither team scores, a *tie-breaker*, which consists of a series of penalty kicks, determines the winner.

Starting the Game. A soccer game begins with a *kickoff* in the center of the field. The opposing captains flip a coin to decide which team will kick off. The other team kicks off to start the second half, when the teams change goals. After a goal, play resumes with a kickoff by the team scored upon.

The kickoff takes place on the *center spot*, a point in the middle of the halfway line. The players line up in their half of the field. No player on the defensive team can enter the center circle until play has started. To start play, the kicking team must move the ball forward at least the distance of its circumference. The player who kicks off may not touch the ball again until another player has touched it.

The Ball in Play. After the kickoff, the ball remains in play unless it completely crosses a goal line or a touch line. There are no time outs in soccer unless the referee calls one after a player has been injured.

The attacking team tries to advance the ball into the opposing team's territory. The attackers then try to pass the ball to a player who is in a good position to score a goal. A player may kick or hit the ball into the goal with any part of the body except the hands and arms.

The defending players constantly shift their positions to break up attacks. They try to cover their opponents, intercept passes, and take the ball away. Hard body contact is permitted only when it results from an attempt to kick the ball or hit it with the head.

Restarts. If the ball goes out of bounds, play is restarted with a *corner kick*, a *goal kick*, or a *throw-in*. The referee, assisted by the linesmen, decides which type of restart is used.

If the ball crosses the goal line without going into the goal, play resumes with either a corner kick or a goal kick. A corner kick, which is made by an offensive player, takes place if a member of the defensive team touched the ball last. The offensive player kicks the ball from the nearest corner of the field. A goal kick occurs if an offensive player touched the ball last. A defensive player restarts play with a kick from inside the goal area nearest the point where the ball went out. The ball must go beyond the penalty area before it can be touched again.

A throw-in takes place if a player knocks the ball over a touch line. An opposing player throws the ball back into play. The thrower must have both feet on the ground, either on the touch line or outside the playing area. The throw must be made with both hands from above the head.

Fouls. A player who repeatedly commits fouls may be put out of the game by the referee. No substitute is allowed for such a player. After most fouls, the referee awards a free kick to the other team. This kick may be a *penalty kick*, a *direct free kick*, or an *indirect free kick*.

A penalty kick is awarded if the defending team commits one of nine fouls within its penalty area. These fouls are (1) deliberately kicking or attempting to kick an opponent, (2) tripping an opponent, (3) jumping so as to endanger another player while trying to get the ball, (4) violently running into an opponent, (5) running into an opponent from behind, (6) striking an opponent, (7) holding an opponent, (8) pushing an opponent, or (9) deliberately touching the ball with the hands or arms. The opposing team takes the kick from the *penalty spot*, which is 12 yards (11 meters) directly in front of the goal. All the players, except the kicker and the opposing goalie, must be outside the penalty area when the kick is made.

A direct free kick may be awarded for one of the nine fouls committed anywhere on the field. This kick is taken toward the opposing team's goal from the point where the foul occurred. Opponents must be at least 10 yards (9 meters) from the ball when it is kicked, but they can try to block it.

An indirect free kick is awarded for dangerous play, such as (1) kicking the ball when the goalkeeper is holding it, (2) *obstructing* (blocking) an opponent, (3) pushing an opponent when the ball is not nearby, or (4) unsportsmanlike conduct. The kicker kicks the ball toward the opposing team's goal, but it must touch at least one other player before entering the goal. All opponents must be at least 10 yards (9 meters) from the ball, but they can attempt to block it.

The referee also awards an indirect free kick if a player is *offside*. Generally, an attacking player is offside when between the ball and the goal line in the opponent's half of the field. However, the player is not offside if (1) two opponents were closer to their

Soccer Terms

Center means to pass the ball into the penalty area from near a touchline.

Charge is the legal use of the shoulder to push an opponent off balance.

Dribbling means to move the ball while running by nudging it along with the feet.

Drop Ball is a way of restarting play after the game has been stopped for a reason other than a foul, such as an injury. The referee drops the ball to the ground between two opposing players.

Half-Volley is a kick made just as the ball bounces off the ground.

Hands is a rule violation that occurs when a player deliberately touches the ball with the hands or arms.

Marking means guarding an opponent.

Obstruction is a violation that occurs when a player deliberately runs or stands in an opponent's path.

Overlap occurs when a defender moves far down the field past an offensive forward to help the attack.

Save occurs when the goalkeeper or another player prevents the ball from going into the goal.

Screen means to maintain control of the ball by keeping the body between the ball and an opponent.

Tackle means using the feet or shoulder to take the ball from an opponent.

Trap occurs when a player uses the feet, thighs, or chest to stop the ball and gain control of it.

Volley is a kick made while the ball is in the air.

Some Soccer Skills Soccer players must control the ball without using their hands. Players use their feet, head, legs, and chest to advance the ball or to pass it to a teammate. Defensive players use their feet to kick or hook the ball from an opponent, a maneuver called *tackling*.

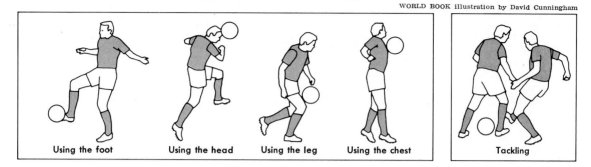

Using the foot   Using the head   Using the leg   Using the chest   Tackling

goal line than the player was, (2) the player moved between the ball and the goal line after a teammate kicked the ball, (3) the ball touched an opponent, or (4) the player received the ball from a corner kick, a goal kick, a throw-in, or a *dropped ball*. The *Soccer Terms* table with this article defines a dropped ball.

Soccer Skills

Soccer requires a variety of skills. They include (1) kicking, (2) passing, (3) heading, (4) dribbling and faking, and (5) tackling.

Kicking is the most important skill in soccer. It involves kicks that attempt to score a goal, put the ball in play, or put the ball into a particular area of the field. A good player can kick the ball accurately in many ways with either foot.

In most cases, kicking the ball with the instep is the most effective method. A player can control the accuracy, distance, and power of a kick better with the instep than in any other way. In certain situations, however, a player might use the outer or inner side of the foot or even the heel.

Soccer players generally try to kick the ball so that it travels just above the field. Players put their non-kicking foot next to the ball. They keep their head down and their eyes on the ball. Then they swing their kicking leg with the toes pointed downward and kick the ball squarely with the instep. After the foot hits the ball, the leg should straighten and continue to move forward. This action makes the ball travel in the right direction and keeps it low.

A player often stops the ball before kicking it. Kicking a moving ball lessens the player's control over the direction of the kick.

Passing the ball among teammates enables a team to move it into scoring position and keep it from the opposition. A player tries to pass the ball so that it travels just above or on the ground. Occasionally, the ball may have to be kicked over the head of a defending player. Short passes generally are more effective than long ones, which give opposing players additional time to intercept the ball.

Heading means hitting the ball with the head. It sometimes is the only legal way a player can reach

Offensive Plays are designed to move the ball into scoring position. The diagrams above show how teamwork and ball control can lead to a goal. By moving the ball quickly, the offensive team pulls the defense out of position, setting up a good shot at the goal. In the diagram on the left, Player 1 near the goal line kicks the ball to Player 2 in the penalty area. Player 2 hits the ball with his head, passing it to Player 3. This player stops the ball with his chest and kicks it to Player 4, who scores a goal. The diagram on the right illustrates an *indirect free kick,* which is awarded after certain violations by the opposing team. A player puts the ball in play by passing to a teammate, who kicks it over the defenders and out of reach of the goalkeeper.

448c

Some Referee Signals The referee enforces the rules during a soccer game. This official stops play after a violation or an injury and uses a hand signal to indicate how the action will resume. The referee holds up a colored card to warn or expel a player for repeated fouling or for unsportsmanlike conduct.

Penalty kick   Direct free kick   Indirect free kick   Goal kick   Corner kick   Warning or expulsion

the ball in the air. A player may use the head to pass the ball, intercept an opponent's pass, or shoot the ball at the goal. Good players can head the ball long distances with great power and accuracy.

When heading, a player jumps up, snaps the head forward, and hits the ball with the forehead. If the ball is hit with the top or back of the head, the impact may stun the player.

Dribbling enables players to keep possession of the ball while running. While dribbling, a player can pass or shoot the ball if an opponent threatens to take it away. Faking makes dribbling more effective. A player may fool an opponent by faking a pass or a shot and then continuing to dribble. Opponents also may be fooled by faking a dribble in one direction and then dribbling in another.

Tackling involves using the feet to kick or hook the ball from an opponent. An ideal tackle involves little or no body contact and leaves the defending player or a teammate in control of the ball. In a *sliding tackle*, a player slides along the ground with one leg extended and takes the ball from an opponent.

Soccer Competition

Soccer is played on several levels throughout the world. Professional teams provide the most popular competition in many countries. Semiprofessional teams compete for pay, but they play only on a part-time basis. Amateur athletes play in interclub soccer competition and receive no pay. Many colleges and high schools include soccer as part of their athletic program.

The Fédération Internationale de Football Association (FIFA) governs soccer in all parts of the world. It consists of the national soccer associations of more than 140 countries. These associations include the United States Soccer Federation (USSF) and the Canadian Soccer Association. Most soccer games, including those in the United States and Canada, are played according to international rules established by the FIFA.

In North America. Two major professional soccer leagues have teams in the United States—the North American Soccer League (NASL) and the Major Indoor Soccer League (MISL). The NASL is made up of 12 teams that play in cities in the United States and Canada. The MISL has teams that play in 14 United States cities. There are also a large number of semiprofessional

and amateur soccer leagues that compete in the United States and Canada.

The USSF holds national and international tournaments. It also sponsors teams that represent the United States in international competition, including the World Cup Championship. In addition, the USSF sponsors a national team for players 16 years old or younger. The United States Youth Soccer Association, a division of the USSF, conducts national, state, and regional championships for youths. The American Youth Soccer Organization, an independent group, holds regional championships and sponsors teams that play foreign teams.

The Canadian Soccer Association holds national and international tournaments. It also conducts national, provincial, and regional championships and sponsors teams that represent Canada in international competition.

In Europe and Latin America. A number of countries in Europe and Latin America have professional or semiprofessional soccer leagues. These leagues consist of a number of divisions for teams of varying ability. At the end of the season, two or three teams from each division may move into a stronger or weaker division, depending on their record. The winner of the top division is the country's national champion.

International Competition includes the World Cup Championship, held every four years. In this tournament, 24 nations compete for the world's championship. All member nations of the FIFA may compete in qualifying rounds held two years before the championship. These rounds determine which 22 teams will join the host nation and the previous champion in the final rounds.

North American Soccer League

Eastern Division

Chicago Sting	New York Cosmos
Montreal Manic	Toronto Blizzard

Southern Division

Fort Lauderdale Strikers	Team America
Tampa Bay Rowdies	Tulsa Roughnecks

Western Division

Golden Bay Earthquakes	Seattle Sounders
San Diego Sockers	Vancouver Whitecaps

1930	Uruguay 4, Argentina 2	(in Montevideo)
1934	Italy 2, Czechoslovakia 1	(in Rome)
1938	Italy 4, Hungary 2	(in Paris)
1950	Uruguay 2, Brazil 1	(in Rio de Janeiro)
1954	West Germany 3, Hungary 2	(in Bern)
1958	Brazil 5, Sweden 2	(in Stockholm)
1962	Brazil 3, Czechoslovakia 1	(in Santiago, Chile)
1966	England 4, West Germany 2	(in London)
1970	Brazil 4, Italy 1	(in Mexico City)
1974	West Germany 2, The Netherlands 1	(in Munich)
1978	Argentina 3, The Netherlands 1	(in Buenos Aires)
1982	Italy 3, West Germany 1	(in Madrid)

Teams from European nations compete annually for three major championships—the Cup Winner's Cup, the European Cup, and the Union of European Football Associations Cup. The European Super Cup Championship matches the winners of the Cup Winner's Cup and the European Cup. Teams representing 10 South American countries compete yearly for the Copa Libertadores. Teams from nations of North America and northern South America play annually for the Champion of Champions Cup. The winners of these two championships play for the Copa Interamericana. Soccer is also an event of the Summer Olympic Games.

History

A game similar to soccer was probably played in China as early as 400 B.C. In the A.D. 200's, the Romans played a game in which two teams tried to score by advancing the ball across a line on the field. The players passed the ball to one another but did not kick it. London children of the 1100's played a form of soccer in the streets.

During the early 1800's, many English schools played a game that resembled soccer. The players added many rules that changed the game as it developed, but each school interpreted the rules differently. In 1848, an association of school representatives met at Trinity College in Cambridge and drew up the first set of soccer rules. In 1863, representatives of English soccer clubs founded the Football Association.

The Newberry Library, Chicago

Soccer Became Popular in England during the late 1800's. Before the construction of large stadiums in the 1900's, crowds of spectators stood along the sidelines.

Soccer began to spread throughout the world in the late 1800's. By 1900, associations had been established in Belgium, Chile, Denmark, Italy, The Netherlands, and Switzerland. In 1904, the national associations founded the Fédération Internationale de Football Association. The Canadian Soccer Association was established in 1912, and the United States Soccer Federation was set up in 1913. In 1930, the first World Cup Championship was played in Montevideo, Uruguay. Since then, the World Cup has been held every four years except during World War II (1939-1945), when the games were suspended.

The first professional soccer league in the United States, the American Soccer League, was formed in 1921 but disbanded in 1929. The present American Soccer League was founded in 1931. The North American Soccer League was established in 1967. During the 1970's, soccer in the United States grew tremendously as a spectator and participant sport.   RICHARD ROTTKOV

See also CHILE (picture); LONDON (Recreation); PELÉ.

Outline

I. The Field Equipment
A. The Field   B. The Ball   C. The Uniform
II. Players and Officials
A. The Forwards   D. The Goalkeeper
B. The Midfielders   E. The Officials
C. The Defenders
III. How Soccer Is Played
A. Starting the Game   C. Restarts
B. The Ball in Play   D. Fouls
IV. Soccer Skills
A. Kicking   C. Heading   E. Tackling
B. Passing   D. Dribbling
V. Soccer Competition
A. In North America   C. International
B. In Europe and Latin   Competition
    America
VI. History

Questions

How is a soccer game restarted if the ball goes out of bounds?

What is the World Cup Championship?

What is a 4-2-4 formation? A 4-3-3?

What organization governs soccer throughout the world?

When does the referee award a *penalty kick*?

What is the most important skill in soccer?

What is a *sweeper*?

How many substitutions can a team make under international soccer rules?

What is *dribbling*? *Tackling*?

When can a player come into contact with the opposing goalkeeper in the goal area?

Additional Resources

CASCIO, CHUCK. *Soccer U.S.A.* Luce, 1975.
DIAGRAM GROUP. *Enjoying Soccer.* Paddington, 1977. A basic handbook for beginners.
ROTE, KYLE, and KANE, BASIL. *Kyle Rote, Jr.'s Complete Book of Soccer.* Simon & Schuster, 1978.
YANNIS, ALEX. *Inside Soccer: The Complete Book of Soccer for Spectators, Players, and Coaches.* McGraw, 1980.

SOCHE, *swah chuh,* also called Yarkand, *yahr KAND* (pop. 10,000 to 50,000), is a trading center in southwestern Sinkiang, an autonomous region of China. It lies about 700 miles (1,100 kilometers) north of New Delhi,

SOCIAL CHANGE

India (see CHINA [political map]). The city has been a station on Asian trade routes since ancient times. It produces carpets, embroideries, cotton, silk, and wool.

SOCIAL CHANGE refers to any significant change in the structure of society. Short-lived changes, such as changes in the employment rate, do not produce social change. Nor do fads, fashions, or temporary changes in ideas and behavior. The election of a new president is not social change. But replacement of the presidency with a dictatorship changes the structure of government and is thus a social change. Most sociologists recognize four main types of social change.

One type of social change involves changes in the number and variety of positions and social roles. When we say that an industrial society is more complex than a peasant society, we mean that it has many new and specialized jobs, such as computer programming, conducting cancer research, and piloting a spacecraft.

A second kind of change occurs in the obligations or duties attached to positions. For example, parents are no longer responsible for educating their children. They give this job to teachers and schools.

These two types of change lead to a third type—new ways of organizing social activities. The establishment of kindergartens occurred partly because the children of working mothers needed care. Other educational changes took place in response to occupational needs. For example, community, or junior, colleges were established for advanced—but not university-level—education.

A fourth kind of social change involves the redistribution of facilities and rewards, such as power, education, income, and respect. In 1950, for example, about half the people in the United States with substandard incomes were nonwhites. Today, about a third of the nation's poor are nonwhites.

Sometimes societies evolve gradually. At other times, they change abruptly, as in times of revolution. Change can result from planning, or it can be unintentional. Every society changes, but not all change at the same rate or in the same direction. Revolutionary change is often accompanied by violence.

Most changes benefit some people more than they benefit others, and they may penalize some people. For this reason, some resistance to change is inevitable. Many social changes have had both beneficial and undesirable consequences.

As change improves conditions, people's expectations grow. They become dissatisfied with current achievements and demand more. Sometimes they demand changes in the law. But when people believe that their grievances cannot be corrected within the system, they call for more radical change—for revolution.

For centuries, people have sought simple explanations for change, often emphasizing single factors. The German social philosopher Karl Marx claimed that the economy is the prime source of social change. Today, scholars believe that such explanations do not account for the complicated events of social change. Many sociologists think that societies are systems. Change in one part of a society, they believe, leads to change in other parts, with no one part having priority. For example, the automobile—a product of technological change—created changes in where people live and in their leisure activities.   HARRIET ZUCKERMAN

See also CULTURAL LAG; CULTURE (How Culture Changes); SOCIAL ROLE; SOCIOLOGY (Social Change).

SOCIAL CLASS is a group of persons in a society that have about the same social standing. Social classes exist because people usually classify one another into more or less distinct groups based on such factors as wealth, power, prestige, ancestry, religion, and occupation. Often, people rank these groups in their minds, considering some "better" than others. Social scientists call the groups *social classes* and describe the process of social ranking as *social stratification*.

All societies seem to have some system of social stratification. That is, there are no "classless" societies. In the United States and other Western democracies, the class system is usually informal, and social scientists disagree on how to classify the groups that seem to exist. Some arbitrarily divide the American people into three classes—upper, middle, and lower. Other social scientists add a fourth class—the working class—between the middle and lower groups, while others substitute the term *working class* for *lower class*.

In the late 1940's, social anthropologist W. Lloyd Warner identified six social classes in a New England community he studied. He called them (1) upper-upper class, (2) lower-upper class, (3) upper-middle class, (4) lower-middle class, (5) upper-lower class, and (6) lower-lower class. The characteristics of each group are described in *Yankee City Series*. Although some sociologists disagree with Warner, his classifications have been widely used by scholars and the public.

In most Western democracies, persons can move from one category to another and there are few clear-cut signs as to which group a person belongs. But in some societies, people are born into a certain social class, and change to another class is difficult if not impossible. A class with such rigid barriers is called a *caste*. A person belongs to the caste of his or her parents. Laws and traditions severely limit the social contacts they may have with members of other castes. India has a more firmly established caste system than any other country. See CASTE; INDIA (Hinduism).

Communism has long had the goal of achieving a "classless" society without distinctions based on rank or birth. But in the Soviet Union and other Communist countries—just as in the non-Communist world—some groups of persons, such as government officials, have much more power, wealth, and prestige than others. See COMMUNISM (Marxism); RUSSIA (Way of Life).

How Persons Are Ranked. Various methods are used to compare and rank individuals and groups. A social scientist may use such objective measures as how much money a person earns. Or members of a group may rank one another, or place themselves on the class ladder. Surveys show that the way persons rank themselves depends on the categories that are used. If they are told to place themselves in either the upper, middle, or lower class, most place themselves in the middle class. But when the working-class category is included, the majority rank themselves in that class. Almost all are unwilling to say they belong to the lower class.

Occupation is one of the best indicators of class, because people tend to agree on the relative prestige they attach to similar jobs. Those at or near the top rung of the prestige ladder usually have the highest incomes, the best education, and the most power. In general, persons who hold positions of leadership and responsibility—such as heads of government and industry—rank at the top. Persons whose jobs require long training and superior intelligence—such as physicians, scientists, college professors, and university-trained professional people—rank next in order of prestige. Persons with low-paying positions that require little training or formal education—such as unskilled laborers—rate at the bottom. People in both capitalist and Communist countries, as well as those in both economically developed and developing countries, rank these jobs almost exactly the same way.

Class Differences. Social status affects a person's behavior, values, and style of life. Upper-class members, for example, are aware of their privileged position and try to preserve it by encouraging marriage within their own class. Persons with higher status usually back conservative political parties and candidates, because they wish to maintain the existing system of inequality. Socially, the upper class is noted for its elegant and refined style of living.

Most members of the middle class enjoy a better-than-average education and standard of living. Middle-class values are usually the dominant values in a society. In the United States, the middle class stresses thrift, self-improvement, and economic success and job advancement. Members of this group believe it is important to own property and to conform to the community's standards on morality and respectability. Generally, they send their children to college, and they are prominent in civic and governmental affairs.

Members of the lower class usually have less formal education and training than those of the middle- and upper-classes, and have unskilled or semiskilled jobs. Because many lower-class members live in poverty or near-poverty, they are more concerned with immediate needs than with long-range goals.

Why Social Classes Exist. Most sociologists who study stratification believe a society must have a system of rewards to encourage some people to undertake the key jobs. Persons who hold these positions usually need much education and training, and often work under great strain. For persons to seek out and work efficiently in such socially crucial occupations, society must see that they are well rewarded. Therefore, these sociologists argue, stratification and unequal reward are necessary for a division of labor with some persons taking greater responsibility than others.

A group of sociologists influenced by the teachings of Karl Marx rejects this interpretation. This group argues that differing rewards are due to variations in power positions. For example, the people who control the resources that people value or who control the police or other instruments of force have the highest income and status. This group suggests that stratification exists in any social organization that involves a chain of command.   SEYMOUR MARTIN LIPSET

See also MIDDLE CLASS; ECONOMIC DETERMINISM.

Additional Resources

BENDIX, REINHARD, and LIPSET, S. M., eds. *Class Status and Power: A Reader in Social Stratification.* Rev. ed. Macmillan, 1966.

BROOM, LEONARD, and others, eds. *The Inheritance of Inequality.* Routledge & Kegan, 1980.
DUBERMAN, LUCILE. *Social Inequality: Classes and Caste in America.* Harper, 1976.
RAINWATER, LEE, and COLEMAN, RICHARD. *Social Standing in America: New Dimensions of Class.* Basic Books, 1978.

SOCIAL CREDIT PARTY. See ALBERTA (History).

SOCIAL DARWINISM is the belief that people in society compete for survival and that superior individuals become powerful and wealthy. Social Darwinism applies Charles R. Darwin's theory of evolution to the development of human society.

Darwin, a British naturalist, published his theory of evolution in 1859 in the book *The Origin of Species* (see EVOLUTION [Darwin's Theory]). Social Darwinism developed as an important social theory during the late 1800's, but it rapidly lost influence in the 1900's. Darwin did not advance or support the social theory, though his name was associated with it.

Social Darwinism tries to explain the differences in achievement and wealth among people. According to the theory, individuals must compete with one another to survive. The principles of *natural selection* favor the survival of the fittest members of society. Such people adapt successfully to the environment, but unfit individuals fail to do so.

Social Darwinism applies the principles of natural selection to *capitalism*, an economic system in which individuals or companies own and control the means of production. Social Darwinists regard capitalism as the natural environment in which people compete for survival. The theory explains and justifies the unequal distribution of wealth and the existence of social classes.

Social Darwinists believe that people best able to survive demonstrate their fitness by accumulating property, wealth, and social status. According to the theory, poverty proves an individual's unfitness or laziness. Some social Darwinists oppose charity and welfare programs because they believe these programs interfere with the laws of nature. Progress can result only from the elimination of the weak members of society and the survival of the strong members.

Herbert Spencer, a British philosopher, first proposed the theory of social Darwinism in the late 1800's. William Graham Sumner, an American sociologist, helped make the theory of social Darwinism popular in the United States.   ALAN P. GRIMES

See also SUMNER, WILLIAM G.

Additional Resources

BARKER, ERNEST. *Political Thought in England, 1848-1914.* 2nd ed. Greenwood, 1980. Reprint of 1928 ed.
HOFSTADTER, RICHARD. *Social Darwinism in American Thought.* Rev. ed. Braziller, 1959.
JONES, GRETA. *Social Darwinism and English Thought: The Interaction Between Biological and Social Theory.* Humanities, 1981.
WILTSHIRE, DAVID. *The Social and Political Thought of Herbert Spencer.* Oxford, 1978.

SOCIAL DEMOCRACY. See DEMOCRACY (Preserving Human Rights).

SOCIAL INSECTS. See ANIMAL (Animals That Live Together); ANT (Life in an Ant Colony); BEE (The Honeybee Colony; Kinds of Bees); TERMITE; WASP.

SOCIAL LEGISLATION. See CHILD LABOR; HOUSING; LABOR MOVEMENT; SOCIAL SECURITY; WOMAN (In the United States and Canada); MEDICAID; MEDICARE.

SOCIAL PSYCHOLOGY is the study of the psychological basis of people's relationships with one another. Social psychologists investigate such processes as communication, cooperation, competition, decision making, leadership, and changes in attitude.

Like other scientists, social psychologists begin their research by developing theories. They then collect evidence to support their theories. For example, the American social psychologist Leon Festinger developed a theory that people become uneasy when they learn new information that conflicts with what they already believe. He suggested that people would do much to avoid this uneasiness, which he called *cognitive dissonance*. To demonstrate Festinger's theory, researchers collected data showing that people who believe they are failures often avoid success, even when they can easily achieve it. Success would conflict with their belief in themselves as failures.

Social psychologists often support their theories through experiments. For example, one study investigated how people's opinions of an essay were affected by the supposed sex of the author. People who believed the writer was a man had a higher opinion of the essay than those who thought the author was a woman. Social psychologists also use other sources of information, including public opinion surveys, recorded observations of behavior, and statistics from government agencies.

Many social psychologists teach and conduct research at colleges and universities. Others work for government agencies, business firms, or other organizations. They may help plan personnel programs or measure the potential sale of new products.

The first textbooks on social psychology were published in the early 1900's. Modern social psychology owes much to the behavioral psychologists of the 1930's, who called for the scientific study of observable behavior. Today, social psychology continues to stress the precise measurement of people's actions.

Another major influence on social psychology was the work of George Herbert Mead and Kurt Lewin. Mead, an American psychologist and philosopher, argued that people's ideas about themselves are developed through social contact. Lewin, a German-born psychologist, investigated how individuals in groups are affected by other members. Both Mead and Lewin claimed that behavior depends primarily on how people interpret the social world. The work of these early researchers continues to influence social psychologists, who study people's perception of themselves and others.   KENNETH J. GERGEN

Related Articles in WORLD BOOK include:

Alienation	Psychology
Group Dynamics	Social Role
Morale	Sociology (Social Behavior)

Additional Resources

ALLEN, BEM P. *Social Behavior: Facts and Falsehoods*. Nelson, 1978.
ARONSON, ELLIOT. *The Social Animal*. 3rd ed. Freeman, 1980. *Readings About the Social Animal*. 3rd ed. 1981.
BERNE, ERIC. *Games People Play: The Psychology of Human Relationships*. Grove, 1964.
RAVEN, BERTRAM H., and RUBEN, J. Z. *Social Psychology: People in Groups*. Wiley, 1976.

SOCIAL ROLE is a set of relationships between a person and members of his or her circle. People's behavior in social roles makes possible the life of a society and its members. For example, an individual in the role of hospital patient follows a physician's instructions and cooperates with the hospital staff. In return, the patient receives food, medicine, and other care from a number of people.

Social roles are learned from a culture, which defines how they should be performed. They are not instinctive. People learn many roles during childhood by observing their parents and other adults. Some roles, such as those of patient or student, are learned by almost all members of a society. Other roles, such as those of physician or teacher, require specialized training.

Because social roles are learned, they differ among different cultures. For example, the major roles of women in some societies are wife and mother. But other societies offer women many roles from which to choose.

Every person occupies many social roles during his or her lifetime. A woman may be a daughter to her parents, a wife to her husband, a mother to her children, and a worker to her employer. Problems may result if the demands of one role interfere with those of another. This situation is called *role conflict*. For example, an employee might need to work overtime to advance his or her career. But such work is likely to conflict with the person's role as a parent.   HELENA ZNANIECKA LOPATA

See also BEHAVIOR; PERSONALITY; SEX (Sex Roles); SOCIAL PSYCHOLOGY.

SOCIAL SCIENCE. Scholars generally identify three categories of knowledge: (1) the natural sciences and mathematics, (2) the humanities, and (3) the social sciences. The natural sciences concern nature and the physical world. The humanities try to interpret the meaning of life on earth rather than to describe the physical world or society. The social sciences focus on our life with other people in groups. They include anthropology, economics, history, political science, sociology, criminology, and the science of law. Some scholars also regard education, ethics, philosophy, and psychology as social sciences. Certain studies in other fields, such as biology, geography, medicine, art, and linguistics, may be said to fall within the broad category of the social sciences.

Relationship to Natural Sciences. Scholars in the social sciences have developed certain ways of studying people and their institutions. Generally these scholars have borrowed from the natural sciences the methods they use to study, simplify, and classify the observed behavior of human society. Their observations of the regularity of human behavior lead them to form *hypotheses* (propositions) and then to test the validity of these hypotheses.

The social sciences are still a comparatively new field of learning. History and geography have existed as separate disciplines for a long time. But attempts to organize human endeavors into systems of economics, sociology, and political science are so new that many scholars doubt that the scientific method can be used with complete success to know and control any aspect of society. They see a wide gulf between the clear and exact nature of the natural sciences and the inexact nature of the social sciences. One of the most powerful tools of the natural sciences is the controlled experiment. Such a method is difficult to use in experiments involving human beings.

Relationship to Humanities. The interdependence of the social sciences and the humanities is important. In a social science, the scholar must note the underlying values of a society, which are stated by the scholars of the humanities. For instance, suppose a political scientist wishes to determine scientifically whether a particular community should have an authoritarian or a representative form of political organization and control. The scholar must first learn the importance the community attaches to such values as the right of the individual to differ with authority, or to have a voice in policy and laws. Then the principles that govern its political action can be formulated.   PAUL R. HANNA

Related Articles in WORLD BOOK include:

Anthropology	History
Archaeology	Law
Civics	Linguistics
Criminology	Philosophy
Economics	Political Science
Education	Psychology
Ethics	Social Psychology
Geography	Social Studies
Geopolitics	Sociology
Government	

SOCIAL SECURITY is a government program that helps workers and retired workers and their families achieve a degree of economic security. Social security, also called *social insurance*, provides cash payments to help replace income lost as a result of retirement, unemployment, disability, or death. The program also helps pay the cost of medical care for people age 65 or older and for some disabled workers. About 36 million Americans—about one in seven persons—receive social security benefits.

People become eligible to receive benefits by working a certain period in a job covered by social security. Employers and workers finance the program through payroll taxes. Participation in the social security system is required for more than 90 per cent of U.S. workers.

Social security differs from *public assistance*. Social security pays benefits to individuals—and their families—who have earned them by working and paying social security taxes. Public assistance, or welfare, aids the needy, regardless of their work records. The government finances public assistance through general taxes. For more information about public assistance programs, see WELFARE.

All industrialized countries as well as many developing nations have a social security system. The Social Security Act of 1935 established the program in the United States. Today, this program has three main parts: (1) old-age, survivors, disability, and health insurance; (2) unemployment insurance; and (3) workers' compensation. Social security began in Canada in 1940. This article deals chiefly with social security systems in the United States and Canada.

Old-Age, Survivors, Disability, and Health Insurance

Coverage. Old-age, survivors, disability, and health insurance (OASDHI) covers over 90 per cent of the workers in the United States, including nearly all workers in private industry and most public employees. The

program does not cover about a third of all state and municipal employees. Other workers not covered include railroad workers, self-employed people who earn less than $400 a year, and some foreign workers who have been admitted temporarily to the United States. The railroad workers and most of the others who are not covered by social security contribute to other retirement and disability funds.

Administration. The federal government administers old-age, survivors, and disability insurance through the Social Security Administration. Health insurance, commonly called *Medicare*, is managed by the Health Care Financing Administration. The Social Security Administration and the Health Care Financing Administration are both agencies of the United States Department of Health and Human Services.

Workers in jobs covered by social security must have a social security card. Each card has a number that enables the Social Security Administration to keep a record of the social security taxes paid by each worker. Any United States citizen may apply for a social security card at a district social security office. Applicants must present proof of age and citizenship.

Old-Age, Survivors, and Disability Insurance (OASDI) forms the foundation of the U.S. social security system. It provides protection for more than 90 per cent of the nation's workers.

Eligibility. Workers or their families become eligible to receive retirement or survivors benefits after the workers earn a specified amount of *work credit* in jobs covered by social security. Work credit is measured in units called *quarters of coverage*. Workers receive a quarter of coverage for every $340 of covered annual earnings, regardless of when during the year they earn that amount. However, workers may receive only four quarters of coverage each year, no matter how much money they earn.

To qualify for benefits, workers must be *fully insured* or *currently insured*. Fully insured workers are those who have earned 40 quarters of coverage. Workers who will reach age 62 before 1991 may become fully insured by earning fewer quarters of coverage, depending on their age. Fully insured workers are entitled to complete old-age, survivors, disability, and health coverage. Currently insured workers are those who have earned at least six quarters of coverage during the 13 quarters before their death or the minimum retirement age. Such workers only qualify for limited survivors coverage.

Workers who become disabled before age 31 may collect disability benefits if they have earned work credit for half the time between their 21st birthday and the time they became disabled. For example, a worker who becomes disabled at age 24 must have $1\frac{1}{2}$ years of work credit to collect benefits. Workers disabled between ages 31 and 42 generally need at least five years of work credit during the 10-year period before they became disabled. Workers disabled at age 43 or older need more than five years of work credit to qualify for benefits.

Benefits. To collect benefits, retired or disabled workers or their survivors must file a claim at a district office of the Social Security Administration. Benefits are paid monthly, except for lump-sum death payments.

Insured workers may collect full retirement benefits if they are 65 or older and their annual earnings do not

U.S. Social Security Programs

This chart shows major social security programs, how they are financed, and the agencies that administer them. The programs pay benefits to individuals—and their families—who have worked and paid taxes for social insurance. Most benefits are based on a worker's average earnings.

David Cunningham

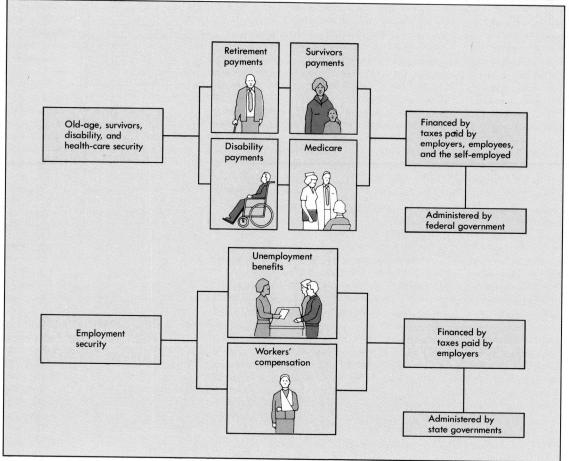

exceed $6,600. At age 70, workers become eligible for full retirement benefits regardless of their income.

Beginning in 2003, the retirement age will increase gradually from 65 to 67. It will rise by two months a year to age 66 by 2009 and then to age 67 by 2027.

Workers also may collect retirement benefits as early as age 62. However, such workers receive a permanently reduced benefit. The amount of the reduction depends on their age at retirement. For example, workers who retire at age 62 collect about 80 per cent of the amount they would have received on retiring at age 65. Beneficiaries ages 62 to 65 may earn no more than $4,920 annually. They lose $1 in benefits for every $2 they earn above that limit.

Starting in 1990, benefits will be reduced $1 for every $3 of income above the base. Workers who retire at age 62 by 2009 will collect about 75 per cent of full benefits, and those who retire at age 62 in 2027 will get about 70 per cent of full benefits.

To collect disability benefits, workers must have a severe physical or mental condition. Such a condition must have lasted at least 12 months or must be expected either to last that long or to result in death. However,

disabled workers must wait five months before they can collect payments.

Social security also provides benefits to the families of retired or disabled workers. A worker's dependent spouse may collect full retirement benefits at age 65 or reduced benefits at age 62. A dependent spouse's benefit equals about 50 per cent of the worker's benefit. Additional benefits are paid to the child of a retired or disabled worker if the child is under 18 and unmarried or is over 18, unmarried, and disabled. However, the child must have become disabled before age 22. A dependent spouse under age 62 may also claim benefits if he or she is caring for such a child. A divorced wife may collect benefits based on her former husband's work record if the marriage lasted 10 years.

When an insured worker dies—either before or after retirement—the worker's dependents may be eligible for a monthly survivors benefit. Payments may be made to a surviving spouse age 60 or older, a surviving unmarried child age 18 or under, or a surviving, disabled, unmarried child age 18 or older who became disabled before age 22. Benefits also may go to a surviving disabled spouse, dependent parents age 62 or older, or a surviving spouse under 62 who is caring for either a disabled child under age 18 or a child under 18 who is collecting benefits. Payments are based on the benefits the worker was receiving at the time of death, or would have received at retirement. In addition, the spouse or child receives a single payment of $255 on the death of the worker.

How Benefits Are Figured. The amount workers receive in OASDI benefits depends on their average lifetime earnings in jobs covered by social security. A worker who has paid the maximum in social security taxes receives a larger benefit than a worker who has paid less. This principle of fair rate of return to each worker is known as the *individual equity goal* of social insurance. However, covered workers with low lifetime earnings collect benefits that are greater in proportion to their contributions than the benefits collected by workers with high lifetime earnings.

Originally, planners expected social security to pay each worker at least as much in benefits as he or she had contributed in taxes. But as the social security system grew, it also began to operate on the *principle of social adequacy*. This principle measures benefits against a minimum standard of living as well as lifetime earnings. Thus, benefits paid to some low-income workers exceed those to which such workers would be entitled if benefits were calculated only on their earnings record. In addition, all people eligible to receive retirement benefits collect a minimum payment, regardless of their earnings. About 70 per cent of the minimum benefits go to elderly women.

When calculating OASDI benefits, the government *wage-indexes* the worker's covered earnings—that is, it adjusts the person's earnings to reflect the rise in wages over his or her working lifetime. The government also automatically adjusts benefits to reflect increases in the cost of living. Benefits increase each year in which the cost of living rises 3 per cent or more. In addition, people who work beyond age 65 without claiming benefits collect a bonus. This bonus provides 3 per cent more in benefits for each year between ages 65 and 72 that such workers did not claim benefits. Between 1990 and 2009, the bonus will increase gradually from 3 per cent to 8 per cent.

Medicare is a program for people age 65 or older and for people under 65 who have received disability benefits for at least two years. It also covers insured workers and their dependents who suffer from chronic kidney disease. Medicare consists of hospital insurance and supplementary medical insurance.

Hospital Insurance helps cover the cost of hospital, nursing, and at-home care. Medicare beneficiaries pay an initial amount of the hospital bill for each period of illness. Hospital insurance then pays the rest of the patient's covered hospital expenses for 60 days and nearly all covered expenses for the next 30 days.

Hospital insurance also pays all covered expenses for the first 20 days of skilled nursing facility care and nearly all covered expenses for the next 80 days. Beneficiaries may be rehospitalized or readmitted to a skilled nursing facility during the illness. In addition, beneficiaries are entitled to up to 100 visits at home by nurses and other health-care workers for a year following their release from a hospital or skilled nursing facility. The hospital and nursing facility, however, must be approved by a Medicare review board.

People entitled to social security or railroad retirement benefits automatically qualify for hospital insurance at age 65, even if they continue to work. However, they must sign up at a social security office to obtain coverage. People age 65 or older who are ineligible for retirement benefits may obtain hospital insurance by paying a monthly premium.

Supplementary Medical Insurance is a voluntary health insurance plan. It helps pay the cost of physicians' services and certain other costs that hospital insurance does not cover.

People covered by medical insurance must pay an initial amount of covered expenses each year. The program then pays 80 per cent of the cost of covered services for the rest of the year. The federal government pays more than two-thirds of the cost of supplementary medical insurance. Most insured members pay the rest through a monthly premium deducted from their social security checks.

Financing OASDHI. A payroll tax shared equally by employers and workers finances old-age, survivors, disability, and health insurance. This tax is called the Federal Insurance Contributions Act (FICA) tax. It is paid on a worker's gross annual wages up to a certain limit, called the *wage base*. Workers who earn more than the wage base pay no additional FICA taxes. In 1983, employers and employees each paid a 6.70 per cent tax on the first $35,700 of earnings. The tax rate for self-employed workers is about $1\frac{1}{2}$ times the rate for employers and employees. In 1983, this rate was 9.35 per cent.

The payroll tax rate is scheduled to rise through the years. In addition, the wage base increases automatically as earnings increase. By 1990, the FICA tax rate for employers and employees will reach 7.65 per cent. At that time, the wage base will reach an estimated $54,000.

All workers covered by social security pay the same percentage of FICA taxes up to the wage base. Thus, workers whose incomes fall below the wage base pay a greater percentage of their total income in social security taxes than do workers with incomes above the wage base.

Employers deduct the FICA tax from workers' pay each pay period, add an equal contribution, and then send the amount monthly or quarterly to the Department of the Treasury. That department distributes most of the money to the Old-Age and Survivors Insurance Trust Fund and the Disability Insurance Trust Fund, and these funds pay the appropriate benefits. The rest of the FICA revenue goes to the Hospital Insurance Trust Fund, which finances Medicare benefits.

Other U.S. Social Security Programs

Unemployment Insurance provides weekly cash payments to workers who have lost their jobs and are looking for employment. Unemployment insurance covers most workers in commerce and industry as well as civilian federal employees. In many states, the program also covers employees of small firms and of state and local government offices.

Federal law requires that the states maintain an unemployment insurance system that meets certain standards. However, the states administer the system and determine the benefits. Unemployment insurance is financed chiefly by a payroll tax on employers. The states determine the rate employers must pay. In a few states, employees also contribute.

To qualify for benefits, an unemployed person must have worked for a certain period in a job covered by unemployment insurance, or must have earned a certain amount of income, or both. Unemployed workers must apply for benefits at a state unemployment office. Such workers also must register for employment and be willing to take a suitable job.

Unemployment benefits vary. Most states base them on the earnings of the worker at the time he or she became unemployed. Benefits generally equal about half the worker's full-time weekly pay, within minimum and maximum limits. A few states pay extra benefits to workers with dependents.

The maximum number of weeks during which workers may collect benefits also varies. Most states provide benefits for up to 26 weeks, but some extend the period to 30 weeks. Some states also extend the maximum benefit period during times of high statewide or nationwide unemployment.

Some workers must pay federal income taxes on unemployment benefits. They are workers who have earned more than $20,000 annually or married workers whose family income exceeds $25,000. These workers also may be required to pay state income tax on their unemployment benefits. See UNEMPLOYMENT INSURANCE.

Workers' Compensation aids people who are injured or who develop a disease as a result of their job. It pays the cost of their medical care and helps replace lost income. In addition, workers' compensation pays death benefits and pensions to the dependents of workers who have been killed on the job. In return for compensation, workers forfeit their right to sue an employer for damages arising from job-related disabilities.

Most workers' compensation programs are administered by a state agency, a private insurance company, or both. Benefits vary by state and depend on the type and duration of the worker's disability and on the worker's weekly earnings. Most states set minimum and maximum limits on benefits and limit the benefit period.

Most states require employers to participate in a workers' compensation program and to pay the entire cost of the program. In some states, however, the programs cover only workers in dangerous jobs. In addition, many states do not cover farm and domestic workers and workers in small firms. See WORKERS' COMPENSATION.

Social Security in Canada

Canada's social security system is similar to the U.S. system. Its goals include both social adequacy and individual equity. The Canadian social security system has three main programs: (1) the Old-Age Security Pension, (2) the Canada Pension Plan, and (3) unemployment insurance.

The Old-Age Security Pension was established to satisfy the principle of social adequacy. It guarantees a minimum retirement income to persons age 65 or older who have lived in Canada at least 10 years. Beneficiaries are paid regardless of their work records.

Benefits, which are paid monthly, automatically rise with increases in the country's cost of living index. During the early 1980's, the Old-Age Security Pension paid beneficiaries more than $225 a month.

The Canada Pension Plan provides additional monthly benefits to retired workers, disabled workers and their children, and the surviving spouse and children of deceased workers. The plan also pays a single death benefit to the estate of a covered deceased worker. Participation in the plan is required for all workers between the ages of 18 and 70 who earn more than $1,800 yearly. Workers in the province of Quebec do not participate in the plan. But they are covered by a similar program, called the Quebec Pension Plan.

The Canada Pension Plan is financed by a payroll tax. Employers and workers each contribute equally at a rate of 1.8 per cent on the first $18,500 of annual earnings. The National Department of Health and Welfare administers the plan.

Retirement benefits are based on workers' earnings and their contributions to the pension plan. Workers must be 65 or older to collect a retirement pension. To qualify for disability and survivors benefits, workers must have contributed to the pension plan for a specified period. Such benefits equal a fixed amount plus a percentage of the retirement pension to which the worker would be entitled. Benefits are adjusted yearly to reflect increases in the cost of living.

Unemployment Insurance covers all Canadian workers except self-employed workers and workers who earn less than a specified amount. It is financed by a payroll tax on employers and employees and by contributions from the federal government. The payroll tax finances the cost of initial benefits and the administration of the program. The federal government pays for excess benefits during certain periods of high nationwide unemployment.

The payroll tax rate is based on weekly earnings. Employers pay a slightly higher rate than employees. The taxes are paid into the Unemployment Insurance Fund, which is administered by the Canada Employment and Immigration Commission.

To qualify for benefits, an unemployed person must be willing to work and must have worked in a covered job for at least 20 weeks during the 52 weeks before filing for benefits. Unemployment benefits amount to about two-thirds of the worker's average earnings during the qualifying period. Benefits are paid for 10 to 50 weeks depending on the worker's earnings during the qualifying period and on the rate of nationwide or provincewide unemployment. In addition, unemployed workers with 20 or more weeks of covered earnings during the qualifying period are eligible for maternity and illness benefits and for a three-week retirement benefit at age 65.

History

Early Social Insurance Programs. The Industrial Revolution of the 1700's and early 1800's led to the development of social insurance in Europe and America. During this period, many people moved from rural areas to cities to work in factories. Most of these workers received low wages, and many labored under dangerous working conditions.

The low wages they received prevented most workers from saving for their old age. Workers who became disabled in job-related accidents or who lost their jobs during business slumps—and their families—suffered great hardships. Many families could no longer afford to support aged or needy relatives. No government assistance programs and few private relief organizations existed because most people of the time believed that poor people were to blame for their own misfortune.

During the late 1800's, Germany began to pioneer the adoption of laws to improve the conditions of workers. It established the first sickness insurance law in 1883 and the first workers' compensation act in 1884. By 1889, Germany had passed the first compulsory old-age and disability insurance program. By the early 1900's, most of the other countries of Europe had enacted similar programs.

The Growth of Social Security. The United States was one of the last major industrialized nations to establish a social security system. In 1911, Wisconsin passed the first state workers' compensation law to be held constitutional. At this time, most Americans believed that the government should not be responsible for caring for the aged, disabled, or needy. But such attitudes changed during the Great Depression of the 1930's. During this depression, many Americans came to realize that economic misfortune could result from events over which workers had no control.

In 1935, Congress passed the Social Security Act. This law became the basis of the U.S. social insurance system. It provided cash benefits only to retired workers in commerce and industry. In 1939, Congress amended the act to benefit the wives and dependent children of retired workers and the widows and dependent children of deceased workers. In 1950, the act began to cover many farm and domestic workers, nonprofessional self-employed workers, and many state and municipal employees.

Social security coverage became nearly universal in 1956, when lawyers and other professional workers came under the system. Congress added disability insurance to the social security system in 1956 and established Medicare in 1965.

Canada's social security system began in 1940, when the Canadian Parliament passed the Unemployment Insurance Act. Parliament amended the act in 1971 to cover nearly all employees. The Canada Pension Plan went into effect in 1966, and the payment of benefits began in 1967. The Quebec Pension Plan was established in 1965.

Recent Developments. During the 1970's, high inflation rates caused hardship for millions of Americans whose main income came from social security. In 1972 Congress introduced an automatic indexing plan, which raised social security benefits each year to reflect increases in the cost of living. It also provided for automatic increases in the wage base to finance the higher benefits. However, a flaw in the indexing plan caused benefits to rise much higher than wages.

In 1977, Congress corrected the indexing flaw, raised payroll tax rates, and increased the wage base to put the system on a sound financial basis. But in the late 1970's, prices increased much faster than wages. This trend caused benefits to rise more rapidly than payroll tax revenues and resulted in a major drain on the Old-Age and Survivors Insurance Trust Fund. Congress eliminated some benefits in 1980 to avoid a further drop in the re-

serves. But the drain continued, and so Congress permitted temporary borrowing from the two other trust funds in 1982.

In 1983, Congress passed legislation that was designed to assure the financial health of the social security system for the next 75 years. The law expanded the categories of workers covered under social security. It required all federal employees hired after Dec. 31, 1983, to join the system. The law also required the participation of about a million employees of nonprofit organizations. The legislation made the benefits of some higher-income retired people subject to federal income taxes. All these changes were expected to help provide $166 billion in additional revenue by the 1990. In addition, the legislation raised the traditional retirement age. Under this provision, the retirement age will rise gradually from 65 to 67 between 2003 and 2027.   ALICIA HAYDOCK MUNNELL

See also MEDICARE; UNEMPLOYMENT INSURANCE; WELFARE; WORKERS' COMPENSATION.

Additional Resources

AARON, HENRY. On Social Welfare. Abt Books, 1980.
FERRARA, PETER J. Social Security: The Inherent Contradiction. Cato Institute, 1980.
PARADIS, ADRIAN A., and WOOD, R. H. Social Security in Action. Simon & Schuster, 1975.
ROBERTSON, A. HAEWORTH. The Coming Revolution in Social Security. Security Press, 1981.
STEIN, BRUNO. Social Security and Pensions in Transition: Understanding the American Retirement System. Macmillan, 1980.
U.S. SOCIAL SECURITY COMMISSION. Social Security Handbook. U.S. Government Printing Office. Pub. annually.

SOCIAL SECURITY ADMINISTRATION (SSA), a United States government agency, administers the nation's social security program. This program provides retirement, disability, and death benefits for 9 out of 10 working Americans and their families. Under the plan, retired or disabled workers or their dependents or survivors receive monthly cash payments. The SSA administers the supplemental security income program, which guarantees an annual income to needy people who are 65 or over, blind, or disabled. It also administers Aid to Families with Dependent Children, which provides financial aid to needy children and to their parents or guardians.

The social security program, created in 1935, began paying benefits in 1940. The SSA was set up in 1953 as part of the Department of Health, Education, and Welfare (now the Department of Health and Human Services). It took over most social security functions of the former Federal Security Agency.

Critically reviewed by the SOCIAL SECURITY ADMINISTRATION

See also SOCIAL SECURITY.

SOCIAL SETTLEMENT. See SETTLEMENT HOUSE.

SOCIAL STRATIFICATION. See SOCIAL CLASS.

SOCIAL STUDIES is a program of study in elementary and high school. It deals with the individuals, groups, and institutions that make up human society.

Social studies includes many of the *social sciences*, the fields of study concerned with people in society. For example, students in social studies classes study anthropology to learn about world cultures. They study sociology to investigate social relationships and groups. The students learn economics to discover how people make and distribute goods. They also study geography to find out where and how people live, history to gain knowledge of the past, and political science to understand different forms of government. In some programs, students also investigate philosophy, psychology, religion, and art.

The term *social studies* first gained widespread use about 1916. That year, the Committee on Social Studies of the National Education Association issued a report on such studies. The committee defined social studies as studies that enable students to understand others and become good citizens.

Goals. A major goal of social studies programs is to provide knowledge of the world and its peoples. Social studies students investigate their own and other cultures to determine the similarities and differences. Early programs concentrated on the cultures of the United States and Western Europe. Today, social studies courses also cover many non-Western cultures.

Educators design social studies programs to teach four chief types of skills: (1) study skills, (2) intellectual skills, (3) group work skills, and (4) social skills. Study skills help students gather information from books, maps, and other materials. Intellectual skills enable them to define and analyze problems. Group work skills help students operate effectively in committees and other groups. Social skills guide them in getting along with others.

Social studies programs are also designed to help students develop certain attitudes and beliefs, such as respect for others and a sense of fairness. However, educators, parents, and community leaders often differ on what values these programs should stress.

Methods. Educators sometimes organize social studies content around key concepts. For example, a teacher may base a teaching unit on the concept of justice, an important idea in political science. Another unit of study might deal with the concept of region, as used by geographers.

Social studies teachers encourage students to ask questions and to seek answers for themselves. This method, sometimes called the *discovery method* or *inquiry method*, teaches young people how to think, rather than what to think.   FRANCIS P. HUNKINS

Related Articles in WORLD BOOK include:

Anthropology	Geography	Political Science
Civics	Government	Social Science
Economics	History	Sociology

SOCIAL SURVEY. See SOCIOLOGY (Surveys).

SOCIAL WAR. See ROMAN EMPIRE (A Century of Revolution).

SOCIAL WELFARE. See WELFARE; PHILANTHROPY.

SOCIAL WELFARE, NATIONAL CONFERENCE ON, promotes discussion of the problems and methods of practical human improvement. It has about 8,000 members, about 1,200 of them agencies or social-welfare organizations. It holds an annual forum and publishes the proceedings. It also publishes a quarterly *Conference Bulletin.* Headquarters are at 22 W. Gay Street, Columbus, Ohio 43215.   Critically reviewed by the
                    NATIONAL CONFERENCE ON SOCIAL WELFARE

SOCIAL WORK is a profession that includes a wide range of social services and programs. Specially trained persons called *social workers* provide counseling, support, and guidance to people who need help. Such assistance enables people to understand themselves and their living conditions and to attain their full potential. Social workers also try to improve living conditions by participating in programs to prevent such problems as crime, child abuse, drug addiction, mental illness, and poor housing.

Most social work is financed by government agencies or private organizations. The majority of social workers are employed in family service agencies, hospitals, clinics, drug abuse centers, nursing homes, settlement houses, schools, prisons, and factories. Some social workers have a private practice and provide counseling for a fee.

Methods of Social Work

Traditionally, social work consists of three basic approaches—*casework, group work,* and *community organization work.* Casework involves direct contact between a social worker and the individuals and families being helped. Group work involves programs in which the social worker deals with several persons at the same time. Community organization work focuses on neighborhoods and their large groups of people. Since the mid-1900's, social workers have increasingly combined the three basic approaches.

Fields of Social Work

There are five major fields of social work: (1) family and child welfare, (2) health, (3) mental health, (4) corrections, and (5) schools.

Family and Child Welfare includes services to families during an emergency, such as the absence of one or both parents from the home. Other critical situations requiring family service include unemployment of the principal wage earner and the illness of one or more members of a family.

Social workers in this field also help families adjust to long-term changes in home life. For example, a counselor may provide guidance to children whose parents are separated or divorced. The Family Service Association of America coordinates family service agencies in communities throughout North America.

Child welfare programs provide such services as adoption, day care, foster child care, and care for handicapped children. Child welfare workers also aid physically or emotionally abused children.

Health. Medical social workers help patients and their families in clinics, hospitals, and other health care facilities. These workers assist physicians by providing information about the social and economic background of patients. For example, such problems as inadequate housing and lack of money for medicine may cause or aggravate illness. Social workers also offer counseling to patients who have been discharged to help them return to everyday life.

Many medical social workers specialize in a particular type of area. These specializations include maternal and child care, the care of dying patients, and counseling victims of a certain disease, such as cancer or kidney failure.

Mental Health. Social work in mental health includes aid to people suffering from mental and emotional stress. Social workers in this field also provide many of the same kinds of services offered by medical social workers. Some receive special training in *psychotherapy,* the treatment of mental or emotional disorders by psychological methods.

Corrections includes programs concerned with the prevention of crime and the rehabilitation of criminals. Social workers in the field of corrections also counsel people who are on probation or parole. Workers in this field give priority to preventive services, such as tutoring and recreation.

Schools. Social work is part of the program in schools on all levels, from nursery school through college. It includes services to students in special schools for the emotionally disturbed and the handicapped. Social workers in schools provide vocational counseling and help with personal problems. They also assist students who have learning difficulties and help them to fulfill their maximum potential.

Other Fields of social work offer assistance in a wide variety of situations. Many social workers help elderly people obtain such services as financial assistance and medical care, which enable them to live as independently as possible. Social workers in clinics and community treatment centers provide counseling to alcoholics and drug abusers.

Some social workers aid people in public housing projects and help find dwellings for families made homeless by urban crises. Social workers employed by corporations and labor unions provide a variety of work-related services, including health counseling and preretirement and retirement planning.

History

The desire to help other people is stressed by the major religions, especially Judaism and Christianity. The Bible tells of ways in which religious individuals assisted the needy. For example, the ancient Jews paid a tax for the benefit of the poor. This tax amounted to a tenth of a person's income. During the Middle Ages, from the late A.D. 400's to the 1500's, various religious groups devoted themselves to healing the sick and feeding the hungry.

Great changes took place in society during the Industrial Revolution, a period of many new inventions and great industrial development that began in the 1700's. The growth of populations and industries, together with the movement of people from rural areas to cities, brought such problems as overcrowding, unemployment, and poverty. Growing numbers of people began to depend on others for help. During the 1800's, many private agencies were established to aid these people.

Working with the needy became a distinct profession in the late 1800's. One agency, the Charity Organization Society, helped the needy in Great Britain, the United States, and Canada. Its counselors, called "friendly visitors," went to people's homes and performed services, some of which were similar to those of present-day social workers.

The New York School of Philanthropy was the first school to train people for jobs with social agencies. This school, now the Columbia University School of Social Work, was founded by the Charity Organization Society in 1898 in New York City. However, the term *social work* did not come into widespread use until the early 1900's. By that time, many state and local governments in the United States had started to provide social services financed by tax funds. The United States govern-

ment created the social security program in 1935, during the Great Depression. Under this program, the government became a major source of public aid. See SOCIAL SECURITY.

Americans who have made important contributions to the development of social work include Jane Addams, Mary E. Richmond, Grace L. Coyle, and Gordon Hamilton. Addams was a leader of the settlement house movement, which established neighborhood centers to provide educational and social services. Richmond wrote the first scientific study of casework techniques in social work, *Social Diagnosis* (1917). Coyle helped develop group practice in social work. Hamilton formulated one of the major approaches to casework. This approach stressed the importance of establishing specific goals for individuals receiving help.

Careers

Social work offers a variety of job opportunities. Most professional social workers deal directly with the people they serve. Others work as administrators, supervisors, planners, or teachers. *Paraprofessional* social workers do not require full professional training. They work as assistants to professional personnel in community centers and agencies, mental health centers, and settlement houses. Many paraprofessional social workers have a part-time position or volunteer their services.

Professional social workers have at least a bachelor's degree in social work. Some jobs require a person to have a master's or doctor's degree in social work. More than 350 colleges in the United States and Canada offer degrees in the subject. Many junior and community colleges have two-year training programs for paraprofessional jobs. In addition, a number of agencies and organizations provide on-the-job training.

Additional information about careers in social work may be obtained from the National Association of Social Workers, 7981 Eastern Avenue, Silver Spring, Md.

Ken Firestone

Casework involves direct contact between the social worker and the individuals and families being helped.

SOCIAL WORKERS, NATIONAL ASSN. OF

20910. In Canada, information about social work careers is available from the Canadian Association of Social Workers, 55 Parkdale Avenue, Ottawa K1Y 1E5, Ont.

EMMA GIORDANO QUARTARO

Related Articles in WORLD BOOK include:

ORGANIZATIONS

Big Brothers/Big Sisters
  of America
Family Service Association
  of America
Jewish Community
  Centers
Junior Leagues

Red Cross
Salvation Army, The
Social Workers, National
  Association of
Travelers Aid
United Way of America

OTHER RELATED ARTICLES

Addams, Jane
Alinsky, Saul D.
Breckinridge, Sophonisba
Child Welfare
Hull House

Lathrop, Julia C.
Riis, Jacob A.
Settlement House
Wald, Lillian D.
Welfare

Additional Resources

EDELWICH, JERRY. *Burn Out: Stages of Disillusionment in the Helping Professions.* Human Services Press, 1980.

FISHER, JACOB. *The Response of Social Work to the Depression.* G. K. Hall, 1980.

GERMAIN, CAREL B., ed. *Social Work Practice: People and Environments, an Ecological Perspective.* Columbia Univ. Press, 1979.

GOTTLIEB, NAOMI, ed. *Alternative Social Services for Women.* Columbia Univ. Press, 1980. Presents a feminist view of social programs for women.

GRANBECK, MARILYN. *Social Work Careers.* Watts, 1977.

LEIBY, JAMES. *A History of Social Welfare and Social Work in the United States.* Columbia Univ. Press, 1978.

SOCIAL WORKERS, NATIONAL ASSOCIATION OF,

is a professional organization devoted to the improvement of social work practices and standards. The organization works to improve the quality of social services to individuals, communities, and the nation. The association was formed in 1955 by the merger of seven organizations. It has 50,000 members in more than 170 chapters in the United States, Puerto Rico, and Europe. Its publications include two quarterly journals, *Social Work* and *Abstracts for Social Workers;* and *The Encyclopedia of Social Work.* The National Association of Social Workers has headquarters at 1425 H Street NW, Washington, D.C. 20005.

Critically reviewed by the NATIONAL ASSOCIATION OF SOCIAL WORKERS

SOCIALISM

is an economic system, a political movement, and a social theory. Most socialists believe that national or local governments, rather than individuals, should own a nation's resources and control their use. Socialism calls for public ownership of land, factories, and other basic means of production.

The idea of *collective ownership* (common ownership) of property dates at least from the time of ancient Greece. In the 300's B.C., the Greek philosopher Plato proposed that a ruling class own everything in common, putting the welfare of the state above all personal desires. Since ancient times, a number of groups have had some form of community ownership of property.

The word *socialism* was first used in the early 1800's.

Alfred G. Meyer, the contributor of this article, is Professor of Political Science at the University of Michigan.

At that time, socialism meant opposition to the selfishness that some people thought was the root of any *capitalist,* or *free enterprise,* system. During the early 1800's, the Industrial Revolution in Western Europe caused severe social problems. For example, many factory owners made their employees work long hours at low pay and under unhealthful conditions. Socialists claimed that public ownership or control of productive resources would assure fairer treatment for all. See IN-DUSTRIAL REVOLUTION (Life During the Industrial Revolution).

Today, socialists disagree on many important points. Some want a strong central government running the economy. Other socialists favor as much local control as possible. Still others believe that there should be no government in a socialist society. Some socialists argue that socialism can be achieved only through revolution and violence. Others believe that socialism must come gradually, within the framework of existing political institutions.

Most countries today have socialist political parties. Many nations have socialist governments, and almost all countries have adopted some of the ideas and methods that have been part of socialist programs. In addition, the countries in which Communist parties control the government are sometimes called *socialist,* but most socialists reject this use of the term.

This article describes what socialism is and how it developed. For more information on socialism and other economic and political institutions, see the WORLD BOOK articles on CAPITALISM; COMMUNISM; DEMOCRACY; ECONOMICS; and GOVERNMENT.

Socialism and Communism

The words *socialism* and *communism* once meant about the same thing—a society based on public ownership of the means of production. Today, people draw sharp distinctions between the two terms.

Members of Communist parties consider socialism as a stage in the development of Communist societies. During this stage, a Communist party is in power in a country, most private property has been eliminated, and the economy is run on the basis of a national production plan. However, the nation is not yet rich enough to give its citizens all the material benefits they need, and the government must *coerce* (force) people to work hard for little reward. In a later stage, the nation will be wealthy enough to satisfy everyone's economic wants. That stage is Communism. Communists claim that coercion by the government will disappear under Communism.

Democratic socialists—that is, socialists in non-Communist countries—do not accept the Communist definition of socialism. Most of them believe that some government coercion is necessary because some people must be forced to be good citizens. Democratic socialists reject most of the methods used by Communist parties, such as revolution and other forms of violence as means of gaining power. Democratic socialists also oppose dictatorial methods of running the state after they are in power. Unlike Communists, democratic socialists believe in democratic processes and do not wish to get rid of all opposition parties. They care more about the fair distribution of goods and services than about rapid economic growth. Democratic socialists also favor democratic methods for determining what goods are to be produced.

Goals and Methods of Socialism

Socialists claim that free enterprise systems are inefficient and wasteful. They believe that capitalism leads to such problems as unemployment, poverty, business cycles, and conflicts between workers and the owners of the means of production. To solve these problems, socialists believe that a nation's wealth must be distributed more equally and justly. They strongly oppose social inequality and discrimination. Socialists aim for a society based on cooperation and brotherhood rather than on competition and self-interest.

Socialism proposes to fulfill its aims by placing the major means of production in the hands of the people, either directly or through the government. Ownership may be by national or local government or by cooperatives. Many socialists favor a *mixed economy*—government ownership of basic industries and private ownership of many other businesses. The private businesses, however, would be regulated by the government.

Socialists believe that a country's resources should be used according to an overall economic plan formulated by manufacturers, farmers, workers, and government officials working together. By such planning, socialists hope to adjust production to the needs of the people. Although the forces of supply and demand may influence production and prices under the socialist economic plan, many decisions regarding how much to produce and what to charge will be made by political authorities.

Socialists disagree over how much wealth should be left in private hands and how to deprive the rich of their excess property. Many socialists call for redistribution of wealth through taxation. They favor laws to help the aged, the unemployed, the disabled and handicapped, widows, dependent children, and other people in need. Many socialists believe that the government should also provide free education and medical service to everyone and should help all citizens obtain safe and sanitary housing at rents they can afford.

Development of Socialism

Early Socialists. During the early 1800's, several writers and reformers criticized industrialism as the cause of great hardship and suffering among working people. Such men as Robert Owen of Great Britain and Charles Fourier and the Comte de Saint-Simon of France made various proposals for setting up communities with ideal social and economic conditions. Owen and followers of Fourier established short-lived cooperative settlements. These socialists were frequently called *utopians*. This term comes from the book *Utopia* (1516) by the English statesman Saint Thomas More. *Utopia* is an account of an ideal society that provides equality and justice for all.

Karl Marx, a German economist and social philosopher, became the most influential socialist of the 1800's. Marx's basic socialist ideas were first expressed in the *Communist Manifesto* (1848), which he wrote with his friend Friedrich Engels. Marx called his socialism *scientific socialism* to distinguish it from utopian socialism. He believed that all history is a series of struggles between the ruling and working classes. Marx taught that

capitalism would be replaced by socialism. He predicted that the ruling class would be overthrown. The victorious working class would then set up a society based on common ownership of the means of production, not on economic privilege. For a fuller discussion of Marx's ideas, see MARX, KARL; and COMMUNISM (Marxism).

The International Socialist Movement. During the late 1800's, several socialist political parties were formed in Europe and North America. In time, these parties became united in an international organization with a single set of beliefs inspired by the writings of Marx. Between 1890 and 1914, the socialist movement grew strong, and socialist parties nearly won control of the government in several countries. But beneath the seeming strength, deep divisions existed. The movement included moderates, radicals, and revolutionaries. In addition, some socialist leaders rejected the doctrines of Marx. The international organization even included groups or parties that were non-Marxist. For example, the Fabian Society, a socialist group in Great Britain, derived its beliefs from Christian ideas and long-established traditions for achieving reforms.

After World War I began in 1914, the international socialist movement collapsed. Socialist leaders had to decide whether they were loyal to the movement or to their country, regardless of who governed it and how. Most socialist leaders decided to place patriotism above their socialist convictions.

Following the Russian revolution of 1917, revolutionary socialists founded new parties, which they called Communist parties. Since then, democratic socialists and Communists have become bitter enemies. Most socialists today are more critical of the writings of Marx than were early socialists. As a result, socialism can no longer be described as a Marxist *ideology* (set of doctrines), though many socialists consider Marx one of many important teachers.

In the United States, for various reasons, socialism has never been so strong as in Europe. In Europe, socialism was largely a working-class movement. But the labor movement began later in the United States and grew slowly. Many scholars believe that labor developed slowly in the United States because the frontier and the untapped wealth of the country provided greater opportunities—even for the poor—than Europe did. Other scholars believe that American ideas of freedom and individualism weakened the appeal of socialism. Some people think that socialism remained weak in the United States because a wide variety of socialist groups sprang up between the 1880's and World War I, and socialists could not develop a unified program.

The Socialist Party has been the most successful socialist political group in the United States. The party reached its greatest strength in 1912, when it had more than 118,000 dues-paying members. In the 1912 presidential election, the Socialist candidate, Eugene V. Debs, received almost 900,000 votes. In the 1920 election, Debs received about 920,000 votes. After Debs's death in 1926, Norman Thomas became the party's leading spokesman. He was the party's candidate in every presidential election from 1928 through 1948.

Since the early 1920's, Socialist strength has greatly declined. The Socialist vote fell to about 2,000 in the

SOCIALISM

1956 presidential election. Since then, the party has not nominated a candidate for President, but it continues to try to spread its ideas. However, a number of small Socialist and Communist parties still nominate candidates.

The United States has basically a free enterprise system, though it has adopted many ideas and methods that have been part of socialist programs. For example, the government regulates and controls many private businesses. It also has set up many social welfare programs to aid the needy, and a few public services are free to everyone. The government strives to maintain employment at as high a level as possible. The government also uses its strong taxing, spending, and credit powers in an attempt to achieve maximum employment, production, and incomes without large increases in prices. But the United States has far fewer socialist features than most other industrialized countries.

Socialism Today. Most socialists are firmly committed to work within the framework of a country's constitution. They seek to cooperate with all parties and regard socialism as representing broad popular concerns, not just those of the workers. Many socialists do not insist on placing all major means of production under public ownership. They are content to place private business under government regulation. Most socialists oppose Communism.

Many countries have socialist parties. In some countries, a socialist party runs the government. In other countries, socialists are members of a coalition government. Political parties whose policies are based on socialist ideas have formed several administrations in Great Britain and Norway since the early 1900's. Socialist parties gained power in France and Greece in 1981. Socialist parties also govern many countries in Africa, the Middle East, and Southeast Asia. Other countries with strong socialist parties include Argentina, Australia, Belgium, Canada, Denmark, India, Israel, Italy, Japan, New Zealand, and West Germany.

No countries today are purely socialist. Even countries governed by Communist parties still have some free enterprise, though most resources are in public hands.   ALFRED G. MEYER

Related Articles in WORLD BOOK include:

Berger, Victor L.	Nationalization
Cooperative	Owen (family)
Debs, Eugene V.	Proudhon, Pierre J.
Engels, Friedrich	Saint-Simon, Comte de
Fabian Society	Syndicalism
Fourier, Charles	Thomas, Norman M.
International, The	Webb (family)

See also *Socialism* in the RESEARCH GUIDE/INDEX, Volume 22, for a *Reading and Study Guide.*

Additional Resources

ELLIS, HARRY. *Ideals and Ideologies: Communism, Socialism, and Capitalism.* Rev. ed. World Publishing, 1972.
ENGELS, FRIEDRICH. *Socialism: Utopian and Scientific.* China Books, 1975. First pub. in 1892.
FORMAN, JAMES. *Socialism: Its Theoretical Roots and Present-Day Development.* Watts, 1972.
HUBERMAN, LEO, and SWEEZY, PAUL. *An Introduction to Socialism.* Monthly Review, 1968.
LAIDLER, HARRY. *History of Socialist Thought.* West, 1980. Reprint of 1927 ed.

SOCIALIZATION, in the behavioral sciences, refers to the complex process by which individuals come to learn and perform behavior expected of them by society. Socialization teaches habits, ideas, attitudes, and values. Behavioral scientists—anthropologists, psychologists, and sociologists—regard socialization as one of the principal ways by which societies perpetuate themselves. Through socialization, culture is transmitted from one generation to the next.

Learning plays an important part in socialization. A person must acquire a wide range of information and skills to participate in the activities of a family, a play group, a school group, a business, or a political system. Besides learning the rules and values of society, an individual must believe in them and support them. On the other hand, people need not accept all the values and rules of their elders. Selective acceptance and rejection account for major changes in social codes. But total rejection of earlier standards destroys social organization. Such rejection may have an unfortunate effect on some individuals, because all persons depend on others to a large degree.

Behavioral scientists study socialization because of three basic characteristics that are common to all human beings. First, human infants cannot live unaided and must depend entirely on others. Second, human beings—strictly speaking—do not have instincts and must learn most of the behavior necessary for survival. Third, because people lack instincts, they must learn to control their relations with one another by living according to shared values and roles.

The family plays a central role in the socialization of the child. From the family, children learn such basic functions as speaking, toilet management, and eating properly. They also learn the basic values, beliefs, and goals of the family. Socialization is deliberate when individuals are told what to do or how to act. But much socialization is unconscious. For example, children learn many basic attitudes and values by observing other persons, especially their parents or older brothers or sisters.

In some societies, socialization takes place almost exclusively in infancy and early childhood. This occurs in most isolated, nonindustrial societies and in those societies with rigid social systems and little change in technology. In modern societies, socialization begins in infancy and continues throughout a person's life. Other agencies, especially the school, have taken over some of the socialization functions of the family. As individuals advance through successive stages of school, they continually discard some attitudes and roles and take on new ones. Other important elements that influence an individual's social behavior include friends and co-workers, religious institutions, television, motion pictures, and various kinds of reading matter.   WILBERT E. MOORE

See also CULTURE; SOCIAL ROLE; SOCIAL PSYCHOLOGY.

Additional Resources

BRIM, ORVILLE G., and WHEELER, STANTON. *Socialization After Childhood: Two Essays.* Krieger, 1976. Reprint of 1966 ed.
BRONFENBRENNER, URIE, and CONDRY, J. C. *Two Worlds of Childhood: U.S. and U.S.S.R.* Sage, 1970.
ELKIN, FREDERICK, and HANDEL, GERALD. *The Child and Society: The Process of Socialization.* 3rd ed. Random House, 1978.
ROSE, PETER I., ed. *Socialization and the Life Cycle.* St. Martin's, 1979.

SOCIALIZED MEDICINE. See Health Insurance, National.

SOCIETY. See Culture; Sociology.

SOCIETY FOR THE ADVANCEMENT OF EDUCATION was organized in 1939 to purchase and publish the journal *School & Society*. The journal publishes information on problems and trends in the field of education. The society has about 900 members. Its headquarters are at 1860 Broadway, New York, N.Y. 10023.

SOCIETY FOR THE PRESERVATION AND ENCOURAGEMENT OF BARBER SHOP QUARTET SINGING IN AMERICA. See Barbershop Quartet Singing.

SOCIETY FOR THE PREVENTION OF CRUELTY TO ANIMALS (SPCA) is the name of many organizations throughout the world that work to foster and promote animal welfare. These anticruelty, or humane, societies help enforce animal protection laws by investigating reports of animal mistreatment. They also maintain shelters and adoption services for lost or unwanted animals. Originally, most anticruelty societies were founded chiefly to protect work animals. Today, these organizations work primarily to protect pets.

The first anticruelty society was founded in 1824 in England. In 1866, Henry Bergh, a New York philanthropist, founded the first such society in the United States, the American Society for the Prevention of Cruelty to Animals (ASPCA). The New York legislature chartered the ASPCA the same year. It became a model for the founding of other anticruelty societies in the United States.

Today, the United States has about 1,000 local anticruelty societies. Many of them maintain animal hospitals and humane education programs. They also perform low-cost birth control operations to prevent pet overpopulation. DUNCAN G. WRIGHT

SOCIETY ISLANDS is a group of islands in the Pacific Ocean. The islands lie slightly northeast of the

WORLD BOOK photo

A Pet Ambulance, such as the one shown above, carries injured, unwanted, or mistreated animals to hospitals and shelters operated by the Society for the Prevention of Cruelty to Animals.

Cook Islands, about 4,200 miles (6,760 kilometers) southwest of San Francisco. Samuel Wallis claimed the islands for Great Britain in 1767. But Louis Antoine de Bougainville claimed them for France in 1768. The group became a French protectorate in 1842, and a colony in 1880.

The Society Islands group consists of 14 islands. Tahiti and Raiatea are the largest islands of the group. The Society Islands cover an area of 646 square miles (1,673 square kilometers), and have a population of about 100,000. For the location of the Society Islands, see Pacific Islands (color map).

Ancient volcanoes on the Society Islands form many high peaks, making the land rough and mountainous. Some of the islands are low atolls, and are used as fishing centers. The capital of the island group is the busy seaport of Papeete, on Tahiti.

The people of the islands are Polynesians. Many of them fish and dive for pearls. EDWIN H. BRYAN, JR.

See also Tahiti.

SOCIETY OF FRIENDS. See Quakers.

SOCIETY OF JESUS. See Jesuits.

SOCIETY OF THE CINCINNATI. See Cincinnati, Society of the.

SOCIETY OF THE SACRED HEART OF JESUS. See Sacred Heart of Jesus, Society of the.

SOCIOBIOLOGY is the study of the biological basis for the social behavior of human beings and other animals. Sociobiologists try to determine the function of various types of behavior in the life of an animal. They also seek to discover how aggression, communication, and other types of social behavior originated and have changed through countless generations.

Social behavior has traditionally been studied by experts in such fields as *ethology* (the study of animal behavior), anthropology, psychology, and sociology. Sociobiologists use information and ideas from these fields, but they examine social behavior primarily in terms of modern theories of genetics and evolution. Many sociobiologists believe that the results of their studies will someday revolutionize sociology and the other social sciences.

Sociobiology is based on the theory that the central process of life is the struggle of genes to reproduce themselves. According to this theory, an organism inherits tendencies to develop certain types of behavior. These behavior patterns increase the animal's chances of transmitting its genes to the next generation.

Sociobiologists believe an animal can pass on its genes not only by reproducing but also by helping related animals, such as brothers and sisters, survive and reproduce. For example, a worker bee may sting an intruder to protect the hive. The act of stinging kills the worker bee but it protects the queen bee, which has many of the same genes. The queen bee will pass on these genes to her offspring. Sociobiologists have discovered that the more closely two animals are related genetically, the more likely one is to sacrifice itself to protect the other. These scientists speculate that self-sacrificing behavior in human beings may also have a genetic basis.

Some biologists argue that sociobiological explanations of social behavior in animals cannot be applied

458a

SOCIODRAMA

to human social behavior. These critics point out that human behavior, unlike animal behavior, is highly changeable and is affected by many cultural and environmental influences. Sociobiologists recognize the importance of such influences. But they insist that human behavior cannot be understood properly without considering genetic factors as well. ARTHUR CAPLAN

Additional Resources

BOCK, KENNETH. *Human Nature and History: A Response to Sociobiology.* Columbia Univ. Press, 1980.

MONTAGU, ASHLEY, ed. *Sociobiology Examined.* Oxford, 1980. Fifteen authorities debate genetic predetermination.

SINGER, PETER. *The Expanding Circle: Ethics and Sociobiology.* Farrar, 1981.

WALLACE, ROBERT A. *The Genesis Factor.* Morrow, 1979.

WILSON, EDWARD O. *Sociobiology: The New Synthesis.* Harvard, 1975.

SOCIODRAMA. See ROLE PLAYING.

SOCIOLOGY is the study of the individuals, groups, and institutions that make up human society. The field of sociology covers an extremely broad range that includes every aspect of human social conditions. Sociologists observe and record how people relate to one another and to their environments. They also study the formation of groups; the causes of various forms of social behavior; and the role of churches, schools, and other institutions within a society. Sociology is a social science and is closely related to anthropology, psychology, and other social sciences.

Most sociological studies deal with the predominant attitudes, behavior, and types of relationships within a society. A society is a group of people who have a similar cultural background and live in a specific geographical area. Each society has a *social structure*, a network of interrelationships among individuals and groups. Sociologists study these relationships to determine their effect on the overall function of the society.

Sociological data can also help explain the causes of crime, poverty, and other social problems. The field of *applied sociology* deals with the use of this knowledge to develop solutions for such problems.

Sociologists formulate theories based on observations of various aspects of society. They use scientific methods to test these theories, but few sociological studies can be conducted in a laboratory under controlled conditions. The sociologist's ability to form indisputable conclusions is also limited by the diverse and changing nature of human beings and society. As a result, many sociological studies are less precise than those in the biological and physical sciences.

What Sociologists Study

Many elements determine the general social conditions of a society. These elements can be classified into five major areas: (1) population studies, (2) social behavior, (3) social institutions, (4) cultural influences, and (5) social change.

Population Studies determine the general social patterns of a group of people living within a certain geographical area. There are two chief kinds of population studies, *demography* and *human ecology.*

Demography is the systematic study of the size, composition, and distribution of human populations. Demographers compile and analyze various statistics, including people's ages, birth and death rates, ethnic backgrounds, migration patterns, and racial distribution. Many demographic studies explain the effects of social conditions on the size and composition of a population. For example, several studies of the 1900's found a direct correspondence between the growth of industrialization and a decline in the death rate.

Human ecology deals mainly with the structure of urban environments and their patterns of settlement and growth. Studies in human ecology explain why and how cities grow and change.

Social Behavior is studied extensively in the field of social psychology. Social psychologists usually work with small groups and observe attitude change, conformity, leadership, morale, and other forms of behavior. They also study *social interaction*, which is the way the members of a group respond to one another and to other groups. In addition, social psychologists examine the results of conflicts between groups, such as crime, prejudice, and war.

In most societies, standards of behavior are passed on from one generation to the next. Social psychologists observe how people adjust their behavior to conform to these standards, a process called *socialization.*

Social psychologists also study *social roles* and *status.* A social role is the function or expected behavior of an individual within a group. Status is a person's importance or rank.

Social Institutions are organized groups of people that perform a specific function within a society. These institutions include business organizations, churches, governments, hospitals, and schools. Each has a direct effect on the society in which it exists. For example,

Major Subdivisions of Sociological Study

Criminology is the study of criminal behavior and the causes of crime. Criminologists also develop methods of crime prevention.

Demography is the study of the size, composition, and distribution of human populations.

Human Ecology deals with the structure of urban environments and their patterns of settlement and growth.

Political Sociology is concerned with how people gain and use power within a political system, and the rise of various political movements.

Social Psychology deals with the individual's social behavior and relationships with others in a society.

Sociolinguistics studies the way people use language in a variety of social situations.

Sociometry deals with the scientific measurement of the relationships among group members. A diagram called a *sociogram* is used to indicate the extent and intensity of each relationship.

Sociology of Education is concerned with understanding how educational institutions transmit cultural attitudes and traditions.

Sociology of Knowledge is the study of a society's myths, philosophies, and sciences and their effect on attitudes and behavior.

Sociology of Law studies the relationships between a society's legal code and various social patterns, such as economic concerns, cultural traditions, and family relationships.

Urban Sociology deals with the social conditions and problems of cities. This field includes the study of race relations and city planning.

University of Chicago (WORLD BOOK photo)

Sociology Students work on various research projects under the guidance of their professors. During class, the students discuss the information they have gained from these studies.

Survey Center, Inc. (WORLD BOOK photo)

Market Researchers often use sociological data and techniques. The woman in the center is being trained by professional sociologists to conduct interviews on consumer buying habits.

the attitudes and goals of an entire society are influenced by the transmission of learning and knowledge in educational institutions. Some branches of sociology study the influence of one particular type of institution. These branches include the sociology of education and the sociology of law.

Each social institution has its own social structure and standards of acceptable behavior. Sociological studies have been conducted in factories, mental hospitals, prisons, and other institutions. Sociologists then compare the social conditions within these institutions with those of the entire society.

Cultural Influences help unify a society and regulate its social life. They also give people a common base of communication and understanding. A society's culture includes its arts, customs, language, knowledge, and religious beliefs. Sociologists study the effect of each of these elements on social conditions and behavior. For example, religious beliefs may determine the moral code of a society. Sociological studies focus on the way this code regulates social behavior and the role it plays in the establishment of a society's laws.

Social Change is any significant alteration in the social conditions and patterns of behavior in a society. Such a change may be caused by fashions, inventions, revolutions, wars, or other events and activities. Technological developments have led to many social changes of the 1900's. A number of sociological studies have concentrated on the changes in education, social values, and settlement patterns that occur in newly industrialized nations.

Methods of Sociological Research

Sociological theories must be tested and verified before they can be considered reliable. Sociologists use three chief methods to test theories. These methods are (1) surveys, (2) controlled experiments, and (3) field observation.

Surveys, sometimes called *public opinion polls*, are the most widely used method of sociological research. They measure people's attitudes about various subjects. Sociologists often use surveys to determine the relationship between a certain viewpoint and such factors as age, education, and sex.

Most surveys are conducted by the use of questionnaires prepared by sociologists. These questionnaires consist of clearly worded questions about the participant's background and his or her opinions on the subject being studied. The sociologist selects the group of individuals to be questioned. This group, called a *sample*, may be chosen at random, or it may be selected to represent a particular segment of the population. The sociologist's staff questions the participants personally or by telephone, or mails the questionnaires to them. In most cases, sociologists use computers to analyze the results of surveys.

Surveys provide information on voting behavior, consumer buying habits, racial prejudice, and many other human attitudes and activities. Surveys are also used by sociologists to pinpoint particular social problems and to evaluate social conditions within a specific community.

Controlled Experiments are used primarily in the study of small groups. Some of these experiments are conducted in a laboratory. In most cases, two or more highly similar groups of people are studied. The groups differ in one principal feature, which is called a *variable*. The variable may be age, sex, economic background, or any other identifiable characteristic. The sociologist observes each group to learn if the variable produces

459

a significant difference in the attitudes and behavior of its members.

For example, a sociologist may theorize that groups of people of the same sex solve problems more effectively than coeducational groups. To test this theory, three groups might be studied. The first group would consist only of women, the second of men, and the third of an equal number of both. The groups must be similar in such factors as age, education, and social background. All the groups receive identical problems and instructions. If the groups composed of members of one sex perform better consistently, the theory has been verified. In most cases, however, sociologists test theories more extensively before forming any general conclusions.

Field Observation usually involves a sociologist's living in the community that he or she is studying. Information is gathered primarily through observation and conversations with members of the community. The sociologist also may participate in various social functions and political activities that occur during the period of study.

The community's institutions and culture are studied, along with the attitudes, behavior, and interactions of its members. The sociologist then draws general conclusions about the community's social conditions and records these findings in a report called a *case study*. Case studies provide reference material for sociologists who are studying similar communities. Such information is also used in *comparative sociology*, a field concerned with examining the similarities and differences of two types of societies.

Field observation provides first-hand information about a group of people, but it is the least reliable method of testing sociological theories. Many conclusions that can be drawn about one community do not apply to other communities. In addition, the sociologist's personal reactions to the individuals being observed may influence the conclusions.

History

Early Sociological Thought. The study of human society dates back to ancient times, but it was not considered a science until the early 1800's. At that time, the French philosopher Auguste Comte created the term *sociology*. Comte developed the theory of *positivism*, which held that social behavior and events could be observed and measured scientifically.

Many sociological theories were suggested during the 1800's. Several of them were *single-factor theories*, which emphasized one factor as the controlling element of the social order. One of the most historically important single-factor theories was *economic determinism*, which was developed by two German social thinkers, Friedrich Engels and Karl Marx. This theory states that economic factors control all social patterns and institutions. It forms much of the basis of Communism.

During the mid-1800's, sociological thought was greatly influenced by the theory of evolution. The British philosopher Herbert Spencer concluded that the development of human society was a gradual process of evolution from lower to higher forms, much like biological evolution.

Development of Social Research. During the late 1800's, many sociologists rejected social evolution and shifted to a more scientific study of society. The French sociologist Émile Durkheim was one of the first social thinkers to use scientific research methods. Durkheim conducted an extensive study of suicide. He collected demographic information from various nations and studied the relationship between their suicide rates and such factors as religion and marital status.

In the early 1900's, the German sociologist Max Weber concluded that sociological theories must be generalizations. He devised a method of study in which he compiled all the typical characteristics of a specific group of people. These characteristics formed what Weber called an *ideal type*. He based general conclusions about the group as a whole on this ideal type.

Several new schools of sociological thought gained prominence during the 1920's. They included *diffusionism, functionalism,* and *structuralism.* Diffusionism stressed the influence that individual societies have on each other. Diffusionists believed that social change occurred because a society adopted various cultural traits of other societies.

Functionalism viewed society as a network of institutions, such as marriage and religion, that are related to and dependent on one another. According to this theory, a measurable change in one institution would cause a change in the others.

Structuralism emphasized the social structure as the major influence on society. Structuralist thinkers developed the idea that social roles and status determined much human behavior.

A sociological theory called *structural-functionalism* also developed during the 1920's. This philosophy, which included elements of both structuralism and functionalism, was advanced in the 1930's by the American sociologist Talcott Parsons. Structural-functionalism dominated sociology until the mid-1900's.

Modern Sociology. During the mid-1900's, sociology became an increasingly specialized field. In general, sociologists shifted from making conclusions about overall social conditions to studying specific groups or types of people within a society. Such groups as business executives, homemakers, and street gangs have been the subject of sociological studies.

Sociologists also began to rely more heavily on scientific research methods. The survey method has been greatly improved, and the use of computers has increased the efficiency of evaluating survey results. Sociologists also have developed better methods of selecting samples.

Social psychology is one of the most rapidly expanding fields of sociology. Sociologists have concentrated on the study of small groups, whose social behavior often reflects that of an entire society. Social psychologists have expanded their use of controlled experiments, which has increased the reliability of their studies.

Changes in lifestyles and social conditions during the 1960's and 1970's have been the subject of many sociological studies. Various theories have been formed on such developments as the drug culture, the youth movement, and the feminist movement.

Since the 1950's, a growing number of sociologists in the United States have called for greater efforts in the field of applied sociology. These men and women believe that sociologists have an obligation to work toward the solution of social problems and the establishment of social justice.

Careers

Most careers in sociology require a master's or doctor's degree. However, persons who have a bachelor's degree in sociology may find positions as interviewers or research assistants. Most sociologists work for educational institutions, but some are employed by government agencies and business organizations.

Colleges and universities employ about 80 per cent of the sociologists with Ph.D.'s. Some of these individuals devote most of their time to research programs and teach only a few classes. Students often gain experience by assisting their professors with research projects. Community colleges and high schools also employ sociology teachers, most of whom have a master's degree.

Government agencies are employing an increasing number of sociologists to study the general conditions and needs of communities. Their findings are used in determining government policies on housing, education, safety, and other matters of civic concern.

Some city governments employ sociologists as *city planners*. These experts study such problems as slum housing, transportation, and traffic congestion. They then propose solutions for the problems and plan future development of the city.

Business companies employ a large number of sociologists in the field of *market research*. Market researchers conduct surveys on consumer buying habits to help firms predict sales of various products. Professional sociologists prepare these surveys, but people with little or no sociological background may conduct the interviews. Some businesses also hire sociologists to study problems concerning employee relations and motivation.

Career opportunities in sociology are also available in various other areas. Further information about careers in sociology can be obtained from the American Sociological Association, 1722 N Street NW, Washington, D.C. 20036.   NEIL J. SMELSER

Related Articles in WORLD BOOK include:

SOCIOLOGISTS

Balch, Emily G.	Merton, Robert K.
Comte, Auguste	Myrdal, Gunnar
Du Bois, W. E. B.	Pareto, Vilfredo
Durkheim, Émile	Parsons, Talcott
Engels, Friedrich	Spencer, Herbert
Frazier, E. Franklin	Sumner, William G.
Johnson, Charles S.	Weber, Max
Marx, Karl	

RELATED STUDIES

Anthropology	Social Psychology
Criminology	Social Science
Demography	Social Work
Ecology	Sociobiology
Psychology	

OTHER RELATED ARTICLES

Alienation	Crime
Assimilation	Criminology
Behavior	Cultural Deprivation
Caste	Cultural Lag
City	Culture
City Planning	Custom
Civil Disobedience	Ethnic Group
Community	Family

Folkway	Racism
Group Dynamics	Research
Juvenile Court	Riot
Juvenile Delinquency	Segregation
Middle Class	Social Change
Minority Group	Social Class
Mores	Social Role
Orphanage	Socialization
Population	Statistics
Poverty	Tribe
Power (social)	Unemployment
Prejudice	Urban Renewal
Public Opinion	Vital Statistics
Public Opinion Poll	

Additional Resources

BERGER, PETER L. *Sociology Reinterpreted: An Essay on Method and Vocation.* Doubleday, 1981.

GIDDENS, ANTHONY. *Central Problems in Social Theory: Action, Structure and Contradiction in Social Analysis.* Univ. of California Press, 1979.

LIGHT, DONALD, JR., and KELLER, SUZANNE. *Sociology.* Knopf, 1979.

MERTON, ROBERT K., and NISBET, ROBERT. *Contemporary Social Problems.* 4th ed. Harcourt, 1976.

SZACKI, JERZY. *History of Sociological Thought.* Greenwood, 1979.

VARADY, DAVID P. *Ethnic Minorities in Urban Areas: A Case Study of Racially Changing Communities.* Kluwer, 1979.

SOCKEYE SALMON. See SALMON (Kinds).

SOCKS. See STOCKINGS.

SOCRATES, *SAHK ruh teez* (469?-399 B.C.), was a Greek philosopher and teacher. His noble life and courageous death, together with his teachings, have made him one of the most admired figures in history. He believed that human nature leads people to act correctly and in agreement with knowledge. Socrates felt that evil and wrong actions arise from ignorance and the failure to investigate why people act as they do. Socrates is credited with saying "the unexamined life is not worth living" and "no man knowingly does evil." Socrates devoted himself completely to seeking truth and goodness.

Socrates' Life. Socrates wrote nothing of his own. Most of our information about his life and teachings comes from *Memorabilia* and *Symposium* by the historian Xenophon; dialogues by the philosopher Plato; *Clouds*, a comedy by Aristophanes; and writings by the philosopher Aristotle. Xenophon and Plato were Socrates' pupils, and Aristotle was a pupil of Plato's. Aristophanes was a leading playwright in Socrates' time.

According to Xenophon, Socrates was a respected teacher chiefly interested in helping people become good. Plato's dialogues tell us that Socrates cared not only about ethics, but also about logic and a theory of *forms*. This theory tried to identify the quality in an object or idea that remains constant and unchangeable. Plato's dialogues contain the most probable account of Socrates' life and teachings. Aristotle seemed to agree generally with Plato's view of Socrates. However, Aristotle claimed that the theory of forms was more characteristic of Plato's philosophy than that of Socrates. In Aristophanes' *Clouds*, Socrates appears as a bumbling, foolish man who supports fantastic theories.

Socrates was born and lived in Athens. He dressed simply and was known for moderation in eating and drinking. He was married to Xanthippe, who, according to tradition, was ill-tempered and difficult to live with. Socrates and Xanthippe probably had at least two children.

Socrates taught in the streets, market place, and gymnasiums. He taught by questioning his listeners, and showing them how inadequate their answers were. He had a following of young men in Athens, but many people mistrusted him because of his unorthodox views on religion and his disregard of public opinion.

Inevitably, Socrates made enemies among influential Athenians. He was brought to trial, charged with corrupting the young and showing disrespect for religious traditions. Socrates defended himself by stating that clear knowledge of the truth is essential for the correct conduct of life. Action, he said, equals knowledge. Thus, virtue can be taught because correct action involves thought. Socrates implied that rulers should be men who know how to rule—not necessarily those who have been elected. Socrates may have appeared dangerous to Athenian democracy, but what he defended were the foundations of that democracy. Plato described Socrates' defense in his dialogue, the *Apology*.

The jury found Socrates guilty and sentenced him to death. The jury may have given Socrates the severe sentence because it resented the unbending pride with which he conducted his defense. He refused several opportunities to escape from prison, and carried out the sentence by calmly drinking a cup of hemlock poison. An account of the death of Socrates appears in Plato's *Phaedo*.

The Socratic Method. Socrates introduced the idea of *universal* (standard) definitions. He believed that although individual people or things vary and are constructed differently, the definitions of how they are similar or vary remain constant. For example, individual dogs differ in shape, color, and size. Yet there are some common characteristics by which we identify these animals as dogs, not as cats or camels. These common characteristics are the universal, to which people must turn when they judge anything.

Socrates believed that the correct method of discovering the common characteristics was by *inductive*

means—that is, by reasoning from particular facts to a general idea. This process took the form of *dialectic* (philosophic) conversation, which became known as the *Socratic method*. Two or more people would begin a discussion with the assumption that each knew the definition of some key term. The conversation first showed that their assumptions were different, and then that the assumptions were inadequate to claim true knowledge. In this way, they proceeded from less adequate to more adequate definitions. They also progressed from definitions that applied to only a few particular examples to a universal definition that applied to all examples. Although they often reached no satisfactory conclusion, their goal was always the same—to gain a true and universal definition.

The Socratic method tended to expose people's ignorance. It showed that many things they assumed to be true were false. Socrates also used *irony* to expose ignorance of key concepts—that is, he claimed to differ from other people only in knowing that he was ignorant. Socrates' insistence on his ignorance reminded others of their own ignorance. J. L. SAUNDERS

See also *Socrates* in the RESEARCH GUIDE/INDEX, Volume 22, for a *Reading and Study Guide*.

Additional Resources

ARMSTRONG, ARTHUR H. *An Introduction to Ancient Philosophy.* 3rd ed. Rowman & Littlefield, 1981. Reprint of 1957 ed. Includes discussion on Socrates.
SANTAS, GERASIMOS X. *Socrates: Philosophy in Plato's Early Dialogues.* Routledge & Kegan, 1979.
SILVERBERG, ROBERT. *Socrates.* Putnam, 1965.
VERSENYI, LASZLO. *Socratic Humanism.* Greenwood, 1979. Reprint of 1963 ed.

SOD HOUSE is a house with walls built of sod or turf in horizontal layers. Sod houses were constructed by early settlers on open plains where there were no trees to supply lumber. For a description of sod houses and how they were built, see WESTERN FRONTIER LIFE (Life in the Country); NEBRASKA (Territorial Days; picture).

SODA is the common name for a group of compounds that contain sodium. These sodium compounds are manufactured from common salt (NaCl), which is made up of sodium and chlorine. See SODIUM.

One common sodium compound is *sodium carbonate*

Metropolitan Museum of Art, N.Y., Wolfe Fund, 1931

Socrates drinks the cup of hemlock to carry out the sentence of death imposed on him by the rulers of ancient Athens. This painting, *Death of Socrates* (1787) by Jacques Louis David, shows Socrates' followers in great despair. Socrates made a toast to the gods and drank the bitter poison. He met death with the same calm and self-control with which he had lived.

(Na_2CO_3), known as *sal soda, washing soda,* and *soda ash.* It comes in crystals or white powder and has a strong alkaline reaction. This means that it neutralizes acids. Sodium carbonate is used in the manufacture of glass, soap, and paper. It is also used as a disinfectant, a cleaning agent, and a water softener.

Sodium bicarbonate ($NaHCO_3$) is a popular soda used in cooking and in medicines. It is also known as *baking soda* or *saleratus.* Baking powder contains sodium bicarbonate, which acts as a leavening agent because it causes bread, biscuits, or pastries to rise in baking. Seidlitz powders also contain sodium bicarbonate. They relieve excess stomach acid. See BAKING POWDER.

Sodium hydroxide ($NaOH$) is a sodium compound known as *caustic soda.* It is widely used in the manufacture of industrial chemicals, rayon, paper, and soap. The compound is also used in the production of aluminum and in petroleum refining.

See also GLASS (Recipes).

SODA WATER. See SOFT DRINK.

SODDY, FREDERICK (1877-1956), was a British chemist who worked on atomic structure. He received the 1921 Nobel prize in chemistry for his research. He and Ernest Rutherford showed that radium breaks down by itself and gives off electrons, helium nuclei, and gamma rays, which are like X rays. Soddy gave the name *isotopes* to atoms of the same element which have different weights (see ISOTOPE). He was born in Eastbourne, Sussex, and studied at Oxford University. He also taught at Oxford.   HENRY M. LEICESTER

SÖDERBLOM, NATHAN. See NOBEL PRIZES (table: Nobel Prizes for Peace—1930).

SODIUM is a silvery-white metallic element that has many important uses. It is a soft metal, and can easily be molded or cut with a knife. Sodium belongs to a group of chemical elements that are called the *alkali metals.*

Where Sodium Is Found. Sodium is the sixth most common chemical element in the earth's crust. It makes up about 2.8 per cent of the crust. Sodium never occurs *pure*—that is, as a separate element—in nature. It combines with many other elements, forming *compounds.* To obtain pure sodium, the metal must be *extracted* (removed) from its compounds.

One of the most familiar sodium compounds is *sodium chloride,* which is common table salt. Sodium chloride can be found in dry lake beds, underground, and in seawater. Countries with the largest deposits of sodium chloride include China, France, Great Britain, India, Russia, the United States, and West Germany.

Such minerals as borax and cryolite contain sodium. Many plants and the bodies of animals contain small amounts of sodium salts. The human body must have a certain amount of sodium to maintain a normal flow of water between the body fluids and the cells. Sodium also plays a part in tissue formation and muscle contraction. A daily diet that includes meat and foods seasoned with table salt supplies enough sodium for the body's normal needs.

Uses. Sodium compounds have many uses in industry, medicine, agriculture, and photography. Manufacturers use *sodium borate* (borax) in making ceramics, soaps, water softeners, and many other products (see BORAX). *Sodium hydroxide* (caustic soda) is an important industrial alkali used in refining petroleum and in making paper, soaps, and textiles. A lead-sodium *alloy* (combination of metals) produces tetraethyl lead, a gasoline compound that improves the performance of automobile engines. *Sodium carbonate* (soda ash or washing soda) is used in the manufacture of *sodium bicarbonate* (baking soda). Many people take sodium bicarbonate to relieve an overly acid stomach. Doctors sometimes prescribe *sodium bromide* as a sedative for tense patients. *Sodium nitrate* (Chile saltpeter) is a valuable fertilizer. Photographers use *sodium thiosulfate* (hypo) to fix photographic images on paper.

Pure sodium also has industrial uses. Some nuclear power plants use it in liquid form to cool nuclear reactors. A few electric power cables have been made of pure sodium metal. Special insulation around the sodium keeps it from combining with air, water, or other substances.

Extracting Sodium. In 1807, the English chemist Sir Humphry Davy became the first person to obtain pure sodium. He used electricity to extract the metal from sodium hydroxide. Manufacturers still use electricity to obtain sodium. The process is called *electrolysis.* In this process, an electric current is passed through a molten sodium compound, such as sodium chloride. The current separates the compound into chlorine gas and sodium metal. See ELECTROLYSIS.

Chemical Properties. Pure sodium is extremely active chemically. Sodium immediately combines with oxygen when it is exposed to the air. As a result, the element loses its shiny appearance and becomes dull. Sodium's bright surface can be seen only after it has been newly cut or extracted.

Sodium weighs less than water. It *decomposes* (breaks up) water, producing hydrogen gas and sodium hydroxide. This chemical reaction is very violent. It produces much heat that often causes the hydrogen to ignite.

The element also reacts quickly with such other nonmetals as chlorine and fluorine, and it forms alloys with many metals. Liquid ammonia dissolves sodium, forming a dark-blue solution. A test for determining whether a material contains sodium is to hold the material in a flame. If sodium is present, the flame will be bright yellow.

Sodium must be handled and stored with extreme care. In laboratories, small amounts are stored under kerosene in airtight bottles. The kerosene prevents air or moisture from reaching the metal. Large quantities of sodium in brick form are stored and shipped in airtight, moisture-free barrels. Sodium is also shipped in sealed tank cars. The metal is melted and poured into the tanks. The sodium hardens during shipping, and must be melted again before it can be removed.

Sodium has the chemical symbol Na. Its atomic number is 11, and its atomic weight is 22.9898. The melting point of sodium is 97.8° C (208° F.), and its boiling point is 892° C (1638° F.).   OTTO THEODOR BENFEY

See also ALKALI; SALT; SALTPETER; SODA.

SODIUM BICARBONATE. See BICARBONATE OF SODA.

SODIUM BORATE. See BORAX.

SODIUM CARBONATE. See SODA; CARBONATE.

SODIUM CHLORIDE. See CHLORIDE; SALT.

SODIUM HYDROXIDE. See CAUSTIC; LYE; SODA.

SODIUM METASILICATE. See WATER GLASS.

SODIUM NITRATE. See SALTPETER; NITRATE.

SODIUM NITRITE. See NITRITE.

SODIUM PENTOTHAL is a drug used to produce sleep during surgery and to help patients discuss their problems during psychiatric treatment. Sodium pentothal has been called a "truth serum" because many people talk less guardedly after taking it. Sodium pentothal is also called *sodium thiopental* and *thiopental sodium. Pentothal Sodium* is a trade name for the drug.

Physicians use large doses of sodium pentothal to produce deep sleep during surgery. Smaller doses may be used to bring on light sleep before surgery to relieve the patient's anxiety. Psychiatrists sometimes give patients even smaller doses of sodium pentothal. Such doses do not produce sleep. But they enable many people to discuss their thoughts and emotions more freely than might otherwise be possible.

Sometimes a physician may be asked to administer sodium pentothal to a person in an effort to obtain information for a police investigation. But the drug cannot be used legally without the person's consent. Courts seldom allow information to be used as evidence if it was obtained after the administration of sodium pentothal. Some people can lie even after receiving the drug. Others tell falsehoods that they believe are true. DONALD J. WOLK

SODIUM SULFATE. See SALT, CHEMICAL.

SODIUM TETRABORATE. See BORAX.

SODIUM VAPOR LAMP. See LIGHTING (Lighting Devices).

SODOM, *SAHD um,* was one of the ancient cities on the plain around the Dead Sea. It is believed that the place where the city stood now lies beneath the waters near the south end of the sea. During early Bible times, the region was so fertile it was compared to the "garden of the Lord" (Gen. 13:10). But later, according to the Old Testament, God destroyed Sodom and the neighboring city of Gomorrah, because the people were wicked.

The Old Testament also tells how Lot, the nephew of Abraham, escaped from Sodom just before it was destroyed. Lot and his wife had been warned by two angels to flee the city and not look back. Lot obeyed, but his wife took a last glance at Sodom. She was immediately turned into a pillar of salt as punishment for her disobedience. WILLIAM A. IRWIN

See also LOT.

SOEHARTO. See SUHARTO.

SOEKARNO. See SUKARNO.

SOFIA, *SOH fee uh* (pop. 965,729; met. area pop. 1,064,712), is the capital and largest city of Bulgaria, and the country's chief economic and cultural center. The city lies in western Bulgaria and is surrounded by the Balkan Mountains and other ranges. For location, see BULGARIA (map).

The Alexander Nevsky Cathedral, built in the late 1800's to celebrate Bulgaria's liberation from Turkish rule, stands in the center of Sofia. The National Museum and the ancient churches of St. George and St. Sofia are in the city's old section. This section has winding, narrow streets, and its small houses are jammed closely to one another. In contrast, modern sections of Sofia have wide avenues and high-rise apartment build-

A. Devaney, Inc.

Sofia is the capital and largest city of Bulgaria. Modern high-rise buildings on Georgi Dimitrov Street, *above,* stand near a Turkish *mosque* (Muslim house of worship) built in the 1500's.

ings. Most of the people of Sofia live in apartments.

Sofia is the site of the National Assembly Building, the National Theater, the National Library, and the former Royal Palace. The University of Sofia and the Bulgarian Academy of Sciences are also located in the city.

About 20 per cent of Bulgaria's industry is in Sofia. Industry and transportation employ more than half the city's workers. Sofia's industries include food processing; the manufacture of textiles and clothing; and the production of machinery, electric equipment, and metals. Farms near Sofia provide fruit, vegetables, and dairy products for the city. Streetcars and buses furnish public transportation.

The Roman Emperor Trajan founded the city in the early A.D. 100's. The Huns, led by Attila, destroyed it in 447. A short time later, Sofia became part of the Byzantine Empire. The Bulgarians conquered the city in 809, but the Byzantines regained control of it in 1018. In 1382, the Turks made Sofia part of the Ottoman Empire. The city again came under Bulgarian rule in 1878, when Russia helped Bulgarian rebels defeat the Turks. Bulgaria became an independent nation that same year, and Sofia was named the capital.

Since 1944, thousands of rural people have moved to Sofia in search of jobs, and the city's population has grown rapidly. To prevent overcrowding, city planners have built apartment buildings and shopping facilities in suburban areas. VOJTECH MASTNY

See also BULGARIA (picture).

SOFT-COATED WHEATEN TERRIER is a breed of dog that originated in Ireland. Irish farmers used it to drive cattle, to guard houses and barns, and to kill rats and other pests. This terrier is related to the Irish and Kerry blue terriers.

Lepreacaun from Juanita Wurzburger

The Soft-Coated Wheaten Terrier Comes from Ireland.

Soft-coated wheaten terrier puppies are dark brown or brownish-red. The adults have a rich wheat-colored coat of soft, wavy hair. The dog's shaggy hair nearly covers its eyes. Most of these terriers have *docked* (cropped) tails. The dogs stand about 19 inches (48 centimeters) high and weigh from 35 to 45 pounds (16 to 20 kilograms).   JOAN MCDONALD BREARLEY

SOFT DRINK is a popular nonalcoholic beverage. Soft drinks are called *soft* to distinguish them from *hard* (alcoholic) drinks. Soft drinks are also called *pop* because the type of bottle caps used before the 1890's made a popping noise when removed. People in various areas call soft drinks *soda pop* or *soda*.

The first soft drink was made in 1807 by a Philadelphia druggist named Townsend Speakman, who flavored carbonated water with fruit juices. Soft drinks became especially popular among young people, but people of all ages drank them. Today, Americans drink an average of 34 gallons (129 liters) of soft drinks per person each year. Popular brands of soft drinks include Coca-Cola, Dr. Pepper, Pepsi-Cola, Royal Crown Cola, and Seven-Up.

How Soft Drinks Are Made. All soft drinks have two main parts, carbonated water and flavoring syrup. Carbonated water is made by first treating and filtering water to remove any minerals and impurities. Carbon dioxide gas is then mixed with the treated water. The gas makes the water bubble and fizz.

Flavoring syrup is a mixture of treated water, one or more sweeteners and acids, plus flavorings and food colorings. The sweetener may be corn syrup, sugar, or a sugar solution. Artificial sweeteners are used in diet soft drinks. Citric acid, phosphoric acid, or some other acid provides a tart taste. Flavorings include fruit juices, oils made from the rinds of citrus fruits, and oils obtained from the roots and leaves of various plants. Cola soft drinks have the flavoring of kola nuts (see KOLA NUT). Artificial food colorings are used in many fruit-flavored soft drinks, such as grape, orange, and strawberry beverages. Caramel, a natural food coloring made from corn, is used in colas, cream sodas, ginger ales, and root beers.

Every soft drink company makes the flavoring syrup for each of its products. It sells the syrup to local bot-tling companies throughout the United States and other countries, and these firms actually manufacture the drinks. Each bottling firm agrees to follow certain formulas established by the soft drink company. These formulas ensure that all the final products taste exactly the same, no matter where they were made. The bottlers distribute the beverages locally.

History. The first artificially carbonated water was made in 1772 by Joseph Priestley, an English chemist. He wanted to make water that resembled the natural bubbling water of mineral springs. At that time, mineral water was a popular remedy for certain illnesses. Priestley's artificial mineral water contained soda, and carbonated water was also called *soda water*. In 1806, bottled soda water was produced and sold by Benjamin Silliman, a chemistry professor at Yale College.

Flavored soda water became popular after Speakman flavored carbonated water with fruit juices in 1807. At first, people bought flavored soda water by the glass at drug stores or soda fountains. It became available in bottles about 1850. The number of soft drink bottling companies in the United States increased from approximately 65 during the mid-1800's to more than 2,000 in the 1970's.

During the 1970's, a sharp rise in the cost of sugar caused an increase in the price of soft drinks. Many people switched to less expensive, noncarbonated soft drinks made from powdered mixes, which became an important part of the industry. Sales of powdered soft drinks in the United States more than doubled from 1974 to 1977.   WILLIAM T. MILLER

SOFT-SHELLED CRAB. See BLUE CRAB.

SOFTBALL is a popular game played by more than 30 million persons throughout the world. Softball resembles baseball, but the rules of the sports differ in several ways. For example, softball pitching must be underhand, and baserunners must remain on base until the ball has left the pitcher's hand. Softball requires less space and equipment, and regulation games last seven innings instead of nine.

Field and Equipment. The infield in softball is smaller than that in baseball. The bases lie 60 feet (18 meters) apart. The pitcher stands 46 feet (14 meters) from home plate in men's games and 40 feet (12 meters) away in women's games.

Softballs are larger than baseballs. They are filled with a soft material called *kapok* or with a mixture of cork and rubber. Softballs have a cover of cowhide or horsehide. Softball bats are made of wood or metal and cannot be thicker than $2\frac{1}{4}$ inches (5.7 centimeters) or longer than 38 inches (97 centimeters). Softball players wear less protective equipment than baseball players do. All players may wear gloves, but only catchers and first basemen may wear padded mitts.

Types of Softball. There are two types of softball games, *slow pitch* and *fast pitch*. Slow-pitch games account for about 80 per cent of the softball competition in the United States. Pitchers in slow-pitch games must throw the ball slowly enough to make it arch on its way to the batter. Slow-pitch teams consist of 10 players—a pitcher, a catcher, and eight fielders. Nine positions are the same as those in baseball. On most teams, the 10th person plays as a fourth outfielder. Many slow-

Pitching a Softball

All softball pitches are thrown underhand. The series of pictures at the right shows a typical right-handed fast pitch. Start with both feet on the pitcher's plate. Then raise the right hand over the head and swing the arm back and down. At the same time, step forward with the left foot, keeping the right foot on the plate. As the right arm swings forward, release the ball and follow through.

WORLD BOOK illustrations by David Cunningham

pitch teams play with balls that measure about 12 inches (30 centimeters) in circumference. Others use 14- or 16-inch (36- or 41-centimeter) balls. Slow-pitch rules prohibit bunting and base stealing.

Fast-pitch teams use a 12-inch ball, and some players can pitch it as fast as 100 miles (160 kilometers) per hour. The teams consist of nine players who play the same positions as those in baseball. Batters may bunt in fast-pitch games, and runners may steal bases after the ball leaves the pitcher's hand.

History. Softball was developed as an indoor game in 1887 by George W. Hancock of the Farragut Boat Club of Chicago. He used a 16-inch ball whose seams looked like ridges because they were turned to the outside. In 1895, Lewis Rober of the Minneapolis Fire Department adapted the game for outdoor play. Rober used a 12-inch ball that had a cover like the one on a

baseball. The present game of softball came from Rober's version of the game.

Until the early 1930's, softball teams followed more than 10 sets of rules. In 1933, the Amateur Softball Association of America (ASA) was founded to govern and promote softball in the United States. The ASA set up a committee that established one set of rules now used by teams in all parts of the world. The International Softball Federation, founded in 1952, governs international competition. It has about 50 member nations, whose teams compete in annual regional, national, and international tournaments.   Don E. Porter

See also BASEBALL.

SOFTWOOD. See LUMBER (Softwood Lumber); TREE (Needleleaf Trees; Needleleaf Forests); WOOD.

SOGDIANA. See ALEXANDER THE GREAT (The Battle of Arbela).

WORLD BOOK diagrams by Arthur Grebetz

A Softball Field

The diagram at the right shows the approximate positions of the players in both slow- and fast-pitch softball. The outfield and the foul territories extend beyond the area shown to the boundaries of the playing area. A detailed diagram of the home-plate area appears below.

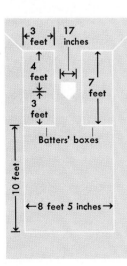

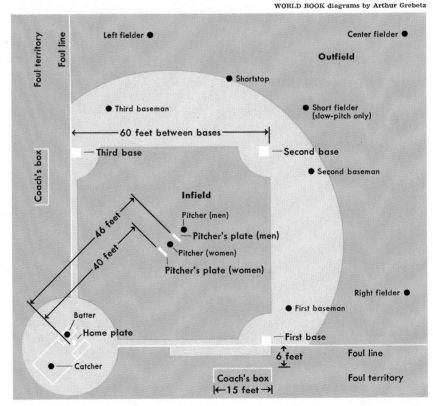

466

SOIL is an important natural resource that covers much of the earth's land surface. All life on earth depends on the soil as a direct or indirect source of food. Plants are rooted in the soil and obtain *nutrients* (nourishing substances) from it. Animals get nutrients from plants or from animals that eat plants. Certain microbes in the soil cause dead organisms to decay, which helps return nutrients to the soil. In addition, many kinds of animals find shelter in the soil.

Soil contains mineral and organic particles, other plant and animal matter, and air and water. The contents of soil change constantly. There are many kinds of soils, and each has certain characteristics, including color and composition. The kind of soil in an area helps determine how well crops grow there. Soil forms slowly and is destroyed easily, and so it must be conserved so it can continue to support life.

Soil scientists, called *pedologists*, use the term *polypedons* for the bodies of individual kinds of soil in a geographic area. Polypedons can be indefinitely large, but some have a surface area of only about 10.8 square feet (1 square meter). Some polypedons measure less than 5 inches (13 centimeters) deep. Others are more than 4 feet (1.2 meters) deep.

Composition of Soils

The mineral and organic particles in soil are called *soil particles*. Water and air occupy the spaces between the particles. Plants and animals live in these spaces, known as *pore spaces*. Plant roots also grow through the pore spaces.

Minerals supply nutrients to green plants. Particles called *sands*, *silts*, and *clays* make up most of the mineral content of soils. Sands and silts are particles of such minerals as quartz and feldspars. Clays consist of illite, kaolin, micas, vermiculite, and other minerals. Trace amounts of many minerals add nutrients, including calcium, phosphorus, and potassium, to the soil. Most soils are called *mineral soils* because more than 80 per cent of their soil particles are minerals.

Plant and Animal Matter consists of organic material in various stages of decay. Many organisms also live in the soil. These soil organisms include plant roots, microbes, and such animals as worms, insects, and small mammals. Bacteria, fungi, and other microbes *decompose* (break down) dead plants and animals. Many soil organisms help mineral and organic particles *aggregate* (come together) and form clumps of soil. Roots and burrowing animals break apart large clumps of soil.

Decaying organic material releases nutrients into the soil. In addition, some organic material combines with mineral particles. Other decaying material forms organic soil particles called *humus*. Most humus is black or dark brown, and it holds large amounts of water. Only 6 to 12 per cent of the volume of particles in most mineral soils is organic. However, these small quantities greatly increase a soil's ability to support plant life. In some soils, called *organic soils*, more than 20 per cent of the soil particles are organic.

Water that enters the soil dissolves minerals and nutrients and forms a *soil solution*. Much of the solu-

S. Pawluk, the contributor of this article, is Professor of Soil Science at the University of Alberta.

tion drains away, but some remains in the pore spaces. Green plants obtain water and some nutrients by absorbing soil solution through their roots.

Air replaces the water that drains from the larger pore spaces. Soil organisms live best in soils that contain almost equal amounts of air and water.

How Soil Is Formed

Soil begins to form when environmental forces break down rocks and similar materials that lie on or near the earth's surface. Pedologists call the resulting matter *parent material*. As soil develops through the centuries, organic material collects, and the soil resembles the parent material less and less. Glaciers, rivers, wind, and other environmental forces may move parent material and soil from one area to another.

Soils are constantly being formed and destroyed. Some processes, such as wind and water erosion, destroy soil. However, few soils appear to change, because their rates of formation and destruction usually balance each other. Significant environmental changes can upset that balance, and changes in the soil may become more apparent.

Soil formation differs according to the effects of various environmental factors. These factors include (1) kinds of parent material, (2) climate, (3) land surface features, (4) plants and animals, and (5) time.

Kinds of Parent Material. The type of parent material helps determine the kinds of mineral particles in a soil. A process called *weathering* breaks down parent material into mineral particles. There are two kinds of weathering, *physical disintegration* and *chemical decomposition*. Physical disintegration is caused by ice, rain, and other forces. They wear down rocks into smaller particles that have the same composition as the parent material. Sand and silt result from physical disintegration.

Chemical decomposition mainly affects rocks that are easily weathered. In this kind of weathering, the rock's chemical structure breaks down, as when water dissolves certain minerals in a rock. Chemical decomposition results in elements and in chemical compounds and elements that differ from the parent material. Some of these substances dissolve in the soil solution and become available as plant nutrients. Others recombine and form clay particles or other new minerals.

The mineral content of parent material also affects the kinds of plants that grow in a soil. For example, some plants, including azaleas and rhododendrons, grow best in soils that contain large amounts of iron.

Effects of Climate. Climate affects the amount of biological and chemical activity in a soil, including the kinds and rates of weathering. For example, physical disintegration is the main form of weathering in cool, dry climates. Higher temperatures and humidity encourage chemical decomposition as well as disintegration. In addition, decaying and most other soil activities require warm, moist conditions. These activities slow down or even stop in cold weather. Therefore, soils in cool, dry climates tend to be shallower and less developed than those in warm, humid regions.

Effects of Land Surface Features also influence the amount of soil development in an area. For example,

SOIL

water running off the land erodes the soil and exposes new rock to weathering. Also, soils on slopes erode more rapidly than those on flat areas. They generally have less time to form and therefore develop less than do soils on flat terrains.

Effects of Plants and Animals. Soil organisms and organic material help soil develop, and they also protect it from erosion. The death and decay of plants and animals add organic material to the soil. This organic material helps the soil support new organisms. Soils can resist erosion if they have a healthy plant cover of vegetation and contain large amounts of organic material.

Effects of Time. Soils that are exposed to intense soil formation processes for long periods of time become deep and well developed. Soils that erode quickly or have been protected from such processes for a long time are much less developed.

Characteristics of Soils

The method and rate of soil formation differs throughout a body of soil. As a result, the soil develops layers. These layers are called *soil horizons*. Soil horizons may be thick or thin, and they may resemble or differ from the surrounding horizons. The boundaries between the layers can be distinct or barely noticeable.

Most soils include three major horizons. The upper two, called the *A* and *B horizons*, are the most highly developed layers. The A horizon is also known as *topsoil*. The lowest horizon, called the *C horizon* or the *subsoil*, is exposed to little weathering. Its composition resembles that of the parent material. Pedologists describe soils by the characteristics of the soil horizons, including (1) color, (2) texture, (3) structure, and (4) chemical conditions.

Color. Soils range in color from yellow and red to dark brown and black. The color of a soil helps pedologists estimate the amounts of air, water, organic matter, and certain elements in the soil. For example, a red color may indicate the presence of iron compounds.

Texture of a soil depends on the size of its mineral particles. Sands are the largest particles. The individual grains can be seen and felt. Silts are just large enough to be seen, and clays are microscopic. Pedologists divide soils into textural classes according to the amounts of sand, silt, and clay in a soil. For example, the mineral portions of soils classified as *loam* contain from 7 to 27 per cent clay and less than 52 per cent sand. In *silty clay*, more than 40 per cent of the mineral particles are clay, and more than 40 per cent are silt.

Texture helps determine how thoroughly water

How Soil Is Formed Soil formation depends on several factors that act together. They include (1) the rock from which the soil forms, (2) the climate, (3) plants and animals, and (4) time. Soils form slowly and continuously. The illustrations below show how a typical soil forms and develops through the centuries.

WORLD BOOK diagrams by Cynthia Fujii

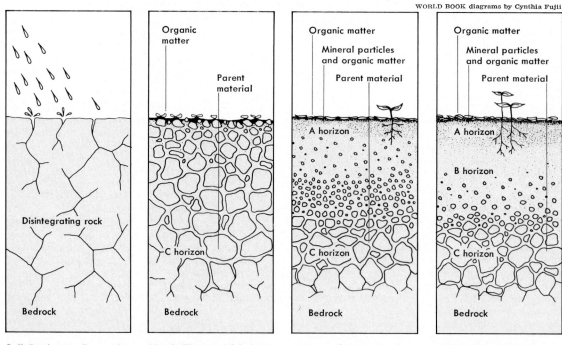

Soil Begins to Form when rain, ice, freezing and thawing, and other environmental forces break down rocks and similar materials. The resulting matter is called *parent material*. This material breaks down further into mineral particles.

Simple Plants and Animals live on rocks that are *decomposing* (breaking down). Plants called lichens produce acids that help decompose the rocks. When the organisms die, organic matter collects among the mineral particles.

Layers Called *Horizons* appear as soil develops. The top layer, or *A horizon*, has more organic matter than the others and becomes deep enough to support plant roots. The lowest layer, or *C horizon*, resembles the parent material.

A Well-Developed Soil can support a healthy cover of vegetation. It also may include a middle layer, called the *B horizon*. This horizon contains minerals that have been washed down in drainage waters from the soil's surface.

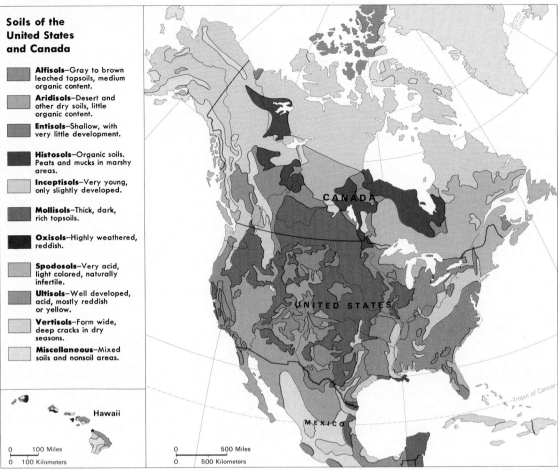

Soils of the United States and Canada

Alfisols—Gray to brown leached topsoils, medium organic content.

Aridisols—Desert and other dry soils, little organic content.

Entisols—Shallow, with very little development.

Histosols—Organic soils. Peats and mucks in marshy areas.

Inceptisols—Very young, only slightly developed.

Mollisols—Thick, dark, rich topsoils.

Oxisols—Highly weathered, reddish.

Spodosols—Very acid, light colored, naturally infertile.

Ultisols—Well developed, acid, mostly reddish or yellow.

Vertisols—Form wide, deep cracks in dry seasons.

Miscellaneous—Mixed soils and nonsoil areas.

Hawaii

0   100 Miles
0   100 Kilometers

0   500 Miles
0   500 Kilometers

CANADA

UNITED STATES

MEXICO

Tropic of Cancer

Arctic Circle

WORLD BOOK map

drains from a soil. Sands promote drainage better than clays.

Structure. When soil particles aggregate, they form clumps of soil that are called *peds*. Most peds range from less than $\frac{1}{2}$ to 6 inches (1.3 to 15 centimeters) in diameter. Their shape and arrangement determine a soil's structure. The ability of peds and soil particles to stick together and hold their shape is called *consistence*.

Most soils contain two or more kinds of structures. Some soils have no definite structure. In some such soils, the peds lack a definite shape or arrangement. In others, the particles do not aggregate.

There are three main kinds of soil structures: (1) platelike, (2) prismlike, and (3) blocklike. Platelike peds are thin, horizontal plates that occur in any horizon. Prismlike peds are column-shaped subsoil structures. Blocklike peds look like blocks with flat or curved sides. Large, flat-sided, blocklike peds commonly occur in subsoils. Small, rounded, blocklike peds make up most topsoils. They contain much organic matter and hold water and nutrients better than do larger peds.

Chemical Conditions. Soils can be acid, alkaline, or neutral. The amounts of acid and alkali in a soil influence the biological and chemical processes that take place there. Highly acid or alkaline soils can harm many plants. Neutral soils support most of the biological and chemical processes, including the process

by which green plants obtain many nutrients. This process is called *cation exchange*. Many nutrients and other elements dissolve in the soil solution, forming positively charged particles called *cations*. The negatively charged clay and humus attract some cations and prevent them from being *leached* (washed away) from the topsoil by drainage waters. The solution that remains in the soil contains other cations. Nutrient cations on the clay and humus and those in the soil solution change places with nonnutrient cations that are on roots. The roots can then absorb the nutrients.

How Soils Are Classified

Pedologists classify soils according to the characteristics of a polypedon. The Soil Survey Staff of the United States Department of Agriculture uses a system that consists of 10 *orders* (groups) of soils. They are (1) Alfisols, (2) Aridisols, (3) Entisols, (4) Histosols, (5) Inceptisols, (6) Mollisols, (7) Oxisols, (8) Spodosols, (9) Ultisols, and (10) Vertisols.

Alfisols develop under forests and grasslands in humid climates. Some agricultural soils are Alfisols.

Aridisols occur in dry regions and contain small amounts of organic matter. Desert soils are Aridisols.

Entisols show little development. They resemble the parent material and occur in many climates.

Histosols are organic soils. They form in water-

469

saturated environments, including swamps and bogs.

Inceptisols are only slightly developed. They are more common in subhumid and humid climates, but also occur in most other kinds of climates.

Mollisols develop in prairie regions. They have thick, organically rich topsoils.

Oxisols are the most chemically weathered soils. They have a reddish color and occur in tropical regions.

Spodosols contain iron, aluminum, and organic matter in their B horizons. They form in humid climates.

Ultisols occur in warm, humid climates. They are moist, well-developed, acid soils.

Vertisols form in subhumid and arid warm climates. They develop wide, deep cracks during dry seasons.

Soil Conservation

The soils of farmlands, grazing lands, and forestlands provide many products and recreational areas. Soil conservationists work to ensure the wise use of these soils for both present and future needs.

Wise use of farmlands involves maintaining a high level of nutrients and organic matter in cultivated soils. Farmers add organic matter to the soil by plowing under certain green plants. They also add fertilizers and rotate crops to replace nutrients that leaching and growing plants remove. In addition, farmers plow and plant their fields in ways that control erosion. See CONSERVATION (picture: Soil Conservation).

Grazing lands that have been overgrazed also suffer from erosion. Overgrazing decreases the amounts of plant life and organic matter in the soil, and the soil erodes easily. Ranchers conserve grazing lands by limiting the time that their herds graze in one area.

Forestlands also must be protected from erosion. In some cases, foresters leave unusable branches and other parts of trees on the forest floor to add organic matter to the soil. They also develop large, healthy groups of trees whose roots protect the soil by holding it in place against wind and water erosion.   S. PAWLUK

Related Articles. See the Natural Resources or Economy section of the various country, state, and province articles. See also the following articles:

Agronomy	Erosion	Loess
Alkali	Farm and	Permafrost
Clay	Farming	Sand
Drainage	Fertilizer	Silt
Dust Bowl	Gardening	Soil Bank
Earthworm	Humus	Soil Conservation
Environmental Pol-	Irrigation	Service
lution (Soil	Loam	Topsoil
Pollution)		

Additional Resources

DONAHUE, ROY L., and others. *Soils: An Introduction to Soils and Plant Growth.* 4th ed. Prentice-Hall, 1977.

HARPSTEAD, MILO L. and HOLE, F. D. *Soil Science Simplified.* Iowa State Univ. Press, 1980.

KEEN, MARTIN L. *The World Beneath Our Feet: The Story of Soil.* Messner, 1974.

SOIL BANK was a United States federal government program designed to reduce crop surpluses by taking croplands out of production. The program consisted of a short-term *acreage reserve plan* and a long-term *conservation reserve plan.* It was adopted in 1956, but was replaced by other programs in the early 1960's.

The acreage reserve plan provided government payments to farmers who agreed to take designated cropland out of production for a year. The conservation reserve plan provided for annual government payments to farmers who agreed to keep land out of production for from three to ten years.
Critically reviewed by the DEPARTMENT OF AGRICULTURE

SOIL CONSERVATION. See CONSERVATION (Soil Conservation); EROSION.

SOIL CONSERVATION SERVICE is an agency of the United States Department of Agriculture. Its professional conservationists help farmers and ranchers prevent soil erosion from water and wind. The service gives assistance through soil-conservation districts and other state and federal agencies. It makes soil surveys, develops conservation plans for individual farms, and helps land users install anti-erosion systems. The agency also manages a national program of flood prevention, drainage and irrigation, and watershed protection. The Soil Conservation Service was established in 1935.
Critically reviewed by the SOIL CONSERVATION SERVICE

SOIL POLLUTION. See ENVIRONMENTAL POLLUTION (Soil Pollution).

SOILLESS AGRICULTURE. See HYDROPONICS.

SOKOL, *SOH kawl,* is an international physical culture and educational organization. It stresses physical fitness and moral strength. The organization has no political or religious connections, and people of any age may join. Sokol was founded in Prague, Czechoslovakia, in 1862. It has chapters in Australia, Canada, the United States, South America, and Western Europe. The American Sokol Organization was founded in 1865 and has about 80 chapters. National headquarters are at 6426 West Cermak Road, Berwyn, Ill. 60402.   Critically reviewed by the AMERICAN SOKOL ORGANIZATION

SOLANUM, *soh LAY num,* is an important group of plants that belong to the nightshade family. More than 1,000 different kinds of herbs and shrubs are included in the group. They grow in many parts of the world, but are especially abundant in tropical regions of North and South America. Some of the plants are cultivated for their showy flowers, others for their edible parts.

The most common species of solanum is the *potato.* Another is the *eggplant.* A few of the other species of the temperate regions are *bittersweet* and *common nightshade.* The *horse nettle* and other spiny troublesome weeds are native to the United States. Several species were once used as medicine, and are still used in China. The fruits of many Indonesian varieties are eaten. The *kangaroo apple* is a common food in Australia and New Zealand.

Scientific Classification. Solanums are genus *Solanum* in the nightshade family, *Solanaceae.*   GEORGE H. M. LAWRENCE

Related Articles in WORLD BOOK include:

Bittersweet	Nightshade
Eggplant	Painted-Tongue
Flowering Tobacco	Potato

SOLAR CELL. See ELECTRIC EYE; SEMICONDUCTOR; SOLAR ENERGY (Capturing Solar Energy; pictures).

SOLAR DAY. See DAY.

SOLAR ECLIPSE. See ECLIPSE.

SOLAR ENERGY is energy given off by the sun. This energy is produced by atomic reactions that take place inside the sun. During these reactions, the sun changes hydrogen atoms into helium atoms. Every second, the sun changes about 657 million short tons (596 million metric tons) of hydrogen into 653 million short tons (592 million metric tons) of helium. The missing 4 million short tons (3.6 million metric tons) of matter is changed into energy. The sun began to give off energy about 5 billion years ago. Scientists believe it will continue to supply energy for at least another 5 billion years.

It is difficult to imagine the huge amount of energy given off by the sun. Suppose that gasoline flowed over Niagara Falls at the same rate that water flows over the falls—5 billion gallons (19 billion liters) per hour. Now suppose that all the gasoline that flowed over the falls for more than 200 million years could be collected. If all that gasoline were burned, it would equal the energy that the sun gives off in an hour.

Scientists and engineers use a unit called a *kilowatt* to measure power. The sun continuously produces 390 sextillion (390 followed by 21 zeros) kilowatts of power. But the sun gives off energy in every direction. As a result, only about 1 two-billionth of the sun's energy ever reaches the upper atmosphere of the earth. Even so, the earth receives more than 1,500 quadrillion (1,500 followed by 15 zeros) kilowatt-hours of power each year. Imagine a loaded coal train that is long enough to reach from the earth to the moon and back five times. If all the coal on this train were burned, it would produce the same amount of energy that reaches the upper atmosphere of the earth from the sun in an hour.

Not all the solar energy that reaches the upper atmosphere gets to the surface of the earth. About 34 per cent is scattered into space by the gases and dust in the atmosphere, or it is directly reflected back by clouds. About 19 per cent is absorbed by the different layers of the atmosphere. This energy creates changes in

the weather. The remaining 47 per cent of the solar energy finally reaches the ground or ocean, where it is absorbed as heat.

More than 700 quadrillion kilowatt-hours of power reach the earth's surface each year. People use more than 50 trillion kilowatt-hours of power to run factories, machines, and vehicles and to heat buildings. These figures show that in 40 minutes the sun delivers to the earth's surface as much energy as people use in a year.

How Solar Energy Affects the Earth. All plants and animals on the earth need the energy of the sun to live. Green plants, by means of a process called *photosynthesis*, store solar energy as food (see PHOTOSYNTHESIS). During photosynthesis, solar energy is changed to chemical energy by plant cells that contain chlorophyll. These cells use the chemical energy to manufacture the compounds that make up the branches, leaves, roots, and other parts of plants. Animals that eat green plants absorb the energy stored by the plants. Even animals that do not eat plants depend on plants for their food energy. Such animals eat other animals that had fed on plants.

Solar energy also causes changes in the earth's weather. The sun's rays are stronger at the equator than they are at the poles. As a result, tropical air becomes warm and rises, and the cooler polar air flows down and replaces it. These currents of air circulate around the earth. Their flow is disturbed by the rotation of the earth and by local changes in the atmosphere. The actions of all these forces on one another

How the Atmosphere Affects the Amount of Solar Energy Reaching the Earth

All the solar energy that strikes the upper atmosphere does not reach the earth's surface. Clouds and particles in the air reflect some energy, and the air itself absorbs some. This diagram shows what percentage of the sun's energy entering the upper atmosphere reaches the earth's surface.

WORLD BOOK diagram

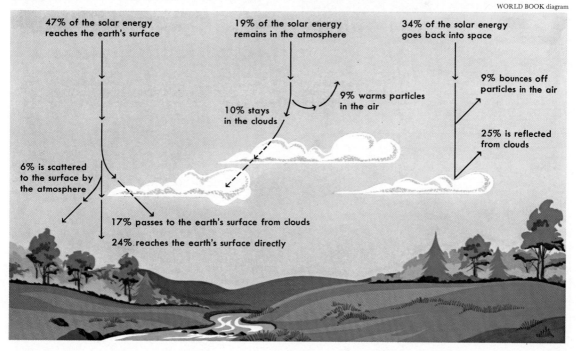

47% of the solar energy reaches the earth's surface

19% of the solar energy remains in the atmosphere

34% of the solar energy goes back into space

9% warms particles in the air

10% stays in the clouds

9% bounces off particles in the air

25% is reflected from clouds

6% is scattered to the surface by the atmosphere

17% passes to the earth's surface from clouds

24% reaches the earth's surface directly

SOLAR ENERGY

produce wind. People use only a small portion of the solar energy that is stored in the wind to power sailboats and windmills.

About a third of the sun's energy that reaches the earth evaporates water from the rivers, lakes, and oceans. The solar energy lifts the water in the form of vapor. Much of this water vapor cools and condenses as it rises. It then falls back to the earth as *precipitation* —rain, snow, or some other form of moisture. About two-thirds of the precipitation falls into the oceans. About a third of it falls on the land. The precipitation that falls on the land either evaporates again or flows into a river that returns it to the sea. Thus, the energy of the flowing water in a stream is a form of stored solar energy. Hydroelectric power stations use a small amount of this stored-up energy to generate electricity.

Capturing Solar Energy. People have been unable to harness much of the tremendous amount of solar energy that reaches the earth because this energy is spread out over such a vast area. The sun simply does not deliver much energy to any one place at any one time. The rate at which any place receives solar energy depends on a number of conditions. These conditions include the time of day, the season of the year, the latitude of the place, and whether the sky there is clear or cloudy. Even on a clear day, with the sun directly overhead, no more than 1,000 watts of power will be received by each square meter of the earth's surface. A square meter is slightly larger than a square yard.

Engineers have built a number of devices to collect solar energy. The simplest one is the *flat-plate* collector, which consists of a metal plate painted black on the side that faces the sun. Black absorbs sunlight more effectively than does any other color. The sunlight absorbed by the plate heats it. One or more layers of plastic or glass cover the plate to keep it from losing heat. The plate also has insulation along its edges and back. The heat produced by solar energy is removed by circulating water or some other fluid through tubes soldered to the back of the plate. Flat-plate collectors have been used to heat houses and to distill fresh water from sea water.

Solar energy can create high temperatures through the use of a device that concentrates the sun's rays. One such device is the *solar furnace*. A *parabolic mirror* concentrates solar energy on a small area in front of the mirror (see PARABOLA). Simple solar furnaces can create temperatures as high as 4900° F. (2700° C). In the late

How Solar Energy Heats a House

Mindy Ross, State University of New York at Albany

Collecting Heat from the Sun. A house heated by solar energy, such as the one shown above, has special *collectors* on its roof to trap sunlight. Each collector, as shown in the diagram below, has a blackened metal plate that absorbs heat from sunlight. When the plate becomes hot, it heats a liquid inside the collector. The glass sheets and fiberglass insulation prevent heat loss.

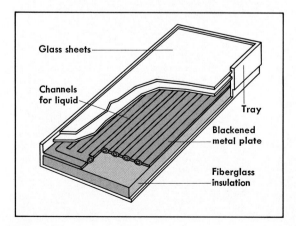

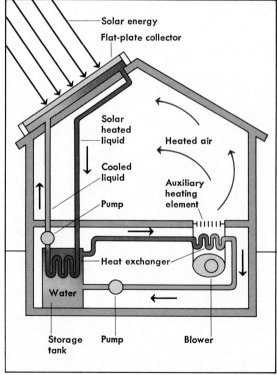

WORLD BOOK diagrams by Arthur Grebetz

Distributing Solar Heat. The liquid heated in the collectors flows to a storage tank, where its heat is transferred to water by a heat exchanger inside the tank. A pump then returns the cooled liquid to the collectors to be reheated. The hot water in the tank is pumped to another heat exchanger, which heats the air blown into the house. On cloudy days, when the collectors cannot trap enough solar energy to produce hot water, an auxiliary electrical heating element is used to warm the house.

Solar Cells convert sunlight into electricity. Panels composed of many cells, *left,* produce enough power for a large building. A single solar cell, *right,* measures about 3 inches (7.6 centimeters) in diameter. It consists of layers of silicon or other semiconductor materials.

1960's, French scientists built a solar furnace in the Pyrenees Mountains that could reach temperatures near 5975° F. (3300° C).

The sun's energy supplies the electric power for nearly all artificial satellites. Devices called *solar cells* or *solar batteries* on the outside of a satellite produce electricity when sunlight shines on them. Solar cells and batteries are made from thin slices of *semiconductor* materials (see SEMICONDUCTOR).

A solar cell has an *efficiency* of about 10 per cent. That is, only about one-tenth of the solar energy that falls on the cell is turned into electric energy. Solar cells make up for low efficiency by their high reliability. A satellite with solar cells has a reliable source of electricity for many years.

Attempts to Harness Solar Energy. The idea of using solar energy to produce high temperatures goes back to ancient times. Some historians believe that Archimedes, a Greek mathematician of the 200's B.C., set fire to Roman ships by concentrating the sun's rays on them with flat mirrors. In 1774, the French chemist Antoine Lavoisier built a solar furnace with a lens about 4 feet (1.2 meters) in diameter. His furnace reached a temperature of 3092° F. (1700° C).

In the 1870's and 1880's, the Swedish-American engineer John Ericsson tried to develop a system to change solar energy into mechanical energy. One of his devices supposedly produced 1 horsepower (746 watts) for each 100 square feet (9.3 square meters) of collecting surface.

Modern research on the use of solar energy started during the 1930's. Developments included the invention of a solar boiler by Charles G. Abbot, an American physicist, and the start of the Godfrey Cabot solar programs at Harvard University and the Massachusetts Institute of Technology. In 1954, the Bell Telephone Laboratories developed the solar battery. That same year, solar-energy scientists in the United States formed the Association for Applied Solar Energy to investigate ways to harness the sun's energy.

During the mid-1970s, shortages of oil and natural gas stimulated efforts in the United States to develop solar energy into a practical power source. In 1974, Congress passed the Solar Energy Research, Development, and Demonstration Act. The act authorized a national solar-energy research program to develop more efficient systems for collecting, concentrating, and storing energy from the sun. Such systems would permit the economical use of solar energy to heat and cool homes and office buildings. They also would enable engineers to build power plants that could convert solar energy into electricity for industrial use.   STANLEY W. ANGRIST

See also SUN.

Additional Resources

BENDICK, JEANNE. *Putting the Sun to Work.* Garrard, 1979. For younger readers.
BUCKLEY, SHAWN. *Sun Up to Sun Down.* McGraw, 1979.
BUTTI, KEN, and PERLIN, JOHN. *A Golden Thread: 2500 Years of Solar Architecture and Technology.* Van Nostrand, 1980.
MICHELS, TIM. *Solar Energy Utilization.* Van Nostrand, 1979.
RAPP, DONALD. *Solar Energy.* Prentice-Hall, 1981.

SOLAR FURNACE. See SOLAR ENERGY (Capturing Solar Energy).

SOLAR HEATING. See SOLAR ENERGY (diagram).

SOLAR PLEXUS is a large network of nerves back of the stomach. It is part of the autonomic nervous system. This system controls all the abdominal *viscera* (internal organs). The nerve threads of the autonomic nervous system connect by branches with the organs of the abdominal cavity.

A blow on a spot between the navel and breastbone, a little to the right, is called the solar plexus punch. A fighter can be knocked out by this punch if it is hard enough. The exact manner in which this occurs has not been determined. The solar plexus first became well known in 1897 as a result of the championship boxing match between James Corbett and Robert Fitzsimmons. Fitzsimmons knocked out Corbett with a blow to the solar plexus.   W. B. YOUMANS

See also NERVOUS SYSTEM.

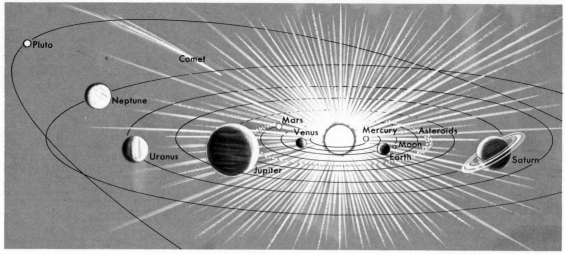

WORLD BOOK illustration by Dick Larson

The Solar System Includes Many Different Objects that travel around the sun. These objects vary from planets much larger than the earth to tiny meteoroids and dust particles.

SOLAR SYSTEM is the sun and all the objects that travel around it. The solar system includes (1) the earth and eight other *planets*, along with the *satellites* (moons) that travel around most of them; (2) planet-like objects called *asteroids;* (3) chunks of iron and stone called *meteoroids;* (4) bodies of dust and frozen gases called *comets;* and (5) drifting particles called *interplanetary dust*, and a drifting gas called *interplanetary plasma*.

The solar system has a circular shape. It is only a tiny part of a *galaxy* (family of stars) called the *Milky Way*. The Milky Way consists of more than 100 billion stars that are somewhat similar to the sun. The Milky Way, which also has a circular shape, is about 100,000 light-years across, and about 16,000 light-years thick at its center. A *light-year* is the distance light travels in one year at a speed of 186,282 miles (299,792 kilometers) per second. The solar system is less than one *light-day* (the distance light travels in one day) across. It is about 30,-000 light-years from the center of the Milky Way. The galaxy turns, and the solar system travels around the center of the Milky Way about every 200 million years.

Many stars in the Milky Way are the centers of solar systems. Some astronomers think many of these systems may have some form of life. The nearest solar system that might have intelligent life is about 100 light-years away. It would take 100 years for a radio message sent from the earth at the speed of light to reach this solar system, and another 100 years for a reply to reach the earth.

Parts of the Solar System

The Sun is the center of the solar system. Its *mass* is more than 750 times as great as that of all the planets combined (see MASS). The huge mass of the sun creates the gravitation that keeps the other objects traveling around the sun in an orderly manner.

The sun continuously gives off energy in several forms—visible light; invisible *infrared, ultraviolet, X,* and *gamma* rays; radio waves; and *plasma* (hot, electrically charged gas). The flow of plasma, which be-comes interplanetary plasma and drifts throughout the solar system, is called the *solar wind* (see SOLAR WIND).

The surface of the sun changes continuously. Bright spots called *plages* and dark spots called *sunspots*, frequently form and disappear. Gases often shoot up violently from the surface. For a complete description of the sun, see the article SUN.

Planets are the second largest objects in the solar system. The four planets nearest the sun—Mercury, Venus, Earth, and Mars—are the smallest planets, although Pluto's size has not been accurately determined. Those four planets are called *terrestrial* (earth-like) planets, and appear to consist chiefly of iron and rock. The earth has one satellite, and Mars has two. Mercury and Venus have no satellites.

The four largest planets—Jupiter, Saturn, Uranus, and Neptune—are called the *major* planets. They are probably made up chiefly of hydrogen, helium, ammonia, and methane. Compared to the terrestrial planets, they contain little iron and rock. Each of the major planets has several satellites. Pluto, the farthest planet from the sun, appears to be somewhat like the terrestrial planets. But because Pluto is so far away, astronomers know little about it and do not include it in either group.

All the planets except Pluto are surrounded by varying kinds and amounts of gases. The earth is the only planet that has enough oxygen surrounding it and enough water on its surface to support life as we know it.

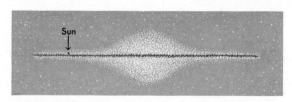

The Milky Way is made up of more than 100 billion stars similar to the sun. Many stars have their own solar systems. This side view of the Milky Way shows the position of the sun in the galaxy.

For a more complete description of the planets, see PLANET and the separate articles on each planet.

Asteroids, also called *planetoids*, are small, irregularly shaped objects. Most asteroids are between the orbits of Mars and Jupiter. Astronomers have figured out the sizes and orbits of about 1,700 of the largest asteroids. Few asteroids are larger than 100 miles (160 kilometers) across, and many are less than 1 mile (1.6 kilometers) across. Astronomers believe that the asteroid belt between Mars and Jupiter includes a large amount of dust that has been created by collisions between asteroids. See ASTEROID.

Meteoroids are small chunks of iron and rock. They are thought to result from collisions between asteroids. Meteoroids also may be formed when comets disintegrate into fragments. Many meteoroids fall into the earth's atmosphere, but most are burned up by friction before they reach the surface of the earth. Meteoroids are called *meteors* while falling through the atmosphere, and *meteorites* if they are found on the earth's surface. See METEOR.

Comets. Most comets have three parts: (1) a solid *nucleus*, or center; (2) a round *coma*, or head, that surrounds the nucleus and consists of dust particles mixed with frozen water, frozen methane, and frozen ammonia; and (3) a long *tail* of dust and gases that escape from the head. Most comets stay near the outside of the solar system. Some come near the sun, where their bright heads and long, shining tails provide a rare and spectacular sight. See COMET.

Formation of the Solar System

Astronomers do not have enough information to describe the formation of the solar system completely. Many ideas have been suggested, but parts of all of them have been proved wrong.

Until the mid-1900's, theories of how the solar system was formed could be based on only five observations. (1) The sun and most other parts of the solar system spin in the same direction on their *axes* (imaginary lines drawn through their centers). (2) Most parts of the solar system travel around the sun in the same direction that the sun spins. (3) Most satellites travel around their planets in the same direction that the planets travel around the sun. (4) Going outward from the sun, the distance between the orbits of the planets increases. (5) The solar system has a circular shape.

The theories that have been suggested to explain the above observations can be divided into two general groups—*monistic theories* and *dualistic theories*. Most astronomers believe that some form of monistic theory will someday be proved correct.

Monistic Theories are based on the belief that the solar system was formed from a single flat cloud of gas. According to some monistic theories, all parts of the solar system were formed from the gas at the same time. Other monistic theories suggest that the sun was formed first, and the planets and other objects came later from the remaining gas. The first monistic theory was proposed in the early 1600's by the French scientist and philosopher René Descartes. In the late 1700's, Pierre Simon de Laplace, also of France, suggested the monistic theory called the *nebular hypothesis*.

Dualistic Theories are based on the belief that the solar system was formed when some huge object passed

near the sun. According to these theories, the force of gravity of the passing object pulled a long stream of gas out from the sun. The planets and other objects were formed from this gas. The first dualistic theory was proposed in the 1700's by the French scientist Comte de Buffon. Buffon believed the passing object was a large comet, which he incorrectly thought was as large as a star. In the early 1900's, Thomas Chamberlin and Forest Moulton, both of the University of Chicago, offered a dualistic theory called the *planetesimal hypothesis*.

Theories Since the Mid-1900's are helping scientists come closer to learning how the solar system was formed. For example, astronomers have discovered that the Milky Way is at least twice as old as the solar system. For that reason, the processes of star formation seen in the galaxy today are probably similar to the processes that formed the sun.

The study of meteorites is producing new information about temperatures, pressures, and other conditions that probably existed during the formation of the solar system. Measurements of the radioactivity of meteorites indicate that they were formed at about the same time as the solar system, about $4\frac{1}{2}$ billion years ago.

The exploration of the moon has provided scientists with a better understanding of how and when the moon was formed. They have learned that the moon was once geologically active, as the earth is today. Rock samples brought back by the Apollo astronauts in the late 1960's revealed that volcanic eruptions occurred on the moon more than 3 billion years ago.

Data collected by space probes during the 1960's and 1970's indicate that the atmospheres and interiors of most of the planets differ greatly from those of the earth. By continuing to study the planets, scientists hope to discover how various chemical elements are spread throughout the solar system. They also hope to learn why some planets have large amounts of carbon dioxide in their atmospheres, and whether the major planets have gaseous or liquid surfaces.

Studies of the sun may lead to the discovery of how the interior of the sun heats its outer atmosphere. They also may help explain why the formation of sunspots reaches a peak about every 11 years.   A. G. W. CAMERON

Related Articles in WORLD BOOK include:

Astronomy	Mars	Pluto
Bode's Law	Mercury	Saturn
Earth (The Birth of	Milky Way	Star
the Solar System)	Moon	Sun
Galaxy	Neptune	Uranus
Gravitation	Planet	Venus
Jupiter		

Additional Resources

Level I
BRANLEY, FRANKLYN M. *The Nine Planets.* Rev. ed. Harper, 1978.
FREEMAN, MAE and IRA. *The Sun, the Moon, and the Stars.* Rev. ed. Random House, 1979.

Level II
BEATTY, J. KELLY, and others. *The New Solar System.* Cambridge, 1981.
COOK, ALAN H. *Interiors of the Planets.* Cambridge, 1981.
GUEST, JOHN. *Planetary Geology.* Halsted, 1980.
WHIPPLE, FRED L. *Orbiting the Sun: Planets and Satellites of the Solar System.* Harvard, 1981.

SOLAR WIND

SOLAR WIND is a continuous flow of gases from the sun. It results chiefly from the expansion of gases in the *corona*, the outermost atmosphere of the sun. The corona's high temperature, which averages about 4,000,000° F. (2,200,000° C), heats the gases and causes them to expand. Many of the gas atoms collide as they are heated. During the collisions, they lose their electrons and become electrically charged particles. These particles, which are called *ions*, make up much of the solar wind.

The solar wind has a velocity of about 310 miles (500 kilometers) per second and a density of about 82 ions per cubic inch (5 ions per cubic centimeter). It is responsible for a variety of occurrences in the solar system. For example, the *magnetosphere*, a region of strong magnetic forces surrounding the earth, is pushed into a teardrop shape by the solar wind as it streams past the earth. The magnetosphere prevents particles of the solar wind from reaching the surface of the earth. The blowing of the solar wind against a comet produces an *ion tail*, which is one of the various types of tails that comets have. Ion tails are long and straight and consist of ionized material that the solar wind has blown off the comet.

In 1959, the Russian *Luna 2* spacecraft confirmed the existence of the solar wind and made the first measurements of its properties. Several American spacecraft have also had equipment that made studies of this wind. The Apollo 11 and Apollo 12 astronauts placed large metal screens called *foils* on the moon to collect solar wind particles. The moon has no magnetosphere, and so the particles reach its surface. The astronauts brought the foils back to the earth for analysis.

Studies of stars other than the sun show that gases also stream away from them. As a result, astronomers believe many stars produce winds, called *stellar winds*, that resemble the solar wind.　　　MORTON S. ROBERTS

See also EARTH (illustration: The Earth Has a Magnetic "Tail"); MAGNETIC STORM.

SOLDER, *SAHD uhr,* is a metal alloy used to join metal surfaces together (see ALLOY). It is also used to mend metal objects. To be effective, the solder must melt more easily than the metals to which it is applied.

There are two types of solder, hard and soft. Hard solders will melt only at high temperatures. The advantage of hard solders is their strength and the fact that they can be pressed or hammered into various shapes without breaking. Some hard solders are drawn out into long threads and others are pressed into sheets. The most common hard solder is silver solder, which consists of silver, copper, and zinc. Other common solders include brasses made up mainly of copper and zinc. Many copper alloys are also used as hard solders.

Soft solders will melt at low temperatures. But they are weak and cannot be hammered without breaking. The most common soft solders include various alloys that consist mainly of tin and lead. These alloys also contain other metals such as antimony, cadmium, bismuth, and silver.　　　WILLIAM W. MULLINS

SOLDIER. See ARMY; ARMY, UNITED STATES; RANK IN ARMED SERVICES.

SOLDIERS' HOMES. See VETERANS ADMINISTRATION (History).

SOLDIER'S MEDAL. See DECORATIONS AND MEDALS.

SOLE is the name of a family of flatfishes which have twisted skulls so that both eyes are on the same side of the body. Soles live in warm seas near shores. Their eyes are small and set close together. The mouth is crooked, and the body flat and oval shaped.

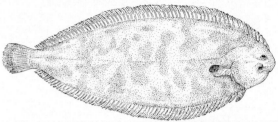

WORLD BOOK illustration by Marion Pahl

A Sole has a flat, oval-shaped body with both eyes on one side of the head. The European sole, *above,* is considered a delicacy.

The *European sole* grows from 10 to 20 inches (25 to 51 centimeters) long, and usually weighs about 1 pound (0.5 kilogram). The *common American sole*, also called *hogchoker*, lives along the eastern coast of North America. It may travel far up rivers. The American sole is often used as food. Some kinds of flounder that live along coasts are also called soles (see FLOUNDER).

Scientific Classification. Soles make up the sole family, *Soleidae.* The American sole is genus *Trinectes*, species *T. manulatus.* The European sole is classified as genus *Solea*, species *S. vulgaris.*　　　LEONARD P. SCHULTZ

SOLENODON, *suh LEE nuh dahn,* is a rare animal that looks like a long-nosed rat. The *yellow-headed solenodon* lives in Cuba and the *brown solenodon* makes its home in Haiti. The solenodon lives in hollow logs and rocky dens, and comes out for food only at night. It scratches for insects with its long claws. The solenodon weighs about 2½ pounds (1 kilogram) and grows about 2 feet (61 centimeters) long, including its stiff, scaly tail, which is 10 inches (25 centimeters) long. It has a long, pointed snout and short, coarse hair. The solenodon is bad tempered, and its saliva may be poisonous.

Scientific Classification. The solenodon is in the solenodon family, *Solenodontidae.* The Haitian solenodon is genus *Solenodon*, species *S. paradoxus.* The Cuban solenodon is *S. cubanus.*

New York Zoological Society

The Rare Solenodon looks like a long-nosed rat. It is a shy animal, and rarely comes above ground in daylight hours.

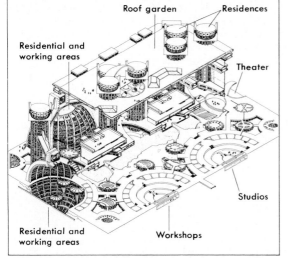

Roof garden — Residences

Residential and working areas

Theater

Studios

Residential and working areas

Workshops

Reprinted from *Arcology* by Paolo Soleri by permission of The M.I.T. Press, Cambridge, Mass.

Soleri's Experimental Cities are designed on many vertical levels to save land. Soleri planned the community of Arcosanti, above, to occupy only a few acres in the Arizona desert. He believes that society must develop such communities to preserve the environment from rapidly growing metropolitan areas.

SOLERI, *soh LEH ree,* **PAOLO** (1919-   ), is an Italian-born architect and urban planner. He became famous for his theories of preserving the environment. Soleri believes that, to protect nature's resources, cities should be built on as little land as possible.

According to Soleri, an urban center should be a single structure surrounded by open land used for agriculture and recreation. He calls such a city an *arcology,* a term formed by combining parts of the words *architecture* and *ecology.* In 1970, Soleri began to build his first experimental city, called Arcosanti, near Prescott, Ariz. He designed Arcosanti for a population of 3,000.

Soleri has also designed other urban environments. As in Arcosanti, all housing, business, and industrial facilities would be located within a single gigantic structure. Such cities would use shuttle systems and moving walkways instead of automobiles. Nuclear and solar power would provide energy. Soleri's designs for these cities indicate his concern for pure geometric forms, and his strong faith in technology and machines.

Soleri was born in Turin, Italy. He moved to the United States in 1947 and settled in Arizona. There he built structures half hidden in the earth. He built some structures by forming the earth into a desired shape, pouring concrete over it, and then removing the earth to expose the interior space.   DAVID GEBHARD

SOLICITOR. See LAWYER.

SOLICITOR GENERAL. See JUSTICE, DEPARTMENT OF; SUPREME COURT OF THE UNITED STATES (Pleading Cases); CANADA, GOVERNMENT OF (The Cabinet).

SOLID, in mathematics, is a geometric figure with the three dimensions of length, breadth, and thickness. Some solids are named from the shapes of their surfaces, such as cubes, cylinders, cones, and spheres. In physics, solid refers to one of the three possible *states* (forms) in which matter may exist. The other states are *liquid* and *gaseous.* The state of each body of matter is classified according to the power of its molecules to resist forces that may change its shape. A solid has a fixed shape, weight, and volume.   HOWARD S. KALTENBORN

Related Articles in WORLD BOOK include:

Cohesion	Cylinder	Matter (Solids)	Prism
Cone	Gas	Mensuration	Pyramid
Cube	Liquid	Molecule	Sphere

SOLID GEOMETRY. See GEOMETRY.

SOLID SOUTH. See RECONSTRUCTION (Effects).

SOLID-STATE PHYSICS deals with the physical properties of solid materials. These properties include magnetism, *luminescence* (giving off light), mechanical strength, and the conduction of electricity and heat. Solid-state physicists try to understand the properties of solids by studying the arrangement and motion of the atoms and electrons that make them up.

The atoms or molecules of most solids are arranged in a repeated pattern called *crystals* (see CRYSTAL). The basic building block of a crystal is the *unit cell,* which is repeated over and over. Physicists beam electrons, X rays, or neutrons at crystals to learn how the atoms or molecules are arranged.

Much of the progress in solid-state physics has been made by preparing extremely pure single crystals of various substances and studying their properties. The detailed structure of the electron distribution of a solid can be determined in this way. The information learned from such relatively ideal materials provides a better understanding of common materials and helps people create new materials with superior properties.

The field of solid-state physics has grown rapidly since about 1946 because of its importance to industry and its scientific interest. More people are involved in it than in any other area of physics. Achievements of solid-state physics include the development of transistors and other devices used in electronic circuits. Solid-state physicists have also made *ferrites* (magnets that do not conduct electricity) used in the memory cores of computers, solid lasers, solar batteries, solid *luminescent sources* (devices that change electricity directly into light), and sensitive detectors for many types of radiation. The electrical, computer, communications, and space industries make use of solid-state technology.

A knowledge of the *quantum theory* is essential in studying solid-state physics. The theory forms the basis of understanding the structure of atoms and molecules and the forces that bind them together to form crystals.

Quantum theory has given an understanding of one of the most remarkable properties to be studied in solid-state physics, *superconductivity.* In normal metals, voltage must be applied and power used to keep an electric current flowing. But in a superconductor, a current will flow indefinitely with no applied voltage. Superconductivity is exhibited by many metals and alloys at extremely low temperatures—for example, a few degrees above absolute zero (−273.15° C, or −459.67° F.).

Solid-state physics is an expanding field of research with many other challenging problems. Some of the problems being studied involve the interaction of light from intense laser beams with matter. Other areas of research include the conversion of electrical energy into light, and improving materials for solid lasers and light sources. Methods of solid-state physics are also being

474c

SOLITAIRE

applied to the transfer of energy and electrical charge in organic systems important in biology.   JOHN BARDEEN

See also SEMICONDUCTOR; TRANSISTOR; INTEGRATED CIRCUIT; QUANTUM MECHANICS; CRYOGENICS; SUPERCONDUCTIVITY; ZONE MELTING.

SOLITAIRE, a bird. See DODO.

SOLITAIRE, *SAHL uh tair*, is the name given to many card games that are played by only one person. Solitaire is usually played with 52 cards.

In one kind of solitaire, the player deals seven cards in a row, the first one faceup and the rest facedown. Then the player deals a card faceup on the second card, and a card facedown on each of the remaining five.

WORLD BOOK photo

In Solitaire, the player stacks the cards into piles by suit and in order, *top*, and by alternate color and rank, *bottom*.

The deal continues until all seven piles have a card facing up.

One card may be placed on a second card if it is one lower in rank and is the opposite color of the second card. Aces rank lowest and are put in a row above the main piles. The object is to stack the cards by suits and in order in the top piles, from ace to king. The top card in any lower pile may be moved to this row if the card before it in the same suit is the last card in a pile. A facedown card that becomes the top card in a lower pile may be turned faceup. The cards that were not dealt into piles are kept facedown. Every third card is turned faceup.   LILLIAN FRANKEL

SOLOMON, the son of David, was the king who brought Israel its greatest prosperity and glory. His mother was Bathsheba, whom King David married after her husband, Uriah, died in battle (see BATHSHEBA; DAVID). In the closing days of David's life, an older son, Adonijah, tried to become his successor to the throne. But David had Solomon anointed as king, and Adonijah had to flee.

Solomon became king about 960 B.C. Soon after he became king, he went up to the sanctuary at Gibeon to pray. The Lord appeared to him and asked him to name whatever blessing he most desired. Solomon requested only one thing: wisdom to know how best to govern his people and encourage them to lead a godly life, in obedience to the Law of Moses. God bestowed upon him not only wisdom, but also wealth, power, and victory over his enemies. He became so renowned that he excited the admiration of other countries.

Shortly after he became king, Solomon began building the Temple of Jehovah. He wanted it to surpass in glory the idolatrous temples of the heathen. He finished it in seven or eight years, and used gold and silver worth as much as $250 million.

Solomon composed remarkable works on natural history and practical philosophy. He also wrote beautiful poetry, such as the Biblical book, Song of Solomon (see SONG OF SOLOMON). The book of Ecclesiastes and a large part of Proverbs are also attributed to Solomon.

The greatness of Solomon's success and prosperity led to pride and self-indulgence. He had about 1,000 wives and mistresses. He indulged their religious preferences by building pagan shrines where they could worship. This action paved the way for the influence of idolatry upon the Hebrew nation. Solomon was also proud of his war chariots and built huge stables in which to quarter his horses. His ships brought goods from India, southern Arabia, and Ethiopia.

After a few decades, the prosperity of Israel dwindled greatly. Economic hardship became widespread, despite almost complete freedom from war and in spite of

Detail of *The Judgment of Solomon* (1649), an oil painting on canvas by Nicolas Poussin; the Louvre, Paris (Giraudon)

Solomon was a king of ancient Israel. A Bible story tells about two mothers who came to him, one with a live baby and the other with a dead baby. Each woman claimed the live child was hers. Solomon ordered the infant cut in half and shared between them. But one of the mothers begged him to give the baby to the other woman rather than kill it. Solomon gave the baby to the first woman. He knew she was the real mother because she cared so much for its safety.

A Village School in the Solomon Islands has several huts, each housing one grade. About two-thirds of the children in the country attend elementary and high school.

friendly relations with all neighboring peoples. Solomon's people finally revolted against high taxes and the system of forced labor that supported his extravagant building projects. His last years were embittered by personal disillusionment and by hostility at home and abroad. After Solomon died, his incompetent son, Rehoboam, could not hold the Hebrew empire together. The Ten Tribes broke away and set up the Northern Kingdom of Ephraim, or Israel.   GLEASON L. ARCHER, JR.

SOLOMON ISLANDS is an island country in the South Pacific Ocean. Its largest islands are Choiseul, Guadalcanal, Malaita, New Georgia, San Cristobal, and Santa Isabel. Its many other islands include Bellona, Rennell, and the Santa Cruz Islands.

The country's largest islands are part of an island chain that is also called the Solomon Islands. However, not all the islands in the chain belong to the country of the Solomon Islands. Bougainville, Buka, and a few smaller islands in the northern part of the chain are part of Papua New Guinea.

The Solomon Islands lies about 1,000 miles (1,610 kilometers) northeast of Australia. It has a land area of 11,500 square miles (29,785 square kilometers). The country spreads over about 230,000 square miles (600,000 square kilometers) of ocean. About 263,000 persons live in the Solomon Islands.

Great Britain ruled the Solomons from 1893 to 1978, when the islands became independent. Honiara, on Guadalcanal, is the capital and largest community of the Solomons. It has a population of about 15,000. The Solomon Islands dollar is the country's basic unit of currency. "God Save Our Solomon Islands" is the national anthem. For a picture of the country's flag, see FLAG (Flags of Asia and the Pacific).

Government. The Solomon Islands is a constitutional monarchy and a member of the Commonwealth of Nations (see COMMONWEALTH OF NATIONS). A prime minister, who is the leader of the political party with the most seats in Parliament, heads the government. An eight-member Cabinet helps the prime minister run the government. Cabinet members are appointed by the prime minister. A 38-member Parliament makes the country's laws. The people elect the members of Parliament to four-year terms. A governor general represents the British monarch in the Solomon Islands.

The Solomon Islands is divided into four districts for purposes of local government. Elected local councils govern the districts.

People. Most Solomon Islanders are dark-skinned people called Melanesians, and more than 90 per cent of them live in rural villages. Many of the people build houses on stilts to keep the dwellings cool. The main foods of the people include chicken, fish, pork, coconuts, and *taro*, a tropical plant with one or more edible rootlike stems.

Although English is the official language of the Solomon Islands, about 90 languages are spoken among the

WORLD BOOK map

Solomon Islands

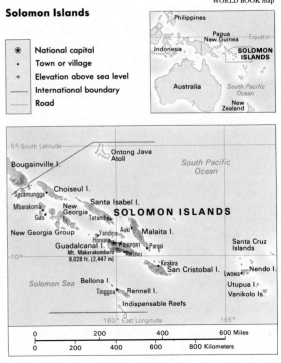

⊛	National capital
•	Town or village
+	Elevation above sea level
	International boundary
	Road

SOLOMON ISLANDS

Melanesians. The islanders also speak *Pidgin English*, which helps them cross language barriers (see PIDGIN ENGLISH). About 80 per cent of the people are Protestants. The other islanders are Roman Catholics or follow local traditional beliefs. The nation has about 350 elementary schools, about 10 high schools, and a technical school. About 200 islanders go to universities in Papua New Guinea and Fiji.

Land and Climate. The country's main islands were formed by volcanoes. They are rugged, mountainous, and covered with tropical plants. The islands range from 90 to 120 miles (140 to 190 kilometers) long and from 20 to 30 miles (32 to 48 kilometers) wide. Each island has a central spine that has mountains up to about 7,000 feet (2,100 meters) high. The land drops sharply to the sea on one side of the island and gently to a narrow coastal strip on the other. Some of the outlying islands are *atolls* (ring-shaped coral reefs).

Rainfall in the Solomon Islands varies from 60 to 200 inches (150 to 500 centimeters) annually. Temperatures range from 70° to 90° F. (21° to 32° C).

Economy. Fish, timber, and *copra* (dried coconut meat) are the main products of the Solomon Islands. Japan buys almost all the fish and timber exported by the country. Food, machinery, manufactured goods, and gasoline are imported from Australia, Great Britain, Japan, Malaysia, and Singapore. The country has good shipping services, but most of its roads are poor. Air routes connect the Solomon Islands with Australia and other neighboring islands. The government publishes a weekly newspaper and broadcasts radio programs in both English and Pidgin English.

History. Scholars believe the Solomon Islands were first settled about 3,000 years ago by people from New Guinea. In 1568, a Spanish explorer named Álvaro de Mendaña became the first European to reach the islands. Few other Europeans went there until the 1700's. From 1870 to 1911, Europeans recruited nearly 30,000 islanders to work on plantations in Fiji and in Queensland, Australia. Some of the islanders were recruited by force and treated harshly. As a result, Great Britain took control of the Solomons in 1893 and made them a protectorate.

Guadalcanal and other islands in the Solomons were the scene of fierce fighting between Allied and Japanese forces in 1942 and 1943, during World War II. The Solomon Islands gained independence from Great Britain on July 7, 1978.   ROBERT LANGDON

See also GUADALCANAL ISLAND; HONIARA; WORLD WAR II (The South Pacific).

SOLOMON ISLANDS are a chain of islands in the South Pacific Ocean. They lie northeast of Australia. For location, see PACIFIC ISLANDS (map). The southern islands of the chain are part of a country that is called the Solomon Islands, and the northern islands are part of Papua New Guinea.

The southern Solomons include Choiseul, Guadalcanal, Malaita, New Georgia, San Cristobal, Santa Isabel, and many smaller islands. They cover 10,983 square miles (28,446 square kilometers). The northern islands include Bougainville, Buka, and a few smaller islands. They cover 4,200 square miles (10,878 square kilometers). Bitter fighting between Japanese and

United States forces took place in the Solomons in 1942 and 1943, during World War II. For more information, see the articles on the countries of SOLOMON ISLANDS and PAPUA NEW GUINEA. See also BOUGAINVILLE; GUADALCANAL ISLAND; WORLD WAR II (The South Pacific).   GEORGE F. DEASY

SOLOMON'S-SEAL is a hardy plant that grows in the temperate zones of North America, Europe, and Asia. Several closely related plants have this name. It gets its name from its thick, creeping rootstalks which bear growth scars that resemble the mystic seal of Solomon.

The plant has a long, arching stem that gives it a graceful appearance. It bears round berries that may be blue or black. Greenish, bell-shaped flowers grow at the bases of the leaves. Solomon's-seal grows best in shady places and rich, moist soil.

Scientific Classification. Solomon's-seal belongs to the lily family, *Liliaceae*. It is genus *Polygonatum*. EARL L. CORE

J. Horace McFarland

Solomon's-Seal is a plant with a long, arching stem. The plant's bell-shaped flowers grow at the base of its leaves.

SOLON, *SOH luhn* (639?-559? B.C.), was a famous lawmaker. He was known as one of the *seven wise men of Greece.*

Solon was born in Athens of a noble family. He first became known as a poet. His poems played a great part in urging the Athenians to regain the island of Salamis, which had long been in foreign hands. He was given command of the forces sent to take back the island, and he quickly conquered it. Afterward, Solon was elected an *archon* (chief government official) of Athens and was given authority to change the laws (see ARCHON).

Athens was badly in need of political and economic reforms. Most of the wealth was in the hands of a few powerful citizens. The farmers had been forced to mortgage their lands and to borrow money, offering themselves and their families as security. Solon immediately passed a law which canceled all these debts and mortgages, and freed those who had become slaves. He also changed the monetary system so that foreign trade was made easier. The only change Solon made in foreign trade was a law prohibiting the exportation of grain.

Solon's constitutional reforms redivided the citizens into four classes, according to income. Citizens of all classes were allowed to become members of the assembly and the public law courts. Solon established a council of 400 to take over the political powers of the Areopagus, and set up popular courts in which citizens could appeal the decisions of the officials (see AREOPAGUS). He kept the old provisions that allowed only the three higher classes to hold public office, and only the highest class to hold the archonship. These provisions continued the oligarchy, but his reforms were a definite step toward democracy.

Solon is said to have made the Athenians promise to keep his laws for 10 years. He then left the state. When he returned 10 years later, he found the country fighting a civil war. Soon afterward, Pisistratus seized control. After opposing Pisistratus, Solon retired from public life.   DONALD KAGAN

SOLSTICE is one of the two moments each year when the sun is at either its northernmost or southernmost position. The sun appears directly overhead at different latitudes during the year because of the tilt of the earth's axis of rotation. The axis is tilted at an angle of 23° 27' to the plane of the earth's orbit around the sun. The *summer solstice* occurs when the sun reaches its most northerly point, directly overhead at the Tropic of Cancer (23° 27' north latitude). At the *winter solstice*, the sun is at its most southerly position, directly over the Tropic of Capricorn (23° 27' south latitude).

The summer solstice occurs on approximately June 21, and the winter solstice on about December 21. In the Northern Hemisphere, the day of the summer solstice is the longest day of the year and marks the beginning of summer. Similarly, the winter solstice occurs on the shortest day of the year and indicates the beginning of winter. In the Southern Hemisphere, summer and winter are reversed.   JAY M. PASACHOFF

See also EQUINOX; SEASON; TROPIC OF CANCER; TROPIC OF CAPRICORN.

SOLTI, *SHOHL tee,* **SIR GEORG** (1912-   ), is a leading symphony orchestra and opera conductor. He has won fame for his interpretations of romantic works, especially the symphonies of Anton Bruckner and Gustav Mahler and the operas of Richard Wagner.

Solti was born in Budapest, Hungary. He worked at the Budapest Opera House from 1930 until World War II began in 1939. From that year until the war ended in 1945, he lived in Switzerland. Solti worked in Germany from 1946 to 1960. He served as music director of the Munich State Opera until 1952, when he was named conductor of the Frankfurt Opera. Solti became con-

Chicago Symphony Orchestra
Sir Georg Solti

ductor of the Royal Opera House in London in 1961 and music director of the Chicago Symphony Orchestra in 1969. He became a British subject in 1971 and was knighted in 1972. Solti became conductor of the London Philharmonic Orchestra in 1979.   KEITH POLK

SOLUBLE GLASS. See WATER GLASS.

SOLUTION is a mixture of two or more individual substances that cannot be separated by a mechanical means, such as filtration. Many solutions include a liquid, but some do not. There are three basic kinds of solutions: (1) liquid, (2) solid, and (3) gaseous.

Liquid Solutions result when a liquid is dissolved in another liquid. They also form when a solid or a gas dissolves in a liquid. Common examples include water mixed with alcohol, and sugar dissolved in coffee. Two liquids that have the ability to form a solution are said to be *miscible*. This ability depends on the chemical properties of the liquids and on such physical conditions as temperature and atmospheric pressure. Some liquid mixtures are more miscible than others. Water and alcohol are completely miscible because any amount of the two substances produces a solution.

Gases and solids that dissolve in a liquid are said to be *soluble*. A given volume of water at a particular temperature dissolves only up to a certain amount of salt. Any additional salt remains as an undissolved solid. This maximum amount of salt that the water can dissolve is called the *solubility* of the salt in water. The substance that is dissolved is called the *solute*, and the substance that dissolves it is the *solvent* (see SOLVENT). The solubility of most solids depends on the chemical properties of the individual substances and on the temperature of the liquid solution. For gases, solubility also depends on pressure.

Solid Solutions, in most cases, form when liquid solutions freeze. For example, a mixture of melted copper and zinc cools to form brass, a solid solution. Sterling silver, another solid solution, results when melted silver and copper are mixed and cooled.

Gaseous Solutions result from the mixture of gases. Air, a gaseous solution, is a mixture of nitrogen and oxygen, plus smaller amounts of argon and carbon dioxide. Gaseous solutions are completely miscible. Physical conditions do not affect the ability of gases to form a solution.   JOHN B. BUTT

SOLVENT is a substance that dissolves another substance to form a solution. The term *solvent* is also used to refer to the substance in a solution that is present in the greater amount. The substance present in the lesser amount is called the *solute*.

Most solvents and the solutions they form are liquids, but there are some solutions of gases or solids. Water is the most common solvent and it forms various solutions. Other common solvents include acetone and alcohol. In most cases, a solvent and the substance it dissolves have similar molecules. For example, water will dissolve acetone or ethanol but not oil, which is dissolved instead by gasoline.

Solvents have many industrial and scientific applications. They are used in the production of cleaning fluids and such coatings as inks and paints. Solvents also are important in the manufacture of nylon, polyethylene, and many other synthetic fibers. In addition, they are useful for *extraction*. This technique involves the transfer of a solute from one solution into a second solvent for further separation. The solute may be a useful by-product or an impurity. Extraction is used in analytical chemistry, chemical purification, and petroleum refining.   J. D. CORBETT

Related Articles in WORLD BOOK include:

Acetone	Carbon	Chloroform	Paint	Turpentine
Alcohol	Disulfide	Furfural	Solution	

SOLZHENITSYN, *SAWL zhuh NEET sihn,* **ALEXANDER** (1918-   ), is a Russian novelist. He was awarded the 1970 Nobel prize for literature.

Alexander Isaevich Solzhenitsyn was born in Kislovodsk. He served four years in the Soviet Army during World War II. In 1945, while still in the army, Solzhenitsyn was falsely accused of a political crime. He was arrested and spent eight years in labor camps and three years in exile.

Alexander Solzhenitsyn
United Press Int.

Solzhenitsyn's novels reflect his prison and war experiences. *One Day in the Life of Ivan Denisovich* (1962) and *The First Circle* (1964) have prison settings. *Cancer Ward* (1966) takes place in a hospital. Using the prison and the hospital as symbols of society, the author dramatizes the contrast between revolutionary ideals and harsh political reality. His heroes express the triumph of dignity over tyranny and suffering.

Solzhenitsyn has also written a historical novel, *August 1914* (1971). The book describes the Russian army's defeat by the Germans at the Battle of Tannenberg in the opening weeks of World War I.

Throughout the 1960's and early 1970's, the Soviet government accused Solzhenitsyn of slandering his country in his writings. The government intensified its attacks on the author following the publication in Paris of volume one of Solzhenitsyn's three-volume *The Gulag Archipelago, 1918-1956* in 1973. The book is a study of the Soviet prison camp system. Volume two of *The Gulag Archipelago* was published in 1975, and volume three in 1976. In 1974, the government revoked Solzhenitsyn's citizenship and deported him. He lived in Switzerland for about two years and then settled in the United States in 1976. Solzhenitsyn described his final years in Russia in the autobiography *The Oak and the Calf* (1975).   THOMPSON BRADLEY

Additional Resources

ERICSON, EDWARD E., Jr. *Solzhenitsyn: The Moral Vision.* Eerdmans, 1980.

FEUER, KATHRYN, ed. *Solzhenitsyn: A Collection of Critical Essays.* Prentice-Hall, 1976.

KODJAK, ANDREJ. *Alexander Solzhenitsyn.* Twayne, 1978.

SOMALIA, *soh MAH lee uh,* is the easternmost country on the mainland of Africa. It stretches along Africa's "horn," facing the Gulf of Aden and the Indian Ocean. Most Somalis are herders who wander over the hot, dry land in search of water and pasture. Somalia has

Somalia

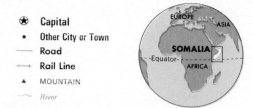

WORLD BOOK map

few towns. Mogadishu, which has about 445,000 people, is the capital and largest town.

Wild animals are plentiful in Somalia. Antelope, cheetahs, and lions roam the grasslands. Crocodiles swim in the country's main rivers, and elephants and hippopotamuses live in the forests along the riverbanks.

Somalia consists of two regions that were once called British Somaliland and Italian Somaliland. These colonies became independent in 1960, and combined to form the nation of Somalia.

Government. Military leaders control Somalia's government. Military officers hold the top posts in both the government and the country's only political party, the Somali Socialist Revolutionary Party. The head of the party also serves as the country's president. A Council of Ministers, appointed by the party's leaders, helps the president carry out the operations of the government. The party's leaders make the country's government policies. A People's Assembly approves the policies. The party's leaders choose the candidates for the assembly. The people vote for or against the candidates in elections.

People. More than 70 per cent of the Somalis are nomads who raise herds of camels, cattle, goats, and sheep. The others live on farms or in Somalia's few towns. Almost all the people are Muslims of the Sunnite branch of Islam. They claim to be related to Muhammad, the founder of Islam. See ISLAM.

The nomads roam over vast stretches of their hot, dry land in search of water and pasture for their herds. Their hard life leaves little time for relaxation. When water and pasture are plentiful, however, they enjoy telling stories and holding poetry contests in the evening around a campfire. They recite long poems about major events, such as battles and victories, or in praise of prized possessions such as camels and horses.

The nomads live in small, collapsible, beehive-shaped huts that have arched wooden braces covered with skins and grass mats. When the grass and water are used up in one spot, they pack their huts and move to a new spot. Their chief food is milk, especially camel's milk. They eat rice and other grains, and mutton. In southern parts of Somalia, the people roast coffee beans in butter oil and eat them boiling hot with milk.

The men and women wrap brightly colored cloth or cotton sheeting around their bodies like a toga. Many of the men wear the *lungi*, a kind of kilt. Many who live in the towns wear trousers and shirts.

Before 1973, Arabic, English, and Italian were the official languages of Somalia. In 1973, the government declared Somali the official language. About 8 per cent of all Somalis can read and write. In 1974, the government temporarily closed most schools. Teachers and students were sent into the countryside to teach the nomads to read and write. The National University, the country's only university, is in Mogadishu.

The Somalis band together in large groups of relatives whose relationships are traced through the men. If members of one group kill or injure a member of another, the attackers' group must pay the victim's group. A man's life is valued at 100 camels, and a woman's at 50. Payment may also be in money.

Land. Narrow plains line the coast in northern Somalia. Behind them, mountains rise nearly 8,000 feet (2,400 meters) above sea level. Farther inland lie high plateaus covered with rich pasture after rainy seasons, and dry plains of thorn bush and tall grasses.

Wide coastal plains in the southern half of Somalia rise gradually toward the west to a plateau cut by plains and valleys. The most important valleys are those of the Giuba and Shabeelle rivers, the only rivers in Somalia that have water all year. Trees line the river banks. Somalia's richest farmland lies between the two rivers. Dry plains cover the rest of the region.

Somalia has an average year-round temperature of 80° F. (27° C). In June and July, the temperature rises to 115° F. (46° C) on the northern coastal plains. That region, the driest in Somalia, receives 2 to 3 inches (5 to 8 centimeters) of rain a year. The southern farmlands receive about 20 inches (51 centimeters).

Economy. Somalia is a developing agricultural country. Bananas, hides and skins, and livestock are its chief products and exports. Sorghum and other grains are grown, but large amounts must be imported. Sugar is also produced. There is little manufacturing. Somalia's minerals, including rich deposits of iron ore and gypsum, have not been mined. Somalia has no railroads, and only about 450 miles (724 kilometers) of its 9,000 miles (14,000 kilometers) of roads are surfaced. Somali Airlines operates domestic and international flights. The government has radio stations in Mogadishu and Hargeysa. Somalia has a few newspapers.

History. Ancestors of the Somalis began migrating from what is now northern Somalia to the south in the 800's and 900's. They were converted to Islam by Arabs who had settled on the coast. The Arabs and Somalis fought many religious wars against the Christian kingdom of Ethiopia between the 1300's and 1500's.

Europeans began to colonize the Somali regions during the mid-1800's. France developed the colony of French Somaliland (now the independent nation of

Facts in Brief

Capital: Mogadishu.

Official Language: Somali.

Area: 246,201 sq. mi. (637,657 km²). *Greatest Distances—* north-south, 950 mi. (1,529 km); east-west, 730 mi. (1,175 km). *Coastline*—1,837 mi. (2,956 km).

Elevation: *Highest*—Mount Surud Ad, 7,894 ft. (2,406 m) above sea level. *Lowest*—sea level along the coast.

Population: *Estimated 1984 Population*—5,362,000; distribution, 66 per cent rural, 34 per cent urban; density, 21 persons per sq. mi. (8 persons per km²). *Estimated 1989 Population*—6,430,000.

Chief Products: *Agriculture*—bananas, grains, hides and skins, livestock, milk, sugar. *Manufacturing*—processed foods.

Flag: The light blue flag has a large white star in the center. The colors come from the United Nations flag. See FLAG (color picture: Flags of Africa).

Money: *Basic Unit*—shilling. See MONEY (table).

Authenticated News Int.

Mogadishu, the Capital of Somalia, has buildings of the Islamic architectural style along its main street, *above*.

479

Djibouti) in the 1860's. The British took over what later became British Somaliland (now northern Somalia) in 1884. In 1889, Italy established control in what is now southern Somalia. During the 1890's, Ethiopian armies seized Ogaden, a Somali territory west of the British and Italian colonies. The Somalis revolted in 1900, but the British crushed the revolt in 1920.

Italian forces conquered Ethiopia in 1936, and joined it to Italian Somaliland. In 1940, during World War II, Italy also seized British Somaliland. But the British drove the Italians from eastern Africa in 1941. The British returned most of Ogaden to Ethiopia in 1948. They retained control of the Haud region of northern Ogaden. In 1950, the United Nations gave Italy its former colony as a trust territory for 10 years, during which Italy agreed to prepare it for independence. By that time, the Somali movement to unite all Somali regions was well established. But in 1955, the British turned over the Haud region to Ethiopia.

The British granted British Somaliland independence on June 26, 1960. On July 1, Italian Somalia also became independent, and the two regions combined to form the Somali Republic. But many Somali people were living in eastern Ethiopia, northern Kenya, and French Somaliland. Somali leaders claimed that these Somalis should also have the right to decide what form of government they wanted. As a result, Somalia's relations with its neighbors became tense. Border fighting with both Ethiopia and Kenya broke out frequently during the 1960's. In 1977, the dispute with Ethiopia led to widespread fighting. Somali inhabitants of Ethiopia's Ogaden region revolted against their Ethiopian rulers. Troops from Somalia aided the rebels. Cuban troops aided the Ethiopians, and Russia provided the Ethiopians with military advisers and equipment. The troops from Somalia withdrew from Ogaden in March 1978, after Ethiopia staged a major offensive. But fighting has continued in Ogaden between Somali rebels and the Ethiopians.

Somalia's president, who had been elected by the people, was assassinated in 1969. Military leaders then seized control of the government. The country has remained under military rule since 1969.   I. M. LEWIS

See also CLOTHING (picture: Traditional Costumes); MOGADISHU.

SOMALILAND. See SOMALIA (History); DJIBOUTI (History).

SOMATIC DEATH. See DEATH (Medical Aspects of Death).

SOMBRERO. See COWBOY (His Clothing); MEXICO (Clothing).

SOMERS, SIR GEORGE. See BERMUDA (History).

SOMERSET, DUKE OF. See EDWARD (VI).

SOMME RIVER, *sawm.* Great battles of World Wars I and II were fought along this stream in northern France. The river rises near the Belgian border, and flows west for 140 miles (225 kilometers) to the English Channel. For location, see FRANCE (physical map). Ocean steamers enter the port of Saint Valéry through the mouth of the Somme. A canal runs beside the Somme from Saint Valéry to Saint Quentin. From Saint Quentin, canals connect with the Oise and Schelde rivers.   EDWARD W. FOX

SOMNAMBULISM. See SLEEPWALKING.

SOMNUS, *SAHM nuhs,* was the god of sleep in Roman mythology. The Greeks called him HYPNOS. He was the son of Erebus and Nyx, the goddess of night. His brother was Mors, the god of death, whom the Greeks called Thanatos. Somnus' son was Morpheus, god of dreams (see MORPHEUS). Somnus and Mors lived in a great cave. The river Lethe flowed nearby, and its gentle murmuring invited sleep. Everything in the dimly lit cave slept. The forms of pleasant dreams floated about, and dark nightmares hid in the cave.   JAMES F. CRONIN

SOMOZA, *suh MOH zuh,* is the family name of three Nicaraguan dictators, a father and his two sons. The Somozas controlled the government, the military, and the economy of Nicaragua from the 1930's until 1979, when a rebellion ended the family's control.

Anastasio Somoza García (1896-1956) ruled Nicaragua for 20 years before he was killed by an assassin. He crushed all opposition and did not allow freedom of expression. He also used his power to become rich.

Somoza was born in San Marcos, Nicaragua, the son of a small rancher. He studied at Peirce Union Business College (now Peirce Junior College) in Philadelphia, then returned to Nicaragua, and became a tax collector. He joined a revolutionary movement led by his wife's uncle, Juan Batista Sacasa. Somoza became minister of war in 1932, after Sacasa was elected president.

In 1934, Somoza gained a reputation as a feared and ruthless man when he ordered Augusto Sandino, a popular guerrilla fighter, killed by the National Guard. In 1936, Somoza drove Sacasa from power. Somoza was elected president later that year in an election controlled by his troops. Somoza resigned as president in 1947, but he forced his successors to rule as he wished. He was elected president again in 1950.

Somoza improved Nicaragua's agriculture, cattle raising, and mining. He balanced the budget and introduced easier credit for farmers. He also expanded port facilities and built new highways, houses, hospitals, power plants, railroads, and schools.

Luis Somoza Debayle (1922-1967) became president of Nicaragua after his father was killed, and served until 1963. He tried to bring about social reforms and loosen the tight military control of Nicaragua. One of his reform laws prevented any member of his family from succeeding him. But the Somoza family hand-picked the man who was elected to succeed him as president. Luis Somoza Debayle was born in León, Nicaragua.

Anastasio Somoza Debayle (1925-1980) served as president of Nicaragua from 1967 to 1972 and from 1974 to 1979. He ruled as a dictator, controlling the government, the military, and the economy as his father did. In the 1970's, many Nicaraguans joined in a rebellion against his rule. In 1979, the rebels forced him to resign from office and leave the country. He was assassinated in 1980 while living in Paraguay.

Somoza was born in León. He graduated from the U.S. Military Academy.   THOMAS G. MATHEWS

See also NICARAGUA (History).

SONAR, *SOH nahr,* is a detection device that uses sound to locate underwater objects. The word *sonar* comes from the words *sound navigation and ranging.* Warships and military aircraft use sonar to locate enemy submarines. Ships also use sonar to determine the depth of the water beneath them. There are two main types of sonar, *active sonar* and *passive sonar.*

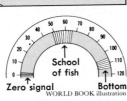

A Fishing Boat uses sonar to detect schools of fish. The sonar sends out a pulse of sound and receives echoes from the fish and the ocean bottom. A meter, *right,* shows the depth of the fish.

WORLD BOOK illustration

Active Sonar sends out a sharp pulse of sound. This sound, which resembles a "ping," is reflected back when it strikes an object. The distance to the object is found by measuring the time taken by the sound to return. Sound travels about 5,000 feet (1,500 meters) per second through water. Therefore, an echo that returns after two seconds has traveled 10,000 feet (3,000 meters)—5,000 feet to the object and 5,000 feet back. This method of finding distance is called *echo ranging.*

Passive Sonar simply listens for sound given off by posssible targets. It can determine the direction in which an object is located, but not its distance. However, a passive sonar system has the advantage of not giving off any sound that another sonar unit might detect. Passive sonar also can help identify a target, because the noise a ship gives off may reveal what type of ship it is. Submarines generally use passive sonar, though they have active sonar as well. Most surface ships must use active sonar because they are too noisy to use passive sonar for detecting submarines.

History. Sonar was developed by British naval scientists following the successful German submarine operations during World War I (1914-1918). The British sent their first detection system to sea in 1921. They called the system *asdic,* after the *Allied Submarine Detection Investigation Committee,* which had first suggested it. The United States used its first sonar system in 1927.

The British and the Americans kept sonar a secret, and so its use surprised the Germans during World War II (1939-1945). Sonar units of that period had only short ranges. They also had to be rotated by hand in order to check in all directions for submarines.

After the war, various navies developed sonar units that rotated automatically. They also improved sonar by increasing its range. Modern sonar units have ranges of more than 10 miles (16 kilometers). Navies also

developed a sonar unit called *variable depth sonar* (VDS). Sometimes a *thermal layer,* a layer of water in which the temperature changes drastically, interferes with normal sonar by reflecting sound. Lowering a VDS unit into the water beneath a thermal layer enables a ship to detect submarines hiding below the layer.

Aircraft also use sonar to detect submarines. Helicopters can lower sonar units on cables into the water. Airplanes can drop small units called *sonobuoys,* which report back to the aircraft by radio.

Fishing ships use sonar to detect schools of fish. Salvage companies use it to locate submerged wrecks. Bats and dolphins navigate by means of a natural sonar system called *echolocation.*   Norman Friedman

See also BAT (How Bats Navigate); DOLPHIN (The Bodies of Dolphins).

SONATA, *suh NAH tuh,* is an instrumental composition with three or four movements with contrasts both in tempo and key, but related in thought. The usual four-movement sonata begins with a brilliant *allegro,* and the second movement is slow, rhythmic, and lyrical (*andante, adagio,* or *largo*). The third movement is usually light and graceful, and may be in dance form, or a *scherzo.* The *finale* (last movement) is in quick, bright tempo. Symphonies, string quartets, and long works for solo instruments use this sonata form. The first movement of the sonata is often in *sonata-allegro* form. It has three sections called the *exposition,* the *development,* and the *recapitulation,* which is almost a repetition of the exposition, but usually shorter.   Raymond Kendall

See also CLASSICAL MUSIC (The Sonata Form).

SONDHEIM, *SAHND hym,* **STEPHEN** (1930-   ), is an American composer and lyric writer who won fame for his musical comedies. Sondheim is known for his witty lyrics, complex melodies, and sophisticated plots.

Sondheim was born in New York City. He began his musical career as a lyric writer with *West Side Story* (1957), for which Leonard Bernstein wrote the music. Sondheim next worked with Jule Styne on *Gypsy* (1959). He wrote both music and lyrics for the first time for *A Funny Thing Happened on the Way to the Forum* (1962).

Sondheim's other musicals include *Anyone Can Whistle* (1964), *Do I Hear a Waltz?* (1965), *Company* (1970), *Follies* (1971), *A Little Night Music* (1973), *Pacific Overtures* (1976), and *Sweeney Todd, the Demon Barber of Fleet Street* (1979). He wrote the music and lyrics for all those shows except *Do I Hear a Waltz?,* for which Richard Rodgers wrote the music.   Ethan Mordden

SONG is a musical composition usually sung by a solo voice. It may be performed with or without accompaniment. Most songs have a simple, lyrical style.

Songs are the oldest musical form and have been found in all cultures. The earliest surviving songs are Latin pieces dating from the 1000's. These early songs were traditional folk songs with a *monophonic style*—that is, with only one part. Between the 1100's and the 1400's, poets and singers called minnesingers and mastersingers in Germany and troubadours and trouvères in France composed works called *art songs.* Their songs glorified romantic love and heroic deeds.

During the 1400's, composers began writing *polyphonic* songs, works with two or more parts. One or more of the parts may have been played on musical instru-

481

ments. About 1650, many French and German composers returned to the monophonic style.

The song reached perhaps its highest level of development in *lieder*, which were art songs written by German composers during the late 1700's and 1800's. The leading composer of lieder was Franz Schubert. Other important composers included Johannes Brahms, Robert Schumann, and Hugo Wolf.

During the 1900's, many American songwriters have composed minor masterpieces for the stage, films, and recordings. The most important of these songwriters include Irving Berlin, George Gershwin, Jerome Kern, Cole Porter, and Richard Rodgers.   ELLEN PFEIFER

Related Articles in WORLD BOOK include:

Carol	Lieder	Spiritual
Chantey	Mastersinger	Troubadour
Folk Music	Minnesinger	Trouvère
Hymn	Popular Music	

SONG OF DEBORAH. See DEBORAH.

SONG OF HIAWATHA is a narrative poem by the American poet Henry Wadsworth Longfellow. The poem describes the life of North American Indians before the arrival of white settlers. Hiawatha, the hero of the poem, is a young chief whose tribe lives in a forest near Lake Superior.

The poem dramatizes Hiawatha's development into the greatest man of his tribe. It describes his marriage to the beautiful princess Minnehaha, and his grief after she dies. It relates how he tries to prepare his people for the coming of white people and Christianity. Finally, the poem tells of Hiawatha's becoming a god of the Northwest Wind.

In *The Song of Hiawatha*, Longfellow showed his deep interest in Indian folklore. He based his hero partly on a real Hiawatha, a Mohawk chief during the 1400's. But the poem emphasizes the legendary and romantic qualities of Indian life, and Longfellow did not intend it to be historically accurate. The poem was published in 1855.   CLARK GRIFFITH

See also LONGFELLOW, HENRY WADSWORTH (Narrative Poems).

SONG OF ROLAND. See ROLAND.

SONG OF SOLOMON is the name of a poetic book in the Old Testament. The book is also called the *Song of Songs* and *Canticles*. For hundreds of years, most persons considered it an allegory that showed God's love for His children by means of a description of human love. Many Jews saw in it the love of God for the people of Israel. Many Christians found in it the love of Christ for the church. Some persons still accept these allegorical interpretations. But most scholars today interpret the book literally. Some consider it a poetic drama whose characters include a girl, her shepherd lover, and King Solomon. Others suggest that the songs were originally part of a pagan spring festival, and were later changed so that they could be included in the Bible. Many scholars regard the book as a collection of love and nature songs written in ancient Israel.   ROBERT GORDIS

SONGBIRD. See BIRD (Calls and Songs). For a list of separate articles on songbirds, see the *Related Articles* at the end of the BIRD article.

SONGHAI EMPIRE was a black trading state in Africa that reached the height of its power during the

The Songhai Empire About 1500

This map shows in dark gray the Songhai Empire at the height of its power. During the reign of Emperor Askia Muhammad, the empire stretched from the Atlantic coast to what is now central Nigeria. The Songhai controlled important trade routes that made the empire the richest in West Africa. The white lines are the boundaries of present-day countries.

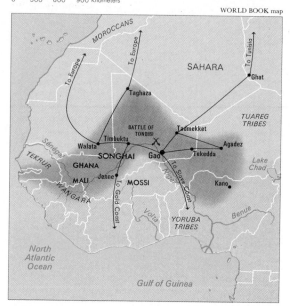

WORLD BOOK map

1400's and 1500's. Songhai began in the 700's, and by the 1400's it had more power and wealth than any other West African empire. Songhai extended from the central area of what is now Nigeria to the Atlantic coast and included parts of what are now Gambia, Guinea, Mali, Mauritania, Niger, Senegal, and Upper Volta. Gao, the capital, stood on the Niger River.

Songhai became powerful chiefly by controlling trade across the Sahara. Most of Songhai's people were farmers, fishers, or traders. The traders exchanged gold and other West African products for goods from Europe and the Middle East.

Two kings, Sunni Ali and Askia Muhammad, strengthened the empire more than any other rulers. Sunni Ali ruled from 1464 until 1492 and began a unified system of law and order, central government, and trade. His army conquered Timbuktu and Jenne, two West African trading centers (see JENNE; TIMBUKTU).

Askia Muhammad, also known as Askia I or Askia the Great, became king in 1493. The empire reached its peak under his rule. Askia reorganized the Songhai government, expanded trade, and encouraged the people to practice Islam, the religion of the Muslims. Askia's three sons deposed him in 1528. The empire ended in 1591 when a Moroccan army defeated the Songhai in the Battle of Tondibi.   LEO SPITZER

See also ASKIA MUHAMMAD; SUNNI ALI; WALATA.

SONIC BOOM is a loud noise caused by an airplane flying at a supersonic speed. To a person on the ground, it may sound like a clap of thunder. The noise results from a shock wave produced by the plane. A shock wave is a pressure disturbance that builds up around a plane flying at a supersonic speed. It results from a change in the air-flow pattern around the plane's leading edges. Sonic booms cannot hurt people, but they may damage plaster walls and break windows.

A plane reaching the speed of sound is said to be crossing the *sound*, or *sonic, barrier*. Captain Charles E. Yeager of the U.S. Air Force became the first person to break the barrier. He did so in a Bell X-1 rocket plane on Oct. 14, 1947.   ROBERT D. ROACH, JR.

See also AERODYNAMICS (Shock Waves and Sonic Booms); YEAGER, CHARLES ELWOOD.

SONNET is a poem of 14 lines with a fixed pattern of meter and rhyme. Its name is an Italian word meaning *a little song*. In the Italian sonnet, the *octave* (the first eight lines) states a theme or experience and the *sestet* (the final six lines) responds to or comments on the theme. The octave rhyme scheme is *abbaabba* (lines one, four, five, and eight rhyme; and lines two, three, six, and seven rhyme). The rhyme scheme of the sestet is often *cdecde*.

During the Italian Renaissance (the A.D. 1200's and 1300's), poets wrote groups of love poems called *sonnet sequences* in this form. Dante addressed sonnets to Beatrice, Petrarch to Laura. The French court poet, Pierre de Ronsard, wrote *Sonnets for Hélène* (1578).

English poets brought back this form from their travels abroad. Sonnets by Sir Thomas Wyatt and Henry Howard, Earl of Surrey, were published in *Tottel's Miscellany* (1557). For his *Amoretti* (1595), Edmund Spenser invented his own rhyme scheme. But the form used by William Shakespeare has been accepted as typically English. It consists of three *quatrains* (four-line stanzas) followed by a *couplet* (two-line stanza), rhyming *abab cdcd efef gg*. By the time Shakespeare's *Sonnets* was published in 1609, the writing of sonnet sequences already was out of fashion.

Few sonnets were written in English during the next 200 years. But in the mid-1600's, John Milton wrote a few great sonnets, including "On His Blindness" (1655). The form was revived during the Romantic period (1798-1832). An example is John Keats' "On First Looking into Chapman's Homer" (1816). Later in the 1800's, Elizabeth Barrett Browning wrote love poems to her husband in the sequence *Sonnets from the Portuguese*. Edna St. Vincent Millay is the best known of recent American poets to write in this exacting and compressed poetic form.   CHARLES W. COOPER

See also SHAKESPEARE, WILLIAM (The Years of Fame; Shakespeare's Poems); POETRY (Form).

SONOMETER, *suh NAHM uh tuhr*, is an instrument used to study the mathematical relations of musical tones. The sonometer, sometimes known as the *monochord*, consists of a tightly stretched string, one end of which passes over a pulley wheel. When plucked, the string vibrates and thus produces sound. The *frequency* (number of vibrations a second) of the tone is increased if the string is made shorter or tighter.   RICHARD H. BOLT

SONS OF LIBERTY was a group of patriotic societies that sprang up in the American colonies before the Revolutionary War. The Sons of Liberty groups began as secret societies, but later came into the open. They fought against the Stamp Tax of 1765. They opposed the importation of British goods after the passage of the Townshend Acts, and later began to demand national independence. They helped other independence moves, including the calling of the Continental Congress.

During the Civil War, a group known as *Copperheads* began to call themselves the *Sons of Liberty*. They were Northern sympathizers with the South, and planned to overthrow the Lincoln government. Their plots were discovered and suppressed.   JOHN R. ALDEN

See also COPPERHEADS.

SONS OF SAINT GEORGE. See GEORGE, SAINT.

SONS OF THE AMERICAN REVOLUTION is a patriotic organization. Its members are male descendants of persons who served in the Revolutionary War, or who contributed toward establishing the independence of the United States. The society is dedicated to perpetuating American ideals and traditions, and to protecting the Constitution. Constitution Day, Flag Day, and Bill of Rights Day were established through its efforts. The society was founded on April 30, 1889. Its official name is the National Society of the Sons of the American Revolution. It has about 22,500 members in the United States, France, Great Britain, and Switzerland. The society has national headquarters at 1000 S. Fourth Street, Louisville, Ky. 40203.

Critically reviewed by the SONS OF THE AMERICAN REVOLUTION

SONTAG, *SAHN tahg*, **SUSAN** (1933-   ), is an American essayist and novelist. Her works strongly influenced experimental art during the 1960's and 1970's.

Sontag is best known for a collection of essays called *Against Interpretation* (1966). In these essays, she argued that people should experience art with their emotions and senses, rather than analyze it intellectually. Her essay collection *Styles of Radical Will* (1969) deals with the effects of drugs and pornography on art. In *On Photography* (1977), she discussed the nature of photography. Several of Sontag's essays on literature and motion pictures were published in *Under the Sign of Saturn* (1980).

© Thomas Victor
Susan Sontag

Sontag has written two novels, *The Benefactor* (1963) and *Death Kit* (1967). In both books, the main characters are cut off from reality because they cannot distinguish between it and their dream worlds. Sontag's short stories were collected in *I, etcetera* (1978).

Sontag was born in New York City. She graduated from the University of Chicago in 1951. Sontag also studied at Harvard University, Oxford University in England, and the Sorbonne in Paris.   EUGENE K. GARBER

SOO CANALS permit ships to pass between Lakes Superior and Huron. They are located on the United States-Canadian border (see MICHIGAN [political map]).

About 85 to 90 per cent of the tonnage on the canals is eastbound. Iron ore and grain make up most of the eastbound cargo. Coal, stone, and oil are the chief products carried on westbound ships. About 56 million short tons (51 million metric tons) of cargo pass through these canals annually. In the early 1970's, the total

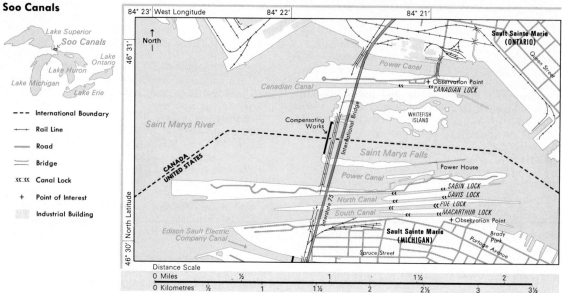

WORLD BOOK map-GJa

tonnage shipped through them was about one-third as much as the cargo tonnage shipped through the Panama Canal. Ice closes the Soo Canals from about mid-November to early April.

The Saint Marys River forms a natural connection between lakes Superior and Huron. Early trappers sometimes "ran the rapids" to cross from one lake to the other. However, they usually carried their canoes and furs around the rough water. In 1798, the Hudson's Bay Company completed a canal with a single lock that permitted canoes and flat-bottomed boats to pass up the river. American troops destroyed the lock during the War of 1812. After 1839, ships were moved around the rapids on rollers. A railroad was built in 1850.

The American Canals. Increasing shipments of iron and copper during the late 1800's created a need for better transportation between lakes Superior and Huron. A federal grant enabled Michigan to complete a canal with a lock in 1855. The U.S. government took over the canal's administration in 1881, and abolished tolls.

The American canals, also called the St. Marys Falls Canal and Locks, are about $1\frac{3}{4}$ miles (2.8 kilometers) long. Davis lock, opened in 1914, and Sabin lock, opened in 1919, are in the North Canal. The South Canal includes MacArthur lock, opened in 1943, and the new Poe lock, opened in 1969. This new lock, 110 feet (34 meters) wide, is the widest of the American canals. It replaced a smaller Poe lock, which was torn down in 1962.

The Canadian Canal. Canada completed its canal in 1895. Until the Davis lock was built, the larger lake ships used the Canadian canal. The Canadian canal, also called the Sault Sainte Marie Canal, is $1\frac{3}{10}$ miles (2 kilometers) long and 150 feet (46 meters) wide.

The 2-mile (3-kilometer) International Bridge carries traffic across the Saint Marys River at Sault Ste. Marie. The bridge opened in 1962.   WILLIS F. DUNBAR

SOOCHOW. See SU-CHOU.

SOONG CHING-LING (1890-1981), MADAME SUN YAT-SEN, was a prominent figure in the Chinese Com-

munist government. She served as a vice-chairman in the government from 1949 to 1975. Soong Ching-ling served as head of a national woman's organization and of the Sino-Soviet Friendship Association after the Communist victory in China. She was awarded the 1951 Stalin peace prize.

Soong Ching-ling was the second wife of Sun Yat-sen, the founder of the Chinese Republic (see SUN YAT-SEN). She worked with him in Japan and later married him there. After his death in 1925, Soong Ching-ling rose to a high position in the Chinese government. When Chiang Kai-shek, the president of the Chinese Nationalist government, broke with the Chinese Communists in 1927, she left China and lived in Moscow (see CHIANG KAI-SHEK). She remained in exile until Communist leaders joined the Kuomintang, the Nationalist Party, in a common front against the Japanese forces that invaded China in 1937.

Soong Ching-ling, the daughter of Charles Jones Soong, was born in K'un-shan, Kiangsu. She attended high school in Shanghai and graduated from Wesleyan College in Macon, Ga.   IMMANUEL C. Y. HSU

SOOT is a black substance found in smoke. Soot is made up of tiny particles of fuel, such as coal, wood, or oil, that have not been burned. These particles are usually considered harmful to people and plant life, but they also have a certain value. Soot contains a great deal of carbon and ammonium salts. The ammonium salts contain a large amount of nitrogen, which is an excellent fertilizer. Soot is therefore useful as a fertilizer.

Soot is used as a *pigment* (coloring matter). The soot found nearest the fire is usually a shining brown powder containing dried tar. This soot is used as a pigment which is called *bister*. The soot found farther from the fire and up higher in the chimney is usually black. It is used as a pigment which is called *lampblack*.

Soot sticks to anything it touches. For this reason, smoke blowing through a city leaves its soot upon buildings and makes them look dingy. In some cities, about 3 per cent of the coal that is burned is converted into soot. This soot formation is a serious waste and has added to the problem of air pollution. RALPH G. OWENS

See also FIRE (What Fire Produces).

SOPHIST PHILOSOPHY, *SAHF ihst,* was an educational movement in the city-states of Greece during the second half of the 400's B.C. The Sophists were migrant teachers who taught grammar and public speaking, which was vital in such ancient democracies as Athens. They were not interested in philosophical thoughts about the nature of the physical universe. Instead, they criticized conventional morality and religion, and described virtue as being successful in the world.

The Sophists believed that law is not part of the nature of things, but is merely custom. Thus, they said, people who are clever enough to evade laws have no moral obligation to obey them. Plato described Socrates as opposing the Sophists because their ideas were vague and contradictory, and especially because their teachings could destroy the social order.

The best-known Sophists included Protagoras, Gorgias, and Antiphon. Protagoras believed that old customs and ceremonies should be followed so society could be held together. Gorgias became known for his intellectually stimulating and skeptical ideas. Antiphon emphasized the difference between civil law and a person's natural search for pleasure in life. He believed people could often serve their own advantage by evading the law and following their natural desires, if they could get away with it. JOSIAH B. GOULD

SOPHOCLES, *SAHF uh KLEEZ* (496?-406? B.C.), was the second in time of the three great Greek writers of tragedy. The others were Aeschylus and Euripides. His tragedies were not concerned with abstract problems of guilt and punishment over several generations, like those of Aeschylus. Instead they dealt with a specific struggle of a strong individual against fate. Where Aeschylus required whole *trilogies* (three plays) to cover one subject, Sophocles wrote single plays.

Bettmann Archive

Sophocles

Sophocles' usual pattern is to show powerful figures who choose a course which the chorus and lesser characters may not approve. This course costs them suffering or death, but it makes them more noble and somehow benefits humanity. Sophocles did not make his figures ordinary in order to criticize conventional morality, as Euripides did. That is why Aristotle said that Sophocles pictured people as they should be, Euripides as they are.

Artistically and in their dramatic construction, Sophocles' plays are more finished than those of Aeschylus or Euripides, and Aristotle regarded his works as models. Sophocles added a third actor, fixed the size of the chorus at 15, and used scene painting. His plays show intrigue and suspense. Of the 100 or more plays Sophocles wrote, seven complete ones have survived. These are *Ajax, Antigone, Trachinian Women, Oedipus Rex, Electra, Philoctetes,* and *Oedipus at Colonus.* Part of a play called *The Trackers* was found in 1907.

Sophocles was a fortunate man. He lived during Athens' greatest period. He won many prizes for his tragedies, and was universally loved. One of his greatest plays, *Oedipus at Colonus,* was written when he was nearly 90. He was born near Athens, and remained there all his life. MOSES HADAS

See also ANTIGONE; DRAMA (Greek Drama); GREEK LITERATURE; OEDIPUS.

SOPRANO, *suh PRAN oh* or *suh PRAH noh,* is a term describing a type of voice. It may also mean a voice part in compositions written for mixed voices. The soprano voice is the highest of four voices. It usually covers more than two octaves above middle C. A woman or a young boy may sing a soprano part. The soprano part is the upper voice part in a harmonic arrangement to be sung by mixed voices. RAYMOND KENDALL

See also OPERA (The Singers).

SORBONNE, *sawr BAHN,* was a world-famous college in Paris. Until 1970, it formed the liberal arts and sciences division of the University of Paris. The name Sorbonne was often used for the university itself.

The Sorbonne is no longer a separate college. In 1970, the French government reorganized the university into 13 units. Three of these units use the Sorbonne buildings for lectures. One of the buildings includes the Sorbonne library, which has more than $1\frac{1}{2}$ million volumes.

The Sorbonne was originally a college of theology. It was founded in the 1200's by the theologian Robert of Sorbon and became one of the best theological schools in Europe. Cardinal Richelieu rebuilt the college in the 1600's. P. A. McGINLEY

SORCERER. See MAGIC (The Magician); WITCHCRAFT.

SOREL, *suh REHL,* Quebec (pop. 20,347), is an industrial and shipping center at the junction of the Richelieu and St. Lawrence rivers. A good port with a deepwater front, it is on the Canadian National Railways. Sorel's industries include shipbuilding and ship-repair plants, steel foundries, lumber mills, and clothing and shirt factories. Sorel has a mayor-council form of government. MURRAY G. BALLANTYNE

SORENSEN, VIRGINIA (1912-), is an American author. She won the 1957 Newbery medal for her children's book *Miracles on Maple Hill,* the story of a 10-year-old girl in the farmland of Pennsylvania. Her story *Plain Girl,* about the life of a small Amish girl, won the Children's Book Award of the Child Study Association of America in 1955.

Sorensen also wrote *Curious Missie* (1953), *The House Next Door* (1954), *Lotte's Locket* (1964), a number of adult novels, and a collection of short stories. She was born in Provo, Utah. ELOISE RUE

SORET, J. LOUIS. See HOLMIUM.

SORGHUM, *SAWR guhm,* is the name of a group of tropical grasses from Africa and Asia. In regions of warm summer climate, farmers grow some of them for forage, syrup, grain, and broom fiber. The common varieties of sorghum have thick, solid stalks and look like corn plants. But their flowers grow in branched clusters at the tips of the stems. Farmers plant and grow sorghums in much the same manner as they do corn. About 20 million acres (8 million hectares) of sorghum are planted in the United States each year, especially

485

J. Horace McFarland

Sorghums furnish sap to make syrup and feed for livestock. Two kinds are Red Top African, *left,* and Milo Maize, *right.*

in the Great Plains region. All sorghums fall into four main groups: (1) grain sorghums, (2) sweet sorghums, (3) grassy sorghums, and (4) broomcorn.

Grain Sorghums are grown especially for their rounded, starchy seeds. The grain serves as a substitute for corn in feeding animals. Some grain sorghums grow as much as 15 feet (5 meters) tall. Plant breeders have produced varieties 2 to 4 feet (0.6 to 1.2 meters) tall that can be harvested with a grain combine. Farmers feed the grain to livestock, or make the entire plant into silage. In India, Africa, and China, the grain is ground and made into pancakes or mush. Common grain sorghums include durra, milo, and kafir (see KAFIR).

Sweet Sorghums, or *sorgos,* have sweet, juicy stems. They are grown especially for the production of sorghum syrup. This syrup is made by pressing the juice out of the stems with rollers and boiling it down to the proper thickness. Animal feed and silage can also be made from sweet sorghums.

Grassy Sorghums are used for green feed and hay. *Sudan grass* is a tall annual sorghum with thin stalks. It grows quickly and may reach 10 feet (3 meters) in height. It serves as excellent summer pasturage (see SUDAN GRASS). *Johnson grass,* a perennial sorghum, grows as a weed in the southern United States. It resembles Sudan grass, but it spreads by creeping rootstocks. Johnson grass is a pest on land needed for cotton or other row crops. But it makes excellent cattle feed.

Broomcorn is a kind of sorghum grown for the *brush* (branches) of the seed cluster.

Scientific Classification. The sorghums belong to the grass family, *Gramineae.* Grain sorghums, sweet sorghums, broomcorn, and Sudan grass are classified as genus *Sorghum,* species *S. vulgare.* Johnson grass is classified as *S. halepense.*   WAYNE W. HUFFINE

SOROPTIMIST INTERNATIONAL is the world's largest service organization for business, executive, and professional women. It has about 60,000 members in clubs in more than 50 countries. Membership is by invitation. The clubs have five main areas of activity: community service, international goodwill and understanding, public affairs, United Nations, and youth activities. The international organization consists of three federations—Soroptimist International of the Americas, Soroptimist International of Europe, and Soroptimist International of Great Britain and Ireland. The first Soroptimist club was chartered in 1921 in Oakland, Calif. The federation of the Americas has its

headquarters at 1616 Walnut Street, Philadelphia, Pa. 19103.   Critically reviewed by SOROPTIMIST INTERNATIONAL

SORORITY is a society of women or girls. In most sororities, the members are college or university students and graduates. Sororities, like fraternities, are often called *Greek-letter societies.* Most sororities form their names by combining two or three letters of the Greek alphabet. The word *sorority* comes from the Latin word *soror,* which means *sister.*

There are four kinds of sororities: (1) *general,* or *social,* (2) *professional,* (3) *honor societies,* and (4) *recognition societies.* General sororities, the most common of the four, encourage high academic standards, carry on charitable and educational programs, and sponsor social activities for their members. On many campuses, they also provide room and board for members in sorority houses. Professional societies consist of persons with the same academic interest, such as education or journalism. Honor societies are for persons with exceptional academic records. Members of recognition societies have done outstanding work in a specific area. Some groups admit both women and men. General sororities in the United States are listed in this article. For the largest professional, honor, and recognition societies, see the article on FRATERNITY.

There are about 40 national general sororities in the United States. They have a total of about 6,000 collegiate *chapters* (local units) and about 10,300 alumnae chapters. Membership totals more than 2,200,000. Twenty-six of the national sororities belong to the National Panhellenic Conference. It and similar organizations promote cooperation among national sororities. Most university and college campuses have an intersorority council, which regulates general sororities.

There are 35 U.S. professional sororities and honor societies. They have more than 3,300 chapters and about 540,000 members. Some groups admit men.

Many school clubs, the forerunners of sororities, were formed during the 1800's. *Adelphean* began as a literary society at Wesleyan College, in Macon, Ga., in 1851. It adopted the name *Alpha Delta Pi* in 1905. *Pi Beta Phi* was organized as I.C. Sorosis at Monmouth College in Monmouth, Ill., in 1867. It was the first organization of college women established on a national basis.

Kappa Alpha Theta was the first group founded as a women's Greek-letter society. It began at DePauw University in 1870. *Gamma Phi Beta,* founded at Syracuse University in 1874, was the first to use the name *sorority.*   Critically reviewed by NATIONAL PANHELLENIC CONFERENCE

SORREL, *SAWR uhl,* is a name given to several plants of the buckwheat family. All the sorrel plants have juicy leaves and stems that contain oxalic acid. This gives them a sour taste.

The common American sorrel is a low-growing plant with three-lobed, arrow-shaped leaves, and spikes of small white, pink, or yellow flowers. *Sheep sorrel, sour sorrel,* and *red sorrel* are some of the names

Kitty Kohout

Sorrel

486

General Sororities in the United States

Name	Members	Chapters*	Year Founded	Where Founded	National Headquarters
Alpha Chi Omega	90,500	388	1885	DePauw University	Indianapolis
Alpha Delta Pi	94,000	530	1851	Wesleyan College	Atlanta
Alpha Epsilon Phi	32,400	48	1909	Barnard College	South Miami, Fla.
Alpha Gamma Delta	66,995	342	1904	Syracuse University	Indianapolis
Alpha Kappa Alpha	75,000	562	1908	Howard University	Chicago
Alpha Omicron Pi	60,000	275	1897	Barnard College	Nashville, Tenn.
Alpha Phi	68,000	349	1872	Syracuse University	Evanston, Ill.
Alpha Sigma Alpha	32,116	174	1901	Longwood College	Springfield, Mo.
Alpha Sigma Tau	18,000	79	1899	Eastern Michigan University	St. Louis
Alpha Xi Delta	70,000	291	1893	Galesburg, Ill.	Indianapolis
Beta Sigma Phi	250,000	11,000	1931	Abilene, Kans.	Kansas City, Mo.
Chi Omega	130,000	357	1895	University of Arkansas	Cincinnati
Delta Delta Delta	110,000	450	1888	Boston University	Arlington, Tex.
Delta Gamma	91,000	384	1873	Oxford, Miss.	Columbus, O.
Delta Phi Epsilon	18,725	85	1917	New York University	Fort Lauderdale, Fla.
Delta Sigma Theta	95,000	600	1913	Howard University	Washington, D.C.
Delta Zeta	93,102	475	1902	Miami University	Columbus, O.
Gamma Phi Beta	70,436	300	1874	Syracuse University	Kenilworth, Ill.
Kappa Alpha Theta	100,000	433	1870	DePauw University	Evanston, Ill.
Kappa Delta	87,765	514	1897	Longwood College	Denver
Kappa Kappa Gamma	103,443	484	1870	Monmouth College (Ill.)	Columbus, O.
Lambda Delta Sigma	11,000	47	1967	Salt Lake City	Salt Lake City
Phi Epsilon Phi	876	38	1937	Oakland, Calif.	Burlingame, Calif.
Phi Mu	73,000	345	1852	Wesleyan College	Atlanta
Phi Sigma Sigma	15,663	73	1913	Hunter College	Coral Gables, Fla.
Pi Beta Phi	118,512	435	1867	Monmouth College (Ill.)	St. Louis
Pi Omicron	1,000	60	1928	(Unreported)	Fort Wayne, Ind.
Psi Psi Psi	2,300	43	1914	Indianapolis, Ind.	Ballwin, Mo.
Sigma Delta Tau	21,184	41	1917	Cornell University	Indianapolis
Sigma Gamma Rho	25,000	300	1922	Butler University	Chicago
Sigma Iota Chi	10,000	5	1903	Alexandria, La.	Pottstown, Pa.
Sigma Kappa	60,000	370	1874	Colby College	Indianapolis
Sigma Phi Gamma	7,702	194	1920	Hartford City, Ind.	Arlington, Tex.
Sigma Sigma Sigma	45,324	226	1898	Longwood College	Woodstock, Va.
Theta Phi Alpha	10,000	45	1912	University of Michigan	Cincinnati
Zeta Phi Beta	45,000	485	1920	Howard University	Washington, D.C.
Zeta Tau Alpha	75,000	390	1898	Longwood College	Indianapolis

*College and alumnae chapters.

Sources: *Baird's Manual of American College Fraternities*, John Robson, Baird's Manual Foundation, Inc., Menasha, Wis., 1977; *Encyclopedia of Associations*, Gale Research Co., Detroit, 1979.

for this plant. The name "red sorrel" comes from the masses of triangular reddish seeds the plant bears.

The common American sorrel is a weed that grows well in acid soil, and its presence in a meadow indicates that the land needs lime.

Scientific Classification. The common American sorrel belongs to the buckwheat family, *Polygonaceae*. It is genus *Rumex*, species *R. acetosella*.　　HAROLD NORMAN MOLDENKE

SORREL TREE, or SOURWOOD, is a beautiful tree of the heath family. It grows in the woods of the southern United States, and as far north as Pennsylvania, Indiana, and Ohio. The name *sourwood* comes from the taste of its leaves and twigs, which hunters, hikers, and campers sometimes chew when they are thirsty. The name *sorrel* comes from an Old French word which means *sour*.

The sorrel tree may reach a height of 50 to 60 feet (15 to 18 meters). It has reddish-gray bark and smooth, oblong leaves. In summer it bears graceful clusters of small, bell-shaped, white flowers, which are soon followed by little downy capsules. In spring the foliage is bronze-green, but in autumn it turns a brilliant scarlet.

The wood is sometimes used to make handles for tools. Leaves of the sorrel tree furnish a black dye.

Scientific Classification. The sorrel tree belongs to the heath family, *Ericaceae*. It is classified as genus *Oxydendrum*, species *O. arboreum*.　　THEODORE W. BRETZ

S O S is the accepted call for help from a ship in distress. It does not stand for anything. It was chosen because it was convenient to send by wireless. It consists of three dots, three dashes, and three dots.

SOTO, HERNANDO DE. See DE SOTO, HERNANDO.

SOU was a small coin in the French money system. It was worth 5 *centimes* (hundredths of a franc). It has not been used since World War II.

SOUL. See RELIGION (A Doctrine of Salvation); PLATO (Plato's Philosophy); REINCARNATION; MYTHOLOGY (Tylor's Theory).

SOULE, JOHN, originated the phrase, "Go West, young man." See GREELEY, HORACE (His Publications).

SOULÉ, PIERRE. See OSTEND MANIFESTO.

SOULÉ, SAMUEL W. See TYPEWRITER (History; picture).

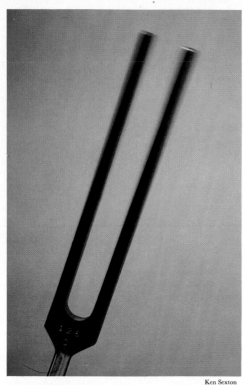

A Male Frog Sounding a Mating Call

Jerry Herman, FPG

Trombonists in a Marching Band

Dennis Hallinan, FPG

Ken Sexton

A Tone-Producing Tuning Fork

All Sounds Are Produced by Vibrations. When a tuning fork is struck, the vibration of its prongs generates a specific tone. A frog croaks by forcing air over its vocal cords, making them vibrate. A trombone produces sound when the player causes the air column inside the instrument to vibrate.

SOUND

SOUND surrounds us all the time. The buzzing of an alarm clock or the chirping of birds may awaken us in the morning. Throughout the day, we hear many kinds of sounds, such as the clatter of pots and pans, the roar of traffic, and the voices of people. As we fall asleep at night, we may listen to the croaking of frogs or the whistle of the wind.

All the sounds we hear have one thing in common. Every sound is produced by vibrations of an object. When an object vibrates, it makes the surrounding air vibrate. The vibrations in the air travel outward in all directions from the object. When the vibrations enter our ears, the brain interprets them as sounds (see EAR [The Sense of Hearing]). Although many of the sounds we hear travel through the air, sound can move through any material. For example, sound travels well through solid earth. You may have read that American Indians used to put their ears to the ground to listen for distant hoofbeats.

Sound has great importance in our lives. First of all, sound makes it possible for us to communicate with one another through speech. Many sounds, such as music and the singing of birds, provide pleasure. The sounds

Alan B. Coppens and James V. Sanders, the contributors of this article, are Associate Professors of Physics at the Naval Postgraduate School.

of radio and television broadcasts bring us entertainment and information. We are warned of danger by such sounds as automobile horns and fire alarms.

How Some Familiar Sounds Are Produced

The Human Voice is produced in the *larynx*, a section of the throat. Two small bands of tissue stretch across the larynx. These bands, called *vocal cords*, have a slitlike opening between them. When we speak, muscles in the larynx tighten the vocal cords, narrowing the opening. Air from the lungs rushes past the tightened cords, causing them to vibrate. The vibrations produce the sound of the voice. The tighter the vocal cords are, the more rapidly they vibrate and the higher are the sounds produced. See LARYNX; VOICE.

Animal Sounds. Birds, frogs, and almost all mammals have vocal cords or similar structures and make sounds the same way that people do. A dolphin produces clicks and whistles in air-filled pouches connected to the *blowhole*, a nostril in the top of its head. The buzzing of bees and flies results from the vibrations of their wings beating against the air. Many other insects produce sounds by rubbing one part of the body against another part. For example, a cricket "sings" by scraping parts of its front wings together.

Some kinds of fishes cluck, croak, grunt, or make other sounds by vibrating a baglike organ, known as a *swim bladder* or *air bladder*, that is located below the backbone. Certain kinds of shellfish produce clicking sounds by striking their claws together. The pistol shrimp makes a sound much like a gunshot by snapping one of its claws.

Musical Sounds are usually pleasing or interesting sounds. Different kinds of musical instruments produce sounds in different ways.

Certain instruments produce sounds when struck. When the membrane of a drum is hit, for example, it vibrates and produces sound. Such instruments as chimes and xylophones have a series of bars or tubes, each of which sounds a particular note when struck.

The sounds of the cello, violin, harp, and piano are produced when a player makes one or more of their strings vibrate. The vibrating strings in turn cause parts of the body of the instrument to vibrate, setting the surrounding air in motion. The strings of cellos and violins are usually stroked with a bow. A musician plucks the strings of a harp. When the keys of a piano are struck, padded hammers hit strings inside the piano, making them vibrate.

Wind instruments, such as the clarinet, flute, and trumpet, generate sounds by the vibration of columns of air inside the instruments. A clarinet has a flat, thin part called a *reed* attached to the mouthpiece. The reed vibrates when a player blows on it, which makes the air column inside the clarinet vibrate. The column of air in a flute vibrates when a musician blows across a hole in the flute's mouthpiece. In a trumpet, the vibrating lips of the player make the air column vibrate.

Noises are unpleasant, annoying, and distracting sounds. Most kinds of noises are produced by vibrating objects that send out irregular vibrations at irregular

intervals. Such noises include the banging of garbage cans, the barking of a dog, and the roar of a crowd. Many machines and devices, such as air conditioners, vacuum cleaners, and the engines of motor vehicles, produce noise. Natural events also create noise. The shaking of the earth generates the rumble of earthquakes. The crash of thunder is produced by violent vibrations of air that has been heated by lightning.

Some noises consist of *impulsive sounds*—that is, vibrations which start suddenly and quickly die. Impulsive sounds include the crack of a gunshot and the pop of a firecracker. A power lawn mower produces a series of impulsive sounds. Such noises as the screech of chalk or a fingernail on a blackboard and the wail of a siren consist of a collection of rapid vibrations that do not blend well. See NOISE.

The Nature of Sound

If you drop a pebble into a still pond, you will see a series of waves travel outward from the point where the pebble struck the surface. Sound also travels in waves as it moves through the air or some other *medium* (substance). The waves are produced by a vibrating object. As a vibrating object moves outward, it compresses the surrounding medium, producing a region of compression called a *condensation*. As the vibrating object then moves inward, the medium expands into the space formerly occupied by the object. This region of expansion is called a *rarefaction*. As the object continues to move outward and inward, a series of condensations and rarefactions travels away from the object. *Sound waves* consist of these condensations and rarefactions.

Sound waves must travel through a medium. Thus,

Terms Used in the Study of Sound

Acoustics is the science of sound and of its effects on people.

Beats are periodic variations in the loudness of a sound. Beats are heard when two tones of slightly different frequencies are sounded at the same time.

Condensation is a region of compression in a sound wave.

Decibel is the unit used to measure the intensity level of a sound. A 3,000-hertz tone of zero decibels is the weakest sound that the normal human ear can hear.

Frequency of sound waves refers to the number of condensations or rarefactions produced by a vibrating object each second.

Hertz is the unit used to measure frequency. One hertz equals one *cycle* (vibration) per second.

Infrasound is sound with frequencies below the range of human hearing.

Intensity of a sound is related to the amount of energy flowing in the sound waves.

Phon is a unit often used to measure the loudness level of tones. The loudness level in phons of any tone is the intensity level in decibels of a 1,000-hertz tone that seems equally loud.

Pitch is the degree of highness or lowness of a sound as perceived by a listener.

Rarefaction is a region of expansion in a sound wave.

Resonance Frequency is approximately the frequency at which an object would vibrate naturally if disturbed in some way.

Sound Quality, also called *timbre,* is a characteristic of musical sounds. Sound quality distinguishes between notes of the same frequency and intensity produced by different musical instruments.

Ultrasound is sound with frequencies above the range of human hearing.

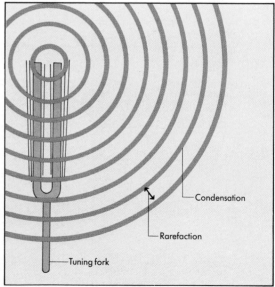

WORLD BOOK diagram by Bill and Judie Anderson

Sound Waves form when a vibrating object causes the surrounding *medium* (substance) to vibrate. As the object moves outward, it produces a region of compression called a *condensation.* As the object then moves inward, a region of expansion known as a *rarefaction* forms. Sound waves consist of the series of condensations and rarefactions generated by the vibrating object.

SOUND

sound is absent in the vacuum of outer space, which contains no material for a vibrating object to compress and expand.

The nature of a particular sound can be described in terms of (1) frequency and pitch, (2) intensity and loudness, and (3) quality.

Frequency and Pitch. The number of condensations or rarefactions produced by a vibrating object each second is called the *frequency* of the sound waves. The more rapidly an object vibrates, the higher will be the frequency. Scientists use a unit called the *hertz* to measure frequency. One hertz equals one *cycle* (vibration) per second (see HERTZ). As the frequency of sound waves increases, the *wavelength* decreases. Wavelength is the distance between any point on one wave and the corresponding point on the next one.

Most people can hear sounds with frequencies from about 20 to 20,000 hertz. Bats, dogs, and many other kinds of animals can hear sounds with frequencies far above 20,000 hertz. Different sounds have different frequencies. For example, the sound of jingling keys ranges from 700 to 15,000 hertz. A person's voice can produce frequencies from 85 to 1,100 hertz. The tones of a piano have frequencies ranging from about 30 to 15,000 hertz.

The frequency of a sound determines its *pitch*—the degree of highness or lowness of the sound as perceived by a listener (see PITCH). High-pitched sounds have higher frequencies than low-pitched sounds. Musical instruments can produce a wide range of pitches. For example, a trumpet has valves that can shorten or lengthen

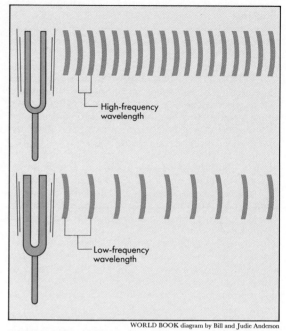

WORLD BOOK diagram by Bill and Judie Anderson

Frequency of sound waves is the number of condensations or rarefactions produced by a vibrating object each second. The more rapidly an object vibrates, the higher will be the frequency. As the frequency increases, the *wavelength*—the distance between any point on one wave and the corresponding point on the next one—decreases. The frequency of a sound determines its pitch. High-pitched sounds have higher frequencies than low-pitched sounds.

Some Common Frequency Ranges

Scientists use a unit called the *hertz* to measure frequency. One hertz equals one *cycle* (vibration) per second. This graph shows the range of frequencies, in hertz, that human beings and some animals can *emit* (give off) and receive. Many animals hear frequencies far above those heard by people.

WORLD BOOK graph

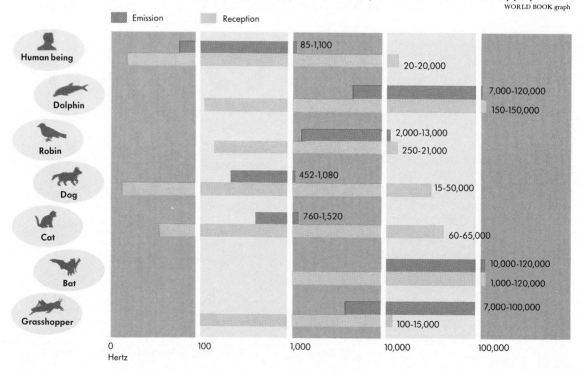

490

the vibrating column of air inside the instrument. A short column produces a high-frequency, high-pitched sound. A long column results in a note of low frequency and low pitch.

Intensity and Loudness. The *intensity* of a sound is related to the amount of energy flowing in the sound waves. Intensity depends on the *amplitude* of the vibrations producing the waves. Amplitude is the distance that a vibrating object moves from its position of rest as it vibrates. The larger the amplitude of vibration is, the more intense will be the sound.

The *loudness* of a sound refers to how strong the sound seems to us when it strikes our ears. At a given frequency, the more intense a sound is, the louder it seems. But equally intense sounds of different frequencies are not equally loud. The ear has low sensitivity to sounds near the upper and lower limits of the range of frequencies we can hear. Thus, a high-frequency or low-frequency sound does not seem as loud as a sound of the same intensity in the middle of the frequency range.

Water waves in a pond get weaker as they travel away from their source. In the same way, sound waves lose intensity as they spread outward in all directions from their source. Thus, the loudness of a sound decreases as the distance increases between a person and the source of the sound. You can observe this effect in a large field by walking away from a friend who is talking at a constant level. As you move farther and farther away, the voice of your friend gets fainter and fainter.

Sound Quality, also called *timbre,* is a characteristic of musical sounds. Quality distinguishes between sounds of the same frequency and intensity produced by different musical instruments.

Almost every musical sound consists of a combination of the actual note sounded and a number of higher tones related to it. The actual note played is the *fundamental.* The higher tones are *overtones* of the fundamental. For example, when a note is produced by a violin string, the string vibrates as a whole and produces the fundamental. But the string also vibrates in separate sections at the same time. It may vibrate in two, three, four, or more parts. Each of these separate vibrations produces an overtone of higher frequency and pitch than the fundamental. The greater the number of vibrating parts is, the higher will be the frequency of the overtone.

The number and strength of the overtones help determine the characteristic sound quality of a musical instrument. For instance, a note on the flute sounds soft and sweet because it has only a few, weak overtones. The same note played on the trumpet has many, strong overtones and thus seems powerful and bright.

How Sound Behaves

The Speed of Sound depends on the medium through which the sound waves travel. The properties of a medium that determine the speed of sound are *density* and *compressibility.* Density is the amount of material in a unit volume of a substance. Compressibility measures how easily a substance can be crushed into a smaller volume. The denser a medium is and the more compressible it is, the slower the speed of sound will be.

In general, liquids and solids are denser than air. But they are also far less compressible. Therefore, sound travels faster through liquids and solids than through air. Compared with its speed through air, sound travels

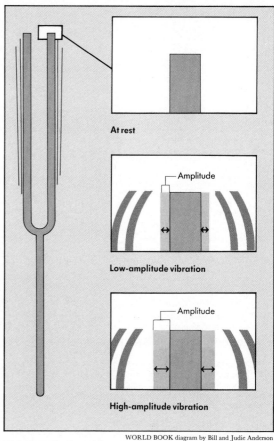

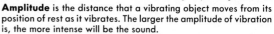

At rest

Low-amplitude vibration

High-amplitude vibration

WORLD BOOK diagram by Bill and Judie Anderson

Amplitude is the distance that a vibrating object moves from its position of rest as it vibrates. The larger the amplitude of vibration is, the more intense will be the sound.

about 4 times faster through water and about 15 times faster through steel. The speed of sound through air increases as the air temperature rises. For instance, sound travels 1,085 feet (331 meters) per second through air at 32° F. (0° C) and 1,268 feet (386 meters) per second through air at 212° F. (100° C).

The speed of sound is much slower than the speed of light. In a vacuum, light travels 186,282 miles (299,792 kilometers) per second—almost a million times faster than sound. As a result, we see the flash of lightning during a storm before we hear the thunder. If you watch a

The Speed of Sound in Various Mediums

Medium	Speed	
	In feet per second	In meters per second
Air at 32° F. (0° C)	1,085	331
Aluminum	16,000	5,000
Brick	11,980	3,650
Distilled water at 77° F. (25° C)	4,908	1,496
Glass	14,900	4,540
Seawater at 77° F. (25° C)	5,023	1,531
Steel	17,100	5,200
Wood (maple)	13,480	4,110

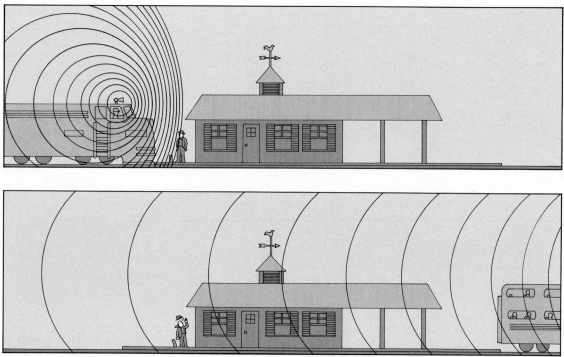

The Doppler Effect is an apparent change in pitch produced by moving objects. For example, the pitch of a train whistle appears higher as the train approaches and lower as the train moves away. As the train approaches, *top,* sound waves from the whistle are crowded together, producing a higher apparent pitch to the listener on the platform. As the train moves away, *bottom,* the waves are spread out, producing a lower apparent pitch. The people on the train hear a uniform pitch.

carpenter hammering on a distant building, you will see the hammer strike before you hear the sound of the blow.

You may have noticed that the pitch of a train whistle seems higher as the train approaches and lower after the train passes and moves away. The sound waves produced by the whistle travel through the air at a constant speed, regardless of the speed of the train. But as the train approaches, each successive wave produced by the whistle travels a shorter distance to your ears. The waves arrive more frequently, and the pitch of the whistle appears higher. As the train moves away, each successive wave travels a longer distance to your ears. The waves arrive less frequently, producing a lower apparent pitch. This apparent change in pitch produced by moving objects is called the *Doppler effect.* To a listener on the train, the pitch of the whistle does not change.

Jet airplanes sometimes fly at supersonic speeds. A plane flying faster than the speed of sound creates *shock waves,* strong pressure disturbances that build up around the aircraft. People on the ground hear a loud noise, known as a *sonic boom,* when the shock waves from the plane sweep over them. See AERODYNAMICS (Shock Waves and Sonic Booms).

Reflection. If you shout toward a large brick wall at least 30 feet (9 meters) away, you will hear an echo. The echo is produced when the sound waves are reflected from the wall to your ears. Generally, when sound waves in one medium strike a large object of another medium—such as the waves in air hitting the brick wall—some of the sound is reflected. The remainder is sent into the new medium. The speed of sound in the two mediums and the densities of the mediums help determine the amount of reflection. If sound travels at about the same speed in both materials and both have about the same density, little sound will be reflected. Instead, most of the sound will be transmitted into the new medium. If the speed differs greatly in the two mediums and their densities are greatly different, most of the sound will be reflected. Sound waves travel much more slowly through air than through brick, and brick is much denser than air. Thus when you shout at the brick wall, most of the sound is reflected. See ECHO.

Refraction. When sound waves leave one medium and enter another in which the speed of sound differs, the direction of the waves is altered. This change in direction results from a change in the speed of the waves and is called *refraction.* If sound waves travel slower in the second medium, the waves will be refracted toward the *normal.* The normal is an imaginary line perpendicular to the boundary between the mediums. If sound travels faster in the second medium, the waves will be refracted away from the normal.

Sound waves can also be refracted if the speed of sound changes according to their position in a medium. The waves bend toward the region of slower speed. You may have noticed that sounds carry farther at night than during a sunny day. During the day, air near the ground is warmer than the air above. Sound waves in the air are bent away from the ground into the cooler air above, where their speed is slower. This bending of the waves results in weaker sound near the ground. At night, air near the ground becomes cooler than the air above. Sound waves are bent toward the ground, enabling sound near the ground to be heard over longer distances.

Diffraction. Sound waves traveling along the side of a building spread out around the corner of the building. When sound waves pass through a doorway, they spread out around its edges. This spreading out of waves as they pass by the edge of an obstacle or through an opening is called *diffraction*. Diffraction occurs whenever a sound wave encounters an obstacle or opening. But it is most evident when the wavelength of the sound wave is long compared with the size of the obstacle or opening. Diffraction enables you to hear a sound from around a corner, even though no straight path exists from the source of the sound to your ears. See DIFFRACTION.

Resonance is the reinforcing of sound. It occurs when a small repeated force produces larger and larger vibrations in an object. To produce resonance, the repeated force must be applied with the same frequency as the *resonance frequency* of the object. Resonance frequency is approximately the frequency at which an object would vibrate naturally if disturbed in some way. It is said that some opera singers can shatter a wineglass by singing a note with a frequency equal to the resonance frequency of the glass. The vibrations produced in the glass get larger and larger until it breaks apart.

You can demonstrate resonance by holding a vibrating tuning fork over a tube that is open at one end and

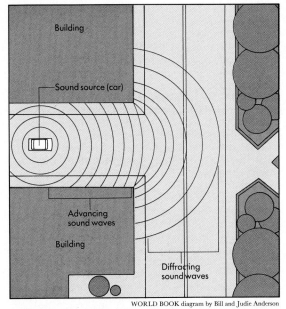

WORLD BOOK diagram by Bill and Judie Anderson

Diffraction is the spreading out of waves as they pass by the edge of an obstacle or through an opening. Diffraction enables the sound produced by the approaching car above to be heard around the corners of the buildings at the intersection.

Refraction of Sound Waves When sound waves leave one medium and enter another in which the speed of sound differs, the waves are *refracted*—that is, their direction is altered. Sound waves can be refracted either away from or toward the *normal,* an imaginary line perpendicular to the boundary between the mediums.

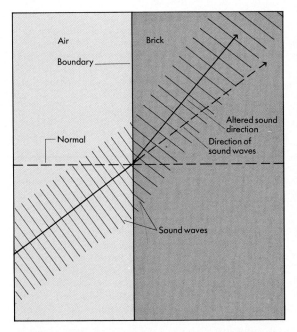

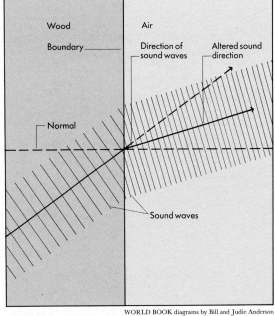

WORLD BOOK diagrams by Bill and Judie Anderson

Refraction Away from the Normal. If sound waves in one medium enter another medium in which the speed of sound is faster, the waves will be refracted away from the normal. For example, sound waves passing from air into brick are refracted away from the normal because sound travels faster in brick than in air.

Refraction Toward the Normal. If sound waves traveling in one medium enter another medium in which the speed of sound is slower, the waves will be refracted toward the normal. For example, sound waves passing from wood into air are refracted toward the normal because sound travels slower in air than in wood.

SOUND

closed at the other end. If the tube is almost exactly one-fourth as long as the wavelength of the sound waves from the fork, the waves will travel down the column of air inside the tube and be reflected from the bottom. The original waves and the reflected waves combine and form wave patterns that appear to stand still. Such patterns are called *standing waves*. When standing waves form in the tube, the air column and the tuning fork are in resonance. The standing waves in the tube cause the surrounding air to vibrate with a larger amplitude, resulting in a louder sound.

Resonance increases the loudness of the sounds produced by many musical instruments. For example, a wind instrument produces resonance in the same way as the tuning fork and the tube. Standing waves are set up in the column of air inside the instrument. The air column resonates with the vibrations at the mouthpiece, amplifying the sound of the instrument.

Beats. When two tones of slightly different frequencies are sounded together, you hear a single sound that gets louder and softer at regular intervals. These periodic variations of loudness are *beats*. Beats are produced because the sound waves of the two tones overlap and interfere with each other.

The interference of the combined waves is called *constructive* if condensations coincide with condensations and rarefactions meet rarefactions. The waves reinforce each other, producing a louder sound. The interference between the waves is *destructive* if condensations coincide with rarefactions. A weaker sound or silence results. If the periods of constructive and destructive interference alternate, the loudness of the sound increases and decreases, producing beats. See INTERFERENCE.

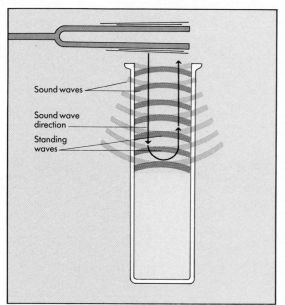

WORLD BOOK diagram by Bill and Judie Anderson

Resonance is the reinforcing of sound. The tuning fork above is in resonance with the air column inside the beaker. Sound waves from the fork travel down the column and are reflected from the water. The original waves and the reflected waves combine and form patterns called *standing waves* that result in a louder sound.

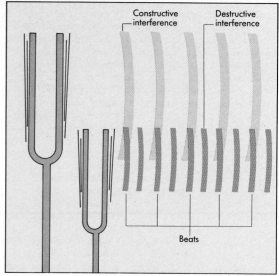

WORLD BOOK diagram by Bill and Judie Anderson

Beats are periodic variations in loudness that occur when the sound waves of two tones overlap and interfere with each other. In *constructive* interference, condensations coincide with condensations, producing a louder sound. In *destructive* interference, condensations meet rarefactions, resulting in a weaker sound.

The number of beats per second, called the *beat frequency*, equals the difference between the frequencies of the two tones. For example, if a 256-hertz tone and a 257-hertz tone are sounded together, one beat will be heard each second.

Working with Sound

Measuring Sound. Scientists use a unit called the *decibel* to measure the intensity level of a sound. A 3,000-hertz tone of zero decibels marks the *threshold of audibility*—the weakest sound that the normal human ear can hear. A sound intensity level of 140 decibels is the *threshold of pain*. Sounds of 140 decibels or more produce pain in the ear, rather than hearing. A whisper amounts to about 20 decibels. Ordinary conversation has an intensity level of about 60 decibels. Loud rock music can produce up to 120 decibels of sound. See DECIBEL.

A unit called the *phon* is often used to measure the loudness level of tones. The loudness level in phons of any tone is the intensity level in decibels of a 1,000-hertz tone that seems equally loud. For example, a tone of 20 decibels with a frequency of 1,000 hertz has a loudness level of 20 phons. A tone of any frequency and intensity that seems equally loud is also assigned a loudness level of 20 phons. For instance, a tone of 80 decibels with a frequency of 20 hertz seems as loud as the 20-decibel tone at 1,000 hertz. Thus, the 80-decibel tone has a loudness level of 20 phons.

Controlling Sound. The science of *acoustics* deals with sound and its effects on people. A major field of acoustics is *environmental acoustics*, which involves control of noise pollution.

We are continually exposed to noise from a variety of sources, such as airplanes, construction projects, industries, motor vehicles, and even household appliances. People exposed to loud noise for long periods may suffer temporary or permanent loss of hearing. Loud sounds of short duration, such as the noise of a gunshot or a firecracker, can also damage the ear. Constant noise—even if it is not extremely loud—can cause fatigue, headaches, hearing loss, irritability, nausea, and tension.

Noise pollution can be controlled in a number of ways. Acoustical engineers have quieted the noise made by many devices. For example, mufflers help reduce the noise from automobile engines. In buildings, thick, heavy walls, well-sealed doors and windows, and various other means may be used to block noise (see INSULATION [Insulation Against Sound]). Industrial workers and other people exposed to intense noise should wear some form of ear protectors to help prevent hearing loss.

Acoustics also involves providing good conditions for producing and listening to speech and music in such places as auditoriums and concert halls. For example, acoustical engineers work to control *reverberation*—the bouncing back and forth of sound against the ceiling, walls, floor, and other surfaces of an auditorium or hall. Some reverberation is necessary to produce pleasing sounds. But too much reverberation can blur the voice of a speaker or the sound of a musical instrument. Engineers use such sound-absorbing items as acoustical tiles, carpets, draperies, and upholstered furniture to control reverberation. See ACOUSTICS.

Using Sound. Sound has many uses in science and industry. Geophysicists often use sound in exploring for minerals and petroleum. In one technique, they set off a

Intensity of Some Common Sounds

The unit used to measure the intensity level of a sound is called the *decibel*. A 3,000-hertz tone of zero decibels is the weakest sound that the human ear can hear. Sounds of 140 decibels or more produce pain in the ear and may damage the delicate tissues.

WORLD BOOK chart

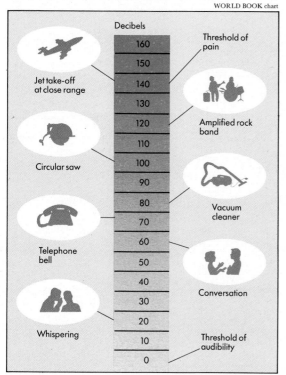

	Decibels	
Jet take-off at close range	160	Threshold of pain
	150	
	140	
	130	
	120	Amplified rock band
	110	
Circular saw	100	
	90	
	80	Vacuum cleaner
	70	
Telephone bell	60	
	50	
	40	Conversation
	30	
	20	
Whispering	10	Threshold of audibility
	0	

small explosion on or just below the earth's surface. The resulting sound waves bounce off underground layers of rock. The nature of each echo and the time it takes for the waves to reach the surface indicate the type and thickness of each rock layer present. Geophysicists can thus locate possible mineral- or oil-bearing rock formations. A device called *sonar* uses sound waves to detect underwater objects (see SONAR). Warships can locate enemy submarines with sonar. Fishing boats use sonar systems to detect schools of fish.

Sound with frequencies above the range of human hearing is called *ultrasound*. It is used to clean watches and other delicate instruments. Manufacturers also use ultrasonic waves to test metals, plastics, and other materials. Physicians can diagnose brain tumors, gallstones, liver diseases, and other disorders with ultrasound. Ultrasonic waves also provide a relatively safe means to check the development of unborn children. See ULTRASOUND.

Scientists and engineers have developed several devices for recording and reproducing sound. These devices include the microphone, the speaker, and the amplifier. A *microphone* changes sound waves into electric signals that correspond to the pattern of the waves. A *speaker* changes electric signals, such as those produced by a microphone, back into sound. An *amplifier* is used in most sound-reproduction systems to strengthen the electric signals and make them powerful enough to operate the speaker. Every phonograph, public address system, radio, tape recorder, and television set has at least one amplifier. See MICROPHONE; SPEAKER; ELECTRONICS (Amplification).

In recording music, engineers sometimes make two or more separate recordings from microphones placed at various points around the source. If these recordings are played back together correctly, they produce *stereophonic sound*. Stereophonic sound has qualities of depth and direction similar to those of the original sound. To reproduce stereophonic sound, a sound system must have an amplifier and a speaker for each of the recordings. See HIGH FIDELITY (Stereophonic Hi-Fi).

The Study of Sound

Early Thought. The study of sound began in ancient times. As early as the 500's B.C., Pythagoras, a Greek philosopher and mathematician, conducted experiments on the sounds produced by vibrating strings. Pythagoras is said to have invented the *sonometer*, an instrument used to study musical sounds (see SONOMETER). About 400 B.C., a Greek scholar named Archytas stated that sound is produced by the motion of one object striking another. About 50 years later, the Greek philosopher Aristotle suggested that sound is carried to our ears by the movement of air. From then until about A.D. 1300, little scientific investigation took place in Europe. But scientists in the Middle East and India developed some new ideas about sound by studying music and working out systems of music theory.

The Wave Theory. The understanding that sound travels in the form of waves may have originated with the Italian artist Leonardo da Vinci about 1500. But European scientists did not begin extensive experiments on the nature of sound until the early 1600's. About that

SOUND

time, the Italian astronomer and physicist Galileo demonstrated that the frequency of sound waves determines pitch. Galileo scraped a chisel across a brass plate, producing a screech. He then related the spacing of the grooves made by the chisel to the pitch of the screech.

About 1640, Marin Mersenne, a French mathematician, obtained the first measurement of the speed of sound in air. About 20 years later, the Irish chemist and physicist Robert Boyle demonstrated that sound waves must travel in a medium. Boyle showed that a ringing bell could not be heard if placed in a jar from which as much air had been removed as possible. During the late 1600's, the English scientist Sir Isaac Newton formulated an almost correct relationship between the speed of sound in a medium and the density and compressibility of the medium.

In the mid-1700's, Daniel Bernoulli, a Swiss mathematician and physicist, explained that a string could vibrate at more than one frequency at the same time. In the early 1800's, a French mathematician named Jean Baptiste Fourier developed a mathematical technique that could be used to break down complex sound waves into the pure tones that make them up. During the 1860's, Hermann von Helmholtz, a German physicist, investigated the interference of sound waves, the production of beats, and the relationship of both to the ear's perception of sound.

Recent Developments. Much of modern acoustics is based on the principles of sound described in *The Theory of Sound*, a book published by the British physicist Lord Rayleigh in 1878. Although many of the properties of sound have thus been long established, the science of acoustics has continued to expand into new areas. In the 1940's, Georg von Békésy, an American physicist, showed how the ear distinguishes between various sounds. During the 1960's, the field of environmental acoustics expanded rapidly in response to growing concern over the physical and psychological effects of noise pollution.

Acoustical research of the 1970's included the study of new uses of ultrasound, and the development of better ultrasonic equipment. During the early 1980's, research included the design of better sound-reproducing equipment and the development of computers that can understand and reproduce speech. Acoustical engineers also studied possible uses of *infrasound*—that is, sound with frequencies below the range of human hearing.

ALAN B. COPPENS and JAMES V. SANDERS

Related Articles in WORLD BOOK include:

PRINCIPLES OF SOUND

Acoustics	Harmonics	Tone
Decibel	Interference	Ultrasound
Doppler Effect	Larynx	Vibration
Ear	Noise	Voice
Echo	Pitch	Waves

SOUND INSTRUMENTS AND DEVICES

Dictating Machine	Motion Picture
Electronics	Oscilloscope
Fathometer	Phonograph
Hearing Aid	Public Address System
High Fidelity	Radio
Loudspeaker	Siren
Microphone	Sonar

Sonometer	Television
Sound-Powered Telephone	Transducer
Speaker	Tuning Fork
Stethoscope	Voder
Tape Recorder	Voiceprint
Telephone	

OTHER RELATED ARTICLES

Aerodynamics (Shock Waves and Sonic Booms)	Frequency Modulation
Bell, Alexander G.	Helmholtz, Hermann
Berliner, Emile	Mach, Ernst
Deafness	Muffler
Edison, Thomas A.	Music
Environmental Pollution (graph: Noise Pollution)	Phonetics
	Singing

Outline

I. How Some Familiar Sounds Are Produced
    A. The Human Voice
    B. Animal Sounds
    C. Musical Sounds
    D. Noises
II. The Nature of Sound
    A. Frequency and Pitch
    B. Intensity and Loudness
    C. Sound Quality
III. How Sound Behaves
    A. The Speed of Sound
    B. Reflection
    C. Refraction
    D. Diffraction
    E. Resonance
    F. Beats
IV. Working with Sound
    A. Measuring Sound
    B. Controlling Sound
    C. Using Sound
V. The Study of Sound

Questions

How does a vibrating object produce sound waves?

Why does sound travel faster through liquids and solids than through air?

How do wind instruments generate tones?

Why do acoustical engineers try to control the amount of reverberation in auditoriums and concert halls?

How can noise pollution affect people?

How did Robert Boyle demonstrate that sound waves must travel in a medium?

Why do sounds carry farther at night than during a sunny day?

How would it be possible for an opera singer to shatter a wineglass by singing?

Why does a note on the flute sound different from the same note played on the trumpet?

Why are sound waves absent in outer space?

Additional Resources

Level I

BRANLEY, FRANKLYN M. *High Sounds, Low Sounds.* Crowell, 1967.

HEUER, KENNETH. *Thunder, Singing Sounds, and Other Wonders: Sound in the Atmosphere.* Dodd, 1981.

KETTLEKAMP, LARRY. *The Magic of Sound.* Rev. ed. Morrow, 1982.

KNIGHT, DAVID C. *Silent Sound: The World of Ultrasonics.* Morrow, 1980.

Level II

CHEDD, GRAHAM. *Sound: From Communication to Noise Pollution.* Doubleday, 1971.

HUNT, FREDERICK V. *Origins in Acoustics: The Science of Sound from Antiquity to the Age of Newton.* Yale, 1978.

KOCK, WINSTON E. *Seeing Sound.* Wiley, 1971.

TANNENBAUM, BEULAH, and STILLMAN, MYRA. *Understanding Sound.* McGraw, 1973.

SOUND is a narrow stretch of water. There are several different kinds of such bodies of water. The word *sound* often describes a fiord or submerged glaciated valley, such as Howe Sound in British Columbia, or Doubtful Sound on South Island in New Zealand. The word sometimes denotes a deep, protected bay formed by the submergence of nonglaciated hilly land below sea level like Hingwha Sound on the southeastern coast of China. *Sound* is also used as a synonym for a strait, or narrow passage of water, between two broad areas of sea. Such straits include Kalmar Sound, separating the island of Öland from Sweden, and The Sound, or Øresund, which separates the Danish island of Sjaelland from Sweden. The word *sund* in the Danish, Norwegian, and Swedish languages means *sound*. J. ROWLAND ILLICK

See also BAY; FIORD; STRAIT.

SOUND BARRIER. See SONIC BOOM.

SOUND EFFECT. See RADIO (Putting a Show on the Air; picture: A Sound-Effects Expert); MOTION PICTURE (Sound; picture: Recording Sound Effects).

SOUND-POWERED TELEPHONE is a communication device that operates only on the power of the sound that enters it. Telephones and most other communication systems operate on electrical power supplied by batteries or electric-power lines. However, the sound-powered telephone has no outside source of power other than that supplied by sound waves.

A sound-powered telephone system consists of two or more identical phone units connected by wires. Each phone consists of a metal diaphragm and a permanent magnet around which a coil is wound. The magnet is placed close to the diaphragm. This forms a type of microphone. When people speak into the microphone, their voices cause sound waves that make the metal diaphragm vibrate. The coil and magnet transform the waves of sound into electrical impulses. These impulses are carried by wires to the other phone units in the system. There the coils and magnets pass on the electrical variations to the receiving diaphragms, causing them to vibrate and thus produce sound.

These telephones can work only over short distances, usually not more than about 15 miles (24 kilometers). Because no amplification is used, the speaker must talk close to the telephone and in a loud voice. But the sound-powered telephone has the advantages of being rugged, reliable, and inexpensive. RICHARD H. BOLT

SOUND SPECTROGRAPH. See VOICEPRINT.

SOUNDING. See FATHOMETER; SONAR.

SOUNDING LEAD. See LEAD, SOUNDING.

SOUNDING ROCKET. See SPACE TRAVEL (Space Probes).

SOUNDPROOFING. See ACOUSTICS; INSULATION.

SOUR GUM. See BLACK TUPELO.

SOURWOOD. See SORREL TREE.

SOUSA, JOHN PHILIP (1854-1932), was a famous American composer and bandmaster. Sousa wrote many kinds of music, including operettas, orchestral suites, songs, waltzes, and a symphonic poem. But his fame rests on his marches, and he became known throughout the world as the "March King."

Sousa took the rather simple form of the military march and gave it a personal style and new rhythmic and melodic vitality. The best-known of his more than a hundred marches include "Semper Fidelis," "The Washington Post," "El Capitan," "Thunderer," "The

High School Cadets," "Liberty Bell," "Manhattan Beach," "Hands Across the Sea," and "The Stars and Stripes Forever." A man of many gifts, Sousa also wrote five novels and an autobiography, *Marching Along* (1928).

Sousa was born in Washington, D.C. His parents could not afford to send him to Europe to study music. But Sousa later said, "I feel I am better off as it is . . . for I may therefore consider myself a truly American composer." After studying violin and harmony, he began his professional career at the age of 17, playing in theater and dance orchestras and touring with a variety show. In 1877, he played in Jacques Offenbach's orchestra when the famous French composer toured the United States. Soon afterward, Sousa wrote an operetta, *The Smugglers*, the first of many that he wrote in the next 35 years. He was one of the first Americans to compose operettas. He wrote the words as well as the music for these. The most successful of Sousa's operettas was *El Capitan* (1896).

Bettmann Archive

John Philip Sousa

Sousa was appointed leader of the U.S. Marine Band in 1880, and made the band into one of the finest in the world. Some of the marches that made him famous were written for the band. In 1892, Sousa obtained his discharge from the Marine Corps and formed his own band.

Sousa gave concerts in America and Europe, playing arrangements of the classics as well as military marches. He was honored wherever he traveled. In England, King Edward VII decorated him with the Victorian Order. In 1900, the American writer Rupert Hughes wrote, "There is probably no other composer in the world with a popularity equal to that of Sousa." In 1910 and 1911, "Sousa's Band" made a triumphal world tour. From 1917 to 1919, Sousa served as bandmaster for the United States Navy. GILBERT CHASE

SOUSAPHONE. See TUBA.

SOUSTER, RAYMOND (1921-   ), is a Canadian poet. He uses direct, simple language to make uncomplicated statements. Most of Souster's poems concern Toronto, where he was born and grew up. He writes about that city with both irony and sympathy.

More than a dozen collections of Souster's poetry have been published. He won the Governor General's Award for the collection *The Colour of the Times* (1964). In 1952, Souster helped found the Contact Press, which publishes the work of modern Canadian poets. He also edited an anthology of Canadian verse, *New Wave Canada: The New Explosion in Canadian Poetry* (1966). Souster wrote a realistic novel, *The Winter of Time* (1949), that was published under the pen name Raymond Holmes. CLAUDE T. BISSELL

SOUTH, THE. See UNITED STATES (Regions).

SOUTH, UNIVERSITY OF THE. See UNIVERSITIES AND COLLEGES (table).

Scenic Cape Town, South Africa's legislative capital and oldest city, lies at the foot of Table Mountain. The Dutch founded the city in 1652 as a supply base for Dutch East India Company ships.

Pete Turner, DPI

SOUTH AFRICA

SOUTH AFRICA is the richest and most highly developed country in Africa. It occupies only about 4 per cent of the continent's area and has only about 6 per cent of its people. Yet the country produces two-fifths of Africa's manufactured goods, nearly half its minerals, and a fifth of its farm products. South Africa generates more than half the continent's electricity and has about two-fifths its automobiles and half its telephones.

South Africa lies at the southern tip of the continent, between the Indian Ocean to the east and the South Atlantic Ocean to the west. The country is nearly three times as large as California and more than twice as large as France. It consists of four provinces—Cape Province, which is sometimes called Cape of Good Hope Province; Natal; the Orange Free State; and the Transvaal. South Africa has three capitals. Parliament meets in Cape Town, the legislative capital. All government departments have their headquarters in Pretoria, the administrative capital. The country's highest court meets in Bloemfontein, the judicial capital.

Johannesburg and Cape Town are South Africa's largest urban centers. More people live within the city limits of Cape Town than live within the city limits of Johannesburg. But the metropolitan area of Johannesburg has a larger population than that of Cape Town. South Africans consider Johannesburg to be the country's largest city.

The landscape varies dramatically throughout South Africa. There are high, sweeping plateaus, towering mountains, and deep valleys. Many picturesque

Leonard M. Thompson, the contributor of this article, is Professor of History at Yale University, coeditor of The Oxford History of South Africa, *and the author of several books about South Africa.*

beaches line the long, fertile coast. In addition to its scenic beauty, much of South Africa has a delightfully mild and sunny climate. Along the coast, such tropical and semitropical fruits as bananas, mangoes, and oranges thrive in the warm sun.

South Africa has one of the world's strongest and fastest-growing economies. It produces more gold and gem diamonds than any other country. It is also a leading producer of asbestos, chromium, copper, manganese, platinum, and uranium. South Africa's farmers produce almost all the food needed by the people. The

Facts in Brief

Capitals: Cape Town (legislative), Pretoria (administrative), and Bloemfontein (judicial).

Official Languages: Afrikaans and English.

Official Name: Republic of South Africa or, in Afrikaans, *Republiek van Suid-Afrika.*

Area (including the Bophuthatswana, Ciskei, Transkei, and Venda; but excluding Walvis Bay): 471,445 sq. mi. (1,221,037 km²). *Greatest Distances*—east-west, 1,010 mi. (1,625 km); north-south, 875 mi. (1,408 km). *Coastline*—about 1,650 mi. (2,655 km).

Elevation: *Highest*—Champagne Castle, 11,072 ft. (3,375 m) above sea level. *Lowest*—sea level along the coast.

Population (including the Bophuthatswana, Ciskei, Transkei, and Venda, but excluding Walvis Bay): *Estimated 1984 Population*—32,199,000; distribution, 52 per cent urban, 48 per cent rural; density, 67 persons per sq. mi. (26 persons per km²). *1970 Census*—21,794,328. *Estimated 1989 Population*—36,253,000.

Chief Products: *Agriculture*—cattle, corn (maize), dairy products, fruits, sheep, sugar, wheat, wine, wool. *Manufacturing*—chemicals, clothing, metals, metal products, processed foods. *Mining*—asbestos, coal, copper, diamonds, gold, platinum, uranium.

National Anthem: "Die Stem van Suid-Afrika" (The Call of South Africa").

Money: *Basic Unit*—rand. For its value in U.S. dollars, see MONEY (table: Exchange Rates).

WORLD BOOK photo by David Goldblatt

A Street Scene in Johannesburg, South Africa's chief in-dustrial center, reflects the country's multiracial population.

country's mines and farms also produce nearly all the raw materials needed by South African industry. South Africa's factories turn out most of the country's cloth-ing, processed foods, machinery, and other manufac-tured goods.

The people of South Africa form one of the most com-plicated racial patterns in the world. The country's government classifies the people into four main groups. These groups are (1) black, (2) white, (3) Colored, and (4) Asian.

The blacks, who are also called *Africans,* make up about 67 per cent of the population. The black people are further divided into subgroups, according to their traditional ethnic divisions.

White people make up about 19 per cent of the popu-lation. They are split into two groups. About three-fifths of all South African whites are *Afrikaners.* Afrikan-ers are chiefly of Dutch, German, and French descent. They speak *Afrikaans,* a language developed from the Dutch language. The remaining two-fifths of the whites are mainly of British descent and speak English as their native language.

Colored people make up about 11 per cent of South Africa's population. The Colored people are of mixed black, white, and Asian descent. Asians account for about 3 per cent of the country's population. The an-cestors of almost all of South Africa's Asians came to the country from India.

South Africa is one of the few countries in the world in which a racial minority controls the government. In South Africa, only whites may vote in parliamentary elections, serve in Parliament, and administer the laws. The government's official policy aims to keep the four racial groups strictly separated politically and socially. The government's goal is the "separate development" of each group. This policy is called *apartheid* (pro-nounced *ah PAHRT hayt*). *Apartheid* is an Afrikaans word meaning *apartness.*

Apartheid laws affect every aspect of life in South

Africa. They determine where a person may live and go to school and what jobs a person may hold.

Almost every country, including the United States, has criticized the South African government's racial policies as a denial of basic human rights. The United Nations (UN) and the World Council of Churches have also denounced apartheid. South Africa has been ex-cluded from taking part in the Olympic Games and many other international sports events.

Most white South Africans support segregation and resent outside criticism of their government. They say that South Africa is not only the most modern country in Africa but also the most stable. They claim that many nonwhites also favor segregation and that blacks in South Africa earn more money and have higher standards of living than do blacks in other coun-tries of Africa. They, also claim that blacks have the opportunity to learn the arts of government and, in time, become independent within their original home-lands. Many people in Western Europe and the United States sympathize with the South African government. They regard the country as a strong defense against Communism and have found it highly profitable to invest in South African businesses.

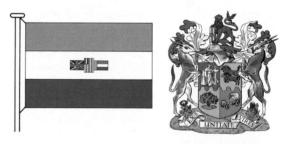

The South African Flag, adopted in 1927, features the British Union Flag and flags of the two former Boer republics.

Coat of Arms. Symbols on the shield represent South Africa's four provinces. *Ex Unitate Vi-res* means *Unity Is Strength.*

WORLD BOOK map

South Africa lies at the southern tip of Africa. It borders the South Atlantic Ocean and the Indian Ocean.

498a

South Africa is a republic, with a president, a prime minister and Cabinet, a Parliament, and a court system. Only white citizens 18 years of age and older may vote in parliamentary elections, and only white persons may serve in Parliament. The table on this page outlines the structure of the white government.

Nonwhite Governments. Apartheid prohibits blacks, Asians, and Coloreds from taking part in the white South African government. Instead, Parliament set up separate organizations for these groups.

The government regards South Africa's black populations as ten separate *nations*, each with its own ancestry and culture. These nations, such as the Xhosa and Zulu, have been assigned reserves in their original homelands. The reserves, called homelands, consist of scattered blocks of land in eastern South Africa. They cover about 13 per cent of the country. As the homelands develop, the government says that it will grant all of them increased powers leading, in time, to independence.

In 1976, the Transkei, a reserve set aside for Xhosa people, became the first homeland to be declared independent by South Africa (see TRANSKEI). Bophuthatswana, the reserve of the Tswana, was declared independent in 1977. Venda, the reserve of the Vhavenda, was declared independent in 1979. Ciskei, a reserve of the Xhosa, was declared independent in 1981. The South African government and the leaders of these four homelands consider the four homelands to be independent nations. But other countries and the United Nations do not recognize the Transkei, Bophuthatswana, Venda, and Ciskei as independent nations. They claim that South Africa actually controls the four homelands.

The Asians have a council called the South African Indian Council. It consists of 40 elected members of the Asian community. The government allows the council to operate the educational system and provide other services in the Asian community. Colored people formerly had a similar council. But in 1975, Colored voters elected council members who had claimed the council had little real power and pledged to dissolve it. Parliament agreed to dissolve the council in 1980.

Political Parties. The National Party has controlled the South African government since 1948. The party stands for apartheid and has the support of most Afrikaners and some English-speaking whites. The main opposition party, the Progressive Federal Party, favors sharp reductions in the country's apartheid laws. South Africa also has several smaller political parties. These parties include the New Republic Party.

The government prohibits interracial political parties. Blacks can form parties within their homelands. Asian parties compete for election to their council.

Namibia, (also called South West Africa), is a former German colony administered by South Africa. It borders South Africa on the northwest. The League of Nations placed the territory under South Africa's control in 1920. The UN has condemned South Africa for applying its apartheid policy there and has voted to end the country's control of the territory. In the late 1970's and early 1980's, representatives of South Africa and the United Nations held discussions about plans that would

Government in Brief

Form of Government: Republic.

Head of State: President, who is elected by Parliament to a 7-year term.

Head of Government: Prime minister, who is usually the leader of the majority party in Parliament. The prime minister and the Cabinet set government policies. Cabinet members head the government departments and must be members of Parliament.

Parliament has a single house, the *House of Assembly*. It has 165 members elected by qualified voters. Members serve 5 years unless Parliament is dissolved sooner.

Courts: The highest court, the Appellate Division of the Supreme Court, hears only appeals. Provincial and local divisions of the Supreme Court hear original cases and appeals from the lowest courts, the magistrates' courts.

Provincial Government: A provincial council, elected by white voters, deals with local matters in each province. An administrator appointed by the president serves as chief executive. Council members and administrators serve 5-year terms.

give independence to Namibia. See NAMIBIA (History).

Armed Forces. South Africa has about 52,000 white men in its army, air force, and navy. In an emergency, an additional 90,000 trained whites can quickly be called into service. White males between 16 and 25 must receive military training. Nonwhites do not have to serve in the military, but some do serve.

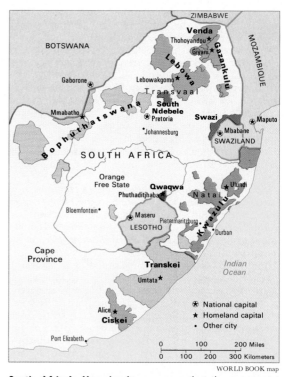

South Africa's Homelands are areas that the government has set aside for the nation's black population groups. The 10 homelands are shown on this map in color and in boldface type.

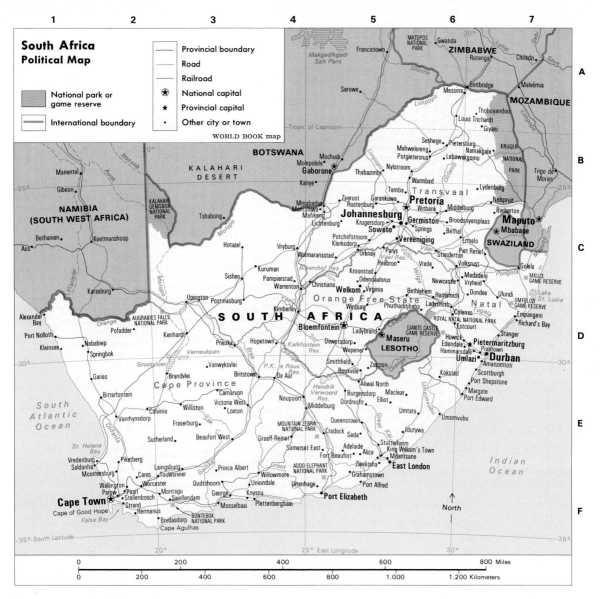

South Africa
Political Map

National park or game reserve

International boundary

- - - Provincial boundary
─── Road
─⊛─ Railroad
⊛ National capital
★ Provincial capital
• Other city or town

WORLD BOOK map

South Africa Map Index

Provinces

Cities and Towns

Source: 1980 census.
* Population of metropolitan area, including suburbs.
*Does not appear on map; key shows general location.

Marvin Newman, DPI

English-Speaking Whites largely control South Africa's businesses and industry. Chiefly of British descent, they still follow many British traditions, such as a love for horse shows, *above*.

Population and Ancestry. In 1984, South Africa had about 32 million persons. About half the people live in urban areas. The country has three cities with more than 500,000 persons. They are Cape Town, Johannesburg, and Pretoria. South Africa has 12 other cities with over 100,000 persons. The country's cities rank among the most modern and beautiful in the world. For more information, see the separate articles on the cities of South Africa listed in the *Related Articles* at the end of this article.

The government divides South Africans into four major racial groups. In order of political and social importance, whites rank first, followed roughly by Coloreds, Asians, and blacks (also called Africans in South Africa). The government issues each citizen a document showing which group he or she belongs to. But no group is "racially pure." For example, many people who are classified as black have some white or Asian ancestry. Many people classified as white have some black or Asian ancestry. By definition, South Africa's Colored people have a mixed ancestry, which varies greatly among individuals. The government classifies individuals on the basis of appearance, known ancestry, and the opinion of other persons in the community.

Whites. About 6 million white persons live in South Africa. Afrikaners make up about three-fifths of the white population. Their ancestors came chiefly from The Netherlands, Germany, and France during the late 1600's and 1700's. Until the 1900's, most Afrikaners lived on farms and were called *Boers*. *Boer* is a Dutch word meaning *farmer*. Today, most Afrikaners live in cities, but they still make up most of the white population in rural areas. English-speaking whites account for about two-fifths of South Africa's white citizens. Their ancestors came chiefly from England, Ireland, and Scotland beginning in the 1800's.

Colored People total about $3\frac{1}{2}$ million. Their ancestors include various peoples. Some were yellowish-skinned hunters and herders who lived in western South Africa when the first white settlers arrived in the 1600's. Some were black and Southeast Asian slaves brought to the country after the whites came. Other ancestors include the early white settlers themselves and passing sailors, soldiers, and travelers.

Asians. Over 1 million Asians live in South Africa. The ancestors of almost all of them came from India between 1860 and 1911. They came to work, under contract, on the sugar plantations in Natal.

Blacks total over 21 million. Their ancestors began to move into what is now eastern South Africa from the north before A.D. 1000.

Languages. South Africa has two official languages —Afrikaans and English. The government uses both languages for official business, and both are taught in white schools. Afrikaans developed from Dutch, but it also has words from other European languages and from Asian and African languages. South African English resembles standard English with many Afrikaans words.

John Rushmer from Carl Östman

Afrikaner Farmers attend a sheep sale. Afrikaners, who are mainly of Dutch, German, and French descent and speak Afrikaans, largely control South Africa's government and agriculture.

E. S. Ross

Blacks make up the largest group of South Africa's population. Nearly half of them, like these Zulu, live in homelands. There, many blacks keep their old customs. For example, the elaborately dressed, red-dyed hair of these women shows they are married.

In their homes, almost all Afrikaners speak only Afrikaans, and almost all other whites speak only English. About 90 per cent of the Colored people speak Afrikaans, and the rest speak English. Asians speak various Indian languages, though most also know English. Blacks speak a variety of Bantu languages. Many blacks also speak a little Afrikaans or English.

Ways of Life. The government's apartheid policy encourages whites, blacks, Coloreds, and Asians to keep and develop their own way of life. The people in each group must live in separate areas, and children must go to separate schools. The groups are also separated in the jobs they may hold. But whites employ large numbers of nonwhites in their homes, industries, and businesses. Each group's way of life thus reflects not only its inherited traditions but also the fact that it must associate with other groups in economic activities.

Differences exist within each racial group as well as between the groups. In each group, some people have better jobs and make more money than others. Even in the black, Asian, and Colored communities—which have many very poor people—there are successful executives and professional persons. Political differences also exist within the groups. For example, most whites vote for politicians who support apartheid, but some vote for candidates who oppose the policy. Some blacks would like to drive the whites out of the country. Yet other blacks believe in cooperating with whites to build a new society without racial bars.

Whites. About 87 per cent of all white South Africans live in urban areas. Most whites have a high standard of living. Their clothing, homes, and social customs resemble those of middle-class Americans and Europeans. Many whites live in luxurious suburban areas of Cape

Town, Durban, Johannesburg, and Pretoria. Most white families in South Africa live in single-family homes, and many have at least one black, Asian, or Colored servant.

Afrikaners and English-speaking whites generally lead separate lives. They live in different sections of a city and belong to different churches and social and professional organizations. Afrikaners hold nearly all the government jobs in South Africa, and they control most of the nation's agriculture. On the other hand, English-speaking whites largely control the nation's businesses and industries.

Colored People. About 75 per cent of South Africa's Coloreds live in cities. The Colored community began in Cape Province, and almost all Coloreds still live there. Colored people have worked for whites for many generations. As a result, they have no traditions of their own and live as much like whites as they can afford. Coloreds would like whites to accept them as equals. Within their group, the lighter a person's skin is, the more highly he or she is regarded. In the cities, most Colored people work as servants, factory laborers, or craftworkers. In rural areas, many work in vineyards or orchards.

Asians. About 85 per cent of all Asians live in cities. The great majority of Indians, who make up almost all the Asian population, live in Natal. Indians have kept many of their old customs. Most Indians are Hindus and largely observe the *caste system* of their religion, which divides them into social classes. Women still wear the traditional *sari*—a long piece of cloth draped around the body. But young people and many men wear Western-style clothing. Most Indians are poor and work in factories or grow vegetables for big-city markets. But a few Indians have become prosperous doctors, industrialists, lawyers, and merchants.

E. S. Ross

A Group of Colored Schoolchildren reflect the mixed ancestry of South Africa's Colored community. Almost all Coloreds live in Cape Province.

498e

Blacks. The government considers every black to be a citizen of his or her particular homeland. But only about 40 per cent of all the blacks live in their homelands. The rest live in cities, on white farms, or near the country's mines. In their homelands, many blacks follow a traditional way of life. They hold traditional ceremonies. The men herd cattle, and the women tend crops. They live in round, thatch-roofed houses, dress their hair in elaborate styles, and wear colorful costumes.

Many black men cannot make a living for their families in the homelands. They must periodically leave their homeland to work in white areas. Generally, their families may not go with them. These migrant laborers spend their lives circulating between the traditional society in which they were born and the mines and factories where they find work. Many other blacks have always lived in cities. In general, they follow Western customs and traditions.

Food and Drink vary among the people of South Africa according to their wealth and customs. Whites enjoy foods much like those eaten by Americans and Europeans. They also eat local specialties, such as *boerewors*, an Afrikaner sausage dish, and *curry*, an Indian dish of eggs, fish, meat, or vegetables cooked in a spicy sauce. The diet of Colored people is like that of whites but less costly. Indians enjoy curry and other traditional dishes. The basic food of blacks is *mealies* (corn), which they eat as a porridge. Many blacks suffer from a shortage of proteins and vitamins.

Popular beverages include coffee, tea, and soft drinks. White people enjoy the fine wines that come from Cape Province. All groups drink beer.

Recreation. South Africans love sports, and the country's mild climate enables them to spend much of their leisure time outdoors. Their favorite games come from England. They include Rugby football—South Africa's national sport—cricket, and association football (soccer). On weekends and holidays, many city dwellers flock to the beaches or tour their country's national parks and game reserves.

Recreation, like other activities, has been affected by apartheid in South Africa. For example, for many years such facilities as restaurants and theaters were—by law—allowed to serve only either whites or nonwhites. Also, all sports events involving both whites and nonwhites were outlawed. In 1979, the government passed a law which allows restaurants and theaters to serve more than one race, but only if they receive permission from the government. Also, since the mid-1970's, some sports competition involving more than one race has been allowed. But most restaurants, sports competitions, and theaters are still segregated.

Education. Students in each racial group attend separate schools. Also, most English- and Afrikaans-speaking white children go to separate schools, but both groups must learn both languages. On a per child basis, the government spends far more money on the education of white children than on that of nonwhites.

White children from age 7 to 16 must attend school. More than 90 per cent go to public schools. The rest attend government-supervised private schools. About 55 per cent of the white children complete high school.

Colored and Asian children aged 7 to 14 must go to school if they live in areas where facilities are available. Many areas have a shortage of schools and classrooms for Coloreds and Asians. More than 99 per cent of the children who go to school attend public schools. The rest attend church-supported schools supervised by the government. About 10 per cent of the Colored children and 25 per cent of the Indian children go on to high school. Until 1981, the law did not require any black children to go to school. That year, a system of requiring black children to attend school was begun. Under it, local government councils may request that the national government require black children in their areas to attend school between the ages of 6 and 15. In the early 1980's, more than 20 per cent of South Africa's black children attended school.

South Africa has 11 universities for whites, 3 for blacks, and 1 each for Coloreds and Asians. Students enrolled at the universities include about 76,000 whites, 5,200 blacks, 4,400 Asians, and 3,600 Coloreds.

Religion. South Africa does not have an *established* (national) church. But most Afrikaners, who largely control the government, belong to the Dutch Reformed Church or to its sister churches. As a result, this church is often identified with the government. Most English-speaking whites belong to the Anglican, Congregational, Methodist, or Roman Catholic churches.

Most Colored people belong to the Anglican, Congregational, Dutch Reformed, Methodist, or Roman Catholic churches. Most Asians are Hindus or Muslims.

About 30 per cent of the black people belong to Christian churches, chiefly the Anglican, Dutch Reformed, Lutheran, Methodist, and Roman Catholic churches. Many other blacks follow traditional African religions. They believe that the spirits of their ancestors affect their lives for good or evil. They try to influence the spirits through animal sacrifices. About 15 per cent of the blacks belong to *independent Christian churches*, which combine Christian and traditional African beliefs.

The Arts. The South African government supports a performing arts council in each province. The councils have English and Afrikaans companies that present ballets, concerts, operas, and plays in small towns as well as big cities. Private black, Asian, Colored, and white companies also perform throughout the country.

South Africa has produced outstanding artists in such fields as ballet, music, painting, and sculpture. But its greatest contribution to the arts has been in literature. Much of South Africa's literature reflects the country's political and social tensions. After the Anglo-Boer War of 1899-1902, such Afrikaner writers as Jan Celliers, C. L. Leipoldt, and C. J. Langenhoven expressed their sorrow over Great Britain's conquest of their land.

Since the 1920's, many South African writers have dealt with racial themes. They include the white authors Nadine Gordimer, Alan Paton, and William Plomer; the Colored novelist Peter Abrahams; and the black writers Ezekiel Mphahlele and Benedict Vilakazi. Over the years, the government has taken measures to prevent artists from criticizing its apartheid policy or from writing on many other subjects. Today, many South African writers cannot publish in their country.

South Africa occupies the southern tip of Africa. It covers 471,445 square miles (1,221,037 square kilometers), excluding Walvis Bay, an area of 434 square miles (1,124 square kilometers) in Namibia that belongs to South Africa. The small, independent country of Lesotho lies entirely within South Africa.

Land Regions

The country has five land regions: (1) the Plateau, (2) the Coastal Strip, (3) the Cape Mountains Region, (4) the Kalahari Desert, and (5) the Namib Desert.

The Plateau covers most of the interior of South Africa. The *Great Escarpment*, a semicircular series of cliffs and mountains, rims the Plateau and separates it from the coastal regions. The escarpment reaches its greatest heights—over 11,000 feet (3,350 meters) above sea level—in the Drakensberg mountain range in the east. The country's highest point, 11,072-foot (3,375-meter) Champagne Castle, rises in the Drakensberg.

The Plateau slopes gradually downward from the escarpment. It has three chief subregions—the Highveld, the Middleveld, and the Transvaal Basin. The *Highveld* occupies all the Plateau except for the northwestern and northeastern corners. It lies mostly between 4,000 and 6,000 feet (1,200 and 1,800 meters) above sea level and consists largely of flat, grass-covered land. In places, flat-topped mountains rise above the plain. The area around Johannesburg is called the *Witwatersrand* or *Rand*. It covers over 1,000 square miles (2,600 square kilometers) and is the world's largest and richest gold field. This area is the nation's chief industrial and business center. Farmers in the Highveld raise cattle, corn, fruits, potatoes, and wheat.

The *Middleveld*, in the northwestern part of the Plateau, averages less than 4,000 feet (1,200 meters) above sea level. It is a dry, flat area and serves largely as ranch country. The *Transvaal Basin* forms the plateau's northeastern part. It also averages less than 4,000 feet above sea level, though it has mountain ranges over 6,000 feet (1,800 meters) high. The area is largely a rolling grassland with scattered thorn trees. Farmers raise citrus and other fruits, corn, and tobacco. Kruger National Park, a world-famous game reserve, lies in the area. Elephants, leopards, lions, zebras, and other wild animals roam freely in the park, which is South Africa's most popular tourist attraction.

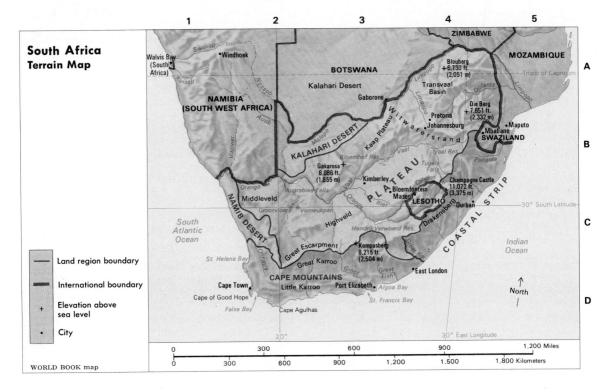

South Africa Terrain Map

WORLD BOOK map

Physical Features

Algoa Bay	D	3
Augrabies Falls	B	2
Bloemhof Reservoir	B	3
Blouberg (Mountain)	A	4
Caledon River	B	4
Cape Agulhas	D	2
Cape Mountains	D	2
Cape of Good Hope	D	2
Champagne Castle (Mountain)	C	4
Coastal Strip	C	4
Die Berg (Mountain)	B	4
Drakensberg (Mountains)	C	4
False Bay	D	2
Gakarosa (Mountain)	B	3
Great Escarpment	C	2
Great Karroo (Plateau)	C	2
Great Fish River	D	3
Great Kei River	C	4
Groot River	D	3
Grootvloer (Salt flat)	C	2
Hendrik Verwoerd Reservoir	C	3
Highveld (Plateau)	C	3
Indian Ocean	C	5
Kaap Plateau	B	3
Kalahari Desert	B	2
Kompsberg (Mountain)	C	3
Limpopo River	A	4
Little Karroo (Plateau)	D	2
Middleveld (Plateau)	C	2
Molopo River	B	3
Namib Desert	C	2
Oilfants River	C	2
Orange River	C	3
Plateau	C	3
Pongola River	B	4
Riet River	C	3
St. Francis Bay	D	3
St. Helena Bay	C	3
South Atlantic Ocean	C	1
Transvaal Basin	A	4
Tugela Falls	B	4
Vaal River	B	3
Vaal Reservoir	B	4
Verneukpan (Salt flat)	C	2
Witwatersrand (Rand) (Ridge)	B	4

498g

Gordon Douglas

South Africa's Magnificent Scenery includes deep valleys, towering mountains, and broad plateaus. Typical Zulu huts, *above,* dot the Zulu homeland of Kwazulu in the Coastal Strip, which extends along the southeast coast. The lofty Drakensberg mountain range rises in the background.

The Coastal Strip extends along the southeast coast from Mozambique to the Cape Mountains Region. Except in the northeast, the region has little low-lying land. In the Durban area, for example, the land rises to 2,000 feet (610 meters) within 20 miles (32 kilometers) of the sea. Chief crops include bananas, citrus fruits, sugar cane, and vegetables. Durban, East London, and Port Elizabeth thrive as resorts, industrial centers, and ports.

The Cape Mountains Region stretches from the Coastal Strip to the Namib Desert. The region's mountains run north to south in the west and east to west in the south. They meet at right angles northeast of the great industrial and port city of Cape Town. Between the mountains and the Great Escarpment lie two dry tablelands—the *Little Karroo* and the *Great Karroo.* There, farmers irrigate wine grapes and other fruits. They also raise wheat and many sheep.

The Namib and Kalahari Deserts. The Namib lies along the Atlantic Ocean north of the Cape Mountains Region and extends into Namibia. The Kalahari lies north of the Middleveld and extends into the country of Botswana. Small bands of hunters roam the deserts, living on the plants and animals they find.

Rivers

South Africa's longest river is the Orange River. It begins in Lesotho and flows westward about 1,300 miles (2,090 kilometers) into the Atlantic. The Vaal River, the Orange's largest branch, rises in southeastern Transvaal. It flows about 750 miles (1,210 kilometers) before joining the Orange in Cape Province. The Limpopo River begins near Johannesburg and winds about 1,000 miles (1,600 kilometers) across eastern South Africa and Mozambique before emptying into the Indian Ocean. South Africa also has many shorter rivers. But sand bars and the shallowness of the water make it impossible for ships to use any of the rivers. See LIMPOPO RIVER; ORANGE RIVER.

Climate

South Africa lies south of the equator, and so its seasons are opposite those of countries in the Northern Hemisphere. Most of South Africa enjoys a mild, sunny climate. But differences in elevation, the wind systems, and ocean currents affect the climate in various areas. For example, the Cape Mountains Region has warm, dry summers and cool, wet winters. Much of the Coastal Strip has hot, humid summers and dry, sunny winters. In the eastern Plateau, summer days are hot, but the nights are cool. In winter, the days are crisp and clear, and the nights are cold. Winter temperatures throughout most of the Plateau often drop below freezing.

Only about a fourth of South Africa receives more than 25 inches (64 centimeters) of rain a year. Most of the rain falls in summer. In general, rainfall decreases from east to west. Parts of the east coast receive over 40 inches (100 centimeters) annually. In the west, the Namib Desert gets almost no rain.

The first European farmers arrived in South Africa in the 1650's. For the next 200 years, the country's economy depended mainly on the raising of livestock and crops. Then in the late 1800's, diamonds and gold were discovered. Mining quickly became the basis of South Africa's economy. Mining also started the country on its way to becoming the industrial giant of Africa.

There have been several reasons for South Africa's spectacular industrial growth. The government actively encourages and provides funds for industrial development. It also seeks foreign investments by advertising the safety of—and the high return on—such investments. As a result, many people in the United States and other countries have put money into South African businesses. The country's growth has also been spurred by its wealth of natural and human resources. South Africa has raw materials needed for industry and a huge labor force, including many skilled managers.

Natural Resources. South Africa has long been famous for its fabulous deposits of gold and diamonds. It also has large supplies of asbestos, chromite, coal, copper, iron ore, manganese, platinum, silver, and uranium (as a by-product of gold). In fact, the country has nearly every useful mineral except oil. Offshore waters provide plentiful fish and help make South Africa a leading fishing country.

South Africa is less fortunate in some other natural resources. Only a third of the farmland receives enough rain to grow crops easily. South Africa also has poor forest resources.

Manufacturing. South Africa's factories produce almost all the country's manufactured goods. The chief products include chemicals, clothing, iron and steel and other metals, metal products, and processed foods. Most factories are in the Cape Town, Durban, Johannesburg, Port Elizabeth, and Pretoria areas. The government offers industrialists financial help and other ben-

efits if they set up new factories on the borders of the black homelands.

Mining. South Africa ranks as one of the world's chief mining countries. It has long produced most of the world's gold. It is also a top producer of asbestos, chromite, copper, diamonds, manganese, platinum, and uranium. South African miners also dig dozens of other minerals.

Ever since its discovery in the 1880's, gold has been the main force behind South Africa's growth. Gold mining has produced enormous income for the country and attracted huge foreign investments. Directly or indirectly, gold mining has led to the development of the railroads and many manufacturing industries in South Africa.

Agriculture. South Africa's farmers produce almost all the food needed by the people. The leading crops include corn, fruits, sugar cane, and wheat. South Africa ranks as one of the world's chief sheep-raising countries, and wool is its main agricultural export. Other farm animals include beef and dairy cattle.

South Africa has two types of farming—that practiced by whites and that practiced by blacks in the homelands. White farmers use modern methods and raise products chiefly for market. Their farms range from fewer than 100 acres (40 hectares) to sheep ranches of more than 10,000 acres (4,000 hectares). The average size is about 2,300 acres (931 hectares).

In the homelands, black farm families produce food mainly for their own needs. The land available for each family averages about 52 acres (21 hectares). Production is extremely low. Critics of the government say productivity is low because the homeland farms are too small and their soils too poor to support the black population. Government officials say the lack of progress results from blacks' refusal to give up their traditional farming methods for modern techniques.

WORLD BOOK photo by David Goldblatt

The Fast-Growing Electronics Industry symbolizes South Africa's modern industrial economy. Workers at this plant are producing equipment for use in underground telephone cable systems.

Marc & Evelyne Bernheim, Woodfin Camp, Inc.

Gold Mining has long provided enormous wealth for South Africa, the world's leading gold producer. Hundreds of thousands of people, most of them blacks, work in the country's gold mines.

Labor Force of South Africa is divided along racial lines. Whites do almost all the high-paid, skilled work. They hold nearly all the executive, professional, and technical jobs in South Africa. Nonwhites do almost all the low-paid, unskilled work. Blacks, who are extremely low-paid, serve largely as manual laborers in factories, on white farms, and in mines. Most Asians and Coloreds serve as domestic or hotel help or work on farms or in factories.

The racial division in the labor force has always existed in South Africa. But over the years, it has been strengthened by social attitudes, differences in education, laws, and government policies. One of these policies is the *job reservation system*, which reserves certain jobs for certain races. As a result of this racial division, South Africa has a shortage of skilled workers and an abundance of unskilled workers. This shortage has led to some easing of the job reservation rules.

Harrison Forman

A Cargo of Corn has been loaded for export at the Port of East London. Corn, or maize, is a leading South African export.

South Africa's Gross National Product

Industry 45%*

Agriculture 7%*

Services 48%*

South Africa's gross national product (GNP) was $70,496,000,-000 in 1981. The GNP is the total value of goods and services produced by a country in a year. The GNP measures a nation's total economic performance and can also be used to compare the economic output and growth of countries.

Production and Workers by Economic Activities

Economic Activities	Per Cent of GDP* Produced	Employed Workers Number of Persons	Per Cent of Total
Manufacturing	25	1,468,400	23
Mining	16	728,500	12
Wholesale & Retail Trade	13	764,700	12
Finance, Insurance, & Real Estate	10	132,400	2
Government	9	838,100	13
Transportation & Communication	9	349,300	5
Agriculture, Forestry, & Fishing	7	1,000,000	16
Construction	4	440,600	7
Utilities	4	48,900	1
Community, Social, & Personal Services	1	540,000	9
Other	2	—	—
Total	100	6,310,900	100

*Based on gross domestic product (GDP). GDP is gross national product adjusted for net income sent or received from abroad.
Sources: International Monetary Fund; Central Statistical Services, Pretoria.

Trade. South Africa's biggest customer and biggest supplier has long been Great Britain. Other trading partners include Japan, the United States, Western European nations, and neighboring African countries. South Africa's chief exports include gold, diamonds, food, metals and minerals, and wool. Machinery and transportation equipment make up nearly half the value of the country's imports. South Africa's other imports include chemicals, food, manufactured goods, and petroleum.

Transportation. South Africa has the best transportation system in Africa. About 200,000 miles (320,000 kilometers) of roads crisscross the country. Of these roads, about 17,000 miles (27,400 kilometers) are surfaced. The government-owned South African Railways operates the country's 14,000 miles (22,500 kilometers) of railroad track. South African Airways, the government-owned national airline, provides domestic and international service. About 15 major overseas airlines also serve the country. South Africa has four large, well-equipped ports—Cape Town, Durban, East London, and Port Elizabeth. A new harbor is also being built at Richards Bay in northern Natal.

Communication. South Africa has 22 daily newspapers, of which 16 are published in English and 6 in Afrikaans. The largest English-language daily, the Johannesburg *Star*, has a circulation of more than 177,-000 copies. *Die Burger*, published in Cape Town, is the largest Afrikaans daily. *Die Burger* sells over 52,000 copies.

The government owns South Africa's 11 radio stations. The country's only television network is also government-owned. Radio and television programs are broadcast in Afrikaans, English, and several Bantu languages. The government runs South Africa's postal, telegraph, and telephone systems.

The Publications Control Board, a government body, reviews all books, films, plays, and other publications. It decides if a publication is obscene, deals excessively with violence or racial conflict, or promotes Communism. The board has prohibited thousands of publications for moral or political reasons.

Rock Painting once flourished among the San, or Bushmen. These yellowish-skinned hunting people lived in South Africa long before the first white settlers arrived in the 1600's. Today, only scattered groups of San survive in remote desert regions of South Africa and neighboring countries. But their excellent rock paintings, which have become of great interest to scientists and tourists, can still be found in caves and rock shelters throughout South Africa.

E. S. Ross

Human-like creatures lived in what is now South Africa as long as 2 million years ago. By at least 2,000 years ago, human beings lived throughout much of the region. They hunted animals and gathered wild plants.

By A.D. 1500, great changes had occurred in the western and eastern parts of South Africa. The western part was thinly occupied by two groups of yellowish-skinned people, who were descendants of the earlier hunting people. One group, the *San*, lived by hunting. The other group, the *Khoikhoi*, raised cattle and sheep. When the Europeans arrived in the 1600's, they called the San *Bushmen* and the Khoikhoi *Hottentots*.

Meanwhile, eastern South Africa had become more heavily populated by brown-skinned people who spoke various Bantu languages. They began to enter the region from the north about A.D. 400. They lived in chiefdoms, raised cattle and sheep, and grew grain.

Settlement by the Dutch. Portuguese sailors became the first Europeans to see South Africa. They sighted it in 1488, when they rounded the Cape of Good Hope in their search for a water route to India.

The first European settlers arrived in 1652. They worked for the Dutch East India Company. The company sent the group, headed by Jan van Riebeeck, to set up a supply base at the present site of Cape Town. The base was to serve as a halfway station where company ships could pick up food and water on the way to and from the East Indies. Soon after the base was set up, the company imported slaves from tropical Africa— and later from Southeast Asia—to work on its farms.

In 1657, the Dutch East India Company began to allow some employees to leave the firm and start their own farms. These people became known as *Boers* (farmers). In 1679, the company also began to offer free passage and land to new settlers from Europe. More Dutch farmers, as well as French and German settlers, joined the Cape Colony. By 1700, whites occupied most of the good farmland around Cape Town. Then they

moved into drier areas and became sheep and cattle ranchers. As the white territory expanded, the Khoikhoi and San population declined. The whites killed some Khoikhoi and San, and many others died of smallpox. Most survivors became servants of the whites.

By 1795, the whites had spread about 300 miles (480 kilometers) north and over 500 miles (800 kilometers) east of Cape Town. The colony had a total population of about 60,000. Nearly 20,000 were whites. The rest consisted of Khoikhoi and San, slaves, and persons of mixed ancestry.

British Rule. In 1795, France conquered The Netherlands. British troops then occupied the Cape Colony to keep it out of French hands. Britain returned the colony to the Dutch in 1803 but reoccupied it in 1806. In 1814, The Netherlands formally gave the Cape to Britain. The first British settlers arrived in 1820.

The Boers soon came to resent British colonial rule. The government made English the only official language in 1828. That same year, the Khoikhoi and Colored people received equal legal rights with whites. In 1834, Britain abolished slavery throughout its empire, which ruined a number of Boer farmers.

Many Boers decided to leave the Cape Colony to get away from British rule. Beginning in 1836, several thousand of them made a historic journey called the *Great Trek*. They loaded their belongings into ox-drawn covered wagons and headed into the interior. They defeated the Bantu-speaking peoples who tried to stop them and settled in what are now Natal, the Orange Free State, and the Transvaal. Britain annexed Natal in 1843. But it recognized the independence of the Transvaal in 1852 and the Orange Free State in 1854.

The Anglo-Boer Wars. In 1870, an incredibly rich diamond field was found where Kimberley now stands. Miners, fortune hunters, and other people from Britain and other countries flocked to the area. Both the British and the Boers claimed the Kimberley area. In 1871,

Britain annexed it. Britain annexed the Transvaal in 1877. Three years later, the Transvaal Boers rose in revolt in the First Anglo-Boer War. They defeated the British in 1881.

In 1886, the fabulous Witwatersrand gold field was discovered where Johannesburg now stands. Miners and other people rushed to the Transvaal. By 1895, these *uitlanders* (foreigners) made up about half the Transvaal's white population. To keep control of the country, the Boers restricted the political rights of the uitlanders, most of whom were British. As a result, tension grew between Britain and the Transvaal.

In 1895, Cecil Rhodes, the prime minister of the Cape Colony, plotted to overthrow the Transvaal government. He sent a force under Leander Jameson to invade the country. But the Boers captured the invaders, and the so-called Jameson Raid failed. Relations between Britain and the Transvaal then grew more strained. In 1899, the Transvaal and the Orange Free State declared war on Britain. The Boers fought bravely against huge odds before they finally surrendered in 1902. The Boer republics then became British colonies.

Meanwhile, all the black African people had come under white rule. Some groups gave in without fighting. Other groups, especially the Zulu, resisted. But in 1879, the British finally defeated the Zulu kingdom. By 1898, all black Africans had lost their independence.

The Union of South Africa. Britain gave colonial self-government to the Transvaal in 1906 and to the Orange Free State in 1907. The Cape Colony and Natal already had self-rule. In 1910, the four colonies formed the *Union of South Africa*, a self-governing country within the British Empire. The country's Constitution gave whites almost complete power.

During World War I (1914-1918), two Boer generals —Louis Botha and Jan Christiaan Smuts—led South African forces against Germany. Botha seized Namibia (then called German Southwest Africa) from Germany in 1915, and Smuts defeated German East Africa in 1917. In 1920, the League of Nations gave South Africa control of Namibia. The two Boer generals also became South Africa's first prime ministers. Botha served from 1910 to 1919, and Smuts from 1919 to 1924.

The Rise of Afrikaner Nationalism. Botha and Smuts had fought the British in the war of 1899-1902. But as prime ministers, they tried to unite *Afrikaners* (as the Boers came to be called) and English-speaking whites. Many Afrikaner authors and religious leaders, however, urged their people to believe they were a nation to themselves. They said Afrikaners had a heroic history, a rich culture, and a God-given mission to rule South Africa. In 1913, J. B. M. Hertzog, another Boer general who had fought the British, founded the National, or Nationalist, Party to promote these ideas.

In 1924, the National Party and the Labour Party joined forces and won control of the government. Hertzog became prime minister. During the next 15 years, he achieved many Afrikaner goals. Afrikaans became an official language in addition to English. Industries were developed to reduce dependence on British imports. In 1931, Britain gave South Africa full independence as a member of the Commonwealth of Nations.

Important Dates in South Africa

c. 2000 B.C. Hunting people lived throughout much of what is now South Africa.

c. A.D. 400 Bantu-speaking farmers began to enter eastern South Africa from the north.

1652 The first Dutch settlers arrived at the site of Cape Town.

1814 The Netherlands gave the Cape Colony to Britain.

1852 The Transvaal became a Boer republic.

1854 The Orange Free State became a Boer republic.

1877 Britain annexed the Transvaal.

1879 Britain defeated the Zulu kingdom.

1880-1881 The Transvaal Boers defeated the British in the First Anglo-Boer War.

1899-1902 Britain defeated the Boers in the Second Anglo-Boer War.

1910 The Union of South Africa was formed.

1920 The League of Nations gave South Africa control of Namibia.

1931 Great Britain gave South Africa full independence as a member of the Commonwealth of Nations.

1948 The National Party came to power.

1961 South Africa became a republic and left the Commonwealth of Nations.

1966 The United Nations voted to end South Africa's control of Namibia.

1971 The International Court of Justice declared South Africa's control of Namibia illegal.

Afrikaner nationalism suffered a setback at the start of World War II (1939-1945). Hertzog wanted South Africa to be neutral. But Smuts wanted the country to join Britain against Germany. Smuts won the bitter debate in Parliament and became prime minister again in 1939. During the war, South Africans fought in Ethiopia, northern Africa, and Europe. In 1946, the United Nations (UN) rejected South Africa's request to annex Namibia.

During the war, D. F. Malan, a strong supporter of Afrikaner nationalism, reorganized the National Party in South Africa. The party came to power, under Malan, in 1948. It began today's apartheid program. In 1949, the Prohibition of Mixed Marriages Act made marriages between whites and nonwhites illegal in South Africa. In 1950, the Group Areas Act provided for separate white and nonwhite residential areas. Other laws gave the South African government extensive police powers.

Opposition to Apartheid. The government had long faced opposition to its racial policies. But opposition grew after the Nationalists came to power. A main opposition group was the African National Congress (ANC). Blacks founded the ANC in 1912 to seek equality. But the group had no success. In the 1950's, the ANC joined with other nonwhite groups and white liberals to force reforms through boycotts, demonstrations, and strikes. The government crushed each campaign, and the movement failed. In addition, ANC members disagreed on methods and goals. In 1959, a dissatisfied group formed the Pan-African Congress (PAC).

The first PAC target was the laws that require blacks to carry *passes* (identity papers). PAC leaders told blacks to appear on March 21, 1960, at police stations without their passes—and so invite arrest. In most places, the police broke up the crowds without incident. But at Sharpeville, near Johannesburg, the police opened fire and killed 69 blacks. The government then banned the ANC and the PAC.

Opposition to apartheid also came from many countries. The government especially resented criticism from Britain and other members of the Commonwealth of Nations. On May 31, 1961, South Africa became a republic and left the Commonwealth. The UN frequently condemned South Africa's racial policies. In 1966, it voted to end the country's control over Namibia. South Africa called the UN action illegal.

In spite of all opposition, the government held to its policies. Since 1958, the government had been headed by Prime Minister Hendrik F. Verwoerd, a man rigidly determined to carry out apartheid. In 1966, a messenger killed Verwoerd as he addressed Parliament. The assassin was insane and apparently had no political motive. Balthazar J. Vorster succeeded Verwoerd.

South Africa Today is still governed by the National Party. But opposition to white rule of South Africa has increased both inside and outside the country. In the early 1970's, black workers staged strikes to protest government policies. In 1971, the International Court of Justice declared that South Africa's control over Namibia is illegal. In 1975, blacks gained control of Angola and Mozambique—two former Portuguese territo-ries near South Africa. They called for an end to white rule in South Africa.

In response to the growing opposition, the South African government sped up its program to make the black homelands in the country independent states (see the *Nonwhite Governments* section of this article). But this action did not end the discontent of many blacks. In June 1976, blacks in Soweto, a town near Johannesburg, rioted to protest against a government policy that required some classes in schools for blacks to be taught in the Afrikaans language. Other riots followed near Johannesburg and in other parts of the country, and many clashes between the rioters and the police took place. About 600 persons, mostly blacks, were killed in the conflicts.

In 1978, Prime Minister Vorster resigned from office. Pieter Willem Botha succeeded him.

In the late 1970's, representatives of the South African government and the UN discussed plans for independence for Namibia. Some discussions were also held in the early 1980's. For details, see NAMIBIA (History).

LEONARD M. THOMPSON

SOUTH AFRICA/Study Aids

Related Articles in WORLD BOOK include:

BIOGRAPHIES

Athlone, Earl of	Kruger, Paulus
Barnard, Christiaan N.	Luthuli, Albert J.
Botha, Louis	Rhodes, Cecil J.
Botha, Pieter W.	Smuts, Jan Christiaan
Broom, Robert	Vorster, Balthazar J.

CITIES

Bloemfontein	Germiston	Pietermaritzburg
Cape Town	Johannesburg	Port Elizabeth
Durban	Kimberley	Pretoria

PHYSICAL FEATURES

Cape of Good Hope	Limpopo River	Vaal River
Kalahari Desert	Orange River	

PROVINCES

Cape Province	Natal	Orange Free State	Transvaal

OTHER RELATED ARTICLES

Africa	Boers	United Nations (The
Afrikaans	Bushmen	Problem of
Language	Hottentot	Southern Africa)
Apartheid	Lesotho	Walvis Bay
Bantu	Namibia	Zulu
Boer War	Transkei	

Outline

I. Government
 A. Nonwhite Governments
 B. Political Parties
 C. South West Africa
 D. Armed Forces

II. People
 A. Population and Ancestry
 B. Languages
 C. Ways of Life
 D. Food and Drink
 E. Recreation
 F. Education
 G. Religion
 H. The Arts

III. The Land and Climate
 A. Land Regions
 B. Rivers
 C. Climate

IV. Economy
 A. Natural Resources
 B. Manufacturing
 C. Mining
 D. Agriculture
 E. Labor Force
 F. Trade
 G. Transportation
 H. Communication

V. History

Questions

What are some reasons for South Africa's spectacular industrial growth?

Into what four racial groups does the government classify the people of South Africa?

What is *apartheid?*

What are the official languages of South Africa?

How does South Africa rank economically among the countries of Africa?

What political party has controlled the South African government since 1948?

How does the way of life differ among South Africa's racial groups?

Who were the first Europeans to settle in South Africa?

How important has gold been to South Africa's economic growth?

What was the *Great Trek?*

Additional Resources

GANN, LEWIS H., and DUIGNAN, PETER. *Why South Africa Will Survive: A Historical Analysis.* St. Martin's, 1981. Argues for the continuation of white control.

NATTRASS, JILL. *The South African Economy: Its Growth and Change.* Oxford, 1981.

PATON, ALAN. *The Land and People of South Africa.* Rev. ed. Harper, 1972. For younger readers.

PRICE, ROBERT M., and ROSBERG, C. G., eds. *The Apartheid Regime: Political Power and Racial Domination.* Univ. of California Institute of International Studies, 1980. Examines the negative effects of South Africa's racial policies.

WILSON, MONICA, and THOMPSON, LEONARD M., eds. *The Oxford History of South Africa.* 2 vols. Oxford, 1969-1971.

SOUTH AMERICA

SOUTH AMERICA, the fourth largest continent, is about twice as large as the United States, but it has only about as many people. Almost half of South America is a wilderness made up of high mountains, empty plains, and tropical forests. Most of the continent's large modern cities are near the coasts.

The continent has some of the world's largest deposits of minerals, rich farmlands, and vast timberlands. However, most South American countries have been slow in developing their natural resources. Millions of South Americans live much as their ancestors did hundreds of years ago. But development projects in parts of South America have led to rapid modernization since the mid-1900's.

Preston E. James, the contributor of this article, is Maxwell Professor of Geography Emeritus at Syracuse University, and the author of Latin America.

Machu Picchu, an Ancient Inca City in Peru

Facts in Brief

Area: 6,883,000 sq. mi. (17,828,000 km²). *Greatest Distances*—north-south, 4,750 mi. (7,644 km); east-west, 3,200 mi. (5,150 km). *Coastline*—24,783 mi. (39,884 km).

Population: *Estimated 1984 Population*—260,000,000; density, 39 persons per sq. mi. (15 per km²).

Elevation: *Highest*—Mount Aconcagua in Argentina, 22,831 ft. (6,959 m) above sea level. *Lowest*—Península Valdés in Argentina, 131 ft. (40 m) below sea level.

Physical Features: *Chief Mountain Ranges*—Andes, Brazilian Highlands, Guiana Highlands. *Chief Rivers*—Amazon, Madeira, Magdalena, Orinoco, Paraguay, Paraná, Pilcomayo, Purús, São Francisco, Uruguay. *Chief Lakes*—Maracaibo, Mirim, Poopó, Titicaca. *Chief Islands*—Falkland Islands, Galapagos Islands, Marajó, Tierra del Fuego. *Chief Gulfs*—Darien, Guayaquil, San Jorge, San Matías, Venezuela. *Largest Deserts*—Atacama, Patagonia. *Largest Waterfalls*—Angel, Cuquenán.

Chief Products: *Agriculture*—bananas, beef, cacao, coffee, corn, cotton, sugar cane, wheat, wool. *Manufacturing and Processing*—automobiles, beverages, canned meats, cement, chemicals, electrical appliances, flour, packaged foods, paper, textiles. *Mining*—bauxite, copper, emeralds, gold, iron ore, lead, manganese, nitrate, petroleum, silver, tin, tungsten, zinc.

J. Barnell, Shostal

Christ of the Andes, on the Argentina-Chile Border

About 40 per cent of the people of South America work on farms, plantations, and ranches. But most of the small farmers cannot raise enough food to feed their families from their small plots of poor land. A relatively few wealthy families own huge areas of fertile land that lies idle. How to put this idle land to use is probably South America's greatest problem. The governments of most South American countries have started or are planning land reform programs. Under these programs, some large estates are being broken up, and the land is given to small farmers.

Manufacturing is growing rapidly in South America. But South American countries still must import many manufactured products. They pay for these goods by exporting agricultural products and minerals. South America exports such agricultural products as bananas, beef, coffee, cotton, sugar, wheat, and wool. The chief mineral exports of South America are bauxite, copper, iron ore, manganese, petroleum, silver, and tin.

Brazil, the largest of the 12 independent South American countries, covers almost half the continent. The other countries in order of size are Argentina, Peru, Colombia, Bolivia, Venezuela, Chile, Paraguay, Ecuador, Guyana, Uruguay, and Suriname. French Guiana, an overseas department of France, lies on the northeastern edge of South America. The Falkland Islands, a British dependency, lie in the South Atlantic Ocean, about 300 miles (480 kilometers) east of the southernmost part of the South American mainland.

South America is part of the cultural region called *Latin America* that also includes Mexico, Central America, and the islands of the Caribbean Sea. For information on the way of life of the people and their education, arts, and history, see LATIN AMERICA.

Independent Countries of South America

Map Key	Name	Area In sq. mi.	In km²	Population	Capital	Date of Independence
L-5	Argentina	1,072,163	2,776,889	29,022,000	Buenos Aires	1816
I-5	**Bolivia**	424,164	1,098,581	6,230,000	La Paz; Sucre	1825
H-7	Brazil	3,286,487	8,511,965	130,440,000	Brasília	1822
K-4	**Chile**	292,135	756,626	11,797,000	Santiago	1818
F-4	Colombia	439,737	1,138,914	30,627,000	Bogotá	1819
G-3	**Ecuador**	109,484	283,561	9,473,000	Quito	1830
E-6	Guyana	83,000	214,969	886,000	Georgetown	1966
J-6	**Paraguay**	157,048	406,752	3,571,000	Asunción	1811
H-4	Peru	496,225	1,285,216	18,502,000	Lima	1821
E-7	**Suriname**	63,037	163,265	392,000	Paramaribo	1975
L-7	Uruguay	68,037	176,215	2,998,000	Montevideo	1828
E-5	**Venezuela**	352,145	912,050	15,842,000	Caracas	1830

Other Political Units in South America

Map Key	Name	Area In sq. mi.	In km²	Population	Status
O-6	Falkland Islands	4,700	12,173	2,000	British dependency
F-7	**French Guiana**	35,135	91,000	67,000	Overseas department of France

Each country and political unit has a separate article in WORLD BOOK.

Populations are 1983 estimates for independent countries and 1983 and earlier estimates for other political units based on the latest figures from official government and United Nations sources.

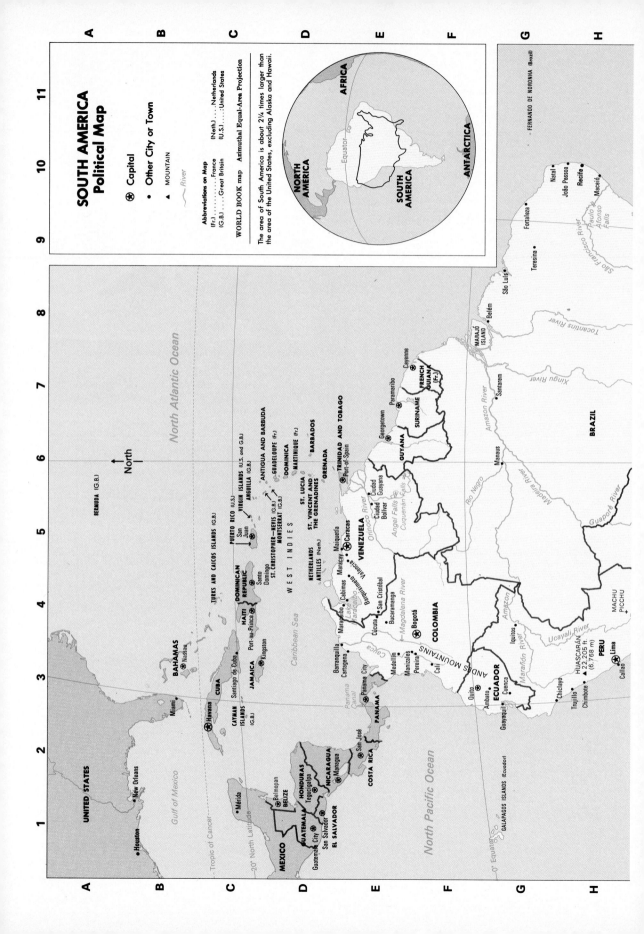

SOUTH AMERICA
Political Map

✴ Capital

• Other City or Town

▲ MOUNTAIN

〜 River

Abbreviations on Map

(Fr.)..........France   (Neth.)....Netherlands
(G.B.)....Great Britain   (U.S.)....United States

WORLD BOOK map   Azimuthal Equal-Area Projection

The area of South America is about 2¼ times larger than
the area of the United States, excluding Alaska and Hawaii.

NORTH AMERICA

Equator

AFRICA

SOUTH AMERICA

ANTARCTICA

North

North Atlantic Ocean

North Pacific Ocean

Gulf of Mexico

Caribbean Sea

WEST INDIES

Tropic of Cancer

20° North Latitude

0° Equator

UNITED STATES

• Houston

• New Orleans

• Miami

MEXICO

• Mérida

BELIZE
• Belmopan

GUATEMALA
✴ Guatemala City

HONDURAS
Tegucigalpa

EL SALVADOR
San Salvador ✴

NICARAGUA
✴ Managua

COSTA RICA
✴ San José

PANAMA
Panama City ✴

Panama Canal

BAHAMAS
• Nassau

CUBA
✴ Havana
• Santiago de Cuba

CAYMAN ISLANDS (G.B.)

JAMAICA
Kingston

HAITI ✴
Port-au-Prince

DOMINICAN REPUBLIC
Santo Domingo

TURKS AND CAICOS ISLANDS (G.B.)

PUERTO RICO (U.S.)
San Juan

VIRGIN ISLANDS (U.S. and G.B.)
ANGUILLA (G.B.)

ST. CHRISTOPHER—NEVIS (G.B.)
MONTSERRAT (G.B.)

ANTIGUA AND BARBUDA
GUADELOUPE (Fr.)
DOMINICA
MARTINIQUE (Fr.)
ST. LUCIA
BARBADOS
ST. VINCENT AND THE GRENADINES
GRENADA

NETHERLANDS ANTILLES (Neth.)

TRINIDAD AND TOBAGO
✴ Port-of-Spain

BERMUDA (G.B.)

COLOMBIA
✴ Bogotá
• Barranquilla
• Cartagena
• Medellín
• Manizales
• Pereira
• Cali
• Cúcuta
• Bucaramanga

VENEZUELA
✴ Caracas
Maiquetía
Maracay
Valencia
Barquisimeto
Maracaibo
Cabimas
San Cristóbal
Ciudad Bolívar
Ciudad Guayana

Maracaibo
Lake Maracaibo

Orinoco River

Angel Falls
Cuquenán Falls

GUYANA
✴ Georgetown

SURINAME
✴ Paramaribo

FRENCH GUIANA (Fr.)
• Cayenne

Rio Negro

ECUADOR
✴ Quito
• Guayaquil
• Ambato
• Cuenca

GALAPAGOS ISLANDS (Ecuador)

PERU
✴ Lima
Callao
• Iquitos
• Chiclayo
• Trujillo
• Chimbote

MACHU PICCHU

HUASCARÁN ▲ 22,205 ft (6,768 m)

ANDES MOUNTAINS

Magdalena River
Cauca
Amazon
Marañón River
Ucayali River
Amazon River
Madeira River
Guaporé River
Rio Negro

BRAZIL

MARAJÓ ISLAND

Belém

Santarém
Manaus

Tocantins River
Xingu River

São Luís
Teresina
Fortaleza
Natal
João Pessoa
Recife
Maceió

FERNANDO DE NORONHA (Brazil)

São Francisco River
Paulo Afonso Falls

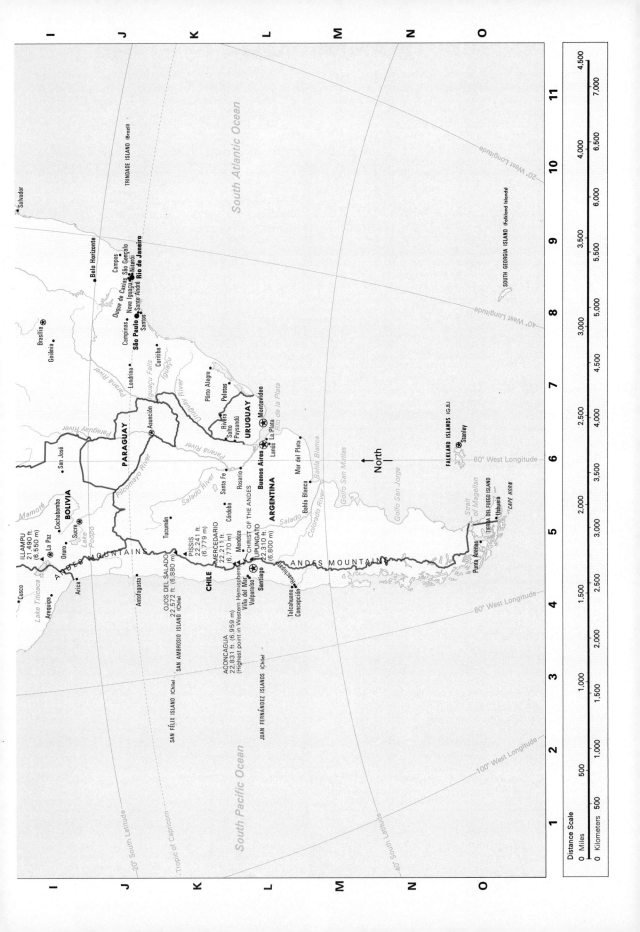

SOUTH AMERICA/Land Regions

The equator crosses South America near the continent's widest point. More than three-fourths of South America lies in the tropics. From the equator southward, the continent narrows sharply. Its southern tip is only about 600 miles (970 kilometers) from Antarctica.

Oceans surround South America except at its northwest corner, where the narrow Isthmus of Panama links the continent to North America. The Pacific Ocean washes South America's western shores, and the Atlantic Ocean borders the continent on the east. The Caribbean Sea is on the north. The Drake Passage separates South America from Antarctica.

The land surface of South America is much like that of North America. High mountains tower in the west, and low mountains form highlands in the east. Great plains cover most of the central area. South America has four main land regions: (1) the Pacific Coastlands, (2) the Andes Mountains, (3) the Central Plains, and (4) the Eastern Highlands.

The Pacific Coastlands lie along the Pacific Ocean, west of the Andes Mountains. Most of the coastlands are less than 50 miles (80 kilometers) wide, and in some places they are only 5 miles (8 kilometers) wide. The northern coastlands in Colombia and Ecuador are swampy and covered by tropical forests. In Peru and northern Chile, the coastlands form a desert. In central Chile, the Pacific Coastlands are a fertile area of farms, grazing lands, and forests. Farther south, the seas flow into the valleys to form the Chilean archipelago, a 1,000-mile (1,600-kilometer) stretch of stormy fiords and cold, rainy islands.

The Andes Mountains rise along the entire western coast of South America. They form the longest mountain range in the world, and only the Himalayas in Asia are higher. Over 50 Andean peaks are higher than 20,000 feet (6,100 meters). These include 22,831-foot (6,959-meter) Mount Aconcagua in Argentina, the highest peak in the Western Hemisphere. Earthquakes often shake parts of the Andes region, and some Andean peaks are active volcanoes. Glaciers move slowly toward the sea in many valleys, especially in the south.

In most places, the Andes region is not more than 200 miles (320 kilometers) wide. It widens to about 450 miles (724 kilometers) in Bolivia, and narrows to less than 20 miles (32 kilometers) in Chile.

In addition to snow-capped peaks and rocky cliffs, the Andes region also has thickly forested slopes, grassy plateaus, and valleys. Andean valleys make up much of Colombia and Venezuela. In Bolivia, a plateau 400 miles (640 kilometers) long lies about 12,500 feet (3,810 meters) above sea level.

The Central Plains, east of the Andes Mountains, cover about three-fifths of South America. The plains consist of four large areas: (1) grassy plains called *llanos* in the Orinoco River basin of Colombia and Venezuela; (2) tropical rain forests called *selvas* in the Amazon River basin of Brazil; (3) partly forested scrublands in the Gran Chaco region that lies largely in Argentina and Paraguay; and (4) productive farmlands and ranch lands of Argentina called the *Pampa*.

The South American central plains are largely unproductive. However, the rich soil and temperate climate of the Pampa make it suitable for farming.

The Eastern Highlands consist of mountains that are much lower than the Andes. The highlands form three separate areas: (1) the Guiana Highlands, (2) the Brazilian Highlands, and (3) the Patagonian Plateau.

The Guiana Highlands rise along Brazil's northern boundary. They are covered mainly by tropical forests, and are less than 5,000 feet (1,500 meters) high.

The Brazilian Highlands, largest of the three areas, cover eastern Brazil. The mountains that rise steeply along the Atlantic coast include 9,482-foot (2,890-meter) Pico da Bandeira, the highest point east of the Andes. Inland, the highlands area is generally one of tablelands and rolling hills, sloping away from the coast. Rich mines, coffee plantations, cattle ranches, and two of South America's largest industrial centers—Rio de Janeiro and São Paulo—are in this area.

The Patagonian Plateau forms flat, rocky tablelands in southern Argentina. These tablelands make up one of the world's largest sheep-grazing areas.

Eastern Highlands   Harald Schultz

Pacific Coastlands   Leon V. Kofod

Andes Mountains   Three Lions

Central Plains   FPG

504

Upper Amazon River   Shostal

Lake Titicaca   Tom Hollyman, Photo Researchers

SOUTH AMERICA/
Natural Features

Rivers. Five great river systems drain the South American continent: (1) the Amazon; (2) the Río de la Plata system, formed by the Paraná, Paraguay, and Uruguay rivers; (3) the Magdalena-Cauca; (4) the Orinoco; and (5) the São Francisco.

The Amazon drains an area of about 2,400,000 square miles (6,220,000 square kilometers), the largest drainage basin in the world. It rises in the Peruvian Andes and flows 4,000 miles (6,437 kilometers) into the Atlantic Ocean. Only the Nile River is longer.

The Río de la Plata system forms the most important inland waterway system in Latin America. It serves Argentina, Bolivia, Brazil, Paraguay, and Uruguay.

The Magdalena and Cauca rivers flow through two long Andean valleys in Colombia. They join, and empty into the Caribbean Sea.

The Orinoco flows along the Colombia-Venezuela border and through the middle of Venezuela to the Atlantic Ocean. More than 400 tributaries give the Orinoco a huge volume of water.

The São Francisco, which is 1,988 miles (3,199 kilometers) long, drains the eastern Brazilian highlands.

Waterfalls. South America's many waterfalls include two of the world's highest. One, Angel Falls, on one of

the headwaters of the Caroní River in southeastern Venezuela, drops 3,212 feet (979 meters). Cuquenán Falls in Venezuela falls 2,000 feet (610 meters). Brazil's many smaller falls include Paulo Afonso Falls on the São Francisco River and Iguaçu Falls on the Brazil-Argentina border. See BRAZIL (picture).

Lakes. South America has few large lakes. The largest is Lake Maracaibo, which covers 6,300 square miles (16,300 square kilometers) in Venezuela. Lake Titicaca on the Bolivia-Peru border is the highest body of water in the world on which steamships operate. It lies in the Andes, 12,507 feet (3,812 meters) above sea level, and covers 3,261 square miles (8,446 square kilometers).

Islands. Several major island groups lie off the coasts of South America. The largest is the Tierra del Fuego group. It is separated from the southern end of the mainland by the stormy Strait of Magellan. Argentina and Chile own these islands. Chile also owns the Juan Fernández Islands, about 400 miles (640 kilometers) west of the mainland in the Pacific Ocean. The Falkland Islands, about 300 miles (480 kilometers) east of the Strait of Magellan in the Atlantic Ocean, are a British crown colony. Both Tierra del Fuego and the Falklands have valuable sheep-grazing lands. The Galapagos Islands are South America's principal islands in the Pacific Ocean. They lie about 600 miles (960 kilometers) off Ecuador, which owns them. The Galapagos Islands, once a pirate hideout, have large colonies of lizards, huge turtles, and birds. Marajó, a flat, grassy island, lies at the mouth of the Amazon River. It is owned by Brazil.

Angel Falls   Ewing Krainin, Photo Researchers

Ushuaia, Tierra del Fuego   Harrison Forman

SOUTH AMERICA/Climate

Most of South America is warm the year around, except high in the Andes Mountains where the climate is always cold. The lowland area in the widest part of the continent, near the equator, is always hot and humid. The narrow southern part of the continent has cool summers and mild winters. Both the summers and winters are much milder than those of most of North America. The seasons south of the equator are opposite to those of North America—summers last from December to March, and winters are from June to September.

Although South America's climate is warm, temperatures usually do not rise as high as summer temperatures in North America. Even in the tropical lowlands of the Amazon River valley, the temperature generally ranges from 70° to 90° F. (21° to 32° C), and rarely reaches 100° F. (38° C). The hottest weather occurs in the Argentine Gran Chaco. The temperature there climbs above 110° F. (43° C) at least once a year.

South America has four regions where rainfall averages more than 60 inches (150 centimeters) a year: (1) the Amazon River valley, (2) the coastal lands of Guyana, French Guiana, and Suriname, (3) the coasts of Colombia and Ecuador, and (4) southwestern Chile.

Rain-bearing winds sweep into South America from both the Atlantic and the Pacific oceans. East of the Andes Mountains, the Atlantic trade winds bring rains to the northern two-thirds of the continent (see TRADE WIND). West of the Andes, in the north, heavy rains drench the coast of Colombia. In the south, the Pacific's moist westerlies keep Chile's central valley well watered in winter. They bring heavy rain to the Chilean archipelago during most of the year.

The cold Peru Current of the Pacific Ocean flows near the continent's southwest coast. It cools the air that blows onto shore at a low level. This cooling of the lower air prevents rain from forming. As a result, the coastal lands in Peru and northern Chile are dry. Cold Atlantic Ocean currents act the same way on the breezes that blow over southeastern South America. As a result the Patagonian Plateau gets little rainfall.

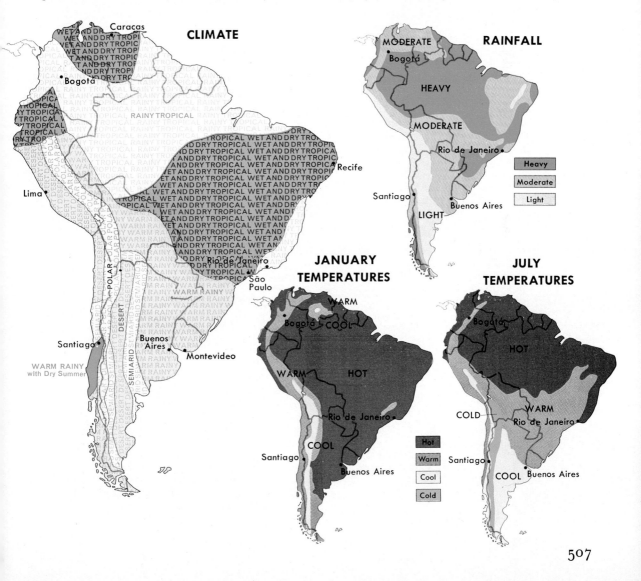

SOUTH AMERICA / Animals

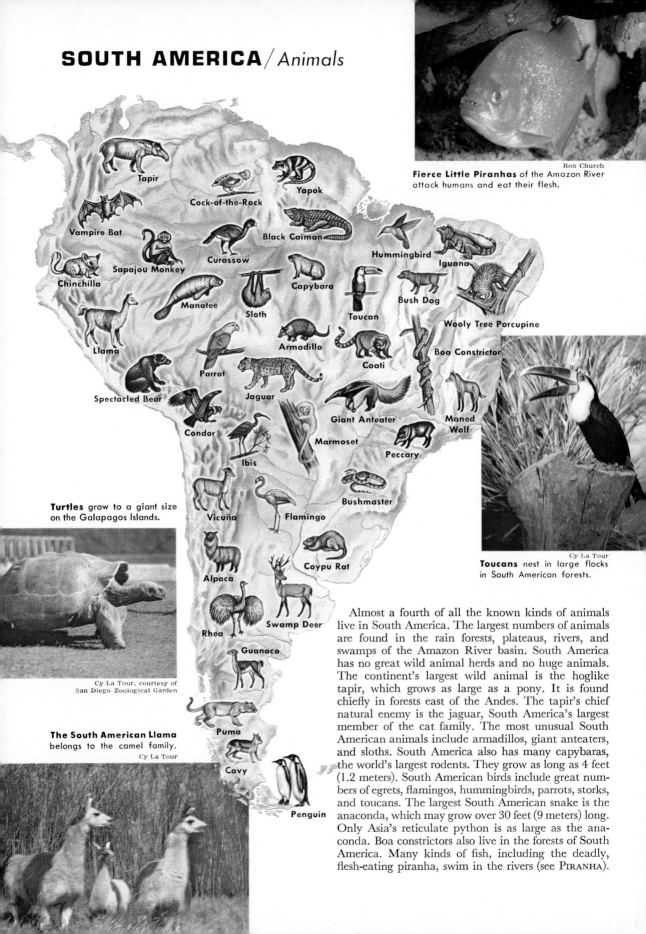

Tapir

Cock-of-the-Rock

Yapok

Vampire Bat

Black Caiman

Curassow

Hummingbird

Iguana

Sapajou Monkey

Chinchilla

Capybara

Manatee

Bush Dog

Sloth

Toucan

Wooly Tree Porcupine

Llama

Armadillo

Parrot

Boa Constrictor

Coati

Spectacled Bear

Jaguar

Maned Wolf

Condor

Giant Anteater

Ibis

Marmoset

Peccary

Bushmaster

Vicuña

Flamingo

Alpaca

Coypu Rat

Rhea

Swamp Deer

Guanaco

Puma

Cavy

Penguin

Ron Church
Fierce Little Piranhas of the Amazon River attack humans and eat their flesh.

Cy La Tour
Toucans nest in large flocks in South American forests.

Turtles grow to a giant size on the Galapagos Islands.

Cy La Tour, courtesy of San Diego Zoological Garden

The South American Llama belongs to the camel family.
Cy La Tour

Almost a fourth of all the known kinds of animals live in South America. The largest numbers of animals are found in the rain forests, plateaus, rivers, and swamps of the Amazon River basin. South America has no great wild animal herds and no huge animals. The continent's largest wild animal is the hoglike tapir, which grows as large as a pony. It is found chiefly in forests east of the Andes. The tapir's chief natural enemy is the jaguar, South America's largest member of the cat family. The most unusual South American animals include armadillos, giant anteaters, and sloths. South America also has many capybaras, the world's largest rodents. They grow as long as 4 feet (1.2 meters). South American birds include great numbers of egrets, flamingos, hummingbirds, parrots, storks, and toucans. The largest South American snake is the anaconda, which may grow over 30 feet (9 meters) long. Only Asia's reticulate python is as large as the anaconda. Boa constrictors also live in the forests of South America. Many kinds of fish, including the deadly, flesh-eating piranha, swim in the rivers (see PIRANHA).

SOUTH AMERICA/*Plants*

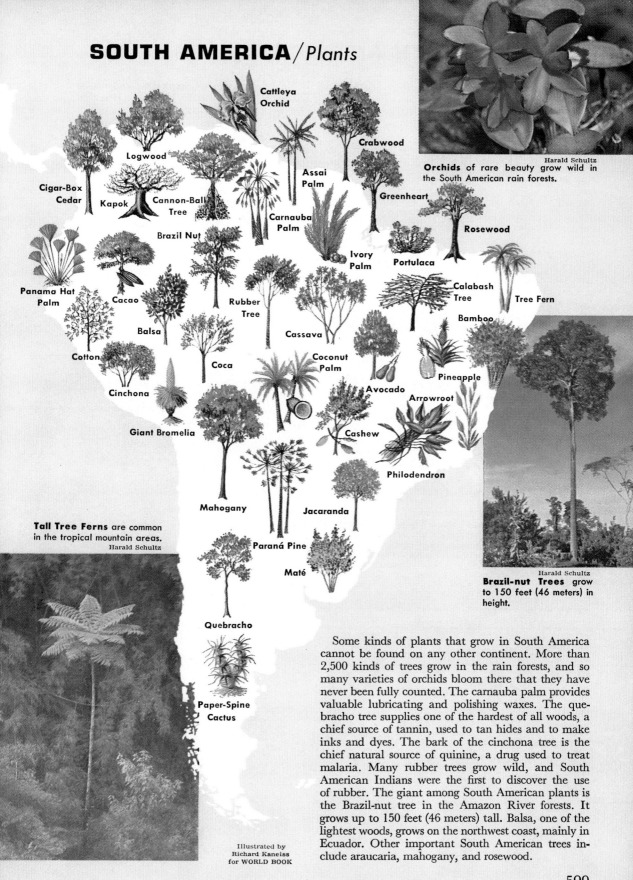

Orchids of rare beauty grow wild in the South American rain forests.
Harald Schultz

Cattleya Orchid

Crabwood

Logwood

Assai Palm

Cigar-Box Cedar

Kapok

Cannon-Ball Tree

Carnauba Palm

Greenheart

Rosewood

Brazil Nut

Ivory Palm

Portulaca

Calabash Tree

Tree Fern

Panama Hat Palm

Cacao

Rubber Tree

Bamboo

Balsa

Cassava

Cotton

Coconut Palm

Pineapple

Cinchona

Coca

Avocado

Arrowroot

Giant Bromelia

Cashew

Philodendron

Tall Tree Ferns are common in the tropical mountain areas.
Harald Schultz

Mahogany

Jacaranda

Paraná Pine

Maté

Harald Schultz
Brazil-nut Trees grow to 150 feet (46 meters) in height.

Quebracho

Paper-Spine Cactus

Illustrated by
Richard Kaneiss
for WORLD BOOK

Some kinds of plants that grow in South America cannot be found on any other continent. More than 2,500 kinds of trees grow in the rain forests, and so many varieties of orchids bloom there that they have never been fully counted. The carnauba palm provides valuable lubricating and polishing waxes. The quebracho tree supplies one of the hardest of all woods, a chief source of tannin, used to tan hides and to make inks and dyes. The bark of the cinchona tree is the chief natural source of quinine, a drug used to treat malaria. Many rubber trees grow wild, and South American Indians were the first to discover the use of rubber. The giant among South American plants is the Brazil-nut tree in the Amazon River forests. It grows up to 150 feet (46 meters) tall. Balsa, one of the lightest woods, grows on the northwest coast, mainly in Ecuador. Other important South American trees include araucaria, mahogany, and rosewood.

SOUTH AMERICA/*Agriculture*

About 40 per cent of the people of South America earn their living on farms or ranches. The average South American farm is small, and barely provides a living for the farm family. Most farms produce simple food crops such as beans, cassava, and corn. Most South American farmers still plow the land with ox-drawn plows and plant seeds by hand. These farmers reap small harvests. As a result, food shortages occur frequently.

South America also has some of the world's largest farms, plantations, and ranches. They are owned by wealthy families, and produce such important exports as bananas, beef, coffee, sugar, wheat, and wool. Sharecroppers and hired laborers do the work. The owners let much good farmland lie idle as meadows or as pastures for their riding horses. The largest farms and ranches spread over the plains, plateaus, and valleys of Argentina and Brazil. On the broad Pampa in central Argentina, cattle graze on many ranches larger than 100,000 acres (40,000 hectares) each. In southern Argen-

tina's Patagonia region, some sheep ranches cover over 1,000,000 acres (400,000 hectares). Brazil has some plantations as large as the state of Oregon.

In most South American countries, government programs have been started to break up large estates into small farms. These land reform programs aim to put much idle land to use and increase food production. However, the landowners must be paid for the land, and the new owners need money to buy seed, fertilizer, and modern machinery. The governments do not have enough money to pay for large-scale land reform programs. The United States has made loans to assist land reform programs in such countries as Argentina, Brazil, Chile, and Venezuela.

A major problem of South America is to find ways of increasing food production to meet the needs of growing populations. Some countries, such as Brazil and Venezuela, operate model farms. These farms show farmers how modern methods can be used to raise larger crops.

Sheep Raising is a major agricultural industry of South America. Some Argentine ranches in the vast sheep raising region of Patagonia cover 1,000,000 acres (400,000 hectares). The Peruvian Indians graze their small flocks on grassy slopes high in the Andes Mountains.

B. Newman, Photo Researchers

Bananas rank among the chief agricultural products of South America. Ecuador exports more bananas than any other country in the world, and Brazil and Colombia are also leading banana exporters. Many of Colombia's bananas are carried in small boats from the plantations to the port of Barranquilla for shipment abroad.
Robert Leahy, Shostal

Three Lions

Modern Machinery and ancient oxcarts often work side by side on the large farms that produce grains for the world market.

Joe Barnell, Shostal

Growing Coffee requires much hand labor. These plantation workers are cultivating trees in the state of São Paulo, Brazil, one of the world's chief coffee-producing areas.

LAND USE

Caracas
Bogotá
FISHING
SCRUBLAND
São Paulo
Rio de Janeiro
Recife
Santiago
FISHING
Montevideo

MOUNTAINS
BARREN
FOREST

South American Cattle are raised on ranches that cover some of the largest grazing lands in the world. Chilled beef is a major export of Argentina and Uruguay.

Authenticated News Int.

South America has some of the world's largest deposits of minerals. These minerals have made possible the development of important manufacturing industries in Brazil, Chile, Colombia, Peru, Uruguay, and Venezuela. Argentina has relatively few minerals except for petroleum. The large Argentine manufacturing industry is built chiefly around factories that process farm and ranch products. Much of South America's mineral wealth remains untouched in mountainous and tropical regions that are hard to reach. However, mining is the most important industry of Bolivia, Chile, and Venezuela. These countries earn most of their income by selling minerals on the world market.

Petroleum is South America's most valuable export. Most of the petroleum that is exported comes from Venezuela, one of the world's leading petroleum-producing countries. Colombia, Ecuador, and Peru also export some petroleum.

Chile is the world's largest copper-exporting country, and ranks as a leader in total copper production. Chile also exports much iron ore and nitrate. It has the world's only deposits of natural sodium nitrate, used largely for fertilizer.

Some of the world's largest iron ore deposits are in Brazil and Venezuela. Brazilian mines also produce large amounts of bauxite and manganese. Bolivia ranks among the world's leading suppliers of tin, and also exports lead, silver, tungsten, and zinc. Peru is a leading silver and lead producer. Colombia is the largest producer of emeralds in the world. Large bauxite deposits are mined in Suriname and Guyana.

South America, like Africa and Australia, has only small deposits of coal. The only country on the continent in which coal is a chief mining product is Colombia, though Brazil, Chile, and Peru mine some coal. Most South American countries import coal to power many of their manufacturing industries. To make up for their small supplies of coal, the larger countries, such as Argentina, Brazil, and Chile, are expanding oil production. They also are building hydroelectric projects.

Fritz Henle, Photo Researchers

Petroleum is South America's most valuable export, and Venezuela produces about two-thirds of it. Oil-pumping derricks operate in Lake Maracaibo.

Mining helps support several South American countries. Bolivia supplies the world market with many minerals, such as tin from this mine at San José.

Thorlichen, Black Star

MINING AND MANUFACTURING

SOUTH AMERICA / *Manufacturing*

Manufacturing has become an important industry in South America, largely since the 1920's. Its most rapid growth came after World War II. When the war ended, the demand for South America's farm and mine exports fell sharply. The governments of several South American countries, especially Argentina, Brazil, and Chile, helped businessmen start factories to make use of locally produced raw materials. Large American and European companies also were invited to open manufacturing branches in South America. As a result, hundreds of factories now operate, and manufacturing centers have been built in several countries. South America's chief manufactured products are textiles and processed foods, such as canned meats, flour, and refined sugar. However, the output also includes many products which previously were imported from Europe or the United States. Among these products are automobiles, cement, chemicals, drugs, electrical appliances, furniture, glassware, machinery, and paper.

Most South American countries aim to build self-supporting economic systems by further expansion of their manufacturing industries. All the South American countries have large resources of manpower. They are handicapped by a lack of the large amounts of money needed for such development. However, the United States and other countries are assisting South America's economic development, largely through long-range programs of international development agencies.

Authenticated News Int.

Hydroelectric Dams supply industrial power in several South American countries that lack large supplies of coal or oil. The Itulinga Dam generates electricity near Rio de Janeiro.

Manufacturing has grown rapidly in many South American countries since the end of World War II. Textiles and processed foods make up the chief products of the factories. Chile's Huachipato steel mill is one of the giants of South American heavy industry.

Authenticated News Int.

Both airplanes and oxcarts are common means of transportation in South America. Railroads and good highways serve the large cities. But in most country areas, horses and oxen pull high-wheeled carts over dirt roads. Millions of South Americans who live in those areas have never ridden in an automobile or even seen a railroad train. Most South Americans have to travel on foot and carry heavy burdens on their backs. Vast forest regions of the continent have no roads at all. In regions with rivers, small boats carry people and goods between the villages. Elsewhere, especially in mountainous areas, pack animals, such as mules or llamas, are used for travel on the rugged trails.

The development of commercial aviation has greatly improved long-distance travel in South America. The airplane solved the problem of crossing high mountains and tropical rain forests that made railroad construction difficult. More than 50 international airlines and many domestic airlines crisscross the continent.

Most of South America's railroads are in Argentina and southeastern Brazil. Argentina, with about 25,000 miles (40,200 kilometers) of railroads, and Brazil, with about 20,000 miles (32,000 kilometers) of railroads, rank among the 10 countries of the world with the greatest railroad mileage. Chile, Colombia, and Uruguay have railroads that connect their important cities. However,

much of the equipment on South America's railroads is old and worn, and service on some lines is poor.

Many South American countries are building new highways to keep pace with their growing automobile and truck manufacturing industries. The continent has about 500,000 miles (800,000 kilometers) of roads. Only about 30,000 miles (48,000 kilometers) of these roads are paved, compared with more than 2 million miles (3.2 million kilometers) of paved highways in the United States. The Pan American highway links the countries of South America (see PAN AMERICAN HIGHWAY).

Steamships provide the most important means of commerce between South American countries and the rest of the world. The largest merchant fleets belong to Peru, which has about 695 ships, and Brazil, with about 625 ships. Argentina and Chile also have large merchant marines, and Colombia, Ecuador, and Venezuela have many ships in coastal trade. Vitória, Brazil, is South America's busiest port.

Communication is one of the basic problems in South America. More than half the people cannot read, and most South Americans cannot afford a telephone, radio, or television set. A majority of South Americans must depend for information on what they hear from people around them. In country areas, the town market place serves as a major communication

Steamships provide South American countries with their most important means of commerce. Brazil and Peru operate South America's largest merchant fleets. Many of the continent's major cities are seaports, such as Valparaíso, Chile.

Joe Barnell, Shostal

The Pan American Highway links the countries of South America, often slicing through thick forests or swamps. This section of the highway is in Chile.

General Secretariat, OAS

center. There, the people gather to talk about local happenings, and to pick up news about national and world events. In the cities, wealthy and middle class people have telephones, radios, and television sets. But even in the cities, many South Americans are too poor to own modern communication devices.

Argentina and Brazil together publish more books and magazines than all the other countries of South America combined. In most countries, the publications are in Spanish, but those in Brazil are in Portuguese. All the South American countries have radio stations, and there are about 30 radio receivers for every hundred people. Television stations broadcast in Argentina, Brazil, Chile, Colombia, Peru, Uruguay, and Venezuela. There are 12 television sets for about every hundred South Americans.

PRESTON E. JAMES

George Holton, Photo Researchers

Small Boats are common means of transportation in many South American areas where rivers serve as roads. Villagers on the upper Amazon River use boats such as these Peruvian craft at Iquitos.

Transportation

Authenticated News Int.

Railroads of South America often operate with old equipment. The old-fashioned trains of this Peruvian line climb over 15,000 feet (4,570 meters) to towns nestled in the Andes Mountains.

Air Transport has greatly improved long-distance travel in South America. Many airlines crisscross the continent, and all the large cities have modern airports.

Pan American World Airways

Map legend:
- Major Railroads
- No Roads
- Inland Waterways
- Major Ports
- Major Airports

Related Articles in WORLD BOOK include:

COUNTRIES

Argentina	Guyana
Bolivia	Paraguay
Brazil	Peru
Chile	Suriname
Colombia	Uruguay
Ecuador	Venezuela

COLONIES AND TERRITORIES

Falkland Islands	French Guiana

LARGE CITIES

Belo Horizonte	Pôrto Alegre
Bogotá	Recife
Buenos Aires	Rio de Janeiro
Caracas	Salvador
Lima	Santiago
Montevideo	São Paulo

ISLANDS

Galapagos Islands
Juan Fernández
Marajó
Tierra del Fuego

MOUNTAINS

Aconcagua	Cotopaxi
Andes Mountains	El Misti
Chimborazo	Ojos del Salado
Cordillera	Pichincha

PLAINS AND DESERTS

Atacama Desert	Pampa
Gran Chaco	Patagonia

PRODUCTS

Balsa	Manganese
Banana	Maté
Bauxite	Nitrate
Cacao	Petroleum
Cattle	Quebracho
Coffee	Rubber
Copper	Silver
Corn	Sugar
Cotton	Tin
Emerald	Wool
Guano	

RIVERS, LAKES, AND WATERFALLS

Amazon River	Orinoco River
Angel Falls	Paraguay River
Cuquenán Falls	Paraná River
Iguaçu River	Purús River
King George VI Falls	Río de la Plata
Lake Maracaibo	São Francisco, Rio
Lake Titicaca	Uruguay River
Madeira River	

OTHER RELATED ARTICLES

Alliance for Progress	Latin America
Cape Horn	Magellan, Strait of
Clothing (pictures:	Pan-American Conferences
Traditional Costumes)	Pan American Highway
El Dorado	Pan American Union
Gaucho	Pan Americanism
Illiteracy (table)	Selva
Indian, American	

Outline

I. Land Regions
 A. The Pacific Coastlands
 B. The Andes Mountains
 C. The Central Plains
 D. The Eastern Highlands
II. Natural Features
 A. Rivers
 B. Waterfalls
 C. Lakes
 D. Islands
III. Climate
IV. Animals
V. Plants
VI. Agriculture
VII. Mining
VIII. Manufacturing
IX. Transportation and Communication

Questions

What are the major causes of food shortages in South American countries?

Which of the South American central plains is suitable for farming? Why?

How is the land surface of South America like that of North America?

What is South America's most valuable export? Which country leads in its production?

What river is the only river in the world that is longer than the Amazon?

How are Argentina, Brazil, and Chile making up for their lack of extensive coal deposits?

Where are most South American railroads?

How do most South Americans in country areas learn about world events?

Why is there little rainfall on the coasts of Peru and northern Chile? What are some of the areas of South America that have heavy rainfall?

Which South American country has the largest area? The smallest area?

When did manufacturing in South America have its most rapid growth? How did the governments of South America aid manufacturing development?

Additional Resources

Level I

BEALS, CARLETON. *The Incredible Incas: Yesterday and Today.* Harper, 1974.

CARTER, WILLIAM E. *The First Book of South America.* Rev. ed. Watts, 1972.

FIDELER, RAYMOND, and KVANDE, CAROL. *South America.* Rev. ed. Fideler, 1978.

JENNESS, AYLETTE, and KROEBER, L. W. *A Life of Their Own: An Indian Family in Latin America.* Crowell, 1975.

SHUTTLESWORTH, DOROTHY E. *The Wildlife of South America.* Hastings, 1974.

Level II

BANNON, JOHN F., and others. *Latin America.* 4th ed. Macmillan, 1977.

BURNS, EDWARD BRADFORD. *Latin America: A Concise Interpretive History.* 2nd ed. Prentice-Hall, 1977.

COLLIER, SIMON D. W. *From Cortés to Castro: An Introduction to the History of Latin America, 1492-1973.* Macmillan, 1974.

ELLIS, JOSEPH A. *Latin America: Its People and Institutions.* 2nd ed. Macmillan, 1975.

FAGG, JOHN E. *Latin America: A General History.* 3rd ed. Macmillan, 1977.

HENNESSY, ALISTAIR. *The Frontier in Latin American History.* Univ. of New Mexico Press, 1978.

ISENBERG, IRWIN, ed. *South America: Problems and Prospects.* Wilson, 1975.

PARRY, J. H. *The Discovery of South America.* Taplinger, 1979.

The South American Handbook. Rand McNally, published annually.

VIGNERAS, LOUIS-ANDRÉ. *The Discovery of South America and the Andalusian Voyages.* Univ. of Chicago Press, 1976.

SOUTH AMERICAN OSTRICH. See RHEA (bird).

SOUTH ARABIA, FEDERATION OF, was a union of 17 small states at the southern tip of the Arabian Peninsula. It included the British-protected state of Aden; the state of Dathina; the emirates of Beihan and Dhala; the sultanates of Audhali, Fadhli, Haushabi, Lahej, Lower Aulaqi, Lower Yafa, Upper Aulaqi, and Wahidi; and the sheikdoms of Alawi, Aqrabi, Mufhahi, Shaibi, and Upper Aulaqi. The federation covered 60,000 square miles (160,000 square kilometers). Great Britain controlled the federation's foreign affairs and defense, and provided economic assistance.

The union was once called the Federation of the Arab Emirates of the South. It was formed in 1959 by six of the states. By 1965, the other 11 states had joined. On Nov. 30, 1967, the federation gained independence as the People's Republic of Southern Yemen (see the *History* section of the YEMEN [ADEN] article).

SOUTH AUSTRALIA is a state in south-central Australia. It faces the Indian Ocean and the Great Australian Bight. For detailed maps, see AUSTRALIA.

The state covers an area of 379,900 square miles (984,000 square kilometers). Much of its land lies from 1,000 to 2,000 feet (300 to 610 meters) above sea level. The Gawler and Flinders mountain ranges rise in the south. The Adelaide and southeastern coastal regions include fertile lands. The Musgrave mountain ranges are in the north. Wheat farms and rolling plains stretch between the northern ranges. The north also has flat sheep-grazing lands. Sandy deserts extend into the center of the state from the north. The *Nullarbor* (treeless) Plain covers much of the western section.

The Murray River is the continent's longest permanently flowing river. It rises near the eastern border of Victoria and flows for 1,609 miles (2,589 kilometers) before it empties into the Indian Ocean near Adelaide. A number of smaller rivers flow into Lake Eyre, which lies in the northeastern section of South Australia.

South Australia's yearly temperature averages 70° F. (21° C). Less than 10 inches (25 centimeters) of rain falls annually in all but the state's southern part.

The state has excellent farming and grazing lands. Shallow lakes produce great quantities of salt. The eastern mountains have deposits of gypsum, ironstone, limestone, manganese ore, opals, and phosphate rock.

The People. South Australia has a population of 1,284,843. Two out of three persons live in the Adelaide metropolitan area. Most of the people of South Australia are of British descent.

By law, children between the ages of 6 and 15 must attend school. Adelaide has a state university and a state school of mines and industries. Flinders University in Bedford Park opened in 1966.

In the southern and eastern sections, people produce large crops of barley, hay, oats, potatoes, and wheat. The Murray River irrigates orchards, orange groves, and vineyards. About 16½ million sheep and 660,000 cattle graze there. The state produces over 173 million pounds (78 million kilograms) of wool annually. Exports include butter, copper, flour, fruits, meats, wheat, wine, and wool.

Industrial products include automobile bodies, chemicals, cotton and woolen goods, electrical equipment, and sheet metal. Mining and quarrying are important. Uranium mining began during World War II.

The state has about 3,900 miles (6,280 kilometers) of railroads and about 62,000 miles (99,800 kilometers) of roads. Port Pirie is the chief port.

Government. The British ruler appoints a governor for the state on the recommendation of the South Australian Parliament. But a premier actually heads the government. The South Australian Legislature consists of a 22-member upper house and a 47-member lower house. The voters elect members of the upper house to six-year terms, and members of the lower house to three-year terms. They also elect 21 members to the Australian Parliament in Canberra. All adult British subjects who live in the state must vote in elections.

History. Matthew Flinders, a British navigator, made the first extensive explorations along the South Australian coast about 1802. In 1836, British settlers founded the first settlement in the area in Adelaide. The discovery of gold in the neighboring colony of Victoria in 1851 brought many new settlers to South Australia. In 1856, South Australians won the right to govern themselves. South Australia joined with five other Australian colonies to form the Commonwealth of Australia in 1901.   C. M. H. CLARK

See also ADELAIDE; GREAT AUSTRALIAN BIGHT; LAKE EYRE; MURRAY RIVER.

SOUTH BEND, Ind. (pop. 109,727; met. area 280,-772), is one of the largest cities in the state. This industrial center lies in north-central Indiana, 90 miles (145 kilometers) east and slightly south of Chicago. It is named for its location at the southernmost point of the Indiana bend in the St. Joseph River (see INDIANA [political map]). Factories make farm machinery and tools, and automobile and airplane brakes and equipment.

The University of Notre Dame and Saint Mary's College are located near South Bend. Bethel College and a branch of Indiana University are also nearby.

In 1823, Alexis Coquillard, a fur trader, founded South Bend. He called it Big St. Joseph Station. The name was later changed to South Bend. The village was incorporated in 1835, and became a city in 1865. It has a mayor-council government.   PAUL E. MILLION, JR.

See also NOTRE DAME, UNIVERSITY OF.

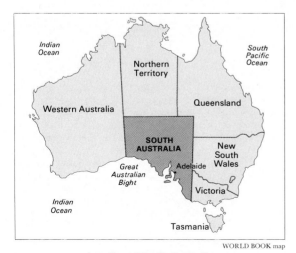

Location of South Australia

Stately Homes in Historic Charleston

SOUTH CAROLINA

THE PALMETTO STATE

SOUTH CAROLINA is the smallest state in the Deep South. In spite of its size, South Carolina is an important manufacturing and farming state. South Carolina produces large amounts of a wide variety of textiles. Among all the states, only North Carolina makes more textiles than South Carolina does. South Carolina raises one of the largest tobacco crops in the United States, and only California grows more peaches than South Carolina does. Columbia is the capital and largest city of South Carolina.

More than half the people of South Carolina live in farm areas, even though manufacturing is the state's chief economic activity. South Carolina still has many features of the South of pre-Civil War days. Graceful buildings erected before the war stand in Beaufort, Charleston, and other cities. Large plantations, once the backbone of the South's economy, remain in parts of South Carolina. The state's many beautiful flower gardens recall the leisurely life of the South before the Civil War.

The eastern part of South Carolina is a lowland that borders the Atlantic Ocean. In the west, the land rises to sand hills, and then to mountains. The people of South Carolina call the eastern part of the state the *Low Country*. They call the western part of the state the *Up Country*.

South Carolina was named for King Charles I of England, in 1629. *Carolina* is a Latin form of *Charles*. The

Lake and Table Rock near the Blue Ridge Mountains

Tom Hollyman, Photo Researchers

Palmetto Trees Along the Atlantic Coast

Louis Schwartz

Facts in Brief

Capital: Columbia.

Government: *Congress*—U.S. senators, 2; U.S. representatives, 6. *Electoral Votes*—8. *State Legislature*—senators, 46; representatives, 124. *Counties*—46.

Area: 31,055 sq. mi. (80,432 km²), including 830 sq. mi. (2,150 km²) of inland water but excluding 138 sq. mi. (357 km²) of Atlantic coastal water; 40th in size among the states. *Greatest Distances*—east-west, 273 mi. (439 km); north-south, 210 mi. (338 km). *Coastline*—187 mi. (301 km).

Elevation: *Highest*—Sassafras Mountain, 3,560 ft. (1,085 m) above sea level. *Lowest*—sea level along the Atlantic Coast.

Population: *1980 Census*—3,119,208; 24th among the states; density, 100 persons per sq. mi. (39 per km²); distribution, 52 per cent rural, 48 per cent urban. *1970 Census*—2,590,713.

Chief Products: *Agriculture*—soybeans, tobacco, beef cattle, eggs, milk, corn, hogs, peaches. *Fishing Industry*—shrimp, crabs. *Manufacturing*—textiles, chemicals, nonelectric machinery, clothing, paper products, electric machinery and equipment, rubber and plastics products, fabricated metal products. *Mining*—stone, clays.

Statehood: May 23, 1788, the eighth state.

State Abbreviations: S.C. (traditional); SC (postal).

State Mottoes: *Animis opibusque parati* (*Prepared in mind and resources*); *Dum spiro spero* (*While I breathe, I hope*).

State Song: "Carolina." Words by Henry Timrod; music by Anne Custis Burgess.

South Carolina (blue) ranks 40th in size among all the states and 11th in size among the Southern States (gray).

word *South* was added in 1730, when North and South Carolina became separate colonies.

Many important Revolutionary War battles were fought in South Carolina. Colonial victories in the Battle of Kings Mountain and the Battle of Cowpens were turning points of the war in the South. South Carolina may have earned its nickname, the *Palmetto State*, as the result of events that occurred during the Revolutionary War. In 1776, colonists in a small fort built of palmetto logs defeated a British fleet that tried to capture Charleston Harbor. The next day, William Moultrie, the colonial commander, saw a column of smoke rising from a burning British ship. The shape of the smoke reminded Moultrie of the palmetto tree, which

grows widely in South Carolina. These events supposedly gave South Carolina its nickname.

South Carolina was the first state to *secede* (withdraw) from the Union before the Civil War. It did so on Dec. 20, 1860. Confederate troops fired the first shot of the Civil War when they attacked Fort Sumter in Charleston Harbor on April 12, 1861.

The contributors of this article are Ernest M. Lander, Jr., Alumni Professor of History at Clemson University; and William D. Workman, Jr., Editorial Consultant for The State *of Columbia, and author of* The Case for the South.

Constitution of South Carolina was adopted in 1895. The state's six earlier constitutions were adopted in 1776, 1778, 1790, 1861, 1865, and 1868.

The constitution has been *amended* (changed) about 350 times. The state legislature or a constitutional convention may propose an amendment. An amendment proposed by the legislature requires approval by two-thirds of the members of both the Senate and House of Representatives. Next, it needs the approval of a majority of the persons voting on it in a state-wide election. To become law, the amendment must then be approved by a majority of members of the state legislature.

A two-thirds vote in each house of the legislature is required to call a constitutional convention. The convention also must be approved by a majority of the persons voting on the issue in a state-wide election.

Executive. The governor of South Carolina is elected to a four-year term but may not serve two terms in a row. The governor is the only elected executive official in South Carolina who cannot serve consecutive terms. The governor receives a yearly salary of $60,000. For a list of all the governors of South Carolina, see the *History* section of this article.

South Carolina voters also elect the lieutenant governor, adjutant general, attorney general, commissioner of agriculture, comptroller general, secretary of state, state treasurer, and superintendent of education. All these officials serve four-year terms.

Legislature, called the *General Assembly*, consists of a 46-member Senate and a 124-member House of Representatives. Voters in 16 senatorial districts elect from 1 to 5 senators, depending on population. Voters in each of the state's 28 representative districts elect from 1 to 12 representatives, depending on population. Senators serve four-year terms, and representatives two-year terms.

Until the mid-1960's, one senator was elected from each of the state's 46 counties. In 1965, a special federal court ordered the legislature to *reapportion* (redivide) the Senate to provide equal representation based on population. The court approved a temporary plan for the 1966 elections, and all senators were elected to two-year terms. In 1968, the court approved the legis-

lature's plan of electing 46 senators from 20 districts. In 1972, the legislature reduced the number of senatorial districts from 20 to 16.

The legislature meets each year, starting on the second Tuesday in January. Sessions have no time limit, but the legislators are paid for only 40 working days. The governor may call special sessions.

Courts. The Supreme Court is South Carolina's highest court. It is a court of appeals, and has a chief justice and four associate justices. The justices are elected by the legislature to 10-year terms. Circuit courts of common pleas and general sessions are the chief trial courts. The legislature elects the state's 16 circuit court judges to four-year terms. Supreme Court justices are usually chosen from among the circuit court judges. Circuit court judges are usually chosen from the legislature.

Magistrates' courts hear minor civil and criminal cases. The magistrates who head the courts are appointed by the governor, with the approval of the state Senate. Most South Carolina counties also have county courts that hear minor civil and criminal cases.

Local Government. County governments in South Carolina are headed by boards of county commissioners, county councils, or similar local boards. County commissioners or council members and their assistants carry out such government functions as enforcing laws and regulating taxes. Many of the county councils appoint professional administrators to direct the county government agencies. Chief county officials in South Carolina include the auditor, clerk of court, county attorney, sheriff, and treasurer.

South Carolina cities and towns operate under charters. Most of the state's larger cities have the council-manager form of government. Most of the smaller cities have the mayor-council form.

Taxation provides about three-fourths of the state government's income. Almost all the rest comes from federal grants and other U.S. government programs. A 4 per cent general sales and use tax provides more than 30 per cent of the state's tax income. A *use tax* is a tax on goods brought into the state from another state. An individual income tax brings in about 20 per cent of

Governor's House, in Columbia, was once part of a state military school. It has been the governor's residence since 1879.
South Carolina State Development Board

Statue of John C. Calhoun, Vice-President and U.S. senator, stands in the lobby of the South Carolina Capitol.
South Carolina Dept. of Parks, Recreation, and Tourism

The State Seal

Symbols of South Carolina. On the seal, a palmetto tree towers over an uprooted oak. The palmetto symbolizes the successful defense in 1776 of the palmetto-log fort on Sullivan's Island against the oaken ships of the British. The figure of Hope carrying a laurel branch across a sword-covered beach represents the wish to remain forever independent. The seal was authorized in 1776. The state flag, adopted in 1777, also bears a palmetto, the state tree.

The State Flag

The State Bird
Carolina Wren

The State Flower
Carolina Jessamine

The State Tree
Palmetto

South Carolina's tax income. A gasoline tax also accounts for about 20 per cent. Funds from the gasoline tax are used to build and maintain highways.

Politics. The Democratic Party has controlled South Carolina politics throughout most of the state's history. Since 1880, non-Democratic presidential candidates have won South Carolina's electoral votes only five times. The state was carried by Strom Thurmond of South Carolina, the States' Rights Democratic (Dixiecrat) Party candidate, in 1948; Senator Barry M. Goldwater of Arizona, a Republican, in 1964; Richard M. Nixon, a Republican, in 1968 and 1972; and Ronald Reagan, a Republican, in 1980. For South Carolina's voting record in presidential elections, see ELECTORAL COLLEGE (table).

The Republican Party gained much strength in South Carolina during the 1950's and 1960's. In 1964, Senator Strom Thurmond of South Carolina resigned from the Democratic Party and became a Republican. In 1974, James B. Edwards became the first Republican to be elected governor of the state in 100 years.

The State Capitol of South Carolina, called the State House, is in Columbia. Columbia has been South Carolina's capital since 1790. Charleston was the capital from 1670 to 1790.

Ellis Sawyer, FPG

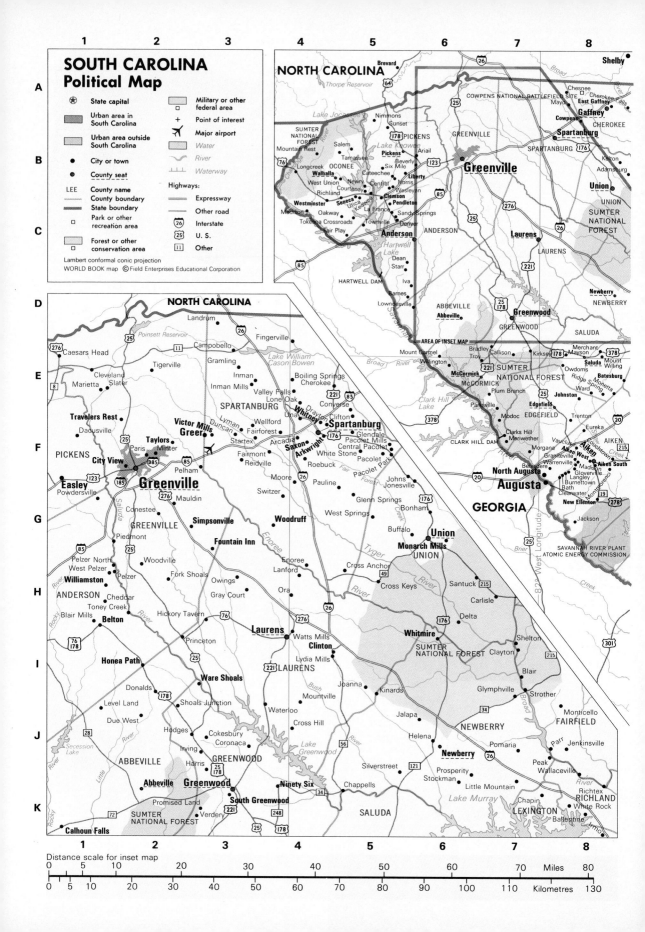

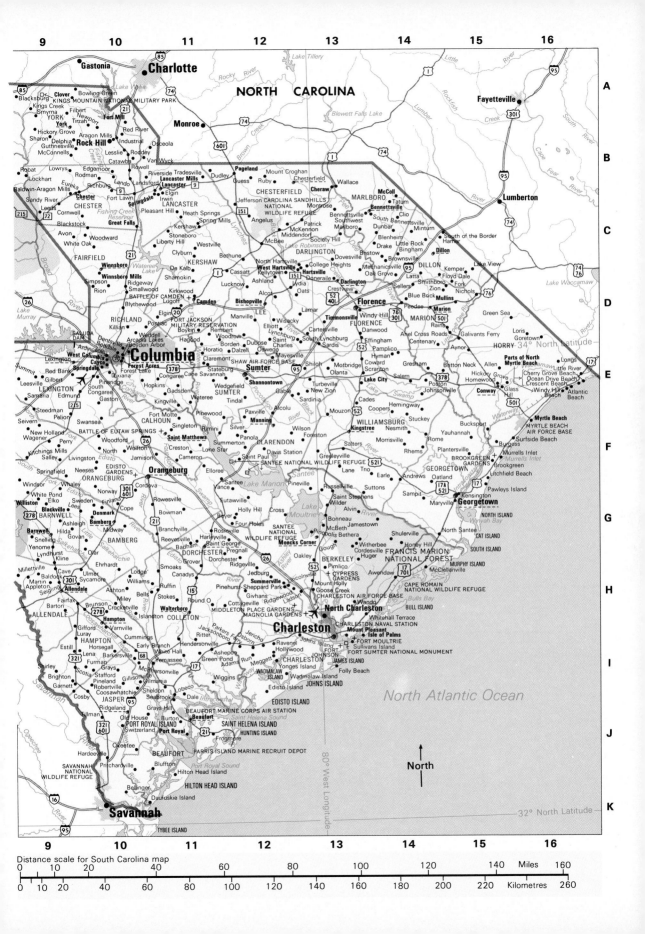

South Carolina Map Index

Population

Metropolitan Areas

Counties

Cities and Towns

Seaport at Charleston is a principal U.S. port on the South Atlantic coast. Cargo passing through the port includes bananas, oil, ore, fertilizer, jute, coal, and tobacco. Georgetown and Port Royal are also important South Carolina port cities.

*Does not appear on map; key shows general location.
'County seat.

Source: 1980 census. Places without population figures are unincorporated areas.

The 1980 United States census reported that South Carolina had 3,119,208 persons. The population had increased by 20 per cent over the 1970 census figure, 2,590,713.

About 52 per cent of South Carolina's people live in farm areas. The state has seven metropolitan areas (see METROPOLITAN AREA). Nearly 2 million South Carolinians, or about three-fifths of the population of the state, live in these areas. Six metropolitan areas are entirely within the state. They are Anderson, Charleston-North Charleston, Columbia, Florence, Greenville-Spartanburg, and Rock Hill. Part of the Augusta, Ga., metropolitan area extends into Aiken County, South Carolina. For the populations of the metropolitan areas, see the *Index* to the political map of South Carolina.

South Carolina's largest cities, in order of size, are Columbia, Charleston, North Charleston, and Greenville. They are the only cities in South Carolina that have a population of more than 50,000 persons. See the separate articles on South Carolina cities listed in the *Related Articles* at the end of this article.

About 76 of every 100 South Carolinians were born in the state, and many are descendants of early settlers. About 99 of every 100 persons in the state were born in the United States. Britons and Germans make up the largest groups born in other countries. About 30 of every 100 persons who live in South Carolina are blacks.

Most South Carolinians are Protestants. Baptists outnumber all other religious groups. Other large religious groups include Methodists and Presbyterians.

Louis Schwartz

Textile Worker inspects yarn. About two-fifths of the persons employed in manufacturing in South Carolina work in the textile industry. The state rebuilt its economy around this industry after the Civil War, and is now a leading U.S. textile producer.

Population

This map shows the *population density* of South Carolina, and how it varies in different parts of the state. Population density is the average number of persons who live in a given area.

Persons per sq. mi.	Persons per km²
More than 100	More than 40
70 to 100	27 to 40
40 to 70	15 to 27
Less than 40	Less than 15

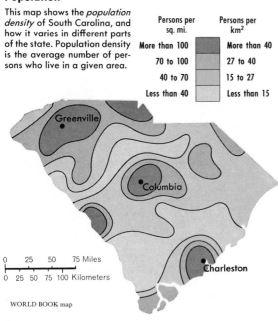

Greenville

Columbia

0   25   50   75 Miles
0   25 50 75 100 Kilometers

Charleston

WORLD BOOK map

South Carolina State Development Board

Paraders and Spectators enjoy the annual Sun-Fun Festival in Myrtle Beach. Other annual events in South Carolina include a steeplechase, stock car races, and a state fair.

Schools. In colonial times, most South Carolina children were educated at home or in private schools. In 1710, the colonial government established semipublic schools called *free schools*. These schools were free to poor children, but other youngsters paid tuition.

In 1811, the state legislature approved a plan to set up free schools in all parts of South Carolina. But not enough money was put aside to run the schools. There were few free schools except in the largest towns. The 1868 constitution called for free public schools for all children. The legislature failed to provide enough money for the schools. Finally, the 1895 constitution provided enough tax support for statewide public schools.

Like other Southern states, South Carolina had separate schools for Negroes and whites for many years. In 1954, the Supreme Court of the United States ruled that public school segregation on the basis of race is unconstitutional. The first racial integration in South Carolina public schools took place in Charleston in 1963. By 1970, South Carolina's school districts had been integrated. Children between the ages of 6 and 16 must attend school. For the number of students and teachers in the state, see EDUCATION (table).

A superintendent of education and a state board of education head the South Carolina public school system. The board has 17 members. The governor appoints one member from the state *at large* (as a whole). The other members are appointed by the state legislators from each of South Carolina's 16 *judicial* (court) circuits. Board members serve four-year terms. The voters elect the superintendent to a four-year term.

Libraries. South Carolina had the first government-supported lending library in the 13 original colonies. The library opened in Charleston in 1698, but closed a few years later. In 1840, the University of South Carolina built the nation's first separate college library building. Today, about 40 public county and *multicounty* (regional) libraries serve all parts of the state.

Museums. The Charleston Museum, founded in 1773, ranks among the oldest museums in the United States. It has natural history and colonial history exhibits, and a planetarium. Bob Jones University in Greenville has a notable collection of paintings on religion. Other art museums include the Columbia Museum of Art and Science and the Gibbes Art Gallery in Charleston.

UNIVERSITIES AND COLLEGES

South Carolina has 24 universities and colleges accredited by the Southern Association of Colleges and Schools. For enrollments and further information, see UNIVERSITIES AND COLLEGES (table).

Name	Location	Founded
Baptist College at Charleston	Charleston	1964
Benedict College	Columbia	1870
Central Wesleyan College	Central	1958
Charleston, College of	Charleston	1770
Citadel, The	Charleston	1842
Claflin College	Orangeburg	1869
Clemson University	Clemson	1889
Coker College	Hartsville	1908
Columbia College	Columbia	1854
Converse College	Spartanburg	1889
Erskine College	Due West	1839
Francis Marion College	Florence	1970
Furman University	Greenville	1825
Lander College	Greenwood	1872
Limestone College	Gaffney	1845
Morris College	Sumter	1908
Newberry College	Newberry	1856
Presbyterian College	Clinton	1880
South Carolina, Medical University of	Charleston	1824
South Carolina, University of	*	*
South Carolina State College	Orangeburg	1896
Voorhees College	Denmark	1897
Winthrop College	Rock Hill	1886
Wofford College	Spartanburg	1854

*For campuses and founding dates, see UNIVERSITIES AND COLLEGES (table).

University of South Carolina's McKissick Memorial Library is on the campus at Columbia. The campus also includes the nation's oldest separate college library building, built in 1840.

Shostal

Woodrow Wilson's Boyhood Home in Columbia was bought by the state in 1929. It is now a museum. The President lived in the house with his parents from 1870 to 1874.

South Carolina State Development Board

South Carolina's mountains, seashore, and historic sites make the state a favorite vacationland. Abundant wildlife in the fields and streams provide exciting action for hunters and fishermen. Visitors also enjoy the state's many beautiful flower gardens.

Tom Hollyman, Photo Researchers

Monument at Kings Mountain Battlefield

Louis Schwartz

Fort Sumter, Site of the Opening Battle of the Civil War

Places to Visit

Following are brief descriptions of some of South Carolina's many interesting places to visit.

Battlegrounds recall South Carolina's part in the Revolutionary War. *Kings Mountain National Military Park* and *Cowpens National Battlefield*, both near Gaffney, mark the sites of major Revolutionary War battles. Other battlefields are marked at *Camden* and at *Eutaw Springs*, near St. Matthews.

Beaches along South Carolina's Atlantic Coast offer swimming and sunbathing. Myrtle Beach is probably the state's most famous seaside resort. Other beaches, from north to south, include Cherry Grove, Ocean Drive, Crescent, Atlantic, Windy Hill, Isle of Palms, Folly, Edisto Island, Hunting Island, and Hilton Head Island.

Forts are among South Carolina's most interesting historic sites. *Fort Sumter*, in Charleston Harbor, is the place where the Civil War began. The fort is now a national monument. *Fort Moultrie*, also in Charleston Harbor, is the site of a brave defense by the colonists against the British during the Revolutionary War. *Fort Johnson*, in Charleston Harbor, is the place where Americans seized tax stamps from the British in 1765 in opposition to the Stamp Act. At *Windmill Point*, near Charleston, Governor Sir Nathaniel Johnson turned back French and Spanish fleets in 1706, during Queen Anne's War (see FRENCH AND INDIAN WARS).

Gardens are among South Carolina's most beautiful attractions. Near Charleston are the famous *Cypress Gardens*, *Magnolia Gardens*, and *Middleton Place Gardens*. Cypress Gardens include a variety of colorful flowers and several lagoons flanked by cypress trees. Magnolia Gardens feature more than 500 varieties of flowers and trees from many lands. Middleton Place Gardens are the oldest landscaped gardens in the United States. They were begun in 1741, and feature azaleas, camellias, and ancient oak trees. The garden area includes exhibits on plantation life of the 1700's and 1800's. *Brookgreen Gardens*, north of Georgetown, cover parts of Brookgreen and three other former rice plantations. These gardens feature South Carolina plants and trees and a park for native South Carolina wildlife. The Brookgreen Gardens displays include a collection of statues. *Edisto Gardens*, in Orangeburg, is a city-owned display of azaleas, camellias, roses, and other flowers.

National Forests. South Carolina has two National Forests—Francis Marion near Charleston, and Sumter, which covers two areas in the Piedmont and one area in the Blue Ridge Mountains.

State Parks and Forests. South Carolina has 47 state parks and historic sites, and 4 state forests. For information, write to Director of Parks, Recreation and Tourism, Edgar A. Brown Building, 1205 Pendleton Street, Columbia, S.C. 29201.

Shostal

Middleton Place Gardens near Charleston

ANNUAL EVENTS

Polo Players Compete in Aiken
W. D. Madewell

Favorite annual events in South Carolina include the Carolina Cup Steeplechase, held in Camden near Easter, and the Southern 500 stock car race, held in Darlington on Labor Day.

Other annual events in South Carolina include the following.

January-June: Polo Games in Aiken (mid-January through Easter); Garden Tours, state-wide (mid-February through May); Canadian-American Days in Myrtle Beach (late March); Heritage Golf Classic at Hilton Head Island (late March); Plantation Tours, throughout the state (March, April); The Governor's Annual Frog Jumping Contest in Springfield (Saturday before Easter); Rebel 500 Stock Car Race in Darlington (April); Outdoor Arts and Crafts Festival in Murrells Inlet (mid-April); Hell Hole Swamp Festival in Jamestown (early May); Iris Festival in Sumter (last week in May); Spoleto Festival U.S.A. in Charleston (May-June); Sun-Fun Festival in Myrtle Beach (second week in June).

July-December: Water Festival in Beaufort (mid-July); Scottish Games and Highland Gathering at Middleton Place Gardens near Charleston (late September); State Fair in Columbia (third week in October); Chitlin Strut in Salley (late November); Colonial Cup in Camden (late November).

Colorful Garden and Mansions near Beaufort
Shostal

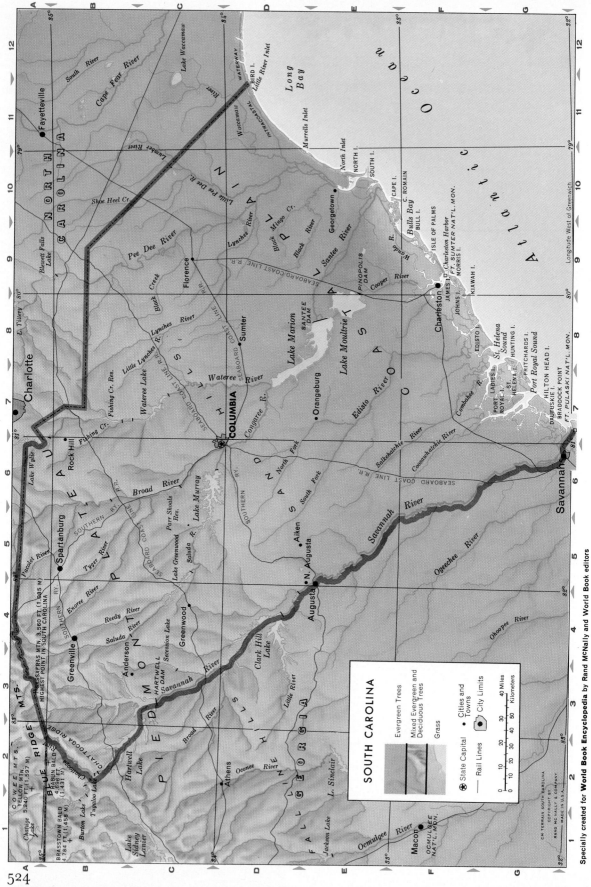

SOUTH CAROLINA

Evergreen Trees

Mixed Evergreen and
Deciduous Trees

Grass

⊛ State Capital ● Cities and Towns
○ City Limits

— Rail Lines

| 0 | 10 | 20 | 30 | 40 Miles |
| 0 | 10 | 20 | 30 | 40 | 50 Kilometers |

CM TERRAIN SOUTH CAROLINA
COPYRIGHT BY
RAND MCNALLY & COMPANY
MADE IN U.S.A.

Specially created for **World Book Encyclopedia** by Rand McNally and World Book editors

NORTH CAROLINA

ATLANTic

Long Bay

Fayetteville

Charlotte

COLUMBIA

Savannah

Augusta
N. Augusta
Aiken

Greenville
Spartanburg
Anderson
Greenwood
Rock Hill

Sumter
Florence
Orangeburg

Georgetown

Charleston

Macon

Athens

GEORGIA

Atlantic Ocean

524

Tom Hollyman, Photo Researchers

Barge Transports Goods near Beaufort, a seacoast town. Harbors line the Atlantic Coastal Plain region and provide shipping facilities for agricultural and industrial products.

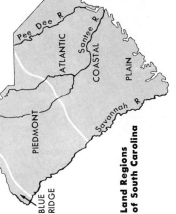

Land Regions of South Carolina

SOUTH CAROLINA / The Land

Land Regions. South Carolina has three main land regions: (1) the Atlantic Coastal Plain, (2) the Piedmont, and (3) the Blue Ridge. South Carolinians call the Atlantic Coastal Plain the *Low Country*, and the Piedmont and Blue Ridge the *Up Country*.

The Atlantic Coastal Plain is a lowland that covers the southeastern two-thirds of South Carolina. It is part of the plain of the same name that stretches from New York to Florida. In South Carolina, the land rises gradually from southeast to northwest. Near the Atlantic Coast, the plain is flat and broken by wide bays and rivers. Swamps cover much of the land near the coast and extend far inland along the rivers. A belt of forest called the *Pine Barrens* covers part of the central Atlantic Coastal Plain. A series of sand hills runs through Aiken, Camden, Cheraw, and Columbia, marking the western edge of the plain. These sand hills form part of an ancient beach, and indicate that the Atlantic Coastal Plain once lay under the ocean.

The Piedmont covers most of northwestern South Caro-

lina. It is part of a land region that extends from New York to Alabama. The *Fall Line* forms the eastern edge of the Piedmont in South Carolina. The Fall Line is a zone where rivers tumble from higher land to the lowlying Atlantic Coastal Plain (see FALL LINE). In the southeast, the South Carolina Piedmont is a rolling upland with elevations from 400 to 1,000 feet (120 to 300 meters) above sea level. The region rises to a hilly area 1,500 feet (460 meters) above sea level at its western edge.

The Piedmont slopes from northwest to southeast, which causes rivers in the region to flow rapidly. The swift-running rivers are a major source of hydroelectric power. This power helps make the Piedmont an important manufacturing area.

The Blue Ridge covers the northwestern corner of South Carolina. It is part of a larger region of the same name that runs from southern Pennsylvania to northern Georgia. The famous Blue Ridge Mountains, part of the Appalachian Mountain system, give the region its

name. The Blue Ridge Mountains of South Carolina are less rugged and more easily crossed than those of North Carolina. Few Blue Ridge peaks in South Carolina rise more than 3,000 feet (910 meters), and all are topped with forests. Sassafras Mountain, the highest point in the state, rises 3,560 feet (1,085 meters) above sea level in the Blue Ridge.

Coastline of South Carolina has many bays and inlets. Measured in a straight line, the coastline totals 187 miles (301 kilometers). If all the coastal area washed by water were measured, the coastline would total 2,876 miles (4,628 kilometers). Important bays and harbors along the coast include, from north to south, Little River Inlet, Winyah Bay, Bull Bay, Charleston Harbor, St. Helena Sound, and Port Royal Sound. The northern part of the coastline, from North Carolina to Winyah Bay, has an almost unbroken beach. South of Winyah Bay, salt-water marshes cover much of the coastal area, and tidal rivers cut far inland. Many islands lie along the coast. They include, from north to

Photos, Tom Hollyman, Photo Researchers

Contour Farming, *above,* in the hilly Piedmont region of South Carolina helps prevent soil erosion. By planting alternate strips of crops that are harvested at different times, the farmer always has a soil-holding crop on the land. Agriculture has been an important activity in South Carolina since the first permanent settlers arrived in 1670. The state's many important farm crops include cotton, corn, peaches, soybeans, and tobacco.

Blue Ridge Mountains, *left,* cover the northwestern corner of South Carolina and give the Blue Ridge region its name. These mountains are less rugged than the Blue Ridge of North Carolina, and are capped with pine and hemlock forests. The region's scenic beauty makes it popular with vacationers. The Blue Ridge region is too mountainous for farming, and most of the people earn their living in manufacturing.

south, Pawley's Island, Bull Island, Isle of Palms, Sullivan's Island, Edisto Island, Hunting Island, Fripps Island, and Hilton Head Island. Parris Island, near Beaufort, is a major U.S. Marine training center.

Rivers, Waterfalls, and Lakes. Many large rivers cross South Carolina from northwest to southeast. The largest is the Pee Dee River, which drains an area of 16,320 square miles (42,269 square kilometers) in North and South Carolina. The Santee River is a close second in size, and the Savannah River is third. Other rivers include the Broad and the Saluda. Every South Carolina river that crosses the Fall Line has a series of rapids or waterfalls. Larger and more beautiful waterfalls may be seen in the Blue Ridge Mountains. South Carolina has no large natural lakes. Dams form many large manmade lakes or reservoirs. The largest is Lake Marion. Other manmade lakes include Greenwood, Wylie, Moultrie, Murray, and Wateree. Clark Hill and Hartwell lakes, on the Savannah River, are shared by South Carolina and Georgia.

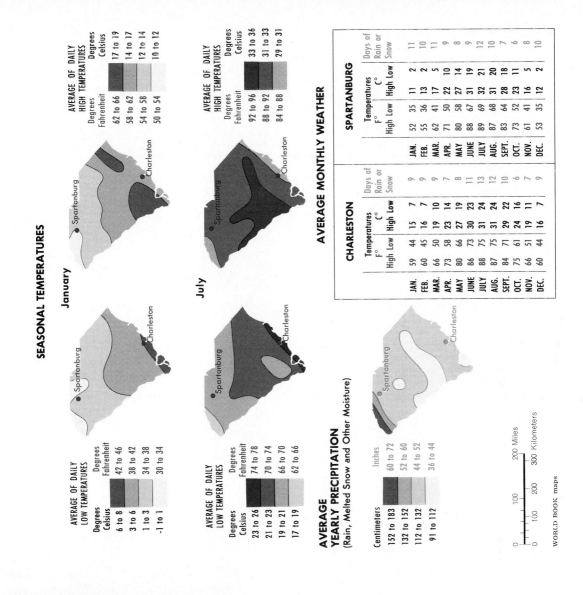

SEASONAL TEMPERATURES

January

AVERAGE OF DAILY LOW TEMPERATURES

Degrees Celsius	Degrees Fahrenheit
6 to 8	42 to 46
3 to 6	38 to 42
1 to 3	34 to 38
-1 to 1	30 to 34

AVERAGE OF DAILY HIGH TEMPERATURES

Degrees Fahrenheit	Degrees Celsius
62 to 66	17 to 19
58 to 62	14 to 17
54 to 58	12 to 14
50 to 54	10 to 12

July

AVERAGE OF DAILY LOW TEMPERATURES

Degrees Celsius	Degrees Fahrenheit
23 to 26	74 to 78
21 to 23	70 to 74
19 to 21	66 to 70
17 to 19	62 to 66

AVERAGE OF DAILY HIGH TEMPERATURES

Degrees Fahrenheit	Degrees Celsius
92 to 96	33 to 36
88 to 92	31 to 33
84 to 88	29 to 31

AVERAGE YEARLY PRECIPITATION
(Rain, Melted Snow and Other Moisture)

Centimeters	Inches
152 to 183	60 to 72
132 to 152	52 to 60
112 to 132	44 to 52
91 to 112	36 to 44

0 100 200	200 Miles
0 100 200 300 Kilometers	

WORLD BOOK maps

AVERAGE MONTHLY WEATHER

CHARLESTON

	Temperatures F° High	F° Low	C° High	C° Low	Days of Rain or Snow
JAN.	59	44	15	7	9
FEB.	60	45	16	7	9
MAR.	66	50	19	10	9
APR.	73	58	23	14	7
MAY	80	66	27	19	8
JUNE	86	73	30	23	11
JULY	88	75	31	24	13
AUG.	87	75	31	24	12
SEPT.	84	71	29	22	10
OCT.	75	61	24	16	6
NOV.	66	51	19	11	7
DEC.	60	44	16	7	9

SPARTANBURG

	Temperatures F° High	F° Low	C° High	C° Low	Days of Rain or Snow
JAN.	52	35	11	2	11
FEB.	55	36	13	2	10
MAR.	62	41	17	5	11
APR.	71	50	22	10	9
MAY	80	58	27	14	8
JUNE	88	67	31	19	9
JULY	89	69	32	21	12
AUG.	87	68	31	20	10
SEPT.	83	64	28	18	7
OCT.	73	52	23	11	6
NOV.	61	41	16	5	8
DEC.	53	35	12	2	10

Warm Summer Weather attracts sunbathers to Myrtle Beach, South Carolina's largest seashore resort. The 312-acre (126-hectare) Myrtle Beach State Park is a year-round vacation spot.

Tom Hollyman, Photo Researchers

SOUTH CAROLINA/Climate

South Carolina has a warm climate. July temperatures average about 81° F. (27° C) in the south and about 72° F. (22° C) in the northwest. January temperatures average about 51° F. (11° C) in the south and about 41° F. (5° C) in the northwest. The state's record high temperature, 111° F. (44° C), was recorded in Blackville on Sept. 4, 1925; in Calhoun Falls on Sept. 8, 1925; and in Camden on June 28, 1954. The record low temperature, –20° F. (–29° C), was recorded at Caesars Head on Jan. 18, 1977.

Yearly *precipitation* (rain, melted snow, and other forms of moisture) in most parts of South Carolina averages about 45 inches (114 centimeters). The mountains receive over 70 inches (178 centimeters) of precipitation annually. South Carolina gets little snow. Annual snowfall ranges from about 7 inches (18 centimeters) in the mountains to light traces of snow in the south.

Manufacturing is South Carolina's chief economic activity. Agriculture ranks second in terms of the value of goods produced. But tourism, a service industry, produces more income than agriculture does. Tourists spend about $2 billion a year in the state. The Piedmont has long been South Carolina's most important manufacturing region. Manufacturing is also important in the Atlantic Coastal Plain. Farms and the tourist trade thrive in many areas in the state.

Natural Resources. South Carolina's most important natural resource is its plentiful water supply. The state also has large forests and abundant wildlife.

Soil. The Atlantic Coastal Plain has some of South Carolina's best soils. Deposits of silt from rivers have left a black loam along the river valleys. A lighter loam covers other parts of the plain. A red soil covers the Piedmont and Blue Ridge.

Minerals. Large deposits of kaolin occur in Aiken County. The Atlantic Coastal Plains region also has deposits of limestone, peat, and sand and gravel. The Piedmont and Blue Ridge areas have clays, gold, granite, mica, sand, silica, talc, topaz, and vermiculite.

Forests cover almost two-thirds of South Carolina. The Low Country has thick forests of hickories, live oaks, magnolias, pines, red and white oaks, and sweet gums. Bald cypresses, black tupelos, cottonwoods, sweet gums, and tulip trees grow in the swamps. Longleaf pines and

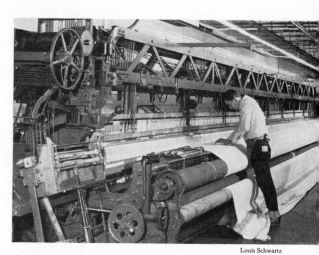

Louis Schwartz

Textiles rank as South Carolina's chief manufactured product. The textile factory above is in St. Stephen.

scrub oaks grow in the sand hills. Piedmont forests have beeches, maples, pines, tulip trees, and white oaks. Hemlocks, pines, and many broadleaf trees cover the Blue Ridge Mountains.

Plant Life. Palmettos, yuccas, and other subtropical plants grow along the South Carolina coast. Thick growths of dwarf white honeysuckle and sweet bay spread over large areas in the Low Country. Spanish moss hangs from many live oak and cypress trees. Other South Carolina plants include Carolina jessamine and the Venus's-flytrap, a rare insect-trapping plant that grows wild only in North and South Carolina. Brilliant patches of azaleas, mountain laurels, and rhododendrons blanket the South Carolina mountains in spring.

Animal Life. White-tailed deer live in the forests near the coast. A few black bears roam the swamps, where alligators sometimes can be seen lying in the sun. Fox squirrels, foxes, and wildcats live in the state's inland forests. Opossums, raccoons, and cottontail rabbits may be seen throughout the state. Short-eared marsh rabbits live along the coast. More than 450 kinds of birds, including wild turkeys, live in South Carolina. Few other states have so many kinds of birds.

People often see bottle-nosed dolphins, sharks, and sperm whales along the South Carolina coast. About 350 kinds of salt-water fishes live in the state's coastal waters and salt marshes. Fresh-water streams and lakes have bass, bream, rockfish, and trout.

Manufacturing accounts for about 89 per cent of the value of goods produced in South Carolina. Goods manufactured there have a *value added by manufacture* of about $9½ billion annually. This figure represents the value created in products by South Carolina industries, not counting such costs as materials, supplies, and fuel. South Carolina's chief manufactured goods, in order of importance, are (1) textiles, (2) chemicals, and (3) nonelectric machinery.

Textiles have a value added of about $2¾ billion yearly. South Carolina ranks second only to North Carolina in textile production. During the 1960's, the state's

Production of Goods in South Carolina

Total annual value of goods produced—$10,711,013,000

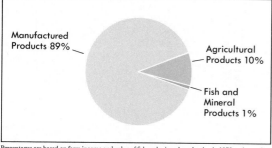

Manufactured Products 89%

Agricultural Products 10%

Fish and Mineral Products 1%

Percentages are based on farm income and value of fish and mineral production in 1979 and on value added by manufacture in 1978. Fish products are less than 1 per cent.
Sources: U.S. government publications, 1980-1981.

Employment in South Carolina

Total number of persons employed—1,241,400

		Number of Employees
Manufacturing	🧍🧍🧍🧍🧍🧍🧍🧍🧍🧍	392,300
Government	🧍🧍🧍🧍🧍🧍	237,300
Wholesale & Retail Trade	🧍🧍🧍🧍🧍🧍	223,900
Community, Social, & Personal Services	🧍🧍🧍🧍	158,000
Construction	🧍🧍	73,000
Agriculture	🧍🧍	54,000
Transportation & Public Utilities	🧍🧍	53,500
Finance, Insurance, & Real Estate	🧍🧍	47,500
Mining	🧍	1,900

Sources: *Employment and Earnings*, May 1981, U.S. Bureau of Labor Statistics; *Farm Labor*, February 1981, U.S. Department of Agriculture. Figures are for 1980.

textile mills began to increase their production of synthetic fabrics. Today, these fabrics rank as South Carolina's leading textile product. South Carolina has about 430 mills. Products of these mills include acrylic, polyester, rayon, silk, wool, plastic and glass fiber yarns; plastic-coated cottons; and rayon and nylon tire cord.

Most of the state's textile mills are in northwestern South Carolina. Important textile-manufacturing centers include Anderson, Greenville, Spartanburg, and York counties.

Chemicals have an annual value added of about $1½ billion. Chemical factories in Charleston, Columbia, Spartanburg, and many other South Carolina cities and towns produce fertilizer. Factories in Aiken, Anderson, Camden, Greenville, Irmo, Rock Hill, Spartanburg, and other cities make synthetic fibers. These fibers are later woven or knitted in other mills throughout South Carolina. The United States government operates a large chemical plant near the Savannah River, south of Aiken. The plant produces chemicals used in national defense and space programs. South Carolina also produces a variety of other chemicals.

Nonelectric Machinery has a yearly value added of about $806 million. The Greenville and Spartanburg areas lead the state in the manufacture of nonelectric machinery. The industry's chief products include textile and other industrial machinery and gas turbines.

Other Products. Clothing ranks fourth in value among the state's manufactured goods. About 315 South Carolina factories make clothing and other textile products.

Most of these factories use textiles woven in the state's mills. Other products manufactured in South Carolina include, in order of value, paper products; electric machinery and equipment; rubber and plastics products; fabricated metal products; lumber and wood products; and stone, clay, and glass products.

Agriculture. Farm products account for about 10 per cent of the value of goods produced in South Carolina. The state's farmers earn about $1 billion a year. South Carolina's 35,000 farms average 186 acres (75 hectares) in size. Farmland occupies about 40 per cent of the state, and about 40 per cent of that is used to grow crops. Most of the rest is covered by forests. South Carolina farmers sell much timber from the forests.

Soybeans are South Carolina's leading cash crop. They have an annual value of about $245 million. The state produces about 40 million bushels of soybeans annually. More South Carolina farmland is used for soybeans than for any other crop.

Tobacco is the state's second leading cash crop. It has a yearly value of about $173 million. South Carolina grows about 58,900 short tons (53,430 metric tons) of tobacco annually, and is a top tobacco-producing state. About a third of South Carolina's counties produce tobacco.

Corn is the third leading cash crop. It has an annual value of about $62 million. The state produces about 41 million bushels of corn yearly. Most of the corn grown in the state is used to feed animals, or in making corn meal, corn syrup, and grits.

Farm, Mineral, and Forest Products

This map shows where the state's leading farm, mineral, and forest products are produced. The major urban areas (shown in red) are the state's important manufacturing centers.

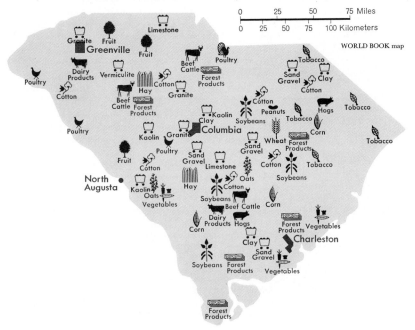

WORLD BOOK map

Webb AgPhotos

Tobacco is a major crop in South Carolina, one of the top tobacco-producing states. The South Carolina tobacco harvester shown above is cutting the entire plant from the ground.

Other Crops. Cotton and peaches are other important South Carolina farm crops. Farmers in most South Carolina counties grow cotton. Lee and Marlboro are the leading cotton counties. South Carolina ranks second only to California in peach production. Other farm crops in South Carolina include apples, cucumbers, forest products, greenhouse and nursery products, hay, peanuts, tomatoes, watermelons, and wheat.

Livestock and Livestock Products. Beef cattle are South Carolina's chief livestock product. Eggs rank second. Other leading livestock products of South Carolina include *broilers* (chickens 9 to 12 weeks old), hogs, milk, and turkeys.

Mining contributes about $122 million annually to the value of goods produced in South Carolina. Granite and limestone are among the state's most valuable mineral products. Granite comes chiefly from the Piedmont. Limestone is mined in the Atlantic Coastal Plain. South Carolina is a leading producer of *kaolin*, a kind of clay; and *marl*, a type of rock used in making cement and fertilizer. The state also ranks as a leading producer of mica and vermiculite.

Fishing Industry. South Carolina has an annual fish catch valued at about $26 million. About 21 million pounds (9.5 million kilograms) of seafood are caught annually. South Carolina ranks high among the states in shrimp caught. Other valuable catches include clams, crabs, groupers, oysters, and snapper.

Electric Power. About 46 per cent of South Carolina's electric power is generated by plants that use nuclear energy. The state has four nuclear reactors. One is in Hartsville, and the others are in Oconee County. Five more reactors were scheduled for completion during the 1980's. Another 46 per cent of South Carolina's electric power is generated by plants that burn coal, oil, or gas. The rest of the state's power is produced by hydroelectric plants.

Transportation. South Carolina has about 61,000 miles (98,200 kilometers) of roads and highways, of which about two-thirds are surfaced. Railroads operate on about 3,000 miles (4,800 kilometers) of track in the state. Eleven railroads provide freight service, and passenger trains serve four cities. The state has about 65 public airports, about 60 private airports, and 3 seaports—Charleston, Georgetown, and Port Royal. The Atlantic Intracoastal Waterway is South Carolina's chief inland shipping route (see ATLANTIC INTRACOASTAL WATERWAY).

Communication. About 20 daily newspapers and about 60 semiweeklies and weeklies are published in South Carolina. The *South Carolina Weekly Journal*, the state's first newspaper, was published for only six months, sometime between 1730 and 1732. Today, the state's largest daily newspapers include the *Anderson Independent*, the *Greenville News*, the *News and Courier* of Charleston, the *Spartanburg Herald and Journal*, and the *State* of Columbia.

South Carolina's first radio station, WSPA, began broadcasting in Spartanburg in 1930. The first television station, WCOS-TV, opened in Columbia in 1953. Today, the state has about 145 radio stations and 25 TV stations.

Indian Days. More than 30 Indian tribes lived in what is now South Carolina before white settlers came. The chief tribes were the Catawba, Cherokee, and Yamasee (or Yemasee). The Catawba belonged to the Siouan Indian language family, the Cherokee to the Iroquoian language family, and the Yamasee to the Muskhogean language family. The Indians lived in semipermanent log shelters. Most of them raised crops.

Exploration and Settlement. In 1521, Francisco Gordillo led a Spanish expedition that explored the Carolina coast. Gordillo came from Spanish-held Santo Domingo in the Dominican Republic. In 1526, Lucas Vásquez de Ayllón, a judge from Santo Domingo Island, tried to establish a colony in what is now South Carolina. He led about 500 men, women, and children from Santo Domingo to the Winyah Bay region. But the colony failed because of disease and bad weather, and the settlers soon returned to Santo Domingo. Between 1562 and 1565, French explorers tried to settle at Port Royal and at another place farther south. They failed, partly because they lacked food.

England claimed the entire North American mainland in the early 1600's. The English based their claim on John Cabot's voyage to America in 1497 (see CABOT). In 1629, King Charles I of England granted North American land to Sir Robert Heath. Part of the grant was a strip of land that included what are now the states of South Carolina and North Carolina. The strip extended to the Pacific Ocean. The land was named *Province of Carolana* (land of Charles). The spelling was changed to *Carolina* in 1663. Heath made no attempts

Important Dates in South Carolina

1521 Francisco Gordillo of Spain explored the Carolina coast.

1670 Englishmen established the first permanent white settlement in South Carolina, at Albemarle Point.

1719 South Carolina became a separate royal province.

1780 American forces won the Battle of Kings Mountain, a turning point in the Revolutionary War.

1788 South Carolina became the 8th state on May 23.

1832 South Carolina passed the Ordinance of Nullification.

1860 South Carolina seceded from the Union on Dec. 20.

1861 The Civil War began on April 12 when Confederate forces fired on Fort Sumter.

1868 South Carolina was readmitted to the Union on June 25.

1877 Reconstruction ended in South Carolina.

1890 Benjamin Tillman, a leader of small farmers, became governor.

1895 South Carolina adopted its present constitution.

1941 The Santee-Cooper Project was completed.

1953 Operations began at the Savannah River Plant of the Atomic Energy Commission near Aiken. The plant, now operated by the Department of Energy, produces nuclear materials.

1964 South Carolina voted for Barry M. Goldwater, the first Republican presidential candidate to carry the state since the Reconstruction.

1970 Three blacks won election to the state legislature. They became the first blacks elected to the General Assembly since 1900.

1974 James B. Edwards became the first Republican to be elected governor since 1874.

526d

HISTORIC
SOUTH CAROLINA

Battle of Kings Mountain, in which the British were defeated, was fought Oct. 7, 1780. It was the turning point of the Revolutionary War in the South.

Blackbeard and other pirates preyed along the South Carolina coast in the early 1700's. Many were hanged from the gallows on Charleston's Execution Dock.

Santee Dam, completed in 1941, harnessed the Santee River to provide hydroelectric power. The dam also made an abandoned canal navigable.

COLUMBIA ★

Rice Was First Raised successfully in North America near Charleston about 1685 by H. H. Woodward, from seed given to him by a ship's captain.

Savannah River Plant near Aiken makes nuclear materials. The plant uses about 750,000 gallons (2,840,000 liters) of water daily.

• Santee Dam

Charleston
•
James Island
Fort Sumter

The Civil War Began on April 12, 1861, when Confederate batteries bombed Fort Sumter in Charleston Harbor. Federal troops evacuated the fort on April 14.

Charleston Water Front in 1760

One of the Nation's First Museums

First Fireproof Building

**First Theater
First Opera Performance**

Charleston's Early Achievements include one of the first museums, founded in 1773; the first fireproof structure, built in 1822; the first opera performance, about 1702; and the first steam locomotive in service, in 1830.

Best Friend of Charleston

to establish settlements in the area of Carolina.

In 1663, King Charles II granted Carolina to eight English noblemen called *lords proprietors*. In 1669, the proprietors sent settlers to America. The settlers arrived in 1670 and set up South Carolina's first permanent white settlement at Albemarle Point, near what is now Charleston. The colonists moved to Oyster Point in 1680, and named the settlement Charles Town. The spelling was changed to *Charleston* in 1783.

Colonial Days. The proprietors wanted to limit self-government in Carolina. They also failed to protect the settlers when enemies threatened the colony. During Queen Anne's War (1702-1713), the colonists turned back French and Spanish forces at Charleston. They successfully defended themselves against attacks by the Yamasee Indians and against several pirate raids between 1715 and 1718. During these battles, the colonists received little help from the powerful proprietors. In 1719, the proprietors rejected laws requested by the colonists. As a result, the colonists rebelled against the proprietors that same year.

The South Carolina region was Great Britain's southern line of defense against French and Spanish attacks. Partly for this reason, King George I bought the South Carolina region from the proprietors in 1719, and made it a royal colony. Britain ruled the colony, but the people were allowed self-government. In 1729, the king bought the North Carolina region, and in 1730 he divided Carolina into two royal provinces—South Carolina and North Carolina. In 1732, the southern part of South Carolina became the colony of Georgia.

During the mid-1700's, many South Carolinians moved from coastal settlements to the Up Country. The Up Country population was also increased by waves of settlers from Pennsylvania and Virginia. By 1775, about 70,000 white persons and about 100,000 Negroes lived in South Carolina. Most of the Negroes were slaves.

The Revolutionary War. During the 1760's, Great Britain passed a series of laws that caused unrest in South Carolina and the other American colonies. Most of these laws set up new taxes or restricted colonial trade. Some South Carolinians, called *Tories*, urged loyalty to Britain in spite of the laws. But the majority of the people, called *Whigs*, favored independence.

The Revolutionary War began in Massachusetts in 1775. South Carolina became the scene of many important battles. In June, 1776, British land and sea forces attacked Charleston. But the colonists defeated the British in the Battle of Sullivan's Island. A second British attack on Charleston was turned back in 1779. The British captured the city in 1780. In August of that year, the British defeated colonial troops under General Horatio Gates at Camden. The British and their Tory allies then controlled most of South Carolina. Colonial victories in the Battle of Kings Mountain (Oct. 7, 1780) and at Cowpens (Jan. 17, 1781) turned the tide of war in the South. In 1781, colonial troops under General Nathanael Greene drove the main British army from South Carolina to Virginia. The South Carolina militia forced smaller British units from the area. Famous leaders of the militia included Francis Marion, called the *Swamp Fox;* Thomas Sumter, called the *Game-*

cock; and Andrew Pickens. The British evacuated Charleston in 1782. During the war, 137 battles or smaller fights took place in South Carolina. Most of them were fought between bands of Whigs and Tories.

On July 9, 1778, South Carolina *ratified* (approved) the Articles of Confederation, the forerunner of the United States Constitution. South Carolina became the eighth state of the Union on May 23, 1788, when it ratified the U.S. Constitution.

Nullification. South Carolina strongly supported state's rights and free trade. The state's people opposed federal tariffs because South Carolina's economy depended heavily on trade with European nations. Tariffs, of course, discouraged this trade. A depression hit the United States in 1819, and South Carolinians blamed federal tariffs for their economic problems. In 1828, Congress passed a law that raised tariffs even higher than before. This law was called the "tariff of abominations." Reaction against the federal government spread throughout the state. In 1828, Vice-President John C. Calhoun, a South Carolinian, wrote the South Carolina Exposition. This document declared that no state was bound by a federal law which the state regarded as unconstitutional. After another high tariff law was passed in 1832, South Carolina adopted an *Ordinance of Nullification.* This ordinance declared the tariff acts of 1828 and 1832 "null and void." President Andrew Jackson threatened to send troops to South Carolina to enforce the law. But Congress passed a compromise tariff bill in 1833, and the state repealed the Ordinance of Nullification. See NULLIFICATION.

The Civil War. Shortly after the nullification crisis, an antislavery movement gained strength in the North. In 1850, a dispute between the North and South arose over whether slavery should be allowed in parts of the West. South Carolina threatened to *secede* (withdraw) from the Union. But little support came from other Southern states, and South Carolina took no further action. On Nov. 6, 1860, Abraham Lincoln, a Northern Republican, was elected President. South Carolina feared Lincoln would use federal power to abolish slavery. On Dec. 20, 1860, South Carolina became the first state to secede from the Union. By the spring of 1861, ten other Southern states had joined the secession movement and had formed the Confederate States of America (see CONFEDERATE STATES OF AMERICA).

The Civil War began on April 12, 1861, when Confederate troops fired on Fort Sumter in Charleston Harbor. Fighting raged along the South Carolina coast throughout the war. A blockade of Charleston Harbor by the Union fleet ruined South Carolina's economy. In 1865, Union troops led by William T. Sherman destroyed many plantations in the state. They also burned Columbia, the capital. About a fourth of the 63,000 troops from South Carolina died during the war.

Reconstruction. During the Reconstruction period after the Civil War, Union troops occupied South Carolina and the other Southern states. The Republican party in the state was made up chiefly of Negroes, southern Union sympathizers called *scalawags*, and northern adventurers called *carpetbaggers*. The Republicans controlled the South Carolina government during part of the Reconstruction period, and had the support of the Union troops. In 1868, South Carolina adopted a new state constitution. The new constitution gave Negroes the right to vote. Congress readmitted South Carolina to the Union on June 25, 1868.

In 1876, Wade Hampton, a Democrat and a Confederate cavalry hero, defeated the Republican candidate for governor. The Republicans challenged the election results, and South Carolina had rival state governments for several months. President Rutherford B. Hayes withdrew the federal troops from South Carolina in March, 1877. Republican power then collapsed, and the Democrats gained control of the state.

Industrial Growth began in South Carolina during the late 1800's. Profits from agriculture had declined greatly after the Civil War. The decline was caused chiefly by competition from many new farms in the western United States. About 1880, South Carolina businessmen began expanding the textile industry. Hydroelectric power, rather than direct water power, became the source of energy for many textile mills. Thousands of poor farmers welcomed the chance to work in the textile mills, even at low wages. A number of textile companies moved from Northern states to South Carolina, partly to take advantage of this inexpensive labor.

During the late 1800's, a group of Democrats called *Tillmanites* gained control of South Carolina politics. The group was led by Benjamin R. Tillman. Before 1890, a group called the Bourbon Democrats ran South Carolina politics. The Bourbon Democrats were lawyers, planters, and businessmen whose strength was in the Low Country. Owners of small farms, especially those in the Up Country, protested the Bourbon rule after farm prices dropped. Tillman campaigned for widespread reforms in state government, and was elected governor in 1890. The Tillmanites rewrote the state Constitution, and all but eliminated Negro voting rights. Tillman became a U.S. senator in 1895, and remained a powerful force in South Carolina politics until his death in 1918.

After the United States entered World War I in 1917, South Carolina's textile mills produced large quantities of cloth for the armed forces. By 1920, the state's textile industry employed about 54,600 workers and was still growing.

The State Governors of South Carolina

	Party	Term		Party	Term
John Rutledge	None	1776-1778	Milledge L. Bonham	Democratic	1862-1864
Rawlins Lowndes	None	1778-1779	Andrew G. Magrath	Democratic	1864-1865
John Rutledge	None	1779-1782	Benjamin F. Perry	Democratic	1865
John Mathews	None	1782-1783	James L. Orr	Democratic	1865-1868
Benjamin Guerard	None	1783-1785	Robert K. Scott	Republican	1868-1872
William Moultrie	None	1785-1787	Franklin J. Moses, Jr.	Republican	1872-1874
Thomas Pinckney	None	1787-1789	Daniel H. Chamberlain	Republican	1874-1876
Charles Pinckney	None	1789-1792	Wade Hampton	Democratic	1876-1879
William Moultrie	Federalist	1792-1794	William D. Simpson	Democratic	1879-1880
Arnoldus Vander Horst	Federalist	1794-1796	Thomas B. Jeter	Democratic	1880
Charles Pinckney	*Dem.-Rep.	1796-1798	Johnson Hagood	Democratic	1880-1882
Edward Rutledge	Dem.-Rep.	1798-1800	Hugh S. Thompson	Democratic	1882-1886
John Drayton	Dem.-Rep.	1800-1802	John C. Sheppard	Democratic	1886
James B. Richardson	Dem.-Rep.	1802-1804	John P. Richardson	Democratic	1886-1890
Paul Hamilton	Dem.-Rep.	1804-1806	Benjamin R. Tillman	Democratic	1890-1894
Charles Pinckney	Dem.-Rep.	1806-1808	John G. Evans	Democratic	1894-1897
John Drayton	Dem.-Rep.	1808-1810	William H. Ellerbe	Democratic	1897-1899
Henry Middleton	Dem.-Rep.	1810-1812	Miles B. McSweeney	Democratic	1899-1903
Joseph Alston	Dem.-Rep.	1812-1814	Duncan C. Heyward	Democratic	1903-1907
David R. Williams	Dem.-Rep.	1814-1816	Martin F. Ansel	Democratic	1907-1911
Andrew Pickens	Dem.-Rep.	1816-1818	Coleman L. Blease	Democratic	1911-1915
John Geddes	Dem.-Rep.	1818-1820	Charles A. Smith	Democratic	1915
Thomas Bennett	Dem.-Rep.	1820-1822	Richard I. Manning	Democratic	1915-1919
John L. Wilson	Dem.-Rep.	1822-1824	Robert A. Cooper	Democratic	1919-1922
Richard I. Manning	Dem.-Rep.	1824-1826	Wilson G. Harvey	Democratic	1922-1923
John Taylor	Dem.-Rep.	1826-1828	Thomas G. McLeod	Democratic	1923-1927
Stephen D. Miller	Democratic	1828-1830	John G. Richards	Democratic	1927-1931
James Hamilton, Jr.	Democratic	1830-1832	Ibra C. Blackwood	Democratic	1931-1935
Robert Y. Hayne	Democratic	1832-1834	Olin D. Johnston	Democratic	1935-1939
George McDuffie	Democratic	1834-1836	Burnet R. Maybank	Democratic	1939-1941
Pierce M. Butler	Democratic	1836-1838	J. Emile Harley	Democratic	1941-1942
Patrick Noble	Democratic	1838-1840	Richard M. Jefferies	Democratic	1942-1943
B. K. Henagan	Democratic	1840	Olin D. Johnston	Democratic	1943-1945
John P. Richardson	Democratic	1840-1842	Ransome J. Williams	Democratic	1945-1947
James H. Hammond	Democratic	1842-1844	Strom Thurmond	Democratic	1947-1951
William Aiken	Democratic	1844-1846	James F. Byrnes	Democratic	1951-1955
David Johnson	Democratic	1846-1848	George B. Timmerman, Jr.	Democratic	1955-1959
Whitemarsh B. Seabrook	Democratic	1848-1850	Ernest F. Hollings	Democratic	1959-1963
John H. Means	Democratic	1850-1852	Donald S. Russell	Democratic	1963-1965
John L. Manning	Democratic	1852-1854	Robert E. McNair	Democratic	1965-1971
James H. Adams	Democratic	1854-1856	John C. West	Democratic	1971-1975
Robert F. W. Allston	Democratic	1856-1858	James B. Edwards	Republican	1975-1979
William H. Gist	Democratic	1858-1860	Richard W. Riley	Democratic	1979-
Francis W. Pickens	Democratic	1860-1862			

*Democratic-Republican

Du Pont Company

Chemical Plants, such as this one in Florence, produce fertilizer and synthetic materials. Chemicals rank among South Carolina's most valuable manufactured goods.

The boll weevil damaged much cotton in South Carolina during the 1920's. Many farmers began raising other crops, including fruits, tobacco, and wheat. But cotton remained the main farm product. The Great Depression of the 1930's caused widespread unemployment in South Carolina. Economic conditions improved as the depression eased in the late 1930's.

The Mid-1900's brought great economic growth to South Carolina as the state shifted from a chiefly agricultural to a more industrial economy. In 1941, the South Carolina Public Service Authority completed the Santee-Cooper navigational canal and power dam between the Santee and Cooper rivers. This $57-million project supplied electric power and helped industry. During World War II (1939-1945), many military bases were established in the state. Some of the bases were made permanent after the war.

In 1953, operations began at the $1,400,000,000 Savannah River Plant of the Atomic Energy Commission near Aiken. This plant, now operated by the Department of Energy, helped South Carolina become a leader in the production of nuclear materials.

During the 1960's, South Carolina industry continued to expand, largely through programs sponsored by the State Development Board. Various companies built manufacturing facilities worth nearly $4 billion.

In the mid-1900's, the Democratic Party lost much of its traditional control of South Carolina politics. In 1948, Governor Strom Thurmond of South Carolina was nominated for President by the States' Rights Democratic (Dixiecrat) Party. Thurmond received the electoral votes of four states—Alabama, Louisiana, Mississippi, and South Carolina. In the 1952, 1956, and 1960 presidential elections, the Democrats barely won South Carolina. Then, in 1964, the state's electoral votes went to the Republican candidate, Barry M. Goldwater, by a large majority. The state also supported Republican Richard M. Nixon for President in 1968. Thurmond, who had been elected to the U.S. Senate in 1954, left the Democratic Party in 1964 and became a Republican. In the mid-1900's, several Republicans were elected to the state legislature and some were elected mayors and city council members.

Since the late 1940's, South Carolina blacks had been voting in growing numbers. During the 1960's, blacks were elected to several local offices, including city council member and school trustee. In 1970, three blacks won election to the state legislature, becoming the first blacks elected to the General Assembly since 1900.

South Carolina schools changed greatly following the 1954 decision of the Supreme Court of the United States prohibiting compulsory school segregation. Traditionally, the state had operated separate schools for blacks and whites. In the 1960's, most of South Carolina's school districts became integrated.

South Carolina Today is encouraging further industrial growth. At the same time, the state has become increasingly concerned about air and water pollution. Pollution has caused special concern where industry is in or near recreation and historic areas.

Tobacco remains a chief crop in South Carolina. Income from tobacco is still high in spite of criticism that cigarette smoking is harmful to health. Increasing soybean production promises continued growth in agricultural income.

Blacks and white Republicans continue to take a larger role in South Carolina politics. More and more black voters are supporting the Democratic Party. As a result, an increasing number of black candidates are being elected and are influencing party policies.

Republicans are offering candidates at almost all levels of government. Many of these candidates are seeking offices traditionally held by Democrats without opposition. In 1972, Nixon carried South Carolina again, and Thurmond won reelection. In 1974, James B. Edwards became the first Republican to be elected governor of the state in 100 years. In 1978, Thurmond was again reelected. Democratic presidential candidate Jimmy Carter won South Carolina's electoral votes in 1976; but in 1980 Ronald Reagan, the Republican candidate, won the votes.   ERNEST M. LANDER, JR.,
                      and WILLIAM D. WORKMAN, JR.

SOUTH CAROLINA/Study Aids

Related Articles in WORLD BOOK include:

BIOGRAPHIES

CITIES

Charleston   Columbia   Greenville

HISTORY

Civil War   Nullification
Confederate States of America   Reconstruction
Fort Moultrie   Revolutionary War
Fort Sumter   in America

PHYSICAL FEATURES

Atlantic Intracoastal Waterway   Piedmont Region
Blue Ridge Mountains   Savannah River

OTHER RELATED ARTICLES

Charleston Naval Base
Congaree Swamp National Monument
Fort Sumter National Monument
Parris Island Marine Corps Recruit Depot

Outline

I. **Government**
   A. Constitution
   B. Executive
   C. Legislature
   D. Courts
   E. Local Government
   F. Taxation
   G. Politics
II. **People**
III. **Education**
   A. Schools
   B. Libraries
   C. Museums
IV. **A Visitor's Guide**
   A. Places to Visit
   B. Annual Events
V. **The Land**
   A. Land Regions   C. Rivers, Waterfalls, and Lakes
   B. Coastline
VI. **Climate**
VII. **Economy**
   A. Natural Resources
   B. Manufacturing
   C. Agriculture
   D. Mining
   E. Fishing Industry
   F. Electric Power
   G. Transportation
   H. Communication
VIII. **History**

Questions

What percentage of South Carolina's people live in rural areas?

Where did the Civil War begin?

Which non-Democratic presidential candidates have won South Carolina's electoral votes since Reconstruction?

What two groups began to take a larger role in South Carolina politics during the mid-1900's?

What school built the first separate college library building in the United States?

When was the Santee-Cooper Project completed?

Who were the *lords proprietors?*

What is South Carolina's chief economic activity?

Where was the state's first permanent white settlement?

What are the three main land regions in the state?

Additional Resources

Level I

BAILEY, BERNADINE. *Picture Book of South Carolina.* Rev. ed. Whitman, 1975.

BURNEY, EUGENIA. *Colonial South Carolina.* Nelson, 1970.

CARPENTER, ALLAN. *South Carolina.* Rev. ed. Childrens Press, 1979.

FRADIN, DENNIS B. *South Carolina in Words and Pictures.* Childrens Press, 1980.

LEE, SUSAN D. and J. R. *Eliza Pinckney.* Childrens Press, 1977.

LYMAN, NANCI A. *The Colony of South Carolina.* Watts, 1975.

STEEDMAN, MARGUERITE C. *The South Carolina Colony.* Macmillan, 1970.

Level II

CHANNING, STEVEN A. *Crisis of Fear: Secession in South Carolina.* Simon & Schuster, 1970.

CLOWSE, CONVERSE D. *Economic Beginnings in Colonial South Carolina, 1670-1730.* Univ. of South Carolina Press, 1971.

HOLT, THOMAS. *Black Over White: Negro Political Leadership in South Carolina During Reconstruction.* Univ. of Illinois Press, 1977.

JONES, LEWIS P. *South Carolina: A Synoptic History for Laymen.* 3rd ed. Sandlapper Press, 1979.

LANDER, ERNEST M., JR. *A History of South Carolina, 1865-1960.* 2nd ed. Univ. of South Carolina Press, 1970.

ROBERTS, BRUCE. *The Faces of South Carolina.* Doubleday, 1976.

SIRMANS, M. EUGENE. *Colonial South Carolina: A Political History, 1663-1763.* Univ. of North Carolina Press, 1966.

WALLACE, DAVID D. *South Carolina: A Short History, 1520-1948.* Univ. of South Carolina Press, 1951.

WOOD, PETER H. *Black Majority: Negroes in Colonial South Carolina, from 1670 Through the Stono Rebellion.* Knopf, 1974.

WRIGHT, LOUIS B. *South Carolina: A Bicentennial History.* Norton, 1976.

SOUTH CAROLINA, UNIVERSITY OF, is a state-supported coeducational institution. Its main campus, in Columbia, S.C., includes colleges of business administration, criminal justice, engineering, general studies, humanities and social sciences, journalism, librarianship, nursing, pharmacy, and social work; schools of law and medicine; and a graduate school. The university also has four-year campuses in Aiken, Conway, and Spartanburg, and five two-year campuses. It grants bachelor's, master's, and doctor's degrees.

The school was chartered in 1801 as South Carolina College. It is one of the oldest state-supported schools in the United States. For enrollment, see UNIVERSITIES AND COLLEGES (table).

Critically reviewed by the UNIVERSITY OF SOUTH CAROLINA

See also SOUTH CAROLINA (Education [picture: McKissick Memorial Library]).

SOUTH CAROLINA STATE COLLEGE is a coeducational college in Orangeburg, S.C. It has schools of arts and sciences, education, home economics, industrial education and engineering technology, and graduate studies. Courses at the college lead to bachelor's and master's degrees.

South Carolina State has cooperative education programs in agriculture and nursing with Clemson University. The college library has a special collection of material written about the American Negro. South Carolina State College was founded in 1896, and took its present name in 1954. For enrollment, see UNIVERSITIES AND COLLEGES (table).   M. MACEO NANCE, JR.

SOUTH CENTRAL STATES. See ALABAMA; ARKANSAS; KENTUCKY; LOUISIANA; MISSISSIPPI; OKLAHOMA; TENNESSEE; TEXAS.

SOUTH CHINA SEA. See CHINA SEA.

Tending Cattle on the Plains of South Dakota

SOUTH DAKOTA

The Sunshine State

SOUTH DAKOTA is a midwestern state of many startling and beautiful contrasts. The wide Missouri River flows southward through the middle of the state. Low hills, lakes formed by ancient glaciers, and vast stretches of fertile cropland lie east of the river. West of the river are deep canyons and rolling plains. The enchanting Black Hills rise abruptly in the southwest. Southeast of the Black Hills are the weirdly beautiful Badlands. South Dakota is often called the *Land of Infinite Variety* because of the many great differences in its landscape.

South Dakota is mainly a farm state. Farms and ranches cover about nine-tenths of the state. Sheep and cattle graze on the sprawling ranches of the western plains, and on smaller farms in the east. Crops are grown on the rich soil of eastern South Dakota. The state is a major producer of beef cattle, hogs, and sheep. It also ranks high in growing barley, flaxseed, oats, rye, spring wheat, and other crops.

Millions of tourists visit South Dakota every year. The Black Hills are one of the most popular vacationlands in the United States. Attractions in the Black Hills include Mount Rushmore National Memorial, also called the *Shrine of Democracy*. Heads of George Washington, Thomas Jefferson, Theodore Roosevelt, and Abraham Lincoln, 60 feet (18 meters) high, have been carved out of a granite mountain. The Mount Rushmore memorial is one of the largest sculptures in the world. Nearby, an even larger statue of the Sioux chief

Crazy Horse is being blasted out of a mountain.

Most of South Dakota's mineral wealth lies in the Black Hills. Gold was discovered there in 1874. Two years later, the rich Homestake *lode* (deposit) was discovered. The Homestake Mine is still one the greatest gold producers in the Western Hemisphere, and South Dakota leads the United States in gold production.

The history of South Dakota reads like an adventure story. It is a tale of daring fur traders, battles between Indians and white settlers, and stampedes for gold. Included in the story of South Dakota's development are such colorful names as Calamity Jane, George A. Custer, Sitting Bull, and Wild Bill Hickok. But the most important figure in the state's history has been the farmer. Courageous South Dakota farmers have clung to their land through droughts, depressions, and blizzards. They have made South Dakota one of the nation's great agricultural states.

South Dakota was named for the Sioux Indians who once roamed the region. The Sioux called themselves *Dakota* or *Lakota*, meaning *allies* or *friends*. The state's sunny climate earned it the nickname of the *Sunshine State*. The coyote is the state animal of South Dakota, which is also known as the *Coyote State*.

The geographic center of the United States is in South Dakota, 17 miles (27 kilometers) west of Castle Rock. Pierre is the capital of South Dakota, and Sioux Falls is the largest city.

528

H. Armstrong Roberts

Mount Rushmore National Memorial near Rapid City

Facts in Brief

Capital: Pierre.

Government: *Congress*—U.S. senators, 2; U.S. representatives, 1. *Electoral Votes*—3. *State Legislature*—senators, 35; representatives, 70. *Counties*—66.

Area: 77,047 sq. mi. (199,551 km²), including 1,092 sq. mi. (2,828 km²) of inland water; 16th in size among the states. *Greatest Distances*—east-west, 380 mi. (612 km); north-south, 245 mi. (394 km).

Elevation: *Highest*—Harney Peak, 7,242 ft. (2,207 m) above sea level. *Lowest*—Big Stone Lake, 962 ft. (293 m) above sea level.

Population: *1980 Census*—690,178; 45th among the states; density, 9 persons per sq. mi. (3 per km²); distribution, 54 per cent rural, 46 per cent urban. *1970 Census*—666,257.

Chief Products: *Agriculture*—beef cattle, hogs, milk, wheat, corn, soybeans, oats. *Manufacturing*—food products, nonelectric machinery. *Mining*—gold, stone.

Statehood: Nov. 2, 1889, the 40th state.

State Abbreviations: S. Dak. or S.D. (traditional); SD (postal).

State Motto: *Under God the People Rule.*

State Song: "Hail, South Dakota." Words and music by Deecort Hammitt.

The contributors of this article are Duncan J. McGregor, State Geologist and Professor of Geology at the University of South Dakota; Everett W. Sterling, former Professor of History at the University of South Dakota; and Anson Anders Yeager, Sr., Associate Editor of the Argus Leader *of Sioux Falls.*

Days of '76 Parade in Deadwood

South Dakota Division of Tourism

South Dakota (blue) ranks 16th in size among all the states, and 4th in size among the Midwestern States (gray).

529

Constitution. South Dakota is still governed under its original Constitution, which was adopted in 1889. However, the document has been *amended* (changed) many times.

A proposed amendment must be placed on the ballot in a regular statewide election. It may be proposed and placed on the ballot in any of three ways: (1) The Legislature may propose it by a majority vote in each house. (2) A group of citizens may propose an amendment by *initiative*. In this method, the citizens submit a *petition* (formal request) signed by at least 10 per cent of the number of persons who voted in the last election for governor. (3) A constitutional convention, approved by a three-fourths majority vote in each house of the Legislature, may propose an amendment. To become law, an amendment must be approved by a majority of the citizens voting on the issue.

Executive. The governor of South Dakota is elected to a four-year term and may not serve more than two terms in a row. The governor receives a yearly salary of $46,750. For a list of South Dakota's governors, see the *History* section of this article.

Other executive officials include the lieutenant governor, secretary of state, attorney general, commissioner of school and public lands, treasurer, and auditor. They are also elected to four-year terms. All may serve an unlimited number of terms.

Legislature consists of a 35-member senate and a 70-member house of representatives. Voters in 25 of the state's 28 legislative districts elect 1 senator and 2 representatives. Voters in the other 3 districts elect from 2 to 5 senators and from 4 to 10 representatives, depending on population. Members of both houses serve two-year terms. The Legislative sessions begin on the second Tuesday in January. Sessions last 35 days in even-numbered years and 40 days in odd-numbered years. The governor may call special sessions.

South Dakota voters can pass laws directly through their power of initiative. In 1898, South Dakota became the first state to adopt the initiative and referendum. If 5 per cent of the state's voters sign a petition for the adoption of a law, the Legislature must pass the measure. It is then put on a statewide ballot. The *referendum* allows voters to accept or reject measures approved by the Legislature. Any law passed by the Legislature must be submitted to the people if 5 per cent of the voters sign a petition asking that a vote on the law be taken. The petition must be completed within 90 days after the adjournment of the Legislature that passed the law. See INITIATIVE AND REFERENDUM.

Courts. The state supreme court is the highest court. It has five judges elected to eight-year terms. Each year, the judges select one of their number to be the chief justice. Voters in each of the eight judicial districts in South Dakota elect at least three circuit court judges to eight-year terms.

Local Government. South Dakota has 66 counties. Two counties—Shannon and Todd—do not have an organized government. Their county functions are administered by adjoining counties. Each organized county is governed by a board of commissioners of three to five members elected to four-year terms. Other elected county officials include the attorney, auditor, coroner, register of deeds, sheriff, and treasurer.

South Dakota has more than 300 cities and towns. The state constitution gives them the power of *home rule*. That is, cities and towns may operate under their own charters and adopt their own form of government. Most cities in South Dakota have the mayor-council form of government.

Taxation. Taxes and licenses bring in more than half of the state government's income. Almost all the rest comes from federal grants. Motor vehicle license fees, and taxes on sales and motor fuels provide most of the state's tax revenue. South Dakota also collects taxes on alcoholic beverages and tobacco. It does not tax property or personal incomes. Only banks and other financial institutions pay corporation taxes.

South Dakota Division of Tourism

Governor's Residence, in Pierre, was built in 1936. The building is located east of the State Capitol and is surrounded by landscaped grounds.

"Great Seal of South Dakota"

The State Seal

Symbols of South Dakota. On the seal, the smelter chimney represents mining, the plowman stands for farming, and the riverboat symbolizes transportation. The seal was adopted in 1889. The state flag, adopted in 1963, has the seal in the center. The gold circle around the seal represents the blazing rays of the sun. The blue field symbolizes South Dakota's clear skies.

Flower illustration, courtesy of Eli Lilly and Company

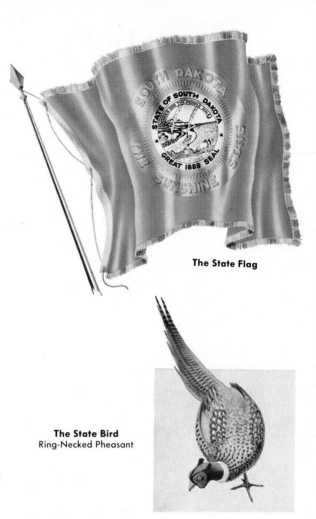

The State Flag

Politics. South Dakota voters have strongly favored the Republican Party throughout most of the state's history. The voters have elected Republicans in most of the elections for governor. South Dakota has voted for the Democratic presidential candidate in only four elections—the elections of 1896, 1932, 1936, and 1964. For South Dakota's electoral votes and for its voting record in presidential elections, see ELECTORAL COLLEGE (table).

During the late 1950's, South Dakota began to show signs of becoming a two-party state. In 1958, for the first time since 1932, the state elected a Democrat, Ralph Herseth, as governor. In the early 1970's, Democrats won most of the chief state offices, including the governorship. During the late 1970's, Republicans regained control of most of the offices.

The State Bird
Ring-Necked Pheasant

The State Capitol stands near the Missouri River in Pierre. The limestone and white marble building was begun in 1905. Pierre has been South Dakota's capital since 1889. Earlier capitals were Yankton (1861-1883) and Bismarck, N. Dak. (1883-1889).

South Dakota Division of Tourism

The State Flower
American Pasqueflower

The State Tree
Black Hills Spruce

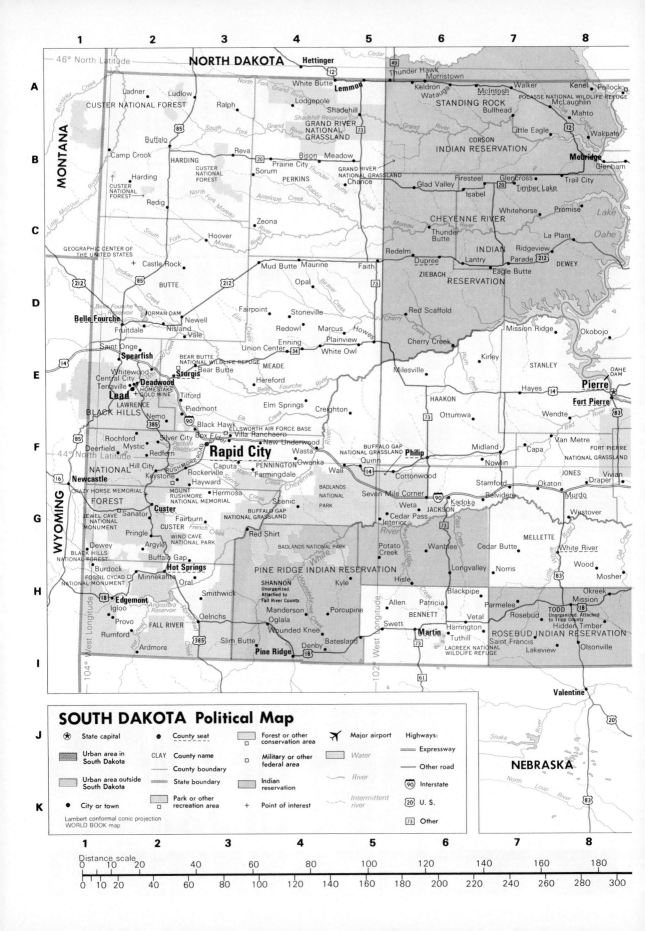

SOUTH DAKOTA Political Map

South Dakota Map Index

Population

690,178 ...Census ... 1980
666,257 ......"...... 1970
680,514 ......"...... 1960
652,740 ......"...... 1950
642,961 ......"...... 1940
692,849 ......"...... 1930
636,547 ......"...... 1920
583,888 ......"...... 1910
401,570 ......"...... 1900
348,600 ......"...... 1890
98,268 ......"...... 1880
11,776 ......"...... 1870

Metropolitan Area

Sioux Falls 109,435

Counties

Aurora .... 3,628. .G 12
Beadle .... 19,195. .E 12
Bennett .... 3,236. .H 6
Bon Homme ... 8,059. .I 13
Brookings .... 24,332. .E 15
Brown .... 36,962. .B 12
Brule .... 5,245. .G 11
Buffalo .... 1,795. .F 10
Butte .... 8,372. .D 2
Campbell ...... 2,243. .B 9
Charles Mix .... 9,680. .H 11
Clark .... 4,894. .D 13
Clay .... 13,135. .I 15
Codington .... 20,885. .C 14
Corson .... 5,196. .B 6
Custer .... 6,000. .G 2
Davison ...... 17,820. .G 13
Day .... 8,133. .C 14
Deuel .... 5,289. .D 16
Dewey .... 5,366. .C 8
Douglas .... 4,181. .H 12
Edmunds ...... 5,159. .B 10
Fall River ...... 8,439. .H 2
Faulk .... 3,327. .C 11
Grant .... 9,013. .C 16
Gregory .... 6,015. .H 11
Haakon .... 2,794. .E 6
Hamlin .... 5,261. .D 15
Hand .... 4,948. .E 11
Hanson .... 3,415. .G 13
Harding .... 1,700. .B 2
Hughes ...... 14,220. .E 9
Hutchinson .... 9,350. .H 13
Hyde .... 2,069. .E 10
Jackson .... 3,437. .G 6
Jerauld .... 2,929. .F 12
Jones .... 1,463. .F 8
Kingsbury ..... 6,679. .E 14
Lake .... 10,724. .F 15
Lawrence ..... 18,339. .E 1
Lincoln ...... 13,942. .H 16
Lyman .... 3,864. .F 9
Marshall ...... 5,404. .A 14
McCook ...... 6,444. .G 14
McPherson .... 4,027. .A 10
Meade .... 20,717. .E 4
Mellette .... 2,249. .G 7
Miner .... 3,739. .F 14
Minnehaha ..109,435. .G 16
Moody .... 6,692. .F 16
Pennington ... 70,133. .F 3
Perkins .... 4,700. .B 4
Potter .... 3,674. .C 9
Roberts ...... 10,911. .A 15
Sanborn .... 3,213. .F 13
Shannon ..... 11,323. .H 4
Spink .... 9,201. .D 12
Stanley .... 2,533. .E 7
Sully .... 1,990. .D 9
Todd .... 7,328. .H 7
Tripp .... 7,268. .H 9
Turner .... 9,255. .H 15
Union .... 10,938. .I 16
Walworth ...... 7,011. .B 9
Yankton ...... 18,952. .I 14
Ziebach .... 2,308. .D 6

Cities and Towns

Aberdeen ..... 25,956. °B 12
Academy .... .H 11
Agar .... 139. .D 9
Akaska .... 49. .C 9
Albee .... 23. .C 16
Alcester .... 885. .I 16
Alexandria .... 588. °G 14
Allen .... .H 5
Alpena .... 288. .F 12
Altamont .... 58. .D 16
Amherst .... .A 13
Andover .... 139. .B 13
Ardmore .... 16. .I 2
Arlington .... 991. .E 15
Armour .... 819. °H 12
Artas .... 43. .A 9
Artesian .... 227. .F 13
Ashton .... 154. .D 12
Astoria .... 154. .E 16
Athol .... .C 12
Aurora .... 507. .E 16
Avon .... 576. .I 13
Badger .... 99. .E 15
Baltic .... 679. .G 16
Bancroft .... 41. .E 14
Barnard .... .A 12
Batesland .... 163. .I 5
Bath .... .B 12
Belle
Fourche ..... 4,692. °D 2
Belvidere .... 80. .G 7
Bemis .... .D 15
Beresford ..... 1,865. .I 16
Big Stone City .... 672. .C 16
Bison .... 457. °B 4
Black Hawk .... 1,608. .F 3
Blunt .... 424. .E 9
Bon Homme Colony ..... .I 14
Bonesteel .... 358. .I 11
Bonilla .... .E 12
Bowdle .... 644. .B 10
Box Elder ...... 3,186. .F 3
Bradley .... 135. .C 14
Brandon .... 2,589. .G 16
Brandt .... 129. .D 16
Brentford .... 91. .C 12
Bridgewater ...... 653. .H 14
Bristol .... 445. .C 13
Britton .... 1,590. °A 13
Broadland .... 49. .E 12
Brookings .... 14,951. °E 15
Bruce .... 254. .E 15
Bryant .... 388. .E 14
Buffalo .... 453. °B 2
Buffalo Gap ...... 186. .H 2
Bullhead .... .A 7
Burbank .... .J 15
Burke .... 859. °I 11
Bushnell .... 76. .E 16
Butler .... 22. .C 14
Camp Crook ..... 100. .B 1
Canistota .... 626. .G 14
Canova .... 194. .G 14
Canton .... 2,886. °H 16
Caputa .... .F 3
Carpenter .... .D 13
Carter .... 7. .H 9
Carthage .... 274. .F 14
Castle Rock .... .D 2
Castlewood ...... 557. .D 15
Cavour .... 117. .E 13
Centerville .... 892. .I 15
Central City ...... 232. .E 2
Chamberlain ... 2,258. °G 10
Chance .... .B 5
Chancellor .... 257. .H 15
Chelsea .... 41. .C 12
Cherry Creek .... .E 6
Chester .... .G 15
Claire City .... 87. .A 15
Claremont .... 180. .B 13
Clark .... 1,351. °D 13
Clayton .... .H 14
Clear Lake ..... 1,310. °D 16
Clearfield .... .I 9
Colman .... 501. .F 15
Colome .... 361. .H 10
Colton .... 757. .G 15
Columbia .... 161. .B 12
Conde .... 259. .C 13
Corona .... 126. .B 15
Corsica .... 644. .H 12
Corson .... .G 16
Cottonwood .... 4. .F 5
Cresbard .... 221. .C 11
Crocker .... .C 13
Crooks .... 594. .G 15
Custer .... 1,830. °G 2
Dallas .... 199. .H 10
Dante .... 83. .I 13
Davis .... 100. .H 15
Deadwood ..... 2,035. °E 2
Dell Rapids ... 2,389. .G 16
Delmont .... 290. .H 13
Dempster .... .D 15
De Smet ...... 1,237. °E 14
Dimock .... 140. .H 13
Doland .... 381. .D 13
Dolton .... 47. .H 14
Draper .... 138. .F 8
Dupree .... 562. °C 6
Eagle Butte ...... 435. .D 7
East Sioux Falls .... .H 16
Eden .... 142. .B 14
Edgemont ..... 1,468. .H 1
Egan .... 248. .F 16
Elk Point ...... 1,661. °J 16
Elkton .... 632. .F 16
Ellis .... .G 15
Ellsworth* ..... 4,766. .F 3
Elm Springs
Colony .... .H 13
Emery .... 399. .G 14
Epiphany .... .G 14
Erwin .... 66. .E 14
Esmond .... .F 13
Estelline .... 719. .E 15
Ethan .... 351. .H 13
Eureka .... 1,360. .A 10
Fairburn .... 41. .G 3
Fairfax .... 225. .I 11
Fairview .... 90. .H 16
Faith .... 576. .C 5
Farmer .... 27. .G 14
Faulkton .... 981. °C 11
Fedora .... .F 13
Ferney .... .C 13
Firesteel .... .B 7
Flandreau ..... 2,114. °F 16
Florence .... 190. .C 14
Forestburg .... .F 13
Fort Pierre ..... 1,789. °E 8
Fort Thompson .... .F 10
Frankfort .... 209. .D 12
Frederick .... 307. .A 12
Freeman ...... 1,462. .H 14
Fruitdale .... 88. .D 2
Fulton .... 108. .G 13
Gannvalley .... °F 11
Garden City ...... 104. .D 14
Garretson .... 963. .G 16
Gary .... 354. .D 16
Gayville .... 407. .I 15
Geddes .... 303. .H 12
Gettysburg .... 1,623. °D 9
Glencross .... .B 7
Glenham .... 169. .B 8
Goodwin .... 139. .D 15
Greenway .... .A 10
Greenwood .... .I 12
Gregory .... 1,503. .H 10
Grenville .... 119. .B 14
Groton .... 1,230. .B 13
Grover .... .D 14
Hamill .... .G 10
Hammer .... .A 15
Harrisburg ...... 558. .H 16
Harrison .... .H 12
Harrold .... 196. .E 10
Hartford ...... 1,207. .G 15
Hayes .... .E 7
Hayti .... 371. °D 15
Hazel .... 94. .D 14
Hecla .... 435. .A 13
Henry .... 217. .D 14
Hermosa .... 251. .G 3
Herreid .... 570. .A 9
Herrick .... 115. .I 11
Hetland .... 66. .E 15
Highmore ..... 1,055. °E 10
Hill City .... 535. .F 2
Hillhead .... .A 14
Hillsview .... 9. .B 10
Hitchcock .... 132. .E 12
Holabird .... .E 10
Holmquist .... .C 14
Hosmer .... 385. .B 10
Hot Springs .... 4,742. °H 2
Houghton .... .A 13
Hoven .... 615. .C 9
Howard .... 1,169. °F 14
Hudson .... 388. .I 16
Humboldt .... 487. .G 15
Hurley .... 419. .H 15
Huron .... 13,000. °E 13
Interior .... 62. .G 5
Ipswich .... 1,153. °B 11
Irene .... 523. .I 15
Iroquois .... 348. .E 13
Isabel .... 332. .B 6
Java .... 261. .B 9
Jefferson .... 592. .J 16
Junius .... .F 15
Kadoka .... 832. °G 6
Kaylor .... .I 13
Keldron .... .A 6
Kenel .... .A 8
Kennebec .... 334. °G 9
Keystone .... 295. .F 2
Kidder .... .A 13
Kimball .... 752. .G 11
Kranzburg .... 136. .D 15
Kyle .... .H 5
La Bolt .... 94. .C 16
Lake Andes .... 1,029. °I 12
Lake City .... 46. .A 14
Lake Norden ...... 417. .E 15
Lake Preston .... 789. .E 14
Lane .... 83. .F 12
Langford .... 307. .B 13
Lantry .... .C 6
La Plant .... .C 8
Lead .... 4,330. .E 2
Lebanon .... 129. .C 9
Lemmon ...... 1,871. .A 5
Lennox .... 1,827. .H 15
Leola .... 645. °B 11
Lesterville .... 156. .I 14
Letcher .... 221. .G 13
Lily .... 38. .C 14
Little Eagle .... .B 7
Long Lake .... 117. .A 11
Loomis .... .G 13
Lower Brule .... .F 10
Lowry .... 22. .C 9
Loyalton .... 6. .C 10
Lyons .... .G 15
Madison ...... 6,210. °F 15
Manderson .... .H 4
Mansfield .... .C 12
Marion .... 830. .H 15
Martin .... 1,018. °I 6
Marty .... .I 12
Marvin .... 52. .C 15
Maxwell Colony .... .H 14
McIntosh .... 418. °A 6
McLaughlin ...... 754. .A 8
Meadow .... .B 5
Meckling .... .I 15
Mellette .... 192. .C 12
Menno .... 793. .H 14
Midland .... 277. .F 7
Milbank .... 4,120. °C 16
Miller .... 1,931. °E 11
Miller Dale
Colony .... .E 11
Mina .... .B 11
Miranda .... .D 11
Mission .... 748. .H 8
Mission Hill ...... 197. .I 15
Mitchell ...... 13,916. °G 13
Mobridge ...... 4,174. .B 8
Monroe .... 170. .H 15
Montrose .... 396. .G 15
Morristown ...... 127. .A 6
Mound City ...... 111. °B 9
Mount Vernon .... 402. .G 13
Murdo .... 723. °G 8
Naples .... 45. .D 14
Nemo .... .F 2
New Effington .... 261. .A 15
New
Underwood .... 517. .F 4
Newark .... .A 13
Newell .... 638. .D 2
Nisland .... 216. .D 2
Norris .... .H 7
North Eagle
Butte* ...... 1,354. .C 7
North Sioux
City .... 1,992. .J 16
Northville .... 138. .C 12
Nunda .... 60. .F 15
Oacoma .... 289. .G 10
Oelrichs .... 124. .H 3
Oglala .... .H 4
Okaton .... .G 7
Okreek .... .H 8
Oldham .... 222. .F 14
Olivet .... 96. °H 14
Onaka .... 70. .C 10
Onida .... 851. °D 9
Oral .... .H 3
Orient .... 87. .D 11
Ortley .... 80. .C 15
Owanka .... .F 4
Parker .... 999. °H 15
Parkston ...... 1,545. .H 13
Parmelee .... .H 7
Peever .... 232. .B 15
Philip .... 1,088. °F 6
Pickstown .... .I 12
Piedmont .... .F 2
Pierpont .... 184. .B 13
Pierre .... 11,973. °E 8
Pine Ridge ..... 3,059. .I 4
Plankinton .... 644. °G 12
Platte .... 1,334. .H 11
Pollock .... 355. .A 8
Porcupine .... .H 4
Potato Creek .... .H 5
Prairie City .... .B 4
Presho .... 760. .G 9
Pringle .... 105. .G 2
Provo .... .H 1
Pukwana .... 234. .G 11
Quinn .... 80. .F 5
Ramona .... 241. .F 15
Rapid City .... 46,492. °F 3
Rapid Valley* .. 3,265. .F 3
Ravinia .... 88. .I 12
Raymond .... 106. .D 13
Red Scaffold .... .D 6
Red Shirt .... .G 3
Redfield .... 3,027. °D 12
Ree Heights .... 88. .E 11
Reliance .... 190. .G 10
Renner .... .G 16
Revillo .... 158. .C 16
Richland .... .J 16
Ridgeview .... .C 7
Rochford .... .F 2
Rockham .... 52. .D 11
Roscoe .... 370. .B 10
Rosebud .... .H 7
Rosholt .... 446. .A 15
Roslyn .... 261. .B 14
Roswell .... 19. .F 14
Rowena .... .G 16
Rumford .... .I 2
Rutland .... .F 15
St. Charles .... .I 11
St. Francis .... 766. .I 7
St. Lawrence ..... 223. .E 11
St. Onge .... .E 2
Salem .... 1,486. °G 14
Scenic .... .G 4
Scotland ...... 1,022. .I 14
Selby .... 884. °B 9
Seneca .... 103. .C 10
Sherman .... 100. .G 16
Silver City .... .F 2
Sinai .... 129. .F 15
Sioux Falls .... 81,343. °G 16
Sisseton .... 2,789. °B 15
Smithwick .... .H 3
South Shore ..... 241. .C 15
Spearfish ...... 5,251. .E 2
Spencer .... 380. .G 14
Spink .... .I 16
Springfield ..... 1,377. .I 13
Stickney .... 409. .G 12
Stockholm .... 95. .C 15
Storla .... .G 12
Strandburg .... 79. .C 15
Stratford .... 82. .C 12
Sturgis .... 5,184. °E 2
Summit .... 290. .C 15
Tabor .... 460. .I 14
Tea .... 729. .H 15
Terraville .... .E 2
Thunder Butte .... .C 6
Thunder Hawk .... .A 5
Tilford .... .E 2
Timber Lake ...... 660. °B 7
Tolstoy .... 97. .C 10
Toronto .... 236. .E 16
Trail City .... .B 8
Trent .... 197. .F 16
Tripp .... 804. .H 13
Tschetter Colony .... .H 14
Tulare .... 238. .D 12
Turton .... 101. .C 13
Tuthill .... .I 6
Twin Brooks .... 87. .C 15
Tyndall .... 1,253. °I 13
Union Center .... .E 4
Unityville .... .G 14
Utica .... 100. .I 14
Vale .... .D 2
Valley Springs .... 801. .G 16
Veblen .... 368. .A 14
Verdon .... 7. .C 13
Vermillion ..... 9,582. °J 15
Viborg .... 812. .I 15
Victor .... .A 15
Vienna .... 90. .D 14
Vilas .... 28. .F 14
Villa
Ranchaero ... 1,666. .F 3
Virgil .... 37. .F 12
Vivian .... .F 8
Volga .... 1,221. .E 15
Volin .... 156. .I 15
Wagner .... 1,453. .I 13
Wakonda .... 383. .I 15
Wakpala .... .B 8
Wall .... 542. .F 5
Wallace .... 90. .C 14
Wanblee .... .G 6
Ward .... 43. .F 16
Warner .... 322. .C 12
Wasta .... 99. .F 4
Watauga .... .A 6
Watertown .... 15,649. °D 15
Waubay .... 675. .C 14
Webster .... 2,417. °C 14
Wecota .... .C 11
Wentworth ...... 193. .F 15
Wessington ...... 327. .E 12
Wessington
Springs ..... 1,203. °F 12
Westport .... 122. .B 12
Wetonka .... 22. .B 11
Wewela .... .I 10
White .... 474. .E 16
White Lake ...... 414. .G 12
White River ...... 561. °G 8
White Rock .... 10. .A 16
Whitehorse .... .C 7
Whitewood .... 821. .E 2
Willow Lake ...... 375. .D 14
Wilmot .... 507. .B 15
Winfred .... 81. .F 14
Winner .... 3,472. °H 9
Witten .... 134. .H 9
Wolf Creek Colony ...... .H 14
Wolsey .... 437. .E 12
Wood .... 134. .H 8
Woonsocket ...... 799. °F 13
Worthing .... 388. .H 16
Wounded Knee .... .I 4
Yale .... 136. .E 13
Yankton ...... 12,011. °I 14
Zell .... .D 12

*Does not appear on map; key shows general location.
°County seat.
Source: 1980 census. Places without population figures are unincorporated areas.

The 1980 United States census reported that South Dakota had 690,178 persons. The state's population had increased about 4 per cent from the 1970 census figure, 666,257.

South Dakota's percentage of urban dwellers ranks among the lowest in the nation. Less than half of the people live in cities and towns. The state has one metropolitan area—Sioux Falls (see METROPOLITAN AREA). For the population of this area, see the *Index* to the political map of South Dakota.

South Dakota has no great manufacturing industries to prompt the growth of large cities. Only Aberdeen, Rapid City, and Sioux Falls have populations of more than 25,000. Most South Dakota towns were established to serve the surrounding agricultural regions, and most lie east of the Missouri River, in the state's chief farming area. Many towns have also grown up in the Black Hills, where mining and the tourist industry prosper. See the separate articles on the cities of South Dakota that are listed in the *Related Articles* at the end of this article.

About 98 of every 100 South Dakotans were born in the United States. Most of those born in other countries came from Canada, Denmark, Germany, Norway, and Russia.

Roman Catholics make up the largest single religious group in South Dakota. Lutherans are the second largest group in South Dakota, followed by Methodists, members of the United Church of Christ, and Presbyterians.

Population

This map shows the *population density* of South Dakota, and how it varies in different parts of the state. Population density is the average number of persons who live in a given area.

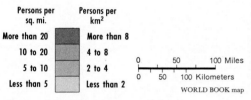

Persons per sq. mi.	Persons per km²
More than 20	More than 8
10 to 20	4 to 8
5 to 10	2 to 4
Less than 5	Less than 2

0   50   100 Miles
0   50   100 Kilometers
WORLD BOOK map

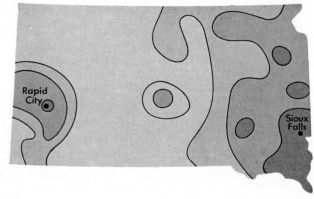

Schools. The first schoolhouse in the South Dakota region opened in 1860 in Bon Homme. The building was torn down after three months, and its logs were used in a stockade built for protection against Indian attacks. The first territorial legislature authorized a public school system in 1862. In 1864, a superintendent of public instruction was appointed.

Today, a seven-member state board of education makes policies for the public school system. The governor appoints the board members, with state Senate approval, to five-year terms. The state superintendent of elementary and secondary education serves as the board's chief administrative officer. Children must attend school between the ages of 7 and 16 or until they complete the eighth grade. For the number of students and teachers in South Dakota, see EDUCATION (table).

Libraries and Museums. South Dakota's first library, the Alexander Mitchell Library in Aberdeen, was established in 1884. Today, the state has about 125 public libraries and 14 bookmobiles.

The University of South Dakota campus in Vermillion has the largest library in the state. The library owns about 300,000 books. The Sioux Falls Carnegie Library has fine collections on art, biography, history, and music. The Historical Resource Center Library in Pierre has excellent materials on the history of South Dakota.

Museums are operated by the W. H. Over Museum at the University of South Dakota in Vermillion and the Museum of Geology at the South Dakota School of Mines and Technology in Rapid City. The Robinson Museum, which houses the collection of the South Dakota Historical Society, is in Pierre. Other museums in Rapid City and Sioux Falls exhibit historic items and Indian arts and crafts. Adams Memorial Museum in Deadwood has many pioneer items on display.

——— UNIVERSITIES AND COLLEGES ———

South Dakota has 13 universities and colleges accredited by the North Central Association of Colleges and Schools. For enrollments and further information, see UNIVERSITIES AND COLLEGES (table).

Name	Location	Founded
Augustana College	Sioux Falls	1860
Black Hills State College	Spearfish	1883
Dakota State College	Madison	1881
Dakota Wesleyan University	Mitchell	1885
Huron College	Huron	1883
Mount Marty College	Yankton	1936
North American Baptist Seminary	Sioux Falls	1858
Northern State College	Aberdeen	1901
Sioux Falls College	Sioux Falls	1883
South Dakota, University of	*	*
South Dakota School of Mines and Technology	Rapid City	1885
South Dakota State University	Brookings	1881
Yankton College	Yankton	1881

*For campuses and founding dates, see UNIVERSITIES AND COLLEGES (table).

SOUTH DAKOTA / *A Visitor's Guide*

About 6 million tourists visit South Dakota yearly. Most of them tour the famous Black Hills and Badlands areas. Visitors can see a large herd of buffaloes in Custer State Park near Custer. South Dakota offers visitors breathtaking scenery, and swimming, fishing, and other recreational facilities.

Places to Visit

Following are brief descriptions of some of South Dakota's many interesting places to visit.

Corn Palace, in Mitchell, is redecorated every fall with murals made of different colors of corn and other grains. Concerts, dances, and many other events are held in the building.

Crazy Horse Memorial, near Custer, is a gigantic sculpture of the great Sioux chief. It was being carved out of a granite mountain by Korczak Ziolkowski from 1947 until his death in 1982. Members of Ziolkowski's family continued the work after his death.

Deadwood, in the Black Hills, was a brawling mining town of the Old West. It has many reminders of its wild early days. Wild Bill Hickok, Calamity Jane, Preacher Smith, and other famous characters are buried in Deadwood's Mount Moriah Cemetery.

"Great Lakes of South Dakota" are formed by four huge dams on the Missouri River. These lakes—Francis Case, Lewis and Clark, Oahe, and Sharpe—offer fishing, boating, and other water sports.

National Forests, Parks, Memorials, Monuments, and Grasslands. South Dakota shares Black Hills National Forest with Wyoming, and Custer National Forest with Montana. The federal government also administers Badlands National Park, Wind Cave National Park, Mount Rushmore National Memorial, and Jewel Cave National Monument. Each has a separate article in WORLD BOOK. Three areas have been designated as national grasslands. These areas—Buffalo Gap, Fort Pierre, and Grand River—offer hiking and camping.

State Parks. South Dakota has 13 state parks. For information, write to Director of Parks and Recreation; Department of Game, Fish and Parks; Anderson Building; Pierre, S. Dak. 57501.

Model of Crazy Horse Memorial near Custer

Deadwood Chamber of Commerce

Mount Moriah Cemetery in Deadwood

Buffalo Herd in Custer State Park

© Robert E. Pelham, Bruce Coleman Inc.

Corn Palace in Mitchell

Cheyenne River Sioux Fair and Rodeo in Eagle Butte

Peter Platten, Cheyenne River Tribal Council

Czech Days Festival in Tabor

All photos from South Dakota Div. of Tourism unless otherwise indicated

Black Hills Roundup in Belle Fourche

Annual Events

Many South Dakota communities stage fairs, plays, pioneer celebrations, and rodeos. The famous Black Hills Passion Play is staged at Spearfish (see PASSION PLAY [picture]). Other outstanding annual events in South Dakota include:

January-July: Schmeckfest (food tasting) in Freeman (March); Czech Days in Tabor (June); Fort Sisseton Historical Festival in Fort Sisseton State Park (June); Long Winter Pageant in De Smet (June-July); Black Hills Roundup in Belle Fourche (July); Sitting Bull Stampede in Mobridge (July); Folk Art Festival in Brookings (July).

August-December: Days of '76 in Deadwood (August); Black Hills Motorcycle Classic in Sturgis (August); Rosebud Indian Reservation Fair and Rodeo in Rosebud (August); Cheyenne River Sioux Reservation Fair and Rodeo in Eagle Butte (August or September); State Fair in Huron (August or September); Corn Palace Festival in Mitchell (September); South Dakota and Open Fiddlers' Jamboree in Yankton (September).

537

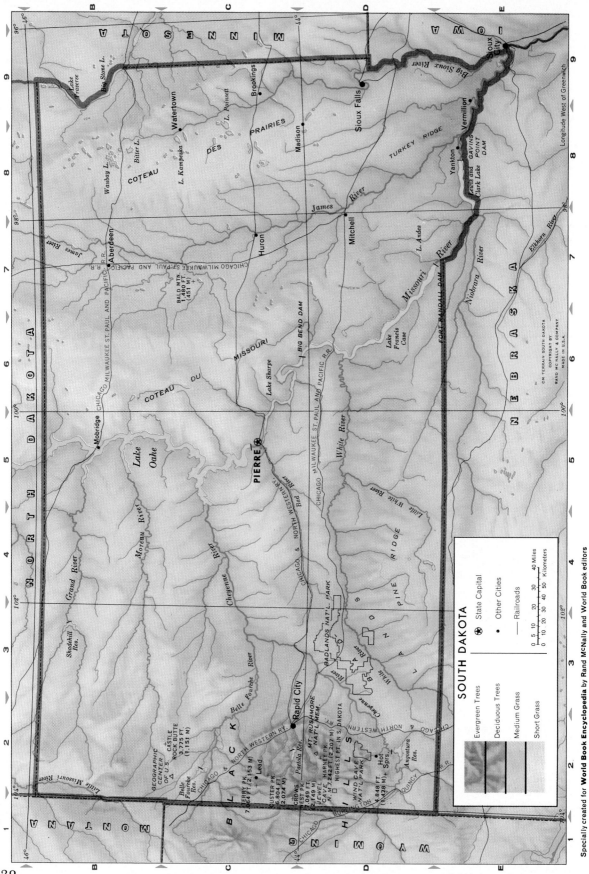

SOUTH DAKOTA

State Capital ⊛
Other Cities •
Railroads ——

Evergreen Trees
Deciduous Trees
Medium Grass
Short Grass

0   5 10   20   30   40 Miles
0 10 20 30 40 50 Kilometers

SOUTH DAKOTA / The Land

The Missouri River flows through the middle of South Dakota from north to south. The river marks the western edge of a series of glaciers that crossed eastern South Dakota during the Ice Age. The glaciers leveled off high places, filled in valleys, and created lakes. As the glaciers spread across the region, they dragged or pushed boulders, rocks, and other materials. When the glaciers melted, they left these materials behind. All the materials deposited by the glaciers or by their melted waters are called *drift*. These materials are either unsorted or laid down in layers. Materials deposited directly by the glaciers are unsorted, and are called *till*.

Land Regions. South Dakota has four major land regions: (1) the Young Drift Plains, (2) the Dissected Till Plains, (3) the Great Plains, and (4) the Black Hills. The Young Drift Plains and the Dissected Till Plains together are known as the *Prairies* or *Central Lowlands*.

The Young Drift Plains extend across most of eastern South Dakota. This region is marked by low, rolling hills and glacial lakes. Most of the region's lakes are near its eastern edge. Early French fur traders called the area the *Coteau des Prairies* (Prairie Hills). The northeastern corner of the Prairie Hills ends abruptly at a 600-foot (183-meter) *escarpment* (steep slope) along the Minnesota River Valley. A 300-foot (91-meter) escarpment marks the western end of the Prairie Hills along the James Basin. This basin occupies the western part of the Young Drift Plains. The basin is a flat to slightly rolling lowland. It extends in a wide belt down the width of the state. The James River winds through the basin. A 300-foot (91-meter) escarpment rises along the basin's western edge.

The Dissected Till Plains cover the southeastern corner of South Dakota. Glaciers left large deposits of till over the region. A deep cover of wind-blown soil particles called *loess* (cut up) the region, giving it a rolling surface.

The Great Plains cover most of the western two-thirds of South Dakota. The Missouri Hills form the eastern edge of the Great Plains. These hills are between the James Basin and the Missouri River. Rolling hills formed by glaciers mark the eastern part of the area.

Rugged ridges and valleys mark the western part. The chief features of the land west of the Missouri are rolling plains, canyons, and *buttes* (steep, flat-topped hills that stand alone). Many of the buttes rise from 400 to 600 feet (120 to 180 meters) above the surrounding plains.

Badlands are common in the Great Plains. Wind and water have worn the soft rocks of these regions into steep hills and deep gullies. The nation's most famous badlands lie southeast of the Black Hills. This area has little plant or animal life. See BADLANDS.

The Black Hills are a low, isolated mountain group in west-central South Dakota. The region has great beauty, with deep canyons and towering rock formations. The Black Hills also have rich mineral deposits, and thick forests of tall pines, spruces, and other trees. The state's highest point—7,242-foot (2,207-meter) Harney Peak—rises in the Black Hills. See BLACK HILLS.

Rivers and Lakes. The Missouri River is the state's most important river. The Missouri and its branches drain all the state except the northeastern corner. The Missouri's western branches include the Cheyenne, Grand, Moreau, and White rivers. The Big Sioux, James, and other rivers join the Missouri in the east.

Most of the state's lakes were formed during the Ice Age by glaciers. A series of glacial lakes stretches

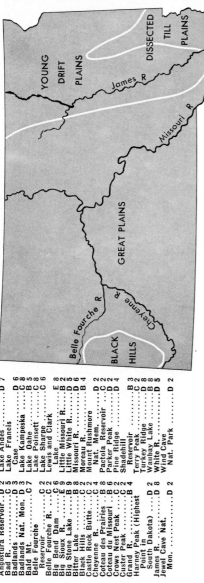

Land Regions of South Dakota

Flocks of Sheep graze in the Great Plains region of western South Dakota. Large-scale ranching in this "short grass country" makes the state a leader in the production of sheep and wool.

Grant Heilman

SOUTH DAKOTA

across eastern South Dakota. The state's biggest lakes are man-made, created by four dams on the Missouri River. The largest lake is Lake Oahe, 250 miles (402 kilometers) long, created by Oahe Dam. Fort Randall Dam created Lake Francis Case, 140 miles (225 kilometers) long. Lake Sharpe, a reservoir formed by Big Bend Dam, is 80 miles (130 kilometers) long. Gavins Point Dam forms Lewis and Clark Lake, 25 miles (40 kilometers) long.

Medicine Lake, near Florence in Codington County, has a salt content of more than 4 per cent, compared with about 3½ per cent for seawater. Its water was once believed to have medicinal qualities.

Badlands National Park, *right,* is a desolate area in southwestern South Dakota. Water and wind have worn away the land, leaving deep ravines, steep ridges, and colorful cliffs. The area is part of the Great Plains region.

Falls of the Big Sioux River are near the city of Sioux Falls. The river flows through the Dissected Till Plains region.

Lake Kampeska, *below,* lies near the center of a broad belt of lakes in South Dakota's Young Drift Plains region.

Towering Granite Boulders, *right,* form the tops of rugged mountains in the Black Hills. This region has many rich mineral deposits.

SOUTH DAKOTA / *Climate*

South Dakota is far from any large body of water. For this reason, the state has great ranges in temperatures. Temperatures over 100° F. (38° C) occur every summer. But even the hottest days are seldom uncomfortable, because the humidity is low. Below-zero temperatures are common on midwinter mornings. Average July temperatures range from 78° F. (26° C) in south-central South Dakota to 68° F. (20° C) in the Black Hills. The state's record high temperature, 120° F. (49° C), was set at Gannvalley (or Gann Valley) on July 5, 1936. Average January temperatures range from 10° F. (−12° C) in the northeast to 22° F. (−6° C) in the southwest. The state's record low, −58° F. (−50° C), was set at McIntosh on Feb. 17, 1936.

South Dakota's annual *precipitation* (rain, melted snow, and other forms of moisture) ranges from about 13 inches (33 centimeters) in the northwest to about 25 inches (64 centimeters) in the southeast. Most of the rain falls in the growing season, from April through September. The heaviest snowfalls occur in February and early March.

SEASONAL TEMPERATURES

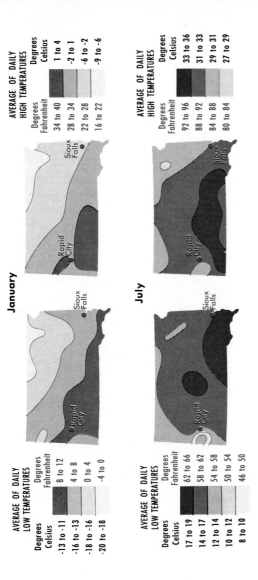

January

AVERAGE OF DAILY LOW TEMPERATURES

Degrees Celsius	Degrees Fahrenheit
-13 to -11	8 to 12
-16 to -13	4 to 8
-18 to -16	0 to 4
-20 to -18	-4 to 0

AVERAGE OF DAILY HIGH TEMPERATURES

Degrees Fahrenheit	Degrees Celsius
34 to 40	1 to 4
28 to 34	-2 to 1
22 to 28	-6 to -2
16 to 22	-9 to -6

July

AVERAGE OF DAILY LOW TEMPERATURES

Degrees Celsius	Degrees Fahrenheit
17 to 19	62 to 66
14 to 17	58 to 62
12 to 14	54 to 58
10 to 12	50 to 54
8 to 10	46 to 50

AVERAGE OF DAILY HIGH TEMPERATURES

Degrees Fahrenheit	Degrees Celsius
92 to 96	33 to 36
88 to 92	31 to 33
84 to 88	29 to 31
80 to 84	27 to 29

AVERAGE YEARLY PRECIPITATION
(Rain, Melted Snow and Other Moisture)

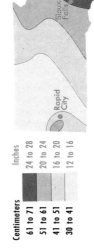

Centimeters	Inches
61 to 71	24 to 28
51 to 61	20 to 24
41 to 51	16 to 20
30 to 41	12 to 16

0	100	200 Miles
0	100 200	300 Kilometers

WORLD BOOK maps

AVERAGE MONTHLY WEATHER

RAPID CITY

	Temperatures				Days of Rain or Snow
	F° High	F° Low	C° High	C° Low	
JAN.	33	9	1	-13	7
FEB.	36	12	2	-11	6
MAR.	43	20	6	-7	9
APR.	57	32	14	0	8
MAY	67	43	19	6	12
JUNE	76	52	24	11	13
JULY	86	59	30	15	9
AUG.	85	57	29	14	8
SEPT.	74	47	23	8	6
OCT.	62	36	17	2	5
NOV.	47	24	8	-4	5
DEC.	37	14	3	-10	5

SIOUX FALLS

	Temperatures				Days of Rain or Snow
	F° High	F° Low	C° High	C° Low	
JAN.	24	4	-4	-16	5
FEB.	30	9	-1	-13	6
MAR.	42	22	6	-6	9
APR.	59	34	15	1	8
MAY	71	45	22	7	10
JUNE	80	56	27	13	11
JULY	88	62	31	17	10
AUG.	85	60	29	16	10
SEPT.	75	49	24	9	7
OCT.	63	37	17	3	6
NOV.	43	21	6	-6	5
DEC.	29	9	-2	-13	6

Early Winter Snow covers a pasture near Hermosa. Cattle can dig through the light snow to get grass. But ranchers must bring food to the herds when heavy snow falls in midwinter.

H. Armstrong Roberts

Agriculture is South Dakota's leading economic activity. Manufacturing ranks second and the tourist industry ranks third. Tourists contribute about $280 million annually to the state's economy.

Natural Resources. South Dakota's most precious natural resource is its fertile soil, the basis of its great agricultural economy. The state also has rich mineral resources. Most of the forest reserves are in the Black Hills. Other plant life and animal life are abundant.

Soil. The soils that cover most of eastern South Dakota developed from glacial materials. These soils are loamy, and range in color from dark brown to black. A belt of loess stretches along the east bank of the Missouri River. A deep deposit of loess also covers the Big Sioux River basin in eastern South Dakota. The soils of eastern South Dakota are good for growing corn, wheat, and other crops. Most of the soils west of the Missouri were formed from the weathering of various shales. These soils make good grazing lands.

Minerals. South Dakota's most important metallic mineral is gold. It is found in the Black Hills. A rich vein of gold ore, the Homestake lode, was discovered at Lead in 1876. This vein has yielded millions of tons of gold ore, and it still has reserves of about $17\frac{3}{4}$ million short tons (16 million metric tons). The gold ore contains some silver. Other metallic minerals in the Black Hills include copper, iron, lead, silver, and uranium. Molybdenum, uranium, and vanadium occur in southwestern and northwestern South Dakota. The northwestern counties have about $2\frac{1}{4}$ billion short tons (2 billion metric tons) of *lignite*, a low-grade coal. Much of western South Dakota lies in the great Williston Basin. This basin is a rich petroleum reservoir that extends across North Dakota and eastern Montana into southern Canada. Other minerals in South Dakota include beryl, clays, feldspar, granite, gypsum, iron ore, limestone, manganese ore, mica, quartz, and sand and gravel.

Forests cover only about 1,700,000 acres (688,000 hectares), or $3\frac{1}{2}$ per cent of South Dakota. Most of the forests lie in the Black Hills. These forests contain chiefly cone-bearing trees, including junipers, ponderosa pines, and spruces. Ashes, cottonwoods, oaks, and other hardwoods are scattered over the rest of the state.

Other Plant Life. The American pasqueflower, South Dakota's state flower, blooms on hillsides in early spring. Black-eyed Susans, goldenrod, mariposa lilies, poppies, sunflowers, and wild orange geraniums grow on the eastern prairies. Cactus plants are common in western South Dakota. Bluebells, forget-me-nots, lady's-slippers, and larkspurs blossom in the Black Hills.

Animal Life. White-tailed deer live in all parts of South Dakota. They are most numerous in the Black Hills and in the woodlands of the Missouri River Valley. Pronghorns roam the land west of the Missouri. Mule deer graze in the rocky butte and canyon areas of the west. Bighorn sheep, elks, and Rocky Mountain goats live in the Black Hills. About 8,000 buffaloes roam in various parts of the state. South Dakota has more buffaloes than any other state.

The ring-necked pheasant, the state bird, is found throughout South Dakota. Hungarian partridges nest in northern parts of the state, and sage grouse in the ex-

treme northwest. Sharp-tailed grouse and prairie chickens are found chiefly west of the Missouri River. Wild turkeys feed in the Black Hills.

Bass, bluegills, crappies, perch, walleyed pike, and other fishes are abundant in the glacial lakes of northeastern South Dakota. Among the fishes in the Missouri River and its branches are bass, catfish, northern pike, paddlefish, sauger, sturgeon, and walleyed pike. People who like to fish catch brook, brown, and rainbow trout in the rivers and lakes of the Black Hills.

Agriculture accounts for about 73 per cent of the value of all goods produced in South Dakota. The state's farm income totals about $2\frac{1}{3}$ billion yearly. South Dakota has about 41,000 farms and ranches. They range in size from about 100 acres (40 hectares) in the southeast to about 75,000 acres (30,000 hectares) in the west. They average about 1,109 acres (449 hectares).

Livestock and Livestock Products provide South Dakota farmers with about three-fourths of their total farm income. The state is a major producer of beef cattle, hogs, lambs, and sheep. Pastures cover about 22 million acres (9 million hectares), or about half the state. Beef cattle graze on the enormous ranches of the western section. The ranchers often ship their calves and yearlings to cattle ranchers called *feeders* in eastern South Dakota or in neighboring states. The feeders fatten the young cattle on grains, and then send them to market.

Production of Goods in South Dakota

Total annual value of goods produced—$3,235,885,000

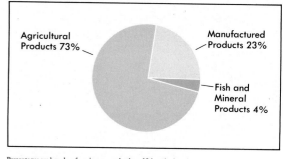

Agricultural Products 73%

Manufactured Products 23%

Fish and Mineral Products 4%

Percentages are based on farm income and value of fish and mineral production in 1979 and on value added by manufacture in 1978. Fish products are less than 1 per cent.
Sources: U.S. government publications, 1980-1981.

Employment in South Dakota

Total number of persons employed—301,100

		Number of Employees
Wholesale & Retail Trade	♟♟♟♟♟♟♟♟♟♟	64,600
Agriculture	♟♟♟♟♟♟♟♟♟♟	64,000
Government	♟♟♟♟♟♟♟♟♟	58,300
Community, Social, & Personal Services	♟♟♟♟♟♟♟♟	50,200
Manufacturing	♟♟♟♟	26,000
Transportation & Public Utilities	♟♟	13,400
Finance, Insurance, & Real Estate	♟♟	11,100
Construction	♟♟	10,700
Mining	♟	2,800

Sources: *Employment and Earnings*, May 1981, U.S. Bureau of Labor Statistics; *Farm Labor*, February 1981, U.S. Department of Agriculture. Figures are for 1980.

Most of South Dakota's sheep come from west of the Missouri River. The state is a leader in wool production. Most of the state's chickens, eggs, geese, and turkeys are produced in the east. South Dakota leads the nation in the production of geese. Farmers also raise dairy cattle throughout the eastern part of the state, and milk is an important product.

Crops are raised on about a fourth of South Dakota's land area. Most of the crops are grown east of the Missouri River. South Dakota is a leading state in the production of alfalfa seed, barley, flaxseed, hay, oats, rye, spring wheat, and sunflowers. Farmers in the southeastern section of the state harvest the most corn and oats. Soybeans are also grown in this area. Most of the flaxseed and much of the barley comes from the northeastern section. Rye and wheat are raised chiefly in the north, and winter wheat is grown in the south. Federal irrigation projects have made the land in some western areas suitable for growing crops. Crops grown on this land include alfalfa, corn, and milo.

Manufacturing accounts for about 23 per cent of the value of all goods produced in South Dakota. Goods manufactured in the state have a *value added by manufacture* of about $726 million yearly. This figure represents the value created in products by South Dakota's industries, not counting such costs as materials, supplies, and fuels.

South Dakota has over 700 manufacturing and processing plants. Most of them employ fewer than 50 persons. Food processing is the leading manufacturing activity, with an annual value added by manufacture of about $198 million. Meat processing and packing is the single most important industry in South Dakota. The largest plant is in Sioux Falls. Other meat processing and packing plants are located in Huron, Mitchell, Rapid City, Wagner, and Yankton. Poultry is dressed and packed in Madison, Sisseton, Watertown, and other cities. Creameries and dairy- processing plants operate in Aberdeen, Mitchell, Rapid City, Sioux Falls, and many other towns. Rapid City and Watertown have flour and feed mills. Feed mills also operate in Sioux Falls.

The manufacture of nonelectric machinery, such as farm and construction equipment, is South Dakota's second leading industrial activity. This production has an annual value added of about $111 million. Madison, Salem, Sioux Falls, and Yankton are the centers of this industry. Other important industries, in order of value, manufacture stone, clay, and glass products; electric machinery and equipment; lumber and wood products; and fabricated metal products.

Mining accounts for about 4 per cent of the value of all goods produced in South Dakota, or about $140 million yearly. About 65 per cent of this total comes from the mining of gold. South Dakota leads the states in gold production and supplies about a third of the nation's output. The Homestake Mine at Lead is one of the largest gold-producing mines in the Western Hemisphere. It has produced millions of ounces of gold since the first ore was mined in 1876. It yields all the gold produced in South Dakota—about 302,000 troy ounces (9,393 kilograms) annually.

Other leading mining products include stone, sand, and gravel. Quarries in Grant County are the state's chief sources of granite. Limestone is taken from extensive deposits in southwestern South Dakota. Sandstone comes from Hanson, Minnehaha, and Tripp counties. Sand and gravel is produced throughout the state.

In 1954, South Dakota drilled its first oil-producing well, in Harding County in the northwestern part of the state. Today, South Dakota has about 85 oil-producing wells in Custer, Dewey, and Harding counties.

Other minerals that are produced in South Dakota include beryllium, clays, feldspar, gemstones, gypsum, iron ore, lithium, mica, natural gas liquids, and silver.

Electric Power. About 70 per cent of South Dakota's electric power comes from hydroelectric projects. The rest is generated by fuel-burning plants. Four huge Missouri River dams—Big Bend, Fort Randall, Gavins Point, and Oahe—supply most of South Dakota's hydroelectric power. The swift streams of the Black

Farm and Mineral Products

This map shows where the state's leading farm and mineral products are produced. The major urban area (shown on the map in red) is the state's important manufacturing center.

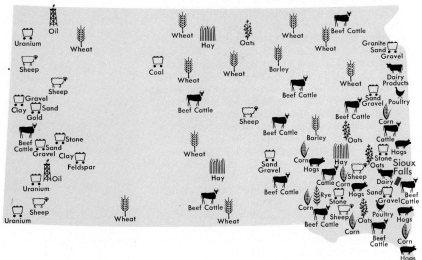

WORLD BOOK map

Hills are also used to generate electric power. See FORT RANDALL DAM; OAHE DAM.

Transportation. The wide Missouri River provided the first great highway into South Dakota. Early explorers, fur traders, and missionaries sailed up the river in canoes or flat-bottomed boats. In 1831, the first steamboat reached the site of what is now Fort Pierre. During the 1870's, gold was discovered in the Black Hills. Prospectors carved trails into the region as they rushed to the gold fields in stagecoaches and oxcarts. In 1872, the first railroad to enter South Dakota reached Yankton. By 1880, two rail lines crossed eastern South Dakota to the Missouri River. A railroad reached the Black Hills in 1886.

Today, five railroads operating on about 2,000 miles (3,200 kilometers) of track in South Dakota provide freight services. No passenger railroads cross the state. South Dakota has about 85,000 miles (137,000 kilometers) of roads and highways. About three-fourths of the roads and highways are surfaced. Commercial airlines serve nine cities and towns. South Dakota has about 140 airports.

Communication. South Dakota's first newspaper, the *Dakota Democrat*, was established in Sioux Falls in 1859. The oldest newspaper still published in the state is the *Yankton Press and Dakotan*. It was founded as the *Weekly Dakotian* in 1861, and became a daily in 1875. South Dakota has 12 daily newspapers, about 110 weeklies, and about 20 periodicals. Daily newspapers with the largest circulations include the *Rapid City Journal* and the *Argus Leader* of Sioux Falls.

The South Dakota School of Mines and Technology established the state's first radio station, WCAT. The station was licensed in Rapid City in 1922. The first television station, KELO, began operating in Sioux Falls in 1953. Today, about 60 radio stations and 19 television stations serve the state.

SOUTH DAKOTA/*History*

Indian Days. Three major Indian tribes lived in the South Dakota region before white explorers first arrived. The Arikara were farmers who made their homes near the mouth of the Cheyenne River, and north of the Cheyenne along the Missouri River. The Cheyenne Indians lived and hunted in the western part of the Cheyenne River area, and also along the White River and in the Black Hills. The Sioux, or Dakota, were hunters and warriors who followed the buffalo herds.

Exploration and Fur Trade. In 1682, Robert Cavelier, Sieur de la Salle, claimed for France all the land drained by the Mississippi River system. This vast territory included what is now South Dakota, because the waters of the Missouri River flow into the Mississippi.

The French-Canadian explorers François and Louis-Joseph La Vérendrye were the first white persons known to have visited the South Dakota area. In 1743, the two brothers buried a small lead plate near the site of present-day Fort Pierre to prove they had been there. Schoolchildren found the plate in 1913, and the South Dakota State Historical Museum now owns it.

540d

HISTORIC SOUTH DAKOTA

Castle Rock

● Deadwood

Rapid City

Geographic Center of the U.S. was located 11 miles (18 kilometers) west of Castle Rock when Alaska became a state in 1959, and 6 miles (10 kilometers) farther west with Hawaiian statehood later that year.

Gold in the Black Hills was discovered in 1874, when General George A. Custer led an expedition to explore the area. The Homestake Mine still leads in U.S. gold production.

The Balloon *Explorer II,* which cast off near Rapid City in 1935, soared to a height of 72,395 feet (22,066 meters). This record stood for 21 years, but has since been broken several times.

Fort Randall Dam, completed in 1956, crosses the Missouri River near Lake Andes. It is 165 feet (50 meters) high and 10,700 feet (3,261 meters) long.

South Dakota Dept. of Highways

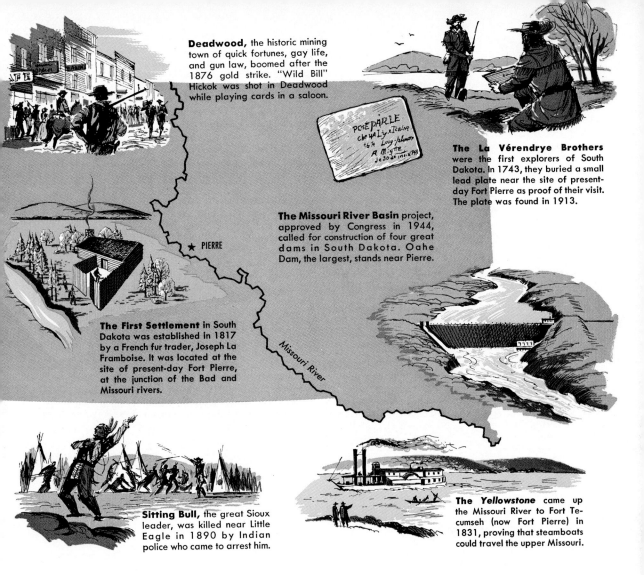

Deadwood, the historic mining town of quick fortunes, gay life, and gun law, boomed after the 1876 gold strike. "Wild Bill" Hickok was shot in Deadwood while playing cards in a saloon.

The La Vérendrye Brothers were the first explorers of South Dakota. In 1743, they buried a small lead plate near the site of present-day Fort Pierre as proof of their visit. The plate was found in 1913.

★ PIERRE

The Missouri River Basin project, approved by Congress in 1944, called for construction of four great dams in South Dakota. Oahe Dam, the largest, stands near Pierre.

The First Settlement in South Dakota was established in 1817 by a French fur trader, Joseph La Framboise. It was located at the site of present-day Fort Pierre, at the junction of the Bad and Missouri rivers.

Missouri River

Sitting Bull, the great Sioux leader, was killed near Little Eagle in 1890 by Indian police who came to arrest him.

The *Yellowstone* came up the Missouri River to Fort Tecumseh (now Fort Pierre) in 1831, proving that steamboats could travel the upper Missouri.

In 1762, France gave its land west of the Mississippi River to Spain. Spain returned it to France in 1800. In 1803, the United States bought this territory, called Louisiana, from France (see LOUISIANA PURCHASE).

About 1785, Pierre Dorion, a French fur trader, arrived in the lower James River Valley, near what is now Yankton. He became the first white man to settle permanently in the South Dakota region.

In 1804, President Thomas Jefferson sent Meriwether Lewis and William Clark to explore the Louisiana Territory and to blaze a trail to the Pacific Ocean. In August, the explorers camped in the South Dakota region for the first time, near what is now Elk Point. They followed the Missouri River through the region. Lewis and Clark passed through again in 1806 on their return from the Pacific. Their reports of the abundant fur-bearing animals in the region attracted an increased number of fur traders. The explorers had also established friendly relations with many Indian tribes.

The most important trading post was built in 1817 at the mouth of the Bad River, on the site of present-

day Fort Pierre. This lonely post became the first permanent settlement in the South Dakota region. It was established by Joseph La Framboise, a French trader.

The first large-scale military action against South Dakota Indians took place in 1823. The Arikara tribe attacked a fur-trading party led by General William Ashley, lieutenant governor of Missouri. The federal government sent troops under Colonel Henry Leavenworth to punish the tribe. The Sioux, traditional enemies of the Arikara, joined in fighting them.

In 1831, the steamboat *Yellowstone* sailed up the Missouri River from St. Louis to Fort Tecumseh (now Fort Pierre). The *Yellowstone* proved that steamboats could travel the upper Missouri. This development further spurred the fur trade in South Dakota. Large cargoes could be shipped in far less time than it took for flat-bottomed boats that were moved by the river currents. The fur trade thrived for several years, but began to decline by 1850. The number of fur-bearing animals had started to decrease, and the demand for furs fell as silk became more fashionable.

Agricultural Settlement. The land that became North Dakota and South Dakota was part of the Missouri Territory between 1812 and 1834. The eastern section later belonged, in turn, to the Michigan, Wisconsin, Iowa, and Minnesota territories. The western section remained part of the Missouri Territory until 1854, when it became part of the Nebraska Territory.

Before the 1850's, all white settlement in the South Dakota region had been along the Missouri River and had been related to the fur trade. Agricultural settlement began in the eastern section during the late 1850's.

In 1857, Congress passed the Minnesota statehood bill. This bill set the new state's western border east of the Big Sioux River. But nothing was done about the rich farmland westward to the Missouri River. Some businessmen and politicians saw a chance to make money. They quickly formed land companies, gained control of choice locations, and laid out townsites. Settlements were established at Sioux Falls, Medary, Flandreau, and other points. In 1858, the Sioux signed a treaty with the government giving up their land in the southeastern corner between the Big Sioux and Missouri rivers. The opening of this land attracted more settlers to the South Dakota region. Yankton, Vermillion, and Bon Homme were founded in 1859.

Territorial Days. Congress created the Dakota Territory in 1861. It consisted of present-day North and South Dakota, and much of Montana and Wyoming. William Jayne was the first governor of the Dakota Territory, and Yankton was the capital.

Indian wars prevented rapid settlement of the terri-

Important Dates in South Dakota

1682 Robert Cavelier, Sieur de la Salle, claimed for France all the land drained by the Mississippi River. This land included the South Dakota region.

1743 François and Louis-Joseph La Vérendrye were the first white men known to have visited the South Dakota region.

1803 The United States acquired South Dakota through the Louisiana Purchase.

1804, 1806 Meriwether Lewis and William Clark passed through South Dakota on their expedition to and from the Pacific Ocean.

1817 Joseph La Framboise established the first permanent settlement in South Dakota at what is now Fort Pierre.

1831 The first steamboat reached Fort Tecumseh (now Fort Pierre).

1861 Congress created the Dakota Territory.

1868 The Laramie Treaty ended Red Cloud's War.

1874 Gold was discovered in the Black Hills.

1889 South Dakota became the 40th state on November 2.

1927 Gutzon Borglum began work on Mount Rushmore National Memorial.

1930's South Dakota suffered its worst drought.

1944 Congress authorized construction of Fort Randall, Oahe, Gavins Point, and Big Bend dams in South Dakota.

1962 Titan missiles became operational in South Dakota.

1963 Minuteman missiles became operational in South Dakota.

1973 A group of armed Indians seized the village of Wounded Knee and occupied it for 71 days.

1980 The U.S. Supreme Court ordered the federal government to pay South Dakota Indian tribes $122\frac{1}{2}$ million for land seized by the government in 1877.

tory during the 1860's. One of the most important wars was Red Cloud's War, named for Chief Red Cloud of the Sioux. The government planned to build a road across the Powder River country to newly discovered gold fields in Wyoming. At the time, Wyoming was part of the Dakota Territory. Red Cloud believed the road would ruin the Indians' hunting grounds. In 1866, the Sioux attacked troops sent to make a survey for the road. The Indians continued their raids until 1868, when the government met their demands. In the Laramie Treaty signed that year, the government agreed to give up its military posts in the Powder River country. The government also promised not to build any roads through the area. The treaty created the Great Sioux Reservation, which covered all the land in present-day South Dakota west of the Missouri River.

In 1874, Lieutenant Colonel George A. Custer violated the Laramie Treaty when he led a military expedition into the Black Hills. The government had ordered him to investigate reports of gold in the mountains. The soldiers discovered gold near the present town of Custer. The news brought a rush of prospectors to the area. In 1876, prospectors discovered far richer deposits of gold in the area between the present towns of Lead and Deadwood. Another stampede of gold seekers followed. The town of Deadwood sprang up as the center of mining operations. It became a brawling, wide-open town, and won a reputation as the most lawless settlement on the frontier. Wild Bill Hickok, Calamity Jane, and other citizens of Deadwood became legends.

The invasion of the Black Hills by white men caused a series of Indian uprisings led by Crazy Horse and Sitting Bull. But in 1876, the Indians signed a new treaty giving up their claims to the Black Hills. Most of the Sioux surrendered and settled on reservations west of the Missouri River. Sitting Bull fled to Canada.

In 1881, Sitting Bull returned to the South Dakota region. He settled on Standing Rock Reservation in 1883. In 1890, a religious movement spread among the Sioux. This movement, called the Ghost Dance, was started by an Indian named Wovoka (see WOVOKA). Army leaders feared the Ghost Dance would lead to another Sioux uprising. They sent Indian police to arrest Sitting Bull, but he resisted and was killed. Some of Sitting Bull's followers fled the reservation and joined Chief Big Foot's band of Sioux on the Cheyenne River. Federal troops caught up with the Indians and took them to a cavalry camp on Wounded Knee Creek. There, the soldiers began to disarm the Sioux. A bloody battle began when someone fired a rifle. The soldiers massacred over 200 Indian men, women, and children. The Battle of Wounded Knee was the last big fight between Indians and white men on the northern plains. See INDIAN WARS (The Sioux Wars).

Statehood. A great land boom followed the discovery of gold in the Black Hills. Thousands came to seek gold. But many more came to farm in other sections of South Dakota. An enormous land rush began in 1878. Between 1878 and 1887, farmers and speculators poured into South Dakota. They acquired more than 24 million acres (9.7 million hectares) of public lands offered by the government. In 1870, the region had a population of less than 12,000. By 1890, the population had soared to 348,600. Most of the settlers came from neighboring states, but many came from Germany, Great

Boom Town of Deadwood sprang up in 1876 after rich gold deposits were found in the Black Hills. The Homestake, one of the richest gold mines in the Western Hemisphere, was established in Lead at that time. It is still in operation.

Britain, Norway, Russia, and other European countries.

Railroad building also boomed during this period. By 1880, two railroads had crossed eastern South Dakota to the Missouri River. In 1886, a railroad reached the Black Hills. Many towns sprang up along the rail lines. During the late 1870's and the 1880's, cattle ranchers entered the open rangeland west of the Missouri. The rush of miners and merchants to the Black Hills and the needs of the Indian agencies and military posts had created a heavy demand for meat.

During the 1870's, a movement began to divide the Dakota Territory into two parts. The major population centers had grown up far apart—in the northeastern and southeastern corners of the territory. The two groups of settlers wanted to develop separate governments. In February, 1889, Congress set the present boundary between South Dakota and North Dakota. It also passed an *enabling act*, which allowed the two regions to set up the machinery to become states (see ENABLING ACT). On Nov. 2, 1889, North Dakota and South Dakota entered the Union as the 39th and 40th states. South Dakotans elected Arthur C. Mellette, a Republican, as their first governor. Pierre became the state capital in 1889, shortly after South Dakota gained statehood.

The Early 1900's. The population of South Dakota had climbed to almost 350,000 by the time it became a state. But little growth occurred during the first 10 years of statehood. A severe drought began in 1889, and lasted until 1897. In 1890, part of the Great Sioux Reservation between the White and Cheyenne rivers was opened to settlement. But few settlers came.

Prosperity returned to South Dakota in the early 1900's. The drought had ended, and prices for farm crops were good. The government opened more new Indian lands in the west, and thousands of settlers poured into the state. Some of this land was offered through great land lotteries. People registered for land and received claims if they were lucky in the lottery drawings. Special trains brought people from all parts of the United States to take part in the lotteries.

By 1910, South Dakota's population had soared to almost 584,000. Between 1900 and 1910, the railroads added more than 1,100 miles (1,770 kilometers) of track in the state. Most of it was laid west of the Missouri River to serve the growing sheep and cattle ranches.

State Experiments. The prosperity and population growth of the first 10 years of the 1900's ended in 1911. Drought again hit the state. In 1915, South Dakota had about the same number of persons it had in 1910.

In 1915, a state law was passed guaranteeing the safety of bank deposits. This law was the first step in a program designed to promote the social and economic welfare of South Dakota's people. Later, the state loaned millions of dollars to farmers. The state also bought a coal mine, built a cement-making plant, and operated an insurance program against damage by hail. By 1932, all except the cement plant had failed because of mismanagement.

The prices of South Dakota's farm products increased after the United States entered World War I in 1917. The value of the state's farmland doubled. The 1920's were years of good rainfall and fine crops. But the state's economy suffered after 1925 because of lower farm prices and bank failures. Then, in 1930, the worst drought and grasshopper plague in South Dakota's history began. Except for some relief in 1932 and 1935, the drought lasted for 10 years. It was accompanied by great dust storms called *black blizzards*. In addition, the entire nation was hit by the Great Depression. Prices for South Dakota's farm products sank lower and lower.

SOUTH DAKOTA

The population of the state also began to decline. In 1930, South Dakota's population had reached a record 692,849. By 1940, it had fallen to 642,961.

The federal government provided money and jobs to help the distressed farmers. The Civilian Conservation Corps (CCC) gave thousands of young men jobs in the forests of the Black Hills. The Works Progress Administration (WPA) provided money to construct bridges, buildings, and other projects. The government also helped farmers plant wheatlands with grasses whose roots reach deep for moisture and hold the soil in place.

The Mid-1900's. During World War II (1939-1945), South Dakota farmers broke production records in supplying food. The increased use of machinery enabled farmers to do more work but, at the same time, made many farmworkers jobless. Thousands of farmworkers moved to towns and cities in search of jobs, but many could not find employment. As a result, large numbers of people—mostly young persons—left the state. To decrease its dependence on farming, South Dakota started a drive to broaden its economy. This effort included developing the Missouri River Basin, increasing tourism, and attracting new industry.

In 1944, Congress authorized the Missouri River Basin Project (now the Pick-Sloan Missouri Basin Program). This huge program was designed to provide electric power, flood control, and irrigation throughout the basin. Part of the project called for construction of four hydroelectric dams on the Missouri River in South Dakota. By 1966, all four dams—Big Bend, Fort Randall, Gavins Point, and Oahe—were producing hydroelectric power. The dams created Francis Case, Lewis and Clark, Oahe, and Sharpe lakes, which became known as the "Great Lakes of South Dakota." These lakes, along with many new highways, attracted additional tourists to the state. Tourism became South

Unloading a Minuteman Missile at a launch site near Newell requires special machinery. Shafts tilt the boxlike container upright. Then, the huge missile is lowered into a pit.

U.S. Air Force

The Governors of South Dakota

	Party	Term
Arthur C. Mellette	Republican	1889-1893
Charles H. Sheldon	Republican	1893-1897
Andrew E. Lee	Populist	1897-1901
Charles N. Herreid	Republican	1901-1905
Samuel H. Elrod	Republican	1905-1907
Coe I. Crawford	Republican	1907-1909
Robert S. Vessey	Republican	1909-1913
Frank M. Byrne	Republican	1913-1917
Peter Norbeck	Republican	1917-1921
W. H. McMaster	Republican	1921-1925
Carl Gunderson	Republican	1925-1927
W. J. Bulow	Democratic	1927-1931
Warren Green	Republican	1931-1933
Thomas "Tom" Berry	Democratic	1933-1937
Leslie Jensen	Republican	1937-1939
Harlan J. Bushfield	Republican	1939-1943
M. Q. Sharpe	Republican	1943-1947
George T. Mickelson	Republican	1947-1951
Sigurd Anderson	Republican	1951-1955
Joseph J. Foss	Republican	1955-1959
Ralph Herseth	Democratic	1959-1961
Archie Gubbrud	Republican	1961-1965
Nils Boe	Republican	1965-1969
Frank L. Farrar	Republican	1969-1971
Richard F. Kneip	Democratic	1971-1978
Harvey L. Wollman	Democratic	1978-1979
William J. Janklow	Republican	1979-

Dakota's second largest industry, after agriculture.

During the 1960's, the government built a number of defense projects in South Dakota. Today, missile sites dot the western part of the state. They are directed from Ellsworth Air Force Base near Rapid City.

In 1972, floodwaters swept across Rapid City and the surrounding area after heavy rains caused Rapid City's Canyon Lake Dam to burst. The flood killed 238 persons and caused an estimated $100 million in damage.

In 1973, the village of Wounded Knee was seized by about 200 armed Indians. The action was designed to protest federal policies concerning Indians, and was also the result of a tribal dispute among the Oglala Sioux. During the occupation, several gunfights broke out between the occupiers and federal authorities. The occupation lasted 71 days and resulted in 2 deaths and over 300 arrests. Government officials promised to study the protesters' complaints.

South Dakota Today. The departure of young people from South Dakota slowed during the 1970's. The state broadened its economy, and new jobs were created in commerce and industry. To continue attracting industries to the state, business leaders point out that South Dakota does not tax personal or corporation incomes. They also call attention to the state's clean air and abundant water supply.

In 1980, the U.S. Supreme Court ordered the federal government to pay $122½ million to eight tribes of Sioux Indians. The payment was for Indian land in the Black Hills seized by the government in 1877.

Also in 1980, the South Dakota legislature approved a plan to purchase abandoned rail lines from the bankrupt Milwaukee Road, a railroad company. The state-owned railroad provides continued service for agriculture and business. The state legislature passed a one-cent increase in the sales tax to provide funds to pay for the purchase.

DUNCAN J. McGREGOR,
EVERETT W. STERLING, and ANSON ANDERS YEAGER, SR.

Related Articles in WORLD BOOK include:

BIOGRAPHIES

Beadle, William H. H.
Calamity Jane
Crazy Horse
Custer, George A.
Gall
Hickok, Wild Bill

La Vérendrye, Sieur de
Lawrence, Ernest O.
McGovern, George S.
Sitting Bull
Spotted Tail
Ward, Joseph

CITIES

Pierre   Rapid City   Sioux Falls

HISTORY

Indian Wars
Lewis and Clark
  Expedition

Louisiana Purchase
Sioux Indians
Western Frontier Life

PHYSICAL FEATURES

Badlands
Black Hills
Fort Randall Dam

Great Plains
Minnesota River

Missouri River
Oahe Dam

OTHER RELATED ARTICLES

Badlands National
  Park
Jewel Cave National
  Monument

Midwestern States
Mount Rushmore National
  Memorial
Wind Cave National Park

Outline

I. Government
  A. Constitution
  B. Executive
  C. Legislature
  D. Courts
II. People
III. Education
  A. Schools
IV. A Visitor's Guide
  A. Places to Visit
V. The Land
  A. Land Regions
  B. Rivers and Lakes
VI. Climate
VII. Economy
  A. Natural Resources
  B. Agriculture
  C. Manufacturing
  D. Mining
  E. Electric Power
  F. Transportation
  G. Communication
VIII. History

  E. Local Government
  F. Taxation
  G. Politics

  B. Libraries and Museums

  B. Annual Events

Questions

What are the "Great Lakes of South Dakota"?
Why is South Dakota sometimes called the *Land of Infinite Variety?*
Why is it so important for South Dakota to expand its industry?
What part of South Dakota was covered by glaciers during the Ice Age?
Who established the first permanent white settlement in what is now South Dakota? When?
What is the state's most precious natural resource?
What is South Dakota's rank among the states in gold production?
What was the first country to claim the region that is now South Dakota? How did the United States acquire this land?
What was the last big fight between Indians and whites on the northern plains?
What were the *black blizzards?*

Additional Resources

Level I

BAILEY, BERNADINE. *Picture Book of South Dakota.* Rev. ed. Whitman, 1980.
CARPENTER, ALLAN. *South Dakota.* Rev. ed. Childrens Press, 1978.
CLEAVER, VERA and BILL. *Dust of the Earth.* Harper, 1975. Fiction.
FRADIN, DENNIS B. *South Dakota in Words and Pictures.* Childrens Press, 1981.
VEGLAHN, NANCY. *South Dakota.* Coward, 1970.
WILDER, LAURA INGALLS. *Little House on the Prairie.* Harper, 1935. *By the Shores of Silver Lake.* 1939. *Little Town on the Prairie.* 1941. All are fiction.

Level II

CLARK, CHAMP. *The Badlands.* Time Inc., 1974.
FARBER, WILLIAM OGDEN, and others. *Government of South Dakota.* 3rd ed. Dakota Press, 1979.
KAROLEVITZ, ROBERT F. *Challenge: The South Dakota Story.* 2nd ed. Brevet Press, 1979.
LAMAR, HOWARD R. *Dakota Territory, 1861-1889: A Study of Frontier Politics.* Yale, 1956.
MILTON, JOHN R. *The Literature of South Dakota.* Dakota Press, 1976. *South Dakota: A Bicentennial History.* Norton, 1977.
PARKER, WATSON. *Gold in the Black Hills.* Univ. of Oklahoma Press, 1966. *Deadwood: The Golden Years.* Univ. of Nebraska Press, 1981.
RÖLVAAG, OLE. *Giants in the Earth: A Saga of the Prairie.* Harper, 1927. Fiction.
SCHELL, HERBERT S. *History of South Dakota.* 3rd ed. Univ. of Nebraska Press, 1975.

SOUTH DAKOTA, UNIVERSITY OF, is a state-supported coeducational school with campuses in Springfield and Vermillion, S. Dak. The main campus, in Vermillion, has a college of arts and sciences and a college of fine arts. It also has a graduate school and schools of business, education, law, medicine, and nursing. Courses lead to bachelor's, master's, and doctor's degrees. The Springfield campus grants associate's and bachelor's degrees. The University of South Dakota was founded in 1882. For the enrollment, see UNIVERSITIES AND COLLEGES (table).   RICHARD L. BOWEN

SOUTH DAKOTA STATE UNIVERSITY is a state-controlled coeducational university in Brookings, S. Dak. It has colleges of agriculture, arts and sciences, education, engineering, home economics, nursing, and phar-

macy; a division of general registration; and a graduate school. The university grants bachelor's, master's, and doctor's degrees. It was founded in 1881 as a land-grant school. For enrollment, see UNIVERSITIES AND COLLEGES (table).   Critically reviewed by
          SOUTH DAKOTA STATE UNIVERSITY

SOUTH GEORGIA. See FALKLAND ISLANDS (Dependencies); ATLANTIC OCEAN (map).

SOUTH ISLAND. See NEW ZEALAND (The South Island).

SOUTH KOREA. See KOREA.

SOUTH MAGNETIC POLE. See EARTH (The Earth's Magnetism); SOUTH POLE.

SOUTH ORKNEY ISLANDS. See FALKLAND ISLANDS (Dependencies); ATLANTIC OCEAN (map).

SOUTH POLE

SOUTH POLE is a term used for several invisible surface points in the Antarctic region. The best known is the *south geographic pole*. But other important south poles include the *instantaneous south pole*, the *south pole of balance*, the *south magnetic pole*, and the *geomagnetic south pole*.

The South Geographic Pole lies near the center of Antarctica at the point where all the earth's lines of longitude meet. Explorer Roald Amundsen of Norway beat Robert Scott of England to the south geographic pole in 1911 by one month. In 1956, the United States established a permanent scientific base at the pole called the Amundsen-Scott South Pole Station.

The Instantaneous South Pole lies at the point where the earth's *axis* (an imaginary line through the earth) meets the surface. The earth wobbles slowly as it turns on its axis, causing the instantaneous south pole to move. This pole takes about 14 months to move counterclockwise around an irregular path called the *Chandler Circle*. The diameter of this circle varies from less than 1 foot (30 centimeters) to about 70 feet (21 meters).

The South Pole of Balance lies at the center of the Chandler Circle. Its position locates the south geographic pole. It has moved about 6 inches (15 centimeters) toward Australia each year since 1900.

The South Magnetic Pole is the point toward which south-seeking compass needles point. This pole may move as much as 5 miles (8 kilometers) in a year. In 1970, the pole was in Wilkes Land, in Antarctica.

The Geomagnetic South Pole lies about 900 miles (1,400 kilometers) from the south geographic pole, toward Vincennes Bay. In the upper atmosphere, the magnetic field of the earth is directed upward and away from this point.

PAUL A. SIPLE

Related Articles in WORLD BOOK include:

Amundsen, Roald	Exploration
Antarctica (Exploration)	(Polar Exploration)
Byrd, Richard E.	Scott, Robert F.
Earth (Earth's Magnetism)	

SOUTH SANDWICH ISLANDS. See FALKLAND ISLANDS (Dependencies); ATLANTIC OCEAN (map).

SOUTH SEA. See BALBOA, VASCO NÚÑEZ DE.

SOUTH SEA BUBBLE. See GEORGE (I) of England; WALPOLE (Sir Robert).

SOUTH SEA ISLANDS. See PACIFIC ISLANDS.

SOUTH SHETLAND ISLANDS. See FALKLAND ISLANDS (Dependencies); ATLANTIC OCEAN (map).

SOUTH VIETNAM. See VIETNAM.

SOUTH WEST AFRICA. See NAMIBIA.

SOUTH YEMEN. See YEMEN (ADEN).

SOUTHAMPTON, *sowth AMP tuhn*, is a major seaport in southern England. The city lies on the River Test, near where the river flows into the English Channel (see GREAT BRITAIN [political map]). It is the largest city in the district of Southampton, which has a population of 201,989.

Docks stand along Southampton's waterfront. The city is a center of cargo shipping and also of passenger traffic by sea between England and continental Europe. Its other industries include the construction and repair of ships, electrical engineering, the production of vehicle parts, and tobacco processing. Landmarks of Southampton include a number of medieval buildings and Bar Gate—part of a wall that encircled the city during the Middle Ages.

The Romans founded a settlement at what is now Southampton shortly after they invaded Britain in the A.D. 40's. The city became a major seaport in the Middle Ages. The *Mayflower*, which carried the Pilgrims to North America in 1620, began its journey at Southampton.

D. A. PINDER

SOUTHAMPTON ISLAND, *sowth AMP tuhn*, is an ice-covered island in Canada's Northwest Territories. It lies in northern Hudson Bay. It is 210 miles (338 kilometers) long and 150 miles (241 kilometers) wide, and covers 15,913 square miles (41,214 square kilometers). About 400 persons live on the island. See CANADA (political map).

SOUTHEAST ASIA includes the peninsula and islands east of India and Bangladesh and south of China. The region consists of Brunei, Burma, Kampuchea (Cambodia), Laos, Malaysia, the Philippines, Singapore, Thailand, Vietnam, and most of Indonesia. Most of Southeast Asia's 384 million people have Chinese or Malay ancestors. About three-fourths of the people live in rural areas. The largest cities are Jakarta, Indonesia; Bangkok, Thailand; Ho Chi Minh City, Vietnam; and Singapore (city), Singapore. Buddhism and Islam are the area's major religions. Most Filipinos are Christians.

Southeast Asia has rich, fertile soil. Its main agricultural products are rubber, rice, tea, and spices. The region's forests produce most of the world's teak. The coastal waters yield large quantities of fish. Parts of the area have rich petroleum deposits and mines that produce large amounts of tin and precious stones. Manufacturing is largely undeveloped except in the large cities.

Europeans, attracted by the area's natural riches, began to take over Southeast Asia in the 1500's. Great Britain, France, The Netherlands, Portugal, Spain, and the United States all have ruled parts of the region. Only Thailand escaped foreign control. After World War II (1939-1945), the Philippines and the major British colonies gained independence peacefully. Elsewhere in Southeast Asia, several groups—including Communists—fought for independence. In 1954, the colony of French Indochina was divided into Kampuchea, Laos, South Vietnam, and Communist North Vietnam. In 1975, North Vietnam conquered South Vietnam after the long and bitter Vietnam War. Communists also gained control of Kampuchea and Laos in 1975.

JOHN F. CADY

For more details on Southeast Asia, see ASIA (Way of Life in Southeast Asia). See also the separate articles in WORLD BOOK for each country in Southeast Asia, and ASSOCIATION OF SOUTHEAST ASIAN NATIONS; INDOCHINA; VIETNAM WAR.

SOUTHEAST ASIA TREATY ORGANIZATION (SEATO) was an alliance of seven nations that signed the Southeast Asia Collective Defense Treaty in Manila, the Philippines, on Sept. 8, 1954. The members were Australia, France, Great Britain, New Zealand, the Philippines, Thailand, and the United States. Pakistan was a member until 1973, when it withdrew. SEATO was dissolved in 1977.

The treaty was proposed by the United States after Communist forces defeated France in Indochina (present-day Vietnam, Laos, and Kampuchea). It was intended to prevent the further expansion of Commu-

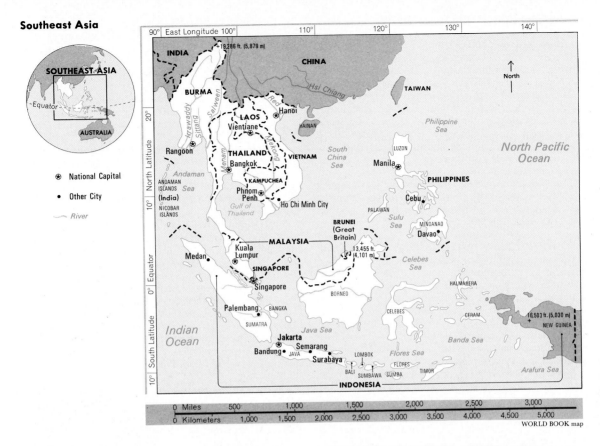

Southeast Asia

SOUTHEAST ASIA

Equator

AUSTRALIA

⊗ National Capital

• Other City

～ River

19,286 ft. (5,879 m)

INDIA

CHINA

BURMA

Hsi Chiang

TAIWAN

North

LAOS
Hanoi
Vientiane
HAINAN

Philippine
Sea

Rangoon

THAILAND   VIETNAM
Bangkok

South
China
Sea

LUZON

Manila

North Pacific
Ocean

PHILIPPINES

Andaman
ANDAMAN
ISLANDS
(India)
NICOBAR
ISLANDS
Sea

KAMPUCHEA
Phnom
Penh
Ho Chi Minh City

Gulf of
Thailand

Cebu

PALAWAN

Sulu
Sea

MINDANAO
Davao

BRUNEI
(Great
Britain)

13,455 ft.
(4,101 m)

Celebes
Sea

HALMAHERA

Medan

Kuala
Lumpur
MALAYSIA

SINGAPORE
Singapore

BORNEO

CELEBES

CERAM

16,503 ft. (5,030 m)

NEW GUINEA

Palembang   BANGKA

SUMATRA

Java Sea

Banda Sea

Indian
Ocean

Jakarta
Bandung   Semarang
JAVA   Surabaya

LOMBOK

Flores Sea

FLORES

Arafura Sea

BALI   SUMBAWA   SUMBA   TIMOR

INDONESIA

0 Miles   500   1,000   1,500   2,000   2,500   3,000
0 Kilometers   1,000   1,500   2,000   2,500   3,000   3,500   4,000   4,500   5,000

WORLD BOOK map

nist influence in Southeast Asia. The SEATO nations agreed to help defend each other—as well as other designated nations—against military aggression in Asia.

SEATO did not develop into a strong alliance, partly because India, Indonesia, and Japan—three of the largest non-Communist nations in Asia—did not join. The SEATO members divided on the extent of the Communist threat and how to meet it. Only four of the SEATO nations—the United States, Thailand, New Zealand, and Australia—sent combat troops to take part in the Vietnam War (1957-1975). LUCIAN W. PYE

SOUTHERN BAPTIST CONVENTION is the largest Baptist organization in the world. It has about 12,750,-000 members. The convention has more than 34,000 churches in 50 states, but most of its members live in the South and Southwest.

The Southern Baptist Convention has 29 state conventions that operate 38 senior colleges, 15 junior colleges, 7 academies, 6 seminaries, and 4 Bible schools. The state conventions also operate hospitals, children's homes, and homes for the aging. The convention supports about 2,300 missionaries in other countries and about the same number in the United States. Many of the denomination's offices are located at 460 James Robertson Parkway, Nashville, Tenn. 37219.

The Southern Baptist Convention was organized in Augusta, Ga., in 1845, after a split among the country's Baptists over whether slaveholders should be appointed as missionaries. For more information about Baptist doctrine and history, see BAPTISTS.

Critically reviewed by the SOUTHERN BAPTIST CONVENTION

SOUTHERN CALIFORNIA, UNIVERSITY OF, is a co-educational private university in Los Angeles. It is one of the largest private universities in the western United States. The university grants degrees in architecture and fine arts; business administration; communications; dentistry; education; engineering; gerontology; international relations; journalism; law; letters, arts, and sciences; library science; medicine; music; performing arts; pharmacy; philosophy; public administration; re-

University of Southern California

The University of Southern California, *above,* covers about 150 acres (60 hectares) southwest of downtown Los Angeles.

545

ligion; social work; and urban and regional planning. It has a full graduate program, a summer session, and evening and extension programs. It also has Air Force and Naval Reserve Officers Training Corps programs.

The university conducts major research programs in many fields. It is especially famous for its communications, engineering, performing arts, science, and world affairs programs and facilities. The university has a materials science center and an international and public affairs center. It also operates a center on Catalina Island for studying marine biology.

The University of Southern California was founded in 1880. It is the oldest major private university in the western United States. For enrollment, see UNIVERSITIES AND COLLEGES (table).

Critically reviewed by the UNIVERSITY OF SOUTHERN CALIFORNIA

SOUTHERN CHRISTIAN LEADERSHIP CONFERENCE (SCLC) is a civil rights organization in the United States. It works to gain equal rights for black Americans and other minority groups through nonviolent civil protest and community development programs. Most SCLC affiliates are church and civil rights groups. Staff membership is open to all, but most SCLC leaders are black Protestant ministers. The SCLC is financed by contributions from individuals and organizations, and by grants from foundations.

Martin Luther King, Jr., and other civil rights leaders founded the SCLC in 1957 to coordinate civil rights work in the South. King headed the organization from 1957 until his assassination in 1968. Headquarters of the SCLC are located at 334 Auburn Avenue N.E., Atlanta, Ga. 30303.   C. ERIC LINCOLN

See also KING, MARTIN LUTHER, JR.; ABERNATHY, RALPH D.; JACKSON, JESSE L.

SOUTHERN CIRCLE. See TROPIC OF CAPRICORN.

SOUTHERN CROSS is a famous *constellation* (group of stars) in the Southern Hemisphere. It is also called the *Crux*, which is Latin for *cross*. The constellation gets its name from the outline of a cross formed by its four brightest stars. The star farthest to the south is a star of the first magnitude. The eastern and northern stars are of the second magnitude, and the western star is of the third magnitude. The four stars are not arranged in the exact form of a cross, and the constellation is sometimes difficult to pick out if one has not seen it before. The upper and lower stars of the constellation, which form the "upright" of the cross, point to the South Pole of the sky.

The Southern Cross appears too far south to be seen in the United States, except for a few places. It was visible in ancient Babylonia and Greece, where people considered it a part of the constellation Centaurus. The

cross has gradually shifted southward in the sky as a result of the earth's *precession* (circular motion of the earth's axis).   I. M. LEVITT

SOUTHERN HEMISPHERE. See HEMISPHERE; SEASON.

SOUTHERN METHODIST UNIVERSITY is a private coeducational school in Dallas. It has schools of the arts, business administration, continuing education, humanities and sciences, law, and theology, and an institute of technology. The university grants bachelor's, master's, and doctor's degrees.

The university was founded in 1911 by the United Methodist Church. It opened in 1915. For the enrollment of Southern Methodist University, see UNIVERSITIES AND COLLEGES (table).   PAUL HARDIN

SOUTHERN RHODESIA. See ZAMBIA (History); ZIMBABWE (History).

SOUTHERN STATES are Alabama, Arkansas, Delaware, Florida, Georgia, Kentucky, Louisiana, Maryland, Mississippi, North Carolina, South Carolina, Tennessee, Virginia, and West Virginia. For information on this region, see UNITED STATES (Regions). See also the articles on the states that make up the region.

SOUTHERN YEMEN. See YEMEN (ADEN).

SOUTHEY, *SOW thee* or *SUHTH ee,* **ROBERT** (1774-1843), was poet laureate of England from 1813 until his death. He is chiefly remembered for a few ballads, including "The Battle of Blenheim" (1798), and for his association with William Wordsworth and Samuel Taylor Coleridge.

Critics consider Southey a better prose writer than poet. He wrote much history and biography, including the *Life of Nelson* (1813). His prose collection *The Doctor* (1834-1847) popularized the fairy tale "The Three Bears." Southey also wrote two long free verse romances, *Thalaba, the Destroyer* (1801) and *The Curse of Kehama* (1810). These works use Muslim and Hindu mythologies, and influenced several poets, including Percy Shelley and Sir Walter Scott.

Detail of an oil portrait on canvas by Sir Thomas Lawrence; South African National Gallery, Cape Town, South Africa

Robert Southey

Southey was born in Bristol. He and Coleridge supported ideals that inspired the American and French revolutions. They planned to establish a utopian community in the United States, but the project failed because of a lack of financial support. Southey later became conservative and supported the English monarchy.   KARL KROEBER

Southern Methodist University

Southern Methodist's central quadrangle has many crisscrossed walks leading to important campus buildings. The dome-topped Dallas Hall faces the quadrangle.

SOUTHWESTERN STATES are Arizona, New Mexico, Oklahoma, and Texas. Arizona and New Mexico are also sometimes considered Rocky Mountain States, as well as Southwestern States. For information on the Southwestern States region, see UNITED STATES (Regions). See also the articles on the states that make up the region.

SOVEREIGN. See POUND.

SOVEREIGNTY. The name "sovereign" was first applied to kings. Everyone in a kingdom was a subject of the king. The king himself was usually *sovereign*, which means *subject to no one.*

Few kings are left in the world, but the idea of sovereignty remains. Today, many countries are considered subject to no one, and therefore sovereign. A sovereign country can conduct its own affairs, enter into treaties, declare war, or adopt any other course of action without another country's consent. Small countries are often sovereign in name only. They shape their policies and conduct their affairs to suit the desires or needs of a stronger country. The United States is a sovereign nation, but the 50 states which compose it do not have full sovereignty.　　　　　　　　　　　　PAYSON S. WILD

SOVIET, *SOH vee eht* or *SAHV ee eht,* is a Russian word which means *council.* Russian revolutionary groups were known as soviets. The first soviets were formed during the Russian workers' revolution in 1905. Soviets were formed throughout Russia after the downfall of the Czar in March 1917. These soviets were councils made up of workers, peasants, and soldiers. These councils rallied groups of people to support the Socialist plan for setting up a Russian government. In 1917, the Bolsheviks (Lenin faction) gained control of the soviets. Since 1922, Russia has been officially known as the Union of Soviet Socialist Republics. Since 1946, the Russian army and navy have been officially known as the Soviet Army and Soviet Navy.　　　　　　　　　WILLIAM B. BALLIS

SOVIET UNION. See RUSSIA.

SOW. See HOG.

SOW BUG. See WOOD LOUSE.

SOW THISTLE is the name of a group of weeds. These weeds grow wild in Europe, and several species have been introduced into the United States, where they have become a nuisance in gardens and fields. The *annual sow thistle* grows 2 to 3 feet (61 to 91 centimeters) high and has a branching stem. It contains a milky juice and its flower heads resemble dandelions. Another type of sow thistle is the *perennial sow thistle.* The sow thistle is one of the most troublesome weeds.

USDA
Sow Thistle

Scientific Classification. Sow thistles belong to the composite family, *Compositae.* The annual sow thistle is classified as genus *Sonchus,* species *S. oleraceus.* The perennial sow thistle is *S. arvensis.*　　　　　　　　　　　　　　LOUIS PYENSON

SOYBEAN is a plant that supplies feed for animals, food for human beings, and raw materials for industry.

Farmers in the United States grow more soybeans than any other cultivated crop except corn and wheat. Soybeans are also the nation's largest single source of vegetable oil and of protein meal for livestock.

The soybean is one of the world's most useful and cheapest sources of protein. It contains about 40 per cent crude protein, compared with 18 per cent for beef and fish. People in many countries eat soybeans instead of such other sources of protein as meat, eggs, and cheese.

The soybean is sometimes known as the *soya,* or *soja, bean.* It is an annual plant and belongs to the same family as peas. Plants in this family are called *legumes.*

The United States grows more soybeans than any other country. Other important producers include Brazil and China. Illinois usually ranks first among the states in the production of soybeans, followed by Iowa. Ontario is the leading soybean producer among the Canadian provinces.

The United States supplies about two-thirds of the world's soybeans. Soybeans are grown on about 68 million acres (27.5 million hectares) of land in the United States. The nation produces about 1.8 billion bushels of soybeans annually. About 40 per cent of the crop is exported to Western European nations, Japan, and other countries.

The Soybean Plant

Soybeans are planted in the spring. After six to eight weeks, small purple or white flowers appear on the plants. The flowers develop for about two weeks and some of them produce pods. Each pod contains two or three *seeds,* also called *beans.* The seeds develop for 30 to 40 days and mature as the leaves of the soybean plant turn yellow and drop to the ground. At maturity, most soybean plants stand from 2 to 4 feet (61 to 122 centimeters) tall.

Many types of soybeans grow in the United States. Scientists developed the types now used by crossing different varieties of the plant. This process produces plants with special characteristics, such as light-colored seeds, resistance to disease, and increased yield.

The soybean plant is covered with short, fine, brown or gray hairs. The pods range in color from light yellow to shades of gray, brown, and black. Soybean seeds are round or oval and may be yellow, green, brown, black, or speckled, depending on variety.

Most soybean varieties grown for commercial processing have yellow or buff-colored seeds. These seeds are about $\frac{1}{4}$ inch (5 to 7 millimeters) in diameter and are processed into soybean meal and oil. About 98 per cent of the soybeans grown in the United States are commercial soybeans. Vegetable-type soybeans are used as whole beans or to produce bean sprouts. Most vegetable-type soybeans have green seeds. These seeds are somewhat larger than those of commercial soybeans.

How Soybeans Are Used

Soybeans are used chiefly in the form of meal and oil. In the United States, soybean seeds are made into these products by a process called *solvent extraction.* First, the seeds are cleaned and dehulled by machines. Then rollers crush the seeds into flakes. Crude oil is *extracted*

International Harvester

Harvesting Soybeans with a combine, *above,* cuts the plants and threshes and cleans the seeds in one operation. Soybeans are harvested in late summer or early fall.

WORLD BOOK illustration by James Teason

The Soybean Plant stands from 2 to 4 feet (61 to 122 centimeters) high. Each of its pods contains two or three seeds, or *beans,* which grow for 30 to 40 days.

(removed) from the flakes by a *solvent,* a substance that can dissolve other substances. After the oil has been removed, the flakes are called *soybean meal* or, more commonly, *soy meal.*

Soy Meal. More than 95 per cent of the crude soybean meal produced in the United States is used to feed animals. The flakes are heated and manufactured into high-protein feed for cattle, hogs, and poultry. Food for house pets also contains soybeans.

Soybean meal is an ingredient of many foods eaten by human beings. It can be finely ground into *soy flour* or coarsely ground into *soy grits.* Soy flour is used in baby food, cereals, and various low-calorie products. Soy grits are used in candy and such processed meats as patties and sausages. Both soy flour and grits go into baked goods and pet foods.

In the 1960's and 1970's, scientists developed a variety of new food products by processing soy flour. A product called *soy protein concentrate* is produced when about a sixth of the nonprotein content is extracted from soy flour. The concentrate is a cream that can be made into a powder or a grainy substance. It is used in baby food, cereals, and processed meats.

Another product, called *isolated soy protein,* is produced when about a fourth of the nonprotein content is extracted from soy flour. This product is used to provide firmness and protein in various processed foods, especially meats.

A number of soy products make up a group of foods called *textured vegetable protein* (TVP). These foods are chemically treated to look and taste like meat so they will appeal to consumers. TVP foods can be mixed with meat or eaten alone. They cost less than meat and contain more protein. TVP products are made of either *extruded soy protein* or *spun soy protein.*

Extruded soy protein is produced when soy flour is *extruded* (pushed) from machines in the same way that toothpaste is squeezed from tubes. The machine shapes the soy flour into small meatlike pieces. The product may be dried before being packaged for sale. Extruded soy protein becomes moist and chewy when the consumer adds water. The food is generally mixed with ground meat.

Spun soy protein is made by spinning isolated soy protein into fibers. Spun soy products resemble such meats as beef, chicken, and ham. They are sold in canned, dried, and frozen form.

Many food items contain soy meal but do not consist entirely of treated soybeans. These products, called *soy derivatives,* include food flavorings, soy milk, and soy sauce. Soy meal is also used in manufacturing such products as fertilizer, fire extinguisher fluid, insect sprays, and paint.

Soy Oil. Crude soybean oil is made into three basic products: (1) technical refined oil, (2) edible refined oil, and (3) lecithin.

548

Food Value of Soybeans

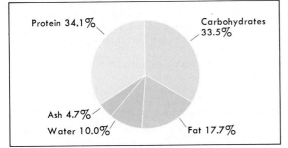

Protein 34.1%

Carbohydrates 33.5%

Ash 4.7%

Water 10.0%

Fat 17.7%

Source: U.S. Agricultural Research Service.

Technical refined oil is produced by putting crude soy oil through several processes. First, manufacturers purify the crude oil by adding a mixture of water and a chemical called an *alkali*. Next, the oil is washed and dried. Then it is bleached by absorbent clay and passed through a filter, producing technical refined oil. This oil is used in manufacturing such products as candles, disinfectants, linoleum, soaps, and varnishes.

Edible refined oil is produced by deodorizing technical refined oil. The technical refined oil is heated and steamed to remove its unpleasant odor and flavor. More than 90 per cent of the crude soybean oil used in the United States is processed into edible refined oil. About half the edible oil goes into making margarine and vegetable shortening. The rest is used in manufacturing cooking oils, mayonnaise, salad dressings, and other food products. Edible refined oil is also an ingredient of a variety of other products, including adhesive tape, carbon paper, various drugs and explosives, and leather softeners.

Lecithin, a sticky substance, is extracted after mixing crude soy oil with water. Soybean lecithin is used in making candy, ice cream, and baking products. It is also used in the manufacture of chemicals, cosmetics, and textiles.

How Soybeans Are Grown

Soybean Farming in the United States is centered in the Midwestern States, but farmers in many Southern States also raise the crop. Soybeans, like corn, thrive in fertile, well-drained soil. A good crop requires at least 20 inches (51 centimeters) of rain during the growing season.

Soybeans are generally planted in May or June. Most farmers plant soybeans in rows 20 to 30 inches (51 to 76 centimeters) apart. The seeds in each row are planted 1 to 1½ inches (2 to 3 centimeters) apart and 1 to 2 inches (2 to 5 centimeters) deep. Farmers control weeds by means of cultivating machines and *herbicides* (chemical weedkillers), and by rotating soybeans with other crops. Like other legumes, soybeans obtain nitrogen from the air, and so they do not require nitrogen fertilizers.

Leading Soybean-Growing States

Bushels of soybeans grown each year*

Illinois	333,700,000 bu.
Iowa	290,840,000 bu.
Missouri	156,430,000 bu.
Indiana	151,330,000 bu.
Minnesota	148,720,000 bu.
Ohio	131,980,000 bu.
Arkansas	108,690,000 bu.
Mississippi	85,170,000 bu.
Louisiana	75,780,000 bu.
Tennessee	57,060,000 bu.

*One bushel equals 60 pounds (27 kilograms). Based on a 4-year average, 1977-1980.
Sources: *Crop Production Annual Summary*, 1979 and 1980, U.S. Department of Agriculture.

Soybeans are grown in few areas of the world. The United States is the leading soybean-growing country. Other important producers include Argentina, Brazil, Canada, China, Indonesia, Mexico, and Russia.

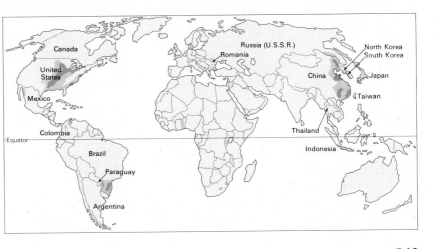

Major soybean producing area

Other soybean producing area

WORLD BOOK map

How Soybeans Are Processed

Soybeans are used chiefly in the form of meal and oil. A process called *solvent extraction* presses the beans into flakes and removes the oil. The flakes and oil are then made into such products as protein meal for livestock and vegetable oil for cooking.

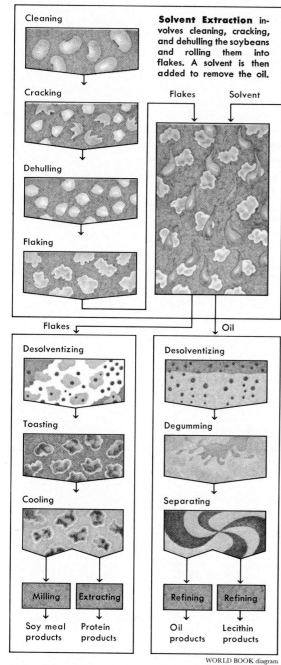

Solvent Extraction involves cleaning, cracking, and dehulling the soybeans and rolling them into flakes. A solvent is then added to remove the oil.

WORLD BOOK diagram

Flake Processing removes the solvent by forcing steam through the flakes. The flakes are then toasted and cooled. The flakes may be milled to make soy meal products, or the protein may be extracted and used in various food products.

Oil Processing removes the solvent by heating the oil until the solvent vaporizes. Water is then added in a process called *degumming,* which helps separate the lecithin from the oil. The oil and lecithin are then refined into various products.

Most farmers harvest soybeans in late summer or early fall. They use a machine called a *combine,* which cuts, threshes, and cleans the seeds in one operation. Farmers sell the harvested seeds to food manufacturers and other buyers, who ship them to processing plants or export terminals.

Diseases and Pests. Soybeans are attacked by about 100 diseases and pests. A fungal disease that infects soybeans is *Diaporthe pod and stem blight.* Bacterial diseases include *bacterial blight* and *bacterial pustule.*

Diaporthe pod and stem blight is carried in soybean seeds. It attacks the pods and stems of plants that are nearing maturity. This fungal disease can be controlled by a special *fungicide,* a chemical that kills fungi. The fungicide is sprayed on the soybeans from an airplane flying as low as 6 to 8 feet (1.8 to 2.4 meters) above the crops.

Bacterial diseases affect soybeans most severely during wet years. The bacteria that cause bacterial blight live in the soil and in diseased soybean plants. They enter healthy plants through the leaves. Wet spots form on the leaves and turn brown. Patches of leaf tissue die and fall out, and the entire leaf may die. Bacterial pustule involves *pustules* (small bumps filled with fluid) that form on the leaves. Several types of soybean plants can resist bacterial diseases.

Many pests attack soybeans, but few are serious threats to the plant. Common pests include the *bean leaf bettle, stinkbug,* and *velvetbean caterpillar.* Farmers control such pests by means of insecticides and by removing dead leaves and other rubbish in which the insects lay their eggs. Scientists have also developed varieties of soybeans that resist most insect pests. Other threats to soybeans include viruses and tiny worms called *nematodes.*

History

Soybeans are one of the oldest crops raised by human beings. Historians believe the plant first grew in Eastern Asia and was cultivated about 5,000 years ago. The ancient Chinese considered soybeans their most important crop and one of the five sacred grains necessary for life.

Soybeans were introduced into Europe during the A.D. 1700's but were not cultivated extensively until the 1900's. In the United States, they were used primarily as forage until the 1900's. Soybeans were first processed into meal and oil in 1911. Most soybean meal was used as fertilizer until the mid-1930's. At that time, the meal became widely used in feed for livestock and poultry. By 1941, soybeans were used chiefly for the production of seeds.

Soybeans are valuable in easing the world food shortage. Soybeans grown on an acre (0.4 hectare) of land can provide about 10 times as much protein as can beef cattle raised on the same land. Soybeans provide more protein than most other vegetables or grains, and so growing soybeans is one of the most efficient uses of land. More and more people are realizing the protein value of the soybean and relying on it to supply their protein needs.

Scientific Classification. The soybean belongs to the family Leguminosae. The cultivated soybean is *Glycine max* (L.) Merrill.   J. E. HARPER

See also JULIAN, PERCY L.

FARR, BARBARA. *Super Soy! Delicious Protein Without Meat.* Keats, 1976.
WOLF, WALTER JAMES, and COWAN, J. C. *Soybeans as a Food Source.* Rev. ed. CRC Press, 1975.

SOYER BROTHERS became leading American artists. Raphael Soyer (1899-   ) and Moses Soyer (1899-1974) were twins whose art remained close in style and subject matter throughout their careers. They became best known for portraying the lives of city working people. Their works reflect their admiration for the realism of the American artists George Bellows, Thomas Eakins, and Robert Henri. The Soyer brothers worked successfully in oils, water colors, pastels, and prints.

The Soyers were born in Borisoglebsk, Russia. They emigrated with their family to the United States in 1912, settling in New York City. The brothers worked within the urban realist movement that developed in the late 1920's. They belonged to a group of artists on New York's lower east side who painted realistic neighborhood scenes. During the Great Depression, the Soyers created sympathetic studies of society's outsiders and downtrodden. Examples include Raphael's *Mission* (1933) and Moses' *Out of Work* (1937).

The Soyers also painted many portraits of their family and artist friends, as well as self-portraits and studies of women and girls. Raphael painted unglamorous, ordinary women and earthy nudes in a style slightly more solid and worldly than his brother's. Moses preferred single figures of girls and young women, whom he portrayed with great tenderness. He showed a special fondness for dancers. Moses' works are more delicate than Raphael's, often showing females lost in thought. Examples of their later work include Raphael's *Avenue of the Americas* (1970) and Moses' *Ballet Studio* (1955).

Office Girls (1936), an oil painting on canvas; Whitney Museum of American Art, New York City

A Painting by Raphael Soyer shows a realistic city street scene. Soyer painted many pictures of unglamorous women in urban settings. His twin brother, Moses, painted similar pictures.

Another brother, Isaac (1902-1981), also painted realistic urban themes.   BESS L. HORMATS

SOYUZ. See ASTRONAUT (table: Important Manned Space Missions); SPACE TRAVEL (Manned Spacecraft [picture]).

SPA. See BATH; MINERAL WATER.

SPAAK, *spahk,* **PAUL-HENRI** (1899-1972), was a European statesman and a leader of the Socialist Party in Belgium. He was elected to Belgium's Chamber of Representatives in 1932. Later, he served in various cabinet posts. He was prime minister in 1938 and 1939 and from 1946 to 1949. He became the first president of the General Assembly of the United Nations in 1946. He helped form the Council of Europe in 1949, and was its first president. Spaak became the Belgian minister of foreign affairs in 1954, and worked to bring about a union of Western European countries. He was a planner of the European Economic Community (Common Market) and Euratom. He was secretary-general of the North Atlantic Treaty Organization (NATO) from 1957 to 1961. Spaak was born in Brussels.   JANE K. MILLER

SPAATZ, *spahts,* **CARL** (1891-1974), was the first Chief of Staff of the United States Air Force. He won this post because of his record as a distinguished combat leader of the U.S. Army Air Forces during World War II (1939-1945).

In 1942, he became commander of the Eighth Air Force in England. He commanded the Northwest African Air Forces in 1943. This combined American-British force supported the conquest of Tunisia and the invasions of Sicily and Italy. Spaatz then led the U.S. Strategic Air Forces in Europe for the final air and ground assault on Germany in 1944 and 1945. See WORLD WAR II (The Air War in Europe).

U.S. Signal Corps

Carl Spaatz

After the victory in Europe, Spaatz went to the Pacific, where his air forces included the B-29's that bombed Japan. He commanded the Army Air Forces in 1946, and was Chief of Staff of the newly independent U.S. Air Force in 1947. Born at Boyertown, Pa., Spaatz was graduated from the United States Military Academy.   ALFRED GOLDBERG

SPACE. See SPACE TRAVEL (What Is Space?).

SPACE COMMAND. See AIR FORCE, UNITED STATES (Space Command).

SPACE COMMUNICATIONS. See COMMUNICATIONS SATELLITE; SPACE TRAVEL (Artificial Satellites).

SPACE MEDICINE. See AEROSPACE MEDICINE.

SPACE NEEDLE. See SEATTLE (The City; picture).

SPACE SHUTTLE. See SPACE TRAVEL.

SPACE STATION. See SPACE TRAVEL.

SPACE SUIT. See SPACE TRAVEL (picture: An Astronaut's Space Suit).

SPACE SURVEILLANCE. See RADAR (In the Military); DEW LINE.

SPACE-TIME. See FOURTH DIMENSION.

NASA

A Solar Wind Experiment on the Moon

NASA

Jim Tuten, Black Star

The Space Shuttle Blasts Off

A Space Probe Photo of Saturn

The Exploration of Space provides knowledge about the moon, the planets, and the stars. Explorers have performed experiments on the moon, and space probes have photographed Saturn and other planets. The space shuttle not only can launch satellites but can also retrieve them.

SPACE TRAVEL

SPACE TRAVEL is humanity's greatest adventure—the chance to explore the moon, the planets, and the stars. Giant rockets lift off with a roaring blast of orange flame. They climb into the blue sky, leaving a white trail. Then they speed out of sight into space, where the sky is always black and the stars always shine. Rockets may carry people on their way to conduct scientific experiments, or they may carry an artificial satellite to explore a distant planet.

Eugene F. Kranz, the contributor of this article, is Flight Operations Director of the U.S. Space Shuttle Program.

The space age began on Oct. 4, 1957. On that day, Russia launched *Sputnik I*, the first artificial satellite to circle the earth. The first manned space flight was made on April 12, 1961, when a Russian cosmonaut, Yuri A. Gagarin, orbited the earth in a spaceship. The next month, U.S. astronaut Alan B. Shepard, Jr., made a 15-minute space flight, but he did not go into orbit. On Feb. 20, 1962, John H. Glenn, Jr., became the first American to orbit the earth.

During the years that followed, many space flights carried people into orbit around the earth. Then, on Dec. 24 and 25, 1968, U.S. astronauts Frank Borman, William A. Anders, and James A. Lovell, Jr., orbited the moon 10 times in their Apollo 8 spacecraft.

Human beings first set foot on the moon on July 20, 1969. U.S. astronaut Neil A. Armstrong stepped out of the Apollo 11 lunar module, *Eagle*, and at 10:56 P.M. E.D.S.T., put his left foot on a rocky lunar plain. After he had walked around for 18 minutes, astronaut Edwin E. Aldrin, Jr., joined him. For about two hours, the two astronauts explored near the lunar module and set up scientific experiments. *Eagle* was on the moon almost 22 hours before Armstrong and Aldrin lifted off to rejoin the command module *Columbia*, piloted by astronaut Michael Collins.

A new era in space exploration dawned on April 12, 1981, when U.S. astronauts John W. Young and Robert L. Crippen took off in the first space shuttle. The space shuttle was the first manned spacecraft designed to be reusable. It permits space flights to be scheduled on a routine basis. On a typical mission, the shuttle rockets into space with its crew, remains in orbit for about a week, and then lands on the earth like an airplane. It can be ready for another flight in about four weeks.

During the years since the space age began, many uses for space travel have been discovered. The space age developed a huge industry called the aerospace industry to design and build space equipment. A new field of medicine called space medicine came into being to study the problems of living and working in space. Weather forecasters receive warning of storms with pictures taken by weather satellites. Telephone calls and television pictures are sent around the world by communications satellites. Signals from navigation satellites enable ship navigators, leaders of scientific expeditions, and search and rescue forces to determine their positions with great accuracy. Scientific satellites and space probes discovered the Van Allen radiation belt around the earth and made many other discoveries.

During the early years of the space age, success in space became a measure of a country's leadership in science, engineering, and national defense. As a result, the United States and Russia competed with one another in developing their space programs. Each of them, for example, sought to build better rockets and spacecraft than the other in order to reach the moon first. But both nations began to realize that they could benefit from working together on selected scientific projects. In 1975, the U.S. and Russia cooperated in their first joint space mission. An Apollo spacecraft piloted by three United States astronauts docked with a Soyuz craft manned by two Russian cosmonauts. The principal area of cooperation between U.S. and Russian space programs has been in space medicine.

Human beings have always wanted to explore the unknown. Many persons believe that we should explore space simply because we have the means to do so. Scientists hope that space travel will answer many questions about the universe—how the sun, the planets, and the stars were formed, and whether life exists elsewhere.

Space Travel Terms

Ablation is the melting away of a spacecraft's heat shield during reentry.

Aerospace includes the atmosphere and the regions of space beyond it.

Aphelion is the point farthest from the sun in the path of a solar satellite.

Apocynthion is the point farthest from the moon in the orbit of a lunar satellite.

Apogee is the point farthest from earth in the orbit of an earth satellite.

Artificial Satellite is a spacecraft that circles the earth or other celestial body. The term is usually shortened to *satellite*, but it then also applies to natural moons.

Astro is a prefix meaning *star*. It also means *space* in such words as *astronautics* (the science of space flight).

Astronaut is a United States space pilot.

Attitude is the position of a spacecraft in relation to some other point, such as the spacecraft's direction of flight, the position of the sun, or the position of the earth.

Biosatellite is an artificial satellite that carries animals or plants.

Booster is the propulsion system that provides most of the energy for a spacecraft to go into orbit.

Burnout is the point in the flight of a rocket when its propellant is used up.

Capsule is a manned spacecraft or a small package of instruments carried by a larger spacecraft.

Cosmonaut is a Russian space pilot.

Eccentricity is the variation of a satellite's path from a perfect circle.

Escape Velocity is the speed a spacecraft must reach to coast away from the pull of gravity.

Exhaust Velocity is the speed at which the burning gases leave a rocket.

Gantry is a special crane or movable tower used to service launch vehicles.

Heat Shield is a covering on a spacecraft to protect the craft and astronaut from high temperatures of reentry.

Hypergol consists of propellants that ignite when mixed together.

LOX or **Liquid Oxygen** is a common oxidizer. It is made by cooling oxygen to $-183°$ C ($-297°$ F.).

Module is a single section of a spacecraft that can be disconnected and separated from other sections.

Orbit is the path of a satellite in relation to the object around which it revolves.

Oxidizer is a substance that mixes with the fuel in a rocket, furnishing oxygen that permits the fuel to burn.

Pericynthion is the point closest to the moon in the orbit of a lunar satellite.

Perigee is the point closest to earth in the orbit of an earth satellite.

Perihelion is the point closest to the sun in the path of a solar satellite.

Period is the time it takes for a satellite to make one revolution.

Propellant is a substance burned in a rocket to produce thrust. Propellants include fuels and oxidizers.

Reentry is that part of a flight when a returning spacecraft begins to descend through the atmosphere.

Rendezvous is a space maneuver in which two or more spacecraft meet.

Revolution is one complete cycle of a heavenly body or an artificial satellite in its orbit.

Spacecraft is an artificially created object that travels through space.

Stage is one of two or more rockets combined to form a launch vehicle.

Thrust is the push given to a rocket by its engines.

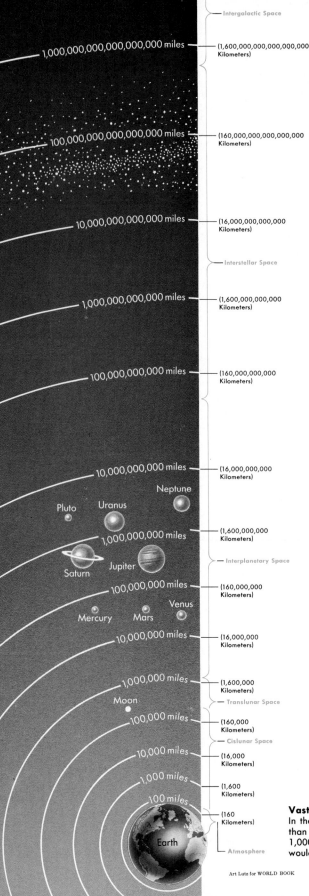

1,000,000,000,000,000,000 miles — (1,600,000,000,000,000,000 Kilometers)

— Intergalactic Space

100,000,000,000,000,000 miles — (160,000,000,000,000,000 Kilometers)

10,000,000,000,000 miles — (16,000,000,000,000 Kilometers)

— Interstellar Space

1,000,000,000,000 miles — (1,600,000,000,000 Kilometers)

100,000,000,000 miles — (160,000,000,000 Kilometers)

10,000,000,000 miles — (16,000,000,000 Kilometers)

Neptune
Pluto   Uranus

1,000,000,000 miles — (1,600,000,000 Kilometers)

— Interplanetary Space

Saturn   Jupiter

100,000,000 miles — (160,000,000 Kilometers)

Venus
Mercury   Mars

10,000,000 miles — (16,000,000 Kilometers)

1,000,000 miles — (1,600,000 Kilometers)

Moon   — Translunar Space

100,000 miles — (160,000 Kilometers)

— Cislunar Space

10,000 miles — (16,000 Kilometers)

1,000 miles — (1,600 Kilometers)

100 miles — (160 Kilometers)

Earth   — Atmosphere

Art Lutz for WORLD BOOK

SPACE TRAVEL / *What is Space?*

Space continues in all directions, and has no known limits. The moon moves through space around the earth. The earth and the other planets circle in space around the sun. The sun and billions of other stars make up a giant *galaxy* whirling through space. Countless other galaxies are scattered throughout space as far as we can see with the largest telescopes.

The Beginning of Space. Space begins where the earth's *atmosphere* (air) is too thin to affect objects moving through it. Near the earth's surface, air is plentiful. But higher above the earth, the air becomes thinner and thinner. Little by little, the atmosphere fades to almost nothing, and space begins. Space usually is said to begin about 100 miles (160 kilometers) above the earth. At this height, a satellite may continue circling the earth for months. But, even there, enough air is still present to slow a satellite and finally cause it to fall. In addition, solar storms in the upper atmosphere may cause satellites to fall sooner than expected.

From Earth to the Moon. The atmosphere continues beyond 100 miles (160 kilometers) above the earth. But it is not like the air near earth. It consists of widely scattered atoms and molecules of gas, and radiation. The radiation consists mostly of electrons, protons, and other subatomic particles. The particles carry electric charges. They are "trapped" in space by the earth's magnetic field. Scientists call the part of the atmosphere that contains these particles the *magnetosphere*.

Space between the earth and moon is called *cislunar* space (*cis* means *on this side*, and *lunar* means *of the moon*). As the moon is approached through cislunar space, earth's gravity becomes weaker and the moon's gravity becomes stronger. The combined gravities of earth and moon are effective to about 1,000,000 miles (1,600,000 kilometers) from earth. This distance is sometimes called *translunar space*.

Space Between the Planets is called *interplanetary space*. The sun's gravity controls interplanetary space. But each planet and moon also has its own gravity. Vast distances separate the bodies that move in interplanetary space. The sun is about 93 million miles (150 million kilometers) from earth. Venus, the closest planet to the earth, approaches only to within about 25 million miles (40 million kilometers) of earth. Interplanetary space reaches far beyond Pluto, the planet most distant from earth. It ends where the sun's gravity is no longer effective—perhaps 50 billion miles (80 billion kilometers) from earth.

To the Stars and Beyond. We find even greater distances in *interstellar space* (space between the stars). *Proxima Centauri*, the nearest star, is over 25 trillion miles (40 trillion kilometers) away. To cover such great distances, a spacecraft would have to travel almost as fast as light. Even then, a round trip to a star could take a space traveler's whole lifetime. Interstellar space reaches distances impossible to imagine. Then *intergalactic space* (space between the galaxies) begins and never ends.

Vast Distances separate the earth from the moon, the planets, and the stars. In the illustration at the left, these bodies appear much closer to the earth than they actually are. If the diagram had been drawn with 1 inch equal to 1,000 miles (or 1 centimeter equal to 630 kilometers), the picture of Pluto would have to be 40 miles (64 kilometers) from that of the earth.

A spacecraft may make several kinds of trips into space. It may be launched into orbit around earth, rocketed to the moon, or sent past a planet. For each trip, the spacecraft must be launched at a particular *velocity* (speed and direction). The job of the launch vehicle is to give the spacecraft this velocity. If the spacecraft carries a crew, the spacecraft itself must be able to slow down and land safely on the earth.

Overcoming Gravity is the biggest problem in getting into space. Gravity pulls everything to earth and gives objects their weight. A rocket overcomes gravity by producing *thrust* (a pushing force). Thrust, like weight, can be measured in pounds or newtons. To lift a spacecraft, a rocket must have a thrust greater than its own weight and the added weight of the spacecraft. The extra thrust *accelerates* the spacecraft. That is, it makes the spacecraft go faster and faster until it reaches the velocity needed for its journey.

Rocket engines create thrust by burning large amounts of fuel. As the fuel burns, it becomes a hot gas. The heat creates an extremely high pressure in the gas. This pressure does two things: (1) it pushes the flaming gas backward and out through the rocket nozzle; (2) it pushes the rocket forward. This forward push on the rocket is the thrust.

Rocket fuels are called *propellants*. Liquid-propellant rockets work by combining a fuel, such as kerosene or liquid hydrogen, with an *oxidizer*, such as liquid oxygen (LOX). The fuel and oxidizer burn violently when mixed. Solid-fuel rockets use dry chemicals as propellants.

Engineers rate the efficiency of propellants in terms of the thrust that 1 pound (0.45 kilogram) of fuel can produce in one second. This measurement is known as the propellant's *specific impulse*. Liquid propellants have a higher specific impulse than most solid propellants. But some, including LOX and liquid hydrogen, are difficult and dangerous to handle. They must be loaded into the rocket just before launching. Solid propellants are loaded into the rocket at the factory, and are then ready to use.

The primary vehicle for research and exploration in the United States space program is the space shuttle. The space shuttle takes off like a rocket, orbits the earth like a spacecraft, and lands like an airplane. It consists of an *orbiter*, an *external tank*, and two *solid rocket boosters*.

The orbiter resembles an airplane. It carries the crew and the *payload* (cargo). The orbiter has three liquid rocket engines near its tail. Propellants are fed to the engines from the external tank. The external tank holds more than $1\frac{1}{2}$ million pounds (680,000 kilograms) of propellant, which consists of liquid hydrogen and LOX. Each solid rocket weighs about 1.3 million pounds (589,000 kilograms) and produces about 2.6 million pounds (1.2 million kilograms) of thrust.

The orbiter's engines, combined with the solid rocket boosters, provide the thrust to launch the space shuttle. After two minutes of flight, the boosters separate from the orbiter. The orbiter continues into space and releases the external tank just before entering orbit.

Returning to Earth involves problems opposite to those of getting into space. The spacecraft must lose

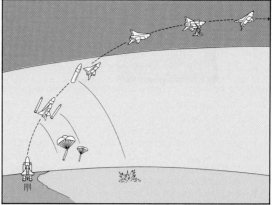

WORLD BOOK illustration by Zorica Dabich

The Space Shuttle Takes Off by using the fuel in its solid rocket boosters and external tank. After the fuel has been used, the boosters return to the earth by parachute and the tank falls into the ocean. In orbit, the spacecraft's payload bay doors are opened for such purposes as releasing or retrieving a satellite.

speed instead of gaining it. The space shuttle orbiter has two smaller engines that are fired to slow down the spacecraft and modify its orbit for the return to earth. These engines are also used for maneuvering during orbit. The orbiter enters the earth's atmosphere at a speed of more than 16,000 miles (25,800 kilometers) per hour. As the spacecraft slows down, friction with the air produces intense heat. The temperature of the wings may reach 2750° F. (1510° C). A *thermal protection system* shields the orbiter from this heat. The thermal protection system consists of more than 25,000 ceramic tiles bonded to the body of the spacecraft. About an hour after the shuttle's engines are fired to bring it out of its orbit, the spacecraft lands on a runway. The shuttle touches down at a speed of about 200 miles (320 kilometers) per hour.

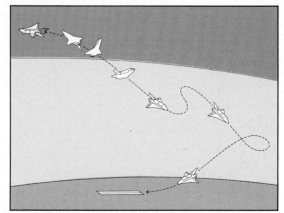

WORLD BOOK illustration by Zorica Dabich

The Orbiter Returns to the Earth by firing two engines that reduce its speed. The spacecraft enters the earth's atmosphere at a speed of more than 16,000 miles (25,800 kilometers) per hour and maneuvers into landing position. It lands on a runway at a speed of about 200 miles (320 kilometers) per hour.

When human beings orbit the earth or travel to the moon, they temporarily live in space. There, they are exposed to conditions that differ greatly from those on the earth. Space has neither air nor the sensation of gravity, and it is subject to extremes of temperature. It also is crisscrossed by dangerous high-energy radiation and particles of stony matter. Astronauts can survive in space only if they are protected from such hazards. They also must be protected from the dangers of sustained high acceleration of the spacecraft, which puts additional pressure on their bodies.

For astronauts to remain healthy in space, their body needs must also be met. These needs include breathing, eating and drinking, elimination of body wastes, sleeping, and exercise and recreation.

Protection Against the Dangers of Space. Engineers working with specialists in space medicine have eliminated or greatly reduced most of the hazards of living in space. They have developed spacecraft and equipment that provide adequate protection under all flight conditions.

The *trajectory* (flight path) of a spacecraft determines in part the amount of pressure on the bodies of the astronauts, especially during launch and reentry into the earth's atmosphere. In determining the trajectory, engineers consider the physical limitations of the human body as well as the structural design of the spacecraft and the orbit it will follow. The trajectory of the space shuttle during launch and reentry limits the effects of acceleration on the crew to about 3 *G's*. Such pressure makes the astronauts weigh about three times as much as they do on the earth. This limit is considered the maximum the astronauts can sustain while enabling them to move their head and arms easily enough to control the spacecraft. Normally, the guidance, navigation, and con-

NASA

The Commander and the Pilot of the space shuttle fly the orbiter from the cabin, *above*. The commander of the first flight was John W. Young, *left*. The pilot was Robert L. Crippen, *right*.

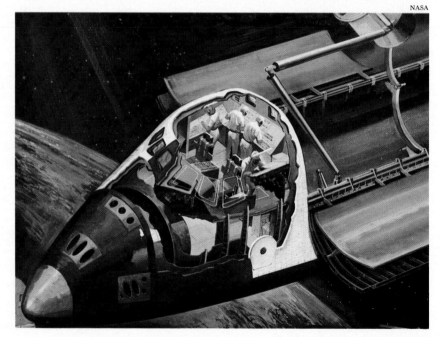

NASA

The Crew's Quarters of the space shuttle can carry up to seven astronauts. It includes cooking and sleeping areas, as well as the astronauts' work stations. Behind the crew's quarters is the payload area.

trol systems of the space shuttle are operated automatically during launch, but the crew can take control in an emergency.

During the early U.S. manned space programs, the astronauts wore pressurized flight suits during launch and reentry in case of a sudden loss of pressure in the cabin. On the space shuttle, pressurized suits are worn only when the astronauts work outside the spacecraft. The shuttle was designed to allow a "shirtsleeve" environment inside. However, the astronauts may wear a *counter pressure garment* during reentry if necessary to help maintain normal blood circulation.

During flight, astronauts are protected from the danger of *micrometeoroids* (particles of space dust) in various ways. The body of the space shuttle has ceramic tiles that shield the spacecraft from high temperatures and a coated felt material that guards against low temperatures. Even if a tiny meteoroid penetrated these materials, the spacecraft's life support and pressurization systems would enable the mission to continue. In case of a hole $\frac{1}{2}$ inch (13 millimeters) or more in diameter, pressure could be maintained long enough to allow the shuttle to land safely on the earth.

When astronauts are working outside their spacecraft, they wear garments that provide oxygen for breathing and maintain proper air pressure and temperature. The garments also protect the astronauts against micrometeoroids. These space suits are made of many layers of strong synthetic materials, including nylon and Teflon.

The space suits and the spacecraft itself also protect astronauts from exposure to high levels of radiation. The radiation in space comes from the sun and from sources outside the solar system. The most dangerous forms of this radiation include atomic particles, such as electrons and protons. They also consist of *ions* (charged atoms) of gas, plus cosmic rays, gamma rays, and X rays. These kinds of radiation can damage the cells of the human body. Exposure to large amounts of high-energy radiation may cause illness or even death.

All spacecraft have a *thermal-control system* to counteract the extreme high and low temperatures of space. This system maintains comfortable temperatures throughout a flight and prevents physical problems that may result from exposure to intense heat or cold.

Scientists have found that the weightlessness of space does not endanger human beings. Astronauts may sometimes experience dizziness and nausea from working under weightless conditions, especially during the first few days of a flight. But such discomforts can be relieved by antimotion drugs. On extended space missions of the future, artificial gravity may be created aboard a spacecraft by slowly spinning the craft.

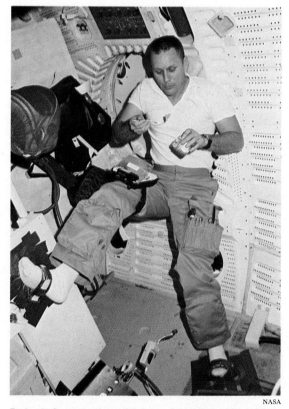

NASA

Eating in Space involves adjusting to the condition of weightlessness. In the photograph above, an astronaut aboard the space shuttle eats his dinner with his feet strapped down.

NASA

An Astronaut's Space Suit provides a life-support system outside the spacecraft. A gas-propelled backpack enables the astronaut to move around the spacecraft for up to six hours.

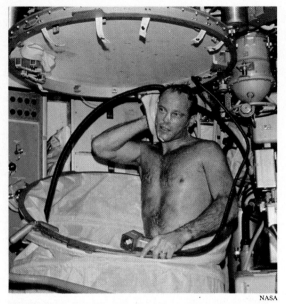

NASA

NASA

Bathing Aboard a Spacecraft requires special equipment. The Skylab astronauts took hot showers in a folding stall equipped with a vacuum system to draw off the wash water.

Recording Medical Information on a spacecraft enables physicians on the earth to determine any abnormal changes in the body that could indicate physical disorders or stress.

Providing for Basic Needs in Space. A manned spacecraft is equipped with life-support systems designed to meet all the body needs of the crew. Portable life-support systems that can be carried in a backpack enable astronauts to work outside their spacecraft.

Breathing. The air in the space shuttle is pure oxygen or a special mixture of oxygen and nitrogen similar to the atmosphere of the earth. The system that supplies the air also controls the amount of moisture in it and removes any impurities.

Eating and Drinking. The food on a space flight must be nutritious, easy to eat, and convenient to store. On the early Apollo missions, the astronauts ate mostly food that was *freeze-dried* (frozen, with the water removed). Such food was supplied in tube-shaped plastic bags and included cream of chicken soup, coffee, and bite-sized pieces of barbecued beef and turkey. The astronauts injected hot water into one end of a bag and mixed the food and water for several minutes. Then they cut off the other end of the bag and squeezed the food into their mouths. On later Apollo flights, the astronauts were provided with freeze-dried foods that they ate with a spoon. These foods included beef stew and scalloped potatoes.

The astronauts' eating conditions were improved for the lengthy missions on the Skylab space station. The Skylab crews warmed up frozen and chilled food in the galley of the space station. The space shuttle orbiter also has facilities for heating food, and the crews use dishes and silverware.

Water for drinking and other purposes is provided by a *water management system*. This system uses devices called *fuel cells* to produce pure, fresh water. The fuel cells also generate electric energy for the spacecraft.

Elimination of Body Wastes. The collection and disposal of body wastes are a special problem in space. The space shuttle orbiter has a *waste collector* that resembles the toilet of an airplane. This device is part of a system that processes urine and collects, dries, and stores solid wastes. The system also processes water that the astronauts have used for washing. The urine and used wash water are transferred to waste storage tanks. When the astronauts are working outside the space shuttle orbiter, they wear a urine collection device under their space suits.

Sleeping. Facilities for sleeping vary according to the size of a spacecraft. In fairly small vehicles similar to the Apollo spacecraft, astronauts had to sleep in the same couches from which they piloted the ship. They strapped themselves to the couches to avoid floating around in the weightless environment. A large spacecraft, such as the space shuttle orbiter, has separate compartments equipped with enclosures that resemble sleeping bags. These enclosures enable astronauts to sleep unstrapped without floating.

Exercise and Recreation. Exercise is important for astronauts, especially on long space flights. The heart, blood vessels, and muscles may weaken because weightlessness involves less work for the body than does fighting gravity. During the Skylab missions, which lasted up to 84 days, the astronauts exercised at least 30 minutes each day. They worked out on a stationary bicycle and on a foot-powered wheel device similar to a treadmill.

Recreation is also essential on long space flights to ensure mental health. Books, games, and tape decks with recorded music provided Skylab crews with entertainment during periods of relaxation.

Taking Medical Measurements. On early space flights, the astronauts wore an *operational bioinstrumentation system* during liftoff and reentry. This system provided medical data to physicians called *flight surgeons*, who specialize in aviation and space medicine. The data obtained from the monitoring devices helped medical specialists learn how the human body reacts to conditions in space. This knowledge enabled physicians to guard against hazards and stresses on later missions. As space flight has become more routine, less use has been made of such monitoring devices.

All manned spacecraft have medical kits that include drugs for such conditions as infections and stomach upsets. During a mission, flight surgeons may diagnose minor illnesses for which they prescribe appropriate drugs. In addition, a crew's work schedule may be adjusted to give them more time to rest if necessary.

Performing Scientific Duties. On a space mission, astronauts carry out a variety of complicated tasks. On the moon, they set up scientific equipment and brought back rock samples for study. The Skylab astronauts collected data on the atmosphere of the sun and on solar flares. They used various devices to make observations of the snow and ice, sources of pollution, and weather conditions on the earth. Space shuttle crews have launched artificial satellites while orbiting the earth. The orbiter also has equipment that is designed to retrieve and repair satellites.

Other experiments conducted during a mission help scientists learn more about the ability of human beings to live and work in space. Skylab crew members did different types of exercises and measured their physical performances to help determine the effects of prolonged exposure to weightlessness. They also drew blood samples and partially processed them for further study by researchers on the earth.

Communications with the Earth. The space shuttle takes off from the John F. Kennedy Space Center in Cape Canaveral, Fla. At the time of liftoff, responsibility for the mission moves to the Lyndon B. Johnson Space Center in Houston. The mission control team there maintains responsibility until landing, when control goes back to the Kennedy Space Center. During a flight, the crew of the shuttle maintains radio contact with the mission control center in Houston.

The mission control center has the major responsibility for planning the space shuttle's launch, orbit, and reentry maneuvers. In addition, mission controllers establish a daily plan that enables the crew to accomplish its flight objectives. A shuttle mission of seven days may have as many as 100 objectives. Primary objectives include launching satellites and providing other services for the shuttle's customers. Secondary objectives involve engineering tests and various performance demonstrations. The mission control center also monitors the spacecraft's systems during the flight and diagnoses problems and suggests solutions.

Radio transmissions from the space shuttle include television pictures and instrument-recorded scientific data. Such information and visual observations are vital to the success of a space mission and to the safety of the crew.

Engineers and scientists at the National Aeronautics and Space Administration (NASA) developed the tracking and communications network for the space shuttle program. The system consists of several ground stations and two orbiting satellites to provide continuous coverage of shuttle flights. The stations and satellites send tracking information about the spacecraft to a computer in the Goddard Space Flight Center in Greenbelt, Md. The computer calculates the orbit and position of the spacecraft.

NASA

Peaks of the Himalaya as seen from the space shuttle are shown in this photograph. The shuttle can be used to observe weather, agricultural, and environmental conditions on the earth.

NASA

A Communications Satellite is prepared for launch by the space shuttle. In this photo, the payload bay doors of the orbiter are open and the satellite is ready to be spring-released.

A launch vehicle is a rocket or a combination of rockets used to launch satellites, space probes, and other spacecraft. The United States uses several launch vehicles with a wide range of lifting power. These vehicles can launch many kinds of spacecraft to various distances. A rocket must burn a large amount of fuel to launch a spacecraft, and so a launch vehicle consists mostly of fuel tanks. The more powerful it is, the larger it must be to hold the needed fuel. See ROCKET.

The Building Block Idea. Engineers use a few basic rockets and rocket engines to build a family of launch vehicles. They call this method the "building block" idea. Here is how it works.

The part of a launch vehicle that provides most of the propulsion for a spacecraft to go into orbit is called the *booster* stage. Atlas boosters orbited U.S. astronauts in the Mercury program. An Atlas combined with an Agena second stage has launched many *Mariner* space probes to Mars and Venus. The combined vehicle is called an Atlas-Agena. The Atlas-Centaur, a more powerful vehicle, combines the Atlas with a Centaur second stage. The Atlas-Centaur has launched heavy satellites, such as the *Orbiting Astronomical Observatories* and the *Intelsat* communications satellites.

The Titan family of launch vehicles combines the Titan booster with the same second stages used by the Atlas. The Titan II launched U.S. astronauts in the Gemini program. The Titan combined with an Agena second stage has launched many military satellites. The Titan-Centaur with two solid-fuel boosters strapped to it has enough power to launch heavy probes to Mars.

Engineers use rocket engines as well as whole rockets for building blocks. For example, the Saturn family of launch vehicles uses three basic engines, the H-1, F-1, and J-2. Saturn vehicles carried the first astronauts to the moon in the Apollo program. These vehicles also orbited the first U.S. space station, *Skylab*. The Saturn 1B has two stages. The first stage uses eight H-1 engines, and the second stage uses one J-2 engine. The more powerful Saturn V consists of three stages. The first stage has five F-1 engines, the second stage five J-2 engines, and the third stage one J-2 engine.

Piggyback Boosters. Sometimes engineers attach solid-fuel rockets to the sides of a liquid-fuel launch vehi-

Launch Vehicles

Launch Vehicle	Stages	Takeoff Thrust		Payload
* Vanguard	3	28,000 lbs.	125,000 N†	50 lbs. (23 kg) in earth orbit
* Jupiter C	4	82,000 lbs.	365,000 N	30 lbs. (14 kg) in earth orbit
Scout	4	107,200 lbs.	476,850 N	410 lbs. (186 kg) in earth orbit, 85 lbs. (39 kg) to moon
* Juno II	4	150,000 lbs.	667,000 N	100 lbs. (45 kg) in earth orbit
* Mercury-Redstone	1	82,000 lbs.	365,000 N	3,000 lbs. (1,400 kg) suborbital
Delta	3	205,000 lbs.	911,900 N	3,900 lbs. (1,770 kg) in earth orbit; 1,050 lbs. (476 kg) to moon
* Mercury-Atlas	1½**	367,000 lbs.	1,632,000 N	3,000 lbs. (1,400 kg) in earth orbit
Atlas-Agena	2½**	400,000 lbs.	1,800,000 N	7,700 lbs. (3,490 kg) in earth orbit; 1,430 lbs. (649 kg) to moon; 1,000 lbs. (450 kg) to Mars or Venus
Atlas-Centaur	2½**	400,000 lbs.	1,800,000 N	10,300 lbs. (4,672 kg) in earth orbit; 2,500 lbs. (1,130 kg) to moon; 2,200 lbs. (998 kg) to Mars or Venus
* Titan II	2	430,000 lbs.	1,910,000 N	8,600 lbs. (3,900 kg) in earth orbit
Titan IIIC	3 or 4	2,400,000 lbs.	10,700,000 N	26,000 lbs. (11,800 kg) in earth orbit; 6,200 lbs. (2,810 kg) to moon
Titan-Centaur	4	2,400,000 lbs.	10,700,000 N	35,000 lbs. (15,900 kg) in earth orbit; 11,500 lbs. (5,216 kg) interplanetary missions
Space Shuttle System	3	6,925,000 lbs.	30,802,000 N	65,000 lbs. (29,500 kg) in earth orbit
* Saturn V	3	7,570,000 lbs.	33,670,000 N	285,000 lbs. (129,300 kg) in earth orbit; 107,000 lbs. (48,530 kg) to moon; 70,000 lbs. (32,000 kg) to Mars or Venus

*No longer in use.
**Half stage is droppable booster engine.
†N is the abbreviation for *newton*, the unit of force in the metric system.

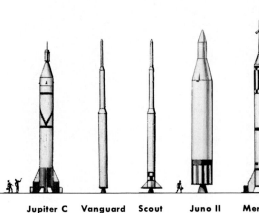
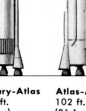

Jupiter C	Vanguard	Scout	Juno II	Mercury-Redstone	Mercury-Atlas	Atlas-Agena	Atlas-Centaur	Titan II
68⅓ ft.	72 ft.	72 ft.	76 ft.	83 ft.	95⅓ ft.	102 ft.	109 ft.	109 ft.
(20.8 m)	(21.9 m)	(21.9 m)	(23.2 m)	(25.3 m)	(29.1 m)	(31.1 m)	(33.2 m)	(33.2 m)

cle to give it extra power. For example, the Titan II liquid-fuel vehicle could lift 8,600 pounds (3,900 kilograms) into a low orbit of the earth. But with two solid-fuel boosters strapped to its sides, Titan can lift 28,000 pounds (12,700 kilograms). This piggyback combination is known as Titan IIIC.

Space Shuttle Systems began to operate in the early 1980's. A space shuttle does the work of a launch vehicle. However, unlike other launch vehicles, it can make more than one flight. For this reason, the shuttle system greatly reduces the cost of space flights. This system is replacing most other large launch vehicles of the U.S. space program.

The shuttle system has three main stages: (1) an orbiter, which has three main engines, (2) an external tank, and (3) two solid rocket boosters. The orbiter lifts off by means of its own engines and the solid rocket boosters. The external tank feeds propellant to the orbiter's engines. After two minutes, the booster rockets separate from the orbiter and return to the earth by parachutes. The boosters can be used again on another flight. The orbiter releases the external tank just before going into orbit. The tank breaks up over the ocean. On most flights, two pilot astronauts operate the orbiter and two astronauts called mission specialists handle the cargo. But the space shuttle can carry a crew of seven astronauts. After the mission has been completed, the orbiter enters the earth's atmosphere and lands on a runway like an airplane.

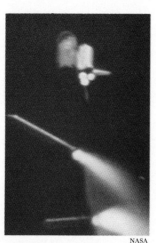

NASA

Solid Rocket Boosters of the space shuttle are released at an altitude of about 27 miles (43 kilometers), after two minutes of flight. The boosters return to the earth by parachute and can be used again on another flight.

WORLD BOOK illustrations

Delta
116 feet
(35.4 m)

Titan IIIC
135 ft.
(41.1 m)

Titan-Centaur
160 ft.
(48.8 m)

Space Shuttle System
184 ft.
(56.1 m)

Saturn V
363 ft.
(110.6 m)

John F. Kennedy NASA Space Center

The Kennedy Space Center lies on the Atlantic coast of Florida. It serves as the primary launch and recovery site of the reusable space vehicle called the *space shuttle.*

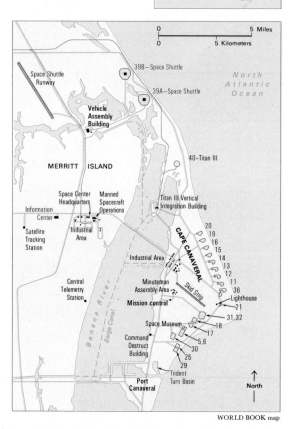

WORLD BOOK map

The equipment needed to launch a space vehicle depends on the vehicle's size. A small sounding rocket, for example, can be launched from a simple stand that has a rail for guiding the rocket. But a huge vehicle such as the space shuttle needs a special launch complex.

The space shuttle is a reusable transport vehicle that is designed to take off like a rocket and land like an airplane. It consists of an orbiter, an external tank for liquid fuels, and two solid rocket boosters. The shuttle orbiter can carry a crew of up to seven astronauts and as much as 65,000 pounds (29,500 kilograms) of equipment into orbit around the earth. Such equipment may include a scientific laboratory or automated space satellites. The orbiter can be used either to place these satellites into earth orbit or to launch them to the planets.

The shuttle orbiter is serviced in the Orbiter Processing Facility at the John F. Kennedy Space Center in Cape Canaveral, Fla. It is then moved into the center's 52-story Vehicle Assembly Building, where it is connected to its large solid rocket boosters and external fuel tank. Next, a giant tractorlike machine called a *crawler* carries the shuttle to one of two launch pads. On the pad, technicians load space satellites or other equipment into the cargo compartment of the orbiter. They also fill the external fuel tank with liquid hydrogen and liquid oxygen for the orbiter's three main engines.

Before the launch, engineers follow a *countdown* (schedule) to be sure that all preparations are completed at the proper time. As the countdown nears its end, a computer takes control. But technicians in the launch control center, who monitor the pad with television cameras, can resume control of the countdown if necessary. Finally, the orbiter's engines ignite and build up thrust. Then the solid rocket boosters are ignited, enabling the shuttle to lift off the pad. The rocket boosters are discarded after about two minutes of flight, and the external tank is released immediately before the orbiter enters earth orbit.

Crawler Transports Space Shuttle to Launch Pad

NASA

Technicians Keep Watch in Launch Control Center

NASA

The NASA Spaceport includes the Vehicle Assembly Building, where the space shuttle's solid rocket boosters, external fuel tank, and airplanelike orbiter are assembled. After assembly, the shuttle is carried by a crawler to one of two launch pads. Fixed and movable service structures at the pad enable technicians to work on the spacecraft until a few hours before launch.

WORLD BOOK illustration by Don Meighan

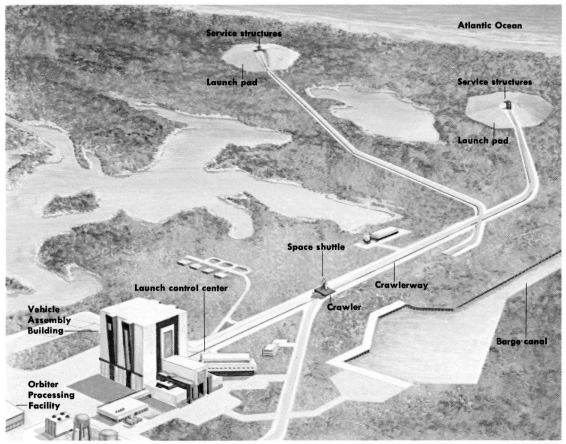

Atlantic Ocean

Service structures

Launch pad

Service structures

Launch pad

Space shuttle

Launch control center

Crawlerway

Crawler

Vehicle Assembly Building

Barge canal

Orbiter Processing Facility

Space Shuttle Lifts Off

NASA

Space Shuttle Approaches Landing Strip on Return

NASA

NASA

Orbiting the Earth at a height of 100 miles (160 kilometers), an astronaut can see blankets of clouds over the ocean, the blue band of the atmosphere curving around the horizon, and the black sky of space. This photo of Gemini 6 was taken during its rendezvous mission with Gemini 7.

Selecting the Orbit is one of the first steps in planning the launch of an earth-orbiting spacecraft. Early manned spacecraft usually orbited less than 200 miles (320 kilometers) high. In this way, they avoided the radiation in the Van Allen belts. A communications satellite may orbit at a much greater distance in order to serve many ground stations.

Most orbiting spacecraft do not stay the same distance from the earth all the time. Their orbits have the shape of a flattened circle called an *ellipse*. One end of the ellipse comes closer to the earth than the other. The point closest to the earth is called the orbiting spacecraft's *perigee*. The farthest point is called the *apogee*. Many scientific satellites follow orbits that have a low perigee and a very high apogee. These satellites can explore a wide range of space.

Satellites may also be launched in various directions around earth. They may circle in an east-west direction, in line with the equator. Or, they may travel north and south, passing over the earth's poles. Most satellites travel in a direction between these extremes.

Launching a Spacecraft. When the launch vehicle blasts off, it lifts the spacecraft straight up for about a minute. Then the vehicle arches into the proper direction for the selected orbit. Finally, the vehicle's last stage fires to give the spacecraft the velocity it needs to go into orbit. The higher the orbit, the lower the speed needed to stay in orbit. For example, a spacecraft in a circular orbit 200 miles (320 kilometers) high must travel more than 17,000 miles (27,400 kilometers) per hour. But to orbit at 22,000 miles (35,400 kilometers),

a spacecraft needs a speed of only about 6,900 miles (11,100 kilometers) per hour. However, a more powerful launch vehicle is needed to put a spacecraft in the higher orbit.

To place a spacecraft in orbit, the launching rockets must be carefully controlled. Each stage must burn for the exact length of time to give the spacecraft the right speed. Sensitive gyroscopes and other special devices guide the vehicle to keep it on course. Some vehicles are controlled by clockwork or magnetic tape devices. Many launch vehicles are controlled electronically from the ground. Signals from the vehicle tell a computer on the ground how the vehicle is working. The computer compares this information with the vehicle's planned operation. The computer then sends signals back to the vehicle to make the necessary corrections in speed or direction.

How a Spacecraft Stays in Orbit. Nothing "holds up" an orbiting spacecraft. Gravity keeps the spacecraft in orbit by pulling down on it. Without gravity, the spacecraft would shoot off into space in a straight line. But gravity pulls the spacecraft out of the straight path and causes it to curve around the earth.

The force of gravity weakens as the distance from earth is increased. Near the earth, a strong gravitational force pulls a spacecraft and causes it to curve. There, the spacecraft must have a high speed. Otherwise it would curve too much and come closer and closer to earth. But at higher altitudes, gravity is not so strong. There, a spacecraft can travel more slowly and still keep from being pulled closer to earth.

Kinds of Earth Orbits

Circular and Elliptical Orbits. The diagram, *right,* shows the difference between circular and elliptical orbits. In a circular orbit, a spacecraft always travels at the same speed and stays the same distance from earth. In an elliptical orbit, a spacecraft's speed and distance from earth change continually. The spacecraft goes fastest at perigee and then slows down as it swings farther from earth. It travels slowest at apogee, but speeds up as it curves back closer to earth.

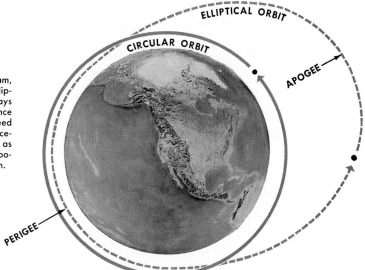

ELLIPTICAL ORBIT

CIRCULAR ORBIT

APOGEE

PERIGEE

An Inclined Orbit forms an angle with the equator, *below, left.* In the diagrams, the red lines show the orbit, and the blue lines represent the spacecraft's path as mapped on the earth. Because the earth rotates, the spacecraft does not pass over the same points on earth during each orbit. As a result, the path of the spacecraft appears as crisscrossed lines on the earth, *right.*

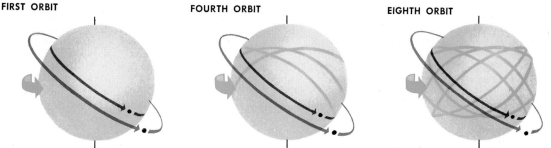

FIRST ORBIT

FOURTH ORBIT

EIGHTH ORBIT

A Polar Orbit carries a spacecraft over the north and south poles, as shown in the diagram, *below, left.* As the earth rotates, the spacecraft passes over different points on earth during each orbit, as shown *below, right.* A polar orbit is especially useful in scientific satellites such as Nimbus. By orbiting almost directly over the poles, Nimbus can photograph the entire earth once a day.

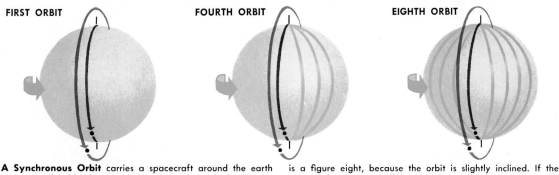

FIRST ORBIT

FOURTH ORBIT

EIGHTH ORBIT

A Synchronous Orbit carries a spacecraft around the earth once every day. The diagram, *below,* shows the path of a Syncom communications satellite. As mapped on earth, the satellite's path is a figure eight, because the orbit is slightly inclined. If the spacecraft were launched directly in line with the equator, it would stay above one spot on earth without moving north or south.

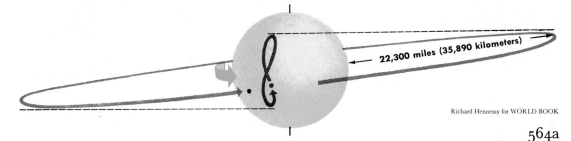

22,300 miles (35,890 kilometers)

Richard Hennessy for WORLD BOOK

564a

This section describes the *Apollo* spacecraft that took U.S. astronauts to the moon in 1969 and the early 1970's. The *Soyuz* spacecraft that carry Russian cosmonauts to orbiting space stations are similar.

The *Apollo* spacecraft were lifted into space atop huge launch vehicles. The spacecraft had the general shape of a cone. They were launched with the narrow end pointing up to reduce air resistance during the flight through the atmosphere. They descended through the atmosphere backwards—with the broad end pointing in the direction of flight. In this way, they lost speed quickly, because the broad end offered great resistance to the air. Spacecraft like the Apollo *lunar module* were not streamlined at all. This spacecraft was designed to operate only near the moon, where there is no air.

The Apollo spacecraft carried (1) life-support systems, (2) communications and navigation equipment, (3) control systems, and (4) reentry and landing equipment.

Life-Support Systems supplied the astronauts with oxygen, food, and water. Oxygen and water were carried in tanks. Food was freeze-dried and stored in meal-size packages. Solid body wastes were sealed into plastic bags and stored aboard the spacecraft. Liquid wastes were released into space.

Communications and Navigation Equipment. The astronauts needed a radio to report to scientists and engineers on the ground. They could answer their questions and ask for directions in an emergency. The Apollo spacecraft carried a television camera so that pictures from space or the moon could be sent to earth during the flight. Navigation equipment included sextants, gyroscopes, and small electronic computers. The astronauts used this equipment to find their position in space and to check their course. *Telemetry* equipment sent information about all spacecraft systems to ground stations (see TELEMETRY).

Control Systems enabled the astronauts to put the spacecraft in any position. They did this by firing tiny rocket motors located at various places on the outside of the craft. By operating these motors, the astronauts could tilt the craft, point it to either side, and roll it right or left. To reenter the atmosphere, the craft had to point a certain way, or else it might have skipped away from earth or descended too fast and burnt up.

Reentry and Landing Equipment. The engines of the propulsion system were used for maneuvering in space. The engines were fired in the opposite direction of orbit to slow the spacecraft down and cause it to fall out of orbit. The *heat shield* protected the astronauts from the intense heat generated when the craft plunged through the atmosphere. It consisted of a thick layer of material covering the broad end of the spacecraft. The material partly melted and partly vaporized during reentry. Air flowing around the spacecraft removed this material, carrying away most of the heat. When the spacecraft had lost enough speed and altitude, parachutes opened and lowered it gently to the earth.

Manned Spacecraft

Four U.S. and two Russian spacecraft are shown *below*. *Vostok* and *Mercury* capsules each carried one space pilot. The *Gemini* capsule carried two astronauts who could change the orbit of the craft. Three astronauts orbited the moon in the *Apollo command module.* Two of them landed on the moon in the *lunar module.* The *Apollo service module* carried a rocket engine used during the flight. The Russian *Soyuz* can carry three cosmonauts.

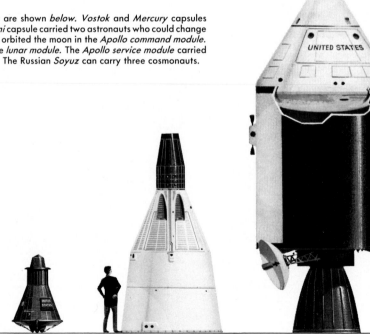

Russian Vostok
About 16 ft.
(4.9 m)

Mercury capsule
6⅞ ft.
(2.1 m)

Gemini capsule
19 ft.
(5.8 m)

Apollo command and service modules
35⅓ ft.
(10.8 m)

NASA

Inside an Apollo Command Module, the pilot moves a control stick to turn the spacecraft. Astronaut Frank Borman is shown lying on his couch during a ground test.

© 1969 Universal Science News Service, Inc.

Inside an Apollo Lunar Module Simulator, astronaut Neil A. Armstrong practices a moon landing. Through a window to his left, he sees a simulated moonscape.

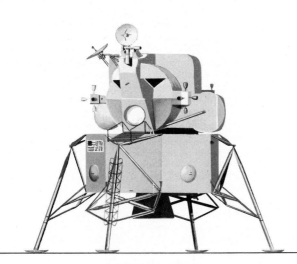

Apollo lunar module
22⅞ ft.
(7 m)

Russian Soyuz
23⅜ ft.
(7.1 m)

565

NASA

The First Persons on the Moon were astronauts Neil A. Armstrong, who took this picture, and Edwin E. Aldrin, Jr., *above,* next to a seismometer. A television camera and an American flag are in the background. The lunar module *Eagle* stands at the right.

Much more power is required to send a spacecraft to the moon than to put it in orbit around the earth. To reach the moon, a spacecraft must reach a speed of about 24,300 miles (39,100 kilometers) per hour. To reach this speed, an Apollo spacecraft was boosted into the sky by a Saturn V rocket. This section describes the Apollo missions of 1969 and the early 1970's.

The three Apollo astronauts, riding in the command module near the top of the vehicle, were forced back on their couches as five engines lifted them from the earth. About $2\frac{1}{4}$ minutes after liftoff, the vehicle was traveling about 6,200 miles (9,980 kilometers) per hour and was about 41 miles (66 kilometers) high. The first stage then separated from the vehicle, and the second stage ignited.

The second stage carried the vehicle about 116 miles (187 kilometers) above the earth and boosted its speed to about 15,400 miles (24,780 kilometers) per hour. Then the second stage separated and the third stage ignited, sending the vehicle into a near-circular "parking" orbit around the earth, 118 miles (190 kilometers) high. While the astronauts were in earth orbit, they checked the spacecraft to make certain it was not damaged during liftoff. The third stage then ignited again, and the astronauts headed for the moon.

Aiming at the Moon. The moon is a moving target. It travels around the earth at more than 2,000 miles (3,200 kilometers) per hour. During a spacecraft's three-day journey, the moon moves more than 165,000 miles (265,500 kilometers). Therefore, a spacecraft must be aimed at a spot that far ahead of the moon—and it must reach this spot at exactly the same time the moon does.

The third stage of the Saturn burned for about $5\frac{1}{2}$ minutes, pushing the spacecraft toward the moon at about 24,300 miles (39,100 kilometers) per hour. After this burn, the command and service module separated from the Saturn stage and turned around. The astronauts then docked with the lunar module (LM), which was still attached to the Saturn third stage. Later, the combined command and service module and LM was disconnected from the third stage.

As the spacecraft sped on, the navigator determined if the craft was on course. Using a *sextant* and a telescope, he measured the angle between a star and some landmark on the earth, or between a star and the moon's horizon. After measuring the angles to three stars, the navigator used a computer to determine the spacecraft's position. At the same time, the mission control center in Houston was plotting the spacecraft's trajectory. If the spacecraft was off course, the mission controllers instructed the crew to make one or more *midcourse corrections.* Small rocket motors were fired to bring the spacecraft to the proper course.

As the spacecraft traveled toward the moon, the earth's gravity slowed it down continuously. When the spacecraft reached a point about 215,000 miles (346,000 kilometers) from the earth, it had slowed to about 2,000 miles (3,200 kilometers) per hour. But at this point— only about 30,000 miles (48,000 kilometers) from the moon—the moon's gravity is stronger than the earth's, and the spacecraft began to pick up speed.

Orbiting the Moon follows the same principles as orbiting the earth. A spacecraft needs a certain speed to orbit at a certain altitude. The Apollo spacecraft had more speed than it needed to go into lunar orbit. Therefore, a rocket engine in the service module fired to slow the spacecraft and put it in orbit. Then two of the three astronauts entered the LM through a hatch.

Landing on the Moon. After the lunar module was carefully checked by the astronauts, it was separated from the command module. The command module, manned by the third astronaut, stayed in lunar orbit. The LM fired its engine and began its descent to the moon. Parachutes and wings could not be used to lower the craft. These devices need air to work, and there is no air on the moon. The LM carried a rocket engine that slowed the descent as the craft neared the surface.

A computer normally guided the LM at the beginning of descent. But the pilot took control as the LM approached the lunar surface. The astronauts could hover above the landing site for about a minute while they made certain that they could land safely. Probes extending from the legs of the LM indicated when it was 5 feet (1.5 meters) above the surface. The men then shut

From Earth to the Moon

The illustration on this page shows the operations involved in sending a spacecraft to the moon. After the lunar module lands (16), the astronauts perform their scientific tasks on the moon. To leave the moon, the lunar module lifts off and docks with the command module. After docking, the lunar module crew moves into the command module. The lunar module is then disconnected and the command module returns to the earth.

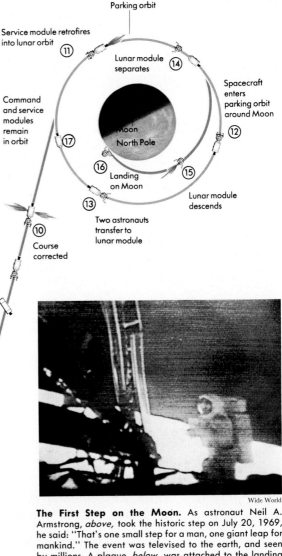

Parking orbit

Service module retrofires into lunar orbit (11)

Lunar module separates (14)

Spacecraft enters parking orbit around Moon

Command and service modules remain in orbit (17)

Moon North Pole

(12)

(16)

(15)

Landing on Moon (13)

Lunar module descends

Two astronauts transfer to lunar module

(10) Course corrected

(9) Third stage separates from spacecraft

(8) Docking with lunar module

(7) Command and service modules turn around

(6) Spacecraft separates

(5) Third stage reignites to send spacecraft to Moon

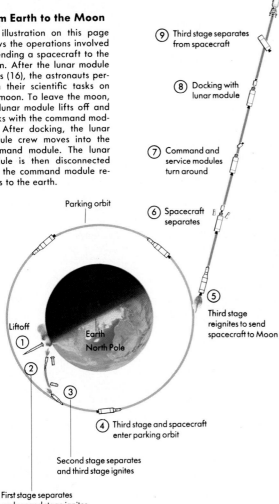

Parking orbit

Liftoff (1)

Earth North Pole

(2)

(3)

(4) Third stage and spacecraft enter parking orbit

Second stage separates and third stage ignites

First stage separates and second stage ignites

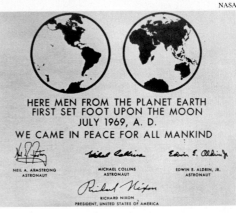

Wide World

The First Step on the Moon. As astronaut Neil A. Armstrong, *above,* took the historic step on July 20, 1969, he said: "That's one small step for a man, one giant leap for mankind." The event was televised to the earth, and seen by millions. A plaque, *below,* was attached to the landing craft's descent stage, which was left on the moon.

NASA

HERE MEN FROM THE PLANET EARTH
FIRST SET FOOT UPON THE MOON
JULY 1969, A. D.
WE CAME IN PEACE FOR ALL MANKIND

NEIL A. ARMSTRONG
ASTRONAUT

MICHAEL COLLINS
ASTRONAUT

EDWIN E. ALDRIN, JR.
ASTRONAUT

RICHARD NIXON
PRESIDENT, UNITED STATES OF AMERICA

off the engine, and the craft landed on the moon.

The astronauts would have been stranded if the LM were damaged beyond repair while landing. The LM had to lift them off the moon because the command module was not designed to land on the moon.

Exploring the Moon. After the Apollo lunar module landed on the moon, the astronauts and the mission controllers in Houston checked the LM to be sure it could get back to the command module. Before leaving the LM, each lunar explorer put on additional garments for protection against the moon's airless environment. A backpack worn outside the LM contained all the systems needed to support life. While the crew was exploring the moon, mission control monitored the LM systems.

The first human beings on the moon were U.S. astronauts Neil A. Armstrong and Edwin E. Aldrin, Jr. Their Apollo 11 lunar module, called *Eagle*, touched down on the rocky plain called the Sea of Tranquility on July 20, 1969. First Armstrong and then Aldrin stepped on the moon's surface. Aldrin described the view of the moon as "magnificent desolation." The astronauts quickly became adjusted to the gravity of the moon, which is only one-sixth as strong as that of the earth's.

Astronauts made six moon landings between 1969 and 1972. The Apollo 12 module, *Intrepid*, landed on the waterless Ocean of Storms on Nov. 19, 1969. It carried astronauts Charles (Pete) Conrad, Jr., and Alan L. Bean. Apollo 14 astronauts Alan B. Shepard, Jr., and Edgar D. Mitchell landed their module, *Antares*, near the Fra Mauro Crater on Feb. 5, 1971. Apollo 15 astronauts David R. Scott and James B. Irwin landed their module, *Falcon*, in the Apennines mountains on July 30, 1971. Apollo 16 astronauts John W. Young and Charles M. Duke, Jr., landed their module, *Orion*, in the Descartes region on April 20, 1972. Apollo 17 astronauts Eugene A. Cernan and Harrison H.

NASA

A Lunar Rover carried Apollo 15 astronauts David R. Scott and James B. Irwin more than 17 miles (27 kilometers) on the moon. The vehicle enabled the men to travel farther from their lunar module than any previous Apollo astronauts. Irwin is shown working with the rover near the landing site. Mount Hadley, in the Apennines range, rises in the background.

Schmitt landed their module, *Challenger*, in the Taurus mountains on Dec. 11, 1972.

An important task of the Apollo astronauts was the recovery of samples from the lunar surface for study. Apollo 11 astronauts collected about 48 pounds (22 kilograms) of surface material. Apollo 15 astronauts Scott and Irwin drilled 10 feet (3 meters) into the moon to obtain some lunar samples. Scott and Irwin became the first astronauts to travel on the moon in a vehicle. They drove their battery-powered *lunar rover* more than 17 miles (27 kilometers). Apollo 17 astronauts Cernan and Schmitt returned with samples that scientists thought might contain evidence of volcanic activity.

The Apollo astronauts also set up a series of scientific experiments called *ALSEP* (*Apollo Lunar Surface Experiment Package*). These experiments were powered by a small nuclear generator and were controlled from the mission control center in Houston for many years after the Apollo program ended. One device—a screen of aluminum foil 1 by 3 feet (30 by 91 centimeters)—captured particles of the solar wind shot out from the sun (see SOLAR WIND). Apollo astronauts also set up instruments called *seismometers* to detect earthquakelike disturbances in the moon. At least one set of vibrations detected by a seismometer was thought to have been caused by a moonquake. After the astronauts were aboard their command modules, they sent the ascent stage of their lunar modules crashing into the moon to create vibrations for the seismometers to detect.

Another device left on the moon was a reflector for a *laser beam* (an extremely intense beam of light). Scientists use it to measure the distance to the moon by timing pulses of light sent from a laser on the earth and reflected back to the earth.

NASA

A Giant Boulder yielded valuable lunar samples to Apollo 17 scientist-astronaut Harrison H. Schmitt, *above*. Astronaut Eugene A. Cernan took this photograph as the two men explored near their landing site in the Taurus Mountains.

NASA

The Lunar Module Blasts Off from the moon in this photo taken from a TV transmission. After liftoff, the lunar module (LM) went into an orbit around the moon that was lower than that of the command module. When the two spacecraft were in the proper positions, the LM went into the same orbit as the command module. The command module then maneuvered to dock with the LM.

When the astronauts lifted off from the moon, they left behind their backpacks, walking boots, and other equipment that was no longer necessary. Leaving these items lightened the load of the LM ascent stage for its trip back up to the command module.

Returning to Earth. The ascent stage of the lunar module lifted off the moon using the descent stage as a launching platform. The LM first went into an orbit that was lower than that of the command module. When the distance and angle between the two spacecraft were just right, the LM engine was fired and the craft soared into the same orbit as the command module, about 69 miles (111 kilometers) above the moon.

The command module pilot maneuvered to dock with the LM. After docking, the pressures in the two craft were equalized, and the hatch between them was opened. The moon samples and the equipment to be returned to the earth were transferred to the command module. All equipment that was not to be returned to the earth was placed in the lunar module. The LM crew then moved into the command module, and the LM was disconnected.

The engine of the service module was fired to push the astronauts out of lunar orbit and send them toward the earth. The trip home resembled the trip to the moon. Before the command module entered the earth's atmosphere, the service module was disconnected.

The command module turned around before it entered the atmosphere. The pressure of the atmosphere against the blunt end helped slow the craft.

The command module had to meet the pressure of the earth's atmosphere at a certain angle to make a safe landing. If the angle was too shallow, the craft would bounce off the atmosphere and go back into space. If the angle was too steep, the friction between the atmosphere and the spacecraft would generate too much heat, and the craft would burn up. During a normal re-entry, the special plastic heat shield on the command module might reach a temperature of 4200° F. (2316° C). The temperature inside the cabin remained at about 80° F. (27° C).

At about 23,300 feet (7,102 meters), special parachutes called *drogues* were released. The drogues slowed and steadied the spacecraft. At about 10,500 feet (3,200 meters), the main parachutes were released. The craft hit the water at about 22 miles (35 kilometers) per hour.

After Apollo 11 returned to the earth, the lunar material, the astronauts, and the equipment that was exposed to the lunar atmosphere were placed in isolation. The purpose of the isolation period, which lasted about 17 days for the astronauts, was to determine whether any germs or other harmful material had been brought from the moon. No harmful material was found.

NASA

After Splashdown, three balloons righted the Apollo 11 spacecraft in the water, and an orange collar helped keep it afloat. On the raft that recovered the spacecraft, the astronauts were scrubbed with disinfectant to kill any germs they might have brought back from the moon.

NASA

The *Skylab 1* Space Station was the first U.S. manned space laboratory. It was orbited about 270 miles (435 kilometers) above the earth in 1973. Astronauts conducted experiments in the station in 1973 and 1974. Skylab disintegrated when it reentered the earth's atmosphere in 1979.

A space station is a special kind of earth satellite. It is designed so that many people can live and work in orbit for a longer time than they could in an ordinary, crowded spacecraft. A space station has living quarters for its crew and carries enough food, oxygen, and water to supply them for weeks or even months. One crew can replace another without disturbing the work of the station. A space station functions as a laboratory for scientists. It may also serve as an assembly base and a stopping-off place for flights to the planets.

There are several ways a space station can be built and launched. One way is to launch a station built in one piece. Russia has used this method to place a number of *Salyut* stations into orbit since the 1970's. Manned Soyuz spacecraft have docked with the stations, and cosmonauts have performed experiments there.

The United States used a similar method to orbit the *Skylab* experimental station in 1973. *Skylab* was a modified third stage of a Saturn V rocket, whose first two stages had placed it in orbit. Astronauts entered *Skylab* from an Apollo spacecraft that had docked with it. Three groups of astronauts conducted experiments in the station in 1973 and 1974. Chiefly because of solar storms, *Skylab* fell from its orbit in 1979 and disintegrated when it reentered the earth's atmosphere.

Another way to build a space station calls for the separate launching of several sections of the station. These sections are then connected in orbit.

An operating space station requires some way to reach it frequently to change crews and to provide fresh supplies and equipment. Since the late 1970's, Russia has used both manned and unmanned spacecraft to carry supplies to cosmonauts on board a *Salyut* station. Each delivery to the station requires a new spacecraft. In 1981, the United States launched its first manned space shuttle. This reusable vehicle could fly back and forth between the earth and a space station.

Space Station Laboratories can be used to study the stars, the sun, the solar wind, and the earth's upper atmosphere and magnetic field. Telescopes in the station can reveal much more about the universe than telescopes on earth. There is no atmosphere to dim an astronomer's view of the stars and galaxies.

Physicists can perform experiments to check the laws of nature and to test scientific theories. For example, they may compare the time kept by atomic clocks in the station to clocks on earth. This experiment would test Einstein's theory of relativity.

Biologists can use a space laboratory to learn more about the growth of plants and animals. On earth, all living things are affected by gravity, by the regular changes of day and night, and even by the attraction of the moon. But many of these forces would not affect living things in a space station. As a result, plants and animals might develop differently.

Stopping-Off Places for Spaceships. The launch into orbit uses up most of a space vehicle's fuel. After reaching orbit, a spaceship could stop at a space station and pick up more fuel. It could then continue its journey deeper into space.

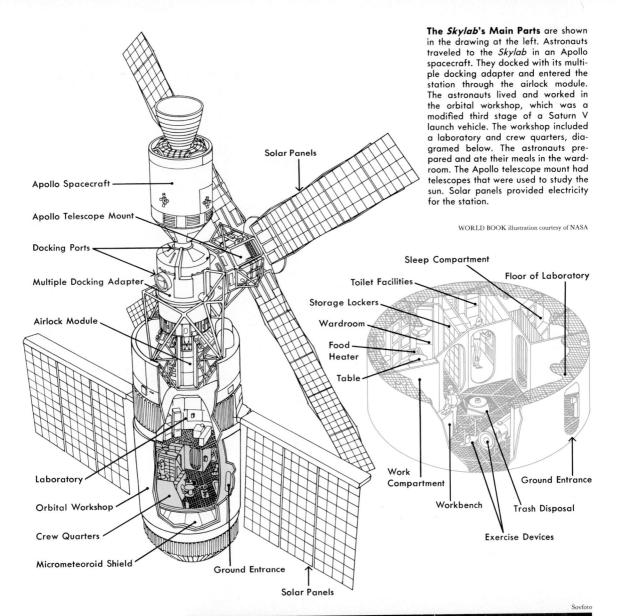

The *Skylab*'s Main Parts are shown in the drawing at the left. Astronauts traveled to the *Skylab* in an Apollo spacecraft. They docked with its multiple docking adapter and entered the station through the airlock module. The astronauts lived and worked in the orbital workshop, which was a modified third stage of a Saturn V launch vehicle. The workshop included a laboratory and crew quarters, diagramed below. The astronauts prepared and ate their meals in the wardroom. The Apollo telescope mount had telescopes that were used to study the sun. Solar panels provided electricity for the station.

WORLD BOOK illustration courtesy of NASA

Apollo Spacecraft
Solar Panels
Apollo Telescope Mount
Docking Ports
Multiple Docking Adapter
Airlock Module
Laboratory
Orbital Workshop
Crew Quarters
Micrometeoroid Shield
Ground Entrance
Solar Panels

Sleep Compartment
Toilet Facilities
Floor of Laboratory
Storage Lockers
Wardroom
Food Heater
Table
Work Compartment
Ground Entrance
Workbench
Trash Disposal
Exercise Devices

Sovfoto

Salyut, an experimental Russian space station, was placed in orbit in 1971. Cosmonauts reached the station in a Soyuz spacecraft like the one pictured in the background. Several teams of cosmonauts visited the station. They conducted experiments to learn how well people can live in space for long periods. The cosmonauts also grew plants and took pictures of the earth. One flight to *Salyut,* the *Soyuz* XI mission, ended in tragedy when the three cosmonauts died while returning to the earth. Their spacecraft hatch did not close properly, and their oxygen leaked into space.

568c

Escaping Earth's Gravity. The moon lies within earth's gravity. But at the moon's distance, the force of gravity is very weak. A spacecraft launched at 25,000 miles (40,200 kilometers) per hour—just 700 miles (1,100 kilometers) per hour greater than that necessary to reach the moon—can escape the influence of earth's gravity. This speed of 25,000 miles per hour (about 7 miles, or 11 kilometers, per second) is called *escape velocity*. It sends the spacecraft into interplanetary space. The craft then comes under the influence of the sun's gravity and goes into an orbit around the sun close to earth's orbit.

The earth itself circles the sun with a speed of 18.5 miles (29.8 kilometers) per second. A spacecraft launched from earth also travels this fast in relation to the sun. The craft's escape velocity is used up in getting away from earth. It does not affect the speed of the spacecraft around the sun. Escape velocity can send the spacecraft into orbit around the sun. But it cannot send the craft to a planet.

Traveling to the Planets. To reach a planet, a spacecraft must be launched from earth at a velocity greater than escape velocity. This extra velocity changes the speed of the spacecraft around the sun. Given the proper velocity, the craft goes into a solar orbit that carries it to the target planet.

The United States and the Soviet Union have launched a number of spacecraft into solar orbit for the purpose of exploring other planets. Such *space probes* may fly past the target planet, go into orbit around it, or land. The probes carry instruments that collect information about the planet and transmit photographs and other data back to the earth. The first space probes to fly past Mars and Venus were launched by the United States in the 1960's. In the early 1970's, Soviet space probes made the first automated landings on these plan-

NASA

A Photograph of Mars by the *Viking II* space probe shows several details of the planet. At the top of the photo is a giant volcano with a cloud of ice trailing from it. A crater can be seen near the bottom of the picture. The photo was taken in early August 1976, about a month before *Viking* landed on Mars.

A Rocket Flight to Mars A spacecraft to Mars must be launched at 7.4 miles (11.9 kilometers) a second—0.4 mile (0.6 kilometer) a second faster than the speed needed to escape the earth's gravity. It must be launched in the same direction the earth moves around the sun. The 0.4 mile a second is added to the 18.5 miles (29.8 kilometers) a second the earth travels around the sun, giving the spacecraft a speed of 18.9 miles (30.4 kilometers) a second. The spacecraft coasts outward until it reaches the orbit of Mars.

WORLD BOOK illustration by Zorica Dabich

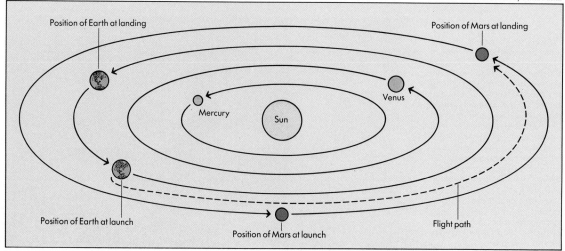

Position of Earth at landing

Position of Mars at landing

Mercury

Venus

Sun

Position of Earth at launch

Flight path

Position of Mars at launch

ets. In addition, space probes have flown by Mercury, Jupiter, and Saturn.

To reach Mars, a spacecraft must be launched at 7.4 miles (11.9 kilometers) per second—0.4 mile (0.6 kilometer) per second faster than escape velocity. Also, the craft must be launched in the same direction the earth moves around the sun. The extra 0.4 mile per second then adds to the 18.5 miles per second the craft has because of the earth's motion. The craft's final speed around the sun is 18.9 miles (30.4 kilometers) per second. At this speed, the spacecraft coasts outward from the sun until it crosses the orbit of Mars.

To reach Venus, a spacecraft must also be launched at 7.4 miles per second. But in this case the craft is launched in a direction opposite to the direction the earth moves around the sun. The extra 0.4 mile per second is therefore subtracted from the 18.5 miles per second, giving the craft a final speed of 18.1 miles (29.1 kilometers) per second. At this speed, the spacecraft moves too slowly to stay near the orbit of earth. It is pulled closer to the sun until it crosses the orbit of Venus.

A spacecraft launched at the minimum velocity necessary to reach a planet travels along a path called a *minimum energy flight trajectory*. This is the course that requires the least power. In practice, planetary spacecraft are usually launched with a velocity greater than the minimum. With the increased speed, they can reach the planet in a shorter time.

Reaching the Stars. Present rocket engines do not have enough power to send spacecraft to even the nearest star. Just to escape from the sun's gravity, a spacecraft must be launched from earth at 14.5 miles (23.3 kilometers) per second. To travel to a star in a reasonable time, the spacecraft must go at a speed close to the speed of light. In the future, such speeds may be reached by advanced rockets using nuclear power.

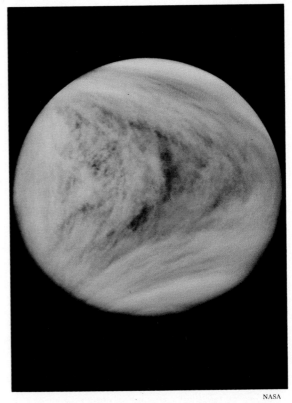

NASA

A Photograph of Venus taken by the *Pioneer Venus 1* space probe from a distance of about 40,000 miles (64,000 kilometers) shows the planet's cloudy atmosphere. Brighter clouds cover the polar regions than the rest of Venus. The planet's clouds move at a speed of about 220 miles (354 kilometers) per hour.

A Rocket Flight to Venus

To reach Venus, a spacecraft must be launched in the opposite direction the earth moves around the sun. It must be launched 0.4 mile (0.6 kilometer) a second faster than the speed needed to escape the earth's gravity. The 0.4 mile a second is subtracted from the 18.5 miles (29.8 kilometers) a second the earth travels around the sun, giving the spacecraft a speed of 18.1 miles (29.1 kilometers) a second. The spacecraft moves toward the sun until it reaches the orbit of Venus.

WORLD BOOK illustration by Zorica Dabich

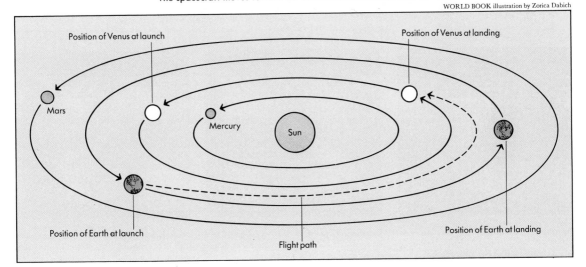

An artificial satellite is a manufactured "moon." It circles the earth in space along a path called an *orbit*. An artificial satellite may be designed in almost any shape, such as a ball, a drum, or a box. It does not have to be streamlined, because there is little or no air where it travels in space. A satellite's size and shape depend on its job. Some satellites, such as the *Echo* balloons, may be 100 feet (30 meters) or more in diameter. But most satellites are much smaller.

Artificial satellites stay in space for varying lengths of time. The lifetime of each satellite depends on its size and its distance from earth. Whenever a satellite swings close to earth, it runs into many air particles that slow it down. To stay in orbit, a satellite must keep a certain speed. If it slows below this speed, it plunges into the atmosphere and burns up because of friction with the air. The slowing of a satellite by air particles is called *decay*. Large satellites in low orbits decay rapidly. Small ones in high orbits decay slowly. For example, the 6-inch (15-centimeter) *Vanguard I* satellite orbits more than 400 miles (640 kilometers) above the earth. This satellite will orbit the earth for hundreds of years.

Most satellites carry some type of radio transmitter and receiver. One kind of transmitter is called a *radio beacon*. It sends signals that enable engineers to track the satellite. *Tracking* means finding the satellite's exact position in space. Another kind of transmitter sends to earth the scientific information gathered by the satellite's instruments. This sending of information is called *telemetry*. Telemetry transmitters usually serve also as beacons. A satellite's receiving equipment is turned on and off by means of signals that engineers beam from earth.

Most satellites stop working long before they fall to earth. Their batteries go dead, or their electronic equipment breaks down. They become "silent" and of no further use. To prevent the potential hazards from the debris of falling satellites, the United States and Russia attempt to bring their satellites out of orbit after they have served their purpose. However, dozens of silent satellites are now circling the earth.

Artificial satellites may be classified according to

NASA

The Solar Maximum Mission (S.M.M.), launched in 1980, was a satellite designed to provide scientists with observations of *solar flares*—violent eruptions on the surface of the sun.

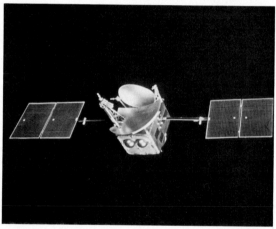

Telesat Canada

Canada's Anik Communications Satellites, such as the one shown above, have improved telecommunications services in the remote, thinly populated northern sections of the nation.

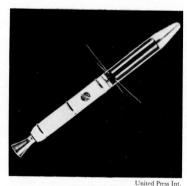

Sovfoto

Sputnik I, the first artificial satellite, was launched by Russia in 1957. Its launch marked the start of the space age.

Explorer I, the first U.S. satellite, went into orbit in 1958. It discovered Van Allen radiation surrounding the earth.

United Press Int.

U.S. Navy

Transit Satellites of the U.S. Navy were the first navigation satellites. The satellite above is the Transit IVB.

Important Satellites

Communications Satellites

Date Launched		Name	Accomplishments
1958	Dec. 18	**Project Score**	Broadcast first voice message from space.
1962	July 10	**Telstar I**	First satellite to relay television programs between United States and Europe.
1963	July 26	**Syncom II**	First synchronous satellite.
1965	Apr. 6	**Early Bird**	First commercial communications satellite.
1967	Jan. 11	**INTELSAT IIB**	First of a series of satellites in stationary orbit; used for television, data, or voice.
1971	Jan. 26	**INTELSAT IVA**	First high-capacity international communications satellite.
1972	Nov. 9	**Anik I**	First Canadian communications satellite.
1974	May 30	**ATS-6**	Brought two-way voice and picture communication to isolated areas.
1977	Dec 14	**CS**	First Japanese communications satellite.
1981	Feb. 21	**Comstar D**	Synchronous satellite; part of a worldwide communications system.

Weather Satellites

Date Launched		Name	Accomplishments
1959	Feb. 17	**Vanguard II**	First satellite to send weather information back to earth.
1960	Apr. 1	**Tiros I**	Took the first detailed weather pictures.
1974	May 17	**SMS-1**	First full-time weather satellite in synchronous orbit.
1975	Oct. 16	**GOES-1**	First weather satellite with enough speed to maintain same observational position over the earth.
1978	June 16	**GOES-3**	Equipped to provide both day and night pictures of the earth's weather patterns.
1980	Sept. 9	**GOES-D**	Designed to take readings of atmospheric moisture and temperature for the purpose of tracking storms.

Navigation Satellites

Date Launched		Name	Accomplishments
1960	Apr. 13	**Transit IB**	First navigation satellite.
1961	June 29	**Transit IVA**	First satellite to use nuclear power.
	Nov. 15	**Transit IVB**	Tested method of using earth's gravity to keep satellites in proper position.
1978	Feb. 21	**NAVSTAR**	First satellite of an 18-satellite system designed to provide navigational positions on a continuous basis.

Scientific Satellites

Date Launched		Name	Accomplishments
1958	Jan. 31	**Explorer I**	First U.S. satellite; discovered Van Allen radiation in space.
1962	Mar. 7	**OSO-I**	First orbiting solar observatory.
	Apr. 26	**Ariel** (U.K. No. 1)	First international satellite; carried U.S. and British instruments.
	Sept. 28	**Alouette**	First Canadian satellite.
1963	Apr. 2	**Explorer XVII**	First satellite to study the atmosphere.
1967	Sept. 7	**Biosatellite II**	Carried living cells, plants, and animals into space and returned them to earth.
1968	Dec. 7	**OAO-II**	First orbiting astronomical observatory.
1972	July 23	**LandSat-1**	Photographed the earth with different wavelengths of light to provide information about earth's natural resources.
1973	June 10	**Explorer XLIX**	Conducted radio-astronomy research on the far side of the moon.
1976	May 4	**Lagoes**	First satellite designed for high-precision geographic measurements.
1977	Aug. 12	**HEAO-1**	Orbiting observatory used to locate objects in outer space that emit X rays.
	Oct. 22	**ISEE's**	A pair of satellites launched by a single rocket to study the effects of the sun on the earth's atmosphere and climate.
1978	Oct. 24	**Nimbus-7**	Collected data for studying the earth's atmosphere and oceans.
	Nov. 13	**HEAO-2**	Transmitted data and photographs of quasars and other cosmic objects that emit X rays.
1979	Feb. 18	**SAGE**	Primarily designed to measure flourocarbon content of the earth's stratosphere.
	Sept. 20	**HEAO-3**	Monitored and analyzed gamma rays and cosmic rays from deep space.
1980	Feb. 14	**S.M.M.**	Designed to study solar flares and the conditions on the sun that cause such eruptions.
1983	Jan. 25	**IRAS**	Collected information on infrared radiation given off by dust clouds, stars, and galaxies.

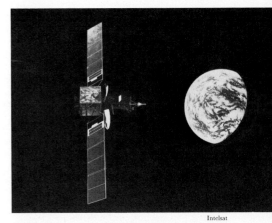

Intelsat

INTELSAT communications satellites relay telephone calls, TV programs, and other communications between the United States and other nations.

NOAA

GOES weather satellites relay pictures of about a fourth of the earth's surface every half hour. The satellites also collect other environmental data.

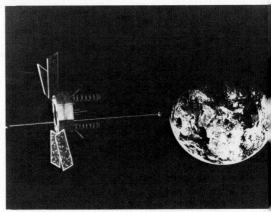

U.S. Navy

NAVSTAR navigation satellites are designed to enable operators of aircraft, ships, and land vehicles to determine their position anywhere in the world.

the jobs they do as (1) weather satellites, (2) communications satellites, (3) navigation satellites, (4) scientific satellites, and (5) military satellites.

Weather Satellites, or *meteorological satellites*, help scientists forecast weather and study how weather is made. The first satellites to do this job were called *Tiros*. These satellites carry television cameras that take pictures of the earth's surface. The pictures show how clouds move. They also show snow and ice on the earth's surface. By studying the pictures, weather forecasters can discover storms forming over the ocean. They can then warn people to prepare for the storms.

Weather satellites also carry instruments called *infrared detectors*. These instruments measure the heat coming from the earth and the clouds. This information helps scientists learn how weather is related to the heating and cooling of the earth.

A Tiros satellite "sees" the earth only part of the time because it always points to a certain spot in space. An advanced weather satellite called *GOES* points its camera toward earth all the time.

Communications Satellites make it possible to send radio messages, telephone calls, and television programs between distant parts of earth. Communications satellites are called *passive* or *active*, depending on the way they work.

The *Echo* balloon is an example of a passive communications satellite. It acts as a mirror for radio waves. A sending station on earth beams waves to the satellite. The waves "bounce" off the satellite and return to

NASA

A Weather Map based on satellite observations and transmitted by computer is pulled from a facsimile machine by a meteorologist. Weather forecasters use such maps in preparing reports.

earth. They then reach a receiving station perhaps thousands of miles from the sending station.

Telstar, Relay, Syncom, and *Early Bird* are active communications satellites. They carry radio receivers and transmitters. Active satellites receive signals from sending stations, *amplify* (strengthen) them, and send them back to earth. Because active satellites amplify the signals, they do not have to be as large as passive satellites. See COMMUNICATIONS SATELLITE.

NASA

An Antenna Receives Video Signals from a weather satellite. The signals go through a rapid photo processing system that produces pictures showing the clouds covering the earth.

GOES-1 DPT   298 1645Z   25 OCT. 75

NASA

A Satellite Photograph of the earth taken from an altitude of about 22,300 miles (35,890 kilometers) shows the pattern of clouds. The land mass in the center of the photo is South America.

Navigation Satellites help pilots and sailors find their exact positions in all kinds of weather. The United States Navy has *Transit* and *NAVSTAR* satellites. Navigators can use them to find their position much as they would use a star. But instead of looking at the satellite, they listen to its radio signals.

Scientific Satellites include several types. *Explorer* and *Monitor* satellites carry a variety of instruments around earth. Some instruments measure radiation, such as that found in the Van Allen belt. Other instruments called *magnetometers* measure the earth's magnetic field. Satellites called *topside sounders* explore the upper parts of the atmosphere. These satellites beam radio waves down into the atmosphere and then measure the reflected signals.

Orbiting observatories are the largest and most complicated of all scientific satellites. The United States uses three types—geophysical, solar, and astronomical. Each type has a standard size and shape. Many kinds of instruments can be built into each one. The *orbiting geophysical observatory* (OGO) explores space near the earth. Scientists use it to study how the earth's magnetic field affects energy coming from the sun. The sun itself is studied with the *orbiting solar observatory* (OSO). This satellite measures radiations that cannot get through the atmosphere to be measured on earth.

The *orbiting astronomical observatory* (OAO) looks deep into space at the stars and galaxies. It too measures rays that never reach the earth.

The United States builds and launches some scientific satellites in cooperation with other countries. The first international satellite, called *Ariel*, carried instruments built by British scientists. The topside sounder *Alouette* was designed and built by Canadian engineers, and then launched by the United States.

Military Satellites. The armed forces can use artificial satellites for communications, navigation, weather forecasting, and mapping. But satellites also have been designed for strictly military purposes. *Reconnaissance satellites*, sometimes called "spy" satellites, can photograph enemy ground forces and warships at sea. *Warning satellites* can guard against surprise missile attacks. They can discover the launching of a missile by measuring the heat of the missile's rocket exhaust. The United States keeps *Vela* satellites in space to detect any "sneak testing" of nuclear bombs in space by other nations.

The United States and the Soviet Union have both promised that they will not place offensive military weapons in space. However, both countries have worked on the development of *antisatellite systems* that can interfere with another nation's satellites. Most military space activities are kept secret.

The Nimbus Scientific Satellite

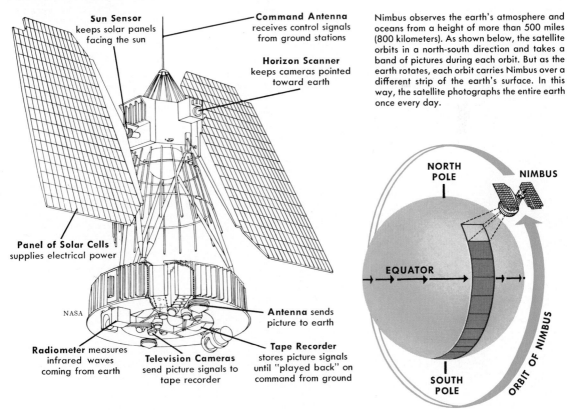

Sun Sensor
keeps solar panels
facing the sun

Command Antenna
receives control signals
from ground stations

Horizon Scanner
keeps cameras pointed
toward earth

Panel of Solar Cells
supplies electrical power

NASA

Radiometer measures
infrared waves
coming from earth

Television Cameras
send picture signals to
tape recorder

Antenna sends
picture to earth

Tape Recorder
stores picture signals
until "played back" on
command from ground

Nimbus observes the earth's atmosphere and oceans from a height of more than 500 miles (800 kilometers). As shown below, the satellite orbits in a north-south direction and takes a band of pictures during each orbit. But as the earth rotates, each orbit carries Nimbus over a different strip of the earth's surface. In this way, the satellite photographs the entire earth once every day.

NORTH POLE

NIMBUS

EQUATOR

ORBIT OF NIMBUS

SOUTH POLE

Space probes are used to explore space at various distances from earth. Four main kinds of probes are: (1) sounding rockets, (2) lunar spacecraft, (3) interplanetary probes, and (4) planetary probes.

Sounding Rockets carry instruments into the upper atmosphere and into space near earth. They are the chief means of exploring regions too close for satellites to orbit. Their instruments may measure the temperature and pressure of the atmosphere as well as radiations from space.

Lunar Spacecraft explored the moon to prepare the way for astronauts to land there. U.S. lunar spacecraft include *Ranger*, *Surveyor*, and *Lunar Orbiter*. In 1964 and 1965, three Rangers took over 17,000 close-up pictures of the moon before crashing into it. The first Surveyor spacecraft landed on the moon in 1966 and sent back pictures of the lunar landscape. The first Lunar Orbiter orbited the moon in 1966. Russian lunar spacecraft include *Luna* and *Zond*. The hidden side of the moon was photographed by *Luna 3* in 1959 and again by *Zond 3* in 1965.

Interplanetary Probes explore space between the planets. They do not reach a specific body in space.

Planetary Probes travel in orbits around the sun. They may fly past the target planet, go into orbit around it, or land. Even at a great distance, a probe's instruments can collect much information about the planet. In 1962, the United States *Mariner II* passed within 22,000 miles (35,400 kilometers) of Venus. It reported that the planet's temperature is about 800° F. (430° C)—too hot for any known animal or plant. In 1965, *Mariner IV* flew as close as 6,118 miles (9,846 kilo-

Jet Propulsion Laboratory

***Viking I* Landed on Mars on July 20, 1976.**

Important Space Probes

Date Launched		Name	Country	Accomplishments
1959	Sept. 12	**Luna 2**	Russia	First probe to strike the moon.
1962	Apr. 23	**Ranger IV**	U.S.A.	First U.S. probe to strike moon; failed to televise pictures to earth.
1964	Nov. 28	**Mariner IV**	U.S.A.	Photographed Mars on July 14, 1965; measured conditions in space.
1966	Jan. 31	**Luna 9**	Russia	Made first soft landing on the moon on Feb. 3; sent 27 pictures to the earth.
	Mar. 31	**Luna 10**	Russia	First spacecraft to orbit the moon; began orbiting on April 3.
1967	June 12	**Venera 4**	Russia	First spacecraft to transmit data on Venus' atmosphere.
	Sept. 8	**Surveyor 5**	U.S.A.	Landed on the moon; sent information on lunar soil back to earth for analysis.
1968	Sept. 14	**Zond 5**	Russia	First probe to orbit the moon and return to a soft landing on earth.
1970	Aug. 17	**Venera 7**	Russia	First spacecraft to transmit data from Venus' surface; landed Dec. 15, 1970.
	Sept. 12	**Luna 16**	Russia	First unmanned spacecraft to return lunar samples; landed on Sept. 20.
1971	May 28	**Mars 3**	Russia	Carried capsule that made first soft landing on Mars; landed Dec. 2, 1971.
	May 30	**Mariner IX**	U.S.A.	First probe to orbit Mars; began orbiting on Nov. 13, 1971.
1972	Mar. 2	**Pioneer X**	U.S.A.	Flew past Jupiter on Dec. 3, 1973, and sent back scientific data; on June 13, 1983, became the first spacecraft to travel beyond all the planets.
1973	Apr. 6	**Pioneer-Saturn**	U.S.A.	Passed close to Jupiter on Dec. 2, 1974, and flew past Saturn on Sept. 1, 1979; sent back scientific data and photos of both planets.
	Nov. 3	**Mariner X**	U.S.A.	First probe to fly by two planets; sent photos and data from Venus on Feb. 5, 1974, and Mercury on March 29 and Sept. 21, 1974, and March 16, 1975.
1975	June 8	**Venera 9**	Russia	First unmanned spacecraft to photograph surface of Venus; landed Oct. 22.
	Aug. 22	**Viking I**	U.S.A.	Sent photos and data from Mars; landed on July 20, 1976.
	Sept. 9	**Viking II**	U.S.A.	Landed on Mars Sept. 3, 1976; sent back photos and scientific data.
1977	Aug. 20	**Voyager 2**	U.S.A.	Flew past Jupiter in July 1979, and flew by Saturn in August 1981; sent back photos.
	Sept. 5	**Voyager 1**	U.S.A.	Passed Jupiter on March 5, 1979, and flew by Saturn on Nov. 12, 1980; made various discoveries about both planets and their moons.
1978	May 20	**Pioneer Venus 1**	U.S.A.	Transmitted radar images of Venus' surface; began orbiting on Dec. 4.
	Aug. 8	**Pioneer Venus 2**	U.S.A.	Entered Venus' atmosphere Dec. 9; measured its density and composition.
	Sept. 9	**Venera 11**	Russia	Made chemical analysis of Venus' lower atmosphere; landed Dec. 25.
	Sept. 14	**Venera 12**	Russia	Sent back data on atmosphere of Venus; landed Dec. 21.
1981	Oct. 30	**Venera 13**	Russia	Sent color photos of Venus and analyzed soil samples; landed March 1, 1982.
	Nov. 4	**Venera 14**	Russia	Landed on Venus four days after *Venera 13* and did similar experiments.

meters) to Mars. The probe reported Mars has a thin atmosphere, no magnetic field, and no radiation belt. In 1967, Russia's *Venera 4* spacecraft transmitted data on Venus' atmosphere. In 1971, the *Mariner IX* probe orbited Mars and photographed most of its surface and its two moons. Also that year, the Russian *Mars 3* craft soft-landed a capsule on the planet.

The United States *Pioneer X* became the first probe to reach Jupiter. In 1973, it sent back data about Jupiter's radiation belt and atmosphere. In 1974, *Mariner X* became the first probe to fly past two planets—Venus and Mercury. Also in 1974, the U.S. *Pioneer-Saturn* probe photographed Jupiter's polar regions. The U.S. *Viking I* and *Viking II* crafts landed on Mars in 1976.

They photographed the planet's surface and analyzed its atmosphere and soil.

The U.S. *Pioneer Venus 1* and *Pioneer Venus 2* probes reached Venus in 1978. They returned data about the planet's atmosphere and weather, as well as radar photographs of its surface. Two Russian probes, *Venera 11* and *Venera 12*, also explored Venus in 1978. The U.S. *Voyager 1* and *Voyager 2* flew past Jupiter in 1979 and took pictures of the planet. Also in 1979, the Pioneer-Saturn craft passed Saturn and photographed the planet and its satellites. Additional data about Saturn's satellites and rings were transmitted by *Voyager 1* in 1980 and by *Voyager 2* in 1981. In 1982, the Russian probes *Venera 13* and *Venera 14* analyzed soil samples of Venus.

Jet Propulsion Laboratory

NASA

Surveyor 1, *left,* made a soft landing on the moon on June 2, 1966. It took about 11,000 pictures of the lunar surface, including the one above.

Mariner IX, *left,* was the first probe to orbit Mars. It photographed a canyon, *above,* from an altitude of 1,225 miles (1,971 kilometers) in 1973.

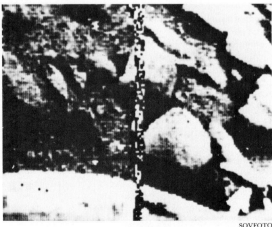

SOVFOTO

Jet Propulsion Laboratory

Russia's Venera 9 space probe, *left,* landed on Venus on Oct. 22, 1975. It took the first closeup photograph of the planet's surface, *above.*

Voyager 2, *left,* flew past Jupiter in July 1979. The space probe took many photographs of the planet, including the one shown above.

572a

The history of space travel could be said to begin more than 300 years ago. In the early 1600's, Johannes Kepler, a German scientist, developed the laws of planetary motion that describe the orbits of bodies in space. Today, these laws are used to determine the orbits of artificial satellites and to plan the flights of spacecraft. See KEPLER, JOHANNES.

In 1687, Sir Isaac Newton published his *Laws of Motion*, which used Kepler's work as a base. Newton's laws, like Kepler's, form a cornerstone of space-flight planning. For example, his third law states that for every action there is an equal and opposite reaction. This law describes why a rocket works. See MOTION (Newton's Laws of Motion); NEWTON, SIR ISAAC.

Early Developments. In 1903, Konstantin E. Tsiolkovsky, a Russian schoolteacher, published the first scientific paper on the use of rockets for space flight. But his work attracted little attention at the time. Several years later, Robert H. Goddard of the United States and Hermann Oberth of Germany succeeded in awakening a scientific interest in space travel. Working independently, these men attacked the technical problems of rocketry and high-altitude research. They earned the title "the fathers of space flight."

In 1919, Goddard explained how rockets could be used to explore the upper atmosphere in his paper "A Method of Reaching Extreme Altitudes." The

Bettmann Archive

A "Moon Train," *above,* was described by the French novelist Jules Verne in 1865. He imagined the spacecraft as a series of cars that would carry travelers between the earth and the moon.

New York Public Library

The Dream of Space Travel has led people to design strange spaceships, *above.* About 1780, a French inventor thought this spaceship might use a balloon, a parachute, and movable wings.

paper also described a way of firing a rocket to the moon. See GODDARD, ROBERT H.

Oberth published *The Rocket into Interplanetary Space* in 1923. In this book, Oberth discussed many technical problems of space flight. He even described what a spaceship would be like. Interest in Oberth's work in Germany led to the formation of the German Society for Space Travel. The members of this society helped develop the first successful guided missiles during World War II. See GUIDED MISSILE (The First Guided Missiles).

In the United States, experimenters formed the American Interplanetary Society in 1930. British scientists founded the British Interplanetary Society in 1933. Members of these groups designed and launched experimental rockets, and promoted the idea of space travel.

High-Altitude Rockets. During the 1930's, rocket research went forward in the United States, Germany, and Russia. Goddard was the chief American researcher, while Oberth led the German experimenters. Leading Russian scientists included F. A. Tsander and I. A. Merkulov. By the early 1930's, both the German and Russian governments were conducting rocket research programs. The United States government did not become interested in high-altitude rockets until the early 1940's.

United Press Int.

The First Successful Liquid-Propellant Rocket was launched in 1926 by Robert H. Goddard, an American scientist, *above*. The rocket burned gasoline and liquid oxygen.

During World War II, German rocketeers under the direction of Wernher von Braun developed the *V-2* guided missile. A number of these missiles were captured by American forces and sent to the United States to be used in research. After the war, Von Braun and some of the other German scientists came to the United States to continue their work on rockets. Others went to Russia.

In the late 1940's, Americans developed two important research rockets, the *Viking* and the *Aerobee*. In 1949, a small rocket called the *WAC Corporal* soared to what was then a record height of 250 miles (402 kilometers). It was launched as a second stage atop a V-2 missile.

Artificial Satellites. In 1955, both the United States and Russia announced plans to launch artificial satellites. The "moons" were to be launched during the International Geophysical Year beginning in 1957.

Then, on Oct. 4, 1957, the Russians launched *Sputnik I*, the first artificial satellite. On Nov. 3, 1957, they launched a second satellite, *Sputnik II*. It carried a dog named Laika, the first animal to soar into space. The United States launched its first satellite, *Explorer I*, on Jan. 31, 1958, and its second, *Vanguard I*, on March 17, 1958. These satellites were much smaller than the Sputniks, because the American launch vehicles were not as powerful as those used by the Russians.

The United States launched many more scientific satellites into orbit and began to make practical use of space. In December of 1958, the United States launched the first communications satellite in a flight

Marshall Space Flight Center, NASA

A Captured German V-2 guided missile from World War II, like those shown at the right, was used to launch a U.S. *WAC Corporal* rocket in 1949. The rocket soared to what was then a record height of 250 miles (402 kilometers).

called *Project Score*. In February 1959, the first weather satellite, *Vanguard II*, sent pictures of clouds to earth. Russia launched far fewer satellites than the United States. But the Russian spacecraft continued to be much larger and heavier than U.S. craft.

Rockets into Outer Space. Early in 1959, first Russia and then the United States launched probes that escaped earth's gravity. Russia's *Luna 1* and the U.S. *Pioneer IV* were aimed at the moon. They zoomed past the moon and went into orbit around the sun as the first artificial *planetoids*. In the following years, both the United States and Russia sent many spacecraft to the moon and the planets, and around the sun.

Human Beings in Space. In the early 1960's, human beings began to travel in space. On April 12, 1961, Russian cosmonaut Yuri Gagarin made a single orbit around the earth. The American astronaut Alan B. Shepard, Jr., on May 5, 1961, rocketed to a height of $116\frac{1}{2}$ miles (187.5 kilometers) in a flight 300 miles (480 kilometers) long. Cosmonaut Gherman Titov made 16 revolutions of the earth on Aug. 6-7, 1961. John H. Glenn, Jr., first American astronaut to orbit the earth, made three revolutions on Feb. 20, 1962. These men were followed by an ever increasing number of astronauts and cosmonauts.

Russian manned flights of the early 1960's maintained an edge over those of the United States. With its powerful launching rockets, Russia could orbit large spacecraft carrying enough life-support equipment to keep a cosmonaut in space for several days. Several cosmonauts made *group flights* in which two pilots orbited earth at the same time in separate spacecraft. In such a flight, Valentina Tereshkova, the first woman to fly in space, orbited earth for almost three days, June 16-18, 1963, during Valery Bykovsky's flight. On Oct. 12,

1964, Russia achieved another first in space by sending three cosmonauts into orbit in one spacecraft, the *Voskhod I*.

Tragedy struck the U.S. space program on Jan. 27, 1967, when three Apollo astronauts were killed in a test of their spacecraft. Virgil I. Grissom, Edward H. White II, and Roger B. Chaffee died when fire and smoke swept their command module during a ground checkout at the John F. Kennedy Space

Sovfoto

Laika, the Russian Space Dog, was the first animal sent into orbit. Laika rode in *Sputnik II* in 1957. Studies of animals in space helped pave the way for manned space travel.

Center. The three men had been scheduled to fly the first manned Apollo spacecraft on Feb. 21, 1967.

The fire probably began with a spark from faulty electrical wiring. The spark ignited items in the cabin of the module, and the fire spread rapidly in the pure oxygen atmosphere of the spacecraft. The tragedy caused a 20-month delay in the first manned Apollo flight. Many safety features were added to the Apollo spacecraft to prevent a similar accident from occurring.

The first known space flight death occurred in April 1967. Cosmonaut Vladimir Komarov was killed when his spacecraft's parachute failed. In June 1971, three more Soviet cosmonauts were killed. The cosmonauts, Georgi Dobrovolsky, Victor Patsayev, and Vladislav Volkov, had completed 24 days orbiting the earth aboard an experimental space station called *Salyut*. The three were found dead in their *Soyuz XI* spacecraft after it had made an apparently normal landing.

NASA

A Walk in Space by Edward H. White II was the first of several space walks in the Gemini program. The astronauts practiced maneuvering to prepare for future work in space.

NASA

How the Earth Looks from the Moon. The Apollo 8 astronauts took this picture while orbiting the moon. They were less than 100 miles (160 kilometers) from the moon and more than 240,000 miles (386,000 kilometers) from the earth. Africa is at the bottom of the lighted area of the earth.

America's first astronaut-in-space project was the Mercury program. The first Mercury flight was made in April 1961, and the last in May 1963. The nation's next steps into space were the Gemini and Apollo programs. The first manned Gemini flight was made in March 1965, and the last in November 1966. The first manned Apollo flight was made in October 1968.

The first human beings on the moon were astronauts Neil A. Armstrong and Edwin E. Aldrin, Jr. Their Apollo 11 lunar module landed on July 20, 1969. Armstrong, Aldrin, and command module pilot Michael Collins left the earth on July 16 and returned on July 24.

For a table of Important Manned Space Missions, see the ASTRONAUT article in WORLD BOOK.

The Space Race. Many persons tried to compare the space accomplishments of the United States and Russia to see which country was "ahead." But differences in the two space programs made comparisons difficult. In the early 1960's, Russia had powerful rockets that could launch heavy spacecraft on long flights. But the United States led in the number of scientific spacecraft it had launched, and in such fields as communications and weather-reporting by satellite.

By the early 1970's, U.S. astronauts had landed on

NASA

Spacelab, a manned space laboratory built by the European Space Agency—a scientific organization of Western European nations—is carried by the space shuttle orbiter in the illustration at the right. The lab was designed for four scientists to conduct experiments in a weightless environment.

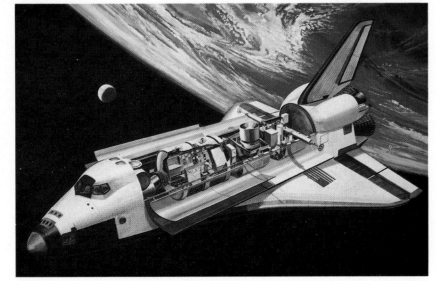

the moon. Unmanned Russian spacecraft had explored the moon and brought soil samples to earth. Manned exploration of the moon by the United States ended in 1972. Both countries experimented with manned space stations that orbited the earth.

In 1975, the United States and Russia undertook their first joint space mission, the Apollo-Soyuz Test Project. On July 17, a three-man U.S. Apollo spacecraft docked with a two-man Soyuz spacecraft launched by Russia. Crew members conducted joint scientific experiments for two days before carrying out separation maneuvers.

In November 1975, the United States and Russia conducted another joint space mission. An unmanned Soviet *Vostok* satellite carried five U.S. biological experiments around the earth for approximately 19 days. The United States participated in another of Russia's biological-satellite projects in August 1977. Similar scientific research projects may be undertaken in the future.

Recent Developments. In the early 1970's, U.S. engineers and scientists began working to develop a reusable manned spacecraft. They sought to design a space vehicle that would take off like a rocket and land like an airplane. On April 12, 1981, the United States launched the *Columbia*, the first such space shuttle. It expected to have three other shuttles in operation by 1985.

The space shuttles were designed to carry artificial satellites, space probes, and other heavy loads into orbit around the earth. Other spacecraft can launch such objects, but only the space shuttles can be reused. Each space shuttle can be used more than 100 times. In addition to launch operations, the space shuttles can retrieve artificial satellites that need servicing. Astronauts aboard the shuttle can work on the satellites and then send them back into orbit. Satellites that cannot be serviced in space can be brought back to the earth and then launched again after they are repaired. The shuttle also could enable crews of astronauts to build and maintain manned space stations and solar power stations in earth orbit.

On the fifth space shuttle mission, in November 1982, the orbiter launched satellites for the first time. The shuttle released two communications satellites—the SBS-3 and the Anik C-3—while traveling at an altitude of about 185 miles (298 kilometers) and a speed of about 17,000 miles (27,400 kilometers) per hour. After launch, booster rockets on the satellites were fired and the satellites climbed to an orbit of about 22,500 miles (36,200 kilometers).

The European Space Agency (ESA), a scientific organization of Western European nations, worked with the United States on the space shuttle program. It agreed to build a manned space laboratory called Spacelab, to be carried by a shuttle orbiting the earth. The laboratory was designed to operate in a weightless environment. It has facilities for four scientists to conduct experiments in such fields as astronomy, manufacturing, medicine, and pharmaceuticals. Spacelab remains attached to the space shuttle orbiter throughout the mission. After the space shuttle returns to earth, the lab is re-

NASA

Ceramic Tiles are bonded to the body of the space shuttle orbiter, *above,* to provide protection against the intense heat produced when the spacecraft reenters the earth's atmosphere.

moved and prepared for its next assignment. ESA and the United States planned to share facilities in the laboratory.

Many countries in addition to those of Western Europe cooperate with the United States in the exploration and practical use of space. Canada and Japan, for example, build satellites and satellite instruments to be launched from American facilities. A number of nations, including Australia and New Zealand, use U.S. sounding rockets for space research. EUGENE F. KRANZ

Related Articles. For information on the astronauts and cosmonauts themselves and on how they are selected and trained, see the ASTRONAUT article. See also the following articles:

BIOGRAPHIES

For a list of WORLD BOOK biographies on astronauts and cosmonauts, see the *Related Articles* at the end of the ASTRONAUT article. See also: GODDARD, ROBERT H.; KUIPER, GERARD PETER; VON BRAUN, WERNHER.

ORGANIZATIONS

American Institute of
  Aeronautics and
  Astronautics
Communications Satellite
  Corporation

European Space Agency
National Aeronautics and
  Space Administration

OTHER RELATED ARTICLES

Aerospace Medicine
Astronautics
Cape Canaveral
Centrifugal Force
Communications
  Satellite
Cosmic Rays
Exobiology

Gravitation
Guided Missile
Heat Shield
Jet Propulsion
Jet Propulsion Laboratory
Jodrell Bank Observatory
Johnson Space Center
Jupiter (Flights to Jupiter)

Meteor
Moon
Orbit
Planet
Radar (In Space Travel)
Radiation
Relativity

Rocket
Solar Energy
Solar System
Telemetry
United Nations (Peaceful
    Uses of Outer Space)

Outline

I. What Is Space?
  A. The Beginning of Space
  B. From Earth to the Moon
  C. Space Among the Planets
  D. To the Stars and Beyond
II. Getting into Space and Back
  A. Overcoming Gravity
  B. Returning to Earth
III. Living in Space
  A. Protection Against the Dangers of Space
  B. Providing for Basic Needs in Space
  C. Taking Medical Measurements
  D. Performing Scientific Duties
  E. Communications with the Earth
IV. Launch Vehicles
  A. The Building Block Idea
  B. Piggyback Boosters
  C. Space Shuttle Systems
V. Launch Operations
VI. Orbiting the Earth
  A. Selecting the Orbit
  B. Launching a Spacecraft
  C. How a Spacecraft Stays in Orbit
VII. Manned Spacecraft
  A. Life-Support Systems
  B. Communications and Navigation Equipment
  C. Control Systems
  D. Reentry and Landing Equipment
VIII. Reaching the Moon
  A. Aiming at the Moon
  B. Orbiting the Moon
  C. Landing on the Moon
  D. Exploring the Moon
  E. Returning to Earth
IX. Space Stations
  A. Space Station Laboratories
  B. Stopping-Off Places for Spaceships
X. Reaching the Planets and the Stars
  A. Escaping Earth's Gravity
  B. Traveling to the Planets
  C. Reaching the Stars
XI. Artificial Satellites
  A. Weather Satellites
  B. Communications Satellites
  C. Navigation Satellites
  D. Scientific Satellites
  E. Military Satellites
XII. Space Probes
  A. Sounding Rockets
  B. Lunar Spacecraft
  C. Interplanetary Probes
  D. Planetary Probes
XIII. Steps in the Conquest of Space
  A. Early Developments
  B. High-Altitude Rockets
  C. Artificial Satellites
  D. Rockets into Outer Space
  E. Human Beings in Space
  F. The Space Race
  G. Recent Developments

Questions

What two men earned the title "the fathers of space flight"?
What is a heat shield?
How far above earth does space begin?
How does a rocket engine produce thrust?
What is a *clean room?*
What was the first international satellite?
At what speed must a spacecraft be launched to reach the moon? To escape earth's gravity?
How do engineers use the "building block idea" to design launch vehicles?
What holds a satellite up?
What space probes photographed the far side of the moon?
What probe was the first to analyze the atmosphere and soil on the surface of Mars?

Reading and Study Guide

See *Space Travel* in the RESEARCH GUIDE/INDEX, Volume 22, for a *Reading and Study Guide.*

Additional Resources

Level I

BERGAUST, ERIK. *The Next 50 Years on the Moon.* Putnam, 1974. *Colonizing the Planets.* 1975.
CIUPIK, LARRY A., and SEEVERS, J. A. *Space Machines.* Raintree, 1979.
COLLINS, MICHAEL. *Flying to the Moon and Other Strange Places.* Farrar, 1976.
HENDRICKSON, WALTER B. *Manned Spacecraft to Mars and Venus: How They Work.* Putnam, 1975.
KERROD, ROBIN. *See Inside a Space Station.* Watts, 1979. *Race For the Moon.* Lerner, 1980.
TURNILL, REGINALD. *Space Age.* Warne, 1980.

Level II

ADELMAN, SAUL J. and BENJAMIN. *Bound For the Stars.* Prentice-Hall, 1981.
CROMIE, WILLIAM J. *Skylab: The Story of Man's First Station in Space.* McKay, 1976.
GATLAND, KENNETH W. *Manned Spacecraft.* Rev. ed. Macmillan, 1976.
GREY, JERRY. *Enterprise.* Morrow, 1979.
MOORE, PATRICK A. *The Next Fifty Years in Space.* Taplinger, 1976.
NICOLSON, IAIN. *The Road to the Stars.* Morrow, 1978.

SPACECRAFT. See SPACE TRAVEL.

SPAGHETTI. See PASTA.

SPAHN, WARREN (1921-   ), became one of the greatest pitchers in baseball history. During his major league career, he won 363 games, more than any other left-handed pitcher. Spahn won 20 or more games in one season 13 times, and he led the National League in games won eight times. He holds the National League record for the most shutouts by a left-handed pitcher, 63.

Warren Edward Spahn was born in Buffalo, N.Y. He played for the Boston (later Milwaukee) Braves from 1942 through 1964. In 1965, Spahn pitched for the New York Mets and San Francisco Giants. He retired after the 1965 season. Spahn was elected to the National Baseball Hall of Fame in 1973.   DAVE NIGHTINGALE

SPAIGHT, *spayt,* **RICHARD DOBBS** (1758-1802), was a North Carolina signer of the United States Constitution. He was a delegate to the Congress of the Confederation from 1783 to 1785. In the Constitutional Convention, he favored election of the President by Congress. Later, he worked for the ratification of the Constitution in North Carolina. He was governor of North Carolina from 1792 to 1795. He served in the U.S. House of Representatives from 1798 to 1801. Spaight was born in New Bern, N.C.   ROBERT J. TAYLOR

The Countryside of Spain consists mostly of plains broken by hills and low mountains. Most of the land has poor soil for growing crops, and so many farmers raise sheep and other livestock. Whitewashed houses with tile roofs, such as the village homes above, are common in rural Spain.

SPAIN

SPAIN is a country in Western Europe famous for its colorful bullfights, sunny climate, and beautiful story-book castles. Until the mid-1900's, Spain was one of the most underdeveloped countries of Western Europe. Most of the people were poor farmers. Then during the 1950's and 1960's, rapid economic development changed Spain into an industrial nation.

Today, more Spaniards work in manufacturing and construction than on farms. About three-fourths of the people live in cities. The standard of living has risen rapidly. Modern urban ways of life have become more popular. Many old customs, such as taking a *siesta* (nap or rest) after lunch, are disappearing.

Spain occupies most of the Iberian Peninsula, which lies in southwestern Europe between the Atlantic Ocean and the Mediterranean Sea. Portugal occupies the rest of the peninsula. Spain's capital and largest city, Madrid, stands in the center of the country.

On Spain's northeastern border, the mighty Pyrenees Mountains separate Spain from France. These mountains once were a great barrier to overland travel between the Iberian Peninsula and the rest of Europe. In contrast, Africa lies only about 8 miles (13 kilometers)

Stanley G. Payne, the contributor of this article, is Professor of History at the University of Wisconsin at Madison and the author of Franco's Spain *and other books about Spain.*

south of Spain across the Strait of Gibraltar, and peoples from northern Africa helped shape Spain's early history. These peoples included Carthaginians and Moors.

Carthaginians ruled much of Spain from the 400's to the 200's B.C. In the A.D. 700's, Moors conquered most of Spain, and they held control for hundreds of years. Ancient Celtic peoples and Greeks also settled in Spain, and the ancient Romans made the peninsula a province of their huge empire.

The Spaniards have had to struggle against many natural handicaps, as well as against invasions by Moors, Romans, and other peoples. Most of Spain is a high, dry plateau called the *Meseta.* Hills and mountains rise throughout the Meseta, and north of it a mountain barrier extends across the peninsula. This rugged landscape makes travel through Spain difficult.

Spain also lacks many raw materials needed by industry, and crops do not grow well in the country's poor soil and dry climate. As a result, the Spaniards have historically produced little that could be offered in trade with other countries. But in spite of their many disadvantages, the proud, strong-willed Spaniards once ruled one of the largest empires in world history.

Spain's rise as a world power started in the A.D. 1000's, when the Spanish people began to drive the Moors from the country. They finally defeated the Moors in 1492. That same year, Christopher Columbus, sailing in Spanish ships, reached America.

Columbus' voyage touched off a great age of Spanish exploration and conquest. The Spaniards built an empire that included much of western South America and

574

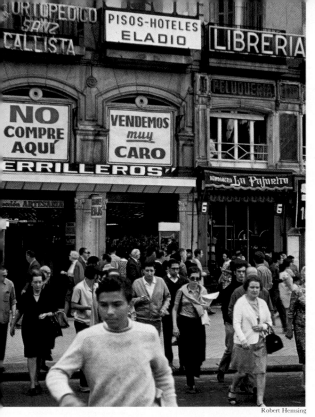

J. Ciganovic from Madeline Grimoldi

Beautiful Castles called *alcazars,* built during the Middle Ages, stand in many Spanish cities. The alcazar above is in Segovia.

Robert Hemsing

The Streets of Madrid, Spain's capital and largest city, are usually crowded with people. Madrid is one of the chief commercial, cultural, and industrial centers of the country.

Michael Kuh, Black Star

Local Festivals are celebrated throughout Spain each year. During the *fiesta* (festival) of San Fermín in Pamplona, *above,* the people run bulls through the streets to the bull ring.

southern North America, as well as lands in Africa, Asia, and Europe. But beginning in the late 1500's, economic difficulties, wars with other countries, and civil wars weakened Spain, and the country lost most of its huge empire. Spain then remained a poor, weak nation until the mid-1900's.

In the late 1930's, a bloody civil war tore Spain apart and brought General Francisco Franco to power as dictator. He controlled the country until his death in 1975. Spain became a democracy after Franco died.

Facts in Brief

Capital: Madrid.

Official Language: Castilian Spanish.

Form of Government: Parliamentary monarchy.

Area: 194,885 sq. mi. (504,750 km²), including Balearic and Canary islands. *Greatest Distances*—east-west, 646 mi. (1,040 km); north-south, 547 mi. (880 km). *Coastline*—2,345 mi. (3,774 km).

Elevation: *Highest*—Mulhacén, 11,411 ft. (3,478 m) above sea level. *Lowest*—sea level along the coast.

Population: *Estimated 1984 Population*—38,576,000; distribution, 77 per cent urban, 23 per cent rural; density, 197 persons per sq. mi. (76 per km²). *1970 Census*—33,956,376. *Estimated 1989 Population*—40,344,000.

Chief Products: *Agriculture*—olives, oranges, wheat, wine grapes. *Manufacturing*—automobiles, cement, chemical products, clothing, ships, steel.

National Anthem: "Himno Nacional" ("National Anthem").

Money: *Basic Unit*—peseta. See MONEY (table); PESETA.

WORLD BOOK map

Spain has an area more than 6 per cent as large as that of the United States, not including Alaska and Hawaii.

575

SPAIN

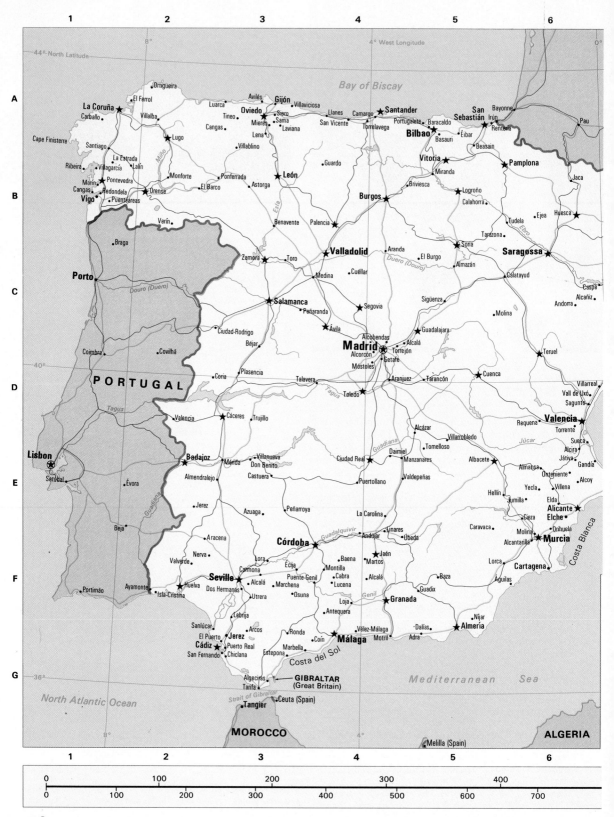

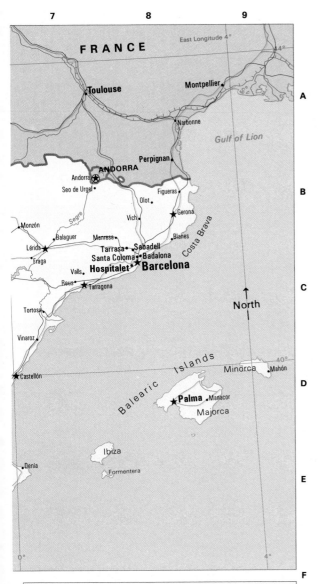

Spain Political Map

⊛	National Capital
★	Provincial Capital
•	Other city or town
▬▬▬	International boundary
———	Major road
———	Rail line

WORLD BOOK maps

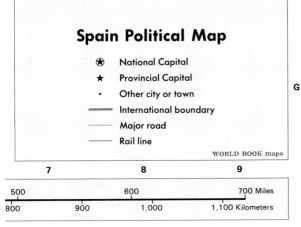

500   600   700 Miles
800   900   1,000   1,100 Kilometers

REGIONS AND PROVINCES OF SPAIN

The table and map below identify the historic regions of Spain and the provinces into which they are divided. Each province is numbered on the map to correspond to its name in the table.

	Population	Area In sq. mi.	In km²
Andalusia (Andalucía)	6,337,121	33,694	87,268
1 Almería	401,077	3,388	8,774
2 Cádiz	973,402	2,851	7,385
3 Córdoba	733,402	5,297	13,718
4 Granada	757,759	4,838	12,531
5 Huelva	413,008	3,894	10,085
6 Jaén	664,270	5,212	13,498
7 Málaga	970,245	2,809	7,276
8 Sevilla	1,423,958	5,416	14,001
Aragon (Aragón)	1,178,664	18,405	47,669
1 Huesca	215,894	6,051	15,671
2 Teruel	157,633	5,716	14,804
3 Zaragoza	805,137	6,639	17,194
Asturias	1,143,871	4,079	10,565
Oviedo	1,143,871	4,079	10,565
Balearic Islands (Baleares)	621,925	1,936	5,014
Baleares	621,925	1,936	5,014
Basque Provinces and Navarre (Vascongadas y Navarra)	2,617,260	6,827	17,682
1 Alava	244,970	1,176	3,047
2 Guipúzcoa	694,313	771	1,997
3 Navarra	495,957	4,024	10,421
4 Vizcaya	1,182,020	856	2,217
Canary Islands (Canarias)*	1,342,773	2,808	7,273
1 Las Palmas*	663,602	1,570	4,065
2 Santa Cruz de Tenerife*	679,171	1,239	3,208
Catalonia (Cataluña)	5,822,652	12,328	31,930
1 Barcelona	4,521,307	2,986	7,733
2 Gerona	452,026	2,273	5,886
3 Lérida	352,415	4,644	12,028
4 Tarragona	496,904	2,426	6,283
Estremadura (Extremadura)	1,096,486	16,063	41,602
1 Badajoz	657,642	8,362	21,657
2 Cáceres	438,844	7,701	19,945
Galicia	2,804,623	11,365	29,434
1 La Coruña	1,081,691	3,041	7,876
2 Lugo	414,491	3,785	9,803
3 Orense	441,632	2,810	7,228
4 Pontevedra	866,809	1,729	4,477
Leon (León)	1,141,860	14,812	38,363
1 León	541,550	5,972	15,468
2 Salamanca	363,312	4,763	12,336
3 Zamora	236,998	4,077	10,559
Murcia	1,249,604	10,106	26,175
1 Albacete	337,780	5,737	14,858
2 Murcia	911,824	4,370	11,317
New Castile (Castilla la Nueva)	5,801,291	27,940	72,363
1 Ciudad Real	492,335	7,625	19,749
2 Cuenca	226,970	6,587	17,061
3 Guadalajara	142,126	4,707	12,190
4 Madrid	4,465,115	3,087	7,995
5 Toledo	474,745	5,934	15,368
Old Castile (Castilla la Vieja)	2,210,487	25,524	66,107
1 Ávila	193,638	3,107	8,048
2 Burgos	359,114	5,509	14,269
3 Logroño	246,491	1,944	5,034
4 Palencia	188,473	3,100	8,029
5 Santander	502,505	2,042	5,289
6 Segovia	152,614	2,683	6,949
7 Soria	105,446	3,972	10,287
8 Valladolid	462,206	3,167	8,202
Valencia	3,487,188	8,998	23,305
1 Alicante	1,091,506	2,264	5,863
2 Castellón	418,550	2,579	6,679
3 Valencia	1,977,132	4,156	10,763

*Does not appear on map; in Atlantic Ocean off northwest Africa.
Source: 1976 official estimates.

SPAIN MAP INDEX

Cities and Towns

(Some population figures include a rural area as well as the city or town.)

Adra ......15,549..G 5
Aguilar* ...14,619..F 4
Águilas ....18,900..F 6
Alacuás* ..21,452..D 6
Albacete ..101,815..E 5
Alcalá [de Guadaira] 39,593..F 3
Alcalá [de Henares] 101,416..D 4
Alcalá [la Real] ...20,184..F 4
Alcantarilla 21,891..F 6
Alcaudete* .12,270..F 4
Alcázar [de San Juan] ....26,930..D 5
Alcira .....35,428..E 6
Alcobendas 50,015..D 4
Alcorcón .112,493..D 4
Alcorsia* ...11,005..C 6
Alcoy .....60,336..E 6
Aldaya* ...18,704..D 6
Alfafar* ...19,045..D 6
Algeciras ..88,006..G 3
Algemesí* .23,623..E 6
Alhama de Murcia* .12,092..F 6
Alhaurín el Grande* .12,952..G 4
Alicante ..219,553..E 6
Almansa ...18,596..E 6
Almazora* .14,515..D 7
Almendralejo ...22,074..E 3
Almería ..121,302..F 5
Almonte* ..12,512..F 2
Almoradí* .12,257..E 6
Almuñécar* 15,419..G 4
Álora* ....14,080..G 4
Amorbieta-Echano* .15,090..A 5
Amposta* ..13,503..C 7
Andoain* ..14,537..A 5
Andújar ...34,459..F 4
Antequera ..40,113..F 4
Aranda [de Duero] ...22,133..C 4
Aranjuez ..31,275..D 4
Archena* ...11,061..E 6
Arcos [de la Frontera] 24,867..G 3
Arganda* ..17,381..D 4
Arteijo* ....13,009..A 1
Aspe* .....14,440..E 6
Astorga ....12,522..B 3
Ávila ......34,263..C 4
Avilés .....85,111..A 3
Ayamonte ..14,027..F 2
Azcoitia* ...10,839..A 5
Azpeitia* ..12,171..A 5
Azuaga ....10,510..E 3
Badajoz ..103,818..E 2
Badalona .201,867..C 8
Baena .....20,138..F 4
Baeza* ....14,952..F 4
Bailén* ....14,269..E 4
Balaguer ..12,241..B 7
Banolas* ..11,171..B 8
Baracaldo 118,136..A 5
Barbastro* 13,415..B 7
Barbate* ..20,092..G 3
Barcelona ..1,754,714..C 8
Basauri ...50,881..A 5
Baza ......20,113..F 5
Beasain ...10,925..A 5
Béjar ......17,128..D 3
Benalmádena* .10,845..G 4
Benavente ..11,584..B 3
Benetúser* 12,516..D 6
Benicarló* .15,626..D 7
Benidorm* .29,673..E 6
Benifayó* .11,014..D 6
Berga* ....12,978..B 8
Berja* ....11,981..F 5
Bermeo* ...18,095..A 5
Betanzos* ..10,845..A 2
Bilbao ....431,071..A 5
Blanes .....18,443..B 8
Boiro* .....15,591..A 1
Bollullos par del Condado* 11,733..F 2
Bueu* .....11,612..B 1
Burgos ...134,682..B 4
Burjasot* ..30,739..D 6
Burlada* ...14,646..A 5
Burriana* ..23,846..D 7
Cabañaquinta* ..21,756..A 3
Cabra .....20,140..F 4
Cáceres ....58,844..D 3
Cádiz ....142,242..G 3
Calahorra ..16,776..B 5
Calatayud ..17,298..C 6
Callosa de Segura* ..13,766..E 6
Calvià* ....17,833..D 8
Camargo ...17,782..A 4
Camas* ....23,840..F 3
Cambados* 11,321..B 1
Campo de Criptana* 13,185..D 5
Candás* ...11,430..A 3
Cangas ....20,607..B 1
Cangas [de Narcea] .20,052..A 3
Caravaca ...19,922..E 5
Carballo ...23,251..A 1
Carcagente* 20,844..E 6
Carlet* ....12,720..E 6
Carmona ..21,548..F 3
Cartagena 158,180..F 6
Castelldefels* ..20,048..C 8
Castellón [de la Plana] ..109,882..D 7
Castrillón* 15,831..A 3
Castro-Urdiales* 12,572..A 5
Catarroja* .17,011..D 6
Cehegín* ..12,365..F 6
Chiclana [de la Frontera] 31,711..G 3
Chipiona* ..11,196..G 3
Chirivella* .22,775..D 6
Cieza .....28,228..E 6
Ciudadela* .16,677..D 8
Ciudad Real 45,247..E 4
Ciudad-Rodrigo .12,530..C 3
Coín ......21,140..G 4
Collado-Villalba* 11,728..C 4
Colmenar Viejo* ...15,950..C 4
Conil* .....11,926..G 3
Córdoba ..255,250..F 4
Coria ......10,558..D 2
Coria del Río* ....20,402..F 3
Cornellá* ..91,110..C 8
Corvera de Asturias* 16,560..A 3
Coslada* ..33,434..D 4
Crevillente* 19,967..E 6
Cuart de Poblet* ..26,281..D 6
Cuenca ....37,088..D 5
Cullera* ...18,700..E 6
Culleredo* .11,177..A 2
Daimiel ....16,986..E 4
Dalías .....25,589..F 5
Denia .....20,664..E 7
Don Benito 26,117..E 3
Dos Hermanas 47,800..F 3
Durango* ..25,738..A 5
Écija ......33,505..F 3
Éibar ......37,838..A 5
Ejea [de los Caballeros] ...14,969..B 6
El Arahal* .15,826..F 3
Elche .....147,614..E 6
Elda ....48,259..E 6
El Ferrol [del Caudillo] 89,212..A 2
Elgóibar* ..13,951..A 5
El Puerto [de Santa María] ..51,600..G 3
El Viso del Alcor* ...12,261..F 3
Ermúa* ...17,692..A 5
Esplugas* .38,110..C 8
Estella* ...11,262..B 5
Estepona ...22,850..G 3
Felanitx* ..12,516..D 8
Fene* ......14,001..A 1
Figueras ...28,102..B 8
Fraga ......10,568..C 7
Fuengirola* 25,616..G 4
Fuenlabrada* ..18,348..D 4
Fuenterrabía* .....10,995..A 5
Galdácano* 23,945..A 5
Gandía ....41,565..E 6
Gavá* .....30,586..C 8
Gerona ....75,600..B 8
Getafe ....116,523..D 4
Gijón .....237,187..A 3
Grado* .....12,734..A 3
Granada ..214,091..F 4
Granollers* 36,366..C 8
Guadalajara 45,162..C 5
Guájar Alto* ....19,234..F 4
Guecho* ...56,238..A 5
Guernica y Luno* .17,271..A 5
Hellín .....22,327..E 6
Hernani* ..28,010..A 5
Hospitalet 280,640..C 8
Huelva ....111,238..F 2
Huércal-Overa* ...12,347..F 5
Huesca ....37,610..B 6
Ibi* ....17,635..E 6
Ibiza* .....20,552..E 7
Igualada* ..30,024..C 8
Inca* ......17,964..D 8
Irún ....51,098..A 5
Isla-Cristina ..15,417..F 2
Jaca ......11,538..B 6
Jaén ......84,114..F 4
Játiva .....22,613..E 6
Jerez .....167,720..G 3
Jerez [de los Caballeros] ..10,096..E 2
Jódar* ....11,335..F 4
Jumilla ....20,165..E 6
La Algaba* 11,156..F 3
La Carolina 16,855..E 4
La Coruña 207,269..A 1
La Estrada 28,318..B 1
La Laguna† 109,061..
Lalín ......20,004..B 2
La Línea* .54,158..G 3
La Llagosta* 11,510..C 8
La Puebla del Río* .12,566..F 3
Laracha* ..11,004..A 1
Laredo* ...11,319..A 4
La Rinconada* ...16,522..F 3
La Roda* ..11,558..E 5
Las Cabezas de San Juan* ...11,044..F 3
La Solana* 13,200..E 4
Las Palmas† 348,776..
La Unión* .13,034..F 6
Laviana ....15,296..A 3
Lebrija ....21,990..F 3
Leganés* .136,990..D 4
Lejona* ...17,845..A 5
Lena ......14,478..A 3
León .....115,176..B 3
Lepe* .....12,625..F 2
Lérida ....102,599..C 7
Linares ....51,648..E 4
Liria* .....12,276..D 6
Llanes .....14,794..A 4
Lluchmayor* ..12,713..D 8
Logroño ...96,622..B 5
Loja ....22,001..F 4
Lora [del Río] ....15,922..F 3
Lorca .....60,513..F 6
Los Palacios y Villafranca* ..21,641..F 3
Luanco* ...12,938..A 3
Luarca ....20,405..A 3
Lucena ....29,373..F 4
Lugo ......68,163..A 2
Madrid .3,201,234..D 4
Mahón ....21,619..D 9
Mairena del Alcor* ...11,410..F 3
Málaga ...411,131..G 4
Manacor ..24,275..D 9
Manises* ..22,230..D 6
Manlleu* ..14,054..B 8
Manresa ...65,469..B 8
Manzanares 15,311..E 4
Marbella ..54,674..G 3
Marchena ..18,510..F 3
Marín .....21,678..B 1
Martorell* .14,667..C 8
Martos .....21,375..F 4
Masnou* ...12,338..C 8
Mataró* ...91,587..C 8
Medina [del Campo] ..17,570..C 4
Medina Sidonia* .14,618..G 3
Mérida ....38,319..E 3
Mieres .....59,136..A 3
Mijas* .....11,271..G 4
Miranda [de Ebro] ...35,354..B 5
Mislata* ...26,100..D 6
Moaña* ....16,445..B 1
Molina [de Segura] ..25,436..F 6
Molíns de Rey* .....19,862..C 8
Mollet* .....28,869..C 8
Moncada* ..16,094..D 6
Moncada* ..23,193..C 8
Mondragón* ..25,679..A 5
Monforte ...19,248..B 2
Monóvar* ..10,729..E 6
Montijo* ...12,039..E 2
Montilla ...21,768..F 4
Montoro* ..11,247..F 4
Monzón ....14,122..B 7
Morón* ....26,047..F 3
Mos* ......12,143..B 1
Móstoles ..76,250..D 4
Motril .....35,471..G 4
Mula* .....14,169..F 6
Murcia ....263,082..F 6
Muros* .....10,737..B 1
Narón* .....26,139..A 2
Navalmoral de la Mata* ...11,589..D 3
Níjar ......12,092..F 5
Novelda* ...18,781..E 6
Noya* ......12,277..B 1
Oleiros* ....11,711..A 2
Olesa de Montserrat* ...12,435..C 8
Oliva* .....18,191..E 6
Olot ....22,941..B 8
Olvera* ....10,923..F 3
Oñate* .....10,765..A 5
Onda* .....16,345..D 6
Ondárroa* .11,774..A 5
Onteniente .26,297..E 6
Orense .....80,048..B 2
Orihuela ...47,754..E 6
Ortigueira ..15,999..A 2
Osuna .....18,983..F 3
Oviedo ...161,944..A 3
Paiporta* ..13,493..D 6
Palafrugell* 13,002..B 8
Palamós* ..11,274..B 8
Palencia ...63,557..B 4
Palma .....282,050..D 8
Palma del Río* .....17,274..F 3
Pamplona .165,277..B 6
Parla* .....30,562..D 4
Pasajes* ...22,501..A 5
Paterna* ...29,656..D 6
Peñarroya [-Pueblonuevo] ..13,579..E 3
Petrel* ....20,348..E 6
Picasent* ..12,435..D 6
Piloña* ....11,301..A 3
Pineda* ....10,750..C 8
Pinos Puente* ..12,292..F 4
Pinto* .....14,320..D 4
Plasencia ..28,574..D 3
Plaza* .....19,070..A 5
Ponferrada .49,915..B 3
Pontevedra 60,535..B 1
Porrino* ...10,892..B 1
Portugalete 54,014..A 5
Pozoblanco* 13,529..E 4
Pozuelo de Alarcón* .23,480..D 4
Prat del Llobregat* ..51,017..C 8
Pravia* ....12,160..A 3
Premiá de Mar* ....16,371..C 8
Priego de Córdoba* 20,560..F 4
Puenteareas 15,609..B 1
Puente-Genil ....25,277..F 4
Puerto Real 21,465..G 3
Puertollano 49,209..E 4
Redondela .24,874..B 1
Reinosa* ..12,534..A 4
Rentería ...46,329..A 5
Requena ...17,732..D 6
Reus ......72,331..C 7
Rianjo* ....11,073..A 1
Ribeira ....21,723..B 1
Ripoll* ....11,496..B 8
Ripollet* ...23,905..C 8
Ronda .....30,099..G 3
Roquetas* ..15,234..F 5
Rota* ......25,702..G 3
Rubí* ......35,855..C 8
Sabadell ..182,012..C 8
Sagunto ...52,424..D 6
Salamanca 133,288..C 3
Sama ......60,141..A 3
San Adrián de Besós* 37,286..C 8
San Andrés del Rabanedo* ....15,057..B 3
San Baudilio de Llobregat* .....65,595..C 8
San Celoni* 10,972..B 8
San Cugat* 29,889..C 8
San Felíu de Guixols* .14,070..B 8
San Felíu de Llobregat* 33,725..C 8
San Fernando ...68,051..G 3
San Fernando de Henares* 12,067..D 4
San Javier* 10,934..F 6
San Juan de Aznalfarache* ...21,925..F 3
San Juan Despí* ..23,736..C 8
San Martín del Rey Aurelio* .28,064..A 3
San Roque* 21,198..G 3
San Salvador del Valle* 13,397..A 5
San Sebastián ....169,622..A 5
San Sebastián de los Reyes* ..27,339..D 4
San Vicente dels Horts* ..18,276..C 8
San Vicente del Raspeig* .19,631..E 6
Sangenjo* ..13,323..B 1
Sanlúcar [de Barrameda] .43,867..G 2
Santa Coloma [de Gramanet] ..137,579..C 8
Santa Comba* .11,362..A 1
Santa Cruz† ..186,237..
Santa María de Barbará* 15,007..C 8
Santa Perpetua de Moguda* 12,419..C 8
Santander 164,999..A 4
Santiago ...84,138..A 1
Santurce-Antiguo* 52,924..A 5
Saragossa (Zaragoza) ...540,308..C 6
Sardanyola* 30,358..C 8
Sarriá* ....12,023..A 2
Segovia ....47,701..C 4
Sestao* ....41,399..A 5
Seville (Sevilla) 590,235..F 3
Siero ......36,688..A 3
Silla* ......13,144..D 6
Silleda* ....11,222..B 1
Sitges* ....11,043..C 8
Socuéllamos* ..12,140..E 4
Soria ......28,308..B 5
Sueca ......22,522..E 6
Tabernes de Valldigna* 15,182..E 6
Talavera [de la Reina] 55,350..D 4
Tarazona ..11,378..B 6
Tarifa .....15,006..G 3
Tarragona 101,619..C 7
Tarrasa ..161,679..C 8
Teo* ....12,056..A 1
Teruel .....24,122..D 6
Tineo ......20,079..A 3
Toledo .....52,988..D 4
Tolosa* ....18,549..A 5
Tomelloso ..26,089..E 5
Torre del Campo* ..10,732..F 4
Torre-Pacheco* 13,364..F 6
Torredonjimeno* ..13,838..F 4
Torrejón [de Ardoz] ..42,266..D 4
Torrelavega 51,175..A 4
Torrente ...46,686..D 6
Torrevieja* 11,028..F 6
Tortosa ....47,246..C 7
Totana* ....16,843..F 6
Tudela .....23,093..B 6
Túy* ....13,452..B 1
Ubeda .....30,223..F 4
Ubrique* ...14,751..G 3
Urnieta* ...12,523..A 5
Utiel* ......11,876..D 6
Utrera .....34,250..F 3
Valdepeñas .23,176..E 4
Valencia ..714,086..D 6
Valladolid 287,230..C 4
Vall de Uxó 25,087..D 6
Valls ......16,710..C 7
Valverde [del Camino] .10,481..F 2
Vejer de la Frontera* 13,301..G 3
Vélez-Málaga ..38,249..G 4
Vendrell* ..10,639..C 6
Vergara* ...15,933..A 5
Vich ....27,615..B 8
Vigo ......230,611..B 1
Viladecáns* 36,270..C 8
Vilaseca* ..15,137..C 6
Villablino .13,851..A 3
Villacarrillo* .12,074..E 5
Villafranca de los Barros* ..12,356..E 2
Villafranca del Panadés* 21,366..C 8
Villagarcía .29,125..B 1
Villajoyosa* 20,428..E 6
Villalba ...16,975..A 2
Villamartín* 12,466..F 3
Villanueva [de la Serena] ..20,740..E 3
Villanueva de Córdoba* 10,842..E 4
Villanueva y Geltrú* ..41,229..C 8
Villarreal ..36,455..D 6
Villarrobledo ....20,084..E 5
Villaviciosa 16,314..A 3
Villena .....27,333..E 6
Vinaroz ....17,049..C 7
Vitoria ....170,870..B 5
Vivero* ....13,215..A 2
Yecla ......23,316..E 6
Zafra* .....12,433..E 3
Zamora ....52,180..C 3
Zaragoza, see Saragossa
Zarauz* ...13,709..A 5
Zumárraga* 12,390..A 5

*Does not appear on map; key shows general location.
†Does not appear on map; in Canary Islands in Atlantic Ocean off northwest Africa.

Source: 1975 official estimates.

General Francisco Franco ruled Spain as a dictator from the end of the Spanish Civil War in 1939 until his death in 1975. Franco and his close advisers made the important decisions about new laws and government policies. Franco established his own political party and outlawed all other political parties in the country.

After Franco's death, Spaniards established a democratic form of government called a parliamentary monarchy. New political parties were allowed to operate, and the people were given a voice in the government. The main government officials are a king, a prime minister, and members of a Cabinet and a parliament.

The King serves as Spain's head of state. He does not have a direct role in the operations of the government, but he has an advisory role in matters of government policies. The king represents the country at important diplomatic and ceremonial affairs. Juan Carlos I, who became king in 1975, played an important part in the process that changed Spain from a dictatorship to a democracy.

The Prime Minister is Spain's head of government. This official heads a Cabinet, which carries out the day-to-day operations of the government. The prime minister is the leader of the political party with the most seats in parliament.

The Parliament of Spain, called the *Cortes*, makes the country's laws. The Cortes is a two-house legislature. It consists of a 350-member lower house called the Chamber of Deputies and a 208-member upper house called the Senate. The people elect the members of both houses to four-year terms.

Local Government. In addition to its territory on the European mainland, Spain includes the Canary Islands and the Balearic Islands. The Canaries lie off the northwest coast of Africa. The Balearic Islands lie off Spain's east coast.

Spain is divided into 50 provinces. Mainland Spain consists of 47 provinces; the Canary Islands, 2; and the Balearic Islands, 1. The national government appoints a governor for each province. The people of each province elect the members of a provincial assembly. Voters in cities and towns elect a city or town council. Each city and town has a mayor. Mayors of communities with more than 10,000 persons are elected by the people. Provincial governors appoint the mayors of smaller communities.

Political Parties. The left-wing Socialist Workers' Party is Spain's largest political party. The right-wing Popular Alliance ranks second in size.

Courts. Spain has two court systems: civil and military. Judges appointed by the national government decide all cases. The civil court system handles most civil and criminal cases. The system consists of a supreme court, 15 appeals courts, 50 provincial courts, and more than 9,000 local courts. Military courts handle cases involving military crimes and civilian crimes classified as military rebellion.

Armed Forces of Spain consist of an army, a navy, and an air force. About 220,000 persons serve in the army, 46,600 in the navy, and 35,700 in the air force. Men 21 to 35 years old may be drafted for two years of military service.

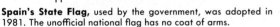

Spain's State Flag, used by the government, was adopted in 1981. The unofficial national flag has no coat of arms.

Coat of Arms was adopted in 1981. The symbols on the shield represent Aragon, Castile, and other historic kingdoms of Spain.

Sygma

Juan Carlos I, *in uniform,* became king of Spain in November 1975. He is shown above with his wife, Queen Sophia, on the day he was sworn in as monarch.

EDISTUDIO, S.A.

Spain's Parliament Building, the Palace of the Spanish *Cortes* (parliament) in Madrid, is the home of the nation's legislature. The building was erected in the mid-1800's.

Most Spaniards were poor rural people before the country's rapid economic development of the 1950's and 1960's. Many of the people owned small farms. Others worked on large estates. The people in each region of the country, such as Andalusia in the south or Castile in central Spain, felt great loyalty to their region. They had little contact with Spaniards in other regions. The nation's greatest unifying force was the Roman Catholic Church. Almost all Spaniards were Roman Catholics, and a Catholic church stood in the center of most villages.

Today, Spain is an industrial nation, and the people live in an increasingly modern urban society. Most Spaniards eat better, dress better, live in better homes, and receive more education and better health care today than ever before. Regionalism and Roman Catholicism remain important forces in Spanish life. But rapid economic and social change has reduced the influence of these forces on many of the people.

Ancestry and Population. People have lived in what is now Spain for more than 100,000 years. At the beginning of recorded history—about 5,000 years ago—a people known as Iberians occupied much of Spain. During the next 4,000 years, other groups came to Spain as conquerors, settlers, or traders. Phoenicians, the first of these groups, were followed by Celts, Greeks, Carthaginians, Romans, Germanic peoples, and Moors. Each group mixed with other peoples in Spain and so helped shape the ancestry of the present-day Spanish people.

Spain has a population of about $38\frac{1}{2}$ million. About three-fourths of the people live in cities. Spain has two cities with more than a million persons. They are Madrid, the nation's capital and largest city, and Barcelona. The country has 46 other cities with populations of more than 100,000 persons. See the separate articles on Spanish cities listed in the *Related Articles* at the end of this article.

Language. Castilian Spanish is the official language of Spain and is spoken by most of the people. There are no *dialects* (local forms) of the language, but pro-

Peter Menzel, Stock, Boston

Modern Apartment Buildings, such as the one above in Barcelona, are common in Spanish cities. Almost all city people live in apartments. Children from this apartment building attend the school connected to it at the left.

nunciation varies slightly from one region to another.

In three northern regions of Spain—Catalonia, the Basque provinces, and Galicia—a second language is used in addition to Castilian Spanish. Many people in Catalonia speak Catalan, a language similar to the Provençal tongue of southern France. Some people in the Basque provinces speak Basque—also called Euskera or Euskara—which is not known to be related to any other language. In Galicia, most people speak a dialect of Portuguese known as Galician. See SPANISH LANGUAGE.

City Life. The standard of living in Spanish cities has risen rapidly since the 1950's, and modern urban ways of life have become increasingly popular. Almost all city people live in apartments, and many of them own rather than rent their dwellings. City people wear the latest Western-style clothing, and they dress up somewhat more than do people in the United States. Almost all city homes have electricity, and a rapidly growing number of families own automobiles and television sets. But the people also suffer from such problems as pollution and traffic jams.

People in the cities still follow a number of age-old customs in addition to the latest trends. For example, most Spanish factories, stores, and offices close for three-hour lunch breaks and then stay open until about 7 P.M. Some Spaniards take a siesta after lunch, though most people no longer follow this old custom. Spaniards enjoy a *paseo* (walk) before their evening meal, which they often do not eat until 10 or 11 P.M. They also go to sidewalk cafes, bars, and clubs, where they visit with friends and drink coffee, soft drinks, or wine.

Country Life in Spain has changed much less than city life. Since the late 1950's, expanded electrical service, improved farming methods, and modern equipment have helped make life easier for Spanish farmers. But

Sabine Weiss, Rapho Guillumette

The Basques of northern Spain are one of the nation's many regional population groups. Each group has folk dances, *above,* and other customs that differ from those of all the others.

agriculture has fallen far behind industry in economic importance, and rural standards of living are much lower than those in the cities. Since the early 1960's, hundreds of thousands of farmers have moved to Spanish cities or to other countries to find work.

Most farmers live in villages or small towns. Every morning and evening they travel the dirt roads between their homes and the fields, either walking or riding in donkey carts. Unlike city people, they take only a short lunch break. But the evening paseo is as popular in rural areas as in the cities. Rural people also enjoy sitting in their town or village square.

Most rural homes are made of clay and stone, which are covered with whitewashed plaster for added protection from the sun. Most houses have gently sloping tile roofs. Many homes rise directly from the street or from a narrow sidewalk, and many have iron grillwork over the windows.

Farmers dress less formally than do city people. Traditionally, the men wear white cotton shirts, black trousers with a sash, and black, round caps called *berets*. The women wear plain dresses or full skirts and blouses.

Food and Drink. Spaniards enjoy seafood, which is inexpensive and plentiful in the coastal waters. They prepare it in a variety of ways. A popular dish is *paella*. It consists of such foods as shrimp, lobster, chicken, ham, and vegetables, all combined with rice that has been cooked with a flavoring called *saffron*. Other favorite dishes include squid, crabs, sardines, and fried baby eels. A popular dish during warm weather is *gazpacho*, a cold soup made of strained tomatoes, olive oil, and spices. It is served sprinkled with bread cubes and chopped cucumbers, onions, and tomatoes.

Popular meats include chicken, goat, lamb, pork,

J. Alex Langley, DPI

An Outdoor Market in Barcelona attracts crowds of shoppers seeking fish and other seafood. Spaniards enjoy seafood dishes, and fishing ranks as a leading Spanish industry.

WHERE THE PEOPLE OF SPAIN LIVE

This map shows the population distribution in Spain and the location of many of Spain's large cities. The most heavily populated areas are shown in the darker colors.

Persons per sq. mi.		Persons per km²
More than 250		More than 97
125 to 250		48 to 97
25 to 125		10 to 48
Less than 25		Less than 10

Major urban areas

■ More than 1,000,000 people

• 250,000 to 1,000,000 people

○ Less than 250,000 people

WORLD BOOK map

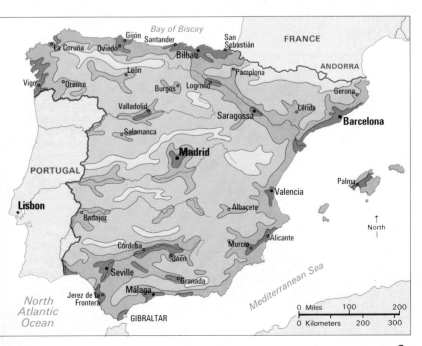

and rabbit. Beef is too expensive for most Spaniards because the country has little good pastureland for cattle. White bread baked in round or oval loaves is eaten plain or with cheese.

Almost every region of Spain produces wine, and most Spaniards drink wine with all meals except breakfast. They also enjoy a drink called *sangría*, which consists of wine, soda water, fruit juice, and fruit. Other popular beverages include soft drinks, strong black coffee, and thick, hot chocolate, which is usually served with deep-fried strips of dough called *churros*.

Recreation. Spaniards spend much of their leisure time outdoors. They like to sit for hours visiting at sidewalk cafes or in town or village squares. Summer vacations at the country's beautiful beaches have become increasingly popular. On weekends, city people often drive into the countryside for picnics or overnight trips.

Soccer is Spain's most popular sport, and many cities have a soccer stadium that seats 100,000 or more fans. Bullfighting is Spain's best-known and most unusual spectacle. Most cities have at least one bull ring, and leading matadors are national heroes.

Religion. About 99 per cent of the people in Spain are Roman Catholics. About 50,000 Protestants and a few thousand Jews also live in Spain.

During most of the period from 1851 to 1978, Roman Catholicism was the state religion of Spain. During that time, the government restricted the rights of non-Catholics in some ways. For example, non-Catholics were not allowed to try to win new followers for their religions, and only marriage ceremonies performed by the Catholic Church were legal. Spain adopted a new Constitution in 1978. Under provisions of the Constitution, Spain has no state religion, and people of all faiths are allowed complete freedom in religious matters.

Religious Holidays. The most important Spanish holiday period is Holy Week, celebrated the week before Easter with parades and other special events. Spaniards also hold celebrations to honor their local *patron* (guardian) saint. Many of these celebrations last several days. People decorate the streets, build bonfires, dance and sing, set off fireworks, and hold parades, bullfights, and beauty contests.

One of the best-known Spanish celebrations is the *fiesta* (festival) of San Fermín, which is celebrated each July in Pamplona. Bulls are turned loose in the streets as part of the festivities. Young men run ahead of the animals to the bull ring, where they hold amateur bullfights.

Education in Spain has improved greatly since 1900. Today, only about 7 per cent of the people 15 years old and older cannot read and write, compared with more than 60 per cent in 1900.

Spanish law requires all children from ages 6 through 13 to attend school. But many children quit school when they reach 14, and the number of students decreases greatly at each successive higher grade.

Students attend primary school for eight years and secondary school for four years. They must take an additional year of special study before entering a university. The government runs most primary and secondary

Michael Kuh, Rapho Guillumette

Spanish Children take part in a Roman Catholic festival in Toledo. Almost all Spaniards belong to the Catholic Church.

schools. But there are also Roman Catholic schools and nonreligious private schools at the primary and secondary levels. Spain has 18 universities, which are attended by about 300,000 students.

Museums and Libraries. The Prado in Madrid, Spain's best-known museum, contains one of the world's finest art collections. It features works by such great Spanish painters as Francisco Goya, Bartolomé Murillo, and Diego Velázquez, as well as by many foreign artists. Madrid's other museums include the Museum of the Americas; the National Archaeological Museum; the Royal Armory; and the Army, Navy, and Municipal museums.

Most of Spain's major cities have museums that exhibit art from the surrounding region. The best known of these museums are the Provincial Museum in Seville and the Museum of Catalan Art in Barcelona. In Toledo, the house of the great painter El Greco has been made into a museum. The museum exhibits many of his works.

Spain's largest library, the National Library in Madrid, has more than 3 million volumes. The Municipal Periodical Library of Madrid owns one of the most complete collections of periodicals in the world. Millions of records and important documents of Spanish history are preserved in the Archives of the Indies in Seville; the General Archives of the Kingdom in Simancas, near Valladolid; and the National Historical Archives in Madrid.

Spain has a rich artistic tradition and has produced some of the world's finest painters and writers. Spanish arts flourished during a golden age in the 1500's and 1600's, when the country ranked among the world's leading powers. Spain's arts then declined somewhat, but a rebirth has occurred during the 1900's.

Literature. The oldest Spanish writings still in existence are *The Poem of the Cid* and *The Play of the Wise Men*. Scholars believe both works date from the 1100's, but they do not know who wrote them. *The Poem of the Cid* describes the deeds of one of Spain's national heroes, El Cid (see CID, THE). Only part of *The Play of the Wise Men* has been preserved. It tells of the visit of the three wise men to the Christ child.

Spanish writers produced some of the country's best-known literature during the golden age. For example, Miguel de Cervantes wrote the novel *Don Quixote*, one of the world's greatest literary works. The playwright Pedro Calderón de la Barca vividly dramatized the dreams and realities of life in his famous play *Life Is a Dream*. Spain's leading writers of the 1900's include the essayists José Ortega y Gasset and Miguel de Unamuno, the playwright Antonio Buero Vallejo, the novelist Camilo José Cela, and the poet Juan Ramón Jiménez. See SPANISH LITERATURE.

Painting. Spain's leading painters during the golden age included El Greco, Murillo, and Velázquez. Goya, one of the first masters of modern art, painted during the late 1700's and early 1800's.

Spain's best-known artist since 1900 has been Pablo Picasso. He created fine sculptures, drawings, graphics, and ceramics in addition to his paintings. Other leading modern Spanish painters include Salvador Dali, Juan Gris, Joan Miró, and Antonio Tàpies.

Architecture in Spain shows the influence of various peoples who once controlled the country. Some aqueducts, bridges, and other structures built by the ancient Romans are still in use, and the ruins of other Roman structures can be seen throughout the country. *Mosques* (houses of worship) built by the Moors stand in some southern cities, though most of these buildings are now Roman Catholic churches. The enormous cathedral in Córdoba was built as a mosque in the 700's. More than 1,000 pillars of granite, jasper, marble, and onyx support its arches. The Moors also built fortified palaces called *alcazars*. The most famous alcazar is the magnificent Alhambra in Granada (see ALHAMBRA).

Spain has about 1,400 castles and palaces, including the alcazars. El Escorial, a combination burial place, church, monastery, and palace, stands about 30 miles (48 kilometers) northwest of Madrid. It was built in the 1500's and is one of the world's largest buildings. The gray granite structure covers almost 400,000 square feet (37,000 square meters) and has 300 rooms, 88 fountains, and 86 staircases. The tombs of many Spanish monarchs are in El Escorial. See ESCORIAL.

About 10 miles (16 kilometers) from El Escorial is the Valley of the Fallen, another burial place and monastery. The burial chamber lies inside a mountain. About 46,000 men who died in the Spanish Civil War are buried there. The body of dictator Francisco Franco is also buried there. A cross 500 feet (150 meters) high, cut

Adeline Haaga, Tom Stack & Assoc.

The Alhambra, a famous alcazar in Granada, is known for the beauty of its inner courtyards, such as the Court of the Lions, above. The Alhambra was built during the 1200's and 1300's.

from a single piece of stone, stands atop the mountain.

The Gothic cathedral in Seville is Europe's second largest church. Only St. Peter's Church in Rome is larger. The Seville cathedral measures 380 feet (116 meters) long and 250 feet (76 meters) wide, and its tower is 400 feet (120 meters) high.

Music. Unlike many other European countries, Spain has produced few leading composers of operas and symphonies. But during the 1600's, Spanish composers created a form of light opera known as *zarzuela*. It combines singing with spoken words. Spain's best-known musicians of the 1900's include the cellist Pablo Casals, the composer Manuel de Falla, and the classical guitarist Andrés Segovia.

Folk singing and dancing have long been popular in Spain, and the people of each region have their own special songs and dances. Musicians provide accompaniment on castanets, guitars, and tambourines. Such Spanish dances as the bolero, fandango, and flamenco have become world famous.

M. Boigne, Rapho Guillumette

The Flamenco, above, is one of the many lively Spanish folk dances. Flamenco dancers are usually accompanied by guitarists.

Spain is the third largest country in Europe. Only France and Russia cover a larger area. Spain occupies more than five-sixths of the Iberian Peninsula, which forms the southwestern tip of Europe. The country also includes the nearby Balearic Islands. Mainland Spain and the Balearics form six major land regions: (1) the Meseta, (2) the Northern Mountains, (3) the Ebro Basin, (4) the Coastal Plains, (5) the Guadalquivir Basin, and (6) the Balearic Islands.

The Meseta is a huge, dry plateau that covers most of Spain. It consists mainly of plains broken by hills and low mountains. Higher mountains rise on the north, east, and south. To the west, the Meseta extends into Portugal. Spain's highest peak, 11,411-foot (3,478-meter) Mulhacén, stands in the Sierra Nevada range on the southern edge of the region.

Poor red or yellowish-brown soil that is unsuitable for raising crops covers most of the Meseta. Forests grow on the mountains and hills, but only small, scattered shrubs and flowering plants can be found on most of the plains. Farmers tend flocks of goats and sheep in the hills and mountains.

Most of Spain's major rivers rise in the Meseta. The longest river, the Tagus, flows 626 miles (1,007 kilometers) from the eastern Meseta through Portugal to the Atlantic Ocean. The Guadalquivir flows 400 miles (640 kilometers) from the southern Meseta to the Atlantic.

The Northern Mountains extend across northernmost Spain from the Atlantic Ocean to the Coastal Plains. The region consists of the Galician Mountains, in the west; the Cantabrian Mountains, in the central area;

and the Pyrenees Mountains, which separate Spain from France, in the east. The Galician and Cantabrian mountains rise sharply from the sea along most of the Atlantic coast. Forests cover many of the slopes in the region, and many short, swift-flowing rivers plunge through the mountains. Like the Meseta, the Northern Mountains have generally poor soil for growing crops, and much of the region is pastureland.

The Ebro Basin consists of broad plains that extend along the Ebro River in northeastern Spain. The Ebro, one of Spain's longest rivers, flows 565 miles (909 kilometers) from the Northern Mountains to the Mediterranean Sea. Its basin is bordered by the Pyrenees to the north, the Meseta to the west and south, and low hills to the east. It is a dry area, but irrigation has turned the basin into an important agricultural region.

The Coastal Plains stretch along Spain's entire Mediterranean coast. The region consists of fertile plains broken by hills that extend to the sea. It is a rich agricultural area. Farmers along the coast, like those in the Ebro Basin, have used rivers that cut through the plains to build irrigation systems.

The Guadalquivir Basin lies in southwestern Spain. It spreads out along the Guadalquivir River to the Atlantic Ocean. The basin is a dry but extremely fertile region in the hottest part of the country. Farmers depend on irrigation to water their crops.

The Balearic Islands lie from about 50 to 150 miles (80 to 240 kilometers) east of mainland Spain in the Mediterranean Sea. Five major islands and many smaller ones make up the group. The three largest islands, in order of size, are Majorca, Minorca, and Ibiza. Majorca is a fertile island with a low mountain range along its northwest coast. Plains stretch from the mountains to hills on the southeast coast. Minorca is mostly flat, with wooded hills in the center. Ibiza is hilly. Both smaller islands are much less fertile than Majorca.

LAND REGIONS OF SPAIN

Spain has six land regions: Northern Mountains, Ebro Basin, Meseta, Guadalquivir Basin, Coastal Plains, and Balearic Islands.

Michael Kuh, Rapho Guillumette

The Meseta is a high plateau that covers most of Spain. Many hills and low mountains rise from the dry plains that stretch across most of the region.

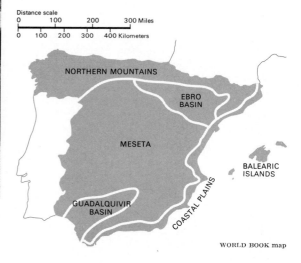

Distance scale

0 — 100 — 200 — 300 Miles

0 — 100 — 200 — 300 — 400 Kilometers

NORTHERN MOUNTAINS

EBRO BASIN

MESETA

GUADALQUIVIR BASIN

COASTAL PLAINS

BALEARIC ISLANDS

WORLD BOOK map

The Snow-Capped Pyrenees Mountains, *above,* which form the eastern end of the Northern Mountains region, separate Spain from France. Villages and small towns lie scattered through the rugged, thinly populated Pyrenees.

SPAIN

Physical Features

Agueda R.	A 2	Luna R.	A 2
Alcanadre R.	A 3	Majorca (I.)	B 4
Alcántara Reservoir	B 2	Mar Menor	
Aragón R.	A 3	(Lagoon)	B 3
Arga R.	A 3	Miño R.	A 1
Bay of Biscay	A 3	Minorca (I.)	B 4
Cabriel R.	B 3	Moncayo (Mt.)	A 3
Cape Creus	A 4	Montes de Toledo	
Cape de Gata	B 3	(Mts.)	B 2
Cape Finisterre	A 1	Montes Universales	
Cape Nao	B 4	(Mts.)	B 3
Cape Ortegal	A 1	Mulhacén (Mt.)	B 3
Cape Palos	B 3	Navia R.	A 2
Cape Peñas	A 3	Odiel R.	B 2
Cape Tortosa	A 4	Peñalara (Mt.)	A 3
Carrión R.	A 2	Perdido (Mt.)	A 3
Cega R.	A 2	Pico de Aneto	
Cordillera		(Peak)	A 3
Cantábrica (Mts.)	A 2	Pisuerga R.	A 2
Duero (Douro) R.	A 2	Pyrenees (Mts.)	A 4
Ebro R.	A 3	Sangonera R.	B 3
El Teleno (Mt.)	A 2	Segre R.	A 4
Gallego R.	A 3	Segura R.	B 3
Genil R.	B 2	Sierra de Gata	
Gibraltar, Strait of	B 2	(Mts.)	A 2
Giguela R.	B 3	Sierra de Gredos	
Guadalope R.	A 3	(Mts.)	A 2
Guadalquivir R.	B 2	Sierra de	
Guadiana R.	B 2	Guadalupe (Mts.)	B 2
Gulf of Almería	B 3	Sierra de Gua-	
Gulf of Cadiz	B 1	darrama (Mts.)	A 3
Gulf of Mazarron	B 3	Sierra de Gúdar	
Gulf of San Jorge	A 4	(Mts.)	A 3
Gulf of Valencia	B 4	Sierra Morena	
Ibiza (I.)	B 4	(Mts.)	B 2
Jabalón R.	B 2	Sierra Nevada (Mts.)	B 3
Jalón R.	A 3	Sil R.	A 2
Jarama R.	A 3	Tajo Reservoir	B 2
Jiloca R.	A 3	Tajo (Tagus) R.	B 2
Júcar R.	B 3	Ter R.	A 4
La Mancha (Plain)	B 3	Tiétar R.	B 2
La Sagra (Mt.)	B 3	Tórmes R.	A 2
Las Marismas		Turia R.	B 3
(Marshes)	B 2	Ulla R.	A 1

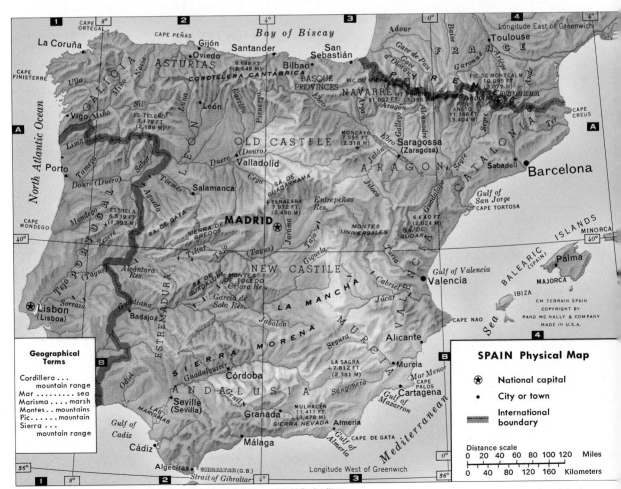

Geographical Terms

Cordillera . . .
   mountain range
Mar . . . . sea
Marisma . . . . marsh
Montes . . mountains
Pic . . . . . . mountain
Sierra . . .
   mountain range

SPAIN Physical Map

⊛   National capital

•   City or town

▬▬   International boundary

CM TERRAIN SPAIN
COPYRIGHT BY
RAND M°NALLY & COMPANY
MADE IN U.S.A.

Distance scale

| 0 | 20 | 40 | 60 | 80 | 100 | 120 | Miles |
| 0 | | 40 | 80 | 120 | 160 | | Kilometers |

J. Alex Langley, DPI

Spain's Sunny Mediterranean Coast has many resort areas, such as the Costa Brava, above, that attract millions of vacationists each summer. Almost all Spain has hot, dry summers.

The Meseta and other inland regions of Spain have dry, sunny weather throughout the year. These regions, which make up most of Spain, have hot summers and cold winters. The average temperature rises above 80° F. (27° C) during July, the hottest month. It falls below 30° F. (−1° C) in January, the coldest month. Summer and winter droughts—broken only by occasional rainstorms—are common, and steady winds often whip up the dry soil. Upper mountain slopes in the Meseta have snow most of the winter.

Mild, rainy winters alternate with hot, dry, sunny summers in the Coastal Plains and the Balearic Islands. The average January temperature rarely falls below 40° F. (4° C), and the average July temperature usually rises to almost 80° F. (27° C). Short, heavy rainstorms are common in winter. But summer droughts last up to three months in some areas. The dry, sunny summers attract millions of vacationists each year to the Balearic Islands and to the Costa Brava, Costa del Sol, and other famous resort areas along Spain's Mediterranean coast.

Winds from the Atlantic Ocean bring mild, wet weather to the Northern Mountains in all seasons. The region has Spain's heaviest *precipitation* (rain, snow, and other forms of moisture). Rain falls much of the time throughout the year, usually in a steady drizzle. There are many cloudy, humid days, and fog and mist often roll in from the sea. The region's heaviest precipitation comes in winter, when the upper mountain ranges usually build up deep snow. In January, the average temperature throughout most of the region rarely falls below 40° F. (4° C), and the average July temperature seldom rises above 70° F. (21° C).

AVERAGE MONTHLY WEATHER

	MADRID						SEVILLE					
	Temperatures				Days of			Temperatures				Days of
	F°		C°		Rain or			F°		C°		Rain or
	High	Low	High	Low	Snow			High	Low	High	Low	Snow
JAN	57	24	14	-4	9		JAN.	67	35	19	2	8
FEB.	61	27	16	-3	9		FEB.	71	35	22	2	9
MAR.	68	30	20	-1	11		MAR.	77	39	25	4	9
APR.	76	34	24	1	9		APR.	84	43	29	6	8
MAY	84	40	29	4	9		MAY	94	48	34	9	5
JUNE	91	47	33	8	6		JUNE	101	55	38	13	2
JULY	96	53	36	12	3		JULY	107	60	42	16	0
AUG.	96	54	36	12	2		AUG.	107	61	42	16	0
SEPT.	89	45	32	7	6		SEPT.	101	56	38	13	3
OCT.	77	37	25	3	8		OCT.	91	48	33	9	5
NOV.	63	30	17	-1	10		NOV.	76	39	24	4	9
DEC.	57	25	14	-4	9		DEC.	68	34	20	1	8

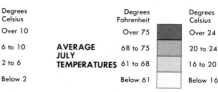

	Inches	Centimeters		Degrees Fahrenheit	Degrees Celsius		Degrees Fahrenheit	Degrees Celsius
AVERAGE YEARLY PRECIPITATION	More than 59	More than 150	**AVERAGE JANUARY TEMPERATURES**	Over 50	Over 10	**AVERAGE JULY TEMPERATURES**	Over 75	Over 24
	39 to 59	100 to 150		43 to 50	6 to 10		68 to 75	20 to 24
	20 to 39	50 to 100		36 to 43	2 to 6		61 to 68	16 to 20
	Less than 20	Less than 50		Below 36	Below 2		Below 61	Below 16

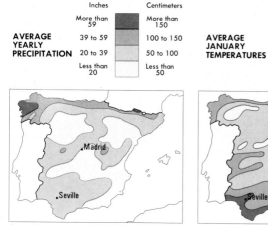

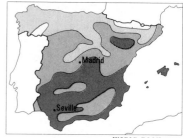

Sources: *Welt-Seuchen-Atlas*, V. III, edited by E. Rodenwaldt and H. J. Jusatz, Hamburg, 1961; and Meteorological Office, London.

WORLD BOOK maps

During the 1950's and 1960's, Spain changed from a poor agricultural country into a modern industrial nation. During this period, the country enjoyed one of the world's highest rates of economic growth as its annual production of goods and services more than tripled. Much of this growth resulted from heavy foreign investment in Spain's industries and from a booming tourist trade.

Between 1950 and the mid-1970's, the percentage of Spain's workers engaged in agriculture fell from about 50 per cent to about 22 per cent. At the same time, the percentage of workers employed in the construction, manufacturing, and mining industries rose from about 25 to 35 per cent. Employment in services, which includes such fields as communication, government, and trade, increased from about 25 to 43 per cent.

By 1970, the value of yearly industrial production in Spain was more than $2\frac{1}{2}$ times that of agricultural production. Although the country had not become a major industrial power, it was no longer a poor, economically backward nation.

Natural Resources. Spain is poor in natural resources. The country has little good farmland, and it lacks many important industrial raw materials.

Spain's most important mineral resource is the high-grade iron ore found in the Cantabrian Mountains. These mountains also contain coal, but the deposits are mostly of low quality. Other minerals found in Spain include copper, lead, manganese, mercury, potash, pyrites, salt, titanium, uranium, and zinc.

Most of Spain has poor soil and limited rainfall, which make it difficult to raise crops. Thick forests once covered much of Spain, but most of the trees have been cut down through the years. Today, few areas of the country have forests.

Manufacturing. Spain ranks among the world's leading producers of automobiles and ships. Other important manufactured products include cement, chemical

A. Gutierreze from Carl Östman

Spanish Steel Mills, such as this one in northern Spain, supply the nation's automobile, shipbuilding, and other important industries. Spain's steel production has increased greatly since the 1950's as part of the rapid industrial growth in the country.

products, shoes and other clothing, and steel. Most of Spain's factories are in the northern provinces, and Barcelona, Bilbao, and Madrid are the country's chief industrial centers. The government controls much of the production in the automobile, steel, and certain other major industries. But most factories in Spain are privately owned and operated.

Many problems threaten the continued growth of Spanish manufacturing. For example, the country's limited natural resources force industrialists to import many raw materials, which raises manufacturing costs. Also, the great majority of factories in Spain are small, employing fewer than 50 workers. Many of these firms use old-fashioned equipment and manufacturing methods, and most of them cannot afford research and development programs. As a result, Spain lags behind other industrial nations in technical development, and manufacturers must hire foreign engineers, scientists, and technicians.

Another problem Spanish manufacturers have is their dependence on investment from outside Spain. Such investment increased more than 500 per cent during the 1960's. Companies and individuals in other countries have been attracted by the low labor costs, low tax rates, and other favorable conditions for investment in Spanish industries.

Agriculture. Almost all the land in Spain is used for farming, either as cropland or as pastureland. But agricultural production in most regions has always been low because of the poor soil, dry climate, and inferior Spanish farming methods. The country does not produce enough food for its people, and so it must import large quantities every year.

Spain's chief farm products are olives, oranges, wheat, and wine grapes. Other important products include barley, cork, corn, lemons, oats, rye, and wool. The

PHOTRI

Olive Orchards are cultivated in the southern Meseta, *above,* and many other regions of Spain. Olives are an important Spanish product, and Spain ranks as a leading olive-growing country.

579

country ranks among the world's leading producers of cork, lemons, olives, oranges, and wine. Grain crops are grown mainly in Spain's northern regions. Farmers in the south and east produce most of the country's grapes, olives, and oranges and other citrus fruits. Sheep are the chief livestock in Spain. Other important farm animals include beef cattle, chickens, goats, and pigs.

About two-thirds of all Spanish farmers own their farms. The rest work as hired hands or tenants on large farms. Less than 1 per cent of all landowners hold about 50 per cent of the farmland in Spain. The poorest 50 per cent of the landowners own only about 5 per cent of the farmland. Small farmers own most of the farmland in the north. In the south, wealthy landlords hold most of the land.

Since about 1960, the government has introduced modern methods and equipment to more and more Spanish farmers. For example, the total area of irrigated farmland increased by a third during the 1960's, and the number of tractors multiplied more than 4 times. Such advances have increased farm production. But agriculture remains the weakest part of Spain's economy, and it lags far behind farming in most other European countries.

Tourism plays an important role in Spain's economy. The tourist industry employs about a tenth of all Spanish workers, and Spain earns more than $2½ billion a year from its tourist trade.

The number of visitors to Spain has increased rapidly —from about 6 million in 1960 to more than 25 million a year in the early 1970's. The Spanish government has encouraged the growth of tourism, and it operates schools that train hotel managers, tour guides, chefs, and other persons involved in the tourist business. The government also closely supervises the quality of services offered tourists.

Most of Spain's visitors come from France, Portugal, West Germany, Great Britain, and the United States. They are drawn to Spain by its resorts on the warm, sunny Mediterranean coast and by its bullfights, castles, and colorful festivals. They are also attracted by prices in Spain, which are lower than in most other countries of Western Europe or in the United States.

Fishing. Spain ranks among the leading fishing countries. About 1¾ million short tons (1.5 million metric tons) of fish are caught a year, chiefly anchovies, codfish, and hake. Much of the catch comes from the waters off Spain's north coast.

Mining. Spain has a wide variety of mineral resources. But the country has only small deposits of most minerals, and mining has steadily declined in importance during the 1900's.

Spain's Gross National Product

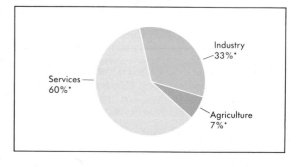

Spain's gross national product (GNP) was $173,299,000,000 in 1981. The GNP is the total value of goods and services produced by a country in a year. The GNP measures a nation's total economic performance and can also be used to compare the economic output and growth of countries.

Production and Workers by Economic Activities

Economic Activities	Per Cent of GDP* Produced	Employed Workers† Number of Persons	Per Cent of Total
Community, Social, & Personal Services	26	1,936,000	16
Manufacturing	19	2,914,600	23
Wholesale & Retail Trade	14	1,859,600	15
Construction	8	1,167,700	9
Agriculture	6	2,577,500	21
Mining	6	427,000	3
Transportation	6	560,500	4
Finance, Insurance, & Real Estate	5	277,700	2
Hotels & Restaurants	4	448,000	4
Utilities	4	80,200	1
Communication	1	98,100	1
Fishing	1	95,100	1
Total	100	12,441,900	100

*Based on gross domestic product (GDP) in 1980. GDP is gross national product adjusted for net income sent or received from abroad.
†Figures are for 1977.
Sources: International Monetary Fund; National Institute of Statistics, Madrid.

J. Ciganovic from Madeline Grimoldi

Oranges, an important Spanish product, are packed in crates for shipment to markets in Spain and many other countries. The orange crop comes mostly from southern and eastern Spain.

Spain is one of the world's leading producers of mercury. The next most important minerals produced in Spain are coal, iron ore, pyrites, titanium, and uranium. The country also mines copper, lead, manganese, potash, salt, and zinc.

Electric Power. The production of electricity in Spain has increased greatly since 1950. But the supply has not kept pace with the demands of Spain's rapidly growing industries.

Spanish power stations produce about 91 billion kilowatt-hours of electricity yearly. About a fourth of the country's electric power comes from hydroelectric stations. Most of the rest of the nation's electric power comes from power plants that burn coal or other fuels. Spain has few nuclear power plants. However, plans call for the rapid development of nuclear plants and for little increase in the production of electricity from other sources.

Foreign Trade. Spain has always imported more goods than it has exported because of its limited natural resources. This situation worsened during the 1950's and 1960's, when Spain's booming economy demanded more and more imported industrial raw materials and machinery. The nation spends almost $3 billion more each year on imports than it earns on exports. But the income from Spain's tourist business makes up for most of this imbalance.

Spain's chief imports include food products, industrial raw materials, and machinery for industry. Its leading exports are cork, fish, mercury, olives, oranges and other citrus fruits, shoes and other clothing, and wine. The nation's main trading partners are France, Great Britain, Italy, The Netherlands, the United States, and West Germany.

Spain has a special trade agreement with the European Common Market, which is made up of Belgium, Denmark, France, Great Britain, Greece, Ireland, Italy, Luxembourg, The Netherlands, and West Germany. This special trade agreement reduces tariffs and other trade barriers between Spain and the Common Market nations.

Transportation. Spain has more than 85,000 miles (137,000 kilometers) of paved highway. Spaniards own about 5⅓ million automobiles. Trucks carry most of the freight transported within the country. The government-owned Iberia Air Lines, Spain's only international airline, flies throughout Spain, to North and South America, and to many Western European cities. Many foreign airlines also serve the country.

More than 12,000 miles (19,300 kilometers) of railroad track crisscross Spain. The government-owned Spanish National Railways operates the railway system and has greatly improved service since the mid-1960's. But railway travel has been declining as more and more Spaniards travel by automobile or airplane.

Spanish ships carry about a third of the freight transported between Spain and other nations. These ships also sail between Spanish ports, carrying about a third of the freight transported within the country. Barcelona and Bilbao are the nation's largest ports.

Communication. The government operates Spain's postal and telegraph services. It also controls all television broadcasting and some of the radio broadcasting in the nation. There are more than 9 million radios and more than 7 million TV sets in Spain. Most homes have a telephone. Spain has about 115 daily newspapers, with a total circulation of about 3½ million copies. The largest daily, Madrid's *A.B.C.*, sells nearly 220,000 copies. More than 3,000 magazines and weekly newspapers are published in the country.

Agriculture and Industry in Spain

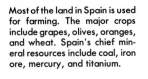

Most of the land in Spain is used for farming. The major crops include grapes, olives, oranges, and wheat. Spain's chief mineral resources include coal, iron ore, mercury, and titanium.

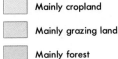

Mainly cropland

Mainly grazing land

Mainly forest

● Manufacturing center

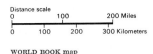

WORLD BOOK map

Early Days. More than 100,000 years ago, people lived in what is now Spain. At the beginning of recorded history—about 5,000 years ago—a people known as Iberians occupied much of Spain. They farmed and built villages and towns. Some of these towns, such as Cartagena and what is now Tarragona, developed into the first cities in Spain.

Phoenicians, who lived on the eastern shore of the Mediterranean, began to establish colonies along Spain's east and south coasts in the 1000's B.C. The Phoenicians carried on a flourishing trade with their colonies. Some of the cities they built, such as Cádiz and Málaga, have lasted to the present day.

Celtic peoples moved into Spain from the north about 900 B.C. and again about 600 B.C. They settled in the northern part of the country. Greeks landed in Spain about 600 B.C. and later established trading posts along the east coast.

During the 400's B.C., the powerful northern African city of Carthage conquered much of Spain. Hannibal, the great Carthaginian general, attacked Roman Italy from Spain during the 200's B.C. But the Romans defeated Hannibal in the Second Punic War (218-201 B.C.) and drove all Carthaginian forces from Spain.

Roman Conquest of Spain began during the Second Punic War. But it took the mighty Roman army almost 200 years to conquer the stubborn, freedom-loving Spanish tribes of every region. Rome also conquered what is now Portugal, and so for the first time the entire Iberian Peninsula came under one government. The peninsula became a Roman province called *Hispania*. Spain's name in Spanish, *España*, comes from *Hispania*.

Spain became a leading province of the Roman Empire, and many Romans went there to live. The Romans built cities in Spain and constructed excellent roads to all regions. They also erected huge aqueducts that carried water from rivers to dry areas. Several of Rome's greatest emperors—including Hadrian and Trajan—were born in Spain. Such outstanding Roman authors as Martial and Seneca also came from Spain.

The Romans introduced Latin into the province, and the Spanish language gradually developed from the Latin spoken by Spaniards. Christianity was also introduced into Spain during Roman rule. It became the official religion of the province—and of the Roman Empire—during the late A.D. 300's. About the same time, the empire split into two parts—the East Roman Empire and the West Roman Empire. Spain became part of the West Roman Empire.

Germanic Rule. During the 400's, invading Germanic tribes swept across the West Roman Empire and helped bring about its collapse in 476. One tribe, the Visigoths, invaded Spain and conquered the entire peninsula by 573. The Visigoths set up a monarchy in Spain that was the first separate and independent government to rule the entire peninsula. The Visigoths, who were Christians, tried to establish a civilization like that of the Romans. But continued fighting among the Visigoth nobles and repeated revolts of the nobles against the kings weakened the nation.

Muslim Control. The Visigoths ruled Spain until the early 700's, when Moors from northern Africa invaded the country. The invasion began in 711, and the Moors conquered almost all the Visigoth kingdom by 718. Only the narrow mountainous region across far northern Spain remained free of Moorish rule.

The Moors were Muslims—that is, followers of the religion of Islam—and many of the Spanish people became Muslims as a result of the Moorish rule. The Muslims had a more advanced culture than did most of medieval Europe. The Muslims had made great discoveries in mathematics, medicine, and other fields of study. They had also preserved many of the writings of the ancient Greek, Roman, and Middle Eastern civilizations. In Spain, the Moors made these works available to European scholars. The Moors also constructed many buildings in Spain, including beautiful *mosques* (houses of worship) and fortified palaces called *alcazars*.

The Moorish government of Spain collapsed during the early 1000's because of fighting among groups of Moors. The country then split into many small Moorish states and independent cities.

Reconquest by the Christian Kingdoms. Groups of Visigoths and other Christians in far northern Spain remained independent following the Moorish conquest. These groups formed a series of kingdoms that extended from Spain's northwest coast to the Mediterranean Sea. During the 1000's, these kingdoms began to expand and push the Moors southward.

Castile, in north-central Spain, became the strongest of the growing Christian kingdoms, and its soldiers

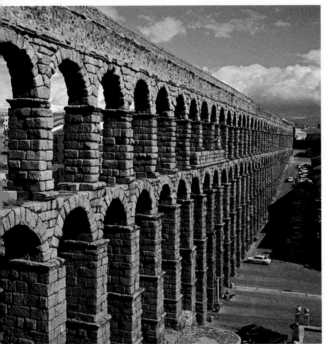

Phillip Sheridan, Tom Stack & Assoc.

Ancient Roman Structures can still be seen in many parts of Spain. The Romans controlled Spain for more than 400 years. During that period, they erected many bridges, buildings, and other structures, including the aqueduct in Segovia shown above.

led the fight against the Moors. A Castilian called El Cid, one of Spain's national heroes, emerged as the champion of the Christian cause (see CID, THE).

During the 1100's, several Spanish kings set up a *Cortes* (parliament) to strengthen their support among the people. Each Cortes brought representatives of the middle class, the nobility, and the Roman Catholic Church into the government. But the Spanish kings gave little or no power to the Cortes.

Also during the 1100's, the region that is now northern Portugal gained its independence from Castile. By the mid-1200's, Portugal controlled all its present-day territory. Meanwhile, Spanish Christians continued to fight the Moors. By the late 1200's, the Muslim territory in Spain had been reduced to the Kingdom of Granada in the south. The Christian kingdoms of Aragon, Navarre, and Castile controlled the rest of what is now Spain. Aragon ruled most of eastern Spain and the Balearic Islands. Navarre ruled a small area northwest of Aragon. Castile controlled the rest of Spain. It remained Spain's largest and most powerful kingdom throughout the 1300's and most of the 1400's.

Union of the Spanish Kingdoms. In 1469, Prince Ferdinand of Aragon married Princess Isabella of Castile. Isabella became queen of Castile in 1474, and Ferdinand became king of Aragon in 1479. Almost all of what is now Spain thus came under their rule.

Ferdinand and Isabella wanted to create a strong, united Spain. They considered the Jews and Muslims in Spain to be a threat to this goal. In 1480, the monarchs established the Spanish Inquisition, a special court that imprisoned or killed people suspected of not following Roman Catholic teachings. The Inquisition continued for more than 300 years. Also in the 1480's, Ferdinand and Isabella began to drive the Muslims from Granada. Their troops defeated the Muslims in 1492. That same year, the last of the Spanish Jews who would not convert to Catholicism were killed or driven from the country. Ferdinand seized the small Kingdom of Navarre in 1512 to complete the union of Spain.

The Spanish Empire. In 1492, while working to unify Spain, Ferdinand and Isabella sent Christopher Columbus on the voyage that took him to America. During the next 50 years, Spanish explorers, soldiers, and adventurers flocked to the New World. Vasco Núñez de Balboa crossed Central America in 1513 and became the first European to see the eastern shore of the Pacific Ocean. Hernando Cortés conquered the mighty Aztec nation of Mexico in 1521. About 1535, the huge Inca empire of western South America fell to Francisco Pizarro. These men and other Spaniards explored much of South America and southern North America.

By 1550, Spain controlled Mexico, Central America, nearly all the West Indies, part of what is now the Southwestern United States, and much of western South America. In the Treaty of Tordesillas, signed in 1494, Spain and Portugal had agreed to a line that divided all of South America between them. But they could not secure the entire continent because England, France, and The Netherlands claimed much of it. See LINE OF DEMARCATION.

While its empire grew in America, Spain seized territories in Europe and Africa. Spanish troops conquered the French province of Rousillon, much of Italy, the Canary Islands, and land in northern Africa.

In 1516, a grandson of Ferdinand and Isabella became King Charles I of Spain. Charles had ruled the Low Countries (what are now Belgium, Luxembourg, and The Netherlands), and he brought these lands into the Spanish kingdom. Charles was the first in a series of Spanish kings from the Habsburg family. The Habsburgs ruled the Holy Roman Empire in central Europe. Charles became Holy Roman emperor in 1519. He ruled the empire as Charles V and Spain as Charles I.

The Spanish Empire reached its height during the reign of Charles's son, Philip II, who became king in 1556. In 1580, Portugal was united with Spain. Spain gained control of the Philippine Islands during the late 1500's. Philip's rule brought the beginning of the golden age of Spanish art, when writers and painters created some of Spain's greatest artistic works. His rule also brought the beginning of the end of the empire.

The Spanish Decline began during the 1500's, soon after Spain reached the height of its power. A series of wars drained the royal treasury and weakened Spain's

Important Dates in Spain

1000's B.C. The Phoenicians began to colonize Spain.

400's B.C. The Carthaginians conquered much of Spain.

200's B.C. The Romans drove the Carthaginians from Spain.

A.D. 400's Germanic tribes took Spain from the Romans.

711-718 The Moors conquered almost all Spain.

1000's Spain's Christian kingdoms began to drive the Moors from Spain.

1479 The kingdoms of Aragon and Castile united, bringing almost all of what is now Spain under one rule.

1492 Spanish forces conquered Granada, the last center of Moorish control in Spain. Christopher Columbus sailed to America and claimed it for Spain.

1512 King Ferdinand V seized the Kingdom of Navarre, completing the unification of what is now Spain.

1556-1598 The Spanish Empire reached its height—and began to decline—under the reign of Philip II.

1588 The English navy defeated the Spanish Armada.

1808 Napoleon's armies conquered Spain.

1808-1813 English, Portuguese, and Spanish forces drove the French from Spain during the Peninsular War.

1810-1825 All Spain's American colonies except Cuba and Puerto Rico revolted and declared their independence. By this time, Spain had lost almost all its empire.

1898 Spain lost Cuba, Puerto Rico, and the Philippines in the Spanish-American War.

1931 King Alfonso XIII fled the country and Spain became a democratic republic.

1936-1939 The Spanish Civil War was fought. It brought General Francisco Franco to power as dictator of Spain.

1950's and 1960's Spain achieved one of the highest rates of economic growth in the world.

1975 Franco died. Spaniards began setting up a new, democratic government to replace his dictatorship.

1978 Spaniards approved a new Constitution based on democratic principles.

1982 Spain joined the North Atlantic Treaty Organization (NATO).

armed forces. Bad weather and poor management—as well as heavy spending—ruined the nation's economy. In addition, the people in several Spanish territories revolted.

Philip hoped to reverse Spain's fortunes by conquering England. In 1588, he launched the great Spanish Armada of 130 ships against England. But the English navy and stormy weather destroyed almost half the Armada.

Spain declined further under the weak rulers who followed Philip. It continued to suffer from revolts in its territories, a ruined economy, and frequent warfare with other countries. Portugal declared its independence in the mid-1600's, and France took several of Spain's northeastern provinces.

French forces continued to attack Spain during the late 1600's. To stop the attacks, King Charles II of Spain named a French duke, Philip of Anjou, as heir to the Spanish throne. Charles had no children of his own. He died in 1700, and Philip of Anjou became King Philip V of Spain. Philip was a grandson of France's King Louis XIV and became the first in a series of Spanish rulers from the French Bourbon family.

The succession of Philip V to the Spanish throne touched off the War of the Spanish Succession (1701-1714). France fought England, The Netherlands, and other European nations that opposed French control of the Spanish crown. France lost the war. Under the peace treaty, Philip remained king of Spain, but Spain lost all its possessions in Europe. In addition, Great Britain received Gibraltar and the Balearic island of Minorca. See SUCCESSION WARS.

Bourbon Reforms. During the 1700's, the Bourbon rulers of Spain carried out many government reforms.

They lowered taxes and collected them more fairly. They also built roads and other public works, and the economy began to grow. Meanwhile, strong ties developed between Spain and France because the rulers of both countries were Bourbons.

Conflict with Great Britain. The 1700's brought Spain into conflict with Great Britain as the two countries challenged each other for colonial power in America. In addition, Spain wanted to regain Gibraltar and Minorca from Britain. As a result of this conflict, Spain became involved with several other European nations in wars with Britain.

Spain also came to the aid of the American Colonies against Britain in the Revolutionary War in America (1775-1783). In 1781, Spanish troops invaded Florida. The Treaty of Paris, which ended the Revolutionary War in 1783, granted Spain control of Florida. It also recognized Spain's control of Minorca, which Spanish troops had taken in 1782. British forces recaptured Minorca in 1798, but Britain returned the island to Spain in 1802.

With the addition of Florida, Spain's American empire reached its greatest extent. But the fighting with Britain had weakened Spain.

French Conquest. Napoleon Bonaparte seized control of France in 1799. At first, Napoleon allied France with Spain. But in 1808, French forces invaded Spain and quickly won control of the government. Napoleon forced Ferdinand VII to give up the Spanish throne and named Joseph Bonaparte, his brother, king of Spain.

The Spanish people bitterly resisted the French occupation. They struck back with a hit-and-run method of fighting called the *guerrilla* (little war), a word used ever since to describe such fighting. This opposition led

SPANISH EMPIRE IN 1588

The Spanish Empire in 1588, at the height of Spain's power, included large areas of the Americas, European and African possessions, and the Philippines. Portugal was united with Spain in 1580, but the Portuguese colonies remained under Portuguese control.

Spanish Empire

Portuguese colonies

Area known to Europeans in 1588

Area unknown to Europeans in 1588

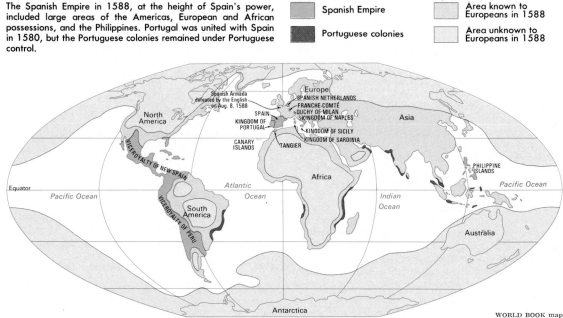

WORLD BOOK map

Launch of Fireships Against Spanish Armada (about 1588), an oil painting by an unknown artist; National Maritime Museum, Greenwich, England

The Defeat of the Spanish Armada in 1588 damaged the prestige of Spain, then the world's most powerful nation. The 130 ships of the Armada sailed against England, and almost half were destroyed. During the fighting, English ships, *right,* launched flaming boats against the Armada, *left.*

to the start of the Peninsular War later in 1808, when Great Britain joined Spain and Portugal against France. The French were driven from the peninsula in 1813.

During the Peninsular War, Spain's Cortes—which had fled from Madrid to southern Spain—drew up a democratic constitution for the country. The new constitution reduced the power of the Roman Catholic Church and increased individual rights and freedoms. But it continued the Spanish monarchy. Supporters of the constitution were known as *liberals*.

Loss of the Empire. King Ferdinand VII returned to the Spanish throne in 1814. He repealed the new constitution and persecuted the liberals. He also tried to regain control of Spain's overseas empire. During the Peninsular War, most of Spain's American colonies had revolted and declared their independence.

In 1820, Spanish troops at Cádiz refused to leave on an expedition to reconquer the American colonies. The mutiny spread quickly into a countrywide military revolt. Ferdinand put down the uprising—with the help of French troops—in 1823. But Spain remained torn politically between Ferdinand's supporters and the liberals. By 1825, Spain had lost all its overseas possessions except Cuba, Puerto Rico, several outposts in Africa, the Philippines, and the island of Guam.

The Reign of Isabella II. In 1833, Ferdinand's daughter succeeded him to the throne as Isabella II. Her reign was opposed by the Carlists, a political group that wanted Ferdinand's oldest brother, Don Carlos, to be king. The liberals supported Isabella. Quarreling among Carlists, liberals, and other political groups

created disorder throughout Isabella's reign. In 1868, a group of army officers led a revolt that quickly gained popular support and forced the queen and her family to leave the country.

Six years of political unrest followed the overthrow of Isabella. A republican government was established in 1873, but a civil war broke out between the Carlists and the liberals. The army overthrew the new government in 1874 and, in 1875, brought Isabella's son back to Spain to become King Alfonso XII. He ruled until his death in 1885.

The Reign of Alfonso XIII. Alfonso XII died six months before his son, Alfonso XIII, was born in 1886. Young Alfonso's mother, María Cristina of Austria, ruled in his place until he became old enough to take the throne in 1902.

Spain's most important remaining colonies, Cuba and the Philippines, rebelled in the 1890's. The United States supported Cuba and declared war on Spain in April, 1898. In August, the Spanish-American War ended with Spain's defeat. Spain gave Cuba its independence and surrendered Guam, the Philippines, and Puerto Rico to the United States. All that remained of the once mighty Spanish Empire were a few tiny outposts in northern Africa. See SPANISH-AMERICAN WAR.

During the late 1800's and early 1900's, the power of the Cortes and the prime minister increased. At the same time, Spanish political parties and trade unions gained more and more power. Control of the government alternated between liberals and conservatives, who favored the traditional Spanish way of life. Radicals, who wanted extreme reforms, and trade union leaders organized continual protests against the government.

Spain remained neutral in World War I (1914-1918) and profited greatly by selling industrial goods to the warring nations. But the war's end caused widespread unemployment in Spain, and Spaniards who had jobs earned low wages. These conditions added to an already growing discontent with Alfonso's rule.

In 1912, Spain gained control over parts of Morocco (see MOROCCO [French and Spanish Control]). But the Moroccans would not submit to Spanish authority. In 1921, they revolted and killed more than 10,000 Spanish troops. This disastrous incident caused bitter disputes in Spain, and these disputes became more intense as the fighting continued in Morocco. Coupled with the nation's political unrest and poor economic conditions, the Moroccan situation led to strikes and violence throughout Spain. In 1923, General Miguel Primo de Rivera headed a military revolt to take over the government and restore order in Spain. Alfonso supported the rebels, and Primo became prime minister with the power of a dictator.

Primo restored order in Morocco and Spain. He also promised to reestablish constitutional government in Spain but repeatedly postponed the move. The army finally turned against Primo in 1930, and he was forced to resign.

Meanwhile, a political movement for a republican form of government gained strength in Spain. The movement consisted of liberals, socialists, and other people who did not want Spain to be a monarchy. Early in 1931, Alfonso called for city elections, to be followed by provincial elections and then a general parliamentary election. In April, the people voted overwhelmingly for republican candidates in the city elections. Alfonso then left the country, though he refused to give up his claim to the throne.

The Spanish Republic. Republican leaders took control of the government after Alfonso left Spain. They called for a parliamentary election to be held in June, 1931. Liberals, socialists, and other republican groups won a huge majority in the Cortes. The new Cortes immediately began work on a democratic constitution, which was approved in December, 1931. That same month, the Cortes elected Niceto Alcalá Zamora, a leading liberal, as the first president of the republic.

The republicans had won control of the government, but political unrest continued in the country. Many Spaniards still favored a monarchy. In addition, the various republican groups were only loosely united. Radical leaders agitated for the overthrow of the government and created uprisings in various sections of the country. The worldwide economic depression of the 1930's added to these difficulties as Spain's exports fell and poverty spread among the people.

The new government reduced the power of the Roman Catholic Church and gave greater power to the trade unions. It took over many of the great estates held by aristocrats and greatly increased the wages of farmworkers. In 1932, the Cortes yielded to demands from nationalists in Catalonia and granted the region limited self-government. Other regions then demanded similar freedom.

The actions of the republican government created opposition among increasing numbers of Spaniards, especially conservatives. The conservatives supported the Roman Catholic Church and wanted Spain to become a monarchy again. The government called for a parliamentary election in 1933. In the election, a newly formed conservative party emerged as the most powerful political force in Spain. This party was the *Confederación Española de Derechas Autónomas* (Spanish Confederation of Autonomous Rightist Parties), called the *CEDA*.

Late in 1934, socialists and Catalan nationalists led an uprising against the government. The uprising quickly spread throughout Spain. Government forces put down the revolt, but they killed more than 1,000 persons in the process. The political division in Spain then widened. Army leaders, monarchists, and Catholic groups made up the Right. Communists, socialists, trade unions, and liberal groups formed the Left.

President Alcalá dissolved the Cortes in February, 1936, and called an election to try to unite the republic. Forces of the Left joined in an alliance called the Popular Front and won the election by a slight margin. Their victory touched off increased violence in Spain. Rightists and Leftists fought in the streets. Armed bands dragged opponents from their homes and murdered them. Political assassinations became common.

Civil War. In July, 1936, Spanish army units stationed in Morocco proclaimed a revolution against Spain's government. Most army units in Spain then rose in revolt, and they soon won control of about a third of the country. The rebels hoped to overthrow the government quickly and restore order in Spain. But Popular Front forces took up arms against the military.

In October, the rebel leaders chose General Francisco Franco as their commander in chief. They also made him head of the revolutionary government, called the Council of National Defense. By this time, the revolt had developed into a full-scale civil war. Franco's forces became known as Nationalists or Rebels. They were supported by Spain's fascist political party, the *Falange Española* (Spanish Phalanx). The forces that fought to save the republic were called Loyalists or Republicans. Both sides killed civilians and prisoners in a violent,

The Monarchs of Spain

In 1469, Prince Ferdinand of Aragon married Princess Isabella of Castile. The princess became Queen Isabella I* of Castile in 1474. Ferdinand became King Ferdinand II of Aragon in 1479. Most of what is now Spain thus came under the rule of the two monarchs. Isabella died in 1504. By the time Ferdinand died in 1516, he had brought all of what is now Spain under his control as Ferdinand V.*

Name	Reign	Name	Reign
Charles I		Charles III	1759-1788
(Holy		Charles IV	1788-1808
Roman		Ferdinand VII	1808
Emperor		Joseph	
Charles V*)	1516-1556	Bonaparte	1808-1813
*Philip II	1556-1598	Ferdinand VII	1814-1833
Philip III	1598-1621	Isabella II	1833-1868
Philip IV	1621-1665	Amadeo	1870-1873
Charles II	1665-1700	Alfonso XII	1875-1885
*Philip V	1700-1724	*Alfonso XIII	1886-1931
Louis I	1724	*Juan Carlos I	1975-
Philip V	1724-1746		
Ferdinand VI	1746-1759		

*Has a separate biography in WORLD BOOK.

bloody conflict that raged across Spain for nearly three years.

The Spanish Civil War drew international attention. Nazi Germany and Fascist Italy supported Franco's forces, and Communist Russia aided the Loyalists. In addition, Loyalist sympathizers from the United States and many other countries joined the International Brigades that Communists formed to fight in Spain.

By the end of 1937, the Nationalists clearly held the upper hand in Spain. They had taken most of western Spain in the summer of 1936 and were gradually pushing the Loyalist forces to the east and north. Russia ended large-scale aid to the Loyalists in 1938, and Franco launched a mighty offensive against Loyalist armies that same year.

Franco entered Madrid, one of the last Loyalist strongholds, in March, 1939. The remaining Loyalist forces surrendered on April 1. Several hundred thousand Spaniards had died in the war, and much of Spain lay in ruins. A dictatorship under Franco had replaced the short-lived republic.

World War II (1939-1945) broke out five months after the Spanish Civil War ended. Officially, Spain remained neutral in the war. But Franco drew closer to Germany after the fall of France in 1940, when it seemed that Germany would win the war. Late in 1942, however, the tide of war began to turn against Germany. Franco then became friendlier toward Britain, the United States, and other Allied countries.

Involvement in the Cold War. In 1945, Russia launched a campaign calling for international opposition to Franco and for the overthrow of his government. Western nations supported this campaign because of Franco's dictatorial policies and because of his support of Germany and Italy in World War II. Nearly all major countries broke off diplomatic relations with Spain in 1945 and 1946.

In 1947, Franco announced that a king would succeed him upon his death or retirement. Franco hoped this announcement would reduce international criticism of his rule. But it was the growing Cold War—the struggle between Communist and non-Communist nations—that finally led the Western powers to ease their stand against Spain during the late 1940's.

Franco strongly opposed the Communist nations, and the United States sought his help to strengthen the defense of Western Europe. In 1953, Spain and the United States signed a 10-year military and economic agreement. Franco allowed the United States to build military bases in Spain, and the United States gave Spain more than $1 billion in grants and loans. The agreement has been renewed for shorter periods ever since, though U.S. aid to Spain has been greatly reduced.

Growth and Discontent. During the 1950's and 1960's, Spain achieved one of the highest rates of economic growth in the world. The nation's automobile, construction, and steel industries boomed, and the Spanish tourist trade flourished. As a result, the standard of living of most Spaniards rose rapidly.

During the mid-1960's, the government began to ease some of its restrictions on personal freedom. In 1966, for example, the government relaxed its strict censorship of the press. But protests against the government erupted. Student demonstrations began in 1968 at the universities of Barcelona and Madrid. During the 1960's

United Press Int.

Francisco Franco was dictator of Spain from 1939 until his death in 1975. This photograph shows him reviewing troops during a parade held in 1970. Prince Juan Carlos, *left,* became king of Spain after Franco died.

and 1970's, people in several Spanish regions protested against the powers of Spain's national government. Some people in the Basque provinces demanded independence for their region. Others did not favor independence, but called for greater control over their government affairs. Some people in the regions of Catalonia, Valencia, Andalusia, and Galicia also called for more control over their government affairs. In the late 1960's, a Basque organization that favored independence began a terrorist campaign against the Spanish government. Under Franco, many Basques and other Spaniards were arrested for revolutionary activities. In 1975, Franco's government executed five terrorists.

Recent Developments. Spain's economy continued to expand throughout the 1970's. But extreme inflation and a lack of technical development slowed down the economic progress of the 1950's and 1960's.

Franco died in November 1975. Spain then entered a period of major political change. Spaniards quickly began a process of establishing a new democratic government to replace Franco's dictatorship.

In 1969, Franco had declared that Prince Juan Carlos would become king of Spain after Franco's death or retirement. Juan Carlos is a grandson of King Alfonso XIII, who left Spain in 1931. Juan Carlos became king two days after Franco died. In 1976, he made Adolfo Suárez González prime minister. Juan Carlos, Suárez, and most other Spaniards favored changing Spain's government from a dictatorship to a democracy.

In 1976, Spain's new government ended Franco's ban on political parties other than his own. In 1977, the government held elections in which several political parties competed for seats in the parliament. This marked the first time since 1936 that the people of Spain were given a choice of candidates in parliamentary elections. In the elections, the Union of the Democratic Center, headed by Prime Minister Suárez, won the most seats in the parliament.

In 1978, Spain's voters approved a new Constitution

587

based on democratic principles. In elections held after the adoption of the Constitution, the Union of the Democratic Center again won the most seats in parliament. In 1981, Suárez resigned as prime minister. Juan Carlos appointed Leopoldo Calvo Sotelo of the Union of the Democratic Center to succeed Suárez.

Spain's democratic government began a process of increasing the local government powers of the country's regions. It provided for the eventual establishment of regional parliaments. In 1980, people in the Basque provinces and Catalonia elected regional parliaments. Since then, the people of some other regions have also elected parliaments. The parliaments have some control over local taxation and other regional matters.

In 1982, Spain joined the North Atlantic Treaty Organization (NATO), a mutual defense organization made up of Western nations.

In elections held in 1982, the left-wing Socialist Workers' Party won the most seats in parliament. Felipe González, the party's leader, became prime minister. The elections gave Spain its first leftist government since 1939.　　　　　　　　　　　　　　STANLEY G. PAYNE

SPAIN/Study Aids

Related Articles. See SPANISH LITERATURE with its list of *Related Articles*. See also:

MONARCHS

Alfonso XIII	Ferdinand V	Philip II
Charles I (Holy Roman	Isabella I	Philip V
Emperor Charles V)	Juan Carlos I	

POLITICAL AND MILITARY LEADERS

Alva, Duke of	Franco, Francisco	Torquemada, Tomás de

EXPLORERS AND CONQUERORS

Alvarado, Pedro de	Jiménez de Quesada,
Balboa, Vasco N. de	Gonzalo
Cabeza de Vaca, Álvar N.	Narváez, Pánfilo de
Columbus, Christopher	Oñate, Juan de
Coronado, Francisco V. de	Orellana, Francisco de
Cortés, Hernando	Pizarro, Francisco
De Soto, Hernando	Ponce de León, Juan

CITIES

Barcelona	Cartagena	Madrid	Toledo
Bilbao	Córdoba	Saragossa	Valencia
Cádiz	Granada	Seville	

HISTORY

Aztec (The Spanish Conquest)	Iberia
Boabdil	Inquisition
Bourbon	Line of Demarcation
Castile and Aragon	Loyola, Saint Ignatius
Cid, The	Monroe Doctrine (Origins)
Colonialism	Spanish-American War
Equatorial Guinea	Spanish Armada
Exploration	Spanish Main
Falange Española	Succession Wars
Granada	Trafalgar

PHYSICAL FEATURES

Bay of Biscay	Mediterranean Sea	Tagus River
Majorca	Pyrenees	

REGIONS AND POLITICAL DIVISIONS

Andalusia	Balearic Islands	Canary Islands

OTHER RELATED ARTICLES

Alcazar	Christmas (In Spain)	Flamenco
Alhambra	Cork	Furniture (Spain)
Andorra	Don Juan	Gaudi, Antonio
Basques	Escorial	Manolete
Bolero	Europe (pictures)	Montserrat
Bullfighting	Flag (picture: His-	Peseta
Castanets	torical Flags of	Spanish
Castle (picture)	the World)	Language

Outline

I. Government
A. The King	D. Local Government
B. The Prime	E. Political Parties
Minister	F. Courts
C. The Parliament	G. Armed Forces

II. People
A. Ancestry and	F. Recreation
Population	G. Religion
B. Language	H. Religious Holidays
C. City Life	I. Education
D. Country Life	J. Museums and Libraries
E. Food and Drink	

III. The Arts
A. Literature	C. Architecture
B. Painting	D. Music

IV. The Land
A. The Meseta	D. The Coastal Plains
B. The Northern	E. The Guadalquivir Basin
Mountains	F. The Balearic Islands
C. The Ebro Basin	

V. Climate

VI. Economy
A. Natural Resources	F. Mining
B. Manufacturing	G. Electric Power
C. Agriculture	H. Foreign Trade
D. Tourism	I. Transportation
E. Fishing	J. Communication

VII. History

Questions

Who were some of the early peoples who lived in what is now Spain?

How does Spain's government promote tourism?

What is the *Meseta?*

What is Spain's official form of government?

When was the golden age of Spanish art?

When did Francisco Franco rule as dictator of Spain?

What is a *paseo?*

When did Spain change from being chiefly an agricultural country into an industrial nation?

When did the Spanish Empire reach its height?

Additional Resources

AMERICAN UNIVERSITY. *Area Handbook for Spain.* U. S. Government Printing Office, 1976.

CARR, RAYMOND F., and FUSI, J. P. *Spain: Dictatorship to Democracy.* 2nd ed. Allen & Unwin, 1981.

CROW, JOHN A. *Spain: The Root and The Flower, A History of the Civilization of Spain and of the Spanish People.* Rev. ed. Harper, 1975.

Fodor's Spain. McKay. Pub. annually.

MORRIS, JAN. *Spain.* Oxford, 1979. A study of the character of the Spanish people.

PAYNE, STANLEY G. *The Spanish Revolution.* Norton, 1970.

SPALATO. See SPLIT.

SPALLANZANI, SPAH luhn ZAH nee, **LAZZARO,** LAHD dzah roh (1729-1799), an Italian experimental biologist, showed that the air carries microscopic life. He also showed that microscopic life in food can be killed by boiling. Spallanzani was the first to watch isolated bacterial cells divide. He found that bats can dodge strings even when blind, and that salamanders can replace damaged limbs. He was born in Scandiano, and took orders in the Roman Catholic Church. He taught at the University of Padua.　　LORUS J. MILNE and MARGERY MILNE

SPAN. See BRIDGE (Arch Bridges).

SPANIEL is a large family of dogs. The American Kennel Club recognizes 10 spaniel breeds: the *American water, clumber, cocker, English cocker, English springer, field, Irish water, Sussex,* and *Welsh springer* spaniels, and the *Brittany.* One toy dog, the *English toy spaniel,* may be related to the others. But another toy dog, the *Japanese chin,* is probably not related to these spaniels.

The spaniel family probably descended from a Spanish dog, and its name comes from the word *Spain.* All spaniels except the toys are sporting dogs. The spaniel has a gentle and friendly disposition, and likes to hunt in the fields. Spaniels are fine companions as well as good hunters. They make excellent pets. All spaniels except the Brittany have long, silky coats. In general, spaniels have long ears; rather large, round eyes; broad, domed skulls; and sturdy bodies and legs. For a description of the unusual Brittany, see BRITTANY.

All the spaniel breeds except the Brittany hunt game in much the same way. They search the ground within gun range of the hunter. When a spaniel smells game, it rushes to *flush* it, or make it fly or run. When the game is flushed and the hunter shoots, the spaniel waits for the command, finds the game, and then brings it back to the hunter.　　MAXWELL RIDDLE

For a list of the separate articles in WORLD BOOK on each spaniel breed, see DOG (table; color pictures: Sporting Dogs).

SPANISH AMERICA is the name sometimes given to the Spanish-speaking parts of Latin America. It includes Central America, except Belize; South America, except Brazil and the Guianas; Mexico; Cuba; Puerto Rico; the Dominican Republic; and certain islands of the West Indies.

See also LATIN AMERICA.

SPANISH-AMERICAN WAR marked the emergence of the United States as a world power. This brief conflict between the United States and Spain took place between April and August 1898, over the issue of the liberation of Cuba. In the course of the war, the U.S. won Guam, Puerto Rico, and the Philippine Islands.

Background of the War

Spanish Misrule. Until about 1860, American expansionists had hoped to acquire Cuba. After the Civil War, interest in annexation dwindled, but Americans continued to be displeased by Spanish misrule. A long and exhausting uprising took place in the 1870's. In 1895, during a depression that made conditions worse, a revolution broke out again and threatened to go on endlessly. The Spanish forces were not powerful enough to put down the insurrection and the rebels were not strong enough to win.

American Intervention. American newspapers, especially the "yellow press" of William Randolph Hearst and Joseph Pulitzer, printed sensational accounts of Spanish oppression, and carried seriously exaggerated reports that a quarter of the population had died. They continually agitated for intervention. Many Americans regarded conditions in Cuba as intolerable and began to demand that the United States intervene. A few felt that the United States should also acquire naval and military bases and become an imperial power.

Bettmann Archive

The Explosion of the *Maine* helped bring on the Spanish-American War. The U.S. battleship blew up on Feb. 15, 1898, at Havana, Cuba. This front page was published two days later.

In November 1897, President McKinley pressured Spain into granting Cuba limited self-government within the Spanish empire. The rebels wanted nothing less than independence, and continued to fight. Meanwhile, pro-Spanish mobs in Havana rioted in protest against self-government. To protect Americans from the rioters, the battleship *Maine* arrived in Havana harbor January 25, 1898. On February 15, an explosion blew up the ship and killed about 260 persons on board. The outraged American public immediately blamed Spain for the explosion, but today many historians believe it was accidental and occurred inside the ship.

"Remember the *Maine*" became a popular slogan but forces already in operation did more to bring about actual war. In March, President McKinley sent three notes to Spain, demanding full independence for Cuba. Spain granted an armistice. On April 19, Congress passed overwhelmingly a joint resolution asserting that Cuba was independent. The resolution also disavowed any American intention to acquire the island, and authorized the use of the army and navy to force Spanish withdrawal. On April 25, the U.S. formally declared that a state of war existed with Spain as of April 21.

Chief Events

Manila Bay. The first important battle of the war took place in the Philippines. The Asiatic Squadron of six ships under Commodore George Dewey sailed from Hong Kong to Manila Bay. On May 1, 1898, it destroyed the entire Spanish fleet of 10 vessels without the loss of an American life or serious damage to any American ship. Then Dewey blockaded Manila harbor while he waited for U.S. troops to arrive.

Cuban Blockade. Meanwhile, the North Atlantic Squadron under Rear Admiral William T. Sampson, had begun a partial blockade of Cuba while scouting in the Caribbean Sea for a fleet that had left Spain under Admiral Pascual Cervera y Topete. Finally, on May 28, American ships located Cervera's fleet, which had anchored in the landlocked harbor of Santiago de Cuba, on the southeastern part of the island. While the navy placed a blockading force outside the harbor, the army hastily prepared to send an expeditionary force to assault Santiago by land.

Land Battles. On June 22, Major General William R. Shafter began landing 15,000 troops at Daiquirí and Siboney, near Santiago. The Spaniards offered little resistance during the landing and deploying of troops. Joyful newspaper reports of this helped make celebrities of the Rough Rider Regiment and its commanders, Colonel Leonard Wood and Lieutenant Colonel Theodore Roosevelt.

General Shafter launched a full-scale two-pronged assault against Santiago on July 1. He sent nearly half of his men against a small Spanish force strongly defending a stone fort at El Caney. The remainder made a frontal assault on the main Spanish defenses at Kettle Hill and San Juan Hill. By nightfall, the Americans had taken the ridges commanding Santiago, but they had suffered 1,600 casualties. Both black and white Americans fought in the campaign. First Lieutenant John J. Pershing wrote: "White regiments, black regiments . . . fought shoulder to shoulder, unmindful of race or color . . . and mindful only of their common duty as Americans."

As soon as Santiago came under siege, the governor of Cuba ordered Admiral Cervera to run the naval blockade to try to save his ships. Cervera led them out on July 3, heading in single file westward along the Cuban coast. The pursuing American naval vessels, commanded by Commodore Winfield S. Schley, sank or forced the beaching of every one of them. Again no serious damage occurred to any American vessel.

After days of negotiations, Santiago surrendered on July 17. On July 25, Major General Nelson A. Miles began an invasion of Puerto Rico which met almost no opposition. Several contingents of U.S. troops arrived in the Philippines. On August 13, they entered and occupied Manila, thus keeping the Filipino patriots out. The cables had been cut, and Dewey did not realize that an armistice had been signed the previous day.

Results of the War

The Peace Treaty. Sentiment grew within the United States to keep the spoils of war, except for Cuba. In the Treaty of Paris, signed Dec. 10, 1898, Spain granted Cuba its freedom. Spain ceded Guam, Puerto Rico, and the Philippines to the United States. The United States, in turn, paid Spain $20 million for the Philippine Islands. See PHILIPPINES (History).

Anti-Imperialism. Many people in the United States did not like their nation's new position as a colonial power. These *anti-imperialists* opposed the annexations. They did not wish to hold subject peoples by force, run the risk of becoming involved in further wars, or face competition from colonial products or workers. Their forces were so strong in the Senate that it ratified the peace treaty by only one vote on Feb. 6, 1899.

Other Results. The United States had to put down a long and bloody insurrection in the Philippines, strengthen its defenses, build more powerful battleships, and reorganize the army to remedy serious weaknesses revealed by the war. The war also showed the need for

The Charge of the Rough Riders at San Juan Hill (1898), an oil painting on canvas by Frederic Remington; Remington Art Museum, Ogdensburg, New York. All rights reserved.

The Rough Rider Regiment won national fame for its charge up Kettle Hill in Cuba in 1898. Lt. Col. Theodore Roosevelt, *on horseback,* led the assault. The charge helped the Americans win the Battle of San Juan Hill and became identified with an attack on that nearby hill.

The Chief Battles of the Spanish-American War took place around Santiago de Cuba. The U.S. Army and Navy played key roles in the war.

— American forces
— Spanish forces
★ Major battle

WORLD BOOK map

a canal through the Isthmus of Panama, which separated the Caribbean Sea from the Pacific Ocean. The Spanish-American War thus led to the building of the Panama Canal.   FRANK FREIDEL

Related Articles in WORLD BOOK include:

Cuba	Puerto Rico
Dewey, George	Roosevelt, Theodore
Maine (ship)	Sampson, William T.
McKinley, William (The	Schley, Winfield S.
Spanish-American War)	Shafter, William R.
Miles, Nelson A.	Wood, Leonard

Additional Resources

BROWN, CHARLES H. *The Correspondents' War: Journalists in the Spanish-American War*. Scribner, 1967.

LAWSON, DON. *The United States in the Spanish-American War*. Harper, 1976. For younger readers.

LINDERMAN, GERALD F. *The Mirror of War: American Society and the Spanish-American War*. Univ. of Michigan Press, 1974.

TRASK, DAVID F. *The War with Spain in 1898*. Macmillan, 1981.

SPANISH ARMADA

SPANISH ARMADA was a fleet of armed ships that tried to invade England in 1588. The Spanish fleet had been called the *Invincible Armada* because the Spaniards thought it could not be defeated. But the English fleet defeated the Armada. The failure of the Armada was a great blow to the prestige of Spain, the world's most powerful country at that time. Spain remained a major power after the battle, but English merchants and sailors challenged the Spaniards with greater confidence throughout the world.

Background to Battle. Bad feeling between Spain and England had existed since the 1570's. Spain was taking gold and silver from lands it had claimed in the Americas, and England wanted some of this wealth. Queen Elizabeth I encouraged Francis Drake and other English seamen to raid Spanish ships and towns.

Religious differences also caused conflict between the two nations. Spain was a Roman Catholic country, and most of England had become Protestant as a result of the Reformation (see REFORMATION). In the 1560's, the English began to aid the Dutch Protestants who were rebelling against Spanish rule (see NETHERLANDS [Freedom from Spain]). In the early 1580's, King Philip II of Spain started planning to send a fleet and army to invade England. He hoped to end the English raids and to make England a Catholic country again.

The Two Fleets. Philip began to assemble the Armada in January 1586. Spain built many new warships and armed its existing ones more heavily. In 1587, Drake raided Cádiz harbor in Spain, and destroyed several ships. The Armada was completed in May 1588, at the Portuguese port of Lisbon, then under Spanish control. Of the 130 ships in the Armada, many were large but slow. Some lacked guns and experienced gunners, and others lacked ammunition. Philip named the Duke of Medina Sidonia, an inexperienced seaman, to command the Armada.

Engraving (1590) by Augustine Ryther of a chart by Robert Adams; National Maritime Museum, London

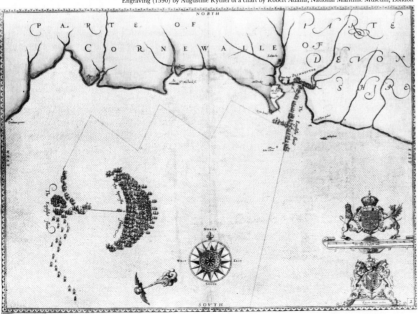

The Spanish Armada was defeated by the English fleet in the English Channel in 1588. This chart shows the two fleets at the beginning of the battle. The Spanish Armada is in a crescent formation against the English ships.

SPANISH BAYONET

Meanwhile, England armed many of its merchant vessels and added them to its fleet. England's fighting ships were smaller, faster, and easier to maneuver than the Spanish vessels. England also had more skillful sailors. Admiral Lord Howard commanded the English fleet, and his squadron leaders included Drake, John Hawkins, and Martin Frobisher.

The Battle. The Armada left Lisbon on May 30, 1588 (May 20 according to the calendar then used in England). It entered the English Channel on July 30 (July 20), and fought long-range gun duels with English warships during the next few days. On August 6 (July 27), the Armada anchored at Calais, France. Medina Sidonia had planned to meet barges carrying Spanish troops from nearby Dunkerque, a port then in The Netherlands. But Dutch gunboats prevented the barges from meeting the Armada.

In the early hours of August 8 (July 29), the English sent eight *fire ships* (vessels filled with gunpowder and set on fire) toward the Armada. The Spanish ships sailed out to sea to escape the flames. Later that morning, about 60 English ships attacked an equal number of Spanish ships off the French port of Gravelines. The English sank two Spanish ships and damaged the rest.

The crippled Armada fled to the North Sea. It returned to Spain by sailing northward around the British Isles. Heavy winds wrecked many ships off the coast of Ireland, and only 67 reached Spain.   VERNON F. SNOW

See also DRAKE, SIR FRANCIS; ELIZABETH I; PHILIP (II) of Spain.

SPANISH BAYONET is the name of a low, slender yucca tree that grows in the southern United States and in Mexico and the West Indies. It may grow to about 25 feet (8 meters) but usually is much smaller. It has long, flat, bayonetlike leaves, $2\frac{1}{2}$ feet (76 centimeters) long and 2 to 3 inches (5 to 8 centimeters) wide. It bears cream-white flowers, sometimes tinted green or purple. The flowers are about $2\frac{1}{2}$ inches (6 centimeters) wide. Several subspecies have leaves with yellow margins or centers. The flowers, which are shaped like deep bowls, grow on erect branched stems about 2 feet (61 centimeters) long. See also YUCCA.

Scientific Classification. The Spanish bayonet belongs to the agave family, Agavaceae. It is classified as genus *Yucca*, species *Y. aloifolia*.   EDMUND C. JAEGER

SPANISH CIVIL WAR. See SPAIN (History).

SPANISH FLY is a beetle, not a true fly. Most Spanish flies live in southern Europe. They are about $\frac{3}{4}$ inch (19 millimeters) long. A substance called *cantharidin* can be extracted from their wing cases. It is used as a *vesicant* (blistering agent) to increase a person's blood circulation and relieve pain.

Scientific Classification. The Spanish fly belongs to the blister beetle family, Meloidae. It is genus *Lytta*, species *L. vesicatrix*.

SPANISH INQUISITION. See INQUISITION; TORQUEMADA, TOMÁS DE.

SPANISH LANGUAGE is the official language of Spain. It is also the official language of most Latin-American countries, and one of the two languages spoken in Puerto Rico. About $14\frac{1}{2}$ million Spanish-speaking persons live in the United States. Most of them reside in Florida and the Southwest. About 297 million persons worldwide speak Spanish, the most popular Romance language (see ROMANCE LANGUAGE).

The Spanish spoken in Spain is often called *Castilian Spanish*. The Spanish used in Latin America is known as *American Spanish*. Castilian Spanish and American Spanish are basically the same but have a few differences in pronunciation and vocabulary.

Many English words come from Spanish. They include *alfalfa, alligator, armada, cargo, cork, lariat, lasso, mosquito, potato, ranch, rodeo, tobacco, tomato, tornado,* and *vanilla.* Some states and many U.S. cities have Spanish names. Among them are *California, Florida, Nevada, Los Angeles, San Antonio, San Francisco,* and *Santa Fe.*

Spanish Pronunciation

Spanish is one of the most phonetic of all languages. That is, its pronunciation follows its spelling closely. See PHONETICS (The Phonetic Ideal).

Vowels. Spanish has only five basic vowel sounds. These sounds are represented by the letters *a, e, i* or *y, o,* and *u.* The following table gives the approximate English sound for each Spanish vowel:

Spanish Vowel	Approximate Sound in English
a	*a* in *father*
e	*e* in *they*
i or *y*	*i* in *machine*
o	*o* in *owe*
u	*oo* in *moon*

Consonants. Spanish has four consonant sounds not found in English. They are *ch, ll, ñ,* and *rr.* Their pronunciation corresponds roughly to the English pronunciation of *ch* in *church; lli* in *million; ny* in *canyon;* and a *trilled* (rolled) *r,* a sound that does not exist in American English. People who speak American Spanish pronounce the consonants *c* (when it is followed by *e* or *i*) and *z* as English-speaking persons pronounce the *s* in *sink.* People who speak Castilian Spanish pronounce them like the *th* in *think.* The letter *h* is not pronounced in Spanish. The consonants *b* and *v* are generally pronounced like a *b.*

Spanish Grammar

Nouns and Adjectives. All Spanish nouns are either masculine or feminine. Most nouns that name male human beings or male animals, or that end in *-o, -l,* or *-r,* are masculine. Most nouns that name female human beings or female animals, or that end in *-a, -d,* or *-ión,* are feminine. For example, *padre* (father), *libro* (book), *papel* (paper), and *calor* (heat) are masculine. *Madre* (mother), *pluma* (pen), *felicidad* (happiness), and *revolución* (revolution) are feminine. Plurals of nouns and adjectives are formed by adding *-s* to those that end in vowels and *-es* to those ending in consonants.

Adjectives must agree in *gender* (masculine or feminine) and in *number* (singular or plural) with the nouns they modify. For this reason, many adjectives have four forms. *Sombrero pequeño* means *small hat, casa pequeña* means *small house, sombreros pequeños* means *small hats,* and *casas pequeñas* means *small houses.*

Verbs. Spanish has 15 commonly used tenses, 8 simple and 7 *perfect,* or compound (see TENSE). The simple tenses are formed by adding endings to the stem of the verb or to the infinitive. The perfect tenses are formed by using the appropriate simple tense of *haber* (to have) followed by a past participle of the verb.

¿adónde va usted? *ah DOHN day VAH oo STAYD,* where are you going?
ayer, *ah YEHR,* yesterday
bien, *BYEHN,* well
bueno, *BWAY noh,* good
buenos días, *BWAY nohs DEE ahs,* good morning
¿cómo está usted? *KOH moheh STAH oo STAYD,* how are you?
¿cómo se llama usted? *KOH moh sayl YAH mah oo STAYD,* what is your name?
gracias, *GRAH syahs,* thanks, thank you
hasta luego, *AH stahl WAY goh,* good-by (until later)
hombre, *OHM bray,* man
hoy, *oy,* today
mañana, *mahn YAH nah,* morning, tomorrow
me llamo Juan, *mayl YAH moh HWAHN,* my name is John
mucho, *MOO choh,* much, a lot
mujer, *moo HEHR,* woman
muy bien, *MWEE BYEHN,* very well
pequeño, *pay KAYN yoh,* small
por favor, *POHR fah BOHR,* please
¿qué hora es? *kay OHR ah EHS,* what time is it?
señor, *sayn YOHR,* sir, Mr.
señora, *sayn YOH rah,* lady, Mrs.
señorita, *sayn yoh REE tah,* young lady, Miss
sí, *SEE,* yes
son las dos, *SOHN lahs DOHS,* it is two o'clock
tengo hambre, *TEHNG goh AHM bray,* I am hungry

Spanish verbs are classified according to the endings of their infinitives. They fall into three groups: *-ar* verbs, such as *andar* (to walk); *-er* verbs, such as *correr* (to run); and *-ir* verbs, such as *vivir* (to live).

Word Order in Spanish is similar to that of English. Two exceptions are the positions of object pronouns and descriptive adjectives in Spanish sentences. Object pronouns usually come before the verb in Spanish. In the English sentence *She greeted us,* the verb (*greeted*) comes before the object pronoun (*us*). In Spanish, this sentence becomes *Ella nos saludó* (*She us greeted*). Descriptive adjectives in Spanish usually follow the nouns they modify. In the English sentence *We live in a white house,* the descriptive adjective (*white*) comes before the noun (*house*). In this sentence becomes *Vivimos en una casa blanca* (*We live in a house white*).

A Spanish sentence is made negative by placing *no* before the verb. An *interrogative sentence* (one which asks a question) is formed by placing the subject after the verb. A Spanish interrogative sentence has an inverted question mark before the first word, and a regular question mark after the last word. This construction enables readers to recognize an interrogative sentence as soon as they begin reading it. The following are the affirmative, negative, and interrogative forms of the English sentence *Charles lives here:* Affirmative—*Carlos vive aquí;* Negative—*Carlos no vive aquí;* Interrogative—*¿Vive Carlos aquí?*

Development

Beginnings. The Spanish language developed from Latin, the language of the Roman Empire. During the 200's and 100's B.C., Roman armies conquered the *Iberian Peninsula* (present-day Spain and Portugal). The Iberians gradually adopted their conquerors' language, *vulgar* (common) Latin.

In the early 400's, Germanic tribes, called Goths, invaded the Iberian Peninsula. The Goths controlled the peninsula until 711, but they had little influence on the language. In 711, the Arabic-speaking Moors conquered all but a small part of the peninsula. They ruled most of the region until the mid-1200's. The Moors added about 700 Arabic words to vulgar Latin. But the language changed little in sound and structure.

Castilian Spanish. Spanish began to emerge as an independent language from Latin in the period from 950 to 1000. Like other languages, Spanish developed several dialects. During the 1200's, the Spanish province of Castile became an important literary, military, and political center. The influence of Castile spread, and the Castilian dialect was soon the accepted form of Spanish in most parts of the Iberian Peninsula.

Two other dialects became separate languages during this period. The *Galician-Portuguese* dialect developed in the western part of the peninsula. It was the basis of Portuguese, which began in the late 1100's (see PORTUGUESE LANGUAGE). The *Catalan* dialect survived in northeastern Spain and grew into the Catalan language.

American Spanish developed in what is now Latin America as Spanish colonists, conquerors, and missionaries began settling there in the 1500's. Spanish gradually replaced many of the Indian languages that were spoken in Latin America, including those of the Aztec, Inca, and Maya.   RICHARD P. KINKADE

See also SPAIN (Language).

Additional Resources

ARMITAGE, RICHARD, and others. *Beginning Spanish: A Cultural Approach.* 4th ed. Houghton, 1979.
CHASTAIN, KENNETH. *Spanish Grammar in Review: Patterns for Communication.* Rand McNally, 1979.
DA SILVA, ZENIA. *Spanish: A Short Course.* 2nd ed. Harper, 1980. Includes tapes.
SPAULDING, ROBERT K. *How Spanish Grew.* Univ. of California Press, 1962.

SPANISH LITERATURE is one of the richest and most varied of all European literatures. The poetry, prose, and drama of Spain are noted for their realism, color, humor, and lyricism.

The geography of Spain helps give special characteristics to the nation's literature. The Pyrenees Mountains and the Mediterranean Sea separate Spain from the rest of Europe. As a result, Spanish writers have kept an individuality somewhat apart from the main currents of European literature. Great rivers and mountain ranges within Spain divide the country into regions. As a result, *regionalism* (concern with a particular area) strongly flavors Spanish literature.

History has also given special features to Spanish literature. The Romans occupied Spain for about 600 years, beginning in the 200's B.C. The main heritage they left to Spain was the Latin language, particularly *vernacular* Latin, the form used by the common people. Vernacular Latin gave birth to three Romance languages that became the most common Spanish dialects—Castilian, Galician-Portuguese, and Catalan (see SPANISH LANGUAGE [Development]). From the A.D. 700's through the 1400's, Christians fought Muslim Moors for control of Spain. This long struggle created a strongly religious patriotism that inspired some of the world's finest religious poetry and prose.

The greatest period of Spanish literature began about the mid-1500's and lasted until the late 1600's. This period, called the Golden Age, brought a flowering of Spanish fiction, poetry, and drama. Spain's greatest and best-known writer, Miguel de Cervantes, the author of *Don Quixote*, lived during this period.

The Middle Ages

Early Medieval Literature. Lyric poetry existed in Spain as early as A.D. 1040. These poems, called *jarchas*, are short refrains added to an Arabic poem called the *muwashaha*. Jarchas were written in Hebrew or Arabic alphabet characters, but the language was a Mozarabic dialect of Spanish (the Mozarabs were Spaniards living under Muslim rule). Jarchas are the oldest form of lyric poetry in a Romance language. Their theme is the sadness of a maiden in the absence of her lover, or simply her longing for love.

Almost all the early Spanish epic poems have been lost. The only one that has survived in nearly complete form is the *Poem of the Cid*, written about 1140. It tells of the adventures of the Castilian hero Rodrigo Díaz. This epic contains stylistic devices similar to those of *The Song of Roland*, a French epic of about 1100. But *The Cid* is more realistic than epics written in other countries during the Middle Ages. It was written only 40 years after the hero's death, so the action of the poem is closer to the actual events that occurred. See CID, THE.

Minstrels called *juglares* who recited epic poems also performed satirical plays called *juegos de escarnio*. Early medieval Spanish drama is not well known. The only play that has survived is a short fragment of a religious drama, *The Play of the Wise Men*, from the mid-1100's.

During the 1200's and 1300's, Spanish lyric poetry came under the influence of the poems of the Provençal troubadours of southern France. The early poetry of two related dialects, Galician and Portuguese, was modeled on Provençal poetry. The Galician-Portuguese works, consisting of short *cantigas* (songs) and longer poems, were collected and preserved in three famous medieval *cancioneros* (anthologies). Gonzalo de Berceo was the first Spanish poet known by his name. In the early 1200's, he wrote a series of poems on the *Miracles of Our Lady* in the tradition of other European poets.

The Castilian king Alfonso X, called *the Learned*, helped promote early Spanish prose. In the mid-1200's, he edited the first collection of Castilian laws, *Las Siete Partidas*. Two long historical works were composed under Alfonso's direction—*Crónica General de España*, a history of Spain; and *Grande e General Historia*, a world history. The king also supported the scientific and philosophical interests of the School of Translators of Toledo, which introduced Ptolemy, Aristotle, and other ancient writers to western Europe. In addition, Alfonso is remembered for his Galician cantigas that were dedicated to the Virgin Mary.

The earliest known prose fiction in Spain included a collection of *apologues* (short stories) in Latin. They were collected in 1100 by Pedro Alfonso under the title *Scholar's Guide*. During the 1200's, several series of tales were translated into Spanish from Arabic and other languages. These works included *Calila e Dimna* (1251) and *Sendebar* (1253). In the early 1300's, Spanish prose began to take on a more distinctive character with the writings of Don Juan Manuel, nephew of Alfonso the Learned. Don Juan Manuel wrote many political and historical works. His greatest achievement was *Count Lucanor*, a collection of *exempla* (tales with a moral).

The poetry of the scholars began to decline during the 1300's. Juan Ruiz, archpriest of the town of Hita in Castile, preserved the verse form of the clerics to some extent in his unique and only work, *The Book of Good Love*. This original poetry offers a picture of many details of Spanish life in the 1300's. The poems tell about food, musical instruments, songs, monastic and tavern customs, and love affairs. Ruiz invented the character of Trotaconventos, a go-between of lovers. The poet's elaboration of the fight between Sir Flesh and Lady Lent is the liveliest development of this topic in all medieval literature.

The 1400's. A panoramic view of the lyric poetry of the 1400's appeared in two cancioneros compiled by Juan Alfonso de Baena and Lope de Stúñiga. The Italian poets Dante, Petrarch, and Giovanni Boccaccio influenced the poetry. The spirit of the Middle Ages survived, however, in many anonymous *romances* (ballads). These romances were lyrical fragments of epic songs, and were meant to be sung or recited. They have been preserved through oral tradition in Spain, South America, and Morocco, and among Sephardic Jews.

Three great poets belong to the 1400's: (1) Iñigo López de Mendoza, better known as the Marquis of Santillana; (2) Juan de Mena; and (3) Jorge Manrique. Santillana wrote sonnets in the Italian style, and elaborate, courtly *serranillas* (pastoral poems). He also wrote an important letter about the poetry of the times. Mena wrote *El Laberinto de Fortuna*, an allegorical work of 300 stanzas inspired by Dante and Petrarch. In the second half of the 1400's, Manrique wrote the *Coplas*, an inspired and artistically structured elegy on the death of his father.

Several events of literary importance took place during the late 1400's. Printing was introduced in Spain, probably in Saragossa in 1473. The first book known to have been printed in Spain was dated 1474 in Valencia. In 1492, Antonio de Nebrija published his *Grammar of the Castilian Language*, the first grammar ever written on the rules of a modern European language. The theater took its first steps toward secularization before 1500. Juan del Encina and Lucas Fernández wrote not only Christmas and Easter plays, but also drama with pastoral and folk dialogue. Other new trends in Spanish literature appeared in such novels as Diego de San Pedro's *Cárcel de Amor* (1492) and the Catalan book of chivalry, *Tirant lo Blanch* (1490). The long novel *Amadís de Gaula*, well known since the 1300's, was printed for the first time in 1508. It was probably written by Garci Ordóñez de Montalvo. See AMADÍS OF GAUL.

The masterpiece generally known as *La Celestina* appeared in the late 1400's. It was first published as an anonymous novel in dialogue form in 16 acts under the title *Comedia de Calisto y Melibea* (1499, although there may have been an earlier edition). This great work was later expanded to 21 acts and titled *Tragicomedia de Calisto y Melibea*. The author of at least 15 acts—and probably of the whole work—was Fernando de Rojas. The work was immediately translated into the main European languages. The classic English version became that of James Mabbe (*The Spanish Bawd*, 1631).

The central character of the famous novel is Celestina, a witchlike go-between who brings together two lovers, Calisto and Melibea. The work combines medieval theology with a Renaissance conception of life. Much of the book's fascination centers on the character of Celestina. The main characters lose their lives one by one. Melibea's father closes the work with a tragic lament that has Biblical overtones. In this lament, he questions the nothingness of his empty world.

The Golden Age (1500-1681)

The spirit of the Italian Renaissance spread through Spanish literature of the 1500's. Beginning in 1530, literary expression was at constant odds with the Inquisition, an effort by the Roman Catholic Church to punish people who opposed church teachings. Many Spaniards were influenced by the Dutch scholar Erasmus of Rotterdam, who worked for reform of the church. His ideas were clearly present in the philosophical writings of Juan Luis Vives and the brothers Alfonso and Juan de Valdés. The beliefs of Erasmus were even in the work of St. Ignatius Loyola, founder of the Society of Jesus (Jesuits).

Poetry. During the early 1500's, Juan Boscán and Garcilaso de la Vega introduced the meters, verse forms, and themes of Italian Renaissance poetry. The Italian influence soon dominated Spanish poetry. But Cristóbal de Castillejo and Gregorio Silvestre, among others, preserved the Castilian tradition of short lines. Spanish poetry is indebted not only to such other Spaniards as Hernando de Acuña and Gutierre de Cetina, but also to the Portuguese Francisco Sá de Miranda and Luiz de Camões. Camões' great epic poem *Os Lusíadas* is a masterpiece in the style of Italian epics.

There were two main poetic schools after the mid-1500's—the Castilian school of Salamanca and the Andalusian school of Seville. Poets of both schools wrote in the style of Petrarch. But a certain serenity and a more cautious use of metaphor characterized the school of Salamanca and its representatives—Fray (Brother) Luis de León, Francisco de Figueroa, and Francisco de la Torre. Poets of the school of Seville included Fernando de Herrera, Francisco de Medrano, Francisco de Rioja, Juan de Jáuregui, and Juan de Arguijo. Through the use of colorful images, they developed a refined artistry in the formal possibilities of language that led to the baroque style of the 1600's.

Another important aspect of Spanish poetry of the 1500's was the lyrical expression of mystics—people who seek union with God through constant meditation. Saint John of the Cross was the major mystic poet. Saint Theresa contributed several prose works, including her autobiography, to mystical literature. Two similar writers were Fray Luis de Granada, author of *The Sinners' Guide* (1567), and Fray Luis de León, a professor at the University of Salamanca who was persecuted by the Inquisition. León wrote religious poetry and the prose masterpiece *The Names of Christ* (1583).

Medieval epics survived in the 1500's, not only in the romances but also in books of chivalry. The epic glorification of people and events also continued in long poems by Luis de Zapata, Luis Barahona de Soto, and Bernardo de Balbuena, and in Alonso de Ercilla y Zúñiga's *La Araucana*. This epic poem told of the conflicts between the Indians of Chile and the Spaniards. All these poets wrote in the Italian narrative style.

Prose. The *pastoral novel* became popular among Renaissance writers, and Spanish novelists produced fashionable works that idealized simple, rural life. *La Diana* (1559?) by Jorge de Montemayor and *La Diana enamorada* (1564) by Gaspar Gil Polo are still well-known Spanish pastoral novels. Cervantes in his first work, *La Galatea* (1585), and Lope de Vega in *La Arcadia* (1598) later followed the vogue of pastoral fiction.

The *picaresque novel* was by far the most important contribution of Spanish Golden Age fiction to world literature. This type of novel presented a picture of society as seen through the eyes of a *pícaro* (rogue). The first important picaresque novel was *Lazarillo de Tormes* (1554), written as the short, anonymous autobiography of a young boy of humble birth. Lázaro makes his way by cunning and treachery while serving a blind beggar, then a greedy priest, and later a starving squire and other representatives of Spanish society. During his account of his wandering life, Lázaro moralizes on the episodes of his struggle. *Lazarillo* became a famous character and inspired many sequels.

The peak of the picaresque novel was attained by Mateo Alemán with *Guzmán de Alfarache* (first part, 1599; second part, 1604). *Guzmán*, another autobiography of a pícaro, is more detailed than *Lazarillo*. Alemán presented a more bitter, pessimistic view of life by showing that neither human nature nor conditions of life can be changed.

The picaresque novel quickly became a tradition. Vicente Espinel wrote *Marcos de Obregón* (1618). López de Ubeda created a female rogue in *La Pícara Justina* (1605). The poet and satirist Francisco de Quevedo wrote the aggressive, skeptical, and sad novel *Life of the Swindler* (1626). Quevedo also became famous for his satire *Visions* (1627) and his moral essays on politics and history.

The counterpart of the realism of the picaresque novel was the idealism of Cervantes' masterpiece, *Don Quixote* (part I, 1605; part II, 1615). This story of a country landowner who considers himself a knight is filled with humor and sadness. Cervantes believed in the noble ideals of his hero and the dream-reality aspect of human life. But he went beyond his times, and gave his characters and themes a quality that extends beyond Spain to all humanity (see DON QUIXOTE). The writings of Cervantes that were most typical of the period were his dramas. But they failed to please audiences of the time, which favored the works of Lope de Vega.

Drama. The Spanish theater developed slowly during most of the 1500's. In 1517, Bartolomé de Torres Naharro published a collection of plays with a prologue on dramatic theory, *Propalladia*. Gil Vicente of Portugal wrote plays in Spanish—*Don Duardos, Amadís de Gaula*, and *La comedia del viudo*. The actor-playwright Lope de Rueda created the *paso*, a short farce that ridiculed the daily life of his time. Juan de la Cueva was the first author to take his plots from Spanish history or from popular narrative songs called ballads.

Lope de Vega emerged in the late 1500's as a unique literary figure of the Golden Age. He wrote for popular audiences, mixing tragic and comic elements. The topics of Lope's dramas had various origins. As the creator of a national drama, he drew on historical events.

SPANISH LITERATURE

He also glorified national heroes. Lope filled many of his plays with the greatness of the spirit of the common people. But he also created rulers who had divine attributes and were concerned with justice. Some of Lope's plays were cloak-and-sword comedies, with love and honor the sources of dramatic conflict. Others were light plays with complicated plots in which his qualities of poet and dramatist stand out. The *bobo* (fool) of earlier comedies became a constant character in Lope's plays in the form of the *gracioso*, the witty counterpart of the hero.

Other dramatists of Lope's school included Tirso de Molina, whose *The Deceiver of Seville* (1630) was the first staging of the Don Juan legend; Guillén de Castro; the Mexican-born Juan Ruiz de Alarcón; Lope's biographer, Juan Pérez de Montalván; Francisco de Rojas Zorrilla; and Agustín Moreto.

The 1600's. At the beginning of the 1600's, the world of art sought new forms of expression. Artists tended toward greater ornamentation and complication in their works. The resulting style was called *baroque* (see BA-ROQUE). In Spain, there were two literary indications of this trend—*conceptismo* and *culteranismo*.

Conceptismo featured a subtle and ambiguous use of figures of speech, including antithesis, parallelism, and metaphor (see FIGURE OF SPEECH). The use of an elaborate metaphor called *concepto* (conceit) was the best example of this trend. Many works of Quevedo and Baltasar Gracián were also examples.

Luis de Góngora led the culteranismo movement, which later became known as *gongorismo*. Góngora created lyric poetry full of color, imagery, and richness in musical linguistic effects. His long and complex poems *Polifemo and Galatea* (1612) and *Las Soledades* (1613), as well as his sonnets, ballads, and short compositions, became models for new developments in literature. Other poets who cultivated culteranismo included Pedro Soto de Rojas; Juan de Tarsis, the count of Villamediana; Luis de Carrillo y Sotomayor; and Sor (Sister) Juana Inés de la Cruz, a Mexican nun.

Drama was also influenced by the baroque style. Pedro Calderón de la Barca succeeded Lope de Vega as the leading Spanish dramatist. He was more profound than his predecessor in the creation of character and the presentation of human problems. Calderón dramatized the dreams and realities of life in a singular work, *Life Is a Dream* (1635). The theme of honor and the conflict between love and jealousy were topics frequently staged by Calderón. His historical comedies and religious dramas showed his versatility. Calderón's work was full of examples of the baroque style. But his *autos sacramentales* (religious plays about the Eucharist) reflected culteranismo combined with the spirit of the Counter Reformation. The Counter Reformation was a reform movement within the Roman Catholic Church following the Protestant Reformation. Calderón used symbolism to express in solemn verse philosophical explorations of life and death, original sin, and free will. Calderón's best-known autos included *The Great Theatre of the World* and *The Feast of Belshezzar*.

The 1700's and 1800's

Neoclassicism. By the end of the 1600's, Spain had declined politically, economically, and artistically.

Spanish Literature from the 1100's

Masters of Spanish literature from the 1100's to the present rank among the greatest literary figures in the world. Spain's Golden Age, a period during the 1500's and 1600's, produced some of the finest drama, poetry, and fiction ever written.

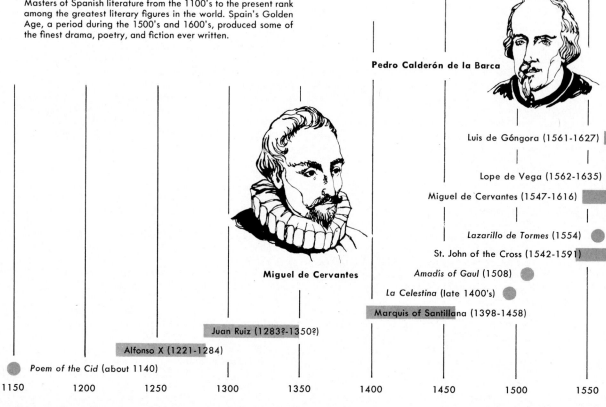

Pedro Calderón de la Barca

Miguel de Cervantes

Luis de Góngora (1561-1627)

Lope de Vega (1562-1635)

Miguel de Cervantes (1547-1616)

Lazarillo de Tormes (1554)

St. John of the Cross (1542-1591)

Amadís of Gaul (1508)

La Celestina (late 1400's)

Marquis of Santillana (1398-1458)

Juan Ruiz (1283?-1350?)

Alfonso X (1221-1284)

Poem of the Cid (about 1140)

1150   1200   1250   1300   1350   1400   1450   1500   1550

Philip V, a Frenchman, became king of Spain in 1700 and began the Bourbon dynasty of rulers. With French rulers in Spain and the beginning of the Age of Reason (Enlightenment) in the rest of Europe, it was inevitable that Spanish literature would assume new directions.

Many writers tried to refine Spanish literature along the lines of French classicism (see CLASSICISM). Benito Jerónimo Feijóo, a Benedictine friar, wrote on almost every branch of learning in his *Teatro Crítico Universal* (8 volumes, 1726-1739) and *Cartas Eruditas y Curiosas* (5 volumes, 1742-1760). Ignacio Luzán also wrote within the framework of the Enlightenment. He supported the new ideas of reason, simplicity, and common sense in his book of literary criticism, *La Poética* (1737). Few Spanish writers of the time wrote novels. The only novel of note was *The History of the famous preacher, Friar Gerund de Campazas* (1758) by the Jesuit José Francisco de Isla. Two of the most important writers in Spain during the 1700's were José Cadalso and Gaspar Melchor de Jovellanos. Cadalso criticized the defects he saw in his countrymen in his best-known collection of essays, *Cartas marruecas* (1789). Jovellanos was a liberal poet, essayist, and economist.

The spirit of the 1700's did not favor lyrical expression. Neoclassicism, a style strongly influenced by Greek and Roman literature, was the most popular trend of the day. However, two of the best poets, Juan Meléndez Valdés and Nicasio Álvarez de Cienfuegos, wrote sentimental works under the influence of the French philosopher Jean Jacques Rousseau and other romantics. These poets were examples of a pre-romantic taste becoming prevalent in Spain. Manuel José Quintana clearly belonged to the neoclassical school. His odes and long poems had a patriotic sentiment that reflected ideas more than emotions. The works of Juan Nicasio Gallego resembled those of Quintana.

Romanticism came late to Spain. It was mainly a response to the more intense romantic impulses in the rest of Europe, and represented little more than a literary fashion (see ROMANTICISM). Spanish liberals brought the new philosophy of art and life with them when they returned from exile in the 1830's after the death of Ferdinand VII.

Ángel de Saavedra, the Duke of Rivas, assured the success of the romantic theater when he staged his drama *Don Álvaro, o La fuerza del sino* in 1835. Antonio García Gutiérrez pleased the public with *El Trovador* (1836). Juan Eugenio Hartzenbusch and Francisco Martínez de la Rosa also wrote for audiences that enjoyed romanticism. The peak of the romantic theater was reached by José Zorrilla. In 1844, he revived the Don Juan myth in *Don Juan Tenorio*, one of the longlasting successes of the Spanish stage. Manuel Tamayo y Baus showed the influence of the high passion typical of romanticism in his historical tragedy *The Madness of Love* (1855) and in *Un drama nuevo* (1867). Manuel Bretón de los Herreros wrote satirical, realistic comedies. Adelardo López de Ayala took his plots from the life of the Spanish middle class. In the late 1800's, romanticism returned in the dramas of José Echegaray, who received the 1904 Nobel prize for literature. His best-known work was *The Great Galeoto* (1881). A concern for social justice, obvious in *Juan José* (1895) by Joaquín Dicenta, highlighted the Spanish stage in the late 1800's.

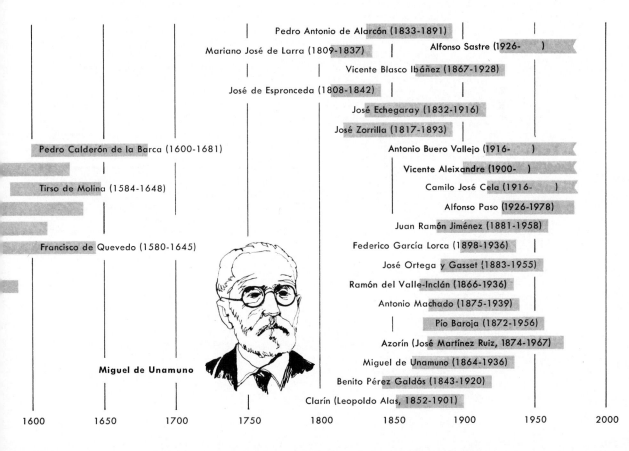

Pedro Antonio de Alarcón (1833-1891)

Mariano José de Larra (1809-1837)

Alfonso Sastre (1926-   )

Vicente Blasco Ibáñez (1867-1928)

José de Espronceda (1808-1842)

José Echegaray (1832-1916)

José Zorrilla (1817-1893)

Pedro Calderón de la Barca (1600-1681)

Antonio Buero Vallejo (1916-   )

Vicente Aleixandre (1900-   )

Tirso de Molina (1584-1648)

Camilo José Cela (1916-   )

Alfonso Paso (1926-1978)

Juan Ramón Jiménez (1881-1958)

Francisco de Quevedo (1580-1645)

Federico García Lorca (1898-1936)

José Ortega y Gasset (1883-1955)

Ramón del Valle-Inclán (1866-1936)

Antonio Machado (1875-1939)

Pío Baroja (1872-1956)

Azorín (José Martínez Ruiz, 1874-1967)

Miguel de Unamuno

Miguel de Unamuno (1864-1936)

Benito Pérez Galdós (1843-1920)

Clarín (Leopoldo Alas, 1852-1901)

1600   1650   1700   1750   1800   1850   1900   1950   2000

SPANISH LITERATURE

Spain's most distinguished poets of the 1800's were José de Espronceda and Gustavo Adolfo Bécquer. Espronceda's long poems *El Diablo Mundo* (1841) and *El estudiante de Salamanca* (on the Don Juan theme) included the richest expression of vibrant Spanish romantic poetry. Bécquer could be called the last of the romantics, but he lived when romanticism as a literary school was already outdated. His collection *Rimas* (1871) shows he was the most sensitive poet of the 1800's.

Two poets, Ramón de Campoamor and Gaspar Núñez de Arce, represented a reaction to romantic sentimentality. Campoamor composed short poems which were philosophical and skeptical. He called them *doloras* and *humoradas*. Núñez de Arce expressed an aggressive patriotism in *Gritos del combate* (1875). Rosalía de Castro wrote delicate lyrics, and her one book in Castilian made her one of the most respected poets of the 1800's.

Romanticism in Catalonia led to a revival of literature in the Catalan language during the last half of the 1800's. It produced such excellent poets as Jacinto Verdaguer and Juan Maragall, and such dramatists as Ángel Guimerá.

Short prose sketches of regional customs and manners developed from romantic literature picturing regional customs and folklore. This type of literature was called *costumbrismo*. Writers who created costumbrista articles included Serafín Estébanez Calderón, known as *El Solitario*. He described typical scenes and people from the province of Andalusia in articles published as *Escenas andaluzas* (1847). Ramón de Mesonero Romanos, who called himself *El Curioso Parlante*, wrote articles about Madrid and published them in three volumes, *Panorama Matritense*. Mariano José de Larra, one of the best prose writers of the 1800's, was similar but more romantic in his attitude. His costumbrista articles, written in the tradition of Quevedo and Cadalso, showed deep concern for Spain. In his critical essays and journalism, often violent, he tried to awaken the nation to its possibilities.

The costumbrista articles gave rise to the Spanish realistic novel which developed in the mid-1800's. Cecilia Böhl de Faber, who wrote under the name of Fernán Caballero, brought costumbrismo to the novel in *La gaviota* (1849). Pedro Antonio de Alarcón wrote about Andalusian characters in his charming story *The Three-Cornered Hat* (1874) and in *The Infant with the Globe* (1880). Juan Valera, one of the most cultured writers of the 1800's, wrote *Pepita Jiménez* (1874) and *Juanita la Larga* (1895). These novels, as well as his literary criticism, reflected his worldly and sophisticated spirit.

Realistic regional novels dominated the second half of the 1800's. José María de Pereda's *Sotileza* (1884) and *Peñas arriba* (1895) were costumbrista novels about life on Spain's northern coast. *Marta y María* (1883) by Armando Palacio Valdés dealt with the conflict of mystic and domestic virtues set against the detailed description of an Asturian city. Emilia Pardo Bazán wrote *Los pazos de Ulloa* (1886), a sparkling narrative of local traditions and politics of the interior of Galicia. *The Cabin* (1898) and *Reeds and Mud* (1902) by Vicente Blasco Ibáñez were tragedies of the swampland near Valencia. Blasco Ibáñez is also known for his two novels inspired by the terror of World War I, *Los cuatro jinetes del Apocalipsis* (*The Four Horsemen of the Apocalypse*, 1916) and *Mare Nostrum* (1918).

The famous literary critic Leopoldo Alas, who wrote under the name of Clarín, created perhaps the best Spanish novel of the 1800's—the carefully structured and sensitive *La Regenta* (1885). But Spain's truly great novelist of the 1800's, and probably of the last 300 years, was Benito Pérez Galdós. He wrote 80 novels and 24 plays. In the five series of novels that make up the *Episodios nacionales*, Pérez Galdós novelized Spanish history from the Battle of Trafalgar (1805) until 1900. Many of his works were novels of ideas in which he dealt with religion and economics. He created profound characterizations—particularly his main female characters—and showed unusual awareness of the depth of human psychology. Pérez Galdós wrote about all levels of society, and his novels provided a clear insight into life in Madrid during the last half of the 1800's. His best novels were *Doña Perfecta* (1876), *El amigo Manso* (1882), *Fortunata y Jacinta* (1886-1887), *Miau* (1888), and *Misericordia* (1897).

The 1900's

The Generation of 1898 was a group of writers who appeared on the literary scene about the time of the Spanish-American War. These writers played an important part in the history of Spanish literature.

In the Spanish-American War, fought in 1898, Spain lost the last parts of its once mighty empire. The corruption of Spain's ruling class and the loss of its overseas colonies led many Spaniards to examine the nation's culture and civilization. The problem was whether Spain's cultural heritage could be adapted to the progress of modern Europe, and if it was original and creative enough to survive. From this examination of the Spanish character and past came a philosophical, historical, and artistic awakening that produced rich artistic expression.

Many types of writers contributed to the national renaissance of creative genius that dominated Spanish letters during the early 1900's. Miguel de Unamuno expressed romantic and existential grief in such essays as *The Tragic Sense of Life* (1912); poetry; and such novels as *Mist* (1914). Unamuno is often considered a forerunner of the philosophical movement called existentialism. The unique prose of Azorín (José Martínez Ruiz) included delicate and melancholic descriptions of Spanish landscape and history (*Castilla*, 1912; and *Doña Inés*, 1925). Pío Baroja became the leading Spanish novelist of the early 1900's. He showed sensitive heroes fluctuating between failure and triumph in such works as *The Tree of Knowledge* (1911) and *Zalacaín el aventurero* (1909). The poetry of Antonio Machado portrayed the severe spirit and landscape of Castile. Ramiro de Maeztu expressed himself in biting journalism. The beautiful prose style of Ramón del Valle-Inclán appeared in such novels as *Sonata de otoño* (1902) and *Divinas palabras* (1920). In such *esperpentos* (satires) as *Luces de bohemia* (1924), Valle-Inclán saw Spain as a grotesque distortion of normalcy.

Spain's literary past was rediscovered, interpreted, and edited and published by a group of scholars at the Center of Historical Studies in Madrid. These scholars included Ramón Menéndez Pidal, Américo Castro, Tomás Navarro Tomás, and José Fernandez Montesinos. They continued the work of Marcelino Menéndez y Pelayo, the great scholar and critic of the late 1800's.

Two fine novelists succeeded the Generation of 1898. Gabriel Miró was extremely lyrical, and Ramón Pérez de Ayala was one of the most intellectual novelists of his day. Noted essayists included the Catalan philosopher and art critic Eugenio d'Ors, and the internationally famous philosopher, historian, and critic José Ortega y Gasset. Among Ortega's works were *The Dehumanization of Art* (1925) and *The Revolt of the Masses* (1930). He and Unamuno became the outstanding Spanish intellectuals of the 1900's.

Poetry. While the Generation of 1898 was trying to discover the spirit of Spain, lyric poetry was undergoing the renewals of *modernism*. This school was inspired by the work of the Nicaraguan poet Rubén Darío and the French Symbolists (see LATIN-AMERICAN LITERATURE [Modernism]). The modernists joined the richness of form, musicality, and expression of the Spanish language with new poetic concepts, and created a new wealth of lyric poetry.

The school of modernism was best represented by Manuel Machado and Gregorio Martínez Sierra. Although short-lived, it inspired many poets whose production has been unequaled during the 1900's in quality and intensity. These writers included Juan Ramón Jiménez, winner of the 1956 Nobel prize for literature.

During the 1920's and 1930's, a number of poets turned to the traditional ballad or to the complex, colorful gongorismo for inspiration. Among those who wrote original and expressive lyric poetry were Pedro Salinas, Jorge Guillén, León Felipe, Gerardo Diego, Federico García Lorca, Dámaso Alonso, Luis Cernuda, and Rafael Alberti. A member of this group, Vicente Aleixandre, won the 1977 Nobel prize for literature.

In the 1930's, Miguel Hernández, Leopoldo Panero, Luis Rosales, Luis Felipe Vivanco, and Germán Bleiberg represented a return to the formal poetry of the Renaissance. But their works reveal the anguish often present in love poetry. Prose writers of note included Ramón Gómez de la Serna and Benjamín Jarnés.

The Spanish Stage during the early 1900's was dominated by Jacinto Benavente, winner of the Nobel prize for literature in 1922. His plays *Bonds of Interest* (1907) and *The Passion Flower* (1913) received international praise. Two brothers, Serafín and Joaquín Alvarez Quintero, wrote amusing and delightful plays on Andalusian life. The plays of José María Pemán and the verse dramas of Eduardo Marquina dealt patriotically with Spanish national themes. The costumbrista plays of Carlos Arniches and the farces of Pedro Muñoz Seca pleased audiences of the time. The drama of this period reached a peak in the lyrical tragedies of García Lorca.

Spanish Literature Today. The Spanish Civil War (1936-1939) caused a break in Spanish literature. Some writers were killed and others were exiled, and the world of letters took some time to recover. But then came Camilo José Cela's novel *The Family of Pascual Duarte* (1942), followed by Carmen Laforet's *Nada* (1944) and Cela's *The Hive* (1951).

Many young authors emerged in the 1950's. Their work, characterized by social realism, was extraordinary. These writers produced the major works of Span-

ish literature from about 1960 to 1980. The novels of Miguel Delibes, Rafael Sánchez Ferlosio, José María Gironella, Juan Goytisolo, Carmen Martín Gaite, and Juan Marsé won international recognition.

The theater was represented by playwrights who wrote in a wide variety of styles. Antonio Buero Vallejo and Alfonso Sastre wrote philosophical plays. Alfonso Paso became popular for his social comedies. Fernando Arrabal gained international attention for his controversial and experimental plays. José Martín Recuerda wrote powerful studies of values in Spanish society.

Poetry since 1939 first followed a direction toward simpler forms of expression with Dionisio Ridruejo and José Luis Cano. Then poetry changed to a nonconformist attitude with Gabriel Celaya, Blas de Otero, and such younger writers as Claudio Rodríguez. Some writers, including the novelists Francisco Ayala and Ramón Sender and the playwright Alejandro Casona, developed their work in exile. Julián Marías, José Luis Aranguren, and José M. Ferrater Mora wrote philosophical and social essays.   GERMÁN BLEIBERG

Related Articles in WORLD BOOK include:

Outline

Questions

What effect did *costumbrismo* have on the novel of the mid-1800's?

What was the Generation of 1898?

What is the significance of the *jarchas* in the history of literature?

Who were the two most important dramatists of Spain's Golden Age?

Why is *The Cid* more realistic than other medieval epic poems?

What are the characteristics of the *picaresque* novel?

What were the contributions of Benito Pérez Galdós to Spanish literature?

How does *conceptismo* differ from *culteranismo*? Why are both characteristic of the baroque style?

Who was Spain's greatest and best-known writer?

Additional Resources

CHANDLER, RICHARD, and SCHWARTZ, KESSEL. *A New History of Spanish Literature.* Louisiana State Univ. Press, 1961.

SPANISH MAIN

DIAZ-PLAJA, GUILLERMO. *A History of Spanish Literature.* New York Univ. Press, 1971.

NORTHUP, GEORGE. *Introduction to Spanish Literature.* 3rd ed. Univ. of Chicago Press, 1960.

WARD, PHILIP. *The Oxford Companion to Spanish Literature.* Oxford, 1978.

SPANISH MAIN was the name English buccaneers and pirates gave to the northern coast of South America. By 1550, Spain controlled the Caribbean Sea, the West Indies, and large areas of the South American mainland. *Spanish Mainland* referred to what are now Colombia and Venezuela. English sailors shortened the name to *Spanish Main.*

SPANISH MOSS is a flowering plant that hangs from trees in the southeastern United States and in tropical South America. Its long, slender, grayish stems look like hair hanging from the trees. It is neither a true moss nor a parasite. The plant has no roots, and absorbs water directly from the air. It has long, narrow leaves and small yellow flowers. Its stems are dried and used to stuff upholstery.

Scientific Classification. Spanish moss belongs to the pineapple family, Bromeliaceae. It is genus *Tillandsia*, species *T. usneoides*.　　　ROBERT W. HOSHAW

See also AIR PLANT.

SPANISH PHALANX. See FALANGE ESPAÑOLA.

SPANISH SAHARA. See WESTERN SAHARA.

SPANISH SUCCESSION, WAR OF THE. See SUCCESSION WARS.

SPARK, MURIEL (1918-　　), is a Scottish author best known for her short novels. Spark fills her fiction with witty dialogue, eccentric characters, and unusual events. These elements are often humorous, but Spark uses them to explore serious moral questions.

Spark's best-known novel is *The Prime of Miss Jean Brodie* (1961). The central character is Miss Brodie, a romantic, domineering teacher at a Scottish girls' school. The analysis of this character reflects Spark's interest in unusual personalities. *The Mandelbaum Gate* (1965) is one of Spark's few long novels. Set in modern Jerusalem, its complex plot involves a large and diverse cast of characters. Spark's other popular short novels include *Memento Mori* (1959) and *The Ballad of Peckham Rye* (1960). She also wrote the political satire *The Abbess of Crewe* (1974) and the comic novel *The Takeover* (1976).

Muriel Sarah Spark was born in Edinburgh, Scotland. She converted to the Roman Catholic Church in 1954. Spark has often dealt with religious issues in her fiction. In addition to her novels, Spark has written poetry, plays, short stories, children's books, and literary criticism. She also has edited the letters of several English writers of the 1800's.　　　CYNTHIA A. DAVIS

SPARK CHAMBER is a device which makes visible the paths followed by electrically charged atomic particles. Nuclear physicists use spark chambers to study these particles, which are too small and travel too fast to be seen by the naked eye. Two Japanese physicists, S. Fukui and S. Miyamoto, built the first practical spark chamber in 1959. Since 1960, the spark chamber has become an important research tool for high energy nuclear physicists. Physicists use it with similar devices called the Wilson cloud chamber and the bubble chamber. But unlike these devices, the spark chamber can be made sensitive for just the short interval that a particle a physicist wants to study is in the chamber.

A spark chamber is made of a series of thin metal plates set parallel in an airtight box that is filled with neon gas. A gap of from 3 to 400 millimeters separates the plates, depending upon the design of the chamber. A typical chamber about 3 feet (91 centimeters) long has 150 plates spaced 6 millimeters apart. Electrical equipment powers the chamber.

The spark chamber is most often used with a device called a *particle accelerator*. This device produces high energy particles that can be studied in the chamber. When a charged atomic particle enters the chamber, it *ionizes* (electrically charges) the neon gas atoms in its path. The particle penetrates the thin metal plates. The ionized gas atoms will conduct electricity, but the atoms that have not ionized will not. An electrical field of 1,000 volts per millimeter of plate separation is applied to alternate plates immediately after the particle ionizes the neon. This electrical field causes a lightninglike spark to jump from plate to plate along the particle's ionized path. The spark can easily be seen and photographed.

Special electronic circuits apply the high voltage to the plates after a selected particle enters the chamber. Physicists can select the particle they wish to study in the chamber. By eliminating unwanted particle *tracks* (paths), the physicist can spend more time studying the important tracks. Physicists learn much about the nucleus of the atom and atomic particles by studying the tracks made by such particles. They have discovered several previously unknown particles with the help of spark chambers.

During the late 1960's and 1970's, physicists developed two devices similar to the spark chamber, the *magnetostrictive chamber* and the *proportional wire chamber*. The construction of both these devices closely resembles that of the spark chamber, but wires are used instead of metal plates. As particles pass through the airtight box of each device, they create electric impulses on the wires. These impulses are read by a computer to determine the paths taken by the particles. Physicists find the proportional wire chamber particularly useful because it can make separate measurements of many more particles per second than a spark chamber can.　　　GERARD K. O'NEILL

See also BUBBLE CHAMBER; PARTICLE ACCELERATOR; WILSON CLOUD CHAMBER.

SPARK PLUG. See IGNITION; AUTOMOBILE (The Electric System; diagrams).

SPARKMAN, JOHN JACKSON (1899-　　), an Alabama Democrat, served in the U.S. Senate from 1947 to 1979. He was the Democratic nominee for Vice-President of the United States in 1952. Sparkman became chairman of the Senate Foreign Relations Committee in 1975. In Congress, Sparkman generally supported the policies of the Democratic Presidents except in civil rights policies. He usually backed Republican Presidents Dwight D. Eisenhower, Richard M. Nixon, and Gerald R. Ford on foreign policy.

Sparkman was born near Hartselle, Ala. He served in the United States House of Representatives from 1937 to 1947.　　　F. JAY TAYLOR

SPARROW is the name of many small, common birds. The name comes from the Anglo-Saxon word

Song Sparrow
Melospiza melodia
Found throughout most of North America
Body length: 5 to 7 inches
(13 to 18 centimeters)

Lark Sparrow
Chondestes grammacus
Found from southern Canada
to El Salvador
Body length: 5½ to 6¾ inches
(14 to 17 centimeters)

House Sparrow
Passer domesticus
Found throughout the temperate
zones of the world
Body length: 5½ to 6¼ inches
(14 to 16 centimeters)

WORLD BOOK
illustrations
by Guy Tudor

spearwa, which probably was a general term for all small birds. Today, it applies especially to many members of the finch family. In America, about 35 species of this family are called *sparrows*. Other sparrows include the *hedge sparrows* of Europe and Asia and European *house* and *tree sparrows*.

Most American sparrows are plain-looking, brownish birds. Many sparrows are noted for their musical songs. Among these are the *song sparrow, vesper sparrow, lark sparrow, white-crowned sparrow, white-throated sparrow, fox sparrow,* and *Lincoln's sparrow.*

Sparrows usually eat seeds, but during the nesting season they also eat insects. The birds build nests on the ground, in clumps of grass, in bushes, or in low trees, but seldom far from the ground. The *chipping sparrow,* or *chippy,* builds its nest in a higher place than other sparrows do. Sometimes the nest may be found in evergreens 25 feet (8 meters) above the ground. The sparrow's nest is a compact, well-built, open structure made of grasses, plant fibers, and sometimes small twigs. The female lays four or five white eggs that are marked with reddish-brown.

American sparrows live almost everywhere. For example, song sparrows live in bushy areas, fox sparrows in forests, swamp sparrows in marshes, vesper sparrows in prairies and sage sparrows in deserts. Those sparrows that live in cold regions usually migrate southward in winter. Some sparrows go to Mexico, others to Central America.

The common house sparrow, often called the *English sparrow* in America, originally lived throughout Europe. It was brought to America in 1850 and now lives in most of the populated regions of Canada, the United States, and northern Mexico.

Scientific Classification. American sparrows belong to the finch family, Fringillidae. The song sparrow is *Melospiza melodia.* Lincoln's sparrow is *M. lincolnii,* and the swamp sparrow is *M. georgiana.* The white-throated sparrow is *Zonotrichia albicollis,* and the white-crowned sparrow is *Z. leucophrys.* The chipping sparrow is *Spizella passerina,* the fox sparrow *Passerella iliaca,* and the vesper sparrow *Pooecetes gramineus.* The sage sparrow is *Amphispiza belli.* Hedge sparrows are in the accentor family, Prunellidae. European house and tree sparrows are in the weaver finch family, Ploceidae. The house, or English, sparrow is *Passer domesticus.*   LEONARD W. WING

See also BIRD (picture: Birds of Urban Areas).

SPARROW HAWK is a bird of prey that lives in Africa, central Asia, and Europe. It resembles the Ameri-

E. V. Breeze Jones, Bruce Coleman Inc.

The Sparrow Hawk preys on sparrows and other small birds. This small hawk lives in Africa, central Asia, and Europe.

595

can Cooper's hawk and the sharp-shinned hawk. The American kestrel is sometimes called the American sparrow hawk, but this bird is actually a type of falcon (see KESTREL).

The male and female sparrow hawk both have a white breast with brown or reddish-brown bars. The tail is gray and has from three to five dark stripes. The male has a gray back and a whitish spot on the back of its neck. The female has a brown back. Sparrow hawks have short, broad wings and a long, slim tail. These features help them swerve in the air to catch prey. The males measure about 12 inches (30 centimeters) long, and the females about 15 inches (38 centimeters).

The bird got its name because it eats mostly sparrows. It also preys on other small birds and small animals. Most sparrow hawks build their nests in evergreen trees, but they occasionally nest in shrubs. The female sparrow hawk lays from three to six whitish eggs spotted with brown.

Scientific Classification. The sparrow hawk belongs to the hawk family, *Accipitridae*. It is genus *Accipiter*, species *A. nisus*.   RICHARD F. JOHNSTON

See also HAWK.

SPARS. See COAST GUARD, UNITED STATES (Women in the Coast Guard).

SPARTA, also called Lacedaemon, LAS *ih DEE muhn*, the capital of Laconia, was at one time the most powerful city-state of ancient Greece. It was famous for its military power and its loyal soldiers. The greatest honor that could come to a Spartan was to die in defense of the country. Endurance, a scorn of luxuries, and unyielding firmness are still spoken of as Spartan virtues.

The Land. Sparta was situated in a lovely, sheltered valley on the bank of the Eurotas River. For location, see GREECE, ANCIENT (color map). It was protected on three sides by mountains. The climate was mild, and the soil was fertile and well watered. Sparta had few mineral resources. Spartans obtained marble and a little iron from nearby Mount Taygetus.

The People belonged to three classes. The Spartans themselves were descended from the Dorians, a people who invaded the Greek peninsula about 1000 B.C. They were the ruling class of Sparta and were the only ones who had full rights of citizenship. They enslaved the earlier Greek peoples of Laconia, the Achaeans and Ionians. These enslaved Greeks, called *helots* (pronounced *HELL ut*) outnumbered the Spartans. Some of the non-Spartan Greeks escaped enslavement. They were not citizens, but they lived in Sparta as free people. This group was known as the *perioeci* (pronounced *PAIR ih EE sigh*). The numbers of the three classes varied widely during Sparta's long history. Some authorities estimate that at the height of Spartan power there were about 25,000 citizens, an unknown number of perioeci, and as many as 250,000 helots.

Way of Life. Spartan citizens could engage only in agriculture. A few aristocrats owned their land, but most citizens held state-owned plots. Citizens who could not make enough from their estate to support their family and pay the taxes lost their land to someone who could make it pay. They also lost their citizenship. It was therefore dangerous to try to rear a large family. The Spartans sometimes left unwanted children in a deep cavern in the mountains to die. Because citizens could not carry on manufacturing or trade, the perioeci took over these pursuits. Some of them grew wealthy.

The helots farmed the soil, and they had to give a fixed amount of produce to their master. The rest, which was often little, went to the helots themselves. The helots bitterly resented their lot, and revolts were not unusual. Once a year the Spartans officially declared war on the helots, so that they could kill any who seemed rebellious without breaking the law against murder.

Every Spartan male belonged to the state from the time of his birth. A boy was left to the care of his mother until he was seven years of age, when he was enrolled in a company of 15 members, all of whom were kept under strict discipline. From the age of seven, every boy had to take his meals with his company in a public dining hall. The bravest boy in a company was made captain. The others obeyed his commands and bore such punishments as he decided they should have.

When the boys were 12, their undergarments were taken away and only one outer garment a year was allowed them. Their beds consisted of the tops of reeds, which they gathered with their own hands and without knives. Spartans did not consider the arts of reading and writing necessary. Boys learned the *Iliad* and songs of war and religion, but leaping, running, wrestling, and wielding a weapon with grace and accuracy were held much more important. Between the ages of 20 and 30, Spartan men served as cadets who policed the country, kept the helots in order, and exacted disciplined obedience from the enslaved people.

At 30, a Spartan male attained full maturity and enjoyed the rights and duties of citizenship. He might marry, attend meetings of the assembly, and hold public office. At 60, his military career ended, and he worked either in public affairs or in training the young.

As a result of this system, the Spartan men became tough, proud, disciplined, and noted for obstinate conservatism and for brevity and directness of speech. From childhood, life was one continuous trial of endurance. All the gentler feelings were suppressed.

Spartan women, on the other hand, lived the freest life of any women in Greece. As girls, they engaged in athletics, and as women, they ran their own households. They engaged in business, and many became wealthy and influential. Aristotle tells us that women owned two-fifths of the land in Sparta.

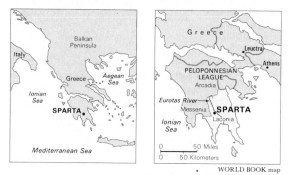

WORLD BOOK map

Sparta was the most powerful city-state of ancient Greece, and the capital of Laconia. By 500 B.C., Sparta had forced nearby city-states to enter the Peloponnesian League.

History. The Dorians who settled in Sparta extended their control over all Laconia at an early date. In the 700's B.C., they conquered Messenia, the rich farming region to the west of Mount Taygetus. Sparta failed to conquer the cities of Arcadia, but forced them to enter the Peloponnesian League. The members of the league were obliged to follow Sparta in war. By 500 B.C., this league included most of the cities in southern and central Greece.

Sparta conquered Athens, the leader of the powerful Athenian Empire, in the hard-fought Peloponnesian War. In 404 B.C., the Athenians were forced to accept a humiliating peace treaty. But the leadership won by Sparta was short-lived. The Spartans ruled over the other Greek states so cruelly that they revolted and threw off the Spartan yoke. At the battle of Leuctra, in 371 B.C., Sparta lost forever its claim to supremacy in Greece. But it remained powerful for the next 200 years. In 146 B.C., Sparta came under the control of Rome.

There is a modern town of Sparta (pop. 11,911) near the site of the ancient city. It was laid out about 1835 and made the capital of the modern political division of Laconia. Excavations have been made on the old site, and much valuable material has been discovered from the early city's history.   DONALD KAGAN

Related Articles in WORLD BOOK include:

Dorians	Lycurgus
Greece, Ancient	Lysander
(The Government of Sparta)	Messenia
Leonidas I	Peloponnesian War

Additional Resources

FITZHARDINGE, L. F. *The Spartans.* Thames & Hudson, 1980.
HOOKER, J. T. *The Ancient Spartans.* Biblio, 1980.
HUXLEY, G. L. *Early Sparta.* Biblio, 1970. Reprint of 1962 ed.
MICHELL, HUMPHREY. *Sparta.* Cambridge, 1952.

SPARTACUS, *SPAHR tuh kuhs* (?-71B.C.), led a great slave revolt against the Roman Empire. The rebellion lasted from 73 B.C. to 71 B.C.

Spartacus was born in Thrace, a region northeast of Greece. He was a member of a group of nomadic herders and later served in the Roman Army. Spartacus deserted the army but was captured and enslaved. The Romans trained him as a gladiator to fight other gladiators and wild beasts in the arena for entertainment (see GLADIATOR).

In 73 B.C., Spartacus and other gladiators rebelled against Roman authority at the town of Capua, in what is now southern Italy. The rebels took refuge on nearby Mount Vesuvius and soon organized an army of about 70,000 runaway slaves. Commanded by Spartacus, the army defeated the Roman forces and gained control over much of central and southern Italy.

In 72 B.C., the rebels divided into two groups. The Romans defeated one group in Italy. Spartacus led the other rebels to victory against a Roman army in Cisalpine Gaul (now northern Italy). In 71 B.C., Spartacus' army returned to the south. Roman forces commanded by Marcus Licinius Crassus defeated the rebel army (see CRASSUS, MARCUS LICINIUS). Spartacus was killed in the battle.   WILLIAM G. SINNIGEN

SPASM. See CRAMP; TETANY.

SPASTIC COLON. See COLITIS.

SPASTIC PARALYSIS is a condition in which there is poor control over the muscles as a result of damage to the *central nervous system* (brain and spinal cord). The damage that causes the condition can occur at or before birth. Spastic paralysis can also develop after birth if an infection such as meningitis damages the brain, or if damage results from strokes, skull fractures, or other injuries.

The part of the central nervous system that is damaged and the amount of damage done determine which muscles are affected and how severely. Sometimes the damage is so slight that the individual may have only a little clumsiness, a slight loss of balance, or a slight speech difficulty. In severe cases, victims cannot walk. Or they may walk on their toes with their feet turned inward, their knees together, and with one leg crossing over in front of the other, in the typical "scissors gait." Spastic paralysis can affect all the muscles. The face, the tongue, and even the muscles that control breathing may be affected. This may result in uncontrollable grimacing, drooling, and difficulty in speaking.

Some persons suffering from spastic paralysis are completely normal, except for their difficulties in controlling the affected muscles. But in other cases, brain injury does affect the individual's intelligence. Even mental retardation may occur. Nevertheless, some persons with spastic paralysis have above-average intelligence.

The damage to the nervous system cannot be cured, but the use of the muscles can be improved through surgery, training, and the use of crutches and braces. Spastic patients can be taught to speak more effectively, to care for themselves, and to earn their own living. In the mid-1970's, surgeons began using brain pacemakers to treat spastic paralysis. The pacemaker electrically stimulates the *cerebellum,* a part of the brain, and helps relieve spastic paralysis in some patients.

The spastic patient should be treated as a normal person, except for the special training that may be required to improve muscle use. For example, spastic children should be encouraged to play with other children. People should understand that spastic paralysis is not a communicable disease, that it is not inherited, and that it is not a form of mental illness. People should not be ashamed of spastic paralysis any more than they should be ashamed of wearing glasses.   MILTON ALTER

See also CEREBRAL PALSY.

SPAVIN, *SPAV uhn,* is a common name for two unrelated diseases which affect the hocks of horses. The hock is the ankle joint of the hind leg. *Bone spavin,* or true spavin, is a bony growth usually on the inner and lower part of the joint. The disease is caused by a lack of certain minerals in the bones. *Bog spavin* is a swelling of a capsule of tissue of the main joint. It is believed to exist at birth and seldom causes any trouble. Both bone spavin and bog spavin are seldom curable. Bone spavin, however, can be treated to end lameness and to keep the growth from enlarging.

SPAWN is the eggs of fishes, mollusks, frogs, and other animals. Usually such eggs are produced in great numbers, particularly by sea animals that are eaten by larger species, or that leave eggs and young to hatch and develop alone. These water animals must produce thousands or millions of eggs to keep from dying out. The eggs of certain fish, particularly the sturgeon, are used to make caviar. The eggs of fishes are also called *roe,* particularly when used as human food. See also CAV-IAR; FISH (How Fish Reproduce); SALMON (The Life of a Salmon); STURGEON. CARL L. HUBBS

SPAYING. See PET (Birth Control); DOG (Social and Moral Responsibilities); CAT (Birth Control).

SPCA. See SOCIETY FOR THE PREVENTION OF CRUELTY TO ANIMALS.

SPEAKEASY. See ROARING TWENTIES (Changing Attitudes).

SPEAKER is an electric device that reproduces sound. Speakers form part of phonographs, radios, tape players, and television sets. They also are part of public address systems and equipment used to amplify sound created by musicians and other performers.

Most speakers have three main parts: (1) a coil of wire called a *voice coil*, (2) a permanent magnet, and (3) a cone-shaped piece of paper or plastic called a *diaphragm*. Electric waves from an amplifier pass through the voice coil and produce varying magnetic forces in the coil. The magnetic forces drive the coil alternately toward and away from the permanent magnet in rapid vibrations. The diaphragm, which is attached to the voice coil, vibrates with it. The vibrations of the diaphragm produce vibrations in the air. The ear hears these air vibrations as sound.

Some equipment has several speakers, each of which reproduces high-, medium-, or low-pitched sounds. A speaker that reproduces only high-pitched sounds is called a *tweeter*. A *squawker* reproduces sounds in the middle range of pitch, and a *woofer* reproduces low-pitched sounds. In general, a system of such specialized speakers provides sound reproduction of higher fidelity than a single speaker. Speakers in high-fidelity systems are mounted in wooden or plastic cabinets. The size and shape of these cabinets determines the tone quality of the sounds made by the speakers. MITCHELL G. HELLER

See also HIGH FIDELITY; RADIO (The Speaker; picture: Main Parts of an AM Transistor Radio).

SPEAKER is the presiding officer in the lower house of several national, state, and provincial legislatures. The duties of the office differ in various legislatures.

In the United States, the speaker of the House of Representatives can wield great power. The speaker is the recognized leader of his or her political party in the House, as well as the presiding officer. The speaker is expected to use the office to promote the party. He or she ranks next after the Vice President in order of presidential succession.

The early speakers considered themselves simply as presiding officers, and tried to be impartial. Henry Clay, elected speaker in 1811, began the practice of using the office for party purposes. The office reached its height as a political force under the strong personalities of Thomas B. Reed, who served as speaker from 1889 to 1891 and again from 1895 to 1899, and Joseph G. Cannon, speaker from 1903 to 1911.

For a time the speaker was considered almost as important as the President. In 1910, the speaker was removed from the Committee on Rules, and the speaker's control over the appointment of committees was taken away. But the speaker is still important in national legislation. One of the strongest speakers since 1910 was Sam Rayburn, who held the office three times between 1940 and 1961. For a list of speakers and other information, see HOUSE OF REPRESENTATIVES.

In Great Britain, a speaker has presided over the House of Commons since at least 1377. The speaker should be a model of impartiality. He or she must rule according to the will of the majority, but never permit the minority to be abused. The House elects each new speaker. It is the custom to reelect the same speaker in all Parliaments until the person dies or retires.

The office of speaker in the House of Commons has great dignity. When the speaker retires, he or she becomes a member of the nobility. GEORGE E. MOWRY

SPEAKER, TRIS (1888-1958), a great American baseball player, was known as the "Gray Eagle" because of his gray hair and his speed in playing the outfield. He won fame with the Cleveland Indians and played in the American League from 1907 to 1928. Speaker had a lifetime batting average of .344, which places him in an all-time outfield with Babe Ruth and Ty Cobb. His highest batting mark was .389 in 1925.

Speaker managed the Indians from 1919 to 1926, winning the World Series in 1920. He was elected to the National Baseball Hall of Fame in 1937. Tristram E. Speaker was born in Hubbard, Tex. ED FITZGERALD

SPEAR ranked as the chief weapon used in the battles of ancient Asia and Europe. The famous Greek poet, Homer, tells how Achilles speared Hector through

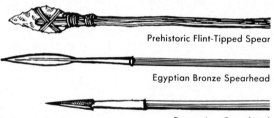

Prehistoric Flint-Tipped Spear

Egyptian Bronze Spearhead

Roman Iron Spearhead

Spearheads were made of various materials. Early ones were made of stone. Later, flint and metal spearheads came into use.

the neck with a "pole heavy with bronze." The early Persians added a sharp spike to the back end of the spear so that both ends could be used. The Romans used a short, heavy spear called a *pilum*. The Gauls fought with a huge, clublike spear. The Illyrian soldiers carried a fine, light javelin. In India, soldiers mounted on charging horses threw the lance, a weapon similar to the javelin. The Bedouins of Arabia were famous for their skill in using the lance on horseback.

Today, the spear is used chiefly in fishing. Eskimos kill seals and fish with spears through holes in the ice. Underwater swimmers often use spear guns with great accuracy. These spear guns shoot spears by means of springs, rubber bands, or compressed gas. JACK O'CONNOR

See also JAVELIN; SPEARFISHING.

SPEARFISH. See MARLIN.

SPEARFISHING is the sport of hunting fish underwater with a spear or a gun that shoots a spear. Spearfishing enthusiasts hunt in rivers, lakes, and oceans in many parts of the world. They use the fish chiefly as food. Some biologists use spearfishing techniques when marking fish for research purposes, but these scientists do not harm the fish.

Basic spearfishing equipment includes a face mask,

An elastic loop propels the pole spear and Hawaiian sling shown below. The rubber-powered spear gun uses rubber loops to fire a spear, and the pneumatic spear gun uses compressed air. The pole spear and Hawaiian sling are about 6 feet (1.8 meters) long. The spear guns are about half as long.

Pole spear

Hawaiian sling

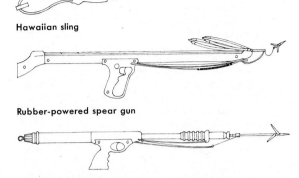

Rubber-powered spear gun

Pneumatic spear gun

Parts of a Rubber-Powered Spear Gun

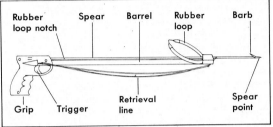

WORLD BOOK illustrations by David Cunningham

a breathing tube called a *snorkel*, swim fins, and one of several kinds of hunting devices. Such devices include (1) pole spears, (2) powered spear guns, and (3) Hawaiian slings.

Pole spears, the simplest spearfishing devices, are fiberglass, metal, or wooden rods that measure up to 10 feet (3 meters) long. They have one or more sharp metal points at one end. The hunter jabs the spear into the fish or shoots it forward by means of an attached elastic loop.

Rubber-powered spear guns are the most widely used devices for spearfishing. A steel spear from 2 to 6 feet (0.6 to 1.8 meters) long rests on top of the barrel of the gun. The spear is held in place by a catch connected to the trigger. The front end of the gun has one or more rubber loops attached to it. The hunter stretches the loops back and hooks them into notches in the spear. When the hunter pulls the trigger, the spear is released and the loops propel it forward with great force. Other types of spear guns are powered by springs, compressed air or gas, or an explosive charge.

Hawaiian slings consist of a short, open tube with an elastic loop fastened across one end. The hunter shoots a steel spear from this device much as a person shoots a pebble from a slingshot. The spear measures about 6 feet (1.8 meters) long, and its shaft fits through the tube and rests against the loop. The hunter grasps the tube with one hand and holds the loop and the spear with the other. To fire the spear, the hunter stretches the loop and releases it.

Spearheads have sharp hooks called *barbs*. The barbs hold the spear in place after it has penetrated a fish. A line attaches a spear to a spear gun and prevents a speared fish from escaping. A spearhead containing an explosive charge is used only to protect the hunter from a shark or to take very large fish.

Most spearfishing enthusiasts can dive to a depth of about 20 feet (6 meters). They must return to the surface for breath after less than a minute. Some skilled divers can go as deep as 100 feet (30 meters) and stay under-

water for about two minutes. A snorkel enables hunters to swim at the surface and spot their prey before diving. Some people who do spearfishing use *scuba* (self-contained underwater breathing apparatus) equipment. Scuba divers breathe air from metal tanks strapped on their backs. They can stay underwater for as long as an hour.

In certain areas of the world, the law prohibits spearfishing with scuba gear. In some areas, powered guns are outlawed. Several states of the United States prohibit spearfishing completely.   ARTHUR H. ULLRICH, JR.

See also SKIN DIVING.

SPEARMINT is a type of mint plant that grows in most of the temperate regions of the world. It yields an oil used in making perfumes, medicine, chewing gum, candies, and mint jelly or sauce. It has smooth, erect stems 1 to 2 feet (30 to 61 centimeters) high, topped with spikes of lavender or white flowers. Most spearmints in the United States grow in Idaho, Indiana, Michigan, Washington, and Wisconsin.

Scientific Classification. The spearmint belongs to the mint family, Labiatae. It is classified as genus *Mentha*, species *M. spicata*.

HAROLD NORMAN MOLDENKE

L. W. Brownell
Spearmint

SPEBSQSA. See BARBERSHOP QUARTET SINGING.

SPECIAL DELIVERY. See POST OFFICE (Speedier Delivery).

SPECIAL DRAWING RIGHTS are reserve assets entered in the books of the International Monetary Fund (IMF) as credits for member nations. A member may use this special account to obtain needed foreign currency from another member. Special drawing rights are often called "SDR's" or "paper gold." They are not real money and have no gold backing, but they have a full guarantee of gold value. Member nations may transfer SDR's among themselves to settle debts.

The IMF created special drawing rights in 1969 to supplement international reserves of gold and national currencies, especially the United States dollar. SDR's represented a more reliable and internationally better controlled medium of exchange. Gold supplies could no longer meet the demand for reserve backing.

In addition, the dollar had two drawbacks. Some Europeans thought its use as an international currency gave the United States too much power in international finance. Some Americans thought a dollar-based exchange placed too much international responsibility on U.S. domestic economic policy.   HARRY G. JOHNSON

See also INTERNATIONAL MONETARY FUND; MONEY (International Finance).

SPECIAL EDUCATION is instruction designed to help both handicapped and gifted children use their full learning ability. The handicapped and gifted youngsters who need such education to get the most from school are called *exceptional children*.

In the past, many people thought the best way to deal with handicapped children was to educate them in separate classrooms or schools. Today, however, many educators believe the handicapped and nonhandicapped should be taught together whenever possible. Isolating handicapped children may give them a sense of inferiority. In addition, the handicapped and nonhandicapped can learn much from each other.

The practice of integrating handicapped children into regular school programs is called *mainstreaming*. Special classrooms or schools are provided only if a student's handicap makes mainstreaming impossible.

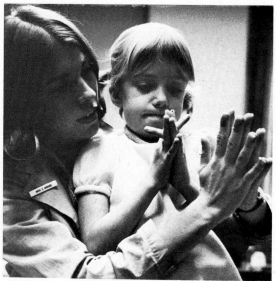

Lynn McLaren, Rapho Guillumette

A Mentally Retarded Child learns to imitate simple movements made by a teacher while playing a game with their hands. Many severely retarded children, aided by specially trained teachers, can learn to dress and feed themselves.

Many handicapped children attend regular classes most of the school day. But they work with a specially trained teacher for short periods each day or several times a week to help overcome their disability. These sessions may be held in a classroom called a *resource room*, which is equipped with such materials as braille typewriters and relief maps for blind students. Other handicapped students attend special classes most of the day but join the rest of the children for certain activities. For example, mentally retarded youngsters may join nonretarded ones for art, physical education, and some other classes.

In the United States, the Education for All Handicapped Children Act of 1975 requires the states to provide free special education for all handicapped children of school age. The law also directs that children be taught in the "least restrictive environment." About 8 per cent of the nation's school-age children need special education because they are physically or mentally handicapped or emotionally disturbed. Another 3 to 5 per cent of the school-age youngsters require special instruction because they are gifted.

Physically Handicapped Children may be crippled; have difficulty hearing or seeing; or suffer from epilepsy, heart disease, or some other serious illness. Many need special education only part of the time because, with certain equipment, they do well in regular classrooms. For example, a child in a wheelchair may need a desk that has been altered. Children who are partially sighted may require books with large print.

Other physical handicaps require especially intensive instruction. Deaf children, for example, need training to learn lip reading and sign language. Many blind children study braille.

Mentally Handicapped Children may be mentally retarded, or they may have normal intelligence but be handicapped by a learning disability.

Mentally Retarded Children learn more slowly than other children. Educators have designed programs to teach mildly retarded students such subjects as reading, writing, and arithmetic. Moderately or severely retarded children must have different special training because they cannot learn to read and write. Special classes teach many such children to care for themselves and to perform useful tasks.

Learning-Disabled Children may have average or even superior intelligence, but they have great difficulty mastering certain skills. Most learning disabilities result from minor disorders of the nervous system. Such disorders interfere with the brain's ability to use information transmitted by the senses.

Many children with learning disabilities have extreme difficulty learning to read, spell, or write, or to solve arithmetic problems. Other learning-disabled youngsters are *hyperactive*. They cannot sit still in class, and they have trouble controlling their behavior. Most such children succeed in regular classes if given special help to overcome their disabilities.

Emotionally Disturbed Children have great problems relating to other people in socially acceptable ways. Some emotionally disturbed children are withdrawn and may not even speak to other people. Other troubled students may argue, fight, or otherwise disrupt classroom activities. Some emotionally disturbed children should be hospitalized for psychiatric care. However, most can attend regular schools if they receive special education and psychological counseling.

Gifted Children may be unusually intelligent or have exceptional ability in art, mathematics, or another area. Special education helps such children develop their talents while they get a well-rounded education. Many schools provide special activities and materials that encourage gifted children to develop at their own rate in regular classrooms.   JEANNETTE E. FLEISCHNER

Related Articles in WORLD BOOK include:

Blindness (Education and Training)	Handicapped (Special Education)
Deafness (Education and Training)	Hyperactive Child
Dyslexia	Learning Disabilities
Education (Special Education)	Mental Retardation (Treatment)

Additional Resources

The Directory for Exceptional Children. 9th ed. Porter Sargent, 1981.

MOPSIK, STANLEY I., ed. *An Education Handbook for Parents of Handicapped Children*, Abt, 1980.

VAIL, PRISCILLA L. *The World of the Gifted Child.* Walker, 1979.

SPECIAL EFFECTS. See MOTION PICTURE (The Cinematographer; pictures: Special Effects); TELEVISION (The Control Room); THEATER (Lighting Methods).

SPECIAL FORCES. See ARMY, UNITED STATES (Special Forces).

SPECIAL LIBRARIES ASSOCIATION is an organization of professional librarians and information specialists whose members serve institutions that require or provide specialized information. Such institutions include businesses, museums, newspapers, research organizations, technical schools, and special departments of public and university libraries. The association works to promote learning through the collection, organization, and distribution of library materials. It also advises institutions on how to organize and operate special libraries.

The Special Libraries Association has about 11,500 members in Canada, the United States, and other countries. Its official journal is *Special Libraries*. It also publishes bibliographic aids in library and information science. The association was founded in 1909. Head-

Eastman Kodak from the State University of New York at Brockport

The Special Olympics features athletic events modeled after those of the Olympic Games. Two happy winners are shown above.

quarters are at 235 Park Avenue S., New York, N.Y. 10003.   Critically reviewed by the SPECIAL LIBRARIES ASSOCIATION

SPECIAL OLYMPICS is an international program that promotes physical fitness and athletic competition for mentally retarded children and adults. The program features a series of sports events modeled after the Olympic Games.

The program includes summer and winter sports: basketball, bowling, diving, floor hockey, Frisbee-disc, gymnastics, ice skating, *poly hockey* (a game similar to floor hockey), skiing, soccer, swimming, track and field, volleyball, and wheelchair events. Participants compete in different divisions depending on their age and ability. They train in programs offered by schools and other institutions. Special Olympic games at local, area, and chapter levels are held every year. Two series of International Special Olympic Games—summer games and winter games— are held every four years.

The Joseph P. Kennedy, Jr., Foundation, which sponsors Special Olympics, founded the program in 1968. Special Olympics headquarters are at 1701 K Street NW, Washington, D.C. 20006.

Critically reviewed by the JOSEPH P. KENNEDY, JR., FOUNDATION

SPECIALTY SCHOOL. See ALTERNATIVE SCHOOL.

SPECIES. See CLASSIFICATION, SCIENTIFIC (Groups in Classification).

SPECIFIC GRAVITY. See DENSITY.

SPECIFIC HEAT of a substance is the amount of heat needed to raise the temperature of a unit mass of the substance (1 pound or 1 gram) by 1 degree. In the metric system, one *calorie* of heat energy will raise the temperature of 1 gram of water 1 degree Celsius. The unit in the English system is the British thermal unit (B.T.U.). One B.T.U. will raise 1 pound of water 1 degree Fahrenheit.   ROBERT LINDSAY

See also BRITISH THERMAL UNIT; CALORIE; HEAT (Changes in Temperature; picture: The Specific Heats).

SPECTACLES. See GLASSES.

SPECTATOR, THE. See ADDISON, JOSEPH.

SPECTROGRAPH. See SPECTROMETER.

SPECTROMETER, *spehk TRAHM uh tuhr,* is an instrument that spreads out light into a spectrum and displays it for study. The atoms or molecules of all substances give off light when heated to high temperatures. The pattern of light given off is different for every substance—that is, no two substances have the same spectrum. Therefore, experts can identify a substance or determine its chemical composition by analyzing the spectrum of the substance.

Spectrometers are used to examine a wide range of materials. Industrial chemists use these instruments to detect impurities in steel and other metal alloys. Spectrometers enable astronomers to study the chemical composition of the stars. Spectrometers are also used to identify chemical substances that have been found at the scene of a crime and to detect pollutants in the air and water.

A typical spectrometer is enclosed by a container that keeps out light not being studied. Light enters through the narrow entrance slit and passes through a *collimating lens.* This lens causes the light to become a beam of parallel light rays. The parallel light then travels through a prism, where it is broken up into a spec-

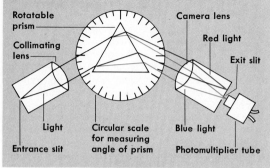

How a Typical Spectrometer Works. Light enters through a narrow slit, as shown in the diagram above. A collimating lens causes the light to become a beam of parallel rays. A prism then spreads the rays into a pattern of different colors, such as blue and red. Only one color of light can pass through the exit slit at a time, and it is focused on the slit by a camera lens. The prism must be rotated to bring the other color into the slit. A photomultiplier tube measures the brightness of light leaving the slit.

trum. A lens focuses the light on the exit slit. Only one color of light can pass through this slit at a time. Therefore, the prism must be rotated to bring the other colors into the exit slit and to scan the entire spectrum. A circular scale records the angle of the prism, so the wavelengths of the light can be determined as they pass through the exit slit.

Some spectrometers have a flat mirror called a *grating*, instead of a prism. The surface of a grating is lined with thousands of narrow, parallel grooves. Upon striking a grating, a parallel beam of light spreads out into a spectrum. See DIFFRACTION (Uses of Diffraction).

There are several kinds of spectrometers, and each type has a different device for studying spectra. A *spectroscope* has a telescope for visual observation of a spectrum. A *spectrograph* photographs a spectrum by recording its image on a photographic plate. A *spectrophotometer* scans a spectrum and measures the brightness of each of its colors. Many spectrophotometers have a *photomultiplier tube* that produces an electric current proportional in strength to the brightness of the light being measured. SANDRA M. FABER

See also LIGHT (The Visible Spectrum); MASS SPECTROSCOPY.

SPECTROPHOTOMETER. See COLOR (Measuring Colors); CRIME LABORATORY (Analyzing the Evidence).

SPECTROSCOPE. See SPECTROMETER.

SPECTRUM. See COLOR (Color in Light); LIGHT (The Nature of Light); SPECTROMETER.

SPECULATION. See COMMODITY EXCHANGE.

SPEECH has several definitions. It may mean the act of speaking, the result of speaking or what is spoken, the language of a nation or group of nations, or the dialect peculiar to a region or locality.

The act of speaking includes conversation, public speaking, debating, forum discussion, reading aloud, storytelling, and acting. It uses the *audible code* and the *visible code*, which are the sounds used by the speaker and the movements or gestures of the face, arms, and other parts of the body that are used for emphasis.

The result of speaking is the content and ideas expressed by the act of speaking. In formal speech, it includes the speech at the time it is given, and any written or printed form in which it may appear.

Language or dialect differs among peoples of various nations and groups of nations, and also within a nation. In the United States, the chief dialects are: (1) eastern (roughly, the New England states and New York City); (2) southern (roughly, the regions south of the Potomac and Ohio rivers [except West Virginia], most of Louisiana, and parts of Texas and Arkansas); and (3) general American (roughly, the rest of the United States).

The average child learns to speak by imitating other people. It is important that a child hear proper speech. Parents should note any speech difficulties, such as lisping or stuttering, in their children. If such difficulties occur, parents should take the child to a competent authority on speech problems. Speech clinics can offer helpful advice. W. HAYES YEAGER

Related Articles in WORLD BOOK include:

Communication	Lisping	Speech
Dialect	Pronunciation	Therapy
Language	Public Speaking	Stuttering

SPEECH, FREEDOM OF. See FREEDOM OF SPEECH.

SPEECH PATHOLOGY. See SPEECH THERAPY.

SPEECH READING. See LIP READING.

SPEECH SPECTROGRAM. See VOICEPRINT.

SPEECH THERAPY is the treatment of speech problems and disorders. Experts in the profession of speech therapy work with children and adults whose speech interferes with communication, calls attention to itself, and frustrates both speaker and listener. These specialists, called speech therapists, evaluate and correct defective speech and teach new speech skills. The field of speech therapy is often called speech pathology, and speech therapists are also known as speech pathologists or speech clinicians.

Types and Causes of Speech Defects. Speech therapists divide speech defects into five main types: (1) articulation problems, such as the inability to produce certain sounds; (2) stuttering, *cluttering* (rapid, slurred speech), and other fluency problems; (3) voice disorders, including problems of pitch, voice quality, and volume; (4) delayed speech, characterized by a child's slow language development; and (5) *aphasia*, the partial or total loss of the ability to speak or understand language.

About 6 per cent of the people in the United States have some kind of speech defect. Of that group, about 60 per cent have articulation problems, 12 per cent have fluency difficulties, and 8 per cent have voice disorders. The remaining 20 per cent have delayed speech, aphasia, or multiple speech problems.

Some speech defects result from a physical condition, such as brain damage, cleft palate, a disease of the larynx, or partial or complete deafness. Other speech defects may be caused by a person's environment. For example, a child who receives little encouragement to talk at home may not develop normal speech skills. Severe emotional conflicts, such as pressure to succeed or a lack of love, can also lead to speech difficulties.

Diagnosis. In many schools, speech therapists test students regularly for speech disorders. If students have a speech problem, they receive therapy at the school, or they go to a speech clinic for treatment. Many physicians, psychologists, and teachers refer people with speech defects to such clinics.

Speech therapists diagnose their patients' speech problems and try to learn their causes. They take detailed case histories and give their patients special speech and hearing tests. A patient may need medical or psychological treatment in addition to speech therapy.

Treatment. The speech therapist first gains the confidence of the patient. For the best results, the individual should enjoy being with the therapist and want to follow instructions.

The method of treatment varies from case to case. The speech therapist must consider the age of the patient, the case history, the type of speech disorder, and the information gained during therapy. The therapist talks to the patient's family, teachers, and others who have close contact. The success of the treatment depends largely on the cooperation of these individuals.

Most children develop speech habits until about the age of 8. Thus, when working with a young patient, the therapist uses methods that help stimulate the development of good speech habits. With older patients, the therapist must use corrective measures. First, the patients must be helped to identify their speech problems and to tell the difference between their speech and normal speech. Many therapists use audio and video recording machines. Patients who mispronounce the ''r'' sound may be able to identify their error by listening to themselves on a tape recorder and by watching the movement of their lips and tongue on a video screen. The therapist pronounces the sound correctly, and the patient hears and sees the difference. During the second stage of treatment, the therapist teaches the patient new speech skills. Tongue exercises and speech drills may be used. After the patients have improved their speech, the therapist teaches them to use their skills in everyday situations.

Speech therapy may be given individually or in groups. Therapists put patients in groups if they think that contact with people who have similar defects will bring rapid improvement. Many persons feel more at home and less self-conscious in a group than when alone with a therapist. They also receive encouragement by listening to others and by hearing the improvement of members of the group. Most patients with complex speech problems, such as aphasia, receive individual therapy. Speech specialists feel that individual attention in such cases achieves faster results than does group therapy. Some patients attend both kinds of sessions.

History. People have studied speech and speech problems for more than 2,000 years. However, little progress in the treatment of speech defects occurred until the 1700's and 1800's. During the 1700's, speech specialists worked mostly with the deaf. Successful teachers of the deaf included Thomas Braidwood, a Scottish mathematician. Braidwood taught his students to talk by starting with simple sounds and then progressing to syllables and, finally, words. The 1800's brought much research into the causes and treatment of stuttering. In 1817, Jean Marie Itard, a French physician, declared that stuttering resulted from a weakness of the tongue and larynx nerves. He recommended exercises to cure stutterers. During the late 1800's, Adolf Kussmaul, a German physician, wrote about the physical and psychological causes of stuttering. Today, speech therapists agree that there is no single cause of stuttering.

Speech therapy became a profession in the early

1900's. In Europe, it was associated with the medical profession. During the 1920's, schools for training speech therapists opened in several European countries. In the United States, speech therapy became closely allied with the fields of education, psychology, and speech. Several colleges opened speech clinics during the 1920's. The organization that became the American Speech and Hearing Association was founded in 1925.

During World War II (1939-1945), many servicemen developed speech defects as a result of war injuries. The need for speech rehabilitation services attracted large numbers of men and women to the profession of speech therapy. Many speech clinics opened, and research increased into speech problems and their causes. Since the end of World War II, the field of speech therapy has expanded rapidly.

Careers. Many universities offer undergraduate and graduate training in speech therapy. Men and women who plan a career in speech therapy should have a master's degree. Those who intend to teach in a college or university or to direct a clinic or research program should have a Ph.D.

Undergraduate students interested in speech therapy take courses in biology, linguistics, psychology, physics, introductory speech correction, and related fields. Graduate training covers five main areas: (1) development of speech, hearing, and language; (2) evaluation of speech production, language abilities, and auditory skills; (3) the nature of speech disorders; (4) treatment procedures; and (5) research techniques.

Most speech therapists work in schools. Others are employed by private institutions, including hospitals, rehabilitation centers, specialized community speech and hearing centers, and university speech clinics. Some therapists conduct research in private institutes. An increasing number of speech therapists are entering private practice. Further information about speech therapy can be obtained from the American Speech-Language-Hearing Association, 10801 Rockville Pike, Rockville, Md. 20852.   HUGO H. GREGORY

See also CLEFT PALATE; LISPING; SPEECH; STUTTERING; APHASIA.

SPEED. See METHAMPHETAMINE.

SPEED. See LIGHT (The Speed of Light); MOTION; SOUND (The Speed of Sound); SPEEDOMETER; VELOCITY; AIRPLANE (Measuring Flying Speed).

SPEED READING is a skill designed to increase the amount of information obtained from material read within a certain period of time. Speed reading has enabled many readers of all ages to double the number of words per minute they can read.

Teachers may use various kinds of methods and machines to increase a person's reading rate. One machine flashes a series of words on a screen at increasing speeds. Another limits the time that the reader can spend on each line of words, according to the desired speed. However, reading speed often depends on (1) the difficulty of the reading material and (2) the purpose in reading it.

Many reading experts criticize speed-reading courses. These experts declare that the reading material used in the courses is too easy and that the comprehension tests are invalid.   STANLEY F. WANAT

SPEEDBALL

SPEEDBALL is a team game that combines elements of soccer and basketball. It is usually played by teams of 11 players each on an outdoor field. The players advance the ball down the field by kicking it or passing it. They may also take one step while bouncing the ball, but they cannot run with it. Points are scored when a player kicks or drives the ball with the body through a goal post, when a player kicks the ball over the crossbar of the goal post, or when a player catches a pass behind the goal line. See also BASKETBALL; SOCCER.

SPEEDOMETER, *spee DAHM uh tuhr*, is an instrument that indicates the speed of an automobile or other vehicle. The dial of a speedometer has numbers and a pointer to indicate the vehicle's speed. The speed is shown in both miles per hour and kilometers per hour in some American-built cars. Speedometers in many cars built in other countries show the speed in kilometers per hour (see KILOMETER).

A speedometer is powered by a flexible shaft that connects to a set of gears in the vehicle's transmission (see TRANSMISSION). The gears take into account the tire size and the axle ratio. When the vehicle moves, the gears in the transmission turn a core inside the shaft. The core is attached directly to a permanent magnet that lies near a *speedcup*. The revolving magnet sets up a rotating magnetic field that pulls the speedcup and its attached pointer in the same direction that the magnetic field is turning. A hairspring keeps the speedcup steady. The pointer on the speedcup comes to rest where the hairspring balances the force of the revolving magnet. When the vehicle stops, the hairspring pulls the pointer to zero. When the vehicle speeds up, the magnet increases its pull on the speedcup. This causes the speedometer to register a higher speed.

A device called an *odometer* registers the total distance traveled by a vehicle. Many speedometers have a *trip odometer* that can be reset to zero at the beginning of a trip. Manufacturers design speedometers so that 1,000 revolutions of the flexible shaft will register 1 mile (1.6 kilometers) on the odometer, and 1,000 revolutions a minute will indicate a speed of 60 miles (100 kilometers) per hour. Speedometers require little care. But dirt and excess grease will make them inaccurate. They should be lubricated about every 10,000 miles (16,000 kilometers). HERBERT O. VOGEL

See also PEDOMETER; TACHOMETER.

SPEEDWRITING is the registered trademark for a widely used shorthand system. It employs letters of the alphabet instead of symbols.

In Speedwriting shorthand, all words are written as they sound. Thus, *you* is written *u; are* is *r; eye* is *i*. In addition, a whole syllable may be represented by a letter or a punctuation mark. The letter *a* expresses the sound of *ate*. Thus, *late* is *la; bait* is *ba*. The letter *r* expresses the sound *re*. Thus, *rebate* is *rba*. The capital letter *C* expresses the sound *ch*. Thus, *check* is written *Ck*. A hyphen represents the final sound of *ment*. Thus, *pigment* is *pg-*.

Brief forms or abbreviations represent 295 frequently used words. All other words are written according to principle. For example, a secretary using Speedwriting writes the sentence, *"Your rebate check will reach you in a few days,"* as:

u rba Ck l rC u n a fu ds

The main advantage of Speedwriting shorthand is that the students need not learn any new symbols.

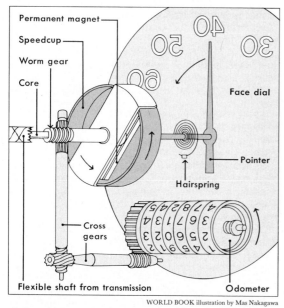

WORLD BOOK illustration by Mas Nakagawa

A Speedometer shows the speed of a vehicle. As the vehicle moves, gears in its transmission turn a core inside a flexible shaft. The core turns a permanent magnet to which it is attached. The magnet rotates a speedcup and pointer on the speedometer dial. The pointer stops when a hairspring balances the force of the magnet. An odometer registers the total distance traveled.

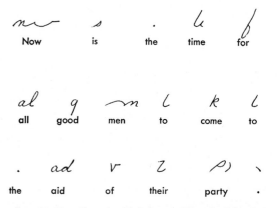

Speedwriting Uses the Alphabet and Standard Symbols.

Therefore, they can take dictation at the rate of about 80 to 100 words per minute after only six to eight weeks of training. They can transcribe their shorthand rapidly and accurately because the notes are in their regular handwriting.

Emma B. Dearborn, a shorthand teacher of Darien, Conn., originated Speedwriting in 1923. BETTY WHITE

See also SHORTHAND (introduction); SHORTHAND MACHINE.

SPEIDEL, *SPY dul*, **HANS** (1895-   ), a German general, served in World War II and became a leader in the postwar West German Army. As chief of staff to

Field Marshal Erwin Rommel in France in 1944, he united the efforts of the German officers fighting against Adolf Hitler. He was important in the series of unsuccessful plots to rid Germany of Hitler. He became commander of the North Atlantic Treaty Organization (NATO) ground forces in Central Europe in 1957. Speidel was born in Metzingen, Württemberg. LESTER B. MASON

SPEKE, JOHN HANNING. See EXPLORATION (table: Explorers of Africa); BURTON, SIR RICHARD FRANCIS; LAKE VICTORIA.

SPELEOLOGY is the scientifc study of caves. Scientists who make such studies are called *speleologists*. Persons who explore and map caves as a hobby are called *spelunkers*. Many cave explorers belong to the National Speleological Society. See also CAVE.

SPELL. See MAGIC (Magic Words).

SPELLING is the way we combine letters to write words. Learning to spell correctly is part of learning a language. The English language has only 26 letters. But the several hundred thousand words of the English language can all be spelled with these 26 letters. Correct spelling, like correct speaking, is more than a sign of a person's education. It helps the person communicate thoughts in writing so others will know quickly and easily what is meant.

Any system of spelling is called *orthography*. The art of spelling and the study of spelling are also called orthography.

To understand how the alphabet works, say out loud the word *bat*. Say the word again, and listen carefully for the three sounds that blend together to make up the spoken word. Now, write the word instead of saying it. First, write the letter that stands for the beginning sound of the word, *b*. Next, write the letter that stands for the middle sound, *a*. Last, write the letter that stands for the final sound, *t*. The letters *b-a-t* repeat in the same order the three original sounds of the spoken word. This is the *spelling* of the word *bat*. Spelling is simply the method of writing letters for spoken sounds. But the historical development of the English language has resulted in many spellings that do not follow the way the words are pronounced.

Learning to Spell

Many persons make spelling more difficult than is necessary. They try to learn their spelling by speaking, as in spelldowns, and forget that writing is the only place in which spelling can possibly matter. They spend time and effort on words that they are unlikely ever to write and whose meanings are vague to them. They emphasize spelling drill and spelling rules, but neglect to work out an effective method of learning to spell new words. They try to learn spelling without developing any interest in the magic of words and the ways people use language to communicate ideas.

Base Words. The first problem in learning to spell is to decide which words are the most important. The average person uses fewer than 25,000 words in speaking, and even fewer in writing. About 2,000 *base words* will satisfy over 90 per cent of the writing needs of the average eighth-grade student. An additional 1,000 base words, or 3,000 in all, will take care of 95 per cent of the writing needs of the average adult. An example of a base word is *danger*. Some words that come from this base include *dangerous* and *endanger*.

The student should first learn to spell the 3,000 base words. Then the student can add the spellings of words used for personal or business reasons. There are two main sources for base words. One is the writing of adults and the other is the writing of children. Many words occur in both groups. Most spelling textbooks include lists of words of both groups.

Thousands of words have been studied to make up the lists of base words. For example, *about* is used by adults and by children as early as the first grade. *Absorb* is used by adults, but is seldom used by children until the eighth grade. *Abrupt* is often used by adults, but is seldom used by young people before high school.

Methods of Study. The difference between good spellers and poor spellers can often be traced to one problem: finding an effective *method* of learning to spell. Good spellers have some method for studying words they want to spell. Poor spellers are frequently helpless with a new word. When they try to learn a new spelling, they usually use poor methods. Here are 10 common steps used by good spellers:

1. Looking at the word.
2. Copying the word.
3. Remembering how the word looks.
4. Listening to the pronunciation of the word.
5. Pronouncing the word.
6. Dividing the word into syllables.
7. Saying the letters of the word in order.
8. Writing the word to get its "feel."
9. Studying the difficult parts of the word.
10. Using the word in a meaningful sentence.

Remembering trick phrases, such as "the princi*pal* is a *pal*," is not a good substitute for an effective learning method. A few spelling tricks, such as remembering "station*ery*" with "pap*er*," may be helpful with particularly hard words. But too many tricks can be confusing.

People who want to improve their spelling can make a combination of the steps listed above that suit them. Few people would use all 10 steps. Once the combination has been selected, it should be tested and changed if necessary. Then the combination can become a regular part of their learning habits. Visualizing the word, or remembering how it looks, should probably be part of everyone's combination. Here is a combination suggested by an authority on spelling:

1. Understand the use, meaning, and pronunciation of the word.
2. Visualize the word.
3. Note the spelling of the word.
4. Write the word carefully and neatly.
5. Check the spelling of the word.
6. Use the word as often as possible in writing.

This combination may not be best for some persons, but it should be useful for most beginners.

Spelling Rules can help improve a person's spelling. But there are often many exceptions to these rules.

Many words come from a base word. For example, the words derived from *develop* include *develops, developed, development, developing,* and *developer*. Each of these new forms is made with a *suffix* added at the end of a word. Here are some rules for spelling suffixes correctly:

1. Drop the final *e* in a word before a suffix beginning with a vowel. For example, *love + ing* is *loving*. An exception is *dyeing*.

absence	benefit	eighth	height	necessary	raise	surgeon
absorption	bicycle	eminent	heinous	night	receipt	sympathize
accommodate	boundary	enough	history	ninth	receive	temperament
ache	bulletin	envelope	hoarse	noticeable	referred	temporary
acquaintance	burglar	everything	hour	occasion	reign	therefore
acquitted	business	exceed	illiterate	occurrence	repeat	tragedy
across	cafeteria	existence	immediately	often	repetition	typical
affidavit	ceiling	expedition	indictment	omitted	rescind	until
again	cemetery	expense	indispensable	optimistic	reservoir	vacuum
aggravate	chauffeur	extraordinary	innocent	origin	restaurant	vegetable
aghast	chocolate	familiar	interfere	original	rheumatism	vengeance
all right	colonel	fascinate	introduce	pageant	rhyme	warrant
ally	column	fasten	laboratory	parliament	ridiculous	wear
already	coming	February	legitimate	perform	sacrifice	week
always	commercial	forfeit	leisure	permanent	schedule	weird
among	committee	forty	library	perseverance	secretary	whether
analysis	confidence	friend	license	picnicking	seize	which
analyze	control	fulfill	literature	pleasant	semester	whole
angel	controversy	genius	magnificent	pneumonia	separate	women
angle	convertible	government	maneuver	possessive	siege	won't
annual	counterfeit	governor	mathematics	prairie	skein	would
answer	courteous	grammar	meant	prejudice	sophomore	writer
appetite	curiosity	gratified	medal	principal	specimen	writing
arctic	dealt	guarantee	millionaire	principle	stationery	written
ascent	desperate	guerrilla	miniature	professor	statistics	wrote
awkward	despise	guess	minute	pursue	strictly	yacht
bachelor	develop	handsome	mortgage	quantity	succeed	
beggar	discipline	hangar	muscle	quiet	sugar	
believe	doctor	harass	mystery	quite	superintendent	

2. Keep the final *e* in a word before a suffix beginning with a consonant. For example, *sure + ly* is *surely*.

3. When a word ends in *y* preceded by a consonant, change the *y* to *i* before adding a suffix (unless the suffix begins with *i*). For example, *plenty + ful* is *plentiful*.

4. When a one-syllable word ends in a consonant preceded by a single vowel, double the consonant before a suffix beginning with a vowel. For example, *run + er* becomes *runner*.

5. When a word has more than one syllable, double the consonant only if the accent of the word is on the last syllable. For example, *admit' + ed* is *admitted*.

Prefixes are added to the beginning of words. Three common prefixes are *dis-*, *mis-*, and *un-*. When they are added to a word beginning with the same letter, there will be two *s*'s or *n*'s. For example, *mis + spell* is *misspell*. When they are added to a word beginning with a different letter, there will be only one *n* or *s*. For example, *un + willing* is *unwilling*.

One of the biggest spelling problems comes from the use of *ei* and *ie*. Some words are spelled with *ei*, such as *receive*. Some words are spelled with *ie*, such as *believe*. A spelling rule to remember is: "Use *i* before *e* except after *c* or when it is sounded like *a*, as in *neighbor* and *weigh*." Exceptions to this rule include *either* and *seize*.

Adding New Words

One way a person can increase the number of words he can spell is to learn the spelling of words derived from a base word. For example, *trust* is a base word. A number of words, such as *mistrust*, *trusting*, and *trustee*, come from this base word. A similar method is to learn the *root meanings* of words. The root of a word is its basic form. For example, the root *port* means *carry*. Knowing this helps to learn the spelling and meaning of such words as *portage*, *import*, *export*, *report*, *porter*, *deport*, *portable*, *comportment*, and *portfolio*.

A more important way of adding new words is to learn the habit of using a dictionary. On seeing a new word, look it up in the dictionary and study its spelling and pronunciation. The dictionary also gives root meanings of words. See DICTIONARY.

Sometimes a word has two or more different spellings. For example, *enrollment* and *enrolment* are both correct spellings. Usually, a dictionary gives the *preferred spelling* first. But this does not mean that the alternate spelling is wrong. There are also many differences between American and British spellings. For example, the American *labor* is the British *labour*. The American *center* is the British *centre*. And the American spelling *connection* is the British *connexion*.

Spelling Demons

Words that people find unusually difficult to spell are called *spelling demons*. They often have an irregular arrangement of letters and need special study. The word *fasten* is a typical spelling demon. Many people who misspell this word write it *fasen*, because the *t* is silent. That is, a person does not sound the *t* in *fasten* when he speaks the word. Another demon is *friend*. People often write it *freind*, because the word has the sound of *e*.

Many spelling demons are *homonyms*, or words that sound alike but have different meanings. For example, *pray* and *prey* are often misspelled because they sound alike. Other homonyms include *bare* and *bear*, *principal* and *principle*, *read* and *red*, and *to*, *too*, and *two*. Failing to pronounce a word accurately and distinctly is a frequent cause of error. The word *government* is an example. If a person says *gov-er-ment*, he may spell the word without the first *n*. Two other examples are *preform* for *perform* and *quanity* for *quantity*.

Simplified Spelling

Many attempts have been made to simplify the spelling of the English language. The aim of most of these plans is to spell a word exactly as it is pronounced. For example, under these plans the word *though* would be spelled *tho*, and the word *knock* would be spelled *nok*.

There have been two chief arguments against such changes. The first is that simplified spelling would destroy the familiar pattern of words and cause confusion. The second is that the pronunciation of words changes continuously. Changes in pronunciation can occur rapidly or slowly. Words would soon become unrecognizable if the spelling were changed to meet each new change in pronunciation. WALTER LOBAN

See also ABBREVIATION; ALPHABET.

SPELLMAN, FRANCIS CARDINAL (1889-1967), was one of the outstanding leaders of the Roman Catholic Church in the United States. His wide acquaintance among church officials throughout the world made his services valuable in special missions for both Presidents Franklin D. Roosevelt and Harry S. Truman. Spellman served as apostolic vicar to the United States armed forces, and made several trips to various battle areas during time of war. Pope Pius XII named him a cardinal in 1946.

United Press Int.
Cardinal Spellman

Spellman was born at Whitman, Mass. He took his college degree at Fordham University, and was ordained a priest in 1916 after studying at the North American College in Rome. His first post was in Boston. From 1925 to 1932 he was in the service of the Papal Secretariat in Rome. He was consecrated a bishop in Rome, and returned to serve as auxiliary bishop of Boston. In 1939, Pope Pius XI named him archbishop of the see of New York. FULTON J. SHEEN

SPELMAN COLLEGE. See UNIVERSITIES AND COLLEGES (table).

SPELUNKER. See SPELEOLOGY.

SPEMANN, *SHPAY mahn,* **HANS** (1869-1941), a German biologist, pioneered in the analysis of embryonic development. Through novel, delicate grafting experiments performed on frog and newt embryos, Spemann discovered *organizers*. These are organ-forming influences exerted on tissues by neighboring embryo parts. He showed that the lens of the eye, for example, is induced to develop by the underlying eye-cup. He won the 1935 Nobel prize for physiology or medicine. Spemann was born in Stuttgart. MORDECAI L. GABRIEL

SPENCER, ANNA GARLIN (1851-1931), was an American reformer, minister, and educator. She supported women's rights, and became active in groups that worked to give women the right to vote. Her book *Woman's Share in Social Culture* (1913) helped call public attention to the ways society can benefit from men and women working together. She also worked to promote world peace, to ban the sale of liquor, and to strengthen family life.

Anna Garlin was born in Attleboro, Mass. She married William H. Spencer, a Unitarian minister, in 1878. In 1891, she became minister of the Bell Street Chapel in Providence, R.I. She was the state's first woman

minister. She later served as associate director of the New York School of Philanthropy, and taught sociology at several universities. LOUIS FILLER

See also WOMAN SUFFRAGE.

SPENCER, HERBERT (1820-1903), was a British philosopher. He is noted for his attempt to work out a philosophy, based on the scientific discoveries of his day, which could be applied to all subjects. In his great work *Programme of a System of Synthetic Philosophy* (1862-1896), Spencer applied his fundamental law—the idea of *evolution* (gradual development)—to biology, psychology, sociology, and other fields.

In his work on biology, Spencer traced the development of life from its lowest recognizable form up to human beings. He believed that the great law of nature is the constant action of forces which tend to change all forms from the simple to the complex. Spencer explained that the mind of human beings has developed in this same way, advancing from the simple automatic responses of lower animals to the reasoning processes of thinking human beings.

Spencer claimed that knowledge was of two kinds: (1) knowledge gained by the individual, and (2) knowledge gained by the race. He said that intuition, or knowledge learned unconsciously, was the inherited knowledge or experience of the race.

Spencer was born in Derby. He was a delicate child. His first interest was biology, but he later turned to engineering. From 1837 to 1846, he worked as an engineer for the London and Birmingham Railway. Later he served as editor of the *Economist*. Spencer left the *Economist* in 1853 to write *Synthetic Philosophy*. He gained a wide reputation as a philosopher, but scientists later proved many of his theories wrong. EUGENE ADAMS

SPENCERIAN WRITING. See HANDWRITING (Later Writing Styles).

SPENDER, SIR STEPHEN (1909-   ), is an English poet. His best-known poetry is a blend of traditional romanticism and thoroughly modern subject matter and attitudes. Thus, he finds in an express train the sort of beauty earlier romantic poets found in waterfalls and sunsets. In "The Express," he wrote:

Ah, like a comet through flame, she moves entranced,
Wrapt in her music no bird song, no, nor bough
Breaking with honey buds, shall ever equal.*

Much of Spender's poetry expresses his radical political views and his compassion for what he sees as the victims of capitalism, such as the children of the poor.

Spender was born in London. He attended Oxford University, and there gained recognition in the 1930's as one of a group of poets led by his friend W. H. Auden. Spender's *Collected Poems* were published in 1954. He also wrote criticism, drama, fiction, translations, and the autobiography *World Within World* (1951). Spender was knighted in 1983. TIM REYNOLDS

*Lines from "The Express" from COLLECTED POEMS 1928-1953 STEPHEN SPENDER, copyright 1955 by Stephen Spender, courtesy Random House, Inc., and Faber & Faber, Ltd.

SPENGLER, *SPEHNG gluhr,* **OSWALD** (1880-1936), was a German philosopher of history. In *The Decline of the West* (1918-1922), he held that the key to history is the law of societies and civilizations, which rise and fall in cycles. Using speculation and insight rather than rigid historical method, he concluded that Western civilization was in a period of decay (see CIVILIZATION [Why Civilizations Rise and Fall]). Spengler was born in Blankenburg. MERLE CURTI

SPENSER, EDMUND (1552?-1599), was a great Elizabethan poet. His epic poem, *The Faerie Queene*, though never finished, is a masterpiece of English literature. Spenser completed only 6 of the 12 *books* (sections) he planned for this work.

Detail of oil portrait by Benjamin Wilson, Pembroke College, Cambridge, England

Edmund Spenser

Spenser's Life. Spenser was born in London. He entered Cambridge University in 1569, and received a B.A. degree in 1573 and an M.A. degree in 1576. At Cambridge, he received a strong background in the classics. He also was influenced there by the anti-Roman Catholic feelings and stern moral beliefs of the Puritans. These influences were later reflected in Spenser's poems. In all his works, he effectively blended themes of paganism with moralistic teachings, and revealed his strong English patriotic feelings. At Cambridge, Spenser became the friend of Gabriel Harvey, one of England's intellectual leaders. Harvey introduced Spenser to the author and courtier Sir Philip Sidney, and both encouraged Spenser in his early writings. Most of these works have disappeared.

In 1580, Spenser became secretary to Lord Grey of Wilton, the governor of Ireland. From 1580 until a month before his death in 1599, Spenser visited England only twice, to supervise publication of *The Faerie Queene.*

Frequent Irish insurrections against English rule kept Spenser so busy that he needed 10 years to write the first three books of *The Faerie Queene*. These books were published in 1590. Spenser dedicated them to Queen Elizabeth, who awarded him a yearly pension.

In 1594, Spenser married Elizabeth Boyle, the daughter of an Irish landowner. They had four children. The second three books of *The Faerie Queene* appeared in 1596. Spenser was appointed sheriff of Cork in 1598, and late that year was sent to England with reports on the Irish uprisings. He became ill in London and died there. A fragment of the seventh book of *The Faerie Queene* was published in 1609.

The Faerie Queene is set in a fairyland, but the characters are realistic. This *allegorical* (symbolic) work is filled with interesting events and scenes of rural Irish life. In writing *The Faerie Queene*, Spenser was influenced by the works of the English poet Geoffrey Chaucer and two Italian epics of the 1500's, Ludovico Ariosto's *Orlando Furioso* and Torquato Tasso's *Jerusalem Delivered*. *The Faerie Queene* also shows the qualities a gentleman should have, reflecting the tradition of the *courtesy book*. The main character in each of the six books gradually develops a desired virtue—holiness, temperance, chastity, friendship, justice, or courtesy. Spenser included both moral and political allegory in

The Faerie Queene. He wrote in a distinctive pattern, now called the *Spenserian stanza*, consisting of eight pentameter lines followed by an alexandrine.

Spenser's Other Poems. Spenser's first major poem, *The Shepheardes Calender* (1579), immediately made his reputation. It consists of 12 *eclogues* (short poems about country life written as dialogues between shepherds). *Colin Clouts Come Home Againe* (1595) shows Spenser's disillusionment with London court life after a visit to England. *Amoretti* (1595) is Spenser's famous *cycle* (series) of 89 love sonnets. *Epithalamion* (1595) has been called literature's greatest poem about marriage. It describes 20 hours in an Irish wedding day, and is a blend of classical and Christian traditions and Irish folklore. THOMAS A. ERHARD

SPERM. See REPRODUCTION.

SPERM WHALE is probably the best known kind of whale. It is also called *cachalot* (pronounced *KASH uh laht*). It became famous in the novel *Moby Dick* by Herman Melville. During the greatest period of U.S. whaling, from the 1830's to the 1860's, Americans hunted sperm whales more than any other kind.

The sperm whale is found in all the oceans. It grows as long as 60 feet (18 meters) and weighs up to 60 short tons (54 metric tons). The huge head makes up a third of the sperm whale's body. The head contains a reservoir of *spermaceti*, a valuable waxy material. *Sperm oil* comes from the head and from the blubber. Another waxy substance, *ambergris*, is found in the intestines of some sperm whales.

Scientific Classification. The sperm whale belongs to the sperm-whale family, Physeteridae. It is genus *Physeter*, species *P. catodon*. RAYMOND M. GILMORE

See also WHALE; SPERMACETI; AMBERGRIS.

SPERMACETI, *SPUR muh SEHT ee* or *SPUR muh SEE tee*, is a waxy material obtained from the enormous head of the sperm whale. The blubber of the sperm whale also contains some of this substance. Spermaceti is used as an ingredient of some salves and face creams. It once was used to make candles. Some spermaceti comes from the bottle-nosed whale and the giant bottle-nosed whale. Spermaceti probably has a function for whales, but no one knows what it is. RAYMOND M. GILMORE

See also SPERM WHALE.

SPERMATOZOA. See FERTILIZATION.

SPERRY, ARMSTRONG (1897-   ), is an American author and illustrator of children's books. Sperry's interest in the sea began in boyhood, and his great-grandfather told him yarns of his adventures as a sea captain in the South Seas. In 1941, Sperry won the Newbery medal for *Call It Courage* (1940).

Sperry was born in New Haven, Conn., and attended the Yale Art School. Later, he studied art in New York City. Sperry lived in the South Pacific for two years. EVELYN RAY SICKELS

SPERRY, ELMER AMBROSE (1860-1930), was an American scientist, inventor, and manufacturer. He is best known for his development of the gyroscope for use in navigation (see GYROSCOPE). Sperry's enterprises included the manufacture of arc lamps in Chicago, of electric railways in Cleveland, Ohio, and gyroscopes in New York City.

Sperry was born in Cortland, N.Y. He studied at the State Normal and Training School and at Cornell University. While still in college, he attracted attention by building an arc lamp with a dynamo to run it. The lamp was much more efficient than any other then used for street lighting, and at the age of 19 Sperry set up his first factory in the city of Chicago where he produced his lamps. Forty years later he returned to the field of lighting and developed the powerful beacon and searchlights later used by many armies and navies. In the meantime, he also developed electrically driven mining equipment, automobiles, and streetcars.

Elmer Sperry

Sperry used the gyroscope in 1911 to develop a new kind of compass for ships. The increase in the amount of steel used in shipbuilding had made magnetic compasses unreliable. Sperry's gyrocompass successfully solved this problem (see GYROCOMPASS). The gyroscopic stabilizer for aircraft, which Sperry devised with his son Lawrence, was successfully demonstrated in 1914. From his gyrocompass, Sperry developed the gyropilot which steers a ship automatically (see AUTOMATIC PILOT). Later he installed giant gyroscopes that could steady the rolling motions of ships. After the United States entered World War I, Sperry developed a number of important instruments for gun control. These inventions increased the effectiveness and range of gunfire and torpedoes. Sperry also produced an aerial torpedo that was controlled by a gyroscope.

Today's naval gunnery methods would be impossible without the inventions that grew out of Sperry's original gyroscope. During World War II it was adapted for use in many complex military instruments, such as naval gunsights. His inventions were equally important for use in navigating aircraft. RICHARD D. HUMPHREY

SPERTUS COLLEGE OF JUDAICA. See UNIVERSITIES AND COLLEGES (table).

SPEYER, DIET OF. See PROTESTANTISM.

SPHAGNUM MOSS. See PEAT MOSS.

SPHALERITE. See ZINC.

SPHENOID BONE. See HEAD.

SPHERE, *sfeer*, is a solid figure that resembles a ball or globe. The name *sphere* comes from a Greek word that means *ball*. In geometry, mathematicians define a sphere as the location in space of all points a certain distance from a fixed point called the *center*. This means that a sphere is a solid figure bounded by a single surface. The surface itself does not have any edges or boundaries. Each point on the surface is the same distance from the center.

Parts. The *radius* of a sphere is the distance from the center to the surface. Or, the radius is any straight line drawn from the center to the surface. The *diameter* of a sphere is twice the radius. Or, the diameter is any straight line, drawn through the center, whose ends stop at the surface. A *secant* is any line that cuts through a sphere. A *chord* is any line that joins two points on the sphere.

If a *plane*, or flat surface, passes through the center of a sphere, the plane produces a *great circle* of the sphere.

The radius and diameter of a great circle are the same as the radius and diameter of the sphere. A great circle cuts a sphere in half. Each half of the sphere is called a *hemisphere*.

Finding the Surface. Here is a formula that you can use for finding the area of the surface of a sphere:

$$\text{Surface} = 4\pi r^2$$

In the formula, the letter r stands for the radius. A convenient value for π is 3.1416. The surface computed with this formula will appear in square units of measure; for example, in square inches or square centimeters.

Finding the Volume. Here is the formula for finding the volume of a sphere:

$$\text{Volume} = \tfrac{4}{3}\pi r^3$$

The letter r stands for the radius. The volume computed with this formula will appear in cubic units; for example, in cubic inches or cubic centimeters.

See also CIRCLE; GEOMETRY (Solid Geometry).

Parts of a Sphere

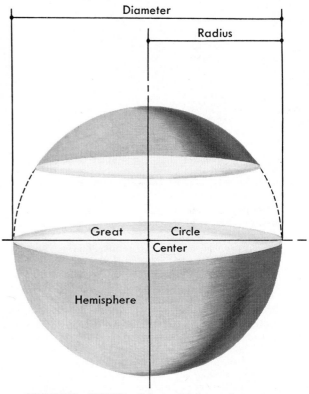

SPHEROID, *SFEER oyd*, is a solid figure that resembles a sphere. It is not perfectly round. The earth is an *oblate* spheroid. It is wider than it is long. A football is a *prolate* spheroid. It is longer than it is wide.

SPHINCTER, *SFIHNGK tuhr*, is a circle of muscle surrounding a body tube. The muscle usually is found near the outlet of the tube. It may be a voluntary or involuntary muscle. The *pyloric sphincter* regulates the flow of food from the stomach into the small intestine. See also MUSCLE. CARL C. FRANCIS

The Great Sphinx at Giza, Egypt, stares with sightless eyes across the desert, as it has for about 4,500 years. The photograph was made after the lower part of the great statue had been uncovered by scientists in 1926. The forefeet are made of huge pieces of stone masonry. In the background are three pyramids—once tombs of Egyptian rulers.

SPHINX, *sfinks*, is an imaginary creature of ancient myths. The Egyptians, Greeks, and peoples of the Near East all had stories about such creatures. According to some stories, the sphinx had a human head, the body of a lion, the tail of a serpent, and the wings of a bird.

The Egyptian Sphinx usually had the head of a man, and the body, legs, feet, and tail of a lion. It had no wings. The sphinx was supposed to represent the god Horus, who guarded temples and tombs. Egyptians made many statues of sphinxes. When Egyptian sculptors made such a statue, they usually made its face resemble the Pharaoh of the time. But some of the statues had heads resembling those of rams and hawks. The Egyptians often lined both sides of avenues with sphinx statues, as in the great temple at Karnak.

The Greek Sphinx usually had the head of a woman. In Greek literature, the sphinx lived on a high rock outside the city of Thebes. When anyone passed by, she asked him a riddle: What has one voice and yet becomes four-footed and two-footed and three-footed? If the traveler could not give the right answer, the sphinx ate him.

When Oedipus passed by on his way to Thebes, the sphinx asked him the riddle. Oedipus replied that the answer was man, because man walks on his hands and feet when he is young, on two feet in the middle of his life, and with a cane or staff in his old age. The sphinx became furious because Oedipus had given the right answer. She howled with rage, and finally threw herself from the rock to her death.

The Great Sphinx that stands at Giza, near the Great Pyramid in Egypt, is one of the most famous monuments in the world. Its head and body are carved from solid rock, and the paws and legs are built of stone blocks. The face is believed to be a portrait of the Egyptian king who built it. No one knows exactly which king built the Sphinx.

The Great Sphinx is 240 feet (73 meters) long and about 66 feet (20 meters) high. The width of its face measures 13 feet 8 inches (4.17 meters). The head has been used as a gunnery target, and desert sands have worn away part of the stone.

Sand covers the base of the Sphinx, and buries it most of the time. Thutmose IV of Egypt cleared it away in the 1400's B.C., and one of the Ptolemies cleared it during Roman times. The sand was cleared away again in 1818, 1886, and 1926.   HOWARD M. DAVIS

See also OEDIPUS.

SPHINX MOTH. See HAWK MOTH.

SPHYGMOMANOMETER. See BLOOD PRESSURE.

SPICA, *SPY kuh,* is a star of the first magnitude in the constellation Virgo. This blue star gives off the light of 2,440 suns. However, Spica is so far away from earth that it takes this light 300 years to reach us. The name *Spica* means *ear of wheat.*

SPICE is the name given to food seasonings made from plants. Spices have a sharp taste and odor. Some spices are valued for their taste, and others for their smell. Common spices include pepper, nutmeg, cloves, ginger, allspice, mace, mustard, and cinnamon.

Spices have little in common except their use. They come from different parts of the various spice plants. For example, cloves come from the bud, cinnamon from the bark, and pepper and nutmeg from the fruit of each plant. Ginger comes from the root and mustard from the seed. Curry, a seasoning made from a combination of spices, is widely used in India.

Spice plants grow in many tropical countries. The Moluccas, or Spice Islands, are a famous source of spices (see MOLUCCAS). Many persons prefer to grow spice plants such as sage, marjoram, thyme, and others in their own gardens. They then dry the plants for later use. Some common spice plants grow indoors if they are placed in pots in sunny windows.

Spices have little food value. But they do increase the appetite and stimulate the organs of digestion. Spices must not be used too generously, for they can sometimes be harmful to the body. Before foods were refrigerated or canned, spices were used to make tainted foods taste better.

Spices have played an important part in history. The cities of Genoa and Venice became powerful because they were at the center of the spice trade with the East. When Columbus and the early explorers set sail across unknown seas, they were interested in discovering an all-water route to the spice lands of the East. Even in modern times, spices are important to us. During World War II, for example, many of the East Indian sources of spice were temporarily destroyed. As a result, U.S. pepper supplies dwindled sharply, and many Americans often had to do without seasoning. Chemists have identified many of the chemical compounds responsible for the taste and odor of spices, and some of these flavors can now be made synthetically. J. B. HANSON

Indonesian Information Office

A Javanese Spice Seller offers a basket of dried mace at the market place.

Related Articles in WORLD BOOK include:

Allspice	Clove	Mustard
Anise	Coriander	Nutmeg
Caper	Curry	Paprika
Capsicum	Dill	Pepper
Caraway	Fennel	Sage
Cardamom	Ginger	Tarragon
Cayenne Pepper	Mace	Thyme
Cinnamon	Marjoram	Turmeric

SPICE ISLANDS. See INDONESIA (The Moluccas).

Avenue of Sphinxes leads to the Great Temple of Amon-Re at Karnak, on the east bank of the Nile River near what is now Luxor, Egypt. King Amenhotep III built the sphinxes about 1400 B.C.

Ewing Galloway

SPIDER

SPIDER is a small, eight-legged animal that spins silk. Spiders are best known for the silk webs they spin. They use their webs to catch insects for food. Even insects that are larger and stronger than spiders cannot escape from the threads of a spider's web.

All spiders spin silk, but some kinds of spiders do not make webs. The bolas spider, for example, spins a single line of silk with a drop of sticky silk at the end. When an insect flies near, this spider swings the line at it and traps the insect in the sticky ball.

All spiders have fangs, and most kinds of spiders have poison glands. A spider's bite can kill insects and other small animals, but few kinds of spiders are harmful to man. In North America, only six kinds of spiders have bites that can harm man. These spiders are the brown recluse spider, the sack spider, the black widow, the brown widow, the red-legged widow, and the varied widow. Of the four "widow" spiders, only the females are known to bite man. Many persons are afraid of spiders. But only hurt or frightened spiders bite human beings.

Spiders are helpful to man because they eat harmful insects. Spiders eat grasshoppers and locusts, which destroy man's crops, and flies and mosquitoes, which carry diseases. Some large spiders eat such animals as mice, birds, lizards, frogs, and fish. Spiders even eat each other. Most female spiders are larger and stronger than male spiders, and often eat the males.

Spiders live anywhere they can find food. They can be seen in fields, woods, swamps, caves, and deserts.

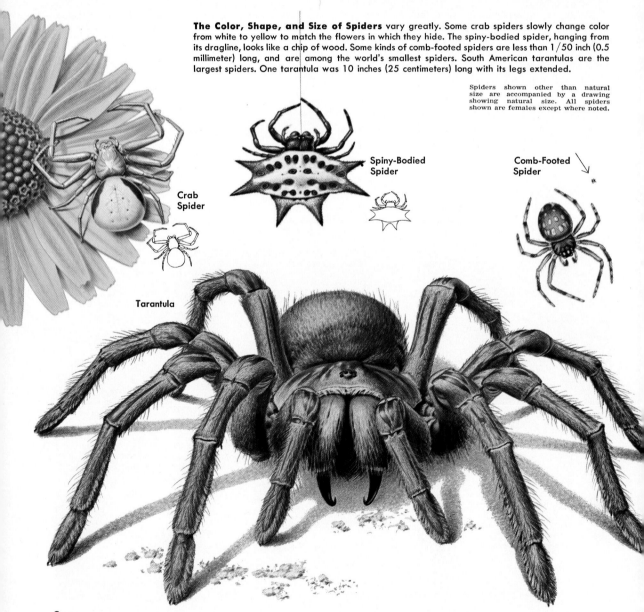

The Color, Shape, and Size of Spiders vary greatly. Some crab spiders slowly change color from white to yellow to match the flowers in which they hide. The spiny-bodied spider, hanging from its dragline, looks like a chip of wood. Some kinds of comb-footed spiders are less than 1/50 inch (0.5 millimeter) long, and are among the world's smallest spiders. South American tarantulas are the largest spiders. One tarantula was 10 inches (25 centimeters) long with its legs extended.

Spiders shown other than natural size are accompanied by a drawing showing natural size. All spiders shown are females except where noted.

Crab Spider

Spiny-Bodied Spider

Comb-Footed Spider

Tarantula

One kind of spider spends most of its life under water. Another kind lives near the top of Mount Everest, the world's highest mountain. Some spiders live in houses, barns, or other buildings. Others live on the outside of buildings—on walls, on window screens, or in the corners of doors and windows.

There are more than 29,000 known kinds of spiders, but scientists believe there may be as many as 50,000 kinds. Some kinds are smaller than the head of a pin. Others are as large as a man's hand. One spider, a South American tarantula, measured 10 inches (25 centimeters) long with its legs extended.

Many persons think spiders are insects. But scientists classify spiders as *arachnids*, which differ from insects in many ways. Spiders have eight legs. Ants, bees, beetles, and other insects have six legs. Most insects have wings and *antennae* (feelers), but spiders do not. Other arachnids include daddy longlegs, scorpions, and mites and ticks.

Scientists classify spiders as either *true spiders* or *tarantulas* according to certain differences in their bodies. Spiders can also be divided according to their way of life. *Web-spinning spiders* spin webs to trap insects. *Hunting spiders* run after insects or lie in wait for them. For the scientific classification of spiders, see the table *Common Kinds of Spiders* at the end of this article.

H. K. Wallace, the contributor of this article, is Chairman of the Department of Zoology at the University of Florida. Willis J. Gertsch, the critical reviewer, is Curator of Arachnids at the American Museum of Natural History, and author of American Spiders. The illustrations throughout this article were prepared for WORLD BOOK *by Jack J. Kunz unless otherwise credited.*

Wolf Spider

Jumping Spider

Spiderlings Travel in Interesting Ways. Baby wolf spiders ride on their mother's back. A young jumping spider travels by *ballooning*. It raises its abdomen so that the wind can pull silk threads from its spinnerets. The wind lifts the spiderling into the air like a balloon on a string.

Black Widow

The Female Black Widow is one of the few spiders that can harm man. It has a red or yellow patch, shaped like an hourglass, on its abdomen.

The Bolas Spider does not trap insects in a web. Instead, it spins a line of silk with a drop of sticky silk at the end. The spider swings the line at an insect and traps it in the sticky ball.

Bolas Spider

The Ogre-Faced Stick Spider traps flying insects in a web of sticky silk. With its four front legs, this spider stretches the web to several times its normal size and captures the insect.

Ogre-Faced Stick Spider

The Purse-Web Spider extends the silk lining of its burrow up the side of a tree to make a tube-shaped web. The spider bites through the tube to seize insects crawling over its web.

Purse-Web Spider

J. KUNZ

613

Spiders may be short and fat, long and thin, round, oblong, or flat. Their legs are short and stubby, or long and thin. Most spiders are brown, gray, or black. But some are as beautifully colored as the loveliest butterflies. Many of these spiders are so small that their colors can be seen only with a microscope.

A spider has no bones. Its tough skin serves as a protective outer skeleton. Hairs, humps, and *spines* (bristles of skin) cover the bodies of most spiders.

A spider's body has two main sections: (1) the *cephalothorax*, which consists of the head joined to the *thorax* (chest); and (2) the *abdomen*. Each of these sections has *appendages* (attached parts). A thin waist called the *pedicel* connects the cephalothorax and the abdomen.

Eyes. A spider's eyes are on top and near the front of its head. The size, number, and position of the eyes vary among different species. Most species have eight eyes, arranged in two rows of four each. Other kinds have six, four, or two eyes. Some species of spiders that live in caves or other dark places have no eyes at all.

Mouth. A spider's mouth opening is below its eyes. Spiders do not have chewing mouth parts, and they eat only liquids. Various appendages around the mouth opening form a short "straw" through which the spider sucks the body fluid of its victim. The spider can eat some of the solid tissue of its prey by *predigesting* it. To do this, the spider sprays digestive juices on the tissue. The powerful juices dissolve the tissue. By predigestion and sucking, a large tarantula can reduce a mouse to a small pile of hair and bones in about 36 hours.

Chelicerae are a pair of appendages that the spider uses to seize and kill its prey. The chelicerae are above the mouth opening and just below the spider's eyes. Each chelicera ends in a hard, hollow, pointed claw, and these claws are the spider's fangs. An opening in the tip of the fang connects with the poison glands. When a spider stabs an insect with its chelicerae, poison flows into the wound and paralyzes or kills the victim.

The fangs of tarantulas point straight down from the head, and the poison glands are in the chelicerae. In

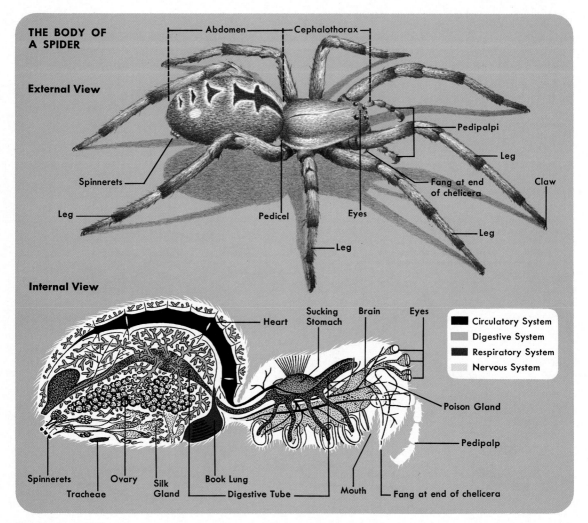

THE BODY OF A SPIDER

External View

Abdomen — Cephalothorax

Pedipalpi

Leg

Spinnerets

Fang at end of chelicera

Claw

Leg

Pedicel

Eyes

Leg

Leg

Internal View

Heart

Sucking Stomach — Brain — Eyes

Circulatory System
Digestive System
Respiratory System
Nervous System

Poison Gland

Pedipalp

Spinnerets

Tracheae

Ovary

Silk Gland

Book Lung

Digestive Tube

Mouth

Fang at end of chelicera

true spiders, the fangs point crosswise, and the poison glands extend back into the cephalothorax.

Spiders also crush their prey with their chelicerae. Some species use their chelicerae to dig burrows in the ground as nests.

Pedipalpi are a pair of appendages that look like small legs. One pedipalp is attached to each side of the spider's mouth, and they form the sides of the mouth opening. Each pedipalp has six *segments* (parts). In most kinds of spiders, the segment closest to the body bears a sharp plate with jagged edges. The spider uses this plate to cut and crush its food. In male spiders, the last segment of each pedipalp bears a reproductive organ.

Legs. A spider has four pairs of legs, which are attached to its cephalothorax. Each leg has seven segments. In most kinds of spiders, the last segment has two or three claws at the tip. A pad of hairs called a *scopula* may surround the claws. The scopula helps the spider cling to such surfaces as ceilings or walls.

When a spider walks, the first and third leg on one

side of its body move with the second and fourth leg on the other side. Muscles in the legs make the legs bend at the joints. But spiders have no muscles to extend their legs. The pressure of the blood in their bodies makes their legs extend. If a spider's body does not contain enough fluids, its blood pressure drops. The legs draw up under the body, and the animal cannot walk.

Spinnerets are short, fingerlike organs with which the spider spins silk. They are attached to the rear of the abdomen. Most kinds of spiders have six spinnerets, but some have four or two. The tip of a spinneret is called the *spinning field*. The surface of each spinning field is covered by as many as a hundred *spinning tubes*. Through these tubes, liquid silk flows from silk glands in the spider's abdomen to the outside of its body. The silk then hardens into a thread.

Respiratory System. Spiders as a group have two kinds of breathing organs—*tracheae* and *book lungs*. Tracheae, found in almost all kinds of true spiders, are small tubes which carry air throughout the body. Air enters the tubes through the *spiracle*, an opening in front of the spinnerets in most kinds of true spiders.

Book lungs are in cavities in the spider's abdomen. Air enters the cavities through a tiny slit on each side and near the front of the abdomen. Each lung consists of 15 or more thin, flat folds of tissue arranged like the pages of a book. The sheets of tissue contain many blood vessels. As air circulates between the sheets, oxygen passes into the blood. Tarantulas have two pairs of book lungs. Most true spiders have one pair.

Circulatory System. The blood of spiders contains many pale blood cells and is transparent. The heart, a long, slender tube in the abdomen, pumps the blood to all parts of the body. As the blood circulates, it flows through open passages instead of closed tubes, such as those of the human body. If the spider's skin is broken, the blood quickly drains from its body. The animal's tough skin often prevents this from happening.

Digestive System. A digestive tube extends the length of the spider's body. In the cephalothorax, the tube is larger and forms a *sucking stomach*. When the stomach's powerful muscles contract, the size of the stomach increases. This causes a strong sucking action that pulls the food through the stomach into the intestine. Juices in the digestive tube break the liquid food into particles small enough to pass through the walls of the intestine into the blood. The food is then distributed to all parts of the body.

Nervous System. The central nervous system of a spider is in the cephalothorax. It includes the brain, and controls the activities of all other parts of the body.

A spider gains knowledge of its surroundings through its sense organs. Most kinds of hunting spiders can see better than web-spinning spiders. But all spiders can see only a short distance. The sense of touch is the most highly developed of the animal's senses. Special hairs on its body serve as organs of touch and perhaps as organs of hearing and smell. Each hair contains a nerve. These nerves send messages to the brain that tell the spider how to respond to changes in its surroundings. Spiders can easily sense vibrations and the presence of certain chemicals.

WORLD BOOK illustrations by Tom Dolan

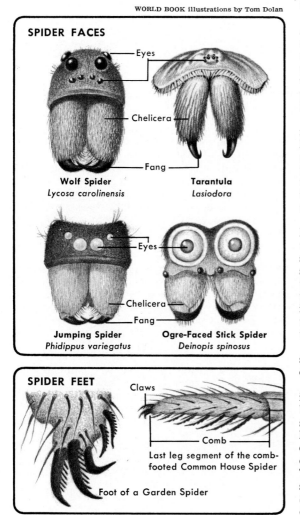

SPIDER FACES

Eyes

Chelicera

Fang

Wolf Spider
Lycosa carolinensis

Tarantula
Lasiodora

Eyes

Chelicera

Fang

Jumping Spider
Phidippus variegatus

Ogre-Faced Stick Spider
Deinopis spinosus

SPIDER FEET

Claws

Comb

Last leg segment of the comb-footed Common House Spider

Foot of a Garden Spider

Jerome Wexler, NAS

Many Kinds of Spiders Spin Bands of Silk to tie up insects caught in webs. The orange garden spider turns its victim over and over, wrapping it in silk from the spider's spinnerets.

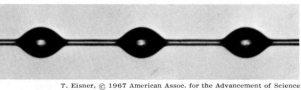

T. Eisner, © 1967 American Assoc. for the Advancement of Science

A Thread of Sticky Silk, enlarged more than 20 times, looks like a beaded necklace. Insects stick to the thread. Oil on the spider's body prevents the silk from sticking to the spider.

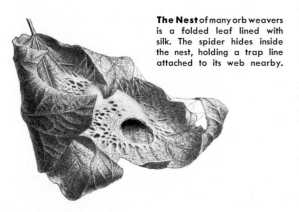

The Nest of many orb weavers is a folded leaf lined with silk. The spider hides inside the nest, holding a trap line attached to its web nearby.

How Spiders Make Silk. Spiders as a group have seven kinds of silk glands. No species of spider has all seven kinds. All spiders have at least three kinds of silk glands, and most species have five. Each kind of gland produces a different type of silk that the spider uses for a particular purpose.

Some silk glands produce a liquid silk that becomes dry outside the body. Other glands produce a sticky silk that stays sticky.

The spinnerets, which spin the silk, work somewhat like the fingers of a hand. A spider can stretch out each spinneret, pull it back in, and even squeeze them all together. Using different spinnerets, a spider can combine silk from different silk glands and produce a very thin thread or a thick, wide band.

The animal also can make a sticky thread that looks like a beaded necklace. To do this, the spider pulls out a dry thread that is heavily coated with sticky silk. Using the claws of one of its hind legs, the spider stretches this thread and lets go of it with a snap. This action causes the liquid silk to form a series of tiny beads along the thread. A spider uses beaded threads in its web to trap jumping or flying insects.

Some kinds of spiders have another spinning organ called the *cribellum*. It is an oval plate that lies almost flat against the abdomen, in front of the spinnerets. Hundreds of spinning tubes cover the spinning field of the cribellum. These tubes produce extremely thin threads of sticky silk.

Spiders with a cribellum also have a special row of curved hairs called a *calamistrum* on their hind legs. Spiders use the calamistrum to comb together dry silk from the spinnerets and sticky silk from the cribellum. This combination forms a flat, ribbonlike silk structure called a *hackled band*. Spiders use hackled bands in their webs, along with the other silk they spin.

How Spiders Use Silk. Spiders, including those that do not spin webs, depend on silk in so many ways that they could not live without it. Wherever a spider goes, it spins a silk thread behind itself. This thread is called a *dragline*. The dragline is sometimes called the spider's "lifeline" because the animal often uses it to escape from enemies. If danger threatens a spider in its web, it can drop from the web on its dragline and hide in the grass. Or the spider can simply hang in the air until the danger has passed. Then it climbs back up the dragline into its web. Hunting spiders use their draglines to swing down to the ground from high places.

Spiders also use silk to spin tiny masses of sticky threads called *attachment discs*. They use the discs to attach their draglines and webs to various surfaces.

Each kind of spider builds a different type of silk nest as its home. Some spiders line a folded leaf with silk to make a nest. Others dig burrows in the ground and line them with silk. Still others build nests in the center of their webs.

Many web-spinning spiders spin sticky bands or wide sheets of silk while capturing their prey. The orb weavers wrap their victims in sheets like mummies so they cannot escape.

The female spider of most species encloses her eggs in an *egg sac*, a bag made of a special kind of silk.

Hunting spiders creep up on their prey or lie in wait and pounce on it. Most kinds of hunters have large eyes and can see their prey from a distance. The powerful chelicerae of hunting spiders help them overpower their victims. Some hunting spiders spin simple webs that stretch out along the ground and stop insects. These spiders are grouped as hunters because they run after the insects that land in their webs.

Jumping Spiders creep up and pounce on their prey. They have short legs, but they can jump more than 40 times the length of their bodies. Jumping spiders are the most colorful of all spiders. Many thick, colored hairs cover their bodies. Most of the males have bunches of brightly colored hairs on their first pair of legs.

Water Spiders are the only spiders that live most of their life underwater. This spider breathes underwater from air bubbles that it holds close to its body. Its underwater nest is a silk web shaped like a small bell. The spider fills the web with air bubbles, which gradually push all the water out of the bell. The animal can live on this air for several months. Water spiders are found only in Europe and parts of Asia. See ANIMAL (How Animals Breathe [picture]).

Tarantulas are the world's largest spiders. The biggest ones live in the South American jungles. Great numbers of tarantulas also are found in the southwestern United States.

Many kinds of tarantulas dig burrows as nests. The *trap-door spider* covers the entrance to its burrow with a lid (see TRAP-DOOR SPIDER). A California tarantula builds a *turret* (small tower) of grass and twigs at the entrance to its burrow. It sits on the tower and watches for insects moving in the nearby grass. See ANIMAL (Animals of the Tropical Forests [picture]); TARANTULA.

Fisher Spiders live near water and hunt water insects, small fish, and tadpoles. These spiders have large bodies and long, thin legs. But because of their light weight, they can walk on the water without sinking. They are sometimes called *nursery-web weavers* because the female builds a special web for her young.

Crab Spiders have short, wide bodies and look like small crabs. They can walk backwards and sidewards as easily as crabs do. Some brightly colored crab spiders hide in flowers and capture bees and butterflies. A few kinds of crab spiders can disguise themselves by changing the color of their bodies to match the color of the flower blossom. *Huntsman spiders* are large, tan crab spiders of the southern United States.

Funnel-Web Spiders hunt only within large webs that they spin in tall grass or under rocks or logs. The bottom of the web is shaped like a funnel and serves as the spider's hiding place. The top part of the web forms a large sheet of silk spread out over grass or soil. When an insect lands on the sheet, the spider runs out of the funnel and pounces on the victim.

Wolf Spiders are excellent hunters. Many kinds have large, hairy bodies, and run swiftly in search of food. Others look and act like other types of spiders. For example, some live near water and resemble fisher spiders in appearance and habits. Others live in burrows, or spin funnel-webs. See ANIMAL (Animals of the Mountains [picture]).

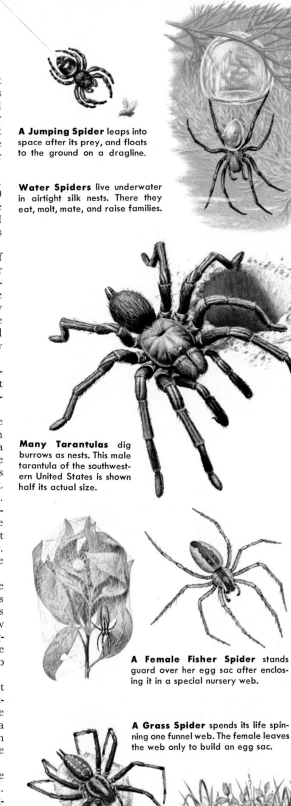

A Jumping Spider leaps into space after its prey, and floats to the ground on a dragline.

Water Spiders live underwater in airtight silk nests. There they eat, molt, mate, and raise families.

Many Tarantulas dig burrows as nests. This male tarantula of the southwestern United States is shown half its actual size.

A Female Fisher Spider stands guard over her egg sac after enclosing it in a special nursery web.

A Grass Spider spends its life spinning one funnel web. The female leaves the web only to build an egg sac.

The Common House Spider spins a loosely-woven tangled web of dry silk, held in place by long threads attached to walls or other supports. The center of the web forms a large insect trap.

Web-spinning spiders, like hunting spiders, live in caves, in grass or shrubs, or in trees. They cannot catch food by hunting because of their poor vision. Instead, they spin webs in the air to trap flying insects. A web-spinning spider does not become caught in its own web. When walking across the web, it grasps the silk lines with a special hooked claw on each foot.

Tangled-Web Weavers spin the simplest type of web. It consists of a shapeless jumble of threads attached to a support, such as the corner of a ceiling. The *cobwebs* found in houses are tangled webs that have collected dust and dirt.

The *cellar spiders* spin tangled webs in dark, empty parts of buildings. One cellar spider that looks like a daddy longlegs has thin legs more than 2 inches (5 centimeters) long.

The *comb-footed spiders* spin a tangled web with a tightly woven sheet of silk in the middle. The sheet serves as an insect trap and as the spider's hideout. These spiders get their name from the comb of hairs on their fourth pair of legs. They use the comb to throw liquid silk over an insect and trap it. The *black widow* is a comb-footed spider (see BLACK WIDOW).

Some spiders spin a tangled web containing a hackled band of dry and sticky silk. The *ogre-faced stick spider*

The Platform Spider spins a silk sheet below a net of criss-crossed threads. Flying insects hit the net and fall onto the sheet.

The Bowl-and-Doily Spider spins a bowl-shaped sheet above a flat sheet of silk. Threads above the bowl stop flying insects.

The Triangle Spider spins a triangular web between two twigs. The web's *hackled bands* of dry and sticky silk trap insects.

The Filmy Dome Spider spins a tangle of threads around a dome-shaped silk sheet, and hangs under the dome. Insects that drop onto the dome are pulled through the webbing by the spider.

The Labyrinth Spider spins a tangled web as its hiding place and an orb web as an insect trap. Several trap lines extend from the center of the orb web to the tangled web.

spins a web that is made up largely of hackled bands. The web is only about as large as a postage stamp. This spider spins a structure of dry silk to hold the sticky web in place. With its four rear legs, the spider hangs upside down from the dry silk. It holds the sticky web with its four front legs. When an insect flies near, the spider stretches the sticky web to several times its normal size and captures the insect.

Sheet-Web Weavers weave flat sheets of silk between blades of grass or branches of shrubs or trees. These spiders also spin a net of crisscrossed threads above the sheet web. When a flying insect hits the net, it bounces into the sheet web. The spider, which hangs upside down beneath the web, quickly runs to the insect and pulls it through the webbing. Sheet webs last a long time because the spider repairs any damaged parts. *Dwarf spiders*, which are less than $\frac{1}{20}$ inch (1.3 millimeters) long, spin small, square sheet webs near rivers and lakes.

Some sheet-web weavers spin two separate sheets as a web. The spider hangs upside down under the top sheet. The sheet beneath the spider probably protects it from attack from below.

Orb Weavers build the most beautiful and complicated of all webs. They weave their round webs in open areas, often between tree branches or flower stems. Threads of dry silk extend from an orb web's center like the spokes of a wheel. Coiling lines of sticky silk connect the spokes, and serve as an insect trap.

Some orb weavers lie in wait for their prey in the center of the web. Others attach a *trap line* to the center of the web. The spider hides in its nest near the web, and holds on to the trap line. When an insect lands in the web, the line vibrates. The spider darts out and captures the insect. Many orb weavers spin a new web every night. It takes them about an hour. Other orb weavers repair or replace damaged parts of their webs.

SPINNING AN ORB WEB

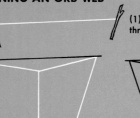

(1) The web hangs from a thread called a *bridge line*.

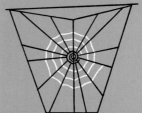

(2) *Foundation lines* limit the area in which the spider spins the round insect trap.

(3) Threads extend from the web's *hub* (center) like the spokes of a wheel.

(4) A line of dry silk coils out from the hub and holds the spokes in place.

(5) The spider spins a coiling line of sticky silk as the trap, and removes the dry line.

WORLD BOOK diagram

Beautiful Orb Weavers include the silk spider, shown half its actual size at the left; the marbled spider, *above right;* and the arrowhead-shaped micrathena, *below right.*

The Orange Garden Spider spins a large orb web that may measure more than 2 feet (61 centimeters) across. The spider spins a zigzagging band of silk across the middle of the web.

Each species of spider has a different life story. Many kinds of spiders live only about a year. Large wolf spiders live several years. Certain kinds of tarantulas live the longest—more than 20 years. Spiders become adults at different times of the year. Some mature in the fall, and then mate and die during the winter. Others live through the winter, mate in the spring, and then die.

Courtship and Mating. As soon as a male spider matures, it seeks a mate. The female spider may mistake the male for prey and eat him. But most male spiders perform courtship activities that identify themselves and attract the females. The male of some species vibrates the threads of the female's web. Some male hunting spiders wave their legs and bodies in an unusual courtship dance.

Before mating, a male spider spins a silk platform. He deposits a drop of sperm from his abdomen onto the platform. Then he fills each of his pedipalpi with sperm. After mating, the female stores the sperm in her body. When she lays her eggs, several weeks or even months later, the eggs are fertilized by the sperm.

Eggs. The number of eggs that a spider lays at one time varies with the size of the animal. A female of average size lays about 100 eggs. Some of the largest spiders lay more than 2,000 eggs. One tiny female cave spider lays only one egg at a time. It is about a fourth the size of her body.

In most species, the mother spider encloses the eggs in a silken egg sac. The sac of each species differs in

Courtship Dances are performed by many male hunting spiders to attract mates. The jumping spider *Peckhamia noxiosa, left,* raises its abdomen into the air and sways from side to side. The wolf spider *Pardosa milvina, right,* waves its front pair of legs.

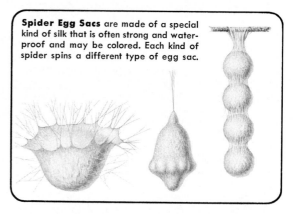

Spider Egg Sacs are made of a special kind of silk that is often strong and waterproof and may be colored. Each kind of spider spins a different type of egg sac.

size and shape. Some species that lay large numbers of eggs make several sacs, and some spin them together into a long chain.

In many species, the mother dies soon after making the egg sac. In other species, she stays with the eggs

---

COMMON KINDS OF SPIDERS

Each of the spiders listed in this table is shown in the pictures with this article.

TRUE SPIDERS

Comb-Footed Spiders (*Theridiidae*)

  Black Widow (*Latrodectus mactans*)
  Comb-Footed Spider (*Mysmena incredula*)
  Common House Spider (*Achaearanea tepidariorum*)

Crab Spiders (*Thomisidae*)

  Crab Spider (*Misumena vatia*)

Fisher Spiders (*Pisauridae*)

  Fisher Spider (*Pisaurina mira*)

Funnel-Web Spiders (*Agelenidae*)

  Grass Spider (*Agelena naevia*)
  Water Spider (*Argyroneta aquatica*)

Hackled-Band Orb Weavers (*Uloboridae*)

  Triangle Spider (*Hyptiotes cavatus*)

Jumping Spiders (*Salticidae*)

  Jumping Spider (*Peckhamia noxiosa*)
  Jumping Spider (*Phidippus variegatus*)

Ogre-Faced Stick Spiders (*Deinopidae*)

  Ogre-Faced Stick Spider (*Deinopis spinosus*)

Orb Weavers (*Argiopidae*)

  Arrowhead-Shaped Micrathena (*Micrathena sagittata*)
  Bolas Spider (*Mastophora cornigera*)

Labyrinth Spider (*Metepeira labyrinthea*)
Marbled Spider (*Araneus marmoreus*)
Orange Garden Spider (*Argiope aurantia*)
Silk Spider (*Nephila clavipes*)
Spiny-Bodied Spider (*Gasteracantha cancriformis*)

Sheet-Web Weavers (*Linyphiidae*)

  Bowl-and-Doily Spider (*Frontinella pyramitela*)
  Filmy Dome Spider (*Linyphia marginata*)
  Platform Spider (*Microlinyphia mandibulata*)

Wolf Spiders (*Lycosidae*)

  Wolf Spider (*Lycosa punctulata*)
  Wolf Spider (*Pardosa milvina*)

TARANTULAS

Purse-Web Spiders (*Atypidae*)

  Purse-Web Spider (*Atypus abboti*)

Tarantulas (*Theraphosidae*)

  Tarantula of South America (*Lasiodora*)
  Tarantula of the United States (*Aphonopelma chalcodes*)

Spiders belong to the phylum *Arthropoda,* and to the class *Arachnida.* They make up the spider order *Araneae.* True spiders belong to the suborder *Labidognatha.* Tarantulas belong to the suborder *Orthognatha.*

To learn how spiders fit into the animal kingdom, see ANIMAL (table: A Classification of the Animal Kingdom).

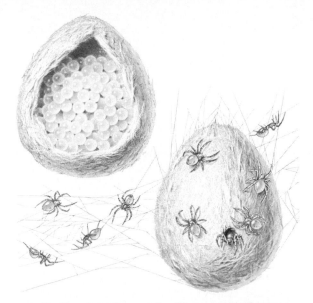

Spiderlings hatch from pearly white eggs inside the egg sac. One by one, they leave the egg sac through a tiny hole that they tear in its side. They immediately begin spinning draglines. Many spiderlings then travel to other areas, usually by ballooning.

Spiderlings hatch inside the egg sac and remain there until warm weather arrives. If the eggs are laid in autumn, the spiderlings stay quietly inside their egg sac until spring. After leaving the egg sac, the spiderlings immediately begin spinning draglines.

Many spiderlings travel to other areas. To do this, a spiderling climbs to the top of a fence post or some other tall object and tilts its spinnerets up into the air. The moving air pulls silk threads out of the spinnerets. Then the wind catches the threads and carries the spiderling into the air like a balloon on a string. This unusual way of traveling is called *ballooning*. A spider may travel a great distance by ballooning. Sailors more than 200 miles (320 kilometers) from land have seen ballooning spiders floating through the air.

Spiderlings *molt* (shed their outer skin) several times while they are growing. A new, larger skin replaces the skin that has grown too tight. Most kinds of spiders molt from five to nine times before they reach adulthood. Tarantulas molt more than 20 times, but dwarf spiders molt only a few times.

Enemies of spiders include snakes, frogs, toads, lizards, birds, fish, and many other animals that also eat insects. Even some insects eat spiders. The wasp, for example, is one of the spider's worst enemies (see WASP [Solitary Wasps]). One group of spiders called *pirate spiders* eats only other spiders. Pirate spiders do not spin webs, but creep into the webs of other spiders and kill them.   H. K. WALLACE

Critically reviewed by WILLIS J. GERTSCH

until they hatch. Some spiders hang the sac in a web. Others attach the sac to leaves or plants. Still others carry it with them. The female wolf spider attaches the sac to her spinnerets, and drags it behind her.

SPIDER / Study Aids

Questions

What is ballooning?
What are some of the ways in which spiders use silk?
How do tarantulas differ from true spiders?
How does an orb weaver know that an insect has landed in its web?
How do spiders differ from insects?
How many kinds of spiders in the United States can harm man?
How does a female wolf spider carry her egg sac?

What is the only food of pirate spiders?
Why are spiders valuable to man?
Why is a dragline often called a spider's "lifeline"?

SPIDER MONKEY is a large monkey noted for using its tail as an extra limb. It can hang by its tail and even pick up objects by curling it around them. This monkey sometimes hangs upside down, with all four limbs and its tail grasping a branch. It resembles a huge spider in this position. These monkeys often use their arms to swing from branch to branch. Only small Asian apes called gibbons can swing through the trees faster.

Spider monkeys are found in the tropical forests of the Western Hemisphere, from central Mexico to central Bolivia. They live in groups of from 2 to 100 monkeys and spend most of their time in high branches, where they eat fruits and nuts. Various species have black, brown, golden, reddish, or tan fur. Adult spider monkeys weigh from 10 to 15 pounds (5 to 7 kilograms) and grow almost 2 feet (61 centimeters) long, not including the tail. Spider monkeys, unlike almost all other monkeys, have only four fingers and no thumb.

Scientific Classification. Spider monkeys belong to the New World monkey family, *Cebidae*. They make up the genus *Ateles*. A common species of spider monkey is *A. paniscus*.   NEIL C. TAPPEN

See also ANIMAL (Animals of the Tropical Forests [picture]); MONKEY (picture).

SPIDERWORT, *SPI der WURT*, is the common name for a group of mostly tropical plants. Some of them are ornamental plants. The leaves of the spiderworts are often grasslike and sometimes striped. The flowers may be blue, purple, or white. They are fragile and may dissolve into watery jelly. They have weak stems.

Some kinds of spiderworts grow erect, and some run along the ground. The *common spiderwort* is the best-known of the erect plants. An example of creeping spiderwort is the *wandering Jew* (see WANDERING JEW). The spiderworts are perennials.

Scientific Classification. Spiderworts belong to the spiderwort family, *Commelinaceae*. The common spiderwort is genus *Tradescantia*, species *T. virginiana*. The wandering Jew is *Zebrina pendula*. PAUL C. STANDLEY

SPIELBERG, STEVEN (1947-   ), is an American motion-picture director. Spielberg directed two popular action films—*Jaws* (1975) and *Raiders of the Lost Ark* (1981). Both movies reflect Spielberg's superb technical knowledge of filmmaking and celebrate his love for the heroic, romantic adventure movies he enjoyed as a child. Spielberg also wrote and directed *Close Encounters of the Third Kind* (1977), and he directed and was co-producer of *E.T.: The Extra-Terrestrial* (1982). These films feature imaginative special effects and a warm, positive vision of friendly and intelligent life visiting from space.

Spielberg was born in Cincinnati. As a teen-ager, he began writing and directing his own films. In 1969, he won awards for a short movie, *Amblin'* (1969), and then began directing television programs for Universal Studios in Los Angeles. He directed a TV film, *Duel* (1972), that won critical praise in the United States and Europe. Spielberg's first theater film was *Sugarland Express* (1974). He also directed *1941* (1979) and was producer and co-writer of *Poltergeist* (1982). CHARLES CHAMPLIN

SPIKENARD, *SPYK nuhrd*, or NARD, is a plant related to the valerians. It comes from India and yields a costly perfume. The root is shaped like an ear of corn. A cluster of thick stems about 2 inches (5 centimeters) long grows from the top of the root. This part is the main source of the perfume. The *American spikenard*, or *Indian root*, is an aromatic herb that grows in southern Canada and the northern United States.

Scientific Classification. The oriental, or "true," spikenard belongs to the valerian family, *Valerianaceae*. It is genus *Nardostachys*, species *N. jatamansi*. The American spikenard belongs to the ginseng family, *Araliaceae*. It is *Aralia racemosa*. HAROLD NORMAN MOLDENKE

SPINA BIFIDA, *SPY nuh BY fuh duh*, is a spinal defect that is present at birth. The term generally refers to the severest form of the condition, *spina bifida manifesta*, also known as *myelomeningocele*.

The spine encloses and protects the spinal cord, a tubelike bundle of nerves. In spina bifida manifesta, several vertebrae in the spine do not develop completely and cannot enclose the spinal cord. A section of the cord sticks out of the resulting gap in the spine, creating a bulge in the victim's back. This section of the cord remains undeveloped, as do the nerves that connect it to the lower part of the body.

Physicians do not know what causes spina bifida manifesta, and it cannot be cured. With proper medical treatment, however, many victims can lead independent, productive lives. About 8,000 babies with the defect are born yearly in the United States.

Spina bifida manifesta involves a number of disabilities that vary in severity among its victims. These people have a lack of feeling in the lower part of the body. They cannot control their bowel and bladder functions, and they suffer paralysis of the legs. Most of them also have *hydrocephalus*, an enlargement of the head. Hydrocephalus is caused by excess cerebrospinal fluid in the brain and may produce mild to moderate mental retardation (see CEREBROSPINAL FLUID).

Treatment of spina bifida manifesta requires a variety of techniques for the different problems involved. The bulge in a victim's back can be eliminated by surgery in which the spinal cord is buried deeper below the skin. Hydrocephalus can be controlled by an operation. A surgeon inserts a tube into the *cerebral ventricles*, which are cavities in the brain in which cerebrospinal fluid collects. The excess cerebrospinal fluid flows through this *shunt* (artificial channel) from the brain into other body cavities, where it is harmlessly absorbed. Physical therapy can strengthen leg muscles and enable many victims to eventually walk unaided or with the aid of braces or crutches. However, patients with extremely severe cases may require wheelchairs. ANGELES BADELL-RIBERA

SPINACH is a popular garden vegetable. It is a slow-growing annual plant that produces a thick cluster of wide, succulent leaves. People eat the leaves raw or cooked. Spinach is related to beets, Swiss chard, and the common weed lamb's-quarters.

Spinach comes from southwest Asia. The Persians once used it as medicine. The English cultivated it as early as 1500, and Americans grew it during the colonial period. Spinach once was a special dish in Europe.

Spinach grows rapidly and matures in the cool season. It is easy to grow. The plant grows best in a fertile, sandy loam. It does not grow well in an acid soil. It withstands frost, but not heat. Gardeners sow the seeds in the spring and harvest the crop in about

William M. Harlow
Spinach Leaves

three months. Another crop can be grown in the fall.

Spinach is high in vitamin value and in minerals. It is an excellent source of vitamins A and C, and a fair source of vitamins of the B complex. It also has a large amount of fiber, and acts as a mild laxative.

Scientific Classification. Spinach plants belong to the goosefoot family, *Chenopodiaceae*. They are genus *Spinacea*, species *S. oleracea*. ERVIN L. DENISEN

See also LAMB'S-QUARTERS.

SPINAL CORD AND SPINAL NERVES. See NERVOUS SYSTEM (The Central Nervous System); SPINE.

SPINAL MENINGITIS. See MENINGITIS.

SPINAL TAP. See CEREBROSPINAL FLUID.

SPINE is the popular name for the *spinal column*, or *vertebral column*. The spine helps support the body of vertebrate animals. It is made up of a column of bones called *vertebrae*. The vertebrae are held in place by strong connective tissue called *ligaments*. There are 33 vertebrae, but some of them grow together in adults. There are 7 *cervical* (neck), 12 *thoracic* (chest region), 5 *lumbar* (lower back), 5 fused *sacral* (hip region), and 4 fused *coccygeal* (tailbone region or coccyx) vertebrae. The first cervical vertebra, the *atlas*, supports the skull. The sacral vertebrae unite with the pelvis (see PELVIS).

Each vertebra has two bony arches that form an opening called the *vertebral foramen*. The openings lie directly over one another, forming a continuous canal called the *vertebral canal*. The spinal cord extends from the lower part of the brain and passes through the canal. A pair of nerves branching off between each vertebra provide communication between the brain and all parts of the body.

The design of the spine provides strength and freedom of motion, yet the delicate spinal cord is protected. Sometimes vertebrae that are fractured in an accident may injure the spinal cord and cause *paralysis* (loss of muscle movement). GORDON FARRELL

Related Articles. See the Trans-Vision three-dimensional

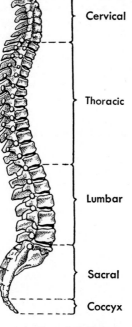

Cervical

Thoracic

Lumbar

Sacral

Coccyx

Divisions of the Spine

color picture with HUMAN BODY. See also:

Cerebrospinal Fluid	Myelitis	Skeleton
Hunchback	Nervous System	Spina Bifida
Meningitis	Scoliosis	

SPINET, *SPIHN iht,* is a keyboard musical instrument that was popular from the 1500's to the 1700's. Many spinets look like miniature grand pianos. Others vary greatly in shape. A spinet operates like a *harpsichord*, though its sound is not as rich (see HARPSICHORD). A spinet has wire strings that are plucked by quills or pieces of leather when the instrument's keys are pressed down. The word *spinet* may have come from the Italian word *spina*, which means *thorn*, and may refer to the instrument's quills. The word *spinet* is also the name of a small upright piano. F. E. KIRBY

See also PIANO (Upright Pianos).

SPINGARN, JOEL ELIAS (1875-1939), was an American literary critic. In 1914, he established the Spingarn medal, which is awarded annually to an outstanding black American. See SPINGARN MEDAL.

Spingarn was born in New York City. He taught literature at Columbia University from 1899 to 1911. His critical works include *A History of Literary Criticism in the Renaissance* (1899) and *The New Criticism* (1911). After 1913, he was a leader of the National Association for the Advancement of Colored People. HENRY LEE MOON

SPINGARN MEDAL awards were instituted by Joel Elias Spingarn, chairman of the board of the National Association for the Advancement of Colored People, in 1914. Gold medals are given each year to the black who, according to a committee appointed by the

Winners of the Spingarn Medal

Year	Medal Winners	Field of Achievement	Year	Medal Winners	Field of Achievement
1915	Ernest E. Just	Research in biology	1954	* Theodore K. Lawless	Dermatology
1916	Charles Young	Organization of the Liberian constabulary	1955	Carl Murphy	Publishing
1917	* Harry T. Burleigh	Creative music	1956	* Jackie Robinson	First black in modern major league baseball
1918	W. S. Braithwaite	Literature	1957	* Martin Luther King, Jr.	Civil rights
1919	Archibald H. Grimke	Politics and literature	1958	Mrs. Daisy Bates	Arkansas NAACP
1920	* William E. B. Du Bois	Founding of Pan-African Congress		Minnijean Brown	First black students to attend Little Rock (Ark.) Central High School
1921	Charles S. Gilpin	Drama		Elizabeth Eckford	
1922	Mary B. Talbert	Helped create Frederick Douglass Shrine		Ernest Green	
1923	* George W. Carver	Agricultural chemistry		Thelma Mothershed	
1924	* Roland Hayes	Concert singing		Melba Patillo	
1925	* James Weldon Johnson	Literature		Gloria Ray	
1926	* Carter G. Woodson	History		Terrence Roberts	
1927	Anthony Overton	Life insurance		Jefferson Thomas	
1928	* Charles W. Chesnutt	Literature		Carlotta Walls	
1929	Mordecai W. Johnson	Education, Howard U.	1959	* Duke Ellington	Creative music
1930	Henry A. Hunt	Education in the South	1960	* Langston Hughes	Literature
1931	Richard B. Harrison	Drama	1961	* Kenneth B. Clark	Psychology
1932	* Robert R. Moton	Educational work	1962	* Robert C. Weaver	Government
1933	Max Yergen	Interracial work in South Africa	1963	* Medgar W. Evers†	Equal rights for blacks in Mississippi
1934	William T. B. Williams	Education, Tuskegee Institute	1964	* Roy Wilkins	Civil rights
1935	* Mary McLeod Bethune	Education	1965	* Leontyne Price	Opera singing
1936	* John Hope†	Education, Atlanta U.	1966	* John H. Johnson	Publishing
1937	* Walter F. White	Civil rights	1967	* Edward W. Brooke	Government
1938	No award given.		1968	Sammy Davis, Jr.	Entertainment
1939	* Marian Anderson	Concert singing	1969	Clarence M. Mitchell, Jr.	Fair housing legislation
1940	Louis T. Wright	Surgery and civic affairs	1970	Jacob Lawrence	Paintings of black life
1941	* Richard Wright	Literature	1971	* Leon H. Sullivan	Equal economic opportunities for blacks
1942	* A. Philip Randolph	Labor and civic affairs	1972	Gordon Parks	Photography, film, literature, music
1943	* William H. Hastie	Equal justice for blacks	1973	Wilson C. Riles	Education
1944	* Charles R. Drew	Medicine	1974	Damon J. Keith	Law
1945	* Paul Robeson	Singing and acting	1975	* Henry Aaron	Baseball
1946	* Thurgood Marshall	Equality before the law	1976	* Alvin Ailey	Modern dance
1947	* Percy L. Julian	Commercial chemistry	1977	* Alex Haley	Literature
1948	Channing H. Tobias	Civil rights	1978	* Andrew J. Young, Jr.	Domestic and international affairs
1949	* Ralph J. Bunche	UN mediator, Palestine	1979	* Rosa Lee Parks	Civil rights
1950	Charles H. Houston†	Law; education	1980	Rayford W. Logan	History; education
1951	Mabel K. Staupers	Equal rights for black nurses	1981	Coleman Young	Government
1952	Harry T. Moore†	Civil liberties	1982	* Benjamin E. Mays	Education; theology
1953	Paul R. Williams	Architecture	1983	* Lena Horne	Entertainment

*Has a separate biography in WORLD BOOK
†Awarded posthumously

The Spingarn Medal has a figure of justice on its face, *left.* The winner's name is engraved on the back, *right.*

board, reached the highest achievement in his or her field in the previous year or over a period of time. See also NATIONAL ASSOCIATION FOR THE ADVANCEMENT OF COLORED PEOPLE; SPINGARN, JOEL E.   HENRY LEE MOON

SPINNERET. See SPIDER (The Spider's Body); RAYON.

SPINNING. See FISHING.

SPINNING is the process of making threads by twisting together plant or animal fibers. It is one of the most ancient arts. For thousands of years, yarn was spun by means of a *spindle.* This consisted of little more than a smooth stick from 9 to 15 inches (23 to 38 centimeters) long. It had a notch at one end for catching the thread, and a stone or baked clay bowl, called a *whorl,* to help make the spindle spin, like a top. The spinner turned the spindle by rolling it against the thigh. Ancient Egyptians used such spindles to make thread for fine cloth.

Ancient spinners in India and South America used finer spindles, usually in a bowl or on the ground. They spun cotton from combed rolls. Wool or flax fibers were wound around a stick called the *distaff.*

The Spinning Wheel, used in Europe as far back as the 1200's, was the first device to give the spindle a spinning movement. The principle was the same as the hand spindle, but the spindle was mounted horizontally. A band or small belt connected to a large wheel passed over a groove in the spindle and turned it. A foot

pedal turned the wheel. A distaff carried the material to be spun. The material was drawn off the distaff by hand, and the fineness of the thread depended on the speed with which the twisting thread was drawn out. For very fine thread, two spinnings were necessary. New England housewives used this early type of spinning wheel in colonial times.

The Spinning Jenny was invented by James Hargreaves in about 1764. This machine could spin more than one thread at a time. But it produced coarse thread rather than fine thread. No one really knows the origin of the term *jenny.* See SPINNING JENNY.

The Water Frame was a cotton-spinning machine patented by Richard Arkwright in 1769. Until then, all cloth had been woven with a linen *warp* (lengthwise threads) since no way had been found to spin cotton for the warp threads. Arkwright's frame drew cotton from the carding machine in a fine, hard-twisted thread suitable for the warp.

The Mule, introduced by Samuel Crompton in 1779, combined the principles of the spinning wheel and the water frame. It was also called the muslin wheel because it was widely used to produce this material. The mule had 48 spindles, and produced unusually fine and uniform yarn.

New spinning machines helped bring about that change in history known as the Industrial Revolution, when machines began to take the place of hand workers. The spinning machines created a demand for more cotton. This need brought about Eli Whitney's invention, the cotton gin. With more thread to weave, the weavers developed better and faster power looms. Then came machines to knit, to make lace, or embroider, to cut out patterns, and finally to sew cloth into finished ready-to-wear garments in large quantities.

Cotton spinning in a present-day factory is a typical example of most spinning. After the raw cotton has been cleaned and arranged into *laps* (bunches) of uniform size, it goes to the carding machines. These machines have huge rollers covered with wire teeth. Here the tangled fibers are straightened out and made to lie in straight, even rows. Then the fibers are rolled over and

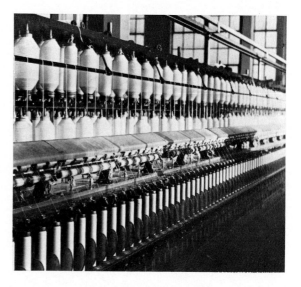

National Gallery of Art, Index of American Design; National Cotton Council

The Old Spinning Wheel, *above,* so common to colonial houses, could make only one thread at a time. It could not compare with a modern spinning machine, *right,* which makes hundreds at a time, and gives threads firmness and strength.

over one another to form *slivers*, which look like loose ropes of soft cotton yarn. A sliver goes through the processes of *drawing*, *slubbing*, and *roving*, by which it is twisted and retwisted and made finer and stronger. Spinning machines perform these operations and give the thread the required twist, firmness, and strength.

New machines have been invented to spin the old natural fibers, such as flax and hemp, and new machines are being made for other fibers, such as kapok and ramie. Machines may someday be developed that will make cloth directly without first spinning thread, but until that time inventors will continue their efforts to improve spinning machines. ELIZABETH CHESLEY BAITY

Related Articles in WORLD BOOK include:

Arkwright, Sir Richard
Colonial Life in America
  (Clothing; pictures)
Cotton (Spinning; picture)
Crompton, Samuel

Hargreaves, James
Industrial Revolution
  (Spinning Machines)
Thread

SPINNING JENNY is a machine for spinning yarn. Like the spinning wheel, it may be operated by a foot treadle or by hand. But the spinning jenny can spin more than one yarn at a time. The idea for multiple-yarn spinning was conceived about 1764 by James Hargreaves, an English spinner. He noticed that the upright spindle of an overturned spinning wheel continued to revolve. In 1770, he patented a machine that could spin 16 yarns at one time. See also HARGREAVES, JAMES (with picture). ERNEST R. KASWELL

SPINOZA, *spih NOH zuh*, **BARUCH,** *buh ROOK*, or BENEDICT (1632-1677), was a Dutch philosopher. He accepted René Descartes' idea that the universe is divided into mind and matter (see DESCARTES, RENÉ). But he saw, as Descartes did not, that if mind and matter are separate substances, they cannot interact. Spinoza decided that they are "attributes" of one substance, God. God, being infinite, has many attributes, but mind and matter are the only two that human minds can know.

Among the consequences of this view is the following: everything that exists, including individual men and women, is a part of God; in God, quite literally, we live and move and have our being. This view upset Spinoza's orthodox contemporaries, both Christian and Jewish, because it was so different from their own. The Jews denounced him and forced him to leave Amsterdam. Spinoza actually was deeply religious, and in many respects was a mystic. He held that people's highest happiness consists in coming to understand and appreciate the truth that they are a tiny part of an all-inclusive, pantheistic God (see PANTHEISM).

Spinoza was born in Amsterdam of Jewish parents. He broke with the Jewish faith after studying Descartes and Giordano Bruno. Spinoza prized independence and freedom of thought so much that he preferred to support himself by grinding lenses rather than accept a university professorship or financial aid. W. T. JONES

See also PHILOSOPHY (The Appeal to Reason).

Culver

Baruch Spinoza

SPINTHARISCOPE, *spihn THAR uh skohp*, or SCINTILLOSCOPE, *sihn TIHL uh skohp*, is an instrument used to observe the flashes of alpha particles emitted from radioactive substances. The instrument consists of a brass tube with a zinc sulfide screen at one end, a lens at the other end, and a speck of radioactive material one millimeter from the screen. Sir William Crookes, an English chemist, developed the instrument in 1903 (see CROOKES, SIR WILLIAM).

SPINY ANTEATER. See ECHIDNA.

SPINY LOBSTER. See LOBSTER (The Body).

SPIRACLE. See BUTTERFLY (The Internal Organs); FLY (Abdomen); INSECT (Respiratory System); SPIDER (Respiratory System).

SPIRAEA, *spy REE uh*, is the name of a genus of herbs and shrubs in the rose family which bear white, pink, or rose-colored flowers. Spiraea grows in the temperate and cold regions of the Northern Hemisphere. Gardeners raise many species of spiraea as ornamental plants.

One of the best known is *Van Houtt's spiraea*, a hardy shrub with thick, deep green foliage. Another is *Thunberg's spiraea*, which has more delicate leaves. The *hardhack*, or *steeplebush*, can be planted in masses. Its flowers grow in narrow, crowded clusters. The *plum-leaved spiraea* is the well-known *bridal wreath* (see BRIDAL WREATH). It may grow more than 6 feet (1.8 meters) high, and has white flowers. Another well-known species is a troublesome weed called *meadow-sweet*. It grows in New England. Spiraeas grow well in good land, but need much water and sunlight.

E. R. Degginger

Meadowsweet Spiraea

Scientific Classification. Spiraea belongs to the rose family, *Rosaceae*. Van Houtt's spiraea is genus *Spiraea*, species *S. vanhouttei*. Thunberg's is *S. thunbergii*. Hardhack is *S. tomentosa*. Bridal wreath is *S. prunifolia*. Meadowsweet is *S. latifolia*. J. J. LEVISON

SPIRE is a term used in architecture to describe the pointed top of a tower or steeple. Most spires narrow to a sharp point high above the roofs of their towers. Many of them have eight sides. The spire developed from the *turret*, a small tower.

In early Christian times, tall peaked turrets were placed on many roofs. In the Middle Ages, it became customary to build turrets on top of large church towers. These turrets gradually became taller and more slender. Some of the greatest spires in the world rise above cathedrals in Europe. The spire of the cathedral of Ulm, Germany, rises 528 feet (161 meters) and is the highest in Europe. The spire of the cathedral at Cologne, Germany, rises 525 feet (160 meters). The spire of Salisbury Cathedral in England rises 404 feet (123 meters). Many famous skyscrapers in New York City and Chicago, especially those built between 1910 and 1930, are topped with spires. ALAN GOWANS

See also COLOGNE (picture: The Spires of the Magnificent Cologne Cathedral).

SPIRILLA. See BACTERIA (The Structure of Bacteria; picture).

SPIRIT. See GHOST; SPIRITUALISTS.

SPIRIT LEVEL. See LEVEL.

SPIRIT OF ST. LOUIS. See LINDBERGH, CHARLES A.

SPIRIT OF '76 is a famous patriotic scene painted about 1875 by the American artist Archibald M. Willard. The scene shows a fife player and two drummers leading American troops during a battle in the Revolutionary War. Willard painted several versions of *The Spirit of '76*. One of them appears in the WORLD BOOK article on REVOLUTIONARY WAR IN AMERICA.

Willard first drew *The Spirit of '76* as a humorous sketch called "Yankee Doodle." The sketch showed three army recruits parading through their training camp playing drums and a fife. Later, Willard painted a serious version of the sketch that was displayed at the Philadelphia Centennial Exhibition of 1876. Willard used friends and relatives as models in the various versions of the painting. EDWARD H. DWIGHT

SPIRITUAL is a type of religious song made famous by blacks of the Southern United States. The spirituals have a strong rhythm and are emotional. They are especially moving when sung by a group. A leader sometimes sings one or two lines alone, and a chorus comes in with the refrain. Spiritual singers often emphasize the rhythm by clapping their hands. Spirituals have been called the only truly American folk songs.

The melodies used in spirituals are sometimes said to have come from Africa. But there are spirituals which have no relation whatever to African songs. These spirituals show a direct relation to the results of evangelistic preaching among the poor whites in the South. These "revivals" also encouraged "white spirituals." The blacks' love for song led them to put their feelings into their singing. Much of the ship loading and plantation work was accompanied by singing of spirituals.

The slaves based most of their spirituals upon characters and stories from the Bible. The manner in which these stories are told in black spirituals shows a colorful imagination and a simple faith. Many slaves thought of themselves as modern children of Israel and looked for a black Moses to deliver them from their bondage. Their songs were warmly appealing and sincere. Among the well-known spirituals are "Go Down, Moses," "Weeping Mary," and "Swing Low, Sweet Chariot."

Spirituals were little known outside the Southern States until after the blacks were freed from slavery. In 1867, William Francis Allen and Lucy McKim Garrison published a collection of black music called *Slave Songs*. The songs included "Climb Jacob's Ladder," "Give Me Jesus," and "I'll Take the Wings of the Morning."

In 1871, spirituals were introduced to other parts of the United States by a group of blacks called the Jubilee Singers, of Fisk University, Nashville, Tenn. They traveled throughout the United States, and to England and Germany, giving concerts to raise money for their school. Within three years they collected $150,000. Other black schools followed their example. The black quartets from Hampton Institute in Virginia and Tuskegee Institute in Alabama became famous.

Spirituals are now one of the best-known forms of American music. Such famous singers as Marian Anderson and Roland Hayes have helped to accomplish this. The influence of spirituals can be heard in the opera *Porgy and Bess* by George Gershwin. RAYMOND KENDALL

See also BURLEIGH, HARRY THACKER.

SPIRITUAL VALUES. See PHILOSOPHY (What Is Good and What Is Evil?); ETHICS.

SPIRITUALISM, in religious philosophy, teaches the existence of a being or reality distinct from matter. This being may be called mind or spirit. Some persons believe that the mind, or spirit, is the only reality. This belief is called *spiritual idealism*.

See also IDEALISM.

SPIRITUALISTS are people who believe that there are spirits of the dead and that some persons can communicate with them. Contact with the dead supposedly is established through persons called *mediums*.

Mediums may contact spirits at public or private gatherings called *séances*. During a séance, the medium and several other persons generally sit at a table. The members of the group may hold or touch hands. They concentrate their thoughts on the dead person whom they wish to contact, in most cases a friend or relative of one of the participants. The spirit of this person supposedly may show its presence by making rapping sounds or by raising or otherwise moving the table. The spirit may throw things about the room or make objects appear, disappear, or float through the air. A medium who carries on such a séance is called a *physical medium*.

Little physical action occurs during a séance conducted by a *mental medium*. Often, the medium enters a trance as the spirit supposedly seizes control of the medium's body and mind. The spirit may speak to the séance through the medium, or it may "write" a message by guiding the medium's hand. Some mediums claim to have a special relationship with one particular spirit. This spirit, called the medium's *control*, speaks through the medium and relays messages from the dead person to the group.

Many scientists and others dispute the claims of spiritualists. It has been shown that mediums trick people at séances into believing that spirits can communicate with the living. Scientists offer explanations for much of what happens at séances. For example, some mediums are ventriloquists. Some use helpers and various types of trick equipment. Others use hypnosis. Many people who attend séances have a strong desire to contact a dead loved one. This desire may make them believe that any message delivered by the medium comes from the spirit world.

Many people believe sincerely in spiritualism. A number of them regard it as an authentic religion based on moral and philosophical principles. Some of these spiritualists also consider themselves Christians. However, several Christian churches declare that any attempt to call a spirit back to the earth is a sin.

Spiritualist Organizations. Some spiritualists are organized into churches. Some groups practice what they call *spiritual healing* of the sick. Some give advice to those who come to them with problems, and others work to spread spiritualism throughout the world.

The chief spiritualist organizations in the United States include (1) the International General Assembly of Spiritualists, (2) the National Spiritual Alliance of the U.S.A., (3) the National Spiritual Association, (4)

the National Spiritualist Association of Churches, and (5) the Progressive Spiritual Church.

History of Spiritualism. Some spiritualist practices date from ancient times. The Old Testament tells that the Hebrew king Saul consulted a medium, the witch of Endor. Through the medium, Saul questioned the spirit of the dead prophet Samuel about an upcoming battle against the Philistines.

The modern spiritualist movement began in 1848 with Katherine and Margaret Fox, two little sisters from Hydesville, N.Y., near Rochester. The girls claimed they had communicated with the spirit of a man who they said had been murdered in their house. The spirit supposedly answered their questions through a code of rapping sounds. The girls' story attracted wide publicity and made them world famous. They later confessed that they had made the sounds themselves by tapping on the floor.

In the late 1800's, the American psychologist William James studied the case of Mrs. Leonora Piper, a Boston homemaker who experienced hypnotic trances. The spirits of such famous persons as the composer Johann Sebastian Bach and the poet Henry Wadsworth Longfellow seemed to compete for control of her mind. In 1964, Mrs. Rosemary Brown, a British kitchen worker, recorded music that she said had just been composed by the spirits of Bach and other composers. Some scientists dismiss such cases as trickery. Others admit that such occurrences cannot be fully explained.

Today, communication with the dead through mediums plays an important part in the religion of many peoples. Among these are groups who live in Africa and on several Pacific islands. They also include some American Indian groups. ERIKA BOURGUIGNON

See also ECTOPLASM; GHOST.

SPIROCHETE. See RELAPSING FEVER.

SPIROGYRA, *spy RUH JY ruh,* is the name of a group of fresh-water green algae that form slimy scum in still water.

See also MICROSCOPE (picture).

SPIROMETER, *spy RAHM uh tuhr,* is a device that doctors use to measure how much oxygen a person's body uses. It also measures how much air the lungs can hold, how well the lungs are working, and the number of times a person breathes each minute.

A spirometer is made up of two cylinders. One cylinder is upside down and rests inside a larger cylinder that is filled with water. The patient breathes through one or more tubes into the inner cylinder. The added air causes the cylinder to rise in the water. When the patient inhales, air is removed from the cylinder and it sinks. A writing arm records these movements on a piece of paper. This record is called a *spirogram.*

The spirometer is most often used to measure a person's *basal metabolic rate* (the amount of oxygen the body uses while at rest). Certain diseases, especially those of the thyroid gland, cause the basal metabolic rate to change. To measure how much air the lungs can hold, the patient first breathes in as deeply as possible, and then exhales as much air as possible into the spirometer. The amount of air that was exhaled is called the *vital capacity.* The vital capacity is less than normal if a person has such disorders as asthma or certain heart diseases. E. CLINTON TEXTER, JR.

SPITSBERGEN. See SVALBARD.

SPITTELER, *SHPIHT uh luhr,* **CARL** (1845-1924), a Swiss poet and writer, won the 1919 Nobel prize for literature. His main theme in the epic poem *Olympic Spring* (1900-1910), and in his other writings, is human suffering. He believed that suffering cannot be overcome, but that it can be reduced by the kind acts of noble people. He was born in Liestal. GOTTFRIED F. MERKEL

SPITZ is a name given to several breeds of small dogs. The American spitz belongs to the spitz family of Arctic dogs, which includes the chow chow, Pomeranian, and Samoyed. The spitz weighs about 25 pounds (11 kilograms), and has a thick white coat, pointed ears, and a sturdy body. Its tail curls up over its back. The spitz is not recognized as a breed by the American Kennel Club. OLGA DAKAN

See also SAMOYED; POMERANIAN.

SPITZ, MARK. See OLYMPIC GAMES (The Modern Games).

SPLEEN is a large, glandlike organ in the body. It helps filter the blood. The spleen lies below the diaphragm, to the left of the stomach and a little behind it. In adults it is about 5 inches (13 centimeters) long and 3 to 4 inches (8 to 10 centimeters) wide, and weighs about 7 ounces (200 grams). It is soft and spongy, crumbles easily, and has a deep violet-red color. The organ is covered by a fold of the *peritoneum,* the membrane that lines the abdominal cavity. The principal cells of the spleen are similar to those of the lymph nodes.

The spleen helps filter foreign substances from the blood, much as a lymph node filters foreign substances from the lymph. Cells in the spleen *engulf* (surround and destroy) these foreign substances. The spleen also serves as a "graveyard" for injured red blood cells. When the body needs extra blood during exercise or hemorrhage, the spleen contracts and squeezes out some of the blood cells it has stored. The spleen may form red blood cells

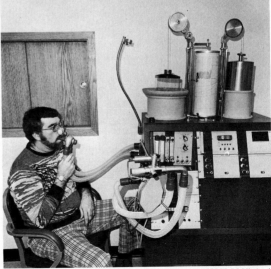

Northwestern Memorial Hospital (WORLD BOOK photo)

A Spirometer, *above,* measures a patient's breathing. A cylinder in the device rises when the patient exhales and sinks when he or she inhales. The movements of the cylinder are recorded on a roll of paper mounted on a rotating drum, *upper right.*

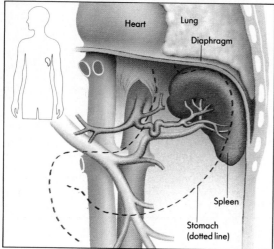

The Spleen is a large, spongy organ that filters foreign substances and damaged cells from the blood. It also stores red blood cells, which can be released into the bloodstream when needed.

in unborn babies, but it does not do so after birth.

The spleen is thought to be only a helper of other glands and organs, for it may be removed from the body without any noticeable ill effects. It is often necessary to remove the spleen. Sometimes, a disease centers in the spleen and causes it to enlarge. In certain other diseases, the spleen works so hard at destroying worn-out red blood cells that it also destroys healthy red cells and causes anemia. Sometimes, it destroys blood platelets, which help in the clotting of blood. When too many platelets are destroyed, the patient may bleed into the tissues. In all these cases, the spleen has to be removed by a surgical operation.   TERENCE A. ROGERS

See also IRON.

SPLICING is a method of joining two ends of rope or wire together without forming a knot. The strands of the ends are unraveled several turns. Then, the strands of one end are twisted around the strands of the other end. See also KNOTS, HITCHES, AND SPLICES (picture).

SPLIT (pop. 235,398) is a city in western Yugoslavia that developed from an ancient Roman town. It lies along the Adriatic Sea (see YUGOSLAVIA [political map]). Its name in Italian is SPALATO. Split was originally built about A.D. 295 within the walls of the palace of the Roman Emperor Diocletian. The remains of the palace still stand in what is now the center of Split. They provide a fine example of Roman architecture. Today, Split is an important seaport and center of industry—especially shipbuilding. Yugoslavia's largest hydroelectric power plant is nearby.   ALVIN Z. RUBINSTEIN

SPLIT INFINITIVE. See INFINITIVE.

SPOCK, BENJAMIN McLANE (1903-   ), an American doctor, became famous for his books on child care. His best-known book, *Common Sense Book of Baby and Child Care* (1946), was translated into more than 25 languages. For later editions, the title was shortened to *Baby and Child Care.* His other books include *Feeding Your Baby and Child* (1955), *Baby's First Year* (1955), *Dr. Spock Talks with Mothers* (1961), *Problems of Parents* (1962), and *Caring for Your Disabled Child* (1965).

In the 1960's, Spock became an active opponent of United States involvement in the Vietnam War. In 1968, he was convicted on charges of conspiring to counsel young men to avoid the military draft. He appealed the verdict. In 1969, the U.S. First Circuit Court of Appeals reversed his conviction.

Spock was born in New Haven, Conn. He graduated from Yale University and received his medical degree from Columbia University.   JOHN A. BARBOUR

SPODE was the family name of three famous English pottery makers, father, son, and grandson.

Josiah Spode (1733-1797), the father, produced blue and white earthenware and transfer-printed willowware. He was apprenticed to Thomas Wheildon, became a master potter, and started his own shop.

Josiah Spode (1754-1827), the son, perfected the formula for bone china (see PORCELAIN [Kinds of Porcelain]). He also designed blue and gold tableware pottery in the style of Oriental porcelains. He was born in Stoke-on-Trent.

Josiah Spode (1776-1829), was the grandson. In 1827, he and William Copeland managed the Spode works, which fell to Copeland at Spode's death. Spode was born in London.   EUGENE F. BUNKER, JR.

SPOHR, *shpawr,* **LOUIS** (1784-1859), was a German violinist, composer, and conductor. His works include the *Violin School* and the opera *Jessonda.* Spohr was born in Brunswick, Germany, and began to study the violin at the age of five. The Duke of Brunswick became his patron eight years later, and Spohr soon became a violin soloist. He started conducting in 1809, and later became court conductor for life in Kassel, Germany.   IRVING KOLODIN

SPOILS SYSTEM is the practice of giving public offices as political rewards for party services. The system is used in many countries. When a new political party comes to power, its leaders place many of their faithful followers in government offices. Many people consider this justifiable when a party places able persons in high offices where policy is to be made. They feel the victorious party must shape policies to satisfy its supporters and be held accountable. However, many people feel the practice is unjustifiable when leaders dismiss able persons from positions not of a policymaking type to make room for others whose chief or only merit consists of their having demonstrated that they are good supporters of the party.

It was once widely thought that the spoils system in the United States first came into general use during the presidency of Andrew Jackson. Recent studies show that President Thomas Jefferson, a Democratic-Republican, followed a policy of not appointing Federalists to government offices. However, Jackson's friend, Senator William L. Marcy of New York, popularized the slogan "to the victor belong the spoils of the enemy."

By 1840, the spoils system was widely used in federal, state, and local governments. In 1883, a civil service law made it illegal to fill some federal offices by the spoils system. Since then, federal civil service legislation has been greatly expanded. Many cities and states also have made education and experience the basis of appointment to public office.   CHARLES O. JONES

See also CIVIL SERVICE (History); GRANT, ULYSSES S. (Political Corruption); JACKSON, ANDREW (The Spoils System); PATRONAGE.

Spokane, Washington's second largest city, is a center of commerce and transportation in the eastern part of the state. The tent-shaped building at the left is the former U.S. pavilion of Expo '74, a world's fair held in 1974.

Photography Unlimited

SPOKANE, *spoh KAN,* Wash. (pop. 171,300; met. area pop. 341,835), is an important commercial center in eastern Washington. It ranks second to Seattle as the state's largest city. Spokane serves as the transportation and distribution center of the *Inland Empire.* This rich agricultural, lumbering, and mining area covers part of eastern Washington, northern Idaho, western Montana, and northeastern Oregon. Spokane lies about 15 miles (24 kilometers) west of the Idaho border. For location, see WASHINGTON (political map).

In 1810, the Canadian North West Company established a fur trading post called Spokane House near what is now Spokane. Permanent settlers came to the area in 1871. They were attracted by the falls of the Spokane River as a possible source of water power. The people named their settlement Spokane Falls. The word *Spokane* is the name of an Indian tribe that lived in the area.

Description. Spokane, the county seat of Spokane County, covers about 52 square miles (135 square kilometers). Two waterfalls in the center of the city furnish hydroelectric power and add to Spokane's scenic beauty. The Pacific Northwest Indian Center in Spokane features manuscripts and displays related to Indian culture, and exhibits of Western art. Other attractions of the city include the Cheney Cowles Memorial Museum, the Fort Wright College Museum, and the Grace Campbell Memorial Museum. Spokane has a symphony orchestra. Educational institutions in the city include Fort Wright College, Gonzaga University, and Whitworth College.

Economy. About 20 per cent of the workers in the Spokane metropolitan area are employed in wholesale and retail trade, more than in any other field. Spokane has about 245 manufacturing plants. The city's leading industries produce, in order of value, primary metal products, food products, printed materials, fabricated metal goods, and lumber and wood products. Spokane has the largest aluminum rolling plant west of the Mississippi River.

Spokane International Airport lies southwest of the city. Passenger and freight trains also serve Spokane.

Government and History. Spokane has a council-manager form of government. The voters elect a mayor and six council members, all to four-year terms. The council hires a city manager to carry out its policies.

Spokane Indians lived in what is now the Spokane area when white men first arrived there in the early 1800's. Spokane Falls was founded in 1871. A railroad first reached the community in 1881, and Spokane Falls also received a city charter that year. The discovery of silver and other minerals in the area attracted new settlers and businesses. A fire destroyed the city's business district in 1889, but the people rebuilt their community. They renamed it Spokane in 1891.

During the late 1890's, Spokane grew as a railroad center. New silver and lead mines opened nearby during the early 1900's and increased Spokane's importance as a mining community. Immigrants from Europe helped boost the city's population from 36,848 in 1900 to 104,402 in 1910. During World War II (1939-1945), Spokane served as a base for training pilots and as a center of aluminum production. The city's population reached 181,608 in 1960, but many people moved to suburban areas during the 1960's and 1970's.

In 1974, Spokane held a world's fair called Expo '74. Many redevelopment projects were carried out before the fair. They included the construction of banks, department stores, and office buildings. Several structures built for the fair became permanent features of Spokane, including an auditorium for the performing arts and a convention center.   JAMES L. BRACKEN

For the monthly weather in Spokane, see WASHINGTON (Climate).

SPONGE

SPONGE, *spuhnj*, is a water animal. At one time, people thought sponges were plants, because sponges are attached to the bottom of the ocean and do not move around. Many sponges look like a type of plant. But zoologists classify sponges as animals.

Sponges make up the animal phylum *Porifera*, which means *pore-bearers*. The surface of the sponge's body is covered with tiny pores.

Most sponges live in the ocean. But there are a few fresh-water *species* (kinds). Sponges can be found both in shallow and in deep water. They inhabit all the seas, but more kinds and numbers of sponges live in the warm

Robert D. Barnes, the contributor of this article, is Professor of Biology at Gettysburg College; and the author of Invertebrate Zoology.

temperate and tropical waters than anywhere else. The largest sponges, including the commercial sponges people use for cleaning, grow in these warmer waters.

Sponges have lived from the earliest ages. Scientists have found remains of sponges in the oldest rocks that bear fossils.

The Body of the Sponge

A sponge does not look like any other animal. Some sponges are shaped like vases or goblets, but most species of sponges have no definite shapes. Some may be thin and flat, while others become round masses. Still others may look like branching shrubbery or treelike bushes. Sponges vary greatly in size. Some grow to less than 1 inch (2.5 centimeters), while others grow to more than 4 feet (1.2 meters).

A sponge has no head, mouth, or internal organs. It depends on a system of water canals in its body to bring in food and oxygen. This system also carries away waste products.

Tiny pores in the surface of the sponge's body lead to the tiny canals. Food and oxygen enter the body through the pores, and are carried through the canals into small chambers. These are called *flagellated chambers*, because each cell that lines them contains a *flagellum* (long thread that whips around to aid movement). The flagellated chambers drain into other small canals. These canals join a network of small canals that eventually lead to the outside through a large opening in the sponge's body called the *osculum*.

A piece of sponge as small as a marble contains thousands of flagellated chambers and canals. Symmetrical sponges with vase-shaped or goblet-shaped bodies have only one osculum. Sponges with bodies that are not symmetrical have many oscula, each providing an exit from the thousands of flagellated chambers and canals. Many zoologists believe that a sponge with many oscula is not a single animal, but a colony made up of many sponges.

The beating, whiplike movements of the flagella circulate water through the sponge. Water enters through the sponge's surface pores. It flows through the flagellated chambers and canals and moves out through the osculum. The water sweeps tiny plants and animals into the sponge and through its body. When these food particles reach the flagellated chambers of the sponge, the cells that line the chambers *engulf* (surround) and digest them.

Sponges have several types of skeletons. Some sponge skeletons consist of tiny needles, called *spicules*. Other skeletons are made of fibers, called *spongin*. Some sponges have skeletons that consist of both spicules and spongin. There are two kinds of spicules in sponge skeletons. Some skeletons have spicules made of *calcium carbonate* (limestone). Others have spicules made of *silica* (glass).

All sponge skeletons form a supporting meshwork throughout the sponge's body. *Glass sponges* contain skeletons made of evenly arranged glass spicules. After

A Sponge Diver gathers live sponges from the bottom of the sea and brings them to his ship to dry. His diving gear enables him to descend 100 feet (30 meters).

SPONGE

Sheepswool and Grass Sponges grow from the same base, *above*. They grow side by side but they are quite different.

The Horny Sponge, or Elephant-Ear, from the Mediterranean Sea has a very fine texture. It is used commercially.

The Glassrope Sponge is a native of the Indian Ocean.

The Velvet Sponge lacks the finer texture of the sheepswool sponge, but it is satisfactory for rougher cleaning work.

Venus's-Flower-Basket has a skeleton of fine lacework.

Fish and Wildlife Service; Ralph Buchsbaum; Visual Education Service; American Museum of Natural History

This Section of a Growing Sponge shows the strange branchlike formation the sponge follows as it enlarges.

This Sponge Growth is like closely twined branches of a gnarled tree.

the sponge cells are removed these beautiful skeletons look like glass wool. The delicate *Venus's-flower-basket* is a glass sponge. Other less attractive sponges leave only the rough spongin fibers after the cells have been removed. Living ocean sponges may be black, brown, gray, or brilliant shades of red, blue, purple, and yellow. Freshwater sponges are green, because *algae* (microscopic plants) live in some of the sponges' cells.

Life Story of the Sponge

The sponge may begin life as a single cell, an egg. This egg divides inside the body of the parent, and keeps dividing until it forms a tiny *larva* (undeveloped animal form) covered with flagellated cells. Then the water circulating through the parent's body sweeps the larva outside the body. The tiny larva is on its own. Its beating, lashing flagella move the larva through the water until it finally settles to the bottom of the ocean and attaches itself to a hard surface. The larva develops into an adult sponge there.

Sponges may also reproduce *asexually* (without eggs). They do this by growing buds and branches that eventually break away from the parent sponge and grow into new sponges on their own.

Sponges have remarkable powers of *regeneration* (regrowth of body parts). Even if much of the body breaks or is cut away, the sponge can replace the broken parts. To test these powers, zoologists have pressed sponges through extremely fine cloths so that all the cells of the sponge separate or divide into small groups. When the zoologists put the cells back into water again, the cells rearrange themselves to form a new sponge.

Commercial Sponges

Most of the so-called *sponges* sold in stores today are not true sponges. They are synthetic materials made to look and to clean like true animal sponges. Skeletons used as true commercial sponges consist of soft, elastic spongin fibers. They are free from impurities and can absorb large amounts of water. These qualities make sponges excellent cleaning tools.

True commercial sponges come from Tarpon Springs off Florida's west coast, and from waters off Key West, the Bahamas, and Cuba. Sponges are also taken from the Mediterranean Sea off the coasts of Egypt, Greece, Tunisia, and Turkey. The silk cup sponge, found off Egypt and Greece, ranks as the most valuable of all commercial animal sponges. Other valuable commercial animal sponges include the elephant-ear, the honeycomb, and the Rock Island wools.

Several different methods are used in sponge fishing. In the deeper waters of the Mediterranean Sea, divers wearing diving suits go down after the sponges. Sometimes sponge-fishing crews use dredges to bring up the sponges. In the shallow waters off the coast of Florida, the *hooking* method is used. In this method, two people go out in a glass-bottom boat. One of them manages the boat while the other does the fishing. They look through the glass bottom of the boat and can see 50 feet (15 meters) or more below the surface. When sponges are sighted, the person who does the fishing lowers a long pole with a pronged hook to where the sponges are. The hook is used to loosen the sponges and bring them to the surface. In the deeper waters of the Gulf of Mexico, people who fish for sponges use diving suits. Sometimes the divers go down 100 feet (30 meters) or deeper to reach the sponges.

The sponges are spread out on deck until the flesh decays. After all the decaying substances are removed, the skeletons are hung in the rigging of the ship to dry. In shallow waters, the catch is kept in *kraals* (pens) along the shore. The high tide fills these pens with water, removing the flesh and leaving the skeleton.

Scientific Classification. Sponges make up the animal phylum *Porifera*. There are three classes of sponges. Sponges with limestone spicules belong to the class *Calcarea*. Glass sponges belong to the class *Hexactinellida*. The largest class is the class *Demospongiae*. These sponges can have glass spicules, spongin fibers, or both types of skeletal materials.

ROBERT D. BARNES

See also FLORIDA (color picture: Diving for Sponges); MARINE BIOLOGY (Marine Biologists); OCEAN (color picture: Benthos).

SPONGE RUBBER. See RUBBER (Sponge Rubber).

SPONTANEOUS COMBUSTION is burning that may occur when heat generated by chemical changes within a substance becomes trapped inside the substance. The substance combines with oxygen in a slow chemical reaction called *oxidation*. Oxidation creates heat that normally is absorbed by the atmosphere. A substance may retain this heat if stored in a place that has poor air circulation. The temperature of the substance then rises, oxidation speeds up, and even more heat is produced. This cycle continues until the substance ignites. Spontaneous combustion occurs most readily in large piles of coal, heaps of oily rags, and damp hay. See also COMBUSTION; FIRE (Kinds of Fire).

HARRIET V. TAYLOR

SPONTANEOUS GENERATION, also called *abiogenesis*, AY by oh JEHN uh sihs, is a theory that certain low forms of living matter came into being from nonliving material. This theory started among the ancient peoples, who believed that such living things as insects and mice came to life from the mud where they were found in large numbers. Ancient peoples also believed that worms came from cheese and wood, and maggots from the juices of decaying meat. Later, scientific experiments disproved this theory. In 1668, an Italian biologist, Francesco Redi, proved that maggots would not breed in meat in which flies were kept from laying eggs. He showed that complex creatures were produced only by others like themselves. Later, when scientists discovered bacteria and other microorganisms, the problem of their beginnings came up again. During the mid-1800's, Louis Pasteur disproved the theory of spontaneous generation. He showed that bacteria would not grow in materials which were sterilized. Today, biologists believe that all complex living matter comes from other living matter.

Some biologists also believe that it is possible that the very lowest forms may have developed through chemical processes from nonliving matter. But no one has ever demonstrated or proved this development under satisfactorily controlled conditions.

GEORGE W. BEADLE

See also LIFE (The Origin of Life [The Theory of Spontaneous Generation]); BIOGENESIS.

SPOON-BILLED CATFISH. See PADDLEFISH.

SPOON RIVER. See ILLINOIS (Rivers and Lakes).

SPOONBILL. See SHOVELER.

SPOONBILL is a wading bird which looks like an ibis. It has an odd, spoon-shaped bill, which it swings from side to side in the water in search of shellfish, water insects, and small crabs. The *roseate spoonbill* lives in the warmer regions of the Americas. The neck and the upper back of this bird are white. The other feathers are rosy pink, turning to red on the outer part of the wings. The roseate spoonbill nests in colonies, and returns year after year to the same place. The nest is a platform of sticks, placed in low trees or shrubs. The female lays 5 to 7 eggs, which are spotted and blotched with olive brown. The finest spoonbill colonies in the United States are on islands in the Gulf of Mexico.

Scientific Classification. The spoonbills belong to the ibis family, *Threskiornithidea*. The roseate spoonbill is genus *Ajaia*, species *A. ajaja*.   ALFRED M. BAILEY

SPORE is a tiny, specialized structure that is able to grow into an organism. Nearly all kinds of plants, plus certain kinds of bacteria and protozoans, form spores. Spores help an organism or its species survive and move from place to place.

Spores vary greatly in size and shape, but most consist of one microscopic cell. Some fungi produce complex, multicelled spores. Spores contain protoplasm and food. Some kinds of spores have a thick wall and can remain *dormant* (inactive) for several months. These two features help such spores withstand harsh weather, chemicals, and other conditions that might otherwise kill the organism. Some spores, called *zoospores*, have tails and can swim. Others may travel on air currents.

Plant Spores. Most kinds of spores are produced by lower plants, which form them in numerous ways. In one common method, the plant grows a structure called a *sporangium* in which the spores develop. Examples of sporangia include the capsules on mosses and the dark spots on bread mold (see MOSS; MOLD). After the spores mature, they *germinate* (start to grow). The protoplasm breaks through the spore wall and begins to develop

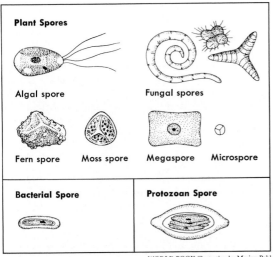

Plant Spores

Algal spore

Fungal spores

Fern spore   Moss spore   Megaspore   Microspore

Bacterial Spore

Protozoan Spore

WORLD BOOK illustration by Marion Pahl

Some Kinds of Spores. Plants, bacteria, and protozoans form spores that vary greatly in size and shape. Most consist of a single cell, although some fungal spores have many cells.

into a new plant. Spore-bearing plants usually produce many spores at a time, but only a few of the spores live and germinate.

Some simple plants, such as certain kinds of algae and fungi, have spores that function like seeds. The mature spores burst out of the sporangium and are widely scattered. If the spores are in a favorable environment, they germinate. They then grow directly into a new alga or fungus. See FUNGI (How a Fungus Lives).

Other lower plants, such as ferns and mosses, produce spores as one stage of their complex reproductive cycle. In most kinds of ferns and mosses, the spores are scattered as are those of the simpler plants. But fern spores and moss spores do not grow directly into a new plant that resembles the parent plant. Instead, they grow into a second kind of plant called a *gametophyte*, which produces *gametes* (sex cells). The gametes unite and, in turn, produce a plant that resembles the original parent plant. This new plant then produces spores, and the cycle begins again. See FERN.

Seed plants have a reproductive cycle somewhat like that of ferns and mosses. However, their spores are produced as a step in the formation of seeds. The female reproductive organ of a seed plant produces spores called *megaspores*, and the male reproductive organ produces spores called *microspores*. Each megaspore remains inside the female reproductive organ and grows into a tiny gametophyte that produces an egg cell. Each microspore grows into a pollen grain, which becomes a gametophyte that produces two sperm cells. After pollination, a sperm cell unites with an egg cell, and a seed begins to develop. See SEED (How Seeds Develop).

Bacterial Spores. Certain types of bacteria form spores as a means of protection. A bacterial spore is a bacteria cell that has developed a thickened cell wall and has become dormant. Some bacterial spores can withstand boiling water and thus hamper the sterilization of various foods.

Protozoan Spores. Certain protozoans form protective spores by a type of cell division. Most of the protozoans are parasites in animals, and they move from animal to animal as spores. One common spore-forming protozoan causes malaria.   DARRELL J. WEBER

See also PLANT (How Plants Reproduce).

SPOROPHORE. See MUSHROOM (Parts of the Mushroom).

SPOROPHYTE. See ALTERNATION OF GENERATIONS; BRYOPHYTE; LIVERWORT.

SPOROZOA. See PROTOZOAN.

SPORT is a term applied to the sudden appearance of certain new hereditary types in plants and animals. Sports are caused by changes in the cells called *mutations* (see MUTATION). The new types are often used as parents to produce new varieties or breeds.

Many plant mutations affect the whole plant. But sometimes the new mutation affects only one branch of the plant. This is known as a *bud sport*. The *variegated* (many-colored) foliage of some plants originated from bud mutations. The navel orange was developed from a bud mutation on an ordinary orange tree. New types of plants produced from sports include the Shirley poppy and the Cupid sweet pea.   J. HERBERT TAYLOR

See also BREEDING.

SPORTING DOGS

SPORTING DOGS. See Dog (table: Breeds of Pure-bred Dogs; pictures: Sporting Dogs).

SPORTS are organized athletic activities played individually or in teams. Most sports can be played by men and women and boys and girls. Many people participate in sports as amateurs for personal enjoyment, the love of competition, or as a healthful form of exercise. Elementary and secondary schools and colleges and universities sponsor teams in many sports, providing student athletes with specialized coaching and equipment. The most skillful athletes may later play professionally.

Sports provide entertainment for people throughout the world. Large crowds attend sporting events in person. Millions of sports fans also follow their favorite teams and athletes by listening to play-by-play accounts of games on radio or watching competition on television.   RICHARD ROTTKOV

Related Articles in WORLD BOOK include:

BALL GAMES

Baseball	Lawn Bowling
Basketball	Little League Baseball
Billiards	Platform Tennis
Bowling	Polo
Cricket	Racquetball
Croquet	Rugby Football
Field Hockey	Soccer
Football	Softball
Golf	Squash
Handball	Table Tennis
Jai Alai	Tennis
Lacrosse	Volleyball

ICE AND SNOW SPORTS

Bobsledding	Ice Skating	Snowmobile
Curling	Iceboating	Tobogganing
Hockey	Skiing	

WATER SPORTS

Birling	Sailing
Boating	Skin Diving
Canoeing	Surfing
Diving	Swimming
Fishing	Water Polo
Rowing	Water-Skiing

OTHER SPORTS

Archery	Horseshoe	Running
Automobile Racing	Pitching	Shuffleboard
Badminton	Hot Rod	Skateboard
Bicycle Racing	Hunting	Skydiving
Boxing	Judo	Spearfishing
Falcon and Falconry	Mountain	Track and Field
Fencing	Climbing	Trapping
Glider	Quoits	Trapshooting
Hiking	Racing	Weight Lifting
Horse Racing	Roller Skating	Wrestling

SPORTS ORGANIZATIONS

Amateur Athletic Union of the United States	National Collegiate Athletic Association
American Bowling Congress	Sokol
Fellowship of Christian Athletes	Women's International Bowling Congress

OTHER RELATED ARTICLES

Balloon	Gymnasium
Cheerleading	Intramural Sports
Commonwealth Games	Olympic Games
Frisbee	Pan American Games
Game	Physical Education

Physical Fitness	Safety (Safety	Sports Medicine
Recreation	in Recreation)	Stadium

See also *Sports* in the RESEARCH GUIDE/INDEX, Volume 22, for a *Reading and Study Guide.*

SPORTS CAR. See AUTOMOBILE (pictures: Sports Cars); AUTOMOBILE RACING (Sports Car Races).

SPORTS MEDICINE is a field that provides health care for physically active people. Its main purpose is to minimize the risk of injury and to treat effectively injuries that do occur. Sports medicine draws on the knowledge of many specialists, including physicians, athletic trainers, physiologists, and physical educators. These experts aid in determining the kind of training needed to help athletes perform to their highest capabilities without injury. They also evaluate coaching methods, the enforcement of regulations to prevent injuries, and the design and use of athletic equipment and facilities.

Many organized athletic teams have an arrangement with a doctor who, as a special service, functions as the team physician. The team physician arranges for pre-season physical examinations and medical attention to members of the team during the season. On many teams, an athletic trainer provides first aid and emergency care. The team physician and athletic trainer work together to provide a rehabilitation program following an injury so the athlete may return to play as quickly as possible. Sports medicine has led to improved diagnosis and treatment of common problems, such as knee injuries and muscle strains, that affect the general public as well as athletes.   KENNETH S. CLARKE

SPOT is a popular sport fish ranging from 6 to 10 inches (15 to 25 centimeters) long and weighing about ½ pound (0.2 kilogram). Spots are silvery above and

WORLD BOOK illustration by Collin Newman, Linden Artists, Ltd.
The Spot Is Named for the Spot on Its Shoulder.

bluish below, with a small dark spot on the shoulder. The upper side has from 12 to 15 yellowish stripes. The spot is caught along the Atlantic and Gulf of Mexico coasts. It has great commercial value as a food.

Scientific Classification. The spot belongs to the croaker family, *Sciaenidae.* It is genus *Leiostomus,* species *L. xanthurus.*   LEONARD P. SCHULTZ

SPOT REMOVING. See DRY CLEANING; CLEANING FLUID.

SPOTSWOOD, ALEXANDER (1676-1740), was a lieutenant governor of colonial Virginia. He took office in 1710. He tried to regulate the fur trade with the Indians, and favored the inspection of tobacco to prevent the export of inferior goods. Spotswood tried to protect the colony from Indian raids. He encouraged settlement along the colony's western frontier and led several expeditions over the Blue Ridge Mountains.

Spotswood quarreled with the council of the Virginia colony over many of his policies. He acquired an estate of about 85,000 acres (34,400 hectares) in Spotsylvania County, and retired there after being removed as lieutenant governor in 1722. He was appointed deputy postmaster general for the colonies in 1730. Spotswood was born in Tangier, Morocco.   JOSEPH CARLYLE SITTERSON

SPOTSYLVANIA COURT HOUSE, BATTLE OF. See CIVIL WAR (Spotsylvania Court House).

SPOTTED ALDER. See WITCH HAZEL.

SPOTTED FEVER. See MENINGITIS (Epidemic Cerebrospinal Meningitis).

SPOTTED FEVER, ROCKY MOUNTAIN. See ROCKY MOUNTAIN SPOTTED FEVER.

SPOTTED TAIL (1823?-1881) was a leader of the Brulé Sioux Indians. He led his band against white settlers in the early 1860's but later supported peaceful relations between the Sioux and the whites.

In 1868, Spotted Tail and other Sioux leaders signed the Laramie Treaty preventing whites from occupying or building roads through Sioux territory. This region included parts of present-day North and South Dakota, Montana, and Wyoming. White miners violated the treaty when they poured into the Black Hills during the gold rush of 1874, and several Indian uprisings resulted. Spotted Tail did not take part in the fighting over the region and he worked for a peaceful solution. In 1876, the Sioux signed a treaty giving up the Black Hills in return for rations, schools, and other goods and services. In 1878, Spotted Tail and his people settled on the Rosebud reservation in what is now South Dakota.

Detail of oil painting on canvas (1887) by Henry Ulke; National Collection of Fine Arts, Smithsonian Institution, Washington, D.C.

Spotted Tail

Spotted Tail was born near Fort Laramie in Wyoming. The Sioux community college in Rosebud, S. Dak., has his Indian name, *Sinte Gleska*. BEATRICE MEDICINE

See also SOUTH DAKOTA (Territorial Days).

SPRAGUE, FRANK JULIAN (1857-1934), was an American electrical engineer and inventor. His inventions ranged from applications of electric power to theoretical problems of motors and generator design. His work on electric-elevator and railroad motors, power supply, and *multiunit* control systems won him the title, "Father of Electric Traction." Sprague was born at Milford, Conn. See also ELECTRIC RAILROAD (History).   ROBERT E. SCHOFIELD

SPRAIN is an injury to a ligament or to the tissue that covers a joint. Ligaments are bands of stringy fibers that hold the bones of a joint in proper position (see LIGAMENT). The tissue that covers the joint is called the *capsule*. Most sprains result from a sudden wrench that stretches or tears the tissues of the ligaments or capsule. Sprains of the ankle and wrist are most common, but a person may sprain any joint.

A sprain is usually extremely painful. The injured part often swells and turns black and blue. Doctors usually prescribe rest and elevation of the injured part.

They may also apply cold compresses first, then warm compresses. They often use elastic bandages to reduce swelling and to provide support for the injured joint.   BENJAMIN F. MILLER

SPRAT is one of the smallest sea fish in the herring family. It is only 3 to 6 inches (8 to 15 centimeters) long, and lives in shoals along the Atlantic and Mediterranean coasts of Europe. Sprats are often mistaken for young herring. But sprats can be recognized by the notched edge on the abdomen. They are a wholesome food. See also HERRING.

Scientific Classification. The European sprat is genus *Clupea*, species *C. sprattus*.   LEONARD P. SCHULTZ

SPRAY GUN. See AIRBRUSH; PAINT (Spray Guns).

SPRAYING is a method of killing garden pests by means of a poisonous mist. Insect poisons are of two sorts, those that kill on contact, and those that the insect must eat in order to die.

Pyrethrum and nicotine sulfate are familiar contact poisons, and are often used on sucking insects. Arsenic salts, such as lead arsenate and calcium arsenate, are familiar stomach poisons used on caterpillars and beetles. Kerosene mixed with soapsuds kills some insects because it stops up their breathing pores.

Whatever the poison used for spraying, it must be made into a fine mist before it reaches the insects. This is done with a special kind of pump called a sprayer or with an *aerosol* (pressurized) container.

There should be little wind at the time when the spraying is done, for wind will blow the poison mist away before it can settle on the insects and their food. Spraying should not be done when there is a likelihood of rain within the next day or two because rain washes off the poison before it can do its work.   W. V. MILLER

See also AEROSOL; FRUIT (Caring for the Crop); FUNGICIDE; INSECTICIDE.

SPREAD-EAGLEISM. See JINGOISM.

SPRING is a natural source of water that flows from the ground. Water from rain and melting snow seeps into the ground. It filters through the pores and cracks in the soil into the layers of rock. The water finally reaches a layer through which it cannot pass. This water held underground is called *ground water* (see GROUND WATER). Gravity may force the water to rise until it finds a way out to the surface to form a spring.

Springs are found in mountains, hills, and valleys.

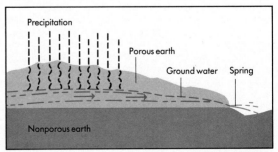

Precipitation

Porous earth

Ground water   Spring

Nonporous earth

WORLD BOOK illustration

A Spring Is Formed when *ground water*, water from rain or snow that has seeped into the ground, finds a way to the surface. When the water reaches ground level, it bubbles out. Springs are often found at a crack or channel in the earth's surface.

SPRING

They are often found at the foot of a cliff or slope or where a crack or fault reaches the surface. Hundreds of springs pour from the walls of the famous Snake River Canyon in Idaho.

The largest springs are found in limestone regions where the water flows underground in cavelike channels. Where such channels reach the surface, great quantities of water may pour from the ground. Famous limestone springs are found in Florida and Missouri.

The temperature of a spring depends on the temperature of the soil or rocks through which its water flows. Ground water that travels close to the surface may produce springs that are warmer in summer than in winter. Springs that come from farther down are always cold. However, deep down in the earth all rocks are hot. In volcanic regions hot rock may even lie close to the surface. As a result, spring water that has traveled from deep in the earth, or has originated in volcanic regions, is often hot.

Many springs contain minerals dissolved from the rock by the moving water. They are known as *mineral springs*. The belief that these springs relieve ailments has popularized them as health resorts. Examples of such health springs can be found in Mount Clemens, Mich., Saratoga Springs, N.Y.; Hot Springs National Park, Ark.; and in France.   M. DANE PICARD

Related Articles in WORLD BOOK include:

Arkansas (Springs)
Florida (Rivers, Lakes, and Springs)
Geyser
Hot Springs
Idaho (Rivers, Waterfalls, Springs, and Lakes)
Mineral Water
Missouri (Springs and Caves)

SPRING is the quality of a material that causes it to "spring" back after being moved. A metal piece that resumes its shape after it has been bent is called a spring. Nearly all springs are made in the shape of a flat or cylindrical spiral, or are otherwise curved. The common materials used for springs are steel and bronze. Most materials have the quality of elasticity, which is the ability to resume a shape after being bent or pulled by an outside force. Although elasticity can be exerted in many ways, springs are usually made to take advantage of the elasticity of torsion, or twist. When a length of wire is coiled, annealed, and hardened in that position, any effort to elongate or compress the coil causes a twist in its material. The spring promptly resists the compressing or stretching motions.

Springs are extensively used in machinery. We have watch springs, shock-absorber springs, door springs, and valve springs. Some springs react slowly in assuming their normal position after being compressed. Others, like the springs in a rifle, move out quickly when they are released. The rate of the return of a spring depends upon the force of return and the amount of material to be moved. Valve springs are the heart of a piston engine. They must retain their elasticity while hot and work for a long time without failure.

Adding alloys such as chromium, nickel, tungsten, and cobalt to steel wire used in springs increases their ability to withstand heat. Stainless-steel springs will perform well at temperatures up to about 500° F. (260° C). An alloy of nickel and chromium has been used at 900° F. (480° C). Jet and gas-turbine engines need springs that are able to withstand even greater temperatures.   LOUIS MARICK

See also AUTOMOBILE (The Suspension System; diagram); ELASTICITY; UPHOLSTERY.

SPRING is the season between winter and summer. The Northern Hemisphere, the northern half of the earth, has spring weather during late March, April, May, and early June. In the Southern Hemisphere, spring weather begins about September and ends by early December. For dates of the first day of spring and other information, see SEASON.

Spring weather begins in much of North America with the melting of winter snow. In the polar regions, spring weather begins later and does not last so long as in the middle parts of the Northern Hemisphere. Tropical regions do not have great seasonal changes.

The number of daylight hours increases during spring, and most spring days have higher temperatures than winter days. Nature awakens in spring, when flowers bloom and hibernating animals leave their winter sleeping places. In many countries, the people have festivals celebrating spring.   JOHN E. KUTZBACH

See also MARCH; APRIL; MAY; JUNE; EASTER (introduction); EQUINOX.

SPRING BEAUTY is the name of a wild flower that grows in forests from Nova Scotia to Georgia and from Saskatchewan to Texas. Its long, narrow leaves grow from a stem 6 to 12 inches (15 to 30 centimeters) high. It has two species. The more common Virginia type bears a white and pink flower with red veins. It blooms so early that many people call it Mayflower or good-morning-spring. The Carolina type has white blossoms.

Scientific Classification. The spring beauty belongs to the purslane family, *Portulacaceae*. The Virginia spring beauty is genus *Claytonia*, species *C. virginica*. The Carolina is *C. caroliniana*.   GEORGE H. M. LAWRENCE

SPRINGBOK, or SPRINGBUCK, is an antelope that lives on the grassy and shrubby open plains of southern Africa. It gets its name from its habit of repeatedly springing up to 10 feet (3 meters) into the air when

The Springbok of Southern Africa is one of the most graceful and nimble members of the antelope family.

frightened, and then racing off at high speed. The springbok resembles the gazelle. A fringe of long white hairs in the middle of its back stands erect when the animal is frightened. Because of this trait, the Portuguese in Angola call this antelope the *goat of the fan*.

Slender and graceful, the springbok stands about $2\frac{1}{2}$ feet (76 centimeters) high and weighs from 70 to 80 pounds (32 to 36 kilograms). It is pale brownish-red, with a white face and white on its underparts and on the inner edges of its legs. Both male and female springboks have curved, lyre-shaped horns. The male horns may be from 14 to 17 inches (36 to 43 centimeters) long.

Wandering herds of springboks at times have ruined crops while seeking food and water. They have even lured whole herds of farm animals away with them. The Dutch settlers of South Africa called them *trekbokken* (traveling bucks). Hunters killed so many of them that large wild herds today can be found only in remote regions of Angola and Botswana.

Scientific Classification. Springboks belong to the cattle family, *Bovid*. They are classified as genus *Antidorcas*, species *A. marsupialis*. VICTOR H. CAHALANE

SPRINGER SPANIEL. See SPANIEL.

SPRINGFIELD, Ill. (pop. 99,637; met. area pop. 187,789), is the state capital and the center of a rich farming region. It lies near a central Illinois coal field, 200 miles (320 kilometers) southwest of Chicago and 100 miles (160 kilometers) northeast of St. Louis (see ILLINOIS [political map]).

Economy. Springfield factories make boilers, earth-moving equipment, electric meters and electronic equipment, farm equipment, flour and cereal products, house and industrial paints, industrial tractors, and mattresses. The city is also a financial and insurance center of central Illinois. Trade shows, cultural events, and sports events are held in the downtown Prairie Capital Convention Center. Lake Springfield, a large artificial lake, furnishes water for industrial purposes and for electric power. The lake also provides recreation.

History. Springfield was founded in 1818, and in 1821 the city was chosen as the seat of Sangamon County. In 1837, it was designated the capital of Illinois, but the state offices were not moved there from Vandalia until 1839. Springfield has a commission form of government.

The original statehouse, associated with Lincoln, Douglas, Grant, and other famous Illinoisans, is now a museum. It has been restored by the state of Illinois, and houses the Illinois State Historical Society. The cornerstone of the present Capitol was laid in 1868.

Abraham Lincoln lived in Springfield from 1837 to 1861. His home still stands at Eighth and Jackson streets, near the city's center. The Lincoln family lived in the two-story frame house from 1844 to 1861. In 1971, the home was designated a national historic site. Lincoln is buried in Springfield's Oak Ridge Cemetery. Larkin G. Mead designed Lincoln's tomb. It was dedicated in 1874. The state maintains the tomb.

The state maintains a Lincoln collection in the Illinois State Historical Library. In New Salem State Park, which is 20 miles (32 kilometers) northwest of Springfield, the pioneer village in which Lincoln lived from 1831 to 1837 has been reconstructed. PAUL M. ANGLE

See also ILLINOIS (picture: Illinois' Capitol); LINCOLN, ABRAHAM (pictures: Lincoln's Tomb, Lincoln's Home).

SPRINGFIELD, Mass. (pop. 152,319), is a commercial, educational, financial, and industrial center in the southwestern part of the state. It lies on the Connecticut River, about 90 miles (140 kilometers) southwest of Boston near the Connecticut border. For location, see MASSACHUSETTS (political map). Springfield and the nearby cities of Chicopee and Holyoke form a metropolitan area with a population of 530,668.

In 1636, a group of English colonists led by William Pynchon bought the site of what is now Springfield from the Agawam Indians. The settlement was named Springfield after Pynchon's birthplace in England.

Description. Springfield, the county seat of Hampden County, covers 33 square miles (85 square kilometers). Many of the city's cultural attractions are within a block called the *Quadrangle*. The Quadrangle includes the Connecticut Valley Historical Museum, the Museum of Science, the George Walter Vincent Smith Museum, and the Springfield Museum of Fine Arts.

A weapons museum forms part of the Springfield Armory National Historic Site. Many sports fans visit the Naismith Memorial Basketball Hall of Fame in Springfield. It was named for James A. Naismith, a Springfield teacher who invented basketball in 1891. Springfield also has a symphony orchestra. The city is the home of American International College, Springfield College, and Western New England College.

The city has more than 200 manufacturing companies. Their chief products include chemicals, clothing, machinery, and metals. Bradley International Airport lies about 15 miles (24 kilometers) south of the city. Freight and passenger trains also serve Springfield.

History. During King Philip's War (1675-1676), Indians burned most of the buildings in Springfield (see PHILIP, KING). But the colonists rebuilt the town, which became a center for farming and trading.

The Continental Army built an armory in Springfield during the Revolutionary War in America (1775-1783). In 1787, a group of farmers led by Daniel Shays tried to capture the armory in a protest against the imprisonment of debtors. Their revolt failed. See SHAYS' REBELLION.

In 1794, the Springfield armory became the first federal United States armory. Many skilled metal workers came to Springfield to work at the armory, and industry began to grow in the town. In 1795, the armory made the first military musket produced in the United States. The Springfield rifle of World War I (1914-1918) and the M1 rifle of World War II (1939-1945) were also developed there.

The coming of the railroad in 1839 contributed to the steady growth of industry and population in the town. Springfield received a city charter in 1852. During the 1850's, it became a major railroad center. The nation's first successful gasoline-powered automobile, the Duryea, made its trial run in Springfield in 1893.

The Springfield armory stopped manufacturing weapons in 1968. Springfield Technical Community College and private industry took over most of its buildings. Several major downtown developments took place in the 1970's. Baystate West, a hotel-office-retail complex in downtown Springfield, opened in 1971.

SPRINGFIELD

The Civic Center, which includes facilities for conventions, cultural groups, and sports events, was completed in 1972. A new Hampden County Hall of Justice opened in 1976. Springfield has a mayor-council form of government.   RICHARD C. GARVEY

SPRINGFIELD, Mo. (pop. 133,116; met. area pop. 207,704), is the commercial center for a large farming, lumbering, and mining district. It is the third largest city in Missouri. Springfield lies at the edge of the Ozark Mountains in southwestern Missouri, about 175 miles (282 kilometers) southeast of Kansas City and 220 miles (354 kilometers) southwest of St. Louis (see MISSOURI [political map]). It is the gateway to the scenic White River region.

Fruit grows in the large orchards nearby. The city has one of the largest dairy processing plants in the United States and is an important poultry market. It also has flour mills, meat-packing plants, electronics equipment plants, machine shops, and trailer factories. The two main lines of the Frisco Railroad intersect in the city, and have large shops there.

Springfield was settled about 1830. It became a town in 1838, and a city in 1847. Colleges in Springfield include Drury College, Evangel College, and Southwest Missouri State University. Lester Cox Medical Center, St. John's Hospital, and the Medical Center for Federal Prisoners are also in the city. Springfield has a council-manager government. The city is the seat of Greene County.   NOEL P. GIST

SPRINGFIELD, Ohio (pop. 72,563; met. area pop. 183,885), is a manufacturing city in west-central Ohio. It lies at the meeting place of Buck, or Lagonda, Creek and the Mad River, about 25 miles (40 kilometers) northeast of Dayton (see OHIO [political map]). Springfield was named for the many springs in nearby cliffs.

Industry in Springfield is highly diversified. Factories in the city produce aircraft-engineering products, awnings, chemicals, diesel engines, electric fans, hoists, incubators, lawnmowers, and lawn sweepers. Other products made in Springfield include leather goods, machine tools, metal caskets, paper-pulp machinery, piano plates, pumps, rigs for drilling wells, roadbuilding machinery, thermometers, trucks, and wire products. These industries have replaced the agricultural-implement plants that made Springfield a world center of farm-machinery production during the late 1800's.

Springfield is the home of Wittenberg University, founded in 1845. It also has a symphony orchestra and an art center. Two railroads provide freight service, and several airlines operate from the municipal airport.

The first settler of the Springfield area was James Demint, who arrived from Kentucky in 1799. Springfield became the seat of Clark County in 1818, and received its city charter in 1850. The city has a commission form of government.   JAMES H. RODABAUGH

SPRINKLER SYSTEM. See FIRE DEPARTMENT (Communication Systems); BISMUTH; ALLOY (Other Alloys).

SPROUTING. See GERMINATION.

SPRUANCE, RAYMOND AMES (1886-1969), was one of the top United States naval commanders during World War II (1939-1945). Many military experts rate him the best American naval combat commander of the war. Spruance helped devise the circular battle formation that made U.S. carrier groups the most effective fighting fleets in history.

Shortly before the United States entered the war in December 1941, Spruance took command of a cruiser division of the Pacific Fleet. In June 1942, he commanded the force sent to stop the Japanese at Midway Island. The United States won the Battle of Midway, which many historians consider the turning point of the Pacific war. The victory established Spruance's reputation as a combat commander, and he was promoted from rear admiral to vice-admiral (see WORLD WAR II [The Battle of Midway]). Admiral Chester W. Nimitz, commander in chief of the Pacific Fleet, made Spruance his chief of staff.

In November 1943, Spruance led the assault on Tarawa in the Gilbert Islands. He was promoted to admiral and in January and February 1944, he commanded the Central Pacific Force in its attacks against the Marshall Islands. In February, Spruance also led an aerial attack on the great Japanese naval base at Truk. During the summer of 1944, he won an overwhelming victory in the Battle of the Philippine Sea and commanded the naval forces in the capture of Saipan and Guam. In 1945, Spruance led the Fifth Fleet in the first carrier strike on Tokyo and directed the capture of Iwo Jima in the Volcano Islands.

After the war, Spruance served as commander in chief of the Pacific Fleet and later as president of the Naval War College. Spruance was born in Baltimore and graduated from the United States Naval Academy in 1907.   DONALD W. MITCHELL

SPRUCE is the common name of a genus of cone-bearing evergreen trees in the pine family. About 40 kinds of spruce trees are native to the Northern Hemisphere. Some spruces grow beyond the Arctic Circle. Others grow as far south as the Pyrenees Mountains in Europe. In North America, they grow as far south as North Carolina and Arizona.

Spruces are more closely related to the firs than to any other cone-bearing tree. But spruces have cones that hang straight downward. Fir trees have cones that stand straight up. The scales on spruce cones remain on the cones. The scales on fir cones fall off when the cones become ripe.

Spruce foliage is also different from that of other cone bearers. Most spruce tree needles are four-sided and less than 1 inch (2.5 centimeters) long. Woody, peg-like projections join the needles to the twig. Fir trees do not have these projections. Spruce trees grow tall. Most are shaped like pyramids. In old trees, the drooping lower branches may brush the ground.

Kinds. The *white*, *black*, and *red* spruces of the East and the *Sitka* and *Engelmann* spruces of the West are the most important commercial spruces in North America. The white and black spruces are named for the general color of the bark and foliage. These spruces are more widely distributed than any other. They grow between Bering Strait on the north, and Maine, New York, and Michigan on the south. The black spruce also grows in high altitudes in Virginia. The trees grow west to British Columbia and Montana.

The white spruce may reach a height of 150 feet (46 meters). The black is a little smaller. The red spruce grows between Nova Scotia and North Carolina, and as far west as Tennessee. The Sitka spruce grows on the

J. Horace McFarland

The Silvery-Blue Foliage of the Blue Spruce makes it one of the most admired of all the American evergreen trees.

The Cones of spruces like the red spruce, *right*, are *pendant* (hang downward). The needles of spruce trees grow in thick spirals around the branches and point in all directions.

Devereux Butcher

Pacific Coast from northern California to Alaska. It sometimes reaches a great height, especially in the swamps or tidewater regions. A number of giant Sitkas are over 300 feet (91 meters) high. The Engelmann spruce grows from British Columbia to New Mexico.

The most important spruce in Europe is the *Norway* spruce. This handsome tree is planted in eastern North America as an ornamental. The so-called *Douglas spruce* (Douglas fir) of Washington, Oregon, and British Columbia, belongs to a different genus, but is related to the spruces. It produces more lumber than any other tree in the world.

Uses. Spruce wood is widely used for wood pulp in the papermaking industry. The timber is strong, light, and flexible, and is well suited for masts and spars of ships. Spruce is also used to make boxes, and forms sounding boards for musical instruments such as pianos.

Spruce wood is also used for interior finishing in houses. Resin, tannin, and turpentine are products of spruce bark. Beer is sometimes made from young spruce twigs. The gum of the black spruce, which is hardened resin, is another product. Dyes have been made from

turpentine, which is a by-product of papermaking.

Scientific Classification. Spruces belong to the pine family, *Pinaceae*. They form the genus *Picea*. The white spruce is species *P. glauca;* the black, *P. mariana;* the red, *P. rubens*. The Douglas spruce, or fir, is genus *Pseudotsuga*, species *P. menziesii*. K. A. ARMSON

See also CONE-BEARING PLANT; TREE (Familiar Broadleaf and Needleleaf Trees [picture]).

SPRUCE BUDWORM is a highly destructive forest insect pest that lives throughout the northern United States and southern Canada. It is a small gray-brown moth with dark markings. During its caterpillar stage, the spruce budworm feeds on the needles of spruce and fir trees.

The adult female moths lay their eggs on spruce and fir trees in midsummer. The eggs hatch into caterpillars, which spend the winter on the trees. In spring, they begin to eat the new buds of the trees. The caterpillars spin cocoons in early summer and emerge as moths. Spruce budworms can kill a tree by eating its needles for three to six years.

The number of spruce budworms has been controlled

Canada/United States Spruce Budworms Program

The Spruce Budworm Caterpillar feeds on the needles of spruce and fir trees. This highly destructive forest insect pest lives throughout the northern United States and southern Canada.

naturally by the insect's limited food supply and by birds and other enemies. However, an outbreak of spruce budworms has occurred about every 30 to 60 years. The insects killed many trees at those times, but their population declined after their food source became exhausted.

Since the 1940's, more than 20 million acres (8 million hectares) of forests in Maine, New Brunswick, and Quebec have been sprayed at least once with pesticides to kill spruce budworms. However, pesticides have not been entirely successful because they kill only part of the spruce budworm population. The survivors thus have a large food supply and can reproduce in great numbers. In addition, environmentalists argue that widespread use of pesticides harms the environment. During the early 1980's, researchers increased their efforts to control spruce budworms through forest management methods and biological controls.

Scientific Classification. The spruce budworm belongs to the order Lepidoptera. It is classified as *Choristoneura fumiferana*. LLOYD C. IRLAND

SPRUCE PARTRIDGE. See GROUSE.

SPUR. See HORSE (Spurs).

SPURGE FAMILY, or EUPHORBIACEAE, *yoo FAWR-bih AY see ee*, is a family of herbs, shrubs, and trees. Many of the plants give us useful products such as castor oil, croton oil, cassava, and rubber. There are about 7,300 different *species* (kinds) in the spurge family. They grow in many regions, especially in the tropics.

Members of the spurge family bear small, inconspicuous flowers, but they sometimes have brilliantly colored flower *bracts* (leaves that look like flower petals). A biting, milky juice is usually found in the plants. Some species in Africa look almost exactly like a cactus when they are not in bloom. The family also includes ornamentals such as the poinsettia.   EARL L. CORE

Related Articles in WORLD BOOK include:

Cassava	Croton	Poinsettia	Snow-on-the-
Castor Oil	Jumping Bean	Rubber	Mountain

SPUTNIK, *SPUHT nihk*, is the name of a series of unmanned earth satellites launched into space by Russia. *Sputnik* is a Russian word meaning *traveler*. Sputnik I, launched Oct. 4, 1957, circled the earth once about every 95 minutes at a speed of 18,000 mph (29,000 kph), until it fell to earth on Jan. 4, 1958. Russia also launched nine much larger sputniks, from November 1957 to March 1961. See also SPACE TRAVEL; JODRELL BANK OBSERVATORY.

SPY is anyone who abandons the uniform or distinctive badge of military service and mingles with the enemy to obtain information of value to the country that person is serving. The international rules of war provide that a soldier in uniform cannot be considered a spy, even if attempting to obtain information within enemy lines. Civilians openly carrying messages through enemy lines are not considered spies if they do not attempt to disguise their identity. To be condemned as a spy, a person must be captured within enemy lines *in disguise*, or while representing to be someone else. Suspected spies must receive a trial. The punishment for wartime spying usually is death.   KARL DETZER

Related Articles in WORLD BOOK include:

André, John	Espionage	Mata Hari
Boyd, Belle	Fifth Column	Rosenberg
Chambers, Whittaker	Hale, Nathan	

SPYRI, *SHPEE ree*, **JOHANNA** (1827-1901), was a Swiss author of children's stories. Her best-known book is *Heidi* (1881), a story of child life in the Swiss Alps. *Heidi's* success encouraged Mrs. Spyri to write more books for and about children. She used the background of her childhood in Switzerland for these books. Her other books include *Cornelli* (1890) and *Vinzi* (1894). She was born in Hirzel, near Zurich.   JEAN THOMSON

SQUAD. See ARMY, UNITED STATES (table: Army Levels of Command).

SQUALL, *skwawl*, is a sudden rise in the wind, often with a marked change in wind direction. Rain and hail may accompany the wind. A squall may be caused by an advancing mass of cold air that violently lifts the warm air in front of it.

SQUANTO (1585?-1622), also called *Tisquantum*, was a Patuxet Indian who befriended the Pilgrims. He helped the Pilgrims survive at Plymouth Colony.

Squanto was born near what is now Plymouth, Mass.

In 1614, he was kidnapped by English fishermen and taken to Spain to be sold as a slave. He escaped to England, where he lived for several years and learned to speak English. He also lived in Newfoundland for a time. Squanto returned home in 1619. He found that the Patuxet tribe had been wiped out by disease and the few survivors had joined the Wampanoag tribe. Squanto also joined the Wampanoag.

In 1621, Squanto met the Pilgrims, who were nearly starving after their difficult first winter at Plymouth Colony. The Pilgrims had angered the Wampanoag by stealing the Indians' corn. Squanto served as an interpreter between the colonists and the Wampanoag chief Massasoit and helped arrange a peace treaty (see MASSASOIT). Squanto then stayed with the Pilgrims and showed them how to plant corn and where to hunt and fish.

Squanto tried to challenge Massasoit's leadership of the Wampanoag. This plot angered the tribe, and Squanto became the enemy of the Wampanoag in 1622. He died from a fever later that year.   NEAL SALISBURY

See also PLYMOUTH COLONY (The First Year).

SQUARE, in geometry, is a plane figure that has four equal straight sides and four right (90°) angles. If each side of a square is 4 inches long, the square can be cut into 4 × 4, or 16, smaller squares that have sides 1 inch long. The *area* of this square equals 16 square inches. In general, the area of a square is expressed in square units. It is found by multiplying by itself the number that represents the length of one side of the square. A square with a side 3 centimeters long has an area of 3 × 3, or 9, square centimeters.

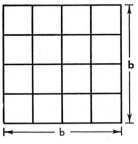

In arithmetic and algebra, the *square* of a quantity is the product of a quantity by itself. For example, 16 is the square of 4, because $4 \times 4 = 16$. If b represents any quantity, the square of b, or $b \times b$, is written b^2. The small 2 that appears to the right of and above the b is called an *exponent*. The exponent 2 indicates that the quantity b is to be taken twice as a factor.

The term *square* also refers to a tool or instrument for measuring and constructing right angles. Carpenters often use a square made in the shape of an L and drafters use a square in the shape of a T.   HOWARD W. EVES

See also POWER; QUADRILATERAL; SQUARE ROOT.

SQUARE DANCING is a type of American folk dancing performed by groups of four couples. The couples may dance in a square formation or in a circle called a *running set*. They may also dance *longways*, in which two lines of couples face each other.

Square dancers follow the directions of a *caller*, who calls out different movements and patterns. Popular calls include "Promenade," "Swing your partner," and "Form a star." The caller may give *singing calls*, in which the directions are sung, or *patter calls*, in which the directions are spoken against a musical background. Most of the music for square dancing is provided by fiddles, banjos, and guitars.

Square dancing is popular throughout the United

Square Dancing is perhaps the most popular form of American folk dancing. The dancers divide themselves into groups of four couples. Then they swing about, bow, join hands, and change partners in this lively type of group dancing.

WORLD BOOK photo

States, especially in rural areas, and different styles have developed in the East and West. Most Eastern square dances are based on simple patterns, with one couple dancing at a time. Western square dances may involve several couples dancing in complex patterns.

Many square dances come from ancient English, Irish, and Scottish folk dances that were brought to America by early settlers. Different communities adapted the calls and movements in various ways. Today, the same square dance may have many variations, which are based on these local adaptations.   MELVIN BERGER

SQUARE DEAL originally referred to fair treatment in dealing playing cards and in handling other transactions. President Theodore Roosevelt used the slogan repeatedly. "When I say 'square deal,'" he wrote, "I mean a square deal to everyone . . ." He declared that he would use his powers as President to safeguard the rights of both capital and labor (see ROOSEVELT, THEODORE [Friend of Labor]).

SQUARE MEASURE is the system used in the measurement of surfaces. The unit for the *area* of a surface is the square. Hence the name of the system. We can describe a table top as being 12 inches long and 10 inches wide, or 12 by 10 inches. But these figures represent only lines, which have just one dimension—that of length.

A plane surface has two dimensions—length and width. They must somehow be combined into a single expression in order to tell how much the table will hold. Thus we describe the area of the same table top as 120 square inches.

Square measure of any square or rectangular plane surface is obtained by multiplying length by width. The reason for this is easily seen if we draw a picture of the table top and mark off its inches. A line should be drawn at every inch along the length and at every inch along the width. The two sets of lines will cross each other. This will give us 120 little squares, each measuring one inch in length and one inch in width. The

measure of each is called a square inch. The areas in square inches, centimeters, feet, meters, and so on, of other geometrical figures are found by special rules. These rules are all based on the one stated above.   E. G. STRAUS

See also METRIC SYSTEM (Surface Measurements; Metric Conversion Table); WEIGHTS AND MEASURES (Surface or Area).

SQUARE ROOT of a number is a second number whose product with itself gives the original number. For example, a square root of 4 is 2, because $2 \times 2 = 4$. The symbol for a square root, called a *radical sign*, is $\sqrt{}$. For example, $\sqrt{25} = 5$ and $\sqrt{4} = 2$. The negative number -2 is also a square root of 4, because $-2 \times -2 = 4$. Each positive number has both a positive and negative square root. These two square roots always have the same numerical value.

Finding Square Roots. The easiest and fastest way to find the square root of a number is to use an electronic calculator. This device, available in pocket-sized models, makes long and tiresome calculations unnecessary. It enables a user to extract square roots by simply pushing certain appropriate buttons or keys. See CALCULATOR.

Another convenient way of finding the square root of a number is to use a *table of square roots*, a *table of squares*, or a *table of logarithms*. If available, these tables give a square root quickly, and it only takes a short time to learn how to use them proficiently. A device called a *slide rule* also provides a useful tool for finding square roots. However, most slide rules can give the square root of a number in only three digits. See LOGARITHMS; SLIDE RULE.

It is possible to compute square roots accurately without the aid of tools. The method described here requires dividing and averaging. It is easy both to learn and to apply.

To find the square root of 40, first determine the number closest to $\sqrt{40}$ in whole numbers. Because $6 \times 6 = 36$ and $7 \times 7 = 49$, it is apparent that 6 is the appropriate number. Begin calculating the square root of 40 with 6. Divide 40 by 6: $40 \div 6 = 6.6$ (to the nearest tenth). Notice that $6 \times 6.6 = 39.6$, or about 40. Now find the average of 6 and 6.6: $\frac{1}{2} \times (6 + 6.6) = 6.3$, and $6.3 \times 6.3 = 39.69$, which is even closer to 40.

To obtain greater accuracy, repeat the procedure. First, divide 40 by 6.3: $40 \div 6.3 = 6.349$. Next, find the average of 6.3 and 6.349: $\frac{1}{2} \times (6.3 + 6.349) = 6.325$. Repeating the procedure a third time, it is found that $40 \div 6.325 = 6.3241106$, and that $\frac{1}{2} \times (6.325 + 6.3241106) = 6.3245553$. This process may be continued indefinitely. In general, in each approximation to the square root, twice as many digits should be kept as in the previous approximation.

Notice that 40 lies between 1 and 100. If the square root of a number that is not in the 1 to 100 range must be found, first divide or multiply the number by 100 to bring it within this range. Consider, for example, finding the square root of 400,000, or $\sqrt{400{,}000}$. Divide 400,000 *twice* by 100. This yields 40, a number within the 1 to 100 range. The square root of 40 has already been determined: $\sqrt{40} = 6.3245553$. Now, multiply the square root of 40 *twice* by 10 (the square root of 100) to obtain the square root of 400,000: $6.3245553 \times 10 \times 10 = 632.45553$. In the same way, $\sqrt{0.4} = 0.63245553$. The square root of 0.4 can be found by multiplying by 100, finding the square root of 40, and dividing by 10.

Square Roots of Negative Numbers. What is the square root of -4? Or, what number multiplied by itself gives a product of -4? If there is such a number, it cannot be positive, negative, or zero. None of these multiplied by itself can give a negative number. But, for convenience in solving certain problems, mathematicians have invented a system of *pure imaginary numbers* whose squares are negative numbers.   HOWARD W. EVES

See also CUBE ROOT; ROOT; SQUARE.

SQUASH is any of more than 40 kinds of gourd-shaped vegetables. The word *squash* refers both to the entire plant and to the fruit, which is the part that people eat. Squashes are closely related to pumpkins. Many plants called pumpkins are actually squashes.

Squashes are highly nutritious. They provide large amounts of vitamins A and C and are low in calories. These vegetables can be cooked in many ways, and one type, Zucchini, is often served raw in salads. Another kind, Banana squash, is commonly used as a baby food. Some cooks substitute the stringy pulp of the Vegetable Spaghetti squash for spaghetti in low-calorie dishes.

Squashes are native to the Western Hemisphere. Indians introduced them to the first European explorers who reached the New World. The name comes from *askutasquash*, an Indian word meaning *eaten raw or uncooked*.

Squashes grow on bushes and vines. The plants have large five-pointed leaves and yellow-orange flowers. The many varieties of squashes have fruits of different colors, shapes, sizes, tastes, and textures. There are two major groups of squashes, *summer squashes* and *winter squashes*.

Summer Squashes grow on bushes. The fruit is picked when it is immature and has a soft rind. If a squash grows too large and ripe, it loses some flavor. Summer squashes should be eaten as soon as possible after harvesting. Common types of summer squashes

include Coczelle, Pattie Pan, White Scallop, Yellow Crookneck, and Zucchini.

Winter Squashes grow on vines or bushes. They are frequently not picked until several days before the first freeze. At this time, the fruit is fully ripe and has a hard rind. Winter squashes can be stored for several months in a cool, dry place before being cooked. Some canned "pumpkin" filling for pumpkin pie actually consists of one or more kinds of winter squashes. Popular winter varieties include Acorn, Banana, Butternut, Hubbard, and Vegetable Spaghetti.

Growing Squashes. Squash plants thrive in any region that has a warm growing season. The seeds should be planted in mounds of rich, well-drained soil. Summer squashes can be harvested in about two months. Winter squashes mature in three or four months.

Squash plants are attacked by several kinds of insects, including cucumber beetles, squash bugs, and squash vine borers. These pests can be controlled with insecticides or by picking them off the plants.

Squash is popular with home vegetable gardeners, but it is not an important commercial crop. The leading squash-producing states are California, Florida, New Jersey, New York, and Texas.

Scientific Classification. Squashes belong to the family Cucurbitaceae. Summer squashes are *Cucurbita pepo*. The winter squash Acorn is also *C. pepo*. Banana squash is *C. maxima*. Butternut squash is *C. moschata*. w. E. SPLITTSTOESSER

See also GOURD; PUMPKIN.

Hubbard

Butternut

Acorn

White Scallop

Zucchini and Yellow Crookneck

WORLD BOOK illustration by Kate Lloyd-Jones, Linden Artists Ltd.

Squash is a nutritious vegetable that grows on bushes and vines. There are more than 40 kinds of squashes, which differ in color, shape, and taste. Some popular types are shown above.

WORLD BOOK photo

Squash is a fast indoor game played on an enclosed court. The players take turns hitting a hard rubber ball with a racket.

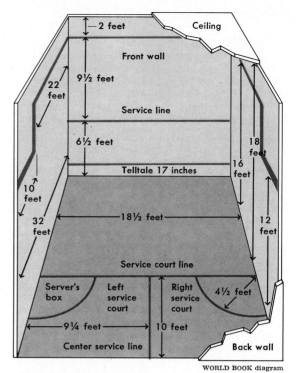

WORLD BOOK diagram

Diagram of a Squash Court

Wilson Sporting Goods Co. (WORLD BOOK photo)

A Squash Racket, *above,* can be up to 27 inches (68 centimeters) long. The ball, *right,* is about the size of a golf ball. The American form of squash uses a solider ball than does the English form.

WORLD BOOK photo

SQUASH, or SQUASH RACQUETS, is an indoor game similar to handball. But squash is played with rackets (or *racquets*) and a hollow, hard black ball about the size of a golf ball. Players use the rackets to hit the ball against the four walls of a court. A variety of shots is possible and the ball travels very quickly.

There are two forms of squash, the American and the English. The American form is played in the United States, Canada, Mexico, and in some South American countries. The English form is mainly played in Europe and in countries that were once part of the British Empire, such as Australia and New Zealand. In *singles* squash under American rules, two competitors play in a cement or wood court 32 feet (10 meters) long and 18½ feet (5.6 meters) wide. The front and side walls are 16 feet (4.9 meters) high, and the back wall is 6½ feet (2 meters) high. An English singles court is 21 feet (6.4 meters) wide. The front wall is 15 feet (5 meters) high, and the back wall is 7 feet (2.1 meters) high. The side walls slant down from 15 feet at the front to 7 feet at the back. *Doubles* squash is played by two teams of two players each on a larger court.

A player may hit the ball against any wall so long as it reaches the front wall before it touches the floor. A player loses a point by missing the ball or by allowing it to bounce twice. A player also loses a point by hitting a ball above an *out-of-court* line on the side, back, and front walls. There is also a metal board called a *telltale* 17 inches (43 centimeters) high at the bottom of the front wall. On English courts, the telltale is 19 inches (48 centimeters) high. A player who hits the telltale loses the point. Under American rules, a 15-point score wins a game. Under English rules, the server must score 9 points to win the game. Generally, the first player or team to win three games wins the match.

Squash originated at Harrow School in England about 1850. The game was introduced into the United States about 1880.   HERBERT H. GROSS

SQUATTER is a person who lives on land but has no deed or other evidence of title to it. In most cases, a squatter may make a valid claim to the land if there is no other person with a legal claim. During the period of the westward movement in the United States, many people moved to lands which had not yet been surveyed and which were not yet for sale (see WESTWARD MOVEMENT [The Frontier Process]). Congress passed special laws which allowed squatters to gain title to the lands they occupied. These laws culminated in the Pre-emption Act of 1841.   HAROLD W. BRADLEY

See also HOMESTEAD ACT; KANSAS (The Struggle Over Slavery); POPULAR SOVEREIGNTY; PRE-EMPTION; SQUATTER'S RIGHTS.

SQUATTER SOVEREIGNTY. See POPULAR SOVEREIGNTY.

SQUATTER'S RIGHTS. During the westward movement in the United States, many *squatters* settled on unsurveyed public land with no title. They did so to avoid buying land or because there was not enough surveyed land to meet the demand. They generally built homes and cleared the land. They believed they had thus earned the right to buy the land at the minimum price when the government sold it. This claim is known as *squatter's rights*. Squatters formed *claim associations* to protect their land before public sales were held. Most Westerners supported the squatters, and Western congressmen backed bills to protect their interests. The Pre-emption Act of 1841 recognized squatter's rights. See also PRE-EMPTION; SQUATTER.   HAROLD W. BRADLEY

SQUETEAGUE. See WEAKFISH.

SQUIB. See NEWSPAPER (Newspaper Terms).

SQUID is a sea *mollusk* (animal with a soft, boneless body) that is similar to the octopus, nautilus, and cuttlefish. Squids live throughout the world. They frequently swim in large groups called *shoals*. These animals are also called SEA ARROWS.

Squids have dark gray bodies with red spots. The body has two fins at the tail end. The head is surrounded by 10 arms, two of which are longer than the others. Each arm has rows of round sucking discs which it uses to catch and hold its prey. The animal has a horny *pen* (shell) inside its body. Squids range in size from less than 1 foot (30 centimeters) to nearly 40 feet (12 meters) in length, including the arms. The giant squid may measure 55 feet (17 meters) long.

The squid's head has two well-developed eyes, a pair of powerful jaws, and a rough *radula* (tongue). A muscular tube, or funnel, lies beneath the head. The squid swims by filling the folds in its body walls with water and forcing it through the tube. This "jet" action makes the animal move. An "ink sac" spurts a dark fluid when a squid flees from an enemy. Squids can also change color to blend with the environment.

Some people eat squid. Fishermen use them for bait. Squids are serious pests to the mackerel and herring fishing industry because they eat large numbers of these and other small fish. The common squid is found from Nova Scotia to Florida. Giant squids swim in Pacific waters near New Zealand and in the North Atlantic.

Scientific Classification. The common squid belongs to the squid family, *Loliginidae*. It is genus *Loligo*, species *L. pealeii*.   R. TUCKER ABBOTT

See also ARGONAUT; CUTTLEFISH; MOLLUSK (picture); NAUTILUS; OCTOPUS; OCEAN (pictures).

The Ten Arms of the Squid Are Used to Catch Fish.

American Museum of Natural History

USDA

The Big Bulblike Root of Squill Is Used in Medicine.

SQUILL is the name of several plants with bulbous roots. They belong to the lily family. One kind of squill, called the *sea onion*, grows around the Mediterranean Sea. It produces bulbs that sometimes weigh as much as 4 pounds (1.8 kilograms). The bulbs of this squill have medicinal value.

Gardeners collect the bulbs of the sea onion in August. They remove the outer husk, slice the bulb, and dry it in the sun. People make a drug from the bulbs. Usually they use it in syrup form or in "tincture of squill." It stimulates the heart and is rather irritating. It particularly affects the stomach, intestines, and bronchial tracts. Sometimes doctors use squill as an expectorant and diuretic. They also treat chronic bronchitis with it, but never when the disease is acute. Red squill is used as a rat poison.

Squill is also the name given the genus *Scilla* in the lily family. It includes 80 or more species that are found in the temperate regions of Europe.

Scientific Classification. The sea onion belongs to the lily family, *Liliaceae*. It is classified as genus *Urginea*, species *U. maritima*.   HAROLD NORMAN MOLDENKE

SQUINT is an abnormal condition of the eyes in which one eye is fixed on one object, and the other eye is fixed on another object. This condition is also known as *strabismus* and *cross-eye*. Normally, the eyes are so located that both eyes see the same object at the same time and in the same place. In strabismus, one eye turns away from its normal position. If this eye turns inward the condition is known as *convergent strabismus*, and if the eye turns outward the condition is known as *divergent strabismus*. If the crossed eye turns upward or downward, the condition is known as *supravergent strabismus*.

The cause of strabismus is not known, except in rare cases where the condition is due to an injury or fall. The tendency to have strabismus is inherited. Strabismus can be corrected in children, especially if the treatment is started early. Treatment of strabismus usually consists of wearing glasses, forced development of the weaker eye, and training in the use of both eyes at the same time. Only 15 per cent of all cases require a surgical operation.   HARRY S. GRADLE

See also CROSS-EYE.

SQUIRE, or **ESQUIRE.** See KNIGHTS AND KNIGHTHOOD.

Ed. Cesar, N.A.S.

Alvin E. Staffan, N.A.S.

Douglas Squirrel and Young

Eastern Gray Squirrel

SQUIRREL is a furry-tailed animal with large, black eyes and rounded ears. Many squirrels are lively animals with long, bushy tails. They scamper about the ground or in trees, and leap from branch to branch. These *tree squirrels* are often seen in parks and woodlands. They include gray squirrels, red squirrels, and flying squirrels. But many kinds of squirrels have short tails and never climb trees. They are called *ground squirrels*, and include chipmunks, marmots, prairie dogs, and woodchucks.

Squirrels live throughout the world except in Australia, Madagascar, and southern South America. One of the smallest squirrels is the African pygmy squirrel, found in western Africa. It weighs about ½ ounce (14 grams) and is 3 inches (8 centimeters) long without the 2-inch (5-centimeter) tail. The marmot is the largest squirrel. It weighs up to 20 pounds (9 kilograms) and grows as long as 30 inches (76 centimeters), including a 10-inch (25-centimeter) tail.

There are more than 300 kinds of squirrels, and they make up the squirrel family, *Sciuridae*. Squirrels are one of the largest families of *rodents* (gnawing animals). Like other rodents, all squirrels have chisel-like front teeth.

Many kinds of squirrels, especially tree squirrels and chipmunks, are easy to tame. They may learn to take nuts and other food from a person's hand. But many squirrels, like most other furry animals, carry the germs

of a disease called *rabies*. Even a tame squirrel may bite or scratch a person and give him rabies.

The word *squirrel* comes from two Greek words that mean *shadow tail*. At first, the word may have been used only for tree squirrels. The large, bushy tails of these animals curl over their backs and seem to keep them in the shade.

The rest of this article is about tree squirrels only. To learn more about the various kinds of ground squirrels, see the WORLD BOOK articles on CHIPMUNK; MARMOT; PRAIRIE DOG; and WOODCHUCK.

Homes. Most kinds of tree squirrels are active, noisy animals. They seem to scold one another continually in a variety of loud chirps, whistles, and noises that sound somewhat like *chirrr*.

Many squirrels have two homes—a warm, permanent one, and a temporary one that is cool enough for hot days. The permanent home may be a den in a hollow tree trunk, or a sturdy nest built on a branch. In Great

───── FACTS IN BRIEF ─────

Common Name	Scientific Name	Gestation Period	Number of Young	Life Span (in captivity)
Flying Squirrel	Glaucomys	40 days	2-6	7-13 years
Fox Squirrel	Sciurus	45 days	2-4	9 years
Gray Squirrel	Sciurus	44 days	2-5	8-15 years
Red Squirrel	Tamiasciurus	40 days	4	8-9 years

Squirrels make up the squirrel family, *Sciuridae*.

SQUIRREL

Britain, a squirrel's nest is called a *dray*. A squirrel's den is lined with dry leaves and strips of bark. During the winter, several squirrels may share one den. A squirrel's permanent nest is made of layers of twigs and leaves packed together to keep out rain, snow, and wind. A temporary nest is only a loose pile of twigs and leaves. It soon falls apart, and a squirrel may have to build several during a summer.

Squirrels move about easily in trees or on rooftops or telephone wires. They spread their legs straight out and leap from place to place. Squirrels use their bushy tails to keep their balance when they jump.

Food. Squirrels eat berries, corn, fruits, nuts, mushrooms, and seeds. They spend much of their time searching for food. A squirrel is especially busy in autumn, when it gathers food and hides it to eat during winter. Squirrels store food in holes in the ground, in trees, or in their dens.

Red squirrels are famous for the many pine cones they cut and store for food. A red squirrel may cut more than a hundred cones from a tree in an hour. Then the animal rushes down to the ground, gathers the cones, and hides them. The hiding place for the cones may be a hollow tree stump. Or the squirrel may pile the cones around a stone or a log and cover them with leaves. When winter comes, the squirrel may have 3 to 10 bushels of cones.

Young. A female squirrel carries her young in her body for 36 to 45 days before birth. She may give birth twice a year, and usually from two to six young are born at a time. Newborn squirrels have no fur, and their eyes are closed. Red squirrels and flying squirrels may open their eyes 26 to 28 days after birth, but gray squirrels may take as long as 37 days. When squirrels are 5 to 8 weeks old, they have all their fur and begin to search for their own food. They start to have their own families when they are about a year old.

Enemies. Man is the greatest enemy of squirrels. Men hunt most kinds of squirrels for sport, but they hunt tree squirrels especially for meat and fur. Other enemies of

The Body of a Squirrel

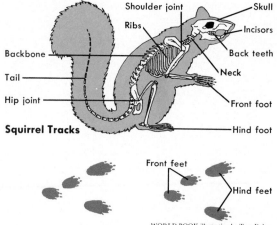

Shoulder joint — Skull
Ribs — Incisors
Backbone — Back teeth
Tail — Neck
Hip joint — Front foot
Squirrel Tracks — Hind foot

Front feet
Hind feet

WORLD BOOK illustration by Tom Dolan

squirrels include bobcats, cats, coyotes, dogs, and foxes. Tree squirrels race for the nearest tree when an enemy comes near. Squirrels may live for 2 to 6 years in the wild. Some have lived for 15 years in captivity.

Kinds of Tree Squirrels. There are three chief groups in the United States and Canada: (1) gray squirrels, (2) red squirrels, and (3) flying squirrels.

Gray Squirrels. Fox squirrels are the largest gray squirrels. Some grow 28 inches (71 centimeters) long, including a 12-inch (30-centimeter) tail. They weigh as much as 3 pounds (1.4 kilograms). Their fur is gray, reddish brown, or black. Fox squirrels are slower and tamer than most other kinds of tree squirrels. They live in the United States east of the Rocky Mountains.

Eastern gray squirrels and western gray squirrels are 16 to 24 inches (41 to 61 centimeters) long, including their tails. They weigh from $\frac{3}{4}$ to $1\frac{1}{2}$ pounds (0.3 to 0.7 kilogram). Most gray squirrels have gray fur on their backs, and whitish fur on their underparts. Eastern gray squirrels live east of the Rocky Mountains, and western gray squirrels live along the Pacific coast. The Kaibab

Kaibab Squirrels, or tassel-eared squirrels, have tufts of fur on their ears. They live in pine forests near the Grand Canyon.

Willis Peterson

Giant Squirrel is the largest tree squirrel. It grows up to 18 inches (46 centimeters) long, with a tail of the same length.

San Diego Zoo Photo

Where Squirrels Live

The black areas on this map show where squirrels are found.

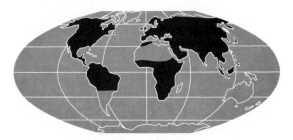

squirrel, a species of gray squirrel rarely seen, lives in the pine forests north of the Grand Canyon.

Red Squirrels are the noisiest and most active of all the squirrels. They always seem to be busy cutting down pine cones and hiding them, scolding one another while they work. These squirrels have reddish fur on their backs and white fur on their underparts. They weigh 5 to 11 ounces (140 to 312 grams). Few red squirrels are over 12 inches (30 centimeters) long, including the tail. The common red squirrel lives throughout most of Alaska and Canada. It also is found in the Northeastern and upper Midwestern United States, in the Appalachian Mountains as far south as South Carolina, and in the Rocky Mountains as far south as New Mexico. A second species of red squirrel, the Douglas squirrel, lives along the Pacific coast from British Columbia to California.

Flying Squirrels are the smallest kind of tree squirrels. Few grow more than 10 inches (25 centimeters) long, including the tail. The flying squirrel has a fold of skin that stretches from its front leg to its rear leg on each side of its body. This skin acts like the wings of a glider, and gives the animal "lift." Some flying squirrels can glide more than 150 feet (46 meters), but 50 to 60 feet (15 to 18 meters) is a more usual distance.

Unlike other kinds of tree squirrels, flying squirrels are usually active only at night. They live throughout the United States and Canada.   DANIEL BRANT

See also CHIPMUNK; FLYING SQUIRREL; GROUND SQUIRREL; MARMOT; PRAIRIE DOG; WOODCHUCK.

SQUIRREL MONKEY is a small, brightly colored monkey that lives in large groups. Some groups have up to 500 monkeys. Bands of squirrel monkeys live in the forests of Central and South America, from Costa Rica to Paraguay. They move swiftly through the trees and on the ground, seeking fruits and insects to eat. They use their long tails for balance when standing or leaping but do not use them for grasping. Most squirrel monkeys grow about 1 foot (30 centimeters) long and weigh less than 2 pounds (0.9 kilogram).

The squirrel monkey has an ash-gray or red-brown back, with shades of gold or olive. Bright yellow or orangish fur covers the lower parts of the limbs. The chest is white or light yellow. The black nose and mouth area contrasts with the white fur around the eyes.

Scientific Classification. Squirrel monkeys belong to the New World monkey family, *Cebidae*. They make up the genus *Saimiri*. A common species is *S. sciureus*.   NEIL C. TAPPEN

SRI INTERNATIONAL is a nonprofit, independent contract research organization. It performs basic and applied research for industry, government, and the pub-

lic. Its staff provides research services in over 100 subject areas, including economics, electronics, engineering, management, the physical and biological sciences, and urban and social systems. SRI International was founded in 1946 as the Stanford Research Institute. It adopted its present name in 1977. Headquarters are at 333 Ravenswood Avenue, Menlo Park, Calif. 94025.

Critically reviewed by SRI INTERNATIONAL

SRI LANKA, *sree LAHNG kuh*, is a beautiful island country in the Indian Ocean. It lies about 20 miles (32 kilometers) off the southeastern coast of India. The country's official name is the *Democratic Socialist Republic of Sri Lanka*. The name *Sri Lanka* (Resplendent Land) comes from a Hindu epic. The country was formerly called *Ceylon*.

Sri Lanka is a land of rich tropical plant life. It has been famous for more than 2,000 years for its spices and precious stones. It ranks third after India and China in tea production, and is a leading rubber producer.

Sri Lanka became an independent nation in 1948 after nearly 450 years of European rule. Colombo, one of the world's busiest seaports, is the capital and largest city.

Government. Sri Lanka is a republic. The president is the head of the government. A prime minister and a Cabinet assist the president. The legislature is a 168-member National State Assembly. All citizens 18 years of age or older may vote.

People. Sri Lanka has six distinct groups of people—Sinhalese, Tamils, Moors, Burghers, Malays, and Veddahs. The *Sinhalese* make up about three-fourths of the population. Their language is called Sinhala and most of them are Buddhists. They are descended from people who came from northern India. About a fifth of the population are *Tamils*, descendants of people who came from southern India. The Tamils are Hindus, and speak Tamil, a southern Indian language. Most of them live in the northern and eastern parts of the country. The

Facts in Brief

Capital: Colombo.

Form of Government: Republic.

Parliament: *National State Assembly*—168 members.

Area: 25,332 sq. mi. (65,610 km²). *Greatest Distances*—north-south, 274 mi. (441 km); east-west, 142 mi. (229 km). *Coastline*—725 mi. (1,167 km).

Highest Elevation: Pidurutalagala, 8,281 ft. (2,524 m).

Population: *Estimated 1984 Population*—15,954,000; distribution, 70 per cent rural, 30 per cent urban; density, 629 persons per sq. mi. (243 per km²). *1981 Census*—14,850,001. *Estimated 1989 Population*—17,701,000.

Chief Products: *Agriculture*—cacao, cinnamon, coconuts, cotton, pepper, rice, rubber, tea, tobacco. *Mining*—aquamarine, graphite, limestone, moonstone, ruby, sapphire, topaz, tourmaline, zircon.

Flag: The gold lion on a crimson field is a symbol of a precolonial Sri Lankan state. The ornaments in the corners of the crimson field are gold bo leaves, which are Buddhist symbols. Vertical green (Muslims) and orange (Tamils) stripes at the left stand for minorities. See FLAG (color picture: Flags of Asia).

Money: *Basic Unit*—rupee. For the value of the rupee in dollars, see MONEY (table: Exchange Rates).

SRI LANKA

Ewing Galloway

At Harvesttime in Sri Lanka, many farmers still use flails to thresh the grain. Some have begun to use machinery.

Sinhalese and Tamils use the Indian *caste* system (see CASTE). The *Moors*, descendants of Arabs, also speak Tamil. Most of them are Muslims. The *Burghers* are descendants of European settlers who intermarried with Sri Lankans. Most of them are Christians and live in cities. The *Malays*, descended from people who came from what is now Malaysia, are Muslims and live mainly in the southwest. The *Veddahs*, descendants of the country's first known residents, live in remote forest regions and practice traditional local religions.

Most Sri Lankans live in villages and work on farms or plantations. They live in houses that have mud walls and thatched roofs.

Most of the men of Sri Lanka wear a *sarong* (a garment wrapped around the waist to form a long skirt) and a long collarless shirt. Some men in the cities wear European-style clothing. Most women wear a *sari* (a straight piece of cloth draped around the body as a long dress) or a *camboy* (a sarong-type skirt and blouse). Rice is the chief food of the people. They usually serve it with fish, vegetable, or meat *curry* (a dish prepared in a spiced sauce).

Religious festivals and *pilgrimages* (journeys) to holy places play a major part in the life of the people. In May, Buddhists celebrate the birth, enlightenment, and death of the Buddha by lighting their houses with candles and colored lamps. Adams Peak, one of the island's

Sri Lanka

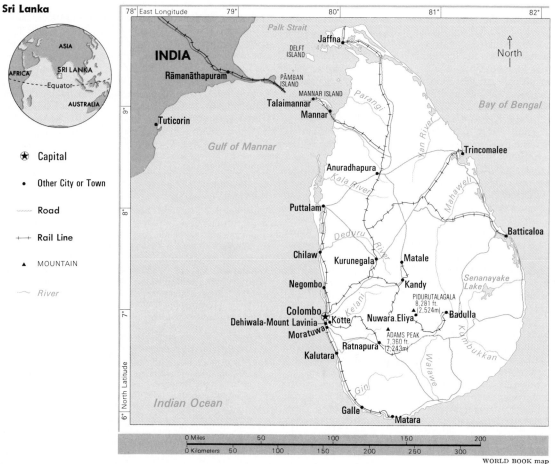

Capital ★

Other City or Town •

Road ----

Rail Line ++++

MOUNTAIN ▲

River ～

WORLD BOOK map

644

Pictorial Parade

A Muslim Mosque in Colombo towers over the shops that line this street. Colombo is Sri Lanka's capital and trading center.

highest mountains, is regarded as holy by most of the people. Buddhists visit a rock on the peak to see a footprint that they believe was made by the Buddha. Many Christians and Muslims also climb to the peak because they believe that Adam lived there after he was cast out of the Garden of Eden.

About 85 per cent of the people can read and write. Education is free and compulsory for children who are from 6 to 14 years of age. Sri Lanka has one university, with campuses in Colombo and three other cities.

Land. The rim of the island is a low coastal plain which runs inland from the northern and eastern shores. The central and southern sections rise to mountains of over 8,000 feet (2,400 meters). Rivers flow from the mountains through the forests and tea and rubber plantations to the coast. An irrigation system supplies farmlands in the dry central lowlands area.

Sri Lanka lies near the equator, but sea breezes keep the temperature about 80° F.(27° C). *Monsoons* (seasonal winds) bring most of the rain, which varies from 40 inches (100 centimeters) a year in the north to 200 inches (510 centimeters) a year on the southwestern mountains.

Economy. Tea accounts for about two-thirds of the country's exports, and rubber for about a sixth. Coconut palms and rice grow well in the coastal plains. But Sri Lanka has to import large quantities of rice to meet its food requirements. Forests produce such valuable lumber as ebony and satinwood. Big rubber plantations lie in the hills, and tea grows on the mountain slopes. The country's mines produce such precious stones as sapphires and rubies, and Sri Lanka leads the world in the production of high quality graphite. See Rubber (table); Tea (table).

History. The Veddahs, a wandering people, were the first known inhabitants of what is now Sri Lanka. Vijaya, a prince from northern India, invaded the island in about 500 b.c. and founded the Sinhalese dynasty. Later, the Tamils of southern India invaded the island and settled in the northern part. From the a.d. 1100's to the 1500's, the island had a Tamil kingdom in the north and a Sinhalese kingdom in the south.

European control of the island began in the 1500's. The Portuguese landed in Colombo in 1505, and ruled most of the island from the end of the 1500's until the Dutch took Colombo in 1656.

British forces captured the island in 1796, and made it the crown colony of Ceylon in 1802. The British planted the first rubber trees, and developed rubber plantations. The colony gained self-government gradually during the 1900's. It became the independent nation of Ceylon within the Commonwealth of Nations on Feb. 4, 1948.

Trouble arose between the Tamils and Sinhalese in the late 1940's over a proposal to make Sinhala the official language. Tamils demanded that Tamil also be an official language. Tension grew after the government made Sinhala the official language in 1956. Rioting broke out in 1958, and a state of emergency was declared. Compromises later provided that Tamil be used for official purposes in many areas.

Prime Minister S.W.R.D. Bandaranaike was murdered in 1959. The following year his widow, Sirimavo Bandaranaike, became the world's first woman prime minister. Dudley Senanayake became prime minister in 1965, but Mrs. Bandaranaike defeated him in 1970. In 1971, thousands of the people, dissatisfied with government economic policies, tried to overthrow the government. Army and police forces put down the revolt. In 1972, the country changed its name from Ceylon to Sri Lanka.

In the 1977 election, J. R. Jayewardene defeated Mrs. Bandaranaike. He became president in 1978 after a constitutional amendment made the president—rather than the prime minister—the head of the government. In 1982, Jayewardene was elected president. B. N. Pandey

Related Articles in World Book include:

Agriculture (picture:	Colombo
Picking Tea Leaves)	Feasts and Festivals
Asia (picture: The	(picture)
Handicrafts Industry)	Sculpture (Ceylon and
Bandaranaike, Sirimavo	Southeast Asia; picture)

SRINAGAR, *sree NUHG uhr* (pop. 586,038), is the capital of India's state of Jammu and Kashmir. The city lies about 170 miles (274 kilometers) northeast of Amritsar in the Vale of Kashmir (see India [political map]). Nearby are the Shalimar Gardens, which were built by the Moguls. British and Indian residents enjoy vacations in houseboats on the nearby lakes or on the Jhelum River, which flows through Srinagar. The city's chief products include rugs, silver articles, wood carvings, paper, and leather goods. Robert I. Crane

SST. See Airplane (Supersonic Airplanes; pictures).

ST. . . . See Saint . . .

STABILE. See Calder, Alexander.

STABILIZER. See Automatic Pilot; Gyroscope; Gyrostabilizer; Airplane (The Tail Assembly).

25 Largest Stadiums in the United States

Name and Location	Seating Capacity
Rose Bowl, Pasadena, Calif.	104,237
University of Michigan Stadium, Ann Arbor	101,701
Superdome, New Orleans	95,427
Memorial Coliseum, Los Angeles	92,604
Neyland Stadium (University of Tennessee), Knoxville	91,249
John F. Kennedy Stadium, Philadelphia	90,000
Stanford (University) Stadium, Palo Alto, Calif.	84,933
Beaver Stadium (Pennsylvania State University), University Park	*83,770
Ohio (State University) Stadium, Columbus	83,112
Memorial Stadium (University of Texas), Austin	*83,053
Pontiac Silverdome, Pontiac, Mich.	80,638
Gator Bowl, Jacksonville, Fla.	80,364
Municipal Stadium, Cleveland	80,322
Rich Stadium, Orchard Park, N.Y.	80,020
Arrowhead Stadium, Kansas City, Mo.	78,094
Camp Randall Stadium (University of Wisconsin), Madison	77,280
Giants Stadium, East Rutherford, N.J.	76,891
Memorial Stadium (University of Nebraska), Lincoln	76,500
Spartan Stadium (Michigan State University), East Lansing	76,000
Tiger Stadium (Louisiana State University), Baton Rouge	75,672
Memorial Stadium (University of California), Berkeley	75,608
Orange Bowl, Miami	75,414
Mile High Stadium, Denver, Colo.	75,123
Kingdome, Seattle, Wash.	*75,000
Rice University Stadium, Houston	*72,500

*Includes temporary seats.

STADIUM, *STAY dee uhm,* is a large structure for spectators built around a playing field or arena.

One of the first stadiums was the foot-race course in Olympia in ancient Greece. Other famous stadiums were in Delphi, Athens, and Epidaurus in Greece and in Ephesus in Asia Minor. Usually terraces shaped like horseshoes enclosed the stadiums to give the spectators a clear view of the field. Seats were often built on the terraces. The famous stadium in Athens was rebuilt and used for the Olympic Games in 1896.

Today's stadium has seats arranged in *tiers* (rows) from which spectators view football and baseball games, track meets, boxing matches, and other public events. Universities have built many stadiums for athletic games. Students and alumni have often paid for memorial stadiums. Some cities have built municipal stadiums where both civic events and sports events are held. Domed stadiums can be used for baseball, football, circuses, conventions, and other events.

The word *stadium* comes from the Greek word *stadion,* which meant the distance between the end pillars of the stadium located at Olympia (about 630 feet, or 192 meters). ELMER D. MITCHELL

See also COLOSSEUM; HIPPODROME; OLYMPIC GAMES.

STAËL, *stahl,* **MADAME DE** (1766-1817), was a prominent French critic and novelist of the early 1800's. Her literary work influenced the growth of romanticism in French literature.

Madame de Staël was one of the first to apply the notion of progress to literature. She felt literature was an extension of society and should reflect social change. In her critical works, such as *On Literature* (1800) and *On Germany* (1810), she emphasized that judgment should be relative, not absolute. *On Germany* introduced the German culture and such great thinkers as Friedrich von Schiller to Europe as a model to imitate.

Her two novels, *Delphine* (1802) and *Corinne* (1807), reflect her own life. They deal with women who disregard public opinion. Their theme, the conflict between the superior person and society, became popular in the romantic movement.

Madame de Staël was born Anne Louise Germaine Necker in Paris. She married Baron Staël-Holstein, Swedish ambassador to France, in 1786, but the marriage ended unhappily. She had a famous love affair with novelist Benjamin Constant. In 1811 she married Albert de Rocca, a Swiss military officer. She traveled extensively in Germany, Italy, and many other countries. She was exiled from Paris several times by Napoleon, who opposed her political beliefs. IRVING PUTTER

STAFF. See MUSIC (Musical Notation).

STAFF is an inexpensive material resembling plaster. Builders use it as an exterior and interior finish for temporary structures. It is made of plaster of Paris and hydraulic cement, mixed in water with dextrine and glycerin. Staff is applied like plaster. See also PLASTERING.

STAFF, GENERAL. See GENERAL STAFF.

STAFFORDSHIRE BULL TERRIER is a powerful, heavyset dog. A member of this breed stands from 14 to 16 inches (36 to 41 centimeters) tall and weighs from 28 to

Missy Yuhl

The Staffordshire Bull Terrier Originated in England.

38 pounds (13 to 17 kilograms). The dog has a broad head and a short, muscular neck. The coat of a Staffordshire bull terrier is short and smooth. It may be black, blue, brown, gray, red, tan, or white, or a combination of those colors.

The breed was developed during the early 1800's by miners of Staffordshire, England. They produced it by mating bulldogs with terriers. Staffordshire bull terriers were once used for dog fighting and for fighting bears and bulls. JOAN MCDONALD BREARLEY

See also AMERICAN STAFFORDSHIRE TERRIER.

STAFFORDSHIRE TERRIER. See AMERICAN STAFFORDSHIRE TERRIER.

STAG. See DEER.

644b

STAG BEETLE is the name of a family of beetles in which some males have oddly enlarged jaws. These jaws look somewhat like the horns of a male deer and have given the beetle its name. In some cases, these "horns" are nearly as long as the body of the insect. Common American species include the *giant stag beetle* of the southern states. It has *mandibles* (jaws) 1 inch (2.5 centimeters) long and a body 1½ to 2 inches (3.8 to 5 centimeters) long. The *pinching bug* of the eastern states is a stag beetle that flies by night. Adult stag beetles eat sap and honeydew. The eggs are laid in cracks in the bark of dead, decaying trees. They hatch into soft white grubs called larvae.

Scientific Classification. The stag beetle belongs to the stag beetle family, *Lucanidae*. The giant stag beetle is genus *Lucanus*, species *L. elaphus*. H. H. ROSS

See also BEETLE (pictures).

STAGBUSH. See BLACK HAW.

STAGE. See THEATER; MOTION PICTURE; DRAMA.

STAGE DESIGNER. See THEATER (Scene Design).

STAGECOACH was a horse-drawn coach used to carry passengers and mail on a regular route. Sometimes it also carried freight. The first long stage line was established about 1670 between London and Edinburgh, Scotland, a distance of 392 miles (631 kilometers).

Stagecoach lines were established in colonial America about 1756. They operated chiefly between Boston, New York, and Philadelphia. In 1785, Congress began mail service by stagecoach. Greater comforts were added to the coaches, such as springs and cushions. Many of the finest stagecoaches were made at Concord, N.H.

Early in the 1800's, travelers from Philadelphia, Baltimore, and Washington traveled to Ohio by the National Road. In elaborate Concord coaches drawn by six horses, they rode along at a brisk 10 miles (16 kilometers) per hour. The trip took two and one-half days. Horses were changed at relay stations every 15 or 20 miles (24 or 32 kilometers). Later, stagecoach lines operated in the West. But the railroads gradually replaced stagecoaches, except in remote regions. FRANKLIN M. RECK

See also WESTERN FRONTIER LIFE (Transportation).

STAGG, AMOS ALONZO (1862-1965), called *Football's Grand Old Man*, gained fame as the oldest active

National Life Insurance Co.

Stagecoaches provided the best transportation for passengers and mail between American cities in the 1700's and early 1800's.

coach in the United States and the man with the greatest number of coaching seasons to his credit. He coached at the University of Chicago for 41 years. After he retired at the age of 70, he coached at College of the Pacific from 1933 to 1946, and at Susquehanna (Pa.) University from 1947 to 1952. He devised many new football developments, including the tackling dummy. Stagg was born in West Orange, N.J. LYALL SMITH

STAHL, GEORG. See CHEMISTRY (The Discovery of Oxygen).

STAIN is a special type of dye used to bring out the grain in wood. Stains are named according to the type of solvent used to dissolve the dye. Water, oil, and alcohol are the chief solvents of stain. Alcohol is considered the best solvent for wood stain because it does not cause the grain to rise above the surface of the wood, as water does. Oil penetrates wood and produces a lustrous finish, but has a tendency to smear into coats of varnish that may be applied over it. FRED FORTESS

STAIN REMOVING. See DRY CLEANING; CLEANING FLUID.

STAINED GLASS is colored glass that has been cut into pieces and reassembled to form a picture or decorative design. The pieces are held together by strips of lead. The picture or design shines brightly when the glass is illuminated. However, light must pass through the glass to create this effect. Therefore, stained glass is used chiefly for windows. A well-made stained-glass window glows and sparkles with color in the rays of the sun.

Colorless glass may be painted or chemically treated to look like stained glass. But authentic stained glass is colored during the glassmaking process. The colors are produced by adding certain metal oxides to the other glassmaking ingredients. For example, cobalt oxide may be added to make blue glass, and copper oxide to make red glass. Most details of stained-glass pictures, such as shadows and facial features, are painted in. But the art of making stained glass is only distantly related to the art of painting. Stained glass achieves its effects mainly through the colors and shapes of the pieces of glass, together with the outlines formed by the lead strips.

How Stained-Glass Windows Are Made

Most stained-glass windows are designed by professional artists. In some cases, the artist also makes the window. In others, skilled craftworkers do this work under the artist's supervision.

The artist first makes a sketch of the picture or design to be portrayed by the window. The sketch serves as a model for a full-sized blueprint of the window. On the blueprint, called a *cartoon*, the artist shows the exact shape and color of each piece of glass. The artist also indicates the location of the lead strips and designates the details to be painted in. The cartoon is then traced onto heavy paper. The artist cuts out the patterns of the individual pieces of glass and marks each one to indicate its color.

Each paper cutout is placed on a sheet of glass of the designated color, and its outline is traced with a glass-cutter. When the glass is snapped, it breaks neatly along the outlines. After all the pieces have been cut out, they are put in place on the cartoon. The artist then paints the details of the window illustration.

The paint used for the details of stained-glass pictures is an enamel—a mixture of powdered glass, iron oxide, and a liquid, such as oil or water. The liquid makes the enamel flow, and the iron oxide gives it a dark brown color. After the artist has painted in the details, the pieces are fired in a special furnace called a *kiln*. The heat bonds the powdered glass and the iron oxide to the surface of the colored glass. After the glass has cooled, the pieces are again put in place on the cartoon.

The pieces of the window are now ready to be joined by means of strips of lead. Lead is used because it is soft and can easily be molded to the shapes of the glass pieces. The lead strips used to join segments of stained glass have a groove along each side and are called *cames*. The two grooves of a came are fitted over the edges of adjoining pieces of glass. Thus, each came joins several pieces. After all the pieces have been joined, the points where the ends of the cames meet

Window (1961) created for the synagogue at the Hadassah-Hebrew University Medical Center in Jerusalem, Israel; © Hadassah Medical Relief Association, Inc.

A Modern Stained-Glass Window by the artist Marc Chagall is one of a series that honors the 12 tribes of Israel. The window above represents the tribe of Zebulun. The fish and ship symbolize predictions in the Bible that the tribe would prosper near the sea.

The Betrayal of Christ by an unknown German artist; Hessisches Landesmuseum, Darmstadt, Germany

A Stained-Glass Window of the 1200's shows Judas Iscariot giving Jesus Christ the kiss that betrayed Jesus to the Romans. During the Middle Ages, the church used such scenes in stained-glass windows to teach people stories from the Bible.

are filled with solder. Putty is forced into the grooves to make them watertight. The finished window is now ready to install.

Large stained-glass windows have a framework of iron bars to hold them in place. The bars divide the window opening into sections. The stained glass for such windows is made in sections that fit the sections of the framework.

History

Early Stained-Glass Windows. The art of making stained-glass windows developed in western Europe during the Middle Ages. From the beginning, the art was closely allied with that of church-building. Stained-glass windows greatly increased the beauty of a church, but they had a more practical purpose as well. Scenes pictured in sparkling light and glowing colors make a strong impression on many people. Stained-glass windows thus became a powerful force in the teaching and encouragement of religion. Most early windows pictured scenes from the Bible or from the lives of saints.

Only fragments of stained glass have survived from the period before the 1000's. Five windows in the cathedral of Augsburg, Germany, are believed to be the oldest stained-glass windows in existence. They date from the last half of the 1000's or the early 1100's. Each of these windows shows a Biblical prophet.

All stained-glass windows made before the mid-1100's

were relatively small. At that time, churches had to have extremely thick walls to support their lofty domes and arches. In addition, window openings had to be small to avoid weakening the walls. During the early 1100's, however, architects began to develop a system of roof supports that greatly reduced the stress on the walls. More space could then be devoted to windows. The church of St. Denis, near Paris, was the first church built in this style of architecture, called Gothic, and the first to have large stained-glass windows. The earliest of these windows were installed in the church in the mid-1100's. During the next 100 years, many Gothic churches were built in Europe, and the art of making stained-glass windows developed rapidly.

Technical Improvements. Most large stained-glass windows of the 1100's had a framework of straight iron bars that divided them into rectangular sections. By the early 1200's, blacksmiths had learned to forge iron bars into curved shapes. Window frameworks then began to have round, as well as rectangular, sections. Round sections of stained glass created beautiful medallion-like patterns in a church window. Huge circular stained-glass windows also became common during the 1200's. These windows were divided into sections by delicate stonework called *tracery*. Because of their flowerlike shape, such windows are known as *rose windows*.

As the Gothic system of roof supports was improved, architects designed churches that had more and larger windows. The Sainte Chapelle, a church built in Paris during the 1240's, has walls made almost entirely of stained glass. The windows are separated only by narrow stone frames and extend from just above the floor to the ceiling, a distance of nearly 50 feet (15 meters). More than 100 large stained-glass windows were installed in the cathedral of Chartres during the 1200's. They include many lovely medallion-style windows and several magnificent rose windows.

The greatest churches of the Middle Ages had many stained-glass windows. But stained glass was expensive, and most churches could afford only a little of it. Then, in the 1300's, craftworkers discovered that colorless glass, if coated with silver nitrate, becomes stained brilliant yellow when fired. The chemical could be applied inexpensively as a solid coating or in patterns. Windows made of this type of stained glass became common in churches during and after the 1300's.

Techniques developed in the 1400's gave artists greater freedom to experiment. One of these techniques involved the use of glass that had only a thin film of color. The film was bonded to the glass during the glassmaking process, but it could be scraped off, exposing the colorless glass underneath. By scraping pictures or designs on the glass, artists produced windows as rich in detail as fine engravings. Also during the 1400's, artists began to use brightly colored enamels to paint elaborate scenes on colorless glass. After the painted glass was fired, it had nearly the same brilliance as stained glass.

Decline and Revival. The techniques developed during the 1400's gradually replaced the traditional methods of making stained glass. To make a decorative window, the artist scraped or painted the picture or design on panes of glass. The panes were then installed in the window framework. This method eliminated the need to build a window from many pieces of colored glass and a number of lead strips. However, the windows looked more like paintings than stained glass. By the 1600's, the art of making stained glass was nearly forgotten.

Interest in the art revived during the 1800's. Artists mastered the old techniques of making stained glass, and churches again began to have large stained-glass windows. At first, the windows were designed to look as nearly like those of the Middle Ages as possible. But by the early 1900's, artists had begun to develop new designs and even new uses for stained glass. John La Farge and Louis C. Tiffany were among the leaders of this movement in the United States. Tiffany invented new types of stained glass and used them not only for windows but also for decorative lampshades.

Today, the creation of stained glass ranks as an imaginative, highly developed art. Gifted artists, such as Marc Chagall and Georges Rouault, have designed superb stained-glass windows for modern religious structures. Some artists use techniques similar to those of the Middle Ages. Others have developed new techniques. For example, many stained-glass windows are now made of thick slabs of colored glass. The slabs are cut to shape and then joined with cement rather than with lead.   JANE HAYWARD

See also GLASS (picture); TRACERY; UNITED NATIONS (picture).

STAINLESS STEEL is the name of a family of alloy steels that resist *corrosion* (rust). As a family, the stainless steels have an easily-maintained, attractive appearance. They show remarkable strength and ductility and are unique in their general resistance to the elements and to most corrosives. Some 30 grades of stainless steels have been developed that have different combinations of strength, ductility, and resistance to corrosion and heat. Most stainless steels used in the home are highly polished, with a silvery appearance, but they do not need this finish to resist corrosion. *Stainless-clad steel* is commonly ordinary steel to which a thin layer of stainless steel has been bonded on one or both sides.

The most familiar use of stainless steel in the home is in kitchen knives, flatware, sinks, pots and pans, and other places where cleanliness and easy maintenance are essential. Stainless-steel equipment is used in hospitals, restaurants, chemical industries, dairies, and food-processing plants. Engineers use stainless steel parts for automobiles, aircraft, and railroad passenger cars. Scientists use microporous stainless steel, made with a nickel alloy, to filter gases, liquids, and small particles.

Chromium is the chief metal alloyed with iron, carbon, manganese, and silicon in making stainless steel. The more common stainless steels usually contain about 8 per cent nickel. One or more of the following elements also may be added to iron to make stainless steel: molybdenum, titanium, columbium, aluminum, nitrogen, phosphorus, sulfur, and selenium. Each of these elements modifies stainless steel so it can be used for a specific purpose.   MAX D. HOWELL

See also HAYNES, ELWOOD; IRON AND STEEL (Stainless Steel).

STAINS, REMOVAL OF. See DRY CLEANING.

STAKED PLAIN. See TEXAS (Land Regions).

STALACTITE, *stuh LAK tite.* The beautiful stone formations that hang down from the walls and roofs of some caves are called *stalactites.* Most stalactites look somewhat like icicles. They usually form in limestone caves. They are caused when water drips through cracks in the roof of the cave and carries the mineral called *calcite* (calcium carbonate) with it. As the water evaporates, it leaves formations of the calcite hanging. Stalactites of basalt rock hang from the roofs of some lava caverns. Similar formations of ice have been found in the ice caves of Arctic regions.

Formations which build up from the floor of a cave are called *stalagmites* (see STALAGMITE). In the United States, excellent examples of stalactites and stalagmites exist in Carlsbad Caverns National Park in New Mexico, in Luray Caverns in Virginia, in Mammoth Cave in Kentucky, and also in Wyandotte Cave in southern Indiana.   ELDRED D. WILSON

See also CALCITE; CAVE; NEVADA (picture).

STALAGMITE, *stuh LAG mite.* Stalagmites are stone formations which rise up from the floors of caves, especially in limestone caverns. They form when water, dripping on the floor from the walls and roofs of the cave, carries with it deposits of calcium carbonate, or calcite. As the water evaporates, the calcite builds up into colorful formations which look like icicles upside down. Similar formations, which hang from the roof, are called stalactites (see STALACTITE). Sometimes stalagmites and stalactites join to form columns or stone curtains against the walls of the cave.   ELDRED D. WILSON

See also CALCITE; CAVE; NEVADA (picture).

Keystone

Joseph Stalin ruled the Union of Soviet Socialist Republics (U.S.S.R.) as dictator from 1929 until 1953.

STALIN, *STAH lin*, **JOSEPH** (1879-1953), was dictator of the Union of Soviet Socialist Republics (U.S.S.R.) from 1929 until 1953. He rose from bitter poverty to become ruler of a country that covers about a sixth of the world's land area.

Stalin ruled by terror during most of his years as dictator. He allowed no one to oppose his decisions. Stalin executed or jailed most of those who had helped him rise to power because he feared they might threaten his rule. He also was responsible for the deaths of millions of Soviet peasants who opposed his program of *collective agriculture* (government control of farms). Under Stalin, the Soviet Union operated a worldwide network of Communist parties. By the time he died, Communism had spread to 11 other countries.

The Soviet people had cause to hate Stalin, and much of the world feared him. But he changed the Soviet Union from an undeveloped country into one of the world's great industrial and military powers. During World War II, the U.S.S.R. was an ally of the United States and Great Britain against Germany. However, Stalin sharply opposed and, on occasion, betrayed his allies even before the war was over. His last years of power were marked by the Cold War in which the nations of the Free World banded together to halt the spread of Communism.

Stalin had little personal charm, and could be brutal to even his closest friends. He seemed unable to feel pity. He could not take criticism, and he never forgave an

Luray Caverns Corp.

Stalactites and Stalagmites in Luray Caverns in Virginia's Shenandoah Valley form beautifully colored columns. The room shown above is called "The Cathedral" because the formations have the appearance of a pipe organ.

Myron Rush, the critical reviewer of this article, is Professor of Government at Cornell University and the author of Political Succession in the U.S.S.R. *and* The Rise of Khrushchev.

opponent. Few dictators have demanded such terrible sacrifices from their own people.

After Stalin became dictator, he had Soviet histories rewritten to make his role in past events appear far greater than it really was. In 1938, he helped write an official history of the Communist party. Stalin had not played a leading part in the revolution of October, 1917 (November by the present Soviet calendar), which brought Communism to Russia. Lenin led the revolution and set up the world's first Communist government. But in his history, Stalin pictured himself as Lenin's chief assistant in the revolution.

Stalin died in 1953. He was honored by having his body placed beside that of Lenin in a huge tomb in Red Square in Moscow. In 1956, Nikita S. Khrushchev strongly criticized Stalin for his terrible crimes against loyal Communists. Later, in 1961, the government renamed many cities, towns, and factories that had been named for Stalin. Stalin's body was taken from the tomb and buried in a simple grave nearby.

Early Life

Boyhood and Education. Joseph Stalin was born on Dec. 21, 1879, in Gori, a town near Tbilisi in Georgia, a mountainous area of southwestern Russia. His real name was IOSIF VISSARIONOVICH DJUGASHVILI. In 1913, he adopted the name *Stalin* from a Russian word meaning *man of steel*.

Little is known about Stalin's early life. His father, Vissarion Ivanovich Djugashvili, was an unsuccessful village shoemaker. He is said to have been a drunkard who was cruel to his young son. Stalin's mother, Ekaterina Gheladze Djugashvili, became a washerwoman to help support the family. The Djugashvilis lived in a small shack. The first three children of the family died shortly after birth, and Stalin grew up as an only child. When Stalin was young, his father left the family and went to nearby Tbilisi to work in a shoe factory. The boy had smallpox when he was 6 or 7, and the disease scarred his face for life.

In 1888, at great sacrifice, Stalin's mother sent him to a little church school in Gori. He spent five years there and was a bright student. He then received a scholarship at the religious seminary in Tbilisi. Stalin entered this school in 1894 at the age of 14. He soon became known among his classmates for reading, debate, and good schoolwork. Some of his classmates later remembered that Stalin held grudges and seldom forgave persons who opposed him.

Stalin studied for the priesthood in the Georgian Orthodox Church. But he was repeatedly punished at the seminary for reading forbidden books. These books included Victor Hugo's novels about social conditions in France, and about French revolutionary movements. Stalin also became interested in the ideas of Karl Marx, a German social philosopher. The people of Tbilisi knew little of Marx and his theories about revolution. But political exiles from Moscow and St. Petersburg (now Leningrad) were beginning to bring Marxist pamphlets to Tbilisi and other smaller cities.

Czar Alexander III died in 1894, and his son, Nicholas II, became czar. Alexander had ruled Russia with complete power. He closely controlled the press, restricted education, and forbade student organizations. Nicholas continued his father's policies, and Russia

Sovfoto

Stalin's Birthplace was a two-room shack in Gori, a town in Georgia in southwestern Russia. A Soviet artist painted this picture of the shack. As a boy, Stalin studied to be a priest.

made important economic and social progress. However, it was difficult to solve the country's social problems. The peasants were demanding more land. They could not raise enough food for the country on their small farms, and, at times, millions of persons faced starvation. The growing class of factory workers was discontented because of long hours and low wages. For a discussion of conditions in Russia at this time, see RUSSIA (History).

In 1898, Stalin joined a secret Marxist revolutionary group. The Tbilisi seminary, like many Russian schools, was a center for the circulation of forbidden revolutionary ideas. In May, 1899, Stalin was expelled for not appearing for an examination. His interest in Marxism probably played a part in his dismissal.

Young Revolutionist. After Stalin left the seminary, he got a job as a clerk at the Tbilisi Geophysical Ob-

IMPORTANT DATES IN STALIN'S LIFE

1879 (Dec. 21) Born in Gori, Russia.
1899 Expelled from Tbilisi seminary.
1901 Joined the Russian Social Democratic Labor party.
1903 Exiled for the first of six times before the October revolution of 1917.
c. 1904 Married Ekaterina Svanidze.
1905 Met Lenin for the first time.
1912 Named by Lenin to Bolshevik party Central Committee.
1917 Named commissar of nationalities after Bolshevik revolution.
c. 1918 Married Nadezhda Alliluyeva.
1922 Appointed general secretary of Communist party.
1928 Began five-year plans to industrialize the U.S.S.R.
1929 Became dictator of the Soviet Union.
1935 Began great purge of Communist party members.
1939 The U.S.S.R. signed a nonaggression pact with Germany.
1941 Named himself premier of the Soviet Union.
1941 Germany attacked the U.S.S.R. during World War II.
1953 (March 5) Died in Moscow.

servatory. Within a year, he began his career as an active revolutionist. In 1900, Stalin helped organize a small May Day demonstration near Tbilisi. He made his first public speech at the demonstration, which was held to protest working conditions.

In March, 1901, the czar's secret police arrested a number of socialists in Tbilisi. The police searched Stalin's room, but he was not there and escaped arrest. He left his job and joined the Marxist revolutionary underground movement that was springing up in Russia. To confuse the police, he changed his name to *Koba*, the name of a hero in a Georgian legend.

In September, 1901, Stalin began to write for a Georgian Marxist journal called *Brdzola* (The Struggle). By this time, he had read revolutionary articles written by Lenin. Stalin's first writings closely imitated the views of Lenin, but lacked Lenin's style or force. In November, 1901, Stalin was formally accepted into the Russian Social Democratic Labor (Marxist) party.

Using various false names, Stalin carried on underground activity in the Caucasus Mountains region. He organized strikes among workers in the Batum oil fields. He helped start a Social Democratic group in Batum and set up a secret press there.

In 1902, Stalin was arrested and jailed for his revolutionary activities. In March, 1903, the several Social Democratic groups of the Caucasus united to form an All-Caucasian Federation. Although Stalin was in prison, the federation elected him to its governing body. In November, 1903, he was transferred from prison and exiled to Siberia. Also in 1903, the Russian Social Democratic Labor party, which included many Social Democratic organizations, split into two major groups. V. I. Lenin headed the *Bolsheviks*, who demanded that party membership be limited to a small body of devoted revolutionists. The other group, called the *Mensheviks*, wanted a wider membership.

Stalin escaped from Siberia in January, 1904. He returned to Tbilisi and joined the Bolsheviks. Stalin met Lenin in Finland in 1905. Shortly before this time, Stalin married Ekaterina Svanidze, the sister of a schoolmate at the Tbilisi seminary. She died of tuberculosis in 1907. They had one son, Jacob, who died during World War II after being captured by the Germans. In 1918 or 1919, Stalin married Nadezhda Alliluyeva, a girl in her late teens who had been his secretary. She died mysteriously in 1932, either a suicide or a victim of Stalin's anger. Stalin and his second wife had a son, Vasily, and a daughter, Svetlana. Vasily, a Soviet air force general, died in an automobile crash after Stalin's death in 1953. Svetlana became a teacher and translator of English. She moved to the United States in 1967.

Between 1906 and 1913, Stalin was arrested and exiled a number of times. He spent 7 of the 10 years between 1907 and 1917 in prison or in exile. In 1912, Stalin was suddenly elevated by Lenin into the small but powerful Central Committee of the Bolshevik party.

In 1913, with Lenin's help, Stalin wrote a long article called "The National Question and Social Democracy." Iosif Djugashvili signed the article *Stalin*, a name he had just begun to use. Also in 1913, Stalin was arrested and exiled for the last time. Before his arrest, he served briefly as an editor of *Pravda* (Truth), the Bolshevik party newspaper.

Germany declared war on Russia in 1914 at the beginning of World War I. Stalin was in exile in Siberia, where he remained until 1917. He was turned down by the army in 1916 because a boyhood blood infection made it difficult for him to bend his left elbow.

By the end of 1916, Russia faced defeat in the war against Germany. Conditions became steadily worse at home. Food shortages in the capital, Petrograd (now Leningrad), led to riots and strikes. Finally, on March 15, 1917, Czar Nicholas II gave up his throne. A *provisional* (temporary) government, run mostly by liberals, was formed the next day. The government released Stalin and other Bolsheviks from exile. They returned to Petrograd on March 25. Stalin took over the editorship of *Pravda* from Vyacheslav Molotov. Lenin became concerned that Stalin did not strongly oppose the provisional government in *Pravda*. Lenin arrived in Petrograd from exile three weeks later and criticized Stalin for not taking a strong Bolshevik stand. Lenin launched a radical program for overthrowing the provisional government. This action led to the Bolshevik seizure of power in November, 1917. The month was October in the old Russian calendar, and the Bolshevik take-over is often called the *October Revolution*.

Rise to Power

The Bolshevik Revolution. During the period before the October Revolution, Stalin was not, as he later claimed, Lenin's right-hand man. He played an important, but not vital, part in the revolution. Lenin worked most closely with Leon Trotsky in the Bolshevik take-over of the government. After Stalin became dictator of the Soviet Union, he had history books rewritten to say that he had led the revolution with Lenin.

Lenin became head of the new government after the revolution, and named Stalin commissar of nationalities. Within a few months, opposition to the new government developed in many parts of the country. Armed uprisings broke out and grew into civil war. Stalin was active on the southern military front. In Stalin's version of history, he repeatedly corrected the mistakes of others. Stalin took credit for a victory at Tsaritsyn, the city later named Stalingrad (now Volgograd). Actually, Stalin's military role there was exaggerated.

During the civil war, the Russian Social Democratic Labor party was renamed the All-Russian Communist party (Bolshevik). Stalin became one of the five members of the newly formed *Politburo* (Political Bureau), the policy-making body of the party's Central Committee. In 1922, the Communist party's Central Committee elected Stalin as its general secretary.

Stalin Takes Over. The Bolsheviks won the civil war in 1920. They then began the task of rebuilding the war-torn country. At first, Lenin and the others were unaware of Stalin's quiet plotting. By the end of 1922, however, Stalin's growing power began to disturb Lenin. Before a series of strokes prevented Lenin from working, he wrote a secret note warning that Stalin must be removed as general secretary. He wrote that Stalin was too "rude" in personal relations and abused the power of his office. Because of his illness, Lenin was unable to carry out his plan to remove Stalin.

United Press Int.

Soviet Farm Workers had to work on government-controlled farms after Stalin began to end private farming in 1929.

Lenin died in 1924. The leading Bolsheviks finally learned of the secret note warning against Stalin, but they ignored it. They accepted Stalin's promise that he would improve his behavior. Instead, Stalin continued to build his own power. He cleverly used this power to destroy his rivals. In December, 1929, the party praised Stalin on his 50th birthday. He had become a dictator.

Dictator of the Soviet Union

The Five-Year Plan. In 1928, Stalin started the first of the Soviet Union's five-year plans for economic development. The government began to eliminate private businesses. Production of industrial machinery and farm equipment became more important, and production of clothing and household goods was neglected.

In 1929, Stalin began to *collectivize* Soviet agriculture. He ended private farming and transferred the control of farms, farm equipment, and livestock to the government. But the farmers resisted his order and destroyed about half of the U.S.S.R.'s livestock and much of its produce. As punishment, Stalin sent about a million families into exile. The destruction of livestock and grain caused widespread starvation. The economy moved forward, but at the cost of millions of lives.

During the 1930's, Stalin adopted a policy of *Russification*. The minority nationalities in the Soviet Union were subject to increasingly strict control by the government. In 1939, the Soviet Union seized a large part of Poland. In 1940, Soviet troops invaded the Baltic countries—Estonia, Latvia, and Lithuania. Stalin tried to destroy the middle classes in these countries. He set up Communist governments and joined them to the Soviet Union. See BALTIC STATES.

The U.S.S.R. and Germany Divided Poland by a treaty signed in September, 1939. Soviet foreign minister Vyacheslav Molotov, *seated*, and German foreign minister Joachim von Ribbentrop, *left*, signed the treaty as Stalin and an aide looked on.

United Press Int.

Rule by Terror. Under the czars, the Russian secret police had often arrested revolutionists and sent them into exile without trial. Stalin set up a police system that was far more terrible. Millions of persons were executed or sent to labor camps. Stalin also turned over many industries to the secret police, who forced prisoners to work in them. Fear spread through the U.S.S.R. as neighbors were ordered to spy on one another. The government broke up families and urged children to inform on their parents to the police.

In 1935, Stalin started a *purge* (elimination) of most of the old Bolsheviks associated with Lenin. During the next few years, he killed anyone who might have threatened his power. He also executed thousands of other Communist party members, including the chiefs and countless officers of the Soviet army. Stalin achieved his purpose. When he decided to cooperate with the German dictator Adolf Hitler in 1939, there was no one left to oppose his policies. Even when the Soviet Union later suffered terrible military defeats from Hitler's army, no political opposition to Stalin was possible.

After World War II ended in 1945, Lavrenti P. Beria, chief of the secret police, became a leading figure in Stalin's government. Police control grew tighter. The bloody purges went on, but in secret rather than in public. No one was safe. Even Politburo members and Communist party leaders were purged and shot in 1949 and 1950. Anti-Semitism, which had been encouraged by Stalin during the 1930's, was now practiced throughout the country.

World War II. By the late 1930's, Adolf Hitler was ready to conquer Europe. Soviet leaders bargained unsuccessfully with the French and the British for a defense agreement against Germany. Then, on Aug. 23, 1939, the U.S.S.R. and Germany suddenly signed a treaty agreeing not to go to war against each other. In a secret part of the treaty, Stalin and Hitler also agreed to divide Poland between themselves.

On Sept. 1, 1939, German troops marched into Poland. On September 3, France and Great Britain declared war on Germany. World War II had begun. Germany quickly conquered western Poland, and the Soviet Union seized the eastern part. On September 28, Germany and the U.S.S.R. signed a treaty which set the boundaries for the division of Poland. The Soviet Union invaded Finland on Nov. 30, 1939, and, after a bitter struggle, took a large portion of that country.

By December, 1940, Hitler began planning an attack on the U.S.S.R. Prime Minister Winston Churchill of Great Britain and President Franklin D. Roosevelt of the United States told Stalin that their secret agents warned of a coming invasion. But Stalin ignored the warnings, as well as those of his own secret service.

In May, 1941, Stalin named himself premier of the Soviet Union. Germany invaded the Soviet Union the next month. In spite of the two extra years that Stalin had to get ready for a war, the country was not prepared. Because of Stalin's purge of the army, the U.S.S.R. did not have enough experienced officers. The country also lacked up-to-date weapons and equipment. The German army approached Moscow, the capital, in October, 1941, and many government officials were moved to Kuybyshev. Stalin remained in Moscow to give hope and courage to the Soviet people. The army finally beat back German attacks on Moscow in the winter of 1941-1942. Stalin reached the height of his popularity during the war.

In March, 1943, Stalin took the military title of Marshal of the Soviet Union. Later in 1943, Churchill, Roosevelt, and Stalin met at Teheran, Iran. The "Big Three" agreed that the United States, Great Britain, and the U.S.S.R. would work together until Germany was defeated. The three leaders met again early in 1945 at Yalta in the Crimea to discuss the military occupation of Germany after the war. For the story of the Soviet Union in the war, see WORLD WAR II.

The Cold War. After the Allies defeated Germany in 1945, Stalin gradually cut off almost all contact between the U.S.S.R. and the West. Stalin used the Soviet army's presence in Eastern Europe to set up Communist governments in Bulgaria, Czechoslovakia, East Germany, Hungary, Poland, and Romania. He also tried unsuccessfully to take over Greece, Iran, and Turkey. The nations of the Free World joined against the Soviet Union and its *satellites* (countries controlled by the U.S.S.R.) to halt the spread of Communism. This struggle became known as the Cold War (see COLD WAR).

Following World War II, Germany was divided into four zones, each occupied by American, British, French, or Soviet troops. Berlin, which lay deep in the Soviet zone, was also divided among the four powers. Stalin refused to cooperate in administering Germany, and in 1948, France, Great Britain, and the United States announced plans to combine their zones into the West German Federal Republic (West Germany). To prevent this action, Stalin tried to drive the Allies out of West Berlin by blockading the city. He hoped the blockade would prevent food and supplies from reaching West Berlin. But the Allies set up the Berlin airlift and supplied the city by airplanes for 11 months. Stalin was defeated, and he ended the blockade of Berlin in May, 1949.

In 1948, Stalin expelled the Yugoslav Communist party from the *Cominform* (Communist Information Bureau), an organization of Communist parties in Europe. Josip Broz Tito, the Communist dictator of Yugoslavia, had refused to allow the Soviet Union to run his country. In 1949, Tito declared Yugoslavia's independence of control by Stalin and the Soviet Union.

Stalin's aggressive policies led the West in 1949 to form the North Atlantic Treaty Organization (NATO), a mutual defense organization.

During the Korean War (1950-1953), Stalin supported the Communist North Korean forces that invaded South Korea. Korea had been divided into two parts after World War II. At first, Soviet troops occupied the northern half, and American troops occupied the southern half, but both sides later withdrew their forces. North Korean troops then launched a surprise attack on South Korea in an attempt to unite the divided country by force. As a result, U.S. troops had to be sent back to Korea. The war ended a few months after Stalin's death. See KOREAN WAR.

Death. Early in 1953, Stalin prepared to replace the top men in the Soviet government. Apparently he was planning another great purge. Then, on March 4, 1953, the Central Committee of the Communist Party announced that Stalin had suffered a brain hemorrhage the night of March 1. Stalin died in Moscow on March 5, 1953.

Critically reviewed by MYRON RUSH

Related Articles in WORLD BOOK include:

Beria, Lavrenti P.	Potsdam Conference
Bolsheviks	Russia
Cold War	Teheran Conference
Khrushchev, Nikita S.	Tito, Josip Broz
Lenin, V. I.	Trotsky, Leon
Marx, Karl H.	World War II
Molotov, Vyacheslav M.	Yalta Conference
Politburo	

Additonal Resources

DEUTSCHER, ISAAC. *Stalin: A Political Biography.* 2nd ed. Oxford, 1967.

GREY, IAN. *Stalin: Man of History.* Doubleday, 1979.

TUCKER, ROBERT C. *Stalinism: Essays in History and Interpretation.* Norton, 1977.

WARTH, ROBERT. *Joseph Stalin.* Twayne, 1969.

STALINABAD. See DUSHANBE.

STALINGRAD. See VOLGOGRAD.

STALINGRAD, BATTLE OF, one of the most important battles of history, marked a turning point in World War II. During the five-month struggle, the Russians kept German troops from capturing Stalingrad (now Volgograd), an important Russian industrial city on the Volga River. The German defeat at Stalingrad ended the Nazis' eastward advance into Russia. The invading German troops had to retreat from the Caucasus oil fields and the lower Don River regions. During the battle, the German army lost about 350,000 soldiers, including about 90,000 prisoners. The prisoners included 24 German generals. Snow and bitter cold took a heavy toll of German troops.

The German Sixth Army launched its drive on Stalingrad on Aug. 21, 1942, from positions about 40 miles (64 kilometers) away on the Don River. By August 23, German tanks had reached the Volga River, north of Stalingrad. Gradually, they forced their way into the city. By November, German forces had isolated Russian troops in four "pockets" along the riverbank in the city. German and Russian units fought hand-to-hand for control of single streets, houses, and factories. When the Volga froze over, Russian troops pushed supplies across on the ice at night.

Russian armies north and south of Stalingrad counterattacked the Germans on November 19. The Russians met west of Stalingrad on November 23, completely surrounding the German units in and near the city.

Nazi dictator Adolf Hitler ordered his generals to continue the battle for Stalingrad. He sent other German units to help the troops in the city, but the relief forces could not break through the Russian lines. The Russians hammered away at the hungry, half-frozen German troops. Finally, German Field Marshal Friedrich von Paulus, Sixth Army commander, surrendered on Jan. 31, 1943.

WILLIAM A. JENKS

See also RUSSIA (World War II; picture); WORLD WAR II (On the Russian Front; picture and map).

STALINO. See DONETSK.

STALLION. See HORSE (table: Horse Terms).

STAMBOLIISKI, ALEXANDER. See BULGARIA (After World War I).

STAMEN. See FLOWER (The Parts of a Flower; pictures).

STAMFORD, Conn. (pop. 102,453; met. area pop. 198,854), is an important business center. The city lies on Long Island Sound, about 35 miles (56 kilometers) northeast of New York City. For location, see CONNECTICUT (political map).

The Stamford area ranks third, behind only New York City and Chicago, as a site for headquarters of the nation's largest corporations. More than 20 of the 500 biggest companies have home offices in the Stamford area. Stamford's leading industries include printing, publishing, and the production of chemicals, electrical equipment, office machines, and textiles. The city has a museum and nature center, opera company, and symphony orchestra. Its recreational facilities include beaches and marinas.

Paugusset and Siwanog Indians lived in what is now the Stamford area before white settlers arrived. In 1640, the Indians sold the land to English colonists who had left another settlement because of religious differences. In 1893, one part of Stamford was incorporated as a city and the other part as a town. The city and town merged in 1949 under a mayor-council form of government.

In the 1970's and early 1980's, urban renewal projects led to a construction boom in downtown Stamford. The projects included a hotel, apartment buildings, office buildings, and a large shopping mall.   JOHN J. SCHMITT

STAMMERING. See STUTTERING.

STAMP is an official mark or seal or a small printed piece of paper with one glued surface. Many documents are not legal until they carry a government stamp. For example, the government may require the payment of a one-dollar tax on a real-estate deed. The collector pastes a revenue stamp of one dollar in value on the deed, as proof that the tax was paid.

The Dutch levied the first stamp taxes in 1624. In 1694, the English used the stamp plan to raise money for carrying on a war with France. The British Stamp Act of 1765 was one of the direct causes of the American colonial revolt against Great Britain.

In 1814, stamp taxes became a part of the fiscal system of the United States. In 1862, the American Congress passed an important stamp law. The law required that legal papers and certain kinds of packages carry government stamps. The purpose of the law was to raise funds to pay some of the expenses of the Civil War. The law was repealed when revenue was no longer needed to pay war expenses. New stamp laws, passed during the Spanish-American War and World War I, helped raise money to pay the costs of war.

Government stamps for raising money are known as internal revenue stamps. Until 1959, the United States government required that such stamps be placed on luxuries such as tobacco and liquor. Some states also tax these luxuries, and require that they be stamped.

During World War II, the United States government offered war savings stamps for sale to citizens. These stamps raised funds for the war. Another kind of stamp, the ration stamp, came into use during World War II. The purpose of the ration stamp was to divide food and clothing equally among civilians. However, people are probably most familiar with the postage stamp.   PAYSON S. WILD

See also INTERNAL REVENUE; POST OFFICE (Stamps and Other Mailing Materials); STAMP ACT; STAMP COLLECTING; TRADING STAMPS.

STAMP ACT. The British Parliament passed the Stamp Act in March, 1765. Its purpose was to raise funds to help support the British army stationed in America after 1763. The act specified that Americans must buy stamps for deeds, mortgages, liquor licenses, law licenses, playing cards, and almanacs. Even newspaper owners and publishers had to purchase stamps for their publications.

The Stamp Act was unpopular throughout the colonies. Societies organized to protest the sale of stamps. In cities and towns the slogan became "no taxation without representation."

The Virginia Assembly declared that the Stamp Act was illegal and unjust. The assembly passed resolutions against taxation by the British Parliament. The Massachusetts House of Representatives invited all colonies to send delegates to a general congress. The colonies which accepted the invitation to attend were New York, New Jersey, Rhode Island, Pennsylvania, Delaware, Connecticut, Maryland, South Carolina, and Massachusetts.

The Stamp Act Congress met in New York in October, 1765. It declared that stamp taxes could not be collected without the people's consent. American resistance forced the British Parliament to repeal the Stamp Act in 1766.   JOHN R. ALDEN

See also ADAMS, JOHN (In New England); REVOLUTIONARY WAR IN AMERICA (The Quartering and Stamp Acts).

STAMP COLLECTING is one of the most popular collecting hobbies in the world. Young persons, old persons, rich persons, and poor persons in every country collect stamps. Stamp collecting has been called "the hobby of kings and the king of hobbies." King George V of England, Franklin D. Roosevelt, and many other famous persons have collected stamps. Students of stamps are called *philatelists*. The name comes from two Greek words, *philos*, meaning *loving*, and *atelos*,

These Three Stamps were used by the British government under the Stamp Act it imposed upon the American colonies.

649

Robert A. Siegel, Inc.

The First Stamps Issued by the U.S. Post Office appeared in 1847. They bore the portraits of George Washington and Benjamin Franklin. Franklin was the first U.S. postmaster general.

meaning *free of tax*, or *paid*. Stamps are signs that the postage, or tax, has been paid.

Origins

Great Britain issued the first stamps to prepay postage on letters on May 6, 1840. These first stamps were a one-penny stamp (now known as "The Penny Black") and a two-pence stamp. Complete envelopes designed by William Mulready were also sold in the same values. But these were discontinued.

The United States did not issue any stamps until 1847. By that time several other countries had already tried the newly invented stamp. Among them were Brazil, Mauritius, and the *cantons* (states) of Switzerland. By 1860 almost every country had adopted stamps as a method of paying postage.

No one knows exactly when stamp collecting started. It probably occurred right after the first stamp was issued. We do know that the first stamp catalog was published in 1864 by an Englishman named Mount Brown. Since then catalogs of stamps have been published in almost every country. A great many books and magazines about stamps have also been published.

People soon discovered that some stamps were harder to find than others, because smaller quantities of them were printed. Collectors traded rare stamps and soon began selling them to each other. Prices rose as more people began collecting stamps. A 5-cent American stamp issued in 1847 was sold for $200,000 in 1975 and resold for $1 million in 1981. A one-penny 1856 British Guiana stamp sold for $850,000 in 1980. Sometimes errors are made in printing stamps. Such stamps are usually rare and may become very valuable. For example, about 100 24-cent United States airmail stamps were issued in 1918 with the airplane mistakenly printed upside down. One of these stamps was sold at auction in 1977 for $62,500.

Ways in Which Stamps Differ

Small differences in stamps mean a great deal to the stamp collector. Stamps which look the same to the beginner might seem entirely different to the expert.

Philatelists study many things, such as the paper and inks used, the way the stamps are separated, the printing process, and postal history.

Paper. The surface of paper may be finished in various ways. Paper with a plain finish is called *wove*. Paper which looks as though it has bars in it when it is held up to the light is known as *laid*. Tiny pieces of colored silk like those in a dollar bill are used in *silk paper*. Pieces of silk so small they can hardly be seen are used in *granite paper*, which is grayish in color.

Sometimes paper is made with a design called a *watermark*, which is pressed into the wet paper with wire. The wire can be laid in any shape wanted. Stamps may look the same on the surface, but have different watermarks. Philatelists consider these as different stamps. The watermark can be seen by holding the stamp up to the light, or by placing it face down in a black dish and pouring watermark fluid on it.

Ink. Stamps are printed with different colored inks. Variations of the color of the basic ink make the stamps different for the collector. For example, a blue stamp differs from an ultramarine stamp.

Printing. A stamp may be printed by one of three methods—*relief*, *planographic*, and *intaglio*. Relief printing is made from a raised design. Planographic printing is made from a design level with the surface, and intaglio is printed from a design cut lower than the surface. The most common forms of planographic printing are *offset* and *lithography*. One form of intaglio printing used for stamps is called *engraving*. The ink is slightly raised, just as it is on an engraved calling card. Another intaglio process is *gravure*. See PRINTING.

Separations. The first stamps had to be cut apart with scissors. Such stamps are called *imperforate*. Soon *perforations* (little holes) were punched between the rows of stamps. Stamps which have a different number of holes per inch along any edge are also considered as different stamps. Sometimes the separations are slits cut with a knife between the stamps, but with no paper punched out. This form is referred to as a *roulette*.

Cancellations. The marks placed on a stamp to show that it has been used are called a *cancellation*. Cancellations show postal history. Used stamps are often left on the envelopes, and early stamps are much more valuable that way. Envelopes with a stamp canceled the first day it was used are called *first day covers*. Collectors now prize such cancellations.

Surcharged Stamps. Countries often change stamps by overprinting (surcharging) something new on an old stamp, instead of issuing a new one. A new value may be printed on an old stamp. When a country is overrun in war, the conquerors often print their names on the stamps of the fallen country.

Special Stamps. Many special types of stamps are issued, in addition to plain postage stamps. A country may honor or commemorate an event or famous person by issuing *commemorative* stamps. The first U.S. commemorative stamp was issued in 1893. It was called the Columbian issue, in honor of the four-hundredth anniversary of the discovery of America. A stamp sold for more than the cost of postage is called a *semipostal*. Such stamps have been issued by many countries, but not by the United States. Extra funds obtained from semipostals have been given to charity, and to help finance fairs, youth clubs, and the rebuilding of a cathedral.

Many types of special stamps are issued by various countries. Among such stamps are airmail, parcel post, official, postage due, provisional stamps for emergen-

A Stamp Collector mounts his stamps in an album. A stamp catalog, *rear*, provides information about various stamps. The collector uses a magnifying glass to examine the details of a stamp. He holds the stamp with tweezers to keep it from being soiled. He uses stamp hinges, *right*, to mount the stamps in his album.

RARE AND UNUSUAL STAMPS

Collectors especially value stamps that are rare or have some unusual feature. A number of stamps, called *errors*, have become valuable because of a printing mistake, such as part of the design being upside down. Some collectors have paid thousands of dollars for one error.

Rare Stamps are highly prized by collectors. Only one known copy exists of this one-penny stamp issued in 1856 in British Guiana.

Early Stamps, such as the French issue from the 1850's shown above, had no perforations. Collectors call these stamps *imperforates.*

An Inverted Center makes this 1918 airmail stamp one of the most valuable errors among all United States stamps.

Robert A. Siegel, Inc.

A Tête-bêche Error occurs when one stamp in a series is printed upside down. The pair shown above was issued in France in 1870.

Souvenir Sheets have been issued periodically by the U.S. Post Office since 1926 to honor major conventions of stamp collectors.

A Plate Block consists of four or more connected stamps with the serial numbers of the plates from which the stamps were printed.

Stamps Showing Birds attract collectors who specialize in beautiful stamps or in issues dealing with the same general subject.

WORLD BOOK photos

A First Day Cover is an envelope bearing a stamp canceled on its first day of issue. On that day, the U.S. Postal Service sells the stamp in only one selected city. The postmark on the example above shows that the first day of issue was Jan. 26, 1973, in Philadelphia. Private companies sell collectors first day covers decorated with specially designed pictures called *cachets*.

Commemorative Stamps honor important events. The Canadian government issued the two stamps at the left in 1967 to commemorate the centennial of the nation's confederation. The United States airmail stamp honored the first astronaut to step on the moon. The stamp on the right was issued to celebrate the 150th anniversary of the birth of the American author Henry David Thoreau.

cies, pneumatic tube, special delivery, and personal delivery. Other types of special stamps include registration, occupation during war, postal savings, newspaper, special handling, and combinations of special services.

Other Reasons for Collecting. Many people like to collect stamps just for the pictures of odd and out-of-the-way places and things. Some people collect stamps of one country only. Others collect only stamps showing birds, or railroads, or ships, or stamps of only one color. The reason for collecting stamps does not matter as long as the collector has fun. CHARLESS HAHN

See also POST OFFICE; STAMP.

Additional Resources

Level I

CETIN, FRANK. *Here Is Your Hobby: Stamp Collecting.* Putnam, 1962.
OLCHESKI, BILL. *Beginning Stamp Collecting.* Walck, 1976.
ZARCHY, HARRY. *Stamp Collector's Guide.* Knopf, 1956.

Level II

CABEEN, RICHARD M. *Standard Handbook of Stamp Collecting.* 3rd ed. Harper, 1979.
The Postal Service Guide to U.S. Stamps. U.S. Postal Service. Published annually. (Earlier editions titled *Stamps and Stories.*)
Scott Standard Postage Stamp Catalogue. Scott Publishing Company. Published annually in 5 vols. (Vol. 5 has title: *Scott Specialized Catalogue of United States Stamps.*)

STAMP WEED. See INDIAN MALLOW.

STANDARD & POOR'S INDEXES are statistics that measure changes in American stock market prices. The indexes help investors decide what securities to buy and sell. They are compiled and published by the Standard & Poor's Corporation, an investment research and advisory company.

The best-known of the Standard & Poor's reports is the Standard & Poor's 500 Index. It reflects stock prices for 500 companies whose shares are traded on the New York Stock Exchange. These companies consist of 400 industrial firms, 40 public utilities, 40 financial institutions, and 20 transportation companies. Altogether, their stocks make up about 80 per cent of the market value of all stocks listed on the exchange. Many investors consider the index more valuable than the Dow Jones Industrial Averages, which are based on stock prices of just 30 companies.

Standard & Poor's analysts compute the 500 Index every five minutes of each business day. They compare current stock prices with average prices during the period 1941-1943, which is called the *base period*. The analysts weight each price according to the total market value of the corporation's publicly owned shares, so that larger companies affect the index more. Current prices are expressed in tenths of average prices during the base period. For example, an index of 120 means that prices average 12 times higher than in 1941-1943.

The Standard & Poor's Corporation also prepares a 100-industry survey, which appears in its weekly publication *The Outlook.* This survey provides stock price statistics on 100 industries, giving an overview of the stock market's strengths and weaknesses. In addition, the company publishes separate indexes daily for transportation stocks, for utility stocks, for financial stocks, and for bonds. WILLIAM G. DEWALD

See also DOW JONES AVERAGES.

STANDARD OF LIVING usually refers to the economic level at which an individual, family, or nation lives. Economists may measure this level by determining the value of the goods and services *consumed* (used) by the individual, family, or nation during a given period. The term *standard of living* may also refer to the goals that people set for themselves as users of goods, services, and leisure. That is, the term may be defined as the level of comfort and happiness that people would like to reach. When their needs and wants have been satisfied, they have achieved their standard of living.

Needs and Wants. Human beings have many needs and wants. Their basic needs have always included food, clothing, and shelter. To these may be added a number of other needs, depending upon the society in which a person happens to live. In many parts of the world, artificial light and artificial heat have become basic needs. In the United States, transportation, leisure, schooling, recreation, and a sense of belonging to something are generally held to be needs. Wants are even less definite than needs. So far as anyone knows, there is no limit to the range of human wants.

When we talk about the standard of living of a nation, it is a little like talking about the "average person." No nation has a general standard of living for everyone, any more than it has an average citizen. The size of the average paycheck is no indication of a nation's standard of living. The cost of living varies over the world. The person who earns $100 a month in one part of the world may live better than one who is paid $100 a week in another place, because the first person's lower wages buy more goods and services.

Economists may estimate a nation's living standard by determining how much income the nation's individuals spend for food, a basic need. A nation in which most individuals must spend 75 per cent or more of their income for food may be said to have a low living standard. A nation in which most individuals spend 25 per cent or less of their income for food may be said to have a high living standard. Economists face several problems when they try to determine what shares of individual income are spent for particular items other than food. A major problem is that many such items are bought by families rather than by individuals.

Area Differences. At present, the world supports about $4\frac{3}{4}$ billion people. At the American standard of grain consumption, only half this number could live. On the other hand, the world could support an additional billion people at present production if everyone went on the Asiatic standard of living. The whole world, with its present population, could be supplied with grain at the European standard of grain consumption before World War II. This would put an end to starvation and misery in Asia, but it would sharply cut the American standard of grain consumption.

The situation is even more striking when it comes to other foods, such as meat or dairy products. The North American standard of living calls for about 3 pounds (1.4 kilograms) of meat per person a week. Europe gets about 2 pounds (0.9 kilogram), and South America about $1\frac{1}{2}$ pounds (0.7 kilogram). Asia and Africa use only $\frac{1}{3}$ pound (0.2 kilogram) per person a week. If the world's animal foods were equally distributed at the present rate of livestock production, each person would get about 1 pound (0.5 kilogram) of meat per week.

The industrial nations—including Canada, Japan, the United States, and many countries of Western Europe—are said to have the world's highest standard of living. More goods per person are consumed there than in other nations. But this measure of living standards does not accurately show how people in industrial nations live. First, it does not show how the consumption of goods actually is divided among the people. Also, this measure does not take into account certain conditions—such as overcrowding and pollution—that may make life unpleasant in parts of these nations. Finally, a high consumption level does not mean that the people's wants have all been satisfied. In general, however, people in industrial nations enjoy more comforts—including better clothing and housing, greater educational opportunities, and more healthful food—than other people. Louis W. Stern

Related Articles in World Book include:

Consumption	Inflation
Cost of Living	National Income
Gross National Product	Technology
Income	Wages and Hours
Industrial Revolution	

STANDARD OIL COMPANY. In 1859, Edwin L. Drake, a retired railroad conductor, drilled the first

commercially successful oil well in the United States near Titusville, Pa. In 1863, John D. Rockefeller and his partners organized Andrews, Clark, and Co., which later became a part of the Standard Oil Company. The new firm built a large oil refinery in Cleveland, and began to sell oil at home and abroad. The new business expanded rapidly. In 1870, Rockefeller and his associates formed the Standard Oil Company of Ohio and began to buy other refineries.

From 1870 to 1882, Rockefeller and his associates bought practically all the refineries in Cleveland, and acquired refineries in other cities. They developed a pipeline system, purchased new oil-producing lands, and created an efficient organization to market their products. To unify the management of the companies and to overcome certain legal difficulties, they transferred the stock of all companies to the newly formed Standard Oil Trust in 1882 (see Trust). Also that year, the Standard Oil Company of New Jersey was chartered as an operating company within the trust.

The creation of the trust made Standard Oil the biggest company in the oil industry. The trust had control of about 90 per cent of the country's refining capacity, and almost as much of its pipelines. But since 1870, Rockefeller and the business practices of Standard Oil had been bitterly attacked by newspapers, magazines, books, state and federal investigating agencies, and many courts. In 1892, the supreme court of Ohio dissolved the trust. All the companies in the trust had to operate separately, as they did before the trust was formed in 1882. In 1899, Standard Oil (New Jersey) amended its charter in an attempt to preserve the vast oil empire and to provide centralized direction for all the companies in the empire. The new company gave its stock in exchange for certificates of companies in the dissolved trust. It held stock in about 20 constituent companies.

The reorganization of Standard Oil of New Jersey

A Measure of Standards of Living

The standard of living for a nation is sometimes measured by dividing its *personal consumption expenditures* by its population. These expenditures represent the value of goods and services purchased by individuals and nonprofit institutions during a given period. However, an accurate comparison of living standards must allow for differences in the purchasing power of money from nation to nation and from year to year. Such a comparison must also allow for differences in the availability of various goods and services. This table lists 20 leading non-Communist nations in personal consumption expenditures per person. The figures for some non-Communist and all Communist countries are not reported in the sources listed below.

Switzerland	$9,605	**Australia**	$6,033
Sweden	$7,379	**Canada**	$5,877
United States	$7,348	**Iceland**	$5,834
France	$7,200	**Japan**	$5,823
Belgium	$7,174	**Great Britain**	$5,776
Luxembourg	$7,007	**Austria**	$5,292
West Germany	$6,812	**Finland**	$4,859
Denmark	$6,811	**Kuwait**	$4,468
Norway	$6,294	**Italy**	$4,008
The Netherlands	$6,268	**New Zealand**	$3,831

Sources: *International Financial Statistics*, January 1982, International Monetary Fund; *Monthly Bulletin of Statistics*, September 1981, UN; *Population and Vital Statistics Report*, October 1981, UN. Figures are for 1980, but 1979 for Kuwait.

made the company one of the richest and most powerful holding companies in the world. In 1906, the federal government, under the Sherman Antitrust Act, brought suit against the combination. In 1911, the Supreme Court of the United States ordered the company to dissolve under the provisions of the Sherman Antitrust Act. This action forced 33 companies of Standard Oil of New Jersey to become separate, independent, competing companies with no corporate connections with each other or with the Standard Oil Company of New Jersey. In 1972, Standard Oil (New Jersey) changed its name to Exxon Corporation.

Today, the five largest of the old Standard Oil companies, ranked in order of sales, are Exxon Corporation, Mobil Corporation, Standard Oil of California, Standard Oil (Indiana), and Atlantic Richfield Company. Exxon is also the largest petroleum company in the world. For the sales, assets, and employees of all the above companies, see MANUFACTURING (table: 100 Leading U.S. Manufacturers).   PAUL H. GIDDENS

See also EXXON CORPORATION; ROCKEFELLER.

STANDARD SCHNAUZER is a powerfully built dog with a wiry coat, shaggy whiskers, and bushy eyebrows. It stands from $17\frac{1}{2}$ to $19\frac{1}{2}$ inches (44 to 50 centimeters) tall and weighs from 35 to 40 pounds (16 to 18 kilograms). Most standard schnauzers have pepper-and-salt (gray) coats, but some are black.

The breed originated in southern Germany during the 1400's. The Germans used the dogs to herd cattle and sheep and to kill rats. Standard schnauzers are

WORLD BOOK photo

The Standard Schnauzer Makes an Excellent Watchdog.

intelligent, alert, and fearless. They make loyal companions and excellent watchdogs. They also have been used for hunting, for carrying messages, and as guide dogs for the blind.   JOAN MCDONALD BREARLEY

See also GIANT SCHNAUZER; MINIATURE SCHNAUZER.

STANDARD TIME is a worldwide system of uniform time zones. This system divides the world into 24 zones. Twenty-three zones are full zones and one zone is divided into two half zones. Each full zone is 15° longitude wide (see LONGITUDE). The difference in time between that of any full zone and its neighbor is exactly one hour. Within each zone, all clocks keep the same time, except for some local variations.

Time Zones. The *local*, or *sun*, time for any specific location depends on its longitude. There is a difference of 4 minutes for each degree of longitude, or a difference of an hour for every 15°. Under standard time, the time kept in each zone is that of the central *meridian*, or longitude line (see MERIDIAN). The central meridians are those 15°, 30°, 45°, and so on, east or west of the prime meridian. In theory, the zone boundaries should extend $7\frac{1}{2}$° on either side of the central meridian. In practice, the boundaries are irregular lines. This is to avoid inconvenient changes in time. For example, in the United States, zone boundaries often are located so that a state will lie entirely within one time zone. The Department of Transportation has the authority to establish limits for time zones in the United States. Canada does not have a federal standard time law. Its time zones generally have the same names as those used in the United States.

The standard U.S. and Canadian time zones are— from east to west—Atlantic, Eastern, Central, Mountain, Pacific, Yukon, Alaska-Hawaii, and Bering. For the boundaries of these zones, see TIME (map).

In summer, the residents of most states advance their clocks one hour to use daylight saving time. An act of Congress, which became effective in 1967, declared that daylight saving time must be used throughout a state or not at all. But an amendment to the act in 1972 allows states that lie in more than one time zone to use daylight time in one zone without using it in the other. See DAYLIGHT SAVING.

History. Before the adoption of standard time, each city in the United States kept the local time of its own meridian. With the growth of railroads, these differences caused difficulties. Railroads that met in the same city sometimes ran on different times. In 1883, the railroads of the United States and Canada adopted a system for standard time. In 1884, an international conference met in Washington, D.C., to consider a worldwide system of standard time. The meridian passing through the English town of Greenwich (now a borough of London) was chosen as the prime meridian. In 1918, Congress gave the Interstate Commerce Commission authority to establish limits for U.S. time zones. Congress transferred this authority to the Department of Transportation in 1967.

Today, nearly all nations keep standard time. Only a few small countries and some other regions keep time that differs by a half hour or by some minutes and seconds from standard time.   WILLIAM MARKOWITZ

See also FLEMING, SIR SANDFORD; TIME.

STANDARDBRED. See HORSE (Light Harness Horses; picture); HARNESS RACING.

STANDARDS, NATIONAL BUREAU OF. See NATIONAL BUREAU OF STANDARDS.

STANDISH, MILES (1584?-1656), came to America with the Pilgrims in the *Mayflower*. He was not a Separatist, and never joined the Pilgrim Church. But he helped the Pilgrims in their plans and in training a militia. See PILGRIM; PLYMOUTH COLONY.

Short but stocky, Standish had red hair and a florid complexion which turned livid when he grew angry. "A little chimney is soon fired," commented one of his enemies. But no one questioned his bravery. Single-handed, he attacked a threatening Indian chief, Witu-wamat, and brought his head back to Plymouth. His watchfulness probably saved the colony from destruction by Indians in its early years.

In 1625, the colonists sent him to England to get a more favorable agreement with the merchants who were financing the colony. He could not accomplish much, partly because of the plague then raging in London. Standish was one of the leaders who assumed the colony's debts. He served as assistant governor from 1624 or perhaps from 1633 on, and as Plymouth's treasurer from 1652 to 1655. He helped found Duxbury, Mass., and moved there about 1632. His statue overlooks the town and Plymouth Bay.

Standish was born in Lancashire, and fought as a young man against the Spaniards in The Netherlands. Henry W. Longfellow's account of him in *The Courtship of Miles Standish* is entirely fictitious (see LONGFELLOW, HENRY W. [Narrative Poems]).   BRADFORD SMITH

STANFIELD, ROBERT LORNE (1914-   ), served as leader of Canada's Progressive Conservative Party from 1967 to 1976. He failed to lead his party to a parliamentary majority in the general elections of 1968, 1972, and 1974. He served as premier of Nova Scotia from 1956 to 1967.

Stanfield was born in Truro, N. S. He graduated from Dalhousie University in 1936 and Harvard University in 1939. In 1948, he became leader of the Nova Scotia Progressive Conservative Party. Stanfield was elected to the Nova Scotia Legislature in 1949. His efforts in encouraging new industry in the province helped him win re-election in 1953, 1956, 1960, and 1967. Stanfield won election to the national House of Commons after the Progressive Conservatives made him their leader. He succeeded former Canadian Prime Minister John G. Diefenbaker.   E. D. HALIBURTON

STANFORD, LELAND (1824-1893), was a railroad builder, a governor of California, and a United States senator. In 1885, he founded Stanford University in memory of his son, with a gift of land and securities. Stanford was born in Watervliet, N.Y. He studied law and started his practice in 1848 in Port Washington, Wis. In 1852, Stanford moved to California and opened a general store. He entered politics and became governor of California in 1862. He helped keep the state loyal to the Union during the Civil War. After his term as governor ended in 1863, Stanford joined others in building the Central Pacific and Southern Pacific railroads. He was president of both railroads. Stanford was a Republican U.S. senator from California from 1885 until his death.   W. H. BAUGHN

STANFORD-BINET TEST. See INTELLIGENCE QUOTIENT.

STANFORD UNIVERSITY is a leading educational and research center in the United States. It has an 8,800-acre (3,600-hectare) campus in Stanford, Calif., about 30 miles (48 kilometers) south of San Francisco. Stanford is a private, coeducational university. It offers undergraduate and graduate courses of study, and about 25 of its graduate programs rank among the top 10 nationally in their fields. Stanford also is known as one of the world's leading centers of research in electronics and physics.

Educational Program. Stanford has schools of business, earth sciences, education, engineering, humanities and sciences, law, and medicine. These schools are divided into about 70 academic departments. The university also sponsors programs of study in Europe, Asia, South America, and Africa.

Undergraduates receive a general education in a wide range of subjects and a specialized education in their chosen field of study. Undergraduates may apply for A.B., B.S., and B.A.S. degrees. Graduate students may apply for A.M., M.S., M.F.A., and Ph.D. degrees or for professional degrees.

Research Program. Stanford University is an important center of research in the physical, biological, social, and technological sciences. The Stanford Linear Accelerator Center (SLAC) is a world center for the study of high-energy physics. The university's medical school is internationally famous for its work on heart transplants, cancer, and *genetic engineering* (altering the genes of a living organism).

The university's Hoover Institution on War, Revolution, and Peace has one of the best collections of books and documents about political, social, and economic movements of the 1900's. This institution was founded in 1919 by Herbert Hoover, a member of Stanford's first graduating class in 1895. Hoover became the 31st President of the United States in 1929.

The Stanford campus is also the home of an industrial park that has about 90 firms. Frederick E. Terman, an electrical engineer who held administrative positions at Stanford University from 1937 to 1965, helped establish the research and manufacturing center in 1951. He supported close ties between the university and industry and persuaded many university faculty members and students to form companies in the Stanford area. A

Stanford University

Stanford University opened in 1891. Its older stone buildings, *above left,* were designed with arches and tiled roofs.

number of these firms have manufactured important electronics devices invented by Stanford faculty members.

History. Stanford University was founded in 1885 by Leland Stanford and his wife, Jane Lathrop Stanford. Leland Stanford built the Central Pacific Railroad. He served as a U.S. senator from California from 1885 until his death in 1893. The Stanfords created the university as a memorial to their son, Leland Stanford, Jr., who died of typhoid fever in 1884. The couple endowed the university with land for a campus and over $20 million.

Stanford opened for classes in 1891. Its academic departments were organized into seven schools in 1948. Since the late 1950's, Stanford University has been ranked as one of the leading educational institutions in the United States.   Critically reviewed by STANFORD UNIVERSITY

For the enrollment of Stanford University, see UNIVERSITIES AND COLLEGES (table).

STANHOPE, PHILIP D. See CHESTERFIELD, EARL OF.

STANISLAS, *STAN is lus,* **SAINT** (1030-1079), is the patron saint of Poland and the city of Kraków, where he served as bishop. He became a saint of the Roman Catholic Church in 1253, and is honored as a martyr. His name is also spelled STANISLAUS.

Saint Stanislas was born at Szczepanowski, Poland. As a priest he took charge of a parish near Kraków. He was named bishop of Kraków by Pope Alexander II. His outspoken attacks against sin in both low and high places earned him the hatred of King Bolesław II of Poland. Bolesław ordered Stanislas killed. The king accompanied the guards who had been ordered to kill Stanislas. When the guards would not obey, the king killed the bishop himself. Saint Stanislas' feast day is celebrated on April 11.   FULTON J. SHEEN

STANISLAVSKI, KONSTANTIN (1863-1938), was the stage name of a well-known Russian director and actor. He tried to create truthful performances by having his actors study the inner lives of the characters as if they were real people. The actor's attempt to live the life of the character became known as the "Stanislavski method."

Konstantin Sergeyevich Alexeyev was born in Moscow. In 1898, with Vladimir Nemirovich-Danchenko, he established the Moscow Art Theater. It became famous for realistic performances of plays by Chekhov, Gorki, and others. Stanislavski's direction of *The Sea Gull* in 1898 gave Chekhov his first success. Stanislavski's fame grew with his writings describing the methods he used in teaching actors and directing plays. His works include *An Actor Prepares* (in English, 1936) and *Building a Character* (in English, 1949).   FREDERICK J. HUNTER

STANLEY, F. A. See STANLEY OF PRESTON, BARON.

STANLEY, WENDELL MEREDITH (1904-1971), an American biochemist, did outstanding research on viruses. In 1935, he isolated the *tobacco mosaic virus* in crystalline form, and showed it to be a protein molecule. Before this discovery, scientists had assumed that viruses were submicroscopic living organisms. Stanley shared the 1946 Nobel Prize for chemistry for preparing enzymes and virus proteins in pure form. He was born in Ridgeville, Ind.   MORDECAI L. GABRIEL

STANLEY AND LIVINGSTONE were two British explorers who excited the Western world with their travels in Africa. Henry Morton Stanley (1841-1904) went to Africa to find David Livingstone (1813-1873) in 1869.

Livingstone was known to be exploring the interior of the continent. But no one had heard from him in several years, and so the *New York Herald* sent Stanley to find him. Stanley's search ended on November 10, 1871, when he met Livingstone at the town of Ujiji, on Lake Tanganyika. Stanley greeted him with the now-famous words: "Dr. Livingstone, I presume?"

Livingstone's Discoveries. David Livingstone was born in Blantyre, Scotland, near Glasgow. He received a medical degree from the University of Glasgow and joined the London Missionary Society. The society sent him to southern Africa. There he worked to convert Africans to Christianity and to end the business of selling captured Africans as slaves.

Livingstone made several difficult journeys into the interior, mapping the land and searching for navigable rivers that British missionaries and traders could use. In 1849, he arrived at Lake Ngami, in what is now Botswana. In 1851, Livingstone traveled to the Zambezi River, on the border between present-day Zambia and Zimbabwe. He became the first European to cross Africa during an amazing journey between 1853 and 1856. On this trip, Livingstone started at the Zambezi and went north and west across Angola to Luanda on the Atlantic Ocean. On the return journey, he followed the Zambezi to its mouth, in what is now Mozambique. In 1855, during the return, Livingstone became the first European to sight Victoria Falls on the Zambezi River. He named the falls for Queen Victoria of Great Britain.

Between 1859 and 1863, Livingstone led a large expedition across Africa's interior. He became the first European to see Lakes Nyasa and Chilwa, in what is now Malawi. During the late 1860's, Livingstone began to explore the Lake Tanganyika region. He learned more about African customs, geography, and the slave trade than any other European of his day. Livingstone's discoveries also led to a great competition among European nations for control of Africa.

Stanley's Explorations. Henry Morton Stanley was born in Denbigh, Wales, and was baptized John Rowlands. He spent most of his youth in a workhouse for orphans. At the age of 17, he sailed as a cabin boy on a ship to New Orleans. There Henry Hope Stanley, a cotton dealer, adopted him. The young Stanley joined the Confederate Army during the American Civil War (1861-1865). He was soon captured. Stanley joined the Union Army to get out of prison but was discharged soon afterward because of poor health. He joined the Union Navy in 1864. In 1865, Stanley deserted and became a newspaper reporter. During the late 1860's, he covered Indian wars in the American West and a British military campaign in Ethiopia. But his best-known assignment was to find Livingstone.

After their meeting, Stanley became interested in Livingstone's hope of finding a source of the Nile River south of the known source in Lake Victoria. Stanley postponed his plans to rush home with news of the great explorer and stayed with him until March 1872.

After Livingstone's death in 1873, Stanley decided to carry on his friend's work in Africa. In 1874, Stanley led an expedition of about 350 people into the interior. The group explored Lake Victoria and other lakes. Then Stanley followed the Congo River all the way west

Exploration of Africa by Stanley and Livingstone

David Livingstone explored central Africa to find the source of the Nile River. He was believed lost until Henry M. Stanley found him at Lake Tanganyika in 1871. In 1874, Stanley set out to trace the course of the Congo River. He began in what is now Zaire and reached the mouth of the river at the Atlantic Ocean in 1877.

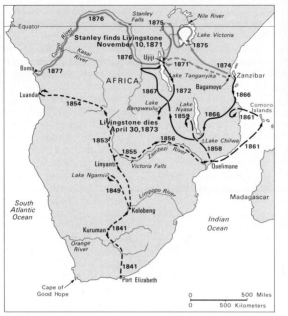

----- Livingstone's first
expedition: 1841-1856

--- Livingstone's second
expedition: 1858-1863

——— Livingstone's third
expedition: 1866-1873

----- Stanley's expedition to
find Livingstone: 1871

——— Stanley's Congo River
expedition: 1874-1877

WORLD BOOK map

Brown Bros.

Sir Henry M. Stanley

Brown Bros.

David Livingstone

to its mouth at the Atlantic Ocean. He reached the ocean in 1877 after many hardships. By then, more than two-thirds of his company had died or deserted.

In Stanley's later years, he continued to explore Africa. He helped establish the Congo Free State, an area ruled by King Leopold of Belgium. In 1888, near Lake Albert, he reached Emin Pasha, a colonial ruler whom African rebels had cut off from civilization. Stanley served in the British Parliament from 1895 to 1900. He was knighted in 1899.   ROBERT I. ROTBERG

See also EXPLORATION (picture); LAKE EDWARD.

Additional Resources

HUXLEY, ELSPETH J. *Livingstone and His African Journeys.* Saturday Review Press, 1974.

STANLEY, HENRY M. *How I Found Livingstone.* Arno, 1970. Reprint of 1872 ed.

STANLEY BROTHERS were two American inventors and manufacturers who built the Stanley steamer, one of the most famous steam-powered automobiles. The brothers were identical twins.

Francis Edgar Stanley (1849-1918) and Freelan Oscar Stanley (1849-1940) were born in Kingfield, Me. In 1884, they formed the Stanley Dry Plate Company to manufacture a formula that Francis had developed for use in dry-plate photography. They patented a dry-plate coating machine in 1886. In 1904, they sold their firm to the Eastman Kodak Company.

Meanwhile, the Stanleys were also experimenting with steam engines, and in 1897 they built the first Stanley steamer. They organized a company to produce and market the cars but sold it, and their manufacturing rights, to the Locomobile Company in 1899. In 1901, the Stanleys bought back their manufacturing rights and formed the Stanley Motor Carriage Company. To gain publicity for their company, they became active in automobile racing. In 1906, one of their cars traveled

128 miles (206 kilometers) per hour, thus becoming the first car to exceed 2 miles (3.2 kilometers) per minute.

Sales of steam cars declined as gasoline-powered automobiles, which were easier to start and operate, became increasingly popular. In 1917, the brothers retired and the Stanley Motor Carriage Company was reorganized under new management. The next year, Francis was killed in an automobile accident. Stanley steamers continued to be manufactured until 1924.   DAVID L. LEWIS

See also AUTOMOBILE (picture).

STANLEY CUP is a trophy awarded annually to the team that wins the National Hockey League (NHL) championship. The champion does not actually receive the trophy. The original cup is kept permanently in the Hockey Hall of Fame in Toronto. The name of the winning team and its players are engraved on a duplicate that is also exhibited at the Hall of Fame except during the Stanley Cup finals. The cup weighs about 32 pounds (14.5 kilograms) and stands $35\frac{1}{4}$ inches (89.5 centimeters) high. It is the oldest trophy in professional sports competition in North America.

Baron Stanley of Preston, a governor general of Canada, donated the trophy in 1893 to be awarded to the annual amateur hockey champion of Canada. Teams in the professional National Hockey Association (reorganized into the NHL in 1917) began competing for the Stanley Cup in 1910.   RICHARD ROTTKOV

See also HOCKEY (table: Stanley Cup Finals).

STANLEY OF PRESTON, BARON (1841-1908), served as governor general of Canada from 1888 to 1893. Stanley, whose given name was Frederick Arthur Stanley, was an enthusiastic sportsman. In 1893, he donated an ice-hockey trophy called the Stanley Cup. Today, the trophy goes to the annual champion of the National Hockey League.

Stanley was born in London. He was elected to the British Parliament in 1865 and served in the Cabinet

658

from 1878 to 1880 and in 1885 and 1886. He became Baron of Preston in 1886. After serving as governor general of Canada, he returned to England and succeeded his brother as the Earl of Derby. He was elected lord mayor of Liverpool in 1895. He became the first chancellor of Liverpool University in 1903. JACQUES MONET

STANLEY STEAMER. See AUTOMOBILE (The First Automobiles [picture]); STANLEY BROTHERS.

STANNOUS FLUORIDE. See TIN (Uses); TOOTHPASTE AND TOOTHPOWDER.

STANOVOY MOUNTAINS, *STAN oh voy,* is a mountain range in Siberia. It extends for about 1,000 miles (1,600 kilometers) from the northern end of Lake Baikal northeast to the Sea of Okhotsk.

STANTON, EDWIN McMASTERS (1814-1869), an American statesman, served as secretary of war in President Abraham Lincoln's Cabinet. He later played a part in President Andrew Johnson's impeachment.

Stanton was born in Steubenville, Ohio, and was educated at Kenyon College. He studied law and was admitted to the bar in 1836. In 1856, he settled in Washington, D.C., and argued many cases before the Supreme Court. President James Buchanan appointed Stanton attorney general in 1860, and Lincoln made him secretary of war two years later.

Stanton was not popular in the war office, and Lincoln did not like him very well. Stanton was outspoken, and made many enemies. But he was an able manager, and gained a reputation for efficiency.

Brown Bros.

Edwin M. Stanton

When Andrew Johnson became President, he and Stanton clashed repeatedly over the treatment of the South. Stanton cooperated with Johnson's enemies in Congress, and when Johnson removed Stanton from the office of secretary of war, the House of Representatives impeached the President. Johnson was acquitted by one vote, and Stanton finally left office in May 1868 (see JOHNSON, ANDREW [Increased Tension]). Stanton died four days after being appointed to the Supreme Court by President Ulysses S. Grant. W. B. HESSELTINE

See also TENURE OF OFFICE ACT.

STANTON, ELIZABETH CADY (1815-1902), was one of the earliest leaders of the women's rights movement. She and Lucretia Mott, another reformer, organized the first women's rights convention in the United States.

Stanton was born in Johnstown, N.Y., and graduated from the Troy Female Seminary (now the Emma Willard School). During the 1830's, she became interested in women's rights and in abolition. She and Henry B. Stanton, an abolitionist

Tamiment Institute Library, New York University

Elizabeth Cady Stanton

leader, were married in 1840. That same year, they went to London for the World Anti-Slavery Convention. However, the delegates voted to exclude women. Elizabeth Stanton discussed the situation with Mott, who also had planned to attend the convention.

In 1848, Stanton and Mott called the nation's first women's rights convention. It was held in Seneca Falls, N.Y., where the Stantons lived. Elizabeth Stanton wrote a Declaration of Sentiments for the meeting, using the Declaration of Independence as her model. For example, the Declaration of Independence states that "all men are created equal." But Stanton wrote that "all men and women are created equal." She also called for woman suffrage.

During the 1850's and the Civil War (1861-1865), Stanton worked for women's rights and for abolition. After slavery was abolished in 1865, she broke with abolitionists who favored voting rights for blacks but not for women. In 1869, Stanton and the women's rights leader Susan B. Anthony founded the National Woman Suffrage Association. Stanton served as its president from 1869 to 1890.

In 1878, Stanton persuaded Senator Aaron A. Sargent of California to sponsor a woman suffrage amendment to the Constitution of the United States. This amendment was reintroduced every year until 1919, when Congress finally approved it. In 1920, it became the 19th Amendment to the Constitution. JUNE SOCHEN

See also MOTT, LUCRETIA COFFIN.

Additional Resources

BANNER, LOIS W. *Elizabeth Cady Stanton: A Radical for Woman's Rights.* Little, Brown, 1980.
CLARKE, MARY S. *Bloomers and Ballots: Elizabeth Cady Stanton and Women's Rights.* Viking, 1972. For younger readers.
LUTZ, ALMA. *Created Equal: A Biography of Elizabeth Cady Stanton.* Farrar, 1973. Reprint of 1940 ed.
WISE, WINIFRED E. *Rebel in Petticoats: The Life of Elizabeth Cady Stanton.* Chilton, 1960. For younger readers.

STAPHYLOCOCCUS, *STAFF uh luh KAHK uhs,* is a common bacterium belonging to a group of round, or spherical, bacteria called *cocci.* Under a microscope, groups of these tiny organisms look like bunches of grapes. Staphylococci live in the air, in water, and on the bodies of human beings and animals. They cause boils and are responsible for a skin infection known as *impetigo.* Some staphylococci grow in foods and cause a type of food poisoning. Others cause pneumonia and blood poisoning. Because of differences in their growth habits, staphylococci have been separated into different strains. Doctors may use antibiotics to treat diseases caused by staphylococci, but some strains have become resistant to these drugs. LOIS G. LOBB

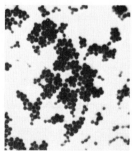

© General Biological Supply House, Inc., Chicago

Staphylococcal Bacteria look like bunches of grapes when seen through a microscope.

See also ANTIBIOTIC; BACTERIA; BOIL; CARBUNCLE; IMPETIGO; TOXIN.

Like Gleaming Jewels, stars sparkle against the night sky. Some are surrounded by hazy clouds of dust. The telescope and camera that were used to make this picture caused circles and cross-shaped "rays" to appear around some stars. Astronomers call this group of stars *the Pleiades.* The inset on the opposite page shows how these stars look when seen without a telescope.

STAR

STAR is a huge ball of glowing gas in the sky. The sun is a star. It is the only star close enough to the earth to look like a ball. The other billions of stars are so far away that they are no more than pinpoints of light—if they can be seen at all.

There are more than 200 billion billion (200,000,000,-000,000,000,000) stars. Suppose that everyone in the world were to count the stars. Each person could count more than 50 billion of them without the same star being counted twice.

Stars are enormous objects. The largest stars would more than fill the space between the earth and the sun. Such stars have a diameter that is about 1,000 times as large as the sun's. The smallest stars are smaller than the earth.

We can hardly imagine the great distances that separate the stars. The star nearest the sun is more than 25 million million miles (40 million million kilometers) away from the sun. But even this great distance

Thornton Page, the contributor of this article, is Research Associate at the National Aeronautics and Space Administration's Lyndon B. Johnson Space Center and the author of several books on astronomy.

is only one-billionth the distance from the sun to the farthest stars.

Stars differ greatly in color and brightness. Some stars look yellow, like the sun. Others glow blue or red. A few stars twinkle brightly, but many are hard to see.

Stars twinkle because starlight comes to us through moving layers of air that surround the earth. The stars shine day and night, but we can see them only when the sky is dark and clear. During the day, sunlight brightens the sky and keeps us from seeing the stars.

At night, the stars seem to move across the sky—as the sun does during the day. This "movement" comes from the spinning of the earth, not from the movement of the stars. The stars themselves do move, but their movement cannot be seen because the stars are so far from the earth. However, the change in position can be determined through precise measurements.

A star is made up mainly of two gases—hydrogen and helium. The star shines because nuclear energy makes these gases very hot. The star continues to shine until it runs out of hydrogen gas, the fuel used to make the nuclear energy. The star may then explode into a huge cloud of gas and dust.

Most stars began shining between 1 million and 10

Minolta Corporation

The Stars of the Pleiades, shown in the above inset, appear in a closely spaced group. The ancient Greeks named these stars for the seven sisters of an ancient story. A stargazer without a telescope can easily see the six brightest stars of the Pleiades.

billion years ago. But new stars are still forming within the clouds of gas and dust of the Milky Way and other galaxies. The sun itself was probably formed in this way, developing from a rotating mass of gas and dust.

People have studied the stars since ancient times. Early farmers watched the stars to know when to plant their crops. Travelers learned to use the stars to tell directions. Ancient peoples made up stories about persons, animals, and other things they saw pictured in certain groups of stars. These groups of stars are called *constellations* (see CONSTELLATION).

The stars have long stood for things of special importance. The Star of David is a sign of the Jewish religion. The Star of Bethlehem recalls the birth of Jesus Christ. Stars appear on the flags of the United States and many other countries. Top performers in motion pictures, television, the theater, and sports are called "stars."

Many starlike objects that we see in the sky are not stars. Some of these objects are planets. Meteors look like falling stars but are really pieces of rock or metal that burn up as they shoot through the air. For more information, see the WORLD BOOK articles on PLANET and METEOR.

STAR TERMS

Absolute Magnitude is a star's brightness if the star were 32.6 light-years from the earth.

Apparent Magnitude is a star's brightness as seen from the earth.

Binary Star is a pair of stars revolving around each other.

Black Hole is a collapsed star that has become invisible. It has so much gravitational force that not even light can escape from it.

Eclipsing Binary is a binary that revolves in such an orbit that one star periodically blocks the other's light.

Hertzsprung-Russell Diagram is a graph that shows the relationship between the absolute magnitude and spectral class of stars.

Light-Year is the distance light travels in one year— 5,880,000,000,000 miles (9,460,000,000,000 kilometers).

Main Sequence, a band of points on the Hertzsprung-Russell diagram, represents the most common kinds of stars.

Neutron Star is a small star that may be made almost entirely of atomic particles called *neutrons.*

Nova is a star that explodes, becomes thousands of times brighter, and then becomes dim again.

Proper Motion is the change in a star's position among other stars.

Spectral Class identifies a star's color and surface temperature.

Supernova is a star that explodes, becomes billions of times brighter for a few weeks, and then becomes dim again.

Variable Star is a star whose brightness changes.

White Dwarf is a small, white star with a large amount of material packed into an extremely small space.

STARS AT A GLANCE

Number: About 200 billion billion stars in the known universe.

Age: Up to 12 billion years. Most stars are between 1 million and 10 billion years old.

Composition: About 75 per cent hydrogen; 22 per cent helium; and traces of most other elements, including— in order of next highest percentages—oxygen, neon, carbon, and nitrogen.

Mass: From $\frac{1}{50}$ the mass of the sun to 50 times the mass of the sun.

Nearest Star Excluding the Sun: Proxima Centauri, 4.3 light-years away.

Farthest Stars: In galaxies billions of light-years away.

Brightest Star Excluding the Sun: Sirius (according to apparent magnitude).

Largest Stars: Have a diameter of about 1 billion miles (1.6 billion kilometers)—about 1,000 times that of the sun.

Smallest Known Stars: Neutron stars that have a diameter of 10 miles (16 kilometers).

Colors: From blue through white, yellow, and orange, to red, depending on the star's surface temperature.

Temperature: *Surface,* from about 50,000° F. (28,000° C) on blue stars to about 5000° F. (2800° C) on red stars; *interior,* more than 2,000,000° F. (1,100,000° C).

Radiations: Heat, light, radio waves, ultraviolet rays, X rays.

Energy Source: Nuclear fusion process and other processes that change hydrogen into helium and energy.

Stars are not spread evenly throughout the universe. They appear in groups called *galaxies*. The sun and all the visible stars belong to a galaxy called the Milky Way. This galaxy has a shape like a pancake with a bulge in the center. The sun and the nine planets—including the earth—lie in the flat portion of the galaxy, about halfway from the center to the edge.

How Many Stars Are There? No one knows exactly how many stars there are. Stars twinkle in every part of the sky, which can be thought of as "surrounding" the earth. On a clear, dark night, a person can see about 3,000 stars—but the person sees only half the sky. A person on the opposite side of the earth could see another 3,000 stars if that half of the sky were dark. Thus, about 6,000 stars can be seen. But these are just the brightest stars—the ones visible without a telescope.

A telescope brings many dim stars into view. For example, a total of about 600,000 stars can be seen through a telescope with a lens 3 inches (7.6 centimeters) in diameter. The largest telescopes make it possible to see about 3 billion individual stars and more than 1 billion galaxies. Astronomers believe these galaxies consist of a total of about 200 billion billion stars.

Only a few stars have names. Ancient stargazers named the brightest stars, such as Betelgeuse and Rigel in the constellation Orion. Today, astronomers use a letter of the Greek alphabet with the name of a constellation to identify a star. For example, Betelgeuse is called *Alpha Orionis* and Rigel is *Beta Orionis*.

The Size of Stars varies from neutron stars that have a diameter of 10 miles (16 kilometers) to giant stars far larger than the sun. The sun itself is a medium-sized star with a diameter of 865,000 miles (1,392,000 kilometers)—109 times that of the earth. Astronomers divide stars into five main groups by size: (1) supergiants, (2) giants, (3) medium-sized stars, (4) white dwarfs, and (5) neutron stars.

Supergiants, the largest known stars, include such stars as Antares and Betelgeuse. Antares has a diameter 330 times that of the sun. Betelgeuse actually expands and shrinks. Its diameter varies from 375 to 595 times that of the sun. The largest supergiants have diameters about a thousand times as large as the sun's.

Giants have diameters about 10 to 100 times as large as the sun's. The diameter of Aldebaran, for example, measures 36 times that of the sun.

Medium-Sized Stars, commonly called *main-sequence* or *dwarf* stars, are about as large as the sun. Their diameters vary from about a tenth that of the sun to about 10 times the sun's diameter. Well-known stars in this group include Altair, Sirius, and Vega.

White Dwarfs are small stars. The smallest white dwarf, van Maanen's Star, has a diameter of 5,200 miles (8,370 kilometers)—less than the distance across the continent of Asia.

Neutron Stars are the tiniest stars. They have as much mass as the sun, but are so compact that they are only about 10 miles in diameter.

The Distance of Stars. The sun is about 93 million miles (150 million kilometers) from the earth. The star nearest the sun, Proxima Centauri, seems like only a pinpoint of light because it is about 25 million million miles (40 million million kilometers) from the earth.

Astronomers measure the distance between stars in units called *light-years*. For example, Proxima Centauri is 4.3 light-years from the sun. A light-year equals 5.88 million million miles (9.46 million million kilometers). This is the distance light travels in one year at a speed of 186,282 miles (299,792 kilometers) per second. Some stars in the Milky Way are as far as 80,000 light-years from the sun and the earth.

The Milky Way's closest "neighbor" is a galaxy 200,000 light-years away. The most distant stars are billions of light-years away from the Milky Way.

The sun belongs to a part of the Milky Way where the distance between stars averages 4 to 5 light-years. In some other parts of the Milky Way, the stars are much closer. In globular clusters, for example, less than one-hundredth of a light-year separates the stars.

Why Stars Shine. A star's energy source lies deep within it. There, hydrogen gas changes into helium gas through a process called *nuclear fusion*. During this process, the mass of helium produced does not wholly equal the mass of hydrogen used up. Some of the material that makes up the original hydrogen changes into energy rather than into helium.

Nuclear fusion creates so much energy that the temperature at the center of the star reaches millions of degrees. From the surface of the star, the energy passes into space in such forms as light, heat, and radio waves. Stars shine until they use up all their hydrogen. Astronomers believe that most stars have enough hydrogen to last billions of years.

Color, Temperature, and Brightness. Starlight has a wide variety of color. Rigel sparkles with a blue light and Vega appears white. Capella's gleam looks yellow

How Large Are the Stars?

This diagram shows the great differences in the sizes of stars. Astronomers divide stars into five groups by size, but the sizes in almost all of these groups vary greatly. Most stars are about the same size as the sun. They may be thought of as being of medium size. Stars called giants have a diameter from 10 to 100 times that of the sun. Supergiants, the largest stars, have a diameter 100 to 1,000 times that of the sun. A few white dwarfs are smaller than the earth. Neutron stars, the smallest stars, are only about 10 miles in diameter.

Main-Sequence Star

White Dwarf

Neutron Star

Giant

Supergiant

WORLD BOOK diagram

THE MILKY WAY GALAXY

The Milky Way is one of more than a billion groups of stars called *galaxies* that are found throughout the universe. Among the billions of stars in the Milky Way are the sun and its planets—including the earth. The ball-like objects in this diagram are clusters of stars called *globular clusters*.

WORLD BOOK diagram by Herb Herrick

and Betelgeuse glows red. Other stars have in-between colors. They include blue-white Sirius and orange-red Arcturus.

A star's color indicates the temperature of its surface. This temperature varies from about 5000° F. (2800° C) for red stars, such as Betelgeuse, to about 50,000° F. (28,000° C) for blue stars, such as Rigel. Stars of other colors have surface temperatures somewhere in between. The sun, a yellowish star, has a temperature of about 10,000° F. (5500° C).

The brightest stars are not always the largest nor the nearest to the earth. Brightness also depends on the amount of light energy that a star sends out. Rigel is smaller and farther from the earth than is Betelgeuse. But Rigel sends out so much more light energy that it looks brighter than Betelgeuse.

Star Motions. Every day, the sun and all the other stars seem to move across the sky, rising in the east and setting in the west. The rising and setting comes from the spinning of the earth, not from the motion of the stars. See EARTH (How the Earth Moves).

Stars do move, but a star's motion produces only a slight change in its position among other stars. Astronomers measure this change, called *proper motion*, by comparing photographs taken at regular intervals. Barnard's Star has the greatest known proper motion. It takes 180 years for this star to move half a degree—an angle equal to the diameter of the moon as seen from the earth. The closer a star is to the earth, the easier it is for astrono-

mers to measure its proper motion. However, most stars are so far away that their proper motion is too small to be measured.

The sun itself moves at a speed of 12 miles (19 kilometers) per second through the Milky Way. In addition, the sun and all the other stars of the Milky Way sweep around the center of the galaxy. This spinning motion of the galaxy gives the sun and the stars near it a speed of 156 miles (250 kilometers) per second.

Star Groups. The Milky Way has more than 100 billion stars. Many of these stars are in smaller groups called star clouds and star clusters. Pairs of stars are called double stars.

Star Clouds look like bright, hazy areas when seen without a telescope. The brightness comes from the millions of stars that make up these areas. Such clouds form a background against which astronomers can see dark clouds of *interstellar* (between-the-stars) dust.

Star Clusters may be either ball-like or of irregular shapes. Ball-like clusters, called *globular clusters*, consist of about thousands of stars. About 100 globular clusters lie around the center of the Milky Way. Irregularly shaped clusters, called *open clusters*, have from 10 to a few hundred stars. These clusters lie within the main "pancake" of the Milky Way.

Double Stars, also called *binaries*, consist of a pair of stars. Many double stars belong to larger groups that include other double stars and single stars. Such groups are called *multiple stars*.

663

Measuring Direction and Position. Stars help map-makers, pilots, and sailors find exact directions and locations. For example, the North Star serves as a guide to the direction north because this star always appears to be in the same place over the North Pole. The earth's spinning motion makes the sky seem to rotate. Observers north of the equator see the stars rotate around a point above the North Pole. The North Star is near this point and seems to move very little.

The North Star also can be used to measure latitude. An observer uses a sextant to measure the angle at which the star appears above the northern horizon. This angle is the same as the observer's latitude. For example, at 45° north latitude, the North Star is at an angle of 45° above the northern horizon.

Pilots and sailors measure their exact position by means of *celestial navigation*. This method depends on the idea that a star is directly over some point on the earth's surface at a given time. The earthly position of a star changes as the star appears to move from east to west. A book called an *almanac* lists the earthly positions of various stars at different times. To determine their location, observers measure the angle of a star with a sextant and note the exact time of the measurement. They then look up the star's earthly position in an almanac. They use the angle of the star to figure out how far their location is from the star's earthly position. By repeating the process with two more stars, they can find their exact location. See NAVIGATION.

Measuring Time. Time is measured in terms of the earth's two basic motions—(1) its spinning motion and (2) its movement around the sun. These motions of the earth cause changes in the position of the sun and of other stars.

The earth's spinning motion makes the sun and other stars appear to move across the sky each day. Ordinary clocks keep *solar time*—time based on the seeming movement of the sun. The period from one midnight to the next is called a *solar day*. Some astronomer's clocks keep *sidereal time*—time based on the seeming movement of the stars. A *sidereal day* is the time it takes for a star to reach the same position in the sky on two nights, one after the other. Because of the earth's motions, the stars seem to move slightly faster than does the sun. As a result, a sidereal day is slightly shorter than a solar day.

The earth's movement around the sun makes the sun change position against the background of the other stars during the year. Scientists measure the length of a *sidereal year* by measuring the time it takes for the sun to reach the same position among the stars. See SIDEREAL TIME.

Learning from the Stars. Understanding the stars helps scientists understand the laws of physics and chemistry. In the early 1900's—even before scientists knew enough about the atom to put it to work—astronomers believed that nuclear energy made stars shine. Today, astronomers seek to explain such mysteries as the high energy of distant galaxies called *quasars* and the "beeping" radio waves from stars called *pulsars*. The answers to these mysteries may lead to a better understanding of the sun and of the earth itself.

HOW STARS HELP IN NAVIGATION

To find the position of their ship, sailors pick three stars and measure the angle that each makes with the horizon. They use an almanac to find the earthly position associated with each of the stars at the time its angle was measured. They then calculate the distance of their ship from each of the three positions. Their ship's location is the place on a map where the three distance lines meet.

WORLD BOOK diagram

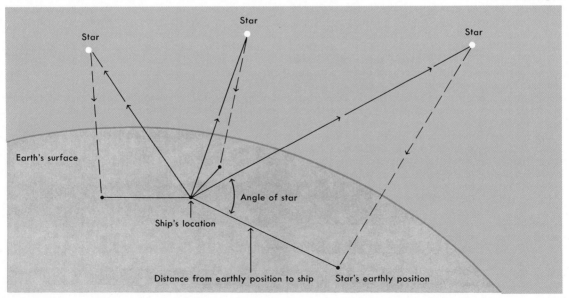

Star

Star

Star

Earth's surface

Angle of star

Ship's location

Distance from earthly position to ship

Star's earthly position

Astronomers classify stars in several ways. For example, stars differ in brightness, color, and size. Stars classified according to these characteristics include main-sequence stars, giants and supergiants, and white dwarfs. Astronomers also group stars according to such features as variations in brightness, the presence of "companion" stars, and the release of radio waves, X rays, and other forms of energy. Stars grouped according to these features include variable stars and binary stars. Other stars and starlike objects give off such unusual radiations that astronomers have not yet completely explained them. Quasars and pulsars are in this mystery group.

Main-Sequence Stars are "ordinary" stars like the sun. They make up about 90 per cent of the stars that can be seen from the earth. They include stars of all star-colors and many degrees of brightness. Main-sequence stars have medium-sized diameters. They are so much smaller than giants and supergiants that they are sometimes called *main-sequence dwarfs*. However, they are much larger than white dwarfs.

Main-sequence stars have a common characteristic. If they were all the same distance from the earth, all stars of the same color would appear about equally bright. Blue stars would be the brightest, followed by white, yellow, and orange stars. Red stars would be the dimmest.

Astronomers use the term *luminosity* for the brightness of a star when viewed from a standard distance. Main-sequence stars get their name from a graph used by astronomers to study the luminosity of stars. Dots on the graph represent stars. The position of each dot indicates a particular star's combination of luminosity and color. The dots that stand for most known stars fall into a broad group. This group extends diagonally across the graph from the high-luminosity blue area to the low-luminosity red area. Astronomers call this grouping of dots the *main sequence*. For more information about the color-luminosity graph—known as the *Hertz-*

sprung-Russell diagram—see the section of this article called *Studying the Stars*.

Giants and Supergiants are larger than main-sequence stars and have a higher luminosity. They also differ in other characteristics, including the pressure and density of their gases (see DENSITY).

Some giants, such as Rigel, shine with a blue light, indicating their high temperature. A high pressure "squeezes" the gases that make up these blue giants. Such stars have a density higher than that of the sun and other main-sequence stars.

Other giants, such as Arcturus, have a red or reddish glow, indicating a low temperature. Red giants are somewhat larger than blue giants. They consist of gases under low pressure, with a density less than that of sunlike stars.

Such supergiants as Betelgeuse also shine with a low-temperature red color. The gases that make up a supergiant spread through so large a space that they may have a lower density than the air we breathe.

White Dwarfs are smaller than main-sequence stars and have a lower luminosity. They shine with a hot, white light. Astronomers believe that gravity within these stars has shrunk them to their small size. Gravity produces extremely high gas pressure and density in white dwarfs. These tiny stars are so dense that a spoonful of their gases would weigh tons if it could be weighed on the earth. White dwarfs include van Maanen's

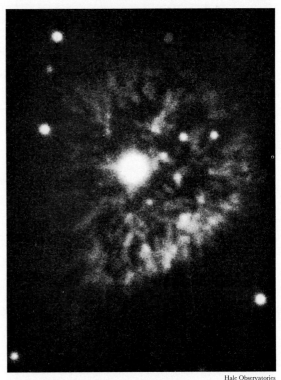

Hale Observatories

An Exploding Star in the constellation Perseus formed the cloud of gas shown above. The explosion's light was seen in 1901. The cloud, too small to be seen until 1916, is still expanding.

The 20 Brightest Stars

Star	Distance (Light-Years)
1. Sirius	8.8
2. Canopus	98
3. Alpha Centauri	4.3
4. Arcturus	36
5. Vega	26
6. Capella	46
7. Rigel	900
8. Procyon	11
9. Betelgeuse	300
10. Achernar	114
11. Beta Centauri	490
12. Altair	16
13. Alpha Crucis	370
14. Aldebaran	68
15. Spica	300
16. Antares	400
17. Pollux	35
18. Fomalhaut	23
19. Deneb	1,600
20. Beta Crucis	490

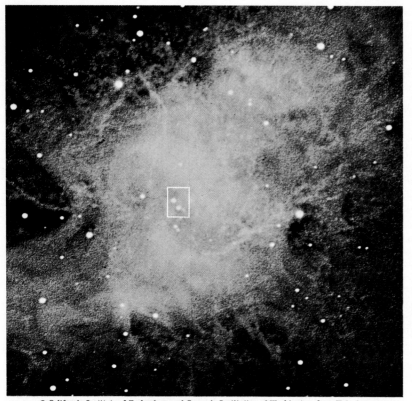

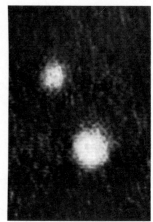

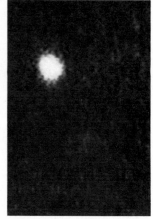

© California Institute of Technology and Carnegie Institution of Washington, from Hale Observatories

The Home of a Pulsar. The Crab Nebula, *above*, is a large cloud of dust and gas. Deep within it, a pulsar sends out its "beeping" radio waves. The pictures at the right show the pulsar, which is located in the above inset. The pulsar's light varies from bright, *top*, to barely visible, *bottom*. This pulsar most likely is the remains of the star that exploded and produced the cloud.

Star and Sirius B, which is a companion star of Sirius.

Variable Stars shine brightly, then dimly, and then brightly again. There are three principal types: (1) pulsating variables, (2) exploding stars, and (3) eclipsing binaries.

Pulsating Variables change in brightness as they expand and contract. The time it takes for such a star to change from bright to dim and back to bright again is called its *period*. Pulsating variables include short-period variables, long-period variables, and irregular variables. Short-period variables are yellow supergiants. Many of them pulsate about once a week. Astronomers also call them *Cepheid* variables because they discovered the first one in the constellation Cepheus. The North Star is a Cepheid variable with a period of about four days. Long-period variables are red giants or supergiants, such as Mira. Many of them have periods that last hundreds of days. Irregular variables do not have a regular period.

Exploding Stars burst unexpectedly with such tremendous energy that they hurl huge amounts of dust and gas into space. One type of exploding star, called a *nova*, becomes thousands of times brighter than normal. This extraordinary brightness may last for a few days or even years, and then the star returns to its dim appearance. Some novae explode again and again after indefinite periods. Another type of exploding star, called a *supernova*, is thousands of times as bright as an ordinary nova. The most famous supernova occurred in the Milky Way in 1054 and produced a huge cloud of dust and gas called the Crab Nebula. See SUPERNOVA.

Eclipsing Binaries are double stars, such as Algol. They consist of a pair of stars that move around each other. The stars move in such a way that one periodically blocks the other's light. This blocking reduces the total brightness of the two stars as seen from the earth. Eclipsing binaries are only one kind of double star. The following section discusses other kinds.

Binary Stars consist of visual binaries and spectroscopic binaries. Either kind may also be an eclipsing binary.

Visual Binaries, when seen through a telescope, look like two stars revolving around each other. One revolution of these stars may take 100 years.

Spectroscopic Binaries look like single stars, even through a telescope. They are named for the *spectroscope*, an instrument that astronomers use to identify them. A spectroscope spreads starlight from a binary star into a *spectrum*, a band of colors similar to a rainbow. Certain features of the spectrum identify the light as coming from a binary. Spectroscopic binaries complete their revolutions around each other in a few days or a few months.

Well-known binaries include Mizar and Alcor, two of the stars in the handle of the Big Dipper. They form a double star that can be seen without a telescope. Through a telescope, Mizar also appears as a visual binary. In turn, both the stars that make up Mizar are spectroscopic binaries. Alcor is also a spectroscopic binary. Thus, Mizar's four stars and Alcor's two make up a total of six stars. Such groups of stars are called *multiple stars*.

Quasars and Mystery Stars. Some stars and starlike objects give off unusually strong radio waves and other kinds of radiation. Such starlike objects include quasars, pulsars, X-ray stars, and infrared stars.

Quasars send out strong radio waves. Astronomers believe they are not individual stars but small, extremely distant galaxies. See QUASAR.

Pulsars, like quasars, give off radio energy. But pulsars "beep," sending out a pulse of radio waves every second or so. Most astronomers believe pulsars are *neutron stars*—stars composed not of atoms but of neutrons, one of the main parts of an atom. A pulsar within the Crab Nebula is believed to be the remains of the star that exploded into a supernova in 1054. See PULSAR.

X-Ray Stars were discovered when scientists sent

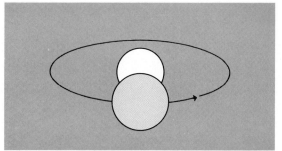

WORLD BOOK diagram

An Eclipsing Binary consists of two stars that vary in total brightness as they revolve around each other. The brightness is greatest when all of both stars can be seen. It is lowest when one star is partially *eclipsed* (blocked) by the other, *above*.

special telescopes above the atmosphere in rockets. Ordinarily, X rays from stars cannot be studied because they cannot get through the earth's atmosphere. The Crab Nebula sends out X rays as well as radio waves, but astronomers are not sure why.

Infrared Stars send out mainly heat. They probably have too low a temperature to give off such forms of energy as light and radio waves. These objects may really be interstellar clouds heated by nearby stars.

STAR/How Stars Produce Energy

Stars produce nuclear energy by changing hydrogen into helium. In a star, hydrogen changes into helium in one of two ways: (1) the proton-proton chain or (2) the carbon cycle. Either way, some of the hydrogen ends up not as helium, but as energy that makes the star shine.

The energy-making process produces chemical by-products as well. It creates carbon, iron, oxygen, silicon, and other elements. The presence of these elements in stars help scientists classify stars into age groups.

The Proton-Proton Reaction gets its name from the nucleus of a hydrogen atom. This nucleus consists of a single atomic particle called a *proton*. In the proton-proton reaction, nuclei of hydrogen atoms collide with one another and combine to produce nuclei of helium atoms.

The Carbon Cycle takes place in steps. First, nuclei of hydrogen atoms collide with carbon nuclei to form nuclei of nitrogen atoms. Then, additional collisions change the nitrogen to oxygen and back to nitrogen. Finally, each nitrogen nucleus breaks down into a carbon nucleus and a helium nucleus. The carbon nucleus then enters the cycle again.

Nuclear By-Products. Collisions between various kinds of nuclei during the nuclear energy-producing process create other elements. The star uses up its hydrogen and builds up its amounts of helium and other elements. Hydrogen and helium make up about 97 per cent of the mass of a star (see MASS). The remaining 3 per cent includes argon, carbon, chlorine, iron, magnesium, neon, nitrogen, oxygen, silicon, sulfur, and other elements.

Hydrogen and helium are the two "lightest" chemical elements. That is, their atoms have less mass than do the other elements. Atoms of such elements as carbon, nitrogen, and oxygen have more mass, and so they are considered "heavier." In a star, the heavier elements are created from the lighter ones during the nuclear energy-producing process.

Star Ages. The fact that stars create heavy elements from lighter ones helps astronomers distinguish between two "generations" of stars. Stars of the "younger" generation contain a larger amount of heavier elements than do stars of the "older" generation.

Many stars end their existence in explosions like the one that produced the Crab Nebula. Such an explosion creates a cloud containing the hydrogen, helium, and heavier elements that made up the former star. In time, the material in the cloud forms a new star. This new, second-generation star thus includes the remains of a star that was rich in the heavier elements. As a result, the new star contains a relatively high amount of those elements.

Astronomers call the younger-generation stars *Population I* stars. They call the older-generation stars *Population II* stars. Population I stars are relatively new stars, such as the sun. They were formed from gas that had been part of earlier stars. Population I stars contain larger amounts of the heavier elements than do Population II stars. Population II stars are older stars that were formed from the first gas clouds in space. These clouds consisted mainly of hydrogen and helium, with few, if any, heavy elements.

666a

The life of most stars lasts billions of years. Most stars began shining between 1 million and 10 billion years ago. Some will keep shining for billions of years. Obviously, no one has ever watched a particular star take shape, change, and finally die. But astronomers have observed many different stars at various stages of their existence. They have also developed theories of star formation based on known chemical and physical laws.

Astronomers get much of their information about the life of a star by studying star clusters. The stars in a cluster probably formed about the same time, and thus are probably all about the same age. Some clusters include many blue giants, and such stars are believed to be young. Other clusters include many red giants that are thought to be old stars. From observation and theory, astronomers have put together the story of how stars probably begin and end their existence.

How Stars Form. A star begins its life as a cloud of interstellar gas and dust. Such clouds can be seen

© California Institute of Technology and
Carnegie Institution of Washington, from Hale Observatories

Stars in the Making. The huge cloud of interstellar dust and gas shown above reflects the light of nearby stars. Such bright clouds make it possible to see small, dark globs of material that are found between the cloud and the earth. Two such dark globs appear in the photograph above—at the upper right and upper left of the cloud. Such globs may be the beginnings of new stars.

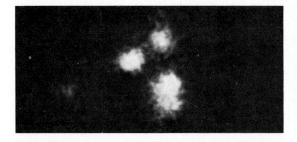
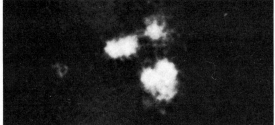

Lick Observatory

Possible New Stars were discovered in a dust-and-gas cloud in the constellation Orion. A photograph taken in 1947, *left,* shows three stars in the cloud. A photograph taken in 1954, *right,* shows what astronomers believe may be two new stars that came to life during the seven-year period. They are so close to two of the original stars that they form single enlarged images in the picture.

as dark patches in front of the bright, distant stars of the Milky Way. The cloud that is to become a star consists mostly of hydrogen mixed with dust. Astronomers believe some of the hydrogen and dust comes from old stars. The cloud may include the remains of a star that exploded, or it may be a collection of gases thrown from the surface of rotating stars.

The first step in the formation of a new star is the contraction of part of an interstellar cloud into a ball. Astronomers have never watched a new star flash into life. But they have discovered several dark, ball-like interstellar clouds that may be new stars beginning to take shape.

Through millions of years, the cloud of gas and dust contracts as gravity pulls it together. As the material pulls together into a ball, the pressure of the gas increases. The gas at the center of the ball becomes extremely hot. When the temperature at the center reaches about 2,000,000° F. (1,100,000° C), the nuclear fusion reaction begins. The hydrogen in the center begins to change into helium and to produce great amounts of nuclear energy. This energy heats the gas that surrounds the center. The gas begins to shine—and a star has come to life.

The kind of star that takes shape depends on the mass of the contracting cloud. A cloud with a mass about $\frac{1}{20}$ that of the sun becomes a red, low-luminosity main-sequence star. A cloud with a mass about 50 times that of the sun becomes a blue, high-luminosity, main-sequence star.

How Stars Change and Die. After a star begins to shine, it starts to change slowly. The speed of its change depends on how rapidly the nuclear energy-producing process takes place inside it. The speed of this process, in turn, depends on the mass of the star. The greater a star's mass, the higher its luminosity and temperature—and the faster it changes. Stars with a mass about 10 times that of the sun take a few million years to change. Smaller stars with a mass about $\frac{1}{10}$ that of the sun take hundreds of billions of years to change.

A star changes because its supply of hydrogen decreases. The star's center contracts, and the temperature and pressure at the center rise. At the same time, the temperature of the outer part gradually drops. The star expands greatly and becomes a red giant.

What happens after a star's red giant phase depends on how much mass the star contains. A star with about the same mass as the sun throws off its outer layers, which can be seen as a glowing gas shell called a *planetary nebula*. The core that is left behind cools and becomes a white dwarf. A star with more than about three times the mass of the sun becomes a supergiant. Elements as heavy as iron are formed inside the star, which then explodes into a supernova. If less than three times the mass of the sun remains after the supernova explosion, it becomes a neutron star. If more than three times the mass of the sun remains, the star collapses and forms an invisible object called a *black hole*. A black hole has so much gravitational force that not even light can escape from it (see BLACK HOLE).

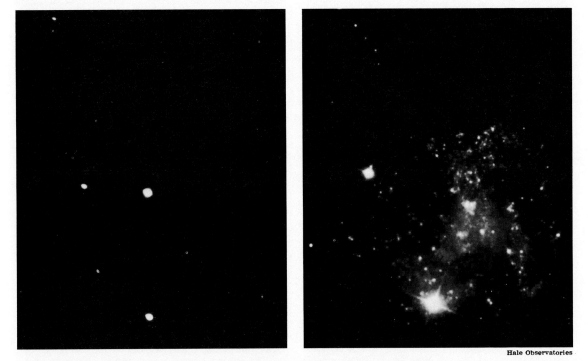

Hale Observatories

A Star Explodes and Dies in these photographs of a supernova and its remains. The photograph at the left shows the exploding star, *center*, at its greatest brightness. The photograph at the right, taken five years later, shows a cloud of gas in the area—but no star.

Astronomers study two main characteristics of starlight—brightness and color. Brightness indicates how much mass the star has. Color indicates the temperature of the star's surface. From a star's brightness and color, astronomers can learn about other important features, such as its size and distance.

This section discusses some of the tools and methods that astronomers use to study stars. For additional information, see the articles on ASTRONOMY (Astronomers at Work) and TELESCOPE.

Measuring Brightness. Astronomers use an instrument called a *photometer* to measure the brightness of stars. They attach the instrument to a telescope. Light from a star enters the photometer and produces an electric current in it. An electrical meter indicates the star's brightness in terms of the strength of the current.

Astronomers compare the brightness of stars by using a number called the star's *magnitude*. The brighter a star is, the lower is its magnitude. A star with a magnitude of 1.00 is brighter than one with a magnitude of 2.00. The brightest stars have magnitudes so low they are less than zero—that is, they are expressed in negative numbers. Thus, a star with magnitude -1.00 is brighter than one of magnitude 1.00, but not so bright as one with a magnitude of -2.00. See MAGNITUDE.

A photometer measures the brightness of a star as it appears from the earth. Astronomers call this brightness the star's *apparent magnitude*. If astronomers know how far away a star is, they can calculate its *absolute magnitude*, which indicates the star's *luminosity* (actual brightness). Absolute magnitude is the brightness the star would appear to have if it were a standard distance -32.6 light-years—from the earth.

Measuring Color. Starlight is a combination of colors. The hottest stars give off more blue light than red light. Stars with lower surface temperatures give off

more red light than blue light. Astronomers measure the intensity of a star's blue and red light by passing the light through color filters and then into a photometer. They use a blue filter to separate the blue light from the other colors. A red filter separates the red light. Astronomers also may measure a star's color with a *spectrograph*. This instrument takes a photograph of the star's spectrum. The photograph indicates how much light of each color is in the starlight.

Astronomers indicate the main color of a star with

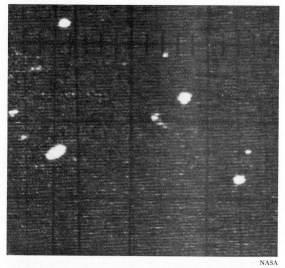

NASA

Star Pictures Taken by Spacecraft are not affected by the earth's atmosphere, and so they contain information that telescopes on the earth cannot gather. The U.S. orbiting astronomical observatory took this picture high above the earth's atmosphere.

Milestones in Star Study

c. 3000 B.C. The earliest recorded astronomical observations were made in China.

c. 100's B.C. Hipparchus, a Greek astronomer, drew up the first catalog of stars that showed their brightness and position.

A.D. c. 150 Ptolemy, an astronomer in Egypt, cataloged more than 1,000 stars and developed a way of using numbers to record the positions of stars.

1572 Tycho Brahe, a Danish astronomer, proved that a supernova he observed was a star. He thus proved wrong an ancient idea that no change in the heavens could occur.

1609-1610 Galileo, an Italian scientist, pioneered the use of a telescope to study stars too faint to be seen with the unaided eye.

1718 Edmond Halley, an English astronomer, checked the positions of stars recorded by Hipparchus and found that some stars had moved. He thus showed that stars had a proper motion.

1780 Sir William Herschel, a British astronomer, made many discoveries about star brightness, binary stars, and clouds of interstellar gas and dust.

1783 John Goodricke, a British astronomer, correctly explained the varying brightness of Algol, the first known variable star, by suggesting that it was an eclipsing binary.

1838 Friedrich Bessel, a German astronomer and mathematician, became the first scientist to measure the distance of a star by parallax.

1850 The American astronomers William and George Bond, father and son, took the first telescopic photograph of a star.

1890's Edward Barnard, an American astronomer, proved that dark clouds of gas and dust exist among the stars of the Milky Way.

1910-1940 Henry Norris Russell, an American astronomer, pioneered in using the ideas of atomic physics to analyze the nature of stars.

1924 Sir Arthur Eddington, a British astronomer, explained the relationship between the mass and the brightness of a star, a key idea in understanding the changing form of stars.

1960 American astronomers at the Palomar Observatory discovered the first *quasar*—a small, distant galaxy—at a spot in the sky known to be a source of strong radio waves.

1967 British radio astronomers discovered the first *pulsar*, an object that sends out strong pulsating radio waves.

1974 Astronomers determined that certain pulsating X-ray sources are binaries in which one of the stars is either a neutron star or a black hole.

one of the following letters: O, B, A, F, G, K, or M. Each letter represents a color group called a *spectral class*. For example, blue stars fall into the "O" spectral class, yellow stars are "G" stars, and red stars are classified "M". The colors and temperatures associated with the spectral classes appear on the Hertzsprung-Russell diagram shown in this section.

The Hertzsprung-Russell (H-R) Diagram illustrates the relationship between star luminosity and spectral class. The diagram was named for the Danish astronomer Ejnar Hertzsprung and the American astronomer Henry Norris Russell. These scientists independently developed the idea for the diagram in the early 1900's. The Hertzsprung-Russell diagram is a graph with absolute magnitude shown vertically and spectral class horizontally. Each point on the graph represents the absolute magnitude and spectral class of a particular star.

The outstanding feature of the diagram is that the

points representing most stars fall close to a diagonal line. For example, most blue stars have a high luminosity, most yellow stars a medium luminosity, and most red stars a low luminosity. Astronomers call this group of points on the diagram the *main sequence*.

The H-R diagram also identifies other kinds of stars. Some red stars have an unusually high luminosity. These are the red giants and supergiants whose high luminosity comes from their tremendous size. Some white stars are much less luminous than white main-sequence stars. These are white dwarfs, which are much smaller than main-sequence stars.

Star Size and Distance. Astronomers have measured the sun's diameter and they have obtained fairly good measurements of the size of a few other stars. These stars are large and relatively close to the earth. But all the other stars are too far away to measure directly. Astronomers calculate the size of these stars from meas-

THE HERTZSPRUNG-RUSSELL DIAGRAM

This diagram helps astronomers classify and study stars. The color bands illustrate spectral classes identified by the letters and temperatures across the top of the diagram. A star is represented on the diagram by a dot located (1) horizontally according to the star's spectral class and (2) vertically according to its absolute magnitude. For example, the sun belongs to spectral class G and has an absolute magnitude of $+5$. This combination puts the sun on the main sequence.

WORLD BOOK diagram

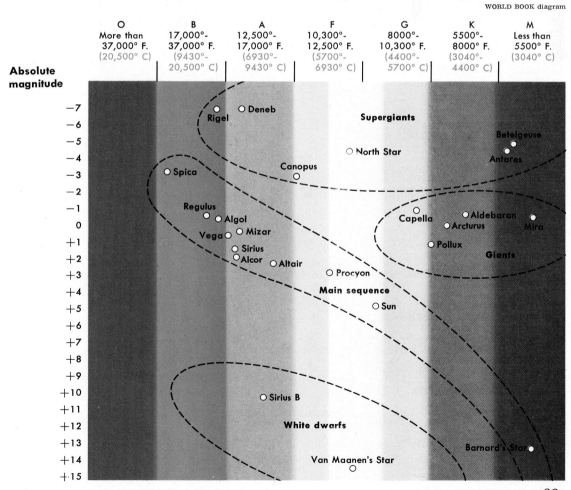

urements of the star's luminosity and temperature.

Astronomers have measured the distance of about 10,000 of the stars nearest the earth by using *parallax*. This method is based on viewing a star from two widely separated places. These places are opposite points along the earth's orbit around the sun. See PARALLAX.

Most stars are too far away for their distance to be measured by parallax. Astronomers measure the distance of such stars in terms of their luminosity by using the H-R diagram. For example, if the star is a main-sequence star, its position on the main sequence is determined according to its spectral type. The diagram indicates the luminosity that corresponds to this spectral type. Astronomers measure the star's spectral type.

They then determine how far the star must be for its measured magnitude to agree with the luminosity indicated by the H-R diagram.

Unsolved Mysteries. Astronomers are working to improve their explanations of quasars, pulsars, and other kinds of mystery stars. They are investigating the effects of star rotation and the mixing of gases within stars. They also want to know more about the exact chemical composition of stars.

Today, astronomers can send instruments into space on rockets or with astronauts. These instruments can measure certain kinds of radiation that are either blocked by or changed by the atmosphere. Measurements made in space may help astronomers solve some star mysteries. They also may reveal new wonders to challenge the astronomer's imagination.   THORNTON PAGE

STAR/*Study Aids*

Related Articles in WORLD BOOK include:

BIOGRAPHIES

Bessel, Friedrich W.	Herschel (Sir William)
Bowditch, Nathaniel	Hipparchus
Cannon, Annie J.	Hogg, Helen Sawyer
De Sitter, Willem	Ptolemy
Eddington, Sir Arthur S.	Rittenhouse, David
Galileo	Russell, Henry N.

STARS

Algol	Mira
Alpha Centauri	North Star
Antares	Nova
Arcturus	Sirius
Betelgeuse	Sun
Capella	Supernova
Deneb	Vega

OTHER RELATED ARTICLES

Astrology	Galaxy	Parallax
Astronomy (maps: The	Maffei Galaxies	Planet
Stars and Constellations)	Magnitude	Pulsar
Binary Star	Meteor	Quasar
Black Hole	Milky Way	Red Shift
Comet	Nebula	Sidereal
Constellation	Neutron Star	Time

Outline

I. Stars in the Universe
  A. How Many Stars Are There?
  B. The Size of Stars
  C. The Distance of Stars
  D. Why Stars Shine
  E. Color, Temperature, and Brightness
  F. Star Motions
  G. Star Groups

II. How People Use the Stars
  A. Measuring Direction and Position
  B. Measuring Time
  C. Learning from the Stars

III. Kinds of Stars
  A. Main-Sequence Stars   E. Binary Stars
  B. Giants and Supergiants   F. Quasars and
  C. White Dwarfs   Mystery Stars
  D. Variable Stars

IV. How Stars Produce Energy
  A. The Proton-   C. Nuclear By-Products
     Proton Reaction   D. Star Ages
  B. The Carbon Cycle

V. The Birth and Death of a Star
  A. How Stars Form
  B. How Stars Change and Die

VI. Studying the Stars
  A. Measuring Brightness   D. Star Size and
  B. Measuring Color   Distance
  C. The Hertzsprung-   E. Unsolved Mysteries
    Russell (H-R) Diagram

Questions

What process makes stars shine?

What two gases compose about 97 per cent of a star?

What do main-sequence stars have in common?

How many years ago did most stars come into existence?

Which star has the largest known proper motion?

What is the difference between a star's apparent magnitude and its absolute magnitude?

What kind of star is so dense that a tiny amount of its material would weigh tons on the earth?

What are some features of the Crab Nebula?

Which stars have a higher surface temperature, red stars or blue stars?

What are Population I stars? Population II stars?

Reading and Study Guide

See *Stars* in the RESEARCH GUIDE/INDEX, Volume 22 for a *Reading and Study Guide*.

Additional Resources

Level I

ADLER, IRVING. *The Stars: Decoding Their Messages.* Rev. ed. Harper, 1980.

ASIMOV, ISAAC. *Alpha Centauri: The Nearest Star.* Morrow, 1976.

BRANLEY, FRANKLYN M. *Sun Dogs and Shooting Stars: A Skywatchers Calendar.* Houghton, 1980.

JOSEPH, JOSEPH M., and LIPPINCOTT, SARAH L. *Point to the Stars.* 2nd ed. McGraw, 1977.

KRASKE, ROBERT. *Riddles of the Stars: White Dwarfs, Red Giants, and Black Holes.* Harcourt, 1979.

MOORE, PATRICK A. *Wonder Why Book of Stars.* Grosset, 1979.

WICKS, KEITH. *Stars and Planets.* Watts, 1977.

Level II

BAADE, WALTER. *Evolution of Stars and Galaxies.* Ed. by Cecilia Payne-Gaposchkin. MIT Press, 1975.

BURNHAM, ROBERT, JR. *Celestial Handbook: An Observer's Guide to the Universe Beyond the Solar System.* Rev. ed. 3 vols. Dover, 1978.

KALS, W. S. *The Stargazer's Bible.* Doubleday, 1980.

KERROD, ROBIN. *Stars and Planets.* Arco, 1979.

REY, HANS A. *The Stars: A New Way to See Them.* 3rd ed. Houghton, 1967.

SULLIVAN, WALTER. *Black Holes: The Edge of Space, The End of Time.* Doubleday, 1979.

STAR, FIVE-POINTED, is the star most widely pictured as a symbol and in art. The five-pointed stars in the Flag of the United States symbolize the Union of the states. Here are directions for drawing a five-pointed star, and for cutting it out of paper.

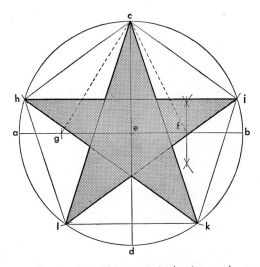

How to Draw a Star. This geometric drawing can be made by drawing a four-inch circle. Draw the horizontal and vertical diameter *ab* and *cd*. Mark the point of intersection *e*. Bisect *eb* and mark the point of intersection *f*. With *f* as a center, and *cf* as a radius, describe an arc cutting *ae*. Mark the point of intersection *g*. With *gc* as a radius and *c* as a center, describe two arcs cutting the circumference at *h* and *j*. With *h* and *j* as centers and the same radius, describe arcs cutting the circumference at *k* and *l*. Form a star by connecting *c* and *l*, *c* and *k*, *h* and *k*, *l* and *j*, and *h* and *j*.

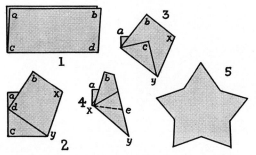

How to Cut a Star. The drawings show how a star may be cut quickly by folding paper. Cut on the dotted line, *x* to *e*.

STAR ANISE. See ILLICIUM.

STAR CHAMBER was an English court of law during the 1500's and 1600's. It tried persons too powerful to be brought before the ordinary, common-law courts. The Star Chamber consisted of men from the King's Council, a group of royal advisers. It passed judgment without trial by jury. The court was so named because it held sessions in the Star Chamber of Westminster Palace. Today, the term *star chamber* refers to an unregulated, secret meeting of any court of justice or official organization.

The Star Chamber was popular for a long time because it protected ordinary people from their oppressors. But eventually it abused its powers. Unlike the com-

mon-law courts, which protected the accused, it used torture to obtain confessions. King Charles I used the Star Chamber to crush opposition to his policies. In 1641, the Long Parliament abolished the court (see LONG PARLIAMENT).   W. M. SOUTHGATE

STAR GRASS is a flower with six starlike blossoms and yellow-green petals. Star grass grows in Kansas, Florida, and Texas, and from Maine to Ontario.

Scientific Classification. The common star grass belongs to the amaryllis family, *Amaryllidaceae*. It is genus *Hypoxis*, species *H. hirsuta*.

STAR MAPS. See ASTRONOMY (The Sky at Different Latitudes; illustrations: The Stars and Constellations); HIPPARCHUS.

STAR OF AFRICA. See GEM (Some Famous Gems).

STAR-OF-BETHLEHEM is a small, hardy plant that belongs to the lily family. It grew first in Italy, but now has become a common garden plant in America. Its flowers form the shape of a six-pointed star. The petal-like parts are white, but have green stripes on the outside. The leaves of the plant are green with white stripes. The flower stalk rises from a coated bulb.

People grow the star-of-Bethlehem in gardens, greenhouses, and window boxes. Its flowers bloom in May and June, and tend to close before nightfall. The bulbs of the star-of-Bethlehem are poisonous.

J. Horace McFarland
Star-of-Bethlehem

Scientific Classification. The star-of-Bethlehem belongs to the lily family, *Liliaceae*. It is genus *Ornithogalum*, species *O. umbellatum.*   ALFRED C. HOTTES

STAR OF DAVID, or SHIELD OF DAVID, is the universal symbol of Judaism. It appears on the flag of the State of Israel, in synagogues, on Jewish ritual objects, and on emblems of organizations. It is made up of two triangles that interlace to form a six-pointed star. The figure itself is an ancient one. Scholars do not know when it became widespread as a Jewish symbol. The figure appeared as early as the 960's B.C. The Hebrew term *Magen David*, which means *Shield of David*, dates from the late A.D. 200's.

The Star of David

LEONARD C. MISHKIN

STAR OF INDIA. See SAPPHIRE.

STAR OF THE SOUTH. See DIAMOND (Famous Diamonds).

STAR-SPANGLED BANNER is the national anthem of the United States. It was written by Francis Scott Key and is sung to music composed by John Stafford Smith. In March 1931, Congress officially approved the song as the national anthem. But the Army and Navy had recognized "The Star-Spangled Banner" as

The Star-Spangled Banner, the flag that inspired Francis Scott Key to write the national anthem, hangs in the Museum of History and Technology in Washington, D.C. Key saw the flag flying over Fort McHenry in Baltimore while he was held prisoner by the British during the War of 1812. The flag, which is 50 feet (15 meters) long, covers an entire wall.

the national anthem long before Congress adopted it.

How the Song Came to Be Written. During the War of 1812, the British forces took prisoner William Beanes of Upper Marlborough, Md., and held him aboard a warship in Chesapeake Bay. Two Americans received permission from President James Madison to communicate with the British in an effort to have Beanes released. The men were Francis Scott Key, a lawyer, and John S. Skinner, both of Washington, D.C. Key and Skinner boarded the warship just as the vessel was preparing to bombard Fort McHenry, which protected the city of Baltimore. The British agreed to release Beanes. But they held all three Americans on a U.S. prisoner-exchange boat at the rear of the British fleet until after the battle ended, so they could not reveal plans of the attack to patriots on shore.

The bombardment started on Tuesday, Sept. 13, 1814, and continued all that day and almost all night.

Key and his friends knew that Fort McHenry had little defense. The prisoners paced the deck all night. Even when dawn came, they did not know who had won the battle because the smoke and haze was so thick.

Suddenly, at 7 o'clock, a break in the mist cleared the view for a moment, and they saw the American flag still flying over the walls of the fort. Key was so excited that he wanted to express his feelings. He pulled an unfinished letter from his pocket and started writing verses. He wrote most of the words of the song in a few minutes. Later that day, the British released the Americans, and Key returned to Baltimore, where he finished the other stanzas.

How the Song Became Famous. The poem was printed on handbills the next morning and distributed in the city. A few days later, actor Ferdinand Durang sang "The Star-Spangled Banner" in Baltimore to the tune of an old English drinking song called "To Anac-

Oh! say, can you see, by the dawn's early light,
What so proudly we hailed at the twilight's last gleaming?
Whose broad stripes and bright stars, thro' the perilous fight,
O'er the ramparts we watched were so gallantly streaming?
And the rockets' red glare, the bombs bursting in air,
Gave proof thro' the night that our flag was still there.
Oh! say, does that star-spangled banner yet wave
O'er the land of the free and the home of the brave?

On the shore, dimly seen thro' the mist of the deep,
Where the foe's haughty host in dread silence reposes,
What is that which the breeze, o'er the towering steep,
As it fitfully blows, half conceals, half discloses?
Now it catches the gleam of the morning's first beam,
In full glory reflected, now shines on the stream.
'Tis the star-spangled banner. Oh! long may it wave
O'er the land of the free and the home of the brave!

And where is that band who so vauntingly swore
That the havoc of war and the battle's confusion
A home and a country should leave us no more?
Their blood has washed out their foul footstep's pollution.
No refuge could save the hireling and slave
From the terror of flight or the gloom of the grave,
And the star-spangled banner in triumph doth wave
O'er the land of the free and the home of the brave.

Oh! thus be it ever when freemen shall stand
Between their loved home and the war's desolation,
Blest with vict'ry and peace, may the Heav'n-rescued land
Praise the Pow'r that hath made and preserved us a nation.
Then conquer we must, when our cause it is just,
And this be our motto, "In God is our trust."
And the star-spangled banner in triumph shall wave
O'er the land of the free and the home of the brave.

---

reon in Heaven." Americans knew the melody as that of a military march of the 1700's, and as a political song named "Adams and Liberty." Durang's performance marked the first time the anthem was sung in public. It became popular immediately, and three months later it was played during the Battle of New Orleans.

By government permission, the United States flag flies continuously over Key's grave at Frederick, Md., and over Fort McHenry. RAYMOND KENDALL

See also ANACREON; BALTIMORE (picture: The Star-Spangled Banner); FLAG (Saluting the Flag); KEY, FRANCIS SCOTT.

STARBUCK ISLAND is an uninhabited coral island in the South Pacific Ocean. For location, see PACIFIC ISLANDS (map). The island covers about 1 square mile (2.6 square kilometers). It was once an important source of guano, which is used as a fertilizer. However, the guano deposits have been depleted. The island was discovered in 1823. In 1979, Starbuck Island became part of the newly formed independent nation of Kiribati. See also KIRIBATI. NEAL M. BOWERS

STARCH is a white, powdery substance found in the living cells of green plants. It can be found in the seeds of corn, wheat, rice, and beans and in the stems, roots, and *tubers* (underground stems) of the potato, arrowroot or *cassava* (tapioca) plants. Starch is a carbohydrate, one of the most important foods. Starchy foods are an important source of energy for human beings and animals. When starch is digested in the body, energy is directly obtained from it.

During *photosynthesis* (the food-making process) in green plants, the energy of sunlight changes water and carbon dioxide into glucose and oxygen. Plant cells can quickly convert glucose into starch. Tiny starch *granules* (grains) are formed in most green leaves during the day. At night, the starch is converted back to sugars, which then move to the root, stem, seeds, fruit, and other parts of the plant. The sugar may be used for growth, or stored again as starch.

Use in Foods. Starch or flour that contains starch are often used in cooking to thicken mixtures. The mixtures usually become pasty or jellylike. When starchy foods such as rice or macaroni are cooked, the starch granules swell and absorb water. Starch does not dissolve in water. Cooked starch is easily broken down in the body by digestive *enzymes* (chemicals). But uncooked starch is too insoluble to be digested easily.

During the cooking of some foods, the starch may change into other substances. For example, slightly scorched starch becomes *dextrin*, a sticky carbohydrate that is used as glue on stamps and envelopes. During bread making a small amount of starch becomes the sugar *maltose*. Maltose is fermented by yeast and changed into carbon dioxide and alcohol. The carbon dioxide forms bubbles in the dough and makes it rise.

Chemists use iodine to test for the presence of starch in food. When a small amount of iodine is added to a starch solution, it becomes blue-black. Under the microscope, starch appears as tiny granules. Cornstarch granules are rounded, irregular *polygons* (many-sided figures) about 10 to 20 microns in diameter. Potato starch granules are oval and may be more than 100 microns in diameter. Rice starch has tiny granules about 3 to 5 microns in diameter. With experience, a person can identify a certain kind of starch by the way it looks under a microscope.

Industrial Uses. Industry manufactures over 5 billion pounds (2.3 billion kilograms) of starch in the United States each year. About half of it is sold as starch and dextrin, and 1½ billion pounds (0.7 billion kilograms) are converted into starch syrup. Most of the starch is used to *size* (stiffen) weaving yarn and to finish the cloth. Starch gives high-quality paper strength and a smooth, glossy finish. Starches are also used in making pasteboard, corrugated board, plywood, and wallboard. A starch called *Amioca* is produced from *waxy maize* (a kind of corn). Amioca produces pastes that are clear and fluid, unlike cornstarch.

To manufacture cornstarch, corn is soaked in warm water and sulfur dioxide for two days. The softened kernels are torn apart and the *germ* (part of the inside) is removed. The kernel fragments are then ground and *screened* (sifted) down to starch and *gluten* (proteins). The starch is then filtered, washed, dried, and packaged.

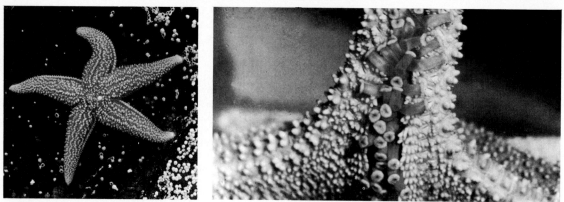

Most Starfish Have Five Arms, *above left,* although some kinds have as many as 50 arms. There are many tube feet on the underside of each arm, *above right.* Each of the tube feet has a tiny suction disk at its tip. The starfish uses its tube feet and suction disks to crawl over the seabed.

Similar processes are used for starch from waxy maize and sorghum.

To make potato starch, the potatoes are washed and ground, and the starch is separated from potato fibers by screening. After further separation, the starch is washed and dried. Arrowroot and tapioca starch may be produced by similar methods.

Wheat starch can be manufactured by *kneading* (mixing) wheat flour into a dough. The starch is washed out of the sticky mass by a stream of water. Rice starch is made by soaking the grain in an alkaline chemical, which dissolves the gluten but not the starch. The starch is then separated and washed.   DEXTER FRENCH

Related Articles in WORLD BOOK include:

Arrowroot	Cornstarch	Sago
Carbohydrate	Dextrin	Tapioca
Cellulose		

STARFISH, or SEA STAR, is a sea animal that has armlike extensions on its body. Most *species* (kinds) have five "arms" and look somewhat like five-pointed stars. However, not all starfish look like stars. Some have such short arms that their body looks like a *pentagon* (five-sided shape). Others have many arms. They are called *sun stars* because their shape resembles the sun and its rays.

Starfish live in all of the world's oceans. But they are not fish. They are members of a group of animals called *echinoderms.* The echinoderm group also includes the brittle star, sea cucumber, sea lily, and sea urchin. See ECHINODERM.

The starfish body has a *central disk* and *arms.* Its mouth, in the middle of the underside of the central disk, leads directly into a large, baglike stomach. On the outside of the body, a groove extends from the mouth to the tip of each arm. Rows of slender tubes, called *tube feet,* line these grooves. The animal uses the suction disk at the end of each tube foot for crawling. These disks grip hard surfaces. The starfish "sees" with a small colored *eyespot* located at the tip of each arm. The eyespot senses light, but cannot form images. The starfish uses its tube feet and a tiny, sensitive *tentacle* located at the tip of each arm to "feel."

Starfish release eggs into the sea through small holes between their arms. The eggs form into tiny swimming larvae. After a while, each larva settles down on the sea bottom and develops into a starfish. Starfish can *regenerate* (grow again) new arms when the old ones are broken off. Even if a starfish is cut in two, each of the pieces will regenerate into a new animal. Most starfish live for three to five years, but some may live as long as seven years.

Many starfish feed on shelled animals such as mussels, clams, and oysters. The starfish can push its stomach out through its mouth. When it feeds on an oyster, it attaches its tube feet to the two halves of the oyster's shell and pulls the shell halves apart, opening a tiny crack between them. Then the starfish pushes its stomach, turned inside out, through the crack. A starfish can slide its stomach through a crack no larger than the thickness of a piece of cardboard. The stomach surrounds the oyster's soft body, slowly digests it, and absorbs the food into the starfish's body. Such starfish are serious pests in the oyster-breeding grounds of the eastern coast of the United States.

Scientific Classification. Starfish belong to the phylum *Echinodermata.* They are classified in the class *Asteroidea.*   ROBERT D. BARNES

See also ANIMAL (pictures: Animals of the Oceans, How Animals Eat); CORAL (How Coral Is Formed).

STARK, JOHANNES (1874-1957), a German physicist, was noted for his discovery of the *Stark effect.* This discovery, the splitting of spectral lines when an emitting atom is in an electrical field, won for him the 1919 Nobel prize in physics. He also noted the change in frequency of light from moving atoms in a gas-discharge tube. This was the first observation of the optical *Doppler effect* from a source other than the stars (see RELATIVITY [General Relativity Theory]).

Stark was born at Schickenhof, Bavaria. He attended schools in Bayreuth and Regensburg. At the University of Munich, he studied physics, chemistry, mathematics, and crystallography. After graduation, he taught in technical high schools at Hannover and Aachen.

In 1917, Stark went as a professor of physics to the University of Greifswald. From there, he went as a professor to the University of Würzburg in 1920. He served as president of a technical institute in Charlottenburg from 1933 to 1939.   CARL T. CHASE

STARK, JOHN (1728-1822), was a leading American general in the Revolutionary War. His crushing defeat of Colonel Friedrich Baum's raiding party of Germans, Tories, Canadians, and Indians near Bennington, Vt., on Aug. 16, 1777, was a turning point of the war. It was a severe setback to General John Burgoyne's campaign to cut the American colonies in half.

Stark's New Hampshire regiment defended the American left wing at Breed's Hill in 1775. He helped cover the 1776 retreat from Canada, commanded units at the battles of Trenton and Princeton, and served in the Rhode Island campaign of 1779. Stark was born in Londonderry, N.H. He served with Rogers' Rangers in the French and Indian War from 1754 to 1763. A statue of Stark represents New Hampshire in the U.S. Capitol in Washington, D.C.   CLINTON ROSSITER

STARLING is a black songbird with pointed wings, a short tail, and a long, sharp bill. Its feathers have a greenish-purple or lilac gloss, and are tipped with buff during the winter. Starlings live in large flocks, sometimes even during the nesting season. The birds make nests in hollow trees, in birdhouses, or in holes in cliffs. The female starling lays from 4 to 6 light-blue eggs.

John Gerard

The Aggressive Starling often steals the nests of other birds for its home. The male has glossy black plumage.

The starling is helpful to farmers because it eats great numbers of harmful insects. But in the fruit season it is a pest because it also eats many berries, cherries, and even apples and pears. Starlings that roost in trees and on buildings are a nuisance to city-dwellers.

The starling came originally from the British Isles and other parts of Europe. In 1890, about 60 starlings were set free in Central Park in New York City. About 40 more were set free in 1891. Millons of starlings now live in the United States.

Scientific Classification. Starlings are members of the starling family, Sturnidae. The starling of North America and much of Europe is *Sturnus vulgaris*.   ALBERT WOLFSON

See also BIRD (color picture: Birds' Eggs).

STARR, ELLEN. See HULL HOUSE.

STARR, RINGO. See BEATLES.

STARS AND BARS. See FLAG (color picture: Flags in American History [Confederate Flags]).

STARS AND STRIPES. See FLAG (Flags of the United States).

STARS AND STRIPES is the name of two unofficial daily newspapers of the U.S. Armed Forces. One is published in Europe, and the other is published in the Pacific area. The two newspapers present news, editorials, and features of interest to military personnel stationed outside the United States. The staffs of the newspapers consist of both civilian journalists and military personnel.

Stars and Stripes appeared briefly during the Civil War. In February 1918, it began as a weekly newspaper, published in Paris by the American Expeditionary Forces serving in World War I. It ended publication in 1919, but reappeared in April 1942, during World War II. *Stars and Stripes* became a daily newspaper in November 1942, as the number of U.S. soldiers involved in the war increased. It was published in several places, including Honolulu, London, Manila, the Mediterranean area, the Middle East, Paris, and Tokyo. Cartoonist Bill Mauldin served on the European newspaper's staff during World War II and became famous for his portrayals of soldiers and war (see MAULDIN, BILL). Since World War II, the two *Stars and Stripes* have continued to serve soldiers stationed outside the United States.   DAVID B. O'HARA

STARTER is a device that sets an engine in motion. Starters use various kinds of power, including human muscle, electricity, compressed air, and even exploding cartridges.

Automobile Starters. The gasoline engines in early automobiles had to be started with a crank. A driver had to pull or spin the crank to make the crankshaft revolve and start the engine. Cranking a car was hard work, especially in cold weather when the oil in the engine was stiff. The engine sometimes backfired and spun the hand crank in the wrong direction. This spin could break a person's arm.

Charles F. Kettering invented the first successful electric starter for automobiles in 1911. It was introduced in the 1912 Cadillac. The chief parts of this starter are the motor and the drive. When the driver turns the ignition key, the key operates the starter switch, and a heavy current from the car's storage battery turns the starter motor. A drive shaft and gear connect the starter motor to the engine's flywheel. When the flywheel turns, the engine's crankshaft revolves, the pistons and rods go up and down, and the engine starts firing. An automatic device then disconnects the starter motor from the engine. Without this disconnecting device, the engine would turn the starter too fast and ruin it.

Diesel Starters. Diesel engines require more starting power than gasoline engines because they work at much higher compression. Some diesel engines use powerful electric starters similar to those for automobile gasoline engines. Railroad locomotive diesels use their generators as electric starters. Many diesels are started by pumping compressed air directly to some of the cylinders. The air drives the pistons until the engine fires of its own accord. A small auxiliary, or helper, engine starts other diesels.

STARTER

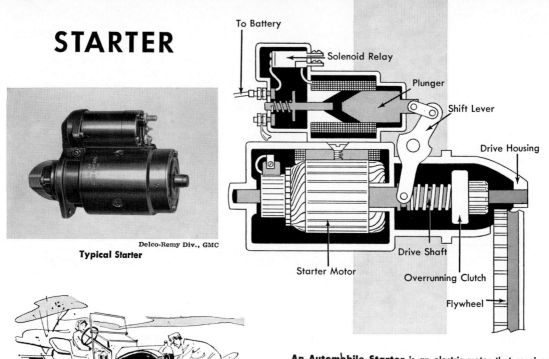

Typical Starter

Delco-Remy Div., GMC

An Autombbile Starter is an electric motor that receives its power from a battery. When a driver engages the starter, the relay connects the motor to the battery. The plunger moves the clutch into position with the engine's flywheel. The revolving starter shaft turns the flywheel, which turns over the engine. The starter then disconnects automatically.

Airplane Starters. Mechanics started the first airplanes by pulling the propeller by hand. Then aircraft engineers developed the *inertia starter*. This has a small flywheel that is set spinning by hand or by an electric motor. When gears engage this flywheel with the engine crankshaft, it turns the engine. Aircraft also use compressed-air starters, exploding cartridges, special hand cranks, and electric-motor starters.   FRANKLIN M. RECK

See also DIESEL ENGINE; GASOLINE ENGINE.

STARVATION occurs when a living thing dies from lack of food or certain kinds of food. Most plants need water, sunlight, and chemicals from the soil. If any of these foods is removed, the plant eventually dies. Human beings need minerals, vitamins, water, and foods such as carbohydrates, fats, and proteins. If they do not receive enough of each, their bodies waste away, and they finally starve.

People need certain foods because body cells do not work properly without them. Without food, a cell must use up its own parts to keep working. During its first few days without food, the body uses *glycogen* (also called *animal starch*) that has been kept in the liver as reserve food. But the main reserves of the body are fat and, later, muscle. As the time without food goes on, the vital cells become so weakened that death occurs.   EWALD E. SELKURT

See also FAST; NUTRITION.

STARVED ROCK STATE PARK. See LA SALLE, SIEUR DE.

STASSEN, HAROLD EDWARD (1907-   ), former governor of Minnesota, served as special assistant for disarmament to President Dwight D. Eisenhower from 1955 to 1958. He was a candidate for the Republican nomination for President in the elections of 1948, 1952, 1964, 1968, 1972, 1976, and 1980.

Stassen was born near St. Paul, Minn., and was graduated from the University of Minnesota. After serving as attorney of Dakota County, he was elected governor in 1938 and was reelected twice. While governor, Stassen revised the civil-service laws and lowered the costs of state government. He supported a labor law that provided a "cooling-off" period before strikes. This brought him national recognition. Early in his third term as governor, Stassen resigned to serve in the Navy.

In 1945, Stassen became a delegate to the San Francisco Conference which founded the United Nations. He was appointed president of the University of Pennsylvania in 1948. Stassen resigned in 1953 to serve as mutual security administrator, and then as foreign operations administrator, a position which controlled American aid to many countries. Stassen resigned as special assistant for disarmament in 1958 to seek the nomination for governor of Pennsylvania, but lost.   RICHARD L. WATSON, JR.

Harold Stassen

Rosenthal, Pix

STATE. See STATE GOVERNMENT; UNITED STATES; NATION.

STATE, DEPARTMENT OF, is the executive department of the United States government that handles U.S. relations with other governments. The head of the department is the secretary of state, the senior member of the President's Cabinet. The secretary and the department advise the President on foreign relations and conditions in other countries.

The department plans United States actions in dealing with other governments. When the President approves these plans, they become the nation's official foreign policy. The department is responsible for carrying out foreign policy. It also coordinates the actions of other executive departments that affect foreign policy.

The department negotiates treaties and agreements with other governments; handles official business with foreign embassies in Washington; speaks for the United States in the United Nations and other international organizations; and arranges for U.S. participation in international conferences. The secretary of state is the official custodian of the Great Seal of the United States, which is affixed to presidential proclamations, treaties, and other official documents (see GREAT SEAL OF THE UNITED STATES). The department also promotes public understanding of United States foreign policy through information services and publications.

Members of the Foreign Service, the operating arm of the department in other countries, represent the United States throughout the world. They deal with officials of other governments and report to the department on developments that affect the United States. These reports give the President and the secretary of state much of the information on which U.S. foreign policy is based. Members of the Foreign Service also issue passports; grant visas to persons visiting or immigrating to the United States; protect U.S. citizens and their property in other countries; and help businesses promote U.S. trade and investment.

Four independent government agencies responsible for foreign-affairs programs receive special guidance from the Department of State. The agencies are (1) the U.S. Arms Control and Disarmament Agency (ACDA), (2) the Peace Corps, (3) the U.S. Information Agency (USIA), and (4) the U. S. International Development Cooperation Agency (IDCA). ACDA formulates United States policy on disarmament and the control of weapons. The Peace Corps works with people in developing nations to help them improve their living conditions. USIA conducts educational and cultural exchanges with other countries and directs information programs to explain U. S. foreign policy and ways of life. IDCA establishes policy and coordinates activities to promote economic and social progress in developing countries. IDCA includes the Agency for International Development (AID), which administers the U.S. foreign aid program, and the Overseas Private Investment Corporation (OPIC). OPIC encourages private investment in developing countries by offering insurance and financial services to investors.

Secretary of State

Responsibilities. The secretary of state is appointed by the President with the approval of the Senate. The secretary is the highest-ranking member of the Cabinet and comes after the Vice-President, the speaker of the House, and the president *pro tempore* of the Senate in order of succession to the presidency.

The secretary is the President's chief adviser on foreign affairs and is responsible for operating the Department of State and carrying out foreign policy. The secretary must identify the major international problems that the United States faces and develop the strategy to deal with them. The secretary serves on the National Security Council and other committees.

Relationship with the President and Congress. The role of the secretary depends on the secretary's relationship with the President. Some Presidents have had strong opinions concerning foreign policy and have formulated their own policy. Secretaries serving such Presidents have had less influence and prestige than those who have served Presidents who were primarily interested in domestic affairs.

The secretary's relationship to Congress is also vital because congressional actions often affect foreign affairs. For example, treaties negotiated by the secretary must be approved by the Senate. The Senate also passes on the appointment of ambassadors and other officials. Congress controls the money that the secretary needs to carry out the administration's policies. In fact, about half the committees in Congress have an impact on foreign policy. To gain congressional support, the secretary must present the administration's foreign policies effectively. The secretary's success with Congress depends mainly on the President's political strength in the country. But the secretary must try to keep partisan politics out of dealings with Congress. Generally, Congress tries to take a *bipartisan* (nonpolitical) attitude in dealing with foreign affairs.

The type of person appointed secretary of state has changed over the years. In the late 1700's and early 1800's, the post often served as a stepping stone to the presidency. Thomas Jefferson, James Madison, James Monroe, John Quincy Adams, Martin Van Buren, and

Department of State

The Department of State advises the President on United States foreign policy. The department's headquarters, *above,* are on C Street, NW, Washington, D.C.

SECRETARIES OF STATE

The post of secretary of state was a stepping stone to the presidency during the early years of the United States. Six secretaries have become President. But none has become President since James Buchanan was elected in 1856.

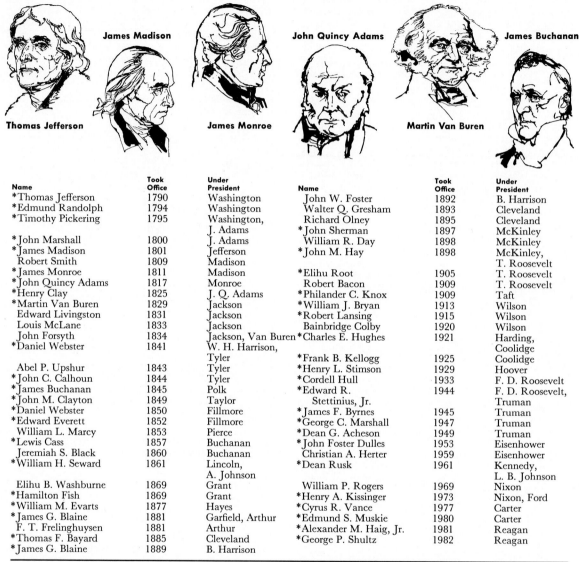

James Madison

John Quincy Adams

James Buchanan

Thomas Jefferson

James Monroe

Martin Van Buren

Name	Took Office	Under President	Name	Took Office	Under President
*Thomas Jefferson	1790	Washington	John W. Foster	1892	B. Harrison
*Edmund Randolph	1794	Washington	Walter Q. Gresham	1893	Cleveland
*Timothy Pickering	1795	Washington, J. Adams	Richard Olney	1895	Cleveland
*John Marshall	1800	J. Adams	*John Sherman	1897	McKinley
*James Madison	1801	Jefferson	William R. Day	1898	McKinley
Robert Smith	1809	Madison	*John M. Hay	1898	McKinley, T. Roosevelt
*James Monroe	1811	Madison	*Elihu Root	1905	T. Roosevelt
*John Quincy Adams	1817	Monroe	Robert Bacon	1909	T. Roosevelt
*Henry Clay	1825	J. Q. Adams	*Philander C. Knox	1909	Taft
*Martin Van Buren	1829	Jackson	*William J. Bryan	1913	Wilson
Edward Livingston	1831	Jackson	*Robert Lansing	1915	Wilson
Louis McLane	1833	Jackson	Bainbridge Colby	1920	Wilson
John Forsyth	1834	Jackson, Van Buren	*Charles E. Hughes	1921	Harding, Coolidge
*Daniel Webster	1841	W. H. Harrison, Tyler	*Frank B. Kellogg	1925	Coolidge
Abel P. Upshur	1843	Tyler	*Henry L. Stimson	1929	Hoover
*John C. Calhoun	1844	Tyler	*Cordell Hull	1933	F. D. Roosevelt
*James Buchanan	1845	Polk	*Edward R. Stettinius, Jr.	1944	F. D. Roosevelt, Truman
*John M. Clayton	1849	Taylor	*James F. Byrnes	1945	Truman
*Daniel Webster	1850	Fillmore	*George C. Marshall	1947	Truman
*Edward Everett	1852	Fillmore	*Dean G. Acheson	1949	Truman
William L. Marcy	1853	Pierce	*John Foster Dulles	1953	Eisenhower
*Lewis Cass	1857	Buchanan	Christian A. Herter	1959	Eisenhower
Jeremiah S. Black	1860	Buchanan	*Dean Rusk	1961	Kennedy, L. B. Johnson
*William H. Seward	1861	Lincoln, A. Johnson	William P. Rogers	1969	Nixon
Elihu B. Washburne	1869	Grant	*Henry A. Kissinger	1973	Nixon, Ford
*Hamilton Fish	1869	Grant	*Cyrus R. Vance	1977	Carter
*William M. Evarts	1877	Hayes	*Edmund S. Muskie	1980	Carter
*James G. Blaine	1881	Garfield, Arthur	*Alexander M. Haig, Jr.	1981	Reagan
F. T. Frelinghuysen	1881	Arthur	*George P. Shultz	1982	Reagan
*Thomas F. Bayard	1885	Cleveland			
*James G. Blaine	1889	B. Harrison			

*Has a separate biography in WORLD BOOK.

James Buchanan all served in the office before being elected President. Other secretaries, such as Henry Clay, Daniel Webster, John C. Calhoun, and William H. Seward, were appointed secretary of state mainly because they were political leaders.

In the 1900's, secretaries have been selected mainly for their experience and ability in foreign affairs. John Hay was a career diplomat. Cordell Hull, who won the Nobel peace prize while secretary of state, had served in both houses of Congress. John Foster Dulles had been a UN delegate and a senator. Both Christian Herter and Dean Rusk had served in the State Department, and Henry A. Kissinger had been President Richard M. Nixon's top White House adviser on foreign policy. Cyrus Vance had served as deputy secretary of defense. Alexander M. Haig, Jr., had been supreme commander of the North Atlantic Treaty Organization forces in Europe.

Organization of the Department

Department headquarters are located in Washington, D.C., on land reclaimed from a swamp near the Potomac River. The area, which was frequently blanketed by fogs, became known as *Foggy Bottom*, and that name is also often applied to the Department of State.

The secretary of state has several main assistants. The deputy secretary of state directs the department in the secretary's absence. The undersecretary for political af-

Department of State

The Department of State handles the foreign affairs of the United States. The departmental seal, *above,* resembles the Great Seal of the United States. The eagle holds an olive branch and arrows, symbolizing a desire for peace but the ability to wage war.

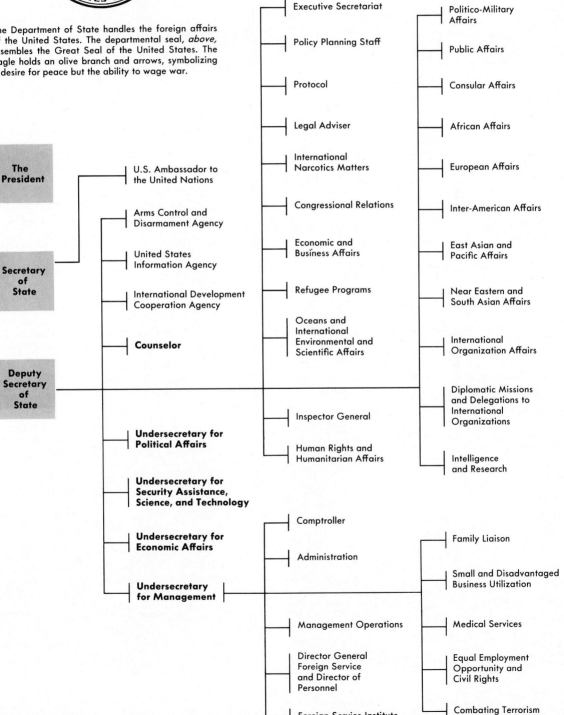

The President

Secretary of State

U.S. Ambassador to the United Nations

Arms Control and Disarmament Agency

United States Information Agency

International Development Cooperation Agency

Counselor

Deputy Secretary of State

Undersecretary for Political Affairs

Undersecretary for Security Assistance, Science, and Technology

Undersecretary for Economic Affairs

Undersecretary for Management

Executive Secretariat

Policy Planning Staff

Protocol

Legal Adviser

International Narcotics Matters

Congressional Relations

Economic and Business Affairs

Refugee Programs

Oceans and International Environmental and Scientific Affairs

Inspector General

Human Rights and Humanitarian Affairs

Comptroller

Administration

Management Operations

Director General Foreign Service and Director of Personnel

Foreign Service Institute

Politico-Military Affairs

Public Affairs

Consular Affairs

African Affairs

European Affairs

Inter-American Affairs

East Asian and Pacific Affairs

Near Eastern and South Asian Affairs

International Organization Affairs

Diplomatic Missions and Delegations to International Organizations

Intelligence and Research

Family Liaison

Small and Disadvantaged Business Utilization

Medical Services

Equal Employment Opportunity and Civil Rights

Combating Terrorism

United States Embassies serve as headquarters for American Foreign Service officials in most countries of the world. The United States embassy in Athens, *left,* houses the State Department delegation to Greece.

fairs is the secretary's chief foreign policy and diplomatic adviser. The undersecretary for economic affairs is the secretary's chief adviser on foreign economic policy. Other senior advisers of the secretary of state are the undersecretary for security assistance, science, and technology; the counselor; and the undersecretary for management.

The Policy Planning Staff is made up of experts with no regular administrative duties. They devote themselves to planning and the coordination necessary to put foreign policy decisions into effect.

Specialized bureaus, usually headed by assistant secretaries, do the department's day-to-day work. Five bureaus, organized on a geographic basis, handle U.S. foreign relations. They are (1) European Affairs (which includes Russia and Canada), (2) Inter-American Affairs, (3) African Affairs, (4) Near Eastern and South Asian Affairs, and (5) East Asian and Pacific Affairs.

The Bureau of International Organization Affairs conducts U.S. relations with the United Nations and other international organizations. The Bureau of Economic and Business Affairs deals with international aviation, energy, finance, food, resources, shipping, tariffs, telecommunications, and trade matters. The Bureau of Intelligence and Research analyzes the information coming into the department and reports on international situations.

The Bureau of Public Affairs informs the public on foreign affairs, distributes a wide variety of printed and audio-visual materials on current U.S. foreign policy, and keeps the official historical record of U.S. foreign relations. The Bureau of Consular Affairs supervises such duties as issuing passports and visas and protecting U.S. citizens abroad. The deputy undersecretary for management administers the budget and personnel. The Bureau of Oceans and International Environmental and Scientific Affairs deals with such matters as conservation, oceans, and outer space.

The Bureau of Human Rights and Humanitarian Affairs helps evaluate human rights issues in the formulation of United States foreign policy. The bureau also promotes communication with foreign governments and international organizations on matters involving human rights.

The American Embassy in Dublin houses the State Department delegation that represents the U.S. government in Ireland.

The Embassy in Buenos Aires is the home of the American Ambassador to Argentina. American flags fly over U.S. embassies.

The assistant secretary for congressional relations handles affairs between the department and Congress. The assistant secretary's office directs the presentation of the department's legislative programs to Congress.

The Executive Secretariat of the department coordinates recommendations for action that come to the secretary and other senior department officials for decision. The Executive Secretariat directs the Operations Center, which maintains a round-the-clock watch on world affairs and keeps top department officials informed.

The chief of protocol advises the secretary in matters of national and international *protocol* (traditional courtesies shown to officials). For example, the chief of protocol handles the arrangements when the head of government of another country visits the President.

The U.S. Mission to the United Nations, in New York City, is part of the department's home organization. The Mission of the U.S. Representative to the Council of the Organization of American States (OAS), in Washington, D.C., is also under the department.

Employees of the Department of State work both in the United States and in other countries. The department has about 6,600 workers in Washington, D.C. About 5,800 employees work in the Foreign Service at more than 260 overseas posts. The Foreign Service also employs about 10,000 citizens of other countries.

History of the Department

Establishment. The Department of State is the oldest executive department of the United States government. During the Revolutionary War, the Continental Congress dealt with other countries through its Committee on Secret Correspondence. This committee was established in 1775 with Benjamin Franklin as its first chairman. In 1777, the group was renamed the Committee for Foreign Affairs.

On Jan. 10, 1781, the Continental Congress created a Department of Foreign Affairs. Robert Livingston became the first secretary of foreign affairs, and John Jay succeeded him in 1784. After the adoption of the Constitution, Congress set up the Department of Foreign Affairs on July 27, 1789, as an executive agency under the President. Congress changed its name to the Department of State on Sept. 15, 1789. The department performed such domestic duties as operating the mint, issuing patents, and taking the census. Most domestic duties have since been transferred to other departments.

President George Washington appointed Thomas Jefferson as the first secretary of state in 1789. But Jay continued as temporary secretary until Jefferson assumed the office in 1790. Under Jefferson, the department had a staff of eight persons. The Foreign Service consisted of legations in London and Paris, an agency at The Hague, and 10 consular offices.

Growth. Before World War II, the department grew slowly. The interests of the United States then centered on domestic matters. Foreign affairs became important only during such crises as the Civil War and World War I. The U.S. shunned alliances with other countries, and the department received scant attention from the public and little support from Congress.

In 1833, separate bureaus were set up to supervise the work of U.S. diplomatic and consular representatives. In 1870, the department's work was spread among nine bureaus and two agencies. The Civil Serv-

ice Act of 1883 and introduction of the merit system enabled the department to hire more highly qualified employees (see CIVIL SERVICE). In 1909 and 1910, the department added four geographic divisions to handle U.S. relations with the rest of the world.

The department's work increased greatly in World War I. Its Washington staff rose to more than 400 in 1918. After World War I, American foreign relations became more important and complex. Congress passed the Rogers Act in 1924 to strengthen the department's overseas organization. In 1939, the Foreign Service absorbed the separate overseas services of the Commerce and Agriculture departments.

World War II and the Cold War expanded department activities still more. The war showed that U.S. security depended on affairs in the rest of the world. Americans felt they must cooperate with other nations to maintain peace. The department took over various war agencies that had gathered information and dispensed aid abroad, and assumed new administrative duties in occupied Germany and Japan. It adopted new economic and military aid programs and set up security arrangements with over 40 nations. In 1946, the Foreign Service was reorganized. The Executive Secretariat was set up in 1947. In 1949 and 1950, the department adopted many of the Hoover Commission's recommendations (see HOOVER COMMISSION).

Between 1954 and 1957, the department integrated its home and foreign services. The office of the Inspector General, Foreign Assistance; the Peace Corps; and the Agency for International Development were established as agencies within the department in 1961. The Inspector General for Foreign Assistance was merged into the department's Office of Inspector General in 1977. The Agency for International Development was transferred to the International Development Cooperation Agency in 1979. The Peace Corps became an independent federal agency in 1981.   Critically reviewed by the DEPARTMENT OF STATE

Related Articles in WORLD BOOK include:

Diplomacy	Foreign Policy
Diplomatic Corps	Foreign Service
Flag (picture: Flags of	International Relations
the U.S. Government)	Presidential Succession
Foreign Aid	

STATE AND LOCAL FISCAL ASSISTANCE ACT. See REVENUE SHARING.

STATE BIRDS. See BIRD (table: State and Provincial Birds); UNITED STATES (table: Facts in Brief About the States); also color picture in each state article.

STATE CAPITALS. See UNITED STATES (table: Facts in Brief About the States).

STATE FAIR. For the date and place of state fairs in the United States, see the Annual Events sections in the various state articles, such as IOWA (Annual Events).

STATE FARM. See COMMUNISM (Communism and the Economy); EUROPE (Farm Organization).

STATE FLAGS. For a description and picture of the flag of each state of the United States, see the picture in each state article. For pictures of all the state flags together, see FLAG (Flags of the States and Territories).

STATE FLOWERS. See FLOWER (table: Flowers of the States); UNITED STATES (table: Facts in Brief About the States); also color picture in each state article.

STATE GOVERNMENT

STATE GOVERNMENT provides many services and regulates many activities for the people of a state. In the United States, a state government maintains law and order and enforces criminal law. It protects property rights and regulates business. It supervises public education, including schools and state universities. It provides public welfare programs, builds and maintains highways, operates state parks and forests, and regulates the use of state-owned land. It has direct authority over local governments—counties, cities, towns, townships, villages, and school districts.

The government in some countries, such as France and Great Britain, operates under the *unitary system*. Under this system, the national government defines and establishes the powers of local governments. The United States has a *federal system*, which divides power between the national and state governments. However, the division of power is subject to dispute. In general, the states reserve the power to take any action that does not conflict with the Constitution of the United States, acts of Congress, or treaties entered into by the national government. See STATES' RIGHTS.

The independent powers of state governments arose during the colonial period. After the Declaration of Independence in 1776, each former British colony called itself a state to indicate its *sovereign* (independent) position. The term *state* generally means an area of land whose people are organized under a sovereign government. Each state gave up some of its powers when it approved the federal Constitution.

Since the founding of the United States, the powers and activities of the national government have greatly expanded. The federal government has become involved in many matters, such as education and housing, that once were handled only by state and local governments. Many of these matters required national action or more financial resources than state or local governments could provide. State and local governments, however, are involved in more areas than ever before. During the 1960's and 1970's, state and local governments increased their expenditures and the number of their employees at a greater rate than the national government. Cooperation among all levels of government has become increasingly important.

State Constitutions

Each state has a constitution that sets forth the principles and framework of its government. Every state constitution includes a bill of rights. Many have provisions on finance, education, and other matters.

The original 13 states had constitutions before the United States Constitution was adopted. Those of Massachusetts and New Hampshire are still in use, though they have been amended often. Constitutional conventions prepared most constitutions now in use.

A state constitution may be amended in several ways. The state legislature may submit a proposed amendment to the people for approval. The Delaware legislature may ratify such an amendment without a popular vote, but only by a two-thirds majority in each of two sessions. In 17 states, the people may suggest an amendment and vote on it in a state election. In some states, constitutional conventions may adopt amendments,

subject to ratification by the people. In other states, a constitutional commission may propose an amendment, which must receive legislative approval before being submitted to the people.

Executive Branch

The Governor elected by the people heads the executive branch in each state. The governor has the power to appoint, direct, and remove from office a large number of state officials. The state constitution authorizes this official to see that the laws are faithfully executed. The governor commands the state militia, grants pardons, and may call the state legislature into special session. He or she directs the preparation of the state budget. In almost all states, the governor may veto bills, and, in some states, may even veto parts of a bill. The governor is also the state leader of his or her political party.

Most state governors serve four-year terms. In four states, the governor holds office for two years. Five state constitutions provide that the governor cannot serve two terms in succession. In approximately 20 states, the governor cannot serve more than two terms in succession. In all states except Oregon, the governor may be removed from office by impeachment and conviction. In most states, a lieutenant governor succeeds a governor who dies in office.

The powers of state governors in the United States have steadily increased. The first state governors had only limited authority because the people had learned to distrust the royal governors appointed by British kings. The office of governor has grown in stature since 1776. Some governors have more power than others. That is, they have more authority to appoint and control subordinate officials. See GOVERNOR.

Other Officers. In most states, the people elect several other executive officials. These officers usually include a lieutenant governor, secretary of state, treasurer, auditor, and attorney general. In some states, the governor or legislature appoints one or more of these officials. In over half the states, a state board of education or the governor appoints a superintendent of public instruction. In about 20 states, the voters elect this official.

The secretary of state administers election laws, publishes legislative acts, and directs the state archives. The attorney general advises the governor on legal matters and prosecutes or defends cases that involve the state. The superintendent of public instruction administers state schools. The treasurer collects and maintains state funds. The auditor receives claims against the state and decides which should be paid. The auditor also examines the financial records of state agencies.

Legislative Branch

The legislature of a state passes laws, levies taxes, and appropriates money to be spent by the state government. It takes part in amending the state constitution and has the power to impeach officials.

Organization. Every state except Nebraska has a *bicameral* (two-house) legislature. Nebraska adopted a *unicameral* (one-house) legislature in 1934. Nineteen states call their legislature the *general assembly*, North Dakota and Oregon call it the *legislative assembly*, and Massachusetts and New Hampshire call it the *general court*. Every upper house is known as the *senate*. Most states call the lower house the *house of representatives*. But

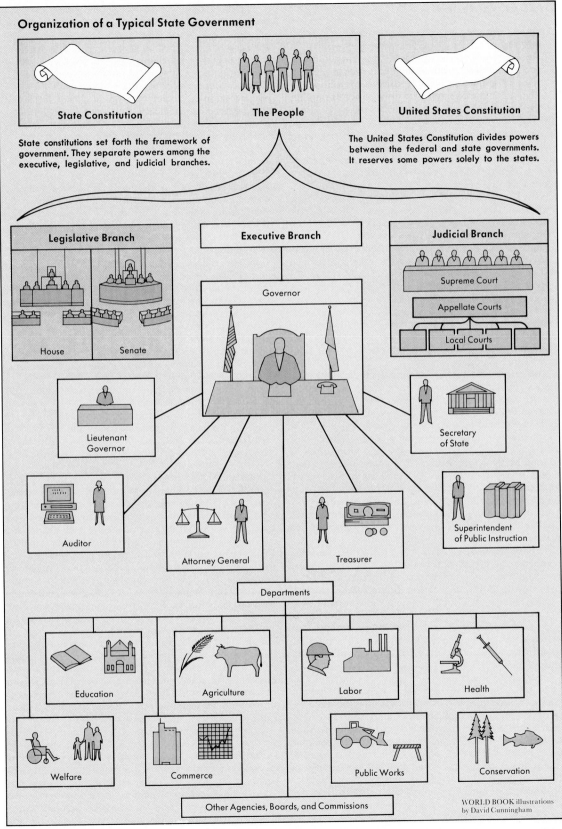

Organization of a Typical State Government

State Constitution

The People

United States Constitution

State constitutions set forth the framework of government. They separate powers among the executive, legislative, and judicial branches.

The United States Constitution divides powers between the federal and state governments. It reserves some powers solely to the states.

Legislative Branch

House

Senate

Executive Branch

Governor

Judicial Branch

Supreme Court

Appellate Courts

Local Courts

Lieutenant Governor

Secretary of State

Auditor

Attorney General

Treasurer

Superintendent of Public Instruction

Departments

Education

Agriculture

Labor

Health

Welfare

Commerce

Public Works

Conservation

Other Agencies, Boards, and Commissions

WORLD BOOK illustrations
by David Cunningham

681

four states use the term *assembly*, and three call it the *house of delegates*. A *speaker* presides over the lower house. The lieutenant governor presides over the senate in about 30 states. In the others, the majority party selects a senate president.

Senators in most states serve four-year terms. They hold office for two years in the other states. In almost all states, members of the lower house serve two-year terms. In four states, they serve four-year terms.

State senates range in size from 20 members in Alaska and Nevada to 67 in Minnesota. The lower houses range from 40 members in Alaska and Nevada to more than 100 in several states.

Salaries of legislators vary. Several states pay more than $25,000 a year. Legislators in some states receive daily payments while the legislature is in session, rather than yearly salaries. Payments vary from $5 a day in North Dakota and Rhode Island to $250 a day in South Carolina. Most states give legislators travel allowances, and many give other allowances.

The legislatures of over four-fifths of the states meet annually. The others meet in regular session *biennially* (every other year). Every legislature may be called into special session by the governor, and more than half the legislatures may also call a special session themselves. The constitutions of most states limit the length of regular sessions.

The legislatures do much of their work through *standing*, or *permanent*, *committees*. The typical legislative chamber has about 15 such committees. Some states have joint committees, which include members from both houses and report proposed bills to both houses. Many states set up *ad interim* (temporary) committees to study particular problems while the legislature is not in session. Many states also have legislative councils that meet between sessions to study problems that may arise at the next session. Legislative assistants and other staff members help write legislation and assist lawmakers in such areas as budget and technology. Many legislatures also have legislative reference services to do research and prepare reports. Electric roll-call machines and other devices have greatly speeded up legislative work. Computers collect and process data about budget items, the status of bills, and other matters. See LEGISLATURE.

Problems of Representation. In most states, the legislature handles the apportionment of representatives. For many years, most legislatures overrepresented rural areas and underrepresented the more heavily populated urban areas. Such unfair apportionment meant that urban voters could elect only about a fourth of the state legislators, though about two-thirds of all U.S. citizens lived in urban areas.

In 1962, in the case of *Baker v. Carr*, the Supreme Court of the United States ruled that individuals could bring questions of unfair districting before a federal court. In 1964, the court ruled that districts in both houses of a state legislature must be substantially equal in population. The court ruled in 1973 that states need not apply the principle of equal population so strictly to their legislative districts as to congressional districts. However, states had to attempt in good faith to make their legislative districts as nearly equal in population as possible. See APPORTIONMENT.

The people in 24 states share legislative power through the *initiative* and *referendum*. They may propose bills by petition and adopt them through referendum votes (see INITIATIVE AND REFERENDUM). Some persons believe that these procedures give the voters a check on their legislature and increase public interest in government. Others maintain that they overburden the voters with decisions they cannot vote on intelligently and that they tend to weaken the legislature's responsibility.

Judicial Branch

State courts settle disputes that come before them under various laws. They handle about nine-tenths of the criminal and civil cases in the United States.

A supreme court heads the judicial system of each state. In a few states, the supreme court is called by another name, such as *court of appeals*. The memberships of state supreme courts range from three to nine judges. About half of the states have supreme courts that have seven judges.

In more than half the states, the voters elect supreme court judges. In several states, the governor or legislature appoints them. In others, such as California and Iowa, the governor appoints the judges, who must later be approved by the voters. Supreme court judges hold office for specified terms in every state except Rhode Island, where they are elected for life. These terms range from 6 years in some states to 14 in New York. Judges serve 8-year or 10-year terms in many states, and up to age 70 in a few states.

Some states have appellate courts to handle some cases that would otherwise go directly to the supreme court. Each state has general trial courts. Most judges in these courts serve four-year, six-year, or eight-year terms. See COURT.

State Services

Education. The states, rather than the federal government, have had the main responsibility for public education. State governments support public schools through taxes, and administer them through local school districts. Most districts supervise their public elementary and secondary schools under a school board elected by the people or appointed by the mayor. State governments set up general standards for schools and their courses of study. The state funds supplement local property taxes that help pay for education. Every state has at least one state university. It also maintains such institutions as agricultural colleges, teacher training schools, junior colleges, and vocational schools.

Public Safety. The state legislatures enact most criminal laws that protect persons and property. State police promote highway safety, preserve the peace, and enforce criminal laws. Each state maintains persons, reformatories, or prison camps. Some states have departments to promote mine safety, pollution control, and sanitation. Each state has a civil defense organization to cooperate with the federal government. The governor commands the state militia, or national guard.

Public Works. Each state has a highway, public works, or transportation department that builds and maintains highways. This department may also supervise the construction of bridges, grade separations, canals, and waterways, and take care of beach protection, flood control, and buildings and grounds. Many toll roads are built and operated by special state turnpike authorities appointed by the governor. All states erect and maintain large numbers of public buildings. Since 1931, the states have built many public works with the aid of subsidies from the federal government.

Recreation. Departments or agencies in the various states manage more than 3,300 state parks and recreation areas. Many parks and recreation areas have been established in state-owned forests. Other areas have been set up as historical monuments. In addition, state highway departments may operate roadside parks for the convenience of motorists.

Health. State departments of health, or boards of health, were first set up in the late 1800's. They supervise and assist local public health agencies. These agencies are responsible for such activities as keeping vital statistics, controlling communicable diseases, and promoting health education, maternal and infant care, sanitation, and hygiene. They have general control over hospitals, nursing, research, and laboratory facilities. State public health work may also include improvement of substandard housing and slum clearance.

Welfare. Aid from the federal government has stimulated state government activities in welfare programs. Each state operates programs that help the poor, aged, delinquent, and unemployed, and the mentally and physically handicapped. States also provide institutional care in hospitals, asylums, reformatories, and various types of homes. Welfare agencies administer the welfare programs in most states.

Conservation activities include protection of water resources through special drainage, irrigation, water supply, and sanitation districts, and soil and forest conservation. State governments carry out their responsibilities through education; extension services; and research on water resources, fish and wildlife, forests, soils, and mineral resources. A director or board heads most conservation departments. Some states have fish and game commissions and forest services.

Agriculture. The states aid agriculture through county agents, soil conservation districts, agriculture extension services, and agricultural colleges. Most states have a department or board of agriculture. In most of these states, the governor appoints the director or board members. In others, the voters elect them. Annual state fairs are held in many states.

Business and Labor. Each state government grants corporations the charters that allow them to do business. It regulates banks, insurance companies, and savings and loan associations. It supervises public utility companies that provide public power, communications, and transportation. All states have workers' compensation laws that provide payments to workers who are injured on the job.

State Finances

The government of a state must have money to pay for the various services the state provides. Most of the money in a state's budget goes into payments for education, highways, public welfare, health and hospitals, insurance trusts for the retirement of employees, and unemployment compensation.

In most of the states, the governor receives the financial requests of the state agencies and submits a total budget to the legislature. The legislature must approve all appropriations. Almost all state constitutions impose debt limitations upon the states.

Grants-in-aid from the federal government rank as the largest single source of state income. In the early 1980's, such grants totaled about $91 billion a year. Other major sources of income include taxes on general sales, motor fuel, alcoholic beverages, tobacco, motor vehicles, individual and corporate incomes, inheritance and gifts, and the use of natural resources.

Traditionally, local authorities have received most of their tax revenues from property taxes. Local governments also rely heavily upon grants-in-aid from the states. They receive these grants upon agreeing to certain conditions, such as meeting standards imposed by the state. State governments also place debt limits upon local governments. See TAXATION.

In 1972, Congress passed the State and Local Fiscal Assistance Act. This revenue-sharing bill created a trust fund for use by state and local governments. A third of each state's share went to the state government, and two-thirds went to local governments within the states. Under legislation enacted in 1980, state revenue sharing was discontinued from Oct. 1, 1980, to Sept. 30, 1981, when it was resumed.

Relations with Other Governments

The federal government has certain constitutional obligations toward the states. It must respect their territorial unity and cannot divide or break up a state without its consent. It must protect the states against invasion and domestic violence. It must guarantee each state a republican form of government.

The United States Constitution also places certain limitations on the states. They may not interfere in foreign relations or make compacts among themselves without the consent of Congress. They may not directly burden or discriminate against interstate commerce. They may not levy import or export taxes. They may not issue paper money or pass laws impairing the obligation of contracts.

The Constitution also places certain obligations on the states in their relations with each other. Each state must give "full faith and credit" to the legal processes and acts of every other state. No state may discriminate in favor of its own citizens against persons coming from other states. The Supreme Court of the United States can ultimately decide disputes between states that cannot be settled by negotiation and agreement. For a more complete description of the provisions, meaning, and interpretation of the Constitution, see CONSTITUTION OF THE UNITED STATES.   DAVID R. BERMAN

Related Articles. See the *Government* and *History* sections of each state article, such as ALABAMA (Government; History). See also the following articles:

STATE MOTTOES. See the Facts in Brief table in each state article, such as ALABAMA (Facts in Brief).

STATE PARKS. See the Places to Visit section of each state article.

STATE POLICE. See POLICE (State Police).

STATE POPULAR NAMES. See UNITED STATES (table: Facts in Brief About the States of the Union).

STATE PRESS is a system of publishing operated by a government or a government-controlled political party. It is the opposite of a *free press*, where individuals publish newspapers and magazines. Freedom of the press is an important element in political freedom. Dictatorships rely on state presses to control public opinion. See also FREEDOM OF THE PRESS.

STATE SEALS. See the picture in each state article.

STATE SONGS. See the Facts in Brief table in each state article, such as ALABAMA (Facts in Brief). See also UNITED STATES (table: Facts in Brief About the States).

STATE TREES. See the color picture in each state article; also UNITED STATES (table: Facts in Brief About the States of the Union).

STATEMENT. See BILL; CHECK.

STATEN ISLAND forms a borough of New York City. The island lies in New York Bay, about 5 miles (8 kilometers) southwest of Manhattan Island (see NEW YORK [political map]). Staten Island has a population of 352,-121.

Ferries link Staten Island with Manhattan. The Verrazano-Narrows Bridge connects Fort Wadsworth on Staten Island with Fort Hamilton in Brooklyn. Three other bridges connect the island with New Jersey. Staten Island covers 64 square miles (166 square kilometers). It is about 14 miles (23 kilometers) long and 7½ miles (12 kilometers) across at its widest point.

Like Manhattan Island, Staten Island was purchased by the Dutch from the Indians in the 1600's. The borough was known as Richmond until 1975, when it was renamed Staten Island. WILLIAM E. YOUNG

See also NEW YORK CITY (Staten Island); RICHMONDTOWN.

Staten Island, *foreground,* and Brooklyn are connected by the Verrazano-Narrows Bridge. The bridge was completed in 1964.
Triborough Bridge and Tunnel Authority

STATEROOM. See SHIP (picture).

STATES-GENERAL, often called *Estates-General,* was the French representative assembly from 1302 to 1789. It was divided into three *estates* (classes). The first estate represented the clergy, the second the nobility, and the third the commoners. In the later Middle Ages, the kings began to invite leaders from each of the three estates to meet and discuss legislative or financial matters. These assemblies did not win the power to make laws for many years.

France's States-General never gained the power that England's parliament held. Its influence was limited because each estate met separately and voted as a unit. By the time of Louis XI, in the late 1400's, the States-General asked the king to govern without it. It never even met during the reign of Henry IV, from 1589 to 1610, and only for a short time under his son, Louis XIII. When he dismissed the States-General, it was not called again until the eve of the French Revolution in 1789, 175 years later.

When the States-General met in 1789, members of the third estate insisted on voting individually, instead of allowing each house to cast one vote. The first and second estates resisted this demand. On June 17, 1789, the third estate declared itself to be the national assembly of France. Three days later, its members swore in the Oath of the Tennis Court that they would not disband until they had written a constitution. Under threats of violence, Louis XVI recognized the national assembly as France's representative government.

The name *States-General* was also used in The Netherlands from 1593 to 1796 for an assembly where each province had one representative and one vote. It became the National Assembly in 1796. The Dutch parliament is now called States-General. EDWIN J. WESTERMANN

See also FRENCH REVOLUTION.

STATES OF THE CHURCH. See PAPAL STATES.

STATES' RIGHTS is a doctrine aimed at protecting the rights and powers of the states against those of the federal government. The 13 American states gave up many powers to the federal government when they ratified the United States Constitution. Only those powers that the Constitution did not grant to the national government were left to the states.

Everyone agrees that the states have rights that the federal government cannot lawfully touch. But the Constitution says that the federal government can make any laws that are "necessary and proper" for carrying its specific powers into effect. This provision makes it difficult to determine exactly what rights the states possess. Therefore, the major issue is not whether the states have rights, but rather who is to decide when these rights are abused.

Early History. Today, most people connect the support of states' rights with the South's position on racial segregation. But historically, the doctrine has been invoked by states in every section of the country whenever they have felt their jurisdiction threatened. One of the earliest instances was the Kentucky and Virginia Resolutions, which made a strong claim for the right of each state to decide this issue for itself. This idea gave rise to the doctrine of *nullification,* which asserts that within its own borders, a state can *nullify* (declare illegal) those acts of the federal government which it considers an invasion of its own rights. The doctrine of nullification was developed by John Calhoun and officially adopted by South Carolina in 1832. See NULLIFICATION.

In 1860 and 1861, 11 Southern states carried the states' rights idea to its most extreme point by seceding from the Union. Their defeat in the Civil War put an end to this particular interpretation of states' rights. But it is still generally agreed that the states have a jurisdiction that the federal government has no right to invade. The task of drawing the exact line of state jurisdiction and deciding whether the federal government has overstepped it is now left to the federal courts. The decisions of the courts can be changed only by the courts themselves, or by an amendment to the United States Constitution.

Later Developments. In the 1950's, supporters of states' rights claimed that decisions of the federal courts weakened the powers of the states. The Supreme Court of the United States declared that state laws ordering segregation in public schools, in public parks, and on public transportation systems violated provisions of the Constitution. It also set aside state antisedition laws and "right to work" legislation. But states' rights supporters claimed that these decisions violated the police powers of the state.

In the controversy over segregation, advocates of states' rights insisted that each state has the right of *interposition*. This doctrine resembles nullification. It asserts that a state has the right to "interpose the sovereignty of a state against the encroachment upon the reserved power of the state." Under this doctrine, a state has the power to overrule a decision of a federal agency if it conflicts with a state law, and all persons in the state must obey the state, not the federal, law.

Congress set up a Commission on Intergovernmental Relations in 1953 to study the extent of federal aid to the states, and the constitutional limits of federal and state powers. In 1955, the commission made its recommendations to the President and Congress. The recommendations covered such fields as agriculture, education, and housing. The commission noted that the Constitution forbids the states to legislate in such fields as interstate commerce, admiralty laws, and currency. The commission also pointed out that the problem of maintaining a federal system arises where both the federal and state governments have a choice of how to act in a given situation.

States' rights parties have run candidates in most presidential elections since 1948. The core of these parties came from conservative Democrats and Republicans who opposed the civil-rights policies of their own parties. One of these groups, the States' Rights Democratic Party (nicknamed the Dixiecrat Party), carried four Southern states in 1948. In 1968, George C. Wallace, the American Independent Party's presidential candidate, also stressed states' rights and carried five Southern states.   DAVID HERBERT DONALD

See also ALABAMA (Early Statehood); CALHOUN, JOHN CALDWELL; DIXIECRAT PARTY; KENTUCKY AND VIRGINIA RESOLUTIONS; WALLACE, GEORGE C.

STATES' RIGHTS DEMOCRATIC PARTY. See DIXIECRAT PARTY.

STATESMAN is a person with a broad general knowledge of government and politics, who takes a leading part in public affairs. Most persons think of statesmen as being concerned with the needs and interests of their country as a whole. In contrast, they think of *politicians* as having only party or political aims. *Elder statesmen*, usually retired from active government, continue to give advice on important issues. Japan developed this system in the *genro*, a council of former government leaders who advise the current government. See also the list of biographies of statesmen at the end of most country articles.

STATIC is a term for a disturbance in a radio or television receiver, usually caused by atmospheric electricity. Static may take the form of crackling and grating noises heard over the radio and white spots seen on a television picture.

Water droplets and dust particles in the air often carry an electric charge. Any motion of electric charges results in radiation at some frequency. If this radiation has a frequency within the radio or television broadcast bands, it will be heard or seen as static.

Ordinarily, the movement of charged particles in the air produces static in the form of a weak, hissing, background noise. However, severe disturbances to the atmosphere, such as lightning, earthquakes, tornadoes, and volcanoes, make the particles move more rapidly and the air vibrate violently. These disturbances thus cause sudden crashes, pops, and other much more prominent static. Certain electric motors and electric sparks from machinery also produce static.   THOMAS D. ROSSING

See also FREQUENCY MODULATION.

STATIC ELECTRICITY. See ELECTRICITY (Static Electricity).

STATICE, *STAT uh see*, is a group of colorful plants used in rock gardens and flower-bed borders. It includes the *thrift* (or *sea pink*) and the *sea lavender*. The thrift has narrow, evergreen leaves that grow in large bunches. Its small pink or white flowers grow in dense, globe-shaped clusters. The sea lavender has wider leaves and purple, rose, white, or yellow flowers. These flowers are often dried and made into bouquets for winter use.

Statices are hardy and grow well in most garden soils. They usually reproduce by seed. Started in a greenhouse in early spring and then planted outside, they have flowers all summer.

Scientific Classification. The statice belongs to the leadwort family, *Plumbaginaceae*. Two common thrifts are classified as genus *Armeria*, species *A. maritima* and *A. pseud-armeria*. Other common statices include *Limonium sinuatum* and *L. latifolium*.   ROBERT W. SCHERY

STATICS is a branch of the science of dynamics. Dynamics deals with the properties of matter and forces. It is divided into two branches—*statics* and *kinetics*. Statics deals with conditions under which material bodies do not change motion when acted upon by various forces. That is, a body at rest will remain at rest, and a body in motion will not change direction or speed of motion. When two or more forces act upon a body so as to produce no change of motion, the forces are said to be in *equilibrium*. Kinetics deals with the changes of motion.   ROBERT F. PATON

See also DYNAMICS.

STATION, RAILWAY. See RAILROAD (picture: During World War II).

STATISTICS

STATISTICS, *stuh TIHS tihks.* Suppose someone handed you records containing the weights of 13,000 newborn babies. Then he asked you to make some conclusions about the weights. Many persons could be puzzled by page after page of nothing but numbers. Great masses of *data* (facts) usually tend to be confusing. But statistics, a branch of mathematics, has ways of simplifying masses of numbers and facts and of presenting them in an understandable form. For example, a statistician could find that the average weight of the newborn boys is 7.35 pounds and that of the girls is 7.13 pounds. Now you have some easily understood conclusions about the weights. In ways such as this, statistics can help you solve many problems.

The word *statistics* appears sometimes as a singular and sometimes as a plural noun. As a plural noun, *statistics* refers to numbers or numerical facts. For example, you can say that "there *are* many statistics in THE WORLD BOOK." As a singular noun, *statistics* refers to the methods used to analyze numerical data, and to draw conclusions from them. You can say that "statistics *is* the art and science of analyzing numerical data."

Uses of Statistics

As a science, statistics began in Germany in the 1700's and 1800's. Governments used statistics to count their citizens and to collect taxes. Governments still use statistics for these and many other purposes, such as planning farm production.

Scientists know that it is unsafe to draw conclusions from small numbers of observations. So they find it necessary to study thousands and even millions of cases. Statistics helps all the sciences—physical, biological, and social—to deal with masses of facts.

Statistics makes vital contributions to business and industry. Statistical methods help to organize business and industrial facts, and uncover the principles and trends at work behind the facts. Advertising, finance, insurance, manufacturing, retailing, and many other fields depend on statistics. Statistics helps politicians plan their campaigns, and the use of statistics forms the basis of public-opinion polls.

How Statistics Works

Solving any problem in statistics involves three steps: (1) definition of the problem, (2) collection of data, and (3) analysis of data.

Definition of the Problem. Beginners in statistics usually learn with surprise that even the simplest problem requires careful definition. Suppose someone asks you to count the words on a printed page. You will discover immediately that you must answer questions about this simple problem. For example, how many words are there in the sentence, "The Civil War (1861-1865) created a new public-school shortage in the U.S."? Do you count abbreviated words? How about hyphenated words and numbers? You must define what you mean by *words* before you begin. Similar questions appear in statistics. Suppose you want to count the population of the United States on Apr. 15, 1960. Whom do you count? Do you include a baby born late that afternoon? A man who died early that morning? A person from another country visiting the United

States? A United States citizen visiting another country? You must define your terms with great care.

Collection of Data. After defining terms, a statistician proceeds to collect data. Sometimes a statistician uses data collected by others, such as census figures or school records. This kind of data is called *derived data.* Sometimes a statistician has to obtain his or her own data, which might consist of laboratory experiments, questionnaires sent to consumers, or personal interviews. Such data is called *original data.*

Analysis of Data. Defining the problem and collecting data have fundamental importance. But a statistician spends most of the time analyzing the data. That is, the statistician tries to find out what the data mean and how they may be interpreted. In some cases, this involves nothing more complicated than computing an average or finding a percentage. In other cases, analyzing the data may require months of labor and the use of giant electronic computers.

Averages

Suppose a statistician received the records of the number of eggs laid in one year by each of 3,131 White Leghorn hens. The statistician usually arranges values such as these in a *table:*

NUMBER OF EGGS	NUMBER OF HENS
0- 29	30
30- 59	36
60- 89	125
90-119	327
120-149	686
150-179	925
180-209	697
210-239	271
240-269	32
270-299	2
TOTAL	3,131

Just a glance at the table makes the pattern clear. You can see that there is a bunching near the middle of the table. The most common egg production lies somewhere between 150 and 179 eggs. It looks as if the most common or most "popular" production is about 165 eggs, or halfway between 150 and 179. Statisticians call this kind of average the *mode.* A study of the actual data from which the table was prepared shows that as many hens laid more than 162 eggs as laid fewer than 162 eggs. This kind of average is the *median.* The median in the table is 162 eggs. If you add together the numbers of all the eggs and divide by 3,131, the number of hens, you will find the *arithmetic average* or *arithmetic mean.* The mean number of eggs is 157. See AVERAGE; MEAN; MEDIAN; MODE.

Frequency Distributions

The egg-production table is called a *frequency table,* because it shows the frequency with which various values occur. A frequency table makes it possible for statisticians to gather thousands of cases into a small space. It also shows immediately the general characteristics of the data. Methods exist for the rapid computation of the mean, median, mode, and other useful numbers from frequency tables.

The values themselves, arranged in a table, form a *frequency distribution.* Many, although by no means all, frequency distributions show the same basic pattern

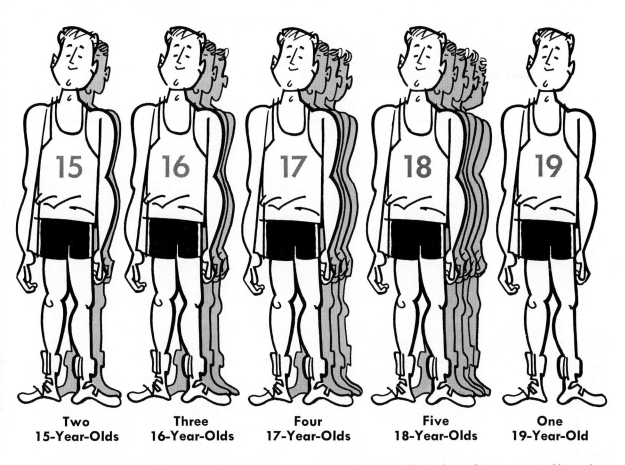

| **Two**
 15-Year-Olds | **Three**
 16-Year-Olds | **Four**
 17-Year-Olds | **Five**
 18-Year-Olds | **One**
 19-Year-Old |

Statistics Can Tell a Great Deal about the ages of the members of this basketball squad. First, you can find the squad's *mean,* or average, age by adding together all the members' ages and dividing by the number of players on the squad. The mean age for the squad is 17 years. Second, you can find the *median* age by listing the ages of all the players from youngest to oldest and finding the age in the middle. The median age for the squad is 17. You can also use statistics to find the *mode* or the age that occurs the most number of times. The mode for the squad is 18, because there are more 18-year-olds than members of any other age.

that appears in the egg-production table. This distribution consists of small frequencies at both ends of the table and large frequencies in the middle. The distribution can be charted, by showing the numbers of cases vertically and the sizes of values horizontally. Here is the chart:

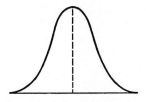

This bell-shaped distribution is called a *normal distribution* or *normal curve.*

Probability

With certain kinds of data, a statistician can tell in advance what values will occur, and how frequently. Suppose you toss a penny over and over again. You expect it to show "heads" half the time and "tails" half the time. If you toss it only three or four times, this may not happen. But as you increase the number of throws, the proportion of "heads" tends to draw more and more closely to the expected value of one half. Suppose you toss four pennies over and over again. Suppose you toss a very large number of pennies a great number of times. You may be surprised to find that the distribution of "heads" and "tails" draws closer and closer to the bell-shaped normal distribution. *Probability,* in statistics, is the measurement of the likelihood of events in numerical terms. The normal distribution, based on pure chance, helps statisticians to make these measurements.

Sometimes a statistician can reason out in advance the relative frequency with which events will occur, such as tossing coins or throwing dice. This is called *a priori probability* (probability *from the first*). But, in many cases, a statistician cannot reason out probability in advance; for example, whether or not a certain patient will recover from diphtheria. But he can reach fairly reliable conclusions as to these probabilities from a study of actual cases. For example, he might find

STATISTICS

that the probability of recovering in diphtheria cases is 78 out of 100. This is called *statistical probability*.

In a normal distribution, the distance you must go above and below the arithmetic mean to include half of the cases is called the *probable error* of the distribution. In any normal distribution, 50 per cent of the cases lie within one probable error of the mean, 82 per cent lie within two probable errors, 96 per cent within three probable errors, 99.3 per cent within four probable errors, and 99.92 per cent within five probable errors.

Statisticians now use a similar measure called the *standard error* more than the probable error. The standard error has certain mathematical advantages. In a normal distribution, 68.27 per cent of the cases lie within one standard error of the mean, 95.5 per cent lie within two standard errors, and practically all the cases (99.7 per cent) lie within three standard errors.

Sampling

Statisticians know that it is risky to draw conclusions from small numbers of observations. Yet usually it is impossible to study all the cases. A statistician must study a group of a hundred, a thousand, or some other limited number of cases. Statisticians call the group they actually study the *sample*. They draw their conclusions from this group. The total number of cases from which they select the sample is called the *universe* or the *population*.

Statisticians can never be completely certain that samples accurately reflect the total number of cases. But, in general, the larger the sample, the more reliable it is in reflecting the total number of cases. The reliability of the sample increases, not in proportion to the number of cases, but in proportion to the square root of the number of cases. To double the reliability, statisticians study four times as many cases. To treble the reliability, they study nine times as many cases.

Statisticians must decide how many cases to study, and which individual cases. They try to select the individual cases carefully. Often they use a *random sample*. A random sample consists of cases selected so that each case in the total number has an equal chance of being included.   ALBERT E. WAUGH

Related Articles in WORLD BOOK include:

Average	Graph	Median
Econometrics	Mean	Mode

Pearson, Karl	Probability	Skew Line
Permutations and Combinations	Public Opinion Poll	Vital Statistics

Additional Resources

FOLKS, J. LEROY. *Ideas of Statistics*. Wiley, 1981.

LARSEN, RICHARD J., and MARX, M. L. *An Introduction to Mathematical Statistics and Its Applications*. Prentice-Hall, 1981.

RIEDEL, MANFRED G. *Winning With Numbers: A Kid's Guide to Statistics*. Prentice-Hall, 1978.

RUNYON, RICHARD P. *How Numbers Lie: A Consumer's Guide to the Fine Art of Numerical Deception*. Lewis, 1981.

STATISTICS, VITAL. See VITAL STATISTICS.

STATUARY HALL is a room in the United States Capitol in Washington, D.C., that houses statues of outstanding citizens from many states. The hall itself is a semicircular domed chamber. It lies near the Great Rotunda on the side of the Capitol leading to the chamber of the House of Representatives.

In 1864, Congress decided that each state should be invited to send two statues to be displayed in the Capitol. The states were asked to contribute statues of distinguished citizens who were "worthy of this national commemoration." Congress set aside the old House of Representatives chamber to hold the statues.

The first statue arrived in 1870. The collection grew over the years. In 1933, architects discovered that the hall was overloaded. Congress then authorized that some of the statues be displayed elsewhere in the Capitol.

By 1971, all 50 states had sent at least one statue to the collection. The statues honor pioneers, political and religious leaders, and other outstanding citizens. Thirty-eight of the statues stand in Statuary Hall itself. The others are located in the Great Rotunda or elsewhere in the building.

Many exciting events in American history took place in what is now Statuary Hall. The House of Representatives met there from 1807 to 1857, except for a period of repair work from 1814 to 1819. The chamber needed the repairs after the British burned the Capitol during the War of 1812. The House met in the hall to choose the President in the contested election of 1824, and elected John Quincy Adams. Millard Fillmore took the oath as President there in 1850.

In honor of the bicentennial celebration of 1976—the 200th anniversary of the founding of the United States —workers redecorated Statuary Hall. They restored the

Architect of the Capitol

Statuary Hall displays statues of outstanding Americans. The hall itself is a semicircular domed chamber in the U.S. Capitol in Washington, D.C. The room looks much as it did in the early 1800's, when the House of Representatives met there.

room to look much as it did when the House of Representatives met there. They uncovered the original mantels and fireplaces, and installed replicas of the red draperies and gas chandelier that hung there.

The floor of Statuary Hall has nine bronze markers. These markers honor the nine Presidents who served in the chamber as representatives when the House met there.

Critically reviewed by the UNITED STATES CAPITOL HISTORICAL SOCIETY

STATUE. See SCULPTURE.

STATUE OF LIBERTY is the large copper statue that stands on Liberty Island (formerly Bedloe's Island) in New York Harbor. Its proper name is *Liberty Enlightening the World*. This statue is one of the largest ever made. France gave the Statue of Liberty to the United States in 1884 as a symbol of friendship and of the liberty that citizens enjoy under a free form of government. The

French people donated about $250,000 for the construction of the statue, and the people of the United States gave about $280,000 for the pedestal. A model of it stands on a bridge over the Seine River in Paris.

Description. The statue represents a proud woman, dressed in a loose robe that falls in graceful folds to the top of the pedestal on which the statue stands. The right arm holds a great torch raised high in the air. The left arm grasps a tablet bearing the date of the Declaration of Independence. A crown with huge spikes, like sun rays, rests on the head. At the feet is a broken shackle symbolizing the overthrow of tyranny.

This statue is one of the most celebrated examples of *repoussé* work, which is a process of hammering metal over a mold in order to shape it. The statue is made of

National Statuary Hall Collection

This table lists the statues of outstanding Americans that each state has placed in the U.S. Capitol and the date each statue was presented. Many of the figures stand in Statuary Hall. Others are located in the east front lobby, in the Great Rotunda, or elsewhere in the building.

State	Statue	Date Presented	State	Statue	Date Presented
Alabama	J. L. M. Curry	1908	Missouri	Thomas H. Benton*	1899
	Joseph Wheeler*	1925		Francis P. Blair, Jr.	1899
Alaska	Edward Lewis (Bob) Bartlett	1971	Montana	Charles M. Russell*	1959
	Ernest Gruening	1977	Nebraska	William Jennings Bryan*	1937
Arizona	John C. Greenway*	1930		J. Sterling Morton	1937
	Eusebio Francisco Kino	1965	Nevada	Patrick A. McCarran	1960
Arkansas	Uriah M. Rose*	1917	New Hampshire	John Stark	1894
	James P. Clarke	1921		Daniel Webster*	1894
California	Thomas S. King	1931	New Jersey	Philip Kearny	1888
	Junipero Serra*	1931		Richard Stockton	1888
Colorado	Florence Rena Sabin*	1959	New Mexico	Dennis Chavez	1966
Connecticut	Roger Sherman	1872	New York	George Clinton	1873
	Jonathan Trumbull	1872		Robert R. Livingston	1875
Delaware	John M. Clayton	1934	North Carolina	Zebulon Baird Vance*	1916
	Caesar Rodney	1934		Charles B. Aycock	1932
Florida	John Gorrie*	1914	North Dakota	John Burke*	1963
	Edmund Kirby Smith	1922	Ohio	James A. Garfield	1886
Georgia	Crawford W. Long	1926		William Allen*	1887
	Alexander H. Stephens*	1927	Oklahoma	Sequoya*	1917
Hawaii	Joseph Damien de Veuster	1969		Will Rogers	1939
	Kamehameha I*	1969	Oregon	Jason Lee*	1953
Idaho	George L. Shoup*	1910		John McLoughlin	1953
	William E. Borah	1947	Pennsylvania	Robert Fulton*	1889
Illinois	James Shields	1893		John Peter G. Muhlenberg	1889
	Frances E. Willard*	1905	Rhode Island	Nathanael Greene	1870
Indiana	Oliver P. Morton	1900		Roger Williams	1872
	Lew Wallace*	1910	South Carolina	John C. Calhoun	1910
Iowa	James Harlan	1910		Wade Hampton	1929
	Samuel J. Kirkwood*	1913	South Dakota	William H. H. Beadle*	1938
Kansas	John J. Ingalls*	1905		Joseph Ward	1963
	George W. Glick	1914	Tennessee	Andrew Jackson	1928
Kentucky	Henry Clay*	1929		John Sevier*	1931
	Ephraim McDowell	1929	Texas	Stephen F. Austin	1905
Louisiana	Huey P. Long*	1941		Samuel Houston*	1905
	Edward Douglass White	1955	Utah	Brigham Young*	1950
Maine	William King	1878	Vermont	Ethan Allen*	1876
	Hannibal Hamlin*	1935		Jacob Collamer	1881
Maryland	Charles Carroll of Carrollton	1903	Virginia	Robert E. Lee*	1934
	John Hanson	1903		George Washington	1934
Massachusetts	Samuel Adams	1876	Washington	Marcus Whitman*	1953
	John Winthrop	1876		Mother Joseph	1980
Michigan	Lewis Cass*	1889	West Virginia	John E. Kenna	1901
	Zachariah Chandler	1913		Francis H. Pierpont*	1910
Minnesota	Henry Mower Rice*	1916	Wisconsin	Jacques Marquette	1896
	Maria L. Sanford	1958		Robert M. La Follette, Sr.*	1929
Mississippi	Jefferson Davis*	1931	Wyoming	Esther Hobart Morris	1960
	James Z. George	1931			

*In Statuary Hall.
Each person listed in the table has a biography in WORLD BOOK.

The Statue of Liberty, a symbol of American democracy and a beacon of refuge for immigrants, stands on Liberty Island in New York Harbor. France gave the Statue of Liberty to the United States in 1884 as a gesture of friendship. The monument rises above Fort Wood, built in the shape of an 11-point star during the early 1800's.

more than 300 thin sheets of copper, with a total weight of about 100 short tons (91 metric tons). The outer layer of copper is supported by an iron framework, which resembles that of an oil derrick. The statue stands 151 feet 1 inch (46.05 meters) high and weighs 450,000 pounds (204,000 kilograms). The torch rises 305 feet 1 inch (92.99 meters) above the base of the pedestal. It gleams at night with powerful incandescent and mercury vapor lights as a symbol of liberty lighting the world. Floodlights from the base of the pedestal shine on the statue.

An elevator carries visitors up the pedestal to the foot of the statue. At this point, an observation balcony affords a magnificent view of the harbor and the city.

Visitors may climb a steep, narrow, spiral staircase from the pedestal as high as the crown on the statue's head. A ladder inside the arm leads to the torch but this is too narrow and steep for public use.

"The New Colossus," a poem by Emma Lazarus, was inscribed on a tablet in the pedestal in 1903. It reads:

Not like the brazen giant of Greek fame,
  With conquering limbs astride from land to land;
  Here at our sea-washed, sunset gates shall stand
A mighty woman with a torch, whose flame
Is the imprisoned lightning, and her name
  Mother of Exiles. From her beacon-hand
  Glows world-wide welcome; her mild eyes
    command
The air-bridged harbor that twin cities frame.

"Keep ancient lands, your storied pomp!" cries she
  With silent lips. "Give me your tired, your poor,
Your huddled masses yearning to breathe free,
  The wretched refuse of your teeming shore.
Send these, the homeless, tempest-tost to me,
  I lift my lamp beside the golden door!"

History. The French historian Édouard de Laboulaye first suggested a monument to symbolize liberty. His friend Frédéric Auguste Bartholdi designed the statue and chose its site. Bartholdi also spent a great deal of time and energy raising funds in France and the United States to bring the plan to completion. Alexandre Gustave Eiffel, who designed the Eiffel Tower in Paris, built the supporting framework.

The people of France presented the Statue of Liberty to the Minister of the United States in Paris, on July 4, 1884. The statue was shipped to the United States in 214 cases aboard the French ship *Isère* in May 1885. The site chosen for the statue was the center of old Fort Wood, on Bedloe's Island, overlooking the ship channel of New York Harbor. President Grover Cleveland dedicated the monument on Oct. 28, 1886. It was unveiled before representatives of both countries.

The floodlights at the base were added in 1916. The statue became a national monument in 1924. It was repaired and strengthened throughout in 1937. Congress changed the island's name to Liberty Island in 1956. The American Museum of Immigration, built inside the statue's base, opened in 1972. The National Park Service maintains the Statue of Liberty National Monument. THOMAS M. PITKIN

See also BARTHOLDI, FRÉDÉRIC A.; EIFFEL, ALEXANDRE G.; LAZARUS, EMMA; LIBERTY ISLAND; UNITED STATES (color picture).

STATUE OF LIBERTY NATIONAL MONUMENT is on Ellis and Liberty islands in New York harbor. The colossal statue by Frédéric Bartholdi stands on Liberty Island. The people of France presented it to the United States on July 4, 1884. Ellis Island was an immigration station until 1954. It became part of the monument in 1965. See also ELLIS ISLAND; STATUE OF LIBERTY.

STATUTE. See LAW (Civil-Law Systems).

STATUTE OF FRAUDS. See FRAUD.

STATUTE OF LIMITATIONS is a law that sets a time limit for the filing of lawsuits. Suits filed after the statute of limitations has passed are barred, no matter how just they may be. Statutes of limitations prevent lawsuits in which the true situation is clouded because of a long lapse of time.

Each state as well as the federal government has its own statute of limitations for different kinds of claims. For example, Illinois has over 20 statutes of limitations. These statutes include limits of one year for libel and slander cases, two years for personal injury lawsuits, 10 years for cases involving written contracts, and 20 years for actions to recover land.

Statutes of limitations also apply to most crimes, limiting the time in which prosecutions must be brought. But serious crimes such as murder are not subject to statutes of limitations. HARRY KALVEN, JR.

STATUTE OF WESTMINSTER. See CANADA, GOVERNMENT OF (International Relations); COMMONWEALTH OF NATIONS (History).

STATUTORY LAW. See CODE; LAW (Civil-Law Systems).

Cutaway View of the Statue of Liberty

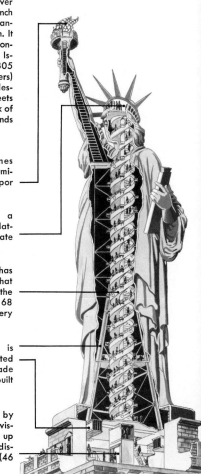

The Statue of Liberty is one of the largest statues ever made. It is 151 feet 1 inch (46.05 meters) from the sandals to the top of the torch. It stands on a granite and concrete pedestal on Liberty Island. The torch towers 305 feet 1 inch (92.99 meters) above the base of the pedestal. The statue, made of sheets of copper over a framework of iron, weighs 450,000 pounds (204,000 kilograms).

Liberty's Torch shines through leaded glass, illuminated by five mercury vapor lamps.

Liberty's Crown has a 25-window observation platform that can accommodate 30 viewers.

Interior of the Statue has two parallel stairways that spiral up from the base to the crown. Each stairway has 168 steps, with rest seats at every third turn of the spiral.

Liberty's Framework is made of iron and is supported by steel columns. It was made by Gustave Eiffel, who built Paris' Eiffel Tower.

Liberty's Base is reached by an elevator which brings visitors from the ground floor up through the pedestal, a distance of about 150 feet (46 meters).

STATUTORY RAPE. See RAPE.

STAUDINGER, HERMANN. See NOBEL PRIZES (Nobel Prizes for Chemistry—1953).

STE. ———. See SAINTE ———.

STEAK. See BEEF; MEAT.

STEAM, *steem,* is water which has been changed into a gas. Steam cannot be seen, for it is colorless. The cloud of vapor which we see beginning about an inch from the spout of a teakettle is not steam. The real steam is in the space that seems vacant, just outside the spout. The cloud we see is water that the cooler air has changed from gas form back into tiny water particles.

Steam can be formed by boiling or by evaporation. At sea level, water boils when it is heated to 100° C (212° F.), the *boiling point.* Water evaporates at lower temperatures. The steam caused by boiling is as hot as the boiling water. The steam caused by evaporation is not hot. Usually the word *steam* refers to hot steam.

When water reaches the boiling point, bubbles of steam begin to rise through it and escape into the air. The temperature will remain at the boiling point until all the liquid has become gas. It requires 100 calories of heat to raise one gram of water from the freezing point

STEAM ENGINE

(0° C, or 32° F.) to the boiling point. To change the same gram of boiling water into steam, without raising its temperature, takes 540 calories of heat. This heat is called the steam's *latent heat.* It is released when the steam changes back to liquid water. Steam can cause more severe burns than boiling water because the steam condenses and releases its latent heat.

Steam fills more space than the water from which it comes. At the moment when boiling stops, the gas is 1,670 times as great in volume as the former liquid. At this stage it is called *saturated steam.* If heated more, it takes up even more space. Then it is known as *super-heated steam.* The steam engine is built around this principle. *Wet steam* supports particles of water still in liquid form. *Dry steam,* however, contains only gas.   LOUIS MARICK

Related Articles in WORLD BOOK include:

Boiling Point	Steam Hammer	Turbine
Evaporation	Steam Shovel	(Steam
Steam Engine	Steamboat	Turbines)

STEAM ENGINE is any engine that is operated by the energy of expanding steam. The steam may be used to push pistons that turn the wheels of powerful locomotives. Or it may be used to spin huge turbines that drive electric generators and giant ocean liners. Large pumps, pile drivers, and many other kinds of powerful machines may also be driven by steam engines.

The development of the steam engine in the 1700's made modern industry possible. Until then, people had to depend on the power of their own muscles or on animal, wind, and water power. One steam engine could do the work of hundreds of horses. It could supply the power needed to run all the machines in a factory. A steam locomotive could haul heavy loads of freight great distances in a single day. Steamships provided safe, fast, dependable water transportation.

How Steam Engines Work

A steam engine does not create power. It uses steam to change the heat energy released by burning fuel into rotary or back-and-forth motion that can do work.

Each steam engine has a *furnace* in which coal, oil, wood, or some other fuel is burned to produce heat energy. In atomic power plants, a reactor serves as the furnace and splitting atoms produce the heat (see NUCLEAR REACTOR). Each steam engine also has a *boiler.* The heat from the burning fuel changes water into steam inside the boiler. The steam expands, or takes up many times the space of the original water. This energy of expansion can be used in two ways: (1) to push a piston back and forth, or (2) to spin a turbine.

Piston Steam Engines have pistons that slide back and forth in cylinders (see PISTON). Various systems of valves allow the steam to enter a cylinder and drive a piston first in one direction and then the other before they exhaust the used steam. These engines are often called *reciprocating* engines, because of the back-and-forth, or reciprocating, motion of their pistons. Steam hammers used to drive piles and to forge metal require this kind of motion (see FORGING; STEAM HAMMER). A locomotive, however, requires rotary motion to turn its wheels. This rotary motion is achieved by attaching a crankshaft to the ends of the pistons. In some types of reciprocating steam engines, called *compound engines*, the steam may flow through as many as four cylinders and operate four pistons.

Steam Turbines produce a rotary motion. A steam turbine has many sets of bladed wheels mounted on a long shaft. The steam enters at one end and spins the bladed wheels as it gushes past them. Steam turbines are used to turn electric generators and ship propellers.

History

Hero, a scientist who lived in Alexandria, Egypt, described the first known steam engine about A.D. 60. The engine consisted of a small, hollow globe mounted on a pipe running to a steam kettle. Two L-shaped pipes were fastened to opposite sides of the globe. When steam rushed out of the two L-shaped pipes, it caused the globe to whirl (see JET PROPULSION [picture: The First Jet Engine]). But this engine performed no useful work. Hundreds of years passed before the first successful steam engines were developed in the 1600's.

How a Steam Engine Works

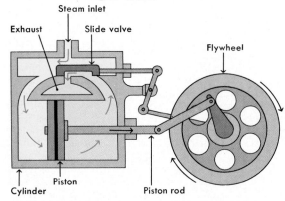

Steam operates the engine by pushing first on one side of the piston and then on the other. A slide valve directs the steam from side to side. In the diagram above, steam enters from the left side of the cylinder and forces the piston to the right. As the piston moves, the piston rod turns the flywheel half a turn.

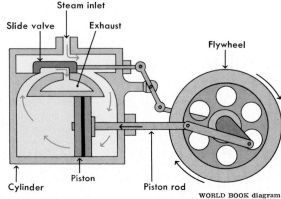

WORLD BOOK diagram

When the piston reaches the right side of the cylinder, *above,* the slide valve moves and directs the steam behind the piston again. The steam forces the piston to the left. The piston rod then pulls the flywheel around to complete one turn. Steam in the left side of the cylinder escapes through the exhaust.

The First Steam Engines operated on the ability of steam to *condense* back into a liquid rather than on its ability to expand. When steam condenses, the liquid takes less space than the steam. If this condensing takes place in a sealed *vessel*, or container, a partial *vacuum*, or sucking action, is created that can do useful work.

In 1698, Thomas Savery (1650-1715), an Englishman, patented the first practical steam engine, a pump to drain water from mines. Savery's pump had no moving parts other than valves operated by hand. These were turned to let steam enter a sealed vessel. Cold water was poured on the vessel to chill it and condense the steam. Then a valve was opened so the vacuum in the vessel could suck water up a pipe.

In 1712, Thomas Newcomen (1663-1729), an English blacksmith, invented another steam-engine pump for mines. Newcomen's engine had a large horizontal beam balanced in the middle like a seesaw. A piston which fitted into a cylinder hung from one end of the beam. When steam was let into the cylinder, it forced the piston up, lowering the other end of the beam. Cold water was then sprayed into the cylinder, the steam condensed, and the vacuum sucked the piston down again. This raised the other end of the horizontal beam, which was attached to the piston of a pump in a mine.

Watt's Engine. When James Watt began his experiments in 1763, the Newcomen engine was the best known. It set Watt to thinking, because it used an enormous quantity of steam and therefore a large amount of fuel. Watt saw that the alternate heating and cooling of the cylinder wasted much heat. He invented an engine in which the condenser and the cylinder were separate. The cylinder always remained hot. This arrangement saved three fourths of the fuel cost, because

very little steam was lost through condensation by entering a cold cylinder.

Watt took out his first patent on a steam engine in 1769, and continued to make improvements in his engines. Perhaps his most important improvement was the use of the *double-action* principle. In engines based on this principle, the steam is used first on one side of the piston, then on the other side. Watt also learned to shut off the steam when the cylinder was only partly filled. This allowed the expansion of the steam already in the cylinder to complete the piston's stroke. Many persons mistakenly believe that Watt invented the steam engine. But he only improved it. He reduced the cost of operating *condensing* engines and made it practical to use these engines for other kinds of work than pumping.

Modern Steam Engines. The main improvement in the years after Newcomen and Watt was to develop engines capable of using high-pressure steam. Watt never experimented in the use of high-pressure steam, because he feared an explosion. The pressures in his engines were not much greater than air pressure, or about 15 pounds per square inch (103 kilopascals). Then, in the late 1700's and early 1800's, an Englishman named Richard Trevithick designed and built the first high-pressure steam engines. One of his first engines operated under 30 pounds (207 kilopascals) of pressure. By 1815, Oliver Evans, an American, had built an engine that used 200 pounds (1,379 kilopascals) of steam pressure. Today, many engines use steam under a pressure of more than 1,000 pounds per square inch (6,895 kilopascals).

Other improvements made in steam engines included the development of the compound engine, and the use of *superheated* steam. In superheating, the temperature of the steam is raised above 700° F. (371° C) without increasing the pressure. This helps keep the incoming steam from condensing on the surfaces of the piston cylinder, because superheated steam does not cool so quickly as ordinary steam. In the late 1800's, the invention of steam turbines marked another big improvement in steam engines. Steam turbines provided an economical source of power to turn electric generators, and to drive the propellers of steamships.   OTTO A. UYEHARA

Related Articles in WORLD BOOK include:

STEAM HAMMER is a power-driven hammer which is used to make heavy forgings. The hammer head is raised by the pressure of steam which is admitted into the lower part of the cylinder. When the hammer reaches the desired height, the steam is released and the hammer falls. Steam admitted into the upper part can be used to increase the speed of the fall. The speed with which the hammer is released also determines its force. Steam hammers vary in weight from 100 pounds (45 kilograms) to 100 short tons (91 metric tons).

Steam drop hammers are raised like ordinary steam hammers. But they differ from other steam hammers in that they fall by their own weight. The steam hammer

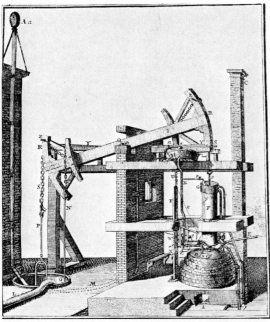

Bettmann Archive

Thomas Newcomen's Steam Engine drove a pump that removed water from mines. This bulky engine of the early 1700's turned only a fraction of the energy it received into useful work.

was invented by the Scottish engineer and manufacturer James Nasmyth in 1839.   ARTHUR C. ANSLEY

See also FORGING; NASMYTH, JAMES; TRIP HAMMER.

STEAM HEATING. See HEATING (Central Heating).

STEAM SHOVEL is a large *excavating* (digging) machine that is powered by steam. It has a large iron or steel scoop with teeth along the front edge. The bottom of the scoop has a hinge, so it can swing open and release its load. The scoop works from a beam that can be moved in any direction. An operator lowers the scoop to the ground and drives it forward and upward, scooping up earth and rock.

In 1838, William S. Otis of Massachusetts developed the first steam shovel. It dug the roadbed for the Western Railroad in Massachusetts. Engineers used steam shovels for projects such as the Panama Canal. Diesel power shovels have now replaced them.   ROBERT G. HENNES

See also CONSTRUCTION EQUIPMENT.

STEAM TURBINE. See TURBINE.

STEAMBOAT is a term used for steam-driven vessels that sail on rivers. It also refers to the smaller vessels on lakes or in the coastal waters of the sea. *Steamship* is used for large vessels such as those sailing on the open sea. In 1787, John Fitch demonstrated the first workable steamboat in the United States. The first financially successful steamboat was Robert Fulton's *Clermont*. In 1807, it steamed the 150 miles (241 kilometers) up the Hudson from New York City to Albany in 32 hours. Steamboats carried passengers on the great rivers before the development of railroads and other faster or more efficient means of transportation. Steamships are still used in many parts of the world.   ROBERT H. BURGESS

Related Articles in WORLD BOOK include:

Clermont	Louisiana (picture)
Fitch, John	Roosevelt, Nicholas J.
Fulton, Robert (with picture)	Ship

STEAMSHIP. See SHIP; STEAMBOAT.

STEARIC ACID, *stee AR ihk*, is a valuable organic fatty acid that comes from many animal and vegetable fats and oils. The acid gets its name from the Greek word *stear*, which means *tallow*.

Stearic acid is prepared commercially by treating animal fats with water at high temperature and at high pressure. It is used for softening rubber, and also in manufacturing wax candles, cosmetics, and soaps.

Stearic acid is a waxy solid that melts at a temperature of about 70° C (158° F.). Its chemical formula is $CH_3(CH_2)_{16}COOH$.   JOHN E. LEFFLER

STEARIN, *STEE uhr ihn*, is a combination of stearic acid and glycerol. Chemically, stearin is an intricate compound of carbon, hydrogen, and oxygen. It is the chief ingredient of mutton and beef fat, and certain vegetable fats such as palm oil. When these substances are boiled, the stearin is crystallized into pearly, waxlike scales which have neither taste nor odor. Stearin is boiled with alkali to form soap. The stearic acid combines with the alkali, and the glycerol is separated as a by-product of the soapmaking. Stearin also yields an oil which is used in making some margarines. See also GLYCEROL; STEARIC ACID.   LEONE RUTLEDGE CARROLL

STEATITE. See SOAPSTONE.

STEEL. See IRON AND STEEL; ALLOY.

STEEL GUITAR. See HAWAII (Dancing and Music).

STEELE, SIR RICHARD (1672-1729), an Irish-born writer, created the popular journalistic essays that were published as *The Tatler*. He worked with Joseph Addison in writing the essays published as *The Spectator*.

The Tatler (1709-1711) dealt in a humorous, good-natured way with family life, the theater, and literature. Steele tried to inform and entertain his readers, especially women, and to develop their taste. Steele did most of the writing in *The Tatler*, though Addison helped him. Addison contributed more essays to *The Spectator* (1711-1712) than his friend did. Steele was a frank, warm person, and his essays are livelier than Addison's (see ADDISON, JOSEPH). Steele later published several less successful series of essays. He also wrote four comic plays. The first play, *The Funeral* (1701), became very popular. His last play, *The Conscious Lovers* (1722), was an example of sentimental comedy, which flourished in English drama during the 1700's.

Steele was born in Dublin. In 1684, he entered the Charterhouse School in London, where he formed his long friendship with Addison, a fellow student. Steele went to Oxford University in 1689, but left without a degree to join the army. He served several terms in Parliament beginning in 1713. He was knighted in 1715.   THOMAS H. FUJIMURA

STEELHEAD. See TROUT (True Trout).

STEELWORKERS OF AMERICA, UNITED (USWA), is one of the largest labor unions in the United States. It is affiliated with the American Federation of Labor and Congress of Industrial Organizations (AFL-CIO). It has locals throughout North America. Its members work in the iron, steel, aluminum, and nonferrous metal industries. For membership, see LABOR MOVEMENT (table).

The union was founded in 1936 as the Steel Workers Organizing Committee (SWOC) of the CIO. The Amalgamated Association of Iron, Steel, and Tin Workers became part of the SWOC in 1936. The present name was adopted in 1942. Since then, four other unions have merged with the USWA. They are the CIO Aluminum Workers of America, in 1944; the International Union of Mine, Mill and Smelter Workers, in 1967; the United Stone and Allied Products Workers of America, in 1970; and the Allied and Technical Workers, District 50, in 1972. The USWA publishes a monthly newspaper, *Steel Labor*. Headquarters are at 5 Gateway Center, Pittsburgh, Pa. 15222.

Critically reviewed by UNITED STEELWORKERS OF AMERICA

STEENBOK. See STEINBOK.

STEEPLECHASING is the sport of horse racing over obstacles. Races are described as being *over brush*, *over timber*, or *over hurdles*, depending on the obstacles used. Jockeys ride thoroughbred horses at breakneck speed in steeplechases. Steeplechasing originated in England, and is the outgrowth of fox-hunting on horseback. The name comes from races hunters staged across country to "yonder church steeple." Organized U.S. steeplechasing began shortly after the Civil War. In addition to races at the major tracks, steeplechase meetings are held by fox-hunting clubs.   JOHN E. COOPER

STEER. See CATTLE.

STEFANSSON, *STEHF uhn suhn,* **VILHJALMUR,** *VIHL hyowl muhr* (1879-1962), an Arctic explorer and author, emphasized that the Arctic region is of great military and strategic importance. Stefansson argued that the region is "warm and friendly" and should be settled and developed.

Stefansson was born in Arnes, Man., and attended the University of North Dakota, the University of Iowa, and Harvard University. In 1905, he became a member of an archaeological expedition to Iceland. Between 1913 and 1918, he led an expedition that explored Canadian and Alaskan Arctic regions.

During World War II, Stefansson served as an adviser to the U.S. Army and Navy. He became Arctic and Antarctic consultant to Dartmouth College in 1947. Later, he moved his 35,000-volume polar library to Dartmouth. He wrote many books, including *The Arctic in Fact and Fable* (1945), *Not by Bread Alone* (1946), and *The Fat of the Land* (1956).   WILLIAM R. WILLOUGHBY

STEFFENS, LINCOLN (1866-1936), was an American author, editor, lecturer, and reformer. He was one of a group of writers known as *muckrakers* because their magazine articles during the early 1900's exposed corruption in government, business, and labor. Starting in 1902 with an exposé of crooked political practices in St. Louis, Steffens went on to write about conditions in many U.S. cities and states.

Joseph Lincoln Steffens was born in San Francisco, and studied at the University of California and in Europe. He began his career with the *New York Commercial Advertiser*. He soon joined *McClure's Magazine*, and there wrote the articles that made him famous. Later, he wrote for the *American Magazine* and *Everybody's Magazine*. He published his *Autobiography* in 1931.   JOHN TEBBEL

STEGOSAURUS. See DINOSAUR (Kinds of Dinosaurs).

STEICHEN, *STY kuhn,* **EDWARD** (1879-1973), was an American photographer who helped develop photography as a creative art. Early in his career, Steichen was a painter as well as a photographer. He became known for the soft, hazy qualities of his photographs of landscapes and people.

Steichen was a member of the Photo-Secession, a group formed in 1902 by Alfred Stieglitz, another American photographer. The group promoted photography as a fine art. Steichen helped Stieglitz publish the magazine *Camera Work*. They also worked together in organizing art exhibits in New York City.

During World War I (1914-1918), Steichen organized an aerial photography unit for the United States Army. After the war, he changed his style of photography and began to take sharp, detailed photographs. From 1923 to 1938, he was chief photographer for two fashion magazines, *Vanity Fair* and *Vogue*. From 1947 to 1962, Steichen directed the photography department of the Museum of Modern Art in New York City. He assembled a famous exhibit there in 1955 called "The Family of Man," which consisted of 503 photographs of people throughout the world.

Edward Steichen was born Eduard Jean Steichen in Luxembourg. His family settled in the United States in 1882.   CHARLES HAGEN

STEIG, *styg,* **WILLIAM** (1907-   ), an American cartoonist and children's author, won the 1970 Caldecott Medal for *Sylvester and the Magic Pebble*. This story tells about a donkey named Sylvester and his adventures after he finds a magic pebble that can grant wishes. Steig wrote and illustrated the story.

Steig was born in New York City. He began his

career in 1930 as a cartoonist and has contributed cartoons to many magazines, particularly *The New Yorker*. His other children's books include *Roland the Minstrel Pig* (1968), *C D B!* (1968), *Abel's Island* (1976), and *Gorky Rises* (1980).

STEIN, GERTRUDE (1874-1946), was an American author who introduced a unique style of writing. She influenced many writers—among them Sherwood Anderson and Ernest Hemingway—who were trying to develop new ways to express themselves.

In her writing style, Stein repeated basic words. Her style is exemplified by her statement, "Rose is a rose is a rose is a rose." She felt that such repetition of words helped communicate the feelings they expressed. Stein believed that punctuation and difficult words distracted the reader from these feelings, and so she used little punctuation and simple words. In her fiction, she placed more importance on revealing the characters' feelings than on telling a story.

Stein was born in Allegheny, Pa., and graduated from Radcliffe College. She studied under the philosopher William James, and his teaching strongly influenced the writing style that she later developed. In 1903, Stein settled in Paris. Her apartment became a gathering place for many writers, musicians, and painters. Stein was one of the first persons to realize the importance of various experimental movements in painting. She encouraged such artists as Henri Matisse and Pablo Picasso in their work, and she became an art critic and collector.

Reprinted with the permission of Joanna T. Steichen
(Museum of Modern Art, New York City)

Greta Garbo, 1928, by Edward Steichen, is a dramatic black-and-white photograph of the famous actress. Steichen produced many sharply defined fashion photographs and portraits.

STEINBECK, JOHN

Stein's best-known book is *The Autobiography of Alice B. Toklas* (1933). She wrote it about herself from the viewpoint of Alice B. Toklas, her friend and secretary. Stein's other works include *Three Lives* (1909), a book of stories; and *Lectures in America* (1935), a collection of lectures on literature, painting, and music. She wrote the text for two operas that were composed by Virgil Thomson, *Four Saints in Three Acts* (1934) and *The Mother of Us All* (1947).

Carl Van Vechten
Gertrude Stein

MARCUS KLEIN

Additional Resources

BRIDGMAN, RICHARD. *Gertrude Stein in Pieces*. Oxford, 1970. Describes and evaluates her work.
BRINNIN, JOHN MALCOLM. *Third Rose: Gertrude Stein and Her World*. Little, Brown, 1959.
HOFFMAN, MICHAEL J. *Gertrude Stein*. Twayne, 1976.
MELLOW, JAMES R. *Charmed Circle: Gertrude Stein and Company*. Phaidon, 1974.

STEINBECK, JOHN (1902-1968), an American author, won the 1962 Nobel prize for literature. Steinbeck became famous for his novels about poor, oppressed California farmers and laborers. His most famous novel, *The Grapes of Wrath*, won the 1940 Pulitzer prize.

John Ernst Steinbeck was born in Salinas, Calif., and the Salinas area provides the setting for most of his fiction. Steinbeck's first novel, *Cup of Gold*, appeared in 1929. *Pastures of Heaven* (1932), his next book, is a collection of related stories. It portrays the people of a farm community near Salinas and their love of the land.

Critics gave Steinbeck serious attention for the first time following the publication of *Tortilla Flat* (1935). This novel vividly describes the life of migrants and poor farmers. *In Dubious Battle* (1936) deals with violent labor strikes in California during the 1930's. The book shows Steinbeck's liberal political views in its sympathetic treatment of the strikers.

Steinbeck continued to express his liberal views in *Of Mice and Men* (1937) and *The Grapes of Wrath* (1939). Both these novels show how people struggle for survival in a hostile social environment.

In *The Grapes of Wrath*, Steinbeck told about the poor Oklahoma farmers, called *Okies*, who migrated to California during the Great Depression of the 1930's. The novel relates how the Joad family loses its farm through a bank foreclosure. The family then makes the difficult journey to California to start a new life. Steinbeck tells how the police and various employers in California mistreat the Joads and other migrant families. Critics at

Philippe Halsman
John Steinbeck

first considered *The Grapes of Wrath* a story of the economic crisis of the 1930's. But years later, critics realized that it portrays everyone's search for human dignity.

Most critics believe Steinbeck's later books rank below his fiction of the 1930's. Perhaps his best-known later novel is *East of Eden* (1952), a symbolic story about the need for love and understanding among people. His other later novels include *Sweet Thursday* (1954) and *The Winter of Our Discontent* (1961). In *Travels with Charley* (1962), Steinbeck described a journey with his pet poodle.

JOSEPH N. RIDDEL

Additional Resources

FRENCH, WARREN. *John Steinbeck*. 2nd ed. Twayne, 1975.
GRAY, JAMES. *John Steinbeck*. Univ. of Minnesota Press, 1971.
KIERNAN, THOMAS. *The Intricate Music: A Biography of John Steinbeck*. Little, Brown, 1979.
MOORE, HARRY. *The Novels of John Steinbeck: A First Critical Study*. 2nd ed. Kennikat, 1968.

STEINBERG, SAUL (1914-   ), is an artist noted for his small-scale pen-and-ink drawings. His work is satirical and full of unexpected images and ideas. He

From the WORLD BOOK Collection

Steinberg's *Sam's Art* shows how the artist uses sharp line and an unusual combination of images to make witty comments about modern life. Much of his work appears in *The New Yorker* magazine.

became noted for funny drawings that had no captions or explanations. In many of these drawings, figures utter "words" indicated by fantastic forms coming from their mouths.

Steinberg likes to draw parades, city crowds, strange animals, railroad stations, and drum majorettes. Some of his drawings of musicians are on music paper. He sometimes uses graph paper as a background and also makes documents resembling diplomas or certificates in which the writing is decorative but illegible. Steinberg was born in Rîmnicu Sărat, Romania. He came to the United States at the age of 28.

ALLEN S. WELLER

STEINBOK, *STINE bahk*, or STEENBOK, is a small antelope that lives in southern and east-central Africa. Its name, taken from the Dutch, means *stone buck*. It has a reddish or pale brownish coat above, and is white below. It stands about 22 inches (56 centimeters) high. Males have straight slender horns seldom more than 4 to 5 inches (10 to 13 centimeters) long. Female steinboks are hornless. Steinboks live in dry grassland, but they can sometimes be found in open woodland.

Scientific Classification. The steinbok is a member of the bovid family, *Bovidae*. The common steinbok is genus *Raphicerus*, species *R. campestris*.   VICTOR H. CAHALANE

STEINEM, GLORIA (1934-   ), is a writer and a leading supporter of the women's liberation movement in the United States. She has campaigned for women's rights in employment, politics, and social life. In 1972, Steinem founded *Ms.*, a magazine published and edited by women. *Ms.* tells women about career opportunities and meaningful ways of life.

Ed Jarecki, *Chicago Daily News*
Gloria Steinem

In 1971, Steinem helped found the National Women's Political Caucus, which encourages women to seek political office and to work for women's rights laws. That same year, she helped establish the Women's Action Alliance, which fights discrimination against women.

Steinem was born in Toledo, Ohio, and graduated from Smith College in 1956. She worked as a magazine and television writer before joining the women's liberation movement in 1968.   CYNTHIA FUCHS EPSTEIN

STEINHEIM MAN. See SWANSCOMBE MAN.

STEINMETZ, CHARLES PROTEUS (1865-1923), was a German-born mathematician and engineer. He is best known for his development of the theory of alternating currents and for his experiments with artificially-created lightning. The disadvantages of poverty, political misfortune, and a crippling deformity did not prevent him from becoming a scientific genius.

Steinmetz established his reputation in the American scientific community in 1892. He prepared an analysis of *hysteresis loss*, a magnetic effect peculiar to alternating current. He was soon invited to join the newly founded General Electric Company, where he spent the remainder of his career in research on electricity. Out of his laboratory, where for some years he lived as well as worked, came many experimental discoveries and inventions.

Steinmetz was born in Breslau, Germany (now Wrocław, Poland). He fled the country in 1888, just before receiving a Ph.D. from Breslau University. He had been threatened with arrest for socialist activity. He came to the United States in 1889. He taught electricity at Union College in Schenectady, N.Y., and wrote several books on electrical theory.   ROBERT P. MULTHAUF

Brown Bros.
Charles Steinmetz

STEINWAY, HENRY ENGELHARD (1797-1871), was a German-born piano maker who founded the Steinway & Sons piano company. Steinway established his firm in New York City in 1853, about three years after he immigrated to the United States. Steinway pianos are famous for their high quality.

In 1855, Steinway introduced the first successful piano with an interior cast-iron frame and a string arrangement called the *overstrung scale*. This arrangement had bass strings that stretched diagonally across the other strings. The frame and diagonal strings greatly improved the sound of a piano and have been used in nearly all pianos made since the 1850's.

Steinway was born near Seesen, in what is now West Germany. His real name was Heinrich Engelhard Steinweg. He received training as a cabinetmaker but began to make pianos in the 1830's.   BARRY W. POULSON

STELLA, FRANK (1936-   ), is an American artist known for his impersonal abstract style. Stella's paintings of the 1960's and early 1970's stand out as the most successful examples of *formalist* art. Formalists believe that art should concern itself exclusively with new techniques of organizing the canvas, plus other innovations in form. Accordingly, Stella has developed a style that relies on geometrical designs and a clean-edged, impersonal application of paint. He avoids any representation of subject matter or any expression of emotion. Stella's *Jasper's Dilemma* appears in the PAINTING article.

Stella has painted many works on large, unusually shaped canvases. The shapes range from rectangles to trapezoids, triangles, and combinations of these and other figures. Stella has also expanded the use of brilliant colors in modern art. Frank Philip Stella was born in Malden, Mass.   JONATHAN FINEBERG

See also ART AND THE ARTS (picture: Creating and Enjoying Art).

STELLER'S SEA COW. See SEA COW.

STELLER'S SEA EAGLE. See EAGLE (Other Kinds; picture).

STEM is the part of a plant that produces and supports buds, leaves, flowers, and fruit. Most stems hold the leaves in a position to receive sunlight needed to manufacture food. The stem also carries water and minerals from the roots to the leaves for use in food production. The sugar made in the leaves is conducted by the stem to other parts of the plant.

All plants have stems except algae, fungi, liverworts, and mosses. However, the stems of various kinds of plants differ considerably in size and appearance. For example, lettuce plants have extremely short stems that are barely visible under the large leaves. California redwood trees have huge stems—their trunks—that may grow 12 feet (3.7 meters) wide and more than 350 feet (107 meters) high.

Most stems grow erect above the ground. A few kinds grow underground or horizontally along the ground. Buds develop on the stem at points called *nodes* and produce branches, leaves, or flowers. The space between each node is called an *internode*.

Kinds of Stems

There are two chief kinds of stems, *herbaceous stems* and *woody stems*. Herbaceous stems have soft tissues, produce small plants, and grow very little in diameter. Most of them live for only one growing season. Such plants as alfalfa, clover, and garden peas have herbaceous stems.

STEM

Woody stems are hard and thick. They have tough, woody tissues and may live for hundreds of years. Each growing season, woody stems develop new tissues that cause them to grow in diameter. Trees and shrubs have woody stems.

Herbaceous Stems. Herbaceous stems consist only of *primary tissues*. Such tissues, which develop from cell division at the tip of the stem, include the *epidermis*, the *phloem*, the *xylem*, and the *parenchyma*.

The epidermis is the outer protective layer of the stem. On many stems, the epidermis has a thin waxy covering that keeps the stem from drying out. Phloem includes living cells that form *sieve tubes*, which carry sugar down from the leaves. Xylem consists mainly of dead tubes that carry water up from the roots to other parts of the plant. Parenchyma is tissue that stores food for a plant.

Herbaceous stems differ in internal structure among various groups of plants. For example, the stems of the two kinds of flowering plants, *monocotyledons* and *dicotyledons*, have a different structure (see PLANT [Flowering Plants]).

Monocotyledonous stems have bundles containing both xylem and phloem scattered throughout the stem. These bundles are surrounded by *ground tissue*, which consists of parenchyma cells.

Dicotyledonous stems have a circular layer of cells called the *cortex*, which lies directly under the epidermis. The cortex consists mainly of parenchyma cells. Bundles of xylem and phloem are arranged in a ring beneath the cortex. The xylem lies toward the inside of the bundle, and the phloem is toward the outside. Dicotyledonous stems also have a band of cells called the *cambium*, which lies between the xylem and phloem within the bundles. The cambium is not active in most herbaceous stems, but it causes woody stems to grow wider. The core of a dicotyledonous stem is called the *pith* and consists of parenchyma cells.

Woody Stems have primary tissues that resemble those of herbaceous dicotyledonous stems. During their first year of growth, woody stems begin to develop *secondary tissues* through cell division in the cambium and in tissue called the *cork cambium*. The secondary tissues support or replace primary tissues by producing wood and bark.

Woody stems increase greatly in diameter because they develop new layers of secondary tissues each year. As the stem grows wider, the epidermis and cortex are pushed outward. These tissues break up and fall away from the stem.

A cross section of a mature woody stem shows circular layers of primary and secondary tissues. These layers, from innermost to outermost, are the (1) primary xylem, (2) secondary xylem, (3) cambium, (4) secondary phloem, (5) phelloderm, (6) cork cambium, and (7) cork. Secondary xylem and secondary phloem result from cell division in the cambium. Phelloderm and cork are produced by cell division in the cork cambium.

Primary xylem and secondary xylem form a core of wood, which makes up the greatest part of a woody stem. Each growing season, the cambium produces a new layer of secondary xylem that can be distinguished from previous layers. These layers are called *growth rings*, or *annual rings*. The approximate age of a stem can be determined by counting its growth rings.

Secondary phloem and phelloderm make up the stem's inner bark. As new layers of secondary phloem develop, they press outward and crush the older phloem into the outer bark. The phelloderm is a layer of parenchyma cells that replaces the cortex.

Outer bark consists of cork, a hard dead tissue that replaces the epidermis as a protective covering. Stems develop new layers of cork yearly. However, the older outer bark wears away or splits apart and falls off as the stem grows wider. Therefore, the thickness of the outer bark of most woody stems does not increase greatly through the years. In the outer bark of older stems, bands of cork alternate with bands of dead

The Structure of Stems   The various kinds of stems differ in structure. Herbaceous stems have only *primary tissues*, which develop from cell division at the tip of the stem. Woody stems have both primary and *secondary tissues*. Secondary tissues cause woody stems to develop wood and bark and to grow thicker. The diagrams below show the internal structures of the two kinds of herbaceous stems and of a woody stem.

WORLD BOOK diagrams by Marion Pahl

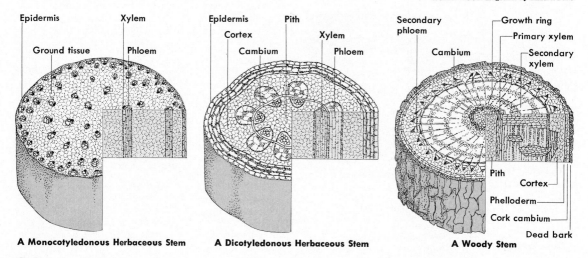

A Monocotyledonous Herbaceous Stem — Epidermis, Xylem, Ground tissue, Phloem

A Dicotyledonous Herbaceous Stem — Epidermis, Pith, Cortex, Xylem, Cambium, Phloem

A Woody Stem — Secondary phloem, Growth ring, Primary xylem, Cambium, Secondary xylem, Pith, Cortex, Phelloderm, Cork cambium, Dead bark phloem that has been pushed outward by the growth of secondary phloem.

Specialized Stems

Some stems perform special functions, such as food storage, reproduction, or protection or support of the plant. Such stems do not look like herbaceous or woody stems. However, specialized stems are true stems because they have nodes on their surface.

Certain specialized stems, including *bulbs, corms, rhizomes,* and *tubers,* are underground stems that can store large amounts of food. Bulbs consist of a short stem surrounded by fleshy leaves. Corms resemble bulbs but have a thicker stem and thinner leaves. Onions and tulips grow from bulbs, and gladiolus plants have corms. Rhizomes are thick stems that grow horizontally. Irises and violets have rhizomes. Tubers are short and swollen. They grow underground at the tip of the stems of such plants as potatoes.

Strawberry plants have *runners,* a kind of specialized stem that is active in reproduction. Runners grow horizontally along the ground and produce new plants at places where their nodes touch the surface. Grape plants and Boston ivy have modified stems called *tendrils,* which coil around or stick to objects, providing support for these climbing plants. The *thorns* of the honey locust are modified stems that protect the plant from animals.

How People Use Stems

Stems provide many foods and are used in a wide variety of products. Such foods as asparagus, bamboo shoots, onions, and potatoes are stems. Sugar is obtained from the stems of sugar cane and sorghum. Sap from the stems of maple trees is used in making maple sugar.

The wood produced by woody stems is used in the manufacture of an enormous range of products, including furniture, paper, and construction materials. Cork from the bark of the cork oak tree is used in making insulation materials, floor coverings, and bottle stoppers. Such fabrics as burlap and linen are produced from fibers in the phloem of some stems. The stems of certain trees provide substances used in making rubber, turpentine, and other products.   RICHARD C. KEATING

Related Articles in WORLD BOOK include:

Bark	Grafting	Rhizome	Tuber
Bulb	Leaf	Root	Wood
Corm	Plant	Sap	

STEM. See SHIP (table: Nautical Terms).

STENDHAL (1783-1842) is the pen name of MARIE HENRI BEYLE, one of the chief figures in the history of the French psychological novel. Stendhal was born in Grenoble. He served in the Napoleonic Wars, and Napoleon I became his great hero. Julien Sorel, the hero of Stendhal's masterpiece *The Red and the Black* (1830), lives a life of action and has great ambition, as Napoleon did. Stendhal's other great novel, *The Charterhouse of Parma* (1839), begins with Napoleon's defeat at the Battle of Waterloo, and tells of political intrigue in Italy.

In his writings, Stendhal was concerned basically with the search for happiness, which he believed could be achieved by the exercise of physical energy and will. Elements of realism and romanticism can be found in his work. He usually neglected other aspects of his nov-

els in favor of analyses of the minute, changing emotional states of his characters.

Stendhal left three partly autobiographical novels unfinished at his death. They are *The Life of Henri Brulard, Lamiel,* and *Lucien Leuwen.*   ROBERT J. NIESS

STENGEL, CASEY (1890-1975), was one of baseball's great managers. He led the New York Yankees to seven world championships, including five straight from 1949 to 1953, and again in 1956 and 1958. Stengel's Yankees were also American League champions from 1955 through 1958, and in 1960. In 1962, Stengel became manager of the New York Mets. A hip fracture forced him to retire in 1965. He was elected to the National Baseball Hall of Fame in 1966. Born Charles Dillon Stengel in Kansas City, Mo., he became a professional player in 1910. During his career, he also managed the Brooklyn Dodgers and Boston Braves.   ED FITZGERALD

STENNIS, JOHN CORNELIUS (1901-   ), a Mississippi Democrat, has been a U.S. senator since 1947. He served as chairman of the Senate Armed Services Committee from 1969 to 1981. The committee plays a powerful role in shaping military budgets.

Stennis is a leading opponent of civil rights legislation. He charged in 1969 that "segregation in the schools exists in many major areas of the North to an equal extent, if not a greater extent than in the South."

Stennis was born near De Kalb, Miss., and graduated from the University of Virginia School of Law. He served in the Mississippi House of Representatives from 1928 to 1932 and was a Mississippi prosecuting attorney for five years before becoming a circuit court judge in 1937.   WILLIAM J. EATON

STENOGRAPHY. See SHORTHAND; SHORTHAND MACHINE.

STENOTYPE. See SHORTHAND MACHINE.

STEPHEN, *STEE vun* (1097?-1154), was an English king whose reign was so full of strife that it is called "The Anarchy." The cause was a disputed succession. Stephen was the son of Adela, daughter of William the Conqueror. The other claimant to the throne was Matilda, daughter of Henry I. Henry had persuaded his barons to pledge allegiance to her before he died in 1135. In 1153, Stephen was finally forced to recognize as his successor Matilda's son, Henry II, the first Plantagenet king (see PLANTAGENET).   ROBERT S. HOYT

STEPHEN is the name of nine popes of the Roman Catholic Church. The church once listed 10 popes named Stephen. But in 1961, it dropped Stephen II from its list of popes. The numbers of the other Stephens were then moved up accordingly. The dates of their reigns are given below. The Roman numerals in parentheses are the old numbers used to name the popes before the first Stephen II was dropped.

Stephen I, Saint (254-257)	Stephen VI (VII) (896-897)
Stephen II (III) (752-757)	Stephen VII (VIII) (928-931)
Stephen III (IV) (768-772)	Stephen VIII (IX) (939-942)
Stephen IV (V) (816-817)	Stephen IX (X) (1057-1058)
Stephen V (VI) (885-891)	

Saint Stephen I (? -257) became famous because of his controversy with Saint Cyprian, bishop of Carthage. Cyprian insisted on rebaptizing converts who had received baptism from heretical ministers. Stephen opposed this practice, and established the enduring principle that baptism when correctly given, even by a non-Catholic, is valid and cannot be repeated. Stephen was born in Rome.

Stephen II (III) (? -757) was the first pope to travel to France. There, he sought the help of the Franks against the Lombards, who wanted to conquer Italy. He consecrated Pepin the Short and his sons as kings of the Franks in 754. In return, they became the protectors of the papacy. In 756, Pepin gave land in central Italy to Stephen that established the Papal States.

Stephen III (IV) (720?-772) excluded lay people from the election of the pope because of political interference by the Italian princes. He was born in Sicily.

Stephen IX (X) (1000?-1058) tried unsuccessfully to prevent the separation of the Eastern and Western churches. He succeeded Victor II as pope in 1057. Stephen was born in Lorraine. GUSTAVE WEIGEL and FULTON J. SHEEN

STEPHEN, GEORGE (1829-1921), BARON MOUNT STEPHEN, was a Canadian financier. He was one of the founders, and the first president, of the Canadian Pacific Railway (now CP Rail). Born in Dufftown, Scotland, he went to Canada in 1850 and became a cloth manufacturer in Montreal. In 1876, he became president of the Bank of Montreal. In 1880, he became a leading member of the company that built the Canadian Pacific, Canada's first transcontinental railway. He moved to England in 1888. WILLIAM R. WILLOUGHBY

STEPHEN, SAINT, was the first Christian martyr. He was stoned to death outside Jerusalem some time after the Crucifixion (Acts 7:59).

Stephen was one of the seven church officers, or deacons, appointed by the apostles. The deacons were to look after the poor. Stephen was a deeply religious man, known for the miracles he performed and for his preaching. Stephen's enemies accused him of teaching disobedience to the customs and rules associated with the law of Moses. He was brought to trial before the high council of the Sanhedrin. Here he made a great speech in his own defense (Acts 7). He said he was not speaking against the sacred Law, but that instead those who attacked him were failing to obey the Law themselves. The mob became furious and attacked him. One witness to his death was Saint Paul, who was not yet converted to Christianity (Acts 8:1). The Roman Catholic Church and the Church of England observe Saint Stephen's Day on December 26. FREDERICK C. GRANT

STEPHENS, ALEXANDER HAMILTON (1812-1883), was vice-president of the Confederate States of America during the Civil War. He was opposed to secession, but he remained loyal to Georgia when the state left the Union in 1861. He served as a delegate to the Montgomery Convention which formed the Confederacy, and he was chosen vice-president of the new government. During the war, Stephens often disagreed with Jefferson Davis, president of the Confederacy, on questions of states' rights.

In February 1865, Stephens led an unsuccessful peace commission which met with President Abraham Lincoln at Hampton Roads (see HAMPTON ROADS CONFERENCE). After the war, he was arrested and imprisoned for six months at Fort Warren in Boston Harbor. Georgia elected him to the United States Senate in 1866, but Congress refused him his seat. He then wrote *A*

Constitutional View of the Late War Between the States (1867-1870). Later, he wrote other books, and became editor of the Atlanta *Southern Sun* in 1871.

Stephens was again elected to Congress in 1872, and served 10 years. He was elected governor of Georgia in 1883, but died a few months after taking office. Stephens was born near Crawfordville, Ga., and was educated at

Brown Bros.

Alexander H. Stephens

the University of Georgia. He had originally intended to become a minister, but he changed his mind, and studied law instead. In 1834, he was admitted to the bar, and two years later became a member of the Georgia state legislature. He opposed vigilance committees, and the "slicking clubs," which were the parent of the Ku Klux Klan. From 1843 to 1859, he served as a congressman from Georgia. Stephens represents Georgia in Statuary Hall in Washington, D.C. W. B. HESSELTINE

STEPHENS, JAMES (1882-1950), was an Irish poet, novelist, and short-story writer. His work is sometimes humorous and playful and sometimes serious, but it is always imaginative and unusual. *The Crock of Gold*, a fantasy-novel, is probably his best-known book. It was first published in 1912. Stephens' interest in Irish folklore is apparent in much of his work, such as his *Irish Fairy Tales* (1920), a book for young people. He also wrote the books of verse *The Hill of Vision* (1912), *Strict Joy* (1931), and *Kings and the Moon* (1938). Stephens was born in Dublin. JOSEPH E. BAKER

STEPHENSON is the family name of two British engineers, father and son. Their inventions helped create the British railway system.

George Stephenson (1781-1848) was called the *Founder of Railways*. His skill in repairing coal-hauling engines in the mines earned him the title of *Engine Doctor*. He finally decided to build a locomotive of his own. His second engine, *Puffing Billy* (1814), embodied his invention, the steam blast. This device increased the draft in the boiler. In turn, the fire became hotter and made steam of a higher pressure. His engine was so successful that it pulled heavy loads of coal for years. His locomotive, *The Rocket* (1829,) traveled at the then unheard-of speed of 30 mph (48 kph). It was a model for later steam locomotives.

Stephenson invented many useful things besides engines, including a miner's lamp, a fishing lamp, and an alarm clock. He became well known for building the Stockton and Darlington Railway from 1821 to 1825. Then he built the difficult Liverpool and Manchester Railway. Here he used his ideas for tunnels, grading, and bridges to make a level roadbed.

Stephenson was born in Wylam, near Newcastle. As a boy, he made models of engines of clay and sticks which later helped him work out some of his great projects. He was consulted on major railway projects in many countries, and spread his original ideas for safety and passenger comfort. With the wealth from his inventions and locomotive factory, he became a philanthropist. His night schools for miners, and libraries, music clubs, recreation rooms, and schools for miners' children, were as original in his day as were his inventions.

Robert Stephenson (1803-1859), the son of George Stephenson, was chiefly noted for the great bridges and viaducts he built. He invented the tubular bridge, and introduced the use of tubular girders in the construction of iron bridges. Stephenson built railways in Germany, Switzerland, Canada, Egypt, and India. Later, he became interested in politics, and served in the House of Commons from 1847 until 1859.

Stephenson was born near the coal mines at Willington Quay. He went to South America as a mining engineer. He returned to England in 1827, and helped his father build *The Rocket*. From 1833 to 1838, Stephenson was chief engineer for the construction of the London and Birmingham Railway. This railway was the first to enter London.   JOHN H. KEMBLE

See also LOCOMOTIVE (picture); ROCKET, THE.

STEPINAC, *STEHP ih nak,* **ALOYSIUS CARDINAL,** *AL oh IHSH ih uhs* (1898-1960), a Yugoslav cardinal of the Roman Catholic Church, became a symbol of resistance to Communism after World War II. At that time, the Communist government of Josip Broz Tito determined to restrict organized religion in Yugoslavia. Stepinac was charged with aiding Germany and Italy during the war. He was tried in October 1946, and sentenced to 16 years of hard labor. He was offered freedom if he would leave the country, but he refused. In 1951, he was released. Pope Pius XII made him a cardinal in 1953. Stepinac was born in Zagreb, Yugoslavia. He worked for the rights of the Croatian people in Yugoslavia. Stepinac became an archbishop in 1937.   JOHN T. FARRELL and FULTON J. SHEEN

STEPPE, *stehp,* is an area covered chiefly by short grasses. Steppes are found in dry areas that have hot summers and cold winters. Most steppes receive an average of from 10 to 20 inches (25 to 51 centimeters) of rain a year—less rain than on a prairie, but more than on a desert. The interior regions of North America and Eurasia have large steppes. In North America, steppes cover most of the Great Plains from northern New Mexico to southern Alberta. In Russia, they extend from the southern Ukraine into central Asia.

Most steppe plants grow less than 1 foot (30 centimeters) high. They do not grow so dense as the tall grasses of prairies. Plants of the North American steppes include blue grama grass, buffalo grass, and small relatives of the sunflower. Until people began to farm those areas, many bison, jack rabbits, prairie dogs, pronghorns, and hawks lived there.

Today, people use steppes to graze livestock and to grow wheat and other crops. Overgrazing and plowing have harmed some steppes. After a steppe has been plowed, strong winds may blow away the loose soil, especially during a drought. A combination of plowing, winds, and drought has caused severe dust storms on the Great Plains (see DUST BOWL).   CLAIR L. KUCERA

STEREO CAMERA. See CAMERA (Stereo Cameras).

STEREOCHEMISTRY. See PLASTICS (table: Terms).

STEREOGRAPH. See AUDIO-VISUAL MATERIALS (Slides).

STEREOPHONIC SOUND. See PHONOGRAPH; HIGH FIDELITY (Stereophonic Hi-Fi); SOUND (Using Sound).

STEREOSCOPE, *STEHR ee uh SKOHP,* is an optical viewing device that makes photographs seem to have three dimensions. An ordinary camera sees things only in a flat plane, and never in the round, the way our eyes usually see things. But two cameras set slightly apart can work like our eyes. They can photograph the same object at the same time. These two photographs are then mounted side by side and viewed through a combination of lenses and prisms called a *stereoscope*. The two views then enter the eyes without strain, and the resulting mental image appears to have three dimensions. The person using the stereoscope sees everything in the round.

A stereoscope with a cabinet of pictures was once a common item. The old-style stereoscope consisted of a rack and handle, a slide, and a pair of screened lens-prisms. The present-day stereoscope is a plastic box with two viewing holes. One popular type has picture slides mounted in a cardboard or plastic disk.

Today, stereoscopes are employed extensively in aerial surveys to map out land elevations. Astronomers use a special type of stereoscope for finding small planets. It is possible to mount two stereophotographs side by side and view them without prisms. The effect is a good picture in the round, but it causes eyestrain.

In 1952, producers introduced "three-dimensional" motion-picture projection. Some types used a large, curved screen and a new kind of sound projection to produce a three-dimensional effect. Others used a stereoscopic principle. Persons watching the film wore special eyeglasses so that each eye saw only the view meant for it. The mental image that resulted had three dimensions.   ROBERT A. SOBIESZEK

See also EYE (Depth Perception); CAMERA (Stereo Cameras); POLARIZED LIGHT.

STEREOTYPING, *STEHR ee uh typ ihng,* is the method of making metal plates for use in printing. In the process, workers set the type and lock it into a steel *chase* (frame). Others brush the face of the type with a thin coating of oil. A prepared sheet of thick, composite paper, called *flong*, is laid on the type and beaten or pressed tightly against it. This sheet takes an impression of the face of the type or *cut* (picture) in the frame. The paper mold thus formed then goes into an oven and bakes until it becomes hard and dry. This mold, which is known as a *matrix*, or *mat*, is placed in a box face up. A worker pours melted stereotype metal, made up of tin, antimony, and lead, over the mold. The stereotype metal hardens at once, forming a solid plate, and the page is printed from this plate.

Introduction of the stereotype process helped speed up newspaper printing. The stereotype plates used on small presses are flat. Those used on rotary presses for newspapers are in the form of half cylinders. It takes only about 15 minutes to make stereotype plates, and they are inexpensive compared to other printing plates. One matrix can produce a number of plates. Country newspapers get some of their subject matter from plants in cities that specialize in making plates and "mats." "Boilerplate" is the slang term for this material. Stereotyping is used mostly in printing newspapers, but it is also used to print magazines, catalogs, and inexpensive books.   EUGENE M. ETTENBERG

See also ELECTROTYPING; TYPE; NEWSPAPER (picture: Making the Printing Plates).

STERILITY

STERILITY, *stuh RIHL uh tee,* refers to the inability to reproduce. It applies to all forms of life, from microorganisms to higher plants, animals, and human beings.

Some antibiotics, such as penicillin, interfere with the reproductive powers of disease-producing bacteria. This keeps the number of bacteria low, and enables the body to overcome disease.

A plant may be sterile because of imperfectly developed reproductive organs. If the stamens and pistils are imperfect or absent, the plant cannot reproduce. Sterility in animals results if the reproductive organs do not develop properly. Certain hybrid animals, such as the mule, cannot reproduce.

Sterility in human beings may have several causes. It may result from defects in the structure of the reproductive organs. Certain diseases affect the reproductive organs and may cause sterility. Improper balance of the hormones produced by the pituitary gland, the thyroid gland, the adrenal glands, and the sex glands may result in failure to produce eggs or sperm. Human beings may intentionally become sterile by undergoing surgical sterilization (see STERILIZATION). STUART ABEL

STERILIZATION, *STEHR uh luh ZAY shuhn,* in medicine and bacteriology, means the killing of germs. Germ killing helps to prevent infection and the spread of disease. Doctors and dentists sterilize their tools before they touch the human body. The bandages and many of the medicines we buy are sterilized before they are packed. Sterilization has been practiced only since the late 1800's. The English surgeon Joseph Lister introduced antiseptic, germ-killing methods into surgery.

Proper sterilization is done by fire, steam, heated air, or certain chemicals. Steam and heated air are the best, for they leave no foreign matter on the sterilized object. Fire is commonly used in the home to sterilize a needle with which to prick a blister or remove a splinter. Steam cabinets are often used to sterilize medical instruments. Heated dry air is used to sterilize oily medicines.

The word *sterilization* is also used to refer to surgical procedures that prevent a female from becoming pregnant or a male from fathering a child. For information on such surgical sterilizations, see BIRTH CONTROL (Methods of Birth Control). GEORGE L. BUSH

See also DISINFECTANT; FOOD PRESERVATION (Canning); PASTEURIZATION.

STERLET. See STURGEON.

STERLING. See POUND.

STERLING SILVER. See SILVER (Uses of Silver).

STERN. See SHIP (table: Nautical Terms).

STERN, ISAAC (1920-), is an American violinist known for his fine artistry. He made his debut with the San Francisco Symphony Orchestra when he was 11 years old. Later, he appeared with the Los Angeles Philharmonic Orchestra and toured the Pacific Coast in a concert series. Stern made his New York City debut in Town Hall in 1937 and played at Carnegie Hall in 1943. He was born in Kreminiecz, Poland (now Kremenets in the Ukraine), and was brought to the United States when he was a year old. DOROTHY DeLAY

STERN, OTTO. See NOBEL PRIZES (table: Nobel Prizes for Physics—1943).

STERNE, LAURENCE (1713-1768), was an English clergyman who suddenly became famous as the author of *The Life and Opinions of Tristram Shandy, Gentleman* (1760-1767).

Tristram Shandy is an unconventional novel of conversations and reminiscences rather than action. Tristram is only about five years old when the story ends. This is partly because the work was never finished, but mainly because Sterne was more interested in other characters —Tristram's family, their friends and servants. The book is lively and extremely witty. Its popularity reflects the growing regard for humor and laughter and for feeling and sentiment during that period. Tristram's Uncle Toby, the simple and good-hearted soldier, climaxed a long line of lovable but comic eccentrics in the literature of the 1700's.

The novel's conversations and incidents do not follow the usual time sequence. Sterne was influenced by the philosopher John Locke. Locke thought that at birth the mind is a blank tablet upon which ideas take form only through the association of experiences gained through our senses. Locke observed that we may sometimes associate ideas that are logically unrelated. These erroneous chains of ideas form the basis of the narrative development in *Tristram Shandy.* Although readers may at first be confused by the way Sterne jumps from one idea to another, the book eventually may seem closer to our own experience of life than more conventional novels. Its method anticipates the stream-of-consciousness novels of James Joyce and Virginia Woolf.

Sterne was born in Clonmel, Ireland. He suffered from tuberculosis and made trips to the milder climate of southern France for his health. These trips inspired *A Sentimental Journey Through France and Italy* (1768). This is an unconventional travel book that tells more about Sterne's love affairs and passing reflections than about the places he visited. IAN WATT

STERNUM. See SKELETON.

STEROID, *STEHR oyd,* is a class of chemical compounds that are important in chemistry, biology, and medicine. They play a very important part in the body processes of living things. Steroids are produced naturally by plants and animals. They are also made commercially. Steroids include sterols, such as cholesterol; bile acids from the liver; adrenal hormones; sex hormones; and poisons in certain toads (see CHOLESTEROL; LIVER).

All steroids are alike in basic chemical structure. But each steroid has a slightly different arrangement of molecules. Because of this difference, steroids have different effects on living things. Also, individual organisms may react differently to the same steroid.

Steroids influence body *metabolism,* the process by which the body changes food into energy and living tissue. In plants, they help form certain vitamins and other important substances. Some steroids are used in medicine to treat diseases. *Digitalis,* a plant steroid, is often used to treat heart failure (see DIGITALIS).

The Sex Steroids include the *estrogens* and *progesterone,* which are given off by the *ovaries* (female sex organs). These steroids are responsible for the female's smooth, soft skin; high-pitched voice; rounded hips; and the development of the breasts. *Contraceptive pills* (pills that help prevent pregnancy) contain powerful synthetic forms of progesterone. Some also contain estrogens (see BIRTH CONTROL).

Androgens are sex steroids that are produced by the

testicles (male sex glands). Androgens are responsible for the male's beard, large muscles, and deep voice. They may even influence personality traits such as aggressiveness, which is considered a male characteristic.

The Adrenal Steroids are present in both sexes. They are produced by the *cortex* (outer layer) of the adrenal gland and are often referred to as *corticosteroids*. There are two main types of corticosteroids—*glucocorticoids* and *mineralocorticoids*. The glucocorticoids, which include *cortisol*, *corticosterone*, and *cortisone*, help regulate protein and carbohydrate metabolism. The mineralocorticoids, chiefly *aldosterone*, influence the mineral and water balance of the body. The glucocorticoids and mineralocorticoids are essential to life. The adrenal cortex also secretes small amounts of the sex hormones, particularly the androgens.

Corticosteroids are extremely effective at reducing inflammation. Doctors use synthetic corticosteroids to treat arthritis, skin diseases, allergies, and many other disorders. Corticosteroids also are prescribed to patients whose adrenal glands have failed. See CORTISONE.

Secretion of Steroids from the ovaries, testes, and adrenal glands is regulated by a small part of the brain called the *hypothalamus*. The hypothalamus controls the release of powerful protein hormones, the *gonadotropins* and *adrenocorticotropic hormone* (ACTH), from the pituitary gland. These hormones cause the ovaries, testes, and adrenal glands to release steroids. The steroids from these organs then affect other body parts and characteristics. GORDON FARRELL

See also HORMONE.

STEROL. See VITAMIN (Vitamin D).

STETHOSCOPE, *STEHTH uh skohp,* is a device physicians use to hear the sounds produced by certain organs of the body, such as the heart, lungs, intestines, veins, and arteries. The stethoscope picks up the sounds made by these organs and excludes other sounds.

The stethoscope consists of a body contact piece, which is placed against the body of the patient, and earpieces, which are placed in the ears of the physician. Hollow rubber tubing connects the body contact piece to the earpieces. Physicians use either a bell, diaphragm, or combination bell-diaphragm body contact piece. The bell type of contact piece picks up low-pitched sounds. The diaphragm type of contact piece picks up high-pitched sounds.

Before the invention of the stethoscope, the physician placed an ear next to the patient's body to hear the sounds made by the organs. René Laënnec, a French physician, made the first stethoscope from a hollow wooden tube in 1816. E. CLINTON TEXTER, JR.

See also LAËNNEC, RENÉ T. H.

STETSON, JOHN BATTERSON (1830-1906), was an American hat manufacturer and philanthropist. He went West in the early 1860's to regain his health, and used his knowledge of Western tastes and hatmaking to design his famous ten-gallon hat. He established a factory in Philadelphia in 1865, and became the leading hat manufacturer in America. Though he had no formal education, Stetson endowed a small academy in De Land, Fla., which later became Stetson University. He was born in Orange, N.J. JOHN B. McFERRIN

STETTIN. See SZCZECIN.

STETTINIUS, *stuh TIHN ee uhs,* **EDWARD RILEY, JR.** (1900-1949), was secretary of state under Presidents

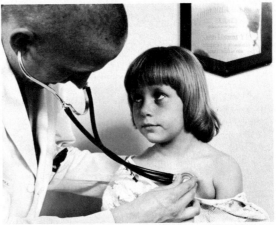

WORLD BOOK photo

A Stethoscope allows a physician to hear various sounds made by the heart, the lungs, and certain other organs.

Franklin Delano Roosevelt and Harry S. Truman. When the national defense program was set up in 1940, Stettinius held key posts. From 1941 to 1943, he was the lend-lease administrator (see LEND-LEASE). As secretary of state in 1944 and 1945, he joined President Roosevelt at the Yalta Conference. He led the U.S. delegation to the 1945 San Francisco Conference, which organized the United Nations. He became rector of the University of Virginia in 1946.

Stettinius was born in Chicago, and attended the University of Virginia. He became vice president of the General Motors Corporation in 1931. In 1938, he took the post of chairman of the board of the United States Steel Corporation. HARVEY WISH

STEUBEN, *STOO buhn* or *SHTOY buhn,* **BARON VON** (1730-1794), FRIEDRICH WILHELM LUDWIG GERHARD AUGUSTIN, was a German soldier who helped the American colonists against England during the Revolutionary War. He sailed to America in 1777. On Benjamin Franklin's recommendation, General George Washington sent him to Valley Forge to train the raw colonial troops. As a major general, Von Steuben led troops against the British at Monmouth and Yorktown. After the war, he became a United States citizen.

Von Steuben was born in Magdeburg, Germany. He joined the Prussian Army and later became aide-de-camp to King Frederick the Great. ROBERT G. L. WAITE

STEVENS was the family name of two American engineers, father and son, who helped to develop the steam engines.

John Cox Stevens (1749-1838) pioneered in developing steam transportation in the United States. His boat *Phoenix*, which operated on the Delaware River to Philadelphia in 1809, became the world's first seagoing steamboat. Stevens experimented in the use of steam engines on railways. A railway on his estate carried the first American-built steam locomotive. Stevens was born in New York City. ROBERT W. ABBETT

Robert Livingston Stevens (1787-1856) became a leader in steamship design and construction. Stevens invented protective devices and was among the first to use high-pressure steam engines in ships. For railroads, he invented the T-shaped rail and the hook-headed railroad spike.

Stevens was born in Hoboken, N.J. He first worked with his father, a rival of Robert Fulton in steamship construction. Robert Stevens also designed an armored ship used by the U.S. government.   ROBERT E. SCHOFIELD

STEVENS, ISAAC INGALLS. See WASHINGTON (Territorial Days).

STEVENS, JOHN PAUL (1920-   ), became an associate justice of the Supreme Court of the United States in 1975. President Gerald R. Ford chose him to replace Justice William O. Douglas, who retired. Stevens had previously served since 1970 as a judge of the U.S. Court of Appeals.

As an appeals judge, Stevens was considered to have moderate, rather than conservative or liberal, views. For example, he made many decisions that supported people's right to privacy from government interference. But he believed that, in some cases, evidence gathered against a person by government wiretaps could be used in court. Stevens also believed that the government should avoid regulating private business and the states as much as possible.

Stevens was born in Chicago. He graduated from the University of Chicago in 1941 and from the Northwestern University School of Law in 1947. Stevens practiced law in Chicago from 1948 until 1970, when he became an appeals judge.   CHARLES E. NICODEMUS, JR.

See also SUPREME COURT OF THE U.S. (picture).

STEVENS, THADDEUS (1792-1868), was an American statesman. He was one of the Republican leaders in Congress who favored harsh treatment for the South after the Civil War.

Stevens served his first two terms in the U.S. House of Representatives from 1849 to 1853. He opposed fugitive slave laws and other measures favorable to the South. He served in the House again from 1859 to 1868, and became one of its dominant figures. He urged emancipation of the slaves and confiscation of the planters' lands. He favored tariffs, banking laws, and railroad subsidies for Northern businesses. Stevens led the movement to impeach President Andrew Johnson.

Stevens was born in Danville, Vt., and graduated from Dartmouth College. He practiced law for many years in Pennsylvania, and championed public schools in the state legislature.   RICHARD N. CURRENT

Brown Bros.
Thaddeus Stevens

STEVENS, THEODORE FULTON (1923-   ), became Republican *whip* (assistant leader) of the United States Senate in 1977. He had served four years in the Alaska House of Representatives before being appointed to the Senate in 1968.

Stevens was born in Indianapolis. He moved with his family to Redondo Beach, Calif., when he was 15 years

old. Stevens left college in 1943, during World War II, to enlist in the Air Force and served until 1946. He then returned to the University of California at Los Angeles and graduated in 1947. He graduated from Harvard Law School in 1950. Stevens practiced law in Washington, D.C., and then in Fairbanks, Alaska, until 1953, when he became the U.S. Attorney for Alaska.

From 1956 to 1961, Stevens held several offices in the Department of the Interior. He then practiced law in Anchorage, Alaska, until 1964, when he won election to the Alaska House. In 1968, Governor Walter J. Hickel appointed Stevens to the United States Senate to succeed Edward L. Bartlett, who had died. In 1970, Stevens was elected to serve the remaining two years of Bartlett's term. He won reelection to a full six-year term in 1972 and was reelected in 1978.   WILLIAM J. EATON

STEVENS, WALLACE (1879-1955), was an American poet. He portrayed human beings as earthbound creatures without hope of an afterlife. As viewed by Stevens, people face at every turn the seeming indifference of nature, the certainty of their own death, and their sense of the moral and physical decay occurring around them. Human beings are rescued from this potentially tragic situation through the use of imagination. Imagination can give meaning to the confusion of reality. It can also discover beauty in indifferent nature and ease the thought of death by marveling at the feeling of being alive. Stevens explored the virtues of the imaginative life in such relatively simple poems as "Sunday Morning" and "The Emperor of Ice Cream," and in such longer, more complex works as "The Man with the Blue Guitar" and "Esthétique du Mal."

Stevens had a unique writing style. His meaning and many of his words are difficult to understand. But his poems are also characterized by an extraordinary richness of language.

Stevens was born in Reading, Pa. His career was unusual in that he turned out his poetry while also succeeding as a lawyer and insurance executive. He was little known as a poet during his lifetime, but became a major influence on other poets after his death. His poetic skills and his recognition of the moral responsibilities of poetry have been models to younger writers. His *Collected Poems* won the 1955 Pulitzer prize for poetry.   CLARK GRIFFITH

STEVENS DAM. See MUD MOUNTAIN DAM.

STEVENSON, ADLAI EWING (1835-1914), was Vice-President of the United States from 1893 to 1897 under President Grover Cleveland. He was the grandfather of Adlai E. Stevenson, the Democratic presidential nominee in 1952 and 1956. Stevenson was an inflationist in a sound-money administration. Largely for this reason, the public was never informed when Cleveland underwent an emergency operation during the business panic of 1893. His advisers feared the panic might increase if there seemed to be any possibility of Stevenson succeeding to the presidency.

Stevenson was nominated for the vice-presidency again in 1900 as the running mate of William Jennings Bryan. But the Democrats lost to William McKinley and Theodore Roosevelt. Stevenson also ran for governor of Illinois in 1908, but was defeated.

Stevenson served in a variety of appointive and elective offices. He was a member of the House of Representatives for two terms. As the first assistant post-

**Adlai E. Stevenson
(1835-1914)**

**Adlai E. Stevenson
(1900-1965)**

master general of the U.S. from 1885 to 1889, he angered Republicans because he shifted jobs to Democrats. He was born in Christian County, Kentucky, and attended Illinois Wesleyan University. IRVING G. WILLIAMS

STEVENSON, ADLAI EWING (1900-1965), was the Democratic nominee for President of the United States in 1952 and 1956. Dwight D. Eisenhower defeated him both times. Stevenson's running mates were John J. Sparkman in 1952 and Estes Kefauver in 1956. Stevenson served as U.S. ambassador to the United Nations from 1961 until his death.

Stevenson was a grandson of Vice-President Adlai E. Stevenson. He was born in Los Angeles, Calif., on Feb. 5, 1900. After graduating from Princeton University, he studied law at Harvard and Northwestern universities. He worked on his family newspaper, the *Bloomington* (Ill.) *Daily Pantagraph*, and practiced law in Chicago. In 1933 and 1934, Stevenson held his first public office, serving as special counsel to the Agricultural Adjustment Administration. Later, during World War II, he was a special assistant to Secretary of the Navy Frank Knox, and led a United States mission on occupation policies in Italy. After the war, he became an alternate delegate to the United Nations.

In 1948, Stevenson was elected governor of Illinois by the largest plurality in the state's history. He was considered by many for his party's 1952 presidential nomination, but he refused to campaign. Nevertheless, the party nominated him after a dramatic convention struggle. During his campaigns, he became noted for his wit, speaking ability, and the high literary quality of his speeches. In 1952, his book *Major Campaign Speeches* was published. He also wrote and published *Call to Greatness* (1954), *What I Think* (1956), *Friends and Enemies* (1959), *Putting First Things First* (1960), and *Looking Outward: Years of Crisis at the United Nations* (1963). His son Adlai III represented Illinois in the U.S. Senate from 1970 to 1981. ARTHUR SCHLESINGER, JR.

STEVENSON, ROBERT (1772-1850), was a Scottish civil engineer noted as a builder of lighthouses. He built 23 lighthouses along the coast of Great Britain, and invented the flashing light now used in lighthouses throughout the world (see LIGHTHOUSE [The Light]). His most noted work is the Bell Rock Lighthouse, which he designed and built with John Rennie. The poet Robert Southey immortalized Bell Rock in his "Inchcape Rock." The lighthouse stands in the North Sea 11 miles (18 kilometers) from Dundee, Scotland. Stevenson was born in Glasgow. The author Robert Louis Stevenson was his grandson. ROBERT W. ABBETT

STEVENSON, ROBERT LOUIS (1850-1894), was a Scottish novelist, essayist, and poet who became one of the world's most popular writers. His exciting adventure stories *Treasure Island* and *Kidnapped* have long appealed to both children and adults. His essays and travel books are considered models of sophisticated English prose style, while the tender, simple poems collected in *A Child's Garden of Verses* are masterpieces of children's literature.

Stevenson's life was as varied and fascinating as his work. He fought illness constantly, writing many of his best books from a sickbed. He traveled widely for his health and to learn about people. He spent his last years on the South Sea island of Samoa, and the Samoans honored him with the title *Tusitala* (Teller of Tales).

Stevenson's Life

Early Life. Stevenson was born on Nov. 13, 1850, in Edinburgh, Scotland. His full name was Robert Lewis Balfour Stevenson. He later adopted the name Robert Louis Stevenson. He was a sickly boy who suffered from a lung disease that later developed into tuberculosis. Young Stevenson loved the open air, the sea, and adventure, but he also loved to read. He preferred literature and history, especially Scottish history which supplied the background for many of his novels.

When he was 17, Stevenson entered Edinburgh University to study engineering, his father's profession. However, he soon gave up engineering for law. He passed his bar examination in 1875, but he did not enjoy law and never practiced it. His real love was writing.

Stevenson began publishing short stories and essays in the mid-1870's. His first book, *An Inland Voyage*, appeared in 1878. It relates his experiences during a canoeing trip through France and Belgium. In *Travels with a Donkey in the Cévennes* (1879), Stevenson describes a walking tour through part of France. Although both books reveal Stevenson's inexperience as a writer, they give signs of the graceful, charming essay style for which he was to become famous.

Marriage. In 1876, Stevenson met Mrs. Fanny Osbourne, a married American woman who was studying art in Paris. Although she was 11 years older than Stevenson and had a son and daughter, Stevenson fell in love with her. In 1879, he followed her to San Francisco in spite of the opposition of his parents. They were married in Oakland in 1880, after her divorce. The long journey from Europe to California severely affected Stevenson's frail health. To speed his recovery, he moved his family to a rough mining camp in the mountains near St. Helena, Calif. Stevenson described his experiences there in *The Silverado Squatters* (1883).

The Stevensons returned to Scotland in 1880. For the next seven years, they moved through Europe from one resort to another, hoping that a change of air would improve Stevenson's health. In 1887, Stevenson returned with his family to the United States, where he entered a sanitarium at Saranac Lake, N.Y.

The South Seas. For Stevenson, the sea had always been bracing. When his health improved, he boldly decided to sail a yacht to the South Seas. He left San Francisco with his wife, widowed mother, and stepson in June 1888, and for the next six years traveled through

Robert Louis Stevenson settled with his family near Apia on Upolu, one of the Samoan islands in the South Seas. There he built a large house which he called *Vailima*. This picture shows Stevenson seated next to his wife Fanny. His mother and stepson Lloyd Osbourne (standing) are shown on the author's right.

the South Sea islands. He came to know the life of the islanders better than any writer of his time.

Eventually, Stevenson decided to settle in the South Seas, the one place that seemed to promise some lasting improvement in his health. He bought some forest land near Apia, Samoa, and built a large house, which he called *Vailima* (Five Rivers). He became a planter and took an active part in island affairs. Stevenson's kindness, understanding, and tolerance gained the affection of the Samoans, who built a road to his house which they called *The Road of the Loving Heart*.

Tragedy clouded Stevenson's last years when his wife suffered a nervous breakdown. This misfortune moved him deeply, affecting his ability to complete his last books. Stevenson's life was beginning to brighten when his wife partially recovered, but he died suddenly of a stroke on Dec. 3, 1894. Local chiefs buried him on top of Mount Vaea, where his gravestone is inscribed with his own poem, "Requiem." Its concluding lines make a fitting epitaph for a gallant adventurer:

> Here he lies where he longed to be;
> Home is the sailor, home from the sea,
> And the hunter, home from the hill.

Stevenson's Writings

Novels. In 1881, Stevenson amused his stepson, Lloyd Osbourne, with a little tale about pirates and the buried treasure of Captain Kidd. It grew into *Treasure Island*, Stevenson's first and most famous novel. The story, first published in a boy's magazine, was revised for book publication in 1883. The boy hero Jim Hawkins, the two villains Long John Silver and blind Pew, and the hair-raising search for the buried treasure have become familiar to millions of readers.

With the publication of Stevenson's second major novel, *The Strange Case of Dr. Jekyll and Mr. Hyde* (1886), his reputation was assured. The story tells of a doctor who takes a drug that changes him into a new person, physically ugly and spiritually evil. As a psychological inquiry into the nature of the evil that exists in all peo-

ple, the novel brilliantly anticipates much modern psychological fiction and is one of the most fascinating horror stories ever written.

Stevenson also published *Kidnapped*, his best long novel, in 1886. Based on considerable historical research, it weaves an exciting fictional story around an actual Scottish murder committed in 1745. The novel displays Stevenson's matchless ability to create adult entertainment out of the materials of children's adventure stories. Because of its length, Stevenson ended *Kidnapped* before the plot was completed. He finally finished the story in 1893 with a sequel, *David Balfour* (published in England as *Catriona*).

The Master of Ballantrae (1889) is set against the background of Scotland's revolt against England in the 1740's. The novel tells a story of bitter hatred between two brothers. *The Master of Ballantrae* begins as a promising psychological study, but suffers from its melodramatic ending.

Stevenson's later novels, far different from his early light-hearted romances, are often bitter in tone. Less popular, they still have merit. The short novel *The Beach of Falesá* (1892), which Stevenson described as "the first realistic South Sea story," was called "art brought to a perfection" by novelist Henry James.

Stevenson wrote three other novels, in collaboration with Lloyd Osbourne—*The Wrong Box* (1889), *The Wrecker* (1892), and *The Ebb Tide* (1894). Stevenson also left two novels unfinished at his death. *St. Ives*, which was completed by Sir Arthur Quiller-Couch, describes the adventures of a French prisoner in Britain in 1813. *Weir of Hermiston*, a story of Scotland in the 1700's, promised to be Stevenson's finest novel.

Other Writings. Stevenson wrote many short stories, some of which were collected into *New Arabian Nights* (1882) and *More New Arabian Nights* (1885). Many of the stories are rich in imagination and fantasy, although the early ones are often written in an artificial style.

Stevenson's concern with prose style is most apparent in his essays, which are among the finest in the language. His observations on people and manners are marked by a delicate fancy. For charm and perceptiveness, they can be compared only to the essays of Charles Lamb and William Hazlitt. Stevenson's most memorable essays were collected in *Virginibus Puerisque and Other Papers* (1881), *Familiar Studies of Men and Books* (1882), and *Memories and Portraits* (1887).

Stevenson wrote several travel books later in his career. The *Amateur Emigrant* (1880, 1895) describes his voyages to the United States; *Across the Plains* (1892) tells of his trip from New York to San Francisco; *In the South Seas* (1890) contains his reflections on his Pacific voyages. All demonstrate Stevenson's extraordinary stylistic quality—the sudden word or phrase that lights a page with meaning.

Stevenson also composed some delightful letters, wrote several volumes of poetry, and collaborated with William Ernest Henley on some unsuccessful dramas. *A Child's Garden of Verses* (1885) reveals the world of a child's imagination with a deceptive simplicity that still appeals to readers young and old. His adult poetry, however, is almost totally ignored today, in spite of occasional pieces of considerable merit.

Stevenson's Place in Literature

Stevenson was both the most popular and the most successful among writers of the late 1800's who developed romance as a reaction to the literary movements of realism and naturalism. If his influence has declined today, it is not necessarily because modern writers are more skillful, but rather that Stevenson's optimistic view of life has become unfashionable.

Stevenson insisted that novels are to adults what play is to children, and that one of the legitimate and necessary functions of literature is to supply adventure for people who lead unexciting lives. A theory of fiction seemingly so limited and naïve might well have produced literary trifles. In fact, it resulted in art of such high quality that the disciplined Henry James once praised Stevenson as "the only man in England who can write a decent English sentence."

Stevenson's faults are obvious. His plots are a bit melodramatic, his pirates rather stagy, and, as he readily admitted, his heroines entirely unreal. But his sure handling of narrative pace, his strong sense of atmosphere, and above all his masterly command of style give his novels and stories enduring vitality. The reading public has never lost its admiration for Stevenson, and it appears likely that as long as there is a taste for romance written with artistry, he will continue to have an audience. Furthermore, there are signs that critics are re-evaluating his works, finding more fine shades of meaning in his writings than they had suspected.

Critically reviewed by FRANK W. WADSWORTH.

See also *Stevenson, Robert Louis*, in the RESEARCH GUIDE/INDEX, Volume 22, for a *Reading and Study Guide*.

Additional Resources

CALDER, JENNI. *Robert Louis Stevenson: A Life Study*. Oxford, 1980.

DAICHES, DAVID. *Robert Louis Stevenson and His World*. Scribner, 1977. Reprint of 1947 ed.

EIGNER, EDWIN. *Robert Louis Stevenson and the Romantic Tradition*. Princeton, 1966.

KIELY, ROBERT. *Robert Louis Stevenson and the Fiction of Adventure*. Harvard, 1964.

STEWARDESS. See FLIGHT ATTENDANT.

STEWART, JAMES (1908-   ), is a lanky American motion-picture actor who speaks with a distinctive drawl. Stewart has appeared in more than 70 movies. He is best known for his roles as an honest, middle-class American who courageously faces some kind of crisis.

Warner Bros.

James Stewart

Stewart won the 1940 Academy Award as best actor for his performance in the comedy *The Philadelphia Story*. His other comedies include *You Can't Take It With You* (1938) and *Harvey* (1950). Stewart played the hero in such Westerns as *Destry Rides Again* (1939), *Winchester '73* (1950), and *The Man Who Shot Liberty Valance* (1962). He played an idealistic young senator in *Mr. Smith Goes to Washington* (1939). He also starred in four suspense movies directed by Alfred Hitchcock—*Rope* (1948), *Rear Window* (1954), *The Man Who Knew Too Much* (1956), and *Vertigo* (1958).

James Maitland Stewart was born in Indiana, Pa. His first movie was *Murder Man* (1935).   ROGER EBERT

STEWART, POTTER (1915-   ), served as an associate justice of the Supreme Court of the United States from 1958 to 1981. On the court, Stewart could not be labeled as either a conservative or a liberal. He voted with the conservative justices on some cases and with the liberals on others. Stewart was born in Jackson, Mich. His father, James Garfield Stewart, became an Ohio supreme court judge. Potter Stewart attended Yale University, Yale University Law School, and Cambridge University. He practiced law in Cincinnati, and was elected to the Cincinnati city council in 1949. He served as a judge of the federal court of appeals from 1954 to 1958.   MERLO J. PUSEY

STEWART, ROBERT. See CASTLEREAGH, VISCOUNT.

STIBNITE. See ANTIMONY; MINERAL (color picture).

STICKLEBACK, *STIK'l BACK*, is a name given to a family of small fishes of the Northern Hemisphere. They are called sticklebacks because some of their fins are made of strong, sharp, separated spines. Instead of having scales, the body is usually covered by hard plates. There are both fresh-water and ocean sticklebacks. The fresh-water ones reach a length of 1 to 3 inches (2.5 to 7.6 centimeters). The ocean sticklebacks grow to be not more than 7 inches (18 centimeters) long. The *brook stickleback* is common in the interior parts of Canada and in the Great Lakes states. These fish, like other sticklebacks, build muff-shaped nests of sticks and roots for receiving the spawn. The male carefully guards the spawn. He also watches over the young for several days after the eggs are hatched. Sticklebacks eat the young of other fish. See also INSTINCT.

Scientific Classification. Sticklebacks make up the stickleback family, *Gasterosteidae*. The three-spined, or *common*, stickleback is classified as genus *Gasterosteus*, species *G. aculeatus*. The brook stickleback is classified as genus *Eucalia*, species *E. inconstans*.   CARL L. HUBBS

STICKSEED

STICKSEED is a weedy plant that grows wild in dry soils throughout most of North America. It is named stickseed because its small, nutlike fruit has barbed prickles that stick to clothing and to the fur or hair of animals. Stickseed has a slender hairy stem, grayish-green leaves, and small blue, lavender or white flowers.

Scientific Classification. Stickseed is in the borage family, *Boraginaceae*. Annual species are genus *Lappula*. Perennials and biennials are genus *Hackelia*. ARTHUR CRONQUIST

STIEGEL, *STEE gel*, **HENRY WILLIAM** (1729-1785), was an early American iron and glass manufacturer. Among his iron products were tin-plate wood stoves that were used widely for many years, and iron castings used by sugar planters and refiners in the West Indies.

In 1762 Stiegel and two associates established the town of Manheim, Pa. There he conducted experiments in glassmaking and soon produced his "Stiegel glass." Some experts regard "Stiegel glass" as the most beautiful glass ever blown, and collectors prize it highly (see GLASSWARE [Stiegel Glass]).

Stiegel was born near Cologne, Germany, and came to Philadelphia in 1750. He had a substantial fortune when he arrived, and he became a prominent landowner and ironmaker. He lived in great style and assumed the title of baron. His extravagant spending, coupled with disturbed economic conditions in the American colonies, brought financial disaster. He was imprisoned for debt in 1774. JOHN B. McFERRIN

See also ANTIQUE (picture: Glass Saltcellar); COLONIAL LIFE IN AMERICA (color picture: Stiegel Glass).

STIEGLITZ, *STEEG lihts*, **ALFRED** (1864-1946), was an American photographer who pioneered in photography as an art form. He also helped introduce and promote modern art in the United States.

During the 1880's and 1890's, Stieglitz became famous for *pictorial photographs*, which featured hazy, romantic scenes. He later produced sharply-focused, realistic photographs of everyday subjects.

In 1902, Stieglitz formed the Photo-Secession, a group of photographers who worked to develop photography as an expressive art. Stieglitz began publishing the magazine *Camera Work* in 1903. It included work by leading photographers, artists, and critics. In 1905, he established a gallery, known as "291," in New York City. It exhibited paintings, sculpture, and other works by leading modern artists of Europe and the United States. During his later years, Stieglitz opened other galleries.

Stieglitz was born in Hoboken, N.J. In 1924, he married the painter Georgia O'Keeffe, whom he often photographed. CHARLES HAGEN

See also PHOTOGRAPHY (History [picture: Expressive Portraits]); O'KEEFFE, GEORGIA.

STIGMA, in botany. See FLOWER (The Pistils; color diagram: Parts of a Flower).

STILETTO. See DAGGER.

STILL. See DISTILLATION.

STILL, ANDREW TAYLOR. See OSTEOPATHY (History).

STILL, CLYFFORD (1904-1980), an American painter, was a leading member of the abstract expressionist movement. He was known chiefly for his imaginative use of large expanses of color, a style called *color field painting*. His paintings contain large, vertical, jagged-edged, flamelike shapes. He combined thickly applied paint with bright, aggressive, sharply contrasting colors to create works that are dramatic and disturbing. The rough surfaces formed by the thick paint suggest rugged natural formations, such as canyons and crevices.

Still was born in Grandin, N. Dak. He used large areas of color in nearly all his works, including those of the 1930's and early 1940's. During that period, he created paintings of the landscape of the Western United States, especially the vast Western plateaus. During the late 1940's, he abandoned the use of recognizable subjects and developed the style associated with his work. GREGORY BATTCOCK

See also ABSTRACT EXPRESSIONISM.

STILLWATER, Minn. (pop. 12,290), is 18 miles (29 kilometers) northeast of St. Paul. It was one of the earliest settlements in the state. It was established in 1839. For many years Stillwater served as an important logging center for lumbering in the nearby pine forests. The city lies on the boundary between Minnesota and Wisconsin near the mouth of the St. Croix River, at a point where the river widens into a lake (see MINNESOTA [political map]). Stillwater is called the *Birthplace of Minnesota*. The convention that formed the territory of Minnesota met there in 1848. The city has a mayor-council form of government. HAROLD T. HAGG

STILT is a wading bird with long, slender legs. These slender legs make it look as if it walks on stilts. The stilts are related to the avocets, and live in both the Eastern and Western hemispheres. The *black-necked stilt*, the only American stilt, is about 15 inches (38 centimeters) long. The upper part of its body is black, and the under part is white. Its long legs are bright red. The stilt builds its nest by lining a low place in the ground

The Art Institute of Chicago,
the Alfred Stieglitz Collection

The Steerage is one of Alfred Stieglitz' best-known photographs. He took this picture of travelers on a ship to Europe in 1907 and considered it one of his best works.

S. A. Grimes

The Stilt Is a Wading Bird with Long, Slender Legs.

with grasses. The female stilt lays 3 or 4 eggs of an olive or buff color, thickly spotted with chocolate tones. The bird lives along shallow ponds in fresh and salt marshes. See also AVOCET.

Scientific Classification. The stilt belongs to the stilt and avocet family, *Recurvirostridae*. The black-necked stilt is genus *Himantopus*, species *H. mexicanus*. ALFRED M. BAILEY

STILWELL, JOSEPH WARREN (1883-1946), commanded all the United States forces in the China-Burma-India theater of war during World War II. He also served as chief of staff to Generalissimo Chiang Kai-shek, supreme commander of the Chinese theater, and was the first American general to command a Chinese army. Stilwell won the nickname of *Vinegar Joe* because of his forthright manner.

Stilwell was sent to Burma in 1942 to assist the Chinese and British troops defending Burma against Japan. When the Allied forces were defeated in Burma, Stilwell retreated to India. In India, he trained several Chinese divisions to recapture Burma and open a line of communication to China. With these forces and a small American force called "Merrill's Marauders," Stilwell opened a route to China late in 1944 (see MERRILL'S MARAUDERS). In June, 1945, Stilwell took command of the U.S. Tenth Army on Okinawa. After the war ended, he held an Army command in the United States.

Stilwell was born in Palatka, Fla. He was graduated from the United States Military Academy in 1904. He studied Chinese, and served as a military attaché in China from 1935 to 1939. MAURICE MATLOFF

STILWELL ROAD. See WORLD WAR II (The China-Burma-India Theater).

STIMSON, HENRY LEWIS (1867-1950), was an American statesman. As secretary of state under President Herbert Hoover, he opposed Japan's seizure of Manchuria in 1931 by a warning known as "The Stimson Doctrine." This stated that the United States would not recognize any changes made there in violation of treaties. Hoover refused to permit him to use an economic boycott against Japan. But, in 1940, as secretary of war under President Franklin D. Roosevelt,

Stimson successfully urged such a boycott. Japan refused to yield to any pressure and struck Pearl Harbor, opening war against the United States. Stimson served as secretary of war from 1940 to 1945 under Presidents Franklin D. Roosevelt and Harry S. Truman.

He was President William Taft's secretary of war from 1911 to 1913 and promoted "dollar diplomacy" to aid defense. Stimson acted as President Calvin Coolidge's mediator in Nicaragua in 1927. He was born in New York City. HARVEY WISH

STIMULANT is a drug that causes an increase in the activity of an organ of the body. The term usually refers to chemicals that excite or increase certain activities of the brain. Some stimulants, such as the amphetamines and caffeine, make a drowsy person more wakeful. They do so by stimulating the central nervous system (see NERVOUS SYSTEM [The Central Nervous System]). A period of depression may follow the stimulation that results from taking an amphetamine.

The body may react to a particular stimulant in different ways, depending on the dosage. For example, a small dose of strychnine, a poison, stimulates the central nervous system. But an overdose of strychnine may cause severe disturbance, convulsions, and death.

Coffee, tea, and some cola drinks contain caffeine. Tobacco contains a stimulant, nicotine. EDWARD F. DOMINO

See also ADRENALIN; AMPHETAMINE; CAFFEINE; DRUG ABUSE; NICOTINE.

STIMULUS. See REFLEX ACTION; PSYCHOLOGY (Behaviorism); LEARNING (How We Learn).

STING. See ANT (The Abdomen; Protection Against Enemies); BEE (Sting); MOSQUITO; SCORPION; WASP.

STING RAY, also called STINGAREE, is a ray, or flattish sea fish. Its long, flexible tail has one or two sharp spines on the back of the tail near the middle. These spines have teeth along their edges. At the base of these teeth are poisonous glands. When bathers disturb or step on the sting ray, it swings its tail upward. In this way, it causes a most painful wound that is nearly as dangerous as a poisonous snakebite. The fish live on sandy to muddy bottoms in all warm shallow parts of

Field Museum of Natural History

The Flat-Bodied Sting Ray, *above,* can inflict a serious wound with the strong, sharp spine on its whiplike tail.

STINKBUG

the ocean and in bays. In South America, small, fresh-water sting rays infest the rivers flowing into the Atlantic Ocean. These sting rays live as far as 2,000 miles (3,200 kilometers) above the mouth of the Amazon River. A sting ray that lives in the waters off Australia reaches a length of 14 feet (4 meters).

Scientific Classification. Sting rays belong to the family Dasyatidae. There are about 50 species. The common sting ray is *Dasyatis centrourus*.   LEONARD P. SCHULTZ

STINKBUG is one of a family of insects that can spray bad-smelling odors. They have scent glands near their hind legs or on their abdomens. When stink-bugs are frightened, they open the glands and spray out a bad odor. Many stinkbugs are brown or green, but some are brilliantly colored. The red and black *harlequin bug* damages cabbage.

USDA
Southern Green Stinkbug

Scientific Classification. Stinkbugs belong to the order Hemiptera. They are members of the stinkbug family, Pentatomidae. The harlequin bug is classified as genus *Murgantia*, species *M. histrionica*. LEWIS J. STANNARD, JR.

STIPULE. See LEAF (The Stipules).

STIRLING ENGINE is an experimental source of power that someday may be used in cars, boats, and other vehicles. It runs more efficiently and produces less air pollution than do most other engines.

A typical Stirling engine has a sealed cylinder that contains a gas—either helium or hydrogen. The gas goes through a cycle of pressure changes by means of a process of alternate heating and cooling. A device called the *regenerator* partially heats the gas at the beginning of the cycle. A heater outside the cylinder provides additional heat by burning a fuel, such as diesel oil, kerosene, or alcohol. At the end of the cycle, the regenerator cools the gas by absorbing its heat.

The gas expands and contracts as it goes through the cycle of pressure changes. In doing so, it causes a power piston to move back and forth inside the cylinder. A rod connects the power piston to a crankshaft that converts the piston's *reciprocating* (back-and-forth) motion to the rotary motion of the drive shaft. This action, in turn, causes a *displacer piston* to move back and forth and force the gas through the regenerator.

Robert Stirling, a Scottish minister, invented the Stirling engine in 1816. Stirling engines have never come into general use because they cost more to build than other types. During the 1960's and 1970's, scientists sought better engines, especially for cars, and conducted research on Stirling engines.   PHILLIP S. MYERS

STITCH. See SEWING (Kinds of Stitches).

STOAT. See ERMINE.

STOCK is a name given to three different garden flowers. The *Grecian stock* bears fragrant lilac or purple flowers which open at evening. This small, branching annual plant comes from southern Europe. Its pods have two noticeable horns on the end. The

Virginian stock is another annual with small white, red, or lilac-colored flowers. It has a short stalk and pods with no horns. The *Brampton*, or *common*, *stock* is about 2 feet (61 centimeters) high. It bears fragrant white, pink, red, purple, or yellow blossoms.

J. Horace McFarland
Stock Blossoms

Scientific Classification. The stocks belong to the mustard family, *Cruciferae.* Grecian stock is genus *Matthiola*, species *M. bicornis.* Brampton stock is *M. incana*. Virginian stock is *Malcolmia maritima.*   DONALD WYMAN

STOCK, CAPITAL, is a right of ownership in a corporation. The stock is divided into a certain number of *shares*, and the corporation issues stockholders one or more *stock certificates* to show how many shares they hold. The stockholders own the company and elect a board of directors to manage it for them.

Stockholders may sell their stock whenever they want to, unless the corporation has some special rule to

How a Stirling Engine Works

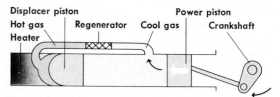

Displacer piston | Power piston
Hot gas | Regenerator | Cool gas | Crankshaft
Heater

A cycle of a Stirling engine begins when the power piston moves toward the displacer piston. This action causes the cool gas between the two pistons to start flowing up to the regenerator.

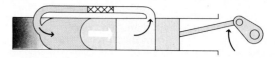

The displacer piston moves toward the power piston, forcing the cool gas through the regenerator to be heated. The heated gas then flows into the space behind the displacer piston.

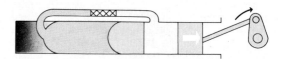

The heater outside the cylinder supplies additional heat to make the gas expand. The expanding gas causes both the displacer piston and the power piston to move in a *power stroke.*

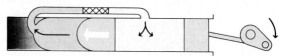

WORLD BOOK diagrams by Arthur Grebetz
The displacer piston returns to its original position, forcing the gas to flow back through the regenerator, which absorbs its heat. The cooled gas then re-enters the space between the pistons.

prevent it. Prices of stock change according to general business conditions and the earnings and future prospects of the company. If the business is doing well, stockholders may be able to sell their stock for a profit. If it is not, they may have to take a loss.

Large corporations may have many thousands of stockholders. Their stock is bought and sold in market places called *stock exchanges*. When a sale is made, the seller signs the certificate. The buyer turns this over to the corporation and gets a new certificate.

When the corporation has made a profit, the directors may divide the profit among the stockholders as *dividends*, or they may decide to use it to expand the business. Dividends may be paid only out of the corporation's profits. When profits are used to expand the business, the directors and stockholders may decide to issue more stock to show that there is more money invested in the business. This new stock will be divided among the stockholders as a *stock dividend*.

Kinds of Stock. The Articles of Incorporation—papers signed when the corporation is formed—may specify the different kinds of stock. *Par stock* must be issued for not less than a set price, called the *par value*, for each share. If the articles provide for *no-par* stock, the directors determine the issuing price of the stock and may change it whenever they wish.

All shares of stock have equal dividend and voting rights unless the articles provide differently. There may be different classes of stock, such as *voting* and *non-voting*. Many articles provide for *common* and *preferred* stock. Preferred stock is entitled to a preference on dividends. That is, the directors must pay a certain amount—usually a percentage of par value—to the holders of preferred stock before they pay anything to the holders of common stock. If the preferred-stock holders share with the common-stock holders in dividends beyond the specified percentage, the stock is called *participating preferred*.

Preferred stock may also be *cumulative*. That is, if there are no dividends given in a year, the preferred-stock holders must be given double their dividend the next year. This is paid before anything is paid to the common-stock holders. It will continue to multiply for as many years as dividends are not paid.

When a corporation goes out of business, it divides its property among the stockholders. This process is called *liquidation*. When a company liquidates, the preferred-stock holders may be given the par value of their stock before the common-stock holders are given anything. This preferred stock is said to be *preferred up to par on liquidation*.   ROBERT E. RODES, JR.

See also the articles INVESTMENT and STOCK EXCHANGE, with their lists of Related Articles.

STOCK CAR. See AUTOMOBILE RACING.

STOCK EXCHANGE is a market place where member *brokers* (agents) buy and sell stocks and bonds of American and foreign businesses on behalf of the public. A stock exchange provides a market place for stocks and bonds in the same way a commodity exchange does for commodities. The stockbrokers receive a small commission on each transaction they make.

How a Stock Exchange Operates

Federal and state laws regulate the issuance, listing, and trading of most securities. The Securities and Ex-

change Commission (SEC) administers the federal laws.

Listing Stocks. Stocks handled by one or more stock exchanges are called *listed stocks*. A company that wants to have its stock listed for trading on an exchange must first satisfy the exchange that it has enough paid-up capital, is a lawful enterprise, and is in good financial condition. Specific listing requirements vary among exchanges. On the New York Stock Exchange a corporation must have 2,000 stockholders who together hold at least 1 million shares, as well as a yearly earning power under competitive conditions of over $2\frac{1}{2}$ million before taxes. Major exchanges suspend trading in certain stocks which no longer meet minimum requirements.

Unlisted securities are sold in *over-the-counter* trading. Most bonds are sold this way. Many unlisted industrial securities are more speculative than listed ones. They are usually not traded on any exchange.

All stocks *fluctuate* (change) in value. Unforeseen circumstances may have lessened the earning power of a company and thus lowered the price that people are willing to pay for shares. Prosperous times or better management may increase values.

Trading. A person who wishes to buy stock places an order with a brokerage house. The broker gets a *quotation* (price) by telephone or telegraph, and relays the order to the firm's partner on the floor of the exchange. The partner negotiates the sale, and notifies the brokerage house. The transaction may take only a few minutes. It is recorded on tape, and sent by *stock ticker* to brokerage firms over a nationwide network.

Each year, investors trade billions of shares worth hundreds of billions of dollars. In the early 1970's, about 2,000 stocks were listed on the New York Stock Exchange. Stock prices often reflect the state of the economy. If business conditions are good, stock prices tend to rise, creating a *bull market*. If conditions are poor, stock prices drop, causing a *bear market*.

New York Stock Exchange

The New York Stock Exchange on Wall Street is often called the *nation's market place*.

STOCK MARKET CRASH

Memberships in exchanges are worth substantial sums of money because only a limited number are available. Each new member must meet a number of requirements and be formally recommended and approved by the exchange's Board of Governors before he or she can buy a *seat* (membership) and operate on the stock exchange. Seat owners generally hold their places personally. The majority of them are partners or voting stockholders in brokerage firms or corporations which are known as *member organizations*. Many firms have more than one member on the Exchange.

Some exchange members, called *specialists*, concentrate on a limited group of securities assigned by the exchange. They also act as agents for other brokers. Others are *odd-lot dealers*, who transact amounts less than the regular trading unit, such as 1 to 99 shares for 100-share units. *Floor brokers*, or "$2 brokers," are unaffiliated with exchange firms, and assist *commission house* (member firm) brokers with their firm orders.

The value of memberships depends largely on current business conditions, the volume of transactions, and the market level of securities. The New York Stock Exchange has 1,366 members and 558 member organizations with about 3,780 offices throughout the nation. The price on this exchange has varied from $17,000 in 1942, during a business recession, to a high of $625,000 in 1929. Memberships on other exchanges may be worth from $1,500 to more than $275,000.

History

The first European stock exchange was established in Antwerp, Belgium, in 1531. The first stock exchange in England was formed in 1773 by the brokers of London. Until that time, people who wished to buy or sell shares of stock had to find a broker to transact their business. In London, these people usually went to a coffeehouse, because brokers often gathered there.

In New York City, brokers met under an old buttonwood tree on Wall Street. They organized the New York Stock Exchange in 1792. The American Stock Exchange, one of the largest in the United States, was formerly called the Curb Exchange because of its origin on the streets of New York City. Other major exchanges operate in Baltimore, Boston, Chicago, Cincinnati, Detroit, Honolulu, Los Angeles, Philadelphia, Pittsburgh, Salt Lake City, San Francisco, and Washington, D.C. Abroad, major stock exchanges are located in Amsterdam, The Netherlands; Brussels, Belgium; Buenos Aires, Argentina; Johannesburg, South Africa; London; Melbourne and Sydney, Australia; Mexico City, Mexico; Milan, Italy; Paris; Rio de Janeiro; Tokyo; and Montreal and Toronto, Canada.   G. KEITH FUNSTON

Related Articles in WORLD BOOK include:

Bears and Bulls	Mutual Fund
Blue-Sky Laws	Philadelphia (Finance)
Bond	Securities and Exchange
Commodity Exchange	Commission
Cornering the Market	Stock, Capital
Dow Jones Averages	Stock Ticker
Investment Banking	Tokyo (picture)
Margin	Wall Street

STOCK MARKET CRASH. See GREAT DEPRESSION (The Stock Market Crash).

710

STOCK TICKER is a teletype machine that records purchases and sales of stock. The machine prints up to 900 characters per minute on a *ticker tape*, a paper tape that is 1 inch (2.5 centimeters) wide. The record of each stock transaction begins with a *stock symbol*. This symbol consists of one or more letters that represent the name of the corporation issuing the stock. The transaction record also includes the number of shares involved and the price at which they were bought or sold.

The New York Stock Exchange introduced stock tickers in 1867. By the early 1900's, about 6,000 tickers were in use in brokerage firms throughout the United States. Since then, most tickers have been replaced by electronic *ticker display devices*, which present stock information on a screen. Today, there are only a few hundred stock tickers in the country, compared with more than 16,000 ticker display devices.

Stockbrokers throughout the United States relay orders to a stock exchange by telephone, teletype, or some other electronic device. At the exchange, another broker buys or sells the stock. An exchange reporter puts the details of the transaction on a computer card, which is placed in one of several electronic *card readers* located on the trading floor. The card reader transmits the data to computers, which convert the information into telegraph signals. A vast telecommunications network carries these signals to tickers and ticker display devices across the country.   CARL L. BOLTON

See also EDISON, THOMAS A. (Early Inventions; picture).

STOCKADE. See PIONEER LIFE IN AMERICA (Indian Attacks).

STOCKHAUSEN, *SHTOHK how zehn,* **KARLHEINZ** (1928-), a German composer, has been a leading force in the development of modern music since the early 1950's. Stockhausen creates music from unusual sounds. His compositions use synthetic electronic sounds and such natural noises as finger snapping, foot scraping, radio static, speech, and street sounds. He sometimes distorts these everyday sounds electronically.

Stockhausen has also experimented with *chance music*, in which the performer determines the order in which the sections of a composition are played. He has scattered the performers throughout a concert hall to produce a live stereo effect called *music in space*.

Experimental works by Stockhausen include *Kontakte* (1960), for electronic sounds, piano, and percussion; and *Spiral* (1968), for a soloist using a short-wave radio receiver. Stockhausen was born in Mödrath, Germany, near Cologne.   JOSEPH BLOCH

See also ELECTRONIC MUSIC.

STOCKHOLDER. See STOCK, CAPITAL.

STOCKHOLM (pop. 658,435; met. area pop. 1,374,-922), is the capital and largest city of Sweden. Stockholm is the heart of Swedish commercial and cultural life, and it serves as an important center for international trade and communications. The city lies on the east coast of Sweden, between Lake Mälaren and the Baltic Sea. For location, see SWEDEN (political map).

The City is built on 14 islands that are connected by about 50 bridges. Careful city planning, and a magnificent natural setting among heavily wooded hills, have made Stockholm one of the world's most beautiful cities. The contrasts of land and water and of old and new architecture add to its charm.

Stockholm covers 14 islands, which are connected by about 50 bridges. The small island of Riddarholmen, *foreground*, is one of the oldest parts of the city. The Riddarholm Church, *right*, dates from the late 1200's and houses the tombs of many Swedish monarchs.

The heart of Stockholm is Gamla Stan (Old Town). This old section is the site of the huge Royal Palace, which dates from the 1700's. Sweden's Parliament building stands north of Gamla Stan in the modern main business and shopping district. Most Stockholmers live in large, modern apartment buildings, many of which are in planned suburban developments.

Stockholm is the home of the University of Stockholm and of Sweden's Royal Ballet, Library, Opera, and Theater. It also has many art galleries and museums. Skansen, a popular park, features an amusement park, a zoo, and an open-air museum.

Thousands of islands of various sizes in the sea east of Stockholm form an archipelago. The islands have many cabins and tiny settlements. Large numbers of people visit the islands the year around for recreation and relaxation.

Economy. Stockholm is the economic center of Sweden. Most of the city's workers have service occupations, and more than a third are employed by the national or local government. Trade and manufacturing also employ many Stockholmers. The city's chief industries include publishing and the manufacture of chemicals, clothing, machinery, metal products, and rubber products. Stockholm is a leading Swedish port and the hub of the nation's air, highway, and railroad travel. Public buses and a subway system serve the city and its suburbs.

History. Stockholm probably was founded in the early 1250's by a Swedish leader named Birger Jarl. He built a castle in the area that is now Gamla Stan. Stockholm grew as a trade center, and the city became the capital of Sweden in 1523.

Through the years, Stockholm expanded and prospered. Like other cities, it developed such problems as congestion and urban decay. But a long tradition of sensible city planning has helped Stockholm deal with many of its problems. For example, the city's population grew rapidly after World War II ended in 1945. During the 1950's and 1960's, residential suburbs were built on land purchased by the city as long ago as 1904. Since the mid-1900's, entire sections of Stockholm have been rebuilt to provide new housing and to replace run-down buildings with new ones. THOMAS J. ANTON

See also SWEDEN (Climate; pictures).

STOCKINGS are articles of clothing that fit snugly over the feet and part or all of the legs. Two forms of stockings, pantyhose and tights, cover the feet and legs and reach to the waist. People wear stockings chiefly for comfort, warmth, and decoration and to protect their shoes from perspiration and foot odor.

How Stockings Are Made. Most pantyhose and women's stockings are *sheer* (transparent). Most tights, men's hose, and children's stockings and some women's stockings are *opaque* (nontransparent). Nearly all sheer stockings are made of some kind of nylon yarn. Almost all opaque stockings are made from cotton, wool, or manufactured fibers, such as nylon, olefin, and acrylic and polyester fibers. Support and surgical hosiery are made of rubber, spandex, and other elastic materials.

There are two basic methods used to make hosiery. Most seamless stockings are made on a *circular machine* that knits each stocking into a tubelike shape. The toe is then closed by hand or machine. Stockings with a seam, called *full-fashioned* hose, are made on a *flat-bed machine*. This machine knits a flat piece of fabric, varying the stitches to shape the leg and foot. Another machine sews the edges together to form a seam.

History. As early as the 400's B.C., people in ancient Greece and some other lands occasionally wore socklike foot coverings for warmth. The stockings were made of fabric and worn inside shoes. During the A.D. 400's, clergymen in western Europe began to wear long, tight stockings as a symbol of purity. By the 1000's, noblemen had also adopted this style of stocking.

Most stockings were made of woven cloth until the 1500's, when wealthy people began to wear hosiery produced by professional hand-knitters. In 1589, William Lee, an English minister, invented a machine that knitted full-fashioned stockings. By the late 1600's, many people wore machine-knitted hose. Manufacturers made most stockings of cotton, silk, or wool until the development of nylon in 1938. JANE SADDLER

See also CLOTHING (Clothing Through the Ages).

STOCKS. See Stock, Capital; Stock Exchange; Investment.

STOCKS are an old device used for punishment. Stocks are a wooden framework with holes for the legs of the victim, and sometimes also for the arms. Persons were placed in the stocks for minor offenses, such as drunkenness, for periods of a few hours to several days. Stocks were commonly used for punishment in American colonial days. In the North, women charged with being "common scolds" were sometimes punished in the stocks. In the South, disobedient slaves were placed in the stocks. Stocks were used until the early 1800's. See also Pillory (with picture). Marvin E. Wolfgang

STOCKTON, Calif. (pop. 149,779; met. area pop. 347,342), is an inland seaport. It lies 78 miles (126 kilometers) east of the Golden Gate of San Francisco Bay (see California [political map]). It was named by its founder, Captain Charles M. Weber, in honor of Commodore Robert Stockton of the U.S. Navy. The channel connecting San Francisco and Stockton is deep enough to accommodate the largest vessels of the American Merchant Marine. Shipments from the port include farm products of the surrounding valley, paper, cedar lumber, and farm machinery. Stockton was chartered as a city in 1850. It is the home of the University of the Pacific, founded in 1851. The city has a council-manager form of government. George Shaftel

STOCKTON, FRANK RICHARD (1834-1902), an American author, wrote humorous, fanciful tales. He first became known for his short fairy stories for children. Stockton's first collection of fairy tales, *Ting-a-Ling*, appeared in 1870. Some of his stories were published in the *St. Nicholas* magazine, which he helped edit from 1873 to 1881. His other collections of stories include *The Floating Prince and Other Fairy Tales* (1881) and *The Bee Man of Orn and Other Fanciful Tales* (1887).

Stockton published his first book for adults, *Rudder Grange*, in 1879. It is a novel of the fantastic adventures of a young couple living in a houseboat. He established his reputation when his best-known short story, "The Lady, or the Tiger?" appeared in 1882. This story, which is famous for its unusual ending, has been translated into many languages. It was followed in 1886 by *The Casting Away of Mrs. Lecks and Mrs. Aleshine*. Stockton was born in Philadelphia. Jean Thomson

STOCKTON, RICHARD (1730-1781), was a New Jersey signer of the Declaration of Independence. He served in the Continental Congress in 1776 and, in the same year, became chief justice of the New Jersey Supreme Court. The British captured Stockton in 1776, and he suffered harsh treatment while imprisoned in New York. Stockton was born in Princeton. New Jersey has placed a statue of him in the U.S. Capitol in Washington, D.C. Clarence L. Ver Steeg

STOCKYARDS. See Meat Packing (Marketing).

STODDARD, WILLIAM OSBORN (1835-1925), was an American author, journalist, and inventor. He was among the first to write that Abraham Lincoln should be elected President of the United States. He served as one of Lincoln's private secretaries from 1861 to 1864. He was United States marshal in Arkansas from 1864 to 1866. Stoddard patented nine inventions and wrote 76 books, including five on Lincoln, 10 on other United

States Presidents, and many novels for boys. He was born in Homer, N.Y. William H. Gilman

STODDERT, BENJAMIN (1751-1813), America's first secretary of the navy, built the Navy up to some 50 vessels and 6,000 seamen. He pushed the purchase of navy yard sites and began basic construction of shore facilities at Portsmouth, N.H.; Charlestown, Mass.; Brooklyn, N.Y.; Philadelphia, Pa.; and Gosport, Va. He served from 1798 to 1801. Stoddert, born in Charles County, Maryland, was a merchant shipper. He served in the Revolutionary War. Richard S. West, Jr.

STOIC PHILOSOPHY flourished from about 300 B.C. to A.D. 300. It began in Greece and then spread to Rome. The Stoic philosophers believed that all people have within themselves reason, which relates each person to all other people and to the Reason (God) that governs the universe. This belief provided a theoretical basis for *cosmopolitanism*—the idea that people are citizens of the world rather than of a single nation or area. This view also stimulated the belief in a natural law that stands above civil law and provides a standard by which human beings' laws may be judged. The Stoics felt that people achieve their greatest good—which is happiness—by following reason, freeing themselves from passions, and concentrating only on things they can control.

The Stoic philosophers had their greatest influence on law, ethics, and political theory, but they also formulated important views on logic, the theory of knowledge, and natural philosophy. Zeno is considered the founder of Stoic philosophy. The early Stoics, particularly Chrysippus, were interested in logic and natural philosophy as well as ethics. The later Stoics, especially Seneca, Marcus Aurelius, and Epictetus, emphasized ethics. Josiah B. Gould

See also Zeno; Epictetus; Marcus Aurelius; Seneca, Lucius Annaeus.

STOKE-ON-TRENT (pop. 249,838), the pottery center of England, lies on the Trent River about 35 miles (56 kilometers) south of Manchester (see Great Britain [political map]). Josiah Wedgwood introduced fine chinaware near Stoke in the 1700's, and potteries still form the main industry for the area. Wedgwood, Spode, and Staffordshire ware all come from the city and nearby towns. This district is the setting for Arnold Bennett's novels of the "Five Towns." Francis H. Herrick

STOKER, BRAM (1847-1912), a British author, wrote *Dracula* (1897), one of the most famous horror stories of all time. Count Dracula, the book's main character, is a nobleman who is really a *vampire* (blood-sucking killer). He lives in Transylvania (now part of Romania), and is several hundred years old. At night, he changes into a huge bat, and flies about the countryside drawing blood from the necks of sleeping victims. Dracula moves to England and terrorizes the people there. He is finally killed by a stake driven through his heart. *Dracula's Guest*, a continuation of *Dracula*, was not published until 1937. Stoker's other books include *The Mystery of the Sea* (1902) and *Famous Imposters* (1910).

Stoker was born in Dublin, Ireland. He was manager for actor Sir Henry Irving, and wrote *Personal Reminiscences of Henry Irving* (1906). James Douglas Merritt

See also Dracula.

STOKES, CARL BURTON (1927-), served as mayor of Cleveland from 1967 to 1971. Stokes was the first black to be elected to head a major American city.

Stokes was born in Cleveland. His family was poor, and Stokes left high school at age 17 to go to work. He served in the Army from 1944 to 1946. After leaving the Army, he finished high school and worked his way through college. He graduated from the University of Minnesota and from Cleveland-Marshall Law School. He became a lawyer in 1957.

Stokes was elected to the Ohio House of Representatives in 1962. He was reelected twice. In 1965, he ran for mayor of Cleveland as an independent, but lost. In 1967, he ran as a Democrat and defeated Republican Seth C. Taft, a grandson of President William Howard Taft. He was reelected to a second two-year term in 1969.

EDGAR ALLAN TOPPIN

STOKOWSKI, *stuh KOW skee,* **LEOPOLD** (1882-1977), was a famous orchestra conductor. During his long and influential career, he extended the range of music played by symphony orchestras. He worked with engineers to improve the quality of recorded sound and sought new ways to bring music to larger audiences.

Houston Symphony Society
Leopold Stokowski

Stokowski was born in London. He was educated at Oxford University and at the Royal College of Music, where he learned to play several instruments. Stokowski moved to the United States in 1905 and became organist and choirmaster at St. Bartholomew's Church in New York City. In 1909, he became conductor of the Cincinnati Symphony Orchestra. From 1912 to 1938, he served as chief conductor of the Philadelphia Orchestra, sharing the last two seasons with Eugene Ormandy. After leaving the Philadelphia Orchestra, Stokowski appeared as guest conductor with orchestras in many countries. In 1962, he founded the American Symphony Orchestra of New York City.

ROBERT C. MARSH

STOL. See V/STOL.

STOLA. See TOGA.

STOMACH is an enlarged part of the alimentary canal. It lies between the *esophagus* and the small *intestine* (see ESOPHAGUS; INTESTINE). In people and most animals, it is a simple baglike organ. In cows, sheep, and other *ruminants* (animals that chew their cud), the stomach has four compartments and is more complicated than a human stomach (see RUMINANT).

A human being's stomach is shaped much like a *J*. In most persons, it is located in the upper left side of the abdomen. But the position can vary. The upper end of the stomach connects with the esophagus. The lower end opens into the *duodenum*, the upper end of the small intestine. The stomach is a muscular organ. This allows it to churn and mix its contents and fit its shape to the amount of food it holds. The average adult stomach can hold a little more than 1 quart (0.9 liter), but the stomachs of individuals differ. For example, people who are tall and thin usually have long, narrow stomachs. Short, stocky people usually have short, wide stomachs.

The Stomach's Work. The stomach serves as a storage place for food, so that a large meal may be eaten at one time. It also helps digest food.

Glands in the stomach wall secrete mucus to lubricate the food. Other glands give off hydrochloric acid and the enzyme pepsin to partially digest the food. The hydrochloric acid kills many *microorganisms* (tiny living organisms such as bacteria) in the food.

The stomach muscles churn the food and digestive juices into a pulpy liquid. Then the muscles squeeze the liquid toward the *pyloric* (intestinal) end of the stomach by ringlike contractions of the muscles. These contractions, called *peristaltic waves*, occur about 20 seconds apart. They start at the top of the stomach and move downward. The *pyloric sphincter*, a ringlike muscle around the duodenal opening, keeps food in the stomach until it is a liquid. Then the pyloric sphincter relaxes and lets some *chyme* (liquid-digested food) pass into the duodenum.

The churning action of the stomach tends to begin at usual mealtimes. When people say their stomach is "growling," they are referring to these peristaltic waves. Sometimes, these movements grow so strong that they squeeze acid gastric juice up into the lower part of the esophagus. This irritates the tissues there and causes discomfort.

The pyloric sphincter allows water to pass through almost as soon as it enters the stomach. But the length of time that the stomach retains food varies. On the mixed diet that most persons eat, the stomach empties in three to five hours.

When food enters the stomach, it contains *ptyalin*, an enzyme in saliva that partially digests starch. This action is stopped by the hydrochloric acid in the stomach. No further digestion of starch occurs until the chyme enters the small intestine. For this reason, salivary ptyalin is not very important to digestion.

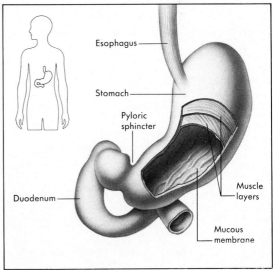

Esophagus

Stomach

Pyloric sphincter

Duodenum

Muscle layers

Mucous membrane

WORLD BOOK illustration by Robert Demarest

The Human Stomach is shaped somewhat like the letter *J*. The cutaway view shows the mucous membrane that lines the organ, and two of the three muscle layers of the stomach wall.

STOMACHACHE

The enzymes secreted in the stomach are *pepsin*, which partially digests proteins and clots milk; and *rennin*, which also clots milk. Rennin is probably important only in infants. Infants also have *gastric lipase*, an enzyme that digests fat in the stomach. In adults, fat digestion occurs in the small intestine.

Although the stomach performs several useful functions, it is not absolutely essential for life. Many persons lead long lives after their stomachs are either partially or wholly removed because of cancer or ulcers.

Stomach Diseases. Many foods irritate the mucous membrane that lines the stomach. Such foods include highly spiced foods, extremely hot foods, and some alcoholic drinks. Rough and dry food that is not well chewed can irritate the stomach. Fear, anger, or constant tension can cause an excessive secretion of stomach juices. This greatly irritates the stomach and the duodenum. If made worse by hastily eaten coarse food, a person can develop ulcers in the stomach or duodenum. Duodenal ulcers almost always result from too much secretion in the stomach. Excessive smoking and drinking of beverages that contain alcohol or caffeine make a person more susceptible to ulcers. Ulcers often heal themselves if the patient eats a simple diet, usually containing milk, and avoids tension. In severe cases, doctors treat ulcers by surgery. TERENCE A. ROGERS

Related Articles. See the Trans-Vision three-dimensional color picture with HUMAN BODY. See also:

Alimentary	Digestive System	Nausea
Canal	Food	Ruminant
Animal (How	Gastritis	Ulcer
Animals Eat)	Gastroscope	Vomiting

STOMACHACHE. See INDIGESTION.

STONE. See BUILDING STONE; ROCK.

STONE, EDWARD DURELL (1902-1978), was an American architect best known for his decorative use of concrete. Stone's most famous buildings are almost completely enclosed in elaborate concrete screens that provide protection from the sun. Many of Stone's buildings were commissioned for commercial, government, and academic clients outside the United States.

Stone was born in Fayetteville, Ark. His early designs show the influence of the German architect Walter Gropius in their geometric shapes, smooth surfaces, and extensive use of glass. This influence appears in such structures as the Museum of Modern Art (1939) in New York City and the Mandel House (1935) in Mount Kisco, N.Y. Stone began designing his best-known buildings during the 1950's. The buildings include the American Embassy (1958) in New Delhi, India; the Huntington Hartford Museum (1964) in New York City; the Kennedy Center for the Performing Arts (1971) in Washington, D.C.; and the Standard Oil Building (1973) in Chicago. NICHOLAS ADAMS

STONE, HARLAN FISKE (1872-1946), served as chief justice of the United States

Wide World

Harlan F. Stone

from 1941 until his death. His years as chief justice on the Supreme Court were marked by changing constitutional views and by division within the court. He became an associate justice in 1925. Although a conservative, Stone often joined Louis D. Brandeis and Oliver Wendell Holmes in upholding liberal measures.

Stone was born in Chesterfield, N.H. He graduated from Amherst College in 1894, and studied at the Columbia University Law School. From 1899 to 1905, he taught law at Columbia. He practiced law in New York City, and became a noted corporation lawyer. Stone served as dean of the Columbia University Law School from 1910 to 1923. He became attorney general of the United States in 1924 and cleaned up scandals in the Department of Justice. MERLO J. PUSEY

STONE, LUCY (1818-1893), helped organize the women's rights movement in the United States. She was one of the first American women to lecture on women's rights and probably the nation's first married woman to keep her maiden name.

Stone was born near West Brookfield, Mass. Few women of her day went to college, but Stone began to teach school at the age of 16 to earn money so she could go. She entered Oberlin College in 1843 and joined the abolitionist movement there. In 1847, she became one of the first Massachusetts women to earn a college degree.

After graduating from college, Stone lectured in the United States and Canada on abolitionism and, later, on women's rights. She viewed slavery and what she considered widespread discrimination against women as linked

Brown Brothers

Lucy Stone

evils of society. Stone helped organize the first national convention on equal rights for women, which was held in Worcester, Mass., in 1850.

In 1855, Stone married Henry Blackwell, a merchant and abolitionist. They omitted the word *obey* from their marriage vows and promised to treat each other equally. Stone continued to use her maiden name and even refused to open mail addressed to Mrs. Henry Blackwell. The phrase *Lucy Stoners* came to refer to women who kept their maiden names after marriage.

In 1869, Stone helped establish the American Woman Suffrage Association, which worked for women's right to vote. The association became a major women's organization. Stone also founded the group's newspaper, *Woman's Journal*. JUNE SOCHEN

See also WOMAN SUFFRAGE (Growth of the Movement).

STONE, THOMAS (1743-1787), was a Maryland signer of the Declaration of Independence. Although he favored independence for the colonists, he urged negotiation with Great Britain instead of war. Stone served in the Second Continental Congress and helped frame the Articles of Confederation. He was elected to the Maryland Senate three times. He died during his third term. Stone was born in Charles County, Maryland, and studied law at Annapolis. RICHARD B. MORRIS

Stone Mountain rises more than 700 feet (210 meters) in a state park near Atlanta, Ga. A skylift carries visitors to the top of the mountain.

STONE AGE is a term used to designate the period in all human cultures when people used stone, rather than metal, tools. The Stone Age began about 2½ million years ago when human beings first began to make crude chopping tools from pebbles. It ended about 3000 B.C., when people began to use bronze (see BRONZE AGE).

Scientists divide the Stone Age on the basis of tool-making techniques into three phases—*Paleolithic, Mesolithic,* and *Neolithic.* The Paleolithic, or Old Stone Age, includes the prehistory of human beings until about 8000 B.C. All Paleolithic peoples were hunters. Mesolithic, or Middle Stone Age, groups were hunters who lived after 8000 B.C. Neolithic, or New Stone Age, peoples were farmers with specialized equipment. Mesolithic and Neolithic peoples lived during the same general period, but in different parts of the world. For more detailed information, see the article PREHISTORIC PEOPLE.

Many peoples were still in the Stone Age when Europeans began their voyages of exploration and discovery in the A.D. 1400's. The aborigines of Tasmania and Australia were using techniques of the Old Stone Age when white explorers discovered them in the 1700's. Explorers found the African Bushmen living in the Middle Stone Age. Islanders of the South Pacific Ocean and most American Indians had progressed to the New Stone Age. A few tribes in New Guinea and Australia are still in the Stone Age.　　　　BRIAN M. FAGAN

See also CITY (How Cities Began and Developed; picture: Neolithic Villages); LAKE DWELLING; TOOL (History of Tools).

STONE FLY is a weak-flying insect. It is not a true fly because it has four wings. True flies have only two wings. Stone flies are usually found in great numbers along the shores of moving water, where they breed. The name stone fly refers to the fact that the *nymphs* (young) live under stones until they mature. Trout and other game fish eat the nymphs. Adult stone flies vary in color to match their surroundings. They may be ½ to 2½ inches (1.3 to 6.4 centimeters) long. They feed on water insects and plants.

Scientific Classification. Stone flies make up the order *Plecoptera.*　　　　E. GORTON LINSLEY

STONE MOUNTAIN is a huge, rounded mass of light-gray granite, about 16 miles (26 kilometers) east of Atlanta, Ga. (see Georgia [physical map]). It is the largest stone mountain in North America. At its highest point it rises over 700 feet (210 meters) above the surrounding terrain. It measures about 2 miles (3.2 kilometers) long and 1 mile (1.6 kilometers) wide. On clear days, it can be seen from 30 miles (48 kilometers) away. Stone Mountain supports an exotic vegetation. A kind of cactus plant grows on thin pockets of soil which lie on top of the solid granite.

In 1923, an ambitious sculpturing project was undertaken on Stone Mountain. It was designed as a memorial to the heroic struggle of the South during the Civil War. That same year, Congress authorized the minting of a Stone Mountain half dollar in connection with the project. Gutzon Borglum was the first sculptor to work on the monument, but he left Stone Mountain and later began working on the famous Mount Rushmore carvings (see BORGLUM, GUTZON). Henry A. Lukeman also worked on the project. The work was discontinued in 1928 because of lack of funds.

In 1958, Georgia purchased 1,613 acres (653 hectares), including Stone Mountain, to establish a state park there. DeKalb County donated another 400 acres (160 hectares). Since then, the state has bought more land, and the area of the park now totals 3,200 acres (1,290 hectares). The park features a lake at the base of

The Stone Fly Is Usually Found Near Brooks or Streams.

British Ministry of Public Buildings and Works

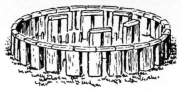

The Monument at Stonehenge, *above,* may have been an ancient astronomical observatory. Scientific studies have shown that the positions of the huge stone slabs indicate the places on the horizon where the sun and moon rise and set about June 21 and December 21. The drawing, *right,* shows what scholars believe was the original arrangement of the stones.

Stone Mountain and a skylift that can carry 50 persons to the top. Other attractions of the park include a beach, a golf course, museums, trails, and a restored plantation.

In 1964, work on the sculpturing project was resumed under the direction of a new sculptor, Walker Kirtland Hancock. The sculpturing of the figures was completed in 1969. The sculpture includes Jefferson Davis, Robert E. Lee, and Stonewall Jackson, on horseback. The figures are so large that when the Lee carving was unveiled, 30 persons could get on the shoulder. A picture of the sculpture appears in the *Visitor's Guide* section of the GEORGIA article.   DAVID J. DE LAUBENFELS

STONE OF DESTINY. See SCONE, STONE OF.

STONECHAT is the name of a small European bird of the thrush family. Its name comes from its peculiar note, a sound like that of two stones struck together.

The male has a black head and throat and chestnut underparts. The female is duller in coloring. The stonechat is restless and active, and usually lives in open, grassy locations. It builds its nest on the ground, under a tuft of grass, and feeds on insect larvae, worms, beetles, and seeds. It lays from four to six greenish-blue, faintly spotted eggs. The bird winters in Africa.

Eric Hosking, NAS
The Stonechat

Scientific Classification.
The stonechat belongs to the thrush family, *Turdidae.* It is genus *Pratincola,* species *P. rubicola.*   LEONARD W. WING

STONECROP. See SEDUM.

STONEFISH. See FISH (picture: Fish Protected by Spines).

STONEHENGE, *STOHN hehnj,* is an ancient monument on Salisbury Plain in Wiltshire, England. It is a group of huge, rough-cut stones. No one knows exactly who placed them there.

In 1950, archaeologists from Edinburgh University discovered two underground holes which had probably served as ritual pits. Charcoal from one of the pits was found to date from 1848 B.C., plus or minus 275 years, after being analyzed by the radio-carbon dating method. Carvings found on the stones in 1953 also indicate that the stones may be more than 3,500 years old. Some stones are of a kind found only in western Wales, about 300 miles (480 kilometers) away. The stones were probably carried to the site.

For hundreds of years, the great stones gradually fell, or people carried them away to make bridges and mill dams. But from the positions of many of the stones still in place, scholars can guess what the monument probably looked like originally. An earth wall about 320 feet (98 meters) in diameter surrounded the monument. Thirty blocks of gray sandstone, each standing about 13½ feet (4 meters) above the ground and averaging 28 short tons (25 metric tons) stood in a circle about 97 feet (30 meters) in diameter. A continuous circle of smaller blocks stood on top of them. Inside was a circle of about 60 blue stones. Inside this circle were two horseshoe-shaped sets of stones, one inside the other, opening toward the northeast. Near the center curve of the inner horseshoe was a flat sandstone block 16 feet (5 meters) long. This was probably an altar, and may have stood upright. A stone marker 80 yards (73 meters) east of the altar was set to cast a shadow on it at dawn of the summer solstice, about June 21. For this reason, some scholars believe that Stonehenge was connected with sun worship.

In 1963, Gerald S. Hawkins of the Smithsonian Astrophysical Observatory calculated the directions of lines joining various stones at Stonehenge. He found that the monument may have served as an accurate astronomical calendar, capable of predicting the seasons of the year and even eclipses of the sun and moon. Using an electronic computer, he found a remarkable correlation between the directions of these lines and the directions of the rising and setting of the sun and moon about 1500 B.C. The chances of such correlations being coincidental is about one in 100 million.

In 1922, the British government began to restore Stonehenge. Some of the scattered stones were put back as they had been originally. The government now takes care of this monument. Woodhenge, also in Wiltshire, is a 3,000-year-old wooden monument similar to Stonehenge.　ROBERT S. HOYT

STONES RIVER, BATTLE OF. See CIVIL WAR (Murfreesboro, or Stones River).

STONEWALL JACKSON. See JACKSON, STONEWALL.

STONEWARE is a hard, nonporous kind of pottery. Stoneware containers are used in restaurants and on farms to store food and in factories to store chemicals. Stoneware also makes durable dishes and pipes. In addition, potters use the material to create statues and other art objects. Stoneware is made by baking a mixture of special clays at extremely high temperatures. Heat

Metropolitan Museum of Art

Stoneware has been a popular type of pottery for many years. The English salt-glazed stoneware figure, *left*, was made about 1750. The American pitcher, *right*, was made in the 1800's.

causes stoneware to become glossy, and so the material does not need to be glazed.

Stoneware was first produced in China during the A.D. 400's. Production was based in the Rhine River region of Germany until about 1671, when the potter John Dwight began manufacturing stoneware in England (see DWIGHT, JOHN). Stoneware was popular among artistic potters in France during the 1800's and was called *grès*. Early settlers in America made stoneware brine containers, milk pitchers, pickle crocks, and other practical items. The manufacture of stoneware eventually was centered in western Pennsylvania and eastern Ohio, where the pottery is still made today.　WILLIAM C. GATES, JR.

See also POTTERY (Types of Pottery).

STOPPARD, TOM (1937-　　), is a major English playwright. His works are noted for their imaginative blend of philosophical themes, witty dialogue, and broad comic technique.

Stoppard first gained fame for *Rosencrantz and Guildenstern Are Dead* (1967). In this play, he used two minor characters from William Shakespeare's *Hamlet* to probe the meaninglessness he saw in human existence. In *Jumpers* (1972), Stoppard mixed acrobatics, murder,

and philosophy. *Travesties* (1974) uses famous literary and political figures to explore questions of art and politics. *Every Good Boy Deserves Favor* (1977) includes a symphony orchestra and deals with Russian dissidents. *Night and Day* (1978) is a realistic play that discusses the role of journalism in the modern world. Stoppard's other plays include *The Real Inspector Hound* (1968), *After Magritte* (1970), and *Dirty Linen* (1976).

Stoppard was born in Zlin (now Gottwaldov), Czechoslovakia. His family moved to England in 1946. Stoppard was a reporter until the early 1960's, when he began writing radio and television plays.　MARDI VALGEMAE

STORAGE BATTERY. See BATTERY.

STORE. See CHAIN STORE; COOPERATIVE; DEPARTMENT STORE; FOOD (Marketing).

STORIED PROVINCE. See QUEBEC (province).

STORK is a large bird with long legs and strong wings. It looks for its food in marshes and swamps, but often nests on roofs and chimneys.

The best-known stork is the *white stork*. It lives in most parts of Europe and Central Asia in the summer and in Africa and northern India in the winter. It is white with black markings on its wings. Its beak is red and its legs and feet are a reddish pink. A pair of storks will return to a nest year after year. Storks eat eels, frogs, reptiles, young birds, and small mammals.

Other storks of the Eastern Hemisphere are the *Japanese stork*, the *black stork*, the *white-necked stork*, and the *adjutant*. The *maguari* and the *jabiru*, a bird 5 feet (1.5 meters) high, are found in South America. The *wood*

Black Star

White Storks seek out cities and towns with chimneys and crannies in which to nest. They rear their families in such high places. A pair of storks will return to a nest year after year.

WORLD BOOK illustration by
Trevor Boyer, Linden Artists Ltd.

The Black Stork has glossy black feathers and a white breast. Adult birds have red bills and legs. Black storks are wilder than white storks, and prefer to live deep in forests.

U.S. Air Force

The Clouds of a Large Storm System, *above,* move across the eastern part of the United States. They were photographed by special cameras on an orbiting weather satellite.

stork of the southern United States, formerly called the *wood ibis,* is also a true stork.

The stork is a respected and protected bird in many places. The Germans and the Dutch like storks because they destroy insects and reptiles. They also believe that the stork brings good luck. The faithfulness of a pair of storks is considered a model of married happiness. The familiar legend that the stork brings the new baby into the home arises from the fact that the bird takes loving care of its own young.

Scientific Classification. The stork belongs to the stork family, *Ciconiidae.* The white stork is classified as genus *Ciconia,* species *C. ciconia.* ALFRED M. BAILEY

See also BIRD (picture: Birds of Europe and Asia); JABIRU; MARABOU.

STORM is a disturbance of the atmosphere. Storms are usually marked by strong winds, rain, snow, or hail, or by a combination of two or more of these. Storms would never occur if the temperature of the air everywhere were equal. The air in low latitudes becomes heated, however, while that in high latitudes is cooled. The air over oceans stays warmer in the winter, and cooler in summer, than that over land. These differences in temperature also result in differences in pressure. Over warm areas the pressure remains relatively low, while over colder areas it is high.

As cold air accumulates in the high latitudes, large masses of it tend to spread out toward the equator. Eventually these large masses break off into separate, wandering masses of cold air which move generally eastward and southward. In the middle latitudes, these masses of cold air usually meet warm air masses that have come up from low latitudes. Wherever warm and cold air masses meet, a struggle develops, which may result in storms. Differences in temperature, pressure, and humidity cause all the many different kinds of storms. GEORGE F. TAYLOR

Related Articles in WORLD BOOK include:

Air	Hurricane	Thunder
Barometer	Lightning	Tornado
Blizzard	Rain	Typhoon
Cloud (Storms)	Sandstorm	Waterspout
Cyclone	Sleet	Weather
Dust Storm	Snow	Whirlwind
Hail	Sunspot	Wind

STORM TROOPS. See HITLER, ADOLF (Birth of the Nazi Party); GESTAPO.

STORMALONG, ALFRED BULLTOP, was a gigantic sea captain in New England folklore. He commanded a huge wooden ship that was so big that the crew rode horseback on deck. Its masts had hinges so they could bend to let the sun and moon pass. Sailors who climbed its rigging as young men came down with gray beards.

Folk tales and a sea song tell about Stormalong's amazing seamanship. For example, he suggested soaping the sides of his ship so it could squeeze through the English Channel. The soap scraped off on the cliffs of Dover, leaving them white. HARRY OSTER

STORMY PETREL. See PETREL.

STORTING. See NORWAY (Parliament).

STORY, JOSEPH (1779-1845), served as an associate justice of the Supreme Court of the United States from 1812 to 1845. As an outstanding member of the Supreme Court, he followed closely in the footsteps of John Marshall (see MARSHALL, JOHN). His *Commentaries,* a series of important legal essays, helped shape American concepts of the common law.

Story was born at Marblehead, Mass., and was graduated from Harvard University in 1798. He began to practice law in 1801 and later served in Congress. He was also a professor of law at Harvard University from 1829 until his death. JERRE S. WILLIAMS

STORYTELLING is one of the oldest forms of folk art. Like dancing and singing, it grew out of people's need to share their emotions and experiences.

Historically, all literature developed from storytelling. Today, storytelling is generally considered one of the most effective ways to introduce children to literature. Most children delight in listening to stories. The experiences with storytelling help many youngsters learn to love literature and may lead to a lifetime habit of reading.

Storytelling as an art means re-creating literature—taking the printed words in a book and giving them life. A good story does more than merely please the listener. By listening, children may learn how to express their own thoughts. Research has shown that storytelling and other oral language activities expand children's language skills significantly. Studies also have shown a close relationship between the ease with which children learn to read and their experience of having stories read to them.

The importance of storytelling is perhaps best expressed by the great Russian poet-storyteller Kornei Chukovsky. In his book *From Two to Five*, he wrote:

"The goal of storytellers consists of fostering in the child . . . compassion and humaneness—this miraculous ability of man to be disturbed by another being's misfortunes, to feel joy about another being's happiness, to experience another's fate as one's own.

"Storytellers take trouble to teach the child in his early years to participate with concern in the lives of imaginary people and animals, and to make sure that in this way he will escape the narrow frame of his egocentric interests and feelings.

"Because it is natural for a child to be on the side of the kind, the courageous, and the unjustly offended when listening to a fairy tale, whether it is Prince Ivan

or Peter Rabbit or the Fearless Spider, our only goal is to awaken, nurture, and strengthen in the responsive soul of the child this invaluable ability to feel compassion for another's unhappiness and to share in another's happiness. Without this, a man is inhuman."

How to Tell Stories

Selection of a story to tell—or to read aloud—is very important. A story should be worth listening to and worth the time it takes to prepare. You can share only what you yourself enjoy and appreciate.

Picture-book stories should be read aloud rather than told, because the illustrations are part of the story. When sharing a picture book with a group of children, hold the book in one hand with the pictures facing the children. Turn the pages with your free hand. You need not memorize the text, but you must know the story well enough to read it by just glancing at the pages. In selecting picture books to use with a group, look for large, clear pictures; flowing language; and a strong story line.

Children up to the age of 6 take pleasure in simple, realistic stories because everyday happenings are still new to them. They also like nursery rhymes, the Peter Rabbit tales of Beatrix Potter, and modern imaginative stories, such as *Where the Wild Things Are* by Maurice Sendak.

Children from 6 to 8 enjoy folk tales. Many folk tales have been published in attractive picture-book editions. Folk tales combine economy of language with plenty of action. They deal with universal truths, and their wisdom is meaningful to children.

Boys and girls older than 8 like tall tales, adventure stories, folk tales, myths and legends. Modern books of fantasy lend themselves to storytelling and reading aloud. Poetry, starting with the rollicking nonsense

Werner Wolf, Black Star

A Storytelling Session fascinates a group of young listeners. This teacher helps the children follow the action of a story in a picture book.

STORYTELLING

verse of Mother Goose for the youngest children, appeals to all youngsters (see POETRY).

Preparation. Before telling a story that has no pictures, read the tale to yourself several times. Visualize how the characters look, the clothing they wear, and how they act. Then imagine the action of the story as if seeing it in a series of pictures.

In preparing a folk or fairy tale, you should distinguish between a traditional tale and a literary tale. A traditional tale has many versions. If you wish, you may retell parts of the story in your own words. However, you should be familiar enough with these tales to express their rhythmic patterns. A literary tale is created by one author. Such stories can achieve their desired effect only if they are told in the author's words. Therefore, you should know these tales thoroughly.

Read the story aloud to get used to the sound of your voice. Listen for basic rhythmic patterns. Feel the mood of the story. Each story has its own mood, which will affect the pace of your telling. Finally, tell the story without the book. While doing this, stand or sit in front of a mirror so you can detect and eliminate any distracting mannerisms. After you feel at home with the story, you are ready to share it with children.

Telling a Story. Stories may be told anywhere—at home, on the playground, in the classroom, or in the library. Whatever the surroundings, the storyteller should give children the feeling that listening to a story is something special.

Make the children as physically comfortable as possible. If you are telling a story to more than two or three youngsters, seat them in a semicircle in front of you. Do not expect children to listen too long. From 15 to 20 minutes is long enough for young children, and 30 minutes is fine for older ones.

With no book between you and the children, you can concentrate on their reactions to the story. You can respond to their mood and adjust your pace to their needs. The children are free to create their own images, making mental pictures that fit the words they hear. It is seldom necessary to explain the meanings of words. But if the children seem puzzled the second or third time they hear an unfamiliar word, substitute an easier word. Let your own pleasure in the story come through as you tell it. Enthusiasm is contagious.

A storyteller should not pry into children's feelings about a story by asking questions that demand responses. You may think children are not listening. But you may be surprised a few weeks later to hear them comment on the story or to ask to hear it again.

History

The Earliest Storytelling probably consisted of simple chants that praised the dawn or the stars, or expressed the joy of being alive. People sang other chants to accompany some task, such as grinding corn or sharpening tools or weapons.

As people began to wonder about the world around them, they created myths to explain natural occurrences. They assigned superhuman qualities to ordinary persons, thus originating the hero tale.

Early storytelling combined stories, poetry, music, and dance. Many people told stories, but in time the best storyteller was chosen to be the entertainer for the community. This person also became the historian for the group, marking the beginning of the profession of storytelling.

The Middle Ages. The storyteller's art flourished during the Middle Ages, from about the A.D. 400's to the 1500's. Storytellers were welcome in royal courts as well as in market places. Traveling storytellers journeyed from country to country. They gathered news and learned the favorite stories of various regions as they traveled. Storytellers exchanged tales so often that it became difficult to trace the origin of many of their stories.

The storytellers of the Middle Ages had thorough training. Ruth Sawyer, a noted American storyteller and author of children's books, described the training of a *troubadour*, a poet-musician of that period. She wrote that a good troubadour was expected "to know perfectly all the current tales, to repeat all the noteworthy theses from the universities, to be well informed on court scandal, to know the healing power of

Illustration from *Roman de Fauvel*, a medieval French manuscript; Bibliothèque Nationale, Paris

Medieval Storytellers traveled throughout western Europe, entertaining royalty. This illustration shows a tale being told by masked comedians and musicians.

herbs and *simples* (medicines), to be able to compose verses to a lord or lady at a moment's notice, and to play on at least two of the instruments then in favor at court.''

No one knows how many storytellers entertained during the Middle Ages. Some writings tell that 426 minstrels were employed at the wedding of Princess Margaret of England in 1290. The many minstrels in the court of Edward I included two women who performed under the names of Matill Makejoye and Pearl in the Egg.

With the invention of movable type about 1440, the influence of the professional storyteller faded as reading replaced listening. Inexpensive *chapbooks* (pamphlets of popular tales) not only provided entertainment but also preserved some of the earliest stories. Oral storytelling survived mainly in rural areas.

The 1800's. During the early 1800's, the brothers Jakob and Wilhelm Grimm awakened a scholarly interest in folk literature with the publication of a collection of German fairy tales. The Grimm collection became probably the best-known work of its kind. The brothers gathered their stories from the common people and faithfully preserved the unique structure and language pattern of the tales. See GRIMM.

Peter Asbjørnsen and Jørgen Moe followed the example of the Grimms and collected Norwegian folk tales (see ASBJØRNSEN, PETER CHRISTEN). In England, Joseph Jacobs searched folklore journals for tales of the British Isles and rewrote them for children.

The 1900's. During the early 1900's, Marie Shedlock, a retired English schoolteacher, made several tours throughout the United States. Shedlock, a gifted storyteller, lectured on the art of storytelling. She emphasized the importance of storytelling as a natural way to introduce children to literature. Her work encouraged organized storytelling that had already begun in Sunday schools, kindergartens, and libraries throughout the United States. In 1903, a group of schoolteachers formed the National Story Tellers' League.

By the mid-1900's, interest in storytelling had declined. However, a revival of storytelling began about 1970. Today, professional storytellers tour the United States and Canada much as storytellers toured during the Middle Ages. In 1972, the National Association for the Preservation and Perpetuation of Storytellers was established in Jonesboro, Tenn. Other local and national storytelling organizations have also been founded.

In many places in North America, storytelling festivals and conferences attract performers, scholars, and enthusiastic audiences. Schools that teach only storytelling have opened in the United States and Canada. Many library schools and schools of education offer courses in storytelling.   ELLIN GREENE

Related Articles in WORLD BOOK. See FOLKLORE with its list of *Related Articles* for some famous stories and characters. See also:

STORYTELLERS

Anderson, Hans C.	Minstrel
Bard	Perrault, Charles
Grimm (family)	Sawyer, Ruth
Mastersinger	Skald
Minnesinger	Troubadour

OTHER RELATED ARTICLES

Ballad	Folklore

Library (picture: Music Helps Tell a Story)	Mythology
	New York City (picture: Traveling Storytellers)
Literature for Children	Nursery Rhyme
Mother Goose	

See the *Books to Read* section of the LITERATURE FOR CHILDREN article. See also the following books:

Additional Resources

PICTURE-BOOK EDITIONS OF FOLK AND FAIRY TALES

ANDERSEN, HANS CHRISTIAN. *The Ugly Duckling*. Tr. by R. P. Keigwin. Illus. by Johannes Larsen. Macmillan, 1955. *The Wild Swans*. Retold by Amy Ehrlich. Illus. by Susan Jeffers. Dial, 1981.

ASBJØRNSEN, PETER C. and MOE, JØRGEN, comps. *The Three Billy Goats Gruff*. Illus. by Marcia Brown. Harcourt, 1957.

BELPRÉ, PURA. *Perez and Martina: A Puerto Rican Folk Tale*. Illus. by Carlos Sanchez. Warne, 1966.

BROOKE, L. LESLIE. *The Golden Goose Book*. Warne, 1905. Four nursery tales: *The Golden Goose, The Three Bears, The Three Little Pigs*, and *Tom Thumb*.

DE PAOLO, TOMIE. *Strega Nona*. Prentice-Hall, 1975.

GÁG, WANDA. *Millions of Cats*. Coward-McCann, 1928.

GRIMM, JAKOB and WILHELM. *The Wolf and the Seven Little Kids*. Illus. by Felix Hoffmann. Harcourt, 1959. *The Seven Ravens*. Illus. by Felix Hoffmann, 1963. *Snow White and the Seven Dwarfs*. Tr. by Randall Jarrell. Illus. by Nancy Ekholm Burkart. Farrar, 1972.

HALEY, GAIL E. *A Story—A Story*. An African Tale. Atheneum, 1970.

JACOBS, JOSEPH. *Tom Tit Tot*. Illus. by Evaline Ness. Holt, 1965.

LANG, ANDREW, ed. *The Twelve Dancing Princesses*. Illus. by Adrienne Adams. Holt, 1966.

The Old Woman and Her Pig: A Folk Tale. Illus. by Paul Galdone. McGraw, 1960.

PERRAULT, CHARLES. *Puss in Boots*. Illus. by Marcia Brown. Scribner, 1952. *Cinderella, or The Little Glass Slipper*. Illus. by Marcia Brown. 1954.

THURBER, JAMES. *Many Moons*. Illus. by Louis Slobodkin. Harcourt, 1943.

TOLSTOY, ALEXEI. *The Great Big Enormous Turnip*. Illus. by Helen Oxenbury. Watts, 1969.

ZEMACH, HARVE. *Mommy, Buy Me a China Doll*. Illus. by Margot Zemach. Follett, 1966.

TRADITIONAL FOLK TALE AND FAIRY TALE COLLECTIONS

ASSOCIATION FOR CHILDHOOD EDUCATION INTERNATIONAL. *Told Under the City Umbrella*. Illus. by Lisl Weil. Macmillan, 1972.

BAKER, AUGUSTA. *The Golden Lynx and Other Tales*. Illus. by Johannes Troyer. Lippincott, 1960.

BELPRÉ, PURA. *The Tiger and the Rabbit and Other Tales*. Illus. by Tomie de Paola. Lippincott, 1965.

BLEECKER, MARY NOEL, comp. *Big Music, or Twenty Merry Tales to Tell*. Illus. by Louis S. Glanzman. Viking, 1946.

CARLSON, NATALIE SAVAGE. *The Talking Cat and Other Stories of French Canada*. Illus. by Roger Duvoisin. Harper, 1952.

CHASE, RICHARD. *Jack Tales*. Illus. by Berkeley Williams, Jr. Houghton, 1943. *Grandfather Tales*, 1948.

COURLANDER, HAROLD. *Terrapin's Pot of Sense*. Illus. by Elton Fax. Holt, 1957.

D'AULAIRE, INGRI and EDGAR PARIN. *East of the Sun and West of the Moon: Twenty-one Norwegian Folk Tales*. Viking, 1969.

DE LA MARE, WALTER. *Tales Told Again*. Illus. by Alan Howard. Knopf, 1959.

FILLMORE, PARKER. *The Shepherd's Nosegay: Stories from Finland and Czechoslovakia*. Ed. by Katherine Love. Illus. by Enrico Arno. Harcourt, 1958.

STORYTELLING

FINGER, CHARLES J. *Tales from Silver Lands*. Illus. by Paul Honoré. Doubleday, 1924.

GÁG, WANDA. *Tales from Grimm*. Coward-McCann, 1936. *More Tales from Grimm*, 1947.

GREENE, ELLIN, ed. *Clever Cooks*. Illus. by Trina Schart Hyman. Lothrop, 1973. *Midsummer Magic*. Illus. by Barbara Cooney. Lothrop, 1976.

GRIMM, JAKOB and WILHELM. *Fairy Tales*. Follett, 1968.

HAVILAND, VIRGINIA, ed. *The Fairy Tale Treasury*. Illus. by Raymond Briggs. Coward, 1972.

JACOBS, JOSEPH. *English Folk and Fairy Tales*. Illus. by John D. Batten. Schocken, 1967.

LANG, ANDREW. *The Blue Fairy Book*. Edited by Brian Alderson. Illus. by John Lawrence. Kestrel Books and Viking Press, 1978.

LESTER, JULIUS. *The Knee-High Man and Other Tales*. Illus. by Ralph Pinto. Dial, 1972.

NIC LEODHAS, SORCHE, pseud. *Heather and Broom: Tales of the Scottish Highlands*. Illus. by Consuelo Joerns. Holt, 1960.

ROSS, EULALIE STEINMETZ, comp. *The Lost Half-Hour*. Illus. by Enrico Arno. Harcourt, 1963.

SAWYER, RUTH. *The Long Christmas*. Illus. by Valenti Angelo. Viking, 1941.

STOUTENBERG, ADRIEN. *American Tall Tales*. Illus. by Richard M. Powers. Viking, 1966.

WIGGIN, KATE DOUGLAS and SMITH, NORA ARCHIBALD, eds. *The Fairy Ring*. Rev. by Ethna Sheehan. Illus. by Warren Chappell. Doubleday, 1967.

WOLKSTEIN, DIANE, ed. *The Magic Orange Tree and Other Haitian Folktales*. Illus. by Elsa Henriques. Knopf, 1978.

LITERARY FAIRY TALE COLLECTIONS

ANDERSEN, HANS CHRISTIAN. *The Complete Fairy Tales and Stories*. Tr. by Erik Christian Haugaard. Doubleday, 1974.

BABBITT, NATALIE. *The Devil's Storybook*. Farrar, 1974.

COLWELL, EILEEN, ed. *The Magic Umbrella and Other Stories for Telling*. Illus. by Shirley Felts. McKay, 1977.

FARJEON, ELEANOR. *The Little Bookroom*. Illus. by Edward Ardizzone. Oxford, 1956.

HOUSMAN, LAURENCE. *The Rat-Catcher's Daughter*. Illus. by Julia Noonan. Atheneum. 1974.

HUGHES, RICHARD. *The Wonder-Dog*. Illus. by Antony Maitland. Morrow, 1977.

KIPLING, RUDYARD. *Just So Stories*. Illus. by Nicholas. Doubleday, 1946.

PERRAULT, CHARLES. *The Glass Slipper: Charles Perrault's Tales of Times Past*. Tr. by John Bierhorst. Illus. by Mitchell Miller. Four Winds, 1981.

PYLE, HOWARD. *The Wonder Clock*. Harper, 1915. *Pepper and Salt*. Harper, 1941.

SANDBURG, CARL. *The Sandburg Treasury*. Illus. by Paul Bacon. Harcourt, 1970.

SINGER, ISAAC BASHEVIS. *Zlateh the Goat and Other Stories*. Illus. by Maurice Sendak. Harper, 1966.

STOCKTON, FRANK. *The Storyteller's Pack: A Frank Stockton Reader*. Scribner, 1968.

YOLEN, JANE. *The Girl Who Cried Flowers and Other Tales*. Illus. by David Palladini. Crowell, 1974.

MODERN PICTURE-BOOK STORIES

BEMELMANS, LUDWIG. *Madeline*. Simon and Schuster, 1939.

BURNINGHAM, JOHN. *Mr. Gumpy's Outing*. Macmillan, 1971.

BURTON, VIRGINIA LEE. *Mike Mulligan and His Steam Shovel*. Houghton, 1939.

DE REGNIERS, BEATRICE SCHENK. *May I Bring a Friend?* Illus. by Beni Montresor. Atheneum, 1964.

ETS, MARIE HALL. *Play with Me*. Viking, 1955.

KEATS, EZRA JACK. *The Snowy Day*. Viking, 1962.

McCLOSKEY, ROBERT. *Make Way for Ducklings*. Viking, 1941.

MUNARI, BRUNO. *Bruno Munari's ABC*. World, 1960.

POTTER, BEATRIX. *The Tale of Peter Rabbit*. Warne, n.d.

RAYNER, MARY. *Mr. and Mrs. Pig's Evening Out*. Atheneum, 1976.

SENDAK, MAURICE. *Where the Wild Things Are*. Harper, 1963.

TRESSELT, ALVIN. *Hide and Seek Fog*. Illus. by Roger Duvoisin. Lothrop, 1965.

WARD, LYND K. *The Biggest Bear*. Houghton, 1952.

WILDSMITH, BRIAN. *Brian Wildsmith's Circus*. Watts, 1970.

YASHIMA, TARO. *Umbrella*. Viking, 1958.

POETRY

BONTEMPS, ARNA, comp. *Hold Fast to Dreams*. Follett, 1969.

CALDECOTT, RANDOLPH. *The Hey Diddle Diddle Picture Book*. Warne, n.d.

COLE, WILLIAM, comp. *The Birds and the Beasts Were There: Animal Poems*. Illus. by Helen Siegl. World, 1963.

DE LA MARE, WALTER, comp. *Come Hither*. Knopf, 1957.

HUGHES, LANGSTON. *The Dream Keeper and Other Poems*. Illus. by Helen Sewell. Knopf, 1932.

LEAR, EDWARD. *The Owl and the Pussycat*. Illus. by Barbara Cooney. Little, 1969.

LEWIS, RICHARD, comp. *Miracles: Poems by Children of the English-Speaking World*. Simon & Schuster, 1966. *Out of the Earth I Sing: Poetry and Songs of Primitive Peoples of the World*. Norton, 1968.

LIVINGSTON, MYRA COHN, ed. *A Time Beyond Us*. Illus. by James J. Spanfeller. Harcourt, 1968.

McCORD, DAVID. *Far and Few: Rhymes of the Never Was and Always Is*. Illus. by Henry B. Kane. Little, 1952. *Speak Up: More Rhymes of the Never Was and Always Is*. Little, 1980.

MILLAY, EDNA ST. VINCENT. *Poems Selected for Young People*. Illus. by J. Paget-Fredericks. Harper, 1951.

MOTHER GOOSE. *The Mother Goose Treasury*. Illus. by Raymond Briggs. Coward-McCann, 1966.

PLOTZ, HELEN, comp. *The Earth Is the Lord's. Poems of the Spirit*. Illus. by Clare Leighton. Crowell, 1965.

READ, HERBERT, ed. *This Way Delight: A Book of Poetry for the Young*. Illus. by Juliet Kepes. Pantheon, 1956.

SILVERSTEIN, SHEL. *Where the Sidewalk Ends*. Harper, 1974.

AIDS FOR THE STORYTELLER

AMERICAN LIBRARY ASSOCIATION. Special Committee of the National Congress of Parents and Teachers and the Association for Library Service to Children of the American Library Association. *Let's Read Together*. 4th ed. A.L.A., 1981. Children's Services Division. *For Storytellers and Storytelling: Bibliographies, Materials and Resource Aids*. A.L.A., 1968.

BAKER, AUGUSTA and GREENE, ELLIN. *Storytelling: Art and Technique*. Bowker, 1977.

CATHON, LAURA E. and others. *Stories to Tell to Children*. 8th ed. Carnegie Library of Pittsburgh, 1974.

COOK, ELIZABETH. *The Ordinary and the Fabulous: An Introduction to Myths, Legends and Fairy Tales for Teachers and Librarians*. 2nd ed. Cambridge, 1976.

FOSTER, JOANNA. *How to Conduct Effective Picture Book Programs: A Handbook*. Westchester Library System, N.Y., 1967.

LARUSSO, MARILYN, ed. *Stories: A List of Stories to Tell and to Read Aloud*. 7th ed. The New York Public Library, 1977.

PELLOWSKI, ANNE. *The World of Storytelling*. Bowker, 1977.

SAWYER, RUTH. *The Way of the Storyteller*. Viking, 1962.

SHEDLOCK, MARIE L. *The Art of the Storyteller*. Dover, 1952.

TASHJIAN, VIRGINIA. *Juba This and Juba That: Story Hour Stretches for Large or Small Groups*. Little, 1969.

STOSS, *shtohs,* **VEIT** (1440?-1533), was a German sculptor. His works have a rich, complex appearance and a clear pattern. Stoss and his fellow German sculptor Tilman Riemenschneider used a late Gothic style. Both used Christian themes almost entirely, but Stoss's work is more dramatic and expressive than Riemenschneider's.

Stoss was born in Germany, and received his early training there. He went to Kraków, Poland, in 1477 and worked there for almost 12 years on what is probably his masterpiece. It is an altar over 42 feet (13 meters) high and 36 feet (11 meters) wide in the Church of St. Mary representing the life of the Virgin. Stoss later settled in Nuremberg, Germany.   ROBERT R. WARK

STOUT. See BEER.

STOUT, REX TODHUNTER (1886-1975), was an American detective-story writer. He created the fat, beer-drinking, orchid-loving detective Nero Wolfe. Wolfe stays home and sends his able assistant Archie Goodwin out for clues. Later, while sitting with a glass of beer and a potted orchid, Wolfe solves the mystery. Wolfe first appeared in *Fer-de-Lance* (1934). Stout's many other Nero Wolfe mysteries include *Too Many Cooks* (1938), *Some Buried Caesar* (1939), *And Be a Villain* (1948), *Death of a Doxy* (1966), and *A Family Affair* (1975).

Stout was born in Noblesville, Ind. He devised a school banking system which he set up in about 400 cities and towns between 1917 and 1927. Profits from the system made him wealthy and enabled him to devote his time to writing. Stout published his first novel in 1929.   PHILIP DURHAM

STOVE. See RANGE.

STOWE, HARRIET BEECHER (1811-1896), is remembered chiefly for her antislavery novel, *Uncle Tom's Cabin* (1851-1852). When most people think of the book's famous characters, Uncle Tom, Little Eva, Topsy, and Simon Legree, however, they are not remembering the book. They are thinking instead of George L. Aiken's play of 1852, or those crude and violent spectacles, the "Tom Shows," which played small towns in the North. Aiken's play and the Tom Shows only faintly suggest Mrs. Stowe's book. *Uncle Tom's Cabin* is melodramatic and sentimental, but it is more than a melodrama. The book re-creates characters, scenes, and incidents with humor and realism. It analyzes the issue of slavery in the Midwest, New England, and the South during the days of the Fugitive Slave Law. The book intensified the disagreement between the North and the South which led to the Civil War. Mrs. Stowe's name became hated in the South.

Other Works. Mrs. Stowe's works, dealing with New England in the late 1700's and early 1800's, are important for anyone who wants to understand the American past. These include *The Minister's Wooing* (1859) and *Oldtown Folks* (1869), both novels; and *Sam Lawson's Oldtown Fireside Stories* (1872), a collection of stories. They present everyday life of the New England vil-

Germanisches Nationalmuseum, Nuremberg, Germany

Madonna and Child, a statue by Veit Stoss, was carved about 1510 in the late Gothic style of sculpture.

Brown Bros.

Harriet Beecher Stowe

lage, and make clear the positive and negative aspects of Puritanism. As in *Uncle Tom's Cabin*, the characters come alive to the reader as soon as they begin to talk.

Of her later books, the most shocking to her contemporaries was *Lady Byron Vindicated* (1870). It told of Lady Byron's separation from her husband, the famous poet, Lord Byron. Mrs. Stowe's account was based on Lady Byron's talk with her in 1856, and is supported by later investigation.

Her Life. Mrs. Stowe was born on June 14, 1811, in Litchfield, Conn., where her father, Lyman Beecher, was minister of the Congregational Church. She was educated at the academy there and at Hartford Female Seminary. From 1832 to 1850 she lived in Cincinnati, Ohio, where her father served as president of Lane Theological Seminary. In 1836, she married Calvin Stowe, a member of the Lane faculty. Her years in Cincinnati furnished her with many of the characters and incidents for *Uncle Tom's Cabin*, which she wrote in Brunswick, Me. After the publication of the book, Mrs. Stowe became famous overnight. On a visit to England, she was welcomed by the English abolitionists.

Mrs. Stowe was the sister of the clergyman Henry Ward Beecher and the reformer and educator Catharine Beecher (see BEECHER).   CHARLES H. FOSTER

See also ABOLITIONIST; UNCLE TOM'S CABIN.

Additional Resources

RUGOFF, MILTON A. *The Beechers: An American Family in the 19th Century.* Harper, 1981.
SCOTT, JOHN A. *Woman Against Slavery: The Story of Harriet Beecher Stowe.* Crowell, 1978.

STRABISMUS. See CROSS-EYE.

STRABO, *STRAY boh* (63 B.C.?-A.D. 24?), was a Greek geographer and historian. He became famous for his 17-volume *Geography*, which described all parts of the known world. These volumes are the best source of geographical information about the Mediterranean countries at the beginning of the Christian Era. Strabo also wrote a lengthy history that is now lost. He was born in Amasia, Pontus. He studied in Rome and Alexandria, and traveled in Arabia, southern Europe, and northern Africa.   J. RUSSELL WHITAKER

STRACHEY, LYTTON (1880-1932), was an English biographer, essayist, and literary critic. His best-known works are biographies—*Eminent Victorians* (1918) and *Queen Victoria* (1921). *Eminent Victorians* is a group of sketches about four famous figures of Victorian England —the educator Thomas Arnold, General Charles Gordon, Henry Cardinal Manning, and the nurse Florence Nightingale. Strachey's biographical portraits are brief but thorough. They provide a clever mixture of fact, imagination, and psychological analysis.

Giles Lytton Strachey was born in London. He formed most of his ideas and lifelong friendships while studying at Cambridge University from 1899 to 1903. Strachey gained a place in the center of London literary life through the wit, elegance, and skeptical nature of his personality and writings. Strachey and his Cambridge friends formed the nucleus of what became known as the Bloomsbury Group (see BLOOMSBURY GROUP). This group included some of the leading English intellectuals of the day. DARCY O'BRIEN

STRADIVARI, *strad uh VAIR ee,* **ANTONIO** (1644?-1737), was one of the leading instrument makers in music history. He used Stradivarius, the Latin form of his name, on the labels of his instruments. Stradivari was probably born in Cremona, Italy. He studied there with Nicolo Amati, a noted instrument maker, and served for a time as Amati's assistant. During his long career, Stradivari made about 1,100 instruments. Of these, about 635 violins, 17 violas, and 60 cellos still exist.

Stradivari's instruments combine excellent wood, outstanding craftsmanship, beautiful shape and proportion, and superb varnish. His masterpieces provide an incomparable blend of strength and sweetness of sound. Stradivari's instruments, like others of his time, were later modified. They were fitted with longer, tilted necks and finger boards; stronger bass-bars; and higher bridges. These changes gave the instruments increased string tension and the structural strength to resist that tension. The modified instruments gained the volume needed to perform in the large concert halls and with the large symphony orchestras of the 1800's and 1900's. ABRAM LOFT

STRAFFORD, EARL OF (1593-1641), THOMAS WENTWORTH, was an English statesman. From 1614 to 1628 he was a leader of Parliament in its struggle with the Stuart kings. He was not a Puritan, however, and gradually drew away from his parliamentary friends as they became more vigorous in their criticism of King Charles I. In 1628, he went over to the king's side and in 1633, became Lord Deputy of Ireland. His administration was extremely harsh.

Wentworth returned to England in 1639. He became one of King Charles' chief advisers in his struggle against Parliament. Parliamentary leaders saw him as the greatest threat to their safety, and in 1640 decided to impeach him. He returned to London on Charles I's guarantee of safety. But, instead of an impeachment, Parliament passed a bill of attainder (see ATTAINDER). Charles, fearing mob violence, signed it, and two days later Strafford was executed. W. M. SOUTHGATE

STRAIGHT TICKET. See VOTING MACHINE; BALLOT.

STRAIN. See STRENGTH OF MATERIALS: ELASTICITY.

STRAIT is a narrow channel of water between two large bodies of water. Many wars have been fought and many treaties negotiated for the control and use of the world's important straits. Well-known straits include the Strait of Gibraltar between the Atlantic Ocean and the Mediterranean Sea, and the straits of Bosporus and Dardanelles between the Mediterranean and Black seas. The Strait of Magellan at the tip of South America is the only strait between the Atlantic and Pacific oceans. SIGISMOND DER. DIETTRICH

See also the separate articles in WORLD BOOK on the various straits, such as GIBRALTAR, STRAIT OF, and MACKINAC, STRAITS OF.

STRAITS SETTLEMENTS, in southeastern Asia, were part of colonial British Malaya. The British East India Company formed the settlements in 1826. They included Singapore, Melaka, Pinang-Wellesley, and the islands of the Dindings district. The mainland of the Dindings district was added to the settlements in 1874. Christmas Island joined the settlements in 1900. The Cocos Islands joined in 1903, and Labuan Island joined in 1907. During World War II (1939-1945), the settlements and Malaya were occupied by the Japanese.

The Straits Settlements colony was dissolved in 1946. Singapore, with Cocos and Christmas islands, became a separate colony, and Labuan Island was added to North Borneo. In 1957, the British ceded Pinang and Melaka to the Federation of Malaya. In 1963, the former Straits Settlements, Malaya, Singapore, Sarawak, and Sabah (North Borneo) merged to form the nation of Malaysia. Singapore became an independent country in 1965. GEORGE F. DEASY

STRAND, PAUL (1890-1976), an American photographer, helped develop photography as an art. Strand took detailed, focused photos that presented subjects

Photograph from the *Mexican Portfolio;* © 1967
Estate of Paul Strand (Art Institute of Chicago)

Plaza—State of Puebla, a photograph taken by Paul Strand in 1933, portrays the beauty of a simple scene in Mexico.

simply and directly. He rejected the hazy, out-of-focus photographic style that had become popular in the late 1800's.

Some of Strand's photographs show the influence of the cubist painters, who emphasized the basic geometric shapes of their subjects. To create a similar effect, Strand took photos of everyday objects, such as bowls and fences, from close and unusual angles. He later took detailed photographs of machines and landscapes.

In 1915, Strand began to take unposed portraits of people he saw on the streets of New York City. He later visited many countries, including Egypt, Ghana, Italy, and Mexico, and photographed the people for a book of pictures on each nation. From 1933 to 1943, Strand worked as a motion-picture cameraman and director. He was born in New York City. CHARLES HAGEN

STRANGLES. See DISTEMPER.

STRASBOURG, *strahz BOOR,* or *STRAS burg* (pop. 253,384; met. area pop. 365,323), is a trading center in France. Its location on the Ill River and its canal link with the Rhine make it a major "ocean port." It stands 250 miles (402 kilometers) east of Paris (see

FRANCE [political map]). Strasbourg's plants produce chemicals, leather, metals, paper, plastics, textiles, and other products.

Strasbourg is an old city with many medieval buildings. The Gothic cathedral, with its famous clock and magnificent rose window, is one of the most beautiful in Europe. Its spire is 466 feet (142 meters) high. Strasbourg University was founded in 1538.

The location of Strasbourg near the German-French border has made the city important commercially, but it has also made it a prize of war for many years. It was a German free town until 1681, when it was united with France. During the French Revolution in 1792, "The Marseillaise," the French national anthem, was written in Strasbourg. After the Franco-Prussian War in 1870, France ceded Strasbourg to Germany. The city became French again after the Treaty of Versailles in 1919. German troops occupied Strasbourg during World War II (1939-1945). Strasbourg has been the headquarters of the Council of Europe since 1949.   EDWARD W. FOX

See also ALSACE-LORRAINE.

STRASSMANN, FRITZ (1902-   ), is a German radiochemist. With Otto Hahn, another German radiochemist, he split the uranium atom in 1938. Strassmann and Hahn bombarded uranium atoms with neutrons and produced an element that they identified as barium. The importance of their work was revealed in 1939 by the Austrian physicists Lise Meitner and Otto R. Frisch. Meitner and Frisch explained that the neutrons had split the uranium atoms into fragments, producing barium and other elements.

Strassmann was born in Boppard, Germany. He taught at a technical high school in Hannover. In 1929, he joined Otto Hahn's laboratory staff in the Kaiser Wilhelm Institute for Chemistry (now Max Planck Institute) in Berlin-Dahlem.   AARON J. IHDE

See also HAHN, OTTO; MEITNER, LISE.

STRATEGIC AIR COMMAND (SAC) is the long-range bomber and missile force of the United States Air Force. Its combat-ready air forces can strike anywhere in the world. SAC includes the Second, Eighth, Fifteenth, and Sixteenth air forces. The command has about 1,300 jet bombers and tanker airplanes. SAC uses several types of missiles, including intercontinental ballistic missiles.

SAC's communications network can mobilize the entire command within seconds after a warning. A bomber force can be on the way to its targets within 15 minutes after a warning. If an enemy attack were to destroy SAC's ground control centers, retaliatory attacks would be directed from an airborne command plane. One of these planes is in the air at all times. SAC was organized in 1946, and has headquarters at Offutt Air Force Base, Nebr. See NEBRASKA (picture: Undergound Command Post).   THOMAS S. POWER

STRATEGIC ARMS LIMITATION TALKS (SALT), a series of meetings between Russia and the United States, began in 1969. The two nations met in an attempt to limit the production of nuclear weapons.

President Lyndon B. Johnson proposed the talks in January, 1967, in an attempt to end the costly arms race between Russia and the United States. At that time, the Russians were trying to overtake the United States in the production of offensive intercontinental ballistic missiles (ICBM's) and submarine-launched

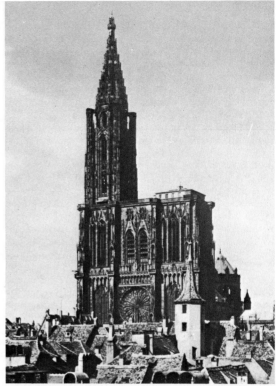

French Government Tourist Office

Strasbourg, a city in eastern France, is famous for its magnificent Gothic cathedral, *above*. This beautiful medieval church, completed in 1439, towers over the city's other buildings.

missiles. Later, the Russians began building an anti-ballistic missile (ABM) system to defend Moscow.

The SALT talks started in November 1969. By then, both Russia and the United States had nearly equal ability to attack each other with nuclear missiles. The first round of meetings was completed in December 1972. The meetings took place in Helsinki, Finland; Vienna, Austria; and Geneva, Switzerland. The second round of SALT meetings, also held in Geneva, lasted from 1973 to 1979.

During a visit by President Richard M. Nixon to Moscow in 1972, the United States and Russia signed two major agreements resulting from the SALT talks. One was a treaty limiting each country's defensive missile system to two ABM sites with no more than 100 missiles at each site. The other pact limited production of certain offensive nuclear weapons for five years. Both agreements went into effect in 1972. In 1979, the two nations signed another SALT agreement, limiting long-range bombers and missiles. But the pact did not take effect because the U.S. Senate refused to ratify it. In 1982, the United States and Russia began a new series of talks in Geneva aimed at reducing the nuclear arms of both nations.   GIL CARL ALROY

Additional Resources

LABRIE, ROGER P., ed. *SALT Hand Book: Key Documents and Issues, 1972-1979.* American Enterprise Institute, 1979.
SMITH, GERARD C. *Doubletalk: The Story of the First Strategic Arms Limitation Talks.* Doubleday, 1980.

STRATEGIC SERVICES, OFFICE OF (OSS), was a secret intelligence agency of the United States government during World War II. William J. Donovan headed the office under the direction of the Joint Chiefs of Staff. It was organized in 1942 to gather and analyze information, and conduct psychological and guerrilla warfare. It was dissolved after the war ended in 1945, and its functions were divided between the Department of State and the War Department. In 1947, the Central Intelligence Agency (CIA) was formed to unify all government intelligence agencies (see CENTRAL INTELLIGENCE AGENCY).   MAURICE MATLOFF

STRATEMEYER, EDWARD (1862-1930), was an American author who created some of the most popular characters in children's literature. In 1906, he founded the Stratemeyer Syndicate, which employed a staff of authors who wrote many of the books. Stratemeyer wrote—or outlined for others to write—over 800 children's books published under more than 60 pen names.

Stratemeyer's best-known books are adventure stories that feature teen-aged heroes and heroines. As Franklin Dixon, he wrote about the Hardy Boys. His other pen names include Victor Appleton for books about Tom Swift, Laura Lee Hope for stories about the Bobbsey Twins, and Arthur Winfield for tales about the Rover Boys. His daughter Harriet created the character of Nancy Drew under the name Carolyn Keene. Stratemeyer was born in Elizabeth, N.J.   ZENA SUTHERLAND

STRATFORD-UPON-AVON is a quiet English market town that has become famous as the birthplace of William Shakespeare. It is one of the oldest towns in England. It lies in the green valley of the River Avon, 8 miles (13 kilometers) southwest of Warwick (see GREAT BRITAIN [political map]). High-peaked Old English style houses line its narrow streets. It is the largest town in the district of Stratford-upon-Avon, which has a population of 99,402.

The house where Shakespeare probably was born has been kept as a memorial. It is always open to visitors. At Shottery, 1 mile (1.6 kilometers) west of Stratford, is the thatched-roof cottage that was the home of Anne Hathaway, Shakespeare's wife. The Guild Hall and grammar school are kept as they were in Shakespeare's day. Visitors also go to Wilmcote, $2\frac{1}{2}$ miles (4 kilometers) northwest of Stratford, to see the cottage of Mary Arden, Shakespeare's mother. Shakespeare and his wife are buried in Stratford's Holy Trinity Church. For pictures of many of these places, see SHAKESPEARE, WILLIAM (Shakespeare's Life).

In 1879, a Shakespeare Memorial was completed on the riverbank above the church. It includes a theater, a museum, and a library that contains valuable books and manuscripts having to do with Shakespeare and his life. The theater burned in 1926, but people immediately donated funds to rebuild it. The new theater was designed by Elisabeth Scott and it opened in 1932. The theater is called the Royal Shakespeare Theatre. The Royal Shakespeare Company performs Shakespeare's plays there. This permanent company includes many of Great Britain's finest actors, actresses, and directors. A Shakespeare Center was opened in 1964 to house the Shakespeare collections and form a meeting place for scholars.   FREDERICK G. MARCHAM

STRATHCONA AND MOUNT ROYAL, BARON OF (1820-1914), DONALD ALEXANDER SMITH, was a Canadian fur trader, railroad builder, financier, statesman, and philanthropist. He was closely associated with the Hudson's Bay Company from 1838 until his death, and became a governor of the company in 1889. He went to Labrador when he was 18 and became a fur trader. Afterwards, he moved to Canada and became interested in the development of the Northwest Territories.

When Manitoba became a province, Smith was elected to the Manitoba Assembly. The next year he was appointed commissioner for the Northwest Territories and was also elected to the Dominion House of Commons, serving from 1871 to 1880 and from 1887 to 1896.

Smith was the chief promoter of the Canadian Pacific Railway (now CP Rail). He served as president of the Bank of Montreal and as chancellor of McGill University. From 1896 to 1906, he acted as Canadian High Commissioner in London. Smith was a man of strong personality, vision, and great charm. Many educational and charitable institutions took advantage of his generosity. He was born in Forres, in what is now Grampian Region, Scotland.   JEAN BRUCHÉSI

STRATIFIED ROCK consists of layers, or *strata*. Each individual layer is called a *stratum*. Most sedimentary rocks, such as shale, sandstone, conglomerate, and limestone, are stratified. See ROCK (Sedimentary Rock).

Originally all strata were more or less horizontal. However, folding of the earth's crust in many places has thrown the rocks out of their former position. The angle at which these layers incline to the horizontal plane is called the *dip*. The dip may range from 0 to 90 degrees (vertical). Sedimentary rocks are stratified on land because rivers and wind spread them in layers. They are stratified on lake and ocean bottoms by currents of the water.   A. J. EARDLEY

STRATOSPHERE is a layer of the earth's atmosphere. It lies between the *troposphere*, the layer nearest the earth, and the *mesosphere*. In the polar regions, the stratosphere begins about 6 miles (10 kilometers) above the earth. Near the equator, it starts about 10 miles (16 kilometers) above the earth. It extends upward to about 30 miles (48 kilometers).

The air in the stratosphere is spread out in horizontal layers. The word *stratosphere* comes from the Latin word *stratus*, meaning *spread out*. There is almost no *convection* (rising of warm air) in the stratosphere, and so very little moisture enters from the troposphere. As a result, clouds rarely form in the stratosphere. But much air from the stratosphere is pulled into the troposphere by low-pressure storm systems there.

The stratosphere is warmer at its top than at its base. The lower 15 miles (24 kilometers) of the stratosphere have a temperature of about $-67°$ F. ($-56°$ C). The temperature rapidly increases to about $28°$ F. ($-3°$ C) at the *stratopause*, the upper layer of the stratosphere. The higher temperatures in the stratopause result from the presence of ozone gas there. Ozone absorbs ultraviolet rays from the sun.   FRANK SECHRIST

See also AIR; TROPOSPHERE; MESOSPHERE; THERMOSPHERE; IONOSPHERE.

STRATTON, CHARLES SHERWOOD (1838-1883), was an American midget who became best known by his circus name, General Tom Thumb. His small, doll-like body was perfectly formed. As a youth, Stratton was only 25 inches (64 centimeters) tall and weighed 15 pounds (6.8 kilograms). He was so bright that at the age of six he was exhibited by P. T. Barnum as though he were a full-grown man.

Charles S. Stratton became internationally famous by the name, General Tom Thumb.

Brown Bros.

Later, Stratton grew to be 40 inches (100 centimeters) tall and weighed 70 pounds (32 kilograms).

Stratton was born in Bridgeport, Conn., to parents of normal height. Barnum persuaded Stratton's parents to let the boy join his museum in New York City in 1842.

Barnum took him to Europe in 1844, where he entertained royalty and caused a sensation. In 1863, Stratton married Lavinia Warren (1841-1919), another one of Barnum's midgets. F. B. KELLEY

See also BARNUM, P. T.

STRATUS is a kind of cloud. See CLOUD (Kinds of Clouds; picture).

STRAUSS, *strows* or *shtrows*, the name of an Austrian family of composers, a father and three sons. They became famous for their waltzes and operettas. All of them were born and lived in Vienna, then considered one of Europe's gayest and most romantic capitals. The Strausses wrote music that captured this "spirit of Vienna."

The Strausses began composing after a musical form called the *Walzer* had developed into a ballroom dance in ¾ time. The four men—particularly Johann Strauss, Jr.—were noted for the waltzes they composed for dancing. In addition, no other composers have rivaled them in the quality of orchestral waltzes intended for concert performance. See WALTZ.

Johann Strauss, Sr. (1804-1849), was the son of a dance- and beer-hall operator. After studying music and becoming a performing violinist and conductor, he began composing waltzes in 1825. He organized his first orchestra in 1826 and toured successfully. In 1845, Strauss was appointed conductor for the Vienna court balls. His many compositions greatly improved the status of dance music. He wrote about 250 pieces, including waltzes, polkas, galops, and marches. He is best known for the "Radetzsky March."

Johann Strauss, Jr. (1825-1899), became known as the "Waltz King," His most famous work was "On the Beautiful Blue Danube." He was the most talented and best-known member of the family.

Strauss became a musician against his father's wishes. In 1844, he formed an orchestra that he combined with his father's orchestra in 1849. After gaining international fame as both a conductor and composer, he turned the orchestra over to his brothers in 1862. Following visits to England, France, and Italy, he traveled to the United States, where he conducted concerts in Boston and New York City in 1872.

Strauss was a great success as a composer of operettas, especially *Die Fledermaus* (*The Bat*, 1874), *A Night in Venice* (1883), and *The Gypsy Baron* (1885). Of his nearly 500 compositions, almost all the most popular ones are concert waltzes that show his gift as a writer of melodies and his brilliance as an orchestrator. Strauss's waltzes include the "Emperor Waltz," "Artist's Life," "Tales from the Vienna Woods," and "Vienna Blood."

Joseph Strauss (1827-1870) was trained as an architect but studied music secretly. He was also a poet, painter, and inventor. He became famous as a conductor of the Strauss family orchestra and composed nearly 300 pieces.

Eduard Strauss (1835-1916) conducted his own orchestra when he was 27. In 1870, he succeeded his brother Johann as director of the Vienna court balls. Strauss wrote many compositions, but he had neither the genius of his father and brother Johann, nor the talent of his brother Joseph. Eduard's son, Johann Strauss III (1866-1939), became a successful conductor of light entertainment music. HERBERT WEINSTOCK

Additional Resources

FANTEL, HANS. *The Waltz Kings: Johann Strauss, Father and Son, and Their Romantic Age.* Morrow, 1972.
GARTENBERG, EGON. *Johann Strauss: The End of an Era.* Pennsylvania State Univ. Press, 1974.
JACOB, HEINRICH EDUARD. *Johann Strauss, Father and Son: A Century of Light Music.* Arno, 1978. Reprint of 1940 ed.
WECHSBERG, JOSEPH. *The Waltz Emperors: The Life and Times and Music of the Strauss Family.* Putnam, 1973.

STRAUSS, LEVI (1829-1902), was an American clothing manufacturer. He founded Levi Strauss & Co., the world's first and largest manufacturer of denim jeans, which are sold under the brand name *Levi's*.

Strauss was born in Buttenheim, Bavaria, in what is now West Germany. He came to the United States in 1847 to join the dry goods business of his two brothers in New York City. In 1853, he opened a San Francisco wholesale business, which later became Levi Strauss & Co.

A Nevada tailor, Jacob Davis, wrote to the firm in 1872 suggesting the company make work pants with rivets to reinforce the seams. Strauss hired Davis, and in 1874 the company began producing riveted blue denim jeans and jackets. Through the years, Levi Strauss & Co. expanded to make other clothing in many fabrics. Today, the company is the world's largest clothing manufacturer. ED CRAY

STRAUSS, *strows* or *shtrows*, **RICHARD** (1864-1949), was a German composer. He is best known for a series of operas he composed to *librettos* (words) by the Austrian poet Hugo von Hofmannsthal. Strauss also became famous as a composer of songs and instrumental works and as a conductor.

Strauss was born in Munich. His first important works for orchestra were tone poems based on narratives from poems or stories. They include, with dates of composition, *Don Juan* (1889), *Death and Transfiguration* (1889), *Till Eulenspiegel's Merry Pranks* (1895), *Thus Spake Zarathustra* (1896), *Don Quixote* (1898), and *A Hero's Life* (1898). Strauss also composed most of his

STRAVINSKY, IGOR FYODOROVICH

almost 150 songs during this period. His best songs rank among the finest ever composed.

Strauss's first operas, *Guntram* (1893, revised 1940) and *Feuersnot* (1901), were unsuccessful. But they reflected the influence of the operas of Richard Wagner and had many of the qualities of Strauss's later operas. Like Wagner, Strauss used a stream of expressive and often complex music throughout each act. *Salome* (1905), Strauss's third opera, was his first success. It outraged many listeners with its *dissonant* (unharmonious) passages. Many listeners feel that the passages reflect the unbalanced mind of the main character.

Ewing Galloway

Richard Strauss

Strauss met Hofmannsthal soon after the première of *Salome*. Their first collaboration, *Elektra* (1908), was an adaptation of the tragedy by the Greek playwright Sophocles. Strauss carried the dissonant style of *Salome* even further in *Elektra*—and created greater controversy. In *Der Rosenkavalier* (1910), Strauss and Hofmannsthal tried to recreate the vanished aristocratic world of Vienna in the 1700's. This work is still Strauss's most popular opera.

Strauss wrote the most elaborate score of his career in *The Woman Without a Shadow* (1917), his next collaboration with Hofmannsthal. Many critics consider this opera Strauss's greatest achievement in musical drama. The work is highly symbolic, with both mortal and supernatural elements. Other works by Strauss and Hofmannsthal include *Ariadne auf Naxos* (final version, 1916), *The Egyptian Helen* (1927, revised 1933), and *Arabella* (first performed in 1933, after Hofmannsthal's death). Strauss's score for *Arabella* contains some of his most delicate and beautiful orchestral writing.

Strauss was one of the finest conductors of his day. He particularly excelled in interpreting the works of his two favorite composers, Wagner and Wolfgang Amadeus Mozart. Strauss held two important conducting positions—conductor of the Berlin Royal Opera from 1898 to 1918 and co-director of the Vienna State Opera from 1919 to 1924.

Strauss wrote five operas after Hofmannsthal's death in 1929. They include *The Silent Woman* (1935) and *Capriccio* (1941). During his last years, Strauss concentrated on a series of small-scale instrumental and vocal pieces. The best-known of these are *Metamorphoses* (1945) and *Four Last Songs* (1948). ROBERT BAILEY

See also HOFMANNSTHAL, HUGO VON.

Additional Resources

DEL MAR, NORMAN. *Richard Strauss: A Critical Commentary on His Life and Works.* 3 vols. Chilton, 1962-1972.

HARTMANN, RUDOLF. *Richard Strauss: The Staging of His Operas and Ballets.* Oxford, 1981.

KENNEDY, MICHAEL. *Richard Strauss.* Dent, 1976. A survey of the life and works of Strauss.

STRAVINSKY, *struh VIHN skih,* **IGOR FYODORO-VICH** (1882-1971), was a Russian-born composer.

He and Arnold Schönberg are often considered the two most important composers of the 1900's.

Schaal, Pix

Igor Stravinsky

Stravinsky was born near St. Petersburg (now Leningrad). He studied composition under the Russian composer Nicholas Rimsky-Korsakov in 1907 and 1908. In 1914, Stravinsky settled in Switzerland. He moved to Paris in 1920 and became a French citizen in 1934. In 1940, he settled in the United States, where he became a citizen in 1945.

Stravinsky first gained international fame for his ballets. He collaborated with the Russian ballet manager Sergei Diaghilev in producing three ballets in Paris—*The Firebird* (1910), *Petrouchka* (1911), and *The Rite of Spring* (1913). At the first performance of *The Rite of Spring*, the ballet's violent and unconventional quality caused the audience to riot. These ballets and a number of others, including *The Wedding* (1923), are based on Russian folklore. Stravinsky's narrated ballet, *The Soldier's Tale* (1918), is also based on Russian folklore. But, unlike his earlier ballets, it is composed in an international cabaret style rather than a Russian style. It is one of several theatrical works in which Stravinsky used a dream as part of the subject matter.

During the early 1920's, Stravinsky began writing in a neoclassical style, using scales, chords, and tone color in a generally clear and traditional way. The period began with *Octet for Wind Instruments* (1923) and ended with *The Rake's Progress* (1951), Stravinsky's only long opera. Stravinsky often chose his models from music of the past. For example, he wrote *The Rake's Progress* in the style of the Austrian composer Wolfgang Amadeus Mozart. In the *Ebony Concerto* (1945), Stravinsky combined elements of the concerto grosso form of the 1600's with modern jazz band orchestration.

During his neoclassical period, Stravinsky wrote three major symphonies—*Symphony of Psalms* (1930), *Symphony in C* (1940), and *Symphony in Three Movements* (1945). He also explored the sonata and concerto forms in such works as *Piano Sonata* (1924) and *Concerto for Violin* (1931).

At first, Stravinsky strongly opposed the 12-tone style of composing developed by Schönberg. But starting in the early 1950's, Stravinsky began a series of works using a modified 12-tone technique. These works included *In Memoriam Dylan Thomas* (1954) for tenor and instruments, the choral *Canticum Sacrum* (1956), and the ballet *Agon* (1957). Stravinsky then composed the choral *Threni* (1958) and *Requiem Canticles* (1966) in a complete 12-tone style. JAMES SYKES

See also SCHÖNBERG, ARNOLD.

Additional Resources

CRAFT, ROBERT. *Stravinsky: Chronicle of a Friendship, 1948-1971.* Knopf, 1972.

SIOHAN, ROBERT. *Stravinsky.* Grossman, 1970. Concentrates on his music.

WHITE, ERIC W. *Stravinsky: A Critical Essay.* Greenwood, 1979. Reprint of 1948 ed. *Stravinsky: The Composer and His Works.* 2nd ed. Univ. of California Press, 1979.

STRAW consists of the dried stems of such grains as wheat, rye, oats, and barley. Straw has many different uses. Farmers use it as bedding for animals, and for soil improvement. Manufacturers use straw to make hats, baskets, saddles, bottle covers, paper, suitcases, and strawboard. In the chemical laboratory, straw is used to produce carbon, phenol oil, pitch, and acetic acid.

Wheat straw makes the best hats. The stalks are pulled out of the ground, cut into short lengths, and laid in the sun. The sun bleaches the straw almost white. The leaves are then pulled off, leaving only the stem, which is bleached again with sulfur. The straw is sorted according to color and is ready for weaving into hats. In some countries, mechanical looms do the weaving. But in many parts of Europe, Japan, and China, the work is done by hand. Some of the best hand-braided straw comes from Tuscany, Italy. Panama hats are not made from a straw, but from the leaf fiber of a tropical tree. Straw differs from hay, which is dried grasses or other plants that are used as feed for animals.   RICHARD W. POHL

STRAWBERRY, a small plant of the rose family, is grown for its tasty heart-shaped fruit. Strawberry plants grow close to the ground and produce small, white flowers that have a pleasant odor. The fruit is greenish white at first and ripens to a bright red. It is a good source of vitamin C and is often eaten fresh. Strawberries are also canned or frozen or used in making jam, jelly, and wine.

Botanists do not classify the strawberry as a true berry. True berries, such as blueberries and cranberries, have seeds within their fleshy tissue. The fleshy part of the strawberry is covered with dry, yellow "seeds," each of which is actually a separate fruit.

Strawberry plants have short roots and a short stem. Leaves grow from the stem in groups of three. The fruit seems to be *strewn* (scattered) among the leaves, and this may be why the plant was first called *strewberry*. It later came to be called *strawberry*.

Strawberries grow wild or are raised commercially in almost every country. Plant breeders have developed hundreds of varieties that are suited for different growing conditions. Important varieties raised in the United

States include the *Albritton, Blakemore, Hood, Pocahontas, Premier,* and *Tioga.* California produces more than three-fourths of the strawberries grown in the United States. Other leading strawberry states include, in order of production, Oregon, Florida, Washington, and Michigan.

Strawberries grow best in a cool, moist climate and thrive in many kinds of soil. They are usually planted in fall or spring and grow only a little during the winter. The plants reproduce by sending out slender growths called *runners.* Roots extend from the runners into the soil and produce new plants that grow fruit. The harvesting season varies, depending on the climate and the type of strawberry. Some types, called *everbearing,* produce fruit throughout the summer and fall. Most strawberry plants bear fruit for five or six years, but the best crops grow during the first one or two years.

Many gardeners raise strawberries because the fruit grows so easily. Several scientific advances have led to increased commercial strawberry production. Plant breeders have developed varieties suited to specific climates. Researchers also have found various methods to control the major diseases and insects that attack strawberries. In addition, many commercial growers use mechanical equipment to plant and harvest strawberries more efficiently. Some growers use large greenhouses to control the environment and improve production.

Wild strawberries were cultivated in ancient Rome. During the 1700's, a hybrid variety was developed in France by breeding wild strawberries brought from North America with others that came from Chile. The first important American variety, the *Hovey,* was grown in 1834 in Massachusetts.

Scientific Classification. The strawberry belongs to the genus *Fragaria* in the rose family, Rosaceae. Common American species include *F. chiloensis, F. vesca,* and *F. virginiana.*   D. L. CRAIG

See also FRUIT (table: Leading Fruits in the United States).

STRAWFLOWER is a tall annual herb with yellow, orange, red, or white flowers. People dry them and use them as winter bouquets. The strawflower originated in Australia, and is now raised in gardens in Europe and America. The plant grows 3 feet (91 centimeters) tall and produces flowers from $1\frac{1}{2}$ to $2\frac{1}{2}$ inches (3.8 to 6.4 centimeters) wide. It grows from seeds.

Scientific Classification. The strawflower belongs to the composite family, Compositae. It is genus *Helichrysum,* species *H. bracteatum.*   ALFRED C. HOTTES

STREAM. See RIVER.

STREAM OF CONSCIOUSNESS. See NOVEL (New Directions in the Novel).

WORLD BOOK illustration by James Teason

Strawberry Plants produce heart-shaped red fruit and tiny white flowers. The delicious fruit can be eaten fresh or made into jam, jelly, and other food products.

J. Horace McFarland

The Strawflower has yellow, orange, red, or white flowers.

STREAMLINING

STREAMLINING is the shaping of a body so that it meets the smallest amount of resistance as it moves through a *fluid* (liquid or gas). The best streamlined shape for a body depends on whether it is to travel slower or faster than sound through the fluid. For *subsonic* (slower than sound) travel, a body should be somewhat blunt and rounded in front, and then taper to a point at the tail. Submarines and subsonic airplanes have this shape. In nature, fish have this type of streamlining. For *supersonic* (faster than sound) travel, a body should have a sharply pointed front. Supersonic airplanes and rockets have this shape.

The Effects of Streamlining

A streamlined object, *left,* offers the least resistance to a fluid flowing past it. A round object, *right,* causes eddy currents that increase its resistance to the flowing fluid.

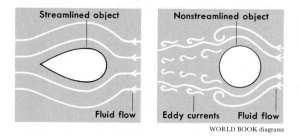

Streamlined object	Nonstreamlined object

Fluid flow   Eddy currents   Fluid flow

WORLD BOOK diagrams

The resisting force acting on a body as it travels through a fluid is called *drag.* The amount of drag depends on how smoothly the fluid flows around the body. The path that any bit of fluid follows around the body is called a *streamline.* If a body is streamlined, the streamlines separate smoothly at the front, pass smoothly around the body, and meet again at the tail. But if the body is not streamlined, the fluid may swirl and twist violently as it passes around the body. These motions are called *eddy currents.* The fluid may separate from the surface of the body and cause a partial vacuum behind it. The amount of drag increases because of the lack of pressure behind the body to balance pressure in front.

The effects of streamlining can be measured in a *wind tunnel.* In the tunnel, air is blown past a body so the drag can be measured. Streamlines can be made visible by adding smoke to the air at several points. When a flat plate is tested in the tunnel, streamlines can be seen curving around the edges of the plate. The air behind it is disturbed, forming eddy currents and a partial vacuum. The drag on the plate is relatively large. The streamlines can be seen following the surface more smoothly on a properly streamlined body. No eddy currents are produced, and there is less drag.

In addition to a body's shape, three other factors affect the drag: (1) the density of the fluid, (2) the amount of the body's area that meets the fluid, and (3) the speed of the body through the fluid. The drag doubles if either the fluid's density or the area of the body meeting the fluid is doubled. Doubling the speed of the body multiplies the drag by four.   WILLIAM L. HULL

See also AERODYNAMICS; WIND TUNNEL.

STREET is a road within a town or city. Streets lead out of the cities and towns, through the surrounding suburban areas, and connect with roads and highways (see ROAD). Streets serve the people who live and work in cities and towns. They also serve the people who come from farms and other nearby places for business and recreation. Some streets are used almost entirely by pedestrians. This is particularly true in some countries that have few automobiles.

Streets called *arterial* streets carry the most traffic and provide routes to the most important sections. Many of them are wider than other streets. Sometimes they are divided in the center to separate the traffic going in opposite directions. *Avenues* and *boulevards* are examples of important arterial streets. *Parkways* run through parks or parklike areas. Most are limited to passenger cars only. *Expressways* and *freeways* carry fast traffic. They are divided in the center, and crossings of other streets are always on different levels. To arrange for these crossings, dry-land bridges, called *grade separations,* are built. At the most important grade separations, ramps are built so that vehicles can get to and from the expressways and the other streets without crossing in front of each other.

There are about 694,000 miles (1,117,000 kilometers) of streets in the United States. This represents about 11 per cent of the nation's total streets, roads, and highways.

How Streets Are Built

Planning. Good street planning begins with a general plan for a beautiful and useful city. This plan shows the areas for businesses, factories, stores, parks, public buildings, and homes. It also includes a layout of streets serving the city and the surrounding suburban communities. Counts of traffic and other studies show where traffic comes from, where it goes, and in what volume. With this information, engineers plan important streets that will take people where they want to go with the least interference. The large number of cross streets, and the need for public transportation, parking space, and sidewalks complicate street planning.

Traffic engineers try to make existing streets as useful as possible. As traffic increases, some streets carry more vehicles than they were first designed to handle. Engineers must then find ways to provide more street space for vehicles to use at faster speeds. Some streets can be widened by moving their edges closer to buildings. Dead-end streets can be connected with other streets, or one-way streets can be created. In larger cities, expressways or freeways may be built.

Cables and pipelines carrying electricity, telephone wires, gas, water, and sewage run under city streets. In large cities subways sometimes run underneath the streets (see SUBWAY).

Draining. Much of the rainfall in cities and towns cannot sink into the ground. So it runs onto the streets. Most streets have gutters along the sides which are lower than the street level. The water runs into the gutters and along them into openings called *catch basins,* which connect with underground sewers. Smaller towns and suburbs sometimes have shallow ditches instead of paved gutters. These ditches may be carried under driveways and cross streets by pipes that are called *culverts.*

WORLD BOOK photo

Maintenance Workers Rebuild a City Street by putting asphalt on the surface, *above.* Some streets need complete reconstruction, but others require only resurfacing. Other streets are repaired by filling in holes or cracks.

Milt and Joan Mann

Stripes Painted on Streets aid public safety by designating lanes and areas for vehicles or pedestrians.

Brent Jones

Snowplows clear streets blocked by snow. Salt or other chemicals may then be spread to melt any ice that remains. The snowplow shown above is removing snow from a residential street.

Milt and Joan Mann

Street Cleaning helps keep streets free of trash, leaves, soot, and other filth. Maintenance crews may use large machines, such as the one shown above, to vacuum and wash streets.

731

STREET

Surfacing. Most city streets are paved with brick, bituminous materials, or concrete. Brick pavements usually are laid on sand spread over the ground or over a concrete foundation. *Bituminous* materials are made of asphalt or tar mixed with stone and sand. They are usually black in color. Concrete is made of cement, sand, gravel, or stone, and water. The pavement, as well as the foundation underneath, is of different thickness depending on the firmness of the ground and the type and volume of traffic expected. Some outlying streets are surfaced with gravel or stone, sometimes topped with a coating of oil, tar, or asphalt.

Intersections. Places where streets meet one another are called *intersections*. When the streets are on the same level, the intersections may be the scene of accidents and traffic jams. Many intersections have traffic signals to regulate the flow of traffic. Sometimes, circles or islands are built to help channel traffic into the correct lanes. These are used especially at wide intersections and where more than two streets meet. Expressways and freeways, with intersecting streets at different levels, have the safest kind of crossings.

Lighting. Good street lighting at night helps reduce crime and traffic accidents. Much of the light on streets comes from the headlights of vehicles, but most communities also have street lights. Many street lights have mercury vapor lamps, which are much brighter than the incandescent lamps used in homes. High-pressure sodium vapor lamps are also widely used for street lighting. These lamps produce a yellow-orange light that is brighter than the light of mercury vapor lamps.

How Streets Are Maintained

Repairing and Resurfacing. Weather and traffic gradually cause the street surface to wear out or become uneven. Most holes and breaks in the surface are filled with the same kind of material from which the streets were built. Cracks and joints in concrete are filled with bituminous materials. Black-top pavements may be sealed with a thin coating of bituminous material to waterproof the pavement and help preserve it.

When most of a street surface wears out or becomes uneven, new material may be added over the entire surface. This is called *resurfacing*. It smooths rough pavements and saves the base for further use. Curbs, gutters, and sidewalks seldom can be raised, and it often is necessary to strip off and replace the old surface. Sometimes the foundation must be repaired also.

On streets which are covered with gravel or stone, the surface must be reshaped from time to time, especially after wet weather. This usually is done with a scraping machine called a *motor grader*. This work, along with the addition of new material at intervals, helps keep the surface smooth.

Clearing Ice and Snow. Rain or sleet may freeze on streets. Then, salt or other chemicals may be spread to melt the ice. Often, these chemicals are mixed with sand or cinders which provide better traction for tires.

In northern climates, snow frequently blocks streets and must be removed or pushed off to one side. This is done with motor graders or with plows fastened to the fronts of trucks. Often, special crews of men are hired to load the snow into trucks so it can be hauled away. The loading is done by hand shovels or by elevating loaders. Elevating loaders are a system of buckets rigged on an endless chain. These "eat" into a snowbank and dump the snow into the trucks. Rotary plows sometimes are used to clear snow. The rotary plows have a big screw on the front. This screw feeds the snow through a spout and into a truck or off to the side of the street.

Cleaning. Streets get dirty from trash, leaves, and cinders. Maintenance crews often use machines

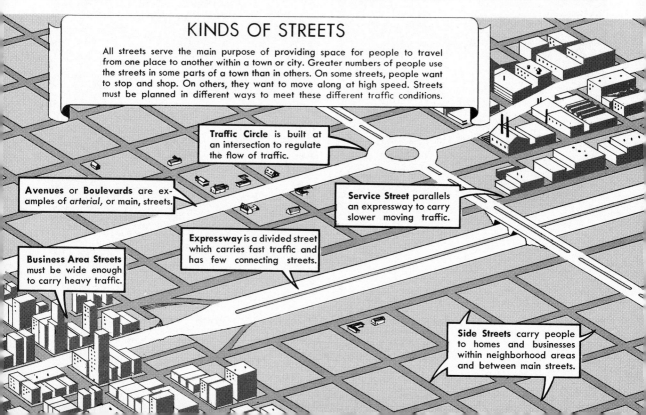

KINDS OF STREETS

All streets serve the main purpose of providing space for people to travel from one place to another within a town or city. Greater numbers of people use the streets in some parts of a town than in others. On some streets, people want to stop and shop. On others, they want to move along at high speed. Streets must be planned in different ways to meet these different traffic conditions.

Traffic Circle is built at an intersection to regulate the flow of traffic.

Avenues or Boulevards are examples of *arterial*, or main, streets.

Service Street parallels an expressway to carry slower moving traffic.

Business Area Streets must be wide enough to carry heavy traffic.

Expressway is a divided street which carries fast traffic and has few connecting streets.

Side Streets carry people to homes and businesses within neighborhood areas and between main streets.

equipped with large brushes to sweep the streets. Some of these machines are like big vacuum cleaners which suck up the dirt and dust. Every once in a while, streets may be flushed with water from trucks. This washes the dirt into the gutters and on into the sewers. Some machines have water, brushes, and vacuum all combined in one. In some places, workers sweep the gutters with a brush and load the dirt into trucks or pushcarts.

How Streets Are Paid For

Most streets are paid for largely from taxes paid by people who live in the cities and towns. A part of every property owner's taxes goes for construction and maintenance of streets. In addition, many of the local, or residential, streets are paid for by special taxes, called *assessments*, on the property served by the streets.

In recent years, cities and towns have received a greater share of the gasoline taxes and license fees collected by the state. The state legislature usually decides how much cities and towns are to be given from such funds. The money usually is divided according to population. Some cities also have their own special license fees and other taxes for street maintenance.

Some state highway departments build and maintain certain arterial streets that are extensions of the roads and highways leading into a city. The federal government also helps pay for some arterial streets. The

MONEY SPENT FOR CITY STREETS IN THE UNITED STATES	
Year	Total
1921	$ 346,000,000
1930	860,000,000
1940	611,000,000
1950	1,144,000,000
1960	3,160,000,000
1970	6,598,000,000
1977 (estimate)	10,294,000,000

Source: Federal Highway Administration.

state and city, or town, provide additional amounts.

Many cities borrow money so that street work can be done sooner than it could if they had to wait until the money were saved up from taxes. The borrowed money is repaid as taxes are collected.

History of Streets

Streets are as old as cities and towns. Greek, Roman, and other ancient cities had some paved streets and many unpaved streets. These streets often were very narrow and winding. Sometimes they were as steep as a flight of stairs. In the 1200's, the rapid growth of towns created a need for paving the main streets. A leader in the movement to pave streets in western Europe in the 1200's was King Philip Augustus of France. He had the street in Paris in front of his palace, the Louvre, paved with stones. Before this, the street was little more than an open sewer. He probably had it paved to overcome the bad odor and to obtain a smooth surface for travel. In England, the first paved street was laid in London in 1417. The laying-out of city streets at right angles to each other, in a gridiron pattern, developed from the feudal town arrangement of the Middle Ages.

In some early American cities, many of the streets may have followed cowpaths of the original farming villages. The streets in some cities were laid out in advance. One of these cities is Washington, D.C., the nation's capital. The Capitol is in the center of the city, with avenues leading out like spokes in a wheel. Other streets form a checkerboard or grid pattern. Circles were built at many points where avenues intersect streets. Supposedly, these circles were planned as places of defense in the event of an enemy attack.

Many early streets in America were surfaced with

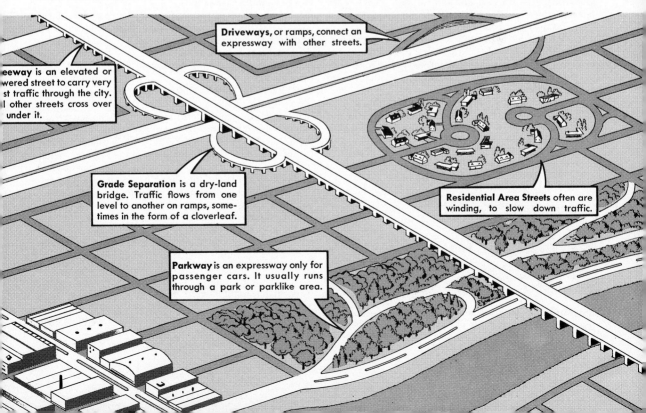

Driveways, or ramps, connect an expressway with other streets.

...eeway is an elevated or ...wered street to carry very ...st traffic through the city. ...l other streets cross over ...under it.

Grade Separation is a dry-land bridge. Traffic flows from one level to another on ramps, sometimes in the form of a cloverleaf.

Parkway is an expressway only for passenger cars. It usually runs through a park or parklike area.

Residential Area Streets often are winding, to slow down traffic.

round, uneven cobblestones and wood blocks. The first successful brick pavement was laid in Charleston, W. Va., in 1873. Stone blocks somewhat thicker and wider than bricks were another early paving material for streets. These still may be seen in use, especially between streetcar tracks. A bituminous pavement was patented in 1834 but was not used generally until many years later. The first concrete pavement was laid in Belle-fontaine, Ohio, in 1893.

Street widths vary from narrow ones like those in downtown Boston and New York City to broad ones like those in Washington, D.C., and Salt Lake City. In recent years, more and more cities have found it necessary to widen old streets and build new expressways to handle the increasing traffic. HENRY A. BARNES

See also ROAD and its list of *Related Articles*.

STREETCAR. The first streetcars were pulled by horses. They were called *horsecars*. Later, a *cable car* was invented. It was pulled by a cable, which was drawn by steam power. The cable ran through a small trench in the surface of the ground. The streetcar attached itself to the cable by means of a gripping device. Therefore it was also called a "grip" car.

In the early 1800's, inventors began trying to use electric power. But for many years the cost of generating electricity was too great to be practical. The invention of the electric generator solved this problem, and by the 1880's a number of electric cars were exhibited. The first commercial electric railway was operated in Lichterfelde, Germany, in 1881. In 1888, Frank J. Sprague opened the first successful electric "street railway" in the United States, in Richmond, Va. Electric cars immediately began to replace cable cars and horsecars.

The modern streetcar gets its power from an overhead line by means of a long trolley pole. The current is generated in a central powerhouse and passes along heavy copper wires which make up the overhead line. The usual type of car has a small trolley wheel, or *shoe*, which rides along the line, conducting the current to the trolley pole, down which it passes to the motors under the car. The current leaves the motors by means of the tracks, and passes back to the central generator to complete the circuit.

The electric motors are attached to the driving axles of the streetcar by gears. The operator of the streetcar controls the speed by regulating the current with a control lever.

Each car has seats for 50 or more people. Straps hang from the ceiling in the front and rear aisles for people who are unable to find a seat.

The streetcar was important in the growth of cities. For years, it was one of the chief means of transportation in such places as Chicago and also in the smaller cities and in towns. The streetcar also was used for transportation between cities and towns in some areas before the automobile came into wide use. Only San Francisco, where there are many steep hills, continues to use the cable car. The trolley bus, introduced in 1913, replaced the streetcar in some cities. It has a bus body and gets its power from an overhead trolley. The trolley bus does not use a track.

By the late 1930's, the streetcar became less important. But some cities continued to use them. Faster, quieter models replaced old cars. FRANKLIN M. RECK

See also CABLE CAR; ELECTRIC RAILROAD.

STREISAND, BARBRA (1942-   ), is an American singer and actress. She became famous for her dramatic interpretation of popular songs. She also gained praise as a comedienne both on the stage and in motion pictures.

Wide World

Barbra Streisand

Barbra Streisand was born in New York City. Her career began in 1961 when she entered a talent contest in a bar then. She won $50 and a nightclub engagement. She made her first Broadway appearance in the musical *I Can Get It for You Wholesale* (1962) and became a star in the musical *Funny Girl* (1964). Her motion-picture debut came in the film adaptation of *Funny Girl* (1968), and she won an Academy Award for her performance. She also starred in the film musicals *Hello, Dolly!* (1969) and *A Star Is Born* (1976). Streisand appeared in non-singing roles in the movie comedies *The Owl and the Pussycat* (1970), *What's Up, Doc?* (1972), and *Up the Sandbox* (1972). JOHN S. WILSON

STRENGTH OF MATERIALS is a term used by engineers to describe how much force a material can resist. Engineers also use the term to describe how a material's shape and size change as a result of force. In addition, strength of materials is the branch of engineering that deals with the study of how materials resist force. When engineers design a building or a machine, they consult publications that list the strength of various materials. These publications aid in the selection of materials that will not fail during use.

How Materials React to Force. The strength of a material depends on its *mechanical properties*, which include elasticity, hardness, and stiffness. Mechanical properties combine differently in every material. As a result, such materials as aluminum, concrete, and steel differ in their ability to resist a particular force. Also, each material differs in its ability to resist various types of force. A bar of cast iron, for example, has greater ability to withstand a force that pushes it together than it does to resist a force that pulls it apart.

When an external force is applied to a material, a

Chicago Transit Authority

The Horsecar of 1878, a forerunner of today's streetcar, was a swaying, noisy car which ran on two rails and was pulled by horses. A small stove, and straw scattered on the floor, kept the passengers warm in cold weather.

force inside the material resists the external force. This internal resistance of a material to such a force is called *stress*. If a material cannot resist an external force, the material changes in shape and size. When a weight is put on the end of a rope, for example, the rope stretches. The actual change in a material—in the above case, the stretching of the rope—is called *strain*. The greater the amount of stress in a material, the greater the amount of strain that will occur in it.

Materials undergo three types of stress: *tensile stress*, *compressive stress*, and *shearing stress*. Tensile stress causes a material to stretch, as with the rope. Compressive stress causes a material to push together. The pillars that support a building undergo compressive stress because the weight of the structure pushes down on them. Shearing stress causes a material to separate into layers by a sliding action. Such an action resembles that of the cards in a deck, which slide apart when they are tilted so the edges are at an angle.

The stresses in a material may combine to resist force. Combined stresses cause *flexure* (bending) and *torsion* (twisting). For example, stresses unite in a springboard when a person stands on it. The person's weight causes tensile stress in the top section of the board, and the fibers there stretch. At the same time, the weight of the individual causes compressive stress in the bottom section of the board. As a result, the fibers there push closer together. This combination of stresses makes the board bend.

How Strength Is Determined. Technicians measure the strength of a material by using special machines that apply force to a sample of the material. First, they determine the material's *elastic limit*, the amount of force it can resist without changing permanently. If the applied force is lower than the elastic limit, the material will return to its original shape and size after the force is removed. But if the force exceeds the elastic limit, the material will change permanently.

Technicians also measure the *ultimate strength* of a material—that is, the maximum force it can resist without breaking. Engineers consider ultimate strength in terms of the number of pounds of force per square inch (kilograms of force per square centimeter) that a material can withstand. For example, a bar of cast iron can withstand about 30,000 pounds per square inch (207,000 kilopascals) of a pulling force without breaking. Laboratory tests for strength are not exact. The results are affected by such factors as a material's age, composition, and moisture.

In constructing a building or a machine, engineers use a material strong enough to resist a heavier load than the one expected. This policy helps ensure that the material will not fail during actual use.

Development of New Materials. During the late 1960's, scientists began the extensive development of *composite materials*. Such a material contains two or more materials. Many composite materials contain a large amount of one substance combined with fibers, flakes, or layers of another. Composite materials have greater strength than many single materials. For example, glass fibers combined with plastics form a material called *fiberglass reinforced plastics*. This material has greater strength than either the glass or the plastics

alone. Manufacturers use fiberglass reinforced plastics to make such products as boat hulls, building panels, and truck parts.

During the early 1970's, scientists increased the development of composite materials that contain fibers. Two of the strongest fibers consist of *boron*, a chemical element, and *graphite*, a form of carbon. Boron fibers and graphite fibers can withstand intense force and high temperatures. These fibers are undergoing research for use in aircraft and rocket parts.

Many materials gain greater strength when produced in the form of *whiskers*, which are extremely thin, tiny crystals of a substance. Whiskers are stronger than fibers because they have fewer flaws than do fibers. One of the strongest types of whiskers is made of sapphire.   R. J. HARKER

See also DUCTILITY; ELASTICITY; METAL FATIGUE.

STREP THROAT is an infectious disease that affects the membranes of the throat and tonsils. It chiefly develops in children from 5 to 12 years of age. The disease is also called *septic sore throat, acute streptococcal pharyngitis*, and *acute streptococcal tonsillitis*.

Strep throat is caused by bacteria of a type called *group A beta-hemolytic streptococci* (see STREPTOCOCCUS). The bacteria generally spread from person to person through droplets of moisture sprayed from the nose and mouth. People called *carriers*, who harbor the streptococci but do not have symptoms of disease, can spread strep bacteria. Laboratory tests can confirm the presence of strep bacteria in material taken from the patient's throat. See DISEASE (Spread of Infectious Diseases).

Symptoms of strep throat include sore throat, fever, headache, and, in some cases, chills, nausea, and vomiting. The patient usually experiences swelling of the tonsils and of the lymph nodes in the neck. The disease disappears rapidly following treatment. Untreated cases may last one to two weeks.

Various complications can follow strep throat. The infection may spread to the ears, sinuses, lungs, bones, or bloodstream. In other cases, patients later develop *rheumatic fever* or a kidney disease called *acute glomerulonephritis* (see RHEUMATIC FEVER; NEPHRITIS). Prompt treatment of strep throat with penicillin can prevent the infection from spreading to other parts of the body. Such treatment also eliminates the risk of rheumatic fever but does not always prevent acute glomerulonephritis. Many doctors advise that other members of the patient's household be tested for the presence of streptococci. Those who are found to be carrying the bacteria are treated with penicillin.   HUGH C. DILLON, JR.

STREPSIPTERA. See INSECT (table).

STREPTOCOCCUS, *STREHP tuh KAHK uhs* (plural, streptococci, *STREHP tuh KAHK sy*), is a *genus* (group) of bacteria that share certain characteristics. Under a microscope, streptococci appear as chains of sphere-shaped

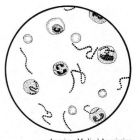

American Medical Association

Streptococcus Germs look like black, beadlike chains.

organisms. Streptococci are classified as *hemolytic* bacteria. These bacteria produce toxins that completely or partially destroy red blood cells. Such destruction is called *hemolysis*.

The *beta-hemolytic streptococci* completely destroy red blood cells in laboratory cultures. Bacteriologists recognize a number of groups of beta-hemolytic streptococci. Members of one of these groups—*group A*—cause most streptococcal diseases in human beings. Group A streptococcal infections include strep throat, impetigo, erysipelas, *septicemia* (blood poisoning), puerperal fever, and scarlet fever. Group A infections can also lead to serious complications, particularly rheumatic fever and a kidney disease called *acute glomerulonephritis* (see RHEUMATIC FEVER; NEPHRITIS).

The *alpha-hemolytic streptococci* partially destroy red blood cells in laboratory cultures. Some of these bacteria are found in the mouth and are associated with tooth decay. A related species, *Streptococcus pneumoniae*, is a major cause of bacterial pneumonia.　　　HUGH C. DILLON, JR.

STREPTOMYCIN, *STREHP tuh MY sihn,* is a drug that fights the bacteria that cause many diseases. It is said to be successful against infections that resist sulfa drugs and penicillin. It is the first drug that has found extensive application in the treatment of tuberculosis. See PENICILLIN; SULFA DRUGS.

Streptomycin is produced by a tiny plant that grows in the soil, a microorganism named *Streptomyces griseus.* In 1939, Selman A. Waksman of Rutgers University began to test microscopic growths to find a substance that could be used against disease germs. The best substance he found was formed by a microbe belonging to the group of actinomycetes, of the genus *Streptomyces.* It was named *streptomycin.*

Streptomycin is given off into a broth in which the microorganisms are grown. The impure drug is separated from the broth first as a solution, then as a solid. Then the drug is purified to small crystals of its salts, which form a white powder.

Chemically, streptomycin is an organic base, and forms several salts. The solid drug can be stored in a refrigerator for six months. Solutions keep their power for a considerable length of time, even when heated.

Streptomycin can be injected into the muscles, under the skin, or it can be taken by mouth or sprayed into the lungs. It is reported to have checked types of streptococcus and staphylococcus, Gram-negative and Gram-positive bacteria, and mycobacteria.

Streptomycin acts by interfering with the growth of the microbes. This effect is *bacteriostatic.* It kills bacteria, a *bactericidal* action. Streptomycin is effective in the treatment of tuberculosis, infections of the urinary passages, typhoid fever, pneumonia, dysentery, undulant fever, and such wound infections as gas gangrene. It may supplement the action of other drugs.　　SELMAN A. WAKSMAN

See also ANTIBIOTIC; WAKSMAN, SELMAN ABRAHAM.

STRESEMANN, *SHTRAY zuh mahn,* **GUSTAV** (1878-1929), a German statesman, was one of the authors of the Locarno Pact (see LOCARNO CONFERENCE). Elected to the Reichstag (the lower house of the German parliament) in 1906, he became the leader of the National Liberal Party and, later, of the German People's Party. In 1923, he became chancellor and foreign minister,

and he secured Germany's admission to the League of Nations in 1926. Stresemann shared the 1926 Nobel peace prize with Aristide Briand. Stresemann was born in Berlin.　　　GABRIEL A. ALMOND

STRESS. See STRENGTH OF MATERIALS; ELASTICITY; ANNEALING.

STRESS is a body condition that may occur when a person faces a threatening or unfamiliar situation. Such situations include illness, the loss of a job, and even a promotion or being elected class president. Stress causes a person's energy and strength to increase temporarily. The body also increases its defenses against diseases. All these bodily changes may help an individual overcome challenges and dangers.

If stress continues for weeks or months, it may damage or exhaust certain organs and lead to various illnesses. Physicians believe that people can help themselves stay in good health by avoiding lengthy stress.

Causes of Stress are called *stressors.* They may include any unusual demand on a person's body or mind.

Illness causes stress because it forces the body to activate its defenses against disease. Stress also results when the body must heal an injury or adapt to such environmental hazards as noise or extreme cold.

In addition, stress may occur when a person must adapt to an unfamiliar situation—whether the change seems favorable or unfavorable. For example, most people experience stress when they welcome a new baby to their family or mourn the death of a close relative. A change in a person's income, marital status, place of residence, or even diet may also trigger stress.

An event that causes great stress for one person may present only a minor difficulty for another. A person's physical condition affects his or her ability to handle stressors. An individual's response also depends on whether he or she feels in control of the situation. A difficulty may cause little stress if a person can predict, overcome, or at least understand it.

How Stress Affects the Body. Stress alters the functioning of most parts of the body, including the brain, the muscles, and the internal organs. These changes increase a person's ability to meet a variety of stressors. In fact, the changes caused by stress may prepare an individual for dangers that are not present. For example, stress heightens certain bodily defenses against germs, whether or not a person is sick.

Stress begins with certain bodily changes that last from a few minutes to a few hours. Their effects include keener senses and increased energy and strength. Other changes develop gradually and may continue for weeks or months if a stressor persists. They heighten the body's ability to check inflammation and to destroy germs and poisons. Stress also causes the body to build up its stores of sugar, which supplies energy.

A part of the brain called the *hypothalamus* regulates the body's responses to stressors. Nerve or chemical signals alert the hypothalamus when a stressor occurs. The hypothalamus then triggers the release of chemical messengers called *hormones* from various glands into the bloodstream.

The short-term changes of stress result chiefly from the hormone *epinephrine*, also called *adrenalin*. This hormone is secreted by the inner part of each adrenal gland. Most long-term changes are set off by *cortisol* and other hormones from the outer part of each adrenal. Hormones from such glands as the pancreas, the pituitary, and the thyroid also play a role in stress.

Stress-Related Illnesses. Prolonged stress may temporarily exhaust the adrenal glands or other organs that help the body maintain enough energy and resist disease. As a result, a person may feel extremely fatigued and have little ability to fight illness. Lengthy stress also weakens the skin and internal membranes. Rashes, ulcers, or other disorders of the skin, stomach, or intestines may result. Other conditions associated with stress include high blood pressure and long-term malfunction of such glands as the adrenals, pancreas, pituitary, and thyroid.

Extremely prolonged and severe stress can lead to potentially fatal conditions. Such conditions include *cardiac arrest* (heart failure) and *shock* (a general weakening of the vital processes).

Physicians recommend three main ways to help prevent stress-related illnesses. (1) Avoid continual stress. A person facing a long series of stressors should plan periods of relaxation. (2) Learn to handle troublesome situations with a minimum of stress. The WORLD BOOK article on HEALTH (Handling Stress) suggests ways to help reduce stress. (3) Pay special attention to your health when stress occurs. A healthful way of life and medical care can prevent a stress-related illness from developing or becoming serious.   HANS SELYE

See also GLAND; HORMONE; SELYE, HANS; TRANSCENDENTAL MEDITATION.

Additional Resources

BROWN, BARBARA B. *Stress and the Art of Biofeedback.* Harper, 1977.
COLEMAN, VERNON. *Stress Control.* Transatlantic, 1980.
MORSE, DONALD ROY, and FURST, M. L. *Stress for Success: A Holistic Approach to Stress and Its Management.* Van Nostrand, 1979.
SELYE, HANS. *The Stress of Life.* Rev. ed. McGraw, 1978.

STRIAE. See ICE AGE (Effects of the Ice Sheets).

STRIKE, in business and industry, is a stopping of work by a group of employees. All or some of a company's employees may be involved. A strike is designed to interrupt the normal flow of goods or services that a company produces or handles. The workers use the strike as their main bargaining weapon. They hope that a strike or the threat of a strike will persuade the company to agree to their demands for higher wages, improved working conditions, or other benefits.

The term *strike* also refers to any stoppage of normal operations or activities to protest an action or condition. During the 1950's and 1960's, some civil rights workers in the United States staged sit-down strikes. They sat down in public places and refused to move to protest racial injustice. Some prison inmates have gone on hunger strikes and refused to eat until officials considered their grievances. In the late 1960's and early 1970's, college students in many countries struck for various kinds of changes. However, strikes are most closely associated with work stoppages in business and industry. This article chiefly discusses such labor strikes.

Functions of Strikes. A strike is a sign of dissatisfaction among a large or small number of workers in a plant or industry. By striking, workers take action to express a grievance or to enforce a demand. In the 1800's and early 1900's, many strikes in the United States resulted from workers' efforts to get employers to recognize unions as their bargaining agents. Today, most strikes involve disputes over wages, hours, and other conditions of employment.

Strikes are an important part of the *collective bargaining* process between workers and employers. In this process, representatives of both parties meet to establish conditions of employment that will be jointly acceptable. There are more than·150,000 collective bargaining contracts in the United States. Most of these agreements are reached—and renegotiated periodically—without strikes. During the 1960's, strikes in the United States accounted for a work loss of only about four hours a year per worker.

Strikes occur occasionally in any society that encourages free collective bargaining. No matter how reasonable the two sides may be, some disagreements will arise between labor and management. During the bargaining process, a strike or the threat of a strike increases the cost of being unreasonable. It encourages each side to seriously consider the other's arguments and demands.

Kinds of Strikes. There are various kinds of strikes. An *authorized strike* is one agreed upon by union officials or a majority of the union members. A *wildcat strike* is a strike called by a group of workers without official union support. Most strikes are *walkouts*, in which the workers leave their jobs. A *sit-down strike* is a strike in which people stop working but do not leave their place of employment. A *sympathy strike* is called by one union in order to support another union that is on strike. A *jurisdictional strike* may result when two or more rival unions claim the right to work on the same job. A *secondary strike* takes place when workers call a work stoppage in an attempt to force their employer to stop doing business with another employer who is involved in a labor dispute.

Generally, nonpublic employees have the right to strike. Similarly, private employers may close their plants in order to keep employees from working. Such action is called a *lockout*. Almost all collective bargaining agreements prohibit strikes and lockouts during the term of a contract. In the United States, federal laws also prohibit or limit certain kinds of strikes. For ex-

Bettmann Archive
Clothing Workers in New York City went on strike for higher wages and better working conditions in 1910.

Striking City Employees, including carpenters, electricians, and transportation workers, picketed San Francisco's city hall in 1976. Strikes by public employees became increasingly common during the 1970's.

Hap Stewart

ample, the Taft-Hartley Act bans jurisdictional strikes, secondary strikes, and sympathy strikes. The Taft-Hartley Act and the Railway Labor Act include provisions to delay strikes that might create a national emergency.

Many states have laws forbidding strikes by employees of the state or local government. But strikes by such public employees as police, teachers, and sanitation workers became common in the 1960's and 1970's. Several states passed laws giving government workers the right to strike. Many labor leaders called for federal legislation to extend the right to all public employees.

Strike Tactics in the United States and other industrial countries have been relatively peaceful for many years. But open warfare, loss of life, and destruction of property were common during the 1800's and early 1900's.

Union members usually follow authorized strike-vote procedures, though occasionally a wildcat strike may occur. Many unions have special strike funds to help support the strikers.

As soon as a strike begins, union members usually set up *picket lines* at entrances to the employer's place of business. The pickets carry signs telling why they are on strike. The purpose of the picket line is to turn away other workers, to discourage customers, and to keep goods from being taken into or out of the plant. Union members usually refuse to cross the picket line of another union.

Strike Settlements. Most strikes are settled through negotiations between representatives of labor and management. A neutral third party may help the parties reach a settlement. In *mediation*, the third party tries to promote discussion, to work out compromises, and to find areas of agreement. A mediator has no power to force a settlement. In *arbitration*, the third party has the power to settle a strike. An arbitrator is given the power of *binding arbitration* through voluntary agreement of the parties involved or by law. Binding arbitration requires both sides to accept the recommendations of the arbitrator.   ABRAHAM J. SIEGEL

Related Articles in WORLD BOOK include:

Arbitration	Lockout
Boycott	National Labor Relations
Federal Mediation and	Board
Conciliation Service	National Mediation Board
Haymarket Riot	Pullman Strike
Homestead Strike	Railway Labor Act
Industrial Relations	Taft-Hartley Act
Labor Movement	

Additional Resources

BROOKS, THOMAS R. *Toil and Trouble: A History of American Labor.* 2nd ed. Delacorte, 1971.
CARTTER, ALLAN M., and others. *Labor Economics: Wages, Employment and Trade Unionism.* 4th ed. Irwin, 1980.
HUTT, WILLIAM H. *The Strike-Threat System: The Economic Consequences of Collective Bargaining.* Arlington House, 1973. Argues against the power to strike.
THE TWENTIETH CENTURY FUND. TASK FORCE ON LABOR DISPUTES IN PUBLIC EMPLOYMENT. *Pickets at City Hall.* The Fund, 1970.

STRINDBERG, AUGUST (1849-1912), a Swedish writer, is one of the key figures in the history of modern drama. His experiments in dramatic form, his dynamic expression, and his brilliant language influenced the development of both naturalism and expressionism in drama. Strindberg also wrote novels, short stories, essays, poetry, and autobiographical works.

Johan August Strindberg was born in Stockholm. After some university training, he became a free-lance journalist in Stockholm. He began writing plays in 1870, and completed a fine historical drama, *Master Olof*, in 1872. He gained fame with the publication of *The Red Room* (1879), a novel about the rackets of Stockholm.

Strindberg returned to playwriting with his famous naturalistic drama *The Father* (1887). This play tells how a wife destroys her husband by forcing him to doubt that he is the father of their daughter. *Miss Julie* (1888), a naturalistic play of social criticism, describes the tragedy of a woman of the Victorian age who loves a man beneath her social class. *The Creditors* (1888) describes the hate and pain which three persons can inflict upon one another.

Detail of a lithograph (1896) by Edvard Munch; the Art Institute of Chicago

August Strindberg

Strindberg suffered much emotional and physical distress following two divorces in the 1890's. But by 1898 he had begun a new style of playwriting with *To Damascus* (parts I and II, 1898; part III, 1904). In this expressionistic trilogy, Strindberg portrayed himself as the "Unknown One," and expressed his lifelong spiritual uncertainty in dreamlike scenes and moods. In the delicate symbolic play *Easter* (1901), however, he faithfully presented traditional Christian principles.

After the cold, brutal domestic drama *Dance of Death* (1901) and the romantic tragedy *The Bridal Crown* (1902), Strindberg again turned to an expressionistic form in *A Dream Play* (1902). This play consists of short scenes and speeches that trace the search for happiness by the daughter of the Indian god Indra. Only one other Strindberg play, *The Spook Sonata* (1907), has less plot and a more pessimistic view of life. *The Spook Sonata* is the strangest and one of the most influential of Strindberg's plays. Its disconnected dialogue, mystical images, and distorted characters had a strong influence on expressionistic drama.   FREDERICK J. HUNTER

See also NATURALISM; EXPRESSIONISM.

Additional Resources

BRUSTEIN, ROBERT. *The Theatre of Revolt: An Approach to the Modern Drama.* Little, Brown, 1964.
JOHANNESSON, ERIC O. *The Novels of August Strindberg: A Study in Theme and Structure.* Univ. of California Press, 1968.
JOHNSON, WALTER. *August Strindberg.* Twayne, 1976.
VALENCY, MAURICE. *The Flower and the Castle: An Introduction to Modern Drama.* Macmillan, 1963.

STRING. See TWINE.

STRING QUARTET. See CHAMBER MUSIC.

STRINGED INSTRUMENT. See MUSIC; ORCHESTRA.

STRIP MINE. See COAL (Surface Mining; pictures).

STROBILE. See CONE-BEARING PLANT.

STROESSNER, *STREHS nuhr*, **ALFREDO,** *ahl FRAY thoh* (1912-   ), led a military overthrow of the government of Paraguay in 1954 and later that year was elected president without opposition. He was reelected in 1958, 1963, 1968, 1973, 1978, and 1983 in government-controlled elections.

Stroessner allowed little opposition to his rule. Some Paraguayans who criticized him were imprisoned, and many others fled the country. Stroessner achieved some political stability and some economic progress for Paraguay. He used loans provided by international agencies to improve the road and water supply systems, increase electric power production, and construct new schools.

Stroessner was born in Encarnación and graduated from the Military College in Asunción. In 1951, Stroessner became the commander in chief of Paraguay's armed forces.   JOHN TATE LANNING

STROKE, or APOPLEXY, is a serious medical condition that occurs if the brain does not receive an adequate supply of blood. The constant circulation of blood provides the brain with oxygen and nutrients. Permanent damage can result if the brain lacks enough blood for as short a time as 3 to 10 minutes.

Stroke ranks as a major health problem in the United States. Every year, over 500,000 Americans suffer strokes. About a third of these attacks are fatal. Most survivors of stroke suffer temporary or permanent disabilities and require extensive medical care.

Causes. Most major strokes result from one of three main causes. These causes, in order of frequency, are (1) cerebral thrombosis, (2) cerebral hemorrhage, and (3) cerebral embolism.

Cerebral Thrombosis occurs when a blood clot forms in one of the major arteries that carries blood to the brain. In most cases, the clot builds up in a blood vessel that has been narrowed by a disease called *arteriosclerosis* (hardening of the arteries). People with

high blood pressure are especially likely to develop arteriosclerosis.

Many persons who suffer cerebral thrombosis have previously had one or more *incipient strokes*. These attacks result from a momentary reduction in blood flow through the narrowed artery. Symptoms may include dizziness, tingling, weakness, slurred speech, and visual problems in one eye. The symptoms may last up to 30 minutes and then disappear completely.

Cerebral Hemorrhage occurs when an artery in the brain ruptures. In many cases, the rupture results from high blood pressure. In other instances, the wall of the artery has an *aneurysm*—a weak spot that swells like a bubble until it bursts. See CEREBRAL HEMORRHAGE.

Cerebral Embolism, like cerebral thrombosis, involves a clot that blocks one of the brain's major arteries. However, the clot forms in another part of the body. It travels through the bloodstream until it clogs one of the arteries that supply the brain. See EMBOLISM.

Effects. The victim of a major stroke may experience weakness and paralysis on one side of the body. Other symptoms include difficulty in speaking or understanding language, and blind spots in vision. In cerebral thrombosis, the symptoms may develop progressively during several hours or days. In cerebral hemorrhage and cerebral embolism, the changes occur very rapidly. In either case, many victims eventually lose consciousness, and a large number die.

Recovery from a stroke depends on how much of the brain has been permanently damaged. In many cases, the stroke does not destroy the entire area of the brain that controls a certain activity. If enough of the area remains undamaged, the victim may be able to learn

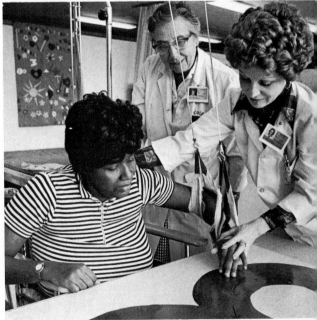

Michael Reese Hospital and Medical Center

Stroke Rehabilitation can help victims return to a relatively normal life. The patient above is learning how to do an exercise that will help her regain the use of a paralyzed arm.

that activity again. Other parts of the brain also can learn to take over some of the jobs previously performed by the damaged area.

Rehabilitation should begin as soon as the patient regains consciousness. At first, treatment consists of stretching contracted muscles and moving the arm and leg on the affected side of the body. This action prevents the muscles and limbs from becoming permanently misshapen. Later, physical therapists use exercises and special equipment to restore strength and mobility in the affected limbs. The physical therapists work under the supervision of physicians called *physiatrists*. Occupational therapists help the patient to regain the functional use of affected limbs and to overcome perceptual problems, such as coordinating hand and eye movements. Many stroke victims must learn again to walk and to care for their bodily needs. If necessary, a speech therapist helps teach the patient to speak again. Most patients can learn to lead productive lives, and some recover almost completely.

Prevention. High blood pressure, also called *hypertension*, is the basic cause of most strokes. Therefore, the control of this condition is the most effective way to prevent strokes from happening. Physicians prescribe various medications and diets to control high blood pressure.

Drugs and surgery can help reduce the risk of a major stroke in persons who have experienced incipient strokes. Daily doses of aspirin can reduce the risk in male patients by slowing the formation of blood clots. Surgery can help both men and women whose incipient strokes resulted from a narrowed internal carotid artery. The internal carotid arteries are the major vessels that carry blood to the brain. In some cases, a surgeon can open the narrowed artery and remove the material that has clogged it.   JAMES A. SCHOENBERGER

See also APHASIA; HYPERTENSION.

Additional Resources

DAHLBERG, CHARLES C., and JAFFE, JOSEPH. *Stroke: A Doctor's Personal Story of His Recovery.* Norton, 1977.
FREESE, ARTHUR S. *Stroke: The New Hope and the New Help.* Random House, 1980.
SARNO, JOHN E. and MARTHA T. *Stroke: The Condition and the Patient.* Rev. ed. McGraw, 1979.

STROMBOLI, *STRAHM buh lee,* is an island in the Tyrrhenian Sea off the northeastern coast of Sicily. The island covers 4.7 square miles (12.2 square kilometers) and has 469 people. It is famous for its volcano, which rises 3,031 feet (924 meters) high. The volcano is one of the few in Europe that are constantly active. Ancient writers reported this activity centuries ago. Disastrous eruptions rarely occur because the lava flows freely instead of building up internal pressure for violent eruptions. For the location of Stromboli, see ITALY (physical map).   SHEPARD B. CLOUGH

STRONG, SIR SAMUEL HENRY (1825-1909), served as the chief justice of the Supreme Court of Canada from 1892 to 1902. He became one of its first members when the court was established in 1875. Strong was a judge of the Court of Chancery from 1869 to 1874. He was knighted in 1893, and sworn into the Imperial Privy Council in 1897. He was born in Poole, Dorsetshire, England.   J. E. HODGETTS

STRONTIUM, *STRAHN shee uhm,* a chemical element, is a soft, silvery, or yellowish metal. It exists as many *isotopes* (atoms with the same atomic number but different atomic weights). Strontium 90 is a dangerous radioactive isotope found in the fallout from some nuclear explosions. In people and animals, the radioactivity of strontium 90 destroys the tissues that produce blood.

Strontium is found in the minerals celestite and strontianite. It combines readily with oxygen, nitrogen, and hydrogen. Strontium nitrate ($Sr[NO_3]_2$) burns with a crimson flame, and is used in flares and fireworks.

Strontium has the chemical symbol Sr. Its atomic number is 38 and its atomic weight is 87.62. It melts at 769° C and boils at 1384° C. It was discovered in 1790 by Adair Crawford of Ireland.   WARREN S. PETERSON

STRUCTURALISM. See LÉVI-STRAUSS, CLAUDE; PSYCHOLOGY (History).

STRUGGLE FOR EXISTENCE. See EVOLUTION (Natural Selection); NATURAL SELECTION.

STRUVE, *STROO vee,* **OTTO** (1897-1963), was an American astronomer. He contributed greatly to knowledge of stellar evolution. Struve was director of the Yerkes Observatory from 1932 to 1947, and of the McDonald Observatory from 1939 to 1947. Struve became professor of astronomy and director of the Leuschner Observatory at the University of California in 1950. He was born in Russia.   HELEN WRIGHT

STRYCHNINE, *STRIHK nihn* or *STRIHK nyn,* is a bitter and poisonous drug obtained from the seeds of plants such as the *nux vomica* tree, found in India and Indonesia. Strychnine comes in colorless crystals. A large dose of strychnine causes a serious case of poisoning, resulting in convulsions. The usual symptoms are twitching, difficulty in swallowing, and a sudden backward bending of the body. If a person has taken strychnine, call a doctor immediately. If the victim is not having convulsions, try to make him or her vomit by touching the back of the throat with the blunt end of a spoon or your finger. The victim should be kept warm and as quiet as possible. Strychnine's chemical formula is $C_{21}H_{22}N_2O_2$.   A. KEITH REYNOLDS

STUART, GILBERT CHARLES (1755-1828), was an American artist. He became famous for his unfinished portrait of George Washington, probably the best-known portrait in America.

Stuart was born near Newport, R.I., and began painting at the age of 13. His early works were simple, thinly painted portraits. In 1775 he went to London for five years to serve as assistant to artist Benjamin West. A Stuart portrait, *The Skater*, was exhibited at the Royal Academy in 1782. This graceful, luminous picture received so much praise that Stuart opened his own portrait studio in London. For the next 10 years, the wealthy of England and Scotland sat for him. But Stuart lived in high style and spent some time in British debtors prisons because of his extravagant living.

In 1792, Stuart returned to the United States. He planned to get money to pay his debts by painting Washington's portrait. Washington sat for three different portraits in 1795 and 1796. The "Vaughan" type is a painting of bust length. "Lansdowne" is a full-length portrait. "Athenaeum" is the familiar unfinished oval of Washington's head. Stuart sold many copies of the portraits that he, his daughter, and others made.

Oil painting on canvas (1778); Redwood Library and Athenaeum, Newport, R.I.

Gilbert Stuart's Self-Portrait shows how he concentrated on facial expression and neglected the background in his works.

Stuart spent the last half of his life as a portrait painter. He became noted for his charm, his ability to complete portraits quickly, and his advice to young artists. "Paint what you see," he told a beginner, "and look with your own eyes." EDWARD H. DWIGHT

For reproductions of Stuart's works, see ADAMS, JOHN; ASTOR; JEFFERSON, THOMAS; MONROE, JAMES; WASHINGTON, GEORGE. See also RHODE ISLAND (A Visitor's Guide).

STUART, HOUSE OF. Stuart is the name of a royal family of England and Scotland. The Stuarts were kings and queens of Scotland from 1371 to 1603, and of England and Scotland from 1603 to 1714. Their rule of the two countries in the 1600's was characterized by their insistence on the Divine Right of Kings (see DIVINE RIGHT OF KINGS).

James VI of Scotland, the son of Mary, Queen of Scots, became king of England at the death of his cousin, Queen Elizabeth I, in 1603. He took the title of James I. His son Charles I succeeded him. Charles's attempt to rule as a dictator brought on the English Revolution. He was beheaded in 1649.

England again became a monarchy in 1660 under Charles II, the son of Charles I. When Charles II died in 1685, his brother, James II, became king. James was determined to rule as a dictator and to restore the Roman Catholic religion in England, even though England was committed to parliamentary government and was strongly anti-Catholic. As a result of this conflict, James was forced to leave the throne in the bloodless revolution of 1688. Parliament gave the crown to his daughter Mary and her husband, William of Orange.

Anne Stuart, Mary's sister, became queen in 1702. She was the last Stuart ruler. During her reign, England and Scotland were united as a single nation known as Great Britain. W. M. SOUTHGATE

Related Articles in WORLD BOOK include:

Anne	England	Mary (II)
Charles (I; II)	(History)	Mary, Queen of Scots
of England	James (I; II)	Scotland (History)

STUART, JAMES EWELL BROWN (1833-1864), was a Confederate cavalry general. "Jeb" Stuart distinguished himself in the first Battle of Bull Run (Manassas). He served with "Stonewall" Jackson at Chancellorsville and commanded Jackson's corps for a short time after Jackson was wounded. In command of all General Robert E. Lee's cavalry, Stuart fought several successful actions in the Wilderness Campaign in 1864. But he had gained his widest fame for his two daring rides "around McClellan." In

Brown Bros.

"Jeb" Stuart

these rides, Stuart took his cavalry all the way around the Union Army.

Stuart became the center of a great controversy following the Battle of Gettysburg. He had taken his command off on an independent operation while General Lee invaded the North, and Stuart's absence deprived Lee of the "eyes" of his army. Stuart was killed at Yellow Tavern, Va., in the battle for Richmond.

Stuart was born in Patrick County, Virginia, and was graduated from the United States Military Academy. He served in Kansas and on the frontier from 1855 to 1861. He resigned from the U.S. Army in 1861, and joined the Confederacy. FRANK E. VANDIVER

STUART, JESSE HILTON (1907-), is an American author known for his writings about the mountain region of Kentucky. Since 1934, Stuart has published more than 30 works, including novels, collections of poetry and short stories, and autobiographies. His major works show his simple, realistic style and his affection for the people of the Kentucky mountains, where he was born and raised.

Stuart's novels include *Taps for Private Tussie* (1943) and *Daughter of the Legend* (1965). Among the collections of his short stories are *Head o' W-Hollow* (1936) and *My Land Has a Voice* (1966). Collections of his poems include *Man with a Bull-Tongue Plow* (1934) and *Hold April* (1962). Stuart described his childhood and family in *God's Oddling* (1960). He based *To Teach, To Love* (1970) on his experiences as a teacher and writer. Stuart was born near Riverton, Ky. JOHN B. VICKERY

STUART, JOHN TODD. See LINCOLN, ABRAHAM (Study).

STUART, MARY. See MARY, QUEEN OF SCOTS.

STUCCO, *STUCK o*, is a plasterlike material applied to outside walls. It forms a hard protective covering. Stucco usually consists of sand, water, and a cementing mixture. Workers usually apply three coats, using trowels. Stucco can be applied in many finishes and colors. See also PLASTERING. GEORGE W. WASHA

STUCK, HUDSON. See MOUNT MCKINLEY.

STUD. See HOUSE (House-Building Terms); CHAIN.

STUDBOOK. See DOG (table; Dog Terms).

STUDEBAKER is the name of a family that became famous as makers of wagons and other vehicles. Their company, Studebaker Corporation, merged with Packard Motors, Inc., in 1954. In 1966, the firm stopped making automobiles. It continued to make automobile parts and other products. In 1967, it merged with Worthington Corporation to form Studebaker-Worthington, Inc.

Clement Studebaker (1831-1901), with his brother Henry, opened a blacksmith and wagon shop in South Bend, Ind., in 1852. The Studebaker Brothers Manufacturing Company was organized in 1868, with Clement as its first president. The company became the largest wagon manufacturer in the country, and had a world market. Studebaker was born in Pinetown, Pa.

John Mohler Studebaker (1833-1917), a brother of Clement Studebaker, moved to California in 1853 during the Gold Rush. There he made wheelbarrows for the miners. When he had saved enough money, he returned to South Bend and bought his brother Henry's interest in the Studebaker firm. John Studebaker became president of the company after Clement died. In 1902, the firm made its first electric-powered vehicles, and in 1904 it began making gasoline-powered cars. By 1920, the Studebaker company was producing automobiles and trucks exclusively. Studebaker was born in Gettysburg, Pa. V. E. CANGELOSI and R. E. WESTMEYER

STUDENT GOVERNMENT is an activity in which students take part in the government of their school, college, or university. This activity usually takes place through a student organization, often called a *student council*. The organization may also be called a *student cabinet, student congress, student legislature,* or *G.O.* (general organization). Most high schools, colleges, and universities have some form of student government.

Students elect representatives to the council or governing board. The council may meet with the faculty and administration to discuss curriculum, student benefits, alumni relations, and other matters of interest to the students. A faculty member may serve as sponsor or adviser. Student government activities include sponsoring scholarship and award programs; coordinating student activities; and organizing assembly programs, conferences, lectures, and other cultural events. Student governments have also fought for students' rights, including an end to racial and sexual discrimination in college admissions. The governments may sponsor student courts, conduct work projects and faculty-evaluation programs, and help manage such student services as cafeterias and health centers. A student government also may organize community projects and travel programs.

About 10,000 high schools in the United States belong to the National Association of Student Councils (NASC), which distributes information about student government. NASC headquarters are at 1904 Association Drive, Reston, Va. 22091.

Several hundred collegiate student organizations belong to the United States National Student Association (USNSA). It sponsors an annual conference and other meetings on student and world problems. USNSA delegates represent U.S. students at international meetings. The association's headquarters are at 2115 S Street NW, Washington, D.C. 20008. Other national student groups are the National Student Lobby, the Coalition of Independent College and University Students, and the National Association of Students in State Colleges and Universities. In addition, there are many state organizations and other special student groups. GORDON J. KLOPF

STUDENT NATIONAL COORDINATING COMMITTEE. See STUDENT NONVIOLENT COORDINATING COMMITTEE.

STUDENT NATIONAL EDUCATION ASSOCIATION. See NATIONAL EDUCATION ASSOCIATION OF THE U.S.

STUDENT NONVIOLENT COORDINATING COMMITTEE (SNCC), also called "Snick," was a civil rights organization in the United States during the 1960's. White and black students founded SNCC in 1960. One of the group's last actions was to change its name to the Student National Coordinating Committee in 1969. In the early 1960's, SNCC organized peaceful protests and demonstrations to speed desegregation in the South. In 1964, SNCC sponsored the Mississippi Project, in which about 800 volunteers helped thousands of blacks register to vote.

Under the leadership of Stokely Carmichael, SNCC abandoned its policy of nonviolence in 1966. It adopted a strong antiwhite attitude, and discouraged white membership. Carmichael criticized the civil rights movement, and called for "Black Power." Carmichael resigned as leader of SNCC in 1967. He denounced the United States during a tour of the world. His successor, H. Rap Brown, continued the strongly militant program started by Carmichael. RICHARD BARDOLPH

See also BLACK AMERICANS (Black Power); CARMICHAEL, STOKELY.

STUDENT PROTEST. See RIOT (During the 1900's); NEW LEFT.

STUDENTS FOR A DEMOCRATIC SOCIETY (SDS) was a radical political organization in the United States during the 1960's. Most of its members were college students or other young people. They opposed what they believed to be the hypocrisy existing in American society.

SDS members believed that American society theoretically supports liberal democratic principles but has failed to correct such injustices as poverty and racial discrimination. SDS strongly opposed U.S. participation in the Vietnam War (1957-1975) and tried to arouse public opinion against the war. The organization also demanded more student influence in the administration of colleges and universities. SDS believed that these institutions do not respond to young people's needs and wishes, and smother their ideas and personalities.

SDS tactics included propaganda and such direct action as student strikes and mass demonstrations. The organization was often accused of using or provoking violence to advance its demands.

SDS was organized in 1962. Many of its ideas came from *Marxism*—the teachings of the German philosopher Karl Marx—and from *anarchism*, the belief that all government and law are evil. But SDS was not united on its ideas and tactics, and internal disputes reduced the effectiveness of the organization. In the late 1960's, SDS split into several factions. MURRAY CLARK HAVENS

STUDIO. See Motion Picture; Radio (How Radio Works); Television (Producing Television Programs).

STUDY is an effort to learn about any subject. Studying is an important part of learning because your achievement in school depends greatly on how much you study. You cannot expect to learn everything you need to know about a subject from a teacher in a classroom. You must also study the subject outside of class. The combination of classroom learning and regular study outside of class determines how well you do in school. Study becomes increasingly important as you move from elementary school to high school and then on to college.

This article offers suggestions on how to develop good study habits. You can use these suggestions to improve your grades in school. Good study habits can also help you learn new job skills or simply investigate a subject that interests you. For more information about study, see the article *How to Do Research* in the Research Guide/Index, Volume 22. It discusses how to use reference books and other resource materials, which are important tools for study.

Where to Study. Every student needs a special place to study. It should have a desk or table and a chair. There should also be enough daylight or artificial light so that you can read for long periods of time without straining your eyes. In addition, a study area should have enough space for your textbooks and such reference books as a dictionary, a general encyclopedia, and an atlas. You should also have a place to store paper, pencils, pens, notebooks, and other study materials.

Most people can study almost anywhere—if the subject fascinates them. But they have difficulty concentrating on something they consider uninteresting. Therefore, your study area should be as free as possible of noise and visual distractions. On the other hand, what distracts one person may not affect another. Some students feel they can study better with soft music in the background. However, others cannot study effectively with music playing. Find out what distracts you and remove it from your study area.

Many students have a problem finding a quiet place to study. You must adapt your study habits to your particular situation. For example, if you have your own room, you could make one corner into an excellent study area. If you share a room with a brother or a sister, both of you could agree to study at the same time in opposite corners. Or you could get up early in the morning and study when your brother or sister is asleep. If your home is too crowded or noisy, you could ask permission to study at the home of a friend or relative who has more space.

When to Study. Students should study regularly throughout the school year. You will remember more about a subject if you study it soon after it has been presented in class. Never wait until just before an exam to start reviewing the work for the entire period to be covered by the test. Anything you learn by such *cramming* is usually soon forgotten.

You may find it helpful to plan a weekly study schedule. Many students write down the times they are in school or are involved with other activities. They then set aside a certain time each day for study. It is easier to keep up with your schoolwork if you have the habit of studying at the same time daily. Two points to consider in developing a study schedule are (1) the best time of day for studying and (2) the length of each study session.

The best time of day for study depends on your personal preferences, the kind of life you lead, and your family situation. Some students prefer to study immediately after arriving home from school. Others have a job or participate in sports and other activities after school, and so they study in the early evening. Still other students study later at night, or in the morning before school, because their home is too noisy early in the evening.

The length of your study sessions depends on your age, your ability as a student, and whether you already have good study habits. If you are still in elementary school or have just begun to develop good study habits, you should probably allow about an hour a day for study. As your schoolwork becomes more difficult, you should plan longer study sessions to keep your homework assignments up to date.

How to Study. Ask yourself two questions before you start to study: "Why am I studying this topic?" "What do I want to learn about it?" You cannot study effectively unless you understand what you are supposed to accomplish. Simply memorizing dates, mathematical formulas, or passages in literature does not make you a good student. If you understand a subject, remembering facts about it becomes much easier.

Many good students sometimes have trouble concentrating on their work. There are several study methods that can help keep your mind from wandering. For example, you should study the most difficult subjects first, when you are the most mentally alert. You should also take breaks between subjects. A short walk or some pushups, stretches, or other simple exercises can help freshen your mind. If you still have trouble concentrating on your studies, work on such tasks as writing out next week's study schedule or reviewing the previous day's work.

There are a number of ways to study more effectively. Some students try to link a fact they want to remember with something they already know. Others use rhymes, mental pictures, and other memory aids called *mnemonic devices* to help recall certain information (see Memory [Improving Memory]). You may find it useful to repeat out loud something you have just learned. Some students like to study in pairs so that they can test each other orally on a subject.

At the end of each study session, test yourself to make sure you understand the major points of the topic. If you are still confused by the topic, study it again at a later session. Do not hesitate to ask your teacher or school counselor for help with a study problem or for general advice about improving your study habits.   Samuel Ball

See also Learning (Efficient Learning); Outline; Reading (Study-Type Reading).

Additional Resources

Apps, Jerold W. *Study Skills for Those Adults Returning to School.* 2nd ed. McGraw, 1981.

Gross, Ronald. *The Lifelong Learner.* Simon & Schuster, 1979.

Kalina, Sigmund. *How to Sharpen Your Study Skills.* Morrow, 1975.

Morgan, Clifford T. *How to Study.* 3rd ed. McGraw, 1979.

STURGEON

New York Zoological Society

The Rock Sturgeon has armor of bony plate to protect its head and body. Sturgeon eggs are used to make caviar.

STURGEON, *STUR jun*, is the common name of a family of large fishes living in the fresh waters and seas of the North Temperate Zone. They are caught for their flesh, which is usually smoked, and for their eggs, which are used in the preparation of caviar. A superior quality of isinglass is obtained from the air bladder of the Russian sturgeon. These fish have slender bodies covered with rows of bony plates. Beneath the long snout there is a small, toothless mouth with thick, sucking lips. There are four *barbels* (fleshy projections) in front of the mouth. The head, like the body, is well protected with plates. A single dorsal fin rises from the back, and the body extends into the long upper part of the tail fin. Most of these fish migrate from salt water into streams in the spawning season, but some species live permanently in fresh waters. Sturgeon suck food into their mouths.

Sturgeon belong to an ancient group of fish. Early ancestors of the sturgeon appeared in the Devonian Period (see EARTH [table]). The fish's sucking mouth and plated body are features that developed later.

One of the best-known sturgeon is the *common sturgeon.* It lives in European waters and along the North American coast from Labrador to the Gulf of Mexico. The largest may be over 10 feet (3 meters) long and weigh over 1,000 pounds (450 kilograms). The *white sturgeon* of the American Pacific Coast is the largest American fish of this group. The *lake* or *rock sturgeon* lives in the Great Lakes and the Mississippi Valley waters. Scientists consider the *beluga,* a sturgeon of Russia, the largest fresh-water fish. It may grow as long as 14 feet (4 meters) and weigh over 3,000 pounds (1,400 kilograms). The beluga produces most European caviar. Another Russian sturgeon, the small *sterlet,* also produces this delicacy. North American sturgeons were abundant once, but overfishing, dams, and pollution have greatly reduced their number.

Scientific Classification. The sturgeon belongs to the sturgeon family, *Acipenseridae.* The common sturgeon is genus *Acipenser,* species *A. sturio;* the white sturgeon, *A. transmontanus;* the lake or rock sturgeon, *A. fulvescens;* the sterlet, *A. ruthenus.* The beluga is genus *Huso,* species *H. huso.*   CARL L. HUBBS

See also CAVIAR; FISH (picture: Fish of Temperate Fresh Waters).

STURGEON, THEODORE (1918-   ), is an American author of fantasy and science fiction. Most of his stories deal with the meaning of love in various kinds of human relationships. Many of his characters are ab-

normal human beings or beings from other worlds. But these characters seem real because Sturgeon describes them with sympathetic understanding.

Sturgeon's most important novel is *More Than Human* (1953). This book tells about a small group of young people who represent an advanced stage of human evolution. Sturgeon's short novel *Killdozer* (1944) reflects his experiences as a civilian bulldozer operator in the Caribbean during World War II (1939-1945). Many of his short stories appear in such collections as *Without Sorcery* (1949), *Caviar* (1955), *Aliens 4* (1959), and *Sturgeon Is Alive and Well* (1971). Sturgeon has also written scripts for television. He was born in New York City.   JUDY-LYNN DEL REY

STURGEON, WILLIAM. See ELECTROMAGNET.

STURGES, PRESTON (1898-1959), was an American motion-picture writer and director. He became famous for films that brilliantly satirize aspects of American life. *The Great McGinty* (1940) satirizes crooked politicians. *Sullivan's Travels* (1941) attacks the false values Sturges saw mirrored in Hollywood. *The Miracle of Morgan's Creek* (1944) and *Hail the Conquering Hero* (1944) deal with small-town politics and the worship of military heroes. Sturges also wrote and directed *Christmas in July* (1940), *The Lady Eve* (1941), and *Unfaithfully Yours* (1948). All show Sturges' skill at writing witty dialogue and creating slapstick comedy.

Sturges was born in Chicago. He wrote several Broadway plays before going to Hollywood in 1932. They include the Broadway comedy hit *Strictly Dishonorable* (1929).   RICHARD GRIFFITH

STURLUSON. See SNORRI STURLUSON.

STURT, CHARLES. See AUSTRALIA (Exploring the New Land).

STUTTERING, or STAMMERING, is a form of defective or disordered speech. Formerly, these words were taken to mean two different defects. *Stuttering* was the repetition of sounds or syllables. *Stammering* was regarded as a continuous *block* that resulted in inability to utter any sound. Present-day specialists in speech correction do not recognize a difference between the terms. The experts use the words interchangeably, but the term *stuttering* is preferred.

An example of one form of stuttering is the inability to say clearly such words as *don't* or *animal.* The stutterer says *d-d-d-don't* and *a-a-a-animal.* A sentence spoken by a stutterer might sound like this: "M-m-m-mother, m-m-m-may Bob-bob-Bobby have a d-d-d-doughnut?"

In stuttering there may also be a spasm of the speech muscles that prevents talking, sometimes almost entirely. Often the difficulty in speaking then results in grimacing and other facial contortions which are caused by contractions of the speech muscles.

No one knows the specific causes of stuttering. Speech experts have various theories as to what causes it and many methods have been used to correct it. Shyness and lack of self-confidence often accompany it, but are not believed to cause it. About 4 to 6 times more males than females stutter. It is most common in young children. If stuttering is not overcome, it may seriously handicap a person both in personal development and in relations with others. Stuttering can become so serious that it makes a vocational failure of even a talented person. It is not associated with any lack of mental ability.

Children often lose *fluency* (smoothness of speech)

744

when they try to speak too rapidly, or if they are upset and excited. The condition is made worse if the speaker is aware of the defective speech. The child strains to avoid the stuttering, and the effort tightens the muscles of the face and throat. This makes the child's speech worse. The speaker may become panicky because of this difficulty, and thus increase the stuttering. The child will gain fluency only by ceasing to struggle and by learning to control the feeling of panic.

There are different ways in which many stutterers can use the voice easily. These include reading in unison, singing, speaking to groups before whom they have self-confidence, and speaking to themselves. In general, pesons who stutter find it very difficult to speak in public or in any situation in which they feel insecure.

Treatment of speech disorders is often a matter of training the mental processes and emotions, as well as retraining the speech of the individual. Each case must be treated individually, according to the person's needs. Children who stutter sometimes outgrow the defect. It is advisable not to call attention to children's stuttering and to exercise calmness and patience when they speak, in order to help them establish fluency and self-confidence.   VIRGIL A. ANDERSON

See also LISPING; SPEECH THERAPY.

STUTTGART, *SHTOOT gahrt* (pop. 583,700), is the capital of the West German state of Baden-Württemberg (see GERMANY [political map]). Stuttgart was formerly capital of the state and kingdom of Württemberg. The city is the center of the printing and publishing industry of southern Germany. Stuttgart lies near the Neckar River. Many buildings in Stuttgart are fine examples of Renaissance architecture.

Bombers hit Stuttgart heavily during World War II because it contained machine-tool, ball-bearing, and internal-combustion engine factories. Many of its famous buildings were damaged. French troops entered Stuttgart on April 21, 1945. The city was in the American zone of occupation after the war. The *Läuderrat* or Council of States for the American zone was established in Stuttgart on Oct. 17, 1945. It was the first German organization above the state level to be established after the war.   JAMES K. POLLOCK

STUYVESANT, *STY vuhs'nt,* **PETER** (1610?-1672), was the last Dutch governor of New Netherland, an area that included land in present-day New York and several nearby states (see NEW NETHERLAND). Stuyvesant was born at Scherpenzeel, near Heerenveen, The Netherlands, the son of a minister. He became a soldier as a young man, and in 1635 entered the service of the Dutch West India Company. In 1643, he became governor of Curaçao and nearby Dutch possessions. The next year, he led an attack against the island of Saint Martin and lost a leg in the battle.

In 1646, Stuyvesant became governor of New Netherland. He arrived in New Amsterdam (now New York City) in May, 1647, and immediately began to make enemies by his harsh methods. But he restored order and business, and made friends with the Indians. His settlement in 1650 with the New England colonists of the eastern boundaries of the Dutch colony angered the Dutch because they thought he gave the Puritans too much territory. Five years later, he captured all New Sweden, which included lands in what are now New Jersey, Delaware, and Pennsylvania. He made New Sweden a part of New Netherland.

Stuyvesant refused to share his power with anybody. When a convention of Long Island citizens demanded a share in the government, he replied, "We derive our authority from God and the West India Company, not from the pleasure of a few ignorant subjects." In 1664, an English fleet ordered the surrender of the city. The citizens refused to support Stuyvesant, and he was forced to give in. Stuyvesant was sent to Holland in disgrace, but he returned to New York after a few years and settled on his *bouwerij* (farm), part of which later became the Bowery of New York City. Stuyvesant died there and lies buried on the site of Saint Mark's Church. He is one of the characters in Washington Irving's *Knickerbocker's History of New York*.   IAN C. C. GRAHAM

See also FIRE DEPARTMENT (History); NEW YORK CITY (History); NEW SWEDEN.

STY is an infection of one of the glands in an eyelid, usually around an eyelash. The infection, which resembles a small boil, is usually caused by a *staphylococcus* bacteria. The germs enter the root of the eyelash, grow there, and form pus. Some experts believe eyestrain is an indirect cause of sties. When people with eyestrain rub their eyes too much, germs from their hands may cause infection. White blood cells in the body usually kill the germs that cause a sty. Then the sty softens, breaks, lets out the pus, and heals. Hot moist applications can make it break more quickly. Sties often come one after another. Doctors can inoculate the patient with a vaccine made from the staphylococcus germs. When sties continue for a long time, doctors may treat them with germ-killing drugs. See also BOIL.   WILLIAM F. HUGHES

STYLE, in literature and the arts, is the way thoughts or ideas are expressed by the writer or artist. See also CLOTHING; FASHION; INTERIOR DECORATION (Style); LITERATURE (Style).

STYRENE. See RUBBER (Synthetic).

STYROFOAM is the trade name of *polystyrene foam*, a plastic manufactured by the Dow Chemical Company. Styrofoam contains millions of tiny air bubbles that make it lightweight and a poor conductor of heat. Styrofoam absorbs water only slightly, and bacteria and molds cannot damage it.

Styrofoam has many household and industrial uses. Manufacturers use it in making such household products as ice chests, disposable drinking cups, and toys. Industry uses Styrofoam as a protective packaging material for such delicate products as radios and television sets. Styrofoam is also used to insulate buildings, freight cars, and trucks.   KENNETH SCHUG

See also PLASTICS (Making Synthetic Resins; The Plastics Industry Grows).

STYRON, WILLIAM (1925-   ), is an American novelist. Although the settings in his fiction are diverse, Styron has usually been called a Southern writer.

New-York Historical Society
Peter Stuyvesant

Styron's frequently powerful, elaborate prose reveals the influence of the Southern writer William Faulkner.

Styron was born in Newport News, Va. His themes reflect the typical Southern writer's concern for the loss or corruption of such traditional values as family stability, religion, and regional culture. In Styron's first novel, *Lie Down in Darkness* (1951), the central character is a young woman from Virginia. She becomes involved in a violent conflict between her parents and runs away from home. She eventually commits suicide, partly as a result of the loss of moral authority represented by the failure of family order.

Styron received the Pulitzer Prize for fiction in 1968 for *The Confessions of Nat Turner* (1967). In the book, Styron as a white Southerner tried to imagine the psychological motivations that drove Turner, a black minister, to lead a bloody slave revolt in Virginia in 1831 (see TURNER, NAT). *Sophie's Choice* (1979) deals with a Polish woman who survives the Nazi concentration camps during World War II (1939-1945). She settles in New York City and has a tragic love affair with an emotionally unstable Jewish man. A young Southern writer narrates the story. Styron also wrote the novelette *The Long March* (1953) and the novel *Set This House on Fire* (1960).   MARCUS KLEIN

STYX, *stihks,* was a dark and dreary river in Greek and Roman mythology. The boatman Charon carried the souls of the dead across either the River Styx or the Acheron River to the Lower World. The gods took their most sacred oaths by the name of the River Styx.

The kingdom of Hades was on the other side of the Styx. After being judged, the dead souls remained in Hades or were sent to the happy Elysian Fields or to the dismal land of Tartarus. A high waterfall in Arcadia, an ancient Greek state, was also called the Styx. People believed its waters were poisonous and that the entry to the Lower World lay behind it.   PADRAIC COLUM

See also CHARON; ELYSIAN FIELDS; TARTARUS.

SUÁREZ, *SWAHrayth,* **FRANCISCO** (1548-1617), was a great Spanish theologian, and a founder of the philosophy of international law. In his famous treatise *On Laws,* he attacked the theory of the divine right of kings, and insisted on the necessity of the consent of the people in a just political order. Suárez saw that the medieval idea of a Christian empire was no longer possible with the emergence of self-governing national monarchies. Suárez was born in Granada. He became a Jesuit in 1564.   JAMES A. CORBETT and FULTON J. SHEEN

SUBCONSCIOUS is a term used to describe mental processes such as thoughts, ideas, and feelings that go on in people's minds without their being aware of them. Psychiatrists, psychoanalysts, and psychologists generally use the term *unconscious* to mean the same thing that most nonmedical persons mean by *subconscious.* Other words that once had the same meaning include *coconscious* and *paraconscious.*

The existence of mental processes that are active in the mind without being conscious was first studied scientifically by the French neurologist Jean Charcot and his pupils in the 1800's. They studied the unconscious by means of hypnosis (see HYPNOTISM). Soon after, doctors realized many mentally ill persons, such as those with hysteria, were influenced by unconscious thoughts and feelings (see HYSTERIA; MENTAL ILLNESS).

The doctor who first realized clearly the importance of unconscious thoughts and feelings in human psychology was Sigmund Freud of Austria. He developed the method of *psychoanalysis* for treating mentally ill patients (see PSYCHOANALYSIS). This method also serves as a way of learning what goes on unconsciously in a patient's mind. By using psychoanalysis, Freud was able to prove that unconscious thoughts and feelings not only produce the symptoms of many types of mental illness, but that they are also of basic importance in the way the minds of normal people work. This knowledge has enabled doctors to make great advances in the treatment of the mentally ill.   CHARLES BRENNER

Related Articles in WORLD BOOK include:

Dream	Nightmare	Sleepwalking
Freud, Sigmund	Phobia	Subliminal
Neurosis	Psychotherapy	

SUBCULTURE. See CULTURE (Characteristics; picture); ADOLESCENT (introduction).

SUBCUTANEOUS TISSUE. See SKIN (Subcutaneous Tissue).

SUBJECT, in grammar. See SENTENCE (Subject and Predicate).

SUBJUNCTIVE MOOD. See MOOD.

SUBLETTE, *SUHB leht,* **WILLIAM LEWIS** (1799?-1845), was an American fur trader and merchant. He was born in Lincoln County, Kentucky, but grew up in St. Charles, Mo. He left Missouri in 1822 to become a trapper. He and his two partners were successful, and in 1831 their fantastic catch brought $170,000. Sublette next operated trading posts on the Platte and Upper Missouri rivers. He helped open the Oregon Trail by using wagons in the Rocky Mountains, and by finding a shortcut, *Sublette's Cutoff.*   HOWARD R. LAMAR

SUBLIMATION, *SUHB luh MAY shuhn,* is the process by which a solid substance changes into a gas, or vapor, without first becoming a liquid. There are a few substances, such as iodine, arsenic, camphor, and dry ice, which change into a gas without first melting. These substances are said to *sublime.* The most familiar example of sublimation can occur when wet clothes are hung out on the line on a winter day when the temperature is below freezing. The water on the clothes freezes and then evaporates into vapor without melting. Solid iodine will change into a vapor when it is warmed without becoming a liquid. Then, when the vapor is cooled, the iodine will change back into crystals. This change of a vapor back into a solid also is part of sublimation.

Sublimation is used in industry to purify substances. When a solid changes directly into a vapor, only the pure substance evaporates and the impurities remain. Pure sulfur (called *flowers of sulfur*), benzoin, and sal ammoniac are made by this process.   RALPH G. OWENS

See also MELTING POINT.

SUBLIMINAL, *suhb LIHM uh nuhl,* refers to stimuli that are so weak or last so short a time that a person is not aware of them. Such stimuli are said to be *subliminal* (below the threshold of consciousness). The consciousness threshold varies from person to person and from time to time, even in the same person. Psychologists have been trying to determine whether subliminal stimuli can influence people, perhaps through the unconscious. Some use has been made of such subliminal stimuli in advertising.   RUSSELL M. CHURCH

An Attack Submarine is designed to search out and destroy enemy ships during wartime. Many attack submarines have nuclear-powered engines and carry torpedoes and guided missiles.

Crew Members Aboard a Submarine eat their meals in the messroom. They have comfortable living quarters and may spend their free time in the ship's library or game room.

SUBMARINE is a ship that travels underwater. Most submarines are designed for use in war—to attack enemy ships or to fire missiles at enemy countries. These ships range in length from about 200 feet (61 meters) to more than 500 feet (150 meters). Their rounded hulls are about 30 feet (9 meters) in diameter. More than 100 crew members live and work aboard such warships.

Some submarines are used for scientific research. These underwater craft explore the ocean depths and gather scientific information. They are smaller than military submarines and carry only a few crew members. See OCEAN (Oceanographic Diving).

In war, a submarine usually attacks from beneath the surface of the water. A submarine must remain underwater to be effective. Early submarines could not stay submerged for long periods. They had to surface every few hours for air for their engines and crews. Enemy planes and ships could then attack them. Today, nuclear submarines can stay underwater for months at a time. Nuclear engines do not need oxygen to operate, and modern submarines can produce all the air their crews need.

A submarine's long, cigar-shaped body enables it to move swiftly underwater. Two hulls protect the submarine from water pressure. An inner hull, called the *pressure hull*, shields the ship from the crushing force of water at great depths. The pressure hull is built of strong, thick steel. The outer hull fits around it. Open-

Norman Polmar, the contributor of this article, is a former editor of the U.S. sections of Jane's Fighting Ships *and the author of* Atomic Submarines *and* Death of the Thresher.

ings in this hull let in water to give the submarine *ballast* (weight) for diving.

A tall, thin structure called the *sail* rises from the middle of a submarine's deck. The sail stands about 20 feet (6.1 meters) high. It holds the periscopes and the radar and radio antennas. The top of the sail also serves as the *bridge*, from where the captain directs the submarine on the surface. Steel fins called *diving planes* stick out from both sides of the sail and from the stern. These diving planes guide the submarine to different depths. A single propeller in the stern drives the submarine. Two rudders mounted above and below the propeller steer the craft.

Kinds of Submarines

There are two main kinds of submarines, *attack submarines* and *ballistic missile submarines*.

Attack Submarines are designed to search out and destroy enemy submarines and surface ships. Most attack submarines in the United States Navy range in length from about 250 to 360 feet (76 to 110 meters). They have about 110 crew members. Most of these submarines have nuclear-powered engines and carry torpedoes and guided missiles.

Attack submarines chiefly hunt enemy submarines. They track and find their targets with *sonar* (for *so*und *na*vigation *a*nd *r*anging), a device that detects sounds underwater. This equipment locates noises from objects in the water. Periscopes and radar are used to identify enemy ships on the surface. See SONAR.

Modern attack submarines fire their torpedoes from four tubes located along the sides of the hull. Torpedoes have *homing devices* that follow the target and guide the

747

Basic Parts of an Attack Submarine

The illustration below shows the basic parts of an attack submarine. A nuclear reactor furnishes the power for the vessel. Steel fins called *diving planes* stick out from both sides of the sail and the stern, and help guide the ship underwater. The rudders, which are mounted on the stern, help steer the submarine. Torpedoes are fired from tubes located along each side of the vessel.

WORLD BOOK illustration by George Suyeoka

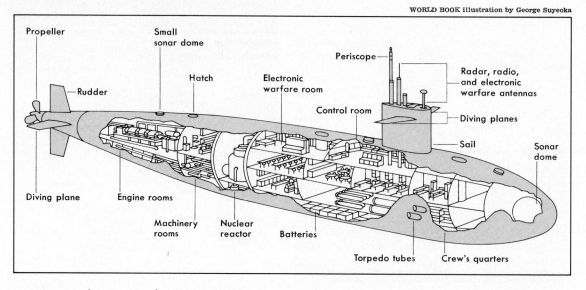

torpedo to it (see TORPEDO). Older submarines had their torpedo tubes in the bow. But in modern submarines, the sonar is located in the bow—far away from the noise of the ship's propeller.

Some submarines can also fire antisubmarine missiles from the torpedo tubes. These short-range ballistic missiles have a nuclear warhead that can destroy submerged submarines from as far away as 30 miles (48 kilometers).

Other submarines can attack surface ships and on-shore targets with *cruise missiles*, which have short wings that open after launching. Cruise missiles can be directed to avoid enemy defenses.

Ballistic Missile Submarines hide in the depths until they attack. Such submarines are larger than attack submarines, measuring from about 380 to 550 feet (115 to 168 meters) long. Their crews number about 150 men. Ballistic missile submarines carry long-range

Basic Parts of a Ballistic Missile Submarine

The illustration below shows the basic parts of a ballistic missile submarine. The exterior of this vessel is similar to that of an attack submarine. But ballistic missile submarines are larger than attack submarines and they carry long-range missiles for bombing enemy cities and military bases on shore. The missiles are launched from tubes through openings at the top of the vessel.

WORLD BOOK illustration by George Suyeoka; adapted from a *Newsweek* illustration by Oliver Williams

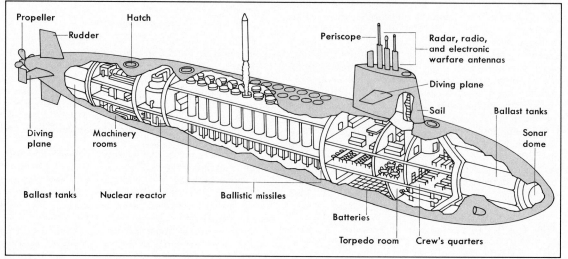

missiles for hitting enemy cities and military bases ashore. The missiles are fired from *silos* (launching tubes) in the submarine's hull. The missiles can strike targets from about 2,900 to 5,000 miles (4,630 to 8,000 kilometers) away. They can carry multiple bombs that can hit several enemy targets at once. Ballistic missile submarines also carry torpedoes for defense against enemy antisubmarine ships.

Special equipment aboard the submarine plots the craft's exact location and determines the path of the ballistic missile to its destination. This equipment, called the *inertial navigation system*, consists of accurate measuring devices linked to computers. The system helps navigate the submarine by recording its starting position on a voyage and its movement in all directions. This information is fed into a guidance system in the missile to provide the precise distance and direction to the target. After launching, the missile's own inertial navigation system guides the weapon to its target. See INERTIAL GUIDANCE.

The Power Plant

The engine of a nuclear submarine consists of a nuclear reactor and a steam generator. The reactor uses uranium for fuel and splits uranium atoms in a controlled process called *fission*. This process produces intense heat. See NUCLEAR ENERGY.

Pipes carry water from the steam generator to the reactor, where the water is heated to about 600° F. (316° C). This superheated water is under pressure, and so it does not boil. Instead, it returns to the steam generator and boils a supply of unpressurized water that turns to steam. The steam spins large *turbines* (wheels), producing power to rotate the propeller shaft and run the ship.

Nuclear engines operate without air, and they consume much less fuel than do other engines. About 4 pounds (1.8 kilograms) of uranium fuel produce more energy than 10 million gallons (38 million liters) of fuel oil.

Some submarines run on diesel engines. However, the U.S. Navy has not built a diesel-powered submarine since 1959. Diesel engines burn fuel oil and need air for combustion. A submarine can use these engines only when on or near the surface. Electric batteries supply power underwater. During World War II (1939-1945), the German Navy equipped submarines with an air tube called a *snorkel*. The snorkel drew air into the submarine when the craft was near the surface. This air replaced oxygen used up by the diesel engines and crew. But the snorkel left a trail through the water and could reveal the submarine's location. Submarines did not become true underwater ships until the development of nuclear power.

How a Submarine Operates

Surface Operation. On the surface of the water, a submarine performs much like any other ship. A submarine can cruise at about 20 *knots* (nautical miles per hour) on the surface. However, modern submarines spend little time above water.

Diving. A submarine dives by flooding its ballast tanks with water. The added weight causes the ship to lose its *positive buoyancy* (ability to stay afloat), and it becomes *neutrally buoyant*. Then the submarine's diving

planes are tilted down and the craft glides smoothly down into the water.

A submarine can dive to a depth of over 100 feet (30 meters) in less than a minute. Only specially designed research submarines can dive deeper than about 5,000 feet (1,524 meters). Their hulls can resist the intense pressure that would crush an ordinary submarine in seconds. The metals used in research submarines are too heavy—and the design techniques are too expensive —for use in combat submarines.

Underwater Operation. A submarine travels underwater somewhat as an airplane moves through the air. The diving planes angle up and down to raise or lower the ship. Two crewmen sit at aircraftlike controls and maneuver the submarine. They push the control wheel forward to make the submarine descend or pull the wheel toward them to make the craft rise. Turning the wheel to the right or left moves the rudder and steers the ship.

A nuclear submarine can travel faster than 30 knots underwater. Its sonar warns of any obstacles in its path, and the inertial guidance system keeps a constant check on its position.

Resurfacing. A submarine is brought to the surface in one of two ways. Water is blown out of the ballast tanks by compressed air, or the diving planes are tilted so the submarine angles up.

Life Aboard a Submarine

Attack submarines of the United States Navy go on patrol for about six months. They frequently stop in ports during the voyage. Ballistic missile submarines stay on patrol for about 60 days and spend almost the entire period underwater. The sailors on both types of submarines have many comforts during their cruise. For example, large air-conditioning units keep the temperature and humidity at comfortable levels. Libraries and game rooms help ease the monotony of life beneath the sea.

On most submarines, every member of the crew works a daily four-hour shift called a *watch*. At the end of his watch, a crewman is relieved and goes off duty for eight hours. He may have to do some maintenance work on the ship but is mostly free to relax or study until he returns to his station. The work assignments vary so that all the crewmen have days off.

Nuclear submarines produce their own air and drinking water. A process called *electrolysis* extracts oxygen from sea water and provides all the air needed for the crew. Chemical filters remove any harmful elements from the air in a submarine. Thick lead plates around the nuclear reactor shield the crew from any dangerous radiation. Machines distill ocean water into pure drinking water.

A submarine returns to port at the end of its cruise. It receives any needed repairs and takes on additional supplies. A ballistic missile submarine also changes crews. Each ballistic missile submarine in the U.S. Navy has two crews, the *blue crew* and the *gold crew*. After one crew completes a patrol, it is replaced by the other. The oncoming crew takes the submarine on another mission. The men returning to shore go on leave and then receive additional training. After the crew of

U.S. Navy

An Early Submarine called the *Turtle* was powered by a hand-cranked propeller and operated by one person. In 1776, the *Turtle* made the first known submarine attack on a warship.

U.S. Navy

The United States Navy's First Submarine, the U.S.S. *Holland,* was powered by a gasoline engine and electric batteries. An American inventor, John P. Holland, launched the vessel in 1898.

an attack submarine completes a patrol, it spends six months in port and in local operations.

History

Early Submarines. The first workable submarine was a wooden rowboat covered with waterproof hides. The builder, a Dutch scientist named Cornelius van Drebbel, demonstrated his invention in England about 1620. Designers constructed many undersea craft during the next century. But little use was made of such ships until the Revolutionary War in America (1775-1783). During that war, David Bushnell, a student at Yale College, designed the *Turtle*, a one-man submarine powered by a hand-cranked propeller. In 1776, the *Turtle* failed in an attempt to sink a British warship in New York Harbor. This mission was the first known attack by a submarine.

In 1800, the American inventor Robert Fulton built the *Nautilus*, a copper-covered submarine 21 feet (6.4

meters) long. Fulton tried to sell the *Nautilus* to France and then to England. However, neither nation showed much interest in the craft, even though it sank several ships in demonstrations.

During the Civil War (1861-1865), the Confederate submarine *Hunley* became the first underwater vessel to sink a ship in wartime. The *Hunley* carried an explosive attached to a long pole on its bow. In 1864, it rammed the Union ship *Housatonic* in Charleston Harbor off the coast of South Carolina. The explosion sank the *Housatonic*, but the *Hunley* went to the bottom with its victim.

In 1898, the American inventor John P. Holland launched a 53-foot (16-meter) submarine powered by a gasoline engine and electric batteries. It could reach a speed of 6 knots submerged. The U.S. Navy bought this ship—its first submarine—in 1900 and named it the U.S.S. *Holland*. Simon Lake, another American inventor, also designed submarines. But his chief accom-

U.S. Navy

German Submarines called *U-boats* sank thousands of merchant ships during World War II (1939-1945). The U-boat shown at the left was captured by the United States during the war.

plishment was the invention of the submarine periscope in 1902. Lake's periscope used magnifying lenses that enabled a submerged submarine to sight distant targets. He also built submarines with wheels so they could roll along the bottom of the sea.

In 1908, Great Britain launched the first diesel-powered submarine. Its engines were more powerful, cost less to operate, and produced fewer dangerous fumes than did gasoline engines. Almost all submarines used diesel engines until the development of nuclear power in the 1950's.

World Wars I and II. During World War I (1914-1918), Germany proved the submarine's effectiveness as a deadly warship. In 1914, the German submarine *U-9* sank three British cruisers within an hour. German submarines, called *Unterseebooten* or *U-boats*, blockaded Britain and took a heavy toll of merchant and passenger ships. U-boats became the terror of the seas by waging unrestricted war on Allied ships.

In May 1915, a German submarine torpedoed the British liner *Lusitania*. Nearly 2,000 passengers, including 128 Americans, died in the attack. Public anger increased in the United States as U-boats sank one American merchant ship after another during the next year. These submarine attacks helped lead to the entry of the United States into the war in April 1917.

During World War II (1939-1945), German submarines sank thousands of merchant ships. The U-boats, equipped with snorkels, hunted in groups called *wolf packs*, which consisted of from 2 to 40 submarines.

The Allies fought to protect their ships from the German submarines. Merchant ships formed large *convoys* (fleets) that were protected by destroyers and other ships. The development of radar and sonar helped locate enemy submarines and reduced the danger of attack.

The U.S. submarines operated chiefly in the Pacific Ocean. They sank over half of Japan's merchant ships and many of its warships. The Navy's submarines also carried troops to raid enemy islands, laid mines in enemy harbors, and performed rescue missions.

Nuclear Submarines. In 1954, the U.S. Navy commissioned the first nuclear-powered submarine, the *Nautilus*. On its first voyage, the *Nautilus* broke all previous submarine records for underwater speed and endurance. In 1958, the *Nautilus* became the first submarine to sail under the ice at the North Pole.

Other United States nuclear submarines also made naval history. In 1960, for example, the *Triton* traveled underwater around the world. Its voyage of 41,500 miles (66,790 kilometers) lasted 84 days. That same year, the *Seadragon* navigated the Northwest Passage, the northern route from the Atlantic to the Pacific.

In the early 1960's, the U.S. Navy developed the first modern ballistic missile submarines. Each of these submarines had 16 missiles in the hull behind the sail. The early missiles carried atomic bombs and could strike targets up to 1,200 miles (1,930 kilometers) away.

In the early 1980's, the U.S. submarine fleet consisted of about 80 attack submarines and about 40 ballistic missile submarines. Major classes of these ships include the *Ethan Allen*, the *George Washington*, the *Lafayette*, the *Los Angeles*, and the *Sturgeon*.

In 1981, the United States commissioned the first *Ohio* class submarine. Ships of this class are the largest and most powerful U.S. submarines ever built. They measure

560 feet (171 meters) long and carry 24 Trident missiles. Each missile has a range of about 4,000 miles (6,400 kilometers) and can hold several individual warheads. Each warhead can be aimed at a separate target.

Russia's ballistic missile submarines are smaller than those of the United States, but their missiles can strike targets up to 5,000 miles (8,000 kilometers) away. Russia has more nuclear-powered submarines than any other nation, and the United States ranks second. Russia also has the largest submarine fleet in the world—about 350 ships. However, many of its submarines are diesel-powered.   NORMAN POLMAR

Related Articles in WORLD BOOK include:

Depth Charge	Guided Missile	Periscope
Diving, Under-	Holland, John P.	Rickover, Hyman G.
water (Diving	New London Naval	World War I
in Vehicles)	Submarine Base	World War II

Additional Resources

Jane's Pocket Book of Submarine Development. Ed. by John E. Moore. Macmillan, 1976.

POLMAR, NORMAN. *The American Submarine.* Nautical & Aviation, 1981.

RÖSSLER, EBERHARD. *The U-boat: The Evolution and Technical History of German Submarines.* Naval Institute Press, 1981.

RUTLAND, JONATHAN P. *See Inside a Submarine.* Watts, 1980. For younger readers.

WHEELER, KEITH. *War Under the Pacific.* Time Inc., 1980.

SUBPOENA, *suh PEE nuh,* or SUBPENA, is a legal notice to appear as a witness and give testimony in court. The name comes from two Latin words, *sub,* which means *under,* and *poena,* which means *penalty.* A person who receives a subpoena must obey it *under penalty* of being held in contempt of court (see CONTEMPT). The *subpoena duces tecum* (Latin for *bring with you under penalty*) requires a person to bring into court specified things, such as papers, books, financial records, or other documents. See also WITNESS.   THOMAS A. COWAN

SUBSIDY, *SUHB suh dee,* is a money payment or other form of aid that the government gives to a person or organization. Its purpose is to encourage some needed activity by furnishing funds, free land, or legal rights that might otherwise be lacking.

In the 1800's, the United States government gave large tracts of land to the railroads on the condition that they would build lines across the continent. Altogether, the railroads received about 160,000,000 acres (64,700,000 hectares) of land in this way. The government also granted subsidies to telegraph and cable companies. In the 1920's, it granted subsidies to ship companies. It gave them generous mail-carrying contracts and allowed them to buy government-owned ships at a fraction of their actual cost. Government air-mail contracts have also aided the airlines since the 1920's.

Federal, state, and local governments award subsidies for a variety of activities. The federal government gives subsidies to farmers in an effort to control farm production and prices. Taxes on goods imported into the United States are indirect subsidies to U.S. manufacturers who make the same kind of goods. Subsidies also help finance many schools. Subsidies are sometimes improperly awarded to gain the political support of those receiving the aid.   ROBERT D. PATTON

See also EDUCATION; TARIFF (Kinds of Tariffs).

SUBSOIL. See SOIL (Characteristics of Soils).

SUBTRACTION

WORLD BOOK photo

SUBTRACTION is a way of taking away a number of things from a larger number. You take them away to find how many things are left. Only *like things* can be subtracted. That is, you cannot subtract apples from pencils.

Suppose you have a set of 8 oranges.

Suppose you want to take away a set of 5 oranges.

You find that you have 3 oranges left.

Learning To Subtract

A question such as "3 from 6 is how many?" is a subtraction problem. To find out how many things are left in a subtraction problem, you can *count* or find the answer by *thinking*.

Subtraction by Counting. Here are two groups of chocolate cupcakes.

How many cupcakes are there in the first group? Count them. There are 6 cupcakes in the first group. Mary took 3 cupcakes from the second group. How many cupcakes are left in the second group? Count them. There are 3 cupcakes left. You counted to find how many cupcakes are left if you take 3 from 6. You discovered that 3 taken from 6 leaves 3.

Subtraction by Thinking. Tommy has 5 pennies.

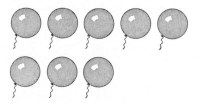

He wants to spend 2 pennies for a pencil. How many pennies will Tommy have left? Cover 2 pennies in the picture. You should be able to tell how many pennies are left by just looking at the picture, without counting. You should learn to *think* "2 from 5 leaves 3." This article will show you the facts you need to know to subtract by thinking. Thinking the answer is a quicker way of subtracting than counting.

You can learn to think the answer to a subtraction problem from what you know about addition. For example, you know that 3 and 2 are 5. This means that if you take 2 from 5, you have 3. You can practice by writing the addition and subtraction facts in groups of four.

3 and 4 are 7	4 from 7 leaves 3
4 and 3 are 7	3 from 7 leaves 4

Subtraction Questions. Subtraction tells you how many things are left when you take away one set of things from another. It also lets you *compare* two sets of things. Suppose Mary has 5 balloons and Sue has 3 balloons.

To compare the two sets of balloons, you must find the *difference* between the two sets. You can find the difference by subtracting. When you subtract 3 from 5, you

SUBTRACTION TERMS

Borrow in subtraction means to change a 10 in the minuend into 1's, to change a 100 into 10's, or to change a 1,000 into 100's, and so on.

Difference. In $12-7=5$, the number 5 is the difference. It means that 12 and 7 are being compared.

Minuend. In $12-7=5$, the number 12 is the minuend.

Minus in subtraction means *less* or *take away*. For example, 12 *minus* 7 is 5.

Remainder. In $12-7=5$, the number 5 is the remainder. It is the answer to the subtraction problem.

Subtraction Fact is a basic statement in subtraction. For example, $16-9=7$ and $4-3=1$ are two subtraction facts.

Subtrahend. In $12-7=5$, the number taken away (7) is the subtrahend.

discover that the difference between the two sets is 2 balloons, or 2.

You can also use subtraction to find out how many more things are needed. Suppose John needs 12 pennies. He has 5 pennies. How many more pennies does he need?

When you subtract 5 from 12, you discover that John needs 7 more pennies to make 12.

Subtraction can tell you (1) how many things are left, (2) what the difference is, and (3) how many more things are needed.

Writing Subtraction. It is best to write your subtraction problems and their answers. This gives you a record of your thinking.

You can make a record with pictures.

The picture shows that 3 taken from 5 leaves 2.

You can write this in numbers and words.

3 from 5 leaves 2

But you must learn to write with numbers and signs.

$$5 - 3 = 2$$

The $-$ sign means to subtract or take away. So $5-3$ means "3 taken from 5." We call the $-$ sign the *minus sign*, and read $5-3$ as "5 *minus* 3." The $=$ sign means that the sets on one side of the $=$ sign are *equal* to the sets on the other side. Here is how it works:

$$5-3 \qquad = \qquad 2$$

There is another way to use numerals and signs.

$$\begin{array}{r} 5 \\ -3 \\ \hline 2 \end{array}$$

Most people use this form when working out problems in subtraction.

Each part of a subtraction problem has a name. When we are subtracting to find out how many things are left, we call the answer the *remainder*. When we are subtracting to compare two groups or to find how many more things are needed, we call the answer the *difference*. We call the number being taken away or subtracted the *subtrahend*. The number from which the subtrahend is taken is called the *minuend*.

$$\begin{array}{r} 5 \\ -3 \\ \hline 2 \end{array}$$ Minuend / Subtrahend / Remainder or Difference

Subtraction Facts. By subtracting one group from another, you discover that $8-5=3$, $6-3=3$, and $12-5=7$. We call these *subtraction facts*.

Each subtraction fact consists of a minuend, a subtrahend, and a remainder, or difference. There are 81 subtraction facts. You can discover each one of them for yourself by counting and taking away one set of things from another. For example, you can practice by crossing off squares as you have seen crossing off done in an earlier example.

The 81 Subtraction Facts

2	3	4	5	6	7	8	9	10
-1	-1	-1	-1	-1	-1	-1	-1	-1
1	2	3	4	5	6	7	8	9
3	4	5	6	7	8	9	10	11
-2	-2	-2	-2	-2	-2	-2	-2	-2
1	2	3	4	5	6	7	8	9
4	5	6	7	8	9	10	11	12
-3	-3	-3	-3	-3	-3	-3	-3	-3
1	2	3	4	5	6	7	8	9
5	6	7	8	9	10	11	12	13
-4	-4	-4	-4	-4	-4	-4	-4	-4
1	2	3	4	5	6	7	8	9
6	7	8	9	10	11	12	13	14
-5	-5	-5	-5	-5	-5	-5	-5	-5
1	2	3	4	5	6	7	8	9
7	8	9	10	11	12	13	14	15
-6	-6	-6	-6	-6	-6	-6	-6	-6
1	2	3	4	5	6	7	8	9
8	9	10	11	12	13	14	15	16
-7	-7	-7	-7	-7	-7	-7	-7	-7
1	2	3	4	5	6	7	8	9
9	10	11	12	13	14	15	16	17
-8	-8	-8	-8	-8	-8	-8	-8	-8
1	2	3	4	5	6	7	8	9
10	11	12	13	14	15	16	17	18
-9	-9	-9	-9	-9	-9	-9	-9	-9
1	2	3	4	5	6	7	8	9

It is best to learn the subtraction facts so that you can recall them without stopping to work them out. You can use them to solve problems right away.

To learn the harder facts, it is sometimes useful to *regroup*. For example, many persons find it easier to subtract numbers from 10. Suppose you wanted to solve the problem $14-7$. You know that 14 is the same as one 10 and four 1's. So you could regroup it like this.

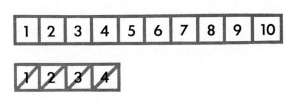

SUBTRACTION

First, you can take away 4. You know that $7-4=3$, so you must still take away 3. Subtracting $10-3$ is easy.

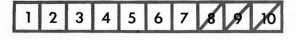

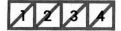

You can see that $10-3=7$. So $14-7=7$.

You can probably invent other ways to help you learn the subtraction facts.

Subtracting Larger Numbers

Subtracting larger numbers is not difficult, if you know the subtraction facts and understand the number system.

Subtracting 10's and 100's. Suppose you have 5 dimes. This is the same as 50¢. Suppose you want to spend 3 dimes on a book. This is the same as 30¢. How much money will you have left? The problem is 5 dimes -3 dimes or 50¢ $-$ 30¢. You can find the answer by counting.

You can also find the answer by using the subtraction facts and thinking.

5 dimes	50¢
-3 dimes	-30¢
2 dimes	20¢

If you know that $5-3=2$, you can see that 3 dimes taken from 5 dimes leaves 2 dimes. A dime is 10¢, so you can see that $50-30=20$. The subtraction fact $5-3=2$ helps you find the answer. *You subtract 10's the same way that you subtract 1's. But you must write the remainder in the 10's place.* And you must remember to write in a zero to show that the remainder is 10's, not 1's.

Subtracting 100's is done in the same way. Suppose you had to subtract 3 dollars from 5 dollars.

5 dollars	500¢	500
-3 dollars	-300¢	-300
2 dollars	200¢	200

You subtract 100's (and 1,000's and so on) the same way that you subtract 1's and 10's. Once again, you can see how the subtraction fact helps you find the answer to the subtraction example.

Subtracting 10's and 1's. Tom had 45 tickets to sell. He sold 23 of them. How many tickets should he have left? That is, what is $45-23$? We call numbers such as 45 and 23 *two-place* numbers, because 45 has two places, four 10's and five 1's; and 23 has two places, two 10's and three 1's.

4 tens and 5 ones	45
-2 tens and 3 ones	-23
2 tens and 2 ones	22

To subtract one two-place number from another, you

754

begin by subtracting the 1's: $5-3=2$. Write the 2 in the 1's place in the remainder.

$$\begin{array}{r} 45 \\ -23 \\ \hline 2 \end{array}$$

Next, subtract the 10's: $4-2=2$. Remember that the $4-2$ stands for 10's, not 1's. Write the 2 in the 10's place in the remainder.

$$\begin{array}{r} 45 \\ -23 \\ \hline 22 \end{array}$$

So Tom should have 22 tickets left.

Here is an example of subtracting *three-place numbers*.

$$\begin{array}{r} 647 \\ -123 \\ \hline 524 \end{array}$$

First, subtract the 1's: $7-3=4$. Write the 4 in the 1's place of the remainder. Next, subtract the 10's: $4-2=2$. Write the 2 in the 10's place in the remainder. Next, subtract the 100's: $6-1=5$. Write the 5 in the 100's place in the answer. Subtracting two- and three-place numbers is easy, but you must remember two things. You must subtract the 1's, 10's, 100's, 1,000's, and so on, *in that order*. Always begin at the right—in the 1's place—and work to the left. Second, you must write your work carefully, so that the numbers of the remainders are in the proper places.

How to Borrow. When you subtract larger numbers, you often cannot solve a problem unless you know how to *borrow*. For instance, look at the example $62-27$. How can you subtract seven 1's from two 1's? Borrowing helps solve this kind of example.

To understand borrowing, you must follow an example step by step. In the example $62-27$, the first step is to write the numbers as 10's and 1's.

You cannot subtract seven 1's from two 1's. *But you can take one of the 10's in the minuend and change it into 1's.* Now you can solve the problem.

6 tens 2 ones	5 tens 10+2 ones	5 tens 12 ones
-2 tens 7 ones	-2 tens 7 ones	-2 tens 7 ones
		3 tens 5 ones

So $62-27=35$. There were too many 1's in the subtrahend to subtract. You "borrowed," or changed a 10 from the 10's part of the minuend into the 1's. This is what borrowing means. You can also borrow 100's, 1,000's, and so on, in solving problems.

You do not have to write out a problem every time you borrow. You can *think* the steps and write in little numbers as a guide. Here is the same example:

$$\begin{array}{r} 62 \\ -27 \end{array}$$

First, you study the example. "I cannot take 7 from 2," you think, "so I must change a 10 to 1's." You draw a line through the 6 in the minuend and write a 5 above it. This means that there are now five 10's in the 10's place instead of six. Next, you write a little 1 just above and to the left of the 2. This means that there are now twelve 1's, instead of two.

$$\begin{array}{r} \overset{5}{\cancel{6}}\overset{1}{2} \\ -27 \\ \hline \end{array}$$

Now you can do the subtraction. "Seven 1's from twelve 1's leave 5," you think, and write a 5 in the 1's place of the remainder. "Two 10's from five 10's leave 3," you think, and write a 3 in the 10's place of the remainder. This completes the example.

$$\begin{array}{r} \overset{5}{\cancel{6}}\overset{1}{2} \\ -27 \\ \hline 35 \end{array}$$

The same method of "borrowing" a 10 can be used for 100's and 1,000's.

$$\begin{array}{r} 628 \\ -361 \\ \hline 7 \end{array}$$

First, you subtract one 1 from eight 1's, and write a 7 in the 1's place of the remainder. But you see that you cannot subtract six 10's from two 10's. You must borrow a 100, or ten 10's, from the six 100's in the minuend.

$$\begin{array}{r} \overset{5}{\cancel{6}}\overset{1}{2}8 \\ -361 \\ \hline 7 \end{array}$$

You draw a line through the 6 in the minuend and write a 5 above it. This means that there are now five 100's in the 100's place, instead of six. Next, you write in a little 1 just above and to the left of the 2. This means that there are now twelve 10's, instead of two. Now you can finish the subtraction. Six 10's from twelve 10's leaves six. You write a 6 in the 10's place of the remainder. Three 100's from five 100's leaves two. You write a 2 in the 100's place of the remainder.

$$\begin{array}{r} \overset{5}{\cancel{6}}\overset{1}{2}8 \\ -361 \\ \hline 267 \end{array}$$

You use the same method for 1,000's. You borrow a 1,000 just as you borrowed a 10 or a 100.

Checking Subtraction

You should always check your work in subtraction to make sure that you have done it correctly.

Checking by Subtraction. One way to check a subtraction problem is to subtract the remainder from the minuend.

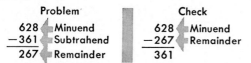

Problem

628	◄ Minuend
−361	◄ Subtrahend
267	◄ Remainder

Check

628	◄ Minuend
−267	◄ Remainder
361	

The new remainder should be the same as the old subtrahend. This checks your work.

Checking by Addition. A good way to check subtraction problems is by addition, because addition is the

opposite of subtraction. You add the subtrahend and the remainder.

Problem

628	◄ Minuend
−361	◄ Subtrahend
267	◄ Remainder

Check

361	◄ Subtrahend
+267	◄ Remainder
628	

The sum of the addition should be the same as the old minuend in the subtraction problem.

Estimating helps you know if your answer is reasonable. Try to estimate the answer *before* you work the problem. Here is an example:

	ESTIMATING
	(Think)
	476 is about 475.
476	254 is about 250.
−254	475 is 400 and 75.
222	250 is 200 and 50.
	75 − 50 is 25.
	400 − 200 is 200.
	The answer should be about 225.

This is almost the exact answer. You can estimate in larger numbers. For example, 476 is about 500, and 254 is about 250. Subtracting 500 − 250 gives you 250. This gives you a good idea of what the answer should be. Estimating the answer before you work a problem will save you time if you make a mistake, because you know about what the answer should be.

Subtraction Rules To Remember

Here are six rules that will help you solve subtraction problems.

1. Remember what subtraction means. You can find the answers to subtraction problems by counting. But it is quicker and easier to *think* the answers.

2. Learning the 81 subtraction facts will help you think the answers to subtraction problems quickly.

3. Subtraction is the opposite of addition. Because of this, addition will help you learn the subtraction facts and check problems.

4. The subtraction facts help you subtract larger numbers to solve problems.

5. You can only subtract quantities of the same kind. That is, you must subtract 1's from 1's and 10's from 10's.

6. Subtraction answers three kinds of questions: how many are left, what is the difference, and how many more are needed.

Other Ways To Subtract

There are several ways of thinking out a subtraction problem. The method we have used is called the "*take-away-borrow*" method. Here is another example:

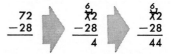

First, you see that you cannot take eight 1's from two 1's. You borrow a 10, making the minuend six 10's and twelve 1's. Then you subtract eight 1's from twelve

755

SUBTRACTION

1's: $12-8=4$. You write the 4 in the 1's place in the answer. Next you subtract two 10's from six 10's: $6-2=4$. You write the 4 in the 10's place in the answer.

Another method is called the *"addition-borrow" method.*

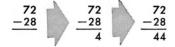

The numbers are the same as in the "take-away-borrow" method, but the *thinking* is different. You see that you cannot take eight 1's from two 1's, and borrow a 10. Instead of subtracting eight 1's from twelve 1's, you think "what *added* to 8 makes 12?" You know that $8+4=12$, so you write the 4 in the 1's place in the answer. Instead of subtracting two 10's from six 10's, you think "what *added* to 2 makes 6?" You know that $2+4=6$, so you write the 4 in the 10's place in the answer.

A third method is called the *"addition-carry"* method.

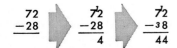

First, you see that you cannot take eight 1's from two 1's. Instead of borrowing, you add ten 1's to the two 1's: $2+10=12$. Next, you think "what *added* to 8 makes 12?" You know that $8+4=12$, so you write the 4 in the 1's place in the answer. Now you think "I added a 10 to the 1's, so I must subtract a 10 from the 10's." To do this, you change the two 10's in the subtrahend to three 10's. You think "what *added* to 3 makes 7?" You know that $3+4=7$, so you write the 4 in the 10's place in the answer.

Fun with Subtraction

Many games that can be played with the addition, multiplication, and division facts can be changed a little for the subtraction facts.

To play a game called *More or Less*, make a pack of 36 cards. Write the numbers from 1 to 18 separately on two sets of cards. This means that there are two cards for each number. Shuffle the cards and place the pile face down. The leader of the game takes the first card and holds it up for the players to see. Suppose it is 14. The first player takes a card from the pile and shows it. Suppose it is 6. He compares it with the 14 card and says "It is less." Then he must tell how much less. In this case, he would say "It is 8 less than 14." He must find the answer by thinking the subtraction. Suppose the next player turns up 17. He compares it with the first card. He must say "It is more. It is 3 more than 14." If a player gives the wrong answer, he is out of the game. When you have gone through the cards once, you can mix them up and go through the game again with new numbers. CHARLOTTE JUNGE

Related Articles in WORLD BOOK include:

Addition	Decimal	Fraction
Algebra (Subtraction)	Numeral System	Mathematics
Arithmetic	Division	Multiplication

Outline

I. Learning To Subtract
   A. Subtraction by Counting   D. Writing
   B. Subtraction by Thinking   Subtraction
   C. Subtraction Questions   E. Subtraction Facts

II. Subtracting Larger Numbers
   A. Subtracting 10's and 100's   C. How to Borrow
   B. Subtracting 10's and 1's

III. Checking Subtraction
   A. Checking by Subtraction   C. Estimating
   B. Checking by Addition

IV. Subtraction Rules To Remember

V. Other Ways To Subtract

VI. Fun with Subtraction

PRACTICE SUBTRACTION EXAMPLES

1. $8-5=$
2. $7-4=$
3. $8-6=$
4. $18-5=$
5. $17-4=$
6. $18-6=$
7. $15-9=$
8. $15-7=$
9. $15-6=$
10. $7-5=$
11. $7-2=$
12. $9-6=$
13. $9-3=$
14. $14-8=$
15. $14-6=$

16. $5-2$
17. $50-20$
18. $8-3$
19. $80-30$
20. $12-3$

21. $120-30$
22. $8-4$
23. $80-40$
24. $6-4$
25. $9-3$

26. $90-30$
27. $7-4$
28. $70-40$
29. $84-22$
30. $95-34$

31. $67-23$
32. $628-115$
33. $843-531$
34. $6725-3513$
35. $52-26$

36. $83-48$
37. $65-39$
38. $625-241$
39. $729-381$
40. $90-36$

41. $923-465$
42. $307-186$
43. $503-280$
44. $700-265$
45. $900-189$

ANSWERS TO THE PRACTICE EXAMPLES

1. 3	6. 12	11. 5	16. 3	21. 90	26. 60	31. 44	36. 35	41. 458
2. 3	7. 6	12. 3	17. 30	22. 4	27. 3	32. 513	37. 26	42. 121
3. 2	8. 8	13. 6	18. 5	23. 40	28. 30	33. 312	38. 384	43. 223
4. 13	9. 9	14. 6	19. 50	24. 2	29. 62	34. 3,212	39. 348	44. 435
5. 13	10. 2	15. 8	20. 9	25. 6	30. 61	35. 26	40. 54	45. 711

SUBURB is a community outside or near a large central city. Since the end of World War II in 1945, suburbs in the United States have grown much faster—both in area and population—than central cities or small towns. In the early 1970's, more Americans lived in suburbs than in central cities. Families with school-age children make up the great majority of suburban residents.

People live in suburbs for various reasons. Many families seek a home, a yard, and freedom from over-crowded, declining city neighborhoods. Others believe their children will have better educational opportunities in the suburbs. Some people move to escape the noise, air pollution, and social conflicts of urban areas.

Most suburban families live in single-family houses, though the number of apartment buildings is increasing. Many suburbs are made up of residents with similar incomes, nationalities, and religions. Black Americans at all income levels find it difficult to obtain suburban homes because of discrimination in the sale and rental of housing.

Many suburban residents travel to the central city to work and for recreational and cultural activities. But there are industrial suburbs as well as primarily residential ones. Many suburban factories, offices, and shopping centers appeared during the 1960's. Most suburbs have their own governments, with a mayor or city manager, a council, and such municipal departments as the police. Other suburbs are governed directly by county officials.

Extensive suburban growth in the United States began in the late 1800's with the development of railroads. People could live in the "country" and ride the train to their jobs in the city. The move to the suburbs has also been helped by federal loans to people who want to buy new homes. During the 1950's and 1960's, general prosperity increased the move to suburbs by middle-income groups. More and more families became able to buy one or two automobiles. Cars are necessary for most suburbanites because of the distances they must travel to work or to shop. Many suburban commuters face the problem of driving on jammed expressways.

The rapid growth of suburbs has created problems for local governments. Many suburbs have difficulty raising money for such services as water, police and fire protection, and especially education. The large number of children in suburbs has made it necessary to provide extensive new educational facilities. Much conflict in suburbs involves the quality of schools and the taxes needed to pay for them. It also involves the handling of controversial social issues.   J. DAVID GREENSTONE

See also CITY; CITY GOVERNMENT; LOCAL GOVERNMENT; METROPOLITAN AREA.

SUBVERSIVE ACTIVITY. See UN-AMERICAN ACTIVITIES COMMITTEE.

SUBWAY is an underground railway. In New York City, London, Paris, and Moscow, the subway system is a great, complicated network of tunnels. London was the first city to have a subway, and now has seven systems that provide quick and cheap transportation to all parts of the city and suburbs. London subways are called *tubes*. Some are so far underground that passengers go down on elevators. The first subway built in London was operated by steam locomotives, and opened in 1863. The first deep-level tube was opened

in 1890, and had electric locomotives. All subways since that time have been operated by electricity. Other major cities, and the years their subways were opened, include: Madrid (1919); Barcelona (1924); Sydney (1926); Tokyo (1927); Buenos Aires (1928); Moscow (1935); Toronto (1954); Milan (1964); Montreal (1966); and Mexico City (1969).

Several large U.S. cities have subway systems. Boston was the first American city to have a subway, opening its line of 1½ miles (2.4 kilometers) in 1897. The subway in New York City is the largest in the world, and is probably the best example of passenger-subway construction. This system is so large that a person can travel from the New Jersey shore, under the city, beneath two rivers into Long Island, without once seeing daylight. The first sections of New York's subway were opened in 1904. Subways also operate in Chicago, Philadelphia, San Francisco, and Washington, D.C.

There are two types of subways. One is called the *open cut*. The construction crew tears out the streets, and builds the subways in deep ditches. If two lines are going to cross, the crew digs one roadbed deeper than the other. They then lay pavement over the subway. The other form of subway, called a *tube*, is constructed by boring through the earth at the desired depth without disturbing the surface. This type of construction is for one or two tracks. The tunnels of an open-cut subway are rectangular. The tunnels of the other subway are usually circular or semicircular. New York City's subway is rectangular and London's is semicircular.

Subways must be built so that ventilation is good. Stale air is carried off through vents. Fresh air may be brought into the system by means of fans.

The cost of construction of a subway is very high. The New York City system cost from $2 million to $3 million per mile ($1.3 million to $1.9 million per kilometer).   FRANKLIN M. RECK

See also ELECTRIC RAILROAD; NEW YORK CITY (Transportation); TUNNEL.

Chicago's Subway runs through a semicircular tunnel over much of its route. This station is one of 20 along 10 miles (16 kilometers) of tunnel.

Chicago Transit Authority

SUCCESSION, PRESIDENTIAL. See PRESIDENTIAL SUCCESSION.

SUCCESSION WARS, *suhk SEHSH uhn*. Wars growing out of disputes over who should *succeed to* (inherit) a throne are called *succession wars*. Four important conflicts in European history are known by this name. They are the War of the Spanish Succession, the War of the Polish Succession, the War of the Austrian Succession, and the War of the Bavarian Succession.

The War of the Spanish Succession began in 1701 and lasted until 1714. Its American phase was known as Queen Anne's War (1702-1713).

Charles II, king of Spain, had no children, and all Europe was interested in the question of who would be his successor. The laws governing succession were so involved, and the claims of the different heirs were so conflicting, that it is almost impossible to say who rightfully should have worn the Spanish crown.

When King Charles II died in Spain on November 1, 1700, he left a will that gave the crown to the French prince, Philip of Anjou. Philip's grandfather, Louis XIV of France, then proclaimed him king of Spain, and declared that the Pyrenees no longer separated the two kingdoms. Since French power was already feared in Europe, other countries were alarmed at the prospect that France might annex the Spanish Empire.

Almost immediately the Grand Alliance was formed by England, The Netherlands, Prussia, Austria, and most of the other states of the Holy Roman Empire. This alliance sought to prevent Philip of Anjou from becoming king of Spain, and to put the Archduke Charles of Austria on the throne instead. War broke out between France and the Grand Alliance. The French were defeated decisively in the battles of Blenheim, Ramillies, Oudenarde, and Malplaquet. The English general, the Duke of Marlborough, and the imperial general, Prince Eugene of Savoy, commanded the forces of the Grand Alliance.

In 1711, Joseph I, the Holy Roman Emperor and ruler of Austria, died. He was succeeded by his brother, the Archduke Charles, who was the allies' candidate for the Spanish throne. It then became clear that the balance of power would be even more seriously threatened if Charles got Spain as well as Austria than it would be if Philip became king of Spain. Charles as ruler of Austria would be in a position where he would control Spain as well as the Holy Roman Empire.

In 1713, Louis XIV used skillful diplomacy to bring about the Peace of Utrecht, under which he obtained fairly favorable terms. His grandson, Philip, was recognized as king of Spain on the condition that Spain and France would never be united. Charles refused to sign the Treaty of Utrecht and did not make peace until a year later. Then he found it necessary to give way and sign the Treaty of Rastatt, which was almost exactly the same as the Peace of Utrecht.

The War of the Polish Succession (1733-1735) was caused when Polish nobles elected Stanislas Leszczyński, father-in-law of Louis XV of France, as king of Poland. Russia and Austria forced the Poles to accept the Elector Augustus of Saxony as king. War followed between France, aided by Spain, and Russia, aided by Austria. The outcome of the war was a damaging blow to French prestige. Augustus of Saxony remained King of Poland.

The War of the Austrian Succession (1740-1748) was known in America as King George's War. It was caused by the death of the Austrian ruler Charles VI, who had no sons and left his dominions to his daughter Maria Theresa. The great powers of Europe had guaranteed that a daughter of Charles could succeed him by the terms of the Pragmatic Sanction. But they broke their words and tried to take Maria Theresa's lands. See PRAGMATIC SANCTION.

The first to attack Maria Theresa was Frederick the Great, king of Prussia, who conquered the province of Silesia. In 1741 he strengthened his hold upon the territory by an overwhelming victory at Mollwitz. France, Spain, Bavaria, Saxony, Sardinia, and Poland joined Prussia, and for a time Maria Theresa was threatened with the loss of her dominions. But she contrived to save her crown and most of her lands by her own great courage and vigorous leadership. Her appeal to the Hungarians won her the powerful support of this chivalrous people. Maria Theresa was further aided by an alliance with the great maritime powers, England and Holland, which crushed the power of France at sea. She separated Frederick the Great from his allies by giving him Silesia. The Treaty of Aix-la-Chapelle, signed in 1748, finally ended the war.

The War of the Bavarian Succession (1778-1779) was a short quarrel between Prussia and Austria over the succession to the throne of Bavaria and the disposition of some Bavarian territory. In 1777, the Elector of Bavaria, Maximilian Joseph, died and left no direct heirs. Austria then attempted to control the affairs of Bavaria and to dictate the succession. This aroused the jealousy of Frederick the Great. Armed forces from Prussia and Austria invaded Bavaria, and war seemed inevitable.

But neither Austria nor Prussia was anxious for war. No battles were fought, and the war is often called "the potato war." Hungry soldiers spent their time searching for food in the fields. Catherine II of Russia mediated peace. In the Treaty of Teschen, signed in 1779, both Austria and Prussia were satisfied with certain territorial gains.   ROBERT G. L. WAITE

Related Articles in WORLD BOOK include:

Blenheim, Battle of
Charles (VI) of the
  Holy Roman Empire
French and Indian Wars
  (Queen Anne's War;
  King George's War)

Louis (XIV)
Maria Theresa
Marlborough, Duke of
Seven Years' War
Utrecht, Peace of

SUCCORY. See CHICORY.

SUCCOT. See SUKKOT.

SUCCULENT, *SUHK yuh luhnt*, is the name for a fleshy plant, such as the cactus, that has large stems or leaves in which to store water. Succulent plants grow in deserts and other dry places in the world where there is little water. Desert plants have large stems or leaves in which to store water.   MARCUS MAXON

See also CACTUS; SEDUM; SPURGE FAMILY.

SU-CHOU, *soo joh* (pop. 300,000-1,000,000), or SOO-CHOW, is an ancient Chinese city known for its canals and *pagodas* (temples). Su-chou lies in a rich agricultural region in Kiangsu Province, between Nan-ching and Shanghai. For location, see CHINA (political map). Su-chou's factories produce chemicals and machinery.

National Film Board

The Sucker has thick lips on the underside of the snout. Its mouth has no teeth, but its throat is lined with thin, comblike spines. Suckers live in lakes and streams.

Skilled craftworkers in the city carve jade and weave silks.   RICHARD H. SOLOMON

SUCKER is the name given to several kinds of fish closely related to the minnow family. Most of them have mouths with thick, fleshy lips that help them suck up animal and plant life on the bottom of lakes and streams. Except for a few kinds in eastern Asia, all the suckers are native to North America. These fish are dull-colored except in the spring, when the males of some species have a rose or orange stripe. The larger kinds of suckers are food fishes. They have a sweet-tasting, but bony, flesh. Large, carplike suckers known as buffalo fishes are caught in the Mississippi Valley.

Scientific Classification. The sucker belongs to the sucker family, *Catostomidae*. The common sucker is genus *Catostomus*, species *C. commersonii*. The bigmouth buffalo fish is *Megastomatobus cyprinella;* the smallmouth buffalo fish, *Ictiobus bubalus;* and the black buffalo fish is classified as *I. niger*.   CARL L. HUBBS

SUCKLING, SIR JOHN (1609-1642), was the most famous member of the *Cavalier poets*, a group associated with the court of King Charles I of England. Suckling's poetry is seldom serious, but its amateur quality has its own charm. Suckling's best verse has a witty and knowing quality, as in:

> 'Tis not the meat, but 'tis the appetite
> Makes eating a delight.

Suckling's plays include *Aglaura* (1637). His short poems were published four years after his death in a collection of his writings titled *Fragmenta Aurea*. Suckling's ability as a literary critic can be seen in "A Ses-

Sempervivum Is an Example of a Succulent Plant.

J. Horace McFarland

sion of Poets" (1637), a verse review of poetry in his day.

Suckling was born in Middlesex, and served in the army. In 1641, he was accused of plotting to gain control of the army for the king. He fled to Paris and died there, perhaps as a suicide.   RICHARD S. SYLVESTER

SUCRE, *SOO kray* (pop. 62,207), is the official capital of Bolivia. However, all the national government offices except those of the Supreme Court are in La Paz, the actual capital. Sucre lies in south-central Bolivia in the *Cordillera Real* (Royal Range) of the Andes Mountains at an altitude of about 8,950 feet (2,728 meters). For location, see BOLIVIA (map).

Sucre is one of the oldest cities in South America and has kept much of its colonial appearance. All the city's buildings are painted white, as they were in the days of the Spanish empire. Sucre's main square has a number of historical structures. They include a highly decorated cathedral built in the 1600's and the Legislative Palace, in which the nation's Declaration of Independence was signed in 1825. One of the oldest universities in the Western Hemisphere, the University of Saint Francis Xavier, is in Sucre. The university was founded in 1624.

Sucre's economy depends largely on the agriculture of the surrounding area. Many of the city's people work on nearby farms or in factories that process the farm products, which include fruits and cereal grains. Others are employed by the government or in such industries as oil refining and cement manufacturing.

Sucre was founded in 1538 by Spanish settlers who called it Charcas. The city's name was later changed to Chuquisaca and then to La Plata. In 1826, it was named Sucre after Bolivia's first president, General Antonio José de Sucre (see SUCRE, ANTONIO JOSÉ DE). The government moved from Sucre to La Paz in 1898, partly because La Paz had better transportation connections with the rest of the country.   NATHAN A. HAVERSTOCK

SUCRE, *SOO kray,* **ANTONIO JOSÉ DE** (1795-1830), liberated Ecuador and Bolivia from Spain and served as the first president of Bolivia. He was one of the ablest generals of his time. His victory at Ayacucho in 1824 put an end to Spanish rule in South America.

When Bolivia became a separate state, Sucre became its first president in 1826. He was an able administrator. He resigned the presidency in 1828 to prevent war with the Peruvians who objected to his friendship with Simón Bolívar (see BOLÍVAR, SIMÓN). Sucre was killed by an assassin in 1830. Bolivia named one of its most important cities in honor of him.

Sucre was born in Cumaná, Venezuela. He joined the revolutionary army when he was 15. He soon became Bolívar's trusted friend and chief lieutenant, and when Bolívar sought to free Ecuador, Sucre scored a victory at Pichincha in 1822. His strategy at Ayacucho freed Upper Peru, now Bolivia (see BOLIVIA [Independence]).   HARVEY L. JOHNSON

SUCROSE is the chemical name for common table sugar. It has the chemical formula $C_{12}H_{22}O_{11}$. It is extracted from sugar beets and sugar cane and is the cheapest pure chemical produced on a large scale. Chemically, sucrose has certain properties of an alcohol, and it will form esters with organic acids (see ESTER). See also SUGAR.   ARTHUR J. ASHE III

SUCTION PUMP. See PUMP (The Lift Pump).

759

Sudan

Capital ✪
Other City or Town ●
Road ──
Rail Line ──
MOUNTAIN ▲
River ～
Cataract ≈

WORLD BOOK map

| 0 Miles | 200 | 400 | 600 | 800 | 1,000 |
| 0 Kilometers | 400 | 600 | 800 | 1,000 | 1,200 | 1,400 | 1,600 |

SUDAN, *soo DAN,* is the largest country in Africa in area. It lies in the northeastern part of the continent, and has a 400-mile (644-kilometer) coastline on the Red Sea. The Sudan is a land with widely differing people and geography. It sprawls across three distinct natural regions, ranging from bleak desert in the north to grassy plains in central Sudan and a great swamp and steaming tropical rainforest in the south.

Most of the people live near the Nile River or one of its branches, or near wells that can supply water for them and their crops. Only *nomads*, who roam in search of water and grazing land for their camels, sheep, goats, and cattle, live in many parts of the sandy north.

In the south, the swamp and the equatorial forest produce little food or cash crops. But big game, including the rare rhinoceros, lions, leopards, elephants, buffalo, giraffe, and other animals, roams there.

The contributor of this article, K. D. D. Henderson, a former member of the Sudan Political Service, is the author of Survey of the Anglo-Egyptian Sudan, The Making of Modern Sudan, *and* Sudan Republic.

The people of the Sudan are sharply divided. Arabic-speaking Muslims make up most of the population in the northern part of the country. They are descendants of African blacks and *Nubians* (brown-skinned people related to the early Egyptians and Libyans). African blacks who belong to several different ethnic groups live in the south. These groups lived in complete isolation from the rest of the world until the early 1800's. Most of the southerners speak their own local languages and practice their own local customs and religions.

The history of this ancient land dates back to Biblical times. The *pharaohs* (rulers) of ancient Egypt carried off valuable supplies of gold, the land's only mineral wealth. The Sudan was invaded and conquered by Egyptians, Romans, and Turks. Later, it was ruled jointly by Great Britain and Egypt for more than 50 years. During this period, it was called *Anglo-Egyptian Sudan.* It finally gained independence on Jan. 1, 1956.

The Sudan's official name in Arabic, the official language, is JUMHURIYAT AS SUDAN AD DIMUQRATIYAH (DEMOCRATIC REPUBLIC OF THE SUDAN). Khartoum, a city on the Nile River in central Sudan, is the country's capital and leading city.

Government. A president heads the government of the Sudan. The people elect the president to a five-year term. The president appoints Cabinet members, who head departments that carry out the operations of the government. The People's Assembly serves as the nation's legislature. The people elect its members to four-year terms. The Sudan is divided into six regions of local government, each of which has an elected legislature. The Sudanese Socialist Union is the country's only political party.

People. Most of the people in the Sudan are farmers or herders. The herders in the north keep camels and those in the south keep cattle.

Arabic-speaking Muslim people make up about two-thirds of the population, and most of them live in the northern two-thirds of the country. Descendants of Nubians and African blacks, they have intermarried

Facts in Brief

Capital: Khartoum.

Official Language: Arabic.

Form of Government: Republic.

Area: 967,500 sq. mi. (2,505,813 km²). *Greatest Distances*—north-south, 1,400 mi. (2,253 km); east-west, 1,075 mi. (1,730 km). *Coastline*—400 mi. (644 km).

Population: *Estimated 1984 Population*—20,944,000; distribution, 71 per cent rural, 29 per cent urban; density, 21 persons per sq. mi. (8 per km²). *1973 Census*—14,113,590. *Estimated 1989 Population*—24,000,000.

Chief Products: *Agriculture*—cassava, corn, cotton, dates, hides and skins, melons, millet, peanuts, sesame, wheat. *Forest Industry*—gum arabic, hardwood. *Manufacturing and Processing*—beer, cement, salt, shoes, soap, textiles.

Flag: Three horizontal stripes of red, white, and black, with a green triangle symbolizing Islam. Adopted in 1970. See FLAG (color picture: Flags of Africa).

Money: *Basic Unit*—Sudanese pound. See MONEY (table: Exchange Rates).

with Arab peoples and adopted their language and religion. Most of these people live in the Nile River Valley and make their living as farmers. Some Beja groups wander about the Red Sea hills with their herds.

Most of the people in northern and central Sudan live in square, flat-roofed houses that are made out of sun-baked bricks. The houses have narrow windows to keep out the heat. The nomads who live on the desert have no permanent homes because they continuously move their herds in search of water and grass. They wear flowing robes as protection from the sun and sand.

About one-third of Sudan's people are African blacks. Most of the blacks live in the southern part of the country south of the great swamp area. Some of these are among the tallest people in the world.

Black tribes lived isolated from the rest of the world for hundreds of years, cut off by the great swamp of central Sudan and the thick rainforests. In the early 1800's, Egyptians and others invaded the swamps and jungles searching for slaves. This made the blacks bitter and suspicious of other people. They have resisted efforts by northerners to convert them to the Islamic faith and to teach them to speak Arabic. Most of these groups speak their own local languages, and practice local religions. They wear little clothing, and live in houses with mud walls and thatched roofs.

Water is scarce in most parts of the Sudan. Because of this, the people dig ditches to store rainwater and bank dirt around their fields to hold rainwater on the fields. In some parts of western Sudan, the people sometimes scoop out the *pith* (soft center) of tree trunks and use the trees as water tanks. The rain runs down the branches into the hollow trunks. The people build big mud saucers at the roots of the trees, so they can haul the water up in leather buckets.

In areas that receive little rainfall, watermelons are important to the people. They go on growing after the rains stop and can be stored and eaten later.

In most parts of the country, the people can make pancakes from sorghum or millet flour and eat this with highly spiced vegetable soups. They add eggs and meat to their soup if they have them. The nomads live on milk most of the time.

About a fourth of the people of the Sudan can read and write. Most of the towns and rural areas have schools, but only about half the school-age children attend classes. The University of Khartoum and the Islamic University of Omdurman are in Sudan. Khartoum also has a branch of Egypt's University of Cairo.

Land. The Sudan has four main natural regions ranging from north to south: (1) the desert region, (2) the steppe region, (3) the savanna region, and (4) the equatorial region.

The *desert region*, in the north, covers about a third of the country. The Libyan and Nubian deserts, which are part of the Sahara, cover most of this region. Vegetation grows only in the Nile River Valley and in a few scattered *oases* (watering places).

The *steppe region* lies in central Sudan. The vast *steppes* (plains) are covered with short, coarse grass and small bushes. The *savanna region* lies south of the steppes. It is an area of tall bushes and thick, green grass (see SAVANNA).

The *equatorial region*, much of it thick tropical forest, covers nearly a third of southern Sudan. The Sudd area, one of the largest marshes in the world, lies in the center of the Upper White Nile basin. The country's chief highland areas lie in the far west, on the Red Sea coast, and around the southern rim of the marsh. Mount Kinyeti rises 10,456 feet (3,187 meters) on the border between the Sudan and Uganda.

The Nile River system flows through the country from south to north. The White Nile and the Blue Nile rivers meet at Khartoum to form the Nile River.

Summers are hot throughout the country, with temperatures of about 100° F. (38° C). Winter temperatures vary from about 60° F. (16° C) in the north to about 80° F. (27° C) in the south. Almost no rain falls in the far north. Rainfall in southern Sudan averages about 40 inches (100 centimeters) a year.

Economy. In most of the Sudan, life centers around the water supply. People are forced to live near the rivers, water holes, and *well fields* (areas containing large amounts of water). Many of the people may spend half of each day at the well. Farmers harvest crops quickly, before the pools of water dry up. The people use water very carefully. Building developments start with plans for dams, cisterns, and other water storage facilities.

Irrigation of such areas as the Gezira Plain, which lies between the Blue Nile and the White Nile, has made the Sudan the world's second largest producer of Egyptian cotton (see COTTON [Egyptian Cotton]). Canals have been built in this area south of Khartoum and Omdurman to distribute water to the fields. The water to irrigate the cotton region is provided by the Sennar Dam, a 3,300-foot (1,010-meter) span that blocks the Blue Nile. The dam creates a reservoir that extends over 93 miles (150 kilometers) up the river.

The competition of *synthetic* (artificial) fabrics and uncertain cotton prices hurt the Sudan. When cotton crops are poor, or cotton prices are low, the economy suffers.

Marc & Evelyne Bernheim, Rapho Guillumette

Ruins in Northern Sudan date from about the A.D. 200's. They stand 35 miles (56 kilometers) from Shandi, north of Khartoum.

SUDAN

United Nations

Women Shoppers in Southern Sudan board a Nile River ferry, carrying purchases home in the earthenware pots.

Sudan's forests provide some hardwood. Nearly 90 per cent of the world's production of gum arabic, which is used in making perfumes and candy, come from forests in the Sudan (see GUM ARABIC). Farmers also produce some cassava, sesame, corn, rice, peanuts, coffee, and sweet potatoes. Of these, only peanuts are grown in sufficient amount to be an important export.

The Sudan has a good network of roads in the north. But in the marshy south, roads are expensive to build and maintain. The country has about 2,800 miles (4,510 kilometers) of narrow-gauge railroads, and about 3,000 miles (4,800 kilometers) of navigable rivers. An airline provides service to the main towns.

History. Egypt invaded what is now northern Sudan many times after about 3000 B.C. A kingdom called Kush existed in the northeastern part of the country from as early as 1500 B.C. to about A.D. 350. It was an important trading and cultural center (see KUSH).

Several Christian kingdoms grew up in the Sudan area during the A.D. 500's. Muslim Arabs captured all of them between the 1100's and the 1500's. In 1504, black-skinned Muslims called Funj established their capital at Sennar, south of what is now Wad Madani. The Funj conquered much of the Sudan, but their power declined during the 1700's. In 1821, Egypt conquered the Funj and gained control of the Sudan (see FUNJ SULTANATE).

In 1881, a Muslim leader named Muhammad Ahmed proclaimed himself *al-Mahdi* (the guide), and led a successful revolt against the Egyptians. His successor, Khalifa Abdullahi, ruled the Sudan until 1898, when British and Egyptian troops reconquered it.

In 1899, Great Britain and Egypt made the Sudan a protectorate. The British appointed a governor general and provided most of the important officials. Some Egyptian nationalists opposed British domination of Sudan. In 1924, Egyptian troops in the Sudan mutinied against the British. The mutiny failed, and most Egyptian officials were expelled from the Sudan. Egypt took no further part in governing Sudan until 1936, when it signed a new agreement with Great Britain.

After World War II, educated Sudanese began to demand independence. In 1953, Great Britain and Egypt agreed on steps leading to self-government for the Sudan. The Sudan officially became an independent country on Jan. 1, 1956, despite the objections of the people living in southern Sudan.

The Sudan was plagued by political unrest and civil war after independence. In 1958, Ibrahim Abboud, an army general, seized control of the government. He dissolved parliament and banned all political parties. Meanwhile, a revolt of blacks in the south against domination by the Arabs had developed into a civil war. Abboud failed to settle the conflict, and he was forced to resign in 1964. The Sudan returned to civilian government. But the new government was unable to settle the unrest in the south and also failed to solve economic problems.

The government of the Sudan changed hands several times during the late 1960's. In 1969, Major General Gaafar al-Nimeiry took control of the government. Leftist military leaders overthrew Nimeiry's government in July, 1971. But Nimeiry regained control a few days after the revolt. Voters elected Nimeiry president in October, 1971, and reelected him in 1977.

In 1972, the government reached an agreement with the leaders of the rebel movement in the south. The agreement provided for some self-government for the south.   K. D. D. HENDERSON

Related Articles in WORLD BOOK include:

Arab League	Nile River	Omdurman
Gordon, Charles G.	Nubia	Port Sudan
Khartoum		

SUDAN GRASS is a hay plant that the Department of Agriculture introduced into the United States in 1909 from Khartoum, Sudan. It was first tested in Texas, and gave excellent results. Farmers planted this grass on vast areas of land in the South and Southwest. Eventually it spread to nearly all parts of the country. It is one of the best drought-resisting plants known to American farmers. Sudan grass has a fibrous root system. It is an annual, which means that seed must be planted every year. Farmers grow the grass for stock feed and for its seed. Sudan hay has a higher feeding value than timothy.

Scientific Classification. Sudan grass is in the grass family, *Gramineae*. It is classified as genus *Sorghum*, species *S. vulgare*, variety *sudanense*.   ROY G. WIGGANS

J. Horace McFarland

Sudan Grass makes excellent forage for livestock. It grows in almost any soil, and also in semiarid land regions.

SUDBURY, Ont. (pop. 91,829; met. area pop. 149,-923), is a world center of nickel production. Mines in and near the city produce about a fifth of the world's nickel supply. Sudbury, often called the *Nickel Capital of the World*, lies about 250 miles (402 kilometers) northwest of Toronto (see ONTARIO [political map]).

Description. Sudbury covers about 124 square miles (321 square kilometers). Most of the city's people have English or French ancestors. Sudbury is the home of Laurentian University, where many classes are taught in both English and French.

Mining ranks as Sudbury's chief economic activity. About two-fifths of the city's workers are employed by companies that mine and process the rich ores found in the area. Nickel and copper are Sudbury's chief products. Iron and such precious metals as gold and platinum are also mined and processed in the area.

History. Huron Indians lived in what is now the Sudbury area before white settlers first arrived. In 1883, the Canadian Pacific Railway established the first permanent settlement there. James Worthington, the head of a railroad construction crew, named the community for the town of Sudbury in Suffolk, England. Also in 1883, the railroad's construction crews discovered the world's richest copper-nickel deposits near Sudbury.

Sudbury's first copper-mining company was formed in 1886. Major mining operations began after 1892, when a practical process for separating copper and nickel was developed. Sudbury was incorporated as a town in 1893. Its population rose from 795 that year to 18,075 in 1930, when it was incorporated as a city.

The world's two largest nickel-mining companies—Inco Limited (formerly the International Nickel Company of Canada, Limited) and Falconbridge Nickel Mines, Limited—were founded in Sudbury during the early 1900's. The city prospered during World War I (1914-1918) and World War II (1939-1945) because of the great demand for nickel. Manufacturers used the metal in making ammunition and armor plating. In 1950, Sudbury had a population of 42,410. In 1960, the city annexed several adjoining townships, and its population jumped to about 80,000.

Through the years, Sudbury's copper and nickel plants have caused much air pollution. In the early 1970's, the provincial government ordered the mining companies to greatly reduce the amount of harmful gases discharged into the air. One mining company built a smokestack that spread the gases over a large area and thus reduced the concentration of pollution in Sudbury. The smokestack, completed in 1972, rises 1,250 feet (381 meters) and is the tallest in the world.

Sudbury has a mayor-council government. The mayor and nine aldermen are elected to two-year terms. The council consists of these officials. GEORGE GRACE

SUDDEN INFANT DEATH SYNDROME, *SIHN drohm,* or SIDS, is an unexplained ailment that results in the death of an apparently healthy baby. In most cases, the baby is found dead a few hours after being put to bed. The cause of death cannot be determined, even with an autopsy. Most of the victims are from 1 to 6 months old. SIDS is also called *crib death.*

Some SIDS cases have actually been observed. The baby suddenly turns blue, becomes limp, and stops breathing. It does not cry out or struggle. Attempts to revive the victim have succeeded in only a few cases.

Sudden infant death syndrome occurs throughout the world. It kills between 6,000 and 7,000 babies a year in the United States. SIDS strikes more boys than girls, and it is more likely to kill premature babies than infants born after a full-term pregnancy. It occurs most often among the poor and in winter. Most victims are asleep when it strikes.

Researchers are working to determine what causes SIDS. They have gathered increasing evidence that victims may be born with a slight defect of the central nervous system. This defect may interfere with the nervous system's ability to control breathing, heart function, or both. MARIE VALDES-DAPENA

SUDERMANN, *ZOO duhr MAHN,* **HERMANN** (1857-1928), was a German dramatist and novelist associated with the naturalism movement. *Dame Care* (1887), his best-known novel, concerns a young man burdened with his father's failure in life. Through sacrifice, the son must master fate's repeated challenges. *Regina* (1890) is a historical novel showing a man's struggle against the prejudices of his community.

Sudermann gained fame in Europe with his plays *Honor* (1889) and *Magda* (1893). In these dramas, he stripped away the pretenses of the middle-class society of the late 1800's. Sudermann's *Lithuanian Tales* (1917) skillfully portray working-class characters and carry a genuine sense of tragedy. Sudermann was born in Matzicken in East Prussia. WALTHER L. HAHN

SUDETENLAND, *soo DAYT uhn land,* is a region located on the slopes of the Sudetes Mountains. It lies in Czechoslovakia, on the borders of Bohemia, Moravia, and Germany. Many Germans once lived in Sudetenland. The treaties of Versailles and St. Germain in 1919 gave the area to Czechoslovakia. The Munich Agreement of 1938 gave the area and other Czech areas to Germany. In 1945, the Allies restored Sudetenland to Czechoslovakia and the Germans were expelled and replaced with Czechs and Slovaks. M. KAMIL DZIEWANOWSKI

SUDETES MOUNTAINS. See CZECHOSLAVAKIA (The Sudetes Mountains).

SUEDE, *swayd,* is a soft leather that has a nap on one side. Suede is made by holding the flesh side of tanned animal hide against a buffing wheel. The rough surface of the wheel raises the nap. Items made from suede include shoes, gloves, hats, and coats.

SUESS, *zyoos,* **EDUARD** (1831-1914), an Austrian geologist, became famous for his work on changes of the earth's surface. His most important book was the four-volume *Face of the Earth* (1885-1901). He served as an assistant at the Hofmuseum in Vienna from 1852 to 1862, and taught at the University of Vienna from 1857 to 1901. He was an inspiring teacher of advanced students. From 1869 to 1896, he served as leader of the Liberal party in the Austrian Parliament. Suess was born in London. CARROLL LANE FENTON

SUET, *SOO iht,* is the hard, white fat around the loins and kidneys of some animals, especially cattle and full-grown sheep. Melted suet forms tallow, which is used in making candles and soap. Beef suet is used for frying and other cooking methods. Many people use suet as bird feed in the winter. JOHN C. AYRES

SUETONIUS, *swih TOH nee uhs* (A.D. 69?-140), a Roman author, wrote a series of biographies of Roman rulers from Julius Caesar to Domitian in his *Lives of the Caesars*. This work is important not only for the information it gives us about these men, but also because it had a great influence on the writing of biography in ancient times and in the Middle Ages. All his other works are lost except his lives of grammarians, orators, and some other literary men.   THOMAS A. BRADY

SUEZ, *soo EHZ* (pop. 381,000), is an Egyptian city at the southern entrance to the Suez Canal. It lies on the Gulf of Suez, about 80 miles (130 kilometers) east of Cairo. For location, see EGYPT (political map).

Suez has been an Egyptian seaport since ancient times. The city became an especially important port and one of Egypt's chief industrial centers after the Suez Canal opened in 1869. Major industries of Suez included oil-refining and fertilizer production.

Suez was heavily damaged during the Arab-Israeli war of 1967. The war hit the city's industries particularly hard. It also forced the closing of the Suez Canal, which sharply reduced the importance of Suez as a port. The Egyptian government reopened the Suez Canal in 1975. It also planned a major reconstruction program for the city.   WILLIAM SPENCER

SUEZ CANAL, *soo EHZ*, is a narrow, artificial waterway in Egypt that extends about 118 miles (190 kilometers) to join the Mediterranean and Red seas. When the canal was opened in 1869, it shortened the route between England and India by 6,000 miles (9,700 kilometers). The canal had been the busiest interocean waterway in the world until it closed during the 1967 Arab-Israeli war. Tankers carrying petroleum and petroleum products had accounted for about 70 per cent of the total tonnage. Egypt reopened the canal in 1975.

The Suez Canal stretches north and south across the Isthmus of Suez, between the cities of Port Said and Suez. It has no locks because there is no great difference between the levels of the Red and Mediterranean seas. Most of the canal can handle only single-lane traffic.

When the canal was constructed, it measured 26 feet (8 meters) deep, 72 feet (22 meters) wide at the bottom, and about 230 feet (70 meters) wide at the surface. It has been widened and deepened several times to handle larger ships and more traffic. Today, the canal is 64 feet (19.5 meters) deep, 302 feet (92 meters) wide at the bottom, and 741 feet (226 meters) wide at the surface.

History. Canals were built to connect the Nile River and the Red Sea hundreds of years before the

Suez Canal

WORLD BOOK map

time of Christ. For a time in the A.D. 600's, the Red and Mediterranean seas were joined by a canal. Napoleon I saw advantages of a waterway across the Isthmus of Suez when he visited Egypt in 1799. But Ferdinand de Lesseps, a French diplomat and canal builder, carried out the plan. He got permission for the project from Muhammad Said (Pasha), the Viceroy of Egypt, in 1854. An International Technical Commission met in 1855 to plan the canal route. By 1858, a company had been organized with a capital stock of about $40 million. Frenchmen and the Ottoman Empire owned most of the stock. Construction began on April 25, 1859, and the canal was opened on Nov. 17, 1869. The Suez Canal Company was given a concession that ended in 1968.

Although Britain gained more from the construction of the canal than any other country, it had no part in building the canal, and bought none of the original shares of stock. However, in 1875, Great Britain bought the shares of the Khedive of Egypt, Ismail Pasha, who had succeeded Muhammad Said (Pasha) as viceroy in 1863. After that, a commission composed mostly of British and French directed management of the canal.

In 1888, an international convention agreed that the canal should be open to all nations in peace and in war. However, Great Britain stationed troops near the canal for its defense in World War I, and kept ships of nations at war with Britain from using the waterway. Axis ships were denied use of the canal in World War II. In 1950, as a result of the Arab-Israeli war (1948-1949), Egypt banned Israeli ships from the canal.

Under the terms of a 1954 agreement with Egypt, British troops left the canal zone in June, 1956. In July, the United States and Great Britain withdrew offers to help finance the Aswan High Dam across the Nile River. This and other factors, including a strong Egyptian nationalist movement, led to the seizure of the canal by Egyptian President Gamal A. Nasser on July 26. Nasser announced that Egypt would use the canal tolls to build the dam. Great Britain, France, and other Western nations protested the seizure.

After years of border clashes, Israel invaded Egypt on Oct. 29, 1956. Great Britain and France attacked Egypt on October 31 in an effort to restore international control of the waterway. United Nations action ended the fighting on November 6. A United Nations police force restored peace in the area. The canal was reopened in March, 1957, under Egyptian management. It was blocked by sunken ships during the Arab-Israeli war in June, 1967. The Suez Canal was not reopened until June, 1975. In 1979, Egypt ended its ban against Israeli use of the canal. In 1980, a tunnel was completed under the canal 10 miles (16 kilometers) north of the city of Suez. Motor vehicles use the tunnel to get from one side of the canal to the other.   WILLIAM A. HANCE

See also DE LESSEPS, FERDINAND MARIE; EGYPT; UNITED NATIONS (The Arab-Israeli Wars).

Additional Resources

FARNIE, DOUGLAS A. *East and West of Suez: The Suez Canal in History, 1854-1956.* Oxford, 1969.
GEORGES-PICOT, JACQUES. *The Real Suez Crisis: The End of a Great 19th Century Work.* Harcourt, 1978.
SCHONFIELD, HUGH J. *The Suez Canal in Peace and War, 1869-1969.* Rev. ed. Univ. of Miami Press, 1969.

SUFFIX. See SPELLING (Spelling Rules).
SUFFRAGE. See VOTING; WOMAN SUFFRAGE.

SUGAR is a food widely used as a sweetener. People sprinkle sugar on such foods as grapefruit and cereal to improve their taste. Some people add it to coffee, tea, and other beverages. In addition, manufacturers include sugar in such foods as ice cream and soft drinks. On the average, each person in the United States uses about 90 pounds (41 kilograms) of sugar yearly.

All green plants produce sugar. But most sugar that people use comes from sugar cane or sugar beets. These plants produce a sugar called *sucrose*. This sugar is the one that people keep in a sugar bowl. Other sources of sugar include cornstarch, milk, maple syrup, and honey.

Sugar belongs to the class of foods called *carbohydrates*. Carbohydrates provide energy for plants and animals. Sugar is *refined* (purified) before it is used for food. The refining process also removes vitamins and other *nutrients* that are necessary for growth and health. As a result, refined sugar serves only as a source of energy.

Many dentists and physicians claim that people eat too much sugar. People who eat large amounts of sugar may become overweight or develop tooth decay or other health problems.

Uses of Sugar

In the Food Industry. Most of the world's sugar crop is used in food. Much of the sugar eaten by people in the United States is contained in *processed* (specially prepared) foods. For example, candy, canned fruit, jams, jellies, and soft drinks all include large amounts of sugar. Sugar is also added to many bakery products to improve their flavor and keep them fresh.

Manufacturers sell sugar in several forms. It is most commonly sold in the form of white *granules* (small grains). Some sugar is ground into powdered sugar and commonly used in cake frostings. Brown sugar, which is often used in baking, is a mixture of molasses-flavored syrup and sugar.

In Other Industries. A small amount of the world's sugar crop is used by nonfood industries to make various products. For example, sugar is used for mixing cement, tanning leather, and making plastics. Some medicines contain sugar, which disguises their unpleasant taste.

Certain products obtained from the sugar-refining process are also made into nonfood items. For example, after sugar has been removed from sugar cane, a material called *bagasse* remains. Bagasse is burned as a source of energy for the sugar factory or is made into paper or wallboard.

Kinds of Sugar

There are two kinds of sugar, *monosaccharides* and *disaccharides*. In pure form, both are white crystals.

Monosaccharides are the simplest carbohydrates. Common monosaccharides include *glucose* and *fructose*. Glucose is the most important carbohydrate in the blood. Fructose, also called *levulose*, is found in fruits and vegetables.

Disaccharides are made up of two monosaccharides. For example, the disaccharide sucrose can be broken down by enzymes into glucose and fructose. Other common disaccharides include *lactose* and *maltose*. Lactose is found in milk and is used in making some medicines. Maltose, which is formed from starch, is used in the production of bread and baby food.

The Sources of Sugar

Sugar Beets and Sugar Cane are the world's main sources of sugar. Sugar beets grow in temperate climates. Sucrose is stored in the plant's fleshy root. Sugar cane is a tall grass plant that thrives in tropical and semitropical climates. It stores sucrose in its stalks. For more detailed information on these sources of sugar, see SUGAR BEET; SUGAR CANE.

Cornstarch and Other Starches are made up of various sugars. Starches can be broken down to form individual sugars by mixing them with acid or enzymes and heating them. For example, the incomplete breakdown of cornstarch produces *corn syrup*, which consists chiefly of glucose and maltose. Corn syrup is used for flavoring such foods as candy and salad dressing. Solid *corn sugar*, which is also formed from cornstarch, is made up primarily of glucose. A liquid called *high-fructose corn syrup* can be produced by a process that converts some of the glucose in cornstarch to fructose. High-fructose corn

Hans & Judy Beste, Tom Stack & Assoc.

Sugar Cane, one of the leading sources of sugar, thrives in tropical and semitropical climates. Most sugar cane is cut and gathered by hand, but some is harvested by machine, *above*.

© John Messineo

Sugar Beets, a major source of sugar, grow in temperate climates. They store sugar in their large, fleshy roots, which are harvested after the leaves of the plants have been removed, *above*.

How Raw Sugar Is Obtained from Sugar Cane

To obtain raw sugar from sugar cane, processors first wash and shred the cane. The cane is then placed in a crushing machine, which forces a sugary juice called *cane juice* from the stalks. After the juice is heated and filtered, an evaporator and vacuum pan remove much of the water from it, forming a syrup. Finally, a centrifuge separates sugar crystals from the syrup, producing raw sugar.

WORLD BOOK diagram by Steven Liska

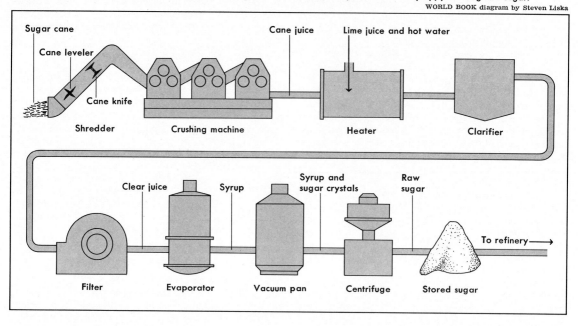

syrup is used in place of sucrose in many baked goods and several soft drinks. See CORN SYRUP; CORNSTARCH.

Honey is the sweet liquid that bees make from the nectar they drink from flowers. Bees collect sucrose from the nectar and convert it into *invert sugar*, an equal mixture of fructose and glucose. Invert sugar is the primary ingredient of honey, which also contains small amounts of vitamins and other nutrients. See HONEY.

Maple Syrup is the concentrated sap of certain maple trees. It consists chiefly of sucrose. However, it gets its characteristic maple taste from various nonsucrose compounds that form during processing. People pour maple syrup on pancakes, waffles, and other foods. Manufacturers use the syrup to flavor certain candies. See MAPLE SYRUP.

Milk. Lactose, also called milk sugar, is found in the milk of all *mammals* (milk-producing animals). It is obtained commercially from skimmed milk and *whey*, a liquid by-product of the cheese-making process.

Molasses is a by-product of sugar-beet and sugar-cane refining processes. It contains 40 to 50 per cent sugar. It is used chiefly in making alcoholic beverages, candy, and livestock feed. The word *molasses* also refers to the extracts of many sugar-bearing plants. For example, the syrup produced by the sweet sorghum plant is called molasses. See SORGHUM (Sweet Sorghums).

Sugar Production

Making Cane Sugar. Sugar cane stalks grow 7 to 15 feet (2 to 5 meters) high. Sugar cane is harvested by hand or by machine. The cut cane is taken to a factory, where the stalks are washed and shredded. They are then placed in a crushing machine or into vats of hot water that dissolve the sugar. Crushing machines burst the cane, squeezing out the sugary liquid from the

stalks. Sprays of water dissolve more sugar from the shredded stalks. The mixture of sugar and water, called *cane juice*, is then taken away for purifying.

Obtaining Raw Sugar. The cane juice, still diluted with water, is heated. Lime is added to the juice to settle out impurities, and carbon dioxide is used to remove the excess lime. Workers then put the clarified juice in huge evaporator tanks, where most of the water is evaporated and the juice becomes thick and syrupy. However, more water must be removed from the syrup so that sugar crystals will form. The syrup is heated in large, dome-shaped vacuum pans to remove excess water. Sugar and sugar syrup scorch easily. But the vacuum lowers the boiling point of the syrup so that it will not scorch even though heating continues.

After large sugar crystals form in the thick syrup, workers put the mixture in a *centrifuge*. This machine spins at extremely high speeds and separates most of the syrup from the crystals. The remaining sugar is called *raw sugar*, and it contains 97 to 99 per cent sucrose. Exporters ship sugar in this form from one country to another.

Refining Cane Sugar. To obtain pure white sugar for table use, the yellowish-brown raw sugar must go through several more steps. The film that gives raw sugar its yellow-brown color is rinsed off. Next, the sugar crystals are dissolved in water, and the solution is poured through filters until it becomes a clear, colorless liquid. The liquid is then evaporated until crystals form again. The crystals are again spun in the centrifuge, and pure white sugar flows from the machine into drying drums. Heated air in the drums absorbs any remaining moisture. The sugar is then packaged for market.

Some of the syrup does not form crystals during the evaporation and spinning process. The process is repeat-

Leading Sugar-Producing Countries

Tons of raw beet and cane sugar produced in 1980

Brazil
9,039,000 short tons (8,200,000 metric tons)

Russia
7,716,200 short tons (7,000,000 metric tons)

India
7,624,700 short tons (6,917,000 metric tons)

Cuba
6,613,900 short tons (6,000,000 metric tons)

United States
5,718,800 short tons (5,188,000 metric tons)

France
4,717,900 short tons (4,280,000 metric tons)

Australia
3,637,600 short tons (3,300,000 metric tons)

Mexico
3,196,700 short tons (2,900,000 metric tons)

West Germany
3,141,600 short tons (2,850,000 metric tons)

China
3,086,500 short tons (2,800,000 metric tons)

Source: U.S. Department of Agriculture.

Leading Sugar-Producing States

Tons of raw beet and cane sugar produced in 1980

Florida
1,070,000 short tons (970,700 metric tons)

Hawaii
1,045,000 short tons (948,000 metric tons)

California
746,000 short tons (676,800 metric tons)

Louisiana
490,000 short tons (444,500 metric tons)

Minnesota
470,000 short tons (426,400 metric tons)

Idaho
407,000 short tons (369,200 metric tons)

North Dakota
274,000 short tons (248,600 metric tons)

Michigan
240,000 short tons (217,700 metric tons)

Colorado
227,000 short tons (205,900 metric tons)

Nebraska
220,000 short tons (199,600 metric tons)

Source: U.S. Department of Agriculture.

---

ed several times to form more white crystals. The remaining syrup is then used to make brown sugar.

Making Beet Sugar. After sugar beets are dug out of the ground, they are shipped to a factory. There, they are washed and cut into thin slices called *cossettes*. The cossettes are placed in diffusers to soak. The soaking removes the sugar from the slices. The cossettes are then dried and mixed with molasses to make cattle feed.

The solution obtained by soaking the cossettes is heated and treated with lime to settle out impurities. Carbon dioxide is added to remove the excess lime in the solution. The juice is then filtered to remove the impurities. The purified solution is called *thin juice*. The juice is evaporated to remove water and crystallize the sugar. From this point, the process for making sugar from sugar beets is the same as for sugar cane. However, in the United States and some other countries, beet-sugar processing is carried out in a single operation. Beet sugar factories produce no raw sugar.

The Sugar Industry

About 97 million short tons (87.7 million metric tons) of sugar are produced throughout the world every year. Brazil leads the world in sugar production, followed by Russia and India. Brazil and India are sugar-cane producing countries. Russia grows large amounts of sugar beets.

The United States produces about 5½ million short tons (5 million metric tons) of sugar a year. Florida ranks first among the states in sugar production, followed by Hawaii and California. The Red River Valley in Minnesota and North Dakota is the largest sugar-beet growing region in the country.

History

Sugar from Sugar Cane. Inhabitants of South Pacific islands grew sugar cane more than 8,000 years ago. The plants were also widely grown in ancient India. Sugar cane is specifically mentioned in records of an expedition by the Macedonian king Alexander the Great to what is now Pakistan in 325 B.C.

The cultivation and refining of sugar cane spread east from India to China about 100 B.C. but did not reach Europe until about A.D. 636. During the early 1400's, Europeans planted sugar cane in northern Africa and on islands in the Atlantic Ocean. Portuguese settlers later planted sugar cane on the west coast of Africa and in Brazil. The Italian navigator Christopher Columbus brought sugar-cane cuttings to islands in the Caribbean Sea in 1493.

The first sugar mill in the Western Hemisphere was built in 1515 in what is now the Dominican Republic. Jesuit missionaries brought sugar cane to Louisiana in 1751. In 1791, the first sugar mill on the North American mainland was built in New Orleans by Antonio Mendez, a Louisiana planter.

Sugar from Sugar Beets. The people of ancient Babylonia, Egypt, and Greece grew sugar beets. In 1744, Andreas Sigismund Marggraf, a German chemist, found that sugar from the sugar beet was the same as that removed from sugar cane. In 1799, Franz Achard, a student of Marggraf's, developed a practical method of removing sugar from sugar beets. Sugar mills then sprang up quickly in Europe and Russia. Beet sugar was first produced in the United States in 1838. E. H. Dyer, an American businessman, established the country's first successful sugar-beet processing factory in Alvarado, Calif., near Oakland.   ROGER E. WYSE

Related Articles in WORLD BOOK include:

Candy	Dextrose	Molasses
Carbohydrate	Glucose	Rillieux, Norbert
Corn Syrup	Maltose	Sucrose

SUGAR BEET is a plant grown for the sugar contained in its large, fleshy root. Sugar beets supply about 40 per cent of the world's commercial sugar. Only sugar cane provides more. Russia is by far the world's largest producer of sugar beets, though France, Italy, the United States, and West Germany also grow substantial quantities of the crop. In the United States, the chief beet-growing states include California, Colorado, Michigan, Minnesota, North Dakota, and Washington.

The sugar beet plant consists of a cluster of dark-green leaves atop a short stocky stem called the *crown.* Beneath the crown is the creamy-white, cone-shaped root, where the plant stores sugar. The enlarged upper part of the root is called the *beet.* The root tapers down to form a thin *taproot,* which extends 2 to 5 feet (0.6 to 1.5 meters) into the soil. The long taproot can obtain water that lies far belowground.

Sugar is manufactured in the plant's leaves by photosynthesis and then transported to the root. Sugar-beet roots weigh from 1½ to 3 pounds (0.7 to 1.4 kilograms). About 15 to 20 per cent of this weight is a sugar called *sucrose.*

Raising Sugar Beets. Sugar beets grow best in regions that have sunny days and cool nights. Farmers plant the seeds in early spring and apply fertilizer early in the growing season. Sugar beets require a large amount of water to prevent them from wilting, and in most growing areas, the plants are irrigated.

Plants grown for sugar are harvested at the end of the first growing season, after the roots have developed. When grown for seed, the plants require a second year of growth. In areas that have mild winters, roots are simply left in the ground after the first growing season. In areas with cold winters, farmers dig up the roots in the autumn, store them over the winter, and then replant them in the spring. During the second year, the plants develop tall, branched stalks with tiny flowers that produce the seeds. In the United States, Oregon is the leading producer of sugar-beet seeds.

A number of diseases and insect pests attack sugar beets. *Leaf spot* and other fungal diseases are troublesome in regions with hot, humid summers. In mild-

Leading Sugar Beet Growing Countries

Tons of sugar beets grown annually

Russia	87,744,000 short tons (79,600,000 metric tons)
France	29,043,000 short tons (26,347,000 metric tons)
United States	23,275,000 short tons (21,115,000 metric tons)
West Germany	21,078,000 short tons (19,122,000 metric tons)
Italy	19,904,000 short tons (13,521,000 metric tons)
Poland	11,464,000 short tons (10,400,000 metric tons)
Turkey	9,700,000 short tons (8,800,000 metric tons)
Great Britain	8,488,000 short tons (7,700,000 metric tons)
Czechoslovakia	7,992,000 short tons (7,250,000 metric tons)
East Germany	7,937,000 short tons (7,200,000 metric tons)

Source: *Production Yearbook, 1980,* FAO.

winter areas, sugar beets may be damaged by such viral diseases as *curly top* and *beet yellows.* During the winter, viruses that cause these diseases are found in various insects and weeds. In the spring, they are transmitted to sugar beets by such insects as aphids and leafhoppers. Farmers control these diseases and pests by planting special disease-resistant varieties of the plants and by applying pesticides.

Harvesting. Sugar beets that are grown for sugar are harvested in late September or early October in most states, though California has a longer growing season. First, a plant is *topped*—that is, its leaves and crown are removed—and then its root is dug up. Both operations are done mechanically. The tops are fed to livestock or are used as fertilizer. The beets are shipped to a factory, where the sugar is extracted. For a detailed description of how sugar is obtained from sugar beets, and for the history of such production, see SUGAR.

Scientific Classification. The sugar beet belongs to the goosefoot family, Chenopodiaceae. It is classified as *Beta vulgaris.*
MYRNA P. STEINKAMP

See also BEET.

SUGAR CANE is a tall grass plant that grows in tropical and semitropical countries. It produces sturdy stalks 7 to 15 feet (2 to 5 meters) high, and about 2 inches (5 centimeters) in diameter. These stalks contain a large amount of sugary juice from which sugar and syrup are made.

Sugar cane grows from a thick, solid rootstock. The numerous stalks have no branches, but have long, narrow leaves that are arranged in two rows. The sugar-cane stalk is divided into several sections, like a bamboo cane. These sections, which are called *internodes,* are connected by joints known as *nodes.* Each node bears a small bud that looks much like a potato eye. The color of the stem varies from yellow to reddish.

South Pacific islanders grew sugar cane more than 8,000 years ago. The plant was also widely grown in ancient India. The cultivation and refining of sugar cane spread from India to China about 100 B.C., but

WORLD BOOK illustration by James Teason
Sugar Beets consist of a creamy-white storage root, *right,* with a crown of large, dark-green leaves, *left.* Sugar makes up 15 to 20 per cent of the weight of the root.

Leading Sugar Cane Growing Countries

Tons of sugar cane produced each year

Brazil
163,623,000 short tons (148,436,000 metric tons)

India
141,978,000 short tons (128,800,000 metric tons)

Cuba
74,957,000 short tons (68,000,000 metric tons)

Mexico
38,030,000 short tons (34,500,000 metric tons)

China
34,966,000 short tons (31,721,000 metric tons)

Pakistan
31,576,000 short tons (28,645,000 metric tons)

Colombia
28,660,000 short tons (26,000,000 metric tons)

United States
28,235,000 short tons (25,614,000 metric tons)

Australia
26,511,000 short tons (24,050,000 metric tons)

Philippines
23,057,000 short tons (20,917,000 metric tons)

Source: *Production Yearbook, 1980,* FAO. Figures are for 1980.

did not reach Europe until about A.D. 636. Colonizers brought sugar cane to America and the West Indies during the 1400's. Today, the leading sugar-cane growing nations include Brazil, India, Cuba, Mexico, and China. Florida, Hawaii, and Louisiana are the leading U.S. cane-producing states.

Growth and Cultivation. Most sugar cane is grown in regions where temperatures generally range between 75°

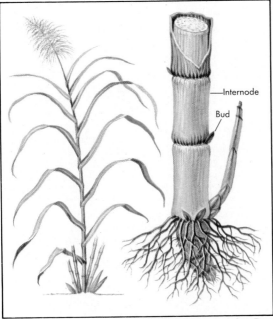

WORLD BOOK illustration by James Teason

Sugar Cane grows in the form of stalks, *left,* which contain a large amount of sugary juice. The stalks are divided into *internodes, right.* Buds grow in the joints between the internodes.

and 86° F. (24° and 30° C) and where rainfall is high. Sugar cane needs about 80 to 120 inches (200 to 300 centimeters) of water a year. In regions with little rainfall, growers irrigate the plants.

Sugar cane is grown chiefly from stem cuttings. Furrows from 5 to 7 feet (1.5 to 2.1 meters) apart are dug in the field. The cuttings are laid in the furrows and covered with soil. The buds on the nodes soon swell and burst, and young stalks emerge from the soil. The leaves appear shortly thereafter, and the stalks develop nodes and internodes a few weeks later.

Harvesting. Most sugar cane is harvested from 8 to 16 months after planting. In some countries, particularly Australia and the United States, machines are used to cut off the cane stalks. But in most other sugar-cane growing areas, workers cut the cane by hand. Each cutter uses a large steel knife that has a blade 5 inches (13 centimeters) wide and 18 inches (48 centimeters) long, with a hook on the back. As the cutters move down the rows, they cut the cane close to the ground, strip off the leaves with the hook, and cut off the top of the stalk at the last matured joint.

The cut stalks are thrown into heaps called *windrows* and then gathered up into carts or railway cars that take them to the sugar factory. The stubble left in the field produces from 2 to 10 additional crops, depending on the location.

For a detailed discussion of how sugar is obtained from sugar cane, see SUGAR (Sugar Production).

Scientific Classification. Sugar cane belongs to the grass family, Gramineae. Its scientific name is *Saccharum officinarum.*   PAUL H. MOORE

See also CUBA (picture); HAWAII (Agriculture); PUERTO RICO (picture); SUGAR.

SUGAR LOAF MOUNTAIN. See RIO DE JANEIRO (picture); EARTH (History of the Earth [color picture]).

SUGAR MAPLE. See MAPLE (The Sugar Maple; pictures); MAPLE SYRUP.

SUGGESTION, in psychology, is the acceptance of an idea by the mind without critical thought. For example, if someone merely makes a throwing motion, many observers will be sure that something actually was thrown. They get this impression because the mind tends to complete a partial picture. Similarly, if a parent touches the forehead of a child who feels ill, the parent may believe that the child has a fever, even though a thermometer would show a normal temperature.

Professional magicians rely on suggestion for most of their effects. If a magician goes through the motion of tossing a coin into a cup, and if people in the audience hear the expected jingling sound, they assume the coin is in the cup. Advertisers use suggestion in many ways. No advertiser would dare guarantee that a person will become popular by using a certain product. But the advertisements may strongly suggest this result.

Children accept suggestions more easily than adults do, because they are less critical and less experienced. Most uneducated or prejudiced people also accept suggestion easily. People are more suggestible when they are worried, tired, or ill.   FRANK J. KOBLER

See also HYPNOTISM; MAGIC; MAGICIAN.

SUHARTO, *soo HAHR toh* (1921-   ), also spelled *Soeharto,* became president of Indonesia in 1968. He and other top military officers seized power from President Sukarno in 1966, after putting down a Communist uprising. Sukarno was allowed to keep the title of president until 1967, when Suharto became acting president. The national assembly elected Suharto president in 1968 and reelected him in 1973, 1978, and 1983. Under Suharto, Indonesia ended border fighting with Malaysia and rejoined the United Nations (UN). Sukarno had withdrawn Indonesia from the UN in 1965.

Suharto was born on the island of Java. As a young man he served in the colonial army The Netherlands kept in Indonesia, then a colony called The Netherlands (Dutch) East Indies. But later, he fought the Dutch for Indonesian independence. After independence, he became lieutenant general in the Indonesian armed forces.

See also INDONESIA (History); SUKARNO.

SUI DYNASTY, *swee*, was a Chinese *dynasty* (family of rulers) that governed from A.D. 589 to 618. Yang Chien, the dynasty's first ruler, brought most of northern and southern China together as an empire after almost 400 years of civil war. Yang Chien died in 604, possibly murdered by his son, Sui Yang Ti, who then ruled.

Yang Ti tried to improve and expand the empire. He built the Grand Canal, a waterway for shipping grain and other products. It extended almost 200 miles (320 kilometers), from Hang-chou to Chen-chiang. Yang Ti failed in attempts to conquer Korea and Manchuria. After the Koreans defeated the Sui army in 612, the Chinese people became dissatisfied with the emperor and revolted. In 615, the Sui army suffered another defeat, by the Eastern Turks, and Yang Ti retreated to the south. He was assassinated in 618. His death marked the end of the Sui Dynasty. The T'ang Dynasty was founded that same year.   EUGENE BOARDMAN

SUICIDE is the act of deliberately killing oneself. Every year, about 28,000 persons in the United States commit suicide. The suicide rate is highest among white, elderly men who live alone. But the number of suicides has been increasing among blacks, children, teen-agers, and women. The individuals most likely to commit suicide are those who have thought about it, threatened to commit it, or attempted it in the past.

Most people who commit suicide do so for personal reasons. The death of a close friend or relative may lead a person to commit suicide. Fear of the future or of failure in school causes some student suicides. Some children commit suicide if they feel that their parents do not love them. Mental illness may also lead to suicide. Some people believe that patients suffering from a hopeless illness should be permitted to kill themselves if they desire. However, the United States and most other nations have laws against helping someone to commit suicide (see DEATH [The Right to Die]).

Society plays a part in some suicides. As a society becomes more complicated, for example, loneliness and job pressures can lead some people to commit suicide. People who feel that they have betrayed the ideals of their society may also kill themselves. Such suicides were common among Japanese warriors, whose ideal was to win in battle. Defeated warriors, who felt that they had betrayed this ideal, committed a suicide ritual called *hara-kiri* (see HARA-KIRI).

A person considering suicide exhibits certain warning signs. The person may express a loss of interest in living or a wish to die. Other signs include listless behavior, insomnia or sleeping too much, severe weight gain or loss of appetite, and headaches. Since the late 1950's, many communities have established suicide prevention centers. People considering suicide can telephone these centers and discuss their problems.   DAVID LESTER

Additional Resources

HEWETT, JOHN H. *After Suicide*. Westminster, 1980. For family survivors and friends.
KIEV, ARI. *The Courage to Live*. Harper, 1979.
KLAGSBRUN, FRANCINE. *Too Young To Die: Youth and Suicide*. Houghton, 1976.

SUIT. People who seek the help of a court of law to enforce their rights are said to "bring suit." Someone who has suffered injury at the hands of another may bring suit for damages. A person may also bring suit to recover property, to collect money, to enforce the terms of a contract, or to accomplish one of many other purposes. A governmental unit may bring suit in the same way as a private person or a corporation. In general, a suit is any civil action brought before a court of law. Criminal cases are not called suits.   THOMAS A. COWAN

See also CLASS ACTION; COURT (How Courts Work); MALPRACTICE SUIT; STATUTE OF LIMITATIONS.

SUITE, *sweet*, is a type of musical composition. Most suites are made up of a number of short works, usually in the same key. These suites generally consist of dance pieces that have contrasting tempos and moods. The suite developed during the 1500's and declined in popularity after about 1750. Johann Sebastian Bach wrote several important suites for harpsichord and for orchestra during the early 1700's.

After the 1800's, the term *suite* also was used to describe several other types of musical compositions. A group of instrumental selections from a ballet or opera is called a suite. For example, music from *The Nutcracker* (1892), a ballet by the Russian composer Peter Ilich Tchaikovsky, was arranged into the *Nutcracker Suite*. A suite can also be a series of descriptive musical pieces. *The Grand Canyon Suite* (1931) by the American composer Ferde Grofé is an example.   R. M. LONGYEAR

SUKARNO, *soo KAHR noh*, (1901-1970), also spelled *Soekarno*, was president of Indonesia from 1945 to 1967. Anti-Communist military leaders took power from him in 1966, after Communists tried to overthrow the government. Sukarno retained the title of president until 1967. Indonesia was officially a "neutral" nation under Sukarno. But his statements and policies showed a leaning toward Communist China and Russia.

Sukarno was born in Surabaya, Java. He formed the Partai Nasional Indonesia (P.N.I.) in 1927, seeking independence from The Netherlands. After independence, Sukarno called for a "guided democracy" for Indonesia. By 1960, he held unrestricted power.

Sukarno brought West New Guinea (now Irian Jaya) under his control. He refused to recognize the Federation of Malaysia, claiming that Sabah should be part of Indonesia. He threatened to crush Malaysia, and began raids on the federation in 1964. He withdrew Indonesia from the United Nations in 1965 after Malaysia was seated on the Security Council.   GEORGE E. TAYLOR

See also INDONESIA (History).

SUKKOT, *su KOHTH*, or FEAST OF TABERNACLES, is a Jewish festival that originally celebrated the end of the harvest season. It begins on the 15th day of the Hebrew month of Tishri, and lasts nine days. Jews in Israel and Reform Jews celebrate it for only eight days. The eighth day of Sukkot is called *Shemini Atzeret*. The ninth is *Simhat Torah* (see SIMHAT TORAH). During the festival, traditional Jews live in a hut called a *sukkah* as a reminder of the huts in which their ancestors lived during their wanderings in the wilderness.

The ancient Hebrews celebrated Sukkot as a festival of thanksgiving, and brought sacrifices to the Temple in Jerusalem. They formed joyous parades carrying *lulabs* (palm branches), *etrogs* (citrons), and myrtle and willow branches. These plants are still used in the celebrations today.

LEONARD C. MISHKIN

Engraving (1723) by Bernard Picart;
courtesy of the Spertus Museum, Chicago

Sukkot is a Jewish festival. This print shows Jews in The Netherlands celebrating Sukkot in the early 1700's. The top scene shows a procession of worshipers carrying traditional Sukkot plants in a synagogue. The lower scenes illustrate the temporary huts called *sukkahs* built for the festival. Sukkahs are decorated with vegetation and are open at the top. Some Jews eat and sleep in them.

SULEIMAN I, *SOO luh MAHN* or *soo lay MAHN* (1494-1566), became known in the Western world as THE MAGNIFICENT, but among his own people as THE LAWGIVER. He was the 10th ruler of the Ottoman Empire. He led armies into Hungary, and stormed the walls of Vienna. In Asia, his armies invaded Persia (Iran) and captured Tabriz and Baghdad. Suleiman's fleets dominated the Mediterranean Sea, the Red Sea, and the Persian Gulf. His sailors held North Africa, and raided the coasts of Spain, France, and Italy. Suleiman took Rhodes from the Knights of Saint John (see KNIGHTS OF SAINT JOHN). He revised the legal system of the Ottoman Empire. Suleiman quarreled with several of his sons, and he executed two of them.

SYDNEY N. FISHER

See also OTTOMAN EMPIRE (History).

SULFA DRUG is any of a group of chemically related antibacterial compounds. Sulfa drugs, also called *sulfonamides* (pronounced *suhl FAHN uh mydz*), were the first drugs to be proved safe and effective against many common bacterial infections. Sulfa drugs played a major role in antibacterial treatment from the early 1930's until the mid-1940's, when penicillin became widely available. The development of sulfa drugs resulted in a sharp decline in the number of deaths caused by many infectious diseases. These drugs contributed remarkably to the saving of lives during World War II (1939-1945). Today, physicians prescribe sulfa drugs chiefly to treat urinary tract infections.

How Sulfa Drugs Work. Normally, sulfa drugs do not actually kill bacteria. Instead, they prevent the bacteria from multiplying. The bacteria are then killed by the body's normal defense mechanisms.

Bacteria that are sensitive to sulfa drugs require a chemical called para-aminobenzoic acid (PABA) in order to multiply. The bacteria convert PABA into folic acid, which is required for many important biological reactions. Sulfa drugs have a chemical structure similar to PABA and are readily absorbed by bacteria that require this compound. The sulfonamides then block the chemical reactions involved in making folic acid, so that the bacteria can no longer divide and multiply.

Human beings also require folic acid for normal cellular growth. However, people obtain folic acid from the diet—as a vitamin—instead of manufacturing it in the body. Therefore, sulfa drugs do not interfere with the body's supply of folic acid.

Uses in Treating Diseases. Sulfonamides are not effective against all bacteria. Therefore, physicians need to identify the type of bacteria causing an infection before they know whether to use a sulfa drug. Sulfa drugs are most commonly taken by mouth, but they may be given by injection or applied directly to the skin.

In the past, sulfa drugs were used in the treatment of such diseases as pneumonia, dysentery, blood poisoning, cellulitis, bubonic plague, and conjunctivitis. The use of sulfa drugs has decreased because more powerful drugs—such as penicillin and other antibiotics—have been developed to treat many bacterial diseases. Also, many bacteria have become resistant to sulfa drugs. Doctors now use sulfa drugs mainly to treat urinary tract infections.

In the late 1960's researchers developed a combination drug consisting of sulfamethoxazole (a sulfonamide) and a compound called trimethoprim. This drug is effective in treating certain bacterial infections not sensitive to sulfonamides alone. Recurrent urinary tract infections, middle-ear infections, and shigellosis are among the diseases that may be successfully treated with this combination drug.

Development of Sulfa Drugs. Knowledge of the sulfonamides dates to 1908. In that year, Paul Gelmo, a German chemist who was looking for better dyes for woolen goods, discovered chemicals that eventually led to sulfa drugs. But it was not until the early 1930's that sulfonamides were used in medicine.

In 1935, a German pathologist named Gerhard Domagk reported that the dye Prontosil killed streptococcal bacteria in mice. Domagk was awarded the 1939

Nobel Prize in medicine for his discovery. Research on Prontosil spread quickly and it was soon observed that Prontosil was broken down to sulfanilamide in the body. Scientists determined that sulfanilamide was the chemical responsible for blocking the growth of the bacteria. Researchers, particularly in France, England, and the United States, investigated thousands of related chemicals before they found the few that were most useful.

A major problem with sulfanilamide and other early sulfa drugs was that they sometimes *crystallized* (solidified) in the urine of the patient, causing kidney damage. To prevent crystallization, doctors instructed patients to drink plenty of liquids and to take sodium bicarbonate. Scientists later developed sulfa drugs that are much more water soluble and, therefore, much less likely to crystallize in the urine. These more soluble drugs, particularly sulfisoxazole, have largely replaced the earlier sulfonamides.   EUGENE M. JOHNSON, JR.

SULFATE is a salt of sulfuric acid. As a rule, sulfates are stable compounds, formed in crystals. Most of them are fairly soluble in water. But such sulfates as barium, strontium, and lead sulfates do not dissolve in water. Heavy spar is a sulfate of barium; gypsum is a sulfate of calcium; celestite is a sulfate of strontium; and Epsom salt is a sulfate of magnesium. Sulfates have important industrial uses. Copper sulfate, or blue vitriol, is used in many industries, including dyeing and calico printing. Iron sulfate is used in making ink and as a medicine. Manganese sulfate is used in calico printing. Zinc sulfate is used in surgery as an antiseptic, in calico printing, and in drying oils for varnishes. Some baking powders contain *alum*, a double sulfate of potassium and aluminum. Every sulfate contains a group of associated atoms of sulfur and oxygen known in chemistry as the *sulfate radical* ($-SO_4$).

See also ALUM; GYPSUM.

SULFIDE is a group of compounds of sulfur with some other elements, usually metals. All sulfides contain the sulfide ion, in which sulfur has the valence of minus 2. The chemical symbol for this ion is S^{--}.

Sulfides are important in chemistry and industry. Hydrogen sulfide, a poisonous gas, is used in the laboratory to test for various metals. Hydrogen sulfide in the air tarnishes silver. Carbon disulfide is a solvent of rubber and sulfur, and a local anesthetic. It has been used to kill animal and insect pests. Deposits of metallic sulfides are important ores of the metals. Examples are the sulfides of zinc (zinc blende), lead (galena), mercury (cinnabar), and copper (chalcocite). Several colored sulfides are pigments in paints.

See also CARBON DISULFIDE; HYDROGEN SULFIDE.

SULFONAMIDE. See SULFA DRUG.

SULFUR is a yellow, solid, nonmetallic element that occurs in and on the earth and elsewhere in the universe. Sulfur has an atomic weight of 32.064, and its atomic number is 16. Its chemical symbol is S. Sulfur has a wide variety of industrial uses.

Sulfur makes up about 0.05 per cent of the earth's crust and about 15 per cent of the earth's core. Sulfur occurs in deposits of volcanic materials and of *pyrite*, a compound of sulfur and iron. Coal, petroleum, natural gas, and such minerals as cinnabar, galena, gypsum, sphalerite, and stibnite also contain sulfur. The atmos-

phere of Venus contains sulfur, and scientists believe the core of Mars consists of pure iron sulfide, another compound of sulfur and iron. Astronomers have discovered several sulfur compounds in interstellar clouds of gas and dust.

All plants and animals need small amounts of sulfur to live. Plants obtain sulfur from the soil. Many foods from plants, including cabbage, onions, and soybean flour, are rich in sulfur.

Uses. Sulfur is used chiefly in the manufacture of many products. However, few of these products actually contain sulfur. For example, most sulfur is used in making sulfuric acid and other sulfur compounds for manufacturing purposes. Manufacturers use these compounds in making such products as chemicals, metals, paper pulp, and textiles.

Products that actually contain sulfur include fertilizers and some types of explosives, fungicides, insecticides, rubber, shampoos, storage batteries, and chemicals used in developing photographic film. In fertilizers, sulfur serves as an important nutrient for plants. Sulfur is also an ingredient of many medicines, including *sulfa drugs* and some drugs used in treating skin diseases. In addition, sulfur may be used in highway construction as a substitute for asphalt.

Forms. Sulfur exists in about 10 forms, called *allotropes*. Each allotrope of sulfur differs in physical and chemical properties. The most stable sulfur allotrope is *orthorhombic sulfur*, which forms pale, shiny crystals. It occurs near volcanoes. Another crystal type of sulfur, *monoclinic sulfur*, forms at temperatures above 93° C and is unstable at room temperature. *Amorphous sulfur*, which stretches like rubber, forms if liquid sulfur is dropped into cold water.

Properties. Sulfur has no taste or odor. It is insoluble in water but dissolves in such liquid chemicals as benzene, toluene, and especially carbon disulfide.

Sulfur melts at 112.8° C and boils at 444.4° C. When heated above 150° C, liquid sulfur becomes thick and *viscous* (syrupy) like honey. Above 250° C, liquid sulfur becomes more fluid again, and its color changes from yellow to red. At its boiling point, sulfur is dark brown. Sulfur vapor condenses into fine grains of powder. These grains are called *flowers of sulfur* because they occur in

Field Museum of Natural History (WORLD BOOK photo)

Sulfur is a yellow, solid, nonmetallic element. It occurs widely in the form of pale crystals, as shown above.

How Sulfur Is Obtained

More than half of the sulfur used today is recovered from sulfur compounds in oil and natural gas through *Claus conversion*. The diagram below shows the basic steps involved in this process.

Separating raw natural gas from crude oil obtained from a well is the first step in recovering sulfur. After the gas has been separated, it is transferred to a cleaning plant. There, a complex purification process removes hydrogen sulfide from the gas.

Conversion of the hydrogen sulfide to sulfur occurs in a *Claus kiln.* Air and water are added to this combustion chamber, and the hydrogen sulfide is heated to form a mixture of sulfurous gases and water vapor. Much of the sulfur condenses to liquid form. The remaining waste gas is removed and incinerated.

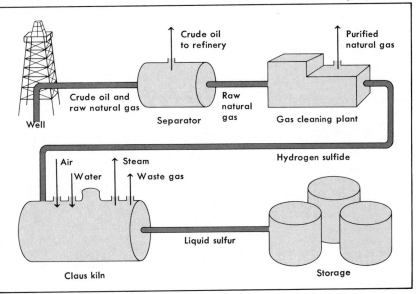

Crude oil to refinery

Purified natural gas

Crude oil and raw natural gas

Well

Separator

Raw natural gas

Gas cleaning plant

Hydrogen sulfide

Air

Water

Steam

Waste gas

Liquid sulfur

Claus kiln

Storage

---

flowerlike patterns. Some liquid sulfur is hardened in cylinder-shaped molds for commercial use. This hardened sulfur is called *roll sulfur.*

Sulfur ignites at 250° C. As it burns, it combines with oxygen to form *sulfur dioxide*, a colorless gas. Sulfur dioxide reacts with certain other substances to form *sulfuric acid* and *sulfurous acid.*

Crystals of orthorhombic sulfur have a density of 2.07 grams per cubic centimeter at 20° C. The monoclinic and amorphous forms of sulfur have a density of about 1.96 grams per cubic centimeter at 20° C.

How Sulfur Is Obtained. Before 1900, many industries obtained sulfur from volcanic deposits, sulfur mines in Sicily, and roasted pyrites. The United States has produced most of the world's sulfur since 1900, mainly in Louisiana and Texas. Other sulfur-producing nations include Canada, Japan, Poland, and Russia.

From 1900 until the mid-1950's, the chief process used to produce sulfur was the *Frasch method.* Herman Frasch, an American chemical engineer, discovered in 1891 that sulfur could be melted underground with superheated steam. In the Frasch process, water is heated under pressure to a temperature above sulfur's melting point. Pumps force the water into the ground, where it melts sulfur into a frothy liquid. Compressed air then forces the liquid sulfur to the surface. Most sulfur produced by the Frasch method is 99 per cent pure. See MINING (diagram: The Frasch Method).

The Frasch method is still widely used, but more than half the sulfur produced today comes from sulfur compounds in oil and natural gas. These compounds are converted to hydrogen sulfide at the well or in a refinery. The hydrogen sulfide is then heated with air and converted to sulfur that is 99.99 per cent pure. This process, called *Claus conversion*, was invented in 1883 by C. F. Claus, an English chemical engineer.

Electric power plants fueled by coal may become an increasingly important source of sulfur. Environmental

protection laws forbid the use of coal unless dangerous amounts of sulfur have been removed from it. This sulfur can be refined for commercial use.   B. MEYER

See also SULFA DRUGS; SULFATE; SULFIDE; SULFUR DIOXIDE; SULFURIC ACID.

SULFUR DIOXIDE is a colorless, poisonous gas with a sharp odor. Sulfur dioxide forms naturally from volcanic activity and from the decay of organic matter. It can be manufactured by burning sulfur or heating metallic sulfur compounds. Sulfur dioxide is also released into the atmosphere by oil refineries and by factories and electric power plants that burn coal or oil. In the air people breathe, the substance can irritate the eyes and respiratory system. It may also dissolve in water droplets to form *acid rain*, which can harm or even kill wildlife and damage buildings. Acid rain also may form when sulfur dioxide in the air is converted into sulfur trioxide. Government regulations in the United States limit the amount of sulfur dioxide that industries can discharge into the air.

Manufacturers combine sulfur dioxide with water to make sulfurous acid, which serves as a bleach and as a food preservative. Sulfur dioxide is also used to prepare such chemicals as sulfites and sulfuric acid. The gas becomes liquid under pressure or at a temperature of $-10°$ C ($+14°$ F). The liquid is a refrigerant. Sulfur dioxide has the chemical formula SO_2.   C. FRANK SHAW III

See also ACID RAIN; ENVIRONMENTAL POLLUTION (Causes).

SULFURIC ACID is a colorless, dense, oily liquid that is extremely corrosive. It plays an important part in the production of many manufactured items in common use. Chemists classify sulfuric acid as a strong mineral acid. Its chemical formula is H_2SO_4.

Sulfuric acid is one of the strongest acids. It can burn the skin and irritate the lining of the nose, windpipe, and lungs. Safety standards established by the United States government protect industrial work-

Some Major Industrial Uses of Sulfuric Acid

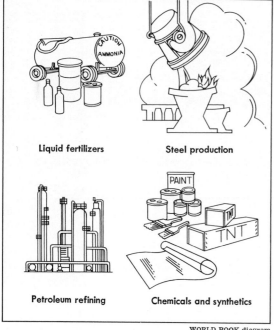

Liquid fertilizers

Steel production

Petroleum refining

Chemicals and synthetics

WORLD BOOK diagram

ers from overexposure to the acid or its fumes.

Uses and Properties. Sulfuric acid is used chiefly in the manufacture of fertilizer. Manufacturers of petroleum products use sulfuric acid in the refining of petroleum. Other manufacturers use it in the production of such items as automobile batteries, explosives, pigments, iron and other metals, paper pulp, and cellulose fibers used in making rayon.

The chemical industry uses sulfuric acid in producing many kinds of organic chemicals. For example, it is used in making alcohol from ethylene. Sulfuric acid reacts with benzene and other compounds to make *sulfonates*, which are used in powerful detergents. It is also used in making some dyes and medicines.

The strength of sulfuric acid makes it useful in producing other acids and in removing soluble materials from minerals. Many metals dissolve in sulfuric acid and form *sulfates* (salts of the acid), which have important industrial uses (see SULFATE).

Sulfuric acid combines quickly with water. The strong chemical attraction of sulfuric acid for water enables it to remove hydrogen and oxygen, the components of water, from many substances. This property makes it useful as a dehydrating agent. The dehydrating action of sulfuric acid can be shown with sugar, which contains carbon, hydrogen, and oxygen. When the acid is poured on sugar, the mixture decomposes and turns into black, foamy carbon "charcoal."

Water and concentrated sulfuric acid react violently when combined, and the mixture becomes boiling hot. Small amounts of acid should be added slowly and carefully to water to prevent splashing. Water should never be added to sulfuric acid because this action causes dangerous spattering.

Some sulfuric acid contains excess *sulfur trioxide*, a chemical that gives off gas when combined with mois-

ture in the air. Chemists call this type of sulfuric acid *oleum* or *fuming sulfuric acid*. It is used in one of the methods of manufacturing sulfuric acid.

How Sulfuric Acid Is Made. Commercial preparation of sulfuric acid was first described in the 1600's. Today, the acid is primarily manufactured from sulfur by two methods—the *contact method* and the *lead-chamber method*, an older process.

The contact method produces purer, more highly concentrated sulfuric acid than does the lead-chamber process. In the contact method, sulfur trioxide is made by passing *sulfur dioxide*, a colorless gas, through a heated tube that contains either vanadium or platinum, each of which acts as a *catalyst* (see CATALYSIS). Next, the sulfur trioxide is dissolved in concentrated sulfuric acid, forming oleum. The oleum is added to water to produce sulfuric acid of any desired concentration.

The lead-chamber method starts with the burning of sulfur to form sulfur dioxide. The sulfur dioxide then reacts with nitrogen compounds called *nitric oxides* in a lead-lined chamber, producing sulfuric acid. This process is inexpensive, but it produces relatively weak acid.

Sulfuric acid can also be produced from sulfur dioxide obtained as a by-product of *roasting* copper and iron pyrites and other sulfide ores. Roasting is a process used in separating and refining metal ores by heating the ores in air.

In the future, electric power plants that burn coal for fuel may provide a practical source of sulfuric acid. The acid could be produced from sulfur dioxide obtained by purifying gases released during coal combustion. However, the many impurities in these gases make it difficult to collect sulfur dioxide in this manner. Also, the remote location of many electric power plants complicates the shipment of the highly corrosive sulfuric acid.   B. MEYER

See also ACID; SULFUR.

SULGRAVE MANOR is an estate in Northamptonshire, England, which is regarded as the home of George

Andy Williams

Sulgrave Manor, *above, is an estate in Northamptonshire, England. Some of George Washington's ancestors lived there.*

774

Washington's ancestors. The Washington family owned it from 1539 to 1610, when Robert Washington and his son Lawrence sold it. Lawrence Washington built the manor house in the 1500's. In 1914, the British government bought the house to celebrate 100 years of peace between Britain and the United States. The house is still fairly well preserved. American patriotic societies helped furnish and restore the interior.   ALAN K. LAING

SULLA, LUCIUS CORNELIUS (138-78 B.C.), reformed the Roman government. He was the first Roman general to use his army against his political opponents. Later politicians, including Julius Caesar, followed this example.

Sulla was a member of a *patrician* (aristocratic) family. In 88 B.C., he was a *consul* (chief government official) and commander of a Roman army. When Mithridates VI, king of Pontus (in Asia Minor) attacked Roman lands in Asia, the Roman Senate put Sulla in command of an army to fight him. But the Assembly overruled the decision, and voted the command to Gaius Marius. Sulla was driven out of Rome. He returned with his army and drove out Marius, then went to fight Mithridates.

In 87 and 86 B.C., Sulla attacked Athens, an ally of Pontus, and defeated two of Mithridates' armies. When Sulla entered Asia, Mithridates asked for and got peace.

Sulla hurried back to Rome, because Marius and other "popular" leaders had returned and killed many of his supporters. Marius was dead when Sulla returned in 83 B.C., but Sulla fought and won a civil war against Marius' followers. As dictator from 82 to 79 B.C., Sulla reorganized the state. He destroyed the power of the *tribunes* (representatives of the people), and gave the Senate control of Rome. After Sulla retired in 79 B.C., most of his reforms were discarded.   HENRY C. BOREN

See also MARIUS, GAIUS.

SULLIVAN, ANNE. See KELLER, HELEN ADAMS.

SULLIVAN, SIR ARTHUR SEYMOUR. See GILBERT AND SULLIVAN.

SULLIVAN, HARRY STACK (1892-1949), was an American psychiatrist who believed that an individual's personality is formed by the person's relationships with others. Sullivan developed what he called the *interpersonal theory* of personality. He divided the formation of personality into six stages: (1) infancy, (2) childhood, (3) juvenile, (4) preadolescence, (5) adolescence, and (6) maturity.

During the first three stages of personality development, according to Sullivan, a person's family, parents, and social environment play an important role. Sullivan considered preadolescence the most important stage in personality development because it determines a person's ability to get along with others. If development at this stage is not successful, the person will lead a relatively lonely life. In adolescence, sex becomes an important factor. Maturity is achieved when an individual forms a relationship of lasting closeness with another person.

Sullivan was born in Norwich, N.Y., and graduated from the Chicago College of Medicine and Surgery. He served as head of the William Alanson White Psychiatric Foundation in Washington, D.C., from 1933 to 1943.   GEORGE H. POLLOCK

SULLIVAN, JOHN L. (1858-1918), was a famous bare-knuckle fighter and world heavyweight boxing

Culver Pictures

John L. Sullivan became one of the most famous boxers in history. He was the world heavyweight champion from 1882 to 1892.

champion. He won the heavyweight title from Paddy Ryan in 1882 in Mississippi City, Miss., on a ninth-round knockout. Sullivan fought his most famous fight with Jake Kilrain in 1889. They fought 75 rounds (2 hours, 16 minutes) before Sullivan won on a knockout. He lost the heavyweight championship to Jim Corbett in 1892. He retired in 1905, and he later appeared on the stage. Sullivan was born in Roxbury, Mass.   LYALL SMITH

SULLIVAN, LEON HOWARD (1922-   ), is a Baptist minister who organizes economic self-help programs for blacks. In 1971, Sullivan became the first black member of the 23-member board of directors of General Motors Corporation. He works to hire and train black men and women for jobs at all levels throughout the company.

Sullivan began his self-help projects in the 1950's. He regarded unemployment as the basic cause of black juvenile delinquency. In 1959, Sullivan led 400 black ministers and their congregations in starting what turned out to be a three-year boycott of about 30 Philadelphia companies. These firms had refused to hire blacks, but opened many jobs to them as a result of the boycott.

In 1962, Sullivan founded Zion Investment Associates. He persuaded members of his Zion Baptist Church —and later other blacks—to give this corporation $10 a month for three years to establish black businesses. The corporation built and manages an apartment complex, a shopping center, a garment manufacturing company, and other businesses—all in Philadelphia. In 1964, Sullivan founded the Opportunities Industrialization Center (OIC) there to provide training and job placement for minority groups. During its first 10 years, OIC trained 217,000 workers and opened centers in more than 100 United States cities. Sullivan was born in Charleston, W. Va.   EDGAR A. TOPPIN

775

SULLIVAN, LOUIS HENRI

SULLIVAN, LOUIS HENRI (1856-1924), ranks with Frank Lloyd Wright and Henry Hobson Richardson as one of America's greatest architects. Sullivan's influence comes from the quality and originality of his designs and his perceptive writings on architectural theory. He was a leader of the Chicago school of architecture.

More than any other architect of the 1800's, Sullivan united the major threads of architecture and engineering with broad theories of nature and social change. Sullivan considered the creation of a building more than a problem of design, a solution of practical needs, or the development of a structural scheme. To him, a building was the expression of a view of humanity, nature, and society. He used ornament, design, utility, and structure to express his philosophy. Sullivan popularized the phrase "form follows function." Through his buildings and writings, he argued that function meant more than satisfying practical needs or arriving at a logical structure. Sullivan declared that a building should be *organic* —that is, it should be an expression of a person's view of nature and society.

Sullivan was born in Boston. He joined the firm of Chicago architect Dankmar Adler in 1879 and became a full partner two years later. Sullivan and Adler seem to have had an ideal relationship. Sullivan was responsible for the design of buildings, and Adler concentrated on solving engineering problems and obtaining clients. Their Chicago Auditorium Building (1886-1889) is considered Sullivan's first original design. In 1890, Sullivan designed the Wainwright Building in St. Louis. It was one of the first buildings to clearly express the vertical thrust of a skyscraper.

Sullivan and Adler separated in 1895, and Sullivan's business success as an architect declined rapidly. After about 1900, he was able to obtain only a few commissions for small Midwestern banks and office buildings. Despite their size, these buildings rank among Sullivan's finest creations. During his later years, Sullivan concentrated much of his effort on writing. His most notable works include *Kindergarten Chats* (1901-1909) and *Autobiography of an Idea* (1924).   DAVID GEBHARD

See also ADLER, DANKMAR; ARCHITECTURE (Early Modern Architecture in America).

SULLIVAN, MARK (1875-1952), was an American author, newspaper columnist, magazine editor, and writer for more than 60 years. He became best known for his syndicated political column, begun in the middle 1920's. He also wrote *Our Times* (1926-1936), a six-volume chronicle of American history. Sullivan, an Irish farmer's son, was born in Avondale, Pa. He began his magazine career on the *Ladies' Home Journal* in 1904. Sullivan joined *Collier's* magazine in 1906, and became its editor in 1914.   JOHN TEBBEL

Richard Nickel

Louis Sullivan, *left,* was one of America's greatest architects. His Wainwright Building, *right,* in St. Louis was one of the first skyscrapers. Sullivan's last works included several small Midwestern banks and office buildings, among them the National Farmers' Bank, *below,* in Owatonna, Minn.

Elmslie

Chicago Architectural Photo Co.

Museum of Fine Arts, Boston

Metropolitan Museum of Art

The Torn Hat by Thomas Sully, *above,* is a study of this American artist's son. The winsome face, torn hat, and simple charm of the boy have made this a favorite among paintings of children. Sully painted the self-portrait, *left,* in the early 1800's.

SULLY, DUKE OF. See FRANCE (Age of Absolutism).

SULLY, THOMAS (1783-1872), an American painter, was noted for his elegant and refined portraits. Sully painted delicate, fragile portraits of women that glowed with life. His portraits of men were elegant but sturdier. Portraits by him appear in the ADAMS, JOHN QUINCY, and HENRY, PATRICK articles.

Sully was born in Horncastle, England, and came to America when he was 9. He began studying painting when he was about 12. Sully settled in Philadelphia in 1808. He visited London in 1809 and 1810, and met the painters Benjamin West and Sir Thomas Lawrence, who greatly influenced his style. Sully enjoyed great success after that and was sent to London in 1838 to paint a portrait of Queen Victoria.　　　FREDERICK A. SWEET

SULLY-PRUDHOMME, *syoo LEE pryoo DAWM,* **RENÉ FRANÇOIS ARMAND** (1839-1907), a French poet, won the 1901 Nobel prize for literature. His early collections of verse, including *Les Épreuves* (1866) and *Les Solitudes* (1869), deal with the sufferings of love. His later poems express the conflicts of science and religion.

He also wrote several books on philosophy and psychology. He was born in Paris.　　　HASKELL M. BLOCK

SULPHUR. See SULFUR.

SULTAN is a title of honor given to Muslim princes and rulers. The word means *sovereign,* but in ancient days it meant merely someone who was stern and mighty. The title has been used since about A.D. 900. The rulers of the Ottoman Empire were called sultans. Today, many sultans have wealth, but few have the power of the ancient princes.　　　SYDNEY N. FISHER

See also OTTOMAN EMPIRE (Government).

SULU SEA is also called the SEA OF MINDORO. It lies between the Philippine Islands and Borneo. The Sulu Sea is surrounded by the Visaya Islands on the northeast, Borneo on the southwest, and the Sulu Islands on the southeast. Straits connect the Sulu Sea with the South China Sea and the Pacific Ocean. The sea has an average depth of 14,600 feet (4,450 meters). Near the western coast of Mindanao, it is more than 16,000 feet (4,880 meters) deep. For location, see PHILIPPINES (color map).　　　F. G. WALTON SMITH

SULZBERGER is the name of two publishers of *The New York Times.* They are Arthur Hays Sulzberger and his son, Arthur Ochs Sulzberger.

Arthur Hays Sulzberger (1891-1968) served as publisher of the *Times* from 1935 to 1961. He succeeded his father-in-law, Adolph S. Ochs (see OCHS, ADOLPH S.).

Under Sulzberger's leadership, the *Times* printed more editorials and technological articles than ever before. Sulzberger also expanded the paper's coverage and analysis of the news. The daily circulation of the *Times* increased by about 40 per cent, and the Sunday circulation nearly doubled.

Sulzberger was born in New York City. He joined the *Times* in 1918 as an assistant to the general manager. He also served as a vice-president before becoming publisher. Sulzberger became chairman of the board in 1957. He retired as publisher in 1961 but continued as chairman until his death. His son-in-law, Orvil E. Dryfoos, succeeded him as publisher.

Arthur Ochs Sulzberger (1926-　　) became publisher of the *Times* in 1963 after Dryfoos' death. Sulzberger published daily columns of opinion by writers from outside the *Times,* and he doubled the weekday space devoted to letters from readers. He expanded coverage of business news and added several regular feature sections. He also combined the operations of the news and Sunday departments. In 1980, under Sulzberger's leadership, the *Times* began printing an edition in Chicago for early-morning distribution in the Midwest.

Sulzberger was born in New York City and worked as a reporter for the *Times* and the *Milwaukee Journal.* He also served as an assistant treasurer of the *Times* before becoming publisher.　　　WILLIAM L. RIVERS

SUMAC, *SHOO mack,* or *SOO mack,* or SUMACH, is a group of about 120 kinds of small trees or shrubs that grow in temperate regions. Many have commercial uses.

Common Sumacs. One of the best known of the North American sumacs is the *staghorn sumac.* It grows from southern Canada to Georgia and Mississippi. It is an attractive flat-topped tree, growing 30 to 35 feet (9 to 11 meters) high. The tree bears small, greenish flowers and tiny red berries. Its leaves are dark green above,

777

SUMAC

J. Horace McFarland

Sumac Has Narrow Leaves and Clusters of Berries.

and pale beneath. In autumn, the leaves turn scarlet, orange, and purple. The branches of immature trees have a velvety down. The berry clusters and leafstalks are hairy. The brittle wood has no practical use.

The *dwarf*, *black*, or *mountain sumac* is as pretty as the staghorn. It grows throughout the eastern United States and from the Mississippi River west to the Rockies. The dwarf sumac is usually a shrub, although in the Tennessee and North Carolina mountains it grows as tall as the staghorn. Its leaves contain much tannin and are used in tanning leather. They also provide a yellow dyestuff. The *smooth-leaved sumac*, which usually grows only about 3 feet (91 centimeters) high, is found east of the Rocky Mountains, from Arizona to British Columbia. The unripe summer berries make a refreshing drink. Some American Indians used the bark, leaves, and berries of the smooth-leaved sumac as a medicine.

Poisonous Sumacs have berries that hang in drooping clusters. The red berries of the harmless sumacs are in dense, erect clusters. The *poison sumac*, also called *poison elder*, has white berries. It grows in swampy land from New England to Minnesota and from Georgia to Texas. *Poison ivy* and *poison oak* have white berries. They are beautiful in autumn, with scarlet and orange foliage. The *varnish tree*, also called the *lacquer tree*, and the *wax tree* grow in Japan, China, and the Himalaya. The lacquer tree provides fine lacquer, and the wax tree is used in making candles.

Scientific Classification. The sumacs belong to the cashew family, *Anacardiaceae*. They make up the genus *Rhus*. The staghorn sumac is species *R. typhina*. The shining sumac is *R. copallina;* the smooth is *R. glabra;* and the poison is *R. vernix.*   J. J. Levison

See also Poison Ivy.

SUMATRA, in Indonesian, Sumatera. See Indonesia (The Islands).

SUMBA. See Indonesia (table: Chief Islands).

SUMBAWA. See Indonesia (table: Chief Islands).

SUMER, *SOO mur,* was a region settled before 3500 B.C. in the lower part of Mesopotamia (now Iraq). The people who settled it probably came from the highlands of present-day Turkey or Iran. They are often pictured with long skirts, shaven heads, and sometimes with beards. Scholars do not know the exact origin of their racial or language group.

The Sumerians developed a brilliant civilization in Mesopotamia. Their small settlements grew into cities and city-states. The more powerful city-states conquered their neighbors and created small kingdoms, including Kish, Lagash, Nippur, Umma, Ur, and Uruk (Warka).

An Ancient Sumerian Grave yielded the headdress and jewelry, *left*, of Queen Shub-ad, who lived about 5,500 years ago. The well preserved, pictorial shell plaque, *right*, came from the grave of a Sumerian king who reigned about 3500 B.C.

University Museum, Philadelphia

778

The Sumerians developed an economy based on farming. They built a great network of irrigation canals to water their fields, and grew barley, date palms, wheat, and many kinds of vegetables. They used domestic animals such as donkeys, goats, and sheep. Their society included priests, soldiers, traders, freemen, and slaves.

The Sumerians invented a system of writing, probably before 3000 B.C. Their *cuneiform*, or *wedge-form*, writing became one of the most important ancient systems of writing (see CUNEIFORM). Thousands of clay tablets and inscriptions that have been preserved tell about the Sumerian government, law, business, and religion. They also show that the Sumerians had some knowledge of mathematics, astronomy, and medicine.

The Sumerians built great temples and palaces in their cities. Skilled workers made beautiful art objects and household equipment out of copper, gold, silver, and stone. They wove fine cloth, and made armor, chariots, spears, and swords for their armies. Many industries were identified with specific towns. Ur was known for its metalworks and Umma for its textiles.

Much of the Sumerian culture was absorbed by Semitic invaders who moved into Mesopotamia and slowly took over the region. By 2000 B.C., the Sumerians had lost political power, but they furnished the base on which the impressive Babylonian and Assyrian civilizations developed.   JOHN WILLIAM SNYDER

See also ASSYRIA; BABYLONIA; UR; HARP (picture).

SUMMA CUM LAUDE. See DEGREE, COLLEGE.

SUMMER is the warmest season of the year. The Northern Hemisphere, the northern half of the earth, has summer weather during late June, July, August, and early September. Summerlike days sometimes occur in mid-autumn (see INDIAN SUMMER). In the Southern Hemisphere, summer weather lasts from late December until early March. For dates of the first day of summer and information about the position of the earth and sun during summer, see SEASON.

In summer, warm southern winds carry moisture north from the Gulf of Mexico to central and eastern North America. These winds can bring warm, humid weather to much of the region east of the Rocky Mountains and as far north as southern Canada. Thunderstorms often develop in and along the northern boundary of this warm, moist air. The highest summer temperatures usually occur in the middle of the continent.   JOHN E. KUTZBACH

See also JUNE; JULY; AUGUST; SEPTEMBER.

SUMMER OLYMPICS. See OLYMPIC GAMES.

SUMMERSIDE, Prince Edward Island (pop. 7,828), is a port and a center for breeding silver foxes. It stands on Bedeque Bay, about 5 miles (8 kilometers) south of Malpeque Bay, which is famous for fine oysters (see PRINCE EDWARD ISLAND [political map]). Summerside is in the richest farmlands of the island. It was once called Green's Shore, but was renamed because it lies on the warmer, or "summer," side of the island. Farm and fish products are shipped from Summerside. The Canadian National Silver Fox Breeders' Association and the Dominion Fox Experimental Station headquarters are there. Summerside has a council-manager form of government.   FRANK MACKINNON

SUMMONS is an order *served* (delivered) by a sheriff or some other officer of a court. The summons notifies the person named in it that a complaint has been made

and that the person must come to court to answer it. In some jurisdictions, the plaintiff's attorney or the court clerk may issue the summons. A summons also may be issued by other governmental agencies, such as congressional committees. See also SUBPOENA; WRIT.

SUMNER, CHARLES (1811-1874), was an American statesman and antislavery leader. After the Civil War, he advocated treating the South harshly. He led the Senate's opposition to President Abraham Lincoln's moderate plans for reconstruction. Later, he also opposed President Andrew Johnson's plans.

Sumner was born in Boston. He was elected United States senator from Massachusetts in 1851. In the Senate, he vigorously attacked the South. In 1856, Sumner made a Senate speech which included several sneering references to Senator Andrew P. Butler of South Carolina. Three days later, Representative Preston S. Brooks (1819-1857), Butler's nephew, attacked Sumner in the Senate, beating him senseless.

Sumner helped found the Republican Party, and during the Civil War was one of the most powerful men in the Senate. He favored freeing the slaves and giving them the right to vote. He opposed President Ulysses S. Grant's plan for annexing Santo Domingo (see GRANT, ULYSSES S. [Foreign Relations]).   W. B. HESSELTINE

SUMNER, WILLIAM GRAHAM (1840-1910), was an American sociologist known for his study of popular traditions and customs. Social groups unconsciously develop ways of doing things that are handed down from generation to generation. Such customs, which Sumner called *folkways*, include rules of etiquette and standards of personal grooming. Sumner used the Latin word *mores* for folkways that reflect ideas of morality, and that a society considers vital to its welfare. Mores include remaining loyal to one's country and preventing close relatives from intermarrying.

Sumner pointed out that folkways vary from society to society. Each society believes its own are the best and most natural. He called this attitude *ethnocentrism*.

Sumner was born in Paterson, N.J. In 1872, he became the first professor of political and social science at Yale University, where he taught until his death. He introduced the ideas of folkways, mores, and ethnocentrism in his book *Folkways* (1906).   IRVING M. ZEITLIN

See also ETHNOCENTRISM; FOLKWAY; MORES; SOCIAL DARWINISM.

SUMO. See JAPAN (Recreation; picture).

SUMP. See GASOLINE ENGINE (Lubrication System).

SUMPTUARY LAW, *SUHMP chu EHR ee.* The word *sumptuary* comes from a Latin word which means *expenditure*. In ancient Greece and Rome, laws limited the amount of money that anyone could spend on private luxuries. Laws of this kind were called *sumptuary laws*.

Similar laws have been common at various times in England, France, Scotland, Spain, and Italy. From the days of Edward III (1327-1377) until the Reformation in the early 1500's, the English Parliament restricted the number of courses of a meal to two, except on holidays. It also regulated the amount that members of each class of society could spend on clothes.   ERWIN N. GRISWOLD

See also BLUE LAWS; PROHIBITION.

SUMTER, FORT. See FORT SUMTER.

SUMTER, THOMAS. See SOUTH CAROLINA (History).

SUN

The Sun Is More Important to People Than Any Other Object in the Sky, though it is only one of billions of stars in the universe. All life on earth—human beings, animals, and plants—depends on the heat, light, and other kinds of energy given off by the sun.

SUN is a huge, glowing ball of gases at the center of the solar system. The earth and the other eight planets travel around it. The sun is only one of billions of stars in the universe. As a star, there is nothing unusual about it. But the sun is more important to people than any other star. Without the heat and light of the sun, there could be no life on the earth.

The *diameter* (distance through the center) of the sun is about 865,000 miles (1,392,000 kilometers), about 109 times the diameter of the earth. Because the sun is about 93 million miles (150 million kilometers) from the earth, it does not appear larger than the moon. But the sun's diameter is 400 times as large as that of the moon. The sun is also almost 400 times farther from the earth than is the moon.

If the sun were the size of a skyscraper, the earth would be the size of a person. The moon would be the size of a cocker spaniel standing next to the person. Jupiter, the largest planet, would be the size of a small building. The nearest star also would be about the size of a skyscraper. But it would be about 7 million miles (11 million kilometers) away.

The sun is nearer the earth than is any other star. For this reason, scientists study it to learn about stars much farther away. The visible surface of the sun consists of hot gases that give off light and heat. Only about one two-billionth of the sun's light and heat reaches the earth. The rest is lost in space.

The temperature of any place on the earth depends on the position of the sun in the sky. The temperature greatly affects the weather of a region. For example, tropical regions near the equator have a hot climate because the sun shines almost directly overhead at noon. Regions near the North and South poles have a cold climate because the sun never rises far above the horizon.

The Egyptians, Greeks, and many other ancient peoples thought the sun was a god. They worshiped the sun, made offerings to it, and built temples to honor it. Many of the early beliefs about the sun began when people tried to explain the sun's movement across the sky.

Today, we know we must have the sun as a source of heat, light, and other kinds of energy. All life on the earth—people, animals, and plants—depends on this energy from the sun. Plants use sunlight to make their own food and in the process give off oxygen. People and animals eat the plants and breathe in the oxygen. In turn, people and animals breathe out carbon dioxide, which plants combine with energy from sunlight and water from the soil to produce more food.

Scientists estimate that the sun and the rest of the objects in the solar system are about 4,600,000,000 years old. They believe that the sun will continue to be a source of our energy needs for at least another 5 billion years.

The contributor of this article is A. G. W. Cameron, Professor of Astronomy at Harvard College Observatory.

The Sun at a Glance

Distance from the Earth: *Shortest*—about 91,400,000 miles (147,100,000 kilometers); *Greatest*—about 94,500,000 miles (152,100,000 kilometers); *Mean*—about 93 million miles (150 million kilometers). Sunlight takes about 8 minutes and 20 seconds to reach the earth, traveling at 186,282 miles (299,792 kilometers) per second.

Diameter: About 865,000 miles (1,392,000 kilometers), approximately 109 times that of the earth.

Volume: About 1,300,000 times that of the earth.

Mass: 99.8 per cent of the mass of the solar system; about 333,000 times that of the earth.

Temperature: *Surface*—about 10,000° F. (about 5500° C); *Center*—about 27,000,000° F. (about 15,000,000° C).

Age: About 4,600,000,000 years.

Rotation Period: About 1 month.

Revolution Period in the Milky Way: About 225 million years.

Chemical Makeup: Hydrogen, about 75 per cent; helium, almost 25 per cent; at least 70 other elements make up the remaining 1 to 2 per cent.

Density: *Convection Zone*—about $\frac{1}{10}$ that of water; *Radiative Zone*—about equal to that of water; *Core*—about 100 times that of water.

Sun

Earth

WORLD BOOK illustration

The Sun is the largest object in the solar system. Its diameter is about 109 times the diameter of the earth, and its volume is about 1,300,000 times that of the earth.

The Size of the Sun. The sun is closer to the earth than is any other star, and so it looks larger than other stars. Compared with the planets in the solar system, the sun is large. For example, the diameter of the sun is about 865,000 miles (1,392,000 kilometers). This distance is about 109 times the diameter of the earth. It is also nearly 10 times the diameter of Jupiter, the largest planet, and about 400 times the diameter of the moon.

Compared with other stars, the sun is only medium-sized. In fact, it is one of many stars that astronomers call *yellow dwarfs*. Some stars have a diameter 10 times as small as that of the sun. Other stars have a diameter as large as 1,000 times that of the sun. Astronomers call these huge stars *supergiants*. One supergiant, Betelgeuse, has a diameter about 460 times that of the sun. If the sun grew to be the size of Betelgeuse, it would swallow up the planets Mercury, Venus, Earth, and Mars.

From the earth, the sun looks like a circle. Astronomers often use the term *disk* for the part of the sun that can be seen from the earth. Some astronomers have measured the disk and found that it is slightly flattened in some places. But other astronomers are not certain how correct these measurements are.

Distance to the Sun. The earth's distance from the sun varies from about 91,400,000 to 94,500,000 miles (147,100,000 to 152,100,100 kilometers). This distance varies because the earth travels around the sun in an orbit that has an *elliptical* (oval) shape. The average distance between the earth and the sun is about 93 million miles (150 million kilometers).

Suppose that the earth's orbit were the same as that of Venus. The earth would be so close to the sun that it would be too hot to support life as we know it. Now suppose that the earth's orbit were the same as that of Mars. The earth would be so far away from the sun that it would probably be too cold to support anything but the sturdiest and simplest forms of life.

Light travels at a speed of 186,282 miles (299,792 kilometers) per second. Light from the sun takes about 8 minutes and 20 seconds to reach the earth. When a spacecraft is escaping from the pull of the earth's gravity, it must travel at a speed of 25,000 miles (40,200 kilometers) per hour. If it could keep this speed on a journey to the sun—and not burn up—the trip would take 154 days, or a little over five months.

The Sun's Brightness. The light and heat of the sun come from its surface. The amount of light and heat stays fairly constant, so that the actual brightness of the sun changes little. The changes in brightness that seem to take place result from weather conditions in the earth's atmosphere. These conditions affect the amount of sunlight that reaches any particular place on the earth. Sometimes a small increase in brightness may result from eruptions of gases on the sun's surface. Most of these eruptions, called *flares*, last from 10 minutes to an hour. But any changes in the total brightness of the sun caused by flares are not visible to the naked eye.

Sunlight contains all the colors of the rainbow. These colors blend to form white light, and so sunlight is white (see COLOR [Color in Light]). But at times, some of the colors become scattered. We see only the remaining colors, and the sunlight appears colored. For example, when the sun appears high in the sky, some of the blue light rays are scattered in the earth's atmosphere. At such times, the sky looks blue and the sun appears to be yellow. At sunrise or sunset, the sun is near the horizon and the light must follow a longer path through the earth's atmosphere. As a result, more of the blue and green rays are scattered in the atmosphere, and the sun looks red. On rare occasions, the sun may look bright green for a moment when only an edge is visible above the horizon. This *green flash* occurs because the red rays are hidden below the horizon and the blue rays are scattered in the atmosphere.

The Sun's Heat. Of course, astronomers cannot measure the sun's temperature directly. They have determined it from indirect measurements on sunlight and from mathematical equations based on known physical laws. Astronomers estimate that the temperature at the sun's center is about 27,000,000° F. (about 15,000,000° C).

The sun's energy is produced at its center and gradually flows to the surface. Midway between the sun's interior and its surface, the temperature is about 4,500,000° F. (about 2,500,000° C). The temperature drops to about 10,000° F. (about 5500° C) at the surface.

When the energy produced at the sun's center reaches the surface, it is sent out into space as radiant energy in the form of heat and light. People once thought this heat and light came from something that was burning. Today, scientists know that the sun's light and heat come from *thermonuclear reactions* in the center of the sun. Such reactions occur when lightweight atoms join and form heavier atoms. For more information about these reactions of the sun, see the section of this article called *How the Sun Produces Energy*.

The Sun's Mass makes up 99.8 per cent of the mass of the entire solar system (see MASS). The mass of the sun is about 1,047 times that of Jupiter, the largest planet in the solar system. The sun's mass is about 333,000 times that of the earth.

Because the sun is so large, the force of gravity on it is much greater than the force of gravity on any of the planets (see GRAVITATION). As a result, objects would weigh more on the sun than they would on any planet. A boy or girl who weighs 100 pounds (45 kilograms) on the earth would weigh about 2,800 pounds (1,270 kilograms) on the sun.

Through the force of gravity, the sun controls the orbits of the planets. The force of gravity also pulls the sun's gases toward the center of the sun. If there were nothing to balance the force of gravity on the sun, the sun would collapse. But it does not collapse because its gases are extremely hot. Hot gases have high pressure and try to expand. The pressure of the gases balances the force of gravity. As a result, the sun keeps its size and shape.

What the Sun Is Made Of. About three-fourths of the mass of the sun consists of hydrogen, the lightest known element. Almost a fourth of the sun's mass consists of helium. Scientists discovered this gas on the sun before they found it on the earth. The word *helium* comes from the Greek word *helios*, meaning *sun*.

Of the 107 elements known on the earth, 92 occur naturally. The others are artificially created. At least 70 of the 92 natural elements have been found on the sun. But all these elements—except hydrogen and helium—make up only between 1 and 2 per cent of the mass of the sun. Scientists were able to identify the elements on the sun by studying the *spectrum* (pattern of colored lines) of light from the sun (see LIGHT [The Visible Spectrum]).

How the Sun Moves. Like the earth, the sun spins like a top. And, just as the earth revolves around the sun, the sun revolves around the center of the Milky Way galaxy.

The earth takes a day to rotate once on its *axis*, an imaginary line through the North and South poles. But the sun takes about a month to spin around once on the axis through its poles. The regions near the sun's equator rotate once in a few days less than a month. The regions near its poles take a few days more than a month to spin around once. This difference occurs because the sun is a ball of gases. A solid body could not rotate at different rates in different parts.

The earth takes a year to revolve around the sun, but the sun takes about 225 million years to make one revolution around the center of the Milky Way. During this period, the sun travels about 10 billion times as far as the distance between it and the earth.

Sun Terms

Chromosphere is the middle region of the sun's atmosphere.

Convection Zone is the outermost third of the sun's interior. It ends just below the sun's surface.

Core is the center of the sun, the region in which nuclear reactions produce the sun's energy.

Corona is the region of the sun's atmosphere above the chromosphere.

Disk is the part of the sun that can be seen from the earth.

Flares are bursts of light on the sun's surface. They release huge amounts of the sun's energy.

Granules are small patches of gas that make up the photosphere of the sun.

Photosphere is the visible surface of the sun, the innermost part of the sun's atmosphere.

Prominences are huge, bright arches of gas that rise from the edge of the disk and flow back into the sun.

Radiative Zone is the middle third of the sun's interior.

Solar Radiation is the sun's energy given off as light and heat and in other forms, including radio waves, ultraviolet rays, and X rays.

Solar Wind is the expansion of gases from the sun's corona.

Spicules are streams of gas that shoot up briefly from the chromosphere.

Sunspots are dark patches on the sun's surface that appear and disappear in regular cycles. A complete sunspot cycle consists of two 11-year periods of sunspot activity.

Heat and Light for Life. All life on the earth depends on the sun for heat and light. The steady flow of heat and light from the sun made possible the development of life on the earth. If the sun's heat and light were to vary, life would be endangered. Sometimes the earth would be too hot for life to exist, and sometimes it would be too cold.

The earth's atmosphere helps trap the heat of the sun. The atmosphere lets sunlight through to the surface of the earth. The light warms the earth, but the heat it creates cannot easily pass through the atmosphere into space. As a result, the earth is warmed by the sun. This behavior of the atmosphere is called the *greenhouse effect* because it resembles the action of the glass roof of a greenhouse. The roof lets sunlight in to heat the plants in the greenhouse, but the heat passes back through the roof very slowly.

Life also depends on the sun for food. All living things—both plants and animals—are part of a process called the *food chain*. The food chain starts with green plants. These plants make their own food through the process of *photosynthesis*. During photosynthesis, plants combine energy from sunlight with carbon dioxide from the air and water from the soil to make food. In the process, the plants give off oxygen. Some plants are eaten by animals, which in turn are eaten by larger animals. Man eats both animals and plants. Man and animals breathe the oxygen that the plants release during photosynthesis. They exhale the carbon dioxide that, in turn, is used by plants. See PHOTOSYNTHESIS.

Sunlight can also be harmful. Too much strong sunlight can burn the skin. The sun can seriously injure the eyes if a person looks at it directly.

Weather. Sunlight has a great influence on the earth's weather. For example, it evaporates water from rivers, lakes, and oceans, and this water later falls as rain or snow. When the water is suspended in the atmosphere, clouds appear. They reflect sunlight back into space. Sunlight also comes to the earth at various angles during different seasons. Clouds, and the angle at which sunlight reaches the earth, result in uneven heating of the earth's atmosphere. This uneven heating causes differences in air pressure. Air moves from high pressure areas to low pressure areas, causing wind and changes in weather. See WEATHER.

The Sun As an Energy Source. Until man learned to develop nuclear energy, he depended entirely on sunlight for his energy needs. Plants used sunlight for photosynthesis. Animals ate the plants, and man used both plants and animals for food, clothing, and shelter.

Man also uses the energy in *fossil fuels*—coal, oil, and natural gas. These fuels come from plants and animals that lived millions of years ago. After the plants and animals died, they were buried by soil deposits in swamplands or on the sea floor. By burning coal, and by refining oil and natural gas, man releases energy from the sun that was stored in the fossils millions of years ago.

In addition, man uses sunlight for power in other ways. For example, the effects of sunlight cause wind, which man uses to power windmills. Sunlight also evaporates water, which falls as rain. The rain forms rivers. Hydroelectric power plants on the rivers use the power of moving water to generate electricity. Solar furnaces use mirrors to focus sunlight to heat water in boilers. Solar energy cells provide power for artificial satellites and spacecraft. See SOLAR ENERGY.

THE GREENHOUSE EFFECT

The atmosphere of the earth traps heat from the sun, much as does the glass roof of a greenhouse. The roof lets sunlight in to heat the plants, but it prevents much of the heat from getting out. In a similar way, the atmosphere lets sunlight through to the surface of the earth. The sunlight warms the earth, but the heat that is created cannot easily pass back through the atmosphere into space.

WORLD BOOK diagram by Herb Herrick

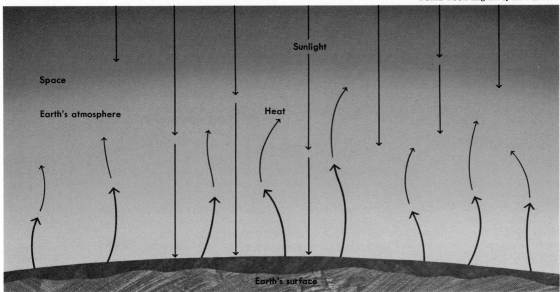

Sunlight

Space

Earth's atmosphere

Heat

Earth's surface

The Metropolitan Museum of Art, New York City;
Design Photographers Int.

Ancient Peoples Built Monuments to the Sun. Most monuments were used to worship the sun, and some also served to tell time. The Egyptians made carvings of the sun and sun worshipers, *left.* The Inca Indians used granite monuments, *above,* as sundials.

Mythology and Sun Worship. Many ancient peoples worshiped the sun as a god. They included the Egyptians in Africa, the Sumerians in Asia, the Greeks in Europe, the Aztec and Maya Indians in North America, and the Inca Indians in South America. Some of these peoples thought an eclipse of the sun was the sun god's way of expressing his anger with them. They believed that prayers and sacrifices calmed his anger.

Many early beliefs about the sun were attempts to explain the sun's movement across the sky from east to west. The Greeks believed that the sun god Helios drove a chariot through the sky. The Egyptians believed that the sun god Re sailed a boat across the sky.

Other peoples who tried to explain the sun's motion included the Eskimos, and the Maoris of New Zealand. The Eskimos thought the sun took a boat trip at night beyond the northern horizon and was responsible for the *aurora borealis,* or northern lights (see AURORA BOREALIS). The Maoris believed that one of their heroes had fought the sun and crippled it, so that it limped across the sky.

Telling Time and Directions. Since ancient times, the sun has played an important part in man's efforts to keep track of time. The length of a day depends on the time the sun takes to return to a particular place in the sky as the earth rotates.

Ancient peoples used several kinds of devices to tell time. Sundials, for example, show the direction of the sun's shadow. The direction changes as the sun moves across the sky. Ancient calendars were based on the phases of the moon. The phases occur because sunlight reflected by the moon is seen from different angles as the moon circles the earth. Many ancient peoples built complicated structures to learn about the sun's motion from north to south and back again as the seasons changed. Such monuments as Stonehenge in England probably kept track of the motions of the moon and the sun (see STONEHENGE).

Today, the sun has an important role in navigating and surveying. Navigators and surveyors carefully measure the position of the sun to find their own position—and various other points—on the earth.

Art, Literature, and Music. Many artists, authors, and composers have put the beauty and warmth of the sun in their work. The Dutch painter Vincent Van Gogh created landscapes that expressed his joy with bright sunshine. The American poet Emily Dickinson wrote a poem called "The Sun," in which she described the rising and setting of the sun. The Russian composer Nicholas Rimsky-Korsakov included a beautiful song, "Hymn to the Sun," in his opera *The Golden Cockerel.*

Circular designs with extending spokes probably represent the sun and its rays. Varieties of this design include the cross, a symbol that appeared even before the time of Jesus Christ; and the *swastika,* a form of a cross (see SWASTIKA).

One Star Among Billions. More than 100 billion stars make up the Milky Way, which is only one of billions of galaxies in the universe. The stars in the Milky Way fan out from the center in wide, curving arms. The arms would give the galaxy a *spiral* (coil) shape if it could be seen from above. The sun is located about in the middle of one of the arms.

Astronomers estimate that the Milky Way was formed between 10 billion and 15 billion years ago. The sun's age of about 4,600,000,000 years makes it one of the fairly young stars in the galaxy. Some stars are much younger than the sun. They were formed during the last few million years.

How the Sun Was Born. Throughout the Milky Way, and in space between the galaxies, are huge clouds of gases and dust. New stars are formed when portions of the gases and dust join together and begin to contract under the force of gravity. The contraction produces heat. As a mass of gases and dust shrinks, some of the heat increases the temperature at the center of the mass. Finally, the temperature at the center becomes so high that thermonuclear reactions begin to occur. These reactions produce energy and cause the mass of gases and dust to shine as a star.

Astronomers believe that the sun was formed from a rotating mass of gases and dust. They think the planets were formed from knots of gases and dust that collected at various distances from the center of the rotating mass. Scientists do not know many details of the birth of the solar system, but study and exploration of space, the moon, and the other planets are helping to increase man's knowledge. Many astronomers believe that planets may also have formed near other stars when those stars came into being.

How Long Will the Sun Shine? The sun gets energy from thermonuclear reactions near its center. These reactions change hydrogen into helium. They release so much energy that the sun could shine for about 10 billion years with little change in its size or brightness. The sun is about 4,600,000,000 years old, and it probably will shine for at least another 5,000,000,000 years.

By studying other stars, astronomers can predict what the rest of the sun's life will probably be like. About 5,000,000,000 years from now, they believe, the center of the sun will shrink and become hotter. The surface temperature will fall slightly. The higher temperature of the center will increase the rate at which hydrogen changes into helium, and the amount of energy given off by the sun will also increase. The outer regions of the sun will expand about 30 to 40 million miles (48 to 64 million kilometers)—about the distance to Mercury, the planet nearest the sun. The sun will then be a red giant star. When the sun is a red giant, the earth's temperature will become too high for life to exist there.

After the sun has used up its thermonuclear energy as a red giant, astronomers believe it will begin to shrink. After the sun shrinks to about the size of the earth, it will become a *white dwarf*.

The sun may throw off huge amounts of gases in violent eruptions called *nova explosions* as it changes from a red giant to a white dwarf. A star that becomes a white dwarf has entered a final stage of its existence.

After billions of years as a white dwarf, the sun will have used up all its energy and lost all its heat. Such stars are called *black dwarfs*. After the sun has become a black dwarf, the planets will be dark and cold. If the earth still has an atmosphere, the gases of the atmosphere will have frozen onto the earth's surface.

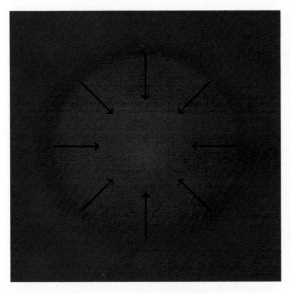

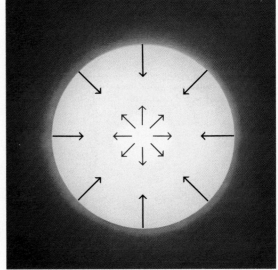

The Sun Was Born About 4,600,000,000 Years Ago. It formed when gravity, *black arrows*, pulled gases and dust in space together. As this mass contracted, the sun's center became so hot that nuclear reactions began, producing the sun's energy.

The Sun Today is a yellow dwarf star. It keeps its size because the intense heat deep within the sun produces pressure, *red arrows*, that balances the force of the sun's gravity. This balance keeps the gases in the sun from pulling any closer together.

784a

The Sun's Interior. The temperature at the *core* (center) of the sun is about 27,000,000° F. (15,000,000° C). There, the material of the sun is more than 100 times as dense as water, but it still consists of gases (see DENSITY). Thermonuclear reactions, which produce the sun's light and heat, occur in this inner third of the sun's interior.

Beyond the inner region is the *radiative zone*, which extends through about the middle third of the sun's interior. In this zone, the temperature is about 4,500,-000° F. (2,500,000° C), and the gases are about as dense as water. Heat normally flows from a hot place to a cooler place, so the drop in temperature causes the energy produced in the center of the sun to flow toward the surface.

The *convection zone* begins about two-thirds of the way from the center of the sun and ends about 137 miles (220 kilometers) below the sun's surface. The temperature in this zone is about 2,000,000° F. (1,100,000° C), and the gases are about a tenth as dense as water. In the convection zone, the gases undergo violent churning motions called *convections* and *turbulence*. These motions help carry the sun's energy to the surface.

The Sun's Surface, or *photosphere*, is about 340 miles (547 kilometers) thick, and its temperature is about 10,-000° F. (5500° C). The photosphere is actually the innermost layer of the sun's atmosphere. It is from 1 million to 10 million times less dense than water.

The photosphere consists of many small patches of gas called *granules*. A typical granule lasts only 5 to 10 minutes, and then it fades away. As old granules fade away, the sun's surface becomes marked with new ones. Scientists believe the granules are caused by waves in the photosphere. The waves are produced by the violent churning motion of the gases in the convection zone.

Astronomers also study other features of the photosphere to learn more about the sun. These features include dark spots on the photosphere called *sunspots*. Sunspots and other features are discussed in detail in the section of this article called *The Sun's Stormy Activity*. In addition, the photosphere is important because it gives off the sun's energy in the form of heat and light. Scientists learn much about the sun when they study the light given off by different parts of the photosphere.

The sunlight given off by the sun's surface is made up of many colors. These colors are not all equally bright. Various elements in the photosphere absorb some of the colors and prevent the sun from giving off

INSIDE THE SUN

Beneath the sun's *photosphere* (surface) are the violently churning convection zone, the radiative zone, and the core, where the sun's energy is produced. This energy flows from the core to the photosphere and then out into space as radiant heat and light.

WORLD BOOK diagram by Herb Herrick

Convection Zone
Temperature, about 2,000,000° F. (1,100,000° C). Density, about 1/10 that of water.

Radiative Zone
Temperature, about 4,500,000° F. (2,500,000° C). Density, about equal to that of water.

Core
Temperature, about 27,000,000° F. (15,000,000° C). Density, about 100 times that of water.

Photosphere
Temperature, about 10,000° F. (5500° C). Density, between 1/1,000,000 and 10/1,000,000 that of water.

those colors. Scientists can see what colors are absorbed by passing sunlight through a glass prism to form a spectrum. Where light has been absorbed, dark lines appear on the spectrum. These lines are called *Fraunhofer lines*, after Joseph von Fraunhofer, a German physicist who studied them during the early 1800's. Each element has its own characteristic pattern of Fraunhofer lines. Astronomers learned what elements are on the sun by comparing the Fraunhofer lines of the sun's spectrum with the lines that various elements show in laboratory experiments.

In photographs of the sun, the region near the edge of the disk does not appear so bright as the central region. This effect is called *limb darkening*. It occurs because light from the central region follows a more direct path to the earth than does light from the edge of the disk. As a result, less of the central light is absorbed by the sun's gases, and more light from deep within the photosphere can be seen. The deeper gases are hotter than those near the surface, and the hotter gases give off brighter light.

Above the Surface. About 100 miles (160 kilometers) above the photosphere, the temperature is about 8000° F. (4400° C). Beyond this point, the temperature rises again. In the *chromosphere* (the middle region of the

sun's atmosphere), the temperature may be about 50,000° F. (27,800° C).

The chromosphere consists partly of streams of gas that shoot up briefly. These gas streams, called *spicules*, are about 500 miles (800 kilometers) thick and shoot as high as 10,000 miles (16,000 kilometers). A spicule lasts up to 15 minutes.

Above the chromosphere is a region called the *corona*, which has an average temperature of about 4,000,000° F. (2,200,000° C). The molecules of the corona are so far apart that the gases of the corona have little heat. If it were possible for an astronaut to be in the corona and shielded from the direct rays of the sun, the astronaut's space suits would have to be heated.

The temperature drops slowly from the corona outward into space. The corona has no well-defined boundary. Its gases expand constantly away from the sun. This expansion of its gases is called *solar wind*.

The temperatures of the chromosphere and the corona are a puzzle to astronomers. Heat flows from hot areas to cooler areas, and yet the photosphere is cooler than the two outer regions of the sun's atmosphere. Astronomers believe that the high temperatures of the chromosphere and the corona result from the turbulence of gases in the convection zone.

Kitt Peak National Observatory

High Altitude Observatory

The Sun's Corona, the outermost region of its atmosphere, can be studied well during a solar eclipse. The sun showed little activity during an eclipse in November 1966, *left.* It displayed prominences and other solar activities during the eclipse of March 1970, *right.*

The sun *radiates* (gives off) energy into space in the form of light and heat. Every second, about 4 million short tons (3.6 million metric tons) of the sun's mass change into energy. The earth gets only about 4 pounds (1.8 kilograms) or about one two-billionth, of the total energy radiated by the sun every second. But this amount is enough to make life possible on the earth.

What makes the sun shine? How can the sun continue to shine if it gives off so much energy every second? People have asked these questions for thousands of years. But only about 1900 did man begin to learn the answers.

Solar Energy Theories. Before men knew the age of the earth and the sun, they tried to explain how the sun produces light and heat. Some believed that the sun was a giant ball of burning coal. Others thought that meteors falling into the sun released the sun's energy. During the 1800's, two physicists, Hermann von Helmholtz of Germany and Lord Kelvin of Great Britain, supported the theory that the sun's energy came from the slow shrinking of the sun. All these theories proved wrong.

Scientists believe that the sun is about 4,600,000,000 years old. Only one source of energy—nuclear energy—could have kept it shining that long. In the early 1900's, a number of scientists formulated theories about nuclear energy.

Sir Arthur Eddington, a British astronomer, showed that the center of the sun has a temperature of many millions of degrees. At this temperature, the nuclei of atoms join together in the process of *thermonuclear fusion*. Two physicists, Hans Bethe of the United States and Carl F. von Weizsäcker of Germany, described this process in the 1930's. These two scientists showed that thermonuclear fusion releases a sufficient amount of the sun's energy to keep the sun shining for billions of years.

The Thermonuclear Furnace. The changing of hydrogen into helium in the sun results in the release of the sun's energy in the form of heat and light. Helium is produced during a set of nuclear reactions. Scientists sometimes speak of these thermonuclear reactions as the "burning" of hydrogen. But such reactions are not "burning" as we think of the chemical process involving, for example, paper or wood.

The most important set of nuclear reactions in the sun is the *proton-proton chain*. These reactions involve protons and neutrons, the two major kinds of particles in the nucleus of an atom. The simplest of these proton-proton reactions has three steps. In the first step, two protons from two hydrogen nuclei fuse together. One of the protons immediately becomes a neutron by a process called *beta decay*. Now the proton and neutron make up the nucleus of a form of hydrogen called *deuterium*. In the second step, the deuterium nucleus captures another proton and becomes a light form of helium. In the third step, two light helium nuclei fuse, forming an ordinary helium nucleus. When they fuse, they give off two protons. The resulting helium nucleus has two protons and two neutrons. But it contains slightly less matter than the six hydrogen nuclei that took part in the process which formed the helium nucleus. Some of the matter that made up these hydrogen nuclei has become the energy that the sun radiates.

Another set of nuclear reactions produces less energy in the sun than do the proton-proton chains. These reactions form the *carbon-nitrogen-oxygen cycle*. In this cycle, protons are added successively to the nuclei of carbon, nitrogen, and oxygen. Carbon becomes nitrogen, and nitrogen sometimes becomes oxygen but more often becomes carbon. Some of the nuclei that have been formed undergo the process of beta decay. After four protons have been added, a helium nucleus is given off.

Hydrogen, the most plentiful element in the universe, makes up about three-fourths of the sun's mass. There is enough hydrogen to keep the sun shining for billions of years.

SUN/*The Sun's Stormy Activity*

A variety of spectacular activities takes place on the surface of the sun. When these activities become somewhat violent, they are called *solar storms*. Some solar storms occur in the form of huge arches of gas called *prominences*. The arches rise from the edge of the disk and flow back into the sun. Other solar storms occur in the form of areas of gas called *sunspots*. They appear and disappear in regular cycles. Still other solar storms take place as bright bursts of light called *flares*. Flares release huge amounts of solar energy.

Solar Magnetism. Astronomers have found that prominences, sunspots, flares, and other stormy activities on the sun occur because of changes in the patterns of *magnetic fields* on the sun. A magnetic field occupies the space around a magnet where magnetism exerts a force. Magnetic fields contain *magnetic lines of force*, or *flux lines*. In a bar magnet, the lines of force form a simple pattern (see MAGNET AND MAGNETISM [picture: Magnets of Different Shapes]).

The sun has a magnetic field that somewhat resembles the pattern of a bar magnet, especially near the sun's poles. But near the sun's equator, the magnetic pattern is always changing because the movement of gases there makes the magnetic field irregular. Atoms of those gases are *ionized*. An ion is an atom or group of atoms that has either gained or lost electrons. Many atoms of gas on the surface of the sun have lost electrons and form a type of gas called a *plasma* (see PLASMA). Particles trapped in a magnetic field usually follow the direction of the magnetic lines of force. But the motion of large quantities of plasma tends to change the direction of these lines. As a result, changes occur in the pattern of the sun's magnetic field, and stormy activity takes place.

Prominences are one of the most interesting features of the sun. Each of these bright arches of gas outlines a long, strong bundle of magnetic lines of force. Prominences shine brightly because their gases have a higher

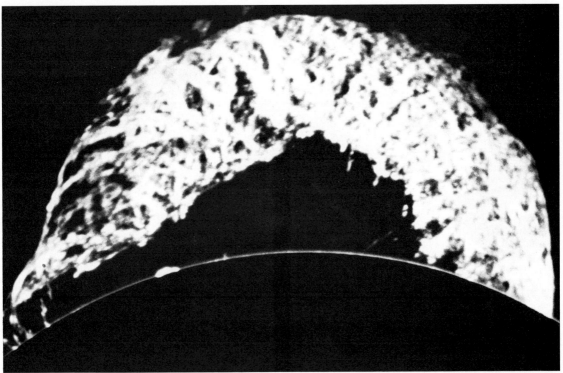

High Altitude Observatory

The Largest Erupting Solar Prominence that astronomers have observed occurred on June 4, 1946. Shown in its early stages above, it became almost as large as the sun itself in about one hour. Within a few hours, the huge prominence had disappeared completely.

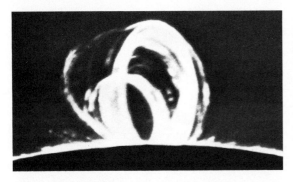

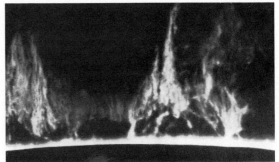

Photos by Sacramento Peak Observatory

Active Solar Prominences have short lives. The loop type of active prominence, *above*, may change rapidly in appearance during a period of only several hours.

Quiescent Solar Prominences may take the form of a hedge-row, *above*, a curtain, or a funnel. A quiescent prominence changes little in appearance during its two- or three-month life.

density and radiate light more efficiently than do the gases in the chromosphere and the corona.

A typical prominence may reach 20,000 miles (32,000 kilometers) above the sun's surface. Its total length may be 120,000 miles (190,000 kilometers), and the gases may be 3,000 miles (4,800 kilometers) thick.

There are two kinds of prominences—*quiescent* and *active*. A quiescent prominence changes little in appearance during its two- or three-month existence. An active prominence changes rapidly during a period of only several hours. Some active prominences erupt and fling their gases rapidly into space.

Sunspots. Sometimes a strong loop of magnetic lines of force extends through the sun's surface. Where the lines cross through the surface, they lower the temperature of the gas. This gas does not shine so brightly as the surrounding gas, and it appears as a dark patch on the sun. These dark patches are called *sunspots*. Because a magnetic loop both leaves and re-enters the surface, two sunspots are associated with the loop. After a

784e

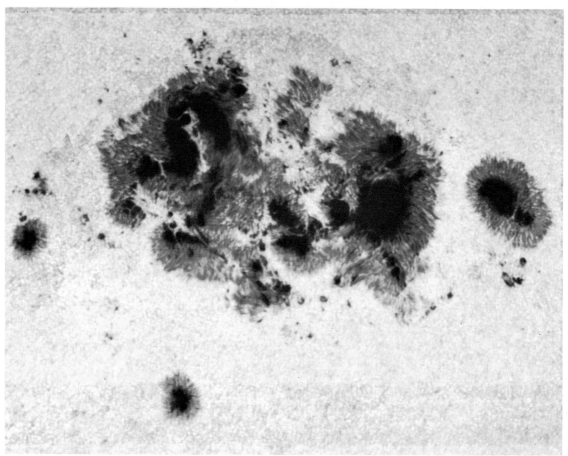

Hale Observatories

Sunspots Appear as Dark Patches on the sun's surface. They are caused by magnetic activity and appear and disappear in regular cycles. A sunspot may measure about 20,000 miles (32,000 kilometers) across. It may then break up into smaller sunspots and form a sunspot group, *above*.

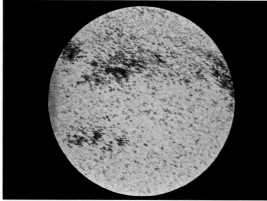

W. C. Livingston, Kitt Peak National Observatory

A Magnetic Picture of the Sun shows active magnetic regions in the northern hemisphere as the sun approaches maximum sunspot activity. Areas of the magnetic picture shown in red indicate south magnetic fields. Areas shown in blue indicate north magnetic fields. The dark colors indicate strong fields.

A SUNSPOT CYCLE

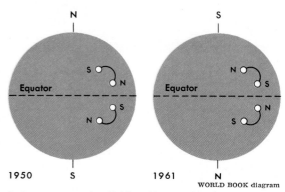

WORLD BOOK diagram

During a sunspot cycle, which lasts 11 years, the number of sunspots first increases and then decreases to a minimum. When the next cycle begins, the magnetic fields of the sun and of the sunspots become reversed. So the sun takes two sunspot cycles—or 22 years—to go through a complete set of magnetic changes.

784f

few days, a magnetic loop may break up into several thinner loops. Each of these loops crosses the surface at a different place. The original sunspot breaks up into several sunspots that form a *sunspot group*. Still later, the magnetic loops spread out and cover a wider area, and their sunspots fade away.

A typical sunspot may have a diameter of about 20,000 miles (32,000 kilometers). Most sunspots have two parts. The inner part, called the *umbra*, may have a diameter of about 8,000 miles (13,000 kilometers)—approximately the size of the earth's diameter. The outer part, called the *penumbra*, may have a diameter of about 12,000 miles (19,300 kilometers). The penumbra is lighter in color than the umbra. Some sunspots have no penumbra because of their small size.

The temperature of the gas in the upper photosphere and in the chromosphere above a sunspot group often rises about 1500° F. (815° C) above its normal temperature. As a result, it radiates more light than do surrounding gases. This light appears in patches called *faculae*, *flocculi*, or *plages*. They are more easily seen near the edge of the disk than near the center of the sun.

The number of visible sunspots varies from about 5 to approximately 100. It takes about 11 years for the number to increase from the minimum to the maximum. This 11-year period is called the *sunspot cycle*.

A sunspot cycle begins when sunspots appear at high solar latitudes. As the cycle continues, more sunspots appear closer to the sun's equator. During a cycle, the north and south magnetic poles of each pair of sunspots are reversed from those of the previous cycle. The north and south magnetic poles of the sun's general magnetic field also become reversed. Thus, the sun takes two sunspot cycles, or 22 years, to go through a complete set of magnetic changes.

Astronomers do not know why sunspot cycles take place. But they know that the cycles are closely connected with other kinds of solar activity. All types of these activities become most intense during the maximum phase of a sunspot cycle. See SUNSPOT.

Flares. After a sunspot group has existed for a long time, the magnetic lines of force usually become jumbled. As a result of the jumbling, magnetic energy is stored in the corona. The energy may be released in a spectacular discharge called a *flare*. In a flare, the magnetic lines of force become reconnected into a simpler pattern. The energy is released in the form of light, heat, and fast-moving atomic nuclei and electrons called *solar cosmic rays*.

A flare may be as small as a sunspot or as large as a sunspot group. The temperature in a flare is about twice as high as the temperature at the sun's surface. Flares radiate much light into space, and astronomers can photograph them against the background light of the sun. Small flares may last about 10 minutes. The largest ones last about an hour.

Large flares produce so many solar cosmic rays that important consequences occur on the earth. For example, the rays disrupt radio communications. They endanger astronauts in space, where the earth's magnetic field is not present to protect the men from such large amounts of radiation. After astronomers learn to predict

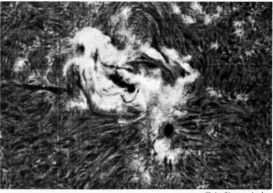

Hale Observatories

Flares Are Spectacular Discharges that release huge amounts of the sun's energy. A flare may be as large as a sunspot group, with a temperature twice that of the sun's surface.

the occurrence of large flares, they will be able to make space travel safer.

Solar Radiation. The sun gives off many kinds of radiation besides visible light and heat. These radiations include *radio waves, ultraviolet rays*, and *X rays*.

Some radio waves of the sun are shorter than the radio waves used in broadcasting. Because they are shorter, they can penetrate the earth's atmosphere. As a result, astronomers can study them to learn about solar storms. Strong bursts of radio waves occur during violent solar activity. Astronomers think these bursts originate in sunspot regions, particularly when flares occur. The bursts last from a few minutes to a few days.

Ultraviolet rays consist of waves of light that are shorter than the waves of violet light on the visible spectrum. They are invisible to the human eye. Ultraviolet rays cause sunburn, and too much exposure to them may cause skin cancer. The atmosphere absorbs much of this radiation. The sun gives off more ultraviolet rays and X rays during periods of violent activity than during calm periods. Flares greatly increase the amount of radiation from the sun.

X rays are another form of solar radiation. The sun's X rays can injure or destroy the tissues of living creatures. The earth's atmosphere shields man from most of this radiation. See X RAYS.

The Solar Wind. The corona is so hot that its gases continually expand away from the sun. This flow of gases continues into space until the gases mix with those near the outer planets of the solar system. The flow of gases is called the *solar wind*. When the solar wind reaches the earth's orbit, it is traveling at 1 million to 2 million miles (1.6 million to 3.2 million kilometers) per hour. The solar wind confines the earth's magnetic field into a specific volume of space called the *magnetosphere*. The boundary of the magnetosphere is about 40,000 miles (64,000 kilometers) from the earth.

Flares increase the speed of the solar wind. The solar wind then presses harder on the magnetosphere and causes magnetic storms on the earth. These storms interfere with radio communications and can make compass needles swing wildly. See SOLAR WIND.

Early Sun Science. Early people believed that the earth was flat and that the sun was a god. During the 400's B.C., the Greek philosopher Anaxagoras realized that the sun must be a large body, far from the earth. He estimated the sun's diameter at 35 miles (56 kilometers). Anaxagoras' ideas disagreed with the religious beliefs of his time. His life was threatened, and he finally was exiled from Athens.

About A.D. 150, the astronomer Ptolemy of Alexandria declared that the earth was a stationary body in the center of the universe. He believed that the sun, moon, planets, and stars all circled the earth.

The true relationship between the earth and the sun became known in the early 1500's. In 1543, the Polish astronomer Nicolaus Copernicus stated that the sun was at the center of the solar system. He said that the earth and the other planets revolved around the sun.

Gradually, astronomers realized that the sun was a star and began to study it more scientifically. In 1904, the American astronomer George Ellery Hale established the Mount Wilson Observatory near Pasadena, Calif. This observatory included instruments for the study of the sun. Hale believed that by studying the sun, scientists could learn much about the other stars. He also made popular the word *astrophysics*, meaning the study of astronomical bodies by using the methods of physics.

Modern Solar Study. The earth receives far more light from the sun than it does from the other stars. To help astronomers study the light more effectively, *solar telescopes* spread it out as much as possible. For example, the solar telescope at the Kitt Peak National Observatory near Tucson, Ariz., produces an image of the sun that is about 32 inches (81 centimeters) in diameter. Even so, turbulence in the earth's atmosphere limits the detail that can be seen on the sun's surface. The smallest

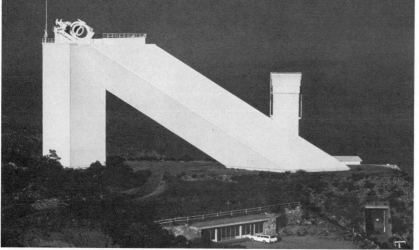

The McMath Solar Telescope rises above the Kitt Peak National Observatory near Tucson, Ariz. About a third of the telescope's 480-foot (146-meter) diagonal shaft is aboveground. The tower behind the observatory houses an instrument called a *solar-vacuum telescope*.

Photos by Kitt Peak National Observatory

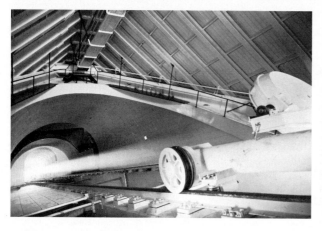

Sunlight streams 480 feet (146 meters) down the shaft of the McMath telescope, *above*, to a mirror 5 feet (1.5 meters) in diameter. The mirror reflects an image of the sun over 2½ feet (0.8 meter) in diameter to the underground viewing room, *right*.

features that can be distinguished are about 500 miles (800 kilometers) across. Other solar telescopes include those at the Sacramento Peak Observatory near Alamogordo, N. Mex.; the High Altitude Observatory in Climax, Colo.; and the University of Hawaii's Institute for Astronomy at Haleakala, on Maui Island.

Astronomers use *solar spectroscopes* to analyze the sun's spectrum. These instruments spread out the colors of the spectrum to help in the study of sunlight.

One special instrument, the *coronagraph*, is used only for solar work. With it, astronomers can photograph the sun's corona without waiting for a total eclipse. The coronagraph is a tube with a disk in the middle to block out the light from the photosphere and chromosphere. With the coronagraph, astronomers can create an "eclipse" whenever they want to study the corona.

Space Age Discoveries. Only the visible light and the radio waves given off by the sun can be studied from the earth. Most solar radiation is best studied from

space. During the 1960's, scientists first used rockets and then satellites in the Orbiting Solar Observatory program to learn about the sun's ultraviolet radiation. The best pictures of the sun's surface were taken from a high-flying balloon that was part of an experiment called *Project Stratoscope. Skylab*, a manned space laboratory launched in 1973, carried a solar telescope.

During the 1960's, astronomers used *space probes* (satellites sent into outer space) to study solar cosmic rays and the solar wind. The Pioneer spacecraft that were sent past the sun, and the Mariner flights to Mars and Venus, provided much information about these features of the sun. The astronauts of the Apollo 11 and Apollo 12 lunar flights conducted experiments to help scientists learn more about the solar wind.

In 1980, the United States launched a spacecraft called *Solar Maximum Mission Satellite*. It showed that sunspots reduce the amount of solar energy that reaches the top of the earth's atmosphere.   A.G.W. CAMERON

SUN/*Study Aids*

Outline

I. Important Facts About the Sun
   A. The Size of the Sun
   B. Distance to the Sun
   C. The Sun's Brightness
   D. The Sun's Heat
   E. The Sun's Mass
   F. What the Sun Is Made Of
   G. How the Sun Moves

II. How the Sun Affects the Earth
   A. Heat and Light for Life
   B. Weather
   C. The Sun As an Energy Source

III. Man and the Sun
   A. Mythology and Sun Worship
   B. Telling Time and Directions
   C. Art, Literature, and Music

IV. The Sun As a Star
   A. One Star Among Billions
   B. How the Sun Was Born
   C. How Long Will the Sun Shine?

V. Regions of the Sun
   A. The Sun's Interior
   B. The Sun's Surface
   C. Above the Surface

VI. How the Sun Produces Energy
   A. Solar Energy Theories
   B. The Thermonuclear Furnace

VII. The Sun's Stormy Activity
   A. Solar Magnetism

   B. Prominences
   C. Sunspots
   D. Flares
   E. Solar Radiation
   F. The Solar Wind

VIII. Studying the Sun
   A. Early Sun Science
   B. Modern Solar Study
   C. Space Age Discoveries

Questions

Why does life on the earth depend on the sun?

What is a *red giant?* A *yellow dwarf?*

Why is sunlight white? Why does it sometimes appear to be colored?

What is the diameter of the sun? How does the sun compare in size with other stars? How does it compare with the earth?

How does the coronagraph help astronomers study the sun?

In what ways do people use the sun as a source of energy?

What are *prominences, sunspots,* and *flares?* Why do they occur?

How old is the sun?

About how far is the earth from the sun?

What two elements make up the largest percentage of the sun's mass?

Reading and Study Guide

See *Sun* in the RESEARCH GUIDE/INDEX, Volume 22, for a *Reading and Study Guide.*

Additional Resources

Level I

FIELDS, ALICE. *The Sun.* Watts, 1980.

FREEMAN, MAE and IRA. *The Sun, the Moon, and the Stars.* Rev. ed. Random House, 1979.

JABER, WILLIAM. *Exploring the Sun.* Simon & Schuster, 1980.

Level II

ASIMOV, ISAAC. *The Sun Shines Bright.* Doubleday, 1981.

EDDY, JOHN A. *A New Sun: The Solar Results from Skylab.* NASA, 1979.

MITTON, SIMON. *Daytime Star: The Story of Our Sun.* Scribner, 1981.

SUN BATH

SUN BATH is the exposure of the body to sunlight or to sun lamps. Sunlight is made up of many different kinds of light rays. *Infrared rays* (heat rays) penetrate deeply into the body. They benefit the circulatory system and the muscles. *Ultraviolet rays* are chiefly absorbed by the skin, and may cause sunburn and tanning. They also cause chemicals in the skin to produce vitamin D, the sunshine vitamin. Sun lamps produce ultraviolet rays. See also INFRARED RAYS; SUN (Heat and Light for Life; Solar Radiation); SUN LAMP; SUNBURN; ULTRAVIOLET RAYS.

SUN BEAR. See BEAR.

SUN DANCE was the most important religious ceremony of many Plains Indian tribes. The Sioux called it the *sun gazing dance*, and performed it annually. They believed it would keep away enemies and famine.

All the scattered hunting bands of the tribe gathered in summer and pitched their tepees in a great camp circle. In the center of this circle they built a large, open enclosure of upright posts and rafters connected to a tall, forked center pole. Within the enclosure, Indian men taking part painted their bodies, fasted, and danced, always facing the sun. The ceremonies lasted several days. The dance itself was simple. The dancers merely rose on their toes to the tune of music played on eagle bone whistles. At the end of the dancing, some of the young men underwent severe tortures in fulfillment of vows. The United States government prohibited the sun dance for several years because of these cruelties. A few tribes, such as the Blackfeet, still perform the sun dance, but without the tortures.   JOHN C. EWERS

See also BUFFALO CEREMONIALS; CROW INDIANS; INDIAN, AMERICAN (picture: Sun Dance).

SUN GOD. See SUN WORSHIP.

SUN LAMP is a common name for a device that gives off artificial ultraviolet radiation. Ultraviolet rays are found in natural sunlight, and they produce a tan on human skin. These rays cannot be seen by the human eye. They have a shorter wave length than the visible violet light. There are two general types of ultraviolet generators, sun lamps and therapeutic lamps. A person can use a sun lamp in the home without the supervision of a physician. Therapeutic lamps require professional supervision, to avoid hazards of overexposure.

The professional therapeutic lamp gives off powerful ultraviolet radiation and can produce a sunburn in a period as short as one-half to one minute. The sun lamp is not as powerful. It requires 10 or 15 minutes to produce a light sunburn.

There are several sources of artificial ultraviolet radiation. The carbon arc is a readily available source. Its ultraviolet radiation is made more intense by impregnating the cores of the carbons with certain salts of metals. The mercury arc inside a quartz tube is a common source. Another source looks like an ordinary large incandescent lamp. Inside the special glass bulb is a small mercury arc in a tiny quartz tube. Also inside the bulb is a tungsten filament. The lamp screws into any ordinary socket of 115-volt alternating current power supply. The light from this source resembles the light from an ordinary incandescent lamp, but it is enriched with ultraviolet radiation.

Direct exposure of the skin to ultraviolet rays from the sun or from artificial sources results in the formation of vitamin D. There is no evidence that ultraviolet radiation increases or improves the tone of the tissues of the body as a whole, stimulates metabolism, acts as a tonic, increases mental activity, or tends to prevent colds as many persons believe.   HOWARD A. CARTER

See also ULTRAVIOLET RAYS.

SUN VALLEY, Idaho (pop. 545), a famous resort, lies in the Sawtooth Mountains of south-central Idaho. For location, see IDAHO (political map). In 1936, Averell Harriman, chairman of the board of directors of the Union Pacific Railroad, picked the site for development as a winter-sports center because of its brilliant sunshine and frequent winter snowfalls. The hotels at Sun Valley are the Sun Valley Lodge and Challenger Inn. Eight electric chair lifts serve over 40 ski runs. Other sports include skating, sleighing, and bowling.   WILLIAM S. GREEVER and JANET GROFF GREEVER

See also IDAHO (A Visitor's Guide).

Sun Valley News Bureau

The Ski Slopes of Sun Valley, in Idaho's Sawtooth Mountains, rank as one of the world's most popular winter sports centers.

SUN WORSHIP developed in some lands as people came to associate the sun with the growing season and with warmth. It developed among agricultural peoples, who needed sunshine for their crops, but not among hunters or seed-gatherers, who did not depend on sunlight for their food supply. Sun worship was important in the cultures of ancient Egypt, Babylonia, Persia, and northern India. The peoples of Scandinavia also worshiped the sun. Teutonic peoples named the first day of the week for the sun.

Sun worship was important to American Indians in the agricultural lands that are now the southeastern and southwestern United States. It also grew up among the Aztec, Inca, and Maya peoples who lived in Central and South America.

Kings and princes in some lands believed themselves to be brothers or children of the sun, and they came to be worshiped as gods. For hundreds of years, the Japanese worshiped their emperor as a descendant of the sun goddess, Amaterasu-O-Mi-Kami.

See also APOLLO; HELIOS; RE; SUN (Man and the Sun; picture).

SUN YAT-SEN, *soon yaht-sen* (1866-1925), a Chinese statesman and revolutionary leader, fought to establish a republic of China. He is generally called the

Father of the Revolution. Sun was too idealistic to be an effective political leader. But his *Three People's Principles* (nationalism, democracy, and socialism) became the guiding principles of the Chinese republic, which was established in 1912.

Sun was born of humble parents in the Chung-shan district of Kwangtung Province. He was educated at mission schools in Hong Kong and Honolulu, and became a doctor. From 1895 to 1911, he traveled widely in the United States, Japan, and Europe to organize sympathy for republican principles and

Brown Bros.

Sun Yat-sen

to seek financial aid for his revolutionary movement against the Manchu dynasty. He was aided by Chinese overseas communities and English, American, and Japanese sympathizers.

The Kuomintang Party, headed by Sun, became a political entity in 1911 after the Wu-han uprising to overthrow the Manchu regime. From 1911 to 1922, Sun tried to unite China and establish a stable government. His party adopted a constitution, and Sun became the temporary president of the Chinese republic in 1912. The political situation at the time was turbulent. To further insure the unity of China, Sun resigned as president in favor of Yüan Shih-k'ai after only six and one-half weeks in office.

His Later Efforts. In 1913, Sun disagreed with Yüan's policies and organized a revolt. He fled to Japan, and the Kuomintang members of parliament were thrown out of office. Once again, the revolutionists assembled to set up a separate government under the 1912 constitution. In 1921, Sun became president of this government in Canton. He was driven out of his capital in 1922, but returned in 1923.

Sun continued to work for the unification of China. After failing to get assistance from Western powers, he turned to Russia. With funds and help from Russia, he reorganized the Kuomintang party and army in 1923. He set up the Whampoa Military Academy, with Chiang Kai-shek as superintendent. Sun died of cancer while attending a conference in Peking in 1925.

In 1929, Sun's body was transferred to a mausoleum erected in his honor in Nan-ching. Politically, he was more effective after his death. His principles became the slogans of his followers. Chiang Kai-shek, during the 1930's and 1940's, achieved the unification under a central government that Sun had sought in vain to accomplish.   IMMANUEL C. Y. HSU

See also CHIANG KAI-SHEK; CHINA (History); SOONG CHING-LING.

SUNBIRD is the common name of a group of tiny tropical birds of Africa, Asia, and Australia. These birds resemble the hummingbirds of the Western Hemisphere in size and in the gay color of the male's feathers. They are larger than most hummingbirds. Their bills are curved instead of straight, like those of the hummingbird. Sunbirds feed on insects, spiders, and flower nectar.

Scientific Classification. Sunbirds belong to the order *Passeriformes.* They are members of the sunbird family, *Nectariniidae.*   ARTHUR A. ALLEN

SUNBURN is a painful inflammation of the skin caused by overexposure to the invisible ultraviolet rays of the sun. It ranges from mild redness that disappears in a few hours to blistering, swollen, scarlet skin that peels before it heals. A severe sunburn can cause chills, dizziness, fever, and weakness.

The seriousness of a sunburn depends on the intensity of the light and the length of time spent in the sun. The sun's burning rays shine most intensely during the summer and between 10 A.M. and 2 P.M. They travel through clouds and water, and so a person can be burned on a cloudy day or while swimming. Sand and snow reflect the rays and increase the chances of being burned on a beach or ski slope.

The skin contains a brown pigment called *melanin,* which partially protects it from sunburn. Blue-eyed blonds, redheads with freckles, and other fair-skinned people have little melanin and burn easily. However, dark-skinned blacks rarely burn because their skin has much more melanin.

Most people can tan without burning if they stay in the sun for only 15 minutes the first day and then increase the time by 10 to 15 minutes daily. Sunburn can also be avoided by covering the skin or by using a lotion containing chemicals that act as a *sun block* or a *sunscreen.* A sun block filters out all the sun's burning rays, and a sunscreen filters most of them.

The best treatment for sunburn is aspirin, which relieves the pain and reduces the inflammation. Cool baths, wet compresses, and medicated creams also provide relief.   YELVA LIPTZIN LYNFIELD

See also SKIN (Burns); SUN LAMP.

SUNDAY is the first day of the week among Christian peoples. It is the day set aside for rest and for worship of God. Sunday was the day sacred to the sun among the old Teutonic peoples, and its name means the "day of the sun." The French call Sunday *dimanche,* the Spanish call it *domingo,* and the Italians call it *domenica.* These three names all come from the Latin words *dies dominica,* which means Lord's Day.

The early Christians lived hard lives, and had to work on Sunday as well as the other days in the week. But they made Sunday a day for special worship, because they believed that the resurrection of Jesus occurred on that day. By the A.D. 300's, both the church and the state officially recognized it as a day of rest in Europe.

In the United States, some states have laws that forbid labor on Sunday. All government agencies and banks are closed on Sundays. A few states and communities have laws that prohibit such amusements as ball games and motion pictures on Sunday. Such laws are called *Blue Laws.*   GRACE HUMPHREY

See also BLUE LAWS.

SUNDAY, BILLY (1862-1935), was a baseball player who became a famous evangelist. He used his baseball background, slangy language, flamboyant manners, and highly developed promotional methods to become the most popular evangelist of the time. He was supposed to have preached to over 100 million persons, and to have converted over a million in his campaigns.

SUNDAY ISLAND

William Ashley Sunday was born in Ames, Iowa. His early years were spent with his grandparents and at an orphans home. Sunday played baseball for major league teams in Chicago, Pittsburgh, and Philadelphia from 1883 to 1890. During these years he was converted and began working with the YMCA. Billy Sunday became a Presbyterian minister in 1903.   L. J. TRINTERUD

Brown Bros.

Billy Sunday

SUNDAY ISLAND. See KERMADEC ISLANDS.

SUNDAY SCHOOL, an observance usually connected with Protestant churches, teaches Bible study and religion. Such schools may have existed as early as the 1500's. But the present-day Sunday-school movement was started in Gloucester, England, by the publisher Robert Raikes. In 1780, he launched his "Ragged School." He tried to aid the children of the poor in his community by teaching them reading, writing, and the principles of religion. The schools received publicity through Raikes' newspaper. With the great "foreign" missionary work of the 1800's and 1900's, the schools spread to all parts of the world. When Raikes died in 1811, 400,000 children were enrolled in Sunday schools. Today, about 42,740,000 children and adults attend more than 437,000 Protestant Sunday schools. The Roman Catholic Church has a similar type of school. Religious study is also offered in Sunday or Sabbath schools operated by Jewish and other religious groups.

In the United States, the Sunday-school movement became widespread after the Revolutionary War. Joanna Graham Bethune, an American social worker, led the movement in the early 1800's. The American Sunday School Union was formed in 1824. Its missionary workers founded Sunday schools throughout the country. The International Sunday School Association served the United States and Canada and in 1922, it became the International Council of Religious Education. It joined the National Council of the Churches of Christ in the United States of America in 1950.

The present-day Sunday school is divided into departments for students of various ages. In a large school, a superintendent directs each department and a teacher is in charge of each class. A uniform course of lessons is widely used in the United States and Canada. It is outlined by the International Council of Religious Education, which also prepares outlines for graded lessons used by many schools. Other features of current Sunday school work are circulation libraries, classes for teachers, conventions, and institutes that help train teachers.

See also RAIKES, ROBERT; RELIGIOUS EDUCATION.

SUNDEW is an unusual plant that traps and digests insects. It gets its name because drops of sticky fluid produced by glands appear on its leaves. In the sunlight, these drops glitter like drops of dew. Sundews live in bogs and marshes throughout the world. The *round-leaved sundew,* the most common kind, thrives in moist, acid soil in all but the southwestern United States. It also grows in some parts of Canada, Europe, and Asia.

The slender stem of the sundew is topped by small white flowers. A cluster of flat, rounded leaves grows at the base of the stem, close to the ground. These leaves are the size of a small coin. They are covered with small red gland-bearing hairs. An insect may easily become stuck to the drops of sticky fluid on the leaves. Then the hairs fold in around the insect and hold it. Fluid covers the insect and suffocates it. The glands produce juices that digest the victim.

Scientific Classification. The sundews are in the sundew family, *Droseraceae.* They form the genus *Drosera.* The round-leaved sundew is genus *Drosera,* species *D. rotundifolia.*   ROBERT W. HOSHAW

See also CARNIVOROUS PLANT; PLANT (picture: Plants That Eat Insects).

SUNDIAL is the oldest known device for the measurement of time. It is based on the fact that the shadow of an object will move from one side of the object to the other as the sun moves from east to west during the day. The sundial is believed to have been used in Babylon at least as early as 2000 B.C.

The earliest description of a sundial comes from Berossus, a Babylonian priest and author of the 200's B.C. His sundial was a hollow half-sphere, or dome, set with its edge flat and with a small bead fixed at the center. During the day the shadow of the bead moved in a circular arc, divided into 12 equal parts. These were called *temporary hours* because they changed with the seasons. *Equal hours* were decided upon about A.D. 1400, when clocks were invented.

A sundial consists of the *plane* (dial face) and the *gnomon* (style). The dial face is divided into hours and sometimes half and quarter hours. The gnomon is a flat piece of metal set in the center of the dial. It points toward the North Pole in the Northern Hemisphere and toward the South Pole in the Southern Hemisphere. The upper edge of the gnomon must slant upward from the dial face at an angle equal to the latitude of the location of the sundial.   ARTHUR B. SINKLER

See also SUN (Man and Sun [picture]).

Robert W. Young, Black Star

A Sundial Tells Time by measuring the angle of a shadow cast by the sun. Many sundials have faces numbered in Roman numerals from 5 A.M. to 8 P.M. When the sun hits the *gnomon,* a flat piece of metal in the center of the dial, it casts a shadow which tells the time. The time on the sundial, *above,* is 2:45 P.M.

SUNDIATA KEITA (? -1255) ruled the Mali Empire from about 1240 to 1255. He helped make it one of the largest and wealthiest empires in West Africa.

Sundiata became a hero of the empire—and is still a hero of the Malinke people of West Africa—because he freed the small state of Kangaba from Ghana. Sundiata reorganized the Kangaba army and, in the Battle of Kirina in 1235, defeated the forces of Sumanguru. Sumanguru was the last of the rulers of what once was the Ghana Empire. As a result of Sundiata's victory, Kangaba became the core of the Mali Empire.

Sundiata built the city of Niani after 1235 and made it his capital. Niani and later capitals lay between salt mines and gold mines on the trans-Saharan trade routes. The Mali Empire became an important trade center after Sundiata gained control of the gold-producing areas. LEO SPITZER

See also MALI EMPIRE.

SUNFISH is a name for several kinds of fish. In the fresh waters of North America, the sunfishes are a group of small, bright-colored food fish, rarely over 10 inches (25 centimeters) long. Their color changes according to conditions of health, food, and temperature. The males become brightly colored in the breeding seasons. They clear out a nest on the bottom of a lake or stream and guard the eggs against intruders. The most widely favored game fish among the sunfishes proper (except for the black basses, which belong to the same family) is the *bluegill*. The pumpkin seed, a kind of sunfish, is found abundantly in brooks and ponds from Maine to Florida, and in the northern part of the Mississippi Valley. It has a roundish body and considerable orange in its color. There is a bright red spot on the ear flap. This fish grows up to 8 inches (20 centimeters) long and weighs as much as 8 ounces (230 grams). People enjoy fishing for it, because it bites with so much vigor. These sunfish are usually caught with worms as a bait. Other species also are common. Some of the smaller, more brilliant sunfish are kept in home aquariums.

The name sunfish also is given to a group of grotesque-appearing ocean fish. Their bodies are scaleless, silvery, and clumsy, and seem to consist of one great head with small fins. They often rest on the surface in sunny weather, with one fin above the water. Ocean sunfish may weigh 1,000 pounds (450 kilograms). They are never eaten. They are not closely related to fresh-water sunfish.

Scientific Classification. Ocean sunfish belong to the mola family, *Molidae*. The common kind is genus *Mola*, species *M. mola*. Fresh-water sunfish belong to the family *Centrarchidae*. The bluegill is genus *Lepomis*, species *L. macrochirus*. The pumpkin seed is *L. gibbosus*. CARL L. HUBBS

See also CRAPPIE; FISH (pictures: Fish of Temperate Fresh Waters [Bluegill; Pumpkin Seed]).

SUNFLOWER is a tall plant known for its showy yellow flowers. There are more than 60 species of sunflowers. The most common type grows from 3 to 10 feet (1 to 3 meters) tall and has one or more heads of flowers. Each head consists of a disk of small, tubular flowers surrounded by a fringe of large yellow petals. A sunflower head may measure more than 1 foot (30 centimeters) in diameter and produce up to 1,000 seeds. The head turns and faces toward the sun throughout the day.

Sunflower seeds are rich in protein. They yield a high-quality vegetable oil used in making margarine and cooking oil. Some varieties of sunflowers have large striped seeds, which are roasted for snack food or blended with other grains to make birdseed. Special *oilseed* varieties produce small black seeds that contain 50 per cent oil. These varieties, first developed by Russian scientists, have made sunflowers the world's second most important oilseed crop. Only soybeans yield more vegetable oil.

Russia produces more sunflower seeds than any other nation. In the United States, production has increased

Gene Wolfsheimer

The Black-Banded Sunfish ranges from New Jersey to Maryland. It grows about 4 inches (10 centimeters) long and has a pearly luster in reflected light. Sunfishes eat insects and shellfish.

John M. Coffman, NAS

The Large, Beautiful Sunflower is raised by farmers in many parts of the world. A sunflower head, *above,* may measure more than 17 inches (43 centimeters) across.

rapidly since the mid-1970's as a result of improved varieties and in response to a growing demand for sunflower oil. The chief sunflower states are Minnesota, North Dakota, South Dakota, and Texas.

Sunflowers originated in North America and were introduced into Europe during the 1500's. Some species come up every year, but the most common ones must be grown annually from seeds.

Scientific Classification. Sunflowers make up the genus *Helianthus* of the composite family, Compositae. The common annual sunflower is *H. annuus*. DAVID E. ZIMMER

SUNFLOWER STATE. See KANSAS.

SUNG DYNASTY, *soong,* ruled China from 960 to 1279. The Chinese made great urban and commercial expansion during this period. Their painting, ceramics, book printing, and philosophy reached a new high point in development. A general, Chao K'uang-yin, founded the Sung dynasty and served as its first emperor. He succeeded in creating a strong, centralized dynasty. The Sungs controlled most of China, except for the northeast section, until 1127. Then the Juchens from Manchuria seized North China. In 1279, the Mongols conquered southern China and ended the dynasty. H. F. SCHURMANN

See also CHINA (The Age of Empire).

SUNNI ALI, *SUN ee AHL ee* (? -1492?), ruled the Songhai Empire in West Africa from 1464 to 1492. He began to absorb the Mali Empire about 1464 and developed Songhai into the most powerful state in the western Sudan.

Sunni Ali conquered many neighboring countries. He captured Timbuktu in 1468 and threw out the Tuareg nomads who had held the city since 1433. About 1475, Sunni Ali conquered Jenne, another important center of trade.

Sunni Ali established law and order in the Songhai Empire and encouraged trade. He disappeared mysteriously in 1492, and historians believe he may have drowned in a flood. LEO SPITZER

See also SONGHAI EMPIRE.

SUNSET BOULEVARD. See LOS ANGELES (Central Los Angeles).

SUNSET CRATER NATIONAL MONUMENT is near Flagstaff, Arizona, and was established in 1930. The volcanic cinder cone for which the monument was named ranks as its chief feature. The monument has a large crater with a brilliantly colored summit and extensive lava flows. It also contains an ice cave that is cold the year around. Ponderosa pine trees grow in the area. For location, see ARIZONA (physical map). For area, see NATIONAL PARK SYSTEM (table: National Monuments). C. LANGDON WHITE

SUNSET LAWS are laws that require certain state government agencies and programs to be reviewed regularly by the state legislature. An agency or program is automatically abolished—that is, its sun will set—if it cannot be proven essential. Even if the agency or program is essential, it may be restructured.

Sunset laws were passed in an effort to eliminate unnecessary agencies and force others to become more efficient. Agencies that are authorized to continue are reviewed on a regular basis, such as every four or six years. A related budgeting technique, also aimed at controlling public spending, is called *zero-base budgeting* (see ZERO-BASE BUDGETING).

In 1976, Colorado, Florida, Louisiana, and Alabama, in that order, became the first states to adopt sunset laws. By 1983, about 35 states had passed such laws. ROBERT T. GOLEMBIEWSKI

SUNSHINE LAWS are laws that require federal, state, and local government agencies to conduct their meetings as openly as possible. These laws permit the public to attend various government meetings. By opening meetings to "let the sunshine in," the laws help discourage secrecy in government.

Sunshine laws originated in 1905, when the Florida Supreme Court ruled that the public could attend city and town government meetings in that state. In 1953, California and New Mexico passed the first state sunshine laws. The problem of secrecy in government reached a height during the Watergate scandal of the 1970's (see WATERGATE). By 1977, all the states had passed sunshine laws. The federal government, through the "Government in the Sunshine Act" of 1976, opened meetings of many agencies to the public.

Sunshine laws vary widely. Some require government agencies to admit the public to almost all their meetings. Others allow preliminary meetings to be closed if the final vote on an issue is held in open session. Many sunshine laws also permit closed meetings on certain topics, such as personnel matters and real estate purchases. ROBERT T. GOLEMBIEWSKI

See also FREEDOM OF INFORMATION ACT.

SUNSHINE SKYWAY is one of the longest overwater crossings in the United States. It stretches 15 miles (24 kilometers) across Tampa Bay in Florida, linking St. Petersburg and Bradenton. It consists of two parallel roadways built over causeways connected by bridges. The first roadway was completed in 1954 and the second in 1971.

SUNSHINE STATE. See FLORIDA; SOUTH DAKOTA.

SUNSPOT is a relatively dark area on the surface of the sun. Sunspots appear dark because they are cooler than the rest of the sun's visible surface. They may have a temperature of only about 7000° F. (4000° C), compared with 11,000° F. (6000° C) for their surroundings. For this reason, sunspots give off less light.

A typical large sunspot may have a diameter of about 20,000 miles (32,000 kilometers)—several times larger than the earth's diameter—and last for months. Such a large spot consists of a dark central region called the *umbra* and a lighter surrounding region known as the *penumbra*. An extremely small sunspot, called a *pore*, has no penumbra. Pores may be several hundred miles or kilometers in diameter and last only for hours.

The number of sunspots and solar latitudes at which they appear vary over a period of about 11 years. This period is called the *sunspot cycle*. At the beginning of a cycle, sunspots appear chiefly between 20° and 40° north and south of the sun's equator. Later, the spots increase in number and occur closer to the solar equator. When they reach a maximum number, they range primarily between 5° and 40° north and south latitude. At the end of the cycle, the number of spots drops to a minimum and the spots occur chiefly between about 5° and 15° north and south latitude.

How Sunspots Form. Sunspots have magnetic fields of a strength up to 3,000 times as great as the average magnetic field of either the sun or the earth. Astronomers believe the cause of sunspots is closely related to this fact. According to the generally accepted explanation, the strong magnetic fields of the sun have the shape of tubes just below the solar surface. The sun rotates faster at its equator than at its poles, and so the tubes are stretched out tightly. "Kinks" then develop in the magnetic tubes and push through the solar surface.

A pair of sunspots appears wherever a kink penetrates, because the kink both leaves and reenters the surface. During an 11-year period, the kinks first push through the solar surface at high latitudes and later at lower latitudes. This change explains the variations in latitude of sunspots during a sunspot cycle.

The two members of a pair of sunspots have opposite magnetic polarities, much like the poles of a magnet. The two spots are called the *preceding spot* and the *following spot* because one "leads" the other in the direction of the sun's rotation. During any given 11-year sunspot cycle, the magnetic polarity of sunspot pairs north of the solar equator is opposite to the polarity of the pairs south of the equator. For example, if the preceding spots in the Northern Hemisphere behave like the north-seeking end of a magnet, the preceding spots in the Southern Hemisphere behave like the south-seeking end. However, during the next sunspot cycle the behavior of the preceding spots is reversed. Thus, a complete sunspot cycle actually lasts about 22 years.

Recent Findings. Astronomers have discovered that the sunspot cycle is only part of a more basic solar activity cycle, which includes *solar flares*, *plages*, and *prominences* (see SUN [The Sun's Stormy Activity]). Such phenomena are closely associated with sunspots and occur in the region around the spots.

In the early 1900's, E. Walter Maunder, a British astronomer, theorized that no sunspots occurred from 1645 to 1715. Research during the 1970's supported the absence of sunspot activity during those 70 years. The existence of that period, called the *Maunder minimum*, indicates that the sunspot cycle may not be as basic a property of the sun as astronomers had thought.

During the 1970's, an increasing number of scientists began to believe that solar activity may have a direct effect on the earth's weather. Further studies may reveal whether the earth's weather patterns are affected by the solar events of an individual sunspot cycle or by solar variations occurring over a much longer period of time. The United States launched a research satellite called *Solar Maximum Mission* in 1980 at the peak of the then-current sunspot cycle. The mission showed that reductions in the amount of solar energy that reaches the earth's atmosphere correspond to the area of the sun covered by sunspots. JAY M. PASACHOFF

See also AURORA BOREALIS; MAGNETIC STORM.

SUNSTROKE is the common name for conditions that result from overheating the body. Doctors usually use the more specific terms *heatstroke* and *heat exhaustion*. Sunstroke is a form of heatstroke caused by being exposed to the sun too much or too long.

Heatstroke usually results when the heat-regulating mechanisms of the body break down. The body maintains its normal temperature in several ways. Among them is the cooling effect that results when sweat evaporates. Researchers found that people who work in excessive heat for a long time sweat less and less. They may stop sweating altogether and their body temperature rises to dangerous levels. Doctors consider true heatstroke a medical emergency because the high body temperatures cause brain damage.

Persons with heatstroke rarely are aware that they have stopped sweating. But they suddenly notice a rapid rise in temperature. The body temperature of a patient may be 112° F. (44° C). The skin feels hot and dry. The patient's breathing is regular, and the pulse is full and pounding. Soon the patient's breathing becomes irregular, the pulse weakens, and coma develops (see COMA).

Victims of heatstroke need immediate treatment. Those who are not treated may die. A doctor should be called at once. The most important thing is to reduce the temperature as quickly as possible. Doctors often place the patient in a bathtub filled with cold water. They apply cold compresses or ice packs to the head and neck. When the patient's temperature drops to about 102° F. (39° C), the drastic cooling measures usually are stopped. Most persons who have had heatstroke become ill quickly when exposed to heat again.

Heat Exhaustion, or *heat prostration*, is less severe than heatstroke. It generally occurs in persons who work near boilers, or in places with high temperatures and humidity. Victims become weak and dizzy and fall into a stupor. They usually perspire freely, and their temperature drops below normal. Their condition is like that of a person in shock (see SHOCK). These persons should be removed to a cooler location. But because of their subnormal temperature, they should be kept warm. Persons who work under conditions that might produce heat exhaustion drink large amounts of water and often take salt tablets to replace salt lost from their body when they sweat. LOUIS D. BOSHES

SUPER BOWL. See FOOTBALL (Professional Competition).

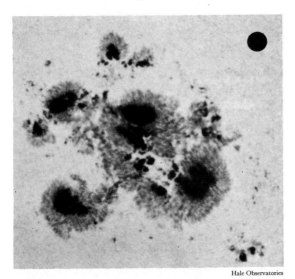

Hale Observatories

Sunspots may cover an area of the sun many times greater than the size of the earth. The black circle, *upper right,* shows the approximate size of the earth compared with that of sunspots.

SUPERCHARGER

SUPERCHARGER is a device that adds power to a gasoline or diesel engine. It does this by compressing, or squeezing, the air fed into the cylinders. The extra air helps the fuel burn more completely, and makes the engine produce more power.

An understanding of how the supercharger works can be gained through an experiment with a drinking glass and a few sheets of paper. Crumple the paper into several large wads. One of the wads will almost completely fill the glass. Next, squeeze the paper wads until they are smaller. Now several wads will fit in the glass.

A cylinder in a gasoline engine is like the drinking glass. It can be filled with a "loose" amount of air like the one larger paper wad. But if the air is squeezed by a supercharger, just as the paper wads were squeezed, then the cylinder can hold several times as much air.

Superchargers are particularly useful on airplane engines. This is because the air pressure decreases as an airplane goes higher. In other words, the air becomes more loosely packed, like the big paper wad. At high altitude the supercharger packs the air tightly to keep the gasoline burning well. Superchargers are sometimes used in boat and automobile engines.

Sometimes gears connected to the engine drive the supercharger. *Turbosuperchargers* are driven by a gas turbine turned by the engine exhaust.

An airplane pilot may shift gears on some superchargers so that the speed of the supercharger may be increased at higher altitudes. Other superchargers have automatic controls to make them go faster when the outside air pressure decreases.   H. S. STILLWELL

See also DIESEL ENGINE; GASOLINE ENGINE.

SUPERCONDUCTIVITY is a phenomenon in which certain metals and alloys conduct electricity without resistance. Superconductivity occurs at temperatures near *absolute zero*, which is $-273.15°$ C. Lead, mercury, and tin become good superconductors at such temperatures. See ABSOLUTE ZERO.

The modern theory of superconductivity was developed by three American physicists—John Bardeen, Leon N. Cooper, and John Robert Schrieffer. They received the 1972 Nobel prize in physics for their work. According to their theory, a superconductor has no electrical resistance because of an *attractive interaction* between its electrons that results in the formation of pairs of electrons. These electron pairs are bound to one another and flow without resistance around impurities and other imperfections. In an ordinary conductor, resistance occurs because its unbound electrons collide with imperfections and then scatter.

Superconductivity is used in the field of electromagnetics. Researchers have developed powerful superconducting magnets, which use much less electricity than ordinary electromagnets do. Superconducting magnets enable physicists to build more efficient *particle accelerators*, which are devices that increase the speed of atomic particles (see PARTICLE ACCELERATOR).

Scientists are experimenting with various other uses for superconducting. For example, researchers are testing superconducting switching devices that control circuits in computers. These devices operate at extremely high speeds and produce almost no heat. Scientists also are seeking materials that superconduct at higher temperatures. Power lines made of such a substance could carry electricity great distances without any loss of current.

The Dutch physicist Heike Kamerlingh Onnes discovered superconductivity in 1911. He made the discovery while measuring the electrical resistance of frozen mercury.   Critically reviewed by LEON N. COOPER

See also BARDEEN, JOHN; CRYOGENICS; CRYOTRON.

SUPERDOME. See NEW ORLEANS (Downtown New Orleans; picture).

SUPEREGO. See FREUD, SIGMUND; PSYCHOANALYSIS.

SUPERHIGHWAY. See ROADS AND HIGHWAYS (Primary Highways).

SUPERIOR, Wis. (pop. 29,571), is a port on Lake Superior, opposite Duluth, Minn. Superior and Duluth form a metropolitan area with 266,650 persons. Superior has one of the largest ore docks in the world. The docks store 550,000 short tons (499,000 metric tons) of iron ore. Superior's grain elevator holds 13 million bushels (354 million kilograms) of grain. It is one of the largest in the United States. Shipbuilding is an important industry in Superior. Superior also has large flour mills, railroad and machinery shops, woodworking factories, canneries, and breweries. The city is the home of the University of Wisconsin-Superior. Fur traders camped on the site of the city in 1662. In 1883, iron ore was discovered in the area. Superior is the seat of Douglas County. It has a council-manager government. For location of the city, see WISCONSIN (political map).   JAMES I. CLARK

SUPERIOR, LAKE. See LAKE SUPERIOR.

SUPERLATIVE. See COMPARISON.

SUPERMAN. See NIETZSCHE, FRIEDRICH.

SUPERMARKET is a large retail store that provides a one-stop food-shopping service. It offers foods of all kinds in one location. Five principal characteristics of a modern supermarket are its large size, the wide variety of foods it offers, its self-service system for shoppers, sales on a cash-and-carry basis, and its many nonfood items. Nonfood items include housewares and kitchen aids, cosmetics and beauty aids, magazines, and, sometimes, hardware, cutlery, and lawn-care materials. Some supermarkets provide snack bars, playgrounds and entertainment facilities for children, and parking areas for cars.

Supermarkets, originally found chiefly in the United States, now are found in many parts of Europe and Latin America.   EDWIN E. HARGRAVE

SUPERNATURALISM. See METAPHYSICS (Doctrines); MYTHOLOGY (introduction).

SUPERNOVA is a star that explodes and becomes billions of times as bright as the sun before gradually fading. At its maximum brightness, a supernova may outshine an entire galaxy. The explosion throws a tremendous cloud of dust and gas into space. The mass of this material may exceed 10 times that of the sun.

Most astronomers believe a supernova results from the death of a star more massive than the sun. When such a star begins to burn out, its core quickly collapses and becomes extremely hot. Runaway nuclear reactions occur in the core, and tremendous energy is suddenly released. Then the star erupts into a supernova.

Most supernovae reach maximum brightness a few days after they explode, and shine intensely for several weeks. Some supernovae fade within months, but others fade more slowly over a period of years. Supernovae also may differ in the amount of material they eject and in the composition of that material. Another difference between such exploding stars is in the type of object they leave behind. After some supernova explosions, a small, dense star composed of neutrons remains. Such a star is called a *neutron star*. After other explosions, an invisible object called a *black hole* is left behind. A black hole has such powerful gravitational force that not even light can escape it (see BLACK HOLE). Astronomers believe that, in some cases, no object of any kind remains after a supernova explodes.

Supernovae probably created many of the heavier elements that make up the earth and other objects of the solar system. Included among these are such commonly known elements as carbon, gold, iron, oxygen, silicon, and uranium. Also, astronomers believe that high-energy cosmic rays originate in supernovae (see COSMIC RAYS).

In 1054, Chinese astronomers observed a supernova so bright that it was visible during the day. It blew off a huge cloud of gas and dust known as the *Crab Nebula*, which still can be seen today. At the center of this nebula is a *pulsar*, a rapidly spinning neutron star that sends out powerful pulses of radio waves. See STAR (picture: The Home of a Pulsar).

Most supernovae are too far from the earth to be seen with the unaided eye. However, astronomers have observed hundreds of them through telescopes. On the average, supernovae may occur as often as once every 15 years in galaxies similar to the Milky Way, the earth's galaxy. But the most recent supernova observed in the Milky Way occurred in 1604.   JAMES W. TRURAN

See also NOVA.

SUPERREGENERATION. See ARMSTRONG, E. H.

SUPERSONIC FLIGHT. See AERODYNAMICS (Shock Waves and Sonic Booms); AIRPLANE (History).

SUPERSTITION is a traditional belief that a certain action or event can cause or foretell an apparently unrelated event. For example, some superstitious people believe that carrying a rabbit's foot will bring them good luck. Others believe that if a black cat crosses their path, they will have bad luck. To yet other superstitious people, dropping a knife or fork on the floor means company is coming. Such beliefs are superstitions because in each case the action and the event it foretells are traditionally thought to be connected.

Superstitions have existed in every human society throughout history. Most people, including highly educated individuals, act superstitiously from time to time. Many persons may joke about avoiding bad luck by knocking on wood or not walking under a ladder. But they have such beliefs anyway. Scholars once believed that all superstitions dated back to humanity's early history. But many superstitions have appeared in relatively recent times. According to a superstition in baseball, for example, a pitcher will give up a hit if anyone mentions that a no-hit game is being pitched.

Countless human activities are involved in superstitions. They include eating, sleeping, working, playing, getting married, having a baby, becoming ill, and dying. Times of danger and uncertainty have brought many superstitions. Superstitions concern animals, clothing, lakes, mountains, names, numbers, the planets and stars, the weather, and parts of the body.

Kinds of Superstitions. Many superstitions deal with important events in a person's life, such as birth,

Well-Known Superstitions

Some superstitions foretell good luck, and others warn of bad luck.

Good Luck

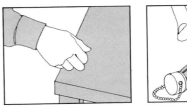

Knocking on wood   Rubbing a rabbit's foot

Bad Luck

WORLD BOOK illustration by David Cunningham

Walking under a ladder   A black cat crossing your path

entering adulthood, marriage, pregnancy, and death. Such superstitions supposedly ensure that a person will pass safely from one stage of life to the next. For example, a person born on Sunday will always have good luck. A bride and groom will have bad luck if they see each other on their wedding day before the ceremony. A pregnant woman must eat the right food, or she will give her child an unwanted birthmark. After a person dies, the doors and windows of the room should be opened so the spirit can leave.

Some superstitions involve a type of magic. One form of such magic comes from the belief that similar actions produce similar results. Many people believe that a newborn baby must be carried upstairs before being carried downstairs. In this way, the child will be assured of rising in the world and having a successful life. According to a Japanese belief, a sick person should be given a potted plant instead of cut flowers. A live plant represents hope for the patient's recovery, but cut flowers soon wither. The same principle appears in the custom of putting money in a purse or wallet being given as a gift. The giver wants to make sure that the purse or wallet will always contain money.

A number of superstitions involve someone's taking a deliberate action to cause something to happen or to prevent something from occurring. Most of these *causal* superstitions involve ensuring good luck, avoiding bad luck, or making something good happen. For example, carrying a silver dollar supposedly brings good luck. Some persons will not start a trip on a Friday, especially if it is the 13th day of the month. Friday and the number 13 are both associated with bad luck. Wedding guests throw rice at the newlyweds to ensure that the marriage will result in many children. Causal superstitions may involve actions intended to give bad luck to someone. Witches supposedly perform some of these actions (see WITCHCRAFT).

Other superstitions foretell an event without any

conscious action by the person involved. Some of these *sign* superstitions foretell good or bad luck. For example, finding a horseshoe or a four-leaf clover means good luck. Breaking a mirror or spilling salt brings bad luck. Other sign superstitions foretell a certain event or condition. A ring around the moon means rain will soon fall. A howling dog means death is near. A person with red hair has a quick temper.

Some sign superstitions may be changed into causal superstitions. If a person hangs a horseshoe over a door, witches cannot enter. If a young woman pins a four-leaf clover to her door, she will marry the first bachelor who comes in the door. In some cases, a person may avoid the bad luck involved in a sign superstition by taking immediate action. For example, someone who has spilled salt may cancel the bad luck by throwing a pinch of salt over the left shoulder.

The Role of Superstitions. Many people scoff at superstitions because they consider such beliefs unscientific. But many scholars believe that some superstitions have a scientific basis. For example, people in England once used tea made from foxglove plants to treat some forms of heart disease. Today, physicians often prescribe digitalis, a drug made from dried leaves of the purple foxglove, for patients with weak hearts.

Some superstitions have a practical origin. For example, many people believe that lighting cigarettes for three persons from one match will bring bad luck. This superstition may have originated among soldiers during World War I (1914-1918). At night, a match that stayed lit long enough to light three cigarettes provided a target for the enemy. Another superstition involves hanging a bag of garlic around a child's neck for protection from illness. The bag has no supernatural power. But its smell keeps away other children—including any with a disease that the wearer of the bag might catch.

Most people have fears that make them insecure. Superstitions help overcome such fears by providing security. They reassure people that they will get what they want and avoid trouble. For example, millions of people believe in astrology and base important decisions on the position of the sun, moon, planets, and stars (see ASTROLOGY). Superstitions will probably have a part in life as long as people fear each other and have uncertainties about the future.   ALAN DUNDES

Related Articles in WORLD BOOK include:

Amulet	Friday	Occultism
Augur	Genii	Omen
Birthstone	Ghost	Palmistry
Blarney Stone	Magic	Pioneer Life in
Divination	Mental Illness	America (Caring
Evil Eye	(History)	for the Sick)
Exorcism	Moon (Legend	Vampire
Fetish	and Folklore)	Voodoo
Fortunetelling	Necromancy	Witchcraft

Additional Resources

JAHODA, GUSTAV. *The Psychology of Superstition.* 2nd ed. Aronson, 1974.

PLANER, FELIX E. *Superstition.* Horizon, 1982. Explores the origin and meaning of superstitions.

SARNOFF, JANE, and RUFFINS, REYNOLD. *Take Warning! A Book of Superstitions.* Scribner, 1978.

SUPERTANKER. See TANKER.

SUPPÉ, *ZOO pay,* **FRANZ VON,** *frahnts fuhn* (1819-1895), was an operetta composer. He produced much music in many forms during his lifetime. But of his great output, only a group of overtures has remained in active use. Such familiar overtures as *Poet and Peasant* (1846); *The Beautiful Galatea* (1865); *Light Cavalry* (1866); *The Jolly Robbers* (1867); *Fatinitza* (1876); *Boccaccio* (1879); and *Morning, Noon, and Night in Vienna* are performed regularly. Suppé was born in or near Spalato (now Split), Yugoslavia.   HERBERT WEINSTOCK

SUPPLY AND DEMAND are economic forces that determine the amount of a product that is produced and its price. The *supply* of a product is the amount of it that businesses are willing to produce and sell. Generally, the higher the price is, the greater the supply will be. Similarly, the *demand* for a product is the amount of it that users would like to buy. Demand also depends on the price, but in the opposite way. Usually, demand is lower at high prices than at low ones. Because the amount that producers actually sell must be the same as the amount that users actually buy, the only price at which everyone can be satisfied is the one for which supply equals demand. This is called the *equilibrium price.*

The supply and demand diagram with this article shows how these economic forces operate. Using the market for onions as an example, the *supply curve SS'* shows the number of pounds that farmers will produce each month at every possible market price. Higher prices encourage farmers to produce more onions, and

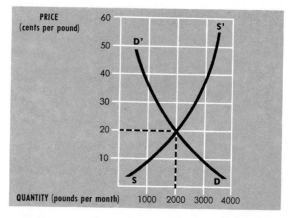

low prices discourage production. Consumers' reactions are shown by the *demand curve DD',* which shows how many pounds of onions customers want to buy each month at every possible price. At low prices, they want a great many onions. At high prices, they use other vegetables instead.

The supply and demand curves cross at a certain price (20¢ a pound in the example). When this is the market price, suppliers will offer just the quantity that users wish to buy. At any higher price, farmers will produce more onions than consumers are willing to buy, and competition among farmers will force the price down. At prices lower than equilibrium, purchasers will demand more onions than are available, and the scarcity of onions will drive the price up.   ROBERT DORFMAN

See also CAPITALISM; ECONOMICS; INTERNATIONAL TRADE; PRICE.

SUPPLY-SIDE ECONOMICS. See ECONOMICS (New Solutions for Old Problems).

SUPRARENAL GLAND. See ADRENAL GLAND.

SUPREME COURT OF CANADA. See CANADA, GOVERNMENT OF (The Supreme Court of Canada).

SUPREME COURT OF THE UNITED STATES is the highest court in the nation. One of its basic duties is to determine whether federal, state, and local governments are acting according to the Constitution of the United States. The Supreme Court does its job by deciding specific legal cases on the basis of established legal rules. Much of the court's work involves rules that are laid down in the Constitution. Although many of these rules are stated in words that are not entirely clear, the Supreme Court must determine their meaning and apply them to the cases presented for decision. For a discussion of the Supreme Court and the Constitution, see GOVERNMENT (Constitutional Government).

A Supreme Court decision has great importance. Once a decision has been reached by the court, all other courts throughout the United States are required to follow the decision in similar cases. In this way, the Supreme Court helps guarantee equal legal justice to all Americans. The court is not required to consider every case that is presented to it. It accepts only a few of them, most of which involve problems of national importance.

The Supreme Court heads the judicial branch of the federal government. It is the only court specifically created by the Constitution. The judicial system of each state is also headed by a supreme court. In some states, the court is known by another name, such as *court of appeals*. For the most part, state courts hear cases concerning state laws. However, the United States Supreme Court may review the decisions of the highest state courts that involve the U.S. Constitution or acts of Congress. This article deals only with the Supreme Court of the United States. For information on the entire federal court system and on the state courts, see the article COURT.

The role of the Supreme Court and its interpretation of the law change occasionally. These changes depend

SUPREME COURT OF THE UNITED STATES

partly on the political, social, and economic beliefs of its members, and partly on the national conditions of the time. In our early days as a nation, for example, the court concerned itself chiefly with the proper division of authority between the federal government and state governments. A major concern today is the protection of the rights and liberties of individuals.

How the Supreme Court Is Organized

Article III of the Constitution provides for the creation of the Supreme Court and states the limits of its jurisdiction. But details of the court's exact organization and the work it can do are left largely to Congress. Congress established the federal court system in the Judiciary Act of 1789.

Membership. The Supreme Court has nine members —a chief justice and eight associate justices. The exact number is set by Congress and has changed through the years. The first Supreme Court had six members. Since 1869, the court has consisted of nine members.

The Constitution sets no qualifications for justices but states that they shall be appointed by the President, with the advice and consent of the Senate. However, all members have had some legal training and experience, and most justices have been prominent judges, lawyers, law teachers, or government officials.

Through the years, the Senate has rejected outright only 11 Supreme Court nominees. About 15 other nominations have been postponed, not acted upon, or withdrawn. In 1969, Clement F. Haynsworth, Jr., of South Carolina became the first nominee since 1930 to be rejected by the Senate. The Senate also rejected G. Harrold Carswell of Florida in 1970. Both men had been nominated by President Richard M. Nixon.

Once appointed, justices may remain in office "during good behavior," and Congress cannot reduce their salary. These provisions protect the justices from political control and help ensure their independence.

Salary and Terms. The court meets regularly in the Supreme Court Building in Washington, D.C. The an-

From "Equal Justice Under Law"

Courtroom of the Supreme Court Building in Washington, D.C., is shown here as the justices see it from the bench. Spectators sit in the rear of the courtroom. The space between the spectators and the bench is reserved for lawyers pleading cases and for other members of the bar. The building, completed in 1935, was designed by Cass Gilbert.

THE SUPREME COURT

Harry A. Blackmun   **W. J. Brennan, Jr.**   **Thurgood Marshall**   **Sandra O'Connor**

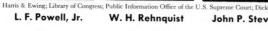
Harris & Ewing; Library of Congress; Public Information Office of the U.S. Supreme Court; Dick Rose, Sygma; United Press Int.; Wide World

Chief Justice Warren E. Burger   **L. F. Powell, Jr.**   **W. H. Rehnquist**   **John P. Stevens**   **Byron R. White**

nual term of the court begins the first Monday in October and usually ends in June.

The chief justice receives $100,700 a year, and each associate justice receives $96,700. A justice 70 years of age, who has served as a justice or judge of the United States 10 or more years, may retire and continue to receive this salary. A justice who has served at least 15 years as a justice or judge may retire at 65.

Authority of the Supreme Court

The Supreme Court declares what the law is only when an actual case comes before it. The case must involve a real dispute between opposing parties. The court does not give legal advice or advisory opinions, even if requested by the President or Congress.

The Constitution permits the court to decide cases "arising under" the Constitution, federal laws, and treaties. The Supreme Court also decides disputes involving the United States or two or more states. The most important of these cases are those that require the court to interpret the Constitution or the laws enacted by Congress.

The Supreme Court has the power to decide whether a federal or state law or executive action is constitutional. This power, known as *judicial review*, is not expressly granted in the Constitution. However, the Constitution by its own terms is the "supreme law of the land." The court has ruled that it must review conflicts between the Constitution and a federal or state law.

The Constitution gives the Supreme Court two types of authority: (1) *original jurisdiction* and (2) *appellate jurisdiction*. The court has original jurisdiction in cases affecting ambassadors or other representatives of foreign countries and in cases in which a state is one of the parties. Cases of this kind go directly to the Supreme

Court. However, they make up only a small fraction of the court's workload.

Most of the work of the Supreme Court comes from its appellate jurisdiction, which is its authority to confirm or reverse the decisions of lower courts. Most cases reviewed by the Supreme Court come from the federal courts of appeals and the highest state courts. The decisions of federal district courts are normally reviewed first by the courts of appeals. But in a few cases, the Supreme Court reviews the decisions of federal district courts directly. It also reviews the decisions of the Court of Appeals for the Federal Circuit and the Supreme Court of Puerto Rico.

The Supreme Court's appellate jurisdiction is further divided into *obligatory jurisdiction* and *discretionary jurisdiction*. In certain cases, the losing party has a right to carry the case to the Supreme Court. Cases of this kind make up the obligatory jurisdiction. The term *appellate jurisdiction* is sometimes used to refer to the court's obligatory jurisdiction only.

Most cases come under the court's discretionary jurisdiction, also called its *certiorari* (pronounced SUR shee uh RAIR ee) jurisdiction. The court has the right to decide which of these cases it will review. Because it cannot possibly review all the cases, it selects the ones it considers to be most important.

The court agrees to hear a case by granting a *writ of certiorari*, a written order calling the case up from a lower court for review. The attorney for the side requesting a review submits a petition for certiorari and a supporting *brief* (written reasons for the appeal). Most appeals are made on grounds that the judge has made an error in declaring the law that applies to the facts of the case. The opposing attorney is given copies of the documents and has a short time to file a brief in opposition. If four

798

U.S. Supreme Court Justices

Name	Term	Appointed By	Name	Term	Appointed By
Chief Justices			* John M. Harlan	1877-1911	Hayes
			William B. Woods	1881-1887	Hayes
* John Jay	1790-1795	Washington	Stanley Matthews	1881-1889	Garfield
* John Rutledge	1795	† Washington	Horace Gray	1882-1902	Arthur
* Oliver Ellsworth	1796-1800	Washington	Samuel Blatchford	1882-1893	Arthur
* John Marshall	1801-1835	J. Adams	* Lucius Q. C. Lamar	1888-1893	Cleveland
* Roger B. Taney	1836-1864	Jackson	David J. Brewer	1890-1910	Harrison
* Salmon P. Chase	1864-1873	Lincoln	Henry B. Brown	1891-1906	Harrison
* Morrison R. Waite	1874-1888	Grant	George Shiras, Jr.	1892-1903	Harrison
* Melville W. Fuller	1888-1910	Cleveland	Howell E. Jackson	1893-1895	Harrison
* Edward D. White	1910-1921	Taft	* Edward D. White	1894-1910	Cleveland
* William H. Taft	1921-1930	Harding	* Rufus W. Peckham	1896-1909	Cleveland
* Charles E. Hughes	1930-1941	Hoover	Joseph McKenna	1898-1925	McKinley
* Harlan F. Stone	1941-1946	F. D. Roosevelt	* Oliver W. Holmes, Jr.	1902-1932	T. Roosevelt
* Frederick M. Vinson	1946-1953	Truman	William R. Day	1903-1922	T. Roosevelt
* Earl Warren	1953-1969	Eisenhower	William H. Moody	1906-1910	T. Roosevelt
* Warren E. Burger	1969-	Nixon	Horace H. Lurton	1910-1914	Taft
			* Charles E. Hughes	1910-1916	Taft
Associate Justices			* Willis Van Devanter	1911-1937	Taft
* James Wilson	1789-1798	Washington	Joseph R. Lamar	1911-1916	Taft
* John Rutledge	1790-1791	Washington	Mahlon Pitney	1912-1922	Taft
William Cushing	1790-1810	Washington	James C. McReynolds	1914-1941	Wilson
* John Blair	1790-1796	Washington	* Louis D. Brandeis	1916-1939	Wilson
* James Iredell	1790-1799	Washington	John H. Clarke	1916-1922	Wilson
Thomas Johnson	1792-1793	Washington	* George Sutherland	1922-1938	Harding
* William Paterson	1793-1806	Washington	Pierce Butler	1923-1939	Harding
* Samuel Chase	1796-1811	Washington	Edward T. Sanford	1923-1930	Harding
Bushrod Washington	1799-1829	J. Adams	* Harlan F. Stone	1925-1941	Coolidge
Alfred Moore	1800-1804	J. Adams	* Owen J. Roberts	1930-1945	Hoover
William Johnson	1804-1834	Jefferson	* Benjamin N. Cardozo	1932-1938	Hoover
H. Brockholst Livingston	1807-1823	Jefferson	* Hugo L. Black	1937-1971	F. D. Roosevelt
Thomas Todd	1807-1826	Jefferson	Stanley F. Reed	1938-1957	F. D. Roosevelt
Gabriel Duvall	1811-1835	Madison	* Felix Frankfurter	1939-1962	F. D. Roosevelt
* Joseph Story	1812-1845	Madison	* William O. Douglas	1939-1975	F. D. Roosevelt
Smith Thompson	1823-1843	Monroe	* Frank Murphy	1940-1949	F. D. Roosevelt
Robert Trimble	1826-1828	J. Q. Adams	* James F. Byrnes	1941-1942	F. D. Roosevelt
John McLean	1830-1861	Jackson	* Robert H. Jackson	1941-1954	F. D. Roosevelt
Henry Baldwin	1830-1844	Jackson	Wiley B. Rutledge	1943-1949	F. D. Roosevelt
James M. Wayne	1835-1867	Jackson	Harold H. Burton	1945-1958	Truman
Philip P. Barbour	1836-1841	Jackson	* Tom C. Clark	1949-1967	Truman
John Catron	1837-1865	Van Buren	Sherman Minton	1949-1956	Truman
John McKinley	1838-1852	Van Buren	* John M. Harlan	1955-1971	Eisenhower
Peter V. Daniel	1842-1860	Van Buren	* William J. Brennan, Jr.	1956-	Eisenhower
Samuel Nelson	1845-1872	Tyler	* Charles E. Whittaker	1957-1962	Eisenhower
Levi Woodbury	1845-1851	Polk	* Potter Stewart	1958-1981	Eisenhower
Robert C. Grier	1846-1870	Polk	* Byron R. White	1962-	Kennedy
Benjamin R. Curtis	1851-1857	Fillmore	* Arthur J. Goldberg	1962-1965	Kennedy
John A. Campbell	1853-1861	Pierce	* Abe Fortas	1965-1969	Johnson
Nathan Clifford	1858-1881	Buchanan	* Thurgood Marshall	1967-	Johnson
Noah H. Swayne	1862-1881	Lincoln	* Harry A. Blackmun	1970-	Nixon
* Samuel F. Miller	1862-1890	Lincoln	* Lewis F. Powell, Jr.	1972-	Nixon
* David Davis	1862-1877	Lincoln	* William H. Rehnquist	1972-	Nixon
* Stephen J. Field	1863-1897	Lincoln	* John P. Stevens	1975-	Ford
William Strong	1870-1880	Grant	* Sandra Day O'Connor	1981-	Reagan
Joseph P. Bradley	1870-1892	Grant			
Ward Hunt	1873-1882	Grant			

*Has a separate biography in WORLD BOOK. †Appointment not confirmed by the United States Senate.

justices vote to grant the petition, the court agrees to hear the case.

The court partially controls its workload by granting only a small percentage of requests for a writ of certiorari. In spite of this procedure, the court has a constantly growing volume of work. Legal experts have proposed the creation of an additional federal appeals court to relieve the Supreme Court's burden.

The Court in Action

Pleading Cases before the Supreme Court is normally done by attorneys who have been admitted to the bar of the court. However, a *litigant* (person engaged in a lawsuit) may argue his or her own case with the court's permission. Most litigants hire and pay their own attorneys. If a litigant has no money, free legal service may be provided. When the U.S. government has an interest in a case before the Supreme Court, it is usually represented by the solicitor general or members of the solicitor general's staff. The attorney general of the United States may also argue important cases.

Deciding Cases. The justices decide a case after they have considered written and oral arguments from each side. During oral arguments, the justices are free to interrupt and to ask questions. After the attorneys' oral arguments, the justices discuss the case *in conference* (in private). The chief justice begins the discussion. Then, in order of seniority, the associate justices give their

799

opinions. After discussion ends, the justices vote in order of seniority. Cases are decided by majority vote.

If the chief justice has voted with the majority, he or she selects a justice to write the *opinion of the court*. This opinion is also called the *majority opinion*. If the chief justice has not voted with the majority, the senior justice of the majority assigns the opinion. A justice who disagrees with this opinion may write a *dissenting opinion*. Justices may write *concurring opinions* if they agree with the conclusion but not with the reasons for reaching it, or if they wish to express similar reasons in their own words. Authors of the opinions announce them in a public session. All opinions are published in the *United States Reports*. The practice of putting opinions in writing requires the justices to explain and justify their decisions. The publishing of opinions also enables the public to study the decisions of the court. This is an important tradition in a free society, and a safeguard against unreasonable use of power.

Effects of Decisions. Supreme Court decisions have far-reaching effects. Once the court decides a case, lower courts must follow the decision in similar cases. The Supreme Court itself usually follows its earlier decisions. The policy of following rules set in previous decisions is known as *stare decisis*. This practice lends stability and predictability to the law.

The Supreme Court, however, is not bound by an earlier decision if it is convinced that an error has been made or that changed circumstances require a different approach. This provides for the court's recognition of social, political, and economic change.

Landmark Decisions

The Marshall Court. Many important and historic Supreme Court opinions were written by John Marshall, one of its most famous justices. He served as chief justice from 1801 to 1835. The Supreme Court during those years is referred to as the "Marshall court."

Marshall's most historic opinion was written in 1803, in the case of *Marbury v. Madison*. His majority opinion stated that the court may rule an act of Congress unenforceable if the act violates the U.S. Constitution. This power of *judicial review* is *implied* (expressed indirectly) but not clearly granted in the Constitution. Some persons have protested vigorously against the court's exercise of judicial review. However, this power has become a basic part of the American constitutional system.

Several other Marshall court decisions also have had far-reaching application. In 1819, in *Dartmouth College v. Woodward*, the court ruled that private charters are contracts. It held that the Constitution protects such charters against violation by the states. This decision strengthened the rights of private property.

Also in 1819, in *McCulloch v. Maryland*, the court supported the doctrine of implied powers. It ruled that the federal government possesses powers in addition to those specifically granted in the Constitution. It said that the United States government has any powers that are necessary and proper in carrying out its specified powers. This decision of the court broadened the scope of the federal government. See MARSHALL, JOHN.

Regulating Commerce. An important concern of the court has been the proper relationship between government and business. The Constitution gives Congress the power to regulate interstate commerce. In 1824, in *Gibbons v. Ogden*, the Marshall court gave a broad interpretation to the word *commerce*. Since the mid-1930's, the court has interpreted the commerce clause in a way that gives Congress wide regulatory powers in matters affecting business. See INTERSTATE COMMERCE.

Civil Rights and Liberties. Through the years, the court's position on civil rights has shifted with changes in public opinion. In 1857, in *Dred Scott v. Sandford*, the court held that blacks were not and could not become U.S. citizens. But the 14th Amendment to the Constitution (1868) made all former slaves citizens and gave them full civil rights. In 1896, in the case of *Plessy v. Ferguson*, the court upheld a law providing for "separate but equal" public facilities for blacks and whites. But in 1954, in *Brown v. Board of Education of Topeka*, the court ruled that racial segregation in public schools is unconstitutional. In the 1969 case of *Alexander v. Holmes County* (Miss.) *Board of Education*, the court ordered that public school systems end segregation "at once." In 1964, in *Heart of Atlanta Motel, Inc. v. United States*, the court upheld the Civil Rights Act of 1964. This act prohibits racial discrimination in many public accommodations.

Several Supreme Court cases in the 1960's dealt with voting rights. In 1962, the court ruled in *Baker v. Carr* that unfair districting of state legislatures could be challenged in federal courts. In other cases, the court ruled that congressional districts must be about equal in population and that state legislatures and local governing bodies must be apportioned on the basis of equal population.

Other decisions have dealt with the rights of persons accused of crimes. In 1964, in *Escobedo v. Illinois*, the court ruled that a confession cannot be used as evidence if it is obtained after the defendant has been denied permission to see a lawyer. In the 1966 case of *Miranda v. Arizona*, the court held that prior to any questioning, the defendant must be informed of his or her constitutional rights, including the right to remain silent. In *Witherspoon v. Illinois* in 1968, the court held that defendants cannot be sentenced to death by juries from which persons who oppose capital punishment have been automatically excluded. In the 1972 case of *Furman v. Georgia*, the court ruled that capital punishment, as then administered in the United States, was unconstitutional. But in the mid-1970's, the court upheld capital-punishment laws in several states.

Several cases of the 1970's dealt with the rights of women and children. In the 1973 cases of *Roe v. Wade* and *Doe v. Bolton*, the court ruled on women's right to have an abortion. It declared that a state may not prohibit abortion, under certain conditions, during the first six months of pregnancy (see ABORTION). In 1975, in *Goss v. Lopez*, the court held that public schools cannot suspend pupils "for more than a trivial period" without notice of the charges against them and a fair hearing. In the 1977 case of *Ingraham v. Wright*, the court ruled that the spanking of students by school officials does not violate the Constitution's ban on "cruel and unusual punishments."

Other important civil rights decisions of the court have dealt with Bible reading and prayers in public schools, freedom of speech and of the press, and pretrial

Powers of the Court, Federal Government, and States

1803 *Marbury v. Madison.* If a law passed by Congress conflicts with the Constitution, the Supreme Court must base its decision on the Constitution. This ruling established the court's power of *judicial review*—that is, its authority to declare laws unconstitutional.

1810 *Fletcher v. Peck.* Georgia could not revoke a land grant after the land had been sold to a third party. The Constitution protects contracts against interference by the states, and a sales agreement is a type of contract.

1819 *McCulloch v. Maryland.* The Constitution gives *implied powers* to the federal government in addition to the *express powers* that are specifically granted. Implied powers are those necessary to carry out express powers.

1819 *Dartmouth College v. Woodward.* New Hampshire could not alter a royal charter and make Dartmouth a state college. A charter is a contract, and the Constitution protects contracts against state interference.

Powers of the President

1952 *Youngstown Sheet and Tube Company v. Sawyer.* The President exceeded his lawful power when he seized the nation's steel mills to prevent a strike during the Korean War.

1974 *United States v. Nixon.* The President cannot withhold evidence needed in a criminal trial. This ruling established that the President's *executive privilege*—the right to keep records confidential—is not unlimited.

1982 *Fitzgerald v. Nixon.* No President may be sued for damages for any official action taken while in office. This immunity applies to civil suits, not to criminal prosecution or other types of judicial action.

Regulation of Business and Industry

1824 *Gibbons v. Ogden.* The powers of the federal government are superior to those of the states in all matters of *interstate commerce* (trade between states).

1905 *Lochner v. New York.* A law limiting bakers to a 60-hour work week was unconstitutional because it violated "freedom of contract" between employer and employee. The court reversed this decision in 1937.

1935 *Schechter v. United States.* The National Industrial Recovery Act of 1933, which provided for fair-competition codes for businesses, was unconstitutional.

1937 *National Labor Relations Board v. Jones and Laughlin Steel Corporation.* The federal government has the power to regulate the local activities of labor unions because these activities may affect interstate commerce.

Election Districts

1962 *Baker v. Carr.* Citizens can challenge unfair election districting before a federal court.

1964 *Reynolds v. Sims.* The U.S. House of Representatives and both houses of a state legislature must follow the rule of "one person, one vote" and create election districts roughly equal in population.

Freedom of Speech and of the Press

1919 *Schenck v. United States.* The government cannot restrict freedom of speech unless the speech creates a "clear and present danger" of violence or some other evil that the government has a right to prevent.

1957 *Roth v. United States.* Freedom of the press, guaranteed by the First Amendment to the Constitution, does not protect publication of obscene material.

1964 *New York Times Co. v. Sullivan.* A newspaper cannot be punished for untrue statements about a public official unless it deliberately published a falsehood.

1971 *New York Times Co. v. United States.* The government could not prevent publication of the *Pentagon papers*, a secret study of the Vietnam War. The court held that the danger to national security did not justify such censorship.

1973 *Miller v. California.* Material can be considered obscene if it fulfills certain requirements established by the court (see OBSCENITY AND PORNOGRAPHY).

School Prayer

1962 *Engel v. Vitale.* Public schools cannot require the recitation of prayers.

Rights of Persons Accused of Crime

1866 *Ex Parte Milligan.* Military courts cannot try civilians outside military areas if civilian courts are available.

1932 *Powell v. Alabama.* If a person on trial for his or her life cannot hire a lawyer, the state must provide one.

1961 *Mapp v. Ohio.* Evidence obtained by illegal means cannot be used in a criminal trial.

1963 *Gideon v. Wainwright.* The states must provide free legal counsel to any person accused of a felony who cannot afford a lawyer.

1964 *Escobedo v. Illinois.* A confession cannot be used as evidence if it is obtained after the accused person has been denied permission to see a lawyer.

1966 *Miranda v. Arizona.* An accused person must be informed of his or her constitutional rights, including the right to remain silent, before being questioned.

1972 *Argersinger v. Hamlin.* The states must provide free legal counsel to any person accused of a misdemeanor that involves a jail term if the person cannot afford a lawyer.

1972 *Furman v. Georgia.* The death penalty, as it was then administered, was cruel and unusual punishment in violation of the Eighth Amendment to the Constitution.

Rights of Women and Minority Groups

1857 *Dred Scott v. Sandford.* Blacks could not be U.S. citizens, and Congress could not prohibit slavery in the U.S. territories. The first part of this ruling was overturned in 1868 by the 14th Amendment. The second part was struck down in 1865 by the 13th Amendment.

1896 *Plessy v. Ferguson.* "Separate but equal" public facilities for whites and blacks did not violate the Constitution. The court reversed this decision in 1954.

1944 *Korematsu v. United States.* The government could lawfully remove persons of Japanese ancestry from areas threatened by Japanese attack during World War II.

1948 *Shelley v. Kraemer.* State or federal courts cannot enforce *restrictive covenants,* which are agreements to prevent real-estate owners from selling their property to members of minority groups.

1954 *Brown v. Board of Education of Topeka* (Kans.). Separate but equal facilities for blacks in public schools do not meet the constitutional requirement for equal protection of the law.

1964 *Heart of Atlanta Motel, Inc. v. United States.* The Civil Rights Act of 1964 is constitutional. This act bans racial discrimination in all public accommodations that affect commerce, including hotels, motels, and restaurants.

1969 *Alexander v. Holmes County* (Miss.) *Board of Education.* Desegregation of all public school systems must take place "at once."

1973 *Doe v. Bolton* and *Roe v. Wade.* The states may not prohibit a woman's right, under certain conditions, to have an abortion during the first six months of pregnancy.

1978 *Regents of the University of California v. Allan Bakke,* also called the *Bakke* case. University and college admissions programs may not use specific quotas to achieve racial balance. But they may give special consideration to members of minority groups.

1979 *United Steelworkers of America v. Weber.* Employers can give preference to minorities and females in hiring and promotion for "traditionally segregated job categories."

---

*Has a separate article in WORLD BOOK.

publicity that is *prejudicial* (unfair) to the accused.

A table with this article describes many of the court's landmark decisions. See also GRANGER CASES.

Controversy on the Court

The Supreme Court has been sharply divided on some cases brought before it. This has been especially true of cases involving questions that have divided the American public, such as minority rights. The court's lack of complete agreement in such cases is not unexpected nor undesirable. It reflects the seriousness of the cases and the presence of different points of view.

Since the Supreme Court was established, a strong debate has continued concerning the extent of its power. One side has insisted that the court should interpret and apply the Constitution to agree with the meaning and intent of those who wrote it. Another group has insisted on a more creative role for the court. They would interpret the Constitution so that it would apply to the new and changing problems of the nation. The second group also draws support from the original intent of the founding fathers, but disagrees as to the scope and meaning of that intent.

The Supreme Court possesses great power over the Constitution and the nation. But this power is based on the respect of the American people. Throughout most of its history, the court has held the streams of government within their proper channels. It has largely succeeded in the delicate task of protecting the rights of unpopular minorities while relying for its support on the approval of the majority.   WILLIAM RAY FORRESTER

Critically reviewed by HARRY A. BLACKMUN

See the separate articles in WORLD BOOK for the justices and the landmark decisions listed in the *tables* in this article. See also CHIEF JUSTICE; CONSTITUTION OF THE UNITED STATES; COURT; ROOSEVELT, FRANKLIN D. (The Supreme Court); SCOTTSBORO CASE; WASHINGTON, D.C. (picture: The Supreme Court Building). For a *Reading and Study Guide*, see *Supreme Court of the United States* in the RESEARCH GUIDE/INDEX, Volume 22.

Additional Resources

ABRAHAM, HENRY J., and DOHERTY, GRACE. *Freedom and the Court: Civil Rights and Liberties in the United States*. 3rd ed. Oxford, 1977.
Congressional Quarterly's Guide to the U.S. Supreme Court. CQ, 1979.
MORGAN, RICHARD E. *The Supreme Court and Religion*. Macmillan, 1974.
PROVINE, DORIS M. *Case Selection in the United States Supreme Court*. Univ. of Chicago Press, 1980.
WOODWARD, BOB, and ARMSTRONG, SCOTT. *The Brethren: Inside the Supreme Court*. Simon & Schuster, 1979.

SURABAYA, *sur uh BAH yuh* (pop. 2,027,913), is the second largest city in Indonesia. It lies along the Kali Mas, a river in eastern Java, about 420 miles (676 kilometers) east of Jakarta (see INDONESIA [color map]). It is a major port and naval base, and has shipbuilding, textile, chemical, and petroleum industries.

SURFACE MEASURE. See AREA; SQUARE MEASURE.

SURFACE TENSION is a force that causes the surface of liquids to behave in certain ways. It causes a liquid to behave as if a thin, elastic film covered its surface. For example, the surface of water can support needles and razor blades if they are placed there carefully.

Surface tension also causes a liquid to rise in a thin tube when the tube is dipped in the liquid. This action is called *capillarity* (see CAPILLARITY).

Because of surface tension, drops of liquid take a spherical shape, which has the smallest possible surface area. For example, raindrops fall as spheres.

Surface tension is caused by *cohesion*, a force that causes the molecules of a substance to be attracted to one another (see COHESION). The molecules of a liquid that are below the surface have molecules pulling on them from all directions. But the molecules on the surface are attracted only by the molecules below and to their sides. The downward and sideward attraction of the molecules creates a constant pull on the surface molecules, causing surface tension.   E. D. GODDARD

SURFACTANT. See DETERGENT AND SOAP.

SURFING is an exciting water sport in which a person rides waves, usually in the ocean. There are 10 recognized forms of surfing. The most popular form is *surfboard riding*, sometimes simply called *surfing*. In this version of the sport, the surfer stands on a board and skims

Catching a Wave, the surfer paddles with his hands to gain speed. When the wave lifts the board, he stands up and puts his weight on his front foot, aiming the board toward the shore.

Surfing requires good balance and quick reflexes. The two men on the right are riding a wave into shore. The man on the left is paddling out to catch another wave. Surfers should be good swimmers.

along the crest of a wave. All forms of surfing require exact timing, and surfers must have sharp reflexes to maintain the balance needed for a successful ride. This is particularly true of surfboard riding, which this article discusses.

To prepare for a surfboard ride, the surfer lies face down on the board and paddles out beyond where the waves begin to form, called the *outside*. When a wave at least 3 feet (0.9 meter) high starts to move toward the shore, the surfer paddles the board just ahead of it. He or she stands up as the wave begins to lift the board and carry it toward the shore. The person shifts his or her weight to steer the board across the *face* of the wave—that is, the smooth water just under the crest.

Expert surfers stand at the front of the board. Less experienced individuals can maintain better control of the board by standing near the center. Skilled surfers may attempt such difficult maneuvers as *360's* (complete circular turns) and *roller coasters* (riding up and down the face of a wave).

All surfboard riders today use a *Simmons board*, which is made of a strong, lightweight plastic called polyurethane. A Simmons board measures 6 to 7 feet (1.8 to 2 meters) long, about 2 feet (0.6 meter) wide, and about 3 inches (7.6 centimeters) thick. It weighs from 10 to 20 pounds (4.5 to 9 kilograms).

Many surfers train for surfboard riding by running on

the beach and by body-surfing. To body-surf, they wait until a high wave starts moving toward the shore. Then they do a *scissors kick*, spreading the legs apart and bringing them together sharply in the direction of the shore. After swimming a few strokes at the crest, surfers put their head down, arch their back, and put their hands along their sides. The wave sweeps them toward shore in this position. As the wave dies out, surfers push their hands out and spread their legs to slow down. The sense of balance gained by body-surfing provides good training for surfboard riding.

Surfing ranks as the oldest sport in the United States. People in what is now Hawaii surfed before Christopher Columbus sailed to the New World in 1492. Today, the sport is popular in many countries, especially the United States, Australia, New Zealand, Great Britain, South Africa, France, Argentina, Mexico, Japan, Brazil, Peru, and Venezuela. The International Council for the Advancement of Surfing sponsors annual world championship competition for both professional and amateur surfers.   GARY FAIRMONT R. FILOSA II

See also HAWAII (picture: Riding the Surf).

Additional Resources

KLEIN, H. ARTHUR. *Surf-Riding*. Harper, 1972. For younger readers.
MADISON, ARNOLD. *Surfing: Basic Techniques*. McKay, 1979.
McGINNESS, LAURIE. *Surfing Fundamentals*. Reed, 1978.

Surfing Terms

Angle means to ride across the face of a wave, either to the left or to the right.

Bellyboard, or **Paipo Board,** is a type of surfboard. Most bellyboards measure less than 3 feet (0.9 meter) long and have the front end slightly turned up.

Blown Out refers to water that strong winds have made too choppy for surfing.

Juice is the energy or power in a wave.

Knee Machine, or **Kneeboard,** is a surfboard about 5 feet (1.5 meters) long. A surfer kneels while riding it.

Shore Break is a wave that breaks close to shore.

SURGEON. See SURGERY; MEDICINE.

SURGEONS, INTERNATIONAL COLLEGE OF, is an organization of qualified surgeons that was founded in 1935 in Geneva, Switzerland. Its purpose is to improve and spread surgical knowledge throughout the world. About 15,000 surgeons in more than 70 countries belong to the organization. There are regional federations in Africa, Asia, Europe, Latin America, North America, and the South Pacific. The organization publishes a monthly journal and bulletin. Headquarters and an International Museum of Surgical Sciences are at 1516 N. Lake Shore Drive, Chicago, Ill. 60610.

Critically reviewed by the INTERNATIONAL COLLEGE OF SURGEONS

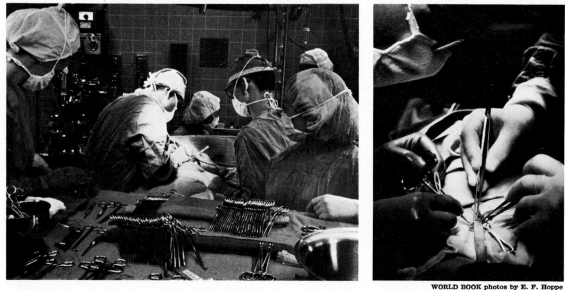

Modern Surgery is a team effort, *left*. A surgeon and his assistant perform the operation, *right*, while nurses keep them supplied with instruments. An anesthesiologist completes the team.

SURGERY is the branch of medicine that deals with the treatment of disease, deformities, or injuries by operations. The doctor who performs the operation is called a *surgeon*. Every physician has some training in surgery and is qualified to perform simple operations. But surgeons are specially trained so that they have the judgment and skill to perform complicated operations. Four or five years of additional training after internship are necessary to qualify physicians to perform general surgery.

The Surgeon's Tools

A surgical operation is complicated. Many persons, medicines, and techniques are used to assure the greatest safety and comfort for the patient and to help the surgeon. The elimination of pain, the prevention of infection, and the use of laboratory tests are important aids to the surgeon. A qualified *surgical team* is essential to the successful performance of an operation. This team usually consists of at least a surgeon, a first assistant, an anesthesiologist, and a nurse.

Anesthesia refers to methods that cause a loss of sensation, particularly a loss of pain sensation. Before the discovery of anesthesia in 1842, surgeons could perform only very short operations because of the extreme pain. They tried to deaden the pain by giving large quantities of alcoholic beverages or by using compounds containing opium. But the relief from pain was not complete and lasted only a short time.

Since the discovery of anesthesia, researchers have studied drugs and gases and developed more satisfactory anesthetics. Numerous *general anesthetics*, such as nitrous oxide, ether, and halothane, are used to put the patient to sleep. These may be used alone or in combination with one another. General anesthesia is also produced by injecting drugs such as sodium pentothal (see SODIUM PENTOTHAL). Sometimes a *local anesthetic*, such as Novocain, which affects only the area near the place of injection, is used (see NOVOCAIN). Local anesthetics injected into the spinal canal produce anesthesia in specific parts of the body. One drug, curare, was used centuries ago by South American Indians (see CURARE). They put the drug on the tips of their arrows to paralyze or kill small animals and birds. Modern surgeons use it to relax the abdominal muscles in many serious operations. See ANESTHESIA.

Antiseptics and Asepsis. Infection once was a great danger in surgery. Even though the surgery was successful, patients often died because of infection. But in 1865, Joseph Lister of Great Britain introduced methods for preventing infection. He used various antiseptics to kill germs in the operating room during the course of an operation. He often sprayed carbolic acid about the room to kill the germs. Later, the method of *aseptic* (completely sterile) surgery was developed. In this method all germs that cause infection are kept out by cleaning and sterilizing all equipment used in the operating room. Instruments and linens are completely sterilized before the operation. Thus, while antiseptics kill germs that are present, asepsis keeps them out altogether. See ANTISEPTIC; LISTER, SIR JOSEPH.

Instruments. A surgeon uses many instruments in the course of a single operation. Sharp instruments include scissors and *scalpels* (knives). There are also holders for needles and sponges, *clamps* to close off blood vessels, *retractors* to hold back folds of skin, and many other instruments.

Modern instruments have advanced the growth of surgery. Perhaps one of the most useful of these, the X-ray machine, is seldom thought of as an "instrument." But this device, which permits the doctor to see inside the human body, is probably one of the most valuable tools for diagnosis. By this means, the surgeon can detect broken bones and diagnose many diseases of the internal organs. A special kind of X-ray machine called a *CAT* (computerized axial tomographic) *scanner* enables the surgeon to view a cross-section of the patient's body. Other instruments are used to examine

804

body cavities. For example, the *bronchoscope* is used to look into the lungs and to perform a *biopsy* (remove small pieces of tissue for diagnosis).

Sutures are threads used to tie severed blood vessels and to close surgical wounds so that the tissues heal better. Modern surgery would be impossible without them. Some kinds of sutures, such as catgut, are absorbed by the body. Others, such as nylon or silk, must be removed after several days. See SUTURE.

Technique. In the early days of surgery, the operator's technique was considered most important. Only the most skilled surgeon could perform an operation in the least possible time. For example, these doctors could perform an amputation in two or three minutes. Modern surgery stresses adequate diagnosis of the disease and proper care of the patient before and after the operation. Thus, the surgeon needs not only knowledge of surgery itself, but also a wide knowledge of physiology, chemistry, and pathology. However, technique remains an important tool in surgery.

Modern techniques enable the surgeon to operate successfully upon all parts of the human body. For example, a present-day surgeon can remove a long section of diseased intestines and sew the remaining intestinal sections together. The body will function normally after the operation. A kidney, or even a major part of the stomach, can be removed by an operation. Surgeons have been able to operate successfully on the heart. In such surgery, a doctor may lift the heart out of the body, operate on it, and then replace it. Extensive surgery on the lungs and ribs is often part of the treatment of tuberculosis. A surgeon can successfully remove an entire lung that has been diseased by cancer. A brain surgeon can remove brain tumors, repair head injuries, and cut nerves to correct certain conditions.

Transplanting organs enables the surgeon to take a healthy organ from one person and use it to replace the diseased organ in another person. But the tissues must be able to exist together, or the patient's body will reject the new organ. See TISSUE TRANSPLANT.

Cryosurgery makes use of extreme cold in surgery. It usually involves freezing tissues. Cryosurgery has been suggested to cure duodenal ulcers. Surgeons sometimes use cold probes on the brain to treat Parkinson's disease. Cold probes are also used to treat detached retinas and remove cataracts. See CRYOBIOLOGY.

Microsurgery is a technique in which the physician operates while viewing the procedure through a microscope or magnifying glass. This technique enables physicians to perform operations on some of the tiniest body structures. For example, surgeons can rejoin extremely small blood vessels and nerves by using microsurgery. Such sugery has led to the successful reattachment of severed fingers, hands, and even arms and legs. Doctors also use microsurgery to operate on the delicate structures in the eye, the kidney, the brain, and many other parts of the body.

A Typical Operation

Perhaps the best way to understand what is involved in a surgical operation is to consider a typical one. After a thorough examination, including laboratory

---

Some Common Surgical Operations

Amputation is the removal of a limb (or part of a limb) or another appendage. Usually performed if a limb is damaged beyond repair, or if a seriously diseased appendage resists treatment and threatens to infect other parts of the body. See AMPUTATION.

Appendectomy is the removal of the vermiform appendix. Commonly performed in cases of appendicitis (see APPENDICITIS).

Cholecystectomy is the removal of the gall bladder. Generally performed if the gall bladder is seriously inflamed or if it contains gallstones that affect the patient's health. See GALL BLADDER.

Colostomy is the creation of an artificial opening in the *colon*, a part of the large intestine. Usually performed if the rectum is diseased or has been removed. Solid body waste passes through an artificial opening made in the wall of the abdomen.

D and C is the *dilation* (stretching) of the opening of the uterus and the *curettage* (scraping) of the inside of the uterus. Commonly performed to diagnose such problems as excessive uterine bleeding or cancer of the uterus. May also be performed to remove placental tissues following childbirth, miscarriage, or induced abortion.

Gastrectomy is the removal of part or all of the stomach. Commonly performed to remove cancerous tissue or peptic ulcers.

Hysterectomy is the removal of the uterus. Usually performed to treat uterine diseases, including cancer. Hysterectomy does not affect sexual desire or function, but it does cause sterility. See HYSTERECTOMY.

Mastectomy is the removal of part or all of a breast. Commonly performed to remove diseased tissue, especially cancerous tissue. *Radical mastectomy* includes the removal of additional muscle and *axillary* (armpit) tissue. See MASTECTOMY.

Nephrectomy is the removal of a kidney. Generally performed to remove cancerous tissue or a kidney that no longer functions properly. Removal of one kidney causes no disability. But removal of both kidneys results in death, unless the patient receives a kidney transplant or undergoes *dialysis* (regular treatments with an artificial kidney machine).

Oöphorectomy is the removal of an ovary. Usually performed to remove diseased tissue, such as a cancerous tumor. Removal of both ovaries causes *menopause* (the end of menstruation) and prevents the patient from having children.

Pneumonectomy is the removal of lung tissue. Commonly performed to remove cancerous tissue; occasionally to remove a long-term abscess or infection. *Total pneumonectomy* is the removal of an entire lung.

Prostatectomy is the removal of part or all of the prostate gland. Commonly performed to remove cancerous tissue or an enlarged prostate that interferes with the flow of urine from the bladder.

Tonsillectomy is the removal of the tonsils. Generally performed in cases of long-term or recurring infection. See TONSILLITIS.

Tracheotomy is the creation of an artificial opening leading from the *trachea* (windpipe) to the outside of the body. Commonly performed to enable a patient with a blocked larynx to breathe.

Vasectomy is the cutting and tying of the *vasa deferentia*, the tubes that carry sperm from the testicles. Usually performed to cause sterility. Vasectomy does not affect sexual desire or function.

tests, the doctor diagnoses the disease as an infected appendix. The patient is brought to the hospital and prepared for the operation. Sedative drugs are given to relax the patient before the operation.

The operating room has been prepared for the patient's arrival by a thorough cleaning and scrubbing. All equipment not to be used for the operation has been removed. A large table is set up near the operating table. This will hold all the sterilized instruments and sponges that the surgeon might need during the operation. A small table on an L-shaped stand is also set up. This fits over both the operating table and the patient. It holds all the instruments and sponges immediately needed by the surgeon. A nurse or an operating room technician has charge of these tables.

The patient is usually put to sleep in a room that is designed for this purpose. The anesthesiologist needs a lot of equipment such as anesthetics, anesthetic machines, masks, sterile syringes, a stethoscope, and an apparatus that measures blood pressure. A tank of oxygen and a mask for giving the gases are always present. Also at hand are small flasks of stimulant drugs.

Meantime the doctors and nurses on the surgical team prepare for the operation. They spend 8 to 10 minutes scrubbing their hands and forearms to remove germs. In addition to this, they wear sterilized rubber gloves because the skin cannot be made completely sterile even with strong antiseptics. The members of the surgical team put on sterilized gowns to cover their clothing and caps to cover their hair. They also wear masks of gauze or other material to cover their mouths and noses so that they will not breathe germs into the area.

Nurses and orderlies bring the patient into the operating room and make the patient comfortable on the operating table. The anesthesiologist takes and records the rate of the patient's pulse, respiration, and blood pressure. A constant check is made on these throughout the operation. Nurses place sheets over the patient in such a manner that the area in which the *incision* (opening) is to be made is left open. This area is thoroughly cleansed, antiseptics are applied, and the area is again draped with sterile sheets. Nurses place the sterile instruments on the tables, and put the small table over the operating table, within easy reach of the surgeon. If gas is the anesthetic, the anesthesiologist places a mask over the patient's face and opens the valves of a complicated machine, thus allowing the patient to breathe the anesthetic. The patient soon feels no pain.

The surgeon starts the operation by making an incision in the skin of the abdomen. The incision is extended through the layer of fat that lies directly beneath the skin. The muscle tissue is pulled back, and retractors are placed in position to hold the tissue out of the way. This exposes the appendix and that part of the intestine to which it is attached.

While working, the surgeon closes the severed ends of small blood vessels with clamps called *hemostats*. Thus very little bleeding takes place during the operation. *Sponges*, which are actually pieces of gauze folded into small pads, are used to remove any surplus blood. The surgeon quickly removes the appendix, ties the stump that remains with a suture and *inverts* (turns)

the stump into the large intestine. Then the "closing-up" procedure begins.

The sponges are removed. The surgeon takes the clamps off the blood vessels and ties the vessels so there will be no bleeding. The retractors are then removed, and the muscles move back into their normal position. The surgeon brings the tissues together with sutures. Finally, the edges of the cut skin are sewed together.

During the course of the operation, the anesthesiologist has been careful to give exactly the right amount of anesthetic to the patient. The various nurses assist the surgeon like members of any well-drilled team.

At the end of the operation, the doctor applies a gauze bandage to the incision area and nurses remove the sheets used for draping. Doctors and nurses return the patient to a hospital bed, and recovery is usually uneventful. Yet such a routine operation would have been impossible a hundred years ago.

Surgical Specialties

As in other branches of medicine, special branches of surgery have developed. These specialties came about because of the need for specialized types of surgery for specific areas of the body. Surgeons in these fields often take additional training. Frequently, new equipment is developed for use in the specialty fields.

Ophthalmology, a specialty in treating diseases of the eyes, has developed a distinct field of surgery. Surgeons cure blindness that results from *cataracts* (a clouding of the eye lens) by removing the lens. They also operate on the muscles of the eye to correct a condition known as cross-eyes. See OPHTHALMOLOGY.

Plastic Surgery can produce exceptional results by removing scars and blemishes. Plastic surgeons often graft skin. World War II gave great impetus to the development of plastic surgery. Soldiers who were seriously disfigured in battle had their deformities corrected by means of surgery. Surgeons made new noses or new ears even though the original ones were completely destroyed. They built new jaws from living bone and cartilage and flesh. See PLASTIC SURGERY.

Gynecology and Obstetrics are related surgical specialties that deal with women's diseases and childbirth, respectively. The Caesarean section in childbirth once resulted in the death of about 86 of every 100 women on whom it was performed. In most modern hospitals, not even two die of every 100 women on whom such operations are performed.

Other Specialty Fields. There are many other fields in which special types of surgery have developed. The *thoracic* surgeon operates on the chest. In *urologic* surgery, the surgeon operates on the kidneys and bladder. The *otolaryngologist* takes care of diseases of the ears, nose, and throat. The *orthopedist* operates on bones. The *proctologist* treats diseases of the lower bowel and anus. *Brain surgeons* and *heart surgeons* need particular skills and training. In each field, new knowledge and techniques have brought great progress.

History

Surgery has been known since ancient times. The first surgeon's tool was probably a piece of flint stone. Some skeletons of Stone Age people show evidence of *trephining*. In this operation, a hole was cut in the head of the patient to relieve pressure from a fracture.

Primitive tribes fixed broken legs with splints. Even in the earliest times, *cautery* (searing the flesh) was used to stop bleeding. Circumcision, performed during certain religious rites, was one of the earliest operations.

Some operations were known to the ancient Babylonians, Greeks, and Romans. Military surgery has been important for two or three thousand years. The early Hindus were expert surgeons. They knew at least 125 different surgical instruments. They also developed plastic surgery to replace noses and ears that had been cut off. In the Middle Ages, surgeons were often confused with barbers. Both performed operations. But only the barber did bloodletting, for the surgeon thought it beneath him. It is from this bloodletting that the red and white striped barber pole developed—the red standing for blood and the white for the bandage.

Among the many famous surgeons of the past was the Frenchman, Ambroise Paré, who lived in the 1500's. He has been called the father of military medicine. He abolished the harmful practice of pouring boiling oil on wounds to sterilize them. John Hunter (1728-1793), a British surgeon, was the founder of experimental surgery. In the United States, Ephraim McDowell (1771-1830) of Kentucky performed the first successful operation to remove a tumor of the ovary in 1809, the beginning of successful abdominal surgery. Crawford Long (1815-1878) of Georgia is credited with having first used ether as an anesthetic in 1842.

Many of the great modern surgeons have been Americans. William Halsted (1852-1922) devised many new surgical procedures and techniques. He introduced the use of sterile gloves in aseptic surgery. Fred H. Albee (1876-1945), an orthopedist, brought bone grafting into practical use. Chevalier Jackson (1865-1958) developed the first practical lighted *esophagoscope*, an instrument used to examine the *esophagus* (the food passage between the mouth and stomach). Other modern surgeons are the famous Mayo brothers, William and Charles, both of whom made many contributions; Harvey Cushing, the great brain surgeon; and Evarts Graham. This pioneer thoracic surgeon in 1933 became the first to successfully remove an entire cancerous lung.

Modern surgery has advanced in five main ways. These are (1) the development of aseptic surgery; (2) the technical improvements in surgical instruments; (3) the increased knowledge of body processes; (4) anesthesia; and (5) the use of chemicals to prevent and treat infections.　　　　　　　　　　WARREN H. COLE

Related Articles in WORLD BOOK include:

BIOGRAPHIES

Barnard, Christiaan N.	Lister, Sir Joseph
Carrel, Alexis	Long, Crawford W.
Crile, George W.	Mayo (family)
Cushing, Harvey	McDowell, Ephraim
DeBakey, Michael E.	Murphy, John B.
Drew, Charles R.	Paré, Ambroise
Kocher, Emil T.	Penfield, Wilder G.

OTHER RELATED ARTICLES

Acupuncture	Laser (In Medicine)
Amputation	Ligature
Anatomy	Mastectomy
Anesthesia	Medicine
Bloodletting	Plastic Surgery
Bronchoscope	Tissue Transplant
Gastroscope	Trephining
Hypothermia	X Rays

SURINAM. See SURINAME.

SURINAM TOAD, *SUR uh nam*, is an odd-shaped toad known for the unusual way it raises its young. The toad is named for Suriname (also spelled Surinam), a country in South America, where it was first discovered.

American Museum of Natural History

The Back of the Female Surinam Toad provides a living place for young toads until they can take care of themselves.

It is flat with a head shaped like a triangle. It has small eyes and no tongue or teeth. The fingers of its front legs are not webbed, but its hind feet have webbed toes.

The Surinam toad lives in the water and has rough, brown skin. At breeding time, the female's skin grows thick and spongy. The female lays each egg while she and her mate turn over in the water. The egg sinks into the skin of the female's back. The young pass the tadpole stage in the mother's back. They come out of the skin when they are about $2\frac{1}{2}$ months old or older.

Scientific Classification. The Surinam toad is in the family Pipidae. It is classified as *Pipa pipa*.　　W. FRANK BLAIR

SURINAME, *SUR uh NAH muh*, is a country on the northeast coast of South America. The country's name is also spelled *Surinam*. Mountainous rain forests cover about 80 per cent of Suriname, and most of the people live in the flat coastal area. Suriname has an area of 63,037 square miles (163,265 square kilometers) and a population of about 392,000. About two-fifths of the people live in or near Paramaribo, the capital, largest city, and chief port. The Netherlands ruled the country during most of the period from 1667 until 1975, when Suriname gained independence. Before it became independent, Suriname was also known as *Dutch Guiana*.

Government. An executive body called the Policy Center heads Suriname's government. It is composed of military and civilian leaders. The commander of the country's army ranks as the most powerful member of the Policy Center. A prime minister heads Suriname's Council of Ministers, which carries out the operations of the

Suriname

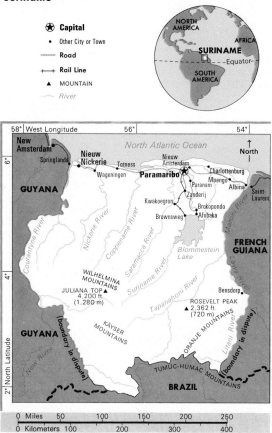

Capital
• Other City or Town
----- Road
+-+-+ Rail Line
▲ MOUNTAIN
~~ River

WORLD BOOK map

Each ethnic group in Suriname has preserved its own culture, religion, and language. Dutch is the nation's official language, but the various groups use a Creole dialect as a common language.

Some Hindustanis in Suriname own and operate small farms, and others are skilled industrial workers. Most Creoles work in government or for businesses. Many Indonesians are tenant farmers, who rent their land.

Blacks in Suriname are called *Bush Negroes*. They are the descendants of a group of black Africans who escaped from slavery in the 1600's. Most Bush Negroes live in the rain forests and follow African tribal customs.

About 70 per cent of Suriname's people can read and write. The law requires children from 7 to 12 years old to attend elementary school, and some go on to high school. Suriname has one university, in Paramaribo.

Land and Climate. Suriname has a narrow coastal area of flat swampland that has been drained for farming. This area extends inland 10 to 50 miles (16 to 80 kilometers) to a sandy plain that rises about 150 feet (46 meters) high. Mountainous rain forests with about 2,000 kinds of trees lie farther inland, and a high grassy *savanna* (treeless plain) runs along the country's southwest border. Rivers flow north through Suriname to the Atlantic Ocean.

The climate is warm and moist, with an average annual temperature of 81° F. (27° C). Annual rainfall averages 76 inches (193 centimeters) in western Suriname and 95 inches (241 centimeters) in Paramaribo.

Economy of Suriname is based on mining and metal processing. The country is a leading producer of bauxite, an ore from which aluminum is made. Raw bauxite and aluminum account for about 90 per cent of Suriname's exports.

Agriculture also has an important part in Suriname's economy. Rice, a major export crop, is grown on about

government. The prime minister is a member of the Policy Center.

People of many ethnic backgrounds live in Suriname. Hindustanis, who are descendants of people from India, make up more than a third of the population. Creoles—people with mixed European and black African ancestry—make up about a third. The rest of the country's people are, in order of number, Indonesians, blacks, American Indians, Chinese, and Europeans.

Facts in Brief

Capital: Paramaribo.

Official Language: Dutch.

Area: 63,037 sq. mi. (163,265 km²). *Coastline*—226 mi. (364 km). *Greatest Distances*—north-south, 285 mi. (459 km); east-west, 280 mi. (451 km).

Elevation: *Highest*—Mt. Juliana Top, 4,200 ft. (1,280 m). *Lowest*—sea level.

Population: *Estimated 1984 Population*—392,000; distribution, 54 per cent rural, 46 per cent urban; density, 5 persons per sq. mi. (2 per km²). *1980 Census*—352,041. *Estimated 1989 Population*—447,000.

Chief Products: Aluminum, bananas, bauxite, rice.

National Anthem: "Opo Kondre Man Oen Opo" ("Get Up People, Get Up").

Flag: The flag has five horizontal stripes of green, white, red, white, and green. A yellow star lies in the center. See FLAG (picture: Flags of the Americas).

Money: *Basic Unit*—guilder.

Leon V. Kofod

Paramaribo is Suriname's capital, largest city, and chief port. Low wooden buildings, *above,* line the streets of the city, a center of business, cultural, and government activity.

808

P. Meyer, Editorial Photocolor Archives

Suriname's Extensive River System is the nation's chief means of transportation. The people use dugout canoes, such as the one shown above, on waterways in the thick rain forests that cover most of the country.

three-fourths of the farmland. Other crops include bananas, coconuts, and sugar. The forests yield a large supply of hardwoods from which Suriname's lumber industry produces logs and plywood.

The country's chief means of transportation is an extensive system of rivers. Suriname has only about 800 miles (1,300 kilometers) of main roads, and railroad service is limited. An international airport operates near Paramaribo. Suriname has three major newspapers, a television station, and five radio stations.

History. Christopher Columbus sighted what is now Suriname in 1498, and Spaniards and Portuguese explored the area during the 1500's. In 1651, British explorers built the first permanent settlement there. They established cotton and sugar cane plantations and brought slaves from Africa to work the land. In 1667,

the Dutch took control of it and in exchange gave the British what became the state of New York.

Suriname's economy suffered in the 1700's because of slave uprisings and Dutch neglect. In the early 1800's, ownership shifted several times between Great Britain and The Netherlands. In 1815, Britain gave up its claim to Suriname, and the Dutch regained control. The Dutch abolished slavery in 1863 and brought laborers from India and Indonesia to work on the plantations. However, plantation farming declined in the early 1900's, and many people moved to urban areas.

Suriname became a self-governing Dutch territory in 1954. During the 1970's, the Creoles led a movement for full independence, which was supported by the Dutch government. But the Hindustanis opposed independence, and racial conflicts occurred in Suriname for the first time. Suriname gained independence on Nov. 25, 1975. It adopted a democratic form of government, in which the people elected a Parliament. Shortly before independence, thousands of Suriname's people emigrated to The Netherlands. The emigration caused a shortage of skilled labor and greatly restricted economic development in Suriname. Early in 1980, a group of noncommissioned officers within Suriname's armed forces seized control of the country's government and abolished the Parliament. Later in 1980, Suriname established a new government in which both civilians and the military hold power. However, the Parliament was not reestablished.   GARY BRANA-SHUTE

See also ALUMINUM (graph); PARAMARIBO.

SURNAME. See NAME (Beginnings).

SURREALISM is a movement in art and literature. It was founded in Paris in 1924 by the French poet André Breton. Like dadaism, from which it arose, surrealism uses art as a weapon against the evils and restrictions that surrealists see in society. Unlike dadaism, however, surrealism tries to reveal a new and higher reality than that of daily life. *Surrealism* is an invented word meaning *super realism*.

The surrealists claim to create forms and images not primarily by reason, but by unthinking impulse and blind feeling—or even by accident. Using these meth-

Europe After the Rain (1942), an oil painting on canvas; Wadsworth Atheneum, Hartford, Conn., Ella Gallup Sumner and Mary Catlin Sumner Collection

Surrealistic Painting combines recognizable forms in unusual ways, creating a feeling of mystery. Max Ernst painted this scene and others that resemble fantastic rocky landscapes.

808a

ods, the surrealists declare that a magical world—more beautiful than the real one—can be created in art and literature. Much of the beauty sought by surrealism is violent and cruel. In this way, the surrealists try to shock the viewer or reader and show what they consider the deeper and truer part of human nature. The movement is not so strong as it once was, but it still influences artists and writers throughout the world.

Leading surrealist painters include André Masson, René Magritte, Salvador Dali, and Max Ernst. The works of Masson feature free, doodlelike brushstrokes. Paintings by Magritte and Dali use carefully drawn realistic forms to create dreamlike images. Ernst often combined both styles. In many of his pictures, strange creatures seem to emerge from patterns of paint spread haphazardly over the canvas.   MARCEL FRANCISCONO

See also DADAISM; BRETON, ANDRÉ; DALI, SALVADOR; ERNST, MAX; FRENCH LITERATURE (Surrealism); MIRÓ, JOAN; PAINTING (Surrealism; pictures).

Additional Resources

HENNING, EDWARD B. *The Spirit of Surrealism.* Indiana Univ. Press, 1979.
JEAN, MARCEL, ed. *The Autobiography of Surrealism.* Viking, 1980.

SURREY, EARL OF (1517?-1547), HENRY HOWARD, is usually linked in literary history with Sir Thomas Wyatt. They are considered the two greatest English poets at the dawn of the English Renaissance. Surrey, a courtier and military commander during the reign of Henry VIII, introduced blank verse into English literature. He and Wyatt also introduced the Italian sonnet form into English poetry. Their poems were first published in *The Book of Songs and Sonnets* (1557). This book is usually called *Tottel's Miscellany.* Surrey was beheaded on a charge of high treason.   PAUL M. KENDALL

SURTAX. See INCOME TAX.

SURTSEY. See VOLCANO (map; table; picture: The Eruption of a Volcano).

SURVEYING is the technique of measuring to determine the position of points, or of marking out points and boundaries. The points may be on, beneath, or even above the earth's surface. Surveying is as old as civilization. It began in Egypt. Every year, after the Nile River overflowed its banks and washed out farm boundaries, the Egyptians fixed new boundaries by surveying.

Types of Surveys depend upon their uses.

The *land survey* is the type with which people are most familiar. It is used to fix boundaries and to find the areas of plots of ground. In Canada and the Western United States, the boundaries and divisions of public lands have been fixed by government surveyors. A *plane survey* is used on small plots of ground only, since it does not take into consideration the curvature of the earth's surface. A *geodetic survey* allows for curvature and is used to find large areas or long boundaries.

The *topographical survey* includes the measuring of altitudes of elevations and depressions for the purpose of making maps. The U.S. Geological Survey makes and publishes topographic maps of the United States.

Engineering surveys are made where buildings, bridges, roads, canals, and other structures are to be built. *Underground surveys* determine where pipes are to be laid or

Chicago Chapter of Illinois Registered Land Surveyors Association

Surveyors Map Boundaries with an instrument called a *transit.* This device, *above,* consists of a small telescope and various attachments that measure angles and determine distances.

tunnels dug. *Nautical,* or *hydrographic, surveys* map out the bed of a river or lake or ocean. By studying riverbeds, people can learn to control the flow of water and erosion. Both have greatly helped navigation.

Aerial survey, or *photogrammetry,* determines distances on the ground by means of photographs taken from airplanes. These photographs include a great amount of detail that a ground observer either cannot or does not get. Aerial surveying is almost always used for topographic mapping of large areas.

Surveying Tools. The most important of all tools used by the surveyor is the *transit.* This is a small telescope set up on a *tripod* (three-legged stand). To it are attached both horizontal and vertical arcs, used to measure horizontal and vertical angles. It has vernier scales by which the surveyor can read very small fractions of degrees (see VERNIER). Both the tripod and the telescope may be made level with attached *spirit levels,* similar to the levels used by carpenters. A *plumb bob* (weight) hangs from the tripod's center and points to the exact spot where the surveying instrument is set up.

Besides measuring and setting out angles, the transit judges distances. With the use of the telescope and levels, the surveyor can also determine where ground must be leveled. Some transits have compasses attached. A surveyor can plot a north-south line simply by pointing a telescope directly north and having a helper place a stake in line with the vertical hair which crosses the center of the telescope.

Surveyors use a long *steel tape* to measure or set out distances. Most steel tapes are 50, 100, or 200 feet long, or 15, 30, or 50 meters long. Surveyors use an *invar tape* when making extremely precise measurements. Invar tapes, which are made of nickel and steel, are less affected by changes in temperature than are steel tapes.

The Basis of Surveying is geometry. Angles and triangles play a very important part in the work. Surveyors must have a thorough knowledge of geometry and trigonometry. They must be able to use delicate instruments with precision and accuracy. For a diagram of how surveying works, see PARALLAX.

Careers in Surveying. Modern surveying is closely connected with the various branches of engineering, especially civil engineering. Surveyors find work to do whenever there are roads, dams, and bridges to be built. They determine the boundaries of the property held by individuals, as well as the boundaries of various political divisions.   B. AUSTIN BARRY

Related Articles in WORLD BOOK include:

Alidade	Level
Base Line	Photogrammetry
Bench Mark	Plane Table
Chain	Public Lands
Chart	Surveyor's Compass
Geodesy	Theodolite

SURVEYOR'S COMPASS is an instrument used for determining magnetic directions. Although engineer's transits often have a compass, the true surveyor's compass has no telescopic sighting device. Pointings are made by open sights similar to rifle sights.

The magnetic needle is the essential part of a surveyor's compass. This piece of hard steel, that is magnetized and balanced, swings in a plane parallel to the horizon. The needle generally pivots on a jeweled bearing to reduce swinging friction to a minimum. The ends of the needle, sharpened to knifelike edges, pass near ruled degree markings. At present, engineers use the surveyor's compass only in surveying land of little value, since this instrument is inferior in precision to the engineer's transit.

A surveyor must allow for the errors of a compass. For example, the balance of the needle on its pivot can be for only one zone of magnetic dip. Lines of magnetic force come up out of the earth as well as from the magnetic poles. Therefore, a free-moving needle will dip as well as swing. The lines of magnetic force from the earth are not constant in direction. They vary from day to day and from hour to hour. Sunspots may cause this variation. The magnetic quality of nearby rocks

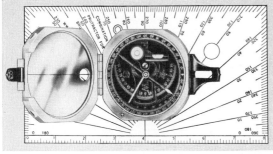

Charles Bruning Co.

A Surveyor's Compass has a mirror on the inside lid which makes it possible to read the compass face while sighting objects.

also will affect the compass needle.   B. AUSTIN BARRY

See also COMPASS.

SURVEYOR'S MEASURE. See WEIGHTS AND MEASURES (Length and Distance; Surface or Area).

SURVIVAL OF THE FITTEST. See NATURAL SELECTION.

SUSA, *SOO zuh*, or SHUSH, was once the capital of the ancient Kingdom of Elam and the Persian Empire. The partly uncovered ruins of this city lie in the province of Khuzistan, in southwestern Iran. Susa appears several times in the Bible, where it is called *Shushan*. The Old Testament story of Esther took place in Susa. The tomb of Daniel is said to be in Susa. Archaeologists found the famous *Code of Hammurabi*, a collection of Babylonian laws, in the ruins of Susa in 1901. Susa flourished until about 640 B.C., when the Assyrians plundered it. Darius I built palaces in the city in the early 500's B.C., and made it one of the capitals of the Persian Empire. Susa declined after Alexander the Great conquered it in the late 300's B.C.   RICHARD NELSON FRYE

See also ESTHER; DANIEL; HAMMURABI.

SUSLOV, *SUS loff*, MIKHAIL ANDREYEVICH (1902-1982), was a leading Russian Communist Party official. He became a member of the party's Central Committee in 1947 and was appointed to the Politburo, the most powerful policymaking body of the party, in 1955. Suslov served as Russian political director in Lithuania from 1944 to 1946. In 1949 and 1950, he was editor of the party's newspaper, *Pravda* (Truth). He was born in Skakhovskoe, Russia.   WALTER C. CLEMENS, JR.

SUSPENDED ANIMATION describes a condition in which the vital functions of the body are stopped for brief periods. Suspended animation occurs in drowning. Rescuers find that the drowned person's breathing has stopped. They cannot feel a pulse nor hear a heartbeat. The person will die unless the rescuers start artificial respiration (see ARTIFICIAL RESPIRATION).

Suspended animation also describes conditions in which a person cannot move and seems to be in a death-like trance. This occurs in some types of mental illness and is called catalepsy (see CATALEPSY). Fakirs can produce this condition in themselves (see FAKIR).

See also CRYOBIOLOGY; TRANCE.

SUSPENSION is a mixture in which the particles of a substance separate from a liquid or gas slowly. Each of the particles consists of many atoms or molecules, and so suspension can be visually recognized as a mixture of two different substances.

There are several types of suspensions. They include (1) a solid in a gas, such as dust and smoke; (2) a liquid in a gas, such as fog and aerosols; (3) a solid in a liquid, such as muddy or soapy water; (4) a gas in a liquid, such as foam; and (5) a liquid in a liquid, such as latex or water-based paints. A suspension that contains extremely small particles is called a *colloid*. The particles in many colloids can only be seen with the aid of a microscope. Homogenized milk with its tiny particles of suspended fat is a common colloid. See COLLOID.

The molecules of a liquid or gas in a suspension move rapidly and collide with the suspended particles. The buffeting effect of these collisions is important in resisting the natural tendency of the particles to settle because of gravity. The rapid, random motion of the suspended particles that results from the collisions is called *Brownian motion*.

A suspension has certain other basic properties. These properties distinguish it from another type of mixture called a *solution*. When a beam of light is shone through a colloidal suspension, such as smoke or dust-filled air, its path becomes clearly visible. This phenomenon, called the *Tyndall effect*, occurs because the suspended particles reflect and scatter light. A solution shows no such effect because its particles are too small to scatter light. Also, a suspension can be separated into its component parts by filtration, but a solution cannot. The size of the particles is again the determining factor. J. D. CORBETT

See also SOLUTION.

SUSPENSION BRIDGE. See BRIDGE.

SUSQUEHANNA RIVER, *SUHS kwuh HAN uh*, is a swift but shallow waterway flowing through one of the most important industrial regions in the eastern United States. The river rises at Otsego Lake in central New York state. It flows southward across Pennsylvania into Maryland, where it empties into Chesapeake Bay at Havre de Grace. For location, see PENNSYLVANIA (physical map). The river is 444 miles (715 kilometers) long. The river's swift current, rock obstructions, and shallow bed discourage shipping. But the Susquehanna has the greatest water-power potential of the rivers in the northeastern United States. E. WILLARD MILLER

SUSSEX, *SUHS ihks*, New Brunswick (pop. 3,972), is the center of a rich farming district about halfway between Saint John and Moncton in Canada (see NEW BRUNSWICK [political map]). Gently sloping hills, fertile valleys, and many small streams make the Sussex region excellent for cattle grazing. Sussex is known for its milk, butter, and soft drinks. The most important small industries in the region are lumbering and the manufacture of ice cream. Once known as Sussex Vale, it was founded by United Empire Loyalists in 1783. Sussex has a mayor-council form of government. W. S. MACNUTT

SUSSEX SPANIEL, *SUHS ihks*, originated in England, and gets its name from the county of Sussex, in southern

WORLD BOOK photo by C. F. Williams
The Sussex Spaniel

England. It is a strong, stocky dog with short legs. The Sussex weighs from 35 to 45 pounds (16 to 20 kilograms). The coat of the Sussex is usually a golden liver color. The Sussex has never been a popular dog in the United States. MAXWELL RIDDLE

SUTHERLAND, GEORGE (1862-1942), served as an associate justice of the Supreme Court of the United States from 1922 to 1938. During the dispute over the validity of New Deal legislation, he voted regularly to hold the measures unconstitutional. In the famous "Scottsboro" case of 1932, his opinion advanced the constitutional rights of persons accused of crime. Sutherland served as a Republican congressman from Utah, and as a United States senator. He was born in Buckinghamshire, England. JERRE S. WILLIAMS

SUTHERLAND, DAME JOAN (1926-   ), an Australian operatic soprano, won acclaim for her brilliant vocal technique. Her voice has a depth and richness not usually associated with the ornate style of her operatic roles. She ranks among the greatest singers of her time for her range, flexibility, and ease of singing in rapid passages of pinpoint precision. She enjoyed great success in London and New York City. Italian opera audiences nicknamed her "La Stupenda," *the stupendous one*.

Joan Sutherland was born in Sydney, and received her early training

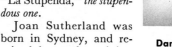

Wide World
Dame Joan Sutherland

there. She moved to London in 1951 and made her operatic debut at the Covent Garden Opera in *Lucia di Lammermoor* in 1959. She first appeared in the United States in 1961. She was made Dame Commander in the Order of the British Empire in 1979. MAX DE SCHAUENSEE

SUTHERLAND FALLS is the fifth highest mountain waterfall in the world. It lies 16 miles (26 kilometers) from the head of Milford Sound, in the Southern Alps of South Island, New Zealand. Its waters plunge down a mountainside in three leaps from a height of 1,904 feet (580 meters). The first leap is 815 feet (248 meters); the second, 751 feet (229 meters); and the third, 338 feet (103 meters). Water from melting glaciers forms the falls. The waters eventually flow into Milford Sound. See also WATERFALL (picture chart). JOHN BELL CONDLIFFE

SUTLEJ RIVER, *SUHT lehj*, is the most easterly of the five waterways of Punjab Province, Pakistan. It ranks as the largest branch of the Indus, the chief river of Pakistan. The Sutlej rises in the plateau of Tibet, nearly 3 miles (5 kilometers) above sea level. The river winds through the Himalaya mountains and crosses northwestern India. Then it flows southwest through Pakistan's Punjab Province. It joins the Indus in the east-central part of Pakistan. The Sutlej is about 950 miles (1,530 kilometers) long. It is a major source of water for the dry Punjab plains. One of the world's highest dams, the Bhakra Dam, rises 740 feet (226 meters) above the river near Bhakra, India. For the location of the river, see PAKISTAN (physical map). J. E. SPENCER

SUTTEE, *suh TEE*, is a Hindu custom once practiced in India. Its name comes from the Sanskrit word *sati*, which means *faithful wife*. By the custom of suttee, a widow allows herself to be burned to death beside her husband's body on the funeral pyre. The pyre is a pile of material that burns easily. No one knows how the custom began. An ancient book states that a widow should lie by her husband's body on the pyre. A few widows, especially wives of kings, refused to leave the pyre and burned to death. In 1829, the British rulers of India made suttee illegal.   WILFRID D. HAMBLY

SUTTER, JOHN AUGUSTUS. See CALIFORNIA (The Gold Rush); SACRAMENTO.

SUTURE, *SOO chuhr*, is the line formed where bones are joined in an immovable joint, as in the skull. It is also the sewing-up of an *incision* (opening) in surgery. Doctors call the material used for sewing an incision a suture, too. This material is made of catgut, fine silk, linen, wire, or nylon. See also LIGATURE.

SUVA, *SOO vah* (pop. 64,000), is the capital and largest city of Fiji, a country made up of more than 800 islands in the South Pacific Ocean. The city lies on the southeastern coast of Viti Levu, Fiji's largest island. For location, see FIJI (map). Suva is Fiji's chief seaport and commercial center. Ships stop at the city to load *copra* (dried coconut meat) and tropical fruit. Many tourist ships also stop there. Factories in Suva make coconut oil and soap. The city's Fiji Museum stands inside the Botanical Gardens. The University of the South Pacific is also in Suva. See also FIJI (picture).   STUART INDER

SUWANNEE RIVER, *suh WAHN ee*, winds for about 190 miles (306 kilometers) through southern Georgia and northern Florida and empties into the Gulf of Mexico. Stephen Foster, who called the river *Swanee*, made it famous with his song, "Old Folks at Home."

The river rises south of Waycross, Ga. It helps drain the Okefenokee Swamp, and flows in a winding course past many small communities. Only very small boats can navigate the Suwannee. In northern Florida, the river forms parts of the boundaries of eight counties. It reaches the Gulf of Mexico at Suwannee Sound, where Hog Island divides the river into two distributaries (see FLORIDA [physical map]).   JOHN H. GARLAND

SUZERAIN, *SOO zuh rayn*, was a feudal lord in medieval times. Today, the term refers to a state which has political control, or *suzerainty*, over another state.

SUZUKI METHOD, *suh ZOO kee*, is a way of teaching children how to play certain musical instruments at a very early age. It is most widely used with the violin but is also applied to such instruments as the cello, flute, and piano. Shinichi Suzuki, a Japanese violinist, developed the method in the 1940's.

The Suzuki method is based on an educational philosophy known as *Talent Education*. According to this philosophy, most children are born with the potential to play a musical instrument, just as they are born with the potential to learn language. Youngsters learn to speak by imitating the speech of their parents and others, and they acquire a large vocabulary before they begin to learn to read. Similarly, Suzuki students listen to recorded music and then learn to play the music on their instruments. The children perform many pieces by heart before they are taught to read music.

The Suzuki teacher instructs the students individually and in groups. Parents play an important role by attending lessons with their child and supervising practice sessions at home. They work closely with the teacher to create an atmosphere that encourages the child to enjoy music.   JOHN D. KENDALL

SVALBARD, *SVAHL bahr*, is a group of islands in the Arctic Ocean, about midway between Norway and the North Pole. The islands belong to Norway, and Svalbard is their Norwegian name. They are sometimes called by their German name, Spitsbergen. Svalbard has five large islands and many smaller ones. The main islands, in order of size, are Spitsbergen, North East Land, Edge Island, Barents Island, and Prince Charles Foreland. Svalbard covers 23,958 square miles (62,050 square kilometers). It is about 700 miles (1,100 kilometers) from the North Pole (see ARCTIC OCEAN [map]; NORWAY [map]). Svalbard has a population of about 3,600. Mining companies, radio and weather stations, and a scientific research station provide jobs. Tourists visit to see Arctic animal and plant life. Svalbard has been the base for many Arctic explorations.

Norse Vikings probably visited the islands. Early Norwegian stories mention Svalbard. In the Middle Ages, the Norwegian kings claimed Svalbard. A Dutch expedition under Willem Barents rediscovered the islands in 1596 (see BARENTS, WILLEM). Henry Hudson saw them in 1607. No one settled on the islands until after the Norwegians began mining coal there in the 1890's. In 1920, other countries formally recognized Norway's claim to the islands.   OSCAR SVARLIEN

SVEDBERG, *SVEHD bar yuh*, **THEODOR,** *TAY oh DAWR* (1884-1971), a Swedish chemist, became famous for developing the ultracentrifuge. This apparatus can spin materials so fast that they have 500,000 times the force of gravity acting upon them. The ultracentrifuge made it possible to determine the molecular weights of proteins and aided the study of the colloidal state. Svedberg is also known for preparing colloidal solutions of metals using an electric arc. He received the 1926 Nobel Prize in chemistry. Svedberg was born in Valbo, near Gävle, Sweden.   K. L. KAUFMAN

SVERDLOVSK, *svehrd LAWFSK* (pop. 1,211,000), is a trading and manufacturing center in the Ural Mountains of Russia. The city is located on the eastern slope of the Ural Mountains, about 1,200 miles (1,930 kilometers) northeast of Moscow (see RUSSIA [political map]). Sverdlovsk is a railroad center and the largest city in the Urals. It has a machine-building industry.

After the Russian Revolution, Czar Nicholas II and his family were reported to have been murdered by the Bolsheviks on July 16, 1918, at Sverdlovsk. The city was then called *Ekaterinburg*.   THEODORE SHABAD

SWAHILI, *swah HEE lee*, are an African people of mixed Bantu and Arab ancestry. The Swahili live along the east coast of Africa, from Somalia to Mozambique. The word *Swahili* means *coast people*. The Swahili language is used throughout East Africa for business and communication among various tribes. It serves as the official language of Kenya and Tanzania. All the Swahili are Muslims.

Historians believe that Arab traders began to settle in East African coastal villages about the time of Christ. The native and Arab cultures gradually mixed and developed into the Swahili civilization. From about 1200 to 1500, many Swahili city-states became thriving commercial centers. They included Kilwa, Lamu, Malindi,

SWAINS ISLAND

Mombasa, and Zanzibar. The Swahili traded gold, ivory, and slaves from the African interior for goods from China, India, and Persia.

During the 1500's and 1600's, the Portuguese looted many Swahili cities and seriously damaged the Swahili trade. Omani Arabs later replaced the Portuguese as rulers of the Swahili. JOHN MIDDLETON

SWAINS ISLAND. See AMERICAN SAMOA.

SWALLOW is a small, graceful bird. It has long, powerful wings, and small, weak feet suited only for perching. It has a large mouth adapted to catching flying insects, which make up nearly all its food. It eats many mosquitoes.

Swallows are found in all parts of the world. Most of them fly long distances to avoid cold or to find a food supply. So far as is known, they *migrate* (travel) by day. They fly together in large numbers, and spend the nights in woods or marshes. Some swallows nest in pairs, and some in colonies. Some make their homes in holes in banks or trees. Others build rough nests of clay or mud on beams of bridges, on rafters in barns, or under the eaves. Several kinds have changed their nesting habits through their contact with human beings.

Female swallows lay 3 to 9 eggs which are pure white, or white spotted with brown. Swallows twitter rather than sing. Some species of swallow have distinctive forked tails, which are called "swallowtails."

The swallows of North America include the *barn swallow*. The barn swallow has a steel-blue back, chestnut-colored breast, and deeply forked tail. Some of these swallows travel as much as 10,000 miles (16,000 kilometers) in yearly migrations. The *cliff swallow* has a square tail and a light-brown patch on its rump. The *tree swallow* often nests in birdhouses. The *bank swallow*, or *sand martin*, is the smallest of the family. The *purple martin* also is a member of the swallow family.

Scientific Classification. The swallows belong to the swallow family, *Hirundinidae*. The barn swallow is genus *Hirundo*, species *H. rustica;* the cliff swallow, *Petrochelidon pyrrhonota;* the tree swallow, *Iridoprocne bicolor;* the bank swallow, *Riparia riparia*. ARTHUR A. ALLEN

See also BIRD (picture: Kinds of Bird Nests). MARTIN; SAN JUAN CAPISTRANO.

SWALLOWING is the process of taking food and saliva from the mouth to the stomach through a tube called the *esophagus* (see ESOPHAGUS). A mucous membrane lines the esophagus so that food can slide down without sticking to the sides. After food has been chewed, it is swallowed. The muscles of the walls of the esophagus perform the swallowing process. These muscles *contract* (shorten). The muscles wave or ripple, normally in a downward direction toward the stomach. This movement is called *peristalsis*. When the muscles in the esophagus cause abnormal wavelike movements upward toward the mouth, vomiting may take place. When the food reaches the lower end of the esophagus, a ringlike muscle opens and allows the food to pass into the stomach.

The presence of certain diseases, or of nervousness, such as stage fright, may cause difficulty in swallowing. Growths, such as tumors or cancers on the esophagus, may also cause the difficulty. In these cases, the esoph-

Tree Swallow
Iridoprocne bicolor
Found throughout North and Central America
Body length: 5 to 6¼ inches (13 to 16 centimeters)

Barn Swallow
Hirundo rustica
Found throughout North and South America, Africa, Asia, and Europe
Body length: 5¾ to 7¾ inches (15 to 20 centimeters)

Bank Swallow
Riparia riparia
Found in North and South America, Africa, Asia, and Europe
Body length: 4½ to 5½ inches (11 to 14 centimeters)

Cliff Swallow
Petrochelidon pyrrhonota
Found throughout most of North and South America
Body length: 5 to 6 inches (13 to 15 centimeters)

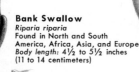

WORLD BOOK illustrations by Albert Earl Gilbert

agus may close. Then food is prevented from entering the stomach.   WILLIAM C. BEAVER

See also ALIMENTARY CANAL.

SWAMMERDAM, *SWAHM ur dahm,* **JAN** (1637-1680), was a Dutch anatomist and zoologist. He pioneered in the study of minute anatomy, especially the anatomy of insects. His observations on the life histories of bees and mayflies are classics, and his work in classifying formed the basis of entomology, the study of insects. He also made important early observations on the physiology of nerves and muscles.

Swammerdam was born in Amsterdam. He studied medicine, and soon began his anatomical studies. Much of his most important work was not published until more than 50 years after his death. But his *Historia Insectorum,* a study of the metamorphoses of insects, the effects on animals of the deprivation of blood, and similar subjects was published in 1669. *Bijbel der Nature,* a report on his observations of red blood corpuscles in animals, was published in 1737.   ROGERS McVAUGH

SWAMP is an area of wet, muddy land covered by trees and shrubs. Swamps occur throughout the world in lowland regions, coastal areas, and near slowly flowing rivers. They differ from marshes, where the plant life consists mostly of grasses.

A wide variety of plants and animals live in swamps. The moist soil supports trees, shrubs, vines, and other plant life. Ponds and streams in swamps provide a home for fish, frogs, and such reptiles as alligators, crocodiles, snakes, and turtles. Many kinds of birds and insects live in swamps, as do such mammals as bears, deer, and rabbits.

There are three major kinds of swamps. *Deepwater swamps* and *shallow-water swamps* have fresh water, and *mangrove swamps* have salt water.

Deepwater swamps lie near rivers that flood in certain seasons. The long wet periods encourage the growth of such tall trees as bald cypresses, elms, oaks, and tupelos. Shorter trees in these swamps include hollies, red maples, and sycamores. Few plants grow on the ground because the thick treetops block out sunlight. Poison ivy and other woody vines climb the tree trunks, and Spanish moss hangs from the branches.

Shallow-water swamps are found mainly in areas where the soil stays extremely moist throughout most of the year. These swamps are covered by shrubs and short trees, including alders, buttonbushes, and willows. Water lilies and other water plants grow in low areas that are always filled with water. Higher areas, called *hummocks,* remain damp but not flooded. Trees, ferns, shrubs, vines, and wildflowers grow there. Algae, lichens, and mosses cover many of the tree trunks.

Mangrove swamps lie along tropical seacoasts. They are named for the mangrove trees that grow there. Pelicans, snails, and various sea animals live in such swamps.

The best-known swamps in the United States are the Dismal Swamp in North Carolina and Virginia, the Everglades in Florida, and the Okefenokee Swamp in Georgia and Florida. Conservationists work to keep many swamps from being drained for use as farmland or as commercial or residential areas.   GEORGE K. REID

See also DISMAL SWAMP; EVERGLADES; MARSH; OKEFENOKEE SWAMP; PONTINE MARSHES.

SWAMP FOX. See MARION, FRANCIS.

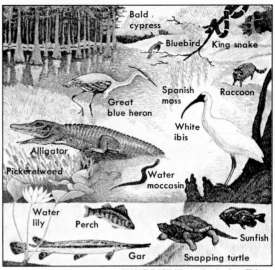

WORLD BOOK illustration by Jean Helmer

Life in a Swamp includes a variety of plants and animals. Trees, shrubs, and other plants thrive in the muddy soil. Many kinds of birds, reptiles, fish, and other animals also inhabit swamps.

SWAMP HICKORY. See BITTERNUT.

SWAMP ROSE MALLOW. See HIBISCUS.

SWAN is a stately water bird closely related to geese and ducks. The swan has snowy white feathers and a long graceful neck. Many poets and composers have written about the swan, and it often appears in legends, as in Richard Wagner's opera, *Lohengrin.* Fairy tales sometimes feature the swan, as in Hans Christian Andersen's "The Wild Swans."

The swan group consists of seven *species* (kinds)

Kenneth W. Fink, NAS

The Whistling Swan is a graceful swimmer. Every fall, flocks of these birds migrate from the Arctic Ocean to coastal bays of the United States, where they spend the winter.

SWAN

that live in various parts of the world. They fly in V-shaped flocks, and utter loud, trumpetlike notes while flying. Swans feed on worms, shellfish, and the seeds and roots of water plants. The birds dip their long, curving necks far into the water in search of food.

The *whistling swan* nests around the Arctic Ocean and the Hudson Bay region. It has decreased sharply in number. In winter, it flies as far south as the Carolinas. Between October and April, flocks of whistling swans fly southward. Observers report they can fly at speeds of 40 to 50 mph (64 to 80 kph). As they fly, the swans fill the air with a wide range of whistling sounds. Whistling swans make their nests out of water plants and line them with down from their bodies. Their nests sometimes stand 2 feet (61 centimeters) high and measure 6 feet (1.8 meters) across. The female lays five to seven white eggs in June. The young, called *cygnets*, are covered with grayish-brown down at first. They become snow-white by the end of a year. The male swan is called a *cob*, and the female a *pen*.

The whistling swan grows a little less than 5 feet (1.5 meters) long. It is white except for a yellow spot between the nostrils and eyes. The legs, feet, and bill are black. The *trumpeter swan*, which was once almost extinct, resembles the whistling swan. It weighs up to 40 pounds (18 kilograms), making it the heaviest flying bird in North America. Its call sounds clear and shrill. The *black-necked swan* is a waterfowl that lives in South America.

Swans of the Eastern Hemisphere include the *European whistling swan*, the *mute swan*, and *Bewick's swan*, which is a smaller bird. The mute swan, considered a royal bird in England since 1462, can be seen in zoos, parks, and estates there. It is said that this swan never uses its voice in captivity. The *black swan*, marked by a scarlet bill banded with white, lives in Australia.

Scientific Classification. Swans belong to the swan, goose, and duck family, *Anatidae*. The mute swan is genus *Cygnus*, species *C. olor*. The black swan of Australia is *C. atratus*. The whistling swan is *Olor columbianus;* the trumpeter swan is *O. buccinator.*   RODOLPHE MEYER DE SCHAUENSEE

SWANSCOMBE MAN was a type of prehistoric man who lived about 275,000 years ago. The only evidence of his existence is three pieces of a skull. They were

The Swan is one of the largest birds, but it swims and flies gracefully. Its beauty has inspired composers, painters, and writers. Four of the seven species of swans are shown below.

Black-Necked Swan
Cygnus melanocoryphus
Found in South America
Body length: 45 inches
(114 centimeters)

Black Swan
Cygnus atratus
Found in Australia
Body length: 40 inches
(100 centimeters)

Mute Swan
Cygnus olor
Found in temperate Eurasia
Body length: 60 inches
(150 centimeters)

Bewick's Swan
Cygnus bewickii
Found in Eurasian tundra
Body length: 48 inches
(122 centimeters)

WORLD BOOK illustrations by Walter Linsenmaier

found at Swanscombe, near London, in the gravel of the River Thames. The first piece was found in 1935. Swanscombe man lived in forested river valleys that provided deer, elephants, hippopotamuses, and rhinoceroses for hunting.

Another skull, more complete than that of Swanscombe man but of about the same age, had been discovered in 1933 at Steinheim, in southern Germany. Most scientists believe the Swanscombe and Steinheim fossils represent early forms of modern human beings—*Homo sapiens* (wise human being). The Swanscombe and Steinheim discoveries suggest that early forms of *Homo sapiens* had replaced Heidelberg man in Europe by about 275,000 years ago, earlier than scientists once thought. Heidelberg man belonged to an earlier species, *Homo erectus* (erect human being). The Swanscombe and Steinheim skulls weigh less, and the brain case is larger, than those of Heidelberg man.   KARL W. BUTZER

SWANSEA, *SWAHN see* (pop. 183,484), is the second largest city in Wales. Only Cardiff has a larger population. Swansea lies about 45 miles (72 kilometers) west of Cardiff, on Swansea Bay. For location, see GREAT BRITAIN (political map).

The city was founded in the 1000's. It became important in the 1800's, after the development of the hard-coal trade and the smelting industry. The use of tin cans for preserving fruits and vegetables brought prosperity to the city. Swansea became the chief British center for the shipping of tin plate. It was once called the "tin plate center of the world." Other industries in Swansea include the refining of nickel, zinc, and petroleum. The city has modern docks which cover 281 acres (114 hectares).   DAVID WILLIAMS

SWASTIKA, *SWAHS tuh kuh*, is an ancient symbol often used as an ornament or a religious sign. The swastika is in the form of a cross with the ends of the arms bent at right angles in a given direction, usually clockwise. The swastika has been found on Byzantine buildings, Buddhist inscriptions, Celtic monuments,

Swastika

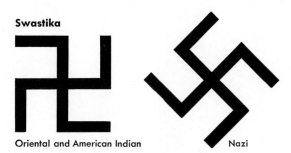

Oriental and American Indian   Nazi

and Greek coins.

Swastikas were widely used symbols among the Indians of North America and South America. The clockwise swastika was adopted in 1920 as the symbol of the National Socialist Party of Germany. As such it came to be one of the most hated symbols in the history of humanity. It came to stand for all the evil associated with the Nazis as they gained control of Europe before and during World War II. After the Allies defeated Germany in 1945, they banned the display of the swastika emblem.   JOSEPH WARD SWAIN

Swaziland

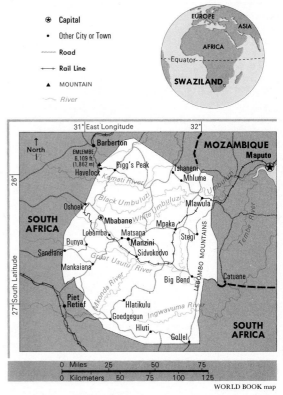

WORLD BOOK map

SWAZILAND, *SWAH zee land,* is a beautiful little country in southern Africa. It is surrounded by the Republic of South Africa on three sides and by Mozambique on the east. Swaziland is about as big as Hawaii.

Swaziland has rich mineral deposits, large forests, and good farm and ranch land. But most of the mines, processing plants, and profitable farms are owned by white people called Europeans. Most of the *Swazi* (black Africans) who live there are peasant farmers.

Swaziland was formerly a British protectorate. It became independent in 1968 as the KINGDOM OF SWAZILAND. Mbabane is the administrative capital and largest town (see MBABANE). Lobamba, a village, is called the traditional, or royal, capital.

Government. Swaziland is a monarchy. The *Ngwenyama* (hereditary leader) rules the country as king, with the assistance of a council of ministers and a legislature. The *Ndlovukazi* (queen mother, or mother of the king) is in charge of national rituals. If the king's mother is dead, one of his wives may act as *Ndlovukazi*.

People. About 9 out of 10 persons in Swaziland are black Africans called Swazi. The Swazi are proud, handsome, courteous people. Most of them farm and raise livestock. Some live in towns and work in factories, offices, and shops. They speak *siSwati*, a Bantu language.

Hilda Kuper, the contributor of this article, is the author of An African Aristocracy: Rank Among the Swazi; The Swazi: A South African Kingdom; *and* Sobhuza II, Ngwenyama and King of Swaziland.

SWAZILAND

Swazi farmers prize their cattle and respect people with large herds. They rarely kill cattle for food, but some are sold for cash or sacrificed at religious ceremonies. When a Swazi man marries, his family gives his wife's family cattle to legalize her status as his wife.

Swazi men may have more than one wife. The ideal family includes a man, his wives, his unmarried children, and his married sons and their families. Each family lives in a separate homestead. For hundreds of years, the homesteads consisted of circular huts built around a cattle pen. Today, many Swazi live in Western-style houses. In homesteads with more than one wife, each wife has her own living quarters. She also has a garden plot where she grows beans, corn, gourds, and other crops. The men and boys tend the cattle.

Traditional Swazi clothing is made of animal skins, leather, or brightly colored cloth. Swazi also wear beautiful beaded ornaments.

Each Swazi man belongs to an *age group* organized by the Ngwenyama. All the men in a particular group are about the same age. Different age groups have special parts in Swazi ceremonies. Three out of four adults in Swaziland cannot read and write. But about 110,000 children attend school there.

More than half the Swazi belong to Christian churches. Most of the rest practice traditional African religions.

About 8,000 Europeans and *Eurafricans* (people of mixed descent) also live in Swaziland. The Europeans own farms, mines, and forests. Many Eurafricans work for Europeans. Others are farmers and craftworkers.

Land. Mountains up to 4,500 feet (1,370 meters) above sea level rise along Swaziland's western border. Vast pine forests cover much of the land there. Temperatures average 60° F. (16° C), and from 45 to 75 inches (114 to 191 centimeters) of rain falls each year. Rolling, grassy midlands lie east of the mountains. More people live in this region than in any other part of the country. Temperatures average 66° F. (19° C) and from 30 to 45 inches (76 to 114 centimeters) of rain falls there each year. Farther east, the land levels off into a low plain covered with bushes and grass. Temperatures average 72° F. (22° C) and only about 20 inches (51 centimeters) of rain falls per year. The high, narrow Lebombo Mountains rise along the eastern border.

Swaziland is one of the best-watered areas in southern Africa. Four main rivers flow eastward across the country. They are the Ingwavuma, Komati, Umbuluzi, and Great Usutu. The rivers supply the water needed to irrigate crops and to run hydroelectric power plants.

Economy. Rich agricultural and mineral resources have enabled Swaziland to develop a varied economy.

Facts in Brief

Capitals: Mbabane (administrative) and Lobamba (traditional).

Official Languages: English and siSwati.

Form of Government: Monarchy.

Area: 6,704 sq. mi. (17,363 km²). *Greatest Distances*—north-south, 120 mi. (193 km); east-west, 90 mi. (140 km).

Elevation: *Highest*—Mount Emlembe, 6,109 ft. (1,862 m) above sea level. *Lowest*—70 ft. (21 m) above sea level.

Population: *Estimated 1984 Population*—618,000; distribution, 90 per cent rural, 10 per cent urban; density, 93 persons per sq. mi. (36 persons per km²). *1976 Census*—494,534. *Estimated 1989 Population*—717,000.

Chief Products: *Agriculture*—corn, sugar cane, cotton, rice, tobacco, citrus fruits, hides and skins. *Manufacturing*—cement, fertilizer, food products, wood products. *Mining*—asbestos, iron ore.

Flag: Five horizontal stripes. The top and bottom stripes are blue (for peace). The wide center stripe is red (for past battles) with a black and white shield, spears, and staff. Between the blue and red stripes are yellow stripes (for natural resources). See FLAG (color picture: Flags of Africa).

Money: *Basic Unit*—lilangeni (plural spelled emalageni).

David Goldblatt, Pix from Publix

The People of Swaziland wear both traditional and European clothing. These Swazis are lined up to vote in Manzini, a leading commercial center.

Swaziland is one of the few African countries that exports more goods than it imports.

Europeans own nearly half the land in Swaziland. They raise most of the cash crops, including citrus fruits, cotton, pineapples, rice, sugar cane, and tobacco. They also raise cattle for meat, skins, and hides. Most of the Swazi graze cattle and grow just enough food for their families. But since the late 1960's, an increasing number of Swazi have begun to raise cash crops.

Since the 1940's, Europeans have planted barren mountainous land in Swaziland with pine and eucalyptus trees. Today, the area has one of the largest artificially created forests in Africa. European-owned mills process wood pulp and other forest products there.

Rich mineral deposits lie in the mountains, and about half the nation's income comes from the European-owned mining industry. Asbestos and iron ore are leading exports. Swaziland also has deposits of coal, gold, tin, *barite* (ore used in making barium), and *kaolin* (clay used in making pottery). About 6,000 Swazi work in the gold mines of South Africa.

Since the late 1960's, a number of small manufacturing firms have developed in Swaziland. They produce cement, fertilizer, food products, and other goods.

Swaziland has about 1,000 miles (1,600 kilometers) of tar or gravel roads. Winding footpaths run between most homesteads. A railroad connects Mbabane with the port at Maputo, capital of Mozambique. Air service links Mbabane with South Africa and Maputo.

History. According to the legends of the Swazi, their ancestors once lived near what is now Maputo. In the late 1700's the Swazi chief Ngwane II led a small band of people over the mountains to what is now southeastern Swaziland. There the Swazi found other African peoples. Ngwane II and the chiefs who ruled after him united several of these peoples with the Swazi.

British traders and *Boers* (Dutch farmers from South Africa) first came to Swaziland in the 1830's. In the 1880's, the settlers discovered gold. Hundreds of prospectors rushed into the region. They asked the Swazi chief and his advisers to sign documents granting them rights to mine minerals and to use land for farming and grazing. The Swazi could not read and did not realize that they were giving up control of the land.

In 1894, the British and Boers agreed that the South African Boer Republic would govern Swaziland. But in 1902, the Boers lost a war with the British, and Great Britain took control of Swaziland. Great Britain ruled Swaziland until the 1960's. In 1967, Swaziland gained control over its internal matters. It received full independence on Sept. 6, 1968. On Sept. 24, 1968, Swaziland became a member of the United Nations.

In 1968, Britain developed a constitution for Swaziland. The constitution established Swaziland as a constitutional monarchy, headed by King Sobhuza II. Many Swazi opposed it because they felt it disregarded Swazi interests and traditions. In 1973, King Sobhuza —at the request of other Swazi leaders—abolished the constitution and suspended the country's legislature. The king began to rule the country with the assistance of a council of ministers. King Sobhuza appointed a commission to produce a new constitution more in keeping with Swazi interests and traditions. A new legislature was established as part of Swaziland's government in 1979. King Sobhuza died in 1982 after a reign of 82 years. One of his wives became acting head of the Swazi government until a new monarch could be selected. HILDA KUPER

SWEAT. See PERSPIRATION.

SWEAT GLAND. See GLAND; PERSPIRATION.

SWEATSHOP. The word *sweatshop* suggests a place of grinding toil. It is a term for makeshift factories where poverty-stricken people—mostly women and children—work at top speed for 12 or more hours a day in an effort to earn a living wage.

The sweatshop, often called the *sweating system*, began when the factory system developed in the early 1800's. Often, factory buildings were not large enough to house all the workers. So factory owners sublet contracts for part of the work. The other manufacturers then set up makeshift factories in dimly lighted and poorly ventilated buildings. They hired workers for low wages and long hours on a piecework basis.

As early as 1830, Americans began to object to sweatshops. But the problem did not become serious until after 1880, when large numbers of immigrants began to come to America. The owners of sweatshops took advantage of the immigrants' ignorance and poverty to get them to work for low wages. The cigar-making and clothing and needlework industries, and some of the mechanical industries, used the sweating system.

In the 1900's, states began to pass laws prohibiting workers from carrying on work outside the factory in industries where sweatshops were most common. They also passed minimum wage laws which made it impractical for factories to sublet work. Laws limiting the number of hours women could work and abolishing child labor were heavy blows to the sweatshop system. Another factor which hastened its decline was the increased interest which women showed in metalworking and other trades where they could not take work outside the factory. Today, there are few sweatshops left in the world. In most countries, such practices have been made illegal. ROBERT D. PATTON

See also CHILD LABOR; WAGES AND HOURS.

Sweatshops employed people for very low pay. Workers put in long hours in makeshift factories under miserable conditions.

Brown Bros.

WORLD BOOK photo by Tore Johnson

The Rugged Wilderness of northern Sweden has long, cold winters and is thinly populated. Most of the people are lumberjacks or miners.

SWEDEN

SWEDEN is a prosperous industrial nation in northern Europe. The Swedes have developed great industries based on their country's three chief natural resources—timber, iron ore, and water power.

The Swedish standard of living is one of the highest in the world. Sweden ranks among the leading European nations in the number of automobiles, telephones, and television sets it has in relation to its population. Another measure of the nation's prosperity is that Swedes spend more money per person on vacations than any other people in Europe. About 350,000 Swedish families, or about a fifth of the nation's families, have country homes where they can enjoy spending weekends and vacations.

Sweden's way of life has often been called the "middle way," because it combines private enterprise with a government that greatly influences the development of the economy. The Swedish government operates one of the most far-reaching social security systems in the world. The government provides free education and largely free medical service. It pays pensions to old people, widows, and orphans. After most Swedes retire, they receive annual pensions of about 60 per cent of their average earnings during their 15 highest paid years. The government also provides health insurance and financial aid for housing.

Sweden is the fourth largest country in Europe, after Russia, France, and Spain. Sweden is a little larger than California, but it is thinly populated and has about one-third as many people as that state. Forests cover more than half of Sweden, and only about a tenth of the country is farmland. Sweden is also a land of beautiful lakes, snow-capped mountains, swift rivers, and rocky offshore islands.

Stockholm, Sweden's capital and largest city, stands on the coast of the Baltic Sea and includes small offshore islands. Almost a sixth of the people of Sweden live in Stockholm or its suburbs.

The northern seventh of Sweden lies inside the Arctic Circle in a region called the *Land of the Midnight Sun.*

The contributors of this article are Torsten Henriksson, former First Secretary of the Swedish Institute in Stockholm; Johan Henrik Norrbin, a Stockholm biology and geography teacher; István Vukovich, Head of the Rural Development Section of the Swedish International Development Authority; and Carl-Christian Wallén, former Deputy Director, Swedish Meteorological and Hydrological Institute.

Sandy Seaside Beaches help make Falsterbo, on the southwestern tip of Sweden, a popular vacation area.

Downtown Stockholm has a modern business area. Automobiles, not permitted on the street level, are parked underground.

There, for periods in summer, the sun shines 24 hours a day. Above the Arctic Circle is part of a wilderness called Lapland. It extends into Finland, Norway, and Russia. For centuries, people called Lapps have led a wandering life with their herds of reindeer.

Sweden, together with Denmark and Norway, is one of the Scandinavian countries. Swedes, Danes, and Norwegians speak similar languages and can usually understand each other. The three Scandinavian nations have close economic and cultural ties.

Facts in Brief

Capital: Stockholm.

Official Language: Swedish.

Official Name: *Konungariket Sverige* (Kingdom of Sweden).

Form of Government: Constitutional monarchy. *Head of State*—King or Queen. *Head of Government*—Prime minister (appointed by the speaker of the parliament). *Parliament* (Riksdag)—349 members (3-year terms). *Political Divisions*—24 counties.

Area: 173,732 sq. mi. (449,964 km²). *Greatest Distances*—north-south, 977 mi. (1,572 km); east-west, 310 mi. (499 km). *Coastline*—4,700 mi. (7,564 km).

Elevation: *Highest*—Mount Kebnekaise, 6,926 ft. (2,111 m) above sea level. *Lowest*—sea level along the coast.

Population: *Estimated 1984 Population*—8,376,000; distribution, 89 per cent urban, 11 per cent rural; density, 49 persons per sq. mi. (19 persons per km²). *1975 Census*—8,208,544. *Estimated 1989 Population*—8,461,000.

Chief Products: *Agriculture*—barley, livestock (cattle, hogs), milk and other dairy products, oats, potatoes, rye, sugar beets, wheat. *Fishing*—cod, herring, mackerel, salmon. *Forestry*—fir, pine, spruce. *Manufacturing*—agricultural machinery, aircraft, automobiles, ball bearings, diesel motors, electrical equipment, explosives, fertilizers, furniture, glass, matches, paper and cardboard, plastics, plywood, precision tools, prefabricated houses, ships, steel, steelware, telephones, textiles, woodpulp. *Mining*—copper, gold, iron ore, lead, uranium, zinc.

National Anthem: "Du gamla, du fria" ("Thou Ancient, Thou Free-Born").

National Holiday: Flag Day, June 6.

Money: *Basic Unit*—krona. One hundred öre equal one krona. For the value of the krona in dollars, see MONEY (table: Exchange Rates). See also KRONA.

Sweden is a constitutional monarchy with a king, a prime minister and Cabinet, and a parliament. Sweden had the same constitution from 1809 to 1975, when a new constitution went into effect.

The 1809 constitution had given the king most of the executive power of the government. The power of the parliament gradually increased, and parliamentary rule was adopted in 1917. Under the 1975 constitution, the king lost most of his remaining executive powers and became merely a ceremonial figure.

King of Sweden is head of state. He attends the opening of parliament and is required to be present at the meeting at which the former prime minister turns over the government to the new prime minister.

Prime Minister and Cabinet hold the executive power in Sweden. The speaker of the parliament nominates as prime minister the leader of the majority party or group of parties in the parliament. The parliament must then confirm the appointment. The prime minister selects the members of the Cabinet.

Parliament of Sweden is a one-house body called the *Riksdag.* The people elect the Riksdag's 349 members to three-year terms. A political party must win at least 4 per cent of the total vote for its candidates to be elected to the Riksdag. A party may also receive a seat in the Riksdag if it wins at least 12 per cent of the vote in any one election district. The Riksdag has the power to remove the entire Cabinet or an individual Cabinet member from office. The prime minister may then call for new parliamentary elections. All persons 18 years and older may vote.

Ombudsmen. The Riksdag appoints an official called an *ombudsman* to investigate complaints by citizens against government actions or decisions. Sweden created this office in 1809, and was the first country to have an ombudsman. The Riksdag appoints a second ombudsman to investigate complaints against military authorities. This office was created in 1915. See OMBUDSMAN.

Politics. Sweden has a large socialist political party called the Social Democratic Party. This party established the country's welfare system. Sweden has three large nonsocialist parties—the Center Party, the Conservative Party, and the Liberal Party. There is also a small Communist Party.

Sweden's political parties receive funds from the national government. The amount of money each party receives is based on the number of seats the party holds in the Riksdag.

Local Government. Sweden's 24 counties have separate governments. Each county is administered by a governor appointed by the government and a council elected by the people.

Courts. District courts serve the towns and counties of Sweden. Regional courts of appeal hear appeals from the district courts. The Supreme Court, the country's highest court, hears final appeals in important civil and criminal cases.

Armed Forces. Swedish men between 18 and 47 are required to serve at least 10 months in the armed forces. The nation's regular army, navy, and air force have a total of about 65,000 members.

Sven Samelius

Sweden's Parliament Building is constructed partly of glass that reflects nearby structures in downtown Stockholm.

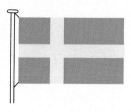

The Swedish Flag, first used in the mid-1400's, was made official in 1663. The colors come from the coat of arms.

Sweden's Coat of Arms features the three small crowns added by King Albert in 1364. It was made official in 1908.

Sweden is nearly 6 per cent as large as the United States, not counting Alaska and Hawaii. The country lies just east of Norway.

WORLD BOOK map

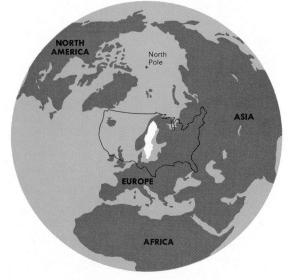

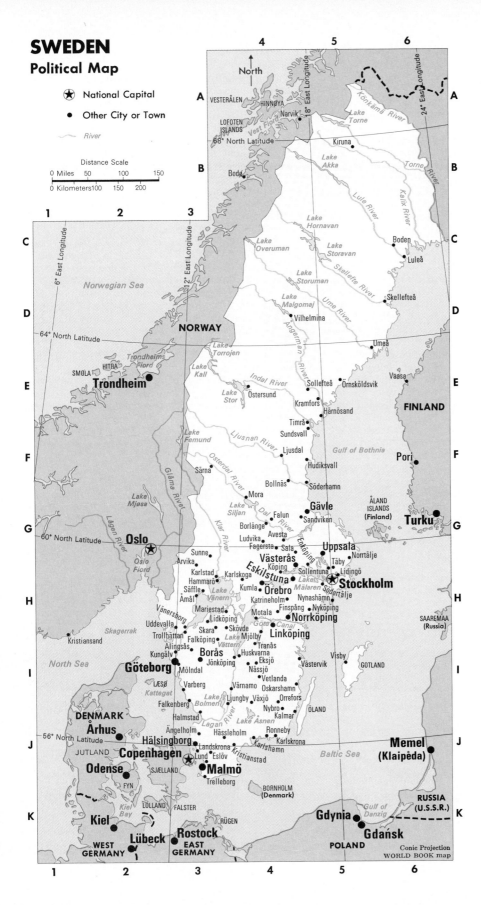

SWEDEN
Political Map

⭐ National Capital

● Other City or Town

〰 River

Distance Scale

0 Miles 50 100 150

0 Kilometers 100 150 200

Cities and Towns†

Ängelholm	.28,804.	J 3
Arvika	....27,277.	H 3
Avesta	...26,904.	G 4
Boden	...28,559.	C 6
Borås	...104,151.	I 3
Borlänge	.45,924.	G 4
Botkyrka*	.73,480.	H 5
Danderyd*	.27,455.	H 5
Enköping	.32,024.	H 5
Eskilstuna	.91,548.	H 4
Eslöv	....26,792.	J 3
Falkenberg	.33,877.	I 3
Falun	...49,150.	G 4
Finspång	.25,070.	H 4
Gällivare*	.25,070.	B 5
Gävle	....87,463.	G 5
Göteborg	.440,082	
	*693,465.	I 3
Gotland*	...54,791.	I 5
Halmstad	.74,990.	I 3
Hälsing-		
borg	...101,105.	J 3
Haninge*	.53,398.	H 5
Härnösand	.27,245.	E 5
Huddinge*	.64,784.	H 5
Hudiksvall	.36,810.	F 5
Järfälla*	.52,227.	H 5
Jönköping	108,568.	I 4
Kalmar	..52,625.	J 4
Karlshamn	.31,981.	J 4
Karlskoga	.37,504.	H 4
Karlskrona	.60,297.	J 4
Karlstad	.72,975.	H 3
Katrine-		
holm	...32,336.	H 4
Kiruna	...30,861.	B 5
Köping	..27,691.	H 4
Kristian-		
stad	...67,922.	J 4
Kristine-		
hamn*	.27,477.	H 4
Kungälv	.28,907.	I 3
Landskrona	37,850.	J 3
Lerum*	..28,982.	I 3
Lidingö	..37,480.	H 5
Lidköping	.34,687.	H 3
Lindesberg*	24,713.	H 4
Linköping	110,779.	H 4
Ljungby	.26,675.	I 3
Ljusdal	..21,767.	F 4
Ludvika	.32,723.	G 4
Luleå	....67,405.	C 6
Lund	....76,970.	J 3
Malmö		
	*453,903.	J 3
Mark*	...30,590.	I 3
Mariestad	.24,706.	H 3
Mjölby	..25,677.	H 4
Mölndal	.47,267.	I 3
Motala	..49,731.	H 4
Nacka*	..55,681.	H 5
Nässjö	..32,412.	I 4
Norrköping	120,647.	H 4
Norrtälje	.39,721.	G 5
Nybro	...21,631.	J 4
Nyköping	.63,327.	H 5
Örebro	...117,036.	H 4
Örnsköds-		
vik	....60,801.	E 5
Orrefors	......919.	I 4
Oskarshamn	28,205.	I 4
Östersund	.55,180.	E 4
Partille*	.26,924.	I 3
Piteå*	..37,210.	D 6
Ronneby	.30,219.	J 4
Sandviken	.43,197.	G 4
Sigtuna*	.27,641.	H 5
Skellefteå	.73,312.	D 6
Skövde	..45,811.	H 3
Söderhamn	31,780.	F 5
Södertälje	.77,829.	H 5
Sollefteå	.26,088.	E 5
Sollentuna	.45,246.	H 5
Solna*	..52,365.	H 5
Stockholm	658,435	
	*1,374,922.	H 5
Strängnäs*	22,828.	H 5
Sundby-		
berg*	..26,041.	H 5
Sundsvall	.94,336.	F 5
Täby*	..44,235.	H 5
Trelleborg	.34,389.	J 3
Tyresö*	.30,870.	H 5
Trollhättan	50,311.	H 3
Uddevalla	.46,483.	H 3
Umeå	....77,458.	E 5
Uppsala	.141,444.	G 5
Vänersborg	34,572.	H 3
Varberg	.43,548.	I 3
Värnamo	.30,075.	I 4
Västerås	.118,141.	H 4
Västervik	.41,437.	I 4
Växjö	...63,045.	I 4
Vetlanda	.28,644.	I 4
Ystad*	..23,789.	J 3

*Does not appear on map; key shows general location.
†Populations of municipalities, which may include rural areas as well as the urban center.
*Population of metropolitan area, including suburbs.
Source: 1977 official estimates.

Conic Projection
WORLD BOOK map

The Swedes are closely related to the Danes and Norwegians. Most Swedes are tall, with fair or brown hair and blue eyes. Since World War II ended in 1945, about 1 million persons from other countries have settled in Sweden.

About nine-tenths of Sweden's people live in cities and towns, mainly in the center and south of the country. About a third of the people live in the three largest cities —Stockholm, Göteborg, and Malmö—and their suburbs. Sweden is one of the most thinly populated countries in Europe, with an average of 49 persons per square mile (19 persons per square kilometer). Only Finland, Iceland, and Norway are less densely populated.

The Lapps, who live in the far north, differ in appearance, language, and way of life from most other Swedes (see LAPLAND). About 10,000 of these short, stocky people live in Sweden. Most Lapps are miners or lumberjacks. About 2,000 of them live as their ancestors did, wandering over the land with their herds of reindeer. About 30,000 Swedes of Finnish origin also live in the north.

Language. Swedish is a Germanic language that resembles Danish and Norwegian. People from all three countries can usually understand each other. Some people of Finnish origin who live in Sweden still speak their own language. The Lapps speak a language related to Finnish. Most Swedes speak some English.

Religion. The Lutheran Church is the state church of Sweden, and about 98 per cent of the people are members. The king must be a member. All Swedes whose parents belong to the Lutheran Church become members automatically at birth. They remain so unless they apply to withdraw. Most Swedes do not attend church regularly, but the churches are full on religious holidays.

Sweden has about 10 other large religious groups, and some of their members belong to the Lutheran Church as well. These groups, in order of size, include the Missionary Union, the Pentecostal Movement, Baptists, and Methodists. Other religious groups in Sweden include Roman Catholics and Jews.

The churches pioneered much welfare work in the country, but the government has taken over most of this work. Swedish churches have a long tradition of missionary activities, particularly the Lutheran Church in India and South Africa.

Food. Sweden is famous for *smörgåsbord*, an assortment of cold and hot foods placed on a large table for self-service. Swedes often eat the foods in a certain order. First they eat cold fish dishes, including anchovies, eels, herring, salmon, sardines, and shrimp. They follow the fish with such cold meats as liver pâté, smoked reindeer, and ham with vegetable salad. Next come small hot dishes, such as meatballs, omelets, sausages, and anchovies or herring cooked in breadcrumbs. Desserts include cheese and fresh fruit, fruit salad, and pastry.

Education. The Swedish government, with the goal of expanding and improving educational services, completely reorganized the nation's school system during the 1960's. Most children receive a free education at schools operated by the government. The government also operates all the universities and most of the technical and other specialized colleges.

Many children under the age of 7 attend kindergartens run by private persons or organizations. The government assists the kindergartens, but attendance is not required.

Children from 7 to 16 must attend a school called

Population

This map shows the population distribution of Sweden. Each of the dots represents 10,000 persons. The three cities shown on the map are the largest in the country.

Distance Scale

| 0 | Miles 100 | 200 | 300 | 400 |

| 0 | Kilometres | 300 | 400 | 500 | 600 |

Stockholm

Göteborg

Malmö   WORLD BOOK map-FHa

Farm Families own about 80 per cent of Sweden's farms, and rent the rest. Most of them live in the southern third of the country. Less than 10 per cent of the labor force are farmers.

WORLD BOOK photo by Nils-Johan Norenlind

a *grundskola*. The grundskola system, which was introduced in 1962, has three three-year divisions. The *junior stage* consists of first grade through third grade, and the *intermediate stage* covers fourth grade through sixth grade. The *senior stage* consists of seventh through ninth grade. In the seventh and eighth grades, students begin to choose their own subjects. In the ninth grade, they select one of nine courses of study. Most pupils continue their general education. Others also learn such practical skills as home economics or workshop methods. Some select special courses in languages, technology, or commerce. Every child in the fourth through seventh grade is required to study English, and about 90 per cent continue English after that.

Following the grundskola, some children go to a secondary school. Since 1966, there have been three kinds of secondary schools. The three-year *upper secondary schools* prepare students to attend a university. The two-year *continuation schools* give courses in social, economic, and technical subjects. The *vocational schools* offer day and evening courses for one to three years in such subjects as industry, handicrafts, and home economics.

Sweden has six universities—in Göteborg, Linköping, Lund, Stockholm, Umeå, and Uppsala. The oldest, the University of Uppsala, was founded in 1477.

Libraries and Museums. Sweden has four general research libraries—the Royal Library in Stockholm and the university libraries in Göteborg, Lund, and Uppsala. The Royal Library, established in the 1600's, has

Vacation Lodges dot much of the Swedish countryside. About 350,000 families own vacation homes. The Swedes spend more money per person on vacations than any other Europeans.

Swedish Schoolchildren visit the public square of the old section of Stockholm. There, in 1520, King Christian II of Denmark executed many Swedes who had rebelled against Danish rule.

Gymnastics are required in Swedish schools. Many adults do these graceful exercises during lunch-hour drills. Music for gymnastics is broadcast daily for housewives.

Swedish Lumberjacks often float logs down rivers to coastal sawmills. About half of Sweden's forests are privately owned, mostly by farmers. Many farmers work part time as lumberjacks.

a large collection of early Swedish manuscripts. Sweden also has about 3,800 public libraries.

Leading museums include the Skansen open-air museum, which exhibits old Swedish houses, and the Nationalmuseum, which has a collection of Swedish sculpture and paintings. Both museums are in Stockholm.

Sports. The Swedes are an athletic people and like outdoor activities. Many spend their vacations by the sea or on the country's offshore islands. Others relax near one of Sweden's many lakes or in the vast wilderness that covers the northern part of the country. Tourists enjoy three-day trips along the Göta Canal, which flows 240 miles (386 kilometers) across southern Sweden. This canal links lakes and rivers, and connects Göteborg with the Baltic Sea.

Cross-country skiing and hockey are the chief winter sports. Every March, thousands of Swedes take part in a ski run called the Vasa Race, held in the province of Dalarna. The run covers 55 miles (89 kilometers). Hunters shoot deer, fox, moose, and various wildfowl. Game fish include pike, salmon, and trout. When the rivers are frozen, people cut holes in the ice and drop their fishing lines through them. The people also like hiking and camping, soccer, swimming, and yachting. Graceful gymnastics called *calisthenics* are popular in Sweden, and are a feature of school training.

Holidays. The main winter festivals in Sweden take place in December. On December 13, the Swedes celebrate St. Lucia Day, the Festival of Light. Before dawn, young girls dress in white with a crown of evergreen leaves. They awaken their families with a traditional song and serve them hot coffee and buns. The main Christmas celebration is on Christmas Eve. Families gather for dinner, which usually includes ham and a fish course. After dinner, everyone receives presents. See CHRISTMAS (picture: On St. Lucia Day).

Midsummer's Eve festivities are held on the Friday between June 19 and 26. The people celebrate the return of summer to Sweden. They stay up most of the night and dance around gaily decorated Maypoles. Flag Day, the national holiday, is June 6. The king presents the national flag to Swedish organizations and societies at a special ceremony.

Social Welfare. The Swedes pay high taxes, but the government provides many welfare benefits. Every family receives an allowance for (1) each child under 16 and (2) each child in a secondary school or university. The government helps newly married couples by providing loans for home furnishings. In some cases of hardship, it pays up to a fourth of a family's rent. The government guarantees every employed person a four-week annual vacation with pay. Some housewives with low incomes receive allowances for vacations with their children.

Swedes who lose their jobs receive unemployment benefits representing a high proportion of their former earnings. The people have largely free medical service. After retirement, most Swedes receive annual pensions of about 60 per cent of their average earnings during their 15 highest paid years. The government also provides pensions for widows, orphans, and children who have lost one parent.

Most Swedish art forms have long been influenced by artistic developments in other parts of Europe. During the 1900's, distinctive Swedish styles have appeared in the fields of architecture and design. Swedish architects and town planners have worked together to create towns and suburbs. These communities have won international fame as models of architectural planning and design.

In 1964, the government set up a system of grants to increase the income of artists who need help. The government also supports three theater schools and a motion-picture school.

The playwright August Strindberg, who wrote *The Father* and *Miss Julie*, was the first Swedish writer to win international fame. The novelist Selma Lagerlöf wrote charming, romantic novels and a classic children's book, *The Wonderful Adventures of Nils*. She was the first Swedish writer to win a Nobel prize.

During the 1600's and 1700's, French painters working in Sweden greatly influenced the development of Swedish painting. Alexander Roslin, who produced brilliant portraits, is the best-known Swedish painter of

The Plays of August Strindberg are performed in most parts of the world. He wrote *Miss Julie*, one of his most famous dramas, in 1888. Strindberg was also a novelist and story writer.
The Royal Dramatic Theater, Stockholm (Swedish Tourist Bureau)

Swedish Motion Pictures are known for their high quality. *The Seventh Seal* and other films directed by Ingmar Bergman are especially outstanding. Bergman writes most of his own scripts.
A. B. Svensk Filmindustri

that period. French impressionism inspired Karl Fredrik Hill and Ernst Josephson in the late 1800's. Some critics consider them Sweden's greatest painters. Today, most Swedish painters follow international trends in abstract art.

The Swedish sculptor Carl Milles worked for many years in the United States, where he achieved a world-wide reputation for outdoor sculptures, particularly fountains. Most other leading Swedish sculptors use abstract forms in their work.

Swedish designers have produced home furnishings of artistic merit. Many homes in the United States are furnished in a style known as *Swedish modern*. Swedish furniture is simple in style, and most of it is made of light-colored wood. Designers use pleasant, bright colors for upholstery and drapery materials. Other Swedish furnishings with international fame for beauty include glassware, pottery, and silverware. Swedish glass vases, bowls, and other products are especially famous for their graceful design and high quality. The towns of Kosta and Orrefors, in southeastern Sweden, are the country's main glassmaking centers.

Fritz Henle, Photo Researchers

Statues by Carl Milles attract many visitors to Millesgården, a park near Stockholm that includes his old home and studio.

Lapp Handicrafts, produced in Lapland in northern Sweden, feature beautifully carved bone and wood.

Pal-Nils Nilsson, J. D. Studios Ltd.

A Great Cultural Movement took place in Sweden during the rule of King Gustavus III (1771-1792). Literature especially flourished. This painting shows the crowning of Gustavus, who wrote poems and plays.

Coronation of Gustavus III by Carl Gustav Pilo. Nationalmuseum, Stockholm

Swedish Industrial Arts, including home furnishings, are known for their simple, graceful design.

J. D. Studios Ltd.

Sweden occupies the eastern part of the Scandinavian peninsula. From Sweden's hilly and, in parts, mountainous border with Norway, the land slopes gently eastward to the Gulf of Bothnia and the Baltic Sea. The country's scenery varies from the unpopulated, treeless Kölen Mountains in the northwest to the fertile plains in the south. Thousands of lakes cover about a twelfth of the country's area.

The long Swedish coastline has sandy beaches in the south, and rocky cliffs in parts of the west and north. Many groups of small islands lie off the coast. Sweden's largest islands are Gotland, a fertile island covering about 1,160 square miles (3,004 square kilometers), and Öland, which covers about 520 square miles (1,350 square kilometers). Both islands are in the Baltic Sea.

Sweden has four main land regions: (1) the Mountain Range, (2) the Inner Northland, (3) the Swedish Lowland, and (4) the South Swedish Highland.

The Mountain Range is part of the Kölen Mountains. Sweden's northern boundary with Norway runs through these mountains, which Norwegians call the Kjølen Mountains. Hundreds of small glaciers cover the higher slopes of the snow-capped range. Sweden's highest mountain, 6,926-foot (2,111-meter) Mount Kebnekaise, is in this rugged region.

The land is completely treeless above about 1,600 feet (488 meters) in the northernmost part of the mountains. There, the climate is too cold for trees. Some birch trees grow on the warmer lower slopes.

The Inner Northland is a vast, thinly populated, hilly region. Great forests of pine and spruce trees cover most of the land, and lumbering is an important industry. Many swift rivers flow southeast across the Inner Northland, and provide much hydroelectric power. The rivers have formed deep, narrow valleys, some of which have long lakes. The valleys broaden toward the coast of the Gulf of Bothnia. Most of the region's people live in these valleys or on the coast.

The Torne River forms part of the boundary between the Inner Northland and Finland. Other rivers in the region include the Lule, the Ume, the Ångerman, and the Dal rivers. Bergslagen, a hilly area rich in minerals, lies south of the Dal River in the southernmost part of the Inner Northland.

The Swedish Lowland has more people than any other part of the country. This region includes the central and southern plains of Sweden. The broad central plains are broken by lakes, tree-covered ridges, and small hills. Farmland covers more than 40 per cent of these plains. Sweden's largest lakes, Vänern and Vättern, are there. Lake Vänern covers 2,156 square miles (5,584 square kilometers), and is one of the largest lakes in Europe. Lake Vättern has an area of 738 square miles (1,911 square kilometers).

The southern plains include some of Sweden's most fertile land. Farmland and beech woods cover most of Skåne, in the far south. It is the most thickly populated and richest farming area of Sweden.

The South Swedish Highland, also called the *Götaland Plateau,* is a rocky upland that rises to about 1,200 feet (366 meters) above sea level. This thinly populated area has poor, stony soils, and is covered mostly by forests. The southern part of the region is flat, with small lakes and swamps.

The Swedish Lowland includes most of Sweden's croplands, such as these fertile plains near Lake Vättern. Many lakes and small hills break up the region's central plains.

Herbert Fristedt from Carl Ostman

LAND REGIONS OF SWEDEN

Distance Scale

0 Miles — 200 — 400

0 Kilometres — 400 — 600

Mountain Range

Inner Northland

• Stockholm

Swedish Lowland

Göteborg•

South Swedish Highland

Malmö•

WORLD BOOK map–FHa

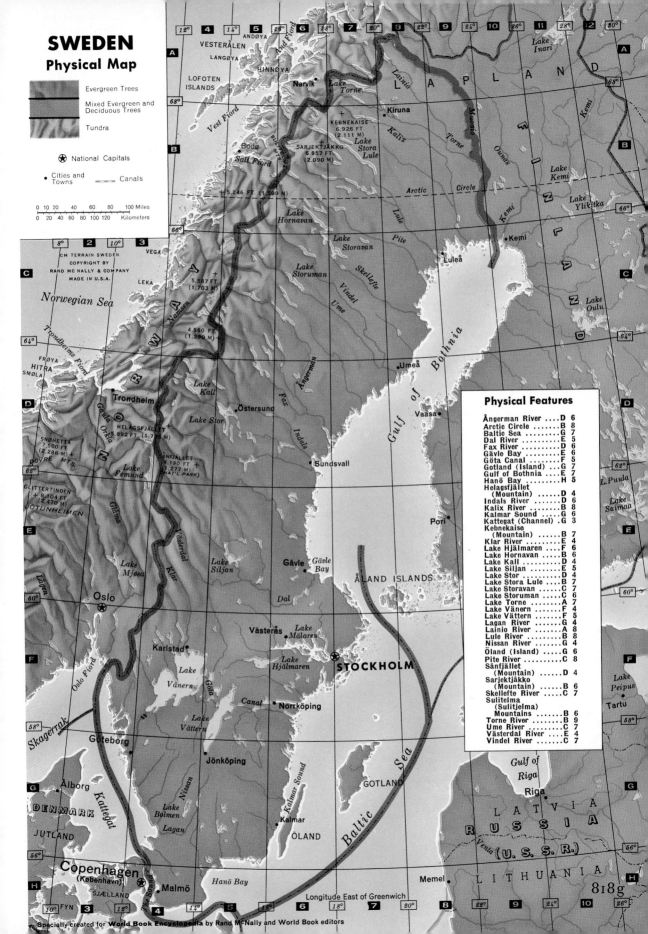

SWEDEN
Physical Map

Evergreen Trees

Mixed Evergreen and
Deciduous Trees

Tundra

★ National Capitals

• Cities and Towns   Canals

Miles: 0 10 20 40 60 80 100 Miles
Kilometers: 0 20 40 60 80 100 120 Kilometers

CM TERRAIN SWEDEN
COPYRIGHT BY
RAND MC NALLY & COMPANY
MADE IN U.S.A.

Physical Features

Ångerman River	D	6
Arctic Circle	B	8
Baltic Sea	G	7
Dal River	E	5
Fax River	D	6
Gävle Bay	E	6
Göta Canal	F	5
Gotland (Island)	G	7
Gulf of Bothnia	E	7
Hanö Bay	H	5
Helagsfjället (Mountain)	D	4
Indals River	D	6
Kalix River	B	8
Kalmar Sound	G	6
Kattegat (Channel)	G	3
Kebnekaise (Mountain)	B	7
Klar River	E	4
Lake Hjälmaren	F	6
Lake Hornavan	B	6
Lake Kall	D	4
Lake Siljan	E	5
Lake Stor	D	4
Lake Stora Lule	B	7
Lake Storavan	C	7
Lake Storuman	C	7
Lake Torne	A	7
Lake Vänern	F	4
Lake Vättern	F	5
Lagan River	G	4
Lainio River	A	8
Lule River	B	8
Nissan River	G	4
Öland (Island)	G	6
Pite River	C	8
Sänfjället (Mountain)	D	4
Sarjektjåkko (Mountain)	B	6
Skellefte River	C	7
Sulitelma (Sulitjelma) Mountains	B	6
Torne River	B	9
Ume River	C	7
Västerdal River	E	4
Vindel River	C	7

Labels on map

VESTERÅLEN
LANGØYA
HINNØYA
LOFOTEN ISLANDS
Narvik
Lake Torne
Kiruna
LAPLAND
Lake Inari
Andøya
And Fiord
Lainio
Vest Fiord
Bodø
Sall Fiord
KEBNEKAISE 6,926 FT. (2,111 M)
SARJEKTJÅKKO 6,857 FT. (2,090 M)
Lake Stora Lule
Kalix
Torne
Maunio
Ounas
Kemi
Lake Kemi
5,246 FT. (1,599 M)
Arctic Circle
Lake Ylikitka
66°
Lake Hornavan
Lule
Pite
Lake Storavan
Skellefte
Vindel
Luleå
Lake Oulu
68°

VEGA
5,587 FT (1,703 M)
LEKA
Lake Storman
Ume
Gulf of Bothnia
Norwegian Sea
Trondheims Fiord
FRØYA
HITRA
SMØLA
4,560 FT. (1,390 M)
Namsen
Trondheim
Umeå
Vaasa
Lake Oulu
Lake Puula
Lake Saimaa

Gaula
Orkla
HELAGSFJÄLLET 5,892 FT (1,796 M)
Lake Kall
Østersund
Lake Stor
Fax
Ångerman
Indals
Sundsvall
SNØHETTA 7,500 FT (2,286 M)
DOVRE MTS.
SÄNFJÄLLET 4,190 FT (1,277 M) (NAT'L PARK)
GLITTERTINDEN 8,104 FT (2,470 M)
JOTUNHEIMEN
Lake Femund
Glåma
Västerdal
Klar
62°

Løgen
Lake Mjøsa
Oslo
Lake Siljan
Dal
Gävle
Gävle Bay
ÅLAND ISLANDS
Pori
60°

Skagerrak
Oslo fiord
Karlstad
Västerås
Lake Mälaren
Lake Hjälmaren
STOCKHOLM
Lake Peipus
Tartu
58°

Göteborg
Lake Vänern
Göta
Canal
Norrköping
Lake Vättern
Jönköping
Gulf of Riga
Riga
LATVIA
RUSSIA (U.S.S.R.)

Ålborg
DENMARK
JUTLAND
Kattegat
Nissan
Lagan
Lake Bolmen
Lake Vättern
Kalmar Sound
Kalmar
GOTLAND
ÖLAND
Baltic Sea
Venta
Memel
LITHUANIA
56°

Copenhagen (København)
Malmö
SJÆLLAND
Hanö Bay
The Sound
Longitude East of Greenwich
FYN
818g

Specially created for World Book Encyclopedia by Rand McNally and World Book editors

SWEDEN /Climate

The climate of Sweden varies greatly between the southern and northern parts of the country. Southwesterly winds from the Atlantic Ocean give southern Sweden pleasant summers and mostly mild winters. Northern Sweden has pleasant summers but cold winters. The Atlantic winds are blocked by the Kölen Mountains, and have less effect on northern Sweden.

In the extreme south, temperatures in January and February, the coldest months, average 32° F. (0° C). In Kiruna, in the far north, temperatures average about 10° F. (−12° C) during these months. In July, Sweden's warmest month, temperatures average from 59° to 63° F. (15° to 17° C) in the south, and 54° to 57° F. (12° to 14° C) in the north. In winter, eastern air masses may lower the temperature to −10° F. (−23° C) in Stockholm, and to −45° F. (−43° C) in the north.

Rainfall is generally greater in the Kölen Mountains and the southern highlands than on the plains that border the Gulf of Bothnia. In the south, snow covers the ground in January and February. The north has snow from mid-October through mid-April.

Pictorial Parade

Cross-Country Skiing is a favorite sport in Sweden, where snow covers the ground from two to six months a year.

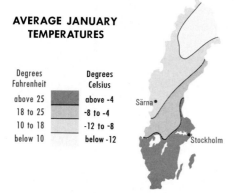

AVERAGE JANUARY TEMPERATURES

Degrees Fahrenheit	Degrees Celsius
above 25	above -4
18 to 25	-8 to -4
10 to 18	-12 to -8
below 10	below -12

Särna
Stockholm

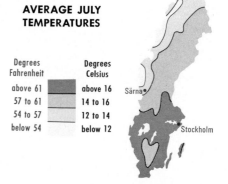

AVERAGE JULY TEMPERATURES

Degrees Fahrenheit	Degrees Celsius
above 61	above 16
57 to 61	14 to 16
54 to 57	12 to 14
below 54	below 12

Särna
Stockholm

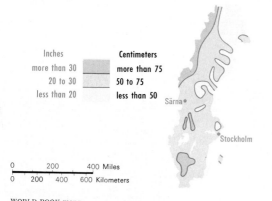

AVERAGE YEARLY PRECIPITATION
(Rain, Melted Snow and Other Moisture)

Inches	Centimeters
more than 30	more than 75
20 to 30	50 to 75
less than 20	less than 50

Särna
Stockholm

| 0 | 200 | 400 Miles |
| 0 | 200 | 400 | 600 Kilometers |

WORLD BOOK maps
Sources: Meteorological Office, London; U.S. Navy

AVERAGE MONTHLY WEATHER

	STOCKHOLM					SÄRNA				
	Temperatures				Days of Rain or Snow		Temperatures			Days of Rain or Snow
	F° High	F° Low	C° High	C° Low			F° High	F° Low	C° High	C° Low	
JAN.	31	23	-1	-5	8	JAN.	19	4	-7	-16	8
FEB.	31	22	-1	-6	7	FEB.	24	5	-4	-15	5
MAR.	37	26	3	-3	7	MAR.	33	11	1	-12	5
APR.	45	32	7	0	6	APR.	42	23	6	-5	7
MAY	57	41	14	5	8	MAY	56	32	13	0	6
JUNE	65	49	18	9	7	JUNE	63	41	17	5	11
JULY	70	55	21	13	9	JULY	69	46	21	8	13
AUG.	66	53	19	12	10	AUG.	65	44	18	7	12
SEPT.	58	46	14	8	8	SEPT.	54	36	12	2	10
OCT.	48	39	9	4	9	OCT.	42	28	6	-2	9
NOV.	38	31	3	-1	9	NOV.	30	19	-1	-7	9
DEC.	33	26	1	-3	9	DEC.	24	11	-4	-12	9

Sweden's economy is based mainly on its three most important natural resources—timber, iron ore, and water power. The large Swedish merchant shipping fleet transports cargoes to and from all parts of the world, and provides an important source of income for the nation. About 90 per cent of Swedish industry is privately owned. For Sweden's rank in the output of various products, see the articles listed under Products and Industry in the *Related Articles* at the end of this article.

Natural Resources. The raw materials for Sweden's industries come chiefly from the country's vast forests and rich deposits of iron ore. Waterfalls, rapids, and dams provide most of the nation's electricity. Although

FARM, MINERAL, AND FOREST PRODUCTS

This map shows where the leading farm, mineral, and forest products of Sweden are produced. Most Swedish agriculture is in the southern parts of the country and on the central plains. The map also shows five important manufacturing centers.

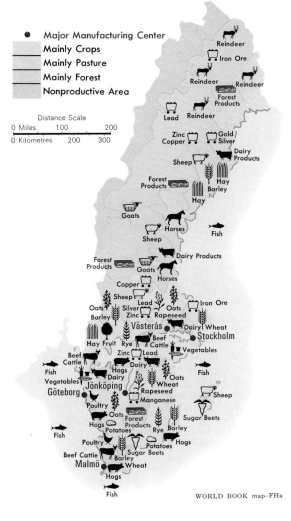

WORLD BOOK map–FHa

Sweden's Gross National Product

Total gross national product in 1979—$83,500,000,000

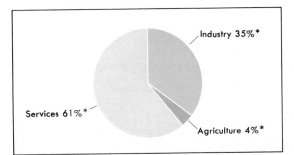

Industry 35%*

Services 61%*

Agriculture 4%*

The gross national product (GNP) is the total value of goods and services produced by a country in a year. The GNP measures a nation's total annual economic performance. It can also be used to compare the economic output and growth of countries.

Production and Workers by Economic Activities

Economic Activities	Per Cent of GDP* Produced	Employed Workers† Number of Persons	Per Cent of Total
Manufacturing	27	961,800	23
Government	25	1,200,000	29
Finance, Insurance, Real Estate, & Business Services	14	192,800	5
Hotels, Restaurants, & Trade	10	562,600	14
Construction & Mining	8	332,100	8
Transportation & Communication	5	273,400	7
Agriculture, Forestry, & Fishing	4	251,400	6
Community, Personal, & Social Services	4	310,800	7
Utilities	3	28,500	1
Total	100	4,113,400	100

*Based on gross domestic product (GDP) in 1978. GDP is gross national product adjusted for net income sent abroad or received from abroad.
†Figures are for 1978.
Sources: National Central Bureau of Statistics, Stockholm, Sweden; *The Planetary Product*, 1979-1980, Dr. Herbert Block.

Sweden Is a World Leader in Paper Production.

Herbert Fristedt from Carl Östman

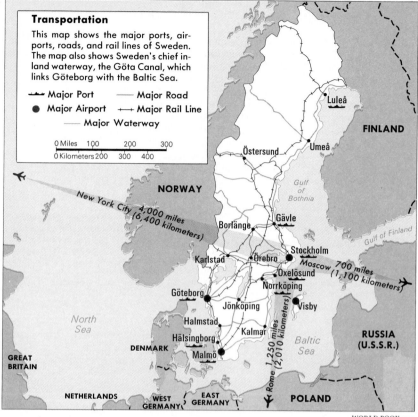

Transportation

This map shows the major ports, airports, roads, and rail lines of Sweden. The map also shows Sweden's chief inland waterway, the Göta Canal, which links Göteborg with the Baltic Sea.

- Major Port
- ● Major Airport
- Major Road
- ┼ Major Rail Line
- Major Waterway

0 Miles 100   200   300
0 Kilometers 200 300 400

Sweden's Major Seaport is Göteborg, which is also the chief shipbuilding center. Shipping and shipbuilding are important sources of income.

John LaDue

most of Sweden is too cold and infertile for farming, farmers produce most of the people's food.

Forests cover more than half of Sweden, and more than a fourth of the nation's exports are lumber or products made of wood. The main lumber regions are in the north and north-central sections, where the most important trees include fir, pine, and spruce. Much lumber is carried to manufacturing plants by truck and railroad. Logs are also floated down the rivers to sawmills on the coast, where some lumber is exported and the rest is sent to industrial centers. Forestry is less important in southern Sweden, even though oak, beech, and other trees cover large areas.

Minerals. Sweden has some of the richest iron ore deposits in the world. Sweden's total iron ore resources have been estimated at about $3\frac{1}{3}$ billion short tons (3 billion metric tons), of which about 60 per cent is near Kiruna in Lapland. The Lapland mines have some of the world's best high-grade ores. Most of the Lapland ore is exported. The Swedish iron and steel industry gets most of its ore from the Bergslagen district, south of the Dal River. The Skellefteå region in northern Sweden has copper, lead, gold, and silver. Some low-grade uranium ore is mined in central Sweden. The country has a few deposits of low-grade coal.

Water Power provides about 65 per cent of Sweden's electricity. The largest hydroelectric power stations are in northern Sweden. Most of them are underground, and can be operated throughout the year. Other im-

portant power stations are in central and southern Sweden, including a large station at Trollhättan.

Farmland covers only about 10 per cent of Sweden. A region called Skåne, in the extreme south, has a good climate and is the most fertile area. Other agricultural areas are in the south and around the lakes in central Sweden. Less than 1 per cent of the Inner Northland region is cultivated.

Manufacturing industries are scattered throughout central Sweden and western Skåne, and along the coast. The iron and steel industry produces high-quality steel, which is used for such products as ball bearings, stainless steel goods for the home, precision tools, and watch springs. Steel is widely used in the engineering industry, which accounts for more than a third of Sweden's total industrial production and for two-fifths of its exports.

Important Swedish engineering products include agricultural machinery, aircraft, automobiles, and ships. Linköping is the chief center of the aircraft industry, and Trollhättan has aircraft engine and diesel motor plants. Stockholm, Göteborg, and Linköping have major automobile plants. Nearly half the automobiles made in Sweden are exported to the United States. Sweden ranks second only to Japan in the number of ships it builds for export. The main shipbuilding centers are Göteborg and Malmö. The electrical engineering industry makes equipment for power supplies and communications, and telephones are an important export.

Sweden produces about 7 per cent of the world's

wood pulp. Other important products based on timber include paper and cardboard, prefabricated houses, plywood, and furniture.

The Swedish chemical industry imports most of its raw materials. The chief products include explosives, fertilizers, plastics, and safety matches. Safety matches were invented in Sweden in 1844, and the country is still one of the world's leading producers.

Agriculture. Dairy farming and livestock raising are the main sources of income for Swedish farmers. Milk and meat are the leading farm products. The chief crops include barley, oats, potatoes, sugar beets, and wheat. Almost all the farmers belong to Sweden's agricultural cooperative movement. The cooperatives collect, process, and market farm products (see COOPERATIVE).

Mining. Sweden's most important mineral is iron ore. The country is a leading producer of this mineral, which accounts for 6 per cent of Sweden's exports. Most of the exported ore comes from mines in Lapland. In summer, the Lapland ore is shipped from the port of Luleå, on the Gulf of Bothnia. In winter, Luleå's harbor is icebound, and the ore must be carried across the mountains to the ice-free port of Narvik in Norway.

Foreign Trade. The value of Sweden's imports is greater than that of its exports. But in most years, income from the country's merchant shipping fleet makes up most of the difference. The chief Swedish exports include engineering products, wood pulp, paper and other wood products, iron ore, and steel. Imports include coal, petroleum, and foodstuffs.

West European nations, including Denmark, West Germany, Great Britain, The Netherlands, and Norway, account for more than 80 per cent of Sweden's exports and more than 75 per cent of its imports. Sweden also has important trade with the United States. Sweden is a member of the European Free Trade Association (see EUROPEAN FREE TRADE ASSOCIATION).

Transportation. The government owns about 95 per cent of Sweden's 8,450 miles (13,600 kilometers) of railways. Only a little more than half are electrified, but electric trains carry about 90 per cent of the total railroad traffic. Ferries connect Swedish railroads with those in Denmark and Germany. Sweden has a network of good roads and highways, and trucks carry almost as much freight as the railroads do.

Stockholm has an international airport at Arlanda. Other important airports serve Göteborg and Malmö. Swedish ships carry raw materials between coastal towns.

Communication. Sweden has about 160 daily newspapers, with a total daily circulation of more than 4 million. *Expressen* of Stockholm, with a circulation of about 455,000, is the largest newspaper in Sweden. Most of Sweden's newspapers are privately owned. Freedom of the press is guaranteed by law, and government censorship is forbidden even in wartime.

The Swedish Broadcasting Corporation, which operates three radio stations and one television channel, is the only broadcasting system. It is run partly by the government, but is nonpolitical. The government does not permit advertising on radio or television.

Sweden's telephone and telegraph services are operated by the government. In the mid-1970's, Sweden had about 590 telephones for every 1,000 persons.

Early Times. Sweden was one of the last regions to lose the ice that covered most of Europe thousands of years ago. The ice had melted by about 6000 B.C., and hunters and fishermen from south of the Baltic Sea settled in the southern tip of Sweden. People moved farther north as the climate improved.

Beginning about 50 B.C., the people traded with the Roman Empire. They exchanged furs and amber for glass and bronze objects and silver coins. The Romans were the first people to make written records about the Swedes. About A.D. 100, the Roman historian Tacitus wrote about the Svear, a Scandinavian people. *Sverige* (Sweden) means *land of the Svear*.

The Swedish Vikings. Beginning about A.D. 800, Scandinavian adventurers called *Vikings* sailed to many parts of the world. They acquired wealth by trade and conquest. Most of the Norwegian and Danish Vikings sailed westward. The Swedish Vikings went eastward across Russia, as far as the Black and Caspian seas. The Swedes traded slaves and furs for gold, silver, and luxury goods. The Viking expeditions lasted until the 1000's. Much of Sweden's trade with the east then came into the hands of German merchants, who settled in the town of Visby on the island of Gotland. See VIKING (The Swedish Vikings); RUSSIA (Early Days).

The Early Kingdom. Christianity was first preached in Sweden in A.D. 829 by Saint Anskar, a Frankish monk. His missionary work began a struggle between Christianity and paganism that lasted about 200 years. The first Christian king of Sweden was Olof Skotkonung, who ruled from the late 900's until the early 1000's. Christianity brought about great changes in Sweden. The clergy founded schools, encouraged the arts, and set down Sweden's laws in writing.

By the 1000's, Sweden, Denmark, and Norway had become separate kingdoms. Sweden began to develop along partly feudal lines (see FEUDALISM). There were three social classes—the clergy, the nobles, and the

Picture Stones were carved by Swedish Vikings, usually as memorial monuments for heroes. This picture dates from the A.D. 700's.
Picture stone from Gotland. Historiska Museet, Stockholm

SWEDEN

Radio Times Hulton Picture Library

Battle of Hangö, during the Great Northern War, ended in victory for Russia's navy over the Swedish fleet in 1714.

peasants. Above them was the king, who was elected by the provincial lawmaking assemblies. In 1249, Sweden conquered much of Finland.

Union with Norway and Denmark. During the 1200's and 1300's, constant struggles took place between the rulers of Sweden and the nobles. In 1388, to oppose the growing German influence in Sweden's affairs, the nobles turned for help to Queen Margrete of Denmark and Norway. The Germans were defeated in

Important Dates in Sweden

c. 6000 B.C. The first settlers came to Sweden.

c. A.D. 800's to 1000's Swedish Vikings attacked other countries, and traded and colonized.

c. 1000 Christianity was introduced into Sweden.

1397 Sweden, Denmark, and Norway were united in the Union of Kalmar.

1523 Gustavus Vasa was elected king and Sweden became independent.

c. 1540 Lutheranism became Sweden's official religion.

1630-1632 Gustavus Adolphus won victories for Sweden in the Thirty Years' War (1618-1648).

1709 Swedish power declined after the Battle of Poltava.

1809 Sweden lost Finland to Russia. A new constitution was adopted.

1814 Sweden gained Norway from Denmark.

1905 Norway dissolved its union with Sweden.

1914-1918 Sweden was neutral in World War I.

1920 All persons at least 21 years old received the vote.

1939-1945 Sweden remained neutral in World War II.

1959 Sweden and six other nations formed the European Free Trade Association.

1963 Nuclear power was used to heat some Swedish homes.

1965 The voting age was lowered to 20 years.

1975 Sweden adopted a new constitution that greatly reduced the power of the king and lowered the voting age to 18.

1389, and the three Scandinavian countries were united under Margrete in 1397. A treaty called the *Union of Kalmar* laid down the conditions of the union between the three countries. This treaty provided for a common foreign policy, but separate national councils and the continuation of existing laws in each country. Except for a few short periods of separation, the union lasted over 100 years.

Under the influence of German merchants, Sweden's economy developed considerably during the 1200's and 1300's. These merchants developed Sweden's mineral resources and controlled Swedish trade. Plague wiped out a large part of Sweden's population in 1350, and caused an economic decline. The German merchants, with their powerful association called the Hanseatic League, increased their control of Swedish trade (see HANSEATIC LEAGUE).

During the late 1400's, the *Riksdag* (parliament) developed into a lawmaking and tax-raising body. Members of a new social class, the merchants, joined the other three classes as members of the Riksdag.

The Beginnings of Modern Sweden. The union with Norway and Denmark continued throughout most of the 1400's. But many struggles took place between supporters and opponents of the union. Gustavus Vasa, a Swedish noble, finally broke away from the union in 1523 after defeating the Danes. He became King Gustavus I of independent Sweden that year. Norway remained under Danish rule.

Gustavus encouraged the followers of Martin Luther, the German religious reformer, to spread their ideas. About 1540, the Lutheran religion became the state religion of Sweden. Gustavus also increased the power of the throne and laid the foundations of the modern Swedish state. He centralized the administration, dealt harshly with revolts, built an efficient army, and encouraged trade and industry. See GUSTAVUS (I).

The Age of Expansion. Beginning in the late 1500's, the Swedes fought a series of wars to gain control of the lands surrounding the Baltic Sea. King Gustavus Adolphus won many victories for Sweden and the Protestant cause in the Thirty Years' War (see THIRTY YEARS' WAR). Sweden gained new possessions in Europe, and these led to continual wars against Denmark, Poland, and Russia. In 1658, under the Treaty of Roskilde, the Swedes forced the Danes to give up their provinces on the Swedish mainland.

Charles XII, who ruled from 1697 to 1718, won many victories, and for a time made Sweden one of the greatest powers in Europe. But in 1709, Czar Peter the Great of Russia defeated the Swedes in the Battle of Poltava. During the next few years, Sweden lost most of its European possessions. See CHARLES (XII).

The Age of Liberty. Charles XII died in 1718. Before agreeing to elect a new king, the Riksdag insisted that any monarch chosen should accept a new constitution. This constitution, which was passed in 1720, transferred many of the crown's powers to the Riksdag. The period of parliamentary government that followed was called the Age of Liberty, and lasted until 1772. That year, an unsuccessful war in Germany and serious economic and political troubles at home resulted in a peaceful revolution that re-established the power of the king.

The Napoleonic Wars. Because of its growing trade with Britain, Sweden became involved in wars against the French Emperor Napoleon in the early 1800's. As a result of these wars, Sweden lost Finland to Russia, but gained Norway from Denmark. In 1809, Sweden adopted a new constitution. In 1818, Jean Baptiste Bernadotte, a French soldier who had become *regent* (acting ruler) of Sweden during the Napoleonic Wars, was elected king of Sweden as Charles XIV. Sweden's present royal family is descended from him.

Industrial Growth. Great economic and social changes occurred during the 1800's. More land was brought into use for farming. But food was often in short supply because of a great increase in the population. There were not enough jobs, and nearly 450,000 persons left Sweden between 1867 and 1886. Most went to the United States and settled mainly in the Midwest.

Emigration decreased after Sweden developed manufacturing, mining, and forest industries. Engineers built many railroads in the 1860's and 1870's, and Sweden's lumber resources were put into use. In 1867, Alfred Nobel, a Swedish chemist, invented dynamite, which speeded the growth of mining. Engineering industries based on iron and steel were developed. By 1900, Sweden had become an important industrial nation.

In 1905, Norway broke away from Sweden. The Norwegians elected a king, and Sweden recognized Norway's independence. See NORWAY (Independence).

Sweden was neutral during World War I (1914-1918) and World War II (1939-1945). After Germany conquered Norway in 1940, Sweden let German troops pass through on their way to Norway. Many Swedes opposed this policy, and Sweden stopped it in 1943.

Sweden Today. Sweden's economy grew tremendously after World War II, and the country now ranks among the world's most prosperous nations. Sweden's high standard of living has been spread to all income groups by means of a government welfare system that has developed since the war. Critics of the system say it makes people so secure that they become bored. Critics also say the system has helped cause high taxation and inflation. But most Swedes support the system.

A new constitution took effect in Sweden in 1975. It greatly reduced the power of the king, and it lowered the voting age from 19 to 18.

The Social Democratic Party controlled Sweden's government from 1932 to 1976, except for a brief period in 1936. A socialist group, it established Sweden's welfare system. In the 1976 parliamentary elections, a coalition of three nonsocialist groups—the Center, Conservative, and Liberal parties—gained control of the government. The coalition government resigned in 1978, and the Liberal Party took control. Parliamentary elections in 1979 re-established the three-party coalition government. In 1981, the Conservative Party withdrew from the coalition. In the 1982 parliamentary elections, the Social Democratic Party regained control of the government.   TORSTEN HENRIKSSON, JOHAN
HENRIK NORRBIN, ISTVÁN VUKOVICH, and CARL-CHRISTIAN WALLÉN

SWEDEN / *Study Aids*

Related Articles in WORLD BOOK include:

BIOGRAPHIES

Bergman, Ingmar	Bergman, Ingrid

Bernadotte, Folke	Linnaeus, Carolus
Bernadotte, Jean B.J.	Milles, Carl W.E.
Berzelius, Jöns J.	Myrdal, Alva R.
Bjoerling, Jussi	Myrdal, Gunnar
Carl XVI Gustaf	Nilsson, Birgit
Charles (Swedish Kings)	Nobel, Alfred B.
Ericsson, John	Nordenskjöld, Nils A.
Garbo, Greta	Oldenburg, Claes
Gustavus	Oxenstierna, Axel G.
Hammarskjöld, Dag	Scheele, Carl W.
Hedin, Sven A.	Siegbahn, Karl M.G.
Lagerkvist, Pär F.	Strindberg, August
Lagerlöf, Selma	Svedberg, Theodor
Lind, Jenny	

CITIES

Göteborg	Malmö	Stockholm

HISTORY

Denmark (History)	Norway (History)
Goths	Vikings

PHYSICAL FEATURES

Baltic Sea	Skagerrak	Torne River

OTHER RELATED ARTICLES

Air Force (Other Major Air Forces)	Clothing (picture: Traditional Costumes)
Christmas (In Denmark, Norway, and Sweden; picture: On St. Lucia Day)	Physical Education (In Modern Times) Scandinavia

Outline

I. Government
II. People

A. Language	E. Libraries and Museums
B. Religion	F. Sports
C. Food	G. Holidays
D. Education	H. Social Welfare

III. Arts
IV. The Land
V. Climate
VI. Economy

A. Natural Resources	E. Foreign Trade
B. Manufacturing	F. Transportation
C. Agriculture	G. Communication
D. Mining	

VII. History

Questions

Who founded Sweden's present royal family?
What is the principal religion of Sweden?
How did Sweden get its name?
Why did many Swedes emigrate in the late 1800's?
What are Sweden's three chief natural resources?
What are Sweden's two largest lakes and islands?
Who was the first Swedish writer to win world fame?
Why are Sweden's forests important to its economy?
What are some of the welfare benefits in Sweden?
What is smörgåsbord?

Additional Resources

AUSTIN, PAUL BRITTEN. *On Being Swedish: Reflections Towards a Better Understanding of the Swedish Character.* Univ. of Miami Press, 1968.
ELSTOB, ERIC C. *Sweden: A Political and Cultural History.* Rowman & Littlefield, 1979.
IMBER, WALTER, and TIETZE, WOLFE. *Sweden.* Binns, 1979.
KOBLIK, STEVEN, ed. *Sweden's Development from Poverty to Affluence, 1750-1970.* Univ. of Minnesota Press, 1975.
KORPI, WALTER. *The Working Class in Welfare Capitalism: Work, Unions, and Politics in Sweden.* Routledge & Kegan, 1978.
SCOTT, FRANKLIN D. *Sweden: The Nation's History.* Univ. of Minnesota Press, 1977.

Brown Bros.
Emanuel Swedenborg

SWEDENBORG, *SWEE duhn bawrg*, or, in Swedish, *SVAY duhn BAWR y*, **EMANUEL** (1688-1772), was a Swedish scientist, inventor, and mystical religious leader. He became an authority on mathematics, astronomy, metallurgy, anatomy, and geology, and was named a member of the Swedish State Council of Mines. He is credited with a number of inventions, and drew plans for a submarine, an airship, and a magazine-type gun, all forerunners of those of today.

Swedenborg, son of a bishop and nobleman, was born in Stockholm. He turned to religion in middle age, although he retained his scientific interests. He wrote a number of books setting forth what he called his "heavenly doctrines." He claimed that they were based on Bible teachings which had been interpreted to him through direct communication with the spiritual world. His views brought him much criticism.

Swedenborg did not intend to found a separate religious body, but, soon after his death in London, some of his followers began to form churches founded on his views. They became known as the Church of the New Jerusalem. F. A. NORWOOD

See also SWEDENBORGIANS.

SWEDENBORGIANS, *SWEE duhn BAWR jee uhns*, look to the formulation of Christian doctrine as set forth by Emanuel Swedenborg, a Swedish theologian. A church based on this doctrine was organized in London in 1787, and in the United States in 1792. Churches in the United States and Canada set up the General Convention of the New Jerusalem in 1817. A separate body, formed in 1890, took the name General Church of the New Jerusalem. Swedenborgians have societies and missions in many parts of the world, usually affiliated with the American bodies or with the Conference of the New Church in Great Britain.

Swedenborg's teachings emphasize one God, the Lord and Savior Jesus Christ, in whom is the Trinity: Father, Son, and Holy Spirit. Swedenborgians believe that the Holy City, New Jerusalem, is symbolic of an ideal human society. They regard Jesus as truly *Immanuel*, or *God with us*. They believe that Swedenborg was called by God to reveal deeper spiritual meanings in scripture, and that, when mankind accepts and practices these truths, Jesus Christ makes his second coming in spirit, not in person. DAVID P. JOHNSON

SWEDISH NIGHTINGALE. See LIND, JENNY.

SWEEPER. See VACUUM CLEANER.

SWEEPSTAKES. See HORSE RACING (Types of Races); LOTTERY.

SWEET ADELINES, INC. See BARBERSHOP QUARTET SINGING.

SWEET ALYSSUM, *uh LIHS uhm*, is a low, spreading plant with clusters of tiny lavender or white flowers. It is a hardy plant that gardeners can sow in early spring. Sweet alyssum usually blooms within six weeks after planting. Some varieties are dwarfed, and others grow about 9 inches (23 centimeters) high.

Scientific Classification. Sweet alyssum belongs to the mustard family, *Cruciferae*. It is classified as genus *Lobularia*, species *L. maritima*. ROBERT W. SCHERY

SWEET BRIAR COLLEGE is a liberal arts college for women at Sweet Briar, Va. It offers courses leading to the A.B. degree. Sweet Briar administers the Junior Year in France, a foreign study program for men and women.

The college was chartered in 1901, and opened in 1906. For enrollment, see UNIVERSITIES AND COLLEGES (table).

SWEET CHERVIL. See CICELY.

SWEET CORN. See CORN.

SWEET FLAG is a tall reedlike plant of the arum family. It grows along brooks and in marshy places in almost all parts of the Northern Hemisphere. Its leaves are flat and 2 to 6 feet (61 to 180 centimeters) long. They are shaped like a two-edged sword. The stems of the sweet flag are almost like the leaves, but are stiffer and bear spikes of small green blossoms near the top. The leaves and stems rise directly from the thick, fleshy underground rootstock. The rootstock is the calamus root. It is used as a tonic and in the manufacture of perfume and other toilet preparations. In Europe, the rootstock is valued as a food.

Scientific Classification. The sweet flag is in the arum family, *Araceae*. It is genus *Acorus*, species *A. calamus*. HAROLD NORMAN MOLDENKE

Sweet Flag, a useful herb, has small flower spikes, *inset*.
L. W. Brownell; Carl L. Howard

John H. Gerard; W. Atlee Burpee Co.
Sweet Alyssum produces clusters of tiny white flowers, *inset*. A low plant, it has long been popular for garden borders.

Leaves of the Sweet Gum, or Red Gum, are among the most brilliant in autumn. The tree is tall and stately.

SWEET GUM, also called RED GUM, is a tall, stately tree. It grows from Connecticut and southern New York to Florida and westward to southern Illinois, Oklahoma, and eastern Texas. Normally, it reaches a height of 80 to 100 feet (24 to 30 meters). When mature, its straight trunk is 3 to 4 feet (91 to 120 centimeters) thick at the base. Sweet gum leaves are deeply lobed, and turn a deep crimson in autumn. The fruit is a brownish, spiny ball that remains on the tree through the winter. The sweet gum is so named because it produces a gummy compound, called *storax*, that is used in making perfumes, adhesives, and salves. Sweet gum wood is fairly hard and heavy. People use it to make veneer, cabinets, and other products.

Scientific Classification. Sweet gum trees belong to the witch hazel family, *Hamamelidaceae*. They are genus *Liquidambar*, species *L. styraciflua*. T. EWALD MAKI

SWEET PEA is a favorite garden flower that belongs to the same family as the kind of pea that we eat. People grow the sweet pea for the beauty and fragrance of its flowers. The sweet pea is one of the special flowers for the month of April. Sweet pea flowers are blue, red, pink, purple, and white. Some look like butterflies. There are more than 1,000 varieties of sweet pea. In some, the flower petals are smooth and velvety. In others, they are crinkled and wavy. The plants may be *dwarf*, which grow close to the ground, or *climbing*, which grow along strings or trellises.

Rich, well-drained soil, plenty of sunshine, and free circulation of air are needed to raise sweet peas. Gardeners should sow the seed in April. They use 1 ounce (28 grams) of seed to 30 feet (9 meters) of row. The plants should be at least 2 inches (5 centimeters) apart in the row, and the rows should be 4 feet (1.2 meters) apart. As soon as the plants appear above ground, the gardener should cultivate the ground. The soil should be stirred lightly every week, preferably after a rain, and the rows should be kept free of weeds. Once a week the plants should be fed with a liquid fertilizer.

The vines should be trained on strings. Wire trellises may absorb too much heat. The flowers should be picked as they open, before they go to seed.

Scientific Classification. Sweet peas belong to the pea family, *Leguminosae*. Common garden sweet peas are genus *Lathyrus*, species *L. odoratus*. DONALD WYMAN

SWEET POTATO is a vegetable of the morning-glory family of plants. Its large, fleshy roots are a popular food. Sweet potatoes are often called *yams*, but yams belong to another family and grow mostly in the tropics.

Sweet potatoes may be yellow or white. Yellow sweet potatoes are grown chiefly in the southern United States. The varieties called *Yellow Jersey* and *Triumph* are dry. *Porto Rico* and *Centennial* sweet potatoes are moist. Most white sweet potatoes come from Africa or Asia. Some kinds of sweet potato plants have pale green vines with small, pointed leaves. Other types have purple vines with large leaves. Sweet potato vines grow from the main stem and lie along the ground.

Sweet potatoes have high energy value and contain vitamins A and C. They may be bought fresh, canned, or *dehydrated* (dried by removing the water). Sweet potatoes first grew in tropical regions of the Western Hemisphere and were raised in colonial Virginia during the early 1600's. They are sometimes used in making alcohol and starch. The American scientist George Washington Carver made 118 products from sweet potatoes (see CARVER, GEORGE WASHINGTON).

Sweet potato plants are grown from roots placed in moist, warm, sandy soil in greenhouses or hotbeds about four weeks before planting time. Stem buds from the roots produce new plants called *slips* that push up through the soil. They are removed and planted 1 foot (30 centimeters) apart in rows 3 to 4 feet (91 to 120 centimeters) apart. The rows are usually ridged to help the water drain. Some hoeing or treatment with weed control chemicals helps the slips grow.

Crops of sweet potatoes should be harvested before frost occurs. The roots must be handled carefully to pre-

Leading Sweet Potato Growing States

Bags of sweet potatoes grown each year*

North Carolina	🥔🥔🥔🥔🥔🥔🥔🥔🥔🥔🥔🥔🥔🥔 4,680,000 bags
Louisiana	🥔🥔🥔🥔🥔🥔🥔🥔 2,470,000 bags
California	🥔🥔🥔🥔🥔 1,647,000 bags
Texas	🥔🥔🥔 741,000 bags
Georgia	🥔🥔 644,000 bags
Alabama	🥔🥔 621,000 bags
Mississippi	🥔🥔 494,000 bags
Virginia	🥔 345,000 bags
South Carolina	🥔 333,000 bags
New Jersey	🥔 275,000 bags

*One bag equals 100 pounds (45 kilograms).
Source: *Crop Production 1981 Annual Summary*, U.S. Department of Agriculture. Figures are for 1981.

The Toothsome Sweet Potato has long been associated with holiday feasts. It has great commercial importance.

vent bruising. They are *cured* (dried) in buildings at temperatures from 80° to 90° F. (27° to 32° C) and then are stored at temperatures of 55° to 60° F. (13° to 16° C).

Sweet potatoes may be affected by diseases caused by tiny plants called *fungi* (see FUNGI). The fungi can be controlled by using disease-free seed, by treating the seeds with chemicals, or by crop rotation.

Scientific Classification. The sweet potato belongs to the morning-glory family, *Convolvulaceae*. It is genus *Ipomoea*, species *I. batatas*. TEME P. HERNANDEZ

See also YAM.

SWEET WILLIAM is a popular garden plant that is native to northern Europe and Asia and to the United States. The plant usually grows about 2 feet (61 centimeters) high and bears dense, round clusters of velvety flowers. The flowers range in color from white to pink, rose, or purple. Some are red with white spots. Cultivated plants may bear double flowers. Gardeners usually cultivate sweet William as a *biennial* (a plant that requires two years to mature).

Scientific Classification. Sweet William is in the pink family, *Caryophyllaceae*. It is genus *Dianthus*, species *barbatus*. H. D. HARRINGTON

Sweet William Blossoms form large velvety clusters at the end of the stem. One cluster may have flowers in many shades.

SWEETBREAD is a tasty meat that comes from certain glands in young animals. The thymus gland in the throat of young calves produces sweetbread that is sold in fine restaurants. The pancreas of older calves is called *stomach sweetbread* or *belly sweetbread*. It is much like the sweetbread of the thymus gland. Butchers divide the thymus gland into the throat sweetbread and the heart, or breast, sweetbread. Heart sweetbread is larger and more tender than throat sweetbread.

The best sweetbread is that taken from baby calves, because the thymus gland gradually shrinks and disappears after the animal grows older. Lamb sweetbread is too small to be sold in markets. JOHN C. AYRES

SWEETBRIER. See EGLANTINE.

SWELLFISH. See PUFFER.

SWIFT is the name of a family that developed one of the world's leading meat-packing companies. Two generations of that family guided Swift & Company (now called Esmark, Inc.) from a small New England firm to world leadership in the industry.

Gustavus Swift

Gustavus Franklin Swift (1839-1903) started working for his brother, a butcher, at 14, and went in business for himself at the age of 17. Before he was 35, he was a cattle exporter and a wholesale meat dealer. Association with the meat business from 1855 until his death made him an expert judge of cattle.

Swift saw the need to eliminate excessive transportation costs. In 1875 he went to Chicago and became the first to slaughter meat there for shipment east. At first this activity had to be confined to the cooler months, but the use of the refrigerator car made it a year-round business.

On April 1, 1885, Swift & Company was formed. Because of the continuous growth of Swift's company in an expanding industry, he had to use unusual methods in raising additional capital. He became famous for his emphasis on cost-cutting and his insistence on the full use of by-products. He was born in Cape Cod, Mass.

Louis Franklin Swift (1861-1937), the oldest son of Gustavus Franklin Swift, became president of Swift & Company when his father died, and served until 1931. Later he served as chairman of the board of directors. Under his leadership, the company established a pension trust and made other advances in labor relations. Swift was active in company expansion plans, opening plants in the United States, and in South America, Australia, and New Zealand. These foreign operations were separated from Swift & Company in 1918, and became Compania Swift Internacional. Louis Swift was born in Sagamore, Mass.

Edward Foster Swift (1863-1932), the second son of Gustavus Franklin Swift, worked closely with his older brother in formulating company policies. He served as vice-president of the company and as president of Compania Swift Internacional and other company affiliates. He was born in Barnstable, Mass.

Charles Henry Swift (1872-1948), the fourth son of Gustavus, succeeded Louis Franklin Swift as chairman of the board of directors of Swift & Company in 1932. He encouraged the branch-house system of distribution, which increased the efficiency of the company's marketing system. He was born at Lancaster, Mass.

Gustavus Franklin Swift, Jr. (1881-1943), the seventh son of Gustavus Franklin Swift, became president of Swift & Company in 1931, and served until 1937. He took a leading part in the organization of the American Meat Institute. He was born in Chicago, Ill.

Harold Higgins Swift (1885-1962), the youngest son of Gustavus Franklin Swift, served as vice-president in charge of industrial relations. He became chairman of the board in 1948 and honorary chairman in 1955. He became a member of the University of Chicago board of trustees in 1914, and served as its chairman from 1922 to 1949. He was a director of the Rockefeller Foundation. He was born in Chicago.   W. H. BAUGHN

SWIFT is a small bird that can fly for many hours with its long, strong wings. Swifts capture their insect food while flying. They almost always return at dusk to the cave, chimney, cliff, or hollow tree where they live in flocks. A chimney swift may fly 135,000 miles (217,000 kilometers) a year. Swifts build nests made of sticks that they cement together with their saliva. Some of these nests are almost entirely made up of saliva. They resemble the bird's nests of east Asia that people eat.

More than 75 different kinds of swifts live in various parts of the world. They are sooty-brown or greenish-black. Some swifts have white throats or rumps. Their song, continually repeated, is little more than short, indistinct sounds.

The chimney swift of eastern North America almost always builds its nest in chimneys. Vaux's swifts of western North America and chimney swifts may roost by the thousands in large chimneys while migrating. They perform spectacular maneuvers in the air as they descend into the chimneys for the night.

Scientific Classification. Swifts make up the swift family, *Apodidae*. The chimney swift is genus *Chaetura*, species *C. pelagica*. Vaux's swift is *C. vauxi*.   LEONARD W. WING

See also ANIMAL (color picture: Animals of the Mountains [Nepalese Swift]); BIRD (picture: How Birds Feed); BIRD'S-NEST SOUP.

SWIFT is the name of certain small lizards that are unusually active. Swifts live on dry land in the western part of North America and in Central America. These lizards have tiny scales with sharp points that often look like spines. There are about 50 different kinds of swifts.

Scientific Classification. Swifts belong to the New World lizard family, *Iguanidae*. They are classified in the genus *Uta* and in the genus *Sceloporus*.   CLIFFORD H. POPE

See also LIZARD.

Swifts Are Strong, Fast Fliers. Some of them can travel over 100 miles (160 kilometers) per hour for short distances. They feed on insects while in the air. Some swifts spend the night in flight.

Swifts Usually Roost on Vertical Surfaces, clinging with sharp toenails and using the tail as a prop, *below.* They rarely perch on branches because their feet and legs are small and weak.
Eric Hosking, Photo Researchers

Treat Davidson, NAS

SWIFT, JONATHAN

SWIFT, JONATHAN (1667-1745), an English author, wrote the story *Gulliver's Travels* (1726), a masterpiece of literature. Swift is called a great *satirist* because of his ability to ridicule customs, ideas, and habits he considered silly or harmful. His satire is often bitter, but it is also often humorous. Swift was deeply concerned about the welfare and about the behavior of his fellow men,

Jonathan Swift by Charles Jervas. National Portrait Gallery, London

Jonathan Swift

and he used his talent to strike out against those men, institutions, and ideas that he considered foolish.

Swift's life was interesting and useful. Swift was a Protestant preacher who became a hero in Roman Catholic Ireland. He wrote many pamphlets to protest the sufferings of the Irish under their British rulers. He was also a friend of important English statesmen and a writer on English political issues.

His Life. Swift was born in Dublin on Nov. 30, 1667. His parents were of English birth. Swift was graduated from Trinity College in Dublin, and moved to England in 1689. He was secretary to the distinguished statesman Sir William Temple from 1689 until 1699, with some interruptions. In 1694, Swift became a minister in the Church of England.

While working for Temple, Swift met a young girl named Esther Johnson, whom he called Stella. He and Stella became lifelong friends, and some persons believe they were married. There is no proof of their marriage, however. Swift wrote long letters to Stella during his busiest days. The letters were published after Swift's death as the *Journal to Stella*.

After Temple died in 1699, Swift became pastor of a small Protestant parish in Laracor, Ireland. He began to play an important part in church life, and his skill as a writer became widely known. He visited England often between 1703 and 1710, conducting church business and winning influential friends. In 1710, he became a powerful supporter of the new Tory government in England. Through his many articles and pamphlets in defense of Tory policies, Swift became one of the most effective public relations men any English administration has ever had.

Queen Anne recognized Swift's political work in 1713 when she made him *dean* (head clergyman) of St. Patrick's Cathedral in Dublin. The queen died in 1714, and George I became king. The Whig Party won control of the government that year. These changes ended the political power of Swift and his friends.

Swift spent the rest of his life—more than 30 years—as dean of St. Patrick's. In many ways, these years were disappointing. Swift was unhappy because his political efforts had amounted to so little. He also missed his exciting friends in England. But it was as dean that Swift wrote *Gulliver's Travels* and that he became the champion of the Irish cause.

Swift's health declined in his last years and finally his mind failed. He died on Oct. 19, 1745. He left his money to start a hospital for the mentally ill.

Gulliver's Travels is often described as a book children read with delight, but which adults find serious and disturbing. However, even young readers usually recognize that Swift's "make-believe" world sometimes resembles their own world. Adults recognize that, in spite of the book's seriousness, it is also amusing.

Gulliver's Travels describes four voyages that Lemuel Gulliver, who was trained as a ship's doctor, makes to strange lands. Gulliver first visits the *Lilliputians* (pronounced *lil eh PEW shuns*)—tiny people whose size and surroundings are only $\frac{1}{12}$ those of normal people and things. The Lilliputians treat Gulliver well at first. Gulliver helps them, but after a time the Lilliputians turn against him and he is happy to escape from them.

Gulliver's second voyage takes him to the country of *Brobdingnag* (pronounced *BROB ding nag*), where the people are 12 times larger than Gulliver and greatly amused by his puny size.

Gulliver's third voyage takes him to several strange kingdoms. The conduct of the odd people of these countries represents the kinds of foolishness Swift saw in his world. For example, in the academy of Lagado, scholars spend all their time on useless projects such as getting sunbeams from cucumbers. Here Swift was satirizing impractical scientists and philosophers.

In his last voyage, Gulliver discovers a land ruled by wise and gentle horses called *Houyhnhnms* (pronounced *HWIN ems*). Savage, stupid animals called *Yahoos* also live there. The Yahoos look like human beings. The Houyhnhnms distrust Gulliver because he resembles the Yahoos. Gulliver wishes to stay in the agreeable company of the Houyhnhnms, but they force him to leave.

Some persons believe Swift was a *misanthrope* (hater of mankind), and that the ugliness and stupidity in his book reflect his view of the world. Other persons argue that Swift was a devoted and courageous Christian who could not have held such bitter opinions about his fellow man. Some of them claim that in *Gulliver's Travels*, Swift is really urging us to avoid the extremes between the boringly perfect Houyhnhnms and wild Yahoos and to lead moderate, sensible lives.

Scholars are still trying to discover all the ways in which real persons, institutions, and events are represented in *Gulliver's Travels*. But readers need not be scholars to find pleasure in the book and to find themselves set to thinking about its distinctive picture of human life.

Swift's Other Works. "A Modest Proposal" (1729) is probably Swift's second best-known work. In this short essay, Swift pretends to urge that Irish babies be killed and eaten. They would be as well off, says Swift bitterly, as those Irish who grow up in poverty under British rule. Swift hoped this outrageous suggestion would shock the Irish people into taking sensible steps to improve their condition.

A Tale of a Tub (1704), on the surface, is a story of three brothers arguing over their father's last will. But it is actually a clever attack on certain religious beliefs and on man's false pride in his knowledge.

In *The Battle of the Books* (1704), a lighter work, Swift imagines old and new books in a library waging war on each other. This work reflected a real quarrel

Engraving by Bernard Lens the elder for the 1710 edition
of *The Battle of the Books.* Newberry Library, Chicago

The Battle of the Books ridicules scholars who argued the relative merits of ancient and modern writers. This picture shows
a battle between ancient and modern books in a library.

Culver

Gulliver's Travels is Swift's most famous book. In its best-
known episode, Gulliver is shipwrecked in the country of Lilliput
where the people are only $\frac{1}{12}$ his size. He awakes to find that
the Lilliputians have tied him down with hundreds of tiny ropes.

between scholars who were proud of being "modern,"
and scholars who believed the wisdom of the ancient
thinkers could not be bettered.

Swift wrote many pamphlets in support of his political views. *The Drapier's Letters* (1724) are probably the
most notable. Swift, in the character of a dry-goods merchant, urged the Irish to boycott the use of copper
money, which England tried to force on them.

Swift could also be very playful. He loved riddles,
jokes, and hoaxes. One of his best literary pranks was
the so-called *Bickerstaff Papers* (1708). In this work, he
invented an astrologer named Isaac Bickerstaff to ridicule John Partridge, a popular astrologer and almanac
writer of the time. Swift satirized Partridge by publishing his own wildly improbable predictions.

Swift wrote a great deal of poetry and light verse.
Much of his poetry is humorous, and it is often sharply
satirical as well. But many of his poems, both comic and
serious, show his love for his friends.

Swift's Personality. Whether Swift hated humanity
or whether he mocked people to reform them is still disputed. However, there are some things Swift clearly
hated and loved. He hated those who attacked religion, particularly when they pretended to be religious

themselves. He also hated the tyranny of one nation
over another nation. Above all, he hated false pride—
the tendency of people to exaggerate their own accomplishments and overlook their own weaknesses. Swift
loved his religious faith. He also loved liberty, simplicity, honesty, and humility. His writings—whether bitter,
shocking, or humorous—ask the reader to pursue these
virtues.   Critically reviewed by EDWARD ROSENHEIM, JR.

See also GULLIVER'S TRAVELS.

Additional Resources

DONOGHUE, DENIS. *Jonathan Swift: A Critical Introduction.*
  Cambridge, 1969.
ROSENHEIM, EDWARD. *Swift and the Satirist's Art.* Univ. of Chi-
  cago Press, 1963.
ROWSE, A. L. *Jonathan Swift.* Scribner, 1975.
VAN DOREN, CARL. *Swift.* Arden, 1981. Reprint of 1930 ed.

SWIGERT, JOHN LEONARD, JR. (1931-1982), a
United States astronaut, served as command module
pilot of the Apollo 13 lunar flight in April 1970. Swigert
made the flight with astronauts Fred W. Haise, Jr., and
James A. Lovell, Jr.

About 56 hours after the flight began, an explosion
caused by a short circuit destroyed the command module's life support and electrical systems. The crew
switched to the lunar module's systems and used them
to return to the earth. The tense return trip ended safely
nearly four days later.

Swigert was born in Denver, Colo., on Aug. 30, 1931.
He served in the Air Force from 1953 to 1956. Swigert
then worked as a civilian test pilot until 1966, when
he became an astronaut. Swigert resigned from the
astronaut program in 1977. In 1982, he won election to
the U.S. House of Representatives from Colorado, but
he died before taking office.   WILLIAM J. CROMIE

SWIMMER'S ITCH. See FLATWORM.

Maurice Schulman, U.S. Olympic Committee

Lee Pillsbury, *Swimming World*

Swimming is an exciting sport and a popular form of recreation. The swimmers at the left dive into a pool at the start of a championship race. The women in the center perform a graceful movement in a sport called *synchronized swimming*. At the right, an instructor teaches children how to swim.

SWIMMING

SWIMMING is the act of moving through water by using the arms and legs. Swimming is a popular form of recreation, an important international sport, and a healthful exercise.

People of all ages—from the very young to the elderly—swim for fun. Throughout the world, millions of people enjoy swimming in lakes, oceans, and rivers. Others swim in indoor or outdoor pools. Many schools, recreation centers, motels, apartment buildings, and private clubs have an indoor or outdoor pool. Thousands of communities provide pools for local residents. Many families even have a pool in their backyard.

During the 1900's, swimming has become a major competitive sport. Thousands of swimmers compete in meets held by schools, colleges, and swimming clubs. The best international swimmers take part in annual meets in many parts of the world. Swimming races have always been a highlight of the Summer Olympic Games, which take place every four years. Many long-distance swimmers attempt such feats as swimming across the English Channel or from the southern California coast to Santa Catalina Island.

Good swimmers can also enjoy a variety of other

Don Van Rossen, the contributor of this article, is Aquatics Director at the University of Oregon.

water sports. Such sports include springboard and platform diving, surfing, water skiing, water polo, scuba diving, and synchronized swimming. In addition, the ability to swim well makes such sports as fishing and boating safer and more enjoyable. Above all, the ability to swim may save a person's life in an emergency in the water.

Swimming is one of the best exercises for keeping physically fit. Swimming improves heart action, aids blood circulation, and helps develop firm muscles.

Water Safety

Swimming, boating, fishing, and other water sports are among the most popular forms of recreation. Yet many people lack knowledge of water safety rules or take dangerous chances. Every year, almost 9,000 persons drown in the United States and about 1,000 persons in Canada. Most of these drownings would not occur if everyone knew how to swim and observed basic water safety rules. The following discussion deals with basic rules and techniques that could save your life or help you save another person's life.

First of all, know how to swim. Many schools provide swimming lessons as part of their physical education program. Adults can learn to swim at public and private pools and at recreation centers.

Never swim alone. Always swim with a companion and know where that person is at all times. Swim only in areas protected by lifeguards. If such an area is not available, be sure that the bottom has no snags, trash,

WORLD BOOK photo

or weeds. If you swim in the ocean or a river, you should know about tides and currents.

Water for diving should be deep and clear. Never dive into unfamiliar waters, and always look carefully for other swimmers before you dive. When swimming, stay away from diving boards and diving platforms.

Whether you are a beginning or experienced swimmer, a knowledge of *survival bobbing* can help you survive an accident or other difficulty in the water. Survival bobbing enables you to float a long time on your stomach while using very little energy. You fill your lungs with air and relax your body. Your arms and legs hang down limply, and your chin flops down to the chest. The air in your lungs holds your back above the water's surface. When you need a breath, you quickly exhale through the nose, lift your face out of the water, and inhale through your mouth. You then return to the restful, floating position. You can raise your mouth higher out of the water for a breath by pressing your hands down or squeezing your legs gently together.

Only a trained lifeguard should attempt a swimming rescue. But even if you are a nonswimmer, you can help a swimmer in trouble. If the person is close by, you can extend a board, pole, shirt, towel, or similar object and pull the swimmer to safety. But be sure to lie down or keep your body low to avoid being pulled into the water. If the swimmer is too far away to reach an object, you can throw a life preserver, a board, or any other object that will float and support the swimmer.

The American Red Cross, the Boys' Clubs of Amer-ica, the Boy Scouts, the Girl Scouts, the YMCA, the YWCA, and various other organizations offer water safety programs. Many of these organizations also teach lifesaving skills to experienced swimmers.

Swimming Kicks and Strokes

Swimmers move their legs, feet, arms, and hands in certain ways to propel themselves through the water easily and quickly. The movements of the legs and feet are called *kicks*. These movements combined with movements of the arms and hands are called *strokes*.

The Basic Kicks. Swimmers use four types of kicks: (1) the flutter kick, (2) the breaststroke kick, (3) the dolphin kick, and (4) the scissors kick. Each of these kicks is used in doing one or more of the strokes described later in this section.

The Flutter Kick is the most popular kick and the easiest for most swimmers to learn. To do the flutter kick, you rapidly whip your legs up and down from the hips, alternating one leg with the other. The legs should be fairly straight, close together, and relaxed. The power to do the flutter kick should come from the thigh muscles.

The Breaststroke Kick begins with your legs fully extended and the toes pointed to the rear. You then bring your heels toward the hips just under the surface of the water. As your feet near the hips, bend your knees and extend them outward. Turn your ankles so the toes also point outward. Then, without pause, push your feet backward and squeeze your legs together until the toes again point to the rear.

The Dolphin Kick resembles the flutter kick. But in the dolphin kick, you move both of your legs up and down at the same time.

The Scissors Kick begins with your body turned to either side. Your legs are together and the toes pointed back. Draw your knees up and then spread your legs wide apart like the open blades of a scissors, moving your top leg forward from the hip. Then snap both legs together to their original position in a scissorslike action.

The Basic Strokes are (1) the front crawl, (2) the backstroke, (3) the breaststroke, (4) the butterfly, and (5) the sidestroke.

The Front Crawl is the fastest and most popular stroke. You move your arms in a steady, circular motion in combination with the flutter kick. One hand reaches forward above the water while the other pulls beneath the water. You breathe by turning your head to one side just as the hand on that side passes your leg. You inhale through the mouth. You exhale through the mouth or nose, but you keep your face in the water while exhaling.

The Backstroke, or *back crawl*, is performed as you lie on your back. It is a restful stroke because your face is always out of the water and breathing is easy. As in the front crawl, each arm alternately moves in a steady, circular motion in and out of the water while your legs do the flutter kick.

The Breaststroke is another restful stroke. It is done in combination with the breaststroke kick. You begin with your face in the water, arms and legs fully extended, and the palms facing outward. You then sweep out your arms as your hands push downward

Basic Swimming Strokes

The Front Crawl

The Backstroke

The Breaststroke

The Butterfly

and outward. The hands continue to circle and come together under the chin. As the hands begin to push down, you lift your head for a breath. Finally, you again extend your arms and legs and glide forward. You then repeat the sequence. You make a breaststroke kick at the end of the stroke as your arms extend for the glide.

The Butterfly is a difficult stroke to learn, but it is smooth and graceful if performed correctly. In this stroke, you swing both arms forward above the water and then pull them down and back to your legs. As your arms start to move toward your legs, you lift your head forward and take a breath. Then you dip your head into the water and exhale as your arms move forward again. You make two dolphin kicks during each complete stroke, one as your hands enter the water and the other as your arms pass under your body.

The Sidestroke is done on your side, whichever side is more comfortable. Your head rests on your lower arm, which is extended ahead with the palm turned downward. The top arm is at your side. The palm of the lower hand presses down in the water until it is beneath the shoulder. At the same time, the top hand slides up to meet the lower hand. The legs do a scissors kick while the lower arm returns to an extended position and the palm of the upper hand pushes toward the feet. You then glide forward before repeating the sequence.

Other Strokes. Swimmers use a number of other strokes besides the basic five. The most important include the *dog paddle* and the *elementary backstroke*. To perform the dog paddle, cup your hands and rotate them in a circular motion underwater, with one hand forward when the other one is back. You do a flutter kick with the dog paddle. Your head remains out of the water throughout the stroke. The elementary backstroke, like the regular

backstroke, is performed on your back. You bring your hands up along the sides of your body to your shoulders. Next you turn out the hands and stretch the fingers outward. Then you push your hands down and glide. Swimmers do the breaststroke kick with this stroke.

Swimming as a Sport

The Federation Internationale de Natation Amateur (FINA) governs international swimming and other water sports at the amateur level. The FINA consists of national associations from about 100 countries. These associations include the Amateur Athletic Union (AAU) of the United States, the Canadian Federation of Amateur Aquatics, the Amateur Swimming Union of Australia, and the Amateur Swimming Association of Great Britain.

The Pool. Swim meets are held in both *long-course* pools, which measure 50 meters (164 feet) long, and *short-course* pools, which measure 22.885 meters (75 feet) long. Long-course pools are divided into 6, 8, or 10 lanes, each of which is 2.4 meters (8 feet) wide. Short-course pools have 6 or 8 lanes. Each lane measures 2.1 or 2.4 meters (7 or 8 feet) wide. In U.S. championship meets, 8 lanes must be used in both long- and short-course pools. The FINA recognizes world records set only in long-course pools.

Water in a regulation pool must be at least 4 feet (1.2 meters) deep and have a temperature of about 78° F. (26° C). Floats called *lane lines* run the length of the pool. They mark lane boundaries and help keep the surface of the water calm.

Kinds of Races. Swimmers participate in five kinds of races—freestyle, breaststroke, backstroke, butterfly, and individual medley. In a freestyle race, a swimmer

WORLD BOOK illustrations by Robert Keys

A Regulation Swimming Pool Swimming pools are divided into lanes for races, one lane for each swimmer in a race. Wall targets, lane lines, and lane markers guide each swimmer. Near each end of the pool, a flag line is hung over the water to warn swimmers in backstroke races that they are approaching the end of the lane.

WORLD BOOK diagram by Arthur Grebetz

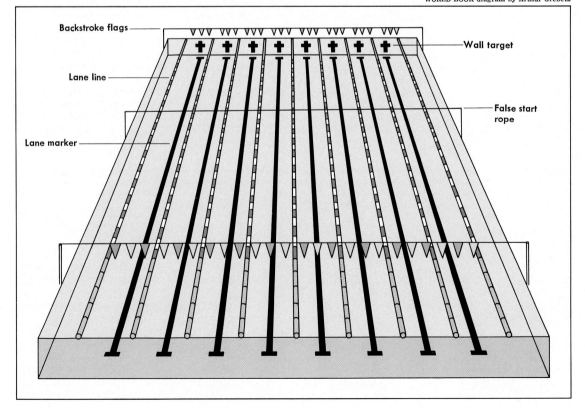

Backstroke flags

Wall target

Lane line

False start rope

Lane marker

833

Team stunt performed by the Santa Clara (Calif.) Aquamaids;
Lee Pillsbury, *Swimming World*

Synchronized Swimming is a water sport in which swimmers *synchronize* (match) graceful, acrobatic movements to music. Competition is divided into solo, duet, and team events.

may choose any stroke. But swimmers always use the front crawl because it is the fastest stroke. In the individual medley, athletes swim an equal distance of each of the four strokes.

In national and international meets, individual free-style races are held at distances of 100, 200, 400, 800, and 1,500 meters. Breaststroke, backstroke, and butterfly events are 100 and 200 meters long. The individual medley covers 200 and 400 meters.

Team *relays* are among the most exciting swimming races. A team consists of four swimmers, each of whom swims an equal distance. Men's and women's teams participate in a 400-meter freestyle relay, a 400-meter medley relay, and an 800-meter freestyle relay. In the medley relay, each member of the team swims a different stroke for 100 meters.

Swim Meets are held at various levels of competition, from local to international. So many swimmers participate in competitive swimming that qualifying times are established for large meets. Swimmers must at least equal the qualifying times for the races that they

hope to enter in order to be eligible for those events.

Large meets have several officials. The chief official is the referee. The referee supervises the other officials and makes sure that the swimmers follow regulations.

Each swimmer in a race is assigned a lane. The swimmers with the fastest qualifying times get the center lanes, and the slowest swimmers receive the outside lanes. The race begins at the sound of the starter's gun or horn. During the race, lane judges watch each swimmer's strokes and the turns at the end of the pool. An illegal stroke or turn disqualifies a swimmer.

In many meets, an electronic timing and judging system determines the order of finish and each swimmer's time to $\frac{1}{1,000}$ of a second. The system begins automatically at the starter's signal. It records the time for each swimmer as the swimmer's hand touches a plate attached to the end of the pool.

Starts and Turns. A swimmer's performance in a race partly depends on the skill used in starting the race and in turning at the end of each lap. At the start of a freestyle, breaststroke, or butterfly race, a swimmer gains time by diving as far as possible through the air before hitting the water. In these races, swimmers dive off a raised starting platform. In backstroke events, they begin in the water with their back to the lane. They hold a starting block attached to the end of the pool. At the starting signal, with their back slightly arched, the swimmers use both feet to push off from the pool's end as forcibly as possible.

Fast turns also save a swimmer time. Freestyle and backstroke swimmers use the *flip*, or *somersault*, turn. In this turn, they make an underwater somersault to reverse their direction after touching the end of the pool. Breaststroke and butterfly swimmers use an *open* turn, in which they keep their head above the water while reversing their direction.

Training. Most young people interested in competitive swimming begin by racing against swimmers in their own age group. In the United States, the AAU has established an age-group program for young swimmers. This program divides swimmers into four groups: (1) age 10 and under; (2) ages 11 and 12; (3) ages 13 and 14; and (4) ages 15 to 18.

Most swimmers in age-group programs work out once or twice a day for five or six days each week. And

Starting a Swimming Race

A skillful start plays an important part in a swimmer's performance in a race. The swimmer first wraps his toes around the edge of the starting block and looks straight ahead, *left*. He swings his arms back, elbows straight, and begins to dive, *center*. Over the water, *right*, he arches his back slightly, lowers his head, and raises his arms. He should hit the water at a slight angle.

Chicago Park District (WORLD BOOK photos)

they follow this schedule for 11 months every year. Their training includes land and water exercises to increase endurance, speed, and strength. They also practice kicks and strokes. To keep up their energy and to help avoid illnesses, all swimmers are advised to eat a well-balanced diet and to get plenty of rest.

Synchronized Swimming is a water sport that combines grace, rhythm, and acrobatic skills. In this sport, swimmers perform certain movements to music that they have selected. They *synchronize* (match) these

movements with the rhythm and the mood of the music.

Synchronized swimming was once called *water ballet*. It began as a form of exhibition swimming at water shows and remains a popular feature of such shows. In 1952, the first international rules were established for synchronized swimming as a sport.

Competition is divided into solo, duet, and team events. A team may have four to eight members. Each

World Swimming Records*

Event	Time	Holder	Country	Made At	Date
Men's Events					
100-meter freestyle	49.36 s.	Ambrose Gaines IV	United States	Austin, Tex.	April 3, 1981
200-meter freestyle	1 min. 48.93 s.	Ambrose Gaines IV	United States	Mission Viejo, Calif.	July 19, 1982
400-meter freestyle	3 min. 48.32 s.	Vladimir Salnikov	Russia	Moscow	Feb. 19, 1983
800-meter freestyle	7 min. 52.83 s.	Vladimir Salnikov	Russia	Moscow	Feb. 14, 1982
1,500-meter freestyle	14 min. 54.76 s.	Vladimir Salnikov	Russia	Moscow	Feb. 22, 1983
100-meter backstroke	55.49 s.	John Naber	United States	Montreal	July 19, 1976
200-meter backstroke	1 min. 59.19 s.	John Naber	United States	Montreal	July 24, 1976
100-meter breaststroke	1 min. 02.53 s.	Steve Lundquist	United States	Indianapolis, Ind.	Aug. 21, 1982
200-meter breaststroke	2 min. 14.77 s.	Victor Davis	Canada	Guayaquil, Ecuador	Aug. 5, 1982
100-meter butterfly	53.81 s.	William Paulus	United States	Austin, Tex.	April 3, 1981
200-meter butterfly	1 min. 58.01 s.	Craig Beardsley	United States	Kiev, Russia	Aug. 22, 1981
200-meter individual medley	2 min. 02.25 s.	Alex Baumann	Canada	Brisbane, Australia	Oct. 4, 1981
400-meter individual medley	4 min. 19.78 s.	Ricardo Prado	Brazil	Guayaquil, Ecuador	Aug. 1, 1982
400-meter freestyle relay	3 min. 19.26 s.	National Team (C. Cavanaugh, D. McCagg, A. Gaines, R. Leamy)	United States	Guayaquil, Ecuador	Aug. 5, 1982
800-meter freestyle relay	7 min. 20.82 s.	National Team (B. Furniss, B. Forrester, B. Hackett, A. Gaines)	United States	West Berlin	Aug. 24, 1978
400-meter medley relay	3 min. 40.84 s.	National Team (R. Carey, S. Lundquist, M. Gribble, A. Gaines)	United States	Guayaquil, Ecuador	Aug. 7, 1982
Women's Events					
100-meter freestyle	54.79 s.	Barbara Krause	East Germany	Moscow	July 21, 1980
200-meter freestyle	1 min. 58.23 s.	Cynthia Woodhead	United States	Tokyo	Sept. 3, 1979
400-meter freestyle	4 min. 06.28 s.	Tracey Wickham	Australia	West Berlin	Aug. 24, 1978
800-meter freestyle	8 min. 24.62 s.	Tracey Wickham	Australia	Edmonton	Aug. 5, 1978
1,500-meter freestyle	16 min. 04.49 s.	Kimberly Linehan	United States	Fort Lauderdale, Fla.	Aug. 19, 1979
100-meter backstroke	1 min. 00.86 s.	Rica Reinisch	East Germany	Moscow	July 23, 1980
200-meter backstroke	2 min. 09.91 s.	Cornelia Sirch	East Germany	Guayaquil, Ecuador	Aug. 7, 1982
100-meter breaststroke	1 min. 08.60 s.	Ute Geweniger	East Germany	Split, Yugoslavia	Sept. 8, 1981
200-meter breaststroke	2 min. 28.36 s.	Lina Kachushite	Russia	Potsdam, East Germany	April 6, 1979
100-meter butterfly	57.93 s.	Mary T. Meagher	United States	Brown Deer, Wis.	Aug. 16, 1981
200-meter butterfly	2 min. 05.96 s.	Mary T. Meagher	United States	Brown Deer, Wis.	Aug. 13, 1981
200-meter individual medley	2 min. 11.73 s.	Ute Geweniger	East Germany	East Berlin	July 4, 1981
400-meter individual medley	4 min. 36.10 s.	Petra Schneider	East Germany	Guayaquil, Ecuador	Aug. 1, 1982
400-meter freestyle relay	3 min. 42.71 s.	National Team (B. Krause, C. Metschuck, I. Diers, S. Hulsenbeck)	East Germany	Moscow	July 27, 1980
800-meter freestyle relay	8 m. 07.44 s.	Mission Viejo Nadadores (M. Linzmeier, S. Habernig, T. Cohen, C. Woodhead)	United States	Brown Deer, Wis.	Aug. 14, 1981
400-meter medley relay	4 min. 05.88 s.	National Team (K. Otto, U. Geweniger, I. Geissler, B. Meineke)	East Germany	Guayaquil, Ecuador	Aug. 6, 1982

*Includes only records set in 50-meter pools.
Source: United States Swimming.

SWIMMING

solo, duet, or team event has two sections—*stunts* and *routines*. Stunts are acrobatic movements. Routines combine stunts with swimming strokes to create various patterns. Routines in international competition have a time limit of five minutes.

More than 30 stunts may be used in international competition. They are divided into two series. The second series is more difficult than the first. Swimmers must perform three stunts from the first series and two from the second.

The *dolphin* is an example of a commonly performed stunt. It is also used in many routines. Swimmers begin the dolphin by floating on their back. They then pull themselves under the water head first, make a complete circle, and return to the floating position. In the *dolphin bent knee* stunt, swimmers bend one knee while they perform the circular movement underwater.

A panel of judges awards points for each stunt and routine. After each stunt, the judges grade swimmers according to the difficulty of the stunt and how well they performed it. The judges give each routine two scores, one for *execution* and one for *style*. The execution score reflects the skill that swimmers showed in performing the stunts and strokes. The style score includes how well the swimmers synchronized their movements with the music.

In water shows and swimming exhibitions, swimmers often base their synchronized routines on a story or a theme. For example, they might act out such a tale as *Alice in Wonderland* with the aid of a narrator. Or they might choose such a theme as the seasons of the year and expressively interpret each season's mood.

History

Ancient peoples may have learned to swim by imitating the way dogs and other animals moved through water. Swimming became a popular form of exercise and recreation in many ancient lands, including Assyria, Egypt, Greece, and Rome. Its popularity declined during the Middle Ages, from the A.D. 400's to the 1500's. Many people feared swimming because they thought bubonic plague and certain other diseases were spread by water. Swimming regained popularity in the 1800's.

Organized swim meets became common during the mid-1800's. At that time, many swimmers used the breaststroke. A faster stroke, the *Australian crawl*, was developed in the late 1800's. Johnny Weissmuller, an American swimmer of the early 1900's, changed this stroke slightly. His version, now called the front crawl, is the fastest, most widely used stroke.

Men's international swim meets began in 1896 in the first modern Olympic Games. Women's meets were added in the 1912 Olympics. That year, Fanny Durack, an Australian, became the first woman to win an Olympic gold medal in swimming. Weissmuller won a total of five gold medals in the 1924 and 1928 Olympics. During his career, he set more than 65 U.S. and world records. Dawn Fraser and Murray Rose, two Australian swimmers, starred in the Olympics in the 1950's and 1960's. Fraser won the women's 100-meter freestyle race in 1956, 1960, and 1964. Rose won the men's 400-meter event in 1956 and 1960, and the 1,500-meter race in 1956. In 1972, Mark Spitz of the U.S. swimming team won seven gold medals, more than any other athlete had ever won in one Olympics.   DON VAN ROSSEN

Related Articles in WORLD BOOK include:

Artificial Respiration	Skin Diving
Diving	Spearfishing
Diving, Underwater	Surfing
Drowning	Swimming Pool
Ederle, Gertrude Caroline	Undertow
Life Jacket	Water Polo
Olympic Games	Water-Skiing
Safety (In Water Sports)	

Outline

I. Water Safety
II. Swimming Kicks and Strokes
  A. The Basic Kicks
  B. The Basic Strokes
III. Swimming as a Sport
  A. The Pool   D. Starts and Turns
  B. Kinds of Races   E. Training
  C. Swim Meets   F. Synchronized Swimming
IV. History

Questions

What contributions did Johnny Weissmuller make to swimming?
How can a nonswimmer help a swimmer in trouble?
What are the five basic swimming strokes?
How do swimmers start in a backstroke race?
What part does music play in synchronized swimming?
What are some basic water safety rules?
Why is swimming a good exercise for keeping fit?
What is a freestyle race?
What is survival bobbing?

Additional Resources

Level I
ORR, CHARLES R., and TYLER, J. B. *Swimming Basics*. Prentice-Hall, 1980.
SCHOLLANDER, DON, and COHEN, J. H. *Inside Swimming*. Regnery, 1974.

Level II
AMERICAN NATIONAL RED CROSS. *Swimming and Aquatic Safety*. Red Cross, 1981.
BESFORD, PAT, comp. *Encyclopaedia of Swimming*. 2nd ed. St. Martin's, 1977.
COUNSILMAN, JAMES E. *The Complete Book of Swimming*. Atheneum, 1977.
WIENER, HARVEY. *Total Swimming: How the Perfect Exercise Can Offer Rewards Both to the Body and to the Inner Self*. Simon & Schuster, 1980.

SWIMMING POOL. Millions of people in the United States and other countries enjoy the fun and recreation provided by swimming pools. Some pools are used for swimming competition. This article discusses backyard pools. For information on pools used in swim meets, see the WORLD BOOK article on SWIMMING.

Manufacturers produce a wide variety of backyard pools. Both the expense and the type of swimming activities planned should be considered when selecting a pool. There are two main kinds of backyard swimming pools, *in-ground pools* and *above-ground pools*.

In-ground pools are pools in which the water is below the surface of the ground. Most of these pools cost at least as much as a new automobile, but they last almost indefinitely. Many in-ground pools are made of concrete or fiberglass. Others consist of a vinyl liner in a shell of steel, aluminum, or special wood. Many in-ground pools have diving boards.

Above-ground pools are pools in which the water is in a metal or plastic frame above the surface of the ground. Such pools are less expensive than in-ground pools. However, they do not last as long. Some above-ground pools are small and shallow, and so they provide only limited opportunities for swimming.

Any backyard pool should have basic equipment. Ladders are necessary for getting into and out of the pool. A filtration system for removing impurities from the water is essential. The pool should also have an automatic *skimmer*, a device that clears the surface of trash. Critically reviewed by the NATIONAL SWIMMING POOL INSTITUTE

SWINBURNE, ALGERNON CHARLES (1837-1909), was one of the major English poets of the 1800's. He shocked Victorian England with his devotion to pleasure and his unorthodox religious and political beliefs. The sensuality of his verse scandalized many readers. Today, Swinburne's life and poetry do not seem so unconventional and shocking as they once did.

Swinburne was born in London. He attended Oxford University but left in 1860 without earning a degree to lead a bohemian life in London. For several years, Swinburne wrote much passionate but carefully composed poetry. His style emphasized long lines with varied meters and complex rhyme schemes. Many of Swinburne's poems were inspired by Elizabethan writers, var-

Drawing and water color (1861) by Dante Gabriel Rossetti; Fitzwilliam Museum, Cambridge, England

Algernon Swinburne

ious French poets, and ancient Greek and Roman writers. Swinburne first gained fame with his verse play *Atalanta in Calydon* (1865) and his collection *Poems and Ballads* (1866).

Swinburne's pleasure-seeking way of life led to his collapse in 1879. For the rest of his life, he lived in the home of a friend, Theodore Watts-Dunton. Swinburne continued to write poetry as well as drama and literary criticism. A powerful wish for death appears in much of his later work. The *Swinburne Letters* was published in six volumes from 1959 to 1962.   AVROM FLEISHMAN

SWINE. See HOG (Hog Terms).

SWINE FLU. See INFLUENZA (Flu Epidemics).

SWING, in music. See JAZZ (The "Swing" Era).

SWISS is a fine, sheer cotton cloth that was first made in Switzerland. The fabric may be plain, figured, or may have woven or paste dots. Swiss may be processed to remain crisp and stiff after washing. It is used in making dresses, aprons, and curtains. It comes in widths of 28, 32, and 36 inches (71, 81, and 91 centimeters) for dresses and aprons. Curtain swiss comes in widths from 36 to 40 inches (91 to 100 centimeters). Wider widths are also available for bedspreads. K. R. FOX

SWISS CHARD is a garden vegetable plant. Its leaves are eaten as greens. Swiss chard is related to the common beet plant. It resembles the beet, except that it does not have a large fleshy root. Swiss chard has a small woody root which cannot be eaten. The vegetable has fleshy leaf-stems, large leaves, and a dark green color. Some varieties of Swiss chard have pale yellow leaves and others have bright red leaves and leaf-stems. The plant has attractive, brilliant colors.

Swiss chard is one of the few garden greens that grow constantly throughout the summer. The seeds are sown in the spring. The large outer leaves are harvested as soon as they develop. Later the inner leaves are taken, and the harvest continues until frost kills the plant.

People grew Swiss chard as long ago as 350 B.C. It is a favorite crop in Switzerland and was introduced in

©Runk/Schoenberger, Grant Heilman

Swiss Chard

the United States in 1806. Massachusetts is one of the leading states in growing Swiss chard.

Swiss chard is an excellent source of vitamin A and contains a fair amount of vitamins of the B complex and C. Like most leafy vegetables, Swiss chard is also rich in minerals.

Scientific Classification. Swiss chard belongs to the goosefoot family, *Chenopodiaceae*. It is genus *Beta*, species *B. vulgaris*, variety *cicla*.   ERVIN L. DENISEN

SWISS CONFEDERATION. See SWITZERLAND (History).

SWISS FAMILY ROBINSON. See WYSS (family).

SWISS GUARDS. This famous body of Swiss soldiers grew out of a group of 250 Swiss who were picked to guard the pope in the late 1400's. In the early 1500's, Pope Julius II secured the position of the Swiss Guards by a treaty with the Swiss cantons of Zurich and Lucerne. According to the terms of the agreement, the cantons supplied 250 men to serve as a bodyguard for the pope from that time on. Since then the pope has always had a body of Swiss Guards around him at the Vatican. But through the years, the number of guards has been reduced and their type of service changed. Today, they are called the Papal Swiss Guard.

Another body of Swiss soldiers, called Swiss Guards, or Switzers, was organized in 1616 to protect King Louis XIII of France. These soldiers served France for 175 years. On August 10, 1792, during the French Revolution, most of them were killed while defending the royal palace in Paris from attack by an angry mob.

The memory of these Swiss Guards is preserved in the famous "Lion of Lucerne," which is carved in the face of a rock in Lucerne, Switzerland. It bears the words, "To the Fidelity and Courage of the Helvetians." See THORVALDSEN, BERTEL (picture).

King Louis XVIII formed a second corps of Swiss Guards in 1815. They were defeated in the Revolution of 1830, and the corps disbanded.   THOMAS E. GRIESS

SWITCH, ELECTRIC. See ELECTRIC SWITCH.

SWITCHBOARD. See TELEPHONE.

SWITHIN, SAINT, also spelled *Swithun*, was a bishop of Winchester, England. He was a faithful adviser to Egbert and Ethelwulf, kings of the West Saxons. Swithin died in 862 and was canonized in the 900's. St. Swithin's Day is July 15. According to an old rhyme, if the weather is fair that day, it will be fair for the next 40 days. If it rains on July 15, it will rain each day for the following 40 days.   FULTON J. SHEEN

SWITZERLAND

Villages Cling to Steep Mountain Slopes in the Swiss Alps. Many of the villages are popular tourist centers that feature winter sports.

SWITZERLAND is a small European country known for its beautiful, snow-capped mountains and freedom-loving people. The Alps and the Jura Mountains cover more than half of Switzerland. But most of the Swiss people live on a plateau that extends across the middle of the country between the two mountain ranges. In this region are most of Switzerland's industries and its richest farmlands. Switzerland's capital, Bern, and largest city, Zurich, are also there.

The Swiss have a long tradition of freedom. About 700 years ago, people in what is now central Switzerland agreed to help each other stay free from foreign rule. Gradually, people in nearby areas joined them in what came to be known as the Swiss Confederation. Various Swiss groups speak different languages. Switzerland has three official languages—German, French, and Italian. The Latin name for Switzerland, *Helvetia*, appears on Swiss coins and postage stamps.

The Swiss show great pride in their long independence. Switzerland has no regular army, but almost all the men receive military training yearly. They keep their weapons and uniforms at home, and can be called up quickly in an emergency. Local marksmanship contests are held frequently.

In the early 1500's, Switzerland established a policy of not taking sides in the many wars that raged in Europe. During World Wars I and II, Switzerland remained an island of peace. Almost all the nations around it took part in the bloody struggles. Switzerland provided safety for thousands who fled from the fighting, or from political persecution. The nation's neutrality

policy helped the Swiss develop valuable banking services to people of countries throughout the world, where banks are less safe. The League of Nations, the major world organization of the 1920's and 1930's, had its headquarters in the Swiss city of Geneva. Today, many international organizations, including various United Nations agencies, have headquarters in Geneva.

Switzerland has limited natural resources, but it is a thriving industrial nation. Using imported raw materials, the Swiss manufacture high-quality goods including electrical equipment, industrial machinery, and watches. They also produce large amounts of cheese and other dairy products and chocolate.

Facts in Brief

Capital: Bern.

Official Languages: German, French, and Italian.

Official Names: Schweiz (in German), Suisse (in French), and Svizzera (in Italian).

Area: 15,941 sq. mi. (41,288 km²), including 523 sq. mi. (1,355 km²) of inland water. *Greatest Distances*—east-west, 213 mi. (343 km); north-south, 138 mi. (222 km).

Elevation: *Highest*—Dufourspitze of Monte Rosa, 15,203 ft. (4,634 m) above sea level. *Lowest*—shore of Lake Maggiore, 633 ft. (193 m) above sea level.

Population: *Estimated 1984 Population*—6,392,000; distribution, 60 per cent urban, 40 per cent rural; density, 401 persons per sq. mi. (155 persons per km²). *1980 Census*—6,365,960. *Estimated 1989 Population*—6,424,000.

Chief Products: *Agriculture*—dairy products, fruits, hay, potatoes, wheat. *Manufacturing*—chemicals, electrical equipment, industrial machinery, precision instruments, processed foods, textiles, watches.

National Anthem: "Swiss Psalm."

National Holiday: Swiss National Day, August 1.

Money: *Basic Unit*—franc. For the value of the franc in dollars, see MONEY (table: Exchange Rates).

The contributors of this article are Heinz K. Meier, Dean of the School of Arts and Letters at Old Dominion University and author of Friendship Under Stress: U.S.-Swiss Relations 1900-1950; *and Norman J. G. Pounds, University Professor Emeritus of History and Geography at Indiana University.*

SWITZERLAND /Government

The government of Switzerland is based on the Swiss Constitution of 1848, which was changed greatly in 1874. The Constitution establishes a *federal republic* in which political powers are divided between the central government and regional governments.

In some ways, the Swiss government is one of the most democratic in the world. A majority of the voters must approve any *amendment* (change) to the Constitution. If 50,000 persons request an amendment, it must be brought to a vote even if the legislature has rejected it. A law must be voted on if, within 90 days after being passed, 30,000 persons or 8 *cantons* (states) request such action. Voters must be at least 20 years old.

Swiss democracy does have one important weakness: most women do not have a voice in local matters. Women have been allowed to vote in national elections only since 1971.

Regional and Local Government. Swiss voters elect executive councils and legislatures in the cantons, half-cantons, and cities. The country's six half-cantons were originally three undivided cantons. They split into separate political units with as much power of self-government as the full cantons. But each half-canton sends only one representative to the national legislature's Council of States, instead of two.

In one canton and in four of the half-cantons, the people vote by a show of hands at an open-air meeting called a *Landsgemeinde*. Similar meetings of voters are held in the small towns and villages.

Politics. Switzerland has many political parties, but there are few differences among the large ones. As a result, the parties cooperate easily. The three largest parties have about the same strength. They are the Catholic Conservative Party, the Radical Democratic Party, and the Social Democratic Party.

Defense. Switzerland has a *militia* (citizens' army) instead of regular armed forces. Swiss men are required to begin a series of military-training periods at the age of 20. They can be called into service until the age of 50. Men whose health or work makes them unable to serve, and those who live out of the country, must pay a special tax.

GOVERNMENT IN BRIEF

Political Divisions: 23 *cantons* (states), 3 of which are divided into half-cantons.

Executive: Federal Council, a 7-member Cabinet elected by the legislature to 4-year terms. They serve in place of a single chief executive.

Head of State: President, elected to a 1-year term by the legislature from among the members of the Federal Council. His duties are largely ceremonial. A man cannot be elected president two years in a row.

Legislature: A two-house Federal Assembly. *Council of States*—46 members. Two members are elected from each canton (one is elected from each half-canton), either by the canton legislature or by the voters. Their terms range from 1 to 4 years. *National Council*—200 members, elected to 4-year terms from election districts based on population.

Courts: *Highest Court*—the Federal Tribunal. It has 26 judges and 12 alternate judges, elected to 6-year terms by the Federal Assembly. Various lower courts are in the cantons.

EPA from Pictorial Parade

Federal Parliament Buildings in Bern are the meeting places of the Council of States and the National Council.

The Swiss Flag was used in an earlier form in 1240 by the region of Schwyz. The cross represents Christianity.

The Coat of Arms of Switzerland, like the Swiss flag, was established with its present dimensions in 1889.

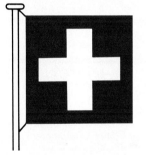

Switzerland, a country east of France, is less than 1 per cent as large as the United States, not counting Alaska and Hawaii.

WORLD BOOK map

839

Even after the Swiss began to join forces about 700 years ago to defend themselves, people from different areas kept their own ways of life. They defended these ways of life in the same spirit of independence that has made Switzerland famous. As a result, the Swiss still differ greatly among themselves in language, customs, and traditions. These differences are apparent from region to region, and even from some small communities to others.

In the past, the local patriotism of the Swiss was so strong that most of them thought of themselves as part of their own local area more than of their country. They considered the Swiss of other areas almost as foreign rivals, and feuds among various areas lasted for hundreds of years. But at most times when their country faced possible danger, the Swiss stood together as one people. Today, strong local patriotism has largely been replaced by national patriotism.

Population. In 1984, Switzerland had an estimated population of 6,392,000. The following table shows some official census figures for Switzerland:

1850	2,392,740	1930	4,066,400
1870	2,655,001	1940	4,265,703
1888	2,917,754	1950	4,714,992
1900	3,315,443	1960	5,429,061
1910	3,753,293	1970	6,269,783
1920	3,880,320	1980	6,365,960

Switzerland has five cities of more than 100,000 persons. They are, in order of size, Zurich, Basel, Geneva, Bern, and Lausanne. None has a population over 500,000. Almost 100 other cities have more than 10,000 persons. About two-fifths of the Swiss people live in rural areas. See the articles on Swiss cities listed in the *Related Articles* at the end of this article.

Language. The Swiss Constitution provides for three *official* languages and four *national* languages. The official languages are German, French, and Italian. As a result, Switzerland has three official names—Schweiz (in German), Suisse (in French), and Svizzera (in Italian). All national laws are published in each of these three languages. The Federal Tribunal, Switzerland's highest court, must include judges who represent each language group.

The four national languages are the three official ones plus *Romansh*, which is closely related to Latin. Romansh is spoken only in the mountain valleys of the canton of Graubünden, by about 1 per cent of the total Swiss population.

About 70 per cent of the people speak a form of German called *Schwyzerdütsch* (Swiss German). They live in the northern, eastern, and central parts of Switzerland. Schwyzerdütsch is almost a separate language, and even people who speak German find it hard to understand. The language and its name vary from place to place. It is called *Baseldütsch* in Basel, and *Züridütsch* in Zurich. But wherever Schwyzerdütsch is spoken, standard German is used in newspapers, books, television and radio programs, plays, and church sermons.

French, spoken in western Switzerland, is the language of almost 20 per cent of the people. Italian is used by nearly 10 per cent, in the south. Both these languages, as spoken by the Swiss, are much like their standard forms in France or Italy.

One difficulty, especially for visitors, is that many place names in Switzerland vary by language. The most complicated example—the city known as *Geneva* to English-speaking people—is called *Genf* in German, *Genève* in French, and *Ginevra* in Italian. English-speaking people know almost all other Swiss cities and towns by their French or German name.

Religion. Switzerland has complete freedom of religion. A little more than half the people are Protestants, and over 45 per cent are Roman Catholics. Of the 26 cantons and half-cantons in Switzerland, 11 are chiefly Protestant and 15 have a Roman Catholic majority.

The Protestant Reformation took a special form in Switzerland. Calvinism developed there and spread to many other countries during the 1500's. As a result, the Protestant movement split into two major camps, Calvinists and Lutherans. See CALVIN, JOHN; REFORMATION (Zwingli and the Anabaptists); ZWINGLI, HULDREICH.

Education. Swiss children are required by canton law to go to school, but the age limits vary. In most cantons, children must attend school from 6 through 14. Instruction is held in the local national language, and each child may also learn one of the other national languages.

Students who plan to attend a university may go to one of three kinds of high schools. These schools specialize in (1) Greek and Latin, (2) Latin and modern languages, or (3) mathematics and science. Other students may go to trade or technical schools while serving an apprenticeship. The students cannot advance in their work without graduating from one of these schools.

Switzerland has seven universities and various other

Population and Language

This map shows the population distribution of Switzerland, and the largest Swiss cities. Each dot represents about 20,000 persons. The map also shows where the national languages are spoken. Most Swiss speak a form of German called *Schwyzerdütsch*.

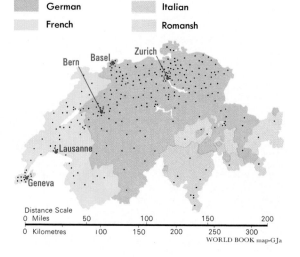

German	Italian
French	Romansh

Distance Scale
0 Miles 50 100 150 200
0 Kilometres 100 150 200 250 300

WORLD BOOK map-GJa

schools of higher learning. The oldest, the University of Basel, was founded in 1460. The University of Zurich, with about 10,000 students, is the largest. University fees are low. At the University of Zurich, for example, students pay only $1.50 per semester hour.

Arts. Most Swiss literature has been written in German. Famous books include two children's classics, *Heidi* by Johanna Spyri and *The Swiss Family Robinson* by the Wyss family. Major Swiss authors of the 1800's were Jeremias Gotthelf, Gottfried Keller, and Conrad Ferdinand Meyer. Carl Spitteler won the Nobel prize in literature in 1919 for his epic poetry and other writings. Later writers of the 1900's include Max Frisch and Friedrich Dürrenmatt, whose plays have been performed in many countries. Charles Ferdinand Ramuz wrote novels in French.

The art movement called *Dadaism* was founded in Zurich in 1916 (see DADAISM). Outstanding Swiss artists of the 1900's include the painter Paul Klee and the sculptors Alberto Giacometti and Jean Tinguely. Le Corbusier won fame in modern architecture.

Several Swiss cities have symphony orchestras. The Orchestre de la Suisse Romande of Geneva became world famous under conductor Ernest Ansermet. An annual music festival in Lucerne attracts thousands of music lovers. Almost every town and village has a singing group that practices weekly for local festivals, and for regional and national singing competitions. Band music and folk dancing in colorful national costumes are also popular. Some mountaineers enjoy yodeling or playing the alpenhorn (see ALPENHORN; YODEL).

Sports. The mountains of Switzerland provide grand opportunities for a variety of sports. About a third of the people ski. Many also enjoy bobsledding, camping, climbing, and hiking in the mountains. Target shooting, stressed by the Swiss military system, is extremely popular. Shooting matches are held frequently. Other favorite sports include bicycling, boating, gymnastics, soccer, swimming, and wrestling. *Hornussen*, a national game somewhat like baseball, is played by two teams. The batter hits a wooden disk with a wooden club 8 feet (2.4 meters) long. Fielders catch the disk with wooden rackets.

William Froelich

Outdoor Flower Markets brighten many busy cities of Switzerland. This market is in Geneva, the third largest Swiss city.

Mort Beebe, Photo Researchers

Local Festivals, *above,* are often held throughout Switzerland. Many people dress in national costumes for these celebrations.

Robert Perron, Photo Researchers

Men Wait to Vote by Hand at an open-air meeting, *left.* The swords held by the men indicate their right to vote.

840a

SWITZERLAND/The Land

Switzerland has three main land regions: (1) the Jura Mountains, (2) the Swiss Plateau, and (3) the Swiss Alps. The two mountain regions make up about 65 per cent of Switzerland's area. But the plateau between them has about four-fifths of the country's population.

The Jura Mountains consist of a series of parallel ridges that are separated by narrow valleys. These ridges extend along Switzerland's western border with France. Within Switzerland, the highest mountain of the range is 5,518-foot (1,682-meter) Mont Tendre. The Jura Mountains are the home of Switzerland's important watchmaking industry. Other industries in the region include dairy farming and lumbering. See JURA.

The Swiss Plateau is a hilly region with rolling plains. It lies from 1,200 to 2,200 feet (366 to 671 meters) above sea level. The movement of ancient glaciers formed many lakes, including Lake Constance and Lake Geneva. Switzerland's richest croplands and grazing lands are in this region, as well as most of the large cities and manufacturing industries. See LAKE CONSTANCE; LAKE GENEVA.

The Swiss Alps are part of the mighty Alps, the

LAND REGIONS OF SWITZERLAND

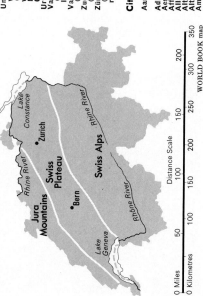

Distance Scale

| 0 Miles | 50 | 100 | 150 | 200 | 250 | 300 | 350 |
| 0 Kilometres | | 100 | 150 | 200 | | 300 | |

WORLD BOOK map

Switzerland Map Index

Cantons†

Aargau	441,000	A 5
Appenzell (Anrovie)	59,600	A 5
Ausser Rhoden‡	46,400	
Inner Rhoden‡	13,200	
Basel (Bâle)	425,400	A 3
Basel-Landt‡	218,500	
Basel-Stadtt‡	206,900	
Bern (Berne)	917,400	B 3
Fribourg (Freiburg)	181,100	B 3
Geneve (Genf)	336,700	B 2
Glarus (Glaris)	35,300	B 5
Graubünden (Grisons)	162,800	B 5
Jura	68,000	A 3
Luzern (Lucerne)	291,600	A 4
Neuchâtel (Neuenburg)	161,100	B 2
St. Gallen (St. Gall)	383,400	A 5
Schaffhausen (Schaffhouse)	68,800	A 4
Schwyz	92,700	A 4
Solothurn (Soleure)	220,500	A 3
Thurgau (Thurgovie)	182,300	A 4
Ticino (Tessin)	261,100	B 4
Uri		
Unterwalden (Unterwald)		
Nidwalden‡	26,600	B 4
Obwalden‡	25,200	
Valais (Wallis)	211,700	B 3
Vaud (Waadt)	520,800	B 2
Zug	73,100	A 4
Zürich (Zurich)	1,112,800	A 4

Cities and Towns

Aarau	*16,000	
	*51,100	A 4
Adliswil	15,500	A 4
Aesch*	8,000	A 4
Affoltern*	17,700	A 4
Allschwil	8,500	A 3
Altdorf*	8,500	B 5
Altstätten	9,500	A 5
Amriswil	7,600	A 5

Arbon	10,900	
Arlesheim*	*14,300	A 5
Arth	8,300	A 4
Baar	14,900	A 4
Baden	13,800	A 4
	*66,800	B 3
Basel	185,300	
	*367,000	A 3
Bellinzona	17,400	
	*33,400	B 4
Belp*	7,300	B 3
Bern	145,500	
	*283,600	A 3
Biberist	*87,900	B 3
Biel	57,700	A 3
Binningen	14,300	A 3
Birsfelden*	13,500	B 3
Bolligen	30,800	B 3
Brig-Gis*	9,900	A 4
Brugg	9,100	A 4
Buchs	9,200	A 5
Bülach	12,000	A 4
Bulle	7,700	B 3
Burgdorf	14,800	A 3
Carouge	12,900	B 2
Cham	9,000	A 4
Chêne-Bougeries	8,500	C 1
Chiasso	8,000	B 4
Chur	32,600	B 5
Davos	11,500	B 5
Delémont	11,600	A 3
Diétikon	22,700	A 4
Dübendorf	20,300	A 4
Ebikon*	8,400	A 4
Einsiedeln	9,800	A 4
Emmen	22,900	A 4
Flawil	8,500	A 5
Fräuten-kon*		
Freid	18,300	A 4
Freid-bach*	9,400	A 4
Fribourg	39,300	A 3
Geneva (Genève)	150,100	
	*322,900	B 2
Goldach	8,400	A 5
Gossau	17,400	A 4
Grenchen	*26,100	A 3
Herisau	17,000	A 4
Horgen	17,400	A 4
Horw*	11,400	A 4
Illnau-Effreti-kon*	14,200	A 4
Interlaken	5,100	B 3
Jona*	11,400	A 4
Kilchberg	7,300	A 4
Kirchberg	6,200	A 3
Kloten	16,000	A 4
Kreuzlingen	34,600	A 5
Kriens	16,100	A 4
Küsnacht	21,300	A 4
Küssnacht	12,100	A 4
La Chaux-de-Fonds	39,000	A 2
Lancy	23,400	B 2
Langenthal	13,300	A 3
Langnau [im Emmental]	*21,800	A 3
La Tour-de-Peilz	9,200	B 2

Lausanne	132,400	
	*227,200	B 2
Le Locle	12,900	A 2
Lenzburg*	7,600	A 4
Liestal	11,700	A 3
Littau	*40,800	A 4
Locarno	15,300	
	*41,200	B 4
Lucerne (Luzern)	63,700	
	*156,500	A 4
Lugano	28,600	
	*68,900	B 4
Lyss	8,400	A 3
Männedorf	7,600	A 4
Martigny	11,000	B 3
Meilen	10,300	A 4
Mendrisio	6,800	G 4
Meyrin	21,800	B 2
Monthey	11,300	B 2
Montreux	20,300	B 2
Morges	*60,300	B 2
Moutier	*18,900	A 3
München-buchsee*	8,300	A 3
München-stein	*8,100	A 3
Münsingen	11,600	B 3
Muri	8,100	B 3
Muttenz	17,100	A 3
Neuchâtel	35,400	
	*59,500	B 2
Neuhausen [am Rheinfall]	*10,900	A 4
Nidau*	8,200	A 3
Nyon	12,400	B 2
Oberwil*	7,600	A 3
Oftringen	8,300	A 4
Olten	17,000	
	*47,000	A 4
Onex*	16,400	B 2
Opfikon*	6,500	A 4
Payerne	7,400	B 3
Pfäffikon	8,100	A 4
Porrentruy	6,600	A 3
Pratteln*	15,800	A 3
Prilly	11,700	B 2
Pully	16,200	B 2
Rapperswil	7,900	A 4
Regensdorf*	11,700	A 4
Reinach	17,400	A 3
Renens	16,600	B 2
Rheinfelden	8,000	A 3
Richterswil*	11,400	A 4
Riehen	20,400	A 3
Romanshorn	7,800	A 5
Rorschach	9,900	A 5
Rüti	*22,900	A 4
Saanen	9,400	B 3
St. Gall	75,400	
	*86,800	A 5
St. Moritz	5,900	B 5
Sarnen	*7,200	B 4
Schaff-hausen	32,400	A 4
Schlieren	12,800	A 4
Schwyz	12,100	A 4
Sierre	12,100	B 3
Sion	23,400	B 3
Solothurn	*34,800	A 3
Spiez	8,900	B 3
Stäfa	9,900	A 4

Steffisburg	12,500	B 3
Suhr	*227,200	A 4
Sursee	7,300	A 4
Thalwil	15,200	A 4
Thônex*	7,600	B 2
Thun	37,000	
	*64,800	B 3
Trimbach	7,300	A 4
Urdorf*	8,800	A 4
Uster	22,500	A 4
Uzwil	27,300	B 2
Vernier	16,000	
Vevey	*60,300	B 2
Volketswil*	17,800	B 4
Wädenswil	11,000	A 4
Wald	10,700	A 4
Wallisellen*	8,500	A 5
Wattwil	18,400	A 5
Weinfelden	14,900	A 4
Wetzikon		B 2
Wil		
Winterthur	86,800	C 3
Wohlen	11,700	B 4
Worb*	11,000	B 3
Yverdon	8,600	A 2
Zofingen	8,800	A 4
Zollikofen	12,000	A 4
Zollikon*	22,300	A 4
Zuchwil		
Zug	*52,000	A 4
	*707,500	A 4
Zurich	379,600	

Physical Features

Aare River		A 3
Bernese Alps		B 3
Bernina Pass		B 6
Birs River		A 3
Bodensee, see Lake Constance		
Broye River		B 2
Chasseral (Mountain)		A 3
Contra Dam*		B 4
Dent du Midi (Peak)		B 2
Diablerets (Mountains)		B 3
Dom (Mountain)		B 3
Doubs River		A 2
Dufourspitze, see Monte Rosa		
Engadine (Region)		B 5
Finsteraarhorn (Mountain)		B 3
Furka Pass		B 4
Giessbach Falls* (Waterfall)		B 4
Glärnisch (Mountain)		B 4
Grand Combin (Mountain)		C 3
Grand Dixence Dam*		B 3
Great Saint Bernard Tunnel		C 3
Hallwil Lake (Hallwilersee)		A 4
Inn River		B 5
Jungfrau (Mountain)		B 3
Jura Mountains		B 2
Lac Léman, see Lake Geneva		
Lake Ageri (Agerisee)		A 4
Lake Biel (Bielersee)		A 3
Lake Brienz (Brienzersee)		B 3
Lake Constance (Bodensee)		A 5
Lake Geneva (Lac Léman)		B 2
Lake Joux / Lac de Joux		B 2
Lake Lugano		C 4
Lake Maggiore		B 4
Lake Morat (Murtensee)		B 3
Lake de Neuchâtel (Lac de Neuchâtel)		B 2
Lake of Lucerne		A 4
Lake of Thun (Thunersee)		B 3
Lake Sarnersee		B 4
Lake Wallen (Wallensee)		A 5
Lake Zug (Zugersee)		A 4
Lepontine Alps (Mountains)		B 4
Lötschberg Tunnel		B 3
Luzzone Dam*		B 4
Matterhorn (Mountain)		C 3
Mauvoisin Dam* (Mountain)		C 3
Monte Rosa (Dufourspitze)		C 3
Penine Alps (Mountains)		C 3
Rhaetian Alps (Mountains)		B 5
Rhine River		B 5
Rhône River		B 3
Saint Gotthard Tunnel		B 4
Simplon Pass and Tunnel		C 3
Splügen Pass		B 5
Staubbach (Waterfall)*		B 3
Tendre, Mont (Mountain)		B 2
Ticino River		B 4
Trümmelbach (Waterfall)*		B 3
Zürich Lake (Zürichsee)		A 4

†Name in German, French, or Italian, according to most spoken language; alternative name in parentheses.
*Population of metropolitan area, including suburbs.
‡Half-Cantons.
*Does not appear on map; key shows general location.
Source, 1978 official estimates.

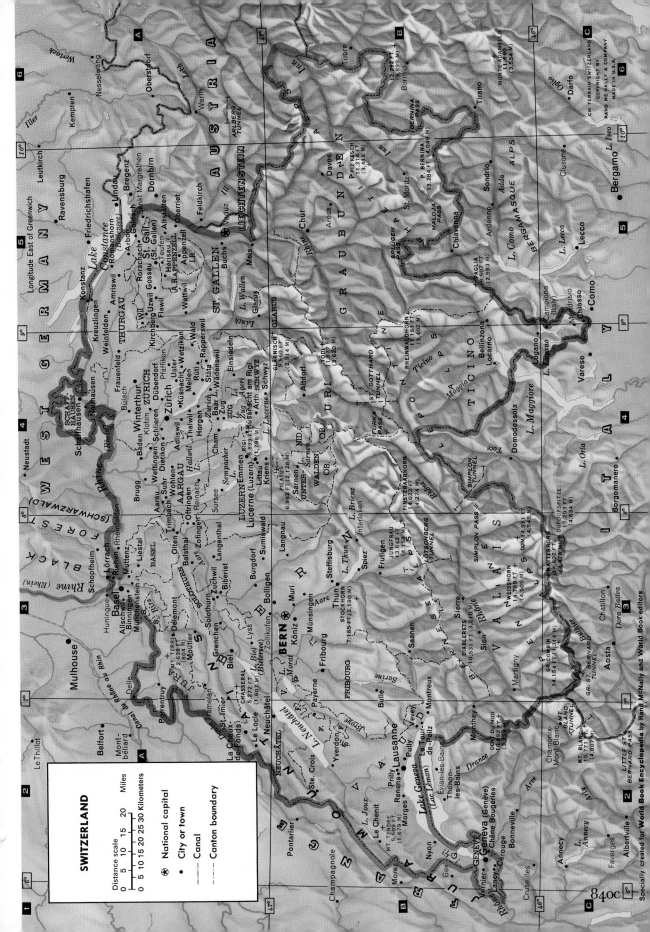

largest mountain system in Europe. This high, rugged region covers about 60 per cent of Switzerland, but less than a fifth of the people live there. There are glaciers as low as 3,500 feet (1,070 meters) above sea level, and snow blankets most of the region from three to five months a year. Much of the region is forested. The forests help prevent snow from sliding down to the valleys, but avalanches sometimes occur.

The upper valleys of the Rhine and Rhône rivers divide the Swiss Alps into a northern and a southern series of ranges. These ranges include the Bernese, Lepontine, Pennine, and Rhaetian Alps. Ancient glaciers carved out sharp peaks, jagged ridges, and steep gorges. Many mountain streams form plunging waterfalls. The highest waterfall is the 1,982-foot (604-meter) Giessbach Falls in the Bernese Alps. The Pennine Alps include Switzerland's highest peak, the 15,203-foot (4,634-meter) Dufourspitze of Monte Rosa. The spectacular beauty of the Swiss Alps attracts tourists from all parts of the world. See ALPS.

Rivers. The Swiss Alps form part of Europe's main drainage divide. They are the source of rivers that flow in all directions. The Rhine and the Rhône rivers rise within 15 miles (24 kilometers) of each other in the Alps, but flow in opposite directions. The Rhine flows into the North Sea, and the Rhône into the Mediterranean Sea. The Inn River winds into the Danube River, which goes into the Black Sea. The Ticino River is a tributary of the Po River, which flows into the Adriatic Sea. See RHINE RIVER; RHÔNE RIVER.

EPA from Pictorial Parade

Ticino, the Southernmost Swiss Canton, is the warmest part of the country. It has hot summers and mild winters.

SWITZERLAND/Climate

The climate of Switzerland varies greatly from area to area because of the wide variety in altitude. In general, temperatures decrease about 3° F. (2° C) with each 1,000-foot (300-meter) increase in elevation, and higher areas receive more rain and snow. Cold air from nearby mountains often settles over lower areas, producing extreme dampness and fog. Fog sometimes covers the entire Swiss Plateau like a sea of clouds. Some low areas may be covered as many as 120 days a year.

January temperatures average from 29° to 33° F. (−2° to 1° C) on the central plateau and in the mountain valleys. In winter, there is colder though drier and sunnier weather above the layer of fog than below it. In summer, the plateau is warm and sunny, but severe storms may occur. July temperatures on the plateau average from 65° to 70° F. (18° to 21° C). Many sheltered valleys sometimes become uncomfortably hot. In summer, the higher slopes are cool or even cold. The canton of Ticino, which extends southward to the Italian plains, has hot summers and mild winters.

The central plateau receives from 40 to 45 inches (100 to 114 centimeters) of *precipitation* (rain, melted snow, and other forms of moisture) a year. Sheltered valleys usually have less. In some high areas, the yearly precipitation totals more than 100 inches (250 centimeters). Above 6,000 feet (1,800 meters), snow covers the ground at least six months a year.

A dry, warm southerly wind called the *foehn* sometimes blows into valleys in the Swiss Alps. It causes rapid changes in temperature and air pressure, which makes many people uncomfortable. This wind also may melt mountain snows earlier than usual, causing severe avalanches.

AVERAGE MONTHLY WEATHER

	BERN Temperatures F° High	BERN Temperatures F° Low	BERN Temperatures C° High	BERN Temperatures C° Low	BERN Days of Rain or Snow		LUGANO Temperatures F° High	LUGANO Temperatures F° Low	LUGANO Temperatures C° High	LUGANO Temperatures C° Low	LUGANO Days of Rain or Snow
JAN.	35	26	2	-3	11	JAN.	43	29	6	-2	7
FEB.	40	27	4	-3	10	FEB.	48	30	9	-1	6
MAR.	48	33	9	1	12	MAR.	56	36	13	2	9
APR.	56	39	13	4	14	APR.	63	43	17	6	11
MAY	64	46	18	8	15	MAY	70	50	21	10	14
JUNE	70	52	21	11	14	JUNE	78	56	26	13	12
JULY	74	56	23	13	13	JULY	83	60	28	16	11
AUG.	73	55	23	13	12	AUG.	82	59	28	15	10
SEPT.	66	50	19	10	11	SEPT.	75	54	24	12	9
OCT.	55	42	13	6	12	OCT.	63	46	17	8	11
NOV.	44	34	7	1	12	NOV.	52	38	11	3	10
DEC.	36	27	2	-3	12	DEC.	45	31	7	-1	8

Source: Meteorological Office, London

Switzerland is a prosperous country with one of the world's highest standards of living. In spite of limited natural resources, the nation's highly specialized industries are extremely profitable. Switzerland has more jobs than its own people can fill. Workers from other countries make up about a fifth of Switzerland's labor force.

Switzerland trades mainly with Western European countries and the United States. The Swiss import more goods than they export. They make up the difference with income from tourism and from banking, insurance, and transportation services to foreign persons or firms.

Natural Resources. Switzerland lacks important deposits of coal, iron ore, petroleum, and other minerals on which heavy industry is based. The country's limited mining activity largely involves salt and such building materials as limestone and sandstone.

Most of the land is too high or too rugged to be good farmland. In addition, the climate is generally better for growing hay and other livestock feeds rather than such crops as wheat and fruit. Crops are raised on only about a tenth of Switzerland's total area, chiefly on the Swiss Plateau. More than 40 per cent of the country consists of meadows or grazing land, much of which can be used only in summer. Forests cover about a fourth of Switzerland.

Switzerland's greatest natural resource is perhaps its rushing mountain rivers. About three-fourths of the electric power produced in Switzerland is generated at hydroelectric power stations on the rivers.

Manufacturing. Switzerland is one of the most industrialized countries in the world. Its manufacturing industries are based on the processing of imported raw materials into high-quality products for export. To keep the cost of materials and transportation as low as possible, these industries specialize in skilled, precision work on small, valuable items. In Switzerland's watchmaking industry, for example, the cost of materials is only about one-twentieth the cost of labor. More than 95 per cent of the watches made in Switzerland are exported.

The Swiss make such engineering products as generators and other electrical equipment, industrial machinery, machine tools, precision instruments, and transportation equipment. Other major products are chemicals, paper, processed foods including cheese and chocolate, and silk and other textiles.

Most Swiss factories are small or medium-sized, because of the stress on quality goods rather than mass production. In addition, hydroelectric power is widely distributed. For these reasons, there are factories in small towns and even in villages throughout the country. The use of hydroelectricity, rather than coal or oil, to power the factories and railroads helps keep the busiest industrial centers almost free of smoke.

Agriculture in Switzerland supplies only about three-fifths of the people's needs. The rest of the nation's food must be imported. Livestock raising is the most important agricultural activity because of the limited cropland resources and the climate. It provides about 75 per cent of Switzerland's farm income, largely through dairy farming. Farmers also raise hogs, goats,

Alan Band Associates

Switzerland's Watchmaking Industry is world famous. Almost all Swiss watches are exported to other countries.

Switzerland's Gross National Product

Total gross national product in 1979—$59,900,000,000

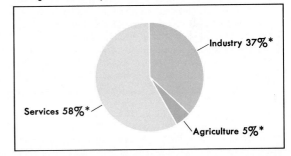

Industry 37%*

Services 58%*

Agriculture 5%*

The gross national product (GNP) is the total value of goods and services produced by a country in a year. The GNP measures a nation's total annual economic performance. It can also be used to compare the economic output and growth of countries.

Production and Workers by Economic Activities

Economic Activities	Per Cent of GDP* Produced	Employed Workers	
		Number of Persons	Per Cent of Total
Manufacturing	31	961,000	32
Hotels, Restaurants, & Trade	20	578,000	20
Finance, Insurance, Real Estate, & Business Services	10	134,700	5
Government	10	226,800	8
Community, Social, & Personal Services	9	450,200	15
Transportation & Communication	7	179,100	6
Construction & Mining	6	182,900	6
Agriculture, Forestry, & Fishing	5	220,400	7
Utilities	2	28,800	1
Total	100	2,961,900	100

*Based on gross domestic product (GDP) in 1975. GDP is gross national product adjusted for net income sent abroad or received from abroad.
Sources: Federal Office of Statistics, Bern, Switzerland; *The Planetary Product, 1979-1980,* Dr. Herbert Block.

and sheep. Most of the dairy cattle graze on the high mountain pastures in summer, and are brought down to the valleys in winter. Much of the milk is used to make cheeses for export. These cheeses include Emmentaler, also known as *Swiss cheese*, and Gruyère.

Swiss farms are small, averaging only 8 acres (3 hectares). Farmers work the land carefully to make it as productive as possible. Crops include fruits, wheat and other grains, and potatoes. Grapes are grown near Lakes Geneva, Lugano, and Maggiore, and in other sunny areas. Olive trees grow in the canton of Ticino.

Tourism. Since the early 1800's, increasing numbers of tourists have come to Switzerland. Today, more than $5\frac{1}{2}$ million tourists from all parts of the world visit the country yearly. The busy tourist industry adds over $350 million to Switzerland's annual national income.

Switzerland has thousands of hotels and inns for tourists. Sports centers in the Alps, including Davos and St. Moritz, attract many vacationers. Skiing is especially popular. Most of the ski runs are free of trees because they are higher than the elevation at which trees stop growing. In summer, guides take tourists mountain climbing. Many visitors come for the healthful clear, dry, mountain air, as well as to enjoy the beauty of the Alps. Water sports on Lake Geneva and other lakes are also popular vacation attractions.

Banking adds more than $150 million a year to the national income. Swiss banks attract deposits from people in many countries. The banks are probably the safest in the world, partly because of the nation's neutrality. A depositor can choose to be identified by a number known only to himself and a few bank officials. In this way, a private fortune can be kept secret. Under Swiss law, a bank employee who violates this secrecy may be fined and imprisoned. But the secrecy may be broken in the investigation of Swiss criminal cases.

Transportation. Switzerland has fine transportation systems in spite of the mountains, which make travel difficult. The government owns and operates almost the entire 3,150-mile (5,070-kilometer) railroad network. Many railroad tunnels cut through the Alps, including the Lötschberg, St. Gotthard, and Simplon tunnels. The 12.3-mile (19.8-kilometer) Simplon Tunnel is one of the longest railroad tunnels in the world.

Switzerland has over 30,000 miles (48,000 kilometers) of hard-surfaced roads and highways. They provide travel even to mountain areas. But roads that wind through the higher mountain passes are open only a few months of the year. Heavy snow makes them unusable except in summer. The $3\frac{1}{2}$-mile (5.6-kilometer) Great St. Bernard Tunnel, opened in 1964, was the first automobile tunnel through the Alps. It links Switzerland and Italy. The 10.14-mile (16.32-kilometer) St. Gotthard Road Tunnel is the longest highway tunnel in the world.

The Rhine River connects Basel, Switzerland's only port, with the North Sea. Large barges can reach Basel, which handles about 8 million short tons (7.3 million metric tons) of cargo a year.

Geneva and Zurich have international airports. The privately owned Swissair, Switzerland's only international airline, flies to about 40 countries.

Communication. Switzerland has more than 450 newspapers. The largest daily newspaper, *Der Blick* of Zurich, has a daily circulation of about 190,000. Over half the more than 100 dailies are published in German, and the others are in French or Italian. A few of the nondaily newspapers are in Romansh.

The Swiss government owns the country's three radio stations and three television stations. Each broadcasts in one of the three official languages. A few programs are in Romansh. The government operates the postal, telegraph, and telephone services.

Raising Dairy Cattle ranks high among Swiss farming activities. Cattle auctions are held on Sundays during the summer.

Thomas Hollyman, Photo Researchers

Skiing Tourists flock to the snowy Swiss Alps. One popular ski resort is Zermatt, near the majestic Matterhorn, *rear*.

George Holton, Photo Researchers

Early Days. Before the time of Christ, a Celtic people called the *Helvetians* lived in what is now Switzerland. They were conquered in 58 B.C. by Roman armies led by Julius Caesar. The region, known as *Helvetia*, became a Roman province. By the A.D. 400's, two Germanic tribes, the Alemannians and the Burgundians, settled there. Another Germanic people, the Franks, defeated these tribes by the early 500's. The Frankish kingdom later expanded and became powerful under Charlemagne, but it broke apart during the 800's. See FRANK.

Most of present-day Switzerland became part of the Holy Roman Empire in 962, when the empire began, and the rest was part of the kingdom of Burgundy. That part came into the empire in 1033. Switzerland consisted of many territories, towns, and villages ruled by local lords, and some communities directly under the emperor. See HOLY ROMAN EMPIRE.

The Struggle for Freedom. By the 1200's, the Hapsburg, or Habsburg, family had gained control over much of Switzerland. The free men of what are now the *cantons* (states) of Schwyz and Uri feared the growth of the Hapsburgs' power. In 1273, Rudolf I became the first Hapsburg to rule the Holy Roman Empire. He began to take control of the two regions. In 1291, Schwyz and Uri decided to fight for freedom. They invited the nearby region of Unterwalden to join them.

Leaders of the three regions met in August, 1291, and signed the Perpetual Covenant, a defense agreement. They declared their freedom and promised to aid each other against any foreign ruler. The Perpetual Covenant was the start of the Swiss Confederation. The confederation came to be known as Switzerland. It took its name from the canton of Schwyz.

—————— **IMPORTANT DATES IN SWITZERLAND** ——————

58 B.C. Roman armies under Julius Caesar conquered Helvetia (now Switzerland).

A.D. 400's Germanic tribes occupied Helvetia.

962 Most of what is now Switzerland became part of the Holy Roman Empire.

1291 Three Swiss *cantons* (states) signed the Perpetual Covenant, which established the Swiss Confederation.

1315-1388 Switzerland defeated Austria in three wars of independence.

1499 Switzerland won independence from the Holy Roman Empire.

1515 The Swiss were defeated by the French in Italy, and began their policy of permanent neutrality.

1648 The Holy Roman Empire recognized Swiss independence.

1798 French forces occupied Switzerland and established the Helvetic Republic under their control.

1815 The Congress of Vienna expanded Switzerland to 22 cantons, and restored the old confederation.

1848 Switzerland adopted a constitution that established federal power over the confederation.

1863 The Red Cross was founded in Switzerland.

1874 Constitutional changes increased federal power.

1920 The League of Nations met at its headquarters in Geneva, Switzerland, for its first session.

1958 Basel became the first Swiss city to let women vote in local elections.

1960 Switzerland helped form the European Free Trade Association.

1963 Switzerland joined the Council of Europe.

1968 Geneva became the first Swiss city to have a woman mayor.

1971 Swiss women received the right to vote in national elections.

By an unknown artist from the *Stumpf Chronicle*. Zentralbibliothek, Zurich, Switzerland

The Battle of Sempach was fought in 1386 against the Austrians during the Swiss wars of independence. That battle, won by the Swiss, is shown in a woodcut dating from 1548.

SWITZERLAND

The Habsburgs ruled Austria, and the Swiss fought several wars of independence against Austrian forces. In 1315, at Morgarten, Swiss peasants trapped and defeated an Austrian army 10 times their strength. Between 1332 and 1353, five more cantons joined the Swiss Confederation. The Swiss again defeated the Austrians at Sempach in 1386 and at Näfels in 1388. See HABSBURG, HOUSE OF.

The wars with Austria were full of dramatic incidents, and many famous stories have been told about Swiss heroes. For two exciting tales, see the articles on TELL, WILLIAM and WINKELRIED, ARNOLD VON.

Independence and Expansion. Switzerland became a strong military power during the 1400's. The Swiss entered several wars to gain land, and won many territories. In three battles in 1476 and 1477, the Swiss defeated Charles the Bold, duke of Burgundy. In 1499, they crushed the forces of Maximilian I, the Habsburg ruler of the Holy Roman Empire. Switzerland won complete independence, though the empire did not officially recognize it until 1648. In 1512 and 1513, the Swiss drove French armies out of northern Italy. Almost all the lands won in these wars of expansion remained under Swiss control for nearly 300 years, and then were admitted into the confederation as cantons.

In 1515, the French defeated the Swiss at Marignano in Italy. The Swiss suffered great losses, and began to question their policy of expansion. Switzerland soon adopted a policy of permanent neutrality, and has stayed out of foreign wars ever since.

Five more cantons joined the Swiss Confederation between 1481 and 1513, making a total of 13. Each canton governed itself as it chose, almost like a separate country. Some cantons were peasant democracies, and others were governed by powerful families or by craftsmen's groups called *guilds*. Many cantons owned nearby territories either by themselves or with other cantons. The confederation had no central government. Delegates from each canton occasionally met in an assembly called the *Tagsatzung* to discuss various matters. But this assembly had no real power.

Religious Civil Wars. The Reformation spread quickly in Switzerland during the early 1500's. Huldreich Zwingli, one of the great leaders of the Protestant movement, preached in Zurich. John Calvin, another great Protestant leader, made Geneva an international center of Protestantism. See REFORMATION.

The Reformation split Switzerland into two armed camps, Protestant and Roman Catholic. The two groups fought in 1529, 1531, 1656, and 1712, but little change in Swiss life resulted.

French Control. In 1798, during the French Revolution, French armies swept into Switzerland and quickly occupied the country. The French set up the *Helvetic Republic*, and gave the new Swiss government strong central power. The Swiss cantons became merely administrative districts of the government.

The great political change caused much confusion and dissatisfaction among the Swiss. As a result, Napoleon of France re-established the 13 Swiss cantons in 1803 and created 6 new ones from their territories. He reduced the power of the central government, and restored much of the cantons' self-government.

After Napoleon's final defeat in 1815, the Congress of Vienna gave Switzerland three more cantons that had been under French control (see VIENNA, CONGRESS OF). The old confederation system was largely restored, with the central government having little power. The Congress of Vienna also guaranteed the neutrality of Switzerland. The European powers at the congress recognized Swiss neutrality as being for the good of all Europe. The neutrality of Switzerland has never since been broken.

The Constitution of 1848. By 1830, many Swiss had begun to demand political reforms—including individual rights and freedom of the press—and greater national unity. Governments were overthrown peaceably in some cantons, but rioting occured in others. The reform movement grew in strength. Seven cantons banded together to oppose the changes, but were defeated in a three-week civil war in 1847.

Switzerland adopted a new constitution in 1848. This constitution set up a representative democracy with a two-house legislature like that of the United States. It established federal power over the confederation and guaranteed religious freedom and other individual rights. The constitution was changed in 1874 to increase the government's powers, especially in military and court matters.

In 1863, Jean Henri Dunant, a Swiss businessman and writer, founded the Red Cross in Geneva. The Red Cross flag was copied from that of Switzerland, with the two colors reversed. See RED CROSS.

Neutrality in the World Wars. World War I began in 1914, and Switzerland immediately declared its neutrality. The fighting nations respected this policy because Switzerland acted in a strictly neutral manner throughout the war. Food imports decreased during the four years of fighting, but Swiss farmers increased their grain production to feed the people. In 1920, Geneva became the headquarters of the newly created League

Expansion of Switzerland—1291 to 1815

■ In 1291		1481 to 1513	
1332 to 1353		1803 to 1815	

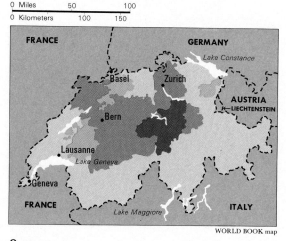

WORLD BOOK map

of Nations, an association of countries organized to prevent war. Switzerland was one of the original members of the League. See LEAGUE OF NATIONS.

After World War II began in 1939, Switzerland again declared its neutrality. German forces did not invade Switzerland. They feared the Swiss would blow up transportation tunnels in the Alps if they did. Switzerland became a major supply link between Germany and its ally Italy. It also represented the United States and other Allied nations in enemy countries. During the war, Switzerland cared for more than 100,000 refugees from a number of countries.

Switzerland did not join the United Nations (UN), which was founded after World War II ended in 1945. The Swiss felt that UN membership, which requires possible military action by member nations, would violate their neutrality policy. But the UN made Geneva its European headquarters, and Switzerland joined most of the UN's specialized agencies.

Switzerland Today still avoids membership in international organizations that might endanger its neutrality—but not so strictly as in the past. Many Swiss, especially young people, have begun to question their nation's policy of neutrality. In 1960, the Swiss helped form the European Free Trade Association, an economic organization of European nations. Switzerland joined the Council of Europe in 1963. This organization of European countries seeks to promote closer unity among its members for economic and social progress, but it has no real power.

A movement to gain political rights for women has made significant progress in Switzerland. In 1958, Basel became the first Swiss city to allow women to vote in local elections. The next year, Vaud became the first canton to grant that right. In 1968, Geneva became the first Swiss city to have a woman mayor. In 1971, Swiss men voted to allow women to vote in national elections. The first women members of Parliament took office in November 1971.

In 1978, Switzerland increased its number of cantons from 22 to 23. It created a new canton called Jura from territory that was part of the canton of Bern. In most of Bern, the majority of people are German-speaking Protestants. But in the part of Bern that became the canton of Jura, most of the people are French-speaking Roman Catholics. Jura was created to give the French-speaking Catholics their own separate canton.

HEINZ K. MEIER and NORMAN J. G. POUNDS

SWITZERLAND/*Study Aids*

Related Articles in WORLD BOOK include:

BIOGRAPHIES

Agassiz (family)	Klee, Paul
Barth, Karl	Kocher, Emil T.
Bernoulli (family)	Le Corbusier
Calvin, John	Mueller, Paul
Dunant, Jean H.	Paracelsus, Philippus A.
Dürrenmatt, Friedrich	Pestalozzi, Johann H.
Euler, Leonhard	Piaget, Jean
Frisch, Max	Piccard (brothers)
Gallatin, Albert	Rousseau, Jean Jacques
Hesse, Hermann	Spyri, Johanna
Jung, Carl G.	Tussaud, Marie G.
Keller, Gottfried	Winkelried, Arnold von

Wyss (family)	Zwingli, Huldreich

CITIES

Basel	Geneva	Lucerne	Zurich
Bern	Lausanne	Saint Moritz	

PHYSICAL FEATURES

Alps	Saint Bernard Passes
Jungfrau	Saint Gotthard Pass
Lake Constance	Saint Gotthard Tunnels
Lake Geneva	Simplon Pass and Tunnel
Lake of Lucerne	Staubbach
Matterhorn	

OTHER RELATED ARTICLES

Clothing (Traditional Costumes)	Helvetians
Europe, Council of	Lake Dwelling
European Free Trade Association	League of Nations
European Monetary Agreement	Tell, William

Outline

I. Government
II. People
  A. Population
  B. Language
  C. Religion
  D. Education
  E. Arts
  F. Sports
III. The Land
  A. The Jura Mountains
  B. The Swiss Plateau
  C. The Swiss Alps
  D. Rivers
IV. Climate
V. Economy
  A. Natural Resources
  B. Manufacturing
  C. Agriculture
  D. Tourism
  E. Banking
  F. Transportation
  G. Communication
VI. History

Questions

What are the three official languages of Switzerland?
Where does the name *Switzerland* come from?
How much of Switzerland do the Alps cover?
What was the first automobile tunnel through the Alps?
Why has Switzerland not joined the United Nations?
How did the Swiss Confederation start?
When did Swiss women receive the right to vote in national elections?
In what region of Switzerland do about two-thirds of the people live?
How does Switzerland keep itself prepared for military defense?
Why are Swiss industrial areas almost free of smoke?

Additional Resources

HUGHES, CHRISTOPHER. *Switzerland.* Praeger, 1975. Examines national political structure as well as that of each canton.
Fodor's Switzerland. McKay. Pub. annually.
KUBLY, HERBERT. *Native's Return.* Stein & Day, 1981. An ethnic and cultural study.
LUCK, JAMES MURRAY, and others, eds. *Modern Switzerland.* SPOSS, 1978.
SCHMID, CAROL L. *Conflict and Consensus in Switzerland.* Univ. of California Press, 1981. A study of the elements that unite a country divided by language and religion.
SCHWARZ, URS. *The Eye of the Hurricane: Switzerland in World War Two.* Westview, 1980.
STEINBERG, JONATHAN. *Why Switzerland?* Cambridge, 1976. Investigates the nation's politics and government, economy, and languages.

SWORD

SWORD, *sohrd*, is one of the oldest of all fighting weapons. Man turned his skill to the art of making weapons almost as soon as he discovered the art of working metals. The earliest swords we know about were those of the Assyrians, Gauls, and Greeks. Their swords were short, two-edged weapons made of bronze. The Roman sword was a short, straight, steel weapon with a sharpened point and two cutting edges.

The *broadsword* is a broad-bladed, single-edged short sword, made for cutting but not for stabbing. The broadsword was once used by regiments of cavalry and Highland infantry in the British army. It was better for attack than defense. The *claymore*, a kind of broadsword, but double-edged and longer, was the national weapon of the Highlanders. The favorite weapon of the East was the *scimitar*, a blade with a decided curve, for which Damascus was noted. Toledo, Spain, made fine swords. The *rapier*, used in the 1500's and 1600's, was a straight two-edged sword, with a narrow, pointed blade. Swords used by cavalry during the 1800's were from 2½ to 3 feet (76 to 91 centimeters) long and weighed about 2½ pounds (1.1 kilograms). The sword gave way to the saber in the United States Army. The saber was made for both cutting and thrusting.

There was less cavalry action in World War I and little chance to use swords. A better weapon for the charges of foot soldiers was the bayonet. This weapon was a blade 1 foot (30 centimeters) or longer attached to the end of the rifle. The sword was also of little use in World War II, when the cavalry units were mechanized.   JOHN D. BILLINGSLEY

See also BAYONET; DAGGER; DUEL; FENCING.

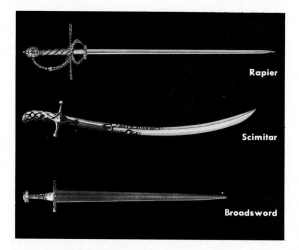

Rapier

Scimitar

Broadsword

SWORD OF DAMOCLES. See DAMOCLES.

SWORDFISH is a large ocean fish with a long, rounded body. It has a long, flattened upper jaw that looks like a sword. The swordfish is given its name because of its jaw. This fish closely resembles the marlins and sailfish, but differs from them because it has a short-based back fin. The swordfish lives in all warm seas. Its average length is 7 feet (2 meters), and it usually weighs about 250 pounds (113 kilograms). Specimens that weigh nearly 1,200 pounds (544 kilograms) and measure as

H. Armstrong Roberts

Swordfish Travel in Pairs during breeding season, and a fishing boat will often hook two of the leaping, speeding sword-nosed fighters. Heavy line and a strong pole are needed for the thrilling, backbreaking fight with a "sword."

long as 15 feet (4.6 meters) have been caught. Swordfish are highly regarded by big-game fishermen. The swordfish is hard to catch because hooks pull out of its tender mouth easily. It is also difficult to get swordfish to take the bait.

Their "swords" are sharp-edged and strong, and half as long as the body. There have been several instances of swordfish charging boats and piercing the hulls.

Commercial fishermen catch swordfish by harpooning them from a pulpit on the bow of a sailboat. The flesh is coarse, but it has a good flavor when cut and cooked as a steak. Swordfish eat squid and menhaden, herring, mackerel, and other fish that travel in schools.

In 1971, the U.S. Food and Drug Administration (FDA) advised the public not to eat swordfish. The agency found that almost all the swordfish sampled contained the mineral mercury in amounts that exceeded safety levels. Scientists have not determined the sources of the mercury, but they believe that some of it comes from industrial wastes.

Two other kinds of fish have pointed, bony spikes much like those of the swordfish. The *marlins* have a long-based but low dorsal fin along the back. The *sailfish* has a long, high, sail-like fin along its back.

Scientific Classification. The swordfish belongs to the swordfish family, *Xiphiidae*. It is classified as genus *Xiphias*, species *X. gladius*.   LEONARD P. SCHULTZ

See also MARLIN; SAILFISH; FISH (picture: Fish of Coastal Waters and the Open Ocean).

SYCAMORE is a shade tree with reddish-brown wood. It grows in fertile lowlands and along streams. It is found in great numbers in the United States from southern Maine to Nebraska and as far south as Texas and Florida. The tree may reach a height of 175 feet (53

Harold M. Lambert from Frederic Lewis

The Sycamore may reach a height of 175 feet (53 meters). It is a popular shade tree for home and park landscaping.

meters) and be 14 feet (4 meters) through the trunk. The bark on the lower trunk is reddish-brown, and the bark on the branches is olive-green. The bark on the branches breaks off in tiny scales. When these scales break off, they show an inner bark that is light cream in color. This light bark gives rise to the phrase "hoary-antlered sycamore." Some sycamores are known as *buttonwoods*, others as *plane trees*.

The sycamore tree can be recognized by its leaves, which are broad and have large teeth. The stem of each leaf is hollow at the base where it encloses the next year's bud. The flowers of the sycamore are of two types, those that bear *stamens* and those that bear *pistils*. Each type of flower grows in separate flower heads on different parts of the same tree. The fruits of the sycamore are borne in small balls which hang from drooping stems. Each ball is made up of many tiny dry fruits which are tightly packed together. The fruits are known as *achenes*.

Scientific Classification. Sycamores belong to the plane tree family, *Platanaceae*. They make up the genus *Platanus*. The most common sycamore tree is *P. acerifolia*.   WILLIAM M. HARLOW

See also TREE (Familiar Broadleaf and Needleleaf Trees [picture]).

SYDENHAM, *SIHD'n um,* **BARON** (1799-1841), CHARLES EDWARD POULETT THOMSON, was a British statesman and governor general of Canada from 1839 to 1841. He succeeded Lord Durham in Canada, and carried through the unification of Upper and Lower Canada. He was born at Wimbledon, England, and worked as a merchant. In 1826 he was elected to Parliament and in 1834 became president of the Board of Trade.   JAMES L. GODFREY

SYDENHAM, THOMAS (1624-1689), an English physician, believed and taught that medicine could be learned only at the bedside of the patient. He was a keen observer, and gave excellent descriptions of gout, scarlet fever, measles, and influenza. He had great faith in the healing power of nature, and he felt that fever was nature's way of fighting the injurious matter that caused disease.

Sydenham was born at Wynford Eagle, Dorset, and received his degree from Oxford University. Success came slowly to him, but eventually he gained recognition as one of the great doctors of his time.

Sydenham prided himself on being a practical physician, and he avoided all theory. He was not interested in the developing sciences of anatomy, physiology, and chemistry, and felt that they were of little use to the practicing doctor. His practical bent is shown by his adoption of quinine for the treatment of fevers, at a time when many doctors opposed this new drug.

Even though he avoided theory, Sydenham developed a theoretical explanation of the origin and spread of epidemics. He believed that changes in the atmosphere acted on ordinary diseases at various times and made them more virulent so that they attacked many people rapidly. This theory was accepted by many physicians for several hundred years.   GEORGE ROSEN

SYDNEY (pop. 2,874,415) is Australia's oldest and largest city and the capital of the state of New South Wales. The city lies on a huge, deep harbor on the southeastern coast (see AUSTRALIA [political map]). This harbor, called Port Jackson, or Sydney Harbour, has made Sydney Australia's busiest seaport. Sydney also ranks as the nation's leading industrial city.

The British founded Sydney as a prison colony in 1788. At that time, many nations sent criminals to distant prison colonies. The colony's first governor, Captain Arthur Phillip, chose the site for its harbor and supply of fresh water. He named it for the British statesman Thomas Townshend, Viscount Sydney.

The City and its suburbs cover about 670 square miles (1,740 square kilometers). Downtown Sydney lies on the south side of Sydney Harbour. The oldest section of the city, an area called the Rocks, lies near the waterfront. During the 1960's, a state redevelopment project restored many historic structures of the Rocks. Before British settlement, this area had many rock formations.

George Street, the city's main street, runs through the center of downtown Sydney. The downtown area includes many towering high-rise buildings. East of the downtown area lies a series of parks, including Hyde Park, the Domain, and the Royal Botanic Gardens. Still farther east is a section of the city called Kings Cross, which includes many nightclubs and restaurants.

The names of many buildings and places in Sydney are reminders of the city's days as a prison colony. Hyde Park Barracks, now Sydney's court building, originally housed male convicts. An island in Sydney Harbour is called Pinchgut because it served as a prison where the inmates often went hungry.

Sydney Harbour Bridge links downtown Sydney with the suburbs on the north shore. Other suburbs spread east, south, and west of the city. Two large recreation areas—Royal National Park and Ku-Ring-Gai Chase—lie just outside the Sydney metropolitan area.

847

SYDNEY

The People of Sydney are called *Sydneysiders*, and most of them have British ancestors. But thousands of other Europeans have settled in the city since the mid-1900's. Sydney also has a few thousand *Aborigines*, the descendants of the first people who lived in Australia (see ABORIGINES).

Most Sydney families own a house and garden in one of the suburbs. However, the number of people living in apartments has increased since about 1960 because of the rising cost of land. Sydney has almost no slums, but some Aborigines live in substandard housing.

The city's mild climate enables Sydneysiders to spend much time outdoors during most of the year. On weekends, thousands of them sail, surf, swim, or water-ski. Sydney has more than 30 beaches, including such surfing beaches as Bondi and Manly. Many Sydneysiders play such games as cricket, Rugby, and tennis.

The Festival of Sydney begins with fireworks on January 1 and lasts the entire month. It features art shows, open-air concerts, and *regattas* (boat races). The Royal Easter Show, held in April, resembles a county fair, with livestock judging and other events.

Cultural Life. Sydney's Opera House, completed in 1973, includes facilities for concerts, opera, and theater. The building has towering, white concrete shells that resemble billowing sails. Many architects consider it one of the finest buildings constructed during the 1900's.

The city has three universities—Macquarie University, the University of New South Wales, and the University of Sydney. The State Library of New South Wales owns a huge collection of books and documents about Australia. The Art Gallery of New South Wales displays works by Australian and European artists.

Economy. Sydney manufactures goods worth more than half the total value of those made in New South Wales. The value of Sydney's production totals almost a third of that of Australia. The city's chief factory products include automobiles, clothing, food products, and textiles. More than 15,000 plants employ over a million workers. Rich cattle- and sheep-raising areas in New South Wales make Sydney an important livestock and wool market as well. Sydney also serves as the banking and business center of New South Wales.

The city is sometimes called the *gateway to Australia.*

Most visitors to the country enter through Sydney. Sydney's Kingsford Smith International Airport ranks as the nation's busiest. Sydney Harbour serves about 4,000 ships and handles about 10 million short tons (9.1 million metric tons) of cargo yearly. The city's chief exports include coal, meat, wheat, and wool.

History. Sydney received its first shiploads of convicts—about 750 men and women—on Jan. 26, 1788. The prison colony grew slowly at first because the convicts knew little about building or farming. About 1800, a farmer named John Macarthur brought the first Merino sheep to the area. This breed created a successful wool industry that attracted many free settlers. By 1842, the population had grown to about 30,000. Sydney was incorporated as a city that year.

In 1848, Great Britain stopped sending convicts to Sydney, but the rich farmland of the area continued to attract settlers. A prospector discovered gold in New South Wales in 1851, and Sydney grew rapidly during the gold rush that followed. By 1891, the population had risen to 383,000.

The city continued to grow steadily during the 1900's. Its population increased to more than a million by the late 1920's, and to nearly 3 million by the early 1980's. Many problems resulted from this rapid growth. As skyscrapers replaced older buildings, for example, downtown streets became increasingly crowded. The people started to show concern about the smog and water pollution created by the many factories in the area. In addition, only about 85 per cent of Sydney's homes had sewers. The remaining 15 per cent dumped their sewage into underground tanks called septic tanks. Such tanks sometimes pollute water supplies. In the mid-1970's, the government began to provide financial aid to help expand the sewage system.   GAVIN SOUTER

See also AUSTRALIA (pictures).

SYLLOGISM. See LOGIC (Deductive Logic).

SYLVESTER is the name of two popes of the Roman Catholic Church.

Sylvester I (?-335), SAINT SYLVESTER, reigned as pope from 314 until his death. According to legend, he healed the Roman emperor, Constantine the Great, of leprosy, and also baptized him. It is certain that Constantine built the basilicas of Saint John Lateran and of Saint Peter in the Vatican while Sylvester was pope. Sylvester was born in Rome.

Fritz Prenzel

Downtown Sydney borders Sydney Harbour. The Sydney Harbour Bridge links the downtown area, *background,* with suburbs to the north. Downtown Sydney has many high-rise buildings. The white, shell-like structure left of the bridge is the Sydney Opera House, a famous landmark.

Sylvester II (950?-1003) was the first Frenchman to become a pope. He reigned from 999 until his death. His ambition was to unite all western Europe into one church and one state. Sylvester was born probably in Aurillac, and was educated in the monastery of Aurillac in Auvergne. He studied mathematics, astronomy, and dialectic.　　　GUSTAVE WEIGEL and FULTON J. SHEEN

SYMBIOSIS, *SIHM by OH sihs*, means *living together*. Any two, different organisms that live together are symbiotic, whether they benefit one another, harm one another, or have no effect at all. The term is often restricted to the idea of mutual benefit. There are three forms of symbiosis: parasitism, commensalism, and mutualism.

In *parasitism*, one organism obtains food and shelter at the expense of another, sometimes destroying the host. An excellent example of parasitism is the hookworm that may live in the intestines of human beings and other animals. See PARASITE.

In *commensalism*, one organism obtains "crumbs" left over from the host's food, and is sheltered by the host. Little, if any, harm is done. For example, the remora attaches itself to the bodies of sharks and sea turtles. It gets free transportation and protection. When the hosts kill prey, the remoras detach themselves to gobble tidbits too small for the hosts (see REMORA).

In *mutualism*, both parties benefit. Human beings have a mutualistic relationship with food crops and livestock. Mutualism occurs naturally when an alga and a fungus grow together to form a lichen which differs from either plant. Each organism benefits from this close association. The fungus, which cannot produce its own food, gets its food from the alga. The alga gets protection from the fungus. See LICHEN.　　　C. BROOKE WORTH

SYMBOL is anything that communicates a fact or an idea or that stands for an object. Some symbols, such as flags and stop signs, are visual. Others, including music and spoken words, involve sounds. Symbols rank among our oldest and most basic inventions.

Almost anything can be a symbol. For example, the letters of the alphabet are among the most important symbols because they form the basis for almost all written and spoken communication. Gestures and sounds made by human beings also symbolize ideas or feelings. A symbol can be used alone or in combination with other symbols.

Uses of Symbols. Individuals, nations, and organizations use symbols every day. Symbols also play an important part in religious life. People throughout the world have agreed on certain symbols that serve as a shorthand for recording and recalling information. Every branch of science, for example, has its own system of symbols. One of these branches, astronomy, uses a set of ancient symbols to identify the sun, the moon, the planets, and the stars. In mathematics, Greek letters and other symbols make up an abbreviated language. Other symbols appear in such fields as commerce, engineering, medicine, packaging, and transportation. Since the 1930's, many nations have been working together to create a system of road and traffic signs that could be universally understood.

All countries have official or unofficial national symbols. A flag, a national anthem, or a national ruler may symbolize a nation. Familiar symbols of the United States also include Uncle Sam and the Statue of Liberty. National symbols for other countries include the maple leaf for Canada, John Bull for Great Britain, and the bear for Russia. Many political parties use symbols for identification. In the United States, a donkey symbolizes the Democratic Party, and an elephant represents the Republican Party.

Most religions use symbols to represent their beliefs. The cross symbolizes not only the death of Jesus Christ, but all Christian beliefs. The Star of David represents the teachings of Judaism.

The armed forces of a nation use symbols to identify their various branches and the rank of each serviceman and servicewoman. Artists and writers often use certain colors, images, or words to express ideas symbolically.

Many rituals have a symbolic nature. Such symbolic acts include coronations, inaugurations, military salutes, and religious sacraments.

Symbols with Different Meanings. Several societies may use the same symbols, but these symbols may stand for different things. In many societies, for example, the color red symbolizes war and violence. But this color also has other meanings. In China, red represents marriage. Among American Indians, it stands for the East. Red symbolizes life in the Shinto religion of Japan, but in France it represents law schools.

A symbol has only the meaning that people have given it. Even a powerful symbol can lose its meaning if the society dishonors or ignores it for a period of time. Throughout early history, many people considered the swastika a good luck charm. But in 1920, the Nazi Party of Germany adopted it as its symbol. The swastika came to represent the Nazi attempt to conquer Europe.

SYMBOLS

A symbol is a sign that stands for an idea or an object. Nations and religions use a variety of pictorial symbols to identify themselves and to express their ideals. The letters of the alphabet are symbols for sounds. People combine letters to form words that also represent ideas and objects. The illustrations in the bottom row show how words can be communicated to blind or deaf people.

WORLD BOOK illustrations by Mas Nakagawa

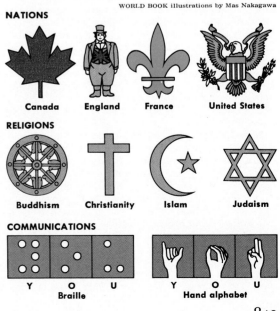

NATIONS

Canada　　England　　France　　United States

RELIGIONS

Buddhism　　Christianity　　Islam　　Judaism

COMMUNICATIONS

Y　O　U
Braille

Y　O　U
Hand alphabet

SYMBOLISM

Today, it ranks as one of the most hated symbols in history. WHITNEY SMITH

Related Articles in WORLD BOOK include:

Advertising (History)
Algebra (Symbols in Algebra)
Alphabet
Cartouche
Color (table: Color in
Religious Symbolism)
Crescent
Easter (Easter
Symbols)
Element, Chemical (tables)
Flag
Heraldry
Indian, American
(Language; pictures)
Insignia
Liberty Cap
Map (Symbols)
Mythology (Mythical
Symbols)
Ranching (picture)
Seal
Swastika

SYMBOLISM is a literary movement started by a group of French poets between 1885 and 1895. Stéphane Mallarmé led the movement, but the poetry of Paul Verlaine was more widely imitated. Leading theorists of symbolism included René Ghil, Gustave Kahn, Jean Moreás, and Charles Morice. Many European poets of the early 1900's followed the symbolist style.

Symbolism gave a spiritual atmosphere to the world by attributing to it a sacred, mystical quality. This central idea comes from the philosophy of Emanuel Swedenborg, a Swedish religious leader. According to him, visible realities are symbols for the invisible world of the spirit. In his sonnet "Correspondences," French poet Charles Baudelaire pictured human beings as walking in "a forest of symbols" which speak to them in words they cannot quite understand.

Symbolist verse usually presents a poetic image that can be interpreted many ways. The symbolists searched for the musical quality in words. They expressed themselves in metaphors and created technical modifications in existing verse forms. Some critics have called the movement decadent because of its obsession with death and its general pessimism. ANNA BALAKIAN

See also DRAMA (Modern); MALLARMÉ, STÉPHANE; RUSSIAN LITERATURE (Symbolism); VERLAINE, PAUL.

SYMPHONIC POEM, *sihm FAHN ihk*, is a fairly long orchestral work in one movement, usually built upon a story. A symphonic poem is sometimes called a *tone poem*. Many symphonic poems follow the form of *sonata-allegro* movements as developed in symphonies, but they are chiefly emotional and dramatic in content. A number of composers who used the free form of symphonic poems developed the *leitmotif* (repeated short melodic phrase or passage) to unify the work. The symphonic poem became popular in the mid-1800's. Franz Liszt and Richard Strauss are noted for their symphonic poems. GRANT FLETCHER

SYMPHONY is a large-scale musical composition for an orchestra. Symphonies are divided into sections called *movements*. Most symphonies consist of four movements, but some have only one and others have as many as six. The first movement of most symphonies is moderately fast. The second movement is the slowest, and the third has a dancelike quality. The fourth movement is a lively or triumphant conclusion.

Symphonies developed from the overtures of Italian operas of the early 1700's. The Austrian composer Joseph Haydn wrote more than 100 symphonies in the late 1700's, and they reflect the development of the symphony into a major musical form. The last four

symphonies of the Austrian composer Wolfgang Amadeus Mozart, written in 1786 and 1788, are examples of especially elegant works called *classical symphonies*.

Many composers of the 1800's and early 1900's modeled their works after one or more symphonies by Ludwig van Beethoven of Germany. For example, his symphonies influenced Hector Berlioz of France; Franz Liszt of Hungary; Anton Bruckner, Gustav Mahler, and Franz Schubert of Austria; Felix Mendelssohn and Robert Schumann of Germany; and Jean Sibelius of Finland. The symphonies of Schumann influenced Johannes Brahms of Germany, Antonín Dvořák of Czechoslovakia, and Peter Ilich Tchaikovsky of Russia.

Leading symphony composers of the 1900's include Sergei Prokofiev, Dimitri Shostakovich, and Igor Stravinsky of Russia; Aaron Copland, Roy Harris, and Charles Ives of the United States; Anton Webern of Austria; and Ralph Vaughan Williams of Great Britain. R. M. LONGYEAR

Each composer discussed in this article has a separate biography in WORLD BOOK. See also ORCHESTRA; SONATA.

SYNAGOGUE, *SIHN uh gahg*, is a Jewish house of worship. Synagogues are believed to have been started during the Babylonian captivity in the 500's B.C. At the time of Jesus, there were synagogues wherever the Jews had settled. Synagogues also served in early days both as courts of law and as places of religious instrucion.

The ancient synagogue was built so that the worshiper, on entering or at prayer, faced in the direction of Jerusalem. The most important articles included the chest, known as the Holy Ark, in which the rolls of Scripture were kept, a lamp that burned all the time to symbolize the presence of God, and candlesticks for use on the Sabbath and festival days. The head of the synagogue was responsible for the conduct of the service. He chose members to lead the prayers, read from the *Torah* (Scriptures), and preached. The congregation was divided by a screen, with the men sitting on one side of it and the women on the other.

The modern synagogue has kept such self-governing features as a board of directors, known in early days as the board of elders. Most synagogues require a quorum of 10 men to begin services. LOUIS L. MANN

See also RHODE ISLAND (picture: Touro Synagogue).

SYNAGOGUE COUNCIL OF AMERICA is the united voice of American Jewry in all matters in which religion plays an important role. It is made up of the six leading national Jewish organizations in the United States, including three rabbinic bodies and three groups of lay persons. The Rabbinical Council of America and the Union of Orthodox Jewish Congregations in America represent Orthodox Jews in the Synagogue Council. The Rabbinical Assembly of America and the United Synagogue of America represent the Conservative Jews. The Central Conference of American Rabbis and the Union of American Hebrew Congregations represent the Reform group. The council was founded in 1926 and has headquarters at 432 Park Avenue South, New York, N.Y. 10016. It cooperates with the U.S. government, the United Nations, and Protestant, Catholic, and other groups on social and moral matters.

Critically reviewed by the SYNAGOGUE COUNCIL OF AMERICA

SYNAPSE. See NERVOUS SYSTEM (The Dendrites).

SYNCHRO-CYCLOTRON, *SIHNG kroh SY kluh trahn*, is a device that accelerates protons or heavier nuclear particles to high energies. Physicists use this type of *particle accelerator* chiefly to study the nucleus of an atom.

The synchro-cyclotron is an improved form of the *cyclotron* (see CYCLOTRON). Both devices are cylindrical machines that use electric fields to speed up particles. Magnetic fields guide the particles around circular paths. However, the synchro-cyclotron accelerates particles to much higher energies than does the cyclotron. It can do so because the frequency of its electric field can be adjusted to remain in step with the spiraling particles. The frequency is *synchronized* with the particles. For this reason, the machine is called a *synchro-cyclotron*.   ROBERT H. MARCH

See also PARTICLE ACCELERATOR; LAWRENCE, E. O.

SYNCHROTRON, *SIHNG kruh trahn*, is an electric device that accelerates electrons and protons to high energies. It is one type of *particle accelerator* that makes particles travel in circular orbits (see PARTICLE ACCELERATOR).

Electrons or protons are released into a synchrotron after they have been sped up in another type of accelerator, usually a *linear accelerator*. In the synchrotron, they travel through a doughnut-shaped vacuum chamber that lies within a ring of magnets. These magnets produce a magnetic field that keeps the particles in the chamber by bending their paths into circular orbits. Each time the particles make a complete orbit, they are accelerated by an electric field located between two magnets. The field alternates in step with the revolutions of the particles, giving them a slight energy boost just as they pass by.

A synchrotron's magnetic field is gradually increased in strength as the particles gain energy. This increase bends the particles into orbits of constant radius and so keeps them in the vacuum chamber until they can be boosted to extremely high energies. When the particles reach the desired energy, they are directed to a solid or liquid target outside the chamber. The collision produces *mesons* and other subatomic particles (see MESON). Physicists study these particles chiefly to learn about the structure of the atomic nucleus and the forces that hold it together.

Vladimir I. Veksler, a Russian physicist, first proposed the idea of a synchrotron in 1944. A similar idea was developed independently in 1945 by the American physicist Edwin M. McMillan. The two scientists based their idea on a principle called *phase stability*. Phase stability ensures that an accelerator's particles remain in step with the electric field when the strength of the magnetic field is gradually increased.

In 1952, Ernest D. Courant, M. Stanley Livingston, and Hartland S. Snyder, all of the United States, developed a method that increased particle-orbit stability. This method, called *strong focusing*, kept the particles in orbits of a constant radius. It enabled scientists to build synchrotrons that would speed up particles to billions of electronvolts (GeV). In 1976, a synchrotron accelerated protons to an energy of 500 GeV at the Fermi National Accelerator Laboratory in Batavia, Ill.   ERNEST D. COURANT

SYNCLINE, *SIHNG klyn*, is the name for the *concave* (down-arched) part of a fold in rock structures. The folds are wrinkles that occurred during the time when the rocks were forming.

SYNCOPE. See ELISION.

SYNDICALISM, *SIHN duh kuh lihz uhm*, was a revolutionary labor movement that achieved its greatest popularity in France during the late 1800's and early 1900's. Its primary goal was to create a society in which associations of workers owned and operated all means of production and controlled the government. Such associations would develop from existing labor unions. The word *syndicalism* came from the French word *syndicat*, which means *union*.

Syndicalists called for the abolition of *capitalism*, the economic system of the United States and most European nations, and for the abolition of national governments (see CAPITALISM). They believed capitalism and these governments benefited private owners at the expense of workers. Syndicalists wanted to replace capitalism and national governments with small associations of workers. These associations would control all resources and industries, handle all political affairs, and form the basis of a free and just society.

Syndicalism rejected political activity as a method of working for its goals. Instead, the movement proposed a general strike of all workers, organized by the associations.

Syndicalism influenced the labor movements in Italy, Spain, and other countries as well as France. In the United States, the Industrial Workers of the World (IWW) adopted syndicalism in 1908 (see INDUSTRIAL WORKERS OF THE WORLD). By the 1920's, however, syndicalism had lost much of its influence on the world's labor movements.   JAMES G. SCOVILLE

SYNDICATE. See CRIME (Organized Crime).

SYNECDOCHE. See METONYMY.

SYNFUELS. See SYNTHETIC FUELS.

SYNGE, *sihng*, **JOHN MILLINGTON** (1871-1909), was an Irish dramatist. Most of his plays are set among Irish peasant characters, and are written in a vigorous poetic language based on folk speech.

Synge had a particular genius for tragicomedy. Like other Irish writers of his time in Ireland, he dealt imaginatively with heroism and the apparent gap between the real and the ideal. This gap forms the theme of *In the Shadow of the Glen* (1903), *The Well of the Saints* (1905), and *The Playboy of the Western World* (1907). Synge wrote two tragedies, *Riders to the Sea* (1904) and *Deirdre of the Sorrows* (performed after his death). In both plays, heroism is tied to the central character's confrontation with mortality.

Synge also wrote verse, and sketches of peasant life in the Aran Islands and other parts of Ireland. He was born in Rathfarnham, a suburb of Dublin.   MARTIN MEISEL

SYNONYM, *SIHN uh nihm*, is a word that has the same, or nearly the same, meaning as another word. It comes from two Greek words meaning *associated* and *name*. There are many cases when one word will serve the same purpose as another, such as *small* boy and *little* boy and *smart* idea and *clever* idea. But although two words may be *synonymous* (used in the same way) in one sense, they may not be synonymous in another sense. For example, *dull* and *stupid* may both be used to describe a person. But one does not use the word *stupid* to describe the *dull* blade of a knife. Synonyms enrich the language by helping the speaker or writer to use words with precise meanings and associations and to avoid the monotony of repetition. GARY TATE

SYNTAX, *SIHN taks*, is a description of the way words are put together to make sentences. It describes the order of the subject and verb, the position of auxiliary words and objects, and the relation of modifiers to the words they modify. See SENTENCE.

Word order is not the same in all languages. In English, we say "I gave Jim the ball." In another language, the order might be "I the ball Jim gave." When we put words together in proper order, we are able to express the meaning we intend. "I was shown a book in black leather by the clerk" is a different sentence from "I was shown a book by the clerk in black leather." The meaning has changed because the syntax has changed.

Syntax is one of the three main divisions of linguistics. The other divisions are *phonology*, the study of the sounds of the language; and *semantics*, the study of words' origins, changes, and meanings. *Morphology* (the study of the formation and structure of words) and syntax are usually considered the main parts of *grammar*. WILLIAM F. IRMSCHER

See also LINGUISTICS (The Components of a Grammar).

SYNTHESIZER is a musical instrument that produces sounds electronically. A person can create and combine many kinds of sounds by operating various controls on a synthesizer. The controls determine such characteristics of the sound as loudness, pitch, and tone color. Most synthesizers are played by means of a keyboard similar to that of an organ.

Many classical, jazz, and rock composers and performers use the synthesizer to imitate the sounds of such instruments as the piano, violin, and snare drum. A synthesizer also can produce sounds like those of the surf, wind, and thunder. However, musicians generally use the instrument for its own unique sound qualities.

Robert A. Moog, an American physicist, invented the first commercially successful synthesizer in 1964. He used controlled levels of voltage to produce different sounds on the instrument. The *digital synthesizer*, which

Tom Wheeler, Moog Music, Inc.

A Synthesizer has many kinds of controls that enable a musician to produce a wide variety of musical and nonmusical sounds.

uses a computer to create and control sounds, was developed in the late 1970's. JON H. APPLETON

See also ELECTRONIC MUSIC.

SYNTHETIC FUELS are fuels that can be substituted for crude oil and natural gas. The chief sources of synthetic fuels, also called *synfuels*, include coal, oil shale, bituminous sands, and biomass.

Coal can be turned into gas and liquid fuels through processes called *gasification* and *liquefaction*. In one method of gasification, mined coal is combined with steam and oxygen to produce a mixture of carbon monoxide, hydrogen, and methane. This gaseous mixture can be used in place of natural gas.

Liquefaction of coal can be carried out by any of several processes. In one process, called *hydroliquefaction*, the carbon molecules in coal are combined with hydrogen gas at high temperatures and under great pressure. This method produces a liquid fuel that can be used in place of crude oil. Through *pyrolysis*, another method of liquefaction, coal is heated rapidly, causing its liquids to evaporate. The vaporized coal tars are then combined with hydrogen to produce liquid fuels.

Oil shale is a soft, fine-grained, sedimentary rock that consists partly of an organic substance called *kerogen* (see SEDIMENTARY ROCK). Kerogen breaks down and releases vapors when heated. These vapors condense into liquid oil. See OIL SHALE.

Bituminous sands, also called *oil sands* or *tar sands*, are saturated with *bitumen*, a gluelike black substance used to produce liquid fuel. The method used to recover bitumen depends on the location of the sands. Bituminous sands mined from deposits that lie near the surface of the ground are heated to distill away the bitumen. Further heating turns the bitumen into oil. Sands found deep underground are heated where they lie in order to melt the bitumen. The bitumen is then pumped through heated pipes to the surface. There, it is heated further to convert the bitumen to oil and other fuels. See BITUMINOUS SANDS.

Biomass is any type of organic matter. All plant and animal matter contains energy that can be recovered by heating or through gasification. Some biomass can be fermented to obtain *methanol*, also known as methyl alcohol, which is mixed with gasoline to produce a fuel called *gasohol* (see GASOHOL).

Synthetic fuels may become important sources of energy because of decreasing supplies of oil and natural gas. The comparatively high cost of producing synfuels hindered their development until the late 1970's, when the prices of oil and gas increased greatly. Several nations, including the United States and Canada, have started programs to promote the production of synthetic fuels. In 1980, the U.S. government established the United States Synthetic Fuels Corporation. This agency was designed to encourage private businesses, through financial assistance and other means, to produce synthetic fuels commercially. ANN BAUGH TIPTON

See also COAL (Coal Research); ENERGY SUPPLY.

SYNTHETICS are artificially created substances in which two or more elements are chemically combined to make a new compound. Synthetics include all plastics and such manufactured fibers as acrylic, acetate, and nylon. Most synthetic substances have been developed when natural products became scarce or inadequate to meet specific industrial needs.

Manufacturers use synthetics in making countless products for the home and industry. For example, they use tough plastics in furniture, machinery parts, and packaging. Synthetic fibers form part of such products as rubber tires, brushes, electric insulating material, and clothing. Other items that can be made *synthetically* (chemically) include gems and various types of foods.

Chemists can give synthetics various properties. Some synthetics are brittle and strong, for example, and others are elastic. Many resist chemicals, insects, mildew, and sunlight. In many ways, synthetics are superior to natural products.

Manufacturers produce most synthetics by combining such raw materials as carbon, hydrogen, nitrogen, and oxygen. The manufacturers change these raw materials into chemical compounds through one of several chemical processes. The most common process is *polymerization*, which involves converting small molecules into much larger ones (see POLYMERIZATION). After the chemical process has been completed, the synthetic may be formed into fibers, a film, or a liquid that can be molded into various shapes. RICHARD F. BLEWITT

Related Articles in WORLD BOOK include:

Acrylic	Linoleum	Resin, Synthetic
Artificial Turf	(History)	Rubber
Fiber (Synthetics)	Nylon	Silicone
Fiberglass	Paint	Styrofoam
Hormone (Man-Made	Plastics	Vinyl
Hormones)	Polyester	

SYNTHETISM. See GAUGUIN, PAUL.

SYPHILIS. See VENEREAL DISEASE; DISEASE (table).

SYRACUSE, *SIHR uh kyoos,* on the southeastern coast of Sicily, was one of the most powerful cities of the ancient Greek world. Greeks from Corinth founded Syracuse about 734 B.C. The city grew rapidly. It became a cultural center under Hiero I, who built an empire in southern Italy.

A democracy was established at Syracuse after Hiero's death. It defeated a strong Athenian force that besieged the city from 415 to 413 B.C. But internal troubles and threats from Carthage brought to power a harsh military ruler—Dionysius I. After Dionysius' death in 367 B.C., Syracuse declined.

About 345 B.C., the Corinthian general Timoleon defeated the Carthaginians and rebuilt the city. During the rule of Hiero II, in the 200's B.C., Syracuse was allied with Rome. But the city later sided with Carthage, and Romans captured it in 212 B.C., after a three-year siege. The mathematician Archimedes aided the defenders during the siege with several defensive devices he invented (see ARCHIMEDES). Syracuse then became the capital of the Roman province of Sicily. In A.D. 878, the Saracens destroyed Syracuse. The town of Siracusa now stands on its site. DONALD W. BRADEEN

SYRACUSE (pop. 170,105; met. area pop. 642,375) is an industrial center of New York. It was once called *Salt City* because it produced so much salt. Syracuse lies near Onondaga Lake, about 150 miles (241 kilometers) west of Albany. For location, see NEW YORK (political map).

Syracuse has about 340 factories that manufacture such products as chemicals, chinaware, drugs, electrical machinery, paper, and transportation equipment. The city is also a market center for nearby farming areas. Passenger trains and several freight railroads serve Syracuse. The Clarence E. Hancock International Airport lies just outside the city.

Syracuse's central location has made the city one of New York's chief convention centers. The Onondaga County War Memorial Convention Complex seats more than 10,000 persons. The annual New York State Fair is held in the city in late August and early September.

Syracuse is the home of Syracuse University and Le Moyne College. Cultural attractions include the Canal Museum, the Everson Museum of Art, the Lowe Art Gallery of Syracuse University, and the Syracuse Symphony Orchestra. A replica of Fort Sainte Marie de Gannentah, a French fort built in 1658, stands near Onondaga Lake. Nearby is the Salt Museum, which features exhibits of the area's earliest industry, the drying of salt.

Iroquois Indians lived in what is now the Syracuse area when Ephraim Webster became the first permanent white settler there in 1786. Webster opened a trading post near the salt springs that surrounded Onondaga Lake. Veterans of the Revolutionary War in America (1775-1783) built a small settlement in the area in 1788. That same year, or in 1789, they established several saltworks.

In 1825, the settlement was named after the ancient Greek city of Syracuse, which also lay near salt springs. Also in 1825, Syracuse was incorporated as a village, and the Erie Canal was completed. The canal, which linked the Atlantic Ocean and the Great Lakes, ran through the village and attracted many merchants to Syracuse. The community soon became a center of the salt industry. Syracuse was chartered as a city in 1848. The coming of railroads in the mid-1800's brought new industries to the area.

During the 1960's and early 1970's, urban renewal projects in Syracuse cleared land for banks, department stores, and office buildings. In 1976, the $24-million Onondaga County Civic Center opened in the city. It combines a 16-story government office building and a cultural center. Syracuse is the county seat of Onondaga County and has a mayor-council form of government. J. LEONARD GORMAN

SYRACUSE, BATTLE OF. See ARMY (table: Famous Land Battles).

SYRACUSE UNIVERSITY is a private coeducational school in Syracuse, N.Y. It has colleges of arts and sciences, engineering, human development, law, and visual and performing arts. The university includes schools of architecture, citizenship and public affairs, computer and information science, education, information studies, management, nursing, public communications, and social work; a graduate school; and a division of continuing education. It grants bachelor's, master's, and doctor's degrees.

The State University of New York College of Environmental Science and Forestry adjoins Syracuse University, and the two schools cooperate in their educational programming. Syracuse University also directs Utica College, a four-year liberal arts school in Utica, N.Y., and several education centers around the world. The university was founded in 1870. For enrollment, see UNIVERSITIES AND COLLEGES (table).

Critically reviewed by SYRACUSE UNIVERSITY

The Syrian Countryside consists of dry plains, fertile valleys, and barren deserts. About half of all the Syrian people live in rural villages. On the plains of northwestern Syria, the villagers build beehive-shaped houses of bricks and sun-dried mud, *above*.

SYRIA

SYRIA, *SEER ee uh,* is an Arab country at the eastern end of the Mediterranean Sea. It is a land of rolling plains, fertile river valleys, and barren deserts. Damascus is Syria's capital and largest city.

Syria is an extremely ancient land with a rich cultural heritage. Some of the oldest known civilizations grew up there. The first alphabet was developed in Syria, and Syrian artists and scholars greatly influenced the cultures of ancient Greece and Rome.

Syria lies along major trade routes linking Africa, Asia, and Europe. Camel caravans followed these routes more than 4,000 years ago carrying goods between Asia and Mediterranean ports. Such Syrian cities as Damascus and Aleppo grew up along the caravan routes and became centers of world trade as early as 2000 B.C.

Syrians have also profited from agriculture. The country lies at the western end of a rich farmland called the *Fertile Crescent* (see FERTILE CRESCENT). Farmers raise chiefly cotton and wheat on the rich Syrian plains.

Most Syrians are Muslim Arabs, but the population also includes many ethnic and religious minorities. About half of all workers are farmers. However, Syrian industries are expanding, and many rural people are moving to the cities to seek industrial jobs.

Government

Syria is a republic. Its Constitution, adopted in 1973, calls the nation a *socialist popular democracy.* Syrians 18 years or older may vote.

National Government. A president is Syria's head of state and most powerful government official. The people elect the president to a seven-year term. A 195-

Robert M. Haddad, the contributor of this article, is Professor of History and of Religion at Smith College and the author of Syrian Christians in Muslim Society: An Interpretation.

member People's Council makes Syria's laws. Voters elect members of the People's Council to four-year terms of office.

Under Syria's Constitution, the president heads the Baath Party, which controls Syrian politics. The party's power rests on its control of the nation's armed forces. The Baath Party is committed to socialism and to the political union of all the Arab countries. Syria has four other legal political parties. They and the Baath Party form a socialist organization known as the *National Progressive Front.*

Local Government. Syria is divided into 13 provinces and the city of Damascus, which is considered a separate unit. The national government appoints all provincial governors and other chief local officials. Each

Facts in Brief

Capital: Damascus.

Official Language: Arabic.

Official Name: Al-Jumhuria Al-Arabia Al-Suria (The Syrian Arab Republic).

Form of Government: Republic.

Area: 71,498 sq. mi. (185,180 km²). *Greatest Distances*—east-west, 515 mi. (829 km); north-south, 465 mi. (748 km). *Coastline*—94 mi. (151 km).

Elevation: *Highest*—Mount Hermon, 9,232 ft. (2,814 m) above sea level. *Lowest*—sea level along the coast.

Population: *Estimated 1984 Population*—10,447,000; distribution, 54 per cent urban, 46 per cent rural; density, 145 persons per sq. mi. (56 per km²). *1976 Census*—7,725,766. *Estimated 1989 Population*—12,649,000.

Chief Products: *Agriculture*—cotton, wheat, barley, fruits and vegetables, tobacco, sugar beets, livestock. *Manufacturing*—textiles, petroleum products, processed foods, cement, glass, soap. *Mining*—oil, natural gas, phosphates, asphalt, iron ore.

National Anthem: "Homat El Diyar" ("Guardians of the Homeland").

Money: *Basic Unit*—pound. See MONEY (table: Exchange Rates).

Damascus is Syria's capital and largest city. Much of Damascus is modern, like the section shown above. But the city is thousands of years old, and some ancient sections still exist.

Björn Klingwall

province also has a people's council made up of elected and appointed members.

Courts. The Court of Cassation is Syria's highest court of appeals for civil, commercial, and criminal cases. Each religious community has its own courts for such matters as marriage, divorce, and inheritance.

Armed Forces. About 178,000 men serve in Syria's army, navy, and air force. All eligible males may be drafted for 30 months of military service.

People

Population and Ancestry. Syria has a population of about $10\frac{1}{2}$ million. Most of the people live in the western part of the country. More than 1 million persons live in Damascus. Syria has four other cities with more than 150,000 persons. They are, in order of size, Aleppo, Homs, Latakia, and Hama.

More than 90 per cent of all Syrians speak Arabic, Syria's official language, and consider themselves to be Arabs. Most of them are descended from people called *Semites* who settled in ancient Syria. Non-Arab Syrians include Armenians and Kurds. Their ancestors came from the north. Most of these Syrians still speak Armenian or Kurdish in everyday life.

Way of Life. About half of all Syrians live in rural villages. Most of the rest live in cities or towns. A few Syrians, called *Bedouins*, are nomads.

Many villagers live much as their ancestors did centuries ago. They farm small plots and build houses of stone or of sun-dried mud bricks. Bedouins live in tents and move about the countryside grazing livestock.

Some of Syria's cities are among the oldest in the world. They have narrow, winding streets and ancient market places. But the cities also have newer sections where life resembles that in most Western cities. The people live in modern houses or apartments and work in such fields as government and industry.

Many Syrian villagers wear traditional clothing, such as billowy trousers and a large cloth head covering. In the cities and towns, many people wear Western-style clothing. Syrians eat bread as their main food. Most also eat dairy products and fresh fruits and vegetables. Lamb dishes are commonly served, and they are always prepared for special occasions. Syrians, like other Arabs, enjoy strong black coffee.

Family ties are close among most Syrians. Many parents share their home with their sons and the sons' families. As in most Islamic cultures, women in Syria traditionally have had little freedom. However, increasing educational opportunities and exposure to Western ideas are gradually improving their position.

Syrians enjoy visiting and conversation as recreation. Listening to transistor radios, watching television, and attending motion pictures are also popular activities, especially in urban areas.

Religion. Muslims make up about 87 per cent of Syria's population. Most of them belong to the Sunni branch of Islam. Christians account for nearly 13 per cent of the people. The Greek Orthodox, Armenian Orthodox, and Syrian Orthodox churches have the most members. More than 150,000 Syrians are *Druses*. They practice a secret religion related to Islam. Syria also has about 4,500 Jews.

Religion, especially Islam, is a powerful political and social force in Syria. Many Syrians feel strong ties to their religious group, and these ties have often hindered national unity.

Syria's Flag, adopted in 1980, bears traditional Arab colors. Two green stars appear on the flag.

The Coat of Arms shows a hawk. This bird was the emblem of the tribe of Muhammad, the founder of Islam.

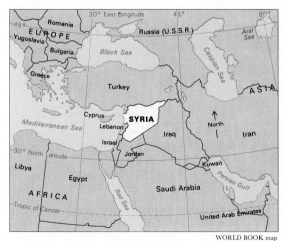

WORLD BOOK map

Syria is a country in southwestern Asia. It lies at the eastern end of the Mediterranean Sea and borders on five other countries.

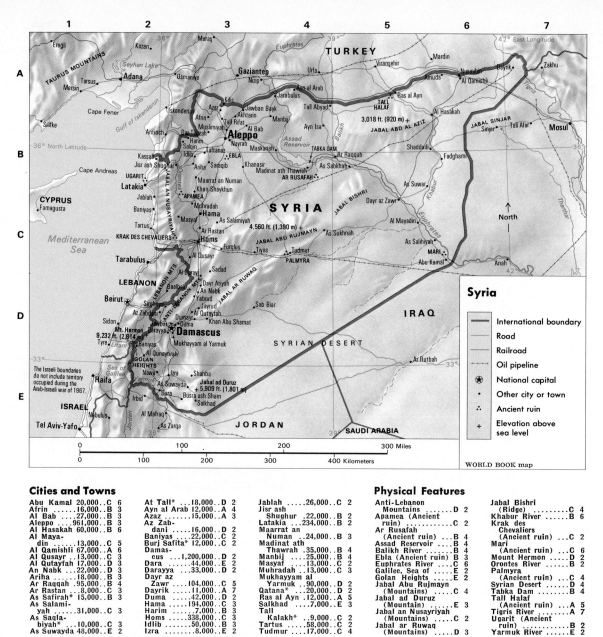

Syria

———	International boundary
———	Road
———	Railroad
———	Oil pipeline
✸	National capital
•	Other city or town
∴	Ancient ruin
+	Elevation above sea level

WORLD BOOK map

The Israeli boundaries do not include territory occupied during the Arab-Israeli war of 1967.

0	100	200	300 Miles
0	100 200	300	400 Kilometers

Cities and Towns

Abu Kamal 20,000..C 6
Afrin ......16,000..B 3
Al Bab ....27,000..B 3
Aleppo ....961,000..B 3
Al Hasakah 60,000..B 6
Al Maya-
din ......13,000..C 5
Al Qamishli 67,000..A 6
Al Qusayr ..13,000..C 3
Al Qutayfah 17,000..D 3
An Nabk ...22,000..D 3
Ariha .....18,000..B 3
Ar Raqqah .95,000..B 4
Ar Rastan ..8,000..C 3
As Safirah* 15,000..B 3
As Salami-
yah ......31,000..C 3
As Saqla-
biyah* ..10,000..C 3
As Suwayda 48,000..E 2

At Tall* ..18,000..D 2
Ayn al Arab 12,000..A 4
Azaz .....15,000..A 3
Az Zab-
dani .....16,000..D 2
Baniyas ....22,000..C 2
Burj Safita* 12,000..C 2
Damas-
cus ....1,200,000..D 2
Dara .....44,000..E 2
Darayya ...33,000..D 2
Dayr az
Zawr ...104,000..C 5
Dayrik ....11,000..A 7
Duma .....42,000..D 2
Hama ....194,000..C 2
Harim ......7,000..B 3
Homs ....338,000..C 2
Idlib .....50,000..B 3
Izra ....8,000..E 2

Jablah .....26,000..C 2
Jisr ash
Shughur .22,000..B 2
Latakia ...234,000..B 2
Maarrat an
Numan ..24,000..B 3
Madinat ath
Thawrah .35,000..B 4
Manbij ....25,000..B 3
Masyaf ....13,000..C 2
Muhradah ..13,000..C 2
Mukhayyam al
Yarmuk ..90,000..D 2
Qatana* ...20,000..D 2
Ras al Ayn .12,000..A 5
Salkhad ....7,000..E 3
Tall
Kalakh* ..9,000..C 2
Tartus ....58,000..C 2
Tudmur ....17,000..C 4

Physical Features

Anti-Lebanon
Mountains ......D 2
Apamea (Ancient
ruin) ....C 2
Ar Rusafah
(Ancient ruin) ...B 4
Assad Reservoir ...B 4
Balikh River ......B 4
Ebla (Ancient ruin) B 3
Euphrates River ...C 6
Galilee, Sea of ...E 2
Golan Heights .....E 2
Jabal Abu Rujmayn
(Mountains) .....C 4
Jabal ad Duruz
(Mountain) .....E 3
Jabal an Nusayriyah
(Mountains) .....C 2
Jabal ar Ruwaq
(Mountains) .....D 3

Jabal Bishri
(Ridge) ....C 4
Khabur River ......B 6
Krak des
Chevaliers
(Ancient ruin) ...C 2
Mari
(Ancient ruin) ...C 6
Mount Hermon ....D 2
Orontes River .....B 2
Palmyra
(Ancient ruin) ...C 4
Syrian Desert .....D 4
Tabka Dam ....B 4
Tall Halaf
(Ancient ruin) ...A 5
Tigris River ....A 7
Ugarit (Ancient
ruin) ....B 2
Yarmuk River ......E 2

*Does not appear on the map; key shows general location.
Sources: 1980 official estimates.

Education. Syrian law requires all children from 6 through 11 years old to go to school. However, about 20 per cent of the children do not attend school because of a shortage of classrooms and teachers. About half of all adult Syrians cannot read or write. Syria has a university in Aleppo, Damascus, and Latakia.

The Arts. Syria's cultural heritage goes back thousands of years. Since ancient times, Syrian craftworkers have been famous for their beautiful glassware, metalwork, and textiles (see GLASSWARE [pictures]). Phoenicians who settled in Syria developed the first alphabet there about 1500 B.C. Basic ideas in architecture, shipbuilding, and ironwork also originated in Syria.

Syria's greatest contribution to the arts has been in literature, the Arabs' supreme art. Two of Syria's finest poets were al-Mutanabbi, who lived in the 900's, and al-Maarri, who lived in the 1000's. During the 900's, the Syrian al-Farabi became one of Islam's leading philosophers. Important Syrian writers of the 1900's include Omar Abu-Rishe, Shafiq Jabri, Nizar Kabbani, and Ali Ahmad Said.

The Land and Climate

Syria can be divided into three main land regions. They are, from west to east: (1) the coast, (2) the mountains, and (3) the valleys and plains.

856

John Launois, Black Star

A Syrian Villager wearing traditional clothing sits at her door-step and prepares vegetables for her family's dinner.

The Coast is a narrow strip of land that extends along the Mediterranean Sea from Turkey to Lebanon. Moist sea winds give the region a mild, humid climate. Temperatures average about 48° F. (9° C) in January and about 81° F. (27° C) in July. About 40 inches (100 centimeters) of rain falls yearly. The coast is one of the few areas in Syria in which crops do not have to be irrigated, and most of the land is cultivated.

The Mountains run mostly from north to south. The region includes the Jabal an Nusayriyah range east of the coast; the Anti-Lebanon Mountains along the border with Lebanon; and the Jabal ad Duruz, a mountain southeast of the Anti-Lebanon range. The western slopes of the Jabal an Nusayriyah and Jabal ad Duruz are well populated, and most of the land is cultivated. The Anti-Lebanon Mountains have a dry, stony surface and are thinly populated.

The mountains catch sea winds blowing inland and force them to drop their moisture on the western side of the mountains. Thus, the western slopes have up to 40 inches (100 centimeters) of rain yearly, but the land

Odile Wertheimer, AAA photo

The Orontes River Valley is one of Syria's main farming regions. It has a dry climate, and farmers rely on irrigation. The water wheel, *far left,* is part of an ancient irrigation system.

to the east remains dry. Temperatures average about 41° F. (5° C) in January and about 72° F. (22° C) in July.

The Valleys and Plains include fertile river valleys, grassy plains, and sandy deserts. The Orontes River and mountain streams water the plains along the eastern edge of the mountains. These plains have rich, productive farmlands and are the home of most of Syria's people. The Euphrates River and its tributaries provide water for a developing agricultural area in the northeast. Most of the rest of Syria is covered by deserts and by dry grasslands where Bedouins graze their livestock.

Little rain falls in the valleys and plains region. Temperatures average about 41° F. (5° C) in January and about 88° F. (31° C) in July.

Economy

Syria is a developing country with great potential for economic growth. The government controls most of the economy, but the majority of farms, small businesses, and small industries are privately owned. Agriculture employs about half the workers and contributes about 20 per cent of the value of all goods and services produced in Syria. Industry employs about 15 per cent of the labor force but accounts for about 25 per cent of the value of goods and services produced.

Natural Resources. Syria's most valuable natural resources are agricultural land and oil. Other important resources include asphalt, iron ore, natural gas, and phosphates. The Euphrates and Orontes rivers provide irrigation water for farmlands. In addition, hydroelectric power is being developed at Syria's huge Tabka Dam on the Euphrates River.

Agriculture. Cotton and wheat are Syria's main crops. Farmers also grow barley and other grains; sugar beets; tobacco; and such fruits and vegetables as grapes, olives, onions, and tomatoes. Bedouins raise cattle, goats, and sheep.

Most Syrian farmers work small plots of land. Some use old-fashioned wooden plows and do many tasks by hand. However, government funds for agricultural development have helped provide modern machinery for many small farms. Syria also has a few large, state-owned farms.

On about 90 per cent of Syria's land, the rainfall is too light and irregular for raising many kinds of crops. Irrigation thus plays a vital role in farming. Water from the Tabka Dam project is expected to nearly double the amount of Syria's irrigated land.

Manufacturing. Textile manufacturing is Syria's largest industry. Syrian brocades and other fabrics have been prized since ancient times. Other important products include cement, chemicals, glass, processed foods, soap, and tobacco products. Syria also has a growing oil-refining industry. The main industrial centers are Damascus, Aleppo, Homs, and Latakia.

Trade. Syria's chief exports, in order, are oil, raw cotton, and woolens and other textiles. Other exports include food products, phosphates, and tobacco. Major imports include food, fuels, machinery, metals and metal products, motor vehicles, and textiles. Syria trades mainly with France, Great Britain, Italy, Russia, the United States, West Germany, Lebanon and other nearby countries, and countries in Eastern Europe.

Transportation and Communication.

Syria has about 5,000 miles (8,000 kilometers) of surfaced roads and about 940 miles (1,510 kilometers) of railroad track. Few Syrians own an automobile, and most people travel by bus or bicycle. Damascus has an international airport. The port of Latakia handles most of Syria's foreign trade. About 40 per cent of all Syrians own a radio, and about 2 per cent own a television set. The country has seven major daily newspapers.

History

Until 1918, Syria included much of what are now Israel, Jordan, and Lebanon and parts of Turkey. This region, often called *Greater Syria*, has a long, colorful past. Throughout history, Syria's rich soil and location on major trade routes have made the country a valuable prize. As a result, Syria was a constant battleground and became part of many empires.

Semitic Settlement.

Unidentified peoples lived in northern Syria before 4500 B.C. However, the first known settlers in Syria were Semites who probably arrived about 3500 B.C. They established independent city-states throughout the region. One city-state, Ebla, flourished in northern Syria sometime between 2700 and 2200 B.C. Ebla was a powerful kingdom with a highly advanced civilization. See EBLA.

Various Semitic groups ruled parts of Syria until 538 B.C. For example, the Akkadians conquered much of northern and eastern Syria during the mid-2300's B.C. About 2000 B.C., the Canaanites moved into the southwest, and the Phoenicians settled along the Mediterranean coast. Phoenician sailors carried Syrian culture throughout the Mediterranean world.

By 1700 B.C., the Amorites ruled much of eastern Syria. The Arameans arrived in Syria about 1500 B.C. Their culture gradually spread through most of Syria. By 1200 B.C., Damascus was a prosperous Aramean city. The Hebrews entered southern Syria during the late 1200's B.C. and introduced the belief in one God into Syrian culture. In 732 B.C., the Assyrians conquered most of Syria. They ruled until 572 B.C., when the Chaldeans took control.

The Age of Non-Semitic Rule.

Persian forces defeated the Chaldeans in 538 B.C. and made Syria part of the Persian Empire. Greek and Macedonian armies under Alexander the Great conquered the Persians in 333 B.C. Alexander and his successors, the Seleucids, spread Greek culture throughout the Middle East. The Seleucid emperors ruled from 312 to 64 B.C. During their reign, trade flourished, and many agricultural advances were made.

Syria fell to the Romans in 64 B.C. Syrians then lived under the Roman system of law for nearly 700 years, first as part of the Roman Empire, then of the East Roman Empire, and finally of the Byzantine Empire. During this period, Christianity was born and developed in a part of Greater Syria called Palestine. It became the state religion of Syria in the A.D. 300's.

The Muslim Arabs.

Muslims from the Arabian Peninsula invaded Syria and drove out the Byzantine forces in 636. Islam gradually replaced Christianity, and Arabic became the common language. Beginning in 661, a vast Muslim empire was governed from Damascus by the Omayyad dynasty. In 750, the Omayyads were overthrown. The Abbasid dynasty gained control of the empire and ruled it from Baghdad.

Christian Crusaders

from Europe invaded Syria during the late 1000's, hoping to regain the Holy Land (Palestine) from the Muslims. Saladin, the Muslim ruler of Egypt, swept into Syria to fight off the crusaders. By the late 1100's, Saladin governed most of Syria.

The Mamelukes and Ottomans.

From 1260 to 1516, Syria was governed by the Mameluke dynasty of Egypt. In 1516, Ottoman Turks conquered Syria and made it part of their huge empire. Ottoman rule lasted about 400 years. During the late 1500's, European explorers discovered sea routes to India. Syria's position as a trade center then declined. By the 1700's, the power of the Ottoman Empire was growing weak. Western ideas began to influence many areas of Syrian life. By 1900, many Syrians were demanding independence.

World War I to Independence.

During World War I (1914-1918), Syrians and other Arabs revolted against the Turks and helped Great Britain fight the Ottoman Empire. The Arabs had agreed to aid Britain in return for its support of Arab independence following the Turks' defeat. After the war ended, however, the League of Nations divided Greater Syria into four states: Syria, Lebanon, Palestine, and Transjordan. In addition, the League gave France a *mandate* to manage Syrian affairs (see MANDATED TERRITORY). Most Syrians resented French control, the presence of French troops, and the division of their land. The French encouraged economic growth and brought many improvements to Syria, but the Syrians demanded independence.

Independence.

France finally withdrew all its troops from Syria in 1946, and Syria gained complete independence. Many Syrians then wanted to reunite Greater Syria. In 1948, however, the United Nations (UN) divided Palestine into a Jewish state (Israel) and an Arab state. Syrian and other Arab forces immediately invaded Israel, but the UN eventually arranged a cease-fire. More than 600,000 Palestinian Arabs fled from their homes in the new Jewish state. They became refugees in nearby Arab countries.

Many Syrians blamed their government for failing to prevent the division of Palestine. In 1949, army officers

John Launois, Black Star

Ruins of Palmyra stand in central Syria. This ancient city thrived more than 2,000 years ago as a major stop for caravans.

c. **2300 B.C.** The Akkadians conquered northern and eastern Syria.

c. **1500 B.C.** The Arameans arrived in Syria.

732 B.C. The Assyrians conquered most of Syria.

538 B.C. Syria became part of the Persian Empire.

333 B.C. Alexander the Great gained control of Syria.

64 B.C. Syria fell to the Romans.

A.D. 637 Muslim Arabs invaded and took control of Syria.

1516 The Ottoman Turks added Syria to their empire.

1914-1918 Syrians and other Arabs revolted against Turkish rule during World War I.

1920 France received Syria as a League of Nations mandate.

1946 Syria gained complete independence from France.

1948 Syrian and other Arab troops invaded Israel. The United Nations (UN) eventually arranged a cease-fire.

1967 Israel defeated Syria, Egypt, and Jordan in a six-day war.

1973 Syria joined several other Arab nations in another war against Israel. Cease-fires ended the fighting.

1976 Syria sent troops into Lebanon in an effort to stop a civil war there.

---

overthrew the government. During the next 20 years, control of the government changed hands many times through military revolts.

In an effort toward establishing Arab unity, Syria joined Egypt in 1958 in a political union called the United Arab Republic (U.A.R.). But Egypt soon threatened to take complete control, and Syria withdrew from the U.A.R. in 1961.

During the early 1960's, Syria's Baath Party rose to power. The government took over most industry and all international trade in Syria. In 1971, Hafez al-Assad, a Baathist leader and air force general, became president of Syria.

The Continuing Arab-Israeli Conflict. During the early 1960's, border clashes between Syrian and Israeli troops occurred frequently. On June 5, 1967, war broke out between Israel and the Arab states of Syria, Jordan, and Egypt. After six days, Israel had won the war and occupied much Arab land. This land included an area called the Golan Heights in the southwestern corner of Syria. Thousands of Arabs fled from Israeli-held territory to neighboring Arab countries.

Fighting between Syria and Israel continued to erupt from time to time in the Golan Heights. Tension between the two nations was increased by the presence in Syria of Arab refugees from Palestine and the Golan Heights. In October 1973, Syria joined other Arab states in another war with Israel. Cease-fires ended most of the fighting by November. However, Syrian and Israeli forces continued fighting until May 1974.

Syria Today plays a key role in the Middle East. In 1976, Syria sent troops into Lebanon with the approval of the Lebanese government then in power in an effort to stop a civil war there. Syrian troops remain in Lebanon as part of an Arab peacekeeping force. Since 1979, that force has included only Syrian troops.

Tension between Syria and Israel has continued into the 1980's. Syria calls for the return of the Golan Heights and the creation of a Palestinian state. In 1981, Israel claimed legal and political authority in the Golan Heights. Syria and many other nations denounced Israel for this action. In 1982, Israel invaded Lebanon and

occupied the country as far north as Beirut. Israel's principal aim was to destroy the political and military capability of the Palestine Liberation Organization, a group that represents Palestinian Arabs. Israel later withdrew its forces to southern Lebanon. In 1983, Israel agreed to remove its troops from Lebanon—but only if the Syrian forces also left. But Syria would not agree to withdraw its troops unless Israel's withdrew first (see LEBANON [History]).

During 1983, there were several direct confrontations between United States and Syrian forces in Lebanon. In late 1982, U.S. troops, along with troops from several other countries, had gone to Lebanon at the request of the Lebanese government to help keep order in that country. In December 1983, the Syrians fired at unarmed U.S. reconnaissance planes as they flew over Syrian-occupied territory. The United States responded by attacking Syrian artillery positions. In a raid on December 4, two U.S. fighter jets were shot down by the Syrians. One U.S. pilot was killed and another, Lieutenant Robert O. Goodman, Jr., was captured. The Syrians released Goodman on Jan. 3, 1984.   ROBERT M. HADDAD

Related Articles in WORLD BOOK include:

Aleppo	Golan Heights
Arabs	Homs
Assad, Hafez al-	Latakia
Bedouins	Middle East
Clothing (picture: Traditional Costumes)	Palestine
Crusades (picture: A Crusader's Fortress)	Palmyra
Damascus	Phoenicia
Druses	Sèvres, Treaty of
Euphrates River	

Outline

I. Government
  A. National Government
  B. Local Government
  C. Courts
  D. Armed Forces

II. People
  A. Population and Ancestry
  B. Way of Life
  C. Religion
  D. Education
  E. The Arts

III. The Land and Climate
  A. The Coast
  B. The Mountains
  C. The Valleys and Plains

IV. Economy
  A. Natural Resources
  B. Agriculture
  C. Manufacturing
  D. Trade
  E. Transportation and Communication

V. History

Questions

What are Syria's main agricultural products?

When did Syria gain full independence from France?

What is the chief religion in Syria?

Who were the first known settlers in Syria?

For what products have Syrian craftworkers been famous since ancient times?

Who is Syria's most powerful government official?

Why was ancient Syria a major trade center?

What is Syria's largest industry?

What are the goals of Syria's Baath Party?

How do Syria's mountains affect the distribution of rainfall in the country?

Additional Resources

COPELAND, PAUL W. *The Land and People of Syria.* Rev. ed. Lippincott, 1972. For younger readers.

DAM, NIKOLAOS VAN. *The Struggle for Power in Syria: Sectarianism, Regionalism, and Tribalism in Politics, 1961-1978.* St. Martin's, 1979.

SYRIAN DESERT

SYRIAN DESERT is a triangular desert plateau that extends northward from the An Nafud desert of northern Arabia. For location, see SAUDI ARABIA (terrain map). It lies roughly between 30 and 36 degrees north latitude. The plateau is from 2,000 to 3,000 feet (610 to 910 meters) above sea level on the west. It slopes downward to the Euphrates River, its eastern boundary. The southern two-thirds of the plateau is rocky. A volcanic zone on the west is dotted with huge boulders of black basalt. The *Jabal Unayzah*, a mountainous area about 3,000 feet (910 meters) high, stands above the central part of the plateau. Deeply cut *wadis* (dry watercourses) wind down from it to the Euphrates.

The northern third of this triangular plateau is a flat sandy plain that forms the natural bridge between Syria and Iraq. A chain of limestone hills rises along the western edge of the plain. The desert contains historic ruins and several towns that have grown up around oases. The famous caravan city in Palmyra is the best known of these towns. Two highways have been built across the desert.   CHRISTINA PHELPS HARRIS

SYRINGA. See MOCK ORANGE.

SYRINGE is a pumplike device. It is a tube, tapered at one end, with a plunger or soft, hollow bulb at the other. The plunger or bulb either creates suction or forces fluid from the syringe. Syringes are used to spray or inject liquids, or to remove them by suction. See also HYPODERMIC INJECTION; INTRAVENOUS INJECTION.

SYRINX. See PAN.

SYRUP. See CORN SYRUP; MAPLE SYRUP; MOLASSES; SORGHUM.

SYSTEM. See BIOLOGY; HUMAN BODY.

SYSTEMATICS. See CLASSIFICATION, SCIENTIFIC.

SYSTEMS ANALYSIS is the study of how the parts of a system work together. A system is any group of people, machines, or other elements that work together to do a certain job.

Systems analysis tries to find the best way for a system to accomplish its task. For example, a high school is a system that includes students, teachers, and classrooms. Systems analysis can develop student schedules that make the most efficient use of the teachers and classrooms. It is used in many fields, including the armed forces, business, economics, government, industry, the sciences, and transportation.

Systems analysis usually uses advanced mathematics to study a system. First, a systems analyst uses mathematical equations to describe the different parts of the system. These equations make up a *mathematical model* of the system. Then the model is analyzed according to the principles of logic (see LOGIC). The analysis of a mathematical model requires the solution of long, difficult mathematical problems. Systems analysts use electronic computers to help find the answers to these problems. The techniques of systems analysis were developed during the late 1930's. The later development of electronic computers resulted in the widespread use of systems analysis.   DONALD G. SAARI

See also MANAGEMENT INFORMATION SYSTEMS.

Additional Resources

FITZGERALD, JERRY, and others. *Fundamentals of Systems Analysis*. 2nd ed. Wiley, 1980.

NEVISON, JOHN M. *Executive Computing: How to Get It Done on Your Own*. Addison-Wesley, 1981.

STEWARD, DONALD V. *Systems and Analysis and Management: Structure, Strategy, and Design*. Van Nostrand, 1981.

WEINBERG, GERALD M. *An Introduction to General Systems Thinking*. Wiley, 1975.

SYSTEMS ANALYST. See SYSTEMS ANALYSIS; COMPUTER (Computer Science).

SYSTOLIC PRESSURE. See BLOOD PRESSURE.

SZCZECIN, *shcheh TSEEN*, or in German, STETTIN (pop. 384,900), is the leading port of Poland. The city lies on the Baltic Sea at the mouth of the Oder River (see POLAND [political map]). Szczecin serves as a port for Czechoslovakia, East Germany, and Hungary, as well as for Poland. The city produces machines, metals, paper, and ships. Szczecin became part of Poland at the end of World War II in 1945. The city had previously formed part of Germany.   ADAM BROMKE

SZELL, *sehl*, **GEORGE** (1897-1970), was a Hungarian-born musician known principally as a symphony orchestra conductor. Earlier in his career, he was equally noted as a composer and pianist. From 1946 until his death, Szell conducted the Cleveland Symphony Orchestra, which he built into one of the world's great orchestras. Szell's extraordinary sense of pitch and rhythm helped make him one of the most respected conductors among musicians.

Szell was born in Budapest. During the 1920's and 1930's, he established himself as a conductor of operas, particularly those of Richard Wagner. He later concentrated on conducting orchestral music. Szell became a United States citizen in 1946.   KEITH POLK

SZENT-GYÖRGYI, ALBERT. See NOBEL PRIZES (table: Nobel Prizes for Physiology or Medicine—1937).

SZILARD, *ZIL ahrd*, **LEO** (1898-1964), an American physicist, pioneered in the development of nuclear energy. With Enrico Fermi, he originated the method of arranging graphite and uranium which made possible the first self-sustaining nuclear reactor in 1942. In July, 1939, Szilard and Eugene Wigner visited Albert Einstein. Einstein then wrote to President Franklin D. Roosevelt and initiated federal support of nuclear energy. Szilard was born in Budapest, Hungary. He became a U.S. citizen in 1943. He and Wigner shared the 1959 Atoms for Peace Award.   CHALMERS W. SHERWIN

SZOLD, *zohld*, **HENRIETTA** (1860-1945), an American social worker, founded Hadassah, the largest Jewish women's organization in the world. She established Hadassah in 1912 and dedicated its activities to improving the living conditions of Jews in Palestine. Szold served as president of Hadassah until 1926. Under her leadership, the organization built many hospitals and schools in Palestine. In 1933, she became director of *Youth Aliyah*, a program sponsored by Hadassah to rescue Jewish children from Nazi Germany and resettle them in Palestine. See HADASSAH.

Szold was born in Baltimore. During the 1880's, she organized Americanization classes for Jews who had emigrated there from eastern Europe. From 1892 to 1916, she served as an editor and translator for the Jewish Publication Society of America. During part of that period, from 1904 to 1910, she also was co-editor of the *American Jewish Year Book*. In 1902, Szold became the first woman to study at the Jewish Theological Seminary of America.   LEON A. JICK